Problems in Political Economy

An Urban Perspective

SECOND EDITION

Edited and with introductions by
DAVID M. GORDON

D.C. HEATH AND COMPANY

Lexington, Massachusetts   Toronto

TO MY PARENTS

ACKNOWLEDGMENTS

This book grew out of a course that I gave at Yale in the fall of 1969 on "The Economics of Urban Problems." Though large, the course allowed me a good deal of contact with my students. As we tried to communicate about this particular set of domestic problems, I became aware of our mutual dissatisfaction with standard curricular fare. We rarely found materials to feed our curiosities. The students had difficulty understanding the similarities and differences among radical, liberal, and conservative analyses of the kinds of problems that we were discussing, and I had trouble developing those comparisons. Often we complained to each other about the sterility of conventional economics.

Especially for their humanity, engagement, and concern, I owe my most important debt to those students with whom I shared my initial frustrations.

In preparing the first edition, I also received valuable help from several supporters — including Sam Bowles, Dinni Gordon, Kay Larson, Joe Persky, and Mike Reich — and from the staff of D. C. Heath.

Since the first edition appeared, I have received countless, invaluable suggestions and reactions from many people throughout the United States. Many of the changes incorporated in this second edition reflect those suggestions and, I hope, help express my debt.

Even more important, I have been buoyed by, and gained support from, a movement that has continued to grow, develop, and challenge all of us. Rather than listing every person to whom I am indebted individually, I would prefer to express a much more meaningful debt to a collectivity. Without the continuing strength of the Union for Radical Political Economics and the movement it reflects, the revision of this reader would neither have been sought nor have made much sense. With URPE, the experience of revision has seemed enormously rewarding.

D. M. G.

CONTENTS

RACE

EDUCATION

POVERTY AND WELFARE

CRIME

7 HEALTH

8

HOUSING

362-374

GENERAL INTRODUCTION

George Kennan once found the perfect simile for America's style of response to new political problems. He was describing United States reaction to its involvement in World War I.

> I sometimes wonder whether . . . a democracy is not uncomfortably similar to one of those prehistoric monsters with a body as long as this room and a brain the size of a pin: he lies there in his comfortable primeval mud and pays little attention to his environment; he is slow to wrath — in fact, you practically have to whack his tail off to make him aware that his interests are being disturbed; but, once he grasps this, he lays about him with such blind determination that he not only destroys his adversary but largely wrecks his native habitat.[1]

Just as the United States suddenly awoke to the European conflict more than fifty years ago, it dramatically uncovered an "urban crisis" in the 1960s. The country had ignored urban problems for years while it contained Communism. But the crisis of events clobbered us over the head. Riots, crime, poverty, congestion, slums, pollution — they all assaulted our slumber.

Tyrannosaurically, the democracy declared war on its urban problems. A barrage of reports and programs boomed from the Washington cannons. Whenever we turned around, another commission professed its wisdom or another agency declared its plans. For wisdom, we read reports from the Kerner Commission on riots, the Eisenhower Commission on violence, the Kaiser Commission on urban housing, the Douglas Commission on urban problems, the Heineman Commission on income maintenance programs, the Crime Commission, and the Commission on hunger. The Ribicoff subcommittee met through seventeen volumes of hearings on the "federal role in urban affairs." City officials competed for press coverage with escalating estimates of the billions necessary to solve their local problems.

For action, we watched Great Society programs proliferate like stepchildren of the New Deal. Almost randomly permuting numbers and letters, planners coined scores of new names for their projects. MDTA, NYC, CEP, and CAMPS would solve our manpower problems. ESEA Title I would help the schools. Armed with 221D-3, we would rebuild the city slums. And HUD, DOT, and OEO would form a domestic Joint Chiefs of Staff, directing the battles from the capital.

By the end of the decade, the government's frantic response to crisis had indeed "wrecked the native habitat." Slums were leveled, but new housing rarely replaced the old. Promises abounded, but performance lagged. Their

[1] George Kennan, *American Diplomacy* (New York: New American Library, 1952), p. 59.

expectations raised, many citizens reacted bitterly to program failures. Many others complained that they had been ignored in the rush of the decade. One remembered that triumphant American general after the battle of Hue in South Vietnam: "We had to destroy the city in order to save it."

Eventually the country tried to forget the crisis. A new administration proclaimed a new calm. In effect, the democracy reclined again in the primeval mud. Describing the mood in Washington in 1970, Richard Sennett wrote: "Now, during the current ascendancy of the 'hardheaded realists,' conservatives in both the Administration and Congress have concluded that the cure for the diseases of previous liberal action programs is 'pragmatic' inaction.... Men of various motives have come to believe in the idea of 'benign neglect.' " [2]

By 1975, indeed, the government in Washington was declaring that the "urban crisis was over." "There was an urban crisis at one time," as the deputy assistant secretary of the urban administration in Washington put it. "But that has changed in the past few years." [3]

Apparently, location and perspective mattered. While the generals in Washington were proclaiming the end to battle, the colonels on the front lines were warning of the smoldering flames. "Hang around until the late 'seventies," the mayor of Boston said. "They'll make the 'sixties looks like a picnic." And the mayor of San Francisco agreed. "Because we walk the edge of the volcanoe," he said, "we have a better understanding of when the next eruption will take place." [4]

Whether or not the volcanoes erupt soon, it seems clear that the problems of our cities remain. One set of liberal responses failed to solve them. Another, more conservative reflex chose to ignore them. The only advantage of the quiet was that we finally had time to reflect on the validity of these public analyses. This book of readings should help contribute to that reflection. The urban crisis persists, however deeply we have buried our heads, and my argument is that neither liberal nor conservative analysis understands its basic source.

Problems in Political Economy

The problems of the urban crisis constitute only a few of the important social problems confronting the United States. (The general economic crisis of the 1970s obviously poses another connected set of problems.) And the reigning liberal and conservative responses to the crisis comprise only two of several general analytic views of social problems. In analyzing any of the problems facing this country, one can view them from a wide variety of academic disciplines and from a number of contrasting analytic and normative perspectives.

Central to the understanding of all these problems are the tools of "political economy" — tools that help us to understand how economic, political, and social institutions determine the allocation of scarce economic resources and goods. Through these allocative patterns, social problems are defined and emerge. Three principal analytic perspectives are typically applied to understand the political economy of those problems in the United States — radical,

[2] Richard Sennett, "Survival of the Fattest," *New York Review of Books,* August 13, 1970.

[3] Quoted in Ernest Holsendolph, "Urban Crisis of the 1960's Is Over, Ford Aides Say," *New York Times,* March 23, 1975, p. 1.

[4] Quoted in Douglas Kneeland, "Mayors Step Up Appeals for Federal Aid to Cities," *New York Times,* March 24, 1975, p. 24.

liberal, and conservative views of society. Each of these three basic perspectives interprets the sources of the problems differently, and each suggests varying solutions.

In general, I hope with this book of readings to exemplify the nature of conflict among these three analytic perspectives and, through that process, to help clarify some basic issues about the nature of the American political economy. I concentrate on the problems of the urban crisis as examples because that concentration permits an indispensable detail of discussion, because so much confusion plagues the public discussion of these problems, and because the liberal and conservative perspectives have had such direct influence on the evolution of public policies toward their solution.

I emphasize the radical analysis of the problems with which this book deals, because that analysis is generally neglected in public discussion and because I think that the radical perspective provides the only valid framework within which to understand their origins, manifestations, and potential solutions. Other books are available that thoroughly outline the liberal and conservative approaches. I intend in this book to suggest a framework within which we can compare perspectives and, redressing historic neglect, to outline the radical analysis of urban problems as fully as possible. Within these narrow covers, the arguments in this book can never be conclusive. I hope that this book will at least begin to suggest some ways to ask questions about our political economy and, second, to reveal the fundamental importance of the radical view.

To encompass the urban crisis, I chose seven critical urban problems that seemed to dominate the substance and tone of the crisis during the 1960s: the urban problems of employment, racism, education, poverty and welfare, crime, health, and housing.[5] These are not our only serious domestic problems, nor are they the only problems with special severity in urban areas. But these seven seemed to dominate public attention as Americans responded to urban problems in the 1960s.

Public concern with these problems often focused exclusively on their virulence in central-city ghettos, especially black slums in the North. In this book, too, I pay special attention to conditions in those ghettos. I do so not because I think the problems exist only there, nor even because I think ghetto conditions demand the most urgent government action. Rather, I try to confront public perceptions of urban problems in terms of the public's own definitions, in order most cogently to suggest a radical explanation of those problems. My interest, it should be clear, involves debate about analysis, not about definition.

A radical analysis of such social problems involves the application of a radical "paradigm" or general set of theories about society. The application of that paradigm requires three stages of argument. First, one argues that the dynamics of the mode of production in capitalist societies tend to produce certain kinds of dominant class and institutional structures. Second, one contends that the nature of those classes and institutions — manifest in different ways in different social settings — "explains" a particular set of social problems, that those problems can be seen as inevitable consequences of the institutions.

---

[5] There are several changes in the list of problems from the first to the second edition. I dropped the problem of the urban environment from the book; it acquired a life of its own and seems separate from the other problems. I added a separate chapter on racism; many suggested that change from the first edition because the problem seemed to thread its way through all the other chapters and required more explicit discussion. In addition, I deleted the chapter on transportation for reasons of length.

Third, one concludes that the problems cannot be "solved" without fundamental changes in those institutions, and that it would require a radically different mode of production to allow the necessary institutional change.

The Scope and Structure of the Book

It would require many volumes adequately to compare perspectives on the urban crisis and to cover all three stages of the radical analysis. In the space available, I am able to pursue only part of the task. In order to pursue the general purposes of this book, I find it convenient to concentrate on the second of the three stages of the radical analysis, on the argument that these problems derive from the basic institutions of our capitalist society. The general radical paradigm has been developed elsewhere, but it has not been extensively *applied* to this particular set of problems. And, perhaps more clearly than any others, these problems dramatically illustrate the differences among perspectives and the usefulness of the radical view.

The most explicit and direct purpose of this book, in short, is *to present seven specific urban problems as inevitable consequences of the American class and institutional structure.*

To fulfill that objective, I organize the readings and introductions on three different levels.

1. To understand the application of a general analytic perspective, one must obviously understand something about the general contours of that perspective. Further, to make some decisions about its relative validity, one must understand something about other interpretations of the same reality. As Thomas Kuhn has written, "To be accepted as a paradigm, a theory must seem better than its competitors." [6]

The book begins at this general level in Chapter 1. The chapter is intended to acquaint the reader briefly with the three principal views about society: the radical perspective applied throughout this book, the liberal perspective ascendant during the 1960s, and the conservative perspective dominant in Washington in the early 1970s. The chapter's readings and introductions outline the basic analytic hypotheses of those perspectives, their respective theories of the State, and their most pervasive normative predispositions. Because the perspectives have been discussed at great length in other works, the chapter covers them somewhat briefly.

2. The next seven chapters analyze the separate problems. To make the boundaries of the analysis clear, I devote some space in each chapter to a summary of definitions and magnitudes. The introductions begin with a summary of facts and figures, and each set of readings begins with a cluster of selections on Impressions, Definitions, and Magnitudes. In each of those initial groups of readings, I include one piece of journalism evoking a qualitative impression of the problem; it seems important to glimpse the problems in human terms before dissecting them analytically. Not all the readings in these sections are by radicals. I chose selections that discussed the dimensions of each problem in the clearest way; often, these definitions were presented by analysts with opinions quite different from my own.

3. Finally, each chapter contains a basic core of analytic discussion. My

[6] Thomas Kuhn, *The Structure of Scientific Revolutions* (Chicago: Phoenix paperbacks, 1964), p. 17.

introductions summarize the general structure of the radical argument, sketching the application of the paradigm to the respective problems. Necessarily, the nature of the application varies from case to case. Further, the introductions note some important differences between the radical interpretations on the one hand and the liberal and conservative analyses on the other — again to permit some comparison of the relative validity of the three perspectives. The readings then elaborate important points of the radical analysis. One should therefore read the introductions first, to understand the general outline of the analysis, and then explore the separate readings within that general framework. I tried wherever possible to include at least one piece that applies the liberal or conservative analyses to underscore the differences between these and the radical perspectives. Each introduction clarifies the purpose of the separate selections.

I conclude each chapter with a bibliography of additional readings. The bibliographies offer some additional references on each problem; they are organized in each chapter by subject. Within each subject heading, the selections are listed in order of increasing difficulty.

In three of the chapters — on employment, education, and health — I added a selection suggesting a vision of how the problem might be "solved" in a completely different institutional context. In most cases, one needs little imagination to envision a solution to the problem; in the case of crime, for instance, one simply seeks a society without any. In these three instances, however, it seemed to me useful to illustrate the human dimensions of possible solutions to the problem.

Further, I added several Editor's Supplements to the readings to summarize some indispensable facts or arguments for which I could not find an appropriate selection.

Finally, it seems important to note that I was not able, either in introductions or with readings, to explore the important interconnections among these seven problems. Each problem is directly related to the other six, and they all have mutual causes and effects; but limited space forced me to outline analyses of each problem quite separately from the others. Above all else, the radical analysis stresses that each problem derives jointly from some mutual structural sources, and that each problem tends inevitably to reinforce the others.

A Political Disclaimer

This book argues that we must radically change the structure of all our institutions before we can effectively solve any of our problems in urban areas. It argues, in effect, that this country needs a revolution to solve its urban crisis. I should make it absolutely clear, however, that the book does not in any way offer insights on the best political means for achieving that revolution. Discussion of that political issue has filled volumes before and will obviously fill more to come. I do not have space in this book to add to the debate.

My aim is merely to contribute to the clarity of our thinking about a group of social problems. Before any of us can effectively debate political strategies for solving those problems, we must be absolutely clearheaded about their origins.

GENERAL PERSPECTIVES... RADICAL, LIBERAL, CONSERVATIVE

"Normal science" means research firmly based upon one or more past scientific achievements, achievements that some particular scientific community acknowledges for a time as supplying the foundation for its further practice. . . . [Such achievements can be called] "paradigms." . . . In the absence of a paradigm or some candidate for paradigm, all of the facts that could possibly pertain to the development of a given science are likely to seem equally relevant. . . . To be accepted as a paradigm, a theory must seem better than its competitors. . . .

— Thomas S. Kuhn[1]

When asked whether or not we are Marxist, our position is the same as that of a physicist or a biologist when asked if he is a "Newtonian" or if he is a "Pasteurian."

There are truths so evident, so much a part of people's knowledge, that it is now useless to discuss them. One ought to be "Marxist" with the same naturalness with which one is "Newtonian" in physics, or "Pasteurian" in biology. . . . The advances in social and political science, as in other fields, belong to a long historical process whose links are connecting, adding up, molding and constantly perfecting themselves.

— Ernesto "Che" Guevara[2]

With readings and introductions, this book seeks to present a radical analysis of some critical urban problems in the United States. The analyses of these separate problems derive from a general radical view of society, from a radical "paradigm" or basic conception of social reality.[3] Like many other "paradigms"

---

[1] *The Structure of Scientific Revolutions* (Chicago: University of Chicago Press, 1962), pp. 10, 15, 17.

[2] "Notes for the Study of the Ideology of the Cuban Revolution," *Studies on the Left,* Vol. 1, No. 3, 1960.

[3] Kuhn's book, from which the first opening quotation was taken, provides a brilliant discussion of the role of paradigms in defining the terms of research in the natural sciences. He speaks some in the book about research in the social sciences. For one interesting discussion of the application of Kuhn's insights to the social sciences and especially to economics, see Paul Sweezy, "Toward a Critique of Economics," *The Review of Radical Political Economics,* Spring 1970.

1

in the social sciences, the radical perspective involves some general analytic and philosophical assumptions about the nature of individuals and their relations in society. One cannot begin to appreciate the implications of succeeding chapters in this book without first understanding the structure of the radical "paradigm" and its differences from other important social perspectives. I try in this introductory chapter to provide the barest skeleton of background for the specific analyses that follow.

I concentrate on three general social perspectives: radical, liberal, and conservative. One can reasonably argue (and radicals often do) that liberal and conservative views of society do not differ fundamentally, but rather that they represent opposite extremes on a continuum of qualitatively similar definitions of social reality.[4] (The views' similarities are discussed further in the concluding remarks of this introduction.) I chose to treat them as separable in this book because their views on the role of the State differ so strongly. In analyzing urban problems, one must pay special attention to varying positions on the potential of government solutions to those problems. A paradigm's postulates about the State therefore assume critical importance.[5]

This chapter focuses on three particular elements of these general perspectives. First, I outline the paradigms' basic analytic hypotheses about social reality, their "positive" preconceptions about the ways in which individuals relate to each other in a social context. Second, I sketch their views of the State, of its role in present societies, and of the role it ought to play in any society. Third, I suggest a few important elements of their "normative" assumptions and values, their criticisms of current societies, and their visions of an "ideal" society. I do not intend that this book should provide elaborate arguments about the "best" kind of society.[6] But I do not believe that analyses of society can be completely objective, free somehow of all normative judgments. With Gunnar Myrdal, I believe that "every study of a social problem, however limited in scope, is and must be determined by valuations. A 'disinterested' social science has never existed and, for logical reasons, can never exist."[7] In order to understand the radical analysis of social problems and its differences with other views of those problems, one must isolate the kinds of normative predispositions that different analysts have carried with them into their work.

In this introduction, I discuss the radical view in the first section and the liberal and conservative perspectives in the second section. In a third section, I briefly describe the reading selections that follow.

I have tried to avoid arguments at this stage of the book about the relative validity of the three perspectives. Although I feel strongly that the radical view provides the clearest understanding of reality and that its normative vision is

[4] Many radicals certainly view the liberal and conservative views as qualitatively similar expressions of a basic orthodox analysis. Furthermore, there is some confusion over the terminology, since modern conservatism derives directly from classical nineteenth-century English "liberalism."

[5] For perhaps the strongest recent statement of these differences, see Milton Friedman, *Capitalism and Freedom* (Chicago: University of Chicago Press, 1962), *passim,* and the selection from the book below.

[6] Obviously I think such discussions are quintessentially important. I simply think that they should be conducted at length, in detail, and with considerable subtlety. I have not had enough space in this book to allow such discussion.

[7] Gunnar Myrdal, *Objectivity in Social Research* (New York: Pantheon Books, 1969), p. 55.

most compelling, I have tried to abstain from criticisms of the two other views in this introduction. I agree with Paul Sweezy about the appropriate basis for choosing among alternative paradigms: "It seems to me that from a scientific point of view the question of choosing between . . . approaches . . . can be answered quite simply. Which more accurately reflects the fundamental characteristics of social reality which is under analysis?"[8] Since the specific analyses in the succeeding chapters deal much more directly with reality than the abstractions of this introduction do, my comments, criticisms, and preferences about the perspectives will appear with the individual analyses.

The Radical View

A modern radical analysis of society draws from, but does not depend exclusively on, the seminal nineteenth-century work of Karl Marx. Marx's analysis of society made original theoretical contributions on both substantive and methodological levels. In his methodological discussions, he insisted that general theories or analytic views of society cannot remain aloof from the course of history, somehow eternally fixed above the evolutions and revolutions of society below. As society changes, so must theories about its nature change. Analysis of society should reflect a dynamic synthesis of theory and reality.[9]

Thoroughly in agreement, modern radicals no longer dwell exclusively on textual exegeses of Marx's writings. As Ernest Mandel puts it, radical economic analysis "endeavours to start from the empirical data of the science of today in order to examine whether or not the essence of Marx's economic propositions remains valid."[10] In sketching the basic features of a radical analysis of American society, I have built from recent radical writings more than from Marx, and from recent historical events more than from the events which Marx perceived.[11]

The underlying analytic framework of the radical "paradigm" involves seven basic clusters of hypotheses about society.

· 1. The analysis argues that the structure and evolution of any society depend principally on the society's dominant mode of economic production. Because basic modes of production differ, capitalist societies differ fundamentally from feudal societies, for instance, and from socialist societies.[12] "By mode of production [Marx] did not refer merely to the state of technique — to what he termed the state of the productive forces — but to the way in which the means of production were owned and to the social relations between men which resulted from their connections with the process of production."[13] As Robert Tucker further elaborates, "In every instance . . . the mode of productive activ-

---

[8] "Toward a Critique of Economics," p. 2.

[9] Indeed, Marx's major criticism of orthodox classical political economists was that they tried to abstract from historical change, that they attempted, in his words, "to blot out all historical differences." ("Introduction to the Critique of Political Economy," in David Horowitz, ed., *Marx and Modern Economics* [New York: Monthly Review Press, 1968], p. 45.)

[10] Ernest Mandel, *Marxist Economic Theory* (New York: Monthly Review Press, 1969), Vol. I, p. 17.

[11] See the bibliography at the end of the chapter for some of these sources.

[12] Marx presented this basic argument most eloquently in Marx and Friedrich Engels, *The Communist Manifesto* (New York: International Publishers, 1948), first published in 1848.

[13] Maurice Dobb, *Studies in the Development of Capitalism,* rev. ed. (New York: International Publishers, 1963), p. 7.

ity has been the definitive fact of the social epoch, the determinant of the character of society in all of its superstructural expressions: political, legal, intellectual, [and] religious." [14]

2. The most important and most distinctive feature of the mode of production in capitalist societies is its organization of labor by means of the wage-contract.

> Thus Capitalism was not simply a system of production for the market — a system of commodity-production as Marx termed it — but a system under which labour-power had "itself become a commodity" and was bought and sold on the market like any other object of exchange. Its historical prerequisite was the concentration of ownership of the means of production in the hands of a class, consisting of only a minor section of society, and the consequential emergence of a propertyless class for whom the sale of their labour-power was their only source of livelihood. Productive activity was furnished, accordingly, by the latter, not by virtue of legal compulsion, but on the basis of a wage-contract. [15]

Recent anthropological evidence has made clear that this basic organization of work and labor originated historically with capitalist societies, that antecedent societies organized work in different ways. Writing about this singular characteristic of production in capitalist societies, Marx himself said, "Without it there is no capital, no bourgeoisie, no bourgeois society." [16]

3. This method of organizing production involves two fundamental and connected economic features — one involving production and the other distribution.

First, *production* itself brings together *workers* — with nothing to offer but their capacity to do work — and *capitalists* — who need laborers to set in motion the means of production that they own. The owners are hiring workers because they may be able to earn a profit from that labor. If production did not result in profit for the employers, then production would not take place. Production is regulated, therefore, by considerations of profit, not by by concern for the usefulness of products and the needs of people. People labor at jobs in the service of their owners' profits, not in the pursuit of their own needs. Capitalists control workers through their control of the means of production. Workers, because they own too little property, must submit to the discipline of a controlling class.

Second, since people cannot produce for themselves, they must buy products in the market place. Capitalism therefore also involves the *distribution* of things that people need through the mechanisms of market exchange. More and more, social needs are expressed through, and reduced to, their quantitative expression in "prices." Whether people need something matters less and less. Whether they can afford it becomes determining.

These two characteristics are integrated through the structure and motion of the whole capitalist system. Workers depend on jobs to support themselves.

---

[14] Tucker, *The Marxian Revolutionary Idea* (New York: W. W. Norton, 1969), p. 15.

[15] Dobb, *Studies*, p. 7.

[16] Marx, *The Class Struggles in France 1848–1850* (New York: International Publishers, n.d.), p. 42. For evidence on earlier societies, see the anthropological discussions in Mandel, *Marxist Economic Theory*, and some of the essays of Karl Polanyi in George Dalton, ed., *Primitive, Archaic, and Modern Economies: Essays of Karl Polanyi* (Garden City, N.Y.: Doubleday, 1968), especially "The Self-Regulating Market and the Fictitious Commodities: Land, Labor and Money."

Their jobs depend on whether or not capitalists can make profits through production. The capitalists cannot realize their profits unless they sell their goods. So they campaign to sell their goods, luring more and more people into the web of market transactions. And as people become more and more dependent on the market, they are less and less able to support themselves. Which means that they must work to support their families. Which replenishes the labor force, keeping wages low and helping maintain the basis for capitalist profits. Around and around these circuits, the system extends itself and deepens its control.[17]

4. This set of connections between production and distribution helps determine the principal dynamic characteristic of the system: the unceasing attempt by owners of capital to increase continuously their stocks of wealth. It is not that capitalists are greedy (although they may be). Capitalists "are driven to expand profits not only because they *want* to," as Richard Edwards has put it, "but also because if they are to remain capitalists, the market *forces* them to do so." [18] The forces of competition among capitalists, whether among small independent shopkeepers or corporate giants, inevitably force owners of capital to protect themselves against their competitors by producing more goods and accumulating more and more profit.[19] As Mandel puts it: "The capitalist mode of production thus becomes the first mode of production in the history of mankind the essential aim of which appears to be unlimited increase in production." [20]

5. With these tendencies, the capitalist system tends more and more to create an opposition between two distinct classes. As people lose control over their own property, they must become workers in order to survive. And as the accumulation of capital leads to an increasing concentration and centralization of wealth, a few capitalists — through their corporations — dominate more and more of our social existence.

While workers depend on corporations for jobs, they must nonetheless do with less if the corporations are to get more. And that provides the potential for conflict between those two classes. Despite that potential, however, the conflicts do not stare us in the face every day. This class relationship is a process, not a simple outcome. As the English historian E. P. Thompson has put it,

> the notion of class entails the notion of historical relationship. . . . We can see a *logic* in the responses of similar experiences, but we cannot predicate any laws. Consciousness of class arises in the same way in different times and places, but never in just the same way.[21]

Many different elements of prevailing ideology in our society have disguised this basic conflict between workers and owners. Those disguises can last only so long, radicals argue, before the system itself rips them off.

[17] For further development of this theme, see Paul Sweezy, *The Theory of Capitalist Development* (New York: Monthly Review Press, 1956).

[18] R. C. Edwards, M. Reich, and T. E. Weisskopf, eds., *The Capitalist System* (Englewood Cliffs, N.J.: Prentice-Hall, 1972), p. 100.

[19] For one discussion of the persistence of this dynamic, even in the age of large corporations, see Paul Baran and Paul Sweezy, *Monopoly Capital* (New York: Monthly Review Press, 1965).

[20] *Marxist Economic Theory,* p. 113.

[21] E. P. Thompson, *The Making of the English Working Class* (New York: Vintage Books, 1967), p. 9.

6. The dynamics of the system tend to generate some basic contradictions with fundamental impact on its further development.

• The continuing development of production leads to continuing mechanization. The division of labor breeds the minute fragmentation of tasks. As Marx himself put it, the division of labor under capitalism tends to convert "the labourer into a crippled monstrosity, by forcing his detail dexterity at the expense of a world of productive capabilities and instincts." [22]

But people have always sought historically, in the radical view, to increase their control over nature and their own destinies. The "mutilation" of our creative potential comes increasingly into conflict with our struggle to control our own lives. Sooner or later, radicals argue, the fragmentation of work is bound to produce some kind of counterreaction. Where and when that reaction becomes manifest depends on time and place. When and if it comes, its impact will be sweeping.

• Capitalism leads more and more to the "objective socialisation of production." [23] People no longer work individually, producing for their own needs. The division of labor under capitalism effects a complete interdependence among people as producers. "The work of each is indispensable to the survival of all, so that each can survive only thanks to the work of thousands and thousands of other men." [24]

But at the same time, capitalism depends on and enforces a totally private, frequently ruthless competition among people. Capitalists must compete with capitalists, workers with workers, through every phase of social activity. Brought into "objective" relationships of social cooperation in production, people are induced subjectively to fight against those cooperative ties. White workers learn to hate black workers, for instance, even though they are thrown together in working situations. The juxtaposition of these two basic dynamics in capitalist societies becomes fundamentally contradictory; they feed upon each other to determine many of the characteristics of capitalist institutions. [25]

• In similar ways, vast increases in productive capacity establish for the first time in history the fundamental irrationality of class conflict in society. Class conflicts have always existed. With the very early precapitalist development of social cooperation in production and with primitive technological innovations, individuals first became capable of producing more with their own labor than was necessary to sustain their own existence — to feed, house, and clothe them and their families. In primitive societies, the village and tribal communities sometimes used this emergent "surplus product" communally, cooperatively

[22] Karl Marx, *Capital* (New York: International Publishers, 1967), Vol. I, p. 360.
[23] Mandel, *Marxist Economic Theory*, p. 170.
[24] *Loc. cit.*
[25] This argument is difficult to formulate but its importance cannot possibly be underestimated. The contradiction's effects pervade capitalist societies. For instance, workers become increasingly cooperative (in this objective sense) in bureaucratic organizations in which everyone works jointly on the "products" of the bureaucracy. But the nature of capitalist institutions cannot permit an equality of cooperation, for that would undercut the class divisions from which capitalists derive their power. So all kinds of new, relatively artificial distinctions develop within the bureaucratic organization to permit objectively cooperative work but to maintain sharp distinctions among workers. Job titles are refined to establish distinct job hierarchies; offices become badges of status; innumerable "ports-of-entry" develop to stratify the work force by initial job level and educational attainment. For more on this example, see the Introduction to Chapter 2, "Employment."

reducing all of their working times and increasing all of their opportunities for leisure. But precapitalist forms of production did not generate very large surplus products, certainly not enough to allow all members of a society to share in very much leisure. Inevitably, some members of society sought to free themselves from work altogether. At different stages of social and economic development and in different ways, some people gained control over the labor of others, providing for themselves by living off the surplus product of those whose labor they controlled. Chieftains lived off the product of their slaves, for instance, while the slaves worked long enough to provide both for themselves and for their rulers. Class conflict grew out of that appropriation of "surplus product." [26] As Mandel puts it, "The producers have never accepted as normal or natural that the surplus product of their labour should be seized by the possessing classes, who thus obtain a monopoly of leisure and culture. . . . The history of mankind is nothing but a long succession of class struggles." [27]

Finally, with capitalist society, the struggles of producers to reclaim some of their surplus product *could* cease. Society begins to produce enough so that *everyone* in society could acquire opportunities for considerable leisure activities. Mandel explains this development:

> It is the capitalist mode of production that, by the extraordinary advance of the productive forces which it makes possible, creates for the first time in history the economic conditions needed for the abolition of class society altogether. The social surplus product would suffice to reduce extensively the working time of all men, which would ensure an advance of culture that would enable functions of accumulation (and management) to be exercised by the whole of society.[28]

But capitalism depends on the private ownership of property and the ability of owners of capital constantly to (try to) accumulate more and more of "surplus product." Some members of society continue to obtain enormous shares of wealth and leisure, while others continue to support both themselves and others with their labor. Class conflicts inevitably continue in capitalist societies.[29] The facts that society now produces enough so that everyone could share adequately in wealth and leisure — without some receiving disproportionate shares — and that class conflicts could therefore potentially cease render those conflicts all the more irrational.

7. Finally, these basic forces defining and driving capitalist societies produce a constantly changing set of social institutions. These institutions largely

[26] This discussion draws heavily on Mandel, *Marxist Economic Theory*, pp. 170–77. Mandel provides plentiful examples of very early class conflicts.

[27] *Ibid.*, p. 175.

[28] *Ibid.*, p. 177.

[29] It has been an essential argument of orthodox liberal and conservative critiques of Marxism that class conflicts have disappeared in advanced capitalist economies like the United States. These arguments emphasize the "happiness" of relatively affluent blue-collar workers. They ignore, first of all, the obvious bloodiness of the fight for union recognition and workers' rights in the United States between 1870 and 1940. And they tend to neglect the extent to which class conflict has been successfully diffused by capitalist institutions into many conflicts among many classes. For further discussion see R. C. Edwards, M. Reich, and D. M. Gordon, eds., *Labor Market Segmentation* (Lexington, Mass.: D. C. Heath, 1975).

determine the nature and content of daily life in capitalist societies, as well as the ways in which the basic forces driving capitalist societies are manifested.[30] Given these institutions, the analysis involves three basic hypotheses about them: first, that the nature and structure of these institutions directly determine the nature of social relations in society; second, that these institutions determine the distribution of power among groups and individuals and therefore determine the specific historical resolutions of class conflicts; and, third, that the most important institutions ultimately benefit those directly included in, or associated with, the capitalist class.[31] When we look at any aspect of our social lives, in short, we must keep in mind its roots in the underlying economic system. The economic system does not determine everything about our lives, in the radical view, but it has enough influence so that we must always take it into account. If we ignore this range of effects, we run the risk of missing the most important sources of the particular problems that we are studying.

The radical view of the State follows from these basic postulates. Since it is discussed in the piece by Sweezy in this chapter, this view can be summarized briefly here. The State, in the radical view, operates ultimately to serve the interests of the controlling class in a class society. Since the "capitalist class" fundamentally controls capitalist societies, the State functions in those societies to serve that class. It does so either directly, by providing services only to members of that class, or indirectly, by helping preserve the system of institutions supporting and maintaining the power of that class. In the United States, government subsidy of defense firms provides a clear example of the former, while government support of, and control over, an educational system that fundamentally supports the "system-defining" institutions illustrates the latter. (All these points will be developed in later chapters.)

The radical analysis of specific social problems flows directly from this general framework. The chapters that follow this introduction provide examples of this analysis, examining seven separate problems associated with the "urban crisis" in the United States. In each chapter I use introductions and readings to provide a specific illustration of this basic view. In different ways, each chapter argues that the problem with which it is concerned flows from the specific evolution of capitalist institutions in the United States. The conclusions of the separate chapters follow precisely: One cannot expect the problems to disappear unless the basic institutions themselves change. And one cannot expect changes in these fundamental institutions unless those classes in conflict with capitalists become strong enough to force such change.

Some of the flavor of these specific chapters depends heavily on the normative elements of the radical perspective, on its criticisms of capitalist societies, and on its vision of a "better" society.

Radicals criticize capitalist society because it evolves irrationally. Its basic mode of production and the structures of its institutions create conflicts that do not need to exist. In the language of economics, it forces "trade-offs" that are not necessary. Radicals argue that capitalism forces a conflict between the aggregate wealth of society (and obviously the enormous wealth of some individuals) and the freedom of most individuals. In another, truly democratic, humanist, and socialist society, radicals argue, conditions could be forged in which increases

---

[30] For further detail, see some of the chapters in Edwards *et al.*, eds., *The Capitalist System.*

[31] See *ibid.* for elaboration of these points.

in aggregate social wealth complement the personal freedom of all individuals.[32]

It should be emphasized in discussing the radical vision that many modern radicals, though socialist, do not view most modern socialist countries with great approval. To many Western radicals, for example, the purposes and the realities of the socialist revolution in China come closer to embodying their ideals than those of the Soviet Union.

In general, radicals envision that socialism can provide a better basis than capitalism for transition toward an "ideal" society in which people could be free to develop themselves as human beings and at the same time to cooperate with others in developing their potential together. This movement would become manifest in many different ways:

• People could become more and more free from the "whip of hunger," liberating themselves from the insecurity and occasional starvation that plague people in capitalist societies.[33]

• People could become more and more free from exploitation by more powerful classes. Socialist development would promote *even* development, with growing equality, rather than the uneven development and sharp inequalities dominating capitalist societies.[34]

• People could become freer from the tyranny of the detailed division of labor. Rather than reducing workers to "fragments of their former selves," socialism could begin to develop everyone's potential to do more and more creative work.[35]

• People could become more and more free to contribute positively to the welfare of fellow members of their communities. In capitalism, radicals argue, people are forced to compete with each other. In the process of socialist transition, they could be free to begin building a better society together.[36]

Comparing capitalism with the socialist process in Cuba, Che Guevara dramatically expressed this sense of direction. Under capitalism, he writes, society is "a dispersed force, divisible in thousands of fractions shot into space like the fragments of a grenade, trying by any and all means, in a fierce struggle with their equals, to achieve a position that would give them support in the face of an uncertain future." [37]

In building toward a truly communist society, Guevara says,

> Man begins to free his thought from the bothersome fact that presupposed the need to satisfy his animal needs by working. He begins to see himself

[32] For a comprehensive bibliography listing many sources for this argument, see Jim Campen, ed., *An Annotated Bibliography on Socialist Alternatives for America* (New York: Union for Radical Political Economics, 1974).

[33] For instance, during the economic crisis of the mid-1970s, many people in countries dominated by capitalist relations either starved or suffered serious malnutrition — as in Bangladesh — while all available reports seem to indicate that there were no serious food shortages in socialist countries like China.

[34] For a development of this theme, see John Gurley, "Maoist Economics Development," *Review of Radical Political Economics,* Winter 1970.

[35] Among many sources, see, for instance, Charles Bettelheim, *Cultural Revolution and Industrial Organization in China* (New York: Monthly Review Press, 1974), excerpt from which appears in Chapter 2.

[36] The early stages of this transformation are brilliantly sketched in William Hinton, *Fanshen* (New York: Monthly Review Press, 1967).

[37] Che Guevara, "Man and Socialism in Cuba," in J. Gerassi, ed., *Venceremos: The Speeches and Writings of Che Geuvara* (New York: Simon & Schuster, 1968), p. 399.

portrayed in his work and to understand its human magnitude through the created object, through the work carried out. This no longer involves leaving a part of his being in the form of labor power sold, which no longer belongs to him; rather it signifies an emanation from himself, a contribution to the life of society in which he is reflected, the fulfillment of his social duty.

We are doing everything possible to give work this new category of social duty and to join it to the development of technology, on the one hand, which will provide the conditions for greater freedom, and to voluntary work on the other, based on the Marxist concept that man truly achieves his full human condition when he produces without being compelled by the physical necessity of selling himself as a commodity.

We will make the twenty-first-century man.[38]

The radical analysis of capitalism and this sense of socialist direction cannot be separated. Radicals argue that theory and practice cannot be divorced. Our knowledge of capitalism helps inform our efforts to change it. And our efforts to change it improve our knowledge. One cannot understand the processes of change in the real world, in this view, without participating in that change. As Mao Tse-tung put it:

If you want knowledge, you must take part in the practice of changing reality. If you want to know the taste of a pear, you must change the pear by eating it yourself. . . . If you want to know the theory and methods of revolution, you must take part in revolution. All genuine knowledge originates in direct experience.[39]

The message for this book is obvious. If we want to change our cities, radicals argue, we cannot simply study them as doctors view an X-ray. We must directly engage in the struggle to change our cities in order clearly to understand the forces tending to assist and oppose that change. And through that struggle, perhaps, we shall come to know and unite with enough people so that we shall finally acquire the strength, the power, and the resolve to transform our urban lives.

The Liberal and Conservative Views

This section briefly surveys the liberal and conservative perspectives. I summarize these paradigms for comparative purposes. In the separate chapters that follow, I present the liberal and conservative analyses in somewhat less detail than I do the radical view. It seems necessary in this introductory chapter simply to provide some general reference points for later discussions.

I will summarize the basic points of the liberal and conservative analyses together, for they begin with the same fundamental hypotheses about social reality. I will discuss their views of the State separately, and their normative predispositions separately, for the two perspectives differ more widely on those levels. I rely primarily on the readings in this chapter to provide the full flavor of each view.

[38] *Ibid.,* pp. 394, 400.
[39] Mao Tse-tung, "On Practice," in *Selected Works* (Peking: Foreign Languages Press, 1964), Vol. I, p. 399.

The liberal perspective has never been quite so clearly formulated as the other two paradigms. It has evolved gradually in the Western world, growing from and through historical experience, rather than springing from the coherent ideas and writings of a single scholar, as the radical perspective does from the works of Marx. Befitting its pragmatic orientations, it has been molded especially by its applications in public policy. Its underlying logical structure has not so often been formulated logically and coherently as it has been suggested or evoked in its specific applications. In some ways, the clearest presentation of liberal postulates about the economy is available in Paul Samuelson's classic introductory textbook, *Economics*.[40] A reasonably clear statement of the liberal's hypotheses about politics and the State can be found in many books presenting the "pluralist" view of democracy in the United States.[41] In some ways, the most precise illustration of the liberal prespective as it has molded public policy and ideology in the United States is presented in a very difficult book written during the 1950s by Robert Dahl and Charles Lindblom, *Politics, Economics and Welfare*.[42]

Conservative analysis has, on the other hand, grown from specific historical roots and has received precise recent formulation. It springs from classical English liberalism of the nineteenth century. It has been forcefully presented by the modern American economist Milton Friedman, especially in his book *Capitalism and Freedom*.[43] And, directly serving the comparative purposes of this book, conservative analysis has been consistently applied to most of the urban problems here discussed in the recent and very influential book by Edward Banfield, *The Unheavenly City*.[44] Since I have included both the conclusion to Banfield's book (to evoke the general approach of the perspective) and Friedman's arguments about the role of the State in the selections, I can rely on them in these introductory summaries of the perspective.

Both liberal and conservative analyses of social problems begin from an underlying view of the society, formulated most rigorously in orthodox economic analysis.[45] This underlying view abstracts from the specific social relations and institutions of a society, taking the existing system of institutions for granted. It then builds from some basic postulates about the behavior of individual decision-making units — like households, workers, or firms — and the ways in which they adjust to the given institutional framework. The analysis postulates

[40] Now in its 10th edition from McGraw-Hill.

[41] Perhaps the best such discussion is Arnold Rose, *The Power Structure: Political Process in America* (New York: Oxford University Press, 1968).

[42] (New York: Harper Torchbooks, 1965). For an interesting history of liberalism in America, see Louis Hartz, *The Liberal Tradition in America* (New York: Harcourt, Brace & World, 1955).

[43] (Chicago: University of Chicago Press, 1962).

[44] (Boston: Little, Brown, 1970). See also its revision, *The Unheavenly City Revisited* (Boston: Little, Brown, 1974). The similarities of Banfield and Friedman's views are not coincidental. Banfield acknowledges his debts to, and agreements with, Friedman often in his book.

[45] The use of the term *orthodox economic analysis* is not intended normatively or pejoratively. It is often used to refer to the dominant traditions in economic theory, extending back to the nineteenth century, preoccupied with marginal analysis at the microeconomic level and with Keynesianism at the macroeconomic level. For a useful discussion of the tradition, see Mark Blaug, *Economic Theory in Retrospect* (Homewood, Ill.: Irwin, 1962). For some further comments, see Maurice Dobb, *Theories of Value and Theories of Distribution* (Cambridge, England: Cambridge University Press, 1973).

specifically that individual units act rationally and are free rationally to maximize their welfare subject to the simplest of constraints. For example, it presumes that consumers are free to choose whatever goods will maximize their welfare, subject to the simple constraint that their expenses not exceed their income. The analysis does not explore the ways in which institutions predetermine the range of goods from which individuals can choose.[46] In political analysis, it tends to imply that voters are free to choose rationally among wide varieties of public alternatives — whether candidates in elections or government programs through representatives.[47] From that beginning, the postulates imply a simple conclusion: final decisions made by individuals accurately reflect their real preferences, about cars or congressmen, for instance, without regard to the institutional context in which those choices are made. The postulates imply that a wide variety of alternative government decisions is possible.

In terms of aggregate social behavior, the liberal and conservative analysis assumes that individual actions combine (or "aggregate," in the technical terms of economics) to produce stable, harmonious social equilibria.[48] This basic postulate involves three separate elements. First, it implies that there is such a thing as an equilibrium in social terms — a conjunction of social forces and relations such that movements away from it will tend to produce countermovements reestablishing the equilibrium. This basic notion dominates economics, where the concept of equilibrium pervades orthodox analysis; sociology, especially in modern applications of "structural-functional" analysis; and much of political science, with its emphases on the stability of political systems. Second, the notion of equilibrium implies that society is relatively free from conflict, that individuals acting privately and independently are capable of combining socially to produce "harmonious" social situations with which few are basically discontented, from which few would like to move.[49] And, third, it tends to imply, more dynamically, that changes in society come gradually, if at all, moving slowly from one harmonious equilibrium to the next.[50]

Given those basic postulates, the two perspectives begin to diverge. Each admits that social problems or difficulties occasionally develop. Each perspective admits, for instance, that the market produces an income distribution in which some earn too little to live, and that, therefore, some way should be found to assist the poorest in society. And each insists that problems develop

[46] J. K. Galbraith has always insisted on this point in his books. See for instance, *The New Industrial State* (Boston: Houghton Mifflin, 1967).

[47] This is especially true of the discussion in conventional economic theory of "public goods" and "public benefits." For the briefest flavor of these discussions, see Otto Eckstein, *Public Finance*, 3rd ed. (Englewood Cliffs, N.J.: Prentice-Hall, 1973), or for a more technical discussion, Richard Musgrave, *The Theory of Public Finance* (New York: McGraw-Hill, 1959).

[48] This tradition extends all the way back to Adam Smith's seminal notion of an "invisible hand" in *The Wealth of Nations* (1776).

[49] Indeed, much of orthodox economic analysis is concerned with arguing that these equilibria represent "optimal" situations, from which it would be impossible to move without the decrease in some individuals' welfare exceeding the gain in others' welfare. For an introduction to these notions, see Samuelson, *Economics*.

[50] This is almost a methodological necessity of the analyses. In order to ensure that the behavior of individual units in a social setting can be adequately and rigorously studied, one must presume that the social setting itself does not change very much in the course of study. The analyses also tend, implicitly, to support the status quo.

from minor imperfections in the basic social mechanisms, principally from in-adequate information or shortsightedness among individuals.[51] But the two perspectives differ sharply on what should be done about such problems.

And this difference draws essentially from their respective analyses of the State. In the liberal view, the State in a modern democracy adequately reflects individual wishes through group representatives. The government is justified in acting, essentially, because it incorporates the preferences of all individuals and because it seeks to advance the interests of all individuals.[52]

In the liberal analysis, there are three principal kinds of government action that society both prefers and requires. First, the government should redistribute income.[53] Second, the government should act when private market mechanisms cannot satisfy consumer preferences effectively.[54] Third, the government should act to provide certain goods that the market mechanism is incapable of pro-viding, like national defense. Armed with these principles, the liberal perspec-tive has motivated and justified a vast increase in government responsibilities in the United States during the twentieth century. Programs have developed to overcome market inefficiencies in housing, for instance, from public construc-tion of low-cost housing to public provision of financial subsidies for those too poor to afford decent housing.   –

In the conservative view, the role of the State should be much more limited. Conservatives tend to have greater faith than liberals in the efficiency and op-timality of the private market mechanism, and to have greater fear than liberals do of both government inefficiency and government infringement on personal liberties. Friedman elaborates these points clearly.

Despite these differences, however, the two perspectives agree on one cen-tral disagreement with the radical view of the State. In neither the liberal nor the conservative perspective does the State serve the interests only of one class, as radicals argue. To conservatives it can barely serve anyone's interest, and to liberals it can effectively serve the interests of all.

---

[51] See the introduction to the chapter on Education for a good example.

[52] This contention has dominated an interesting series of conflicts between two schools of political analysis in this country. On the one hand, "pluralists" have argued the liberal view that the government represents in this country. On the other hand, fol-lowing the original contribution of C. Wright Mills, some radicals have argued that a "power elite," dominated by the capitalist class, has controlled the government, ensuring that it represents the interests almost exclusively of that class. For a recent summary of the pluralist view, see Rose, *The Power Structure.* For the "power elite" argument, see Mills, *The Power Elite* (New York: Oxford University Press, 1956), and G. William Dom-hoff, *Who Rules America?* (Englewood Cliffs, N.J.: Prentice-Hall, 1967). For a collection of essays from both sides, see Domhoff and Hoyt Ballards, eds., *C. Wright Mills and the Power Elite* (Boston: Beacon Press, 1968).

[53] The argument presumes that the final pattern of redistribution will reflect aggregate social preferences (and therefore all individual preferences) about the shape of the in-come distribution.

[54] The classic example of this in economics is the example of pollution from a chim-ney stack. A firm does not have to consider the "social costs" of soot from the chimney (costs to others of cleaning clothes, for instance). It bases its production solely on its private, internal costs. Theoretically, if it were forced to pay the social costs too, it would produce less or install machinery to eliminate the pollution. Thus, the analysis justifies government intervention in the form of a pollution tax or pollution-abatement incentive. For a summary and criticism of this traditional argument, see E. J. Mishan, *The Costs of Economic Growth* (New York: Praeger, 1967).

The liberal and conservative perspectives also differ sharply with each other on normative grounds, although the differences seem more precisely disagreements of temperament than of basic principle. Conservatives tend to place the highest priority on individual freedom and social order, while liberals tend to place their highest priority on individual equality and social justice.[55] Liberals seem more willing to countenance both rapid social change and extensive government involvement in the private sector. Both differ completely from the radical perspective in one important respect: each tends to regard capitalism as the "best" economic mode of production because it affords, they argue, the maximum feasible individual freedom. Each perspective envisions as its "ideal" society a perfectly functioning capitalist democracy. Each imagines that we can come extremely close to that ideal without major changes in current capitalist institutions (although conservatives would certainly prefer a much less powerful government than we have in the United States). These normative views inform their specific analyses of the problems discussed in succeeding chapters.

The Readings

Each of the readings in this chapter helps elaborate these three general perspectives.

The first three selections develop the radical view. In the first, David M. Gordon provides a general background for the radical analysis of the urban problems discussed in this book. The selection traces the major forces and institutions in modern capitalist America that *frame* and *limit* social behavior and individual possibilities. The second selection, by Stephen Hymer and Frank Roosevelt, briefly summarizes some of the central postulates of Marxian economics on which the radical analysis builds. In particular, it emphasizes some of the most important differences between Marxian economics and orthodox economics. In the third selection, originally written in 1942, Paul Sweezy exposits the radical view of the State. Sweezy writes in a style from a somewhat earlier era, quoting extensively from Marx himself. The points that he makes have been extended by many radicals writing more recently, however, and this selection serves as a clear introduction to this strand of the radical analysis.

The selections by Arthur Okun and Walter W. Heller represent the liberal view. Okun clearly states the central dilemma that liberals constantly confront — the problem of balancing considerations of efficiency and equity. The balance that they strike, from period to period, largely determines the specific policies they pursue to address individual problems.

Heller's piece provides an exposure to the liberal view of the state. He summarizes the economic arguments underlying that perspective. He suggests that government officials have a choice among a nearly infinite variety of social outcomes and that, despite the technical problems involved in such choices, government actions will accurately reflect the will of the people.

Edward C. Banfield and Milton Friedman present the conservative view with vigor. Banfield's discussion of urban problems — from the concluding chapter of his book — reveals the conservative opposition to "ameliorative" government

---

[55] On all of these values and their precise philosophic foundations, see Robert Wolff, *The Poverty of Liberalism* (Boston: Beacon Press, 1968). See also the selection by Okun in this chapter.

policies. He contends that urban problems are not anywhere nearly as serious as many believe, and that government intervention is more likely to make things worse than better. Friedman outlines the conservative view of the State, upon which Banfield partly builds. Friedman argues that there are narrow boundaries to the actions that a government should consider in a market economy. Beyond those limits, he suggests, the government should never interfere with the market mechanism and the freedom of individual citizens.

DIGGING UP THE ROOTS: THE ECONOMIC DETERMINANTS OF SOCIAL PROBLEMS

David M. Gordon

This short essay provides a basic summary of the forces that, in the radical view, frame our present social problems. While not relying on the formal language of the radical approach to the analysis of history, it nonetheless represents a direct application of that methodology.

The article is reprinted almost in its entirety from *The Social Welfare Forum, 1974.*

Gordon teaches economics in the Graduate Faculty of the New School for Social Research.

It is my belief that we cannot fully understand social problems by analyzing them as discrete, isolated phenomena. We must view them as symptoms of some common institutional causes, as functions of systemic environmental forces. The most important of these forces, in my view, are economic.

This argument builds upon four basic hypotheses:

1. Our economy, dominated by large corporations and the laws of private property, speeds through time propelled by some underlying and enduring behavioral principles, by some fundamental laws of motion.
2. As it races along, the economy also creates and shapes institutions with characteristic forms, functions, and biases.
3. Taken together, these driving forces and induced institutions constitute the dominant (or determining) causes of most of the serious individual and social problems that we see around us.[1]

4. Consequently, those serious individual and social problems cannot themselves be eradicated or more than marginally resolved without fundamental changes in our dominant economic forces and institutions.

Our Historical Legacies

Our historical perspectives are almost always contained, as the English historian E. P. Thompson puts it, within our living memories of time past.[2] Our specific memories fade quickly. On the other side of the historical dissolve, there stands the past, a lifeless, static concept full of myth, distortion, and elision. Facing this lifeless, monumental concept of the past, we tend to assume that most of our present circumstances have always pertained; everyone has always lived as we currently live; everyone has always faced the same kinds of problems we currently endure.

We should begin to penetrate the fog obscuring our historical experiences as people in a social world. When we do so, we will begin to appreciate the historical contingency of our present social arrangements. Many of the institutions and ideologies we take for granted actually emerged in the relatively recent past as companions to the rise of modern economic systems. A quick review of these corollaries will help clarify the origins and therefore also the functions of many of our economic institutions.

1. The very dominance of economic forces itself emerged with the rise of capitalism as an economic mode. Accumulation of capital, as either a private or a social goal, had never before been so eagerly sought. Our determination to base most of our social judgments upon the ruthless economic criteria of

Source: From *The Social Welfare Forum, 1974,* official proceedings of the 101st Annual Forum, National Conference on Social Welfare. Copyright © 1975 National Conference on Social Welfare, published by Columbia University Press 1975. Reprinted with permission of Columbia University Press.

[1] This hypothesis is not equivalent to a rigid economic determinist view that everything in society is uniquely and singularly defined by economic structures. The hypothesis suggests that economic structures and forces constitute such important sources of social problems that they must be considered as more important than other sources.

[2] See E. P. Thompson, *The Making of the English Working Class* (New York: Vintage Books, 1967).

"efficiency" in order to sustain growth became the legacy of those pioneering grand acquisitors who launched the thousand accumulating ships.[3]

2. Individualism also grew hand in hand with the spread of economic markets. In order to appreciate the gains available through the market exchange of equivalents, individuals had to learn to identify with the goods or income they were able to obtain through market transactions. In order for employers to be able to expand their wealth through factory production, they had to be able to draw on pools of workers who themselves appeared as "wage-laborers," severed from the communal economic base upon which they had formally relied, "free" to support themselves by selling their power to work as individuals in the labor market.[4] Mark Kennedy writes:

> Early or late, individualism . . . came eventually to find social expression . . . in economy as new institutions of private property, the market, entrepreneurship, rational accounting, and the redivision of labor along new social lines. . . . On every side, with each new expression of individualism, the society based earlier on the ethic of shared responsibility for individual conduct vanished from the scene. When fealty was for sale, altruism was dead. . . .[5]

3. The forward march of economic forces into the nineteenth century began increasingly to destroy or recast the community institutions upon which societies had formerly been built. Large industrial cities forged a greater separation between the locations of work and residence. Encouraged to become "mobile" factors of production, workers were induced, or forced, by shifting economic incentives to abandon their ties with the place and spirit of their abiding social relationships. This transition from *Gemeinschaft* to *Gesellschaft*, as the sociologists put it, reinforced the disintegration of communities' concerns for the welfare of every citizen.[6] People were left to wander in the big cities by themselves.

4. With the spread of the factory system, peoples' lives changed dramatically. Industrial technology caused even more fragmentation and specialization of work. Workers lost control over their conditions of work and the distribution of their products. Workers became less and less capable of doing general work and performing managerial tasks as they became more and more dexterous at repetitive, minute, specialized tasks. As an early English textile manufacturer reflected with some relief in 1806, workers "trained up in a manufactory are not likely to set up for themselves." [7]

5. With the growth of an extended and interdependent economic system which at least theoretically improved producers' access to consumers, employers faced the problem of legitimizing their own control over the profits from market exchange. Recent studies suggest that the factory system arose not so much because new inventions demanded it but because employers saw it as the best way of securing for themselves a role in production. As the Harvard economist Stephen Marglin says,

> The capitalist division of labor . . . was the result of a search not for a technologically superior organization of work, but for an organization which gave to the entrepreneur an essential role in the production process, as integrator of the separate efforts of his workers into a marketable product.[8]

The eminent economic historian N. S. B. Gras agrees:

> [The factory] was purely for purposes of discipline, so that workers could be effectively controlled, under the supervision of foremen, under

---

[3] In other words, the capitalist epoch witnesses for the first time in history an historical dynamic in which the intrinsic desire of property owners to expand their wealth for the sake of expanding their wealth dominates social structures and social change. In the feudal period, there were propertied classes, but the causes and consequences of their mode of property accumulation were different. On these issues, see Etiénne Balibar, "The Basic Concepts of Historical Materialism," in Louis Althusser and Etiénne Balibar, *Reading Capital* (New York: Pantheon Books, 1970), pp. 199–308.

[4] The enclosure movements in England, for instance, helped create such pools of wage laborers who, having lost their own property, were "free" to work in order to survive.

[5] Mark Kennedy, "Beyond Incrimination," *Catalyst,* Summer 1970, pp. 6–7.

[6] See Raymond Williams, *The Country and the City* (New York: Oxford University Press, 1973), for a sensitive discussion of these developments, particularly in England.

[7] Quoted in Stephen A. Marglin, "Long, Long Time on the Way" (Cambridge, Mass.: Harvard University, 1973; mimeographed), pp. 1–21.

[8] Stephen A. Marglin, "What Do Bosses Do?" *Review of Radical Political Economics,* Summer 1974, p. 62.

one roof or within a narrow compass. They could be started to work at sunrise and kept going to sunset. . . .[9]

And once that mode of hierarchy acquired strong roots, its trees and branches proliferated. Bureaucracies and structured job ladders grew naturally as extensions of these first basic principles of specialization to guarantee legitimacy and control.

6. Markets spread, and the factory brought specialization of work tasks. The two developments together exposed workers for the first time to a new kind of economic insecurity. There had always been droughts and blights — and thus insecurity borne of natural disasters. Now workers, more and more exclusively dependent on wages for survival, were finding themselves without work as a result of the anarchic growth and contraction of production itself. This insecurity brought new dangers because workers had neither their traditional communities nor varied truck farming and household manufacture to sustain them through periods of unemployment. Norman Ware makes this point in discussing the factory's invasion of the American boot and shoe industry in the middle of the nineteenth century:

> The panic of 1837 was less distressing in its results for the Lynn shoemakers than it would have been at a later period because of the still primitive nature of the industrial situations. With a garden, a pig, and some fishing tackle the shoemaker "could bid defiance to financial tempests." . . .[10]

"From 1855, or a little later," Ware continues, "the workmen began to leave the little shops to work in the factories, and in a few years vacant 'ten-footers' were seen all over Lynn." [11] They had left their small plots for the factory cities where, with each new depression, as Leon S. Marshall puts it, "bread lines were common in every large city." [12] Economic insecurity became the source of a totally new kind of dependence.

[9] Quoted in Harry Braverman, *Labor and Monopoly Capital* (New York: Monthly Review Press, 1974).

[10] Norman Ware, *The Industrial Worker, 1840–1860* (New York: Quadrangle Books, 1964), p. 40.

[11] *Ibid.*, p. 46.

[12] Leon S. Marshall, "The English and American Industrial City of the Nineteenth Century," in Alexander Callow, ed., *American Urban History* (New York: Oxford University Press, 1969), p. 152.

The Current Forces and Institutions

Once reminded of some important elements of our history, we can better understand the basic economic forces and institutions shaping the present:

1. The basic directions in which our society travels are charted at the pinnacles of corporate skyscrapers. The corporate expansions and contractions wag the tail of the national economy. After the wave of mergers in the 1960s the 200 largest manufacturing corporations controlled 60 percent of all manufacturing assets, and their share continues to grow.[13] Whatever their executives may say about "corporate responsibility," private profits and capital accumulation remain their gospel.

2. For those large corporations to be able to grow continually, two conditions must be satisfied. The markets in which they sell their commodities must become more and more extensive, and/or new commodities must be brought onto the market, inducing people to satisfy new needs by purchasing those commodities.

The first condition has been continuously fulfilled by the growth of the world market and the dramatic emergence of the multinational corporation. And with this extension of the world market, the multinational corporations have begun to transcend their reliance on the support of any individual nation state. We are losing our leverage on the corporations; if we seek to apply pressure on them to increase wages or equalize opportunities, they can simply shift their resources to another country.

The second condition is being continuously fulfilled by the creation of new products and the marketing of new services. More and more food is processed, for instance, exposing to market dominance the activities of cooking and preparing at home. And as these products and services are more and more dominated by the calculus of exchange, we lose more and more of our independence. Those without the cash to buy the goods and services are left behind completely.

3. As corporations spread their activities and augment their power, the private economy contributes to increasingly divergent or uneven development. Large corporations, with huge stocks of capital to invest, want to avoid unnecessary risks. They naturally choose to pour their money into safe invest-

[13] See the compilations in Ralph Andreano, ed., *Supercorporation, Superconcentration* (Andover, Mass.: Warner Publications, 1973).

ments. As Stanford economist John G. Gurley writes, "it is almost always most profitable, from a private business point of view, to build on the best." [14] And "building on the best" — locating a factory near a skilled labor force, making loans to people who are economically secure — ensures efficiency at the cost of inequality. As Gurley concludes, "capitalist development, even when most successful, is always a trickle-down development." [15]

Despite all the apparent government efforts to apply more progressive tax schemes, to offset privately generated inequalities, the tendencies toward uneven development have prevailed. In the early 1950s, the wealthiest one percent of American families controlled about 25 percent of aggregate personal wealth.[16] By the early 1960s, their share had increased to over 30 percent.[17]

4. The quest for profits leads to automation and technological change. Again the corporations build on the best, developing sectors with already high productivity and high wages. Wage differentials widen between the advanced and backward sectors. The specialization and fragmentation of work tasks intensify. Strong tendencies toward further unemployment also emerge, tendencies which have been overcome in this country since the Second World War only by the huge military budget, the lengthening of the average number of years which children spend in school, and earlier retirement for many older workers. Despite our affluence, nonetheless, the threat of insecurity and unemployment remains. The private sector does not consider full employment as one of its principal responsibilities.

5. All these tendencies together have created some important structural divisions in our economy. The core industries, dominated by the largest corporations, become more and more concentrated, profitable, capital-intensive, and technologically advanced. The peripheral industries remain competitive and unstable, with small firms, lower profits, lower wages, low skill requirements, and backward

technology. The firms in the core industries can begin, as Robert Averitt puts it, "to act upon the assumption that they have eternal life." [18] The small firms in the peripheral industries face the hell and damnation of perpetual market instability and potential bankruptcy.

Along with these industrial divisions have arisen some fundamental structural differences between labor markets. In the "primary labor market," workers enjoy stable jobs, secure and sheltered incomes, higher wages, and more favorable working conditions. In the "secondary labor market," workers are fated to insecure jobs, lower wages, almost no promotion or training opportunities, the recurrent threat of dismissal, and the prevailing reality of miserable working conditions. These structural differences between labor markets do not grow out of the differences in skills or attitudes among groups of workers, but emerge as relatively simple functions of the more fundamental differences between firms and industries.

[The original article proceeds with an analysis of a variety of social problems, which parallels the subsequent chapters in this reader. In the case of each of these problems, the article argues that the forces outlined in the preceding section lie at the roots of that problem. The article then turns to a discussion of the implications of that analysis.]

Preconditions for Digging Up the Roots

The economic roots of our social problems are obviously basic. In order to conceive of a set of economic preconditions that would help overcome these problems instead of creating and reinforcing them, we must specify an economy whose tendencies move in very different directions from our own.

• Basic decisions about investment and accumulation must be based upon social need rather than upon the private profit calculation of corporate executives.

• One of the basic social priorities that dominate our investment decisions must emanate from a determination to guarantee a truly decent standard of living for everyone.

• We must seek to promote an even development among classes and regions, refusing to tolerate enduring inequalities.

[14] John G. Gurley, "Capitalist and Maoist Economic Development," in Mark Selden, ed., *America's Asia* (New York: Vintage Books, 1971), p. 331.

[15] *Ibid.*

[16] See Robert Lampman, *The Share of Top Wealth-Holders in National Wealth* (New York: National Bureau of Economic Research, 1962).

[17] See Dorothy S. Projector and Gertrude S. Weiss, *Survey of Financial Characteristics of Consumers* (Washington, D.C.: Federal Reserve Board, 1966).

[18] Robert Averitt, *The Dual Economy* (New York: W. W. Norton & Co., 1968), p. 7.

• We must seek to organize work in ways that erode hierarchies of authority and that increase the variety and satisfaction for workers on their jobs.

• Through all of these tendencies, and in addition to them, we must seek wherever possible to promote equalities of outcomes, rather than opportunities, among people in their working and living experiences.

Defusing Resistance

Ah, but that's impossible! Quit being utopian! Start getting practical!

To these probable responses two comments seem necessary.

First, if we do not seek to establish an economic structure which promotes these tendencies, I do not believe we can seriously expect to solve any of our major social problems. Each of these tendencies represents, in my view, a necessary precondition for solving our social problems. No one development by itself would be sufficient. We must start moving in each of those directions if any one of them is to help.

Second, these suggestions are not utopian. We are capable of organizing societies which satisfy these principles. Our habituated resistance to these objectives is itself founded on popular myths:

1. Many would reply that we must keep growing as rapidly as possible in order to realize a decent standard of living for those who are poor. But if we divided our present national income equally, an average family of four would receive about $20,000 a year.[19] The goods are certainly there; it is a question of how we choose to distribute them.

2. Many would reply that we need inequalities in income in order to provide incentives for people to produce the goods we need. Those assertions presume our current institutions and organization of work. But if community institutions recovered some of their former strength and jobs became more rewarding, nonmonetary incentives could certainly, in the long run, grow stronger and stronger.[20]

---

[19] The average family of four would receive $20,000 if the more than $1 trillion in national income were divided equally among all 200 million people.

[20] See the discussion in Carl Riskin, "Work Incentives in China," *Working Papers*, Winter 1974.

3. Many would reply that we must retain our organization of work, with all its specialization and fragmentation, to be able to sustain our levels of output. If we develop less specialized technologies or more varied job structures, we will have to sacrifice our standard of living. But every recent study of job design has found that workers would produce more, not less, if their job assignments were more varied, flexible, and enriched. There is every empirical indication that our economy would make more efficient use of our resources, not less, if we began to move away from our present mode of hierarchical, specialized, and fragmented work.[21]

4. Many would reply that we must accept the present scale of our cities, factories, and bureaucracies because they provide us with "economies of scale." The economic objectives I have outlined, they say, would require organizing society around smaller economic and political units, and that would force us to sacrifice efficiency. Once again, evidence suggests that this conventional view is wrong. Every available study suggests that our cities, our plants, our farms, and our bureaucracies do not need to be anywhere nearly as large as they are in order to make best use of our resources. They have developed to their present size largely in order to permit better control of economic decisions by the dominant corporations.

But We Are Few and the Tasks Are Great

Many have internalized a final kind of objection to these suggestions. We are few, and the tasks of fundamentally restructuring our society are immense. How can we possibly begin to move in those directions?

We must begin to see ourselves — all of us — as victims of the same institutions, the same economic structures, the same economic laws of motion. Without that shift in perspective, we become accomplices in the perpetuation of our immediate problems.

Many people are rebelling against our institutions. If we care about solving our most pressing social problems, we should join them.

---

[21] See the summary evidence in Paul Blumberg, *Industrial Democracy* (New York: Schocken Books, 1969).

THE MARXIAN PARADIGM

Stephen Hymer and Frank Roosevelt

This brief excerpt from a longer piece provides a glimpse of the fundamental tenets of the Marxian paradigm upon which most radicals draw in their critique of capitalism. It argues that orthodox social scientists commit a basic error in their analyses of capitalist societies by mistaking the apparent freedom-of-exchange relationships for the more basic relationships of these societies. These more basic social relationships, Hymer and Roosevelt argue, derive from the authoritarian character of capitalist control over the process of production.

This excerpt comes from a longer contribution to a symposium on Assar Lindback's book, *The Economics of the New Left.* The symposium appeared in the *Quarterly Journal of Economics.*

Stephen Hymer, at the time a professor of economics in the Graduate Faculty of The New School for Social Research, was tragically killed in an automobile accident in 1974. Frank Roosevelt, formerly a graduate student in economics at The New School, now teaches economics at Vassar College.

The Marxian system begins with the process of production. In every mode of production, labor and means of production are united to produce output. But it is the specific manner in which this union is accomplished that distinguishes the different socio-economic formations from one another. Under capitalism they are united through the wage-labor contract under which the laborer alienates his labor power and agrees to submit to the control of the capitalist or his representative during the process of production.

In the market the laborer was a "free agent" who owned his own labor power and dealt with the capitalist on equivalent footing in pursuit of his own private interest. The bargain completed, however, he finds himself no longer free or equal or a property owner or an individual but a subordinate in an authoritarian hierarchy working with and on materials he does not own in a collective process of production.

The dualism between freedom in the marketplace and authoritarianism in the workplace is the essential characteristic of capitalist society. If the marketplace furnishes the economist with the model to justify capitalism in terms of freedom, equality, possession, and individualism, the actual conditions of work furnish the New Left with the critique of capitalism (with its nonfreedom and nonequality) as well as the clues to a future society (with a nonpossessive and nonindividualistic organization of work).

When the worker sells his labor, he in effect surrenders his freedom; but this does not mean that he passively accepts capitalist production. The laborer's daily work is involuntary, and so each day involves a struggle between capital and laborer. The capitalist tries to get the worker to do something he or she does not want to do; the worker tries to resist doing it. In Volume I of *Capital,* Marx analyzes the capitalist system of production in terms of this constant struggle, showing the forms of resistance put up by the workers and the types of pressure (e.g., organization, introduction of machinery, social legislation) devised by the capitalist to maintain control over the workers' labor time. These problems, which lie outside the market sphere, are hardly touched on at all in the modern economics curriculum. Although detailed and explicit discussion of them can be found in the literature of corporate organization, personal relations, industrial sociology, and psychology, they are always approached from the point of view of control rather than resistance. One of the tasks of radical social scientists is to turn this literature on its head and develop counter-organization theories in continuation of Marx's work.

How does the market fit into this? In the market numerous buyers and sellers confront each other under more or less competitive conditions and exchange commodities according to the laws of supply and demand. This aspect has been extensively ana-

Source: "Comment," by Stephen Hymer and Frank Roosevelt, from "Symposium: Economics of the New Left," *Quarterly Journal of Economics* LXXXVI, November 1972. Reprinted with permission.

lyzed by economists. But they have neglected a second aspect: the constraints placed on the market outcomes by the need to maintain the capitalist nature of production. Volume II of *Capital* attempts to deal with this problem by showing how the circular flow of goods and money reproduces the capital-labor relation — i.e., results in a distribution of income and wealth such that the capitalists end up again owning the means of production and the laborers end up again having to sell their labor in order to live. The wage must be sufficiently high to maintain the laborer but not high enough to allow him to become a capitalist. For example, if wages rise and eat into profits, investment dries up, growth slows down and unemployment results. This exerts a downward pressure on wage demands, restores the rate of profit, and allows the capitalist system to go on.

When we examine the interconnections between markets and production, it becomes clear that we cannot restrict our methodology to the economic plane alone — consideration must be given to the political and ideological planes as well. It is only by breaking the ties that bind circulation and production together that economists can ignore the relations between economic and political power.

Since capitalism requires unequal relations of dominance and subordination in production, the game of the market must be a loaded game. The players begin with unequal endowments of wealth and education and at the end of play find themselves in much the same relative position as before. Of course a certain degree of mobility exists: a small number of people change ranks; but in cycle after cycle over the last two hundred years, the pyramid has remained a pyramid. In each round the top 10 percent of the population gets from 30 to 40 percent of the take, the bottom two thirds get only one third. The players are then ready to play again in production — the poor to work, the middle to manage, the rich to accumulate. . . .

Much force was needed to bring this system into being. Though economists have generally overlooked its brutal origins during the period of primitive accumulation in the sixteenth and seventeenth centuries, we can today see in the underdeveloped countries a replay of the violence of modernization. Pacification of the countryside, the police state, the pass system are the seeds and fertilization from which a free market is growing in the "backward" areas.

Once free markets are established, force takes on more respectable forms. One of these respectable forms is the education system where people are trained to accept competition, discipline, authoritarianism, rigid schedules in preparation for life in capitalist production. This form of coercive socialization has been of particular interest to the New Left and is being extensively investigated by radical economists using the tools of class analysis rather than the market methodology of human capital.

Another respectable form of coercion is the propagation of ideologies that disguise the nature of human relations in our society. In our view, economics is one of the most important of these ideologies. By concentrating on market relations that mask the real nature of the transaction between capital and labor, economists have mystified the economic processes in our society and hindered the development of analytical tools for going beyond them.

While economists have focused on the relation between things — e.g., the price of apples in terms of bananas — Marx has pierced the veil of the market to discover its connection to the relations between people. Having started from an analysis of production in Volume I of *Capital* and traced through its connection with circulation in Volume II, he returns in Volume III to the various forms capital assumes on the surface of society (in the actions of different capitals upon one another, in competition) and in the ordinary consciousness of the agents of production. In production, the capitalist is acutely conscious of the relation between himself and the laborer — but in circulation he is more concerned with his competitive relations with other capitalists. This concern leads to various illusions about the nature of the economy that serve in part to maintain the system by confusing the issues and in part to undermine the system by rendering it unable to handle continued economic progress. We cannot here describe these illusions in detail. We can only mention in passing the basic bias in the market relation in exaggerating the role of capitalist cunning and entrepreneurship and downgrading the importance of labor cooperation in advancing civilization. It is because of this set of blinders, according to Marx, that "The capitalist mode of production is generally, despite all its niggardliness, altogether too prodigal with its human material, just as, conversely, thanks to its method of distribution of products through commerce and manner of competition, it is very prodigal with its material means, and loses for society what it gains for the individual capitalist." [1] . . .

The Marxian paradigm offers an alternative perspective [to orthodox economics] and produces a different set of answers. It shows that capitalism, because it is based on private property and promotes

an individualist point of view, places strict limits on how much government interference it will tolerate. It argues that as the system advances, the contradiction between its social nature and its private organization becomes increasingly intense. And it recommends that we supersede the mode of production based on wage labor by striving consciously to control our own everyday life in production as well as in consumption.

[1] *Capital,* Vol. III (New York: International Publishers, 1967), pp. 86–87.

THE RADICAL THEORY OF THE STATE

Paul Sweezy

This selection from Sweezy's book, *The Theory of Capitalist Development,* expounds the basic radical view of the State and its role in class society. The excerpt comes from a longer chapter on the State in the revised version of Sweezy's book, which was originally published in 1942. In contrast to liberal views, the radical theory argues that the State serves the interest of the dominant class in society. It does this both by providing services directly to members of that class and by helping stabilize the institutional system within which that class flourishes.

Sweezy has been a leading Marxist in the United States since the 1930s, when he received his Ph.D. in economics from Harvard. He has written widely, coauthored *Monopoly Capital* (with Paul Baran), and coedits the radical journal *The Monthly Review.*

The Primary Function of the State

There is a tendency on the part of modern liberal theorists to interpret the state as an institution established in the interests of society as a whole for the purpose of mediating and reconciling the antagonisms to which social existence inevitably gives rise. This is a theory which avoids the pitfalls of political metaphysics and which serves to integrate in

Source: Reprinted by permission of Monthly Review Press, 116 W. 14th Street, New York, N.Y. Copyright © 1942 by Paul M. Sweezy.

a tolerably satisfactory fashion a considerable body of observed fact. It contains, however, one basic shortcoming, the recognition of which leads to a theory essentially Marxian in its orientation. A critique of what may be called the class-mediation conception of the state is, therefore, perhaps the best way of introducing the Marxian theory.[1]

The class-mediation theory assumes, usually implicitly, that the underlying class structure, or what comes to the same thing, the system of property relations is an immutable datum, in this respect like the order of nature itself. It then proceeds to ask what arrangements the various classes will make to get along with each other, and finds that an institution for mediating their conflicting interests is the logical and necessary answer. To this institution powers for maintaining order and settling quarrels are granted. In the real world what is called the

[1] Among the most important Marxist writings on the state the following may be mentioned: Engels, *The Origin of the Family, Private Property and the State,* particularly Ch. IX; Lenin, *The State and Revolution;* Rosa Luxemburg, "Sozialreform oder Revolution?" *Gesammelte Werke,* Vol. III. An English translation of the latter work is available (*Reform or Revolution?,* Three Arrows Press, N.Y., 1937), but it is unfortunately not a very satisfactory one. A reasonably adequate survey of a large body of Marxist literature on the state is contained in S. H. M. Chang, *The Marxian Theory of the State* (1931).

state is identified as the counterpart of this theoretical construction.

The weakness of this theory is not difficult to discover. It lies in the assumption of an immutable and, so to speak, self-maintained class structure of society. The superficiality of this assumption is indicated by the most cursory study of history.[2] The fact is that many forms of property relations with their concomitant class structures have come and gone in the past, and there is no reason to assume that they will not continue to do so in the future. The class structure of society is no part of the natural order of things; it is the product of past social development, and it will change in the course of future social development.

Once this is recognized it becomes clear that the liberal theory goes wrong in the manner in which it initially poses the problem. We cannot ask: Given a certain class structure, how will the various classes, with their divergent and often conflicting interests, manage to get along together? We must ask: How did a particular class structure come into being and by what means is its continued existence guaranteed? As soon as an attempt is made to answer this question, it appears that the state has a function in society which is prior to and more fundamental than any which present-day liberals attribute to it. Let us examine this more closely.

A given set of property relations serves to define and demarcate the class structure of society. From any set of property relations one class or classes (the owners) reap material advantages; other classes (the owned and the non-owners) suffer material disadvantages. A special institution capable and willing to use force to whatever degree is required is an essential to the maintenance of such a set of property relations. Investigation shows that the state possesses this characteristic to the fullest degree, and that no other institution is or can be allowed to compete with it in this respect. This is usually expressed by saying that the state, and the state alone, exercises sovereignty over all those subject to its jurisdiction. It is, therefore, not difficult to identify the state as the guarantor of a given set of property relations.

If now we ask where the state comes from, the answer is that it is the product of a long and arduous struggle in which the class which occupies what is for the time the key positions in the process of production gets the upper hand over its rivals and fashions a state which will enforce that set of property relations which is in its own interest. In other words any particular state is the child of the class or classes in society which benefit from the particular set of property relations which it is the state's obligation to enforce. A moment's reflection will carry the conviction that it could hardly be otherwise. As soon as we have dropped the historically untenable assumption that the class structure of society is in some way natural or self-enforcing, it is clear that any other outcome would lack the prerequisites of stability. If the disadvantaged classes were in possession of state power, they would attempt to use it to establish a social order more favorable to their own interests, while a sharing of state power among the various classes would merely shift the locale of conflict to the state itself.

That such conflicts within the state, corresponding to fundamental class struggles outside, have taken place in certain transitional historical periods is not denied. During those long periods, however, when a certain social order enjoys a relatively continuous and stable existence, the state power must be monopolized by the class or classes which are the chief beneficiaries.

As against the class-mediation theory of the state, we have here the underlying idea of what has been called the class-domination theory. The former takes the existence of a certain class structure for granted and sees in the state an institution for reconciling the conflicting interests of the various classes; the latter, on the other hand, recognizes that classes are the product of historical development and sees in the state an instrument in the hands of the ruling classes for enforcing and guaranteeing the stability of the class structure itself.

It is important to realize that, so far as capitalist society is concerned, "class domination" and "the protection of private property" are virtually synonymous expressions. Hence when we say with Engels that the highest purpose of the state is the protection of private property,[3] we are also saying that the state is an instrument of class domination. This is doubtless insufficiently realized by critics of the

---

[2] Many theorists recognize this up to a point, but they believe that what was true of past societies is not true of modern society. In other words, capitalism is regarded as the final end-product of social evolution.

[3] *Origin of the Family, Private Property and the State,* Kerr, ed., p. 130.

Marxian theory who tend to see in the notion of class domination something darker and more sinister than "mere" protection of private property. In other words they tend to look upon class domination as something reprehensible and the protection of private property as something meritorious. Consequently, it does not occur to them to identify the two ideas. Frequently, no doubt, this is because they have in mind not capitalist property, but rather private property as it would be in a simple commodity-producing society where each producer owns and works with his own means of production. Under such conditions there are no classes at all and hence no class domination. Under capitalist relations, however, property has an altogether different significance, and its protection is easily shown to be identical with the preservation of class dominance. Capitalist private property does not consist in things — things exist independently of their ownership — but in a social relation between people. Property confers upon its owners freedom from labor and the disposal over the labor of others, and this is the essence of all social domination whatever form it may assume. It follows that the protection of property is fundamentally the assurance of social domination to owners over non-owners. And this, in turn, is precisely what is meant by class domination, which it is the primary function of the state to uphold.

The recognition that the defense of private property is the first duty of the state is the decisive factor in determining the attitude of genuine Marxist socialism towards the state. "The theory of the Communists," Marx and Engels wrote in the *Communist Manifesto*, "can be summed up in the single sentence: Abolition of private property." Since the state is first and foremost the protector of private property, it follows that the realization of this end cannot be achieved without a head-on collision between the forces of socialism and the state power.[4]

---

[4] The treatment of the relation between the state and property has of necessity been extremely sketchy. In order to avoid misunderstanding, the following note should be added. The idea that the state is an organization for the maintenance of private property was by no means an invention of Marx and Engels. On the contrary, it constituted the cornerstone of the whole previous development of political thought from the breakdown of feudalism and the origins of the modern state. Bodin, Hobbes, Locke, Rousseau, Adam Smith, Kant, and Hegel — to mention but a few outstanding thinkers of the period before Marx — clearly recognized this central function of the state. They believed private property to

The State as an Economic Instrument

The fact that the first concern of the state is to protect the continued existence and stability of a given form of society does not mean that it performs no other functions of economic importance. On the contrary, the state has always been a very significant factor in the functioning of the economy within the framework of the system of property relations which it guarantees. This principle is generally implicitly recognized by Marxist writers whenever they analyse the operation of an actual economic system, but it has received little attention in discussions of the theory of the state. The reason for this is not difficult to discover. The theory of the state has usually been investigated with the problem of transition from one form of society to another in the foreground; in other words, what we have called the primary function of the state has been the subject of analysis. Lenin's *State and Revolution* — the title clearly indicates the center of interest — set a precedent which has been widely followed. Consequently, the theory of the state as an economic instrument has been neglected, though evidently for our purposes it is necessary to have some idea of the essentials of Marx's thinking on the subject.

Fortunately Marx, in his chapter on the length of the working day,[5] provides a compact and lucid analysis of the role of the state in relation to one very important problem of capitalist economy. By examining this chapter in some detail we can deduce the guiding principles of Marxist teaching on the role of the state within the framework of capitalist property relations.

The rate of surplus value, one of the key variables in Marx's system of theoretical economics, depends

---

be the necessary condition for the full development of human potentialities, the *sine qua non* of genuine freedom. Marx and Engels added that freedom based on private property is freedom for an exploiting class, and that freedom for *all* presupposes the abolition of private property, that is to say the achievement of a classless society. Nevertheless, Marx and Engels did not forget that the realization of a classless society (abolition of private property) is possible only on the basis of certain definite historical conditions; without the enormous increase in the productivity of labor which capitalism had brought about, a classless society would be no more than an empty Utopia.

[5] *Capital* I, Chapter x. [Ed.: Sweezy's citations refer to the three-volume edition of *Capital* published by Charles Kerr and Company, Chicago, 1933.]

on three factors: the productivity of labor, the length of the working day and prevailing subsistence standards. It is therefore a matter of importance to discover the determinants of the length of the working day. This is clearly not a question of economic law in any narrow sense. As Marx put it,

> Apart from extremely elastic bounds, the nature of exchange of commodities itself imposes no limits to the working day, no limit to surplus labor. The capitalist maintains his rights as a purchaser when he tries to make the working day as long as possible.... On the other hand ... the laborer maintains his right as a seller when he wishes to reduce the working day to one of definite normal duration. There is here, therefore, an antinomy, right against right, both equally bearing the seal of the law of exchanges. Between equal rights force decides. Hence it is that in the history of capitalist production, the determination of what is a working day presents itself as the result of a struggle, a struggle between collective capital, i.e. the class of capitalists, and collective labor, i.e. the working class.[6]

After describing certain forms, both pre-capitalist and capitalist, of exploitation involving the duration of the working day, Marx examines "The Struggle for a Normal Working Day" in the historical development of English capitalism. The first phase of this struggle resulted in "Compulsory Laws for the Extension of the Working Day from the Middle of the 14th to the End of the 17th Century."[7] Employers, straining to create a trained and disciplined proletariat out of the available pre-capitalist material, were frequently obliged to resort to the state for assistance. Laws extending the length of the working day were the result. For a long time, however, the extension of the working day was a very slow and gradual process. It was not until the rapid growth of the factory system in the second half of the eighteenth century that there began that process of prolonging hours of work which culminated in the notorious conditions of the early nineteenth century:

> After capital had taken centuries in extending the working day to its normal maximum length, and then beyond this to the limit of the natural day of 12 hours, there followed on the birth of machinism and modern industry in the last

third of the 18th century a violent encroachment like that of an avalanche in its intensity and extent.... As soon as the working class, stunned at first by the noise and turmoil of the new system of production, recovered in some measure its senses its resistance began.[8]

The beginnings of working-class resistance ushered in the second phase of the development: "Compulsory Limitation by Law of the Working Time, The English Factory Acts, 1833 to 1864."[9] In a series of sharp political struggles, the workers were able to wring one concession after another from their opponents. These concessions took the form of laws limiting hours of work for ever wider categories of labor, until by 1860 the principle of limitation of the working day was so firmly established that it could no longer be challenged. Thereafter progress pursued a smoother course.

The limitation of the working day was not simply a question of concessions by the ruling class in the face of a revolutionary threat, though this was undoubtedly the main factor. At least two other considerations of importance have to be taken into account. Marx noted that,

> Apart from the working class movement that daily grew more threatening, the limiting of factory labor was dictated by the same necessity which spread guano over the English fields. The same blind eagerness for plunder that in the one case exhausted the soil had, in the other, torn up by the roots the living forces of the nation.[10]

Moreover, the question of factory legislation entered into the final phase of the struggle for political mastery between the landed aristocracy and the industrial capitalists:

> However much the individual manufacturer might give the rein to his old lust for gain, the spokesmen and political leaders of the manufacturing class ordered a change in front and of speech toward the workpeople. They had entered upon the contest for the repeal of the Corn Laws and needed the workers to help them to victory. They promised, therefore, not only a double-sized loaf of bread, but the enactment of the Ten Hours Bill in the Free Trade millennium ...[11]

---

[6] *Ibid.*, p. 259.
[7] Chapter x, Section 5.

[8] *Capital* i, pp. 304–5.
[9] Chapter x, Section 6.
[10] *Capital* i, pp. 263–4.
[11] *Ibid.*, pp. 308–9.

And after repeal of the Corn Laws had gone through, the workers "found allies in the Tories panting for revenge." [12] Thus factory legislation derived a certain amount of support from both sides to the great struggle over free trade.

Finally Marx concluded his treatment of the working day with the following statement:

> For "protection" against "the serpent of their agonies" the laborers must put their heads together and, as a class, compel the passing of a law, an all-powerful social barrier that shall prevent the very workers from selling, by voluntary contract with capital, themselves and their families into slavery and death. In place of the pompous catalogue of the "inalienable rights of man" comes the modest Magna Charta of a legally limited working day, which shall make clear "when the time which the worker sells is ended, and when his own begins." *Quantum mutatus ab illo!* [13]

What general conclusions can be deduced from Marx's discussion of the working day? The principle of most general bearing was stated by Engels. Answering the charge that historical materialism neglects the political element in historical change, Engels cited the chapter on the working day "where legislation, which is surely a political act, has such a trenchant effect" and concluded that "force (that is, state power) is also an economic power" and hence is by no means excluded from the causal factors in historical change.[14] Once this has been established, it is necessary to ask under what circumstances and in whose interest the economic power of the state will be brought into action. On both points the analysis of the working day is instructive.

First, the state power is invoked to solve problems which are posed by the economic development of the particular form of society under consideration, in this case capitalism. In the earlier period a shortage of labor power, in the later period over-exploitation of the laboring population were the subjects of state action. In each case the solution of the problem required state intervention. Many familiar examples of a similar character readily come to mind.

Second, we should naturally expect that the state power under capitalism would be used first and foremost in the interests of the capitalist class since the state is dedicated to the preservation of the structure of capitalism and must therefore be staffed by those who fully accept the postulates and objectives of this form of society. This is unquestionably true, but it is not inconsistent to say that state action may run counter to the immediate economic interests of some or even all of the capitalists provided only that the overriding aim of preserving the system intact is promoted. The legal limitation of the working day is a classic example of state action of this sort. The intensity of class antagonism engendered by over-exploitation of the labor force was such that it became imperative for the capitalist class to make concessions even at the cost of immediate economic advantages.[15] For the sake of preserving domestic peace and tranquility, blunting the edge of class antagonisms, and ultimately avoiding the dangers of violent revolution, the capitalist class is always prepared to make concessions through the medium of state action. It may, of course, happen that the occasion for the concession is an actual materialization of the threat of revolution.[16] In this case their purpose is to restore peace and order so that production and accumulation can once again go forward uninterruptedly.

Let us summarize the principles underlying the use of the state as an economic instrument within the framework of capitalism. In the first place, the state comes into action in the economic sphere in order to solve problems which are posed by the development of capitalism. In the second place, where the interests of the capitalist class are concerned, there is a strong predisposition to use the state power freely. And, finally, the state may be used to make concessions to the working class provided that the consequences of not doing so are sufficiently dangerous to the stability and functioning of the system as a whole.

---

[12] *Ibid.*, p. 311.

[13] *Ibid.*, p. 330.

[14] Letter from Engels to Conrad Schmidt, 27 October 1890. *Selected Correspondence,* p. 484.

[15] This example makes clear the concession character of state action favoring the working class, since it could not possibly be maintained that the workers had a share in state power in England at the time the main factory acts were passed. In this connection it is sufficient to recall that the Reform Act of 1832 contained high property qualifications for voting and it was not until 1867 that the franchise was next extended. By this time the most important victories in the struggle for factory legislation had already been won.

[16] For example, Marx remarked that in France, "the February [1848] revolution was necessary to bring into the world the 12 hours' law." *Capital* I, p. 328.

EQUALITY AND EFFICIENCY: THE BIG TRADEOFF

Arthur M. Okun

Arthur Okun develops in this selection a clear statement of the liberal view of social problems. He argues that compromise is inevitable in societies that seek to blend capitalism and democracy. Capitalism must be preserved, Okun says, to guarantee that "self-interest — even 'greed' — is harnessed to serve social purposes." But capitalism tends to create inequalities, he admits, and some suffer absolute deprivation. So he suggests that the pursuit of equality is also necessary — and therefore the messy task of compromise. With that kind of compromise, Okun seeks a place in the sun for liberals between the rigorous adherence to free-market capitalism advocated by conservatives and the systemic attacks on capitalism levied by radicals. Can the compromises work? Okun argues that they can. Economic misery and deprivation are not inevitable, he suggests; we "can essentially end poverty in our affluent society." While we can never finally evade the conflict between equality and efficiency, Okun admits, he argues that we can "put some rationality into equality and some humanity into efficiency."

This essay was written for *The New York Times Magazine* with the title "Equal Rights but Unequal Incomes." It is based on Okun's book, *Equality and Efficiency — The Big Tradeoff,* and most of its themes are further developed in that work.

Okun has been one of the leading liberal economic advisers to the U.S. Government for more than a decade. He served as Chairman of the Council of Economic Advisers and is currently a Senior Fellow at the Brookings Institution in Washington, D.C.

We have a split-level society — one of equal rights but unequal incomes. Our laws bestow upon us the rights to obtain equal justice, to exercise freedom of speech and religion, to vote, to take a spouse and procreate, to be free in our persons in the sense of immunity from enslavement, to leave America if we want, to benefit from public services such as the police and sanitation departments and the schools. These rights are distributed equally and free of charge, not on the basis of one's ability, education,

Source: *The New York Times Magazine,* July 4, 1976. © 1976 by The New York Times Company. Reprinted by permission.

income or looks. They may not even be bought or sold for money. They confer on Americans membership in a social and political club in which no one is more equal than anyone else.

But the economic club operates under entirely different rules, with rewards and penalties that necessarily generate unequal incomes. In the pursuit of efficiency and material progress, our economic institutions prod us to outdo our neighbors and insist that we must succeed — or suffer. The rewards and penalties of the marketplace create such glaring disparities that the rich can feed their pets better than the poor can feed their children. Thus the society is marked and marred by the conflict between equality and efficiency, between the principles of democracy and the practices of capitalism.

Yet I believe that, for all its faults, the mixed system — equal rights and unequal incomes — reflects a sensible willingness to compromise rather than a hypocritical double standard. If we understand our split-level structure and use that understanding to make the American economic system more humane, democratic capitalism can have a bright future.

Our economic rules are meant to encourage effort and channel it into socially productive activity. In principle, the best-paying jobs are those adding the greatest value to products sold in the marketplace. Pursuing their own choices, workers respond to the signals of what society values most and is willing to pay for. In their search for profits businesses naturally expand the output of an item for which buyers will pay more than the cost of production. It was in 1776, interestingly, that Adam Smith described this incentive system in his theory of the "invisible hand." Through the market, self-interest — even "greed" — is harnessed to serve social purposes in an impersonal and automatic way. Because producers seek profits, they draw resources into those uses for which consumers will pay the most. They have the incentive to make what the consumer wants and to make it in the least costly way. Nobody is obliged to evaluate what is good for the economy; if he merely pursues his own economic self-interest, he will automatically serve the social interest.

This snapshot of the capitalist economy is, of course, heavily retouched and idealized. Over the years, society has found it necessary to treat the blemishes of real-world private enterprise in many ways — regulation and consumer information to guard against the nefarious or careless producer, special rules for "natural monopoly" situations such as telephones and electric power, where competition cannot work, curbs on productive processes that would despoil the environment or jeopardize public health and safety, and provision of public services that, though vital, do not meet the market's test of profitability. And despite these efforts, the system remains blemished by monopoly, misinformation, misplaced costs and benefits, and, recurrently, by that greatest of all inefficiencies, too much unemployment.

Yet the resemblances between the contemporary American economy and the glorified model are more striking than the contrasts. Most products we buy are made in response to the drive for profit, and most markets are sufficiently competitive to offer some genuine choices among brands and sellers. More often than not, growth and success are the result of the consumers' vote of confidence. From the telegraph and the light bulb to the Xerox machine, frozen food and permanent-press sheets and shirts, most innovations that have raised the American standard of living have been the creatures of a profit-oriented market system. Despite the "hidden persuaders" of Madison Avenue, nearly half of newly introduced, advertised products are rejected by the consumer and are removed from the shelves. And for all of this, corporate profits after taxes take about a nickel out of each dollar of our national product, and all the smaller capitalists who own unincorporated businesses, farms and professional practices take roughly another dime.

Many elements contributed to the American saga of economic progress. Our vast continent teemed with unexplored natural resources; our immigrants (apart from our shame of slavery) came as volunteers driven by venturesomeness and ambition; our social environment was not ossified by feudal hierarchies or medieval traditions. We were a wonderful laboratory for an experiment with Smith's free-market system. Politically we opted to conduct that experiment, and it worked.

The result of the system has been a high standard of living for most Americans. A family with an income at the national average of about $14,000 a year today has a command over goods and services that would have put it well into the top 10 percent of the pyramid in 1948; a family with a $7,000 income — half the average — has a living standard matching that of the average family of 1948. Judged purely as a system of productive efficiency, contemporary American capitalism has to get a high grade. It needs a tune-up, and perhaps even an overhaul, but not a trade-in.

Most Americans want that productive efficiency — a large and growing volume of goods and services. That public consensus becomes especially evident during recessions, like the one we've recently experienced, when a temporary setback in our standard of living has caused anguish from Maine to Hawaii. Only in the eyes of an antimaterialistic minority is the quality of American life impaired by the quantity of our goods. Most of us consider ourselves sensible enough to use our purchasing power to improve the quality of our lives. For the majority, living in one's own home (as two-thirds of American families do) with a garden and an air-conditioner is a characteristic of the good life.

Whether we are truly made better off by the production of more big cars, more cigarettes and more whisky is a real question. But who should answer that question? Society should ban the sale of products, like heroin, that pose a clear and present danger. But on matters of taste, society should — as it does — let each family make its own choices. Indeed, to most of us, the right to select the items for our market baskets, out of a reasonable list of choices, is an essential element of personal freedom. So is the right to pick our job. The protection of these freedoms is one of the fringe benefits of the market system, along with its productive efficiency.

Another benefit is the limitation on the power of bureaucracy to use economic sanctions against those who disagree with the Government. As an entry on some of the enemies lists compiled during the Nixon Administration, I shudder to imagine my income and status during that era if the Federal Government had been the only employer. Our present economic system guarantees some supply of dissent and criticism. In our profit-seeking newspapers, Seymour Hersh can expose the excesses of the C.I.A., and Bob Woodward and Carl Bernstein can unlock the mystery of Watergate.

In these various ways, capitalism does have *something* to do with freedom. It is impressive that no nation with a fully centralized economy has ever had a free press or a free election. But the capitalism-and-freedom connection is often grossly oversold as an argument against any humanizing and equalizing reform. In fact, coercion by Government — as well as freedom — is part of the recipe for a private-enterprise economy. It relies on promarket laws to enforce contracts, ban fraud and require observance of keep-off signs on private property. These laws are necessary and sensible, but nonetheless encroach on freedom as much as do many antimarket Government bans and regulations. Moreover, the preservation of freedom does not require the preservation of every present feature of U.S. capitalism. It does not depend on whether the dividing line between socialized and private industries is drawn at highways, airports, airlines or steel. Nor does it depend on tax breaks for real-estate deals and family trusts. And it certainly does not depend — contrary to the rhetoric of the Secretary of the Treasury — on cutting the ratio of Federal spending to G.N.P. below the present 23 percent figure. Clearly, personal freedoms have been scrupulously protected in Scandinavian countries with huge budgets and have been obliterated by Fascist regimes that espoused fiscal prudence and private enterprise.

The big liability on the balance sheet of capitalism is, of course, the lopsided distribution of its income and wealth — invidious, inhumane and unesthetic. Individuals get their incomes by using or selling their property, by employing labor or by selling their labor to other employers. If their property commands high interest and profit rates and if their skills are deemed valuable, then they get high incomes. But if what they have to sell has no ready and eager market, they wind up at the bottom of the income pyramid. And so the top 1 percent of all families get more income than the entire bottom 15 percent. Moreover, because high incomes permit saving and investing, the top 1 percent have accumulated more wealth than the bottom 70 percent.

This imbalance cannot be defended ethically as the outcome of fair races in which the prizes go to those who make the greatest contribution. First, even if the system is functioning competitively and honestly, the races aren't completely fair. Some people get head starts through family advantages while others suffer handicaps that are no fault of their own. Second, successes and failures in the marketplace cannot be equated with individual merit or demerit. The buggy-whip manufacturer who went broke be-

cause of the invention of the automobile had not become less deserving or less productive or less ambitious. Although such penalties may be needed to drive talents and funds away from obsolete products, the results are ethically regrettable. And the successes are the product of a whole social system, not merely the individual's contribution. Henry Ford's mass-produced automobile was a big winner in a country with a high average income, the width of a continent for unimpeded driving, an alert and ambitious work force and a Government that could protect travelers and enforce rules of the road. An Afghan with the same idea might have died penniless.

Finally there is no excuse for inhumane penalties for losers. Whether or not gladiatorial contests were "fair" it was barbaric to feed the losers to the lions. And it is barbaric to starve the losers in the races of an affluent society. Even when the last-place entries do not exert their full effort, impoverishment is not necessarily the most effective way to get them to try harder in the future. We might learn something from primitive hunting societies that gave their slackers an equal share of the catch, but made them eat apart from the rest of the community or gave them a public scolding for goofing off. Or our social rules might draw from our family rules, which only occasionally invoke material rewards and penalties. Indeed, families typically spend more of their time, effort and money on members with physical, mental or emotional handicaps than on those who function well. We don't regard that as an unfair or perverse incentive system. There is an equally strong case for trying to rehabilitate and motivate the losers and even the slackers in the community — although the process is bound to be costly.

In general, the ethical case for unequal incomes is about as weak as the esthetic case for lawn mowers. But a violin won't cut the grass and the principle of equal sharing wouldn't maintain our standard of living. However attractive it might be ethically to establish the principle of one-person, one-income — along with one-person, one-vote and one-person, one-spouse — it would invite economic disaster. If extra income were not offered as an incentive for extra production, then Adam Smith's "invisible hand" would be paralyzed. That means society would need a brand-new set of signals and incentives for work effort and production.

At this point, I see no reliable substitute for the prizes and penalties of the marketplace. Idealistically, altruism looks great; but realistically its demonstrated scope for motivating human behavior is limited. Blind allegiance to the leader or to the state can be an effective motivator, but the consequences are a lot worse than inequality of income. In the absence of some revolution or breakthrough in human motivation and group organization, a commitment to full equality of income would impose the very high price of a less productive and less efficient society. For the vast majority, an equal slice of a shrunken pie would be no bargain. If, for example, full equality of income cost us a generation's worth of economic growth (an optimistic guess, in my judgment), four-fifths of our citizens would be made worse off by that trade. Compared with the alternatives, we are better off living with some economic inequality, although it is ethically unappealing, because it is the most practical route to greater economic benefits for the vast majority.

That verdict does not mean that we must accept all the inequality generated by the market. The distribution of income can be and is adjusted by social action. Our main technique of equalization is a readjustment of incomes away from the well-to-do through progressive taxes and to the poor through "transfer" payments such as Social Security, welfare and food stamps. Federal transfer payments provide more than half of the available incomes of those below the statistical poverty line (currently, a little over $5,000 for a nonfarm family of four) and lift millions more above the line. In trying to promote economic equality, we accept some net cost of inefficiency. When we tax the rich by a dollar to help the poor, the latter cannot get a full dollar's worth of benefits. It costs something to collect taxes, to enforce the laws and to administer the programs of aid. Cheating on taxes and on transfer benefits also imposes a cost. Generous benefit payments to the poor may lead some people to work less. Finally, the rich will save and invest somewhat less when their take-home profits are cut by high taxes.

In short, when we carry money from rich to poor through Government programs, we generally have to use a leaky bucket. We can't expect perfection, although we ought to hold the leaks to a minimum. A 20 percent leakage may be quite tolerable (as well as irreducible in some cases) in view of the humanitarian benefit of the 80 percent that doesn't leak out. Many insidious attacks on transfer benefits really prove only that the programs don't meet a standard of zero leakage — and that is an impossible standard of perfection. Despite the leakages, the tax-transfer reshuffle is the best method of equalization we have.

The leaky bucket can essentially end poverty in our affluent society. When that objective was taken more seriously, the number of people with incomes below the poverty line was reduced from 40 million in 1961 to 24 million in 1969; it has changed little since then. The widespread myth that the poverty problem is intractable comforts those who don't want to share the bill for solving it.

Our most successful antipoverty program is retirement benefits for the aged. Nearly all people retiring at age 65 currently are entitled to Federal pensions that can buy an above-poverty-line market basket. Their benefits are generally far greater than the private annuity their payments of Social Security taxes would have brought. The system produces a huge redistribution from today's young to today's aged, but nobody makes a big deal out of that reshuffle; the young, knowing that their turn will come, do not gripe too much; and the aged cash their Social Security checks without guilt, viewing them as a right they have paid for.

Four million families with heads under age 65 were living on incomes below the poverty line in 1974, and they included 10 million children under 18. For most of this group, unlike the aged, the work disincentive of some programs could spring a huge leak in the bucket. For example, the leakage would be enormous if the Government simply made up the difference between the poverty-line of $5,000 and the actual income of an average-sized poor family. No working member of such a family would continue at his or her miserable job if offered a $5,000 grant with full-time leisure. To preserve work incentives, an efficient system of cash aids must allow poor people to keep a significant fraction of any additional income that they earn from jobs — just as an efficient tax system must let the rich keep a significant part of their high incomes. Designing a sound program is difficult. Should society provide systematic cash support without requiring *some* work effort? If work effort is required, how can it be accompanied by a guarantee of work opportunity, as it logically must be? The most baffling questions concern fatherless families, which include more than half of all poor children. For families headed by mothers — separated, divorced, widowed or never married — would a work requirement deprive the children of maternal care? Would one that exempted mothers with children under school age encourage the creation of more deprived kids? The nasty fact is that society cannot afford to remove the economic penalties that discourage women from getting into dependent positions and that discourage their men from putting them there. But neither can a proud and affluent democratic nation afford to starve the children of broken families.

These problems have no easy solution; but there is plenty of room for improvement over the existing welfare system, which provides neither adequate aid nor adequate work incentives. In particular, the problem of the fatherless family is accentuated by the widespread denial, under the present system, of welfare aid to intact families. According to public-opinion surveys, a majority of Americans would support Federal cash grants to low-income families that preserved work incentives and backed them up with work opportunities. Welfare reform belongs at the top of the nation's agenda for social progress.

While the tax-transfer shuffle requires equality and efficiency, some social reforms promote *both* equality and efficiency. One example is the ending of sexual and racial discrimination in jobs. When, through discrimination, black or female workers are excluded from highly productive jobs for which they are qualified, they are forced, in effect, to function with one of their hands tied behind their backs. That is a source of inefficiency as well as of inequality. Society opted for equal-employment opportunity a decade ago, placing fair play for workers above the right of employers to discriminate. Measured against our hopes, the rate of progress has been disappointing; but measured against where we started, it has been impressive, both in raising incomes and in proving that public action can change private behavior with virtually no expenditure of public funds. The achievements so far have added at least $10 billion a year to our gross national product. An intensified effort to eliminate job discrimination could give us a good-sized bonus in G.N.P. as well as a bonus of pride and justice.

Elimination of the disadvantages of the poor in trying to borrow money could also increase efficiency and equality of both income and opportunity. When low-income groups are deprived of access to funds, society suffers an inefficiency. This disadvantage curbs investment by the poor in businesses and homes; it limits their ability to accept apprenticeship jobs and educate their children. The unequal access to capital contributes to the vast differences in rates of college attendance by income class. Male high-school graduates in the bottom socioeconomic quarter of the population tend to go on to college at a rate that is 25 percentage points lower than the rate for male high-school graduates in the top quarter — even when the graduates compared are of *equal* academic ability. (For female graduates, the figure is 35 percentage points.)

In all fairness banks cannot be asked to take the chances of lending to the poor — it is very risky to take the i.o.u.'s of people who lack the collateral and the income to insure their ability to repay their debts. The Federal Government can and must assume these risks. As an example, it might narrow the huge educational-financing gap by establishing a voluntary social-insurance program that would function in a way that mirrors the present old-age program. Young people from lower-income families could get adequate Federal loans to finance their education, repaying them later with a supplementary tax on their postgraduate incomes.

In general, we should strive for greater equality of opportunity — fairer races. Under the existing system of silver spoons and lead weights, the sons of families in the top fifth of the socioeconomic pyramid have average incomes 75 percent higher than those coming from the bottom fifth. Narrowing that differential is an urgent and feasible objective for a capitalistic democracy.

In our split-level system, money, unfortunately, buys a great many things that are not supposed to be for sale in a democracy. Whenever money buys better legal representation for the wealthy, one of our most sacred rights, equality before the law, is violated. Whenever the poor do not have access to adequate health care, the market is granted power over life and death. Whenever money buys political power and influence, the principle of one-person, one-vote is compromised. The uses of money to counterfeit rights can fill a chamber of horrors. Tax reform has been ignored by some liberal politicians who would not risk antagonizing wealthy potential campaign contributors; the regional and industrial interests of Howard Hughes have been protected by contributions to both political parties; again and again, 200,000 milk producers have used intensive lobbying and big campaign contributions to beat 200 million consumers in the arena of politics.

A great many actions are required to take our cherished rights off the auction block — once and for all. The recent reform of election-campaign financing is an encouraging first step; it may turn out to be the most important piece of *economic* legislation of our generation. Next, we need a code of fair play for relations between public officials and lobbying groups, one that distinguishes the legitimate persuasion of ideas from the purchase of favors. We need an enormous and costly expansion of legal services for advising and defending the poor, one that honors our commitment to equality before the law. We need additional Government support for voluntary associations of consumers to countervail the super-rich and the special-interest producer groups.

Democratic capitalism is a workable compromise if people see it as a compromise and want to make it work. That means facing the issues of equality as matters of *more* or *less* rather than *all* or *none*. It means recognizing that "profits" and "rich" are neither dirty nor sacred words. It means developing specific measures that offer greater equality at a low cost of inefficiency or shrinkage of the national economic pie. With such measures, we can establish a right to a decent standard of living, end the transgression of money on rights, and reduce the handicaps in the races for jobs and funds. And we can do all that within the framework of efficiency and private enterprise.

Obviously we cannot do all this costlessly or even cheaply. In combination, the measures that I have espoused would add significantly to the Federal budget — and we cannot afford a major expansion today. But economic growth and prosperity can once again swell the revenues of the Federal Government (with tax rates unchanged). Indeed, we need the productive efficiency of a market system to help finance equalization programs without an extra tax burden on the majority of Americans. Progress toward the goal can be swifter if we forgo tax cuts as a regular and steady diet, if we close tax loopholes that now

benefit the wealthy (to the tune of perhaps $15 billion a year), and if we shift resources within the Federal budget (perhaps another $15 billion a year) by putting top priority on equalization programs. If we set the goal of the elimination of poverty, we can move in that direction with welfare reform and continuing improvements in Social Security, food stamps, health-care aid and job-creating programs. We will need to set priorities; we will need to pace ourselves; but we will move with a sense of direction and of mission. And when we reach that target, we should raise our sights further by setting half of the nation's average income as the basic minimum of a decent existence — a standard that is now out of reach of about one-fifth of our families.

Unequal incomes would still determine who can buy beachfront condominiums, second cars and college slots for academic underachievers. But they would not block access to first homes, first cars and college slots for solid students; or would they confer vastly unequal power over legislators and juries. As the British egalitarian R. H. Tawney once stated his reasonable goal: "Differences of remuneration between different individuals might remain; contrasts between the civilization of different classes would vanish."

And that goal can best be reached by modifying and strengthening democratic capitalism. By preserving our basic institutional framework, we can build on its capacity to adapt gradually — and that adaptability is one of its greatest virtues. The vending-machine society espoused by the right would be brittle and inhumane; the collectivized economy proposed by the left would be bureaucratic and inefficient. All things considered, capitalism and democracy, though polar opposites in some respects, really need each other — to put some rationality into equality and some humanity into efficiency.

REFLECTIONS ON PUBLIC EXPENDITURE THEORY

Walter W. Heller

This selection reflects several important features of the liberal theory of the State, although it does not seek rigorously to formulate that theory. It illustrates the general theory especially in its emphasis on the nearly infinite number of options open to the government and in its belief that the State can represent all groups in society rather than the interests of only one class. As Heller puts it, the liberal view expects that the government can achieve "any combination of Government services, income redistribution, and economic redistribution and economic stability we set our sights on" — all this regardless of the structure of economic institutions and the relative power of competing groups.

The selection comes from a slightly longer piece included in *Private Wants and Public Needs*. It offers a simple and discursive expression of the basic theory of public expenditure dominating liberal economic thought in this country, more rigorously formulated in Richard Musgrave, *The Theory of Public Finance*.

A leading liberal academic economist, Heller teaches at the University of Minnesota. He served as chairman of the Council of Economic Advisers under President John F. Kennedy, playing a leading role in the establishment of "The New Economics" as a dominant strain in government policy.

What does the economist have to offer a perplexed public and its policymaking representatives on the theory of Government functions as they affect the budget? The cynic's offhand answer, "not much," may be close to the mark if one demands definitive rules of thumb for determining the precise scope of Government functions and level of Government expenditures. But if, instead, the demand is for economic guidelines to aid the budgetary decisionmaker (1) in blending rationally the service, stabilization, and income-transfer functions of Government, (2) in identifying those deficiencies in the private-market mechanism which call for Government budgetary action or, more broadly, those activities where Gov-

ernment use or control of resources promises greater returns than private use or control, and (3) in selecting the most efficient means of carrying out Government functions and activities (whether by Government production, contracts with private producers, transfer payments, loans, guaranties, tax concessions, and so forth) — if this is the nature of the demands on him, the economist is prepared to make a modest offering now and to work along lines that promise a greater contribution in the future.

In a sense, this paper is a progress report designed to show where the economist can already offer some useful counsel, to indicate some of the lines along which promising work is being done, and to suggest certain limitations or constraints within which the economic criteria for dividing resources between public and private use must be applied.

A Basic Framework

As a first step in the search for economic guideposts, we need to disentangle, classify, and define the basic objectives and functions of Government that shape its budgetary decisions. Fortunately, Prof. Richard A. Musgrave has developed a conceptual framework for this task in his "multiple theory of budget determination." [1]

The component functions of the budget as he brings them into focus are: (1) The service, or want-satisfying, function: to provide for the satisfaction of those individual wants which the market mechanism cannot satisfy effectively (e.g., education and conservation) or is incapable of satisfying (e.g., defense and justice); (2) the income-transfer or distributional function: to make those corrections in the existing income distribution (by size, by occupational groups, by geographical area, etc.) which society desires; and (3) the stabilization function: to join with monetary policy and other measures to raise or lower

[1] See, for example, "A Multiple Theory of Budget Determination," *Finanzarchiv* 1957, vol. 13, no. 3, pp. 333–343, and the relevant chapters of his treatise, *The Theory of Public Finance* (New York: McGraw-Hill, 1959).

the level of aggregate demand so as to maintain full employment and avoid inflation. The first function is of dominant interest [here] and the succeeding sections of the paper return to it. But several general implications of the Musgrave system as a whole deserve attention before turning to specifics.

Musgrave's formulation helps unclutter our thinking on the component parts of the budget decision. It drives home the significant point that our decisions on how much and what kind of want-satisfying services to provide by Government budgets need not be tied to our demands on the budget for correction of either the existing patterns of income distribution or the level of aggregate demand. If we prefer, we can have a small budget for services (financed by taxes levied on the benefit principle) combined with a big budget for redistributive transfers of income (financed by taxes levied on the ability principle), or vice versa; and either combination can be coupled with either a deficit to stimulate demand and employment or a surplus to reduce demand and check inflation. In this respect, it is reminiscent of Samuelson's "daring doctrine" that by appropriate fiscal-monetary policy "a community can have full employment, can at the same time have the rate of capital formation it wants, and can accomplish all this compatibly with the degree of income-redistributing taxation it ethically desires." [2] Musgrave, in turn, points the way to achieving any combination of Government services, income redistribution, and economic redistribution, and economic stability we set our sights on. . . .

Economic Determinants of the Proper Sphere of Government Activity

Given a framework for straight thinking about budget functions, the economist is brought face to face with two questions that come closer to the central problem of the proper sphere of Government activity. First, where competitive bidding via the pricing mechanism is inapplicable, how are the preferences of voters for governmental services to be revealed, measured, and appropriately financed? Second, waiving the question of measurement of preferences, where would the line between public and private

control over resources be drawn if economic efficiency were the only criterion to be implied?

On the first question, insofar as it relates to individual preferences for public goods, economists have agreed on the nature and difficulty of the problem, have made some intriguing suggestions as to its solution, and have concluded that it is next to insoluble. The key difficulty is that the voting process, unlike the pricing process, does not force the consumer of public goods to show his hand. The essence of preference measurement is the showing of how much of one good or service the consumer is willing to forgo as the price of acquiring another. But the amount of a public good or service (say, of defense, police protection, or schooling) available to the voter is independent of the amount he pays in taxes or the intensity of his demand for it. [3] Unless and until we devise a reliable and reasonably accurate method of detecting specific voter preferences in some detail, our definition of the proper sphere of government activity will have to rely chiefly on the informed judgment and perception of those whom we vote into legislative and executive office. [4]

This being the case, the economist's task is to contribute what he can to this informed judgment and perception. In effect, the economist's job becomes one of telling the voters and their representatives what their preferences as to governmental activities would be if they were guided by the principle of economic efficiency. In doing so, the economist is not proposing that decisions as to what kinds of activities should be assigned to government — what wants should be satisfied and resources should be redirected through government action — should be made on economic grounds alone. He is fully aware that values such as those of political and economic freedom play a vital role in these decisions. But he can perform the valuable service of identify-

---

[2] Paul A. Samuelson, "The New Look in Tax and Fiscal Policy," in *Federal Tax Policy for Economic Growth and Stability,* Joint Committee on the Economic Report, Washington, November 9, 1955, p. 234.

[3] For an illuminating exploration of ways and means to get at a more valid and clear-cut expression of voter preferences for government services, see the pioneering work by Howard R. Bowen, *Toward Social Economy,* New York, 1948, especially ch. 18, "Collective Choice." In this chapter Bowen explores both voting and polling techniques for ascertaining those individual tastes and preferences which cannot find expression in, or be measured by, the market mechanism.

[4] Insofar as voter wants in the public sphere go beyond individualistic preferences to general welfare choices . . . the problem changes form, but the desirability of sharper definition of voter preferences remains undiminished.

ing those deficiencies in the market mechanism and those inherent economic characteristics of government which make it economically advantageous to have certain services provided by government rather than by private initiative. In other words he can show where government intervention in resource allocation and use promises a greater return per unit of input than untrammeled private use.

The economist recognizes, of course, that there are areas in which he is necessarily mute, or at least should not speak unless spoken to. These are the areas of pure public goods, whose benefits are clearly indivisible and nonmarketable, and no amount of economic wisdom can determine the appropriate levels of output and expenditure.[5] In the realm of defense, for example, one successful Russian earth satellite or intercontinental ballistics missile will (and should) outweigh 10,000 economists in determining the appropriate level of expenditures. At most, the economist stands ready to offer analysis and judgments as to the critical levels of defense expenditures beyond which they threaten serious inflation in the absence of drastic tax action or curtailment of civilian programs, or, given that action, threaten impairment of producer incentives and essential civilian programs.

A much more fruitful activity for the economist is to demonstrate the economic advantage offered by government intervention, budgetary and otherwise, in those intermediate service areas where benefits are at least partially divisible and marketable. A number of economists have made useful contributions on this front.[6] In what situations does economic logic point to government intervention to correct the market mechanism's allocation of resources in the interests of greater efficiency in their use?

1. Where there are important third-party benefits

[usually known as neighborhood effects, external effects, or externalities] which accrue to others than the direct beneficiary of the service, as in the case of education, disease prevention, police and fire protection, the market price and demand schedules underestimate the marginal and total social benefits provided by the service in question. By and large, the direct beneficiaries are the only ones who enter the private market as buyers, with the result that the services would be undervalued, underpriced, and underproduced unless Government entered the transaction. Government is the instrument for representing the third-party beneficiaries and correcting the deficiency of the market place (though this is not to deny that private religious and philanthropic organizations, for example, also represent third-party beneficiaries and operate on budget rather than market principles).

2. Just as there may be indirect benefits not reflected in market demand, there may be indirect costs inflicted on society which do not enter the private producer's costs and therefore do not influence market supply. Classic examples are the costs of smog, water pollution, denuding of forests, and the like. In these areas, private output will exceed the optimum level unless government corrects the situation either by regulation or by a combination of expenditure and charge-backs to the private producers involved.

3. Where a service is best provided, for technical reasons, as a monopoly (e.g., postal service, electricity, railroad transportation), the Government is expected to step in either by regulation or operation to avoid costly duplication and improve the quality of service. Ideally, its function would also be to guide prices toward levels consistent with optimum output. Involved here is the problem of the decreasing cost industry, where efficient plant size is so large relative to total demand that average cost decreases as output increases, and the market solution of the output and price problem will not result in best use of the productive assets. To push production to a point representing an ideal use of resources may require, if not Government operation, a subsidy financed out of tax revenues.

4. Government may enjoy some advantages in production or distribution which make it an inherently more efficient producer of certain services. Here, the classic case is highways, streets, and sidewalks. By providing them free to all comers, Government effects substantial savings in costs of distribution

[5] No attempt is made here to define a public good. Samuelson (in "The Pure Theory of Public Expenditures," *The Review of Economics and Statistics,* November 1954, vol. 36, p. 387) has defined "collective consumption goods" as those in which one individual's consumption of the good leads to no diminution of any other individual's consumption of that good. . . .

[6] See, for example, O. H. Brownlee and E. D. Allen, *Economics of Public Finance,* second edition, New York, 1954, ch. 10, "The Role of Government Expenditure." See also Max F. Millikan, "Objectives for Economic Policy in a Democracy" (especially pp. 62–68), and Robert Dahl and Charles E. Lindblom, "Variation in Public Expenditure," both in *Income Stabilization for a Developing Democracy,* Max F. Millikan, editor, New Haven, 1953.

since it does not have to meter the service and charge a price for each specific use. In this category we might also fit projects, such as the initial development of atomic energy, which involve such great risks and huge accumulations of capital that the private market does not have the financial tools to cope with them.

Alternative Means of Carrying Out Government Functions

Given the decisions as to the appropriate sphere of Government activity (on the basis not merely of considerations of greatest economic gain but also of value preferences), there remains the problem of choice among alternative methods to implement these decisions, to achieve given aims and satisfy expressed public wants. This choice will affect the budget in different ways. It may increase expenditures, decrease revenues, establish contingent liabilities, or perhaps have no effect on the budget at all (except for a small amount of administrative expenses involved in the supervisory and regulatory activities). Since the operational question is not merely what functions and activities Government should carry out, but what budgetary principles and expenditure levels these lead to, the problem of implementation must be included in any applied theory of public expenditures.

Here, the economist's role is to determine the most efficient method of providing the service or otherwise influencing resource allocation. He is concerned with minimizing costs, i.e., achieving the stated objective with a minimum expenditure of resources. Needless to say, other considerations will also influence the selection among alternative means, as even a brief consideration of the types of choices involved in the implementation process will make clear.

What are these choices? Take first the case of direct satisfaction of individuals' public wants. Should the Government produce the desired public goods or obtain them from private industry by purchase or contract? To accomplish redistributive ends, should the Government provide transfers in cash or transfers in kind? [7] Should Government rely on public produc-

tion of educational services, or should it consider private production combined with earmarked transfers of purchasing power to parents? Thus far, the choices all involve direct budgetary expenditures, the level of which differs, at least marginally, depending on the relative efficiency of the method chosen. But in making his choice, the policymaker must consider not merely the direct costs of providing the service but whether one method involves more or less disturbance of private market incentives and patterns of production than another, whether it involves more or less interference with individual freedom (which is largely a function of the extent of Government expenditures and intervention but certainly in part also a function of the form of that intervention), and so on.

Another set of choices may take the item off of the expenditure side of the budget entirely, or leave it there only contingently. Should such subsidies as those to promote oil and gas exploration, stimulate foreign investment, expand the merchant marine, promote low-cost housing, and increase the flow of strategic minerals take the form of (1) outright subsidies or above-market-price purchase programs, (2) Government loan programs, (3) Government guaranties, or (4) tax concessions? The choice will clearly involve quite different impacts on Government expenditures.

In many of these cases, the economist can be helpful with his efficiency criterion. But one would be naive to think that efficiency alone dictates the choice. The economist may show that a direct subsidy could stimulate a given amount of private direct investment abroad or a given amount of exploration for oil and gas, with a much smaller cost to the budget than is implicitly required in the tax concession method of achieving the same end. Yet, the costlier tax concession method may be preferred for two simple reasons: (1) it is virtually self-administering, involving no administrative hierarchy to substitute its authority for relatively free private decisions, and (2) it does not involve an increase in the expenditure side of the budget, a fact which has certain attractions to the Executive and Congress.

As yet, no clear boundary lines have been drawn among the various forms of Government intervention

[7] One involves so-called resource-using (also called factor-purchase or exhaustive) Government expenditures, i.e., payments in exchange for current goods and services rendered, with direct control of resources remaining in

public hands. The other involves transfer payments, i.e., payments made without any provision of current goods and services in return, with direct control over resources passing into private hands.

to mark off those that properly belong within the scope of public expenditure theory. But this illustrative review of the various choices makes clear that some forms of Government activity which are not reflected in expenditures at all (tax concessions) or only contingently (guaranties) are an integral part of such expenditure theory. In fact, there may be a stronger case for embracing these in expenditure theory than many Government activities which require budgetary outlays but are conducted on the pricing principle, i.e., Government enterprise activities.

Economists are conducting some provocative inquiries into questions of alternative methods of carrying out Governmental programs in areas where the answers had heretofore been taken for granted. For example, the transfer of schooling to a private production and Government transfer payment basis has been urged by Professor Milton Friedman as a more efficient means of providing the desired service.[8] ... Once fairly conclusive findings are devised as to the methods most likely to minimize costs, there remains the vital task of blending these findings with the nonmonetary values that would be gained or lost in the process of transferring from public to private production.

Some Constraints on the Application of Specific Economic Criteria

Repeatedly in this discussion, the note has been sounded that, in determining the level of Government activity, the policymaker cannot live by economics alone. More particularly, we need to guard against setting up our economic guides solely in terms of those considerations which lend themselves to sharp economic analysis and definition. In other words, the role of both economic and noneconomic constraints must be given full weight.

The former include a host of considerations relating particularly to economic motivation in Government versus private undertakings. Government may, for example, have a decided edge in the efficiency of distribution or be able to achieve a better balancing of social costs and social benefits in a variety of fields. Yet, there may be important offsets to these economic advantages in terms of (1) bureaucracy, (2) lack of the profit criterion to gage the results of Government activities, and (3) undesigned or unintended (presumably adverse) economic effects of taxation.[9]

The latter factor, in particular the fact that tax financing of public services involves breaking the link between an individual's cost of a given service and his benefit from it, may involve important offsets to economic advantages otherwise gained by Government expenditure. Thus far, to be sure, no dire consequences of the disincentive effects of taxation have been firmly proved, but changes in the form of private economic activity to minimize taxes are certainly a cost that must be weighed when netting out the balance of economic advantage in Government versus private performance of services.

Beyond the economic factors, one encounters an even more basic and less manageable constraint, namely that of freedom of choice. Thus, it is quite conceivable that following the kinds of economic criteria discussed earlier in the paper would take us considerably farther in the direction of Government spending and control over resource allocation than we would wish to go in terms of possible impairment of economic and political freedom. This consideration enters importantly not merely in decisions as to the proper range of Government activity but also in choosing among alternative methods of providing Government services.

This is not to imply that all value considerations run counter to the expansion of the Government sector of our economy. Such expansion may serve a number of social values, such as greater equality of income and opportunity, a more acceptable social environment, and so on.[10]

---

[8] See Milton Friedman, "The Role of Government in Education," in *Economics and the Public Interest*, Robert A. Solo, editor, New Brunswick, 1955, pp. 123–144. In his prescription, Friedman would, of course, have Government regulate the private schools to the extent of insuring that they meet certain minimum standards in their programs and facilities.

[9] These less sharply defined economic effects have to be balanced, of course, against comparable and perhaps offsetting drawbacks in the market mechanism. For an exploration of some of these factors, both in the private and the public sphere, see Robert A. Dahl and Charles E. Lindblom, *Politics, Economics, and Welfare*, New York, 1953, especially pt. V. See also C. Lowell Harriss, "Government Spending: Issues of Theory and Practices," *Public Finance*, vol. 12, 1957, pp. 7–19.

[10] This type of consideration is examined in William Vickrey, "An Exchange of Questions Between Economics and Philosophy," in *Goals of Economic Life*, edited by A. Dudley Ward, New York, 1953, pp. 148–177. See also Max F. Millikan, *op. cit.*

To get all of these considerations into the decision-making equation on private versus public provision of a particular service, or on the choice among alternative forms of providing the service, requires a wisdom which goes well beyond the field of economics. Perhaps this explains why so few economists enter politics.

THE UNHEAVENLY CITY REVISITED

Edward C. Banfield

The following selection illustrates the general conservative approach to the problems discussed in this book of readings. It comprises the concluding chapter of the revised edition of Banfield's influential book on urban problems — with the same title as this selection. Throughout the rest of the book, Banfield carefully outlines a conservative analysis of almost all the problems discussed in succeeding chapters in this reader. In the concluding chapter reprinted here, he summarizes the important points of his book. Banfield's advocacy of passive restraint and benign neglect helped provide legitimacy for the Nixon and Ford administrations' proclamations that "the urban crisis is over."

Banfield is a university professor at the University of Pennsylvania, where he teaches political science. He has written many books on urban politics and problems, including *City Politics* (with James Q. Wilson).

It is probable that at this time we are about to make great changes in our social system. The world is ripe for such changes and if they are not made in the direction of greater social liberality, the direction forward, they will almost of necessity be made in the direction backward, of a terrible social niggardliness. We all know which of those directions we want. But it is not enough to want it, not even enough to work for it — we must want it and work for it with intelligence. Which means that we must be aware of the dangers which lie in our most generous wishes.

— Lionel Trilling

Source: From *The Unheavenly City Revisited,* by Edward C. Banfield, by permission of Little, Brown and Co. Copyright © 1968, 1970, 1974 by Edward C. Banfield.

The quotation at the head of the article is from *The Liberal Imagination* (Garden City, N.Y.: Anchor Books, 1953), pp. 214–215.

It is impossible to avoid the conclusion that the serious problems of the cities will continue to exist in something like their present form for another twenty years at least. Even on the most favorable assumptions we shall have large concentrations of the poor and the unskilled, and — what, to repeat, is by no means the same thing — the lower class in the central cities and the larger, older suburbs. The outward movement of industry and commerce is bound to continue, leaving ever-larger parts of the inner city blighted or semi-abandoned. Even if we could afford to throw the existing cities away and build new ones from scratch, matters would not be essentially different, for the people who move into the new cities would take the same old problems with them. Eventually, the present problems of the cities will disappear or dwindle into relative unimportance; they will not, however, be "solved" by programs of the sort undertaken in the past decade. On the contrary, the tendency of such programs would be to prolong the problems and perhaps even make them worse.

For the most part, the problems in question have arisen from and are inseparably connected with developments that almost everyone welcomes: the growth and spread of affluence has enabled millions of people to move from congested cities to new and more spacious homes in the suburbs; the availability of a large stock of relatively good housing in the central cities and older suburbs has enabled the Negro to escape the semi-slavery of the rural South and, a century late, to move into industrial society; better public health measures and facilities have cut the deathrate of the lower class; the war and postwar baby boom have left the city with more adolescents and youths than ever before; and a wide-spread and general movement upward on the class-cultural scale has made poverty, squalor, ignorance, and brutality — conditions that have always and everywhere been regarded as inevitable in the nature of things — appear as anomalies that should be removed entirely and at once.

What stands in the way of dealing effectively with these problems (insofar as their nature admits of their being dealt with by government) is mainly the virtues of the American political system and of the American character. It is because governmental power is widely distributed that organized interests are so often able to veto measures that would benefit large numbers of people. It is the generous and public-regarding impulses of voters and taxpayers that impel them to support measures — for example, the minimum wage and compulsory high school attendance — the ultimate effect of which is to make the poor poorer and more demoralized. Our devotion to the doctrine that all men are created equal discourages any explicit recognition of class-cultural differences and leads to "democratic" — and often misleading — formulations of problems: for example, poverty as lack of income and material resources (something external to the individual) rather than as inability or unwillingness to take account of the future or to control impulses (something internal). Sympathy for the oppressed, indignation at the oppressor, and a wish to make amends for wrongs done by one's ancestors lead to a misrepresentation of the Negro as the near-helpless victim of "white racism." Faith in the perfectibility of man and confidence that good intentions together with strenuous exertions will hasten his progress onward and upward lead to bold programs that promise to do what no one knows how to do and what perhaps cannot be done, and therefore end in frustration, loss of mutual respect and trust, anger, and even coercion.

Even granting that in general the effect of government programs is to exacerbate the problems of the cities, it might perhaps be argued that they have a symbolic value that is more than redeeming. What economist Kenneth Boulding has said of national parks — that we seem to need them "as we seem to need a useless dome on the capitol, as a symbol of national identity and of that mutuality of concern and interest without which government would be naked coercion" [1] — may possibly apply as well to

Freedom Budgets, domestic Marshall Plans, and other such concoctions. That government programs do not succeed in reducing welfare dependency, preventing crime, and so on, is not a weighty objection to them if, for want of them the feeling would spread that the society is "not worth saving." There is an imminent danger, however, that the growing multitude of programs that are intended essentially as gestures of goodwill may constitute a bureaucratic juggernaut which cannot be stopped and which will symbolize not national identity and mutual concern but rather divisiveness, confusion, and inequity. If a symbol is wanted, a useless dome is in every way preferable.

That government cannot solve the problems of the cities and is likely to make them worse by trying does not necessarily mean that calamity impends. Powerful accidental (by which is meant, nongovernmental and, more generally, nonorganizational) forces are at work that tend to alleviate and even to eliminate the problems. Hard as it may be for a nation of inveterate problem-solvers to believe, social problems sometimes disappear in the normal course of events.

One powerful accidental force at work is economic growth. Because capital tends to increase by geometric progression, a rich country becomes exceedingly rich in the space of a few years. If real per capita productivity grows at 2.2 percent per year and if the current trend toward reduced fertility continues (the norm being two children) the population by the end of the century, about 270 million, will produce and consume almost two and one-half times as much as at present. By the year 2040, the population will be approaching stability at about 320 million and will produce about seven times as much as at present.[2] These are by no means implausible assumptions, but even on more conservative ones the end of poverty, in the sense of hardship, is in sight.[3]

---

[1] Kenneth Boulding, book review in the *Journal of Business* (January 1963): 121.

[2] The projections are from Denis F. Johnston, "The Future of Work: Three Possible Alternatives," *Monthly Labor Review* (May 1972): 9.

[3] *The Manpower Report of the President* (Washington, D.C.: G.P.O., March 1973) says (p. 63): ". . . if the average net annual reduction in the absolute number in low-income groups (about 1.1 million persons per year, 1959 to 1971) can be maintained in the future, the result would be the virtual elimination of the low-income group (as presently defined) in about two decades." The report adds, however, that it may be difficult to sustain this rate of progress because the smaller low income group is likely to consist of more difficult cases. In the opinion of

As this suggests, a second — and interacting — accidental force of great importance is demographic change. The baby boom that occurred after the Second War resulted in the 1960's in an unprecedented number of teen-agers. The birthrate has since fallen sharply because couples took to marrying later and having fewer children; after 1975 the number and proportion of young people in the population will probably cease to grow for about thirty years. With fewer children to support and educate, there will be more money to devote to other things. (Schools are by far the biggest item of local expenditure; the decrease in the number of children will therefore do much to relieve the "fiscal crisis" of the cities.) The problem of maintaining order will be reduced only slightly; after 1975 the proportion of males ages 15 to 24 to the total population will remain for three decades about the same as it was in 1965.[4]

A third such force — perhaps the most important of all — is the process of middle- and upper-class-ification. For the reasons that were given in Chapter Ten [of Banfield's book], it is problematic, to say the least, whether the lower class will be absorbed into the outlook and style of life of the "mainstream." With this small but nevertheless important exception, it seems highly probable that there will continue to be a general upward movement all along the class-cultural scale. This will mean a softening of manners, better performance in schools, and less violence of the sort that serves to emphasize mascu-

linity by acts of daring and aggression. "As the larger culture becomes more cerebral," Wolfgang and Ferracuti write, "the refined symbolic forms of masculinity [for example, debating societies, musical virtuosity, and literary talent] should be more fully adopted."[5]

Middle- and upper-class-ification also implies a reduction in racial prejudice and discrimination. This should proceed with gathering momentum because of the operation of what Gunnar Myrdal, in *An American Dilemma*, called "the principle of cumulation."

> White prejudice and discrimination keep the Negro low in standards of living, health, education, manners and morals. This, in turn, gives support to white prejudice. White prejudice and Negro standards thus mutually "cause" each other. . . . Such a static "accommodation" is, however, entirely accidental. If either of the factors changes, this will cause a change in the other factor, too, and start a process of interaction where the change in one factor will continuously be supported by the reaction of the other factor.[6]

It is impossible to judge how much effect these accidental forces will have on the lower class. Rapid economic growth and the prospect of high returns to investment in the "human capital" represented by oneself or one's children may, as suggested in Chapter Ten [of Banfield's book], encourage rapid mobility from the lower class. Conceivably, however, increasing affluence might have an opposite effect: generous welfare programs, for example, may destroy more incentives to provide for the future than better job and other opportunities create; moreover, the diffusion of more present-oriented ways in the middle and upper classes might lessen any pressure that lower-class people feel to change their ways or even discourage them from doing so. An increase in the absolute (if not the relative) size of the lower class is by no means out of the question. Unless the increase were very large, however, it would not necessarily lead to a radical worsening of the situation or precipitate a crisis in the life of the nation. Moreover, if an increase is not out of the question, neither is a decrease.

Robert J. Lampman, "it appears unlikely that poverty will be completely eliminated before 1980 unless some new and extraordinary measures are taken." *Ends and Means of Reducing Income Poverty* (Chicago: Markham Publishing Company, 1971), p. 132.

[4] Johnston, "The Future of Work," p. 7, projects dependency ratios (number of persons not in the labor force divided by number who are) as: 1960 (actual), 1.50; 1970 (actual), 1.39; 1980, 1.19 (assuming the two-child norm of the Census's Series E); and 2000, 1.10 (on the same assumption).

For estimates of the effect of changes in age structure on arrest rates, see Peter A. Morrison, "The Effects of Changing Age Structure," *Dimensions of the Population Problem in the United States* (Santa Monica, Calif.: The Rand Corporation, Monograph R-864-CPG, August 1972), p. 17. The estimates used in the text of the numbers of young males in the future population are from Irene B. Taeuber, "Growth of Population in the United States in the Twentieth Century," in U.S. Commission on Population Growth and the American Future, Charles F. Westoff and Robert Parke, Jr., eds., *Demographic and Social Aspects of Population Growth*, vol. I of Commission Research Reports (Washington, D.C.: G.P.O., 1972), p. 70.

[5] Marvin E. Wolfgang and Franco Ferracuti, *The Subculture of Violence* (London: Tavistock Publications, 1967), p. 306.

[6] Gunnar Myrdal, *An American Dilemma* (New York: Harper, 1944), pp. 75–76.

Although the *objective* situation does not warrant the alarmist tone of much that is said and written about the city, the *subjective* one may. However much the accidental forces may reduce the *real* importance of the problems that have been under discussion, they may have no impact on their *seeming* importance. Indeed, this is likely to grow, for some of the very same factors that improve the objective situation also raise people's standards and expectations, thus leaving the subjective situation no better — and perhaps even worse — than it was to begin with. What people *think* a situation is may (as sociologist Robert K. Merton has pointed out) become an integral part of that situation, and therefore a factor in its subsequent development. A false public definition of the situation may, as Merton says, evoke new behavior that makes the originally false definition come true, thus perpetuating a "reign of error."[7] In short, wrong public definitions of urban problems may lead to behavior that will make matters worse despite the ameliorating influence of the accidental forces.

This possibility is most painfully apparent in the case of the Negro. That racial prejudice has long been declining and may be expected to continue to decline at an accelerating rate counts for little if the Negro *thinks* that white racism is as pervasive as ever; that his opportunities to improve his position by acquiring skills are at last fairly good counts for little if he *thinks* that "massive" government welfare, housing, and other programs — and *only* these — can help him. If he misperceives the situation in these ways, he is likely to do things that are counterproductive (for example, to cut himself off from "white" schools, jobs, and politics and to enter the fantasy world of black separatism). Such a course, if carried far enough, may validate his original (false) hypothesis — that is, he may become in fact as dependent upon government programs as he (wrongly) supposed himself to be and may revive the fact of white prejudice by giving it some objective grounds to feed upon.

Nothing could be so tragic and ironic as the acceptance of a false public definition of the situation that proves to be a self-fulfilling prophecy of racial hatred. Even if nonracial factors had not in recent years superseded the racial ones as the Negro's

main handicap, it would be well to pretend that they had, for a self-fulfilling prophecy of the unimportance of racial factors would be as great a blessing as its opposite would be a curse.

Except as they create, or reinforce, counterproductive public definitions of problems and thereby encourage a "reign of error," wrong governmental measures are not likely to lead to catastrophe or even to any very significant worsening of the situation. Most wrong measures will lead to nothing worse than some additional waste and delay, usually a trivial amount. (One gets a sense of how unimportant even "important" governmental actions may be from one economist's estimate that the elimination of monopoly in the United States in 1929 would have raised income by no more than 1/13 of 1 percent, and from the estimate of another that benefits attributable to better resource allocation by virtue of the Common Market would also be much less than 1 percent.[8]) The governmental measures having the largest effect upon the city since the turn of the century are probably subsidization of truck and automobile transportation and subsidization of home ownership for the well-off; these measures certainly hastened the departure of the white middle class from the central city and, a fortiori, the entry of the poor — especially the black poor — on a large scale, but they did not significantly change the pattern of metropolitan growth; this was determined by accidental forces — the demographic, technological, economic, and class-cultural imperatives described in Chapters Two and Three [of Banfield's book].

Although it is easy to exaggerate the importance, either for good or ill, of the measures that government has adopted or might adopt, there does appear to be a danger to the good health of the society in the tendency of the public to define so many situations as "critical problems" — a definition that implies (1) that "solutions" exist or can be found and (2) that unless they are found and applied at once, disaster will befall. The import of what has been said in this book is that although there are many difficulties to be coped with, dilemmas to be faced, and afflictions to be endured, there are very few problems that can be solved; it is also that although much is seriously wrong with the city, no disaster impends unless it be one that results from public

[7] Robert K. Merton, *Social Theory and Social Structure* (New York: The Free Press, 1949), p. 181.

[8] Harvey Leibenstein, "Allocative Efficiency vs. 'X-Efficiency,'" *American Economic Review*, 56 (June 1966): 392–393.

misconceptions that are in the nature of self-fulfilling prophecies.

Insofar as delusory and counterproductive public definitions of the situation arise from biases that lie deep within the culture (for example, from the impulse to DO SOMETHING! and to DO GOOD!), they are likely to persist in the face of all experience. To exhort the upper classes to display more of the quality that Trilling calls moral realism would be to offer a problem-begging "solution," since the very want of moral realism that constitutes the problem would prevent their recognizing the need of it.

The biases of the culture limit the range of possibilities, but they do not determine fully how the public will define the situation. This definition is in large part the result of a process of opinion formation that goes on within a relatively small world of officials, leaders of civic associations and other interest groups, journalists, and social scientists, especially economists; from this small world opinion is passed on to the public-at-large through the mass media, books, classroom instruction, campaign oratory, after-dinner speeches, and so on. Needless to say, a vast amount of misinformation, prejudice, and illogic enters into the process of opinion formation. (The agony of the cities, someone has remarked, is what the network executive and his fellow-commuters on the Long Island Railroad see out the window as they make their agonized way to and from their offices in Manhattan.) Within the past decade or two, developments have occurred that could make for a more realistic view of the urban situation — for example, the number of technically trained persons working on urban problems has increased greatly, their resources for gathering and manipulating data and the analytical apparatus that they can bring to bear upon policy questions are much improved, and what they have to say is taken much more seriously by politicians and administrators and therefore also by journalists.[9] It would not be surprising if the con-

ventional wisdom were to be very much revised in the next decade or two as a consequence of these developments. Turnover within the small world of opinion-makers is rapid, and the young newcomers in that world tend to be open to new ideas and even in search of them. Because communication within the small world and between it and the public-at-large is excellent, a new definition of the situation, once formulated, could catch on very quickly.

It would be pleasant to be able to end this discussion on that relatively optimistic note. Unfortunately, another side to the matter requires mention. Technically trained persons have their own characteristic biases, and if their view of the city is different from that of the commuter on the Long Island Railroad it is not necessarily more realistic. Moreover, as the technician comes to play a more important part in policy-making he is bound to come more and more under the discipline of large organizations, especially foundations and government agencies, whose maintenance and enhancement depend in some way upon the elaboration of an alarmist, or at any rate expansionist, public definition of the situation. That young newcomers to the small world of opinion-makers tend to be open to new ideas is not altogether reassuring either, for they may tend to accept new ideas *just because* they are new. To the pessimist, the prospect is that a new conventional wisdom about the problems of the city, the product of many millions of dollars' expenditure on research, cast in the language of systems analysis and the computer, will only compound the existing confusion. The optimist, however, will see reason to believe that facts, rational analysis, and deliberation about the nature of the public interest will play a somewhat larger part than hitherto in the formation of both opinion and policy.

9 For a description and analysis of the use of sophisticated problem-solving techniques in two cities (San

Francisco and Pittsburgh), from which pessimists will probably take more comfort than will optimists, see Garry D. Brewer, *Politicians, Bureaucrats, and the Consultant, A Critique of Urban Problem Solving* (New York: Basic Books, 1973).

THE ROLE OF GOVERNMENT IN A FREE SOCIETY

Milton Friedman

This selection expounds the conservative theory of the State. In it, Friedman argues strongly against active government intervention in the private market system. His positions derive in important ways from the views of classic nineteenth-century English "liberalism," from the views of philosophers like John Stuart Mill. (He uses the word *liberal* in that classical sense.)

The selection is Chapter II of Friedman's book *Capitalism and Freedom*. Throughout that book, the author offers a variety of arguments reflecting conservative economic views of economy and society. His book is perhaps the most important recent exposition of such views.

Friedman teaches economics at the University of Chicago, is one of the most widely respected technical economists in the United States, and also writes a regular column on economics for *Newsweek*.

A common objection to totalitarian societies is that they regard the end as justifying the means. Taken literally, this objection is clearly illogical. If the end does not justify the means, what does? But this easy answer does not dispose of the objection; it simply shows that the objection is not well put. To deny that the end justifies the means is indirectly to assert that the end in question is not the ultimate end, that the ultimate end is itself the use of the proper means. Desirable or not, any end that can be attained only by the use of bad means must give way to the more basic end of the use of acceptable means.

To the liberal, the appropriate means are free discussion and voluntary co-operation, which implies that any form of coercion is inappropriate. The ideal is unanimity among responsible individuals achieved on the basis of free and full discussion. This is another way of expressing the goal of freedom emphasized in the preceding chapter.

From this standpoint, the role of the market, as already noted, is that it permits unanimity without

conformity; that it is a system of effectively proportional representation. On the other hand, the characteristic feature of action through explicitly political channels is that it tends to require or to enforce substantial conformity. The typical issue must be decided "yes" or "no"; at most, provision can be made for a fairly limited number of alternatives. Even the use of proportional representation in its explicitly political form does not alter this conclusion. The number of separate groups that can in fact be represented is narrowly limited, enormously so by comparison with the proportional representation of the market. More important, the fact that the final outcome generally must be a law applicable to all groups, rather than separate legislative enactments for each "party" represented, means that proportional representation in its political version, far from permitting unanimity without conformity, tends toward ineffectiveness and fragmentation. It thereby operates to destroy any consensus on which unanimity with conformity can rest.

There are clearly some matters with respect to which effective proportional representation is impossible. I cannot get the amount of national defense I want and you, a different amount. With respect to such indivisible matters we can discuss, and argue, and vote. But having decided, we must conform. It is precisely the existence of such indivisible matters — protection of the individual and the nation from coercion are clearly the most basic — that prevents exclusive reliance on individual action through the market. If we are to use some of our resources for such indivisible items, we must employ political channels to reconcile differences.

The use of political channels, while inevitable, tends to strain the social cohesion essential for a stable society. The strain is least if agreement for joint action need be reached only on a limited range of issues on which people in any event have common views. Every extension of the range of issues for which explicit agreement is sought strains further the delicate threads that hold society together. If it goes so far as to touch an issue on which men feel deeply yet differently, it may well disrupt the society. Fundamental differences in basic values can seldom if ever be resolved at the ballot box; ultimately they can only be decided, though not resolved, by conflict. The religious and civil wars of history are a bloody testament to this judgment.

The widespread use of the market reduces the strain on the social fabric by rendering conformity unnecessary with respect to any activities it encompasses. The wider the range of activities covered by the market, the fewer are the issues on which explicitly political decisions are required and hence on which it is necessary to achieve agreement. In turn, the fewer the issues on which agreement is necessary, the greater is the likelihood of getting agreement while maintaining a free society.

Unanimity is, of course, an ideal. In practice, we can afford neither the time nor the effort that would be required to achieve complete unanimity on every issue. We must perforce accept something less. We are thus led to accept majority rule in one form or another as an expedient. That majority rule is an expedient rather than itself a basic principle is clearly shown by the fact that our willingness to resort to majority rule, and the size of the majority we require, themselves depend on the seriousness of the issue involved. If the matter is of little moment and the minority has no strong feelings about being overruled, a bare plurality will suffice. On the other hand, if the minority feels strongly about the issue involved, even a bare majority will not do. Few of us would be willing to have issues of free speech, for example, decided by a bare majority. Our legal structure is full of such distinctions among kinds of issues that require different kinds of majorities. At the extreme are those issues embodied in the Constitution. These are the principles that are so important that we are willing to make minimal concessions to expediency. Something like essential consensus was achieved initially in accepting them, and we require something like essential consensus for a change in them.

The self-denying ordinance to refrain from majority rule on certain kinds of issues that is embodied in our Constitution and in similar written or unwritten constitutions elsewhere, and the specific provisions in these constitutions or their equivalents prohibiting coercion of individuals, are themselves to be regarded as reached by free discussion and as reflecting essential unanimity about means.

I turn now to consider more specifically, though still in very broad terms, what the areas are that cannot be handled through the market at all, or can be handled only at so great a cost that the use of political channels may be preferable.

Government as Rule-Maker and Umpire

It is important to distinguish the day-to-day activities of people from the general customary and legal framework within which these take place. The day-to-day activities are like the actions of the participants in a game when they are playing it; the framework, like the rules of the game they play. And just as a good game requires acceptance by the players both of the rules and of the umpire to interpret and enforce them, so a good society requires that its members agree on the general conditions that will govern relations among them, on some means of arbitrating different interpretations of these conditions, and on some device for enforcing compliance with the generally accepted rules. As in games, so also in society, most of the general conditions are the unintended outcome of custom, accepted unthinkingly. At most, we consider explicitly only minor modifications in them, though the cumulative effect of a series of minor modifications may be a drastic alteration in the character of the game or of the society. In both games and society also, no set of rules can prevail unless most participants most of the time conform to them without external sanctions; unless, that is, there is a broad underlying social consensus. But we cannot rely on custom or on this consensus alone to interpret and to enforce the rules; we need an umpire. These then are the basic roles of government in a free society: to provide a means whereby we can modify the rules, to mediate differences among us on the meaning of the rules, and to enforce compliance with the rules on the part of those few who would not otherwise play the game.

The need for government in these respects arises because absolute freedom is impossible. However attractive anarchy may be as a philosophy, it is not feasible in a world of imperfect men. Men's freedoms can conflict, and when they do, one man's freedom must be limited to preserve another's — as a Supreme Court Justice once put it, "My freedom to move my fist must be limited by the proximity of your chin."

The major problem in deciding the appropriate activities of government is how to resolve such conflicts among the freedoms of different individuals.

In some cases, the answer is easy. There is little difficulty in attaining near unanimity to the proposition that one man's freedom to murder his neighbor must be sacrificed to preserve the freedom of the other man to live. In other cases, the answer is difficult. In the economic area, a major problem arises in respect of the conflict between freedom to combine and freedom to compete. What meaning is to be attributed to "free" as modifying "enterprise"? In the United States, "free" has been understood to mean that anyone is free to set up an enterprise, which means that existing enterprises are not free to keep out competitors except by selling a better product at the same price or the same product at a lower price. In the continental tradition, on the other hand, the meaning has generally been that enterprises are free to do what they want, including the fixing of prices, division of markets, and the adoption of other techniques to keep out potential competitors. Perhaps the most difficult specific problem in this area arises with respect to combinations among laborers, where the problem of freedom to combine and freedom to compete is particularly acute.

A still more basic economic area in which the answer is both difficult and important is the definition of property rights. The notion of property, as it has developed over centuries and as it is embodied in our legal codes, has become so much a part of us that we tend to take it for granted, and fail to recognize the extent to which just what constitutes property and what rights the ownership of property confers are complex social creations rather than self-evident propositions. Does my having title to land, for example, and my freedom to use my property as I wish, permit me to deny to someone else the right to fly over my land in his airplane? Or does his right to use his airplane take precedence? Or does this depend on how high he flies? Or how much noise he makes? Does voluntary exchange require that he pay me for the privilege of flying over my land? Or that I must pay him to refrain from flying over it? The mere mention of royalties, copyrights, patents; shares of stock in corporations; riparian rights, and the like, may perhaps emphasize the role of generally accepted social rules in the very definition of property. It may suggest also that, in many cases, the existence of a well specified and generally accepted definition of property is far more important than just what the definition is.

Another economic area that raises particularly difficult problems is the monetary system. Government responsibility for the monetary system has long been recognized. It is explicitly provided for in the constitutional provision which gives Congress the power "to coin money, regulate the value thereof, and of foreign coin." There is probably no other area of economic activity with respect to which government action has been so uniformly accepted. This habitual and by now almost unthinking acceptance of governmental responsibility makes thorough understanding of the ground for such responsibility all the more necessary, since it enhances the danger that the scope of government will spread from activities that are, to those that are not, appropriate in a free society, from providing a monetary framework to determining the allocation of resources among individuals. We shall discuss this problem in detail in chapter iii [of Friedman's book].

In summary, the organization of economic activity through voluntary exchange presumes that we have provided, through government, for the maintenance of law and order to prevent coercion of one individual by another, the enforcement of contracts voluntarily entered into, the definition of the meaning of property rights, the interpretation and enforcement of such rights, and the provision of a monetary framework.

Action Through Government on Grounds of Technical Monopoly and Neighborhood Effects

The role of government just considered is to do something that the market cannot do for itself, namely, to determine, arbitrate, and enforce the rules of the game. We may also want to do through government some things that might conceivably be done through the market but that technical or similar conditions render it difficult to do in that way. These all reduce to cases in which strictly voluntary exchange is either exceedingly costly or practically impossible. There are two general classes of such cases: monopoly and similar market imperfections, and neighborhood effects.

Exchange is truly voluntary only when nearly equivalent alternatives exist. Monopoly implies the absence of alternatives and thereby inhibits effective freedom of exchange. In practice, monopoly frequently, if not generally, arises from government support or from collusive agreements among individuals. With respect to these, the problem is either to avoid governmental fostering of monopoly or to stimulate the effective enforcement of rules such as those embodied in our anti-trust laws. However, monopoly may also arise because it is technically efficient to have a single producer or enterprise. I venture to suggest that such cases are more limited than is supposed but they unquestionably do arise. A simple example is perhaps the provision of telephone services within a community. I shall refer to such cases as "technical" monopoly.

When technical conditions make a monopoly the natural outcome of competitive market forces, there are only three alternatives that seem available: private monopoly, public monopoly, or public regulation. All three are bad so we must choose among evils. Henry Simons, observing public regulation of monopoly in the United States, found the results so distasteful that he concluded public monopoly would be a lesser evil. Walter Eucken, a noted German liberal, observing public monopoly in German railroads, found the results so distasteful that he concluded public regulation would be a lesser evil. Having learned from both, I reluctantly conclude that, if tolerable, private monopoly may be the least of the evils.

If society were static so that the conditions which give rise to a technical monopoly were sure to remain, I would have little confidence in this solution. In a rapidly changing society, however, the conditions making for technical monopoly frequently change and I suspect that both public regulation and public monopoly are likely to be less responsive to such changes in conditions, to be less readily capable of elimination, than private monopoly.

Railroads in the United States are an excellent example. A large degree of monopoly in railroads was perhaps inevitable on technical grounds in the nineteenth century. This was the justification for the Interstate Commerce Commission. But conditions have changed. The emergence of road and air transport has reduced the monopoly element in railroads to negligible proportions. Yet we have not eliminated the ICC. On the contrary, the ICC, which started out as an agency to protect the public from exploitation by the railroads, has become an agency to protect railroads from competition by trucks and other means of transport, and more recently even to protect existing truck companies from competition by new entrants. Similarly, in England, when the railroads were nationalized, trucking was at first brought into the state monopoly. If railroads had never been subjected to regulation in the United States, it is nearly certain that by now transportation, including railroads, would be a highly competitive industry with little or no remaining monopoly elements.

The choice between the evils of private monopoly, public monopoly, and public regulation cannot, however, be made once and for all, independently of the factual circumstances. If the technical monopoly is of a service or commodity that is regarded as essential and if its monopoly power is sizable, even the short-run effects of private unregulated monopoly may not be tolerable, and either public regulation or ownership may be a lesser evil.

Technical monopoly may on occasion justify a *de facto* public monopoly. It cannot by itself justify a public monopoly achieved by making it illegal for anyone else to compete. For example, there is no way to justify our present public monopoly of the post office. It may be argued that the carrying of mail is a technical monopoly and that a government monopoly is the least of evils. Along these lines, one could perhaps justify a government post office but not the present law, which makes it illegal for anybody else to carry mail. If the delivery of mail is a technical monopoly, no one will be able to succeed in competition with the government. If it is not, there is no reason why the government should be engaged in it. The only way to find out is to leave other people free to enter.

The historical reason why we have a post office monopoly is because the Pony Express did such a good job of carrying the mail across the continent that, when the government introduced transcontinental service, it couldn't compete effectively and lost money. The result was a law making it illegal for anybody else to carry the mail. That is why the Adams Express Company is an investment trust today instead of an operating company. I conjecture that if entry into the mail-carrying business were open to all, there would be a large number of firms entering it and this archaic industry would become revolutionized in short order.

A second general class of cases in which strictly voluntary exchange is impossible arises when actions of individuals have effects on other individuals for which it is not feasible to charge or recompense them. This is the problem of "neighborhood effects." An obvious example is the pollution of a stream. The man who pollutes a stream is in effect forcing others to exchange good water for bad. These others might be willing to make the exchange at a price.

But it is not feasible for them, acting individually, to avoid the exchange or to enforce appropriate compensation.

A less obvious example is the provision of highways. In this case, it is technically possible to identify and hence charge individuals for their use of the roads and so to have private operation. However, for general access roads, involving many points of entry and exit, the costs of collection would be extremely high if a charge were to be made for the specific services received by each individual, because of the necessity of establishing toll booths or the equivalent at all entrances. The gasoline tax is a much cheaper method of charging individuals roughly in proportion to their use of the roads. This method, however, is one in which the particular payment cannot be identified closely with the particular use. Hence, it is hardly feasible to have private enterprise provide the service and collect the charge without establishing extensive private monopoly.

These considerations do not apply to long-distance turnpikes with high density of traffic and limited access. For these, the costs of collection are small and in many cases are now being paid, and there are often numerous alternatives, so that there is no serious monopoly problem. Hence, there is every reason why these should be privately owned and operated. If so owned and operated, the enterprise running the highway should receive the gasoline taxes paid on account of travel on it.

Parks are an interesting example because they illustrate the difference between cases that can and cases that cannot be justified by neighborhood effects, and because almost everyone at first sight regards the conduct of National Parks as obviously a valid function of government. In fact, however, neighborhood effects may justify a city park; they do not justify a national park, like Yellowstone National Park or the Grand Canyon. What is the fundamental difference between the two? For the city park, it is extremely difficult to identify the people who benefit from it and to charge them for the benefits which they receive. If there is a park in the middle of the city, the houses on all sides get the benefit of the open space, and people who walk through it or by it also benefit. To maintain toll collectors at the gates or to impose annual charges per window overlooking the park would be very expensive and difficult. The entrances to a national park like Yellowstone, on the other hand, are few;

most of the people who come stay for a considerable period of time and it is perfectly feasible to set up toll gates and collect admission charges. This is indeed now done, though the charges do not cover the whole costs. If the public wants this kind of an activity enough to pay for it, private enterprises will have every incentive to provide such parks. And, of course, there are many private enterprises of this nature now in existence. I cannot myself conjure up any neighborhood effects or important monopoly effects that would justify governmental activity in this area.

Considerations like those I have treated under the heading of neighborhood effects have been used to rationalize almost every conceivable intervention. In many instances, however, this rationalization is special pleading rather than a legitimate application of the concept of neighborhood effects. Neighborhood effects cut both ways. They can be a reason for limiting the activities of government as well as for expanding them. Neighborhood effects impede voluntary exchange because it is difficult to identify the effects on third parties and to measure their magnitude; but this difficulty is present in governmental activity as well. It is hard to know when neighborhood effects are sufficiently large to justify particular costs in overcoming them and even harder to distribute the costs in an appropriate fashion. Consequently, when government engages in activities to overcome neighborhood effects, it will in part introduce an additional set of neighborhood effects by failing to charge or to compensate individuals properly. Whether the original or the new neighborhood effects are the more serious can only be judged by the facts of the individual case, and even then, only very approximately. Furthermore, the use of government to overcome neighborhood effects itself has an extremely important neighborhood effect which is unrelated to the particular occasion for government action. Every act of government intervention limits the area of individual freedom directly and threatens the preservation of freedom indirectly for reasons elaborated in the first chapter [of Friedman's book].

Our principles offer no hard and fast line how far it is appropriate to use government to accomplish jointly what it is difficult or impossible for us to accomplish separately through strictly voluntary exchange. In any particular case of proposed intervention, we must make up a balance sheet, listing separately the advantages and disadvantages. Our principles tell us what items to put on the one side and what items on the other and they give us some basis for attaching importance to the different items. In particular, we shall always want to enter on the liability side of any proposed government intervention, its neighborhood effect in threatening freedom, and give this effect considerable weight. Just how much weight to give to it, as to other items, depends upon the circumstances. If, for example, existing government intervention is minor, we shall attach a smaller weight to the negative effects of additional government intervention. This is an important reason why many earlier liberals, like Henry Simons, writing at a time when government was small by today's standards, were willing to have government undertake activities that today's liberals would not accept now that government has become so overgrown.

Action Through Government on Paternalistic Grounds

Freedom is a tenable objective only for responsible individuals. We do not believe in freedom for madmen or children. The necessity of drawing a line between responsible individuals and others is inescapable, yet it means that there is an essential ambiguity in our ultimate objective of freedom. Paternalism is inescapable for those whom we designate as not responsible.

The clearest case, perhaps, is that of madmen. We are willing neither to permit them freedom nor to shoot them. It would be nice if we could rely on voluntary activities of individuals to house and care for the madmen. But I think we cannot rule out the possibility that such charitable activities will be inadequate, if only because of the neighborhood effect involved in the fact that I benefit if another man contributes to the care of the insane. For this reason, we may be willing to arrange for their care through government.

Children offer a more difficult case. The ultimate operative unit in our society is the family, not the individual. Yet the acceptance of the family as the unit rests in considerable part on expediency rather than principle. We believe that parents are generally best able to protect their children and to provide for their development into responsible individuals for whom freedom is appropriate. But we do not believe in the freedom of parents to do what they will with other people. The children are responsible individuals in embryo, and a believer in freedom believes in protecting their ultimate rights.

To put this in a different and what may seem a more callous way, children are at one and the same time consumer goods and potentially responsible members of society. The freedom of individuals to use their economic resources as they want includes the freedom to use them to have children — to buy, as it were, the services of children as a particular form of consumption. But once this choice is exercised, the children have a value in and of themselves and have a freedom of their own that is not simply an extension of the freedom of the parents.

The paternalistic ground for governmental activity is in many ways the most troublesome to a liberal; for it involves the acceptance of a principle — that some shall decide for others — which he finds objectionable in most applications and which he rightly regards as a hallmark of his chief intellectual opponents, the proponents of collectivism in one or another of its guises, whether it be communism, socialism, or a welfare state. Yet there is no use pretending that problems are simpler than in fact they are. There is no avoiding the need for some measure of paternalism. As Dicey wrote in 1914 about an act for the protection of mental defectives, "The Mental Deficiency Act is the first step along a path on which no sane man can decline to enter, but which, if too far pursued, will bring statesmen across difficulties hard to meet without considerable interference with individual liberty."[1] There is no formula that can tell us where to stop. We must rely on our fallible judgment and, having reached a judgment, on our ability to persuade our fellow men that it is a correct judgment, or their ability to persuade us to modify our views. We must put our faith, here as elsewhere, in a consensus reached by imperfect and biased men through free discussion and trial and error.

Conclusion

A government which maintained law and order, defined property rights, served as a means whereby we could modify property rights and other rules of the economic game, adjudicated disputes about the interpretation of the rules, enforced contracts, pro-

[1] A. V. Dicey, *Lectures on the Relation between Law and Public Opinion in England during the Nineteenth Century* (2d ed.; London: Macmillan & Co., 1914), p. li.

moted competition, provided a monetary framework, engaged in activities to counter technical monopolies and to overcome neighborhood effects widely regarded as sufficiently important to justify government intervention, and which supplemented private charity and the private family in protecting the irresponsible, whether madman or child — such a government would clearly have important functions to perform. The consistent liberal is not an anarchist.

Yet it is also true that such a government would have clearly limited functions and would refrain from a host of activities that are now undertaken by federal and state governments in the United States, and their counterparts in other Western countries. Succeeding chapters [of Friedman's book] will deal in some detail with some of these activities, and a few have been discussed above, but it may help to give a sense of proportion about the role that a liberal would assign government simply to list, in closing this chapter, some activities currently undertaken by government in the U.S., that cannot, so far as I can see, validly be justified in terms of the principles outlined above:

1. Parity price support programs for agriculture.
2. Tariffs on imports or restrictions on exports, such as current oil import quotas, sugar quotas, etc.
3. Governmental control of output, such as through the farm program, or through prorationing of oil as is done by the Texas Railroad Commission.
4. Rent control, such as is still practiced in New York, or more general price and wage controls such as were imposed during and just after World War II.
5. Legal minimum wage rates, or legal maximum prices, such as the legal maximum of zero on the rate of interest that can be paid on demand deposits by commercial banks, or the legally fixed maximum rates that can be paid on savings and time deposits.
6. Detailed regulation of industries, such as the regulation of transportation by the Interstate Commerce Commission. This had some justi-

fication on technical monopoly grounds when initially introduced for railroads; it has none now for any means of transport. Another example is detailed regulation of banking.
7. A similar example, but one which deserves special mention because of its implicit censorship and violation of free speech, is the control of radio and television by the Federal Communications Commission.
8. Present social security programs, especially the old-age and retirement programs compelling people in effect (a) to spend a specified fraction of their income on the purchase of retirement annuity, (b) to buy the annuity from a publicly operated enterprise.
9. Licensure provisions in various cities and states which restrict particular enterprises or occupations or professions to people who have a license, where the license is more than a receipt for a tax which anyone who wishes to enter the activity may pay.
10. So-called "public-housing" and the host of other subsidy programs directed at fostering residential construction such as F.H.A. and V.A. guarantee of mortgage, and the like.
11. Conscription to man the military services in peacetime. The appropriate free market arrangement is volunteer military forces; which is to say, hiring men to serve. There is no justification for not paying whatever price is necessary to attract the required number of men. Present arrangements are inequitable and arbitrary, seriously interfere with the freedom of young men to shape their lives, and probably are even more costly than the market alternative. (Universal military training to provide a reserve for war time is a different problem and may be justified on liberal grounds.)
12. National parks, as noted above.
13. The legal prohibition on the carrying of mail for profit.
14. Publicly owned and operated toll roads, as noted above.

This list is far from comprehensive.

BIBLIOGRAPHY

I.   RADICAL PERSPECTIVES

A.   General Perspectives on Problems

Richard C. Edwards, Michael Reich, and Thomas E. Weisskopf, eds. *The Capitalist System,* 2nd ed. Englewood Cliffs, N.J.: Prentice-Hall, 1977.

David Mermelstein, ed. *Economics: Mainstream Readings and Radical Critiques,* 3rd ed. New York: Random House ,1976.

B.   An Introduction to Marxian Political Economy

E. K. Hunt and Howard Sherman. *Economics,* 2nd ed. New York: Harper & Row, 1975.

Paul Sweezy. *The Theory of Capitalist Development.* New York: Monthly Review Press, 1942.

Ernest Mandel. *Marxist Economic Theory,* Vols. I and II. New York: Monthly Review Press, 1968.

H. Selsam *et al.,* eds. *The Dynamics of Social Change.* New York: International Publishers, 1970. A useful introductory collection of important selections from the writings of Marx and Engels.

C.   The State

Ralph Miliband. *The State in Capitalist Society.* New York: Basic Books, 1969.

James O'Connor. *The Fiscal Crisis of the State.* New York: St. Martin's Press, 1973.

D.   Detailed Bibliography

The Union for Radical Political Economics. *Reading Lists in Radical Political Economics.* Volume 3. (New York: URPE, 1977). A collection of readings lists from courses on many different problems. Available from URPE, 41 Union Square West, Room 901, New York, N.Y. 10003.

II.   LIBERAL AND CONSERVATIVE PERSPECTIVES

A.   Urban Problems

Edward C. Banfield. *The Unheavenly City Revisited.* Boston: Little, Brown, 1974. A conservative approach.

Dick Netzer. *Economics and Urban Problems: Diagnosis and Prescription.* New York: Basic Books, 1970. A liberal approach.

B.   An Introduction to Orthodox Economics

Paul Samuelson. *Economics,* 10th ed. New York: McGraw-Hill, 1977.

Robert Heilbroner and Lester C. Thurow. *The Economic Problem,* 4th ed. Englewood Cliffs, N.J.: Prentice-Hall, 1975.

C.   The State

Otto Eckstein. *Public Finance,* 3rd ed. Englewood Cliffs, N.J.: Prentice-Hall, 1973. Introductory level.

Richard Musgrave. *The Theory of Public Finance.* New York: McGraw-Hill, 1959. More technical than Eckstein, but covers the same ground.

III.   COMPARISONS AMONG PARADIGMS — METHODOLOGICAL PERSPECTIVES

Thomas Kuhn. *The Structure of Scientific Revolutions,* 2nd ed. Chicago: University of Chicago Press, 1969. On competition between paradigms in the natural sciences.

Maurice Dobb. *Theories of Value and Distribution Since Adam Smith.* Cambridge, England: Cambridge University Press, 1973. Chapter 1. On different approaches to the objects of economic analysis.

Gunnar Myrdal. *The Political Element in the Development of Economic Theory.* London: Routledge & Kegan Paul, 1953. Argues that "political" views always invade social scientific analysis.

EMPLOYMENT

We mold men to jobs, not jobs to men.

— Corporate personnel officer[1]

I told him that the reason I wasn't too sure if I wanted the job was because they weren't paying enough money, and plus I was looking for a job with a future. I don't want to work where I can see I wasn't going to make no kind of progress or build myself up with no kind of background or nothing.

— 19-year-old black high school graduate[2]

The millions of workers in the United States are burdened by different kinds of employment problems — with varying symptoms and causes. It could hardly be otherwise. As Elliot Liebow has put it, "The centrality of work . . . is not new to human experience." [3] Employment dominates the ways we spend our time, the ways we earn our living, and the contributions we make to the world. Although I have chosen to discuss the problems of only one group of American workers in this chapter — the underemployed — I do not intend to imply that all other groups of workers are free from such characteristic fates as exploitation on the job or severe alienation. I hope to illustrate the ways in which employment problems derive from the basic structure of capitalist institutions. The analysis could easily be transposed to other equally important labor market issues, problems, or groups.[4]

This chapter concentrates on the problem of "underemployment" in the United States, especially as that problem has been perceived and defined by the American public since the late 1960s. In the public view, the problem of underemployment seemed most entrenched and complicated in Northern central–city ghettos, particularly among black ghetto workers. Many policies and programs arose throughout the sixties to help solve ghetto employment prob-

[1] Quoted in Peter Doeringer and Michael Piore, *Internal Labor Markets and Manpower Analysis* (Lexington, Mass.: D. C. Heath, 1971), Chapter 5.

[2] Quoted in Herb Goro, *The Block* (New York: Random House, 1970), p. 143.

[3] Elliot Liebow, "No Man Can Live with the Terrible Knowledge That He Is Not Needed," *New York Times Magazine,* April 5, 1970, p. 29.

[4] Some of this additional analysis is provided in Chapter 1, "General Perspectives."

lems. Despite their obviously benign intentions, none of them seemed to do any good. By the end of the decade, Congress was beginning to wonder if federal programs should be continued at all; according to one newspaper report in early 1970, "Friends as well as foes agree that only a small proportion of the 6.4 million persons who were in the programs have really been helped."[5] Private corporations that had rushed into special training programs for "disadvantaged" workers were also backing off; many believed that they had acted too impulsively and that training ghetto workers "was not something they were very good at."[6] Since the early 1970s, this disillusionment has continued.[7]

This chapter indicates that such failures should have been expected. As Chapter 1 made clear, the radical analysis of problems like underemployment views them as natural consequences of the basic set of institutions dominating capitalist societies like the United States. The manpower programs of the 1960s did not seek to change the structure of those institutions and were therefore likely to have marginal effects. In presenting the outline of that argument in this introduction, I have divided the discussion into four sections: first, the definition of urban underemployment; second, a summary of the liberal and conservative analyses of those problems; third, an elaboration of the radical analysis of ghetto employment problems; and, finally, an introduction to the purpose and contents of the reading selections that follow.

Problem Definitions and Magnitudes

As the public became more concerned about employment problems in central-city ghettos during the 1960s, it revised its basic definitions of labor market disadvantage.[8] Earlier, public policy had sought to help the "unemployed" — those who wanted to work but could not find a job. Those who were employed seemed satisfied, at least, and those who were not looking for work were presumably, for health or family reasons, incapable of working. The unemployment rate seemed a perfectly adequate measure of the severity of employment problems.[9] But several developments during the decade forced attention on a new set of problems. Greater prosperity had solved the employment problems of many workers who had formerly been unemployed.[10] The civil rights movement and ghetto riots had focused concern on the difficulties of blacks, espe-

[5] *The New York Times,* February 20, 1970, p. 20.

[6] *The New York Times,* March 1, 1970, p. 42.

[7] Since the 1970s, in fact, the public has become preoccupied by the more general employment problems of the economic crisis wracking the entire capitalist world economy. For general analyses of that economic crisis, see URPE, *Radical Perspectives on the Economic Crisis,* rev. ed. (URPE, 1975), 1977; or David Mermelstein, *The Economic Crisis Reader* (New York: Random House, 1975).

[8] For more detail, see David M. Gordon, *Theories of Poverty and Underemployment* (Lexington, Mass.: D. C. Heath, 1972), Chapter 1.

[9] Unemployment is defined as the percentage of the total labor force that is not employed. The labor force includes those who are employed and those who say that they are looking for work. Those who are neither employed nor looking for work are considered "not in the labor force." For further discussion of these categories and their historical justification, see Seymour Wolfbein, *Employment and Unemployment in the United States* (New York: Science Research Associates, 1964).

[10] During the 1960s, for instance, the unemployment rate had dropped from nearly 7 percent to roughly 3.5 percent before it began to rise again in 1969.

cially those in the central cities.[11] And the continuing evolution and frequent failure of manpower programs produced new impressions of success and failure that affected objectives and priorities.[12]

By the end of the decade, analysts and government officials began to use the concept of "underemployment" to evoke the new set of problems with which they had become preoccupied. The concept encompassed those who were unemployed, those who were working full time at very low wages, those who wanted to work full time but could find only part-time work, those who wanted to work but had dropped out of the labor force, and those who seemed so unattached to primary labor market institutions that they were often missed by the surveys upon which employment statistics were based.[13] The concept focused on the problems of a large group of disadvantaged workers, often described as "secondary workers" or the "underclass," who were frequently able to find work but earned low wages, worked intermittently, and could rarely hope for occupational advancement. While unemployment rates, measured by traditional statistical categories, were often around 15 percent in central-city ghettos, by the mid-1970s underemployment rates soared as high as 50 to 60 percent.[14]

The three defining characteristics of "underemployed" workers were their low wages, their relatively underdeveloped skills, and their frequently unpredictable patterns of work.[15] Each of these characteristics reinforced the others, joining to form a self-perpetuating cycle of underemployment. If a worker earned low wages, for instance, he or she was often likely to quit the job — to search for higher-paying work, to hustle on the "illegitimate" job market, or to collect relief. This would gradually establish a pattern of unstable employment. This record of instability would often prevent the worker from qualifying for jobs in which employers consider stability important, and in which increasing job tenure sometimes leads to the acquisition of significant skills on the job. It would make the worker undesirable to any but the lowest-wage employers. The employee would be back where he/she began, and the pattern of job instability would be perpetuated.

This new focus on the underemployed raised many new and perplexing questions for labor market analysts. Why were so many people finding it so difficult to find decent jobs? Would some simple solutions like improving job information help? Or would more dramatic efforts to improve the skills of the underemployed be required? Or would it also be necessary to change the structures of jobs available in the labor market? And could any of these changes be effected without requiring major structural changes in the entire economic system? Tentative answers to many of these questions have been filling shelves of books.[16]

---

[11] The Riot Commission Report crystallized many of these influences. See *Report of the National Advisory Commission on Civil Disorders* (New York: Bantam, 1968).

[12] For a discussion of these programs, see Sar A. Levitan and Garth L. Mangum, *Federal Training and Work Programs in the Sixties* (Ann Arbor: Institute of Labor and Industrial Relations, 1969).

[13] For further discussion, see the selection by Spring, Harrison, and Vietorisz, and the Editor's Supplement in this chapter.

[14] *Ibid.*

[15] For perhaps the best impressionistic account of these characteristics and their interactions, see Elliot Liebow, *Tally's Corner* (Boston: Little, Brown, 1967).

[16] For a summary of most of this work and its implications, see Gordon, *Theories of Poverty and Underemployment,* entire.

Liberal and Conservative Views

Public policies responding to these new perceptions followed directly from conventional analyses of employment problems. As is true with many other problems in this book, liberal and conservative perspectives agree on underlying analytic assumptions but tend to differ on policy prescriptions. In this section, I first summarize the common analytic assumptions and then describe the policy differences.

The analyses begin from basic orthodox economic analysis and its postulates about the distribution of income from labor. According to those postulates, a worker's wages in the labor market tend to vary with his/her marginal product in competitive equilibrium.[17] Those with higher marginal productivities will earn relatively high incomes, while those with lower productivities will earn less. According to a recent reformulation of these basic theories, a worker's wages can be viewed as a return on the amount of money invested in his/her training, or, as the new perspective puts it, a return to investment in "human capital."[18] Human capital analysis emphasizes that educational investments while workers are in school and firm investments in on-the-job training are analytically comparable, for each represents a capital investment designed to increase a worker's productivity. If some workers have low productivities, the analysis assumes that either they or society think that returns to investments in their productivities would be too low to warrant the expenditure. If some jobs do not provide on-the-job training, the analysis implies that employers would not find it profitable to invest in worker training in those economic circumstances.[19]

The implications of this kind of analysis for underemployment seemed clear for a while. Lester Thurow put it simply in 1969: "If an individual's income is too low, his productivity is too low. His income can be increased only if his productivity can be raised."[20] Since most economists thought that "productivity" consists of general skills acquired through schooling and specific skills acquired on the job, this analysis helped stimulate most of the innovations in manpower programs during the 1960s. Wide varieties of public efforts were designed to stimulate training: institutional vocational training; financial incentives to firms to provide more on-the-job training to disadvantaged workers; job referral services to steer workers toward the most stable job opportunities; various programs to improve worker motivation and stability.[21]

After a while, many economists began to feel uneasy with this unqualified kind of analysis. Many training programs designed to provide skills to disadvantaged workers appeared to make little difference. It began to appear that many workers failed to qualify for decent jobs because employers "thought"

---

[17] One can begin reading about these theories at the beginning, with the discussion on income distribution in Paul Samuelson, *Economics,* 10th ed. (New York: McGraw-Hill, 1977).

[18] For a basic statement of human capital analysis, see Gary Becker, *Human Capital,* 2nd ed. (New York: National Bureau of Economic Research, 1974) or Gary Becker, *Human Capital and the Personal Distribution of Income* (Ann Arbor: University of Michigan Press, 1967).

[19] For an application of these concepts to the specific problems discussed in this chapter, see Lester Thurow, *Poverty and Discrimination* (Washington, D.C.: Brookings Institution, 1969).

[20] *Ibid.,* p. 26.

[21] The list of such programs is too long to cover here. See Levitan and Mangum, *Federal Training and Work Programs of the Sixties,* for more detail.

that they would not stay on those jobs very long — that "productivity" consisted of general behavioral characteristics like "job stability" as much as it consisted of stocks of manifest skills like cognitive ability or manual dexterity.[22]

This set of perceptions led to a new policy emphasis on informational programs rather than training programs. If employers were rejecting applicants because employers "thought" those applicants would be unstable, then it might be important to provide employers with the most accurate possible information about those potential workers. And if employees could get better jobs if they were able to find those employers who wanted workers with exactly their "stability characteristics," better information about available jobs might help steer the underemployed to the best jobs that they could hope to find.[23]

Most orthodox economists could agree on many of those analytic perspectives. Liberals and conservatives tend to disagree about the ways in which they suggest their application to public policy.

Conservatives emphasize two basic points. First, they suggest that individuals have many opportunities to solve their own problems by improving their own productivities. They can stay in school longer, work more steadily, and stay on jobs longer to learn new skills. If they do not, then they have no one to blame but themselves.[24] Second, conservatives usually argue that government interference with market mechanisms will only make matters worse. For instance, they often argue that the government imposition of a minimum wage means that some workers, plagued with very low productivities, will not be able to sell their labor at a wage low enough to make their employment profitable for employers.[25] This kind of argument obviously reflects the more general conservative emphasis on the sanctity of the "free market."

Liberals build toward different kinds of policy prescriptions from the same analytic framework. Liberals argue that many structural factors — social, economic, and institutional forces — explain the low skills and employment problems of many workers. Because they feel that those forces will not quickly adjust if some individuals simply acquire a few more skills, they tend to argue that the government should speed up the process of adjustment.

This argument leads to two main policy emphases. First, unlike conservatives, liberals suggest that individuals are not to blame for their individual problems and that society has a responsibility to provide the basis for an increasing equality of outcomes. Second, again in contrast with conservatives, liberals argue that the government should directly address the sources of individual problems. During the 1960s, many liberals thought that individual problems lay in the inadequacy of their previous training; liberals therefore led the advocacy of expanded government training programs. During the 1970s, liberals have tended more and more to suspect that the principal source of individuals' un-

[22] Many of these new perceptions appeared in technical journals, but the Feldstein article below reflects some of this new analysis.

[23] This new emphasis worked its way into federal manpower policy in the early 1970s, when many experiments aimed at improving labor market information were instituted.

[24] This is one of the principal implications of the application of human capital analysis to the employment problems. If workers do not have enough human capital to be very "productive," then they should invest more in their own stocks of human capital. See Becker, *Human Capital*.

[25] Edward Banfield develops some of this argument in *The Unheavenly City Revisited* (Boston: Little, Brown, 1974), Chapter 5; and Martin Feldstein develops a parallel argument about unemployment insurance in the selection included in this chapter.

deremployment problems lay in the limited numbers of decent jobs. By 1976, most liberal politicians had reached a consensus around government programs to "guarantee" full employment by government provision of public employment.[26]

The Radical View

A radical analysis of underemployment begins with the same description of reality. It simply explains that reality in entirely different ways.

In general, echoing the discussion in Chapter 1, the radical analysis views such problems as inevitable consequences of basic capitalist institutions. Those institutions serve the interests of the dominant capitalist class and define the status of workers in the labor market. In contrast to orthodox postulates about the process of income determination and distribution, the radical analysis offers a very different view of wage and status determination.

In the radical analysis, there are two stages in the determination and distribution of income. First, a complex set of social, economic, and technological forces determine a given worker's total productivity; this can vary with the worker's skills and the characteristics of the job in which he works. Then, the relative power of employers and employees determines the share of the worker's total product paid to the worker in wages. He receives some of the product as wages and the employer receives the rest as "surplus value." The worker's final wage thus depends *both* on his productivity *and* on the relative power of the class or group with which he is identified. Employers seek constantly either to increase or to maintain their relative share of total product. At the same time, they hope to provide workers enough return so that the working class does not revolt in response to its oppression or impoverishment. Ernest Mandel summarizes these general propositions.

> In fact, it is not the absolute level of wages that matters to capital. . . . What matters to capital is the possibility of extracting more surplus labour, more unpaid labour, more surplus value, more profit from its workers. The growth in the productivity of labour, which makes possible the growth of relative surplus value, implies the possibility of a slow rise in real wages . . . on condition that the equivalent of these increased real wages is produced in an ever shorter period of time, i.e. that wages rise less quickly than productivity. . . .
>
> The rise in real wages does not follow *automatically* from the rise in the productivity of labour. The latter only creates the *possibility* of such a rise, within the capitalist framework, provided profit is not threatened. For this potential increase to become actual, two interlinked conditions are needed: a favourable evolution of "relations of strength in the labour market" . . . and effective organization . . . of the wage workers which enables them to abolish competition among themselves and so to take advantage of these "favourable market conditions." [27]

Over time in capitalist societies, workers are drawn together in large work places and, as Marx and Engels predicted, are increasingly likely to perceive their common interests and unite around those interests to demand a larger

[26] See, for instance, the article by Hubert Humphrey in the *Annals* of the American Academy of Political and Social Science, March 1975.

[27] Ernest Mandel, *Marxist Economic Theory* (New York: Monthly Review Press, 1969), p. 145.

share of total product and better working conditions.[28] In societies based on democratic traditions, the capitalist class cannot easily suppress those worker demands. Instead, the capitalist class is likely to seek to promote class divisions *within* the working class in order to weaken the unity of worker protest. The more labor is internally divided and competes among its separate strata, the less unified it will be in its demands of employers.[29] It will always be in the interests of employers to promote or preserve such intra-class stratifications.

These general propositions are intended to apply to any capitalist economy.[30] Their specific manifestations will vary from country to country and from time to time, depending on the relative stage of economic development of different societies and on their peculiar historical traditions. As Chapter 1 explained, these characteristic patterns are "specified" by the unique features of individual economies. To understand the implications of these basic propositions for ghetto underemployment in the United States, it is necessary to examine the specific structure and history of labor market institutions in this country.

In the United States over the past fifty years, according to the radical argument, the labor market has been dominated by tendencies toward "labor market segmentation" — toward the increasing compartmentalization of the labor market into sectors featuring different kinds of labor processes.[31]

The most important of these tendencies toward segmentation, for the purposes of this book, involves the emergence of a "dual labor market."

It seems important to emphasize two main points about the tendencies creating a dual labor market:

1. Underlying the development of the dual labor market lies a sharp split between two different kinds of working situations. One kind of working experience involves what we call the "primary labor process." The other involves the "secondary labor process." Work is organized in different ways in the two processes.

The primary labor process is structured internally. There are job ladders, promotional channels, customary practices, a variety of jobs, and some jobs with decent wages. The secondary labor process is unstructured. There are no job ladders, few opportunities for promotion, unpredictable working relationships, primitive capital equipment, little variety in the range of jobs available, and uniformly low wages.[32]

2. There have been powerful tendencies reproducing this distinction between primary and secondary jobs, building together to create differences at the level of labor markets.

[28] They made this argument first in *The Communist Manifesto* (New York: International Publishers, 1948).

[29] This obviously has implications for interpretations of trade union history in the United States. The craft unions were clearly more acceptable to employers than were the industrial unions because the former tended to promote stratification. See Stanley Aronowitz, *False Promises* (New York: McGraw-Hill, 1973), Chapter 4.

[30] For further discussion at this level of abstraction, see Samuel Bowles and Herbert Gintis, *Schooling in Capitalist America* (New York: Basic Books, 1975), Chapter 3; and Bertram Silverman and Murray Yanowitch, eds., *The Worker in "Post-Industrial" Society* (New York: Random House, 1974).

[31] See the piece by Reich, Gordon, and Edwards in this chapter, and Richard C. Edwards, Michael Reich, and David Gordon, eds., *Labor Market Segmentation* (Lexington, Mass.: D. C. Heath, 1975).

[32] See the piece by M. Piore in this chapter, and Gordon, *Theories of Poverty and Underemployment,* Chapters 4–5.

• The American industrial structure has become more and more divided.[33] On the one hand, the largest corporations have come to dominate many "concentrated" industries. Those corporations have the capital resources to change their work processes, develop job ladders, invest in many kinds of job training programs, stabilize their work forces, and partially reward unions for cooperative behavior.[34] On the other hand, there remain many "competitive" or "peripheral" industries. In these sectors, firms are small, pushed to the margin by competition, too penniless to be able to invest in new work processes or new mechanisms for controlling workers. Unions may develop in these peripheral sectors, but they can rarely transform their militance into real power because they might easily put their individual employers out of business.[35]

• Many government programs increase the costs to peripheral employers of changing their work processes.[36] Various social security and unemployment compensation benefits make it more expensive than before to maintain a stable work force. Those who can afford those programs — mostly the larger corporations — face growing incentives to keep their employees on the job longer (in order to spread out the extra costs of employers' contributions to those programs). Those firms that cannot afford the extra contributions are more and more likely to rely on a work force that comes and goes frequently, which exhibits "unstable" characteristics.

• As labor unions have increased their strength in some sectors, they have begun to acquire the power to protect their working conditions and to impede employer "speed-up" and harassment.[37] This has tended, other things equal, to push employers to substitute "disciplined" machines for "undisciplined" workers. This has created a dynamic, in the "core" industries, through which each increment of extra output generates fewer and fewer jobs. The processes in those industries have become more and more capital-intensive. In contrast, "peripheral" firms are unable to invest in capital-intensive technologies, largely because they cost so much. Their production processes remain relatively labor-intensive. As a result, the production processes in the two sectors become increasingly divergent.

• America has become a bureaucratic society. Corporations have developed large administrative structures to solve many of their problems. These administrative structures have relied more and more on new methods for hiring and controlling workers. They emphasize rationalization, rather than force; status incentives rather than piece-rate incentives; educational credentials rather than union credentials. In many white-collar jobs, these new processes tend to dominate the work process and further divide those primary jobs from the particularistic, unpredictable, and unstructured processes of the secondary labor market.[38]

• All these differences are reflected as differences among *labor markets.*

[33] See Robert Averitt, *The Dual Economy* (New York: Norton, 1968).

[34] Two major examples of such industries in the U.S. are the auto industry and the steel industry.

[35] The textile industry and several divisions of the food processing industry provide two important examples of this sector.

[36] See the piece by Piore in this chapter.

[37] See the piece by Reich, Gordon, and Edwards in this chapter.

[38] See Harry Braverman, *Labor and Monopoly Capital* (New York: Monthly Review Press, 1974); Bowles and Gintis, *Schooling in a Capitalist America,* Chapters 4–5; and Richard C. Edwards, "Labor Market Structure and the Social Relations of the Firm," in Edwards *et al., Labor Market Segmentation.*

Some people — from certain class backgrounds, with certain skin colors, living in certain areas — are able to gain access to primary jobs. Informal labor market institutions and stratified schools smooth their passage to and between those jobs. Other people — from lower-class backgrounds, with darker skin colors, living in different areas — are institutionally channeled into secondary jobs. Their schools, community institutions, and government programs grease the skids, tending to recycle them through the same kinds of employment.[39] Movement *among* labor market segments becomes more and more unlikely.

With these underlying developments, radicals argue, one can begin to look at the problems of underemployment in a substantially different way. Several critical points follow in order.

First, there are only so many "good" jobs in the economy. As output increases, the corporate sector tends to translate each extra dollar of output into relatively fewer and fewer good jobs.[40] Unless the government began to transform the power of the largest corporations, it appears unlikely that the private sector will autonomously generate growing numbers of good jobs by itself.

Second, access to good jobs is mediated by many customary, bureaucratic, and impersonal criteria. It is not always true that the people with the most "productive" skills get those jobs. Often, people with the right skin color, proper class background, congenial bearing, appropriate educational credentials, or "manageable" personality are most likely to pass through the maze of bureaucratic barriers.[41]

Third, given the relatively fixed numbers of good jobs and the relatively rigid procedures for obtaining them, there is little that an individual with the "wrong" characteristics and background can do to obtain a good job. "Productive" skills are beside the point, to a large extent, and so is a worker's attitude. What matters is what employers want, and they may simply not want workers with certain characteristics.[42]

Fourth, and finally, the combination of all these factors tends to lock certain groups of workers into secondary labor markets — in what, by any standards, are "bad" jobs. Good jobs move away from their communities. Deteriorating communities impede their struggle for skills and job access. Skin color and class background "screen" them out of certain jobs. Their best efforts may often fail to improve their status, earnings, or job security. Their individual qualities had little to do with where they've got, and potential changes in their individual qualities will have little to do with where they may get.

---

[39] See the piece by Harrison in this chapter.

[40] As Braverman (*Labor and Monopoly Capital*) points out, corporations have developed machines that separate workers from each other and tend to erode communication among workers. This kind of automation serves the central function of helping corporations gain more and more control over the production process. As a result, more and more jobs are eliminated.

[41] See Bowles and Gintis for much more detail.

[42] Orthodox economists would argue that, if workers' skills improved enough, the job structure — the demand for labor — would adjust to the changes in supply, providing more jobs for these workers. But the radical argument suggests that corporations cannot afford to abandon many of these fixed job structures; they serve fundamental functions — providing incentives to workers, dividing workers into strata and segments, controlling the spread of unionization — upon which corporations fundamentally depend. They do not dare to change their job structures for fear of losing some of their central control over production. For a basic elaboration of this central argument, see David M. Gordon, "Capitalist Efficiency and Socialist Efficiency," *Monthly Review,* July–August 1976.

As this process of segmentation has set in, radicals would argue that it has had a fundamental effect on the attitudes of "disadvantaged" workers. Traditionally, disadvantaged workers in this country have been recent migrants (from Europe or from the South); they have been willing to work patiently at menial work because those jobs offered higher wages, better working conditions, or better prospects than jobs in their previous social settings. The act of migration had fostered a basic optimism about their or their children's prospects. But a new generation of Northern-born ghetto workers has now entered the labor force, starting at the lowest rungs of the occupational ladder. They have not migrated and cannot build from that hopeful act. I have called this the "promised land" effect, after Claude Brown's book *Manchild in the Promised Land.* Brown compares the attitudes of black migrants from the South with those of blacks born, raised, and initiated in Northern ghettos:

> Going to New York was good-bye to the cotton fields, good-bye to "Massa Charlie," good-bye to the chain gang, and, most of all, good-bye to those sunup-to-sundown working hours. . . .
> Before the soreness of the cotton fields had left Mama's back, her knees were getting sore from scrubbing "Goldberg's" floor. Nevertheless, she was better off; she had gone from the fire into the frying pan.
> The children of these disillusioned colored pioneers inherited the total lot of their parents — the disappointments, the anger. To add to their misery, they had little hope of deliverance. For where does one run to when he's already in the promised land? [43]

Without "hope of deliverance," these workers are looking at their jobs more realistically than previously disadvantaged workers. They find that, besides earning low wages, they have few chances for rising occupationally. In the sectors of the labor market to which they seem limited, it does not matter if they move in and out of jobs or the labor force, because it appears that neither their skills nor their work histories affect their chances for better jobs. And so, it seems to them to make little difference if they continue in school or work diligently on the job. They place little value in work, they often earn more by "hustling," and they assume that rewards in the labor market do not correspond to their merit or abilities. In these sectors of the labor market, indeed, their perceptions seem accurate. As Liebow points out:

> Both the employee and employer are contemptuous of the [secondary] job. The employee shows his contempt by his reluctance to accept it or keep it, the employer by paying less than is required to support a family. . . . With few exceptions, jobs filled by the streetcorner men are at the bottom of the employment ladder in every respect, from wage level to prestige.[44]

Older workers, with different histories and different time horizons, were apparently willing to tolerate those jobs. Younger workers in the ghetto, it now appears, will not.[45]

[43] *Manchild in the Promised Land* (New York: Macmillan, 1965), pp. 7–8.
[44] *Tally's Corner,* p. 58.
[45] Their refusals have obviously also become more feasible with the increasing prevalence of extralabor market income opportunities — through crime or public assistance. See Harrison in this chapter.

Given those attitudes, it seems clear that training programs will not work for ghetto workers — regardless of their subtlety and sophistication — unless the programs manifestly guarantee entirely different kinds of job opportunities to those workers. Many younger workers are no longer interested in training themselves if training permits a barely improved job with barely higher wages and inconsequential opportunities for training and advancement on the job. These workers clearly want jobs in the "primary" labor market, jobs that pay decent wages, and jobs that offer opportunities for rapid and guaranteed promotion. To the extent that many of these younger workers are black, they obviously insist on equal opportunities with whites for landing those jobs. All the varieties of government programs that offer them less than this end up offering them nothing.[46]

In a long interview with Herb Goro for *The Block,* a nineteen-year-old black high school graduate clearly expressed most of these attitudes:

> I want a respectable job — clean, I was explaining it to my counselor why I wanted a job in the hospital, he came out and — bang, out of his mouth — he came out and said, "Why don't you get a job with the Sanitation Department? Why don't you be a delivery boy or something like that?" You know, I told him, I said, "Why do you think I went to school twelve years, to become a delivery boy? You must be kidding." He said, "You want a job, right?" I said, "Well, if that's the case I don't need no job. I was doing pretty good without that before, you know." ... You see, my thing was that being I was black and he was white, he just didn't want me to get in a clean hospital or decent place to work. He wanted me to work out there in the Sanitation Department where people could laugh at me, you know, and say, well, "He's a Sanitation man, he's got to sweep the streets. He got a high school diploma and he's sweeping the streets. He's just a fool" — you know, like that ...
>
> I'm concerned about respect, that's what I'm concerned about. And I'm concerned about a job with respect and salary ... I mean I make more than $1.50 shooting dice. ...[47]

The pieces by Piore; Bluestone; Harrison; and Reich, Gordon, and Edwards in this chapter develop almost all these points in further detail. For the purposes of this introduction, a simple summary can suffice. Important historical changes in the American labor market have created an increasingly segmented labor market. Denied access to limited pools of "good" jobs, ghetto residents will continue their marginal attachment to the labor market, impatiently rejecting traditional kinds of lower-class jobs. The cycle of underemployment follows its course. Only some fundamental changes in the entire structure of labor market institutions in this country could break the vicious circle. We need more good jobs. The private sector will not provide them. We shall have to provide them ourselves.

The Readings

The first group of readings provides Impressions, Definitions, and Magnitudes. The brief vignette from Elliot Liebow's book *Tally's Corner* evokes the

---

[46] For a general review of the impact of government training programs in the 1960s, see Bennett Harrison, *Education, Training, and the Urban Ghetto* (Baltimore: Johns Hopkins Press, 1972).

[47] Quoted in Goro, *The Block,* p. 156.

frustration that many disadvantaged workers feel about their jobs. The selection by William Spring, Bennett Harrison, and Thomas Vietorisz reviews the concept of underemployment and sketches its magnitudes in the largest central-city ghettos. (Their piece was written before the economic crisis of the mid-1970s; the scale was much smaller than it was later to become.) An Editor's Supplement pulls together some aggregate estimates of the numbers of underemployed in the United States.

The second group of readings represents the different analytic perspectives on employment problems. The selection by Richard H. Leftwich elaborates the basic orthodox economic theory of the distribution of income from labor, discussing the determinants of marginal productivity as it varies among workers. The essay by Martin Feldstein represents the more recent orthodox response, most commonly echoed among conservative economists, to the problems of underemployment. It emphasizes many of the government mechanisms that interfere with the "free market." The next four pieces develop some strands of the radical interpretation of the problems of underemployment. Michael J. Piore presents the basic theory of the dual labor market and summarizes some of its implications. Barry Bluestone reviews the industrial dimensions of duality, focusing on the sharp differences between core industries and peripheral industries. Bennett Harrison explores some of the institutions reinforcing the behavioral mechanisms of the secondary labor market. Michael Reich, David M. Gordon, and Richard C. Edwards, finally, present the more general historical and theoretical basis for the radical theory of labor market segmentation into which, for many, the dual labor market analysis fits.

A third group of readings reviews some of the policy implications of this analysis. Lloyd Ulman, an orthodox economist, reviews the public experience with manpower training programs during the 1960s. He argues that, despite many failures, there are still important uses for such programs today. David Wellman puts some of those well-meaning training programs of the 1960s into a more radical perspective. Many of the programs sought to "improve the attitudes" of young ghetto workers. Wellman shows that those attitudes were based on remarkably clear perceptions of the real dimensions of labor market opportunities and the illusory character of intangible program promises. Barry Bluestone and Bennett Harrison present a radical critique of increasingly popular liberal programs for public employment programs. They agree that public employment is a necessary development, but they criticize conventional liberal proposals for failing to "capitalize" their public employment ventures; such programs, they argue, condemn public employment to insignificance.

A final selection presents a vision of a wholly different relationship between employment and society. Charles Bettelheim reports on some of the developments in work in China after the Cultural Revolution of the 1960s. His report suggests that work in China, rather than being subjected to the pursuit of profit, is increasingly structured by the needs and desires of workers. We talk about the need for "good jobs" in our capitalist society but can do little to fulfill that need as long as corporations control the economy. The Chinese have learned not only to talk about "good jobs" but also to create them

TALLY'S JOB

Elliot Liebow

This very simple little anecdote comes from the chapter on "Men and Jobs" in Liebow's classic study of streetcorner life in the ghetto, *Tally's Corner*. Tally's attitude about his job — a regular, relatively well-paying, semiskilled job — reflects increasingly strong feelings among disadvantaged workers in this country about relative occupational status and prestige. It also illustrates the extraordinary importance of employment in establishing the tenor of workers' lives.

Tally and I were in the Carry-out. It was summer, Tally's peak earning season as a cement finisher, a semiskilled job a cut or so above that of the unskilled laborer. His take-home pay during these weeks was well over a hundred dollars — "a lot of bread." But for Tally, who no longer had a family to support, bread was not enough.

"You know that boy came in last night? That Black Moozlem? That's what I ought to be doing. I ought to be in his place."

"What do you mean?"

"Dressed nice, going to [night] school, got a good job."

"He's no better off than you, Tally. You make more than he does."

"It's not the money. [Pause] It's position, I guess. He's got position. When he finish school he gonna be a supervisor. People respect him. . . . Thinking about people with position and educa-

Source: From *Tally's Corner: A Study of Negro Streetcorner Men,* by Elliot Liebow, by permission of Little, Brown & Co. Copyright © 1967 by Little, Brown & Company (Inc.).

tion gives me a feeling right here [pressing his fingers into the pit of his stomach]."

"You're educated, too. You have a skill, a trade. You're a cement finisher. You can make a building, pour a sidewalk."

"That's different. Look, can anybody do what you're doing? Can anybody just come up and do your job? Well, in one week I can teach you cement finishing. You won't be as good as me 'cause you won't have the experience but you'll be a cement finisher. That's what I mean. Anybody can do what I'm doing and that's what gives me this feeling. [Long pause] Suppose I like this girl. I go over to her house and I meet her father. He starts talking about what he done today. He talks about operating on somebody and sewing them up and about surgery. I know he's a doctor 'cause of the way he talks. Then she starts talking about what she did. Maybe she's a boss or a supervisor. Maybe she's a lawyer and her father says to me, 'And what do you do, Mr. Jackson?' [Pause] You remember at the courthouse, Lonny's trial? You and the lawyer was talking in the hall? You remember? I just stood there listening. I didn't say a word. You know why? 'Cause I didn't even know what you was talking about. That's happened to me a lot."

"Hell, you're nothing special. That happens to everybody. Nobody knows everything. One man is a doctor, so he talks about surgery. Another man is a teacher, so he talks about books. But doctors and teachers don't know anything about concrete. You're a cement finisher and that's your specialty."

"Maybe so, but when was the last time you saw anybody standing around talking about concrete?"

THE CRISIS OF THE UNDEREMPLOYED

William Spring, Bennett Harrison, and Thomas Vietorisz

This selection provides a basic review of the problem of underemployment. Underemployment is provisionally defined, and some of its magnitudes are sketched. More detail is provided in the following Editor's Supplement.

William Spring has worked as a staff member of the U.S. Senate Committee on Employment, Manpower and Poverty. Bennett Harrison teaches urban planning and economics at the Massachusetts Institute of Technology. Thomas Vietorisz teaches economics at the New School for Social Research.

What is wrong with the economies of America's big cities is at best poorly measured by the conventional unemployment rate published monthly by the U.S. Department of Labor and dutifully reported in the press and on television. The problem is that even those who work — or a very large proportion of them — do not and cannot earn enough money to support their families. They work for a living but not for a living wage. Many have long known this fact; certainly, the poor themselves. Now we have documentary evidence that will help bring the picture into focus for others. This lack of perception, this inability of the nation to understand the nature of the problem itself helps to explain our failure to come to the rescue of the cities.

The evidence consists of startling findings now available from surveys conducted by the Census Bureau in 51 urban areas as part of the 1970 Census, findings that should eventually lead to better solutions than welfare or income maintenance and should in the long run contribute substantially to the nation's over-all economic prosperity.

Within the neighborhoods covered by these surveys, more than 60 per cent of all workers did not earn enough to maintain a decent standard of living for their families, and 30 per cent could not even earn a poverty-level income. Of course, many of these areas are among the most depressed portions

of the city, and do not represent the whole. If half of the *entire* city population were earning less than subsistence, what is now a crisis would long ago have become a catastrophe. But the samples cover much more than the misery in the ghetto proper. They report on conditions that affect at least a third of the total city population. Thirteen million people in all live in the areas surveyed, 49.5 per cent of them black; 47.9 per cent white, including 11.8 per cent of Spanish background; and 2.6 per cent of other racial or ethnic origin. The figures reveal economic conditions of a submerged group that spreads out from the black and brown ghettos into the neighborhoods of the white working class.

The basic findings emerge from an analysis of the Census Employment Survey (C.E.S.), designed by the Bureau of Labor Statistics (B.L.S.). Some 68 volumes of raw statistics from the C.E.S. have been published, but the Administration has chosen not to analyze the numbers, or even to calculate the simplest indexes of economic well-being for these 51 cities. Consequently, the staff of and consultants to Senator Gaylord Nelson's Subcommittee on Employment, Manpower and Poverty have undertaken the task of digging through these invaluable statistics to develop a picture of the state of the inner-city economy in 1970. This effort has culminated in the measurement of "subemployment" — the key to understanding what the urban crisis is all about.

Unemployment — Subemployment

The development of the new subemployment concept began in 1966 when former Secretary of Labor Willard Wirtz decided to take a close look at the relation between the job market and poverty in the nation's inner cities. His staff conducted door-to-door sample interviews in 10 ghettos in eight major cities. In 1967 the B.L.S. set up a task force under the direction of William Milligan to carry on research in a number of large ghettos. The team experimented with new ways of interviewing the poor, new kinds of questions, new insights from academic research, and it made use of the experience gained in administering the 1966 survey. In 1970, Milligan's group managed to have its questionnaire added to the regular Decennial Census form in 51 large cities and 9 rural counties. (Shortly after completing its work on the survey, the group was disbanded by the Nixon Administration.)

The failure of the social and economic system to provide people with adequate wages is hidden from view under the surface of traditional unemployment statistics. These statistics are excellent for measuring fluctuations in the economy but they do not go far enough as measures of the labor market. To gauge the degree of labor-market failure, it is necessary to know not only the magnitude of overt unemployment, but also the extent of worker discouragement ("discouraged workers" are those who have given up looking for jobs); the number of people who can find only part-time work; and the number who hold jobs but at inadequate pay. The subemployment index attempts to encompass all these factors.

In 1970, nationwide unemployment amounted to 4.9 per cent of the labor force (since then, it has hovered close to the 6 per cent mark month after month). In the C.E.S. central-city survey areas, the unemployment rate in 1970 was 9.6 per cent. This is *very* high. In France, the labor unions took to the streets last February when unemployment reached 2.6 per cent. But as high as it is here, the employment rate alone falls far short of revealing the full extent of urban crisis. When we look at the official definition of unemployment, we note that one cannot be "unemployed" unless one is currently looking for a job. It does not count those people who have given up looking for jobs after failing repeatedly to find work.

How many such discouraged nonseekers are there? The C.E.S. enables us to make a dependable estimate. For example, in New York City, the conventional unemployment rate in 1970 averaged 8.1 per cent in the survey areas (compared with 4.4 per cent for the labor force of the city as a whole), but jumped to 11 per cent when the discouraged workers were added.

This adjustment begins to give us a picture of realities of economic life at the bottom of a city's social structure. But to this we must now add another category — part-time employed workers who would like to work full time but cannot find full-time jobs. The C.E.S. survey carefully separates people who *wanted* to work only part time from those who wanted to work full time, and in this way adds (again, for New York) another 2.3 percentage points to our emerging index of urban poverty. In other words, adding together the officially unemployed, the discouraged jobless and the involuntary part-time workers, we can now account for at least 13.3 per cent of the labor force in the New York City sample areas.

Our adjustments have nearly doubled the official unemployment figures for the sample areas and tripled the national rate of unemployment. But, still, they are far from complete. The last and most important part of the index is the worker who has a full-time job but does not earn enough to make ends meet.

What is meant by "making ends meet"? What exactly *is* poverty? Where does one draw the line between a decent minimum and an indecent destitution?

The answer is not to be found in any simple set of criteria. Families know whether they are just poor or destitute, and act differently, according to their feelings. Poor families struggle; many of the destitute surrender. Once a family surrenders, it does not help to point out that it is "well off by the standards of Calcutta." The family does not live in Calcutta, but only a stone's throw from Fifth Avenue. Nor does it help to point out that it can provide its needed protein, vitamins and calories by eating beans or dog food, even if that is technically correct. The destitute will not act in ways that affront their basic humanity.

Can we identify the watershed "decent" and "indecent" standards of living? The most careful (and reputable) attempt has been an item-by-item enumeration of consumption needs undertaken by the B.L.S. Since 1967, it has published a three-level list of family income needs under conditions as they exist in different cities in the United States — the lower-level income before taxes amounted to $7,183 for a family of four in New York City in the spring of 1970. In the fall of 1971, it was $7,578. (The bureau placed the middle level for an urban family of four at $12,585 in 1971, the upper level at $19,238.)

The question of the line between decent poverty and destitution is clouded by the existence of an official poverty line. In 1964 when the Social Security Administration went about defining a poverty line for the War on Poverty, it began with a Department of Agriculture estimate of the absolute minimum needed to feed a family of four a survival diet and multiplied by three. Food, it figured, ought to be about one-third of a poor family's expenditures. The administration came out with a figure of $3,128 for a family of four at 1963 prices; it set the official line at $3,000. Since then, the poverty line has been adjusted annually upward in line with the Cost of Living Index. The level reached $4,000 in the fall of 1971, but, still, it does not represent a true measure of need.

The B.L.S. lower family-income figure of $7,183 is much sounder. It has been recognized as such by the Congress, which, in passing the Child Development program last fall, wrote the B.L.S. figure into the legislation as the level below which services ought to be provided for a nominal fee. In extending authority for wage and price control last December, Congress prohibited controlling annual wages below the B.L.S. lower amount.

That amount is based on actual minimum costs of living in the urban areas studied. In 1970, the average family of four in New York City, to meet the B.L.S. lower standard, had to pay about $28.65 a week in various Federal, state and local taxes, or $1,490 a year; $100 a month for rent (only enough for a barely habitable apartment) or $1,200 a year. To keep it up — that is, pay for repairs, cleaning materials, curtains, furniture repair, etc., the family would run into costs of at least $15 a month, or $183 a year. Other living expenses: $40.20 a week for food, or $2,091 a year; $8.32 a week for transportation, or $433 a year — which includes the cost of necessary public transportation for the family plus the cost of buying and operating a six-year-old car; $15.59 a week for medical bills, or $811 a year; $7.25 a week, or $377 a year, for other family consumption such as movies, recreation, TV's, radios, cigars, pipe tobacco, etc.; and $6.88 a week, or $347 a year, for other costs such as life-insurance premiums and charitable contributions. The expenses vary, of course; one category may be higher one month, and lower the next. But the B.L.S. researchers who checked prices in the city found total annual expenses, for living at the lower level, to be $7,183.

If we accept the B.L.S. figure of $7,183 as the least a family of four must earn to keep its head above water in New York City in 1970 (the B.L.S.'s national urban average for 1970 was $6,960), what does this require for the family's income earner? If he or she works 50 weeks a year, 40 hours a week (which is itself unlikely in the inner city), the answer is $3.50 an hour. Here is where we find the final link in our chain of employment statistics. For when we add those individuals who earn less than $3.50 an hour to the discouraged nonseekers, the involuntary part-timers and the officially unemployed, the statistics take a horrifying leap. In the seven New York City sample areas, the subemployment rate rises to between 39.9 per cent and 66.6 per cent of the labor force. Indeed, the average for all the sampled areas in the country comes to 61.2 per cent.

That the problem extends beyond the hard-core ghettos is demonstrated by statistics gathered for a recent New York City Planning Commission survey of industrial zones in all five boroughs of the city. The evidence shows that 60 per cent of all manufacturing establishments in the city pay median wages below the $3.50 threshold. If the median wage of an establishment is under $3.50, then more than half of its workers must be earning less than that amount.

Suppose — one may ask — that more than one member of the family works? Does each member need $3.50 an hour for the family to achieve the threshold of decent poverty? It is true that, nationwide, the *average* family has 1.7 full-time equivalent workers. But the majority of *low-income* families in America are unable to *find* enough work to occupy more than one "full-time-equivalent" member. In 1970, the average number of "full-time-equivalent" workers per low-income family was *less than one!* In other words, one person (usually the male head) worked nearly (but not totally) full time, or several family members worked, but very sporadically. It is therefore useless — and cynical — to tell those for whom jobs do not exist that they could relieve their poverty if only they would be more willing to work. Indeed, the proportion of C.E.S. four-person ghetto families — and just four-person families — with gross earnings of less than $7,000 in 1970 was also 69 per cent.

Even if we set the threshold level of subsistence at the official poverty line of $2 an hour, the Census Employment Survey shows that the seven New York City sample areas still had subemployment rates ranging from 19.3 to 25.9 per cent (the 51-city average was 30.5 per cent). Thus, even if we suppose that it takes only $2 an hour (or $4,000 a year) to hold a family of four together, we still have not solved the problem because the main reason for poverty in New York — and by extension elsewhere — is simply that not enough people can earn even this meager amount.

The Consequences of High Subemployment

How do people in the central cities survive? They struggle for what income they can get: from jobs where possible; from welfare where necessary. They line up for manpower training programs, especially those that pay stipends. The money helps, but the training seldom leads to jobs at decent pay (a recent study of manpower programs in four cities concluded that ". . . the average enrollee who worked following training [and not all the 'graduates' were so fortunate] was still earning at a rate of $3,000 per year"). The Employment Service cannot make much difference either, given the structure of the job market; 40 to 60 per cent of Employment Service non-agricultural placements in 1970 were in jobs paying less, on the average, than the minimum wage. Since "legitimate" pursuits do not yield adequate incomes, there is inevitably a good deal of economic crime. When great numbers of young workers are unable to earn enough to support wives and children in basic decency, they become demoralized and families fall apart and the welfare rolls soar. Property is not kept up, because it cannot be. Neighborhoods deteriorate, the circle of poverty and despair closes on itself and it eventually creates an enormous drag on the entire economy.

This *is* the urban crisis. And it is the subemployment rate which helps us to see the connection between the structure of the labor market and continued poverty and despair — a connection that is masked by the conventional unemployment rate. Last January, on the C.B.S. Evening News, commentator Eric Sevareid suggested that the measured unemployment rate actually overstates the severity of our labor market problems, presumably because it gives equal weight to women and teen-age workers, whose unemployment Sevareid (and many others) apparently believes to be less socially consequential than the unemployment of adult men. In fact, as we have seen, the conventional unemployment rate seriously *understates* the extent of our difficulties. Subemployment — the inability to make a living in our big cities — is from three to six times as great as simple unemployment.

These differences are hardly academic. So long as official statistics made it appear that only 5 to 10 per cent of the labor force was in trouble, even in the ghetto — or in other words, that 90 to 95 per cent were doing all right — it was possible for some to attribute the rise in the welfare rolls to laziness and immorality, and for others to perceive the fragility of the black family as a cause rather than as what is now easily seen to be a virtually inevitable consequence of sporadic low-paying employment and poverty.

In formulating an antipoverty strategy, the Government in the nineteen-sixties ignored the question of inner-city job supply, pay scales and the labor market. Its programs were built on the assumption that the cause of poverty lay in the disadvantaged condition of individuals, not in the failure of the job market. Thus, Head Start for the children, anti-discrimination and legal services for the grown-ups, community health service for the sick and, through Community Action and Model Cities agencies, a voice in city affairs for everybody. All these programs were expected to make more of a difference.

That they have made urban poverty somewhat less oppressive, that they encouraged the poor to organize and that they provided help to thousands of individuals cannot be doubted. But they have not begun — and cannot begin — to reach to the heart of the matter.

COUNTING THE UNDEREMPLOYED

Editor's Supplement

As the preceding selection argues, employment problems in the United States are more serious than official unemployment rates indicate. Rather than thinking exclusively about the *"unemployed,"* many have argued, we should focus our attention on the *underemployed.*

Almost all definitions of *underemployment* include four separate components:

1. Many people are actually *unemployed,* looking for work but unable to find a job;
2. Others are *"discouraged workers,"* unemployed and wanting work but not actually looking for a job because they believe no jobs are available;
3. Others work part-time *involuntarily,* actually wanting full-time work but unable to find it; and
4. Many work in jobs providing inadequate incomes, unable to support a decent standard of living on their wages.

This supplement provides data on the magnitude of underemployment in this country. It presents the most recent available figures for the nation as a whole. In developing a range of estimates of underemployment for the United States, it provides a "lower," "middle," and "higher" figure.

Definitions

Almost all studies begin with some "official" government definitions of labor force attachment among the noninstitutional population sixteen years or older.[1]

A person is officially "employed" if he/she performed paid work during the survey period or was not at work because of illness or temporary absence.

[1] For a detailed review of most of these definitions, see Stanley Moses, "Labor Supply Concepts: The Political Economy of Conceptual Change," *Annals* of the American Academy of Political and Social Science, March 1975; and Thomas Vietorisz, Robert Mier and Jean Giblin, "Subemployment: Exclusion and Inadequacy Indexes," *Monthly Labor Review,* May 1975.

A person is officially "unemployed" if he/she did not work during the survey period, was available for work at that time, *and* had looked for work at some time during the past four weeks. This category of unemployment, therefore, does not include those who are not working, could work, *but have not been looking for a job.*

The official "labor force" includes the employed and the unemployed. It therefore excludes people who work as unpaid household workers, those who work as volunteers, and those who are not working because of longer-term disabilities.

The "not in the labor force" category includes all those in the noninstitutionalized population sixteen years and over who are not included in the above categories.

"Full-time" work is defined as involving thirty-five hours a week or more. "Part-time work" involves fewer than thirty-five hours.

Unemployed Workers

Table 1 summarizes recent data on unemployment in the United States. The table shows that, even by official definitions of unemployment, millions of Americans were looking for work in 1975 and could not find it. Comparing the years of 1965 and 1975, almost two-and-one-half times as many Americans were unemployed in 1975 than ten years earlier.

Table 2 presents some data on the incidence of unemployment among different groups of American workers. Women, blacks, teens, and minority teen-

TABLE 1.   Counting the Unemployed

	1965	1975
Unemployed	3,366,000	7,830,000
Civilian Labor Force	74,455,000	92,613,000
Unemployment Rate	4.5%	8.5%

Source: Employment and Training Report of the President, 1976 (Washington, D.C.: U.S. Government Printing Office, 1976), p. 211.

TABLE 2.   The Incidence of Unemployment, 1975

	Unemployment Rate (%)	
	Total	Metropolitan Poverty Areas
Adult white males	6.2	9.7
Adult white females	7.5	8.6
Adult black males	12.4	15.8 *
Adult black females	12.1	12.3 *
Adult Spanish males	9.7	n.a.
Adult Spanish females	11.6	n.a.
White teens	17.9	26.2
Black teens	39.4	45.5 *
Spanish teens	27.7	n.a.

* The figures for blacks in metropolitan poverty areas are for "Negroes and other races."

Source: Employment and Training Report of the President, 1976 (Washington, D.C.: U.S. Government Printing Office, 1976), pp. 220, 223, and 227.

agers all find it substantially more difficult to find work than do adult white men. The unemployment rate among black teens was, for instance, six-and-one-half times greater in 1975 than the unemployment rate for adult white males.

Discouraged Workers

Many people assume, with good reason, that they would have trouble finding a job if they looked, so they do not look. When the census taker comes to the door, these people are regarded, for official purposes, as "not in the labor force." As "discouraged workers," they should certainly be counted as part of the problem of underemployment in this country. If more and better jobs were available, these discouraged workers would take them. As many have put it, these are the "hidden unemployed."

Several different tabulations of discouraged workers have been proposed. At the low end, some define discouraged workers as those who are not in the labor force, who "want a job now," but who are not looking because they "think they cannot get a job." At the high end, others include all those not in the labor force who "want a job now" but who are not looking for a wide variety of reasons. In between, one might include some of those not in the labor force who "want a job now" and exclude others. Applied to government data for 1975, these different definitions of discouraged workers generate a "low" estimate of

1,082,000, a "middle" estimate of 2,619,000, and a "high" estimate of 5,196,000.[2]

Involuntary Part-Time Workers

Many people would work full-time if they could find adequate full-time jobs. Discouraged from that search, they settle for part-time work. When the census taker comes to the door, they are counted as the part-time employed. When they are asked about the reasons they are working part-time, however, they acknowledge that they would prefer full-time work. Given those census data on the "involuntary part-time," we know that these workers should be counted among the underemployed.

In 1975, according to official government data, there were 3,748,000 involuntary part-time workers.[3]

Low-Wage Workers

There is one final component of the problem of underemployment. Though last, it is hardly the least. It involves the ability of workers to provide an adequate standard of living for themselves and others in their household. If a job pays too little in wages or salaries even though full-time, then it provides an inadequate basis for family support. Those who work in those jobs, by this standard, are also underemployed.

While many observers accept this general notion of earnings inadequacy, there has been considerable controversy about its statistical application. Two main issues have dominated the debate. First, which workers should be counted — only the heads of households, or all those in the household who make a significant contribution to family income? Second, what is an adequate standard of living for a household — the "poverty standard" or the "lower-level" family income standard?

The first issue poses a simple question. In con-

[2] These numbers come from Employment and Training Report of the President, 1976 (Washington, D.C.: U.S. Government Printing Office, 1976), p. 230. The low estimate includes those who are not in the labor force, "want job now," and "think cannot get job." The middle estimate includes those who are not in the labor force, "want job now," and (a) "think cannot get job"; (b) aren't looking for reasons of "ill health, and disability"; and (c) aren't looking for "all other reasons." The high estimate includes all not in the labor force who "want job now."

[3] These numbers come from Ibid., p. 256.

sidering the nation's job structure, should we take current family structures for granted? If we do, then we could feel reassured as long as the wages of all working family members add up to an adequate standard. But we would have good reasons for arguing that people should not be pinned to their families because they cannot earn adequate incomes to support themselves. Many women face the forced choice between an unhappy marriage and adequate income, on the one hand, and separation/divorce and inadequate income, on the other. Many have argued, quite reasonably, that all jobs should provide the potential for adequate support for an average family no matter who works in them.

The second issue poses simple problems of definition. What do we describe as an adequate standard of living? For reasons presented in detail in Chapter 5, many argue that the government's official "poverty" standard significantly understates the needs of families for minimum subsistence. In 1974 prices, it would have required $5,008 for a family of four to achieve the "poverty standard" and $9,198 to achieve the "lower level" adequacy standard.[4]

Building from those debates, we can develop some provisional estimates of this component of underemployment. We can take as our lower estimate of the low-wage underemployed the number of heads of households who work full time at wages that provide an annual income less than the "poverty standard" for their family size. We can take as our higher estimate the number of workers, whether heads of household or not, who work full time at wages that pro-

[4] See the details in the Editor's Introduction to Chapter 5.

vide an annual income less than the "lower-level" adequacy standard. We could take as our middle estimate either of the other two alternatives — heads of household earning less than the "lower-level" standard or all workers earning less than the poverty standard. For convenience in this supplement, I have taken an average of the two figures.

Table 3 summarizes the figures and clarifies the relationship of the data to our lower, middle, and higher estimates of the low-wage underemployed.[5]

[5] Since the government does not directly provide these data, it was difficult to piece together these numbers. In general, they were obtained by applying the relevant "poverty standards" by family size to the size distribution of income by relevant family size. The income data were not available for 1975 at the time of writing but 1973 data were used on the assumption that the real-dollar shape of the income distribution had hardly changed at all between 1973 and 1975. (Real workers' earnings remained almost exactly constant through that period. For evidence on the constancy of the distribution from 1973 to 1974 available at the time of writing, see U.S. Bureau of the Census, "Money Income and Poverty Status of Families and Persons in the United States: 1974 (Advance Report)," *Current Population Reports*, Series P-60, Number 99, July 1975.) The basic income distribution data for all the calculations came from U.S. Bureau of the Census, "Money Income in 1973 of Families and Persons in the United States," *Current Population Reports*, Series P-60, Number 97, January 1975. The "poverty" level budgets by family size were taken from U.S. Bureau of the Census, "Characteristics of the Low-Income Population: 1973," *Current Population Reports*, Number 98, January 1975, p. 162. The "lower-than-moderate" budget levels by family size came from Edna B. Branch, "Urban Family Budgets Updated to Autumn 1974," *Monthly Labor Review*, June 1975; they were backcast to 1973 price levels by the 1973–1974 change in the Consumer Price Index.

TABLE 3.   Counting the Full-Time Working Poor, 1975

	"SSA Poverty Standard"	"BLS Lower-than-Moderate Standard"
Heads of Households	LOW ESTIMATE 3,234,000	MIDDLE ESTIMATE 7,066,000
% of group	7.7	16.8
All Full-Time Workers	MIDDLE ESTIMATE 7,227,000	HIGH ESTIMATE 15,274,000
% of group	12.7	26.9

In this table, "full-time" is defined as those who worked full-time for 50–52 weeks during the year.

Sources: See footnote 5.

TABLE 4.   Counting the Underemployed, 1975
(All numbers in thousands)

	Low Estimate		Middle Estimate		High Estimate	
	Number	*%*	*Number*	*%*	*Number*	*%*
Expanded Labor Force	93,695	100.0	95,232	100.0	97,809	100.0
1. Unemployed	7,830	8.4	7,830	8.2	7,830	8.0
2. Discouraged Workers	1,082	1.2	2,619	2.7	5,196	5.3
3. Involuntary Part-Time	3,748	4.0	3,748	3.9	3,748	3.8
4. The Working Poor	3,234	3.5	7,146	7.5	15,274	15.6
Total Underemployment	15,894	17.0	21,343	22.4	32,048	32.8

(Totals do not add to total percentages due to roundings.)

Sources: The Expanded Labor Force adds Row 2 to the official labor force estimate from Table 1.
The Unemployed data come from Table 1.
The Discouraged Workers data are cited in footnote 2.
The Involuntary Part-Time data are cited in footnote 3.
The Working Poor data come from Table 3.

Underemployment — A Cumulative Estimate

Table 4 pulls together these estimates of the four different components of underemployment. It presents those estimates in three different columns — for lower, middle, and higher estimates.

Those numbers clearly underscore the seriousness of employment problems in this country. Even according to the low estimate, 15.9 million Americans are underemployed. If we accepted the high estimate, we would consider 32.0 million Americans, or 32.7 percent of the total (expanded) labor force as underemployed. Neither the economy nor the government, obviously, is living up to the promises of "full employment."

Some Find It Hardest. . . .

As both the Editor's Introduction and the preceding selection by Spring, Harrison, and Vietorisz noted, some people are much more likely to suffer problems of underemployment than others are. Women and minority workers find it harder than white males do to find adequate employment. Those living in central-city ghettos find it especially difficult to find decent jobs.

Since the country often seeks to ignore many of these especially severe employment problems, its government does not normally collect data that adequately measure their severity. Table 5 provides an estimate of the problems of two of those groups — patching together some estimates of the underemployment of women and blacks. (For some figures on underemployment in central-city poverty areas, see the preceding selection by Spring, Harrison, and Vietorisz.) Table 5 suggests that at least one-quarter and perhaps as many as one-half of all black workers are underemployed. It also indicates that at least one-sixth and perhaps as many as two-fifths of all women workers are underemployed.

. . . And Others Are Never Found

All these numbers focus on a specific population: those who are over sixteen, are not in the Armed Forces, are not in institutions, and can be found by the census takers. The fact that most observers count only those people does not necessarily mean that others excluded from that count do not also suffer employment problems.

Now that the United States has a "volunteer" army, it seems obvious that many who choose to enter military service do so because they cannot find decent employment in civilian occupations. In 1975, more than two million worked in the Armed Forces.[6] Although data do not specifically provide information on the "reasons for armed service," it seems reasonable to assume that from one-tenth to one-half of those in the Armed Forces join the services because they would otherwise be "underemployed" in the civilian sector. That would add from 200,000 to one million to our totals.

Many others are captive in prisons and mental in-

[6] See *Employment and Training Report,* p. 211.

TABLE 5. Some Find It Hardest
Underemployment among Blacks and Women, 1975 (All numbers in thousands)

BLACKS

	Low Estimate		Middle Estimate		High Estimate	
	Number	*%*	*Number*	*%*	*Number*	*%*
Expanded Labor Force	10,835	100.0	11,295	100.0	12,049	100.0
1. Unemployed	1,459	13.4	1,459	12.9	1,459	12.1
2. Discouraged Workers	306	2.8	766	6.8	1,520	12.6
3. Involuntary Part-Time	638	5.9	638	5.6	638	5.3
4. The Working Poor	615	5.7	1,266	11.2	2,523	21.0
Total Underemployment	3,018	27.8	4,129	36.6	6,140	51.0

Note: Numbers are for "Negroes and other races."

WOMEN

	Low Estimate		Middle Estimate		High Estimate	
	Number	*%*	*Number*	*%*	*Number*	*%*
Expanded Labor Force	37,720	100.0	38,746	100.0	40,457	100.0
1. Unemployed	3,445	9.1	3,445	8.9	3,445	8.5
2. Discouraged Workers*	722	1.9	1,748	4.5	3,459	8.5
3. Involuntary Part-Time**	1,855	4.9	1,855	4.8	1,855	4.6
4. The Working Poor	635	1.7	2,702 ***	7.0	7,964	19.7
Total Underemployment	6,657	17.7	9,750	25.2	16,723	41.3

Note: Totals do not add to total percentages due to rounding.
  * This set of figures involves some approximation through interpolation.
 ** This figure involves a minor adjustment for agricultural workers.
*** This is the one case where the two alternative "middle" estimates are significantly different from each other; this number, therefore, has an elusive substantive meaning.

Sources: Same as for Table 4.

stitutions. The U.S. Bureau of Labor Statistics reports that "comprehensive data on the labor force status of offenders are not presently available." [7] Based on sources cited in Chapter 6, however, it seems reasonable to estimate that between one and one-half and three million people are in local, state, or federal prisons and mental institutions at any one time in the United States.[8] As some of the selections in Chapter 6 also argue, many criminals resort to crime

[7] *Ibid.*, p. 199.
[8] The estimates cited by Goldfarb in "Jails" suggest, for instance, that there may be as many as 450,000 inmates in local jails at any one time alone, and that doesn't even begin to count state and federal prisons, or various mental institutions.

because they face underemployment in the "legitimate" labor market. As some of the material in Chapter 7 argues, many people suffer "mental illness" because of the problems they encounter finding work or working at low-wage jobs. Based on those arguments, it seems reasonable to add from 200,000 to one million of this group to our totals.

Finally, the census takers never find many people. Especially in deep back country and deep in the ghettos, census takers never find many of our most invisible people. There has long been a debate over the numbers and employed status of the "missing" people. Some estimates for the 1970 Census calculate that at least five million people were not found and that those "omitted" were disproportionately

TABLE 6.   A Final Count of the Underemployed

	Low Estimate		Middle Estimate		High Estimate	
	Number	%	*Number*	%	*Number*	%
Expanded Labor Force	93,695	100.0	99,232	100.0	103,809	100.0
1. Unemployed	7,830	8.4	7,830	7.9	7,830	7.5
2. Discouraged Workers	1,082	1.2	2,619	2.6	5,196	5.0
3. Involuntary Part-Time	3,748	4.0	3,748	3.8	3,748	3.6
4. The Working Poor	3,234	3.5	7,146	7.2	15,274	14.7
5. Armed Forces	—	—	200	0.2	1,000	1.0
6. Prisons and Mental Institutions	—	—	200	0.2	1,000	1.0
7. Omitted by Census	—	—	200	0.2	1,000	1.0
Total Underemployed	15,894	17.0	21,943	22.1	35,048	33.8

Sources: 1–4 same as Table 4.
For 5–7, see footnotes 6–8 respectively.

among the poor.[9] For the purposes of this supplement, it seems plausible to estimate that at least two million of the "missing" population are of productive age and that somewhere between 200,000 and one million of those two million are underemployed.

Taking into account these additional groups of underemployed people, we now have a new, much higher estimate of the underemployed in this country. Table 6 adds these new data to those of Table

[9] See U.S. Bureau of the Census, "Coverage of Population in the 1970 Census and Some Implications for Public Programs," *Current Population Reports,* Series P-23, Number 56, August 1975, pp. 2, 8.

4. The low estimate continues to ignore the "hidden" underemployed. The middle estimate takes the bottom of the range of estimates of "hidden" underemployment suggested in this section. The higher estimate takes the top of the range.

The totals in Table 6 present some final estimates of the magnitude of underemployment in this country. If we took seriously the task of providing decent full-time employment in this country for all who wanted and needed it, we would have to improve the employment status of at least 15.9 million Americans — and conceivably as many as 35 million. That effort obviously requires more than a few manpower training programs and some pious hopes.

PERSONAL INCOME AND MARGINAL PRODUCTIVITY

Richard H. Leftwich

This selection comes from a standard economics textbook. It elaborates the basic orthodox analysis of the distribution of income, arguing that incomes reflect the marginal productivities of workers. This analytic perspective informs most government efforts to improve the skills of the poor. It also clearly illustrates the basic satisfaction of liberal and conservative analyses with the capitalist system. Leftwich concludes: "Redistribution can be accomplished within the framework of the price system and the private enterprise economy."

Leftwich is a professor of economics at Oklahoma State University.

Individual Income Determination

The principles of individual determination and of income distribution in a private-enterprise economic system are called *the marginal productivity theory*. These principles were set out in previous chapters, but we shall draw together and summarize them here.

The principles of income determination where pure competition prevails, both in product markets and resource markets, were developed in Chapter 14 [of Leftwich's book]. The owner of a given resource is paid a price per unit for the units employed equal to the value of marginal product of the resource. The price of the resource is not determined by any single employer or by any single resource owner. It is determined by the interactions of all buyers and all sellers in the market for the resource.

If for some reason the price of a resource should be less than the value of its marginal product, a shortage will occur. Employers want more of it at that price than resource owners are willing to place on the market. Employers, bidding against each other for the available supply, will drive the price up

until the shortage disappears and each is hiring (or buying) that quantity of the resource at which its value of marginal product equals its price.

A price high enough to create a surplus of the resource will set forces in motion to eliminate the surplus. Employers take only those quantities sufficient to equate its value of marginal product to its price. Resource owners undercut each other's prices to secure employment for their unemployed units. As price drops, employment expands. The undercutting continues until employers are willing to take the quantities that resource owners want to place on the market.

Where some degree of monopoly [1] exists in product markets, these principles are altered to some extent. Monopolistic firms employ those quantities of the resource at which its marginal revenue product is equal to its price. Thus, the price per unit received by owners of the resource is less than its value of marginal product, and the resource is exploited monopolistically.

Some degree of monopsony in the purchase of a given resource will cause it to be paid still less than its marginal revenue product. The monopsonist, faced with a resource supply curve sloping upward to the right, employs that quantity of the resource at which its marginal revenue product is equal to its marginal resource cost. Marginal resource cost is greater than the price paid for the resource. Monopsonistic exploitation of the resource occurs to the extent that its marginal revenue product exceeds its price. If the resource purchaser is also a monopolist, marginal revenue product of the resource will in turn be less than its value of marginal product, and the resource will be exploited monopolistically as well as monopsonistically.

As we noted in Chapter 2 [of Leftwich's book] an individual's income per unit of time is the sum of the amounts earned per unit of time from the employ-

[1] Again, we use the term to refer to all cases in which the firm faces a downward-sloping product demand curve. They include cases of pure monopoly, oligopoly, and monopolistic competition.

ment of the various resources which he owns. If he owns a single kind of resource, his income will be equal to the number of units placed in employment multiplied by the price per unit which he receives. If he owns several kinds of resources, the income from each one can be computed in the same manner; and then all can be totaled to determine his entire income.

Causes of Income Differences

With reference to the determinants of individual[2] incomes, it becomes clear that differences in incomes arise from two basic sources: (1) differences in the kinds and quantities of resources owned by different individuals and (2) differences in prices paid in different employments for units of any given resource. The former are the more fundamental. The latter arise from various types of interference with the price system in the performance of its functions and from any resource immobility which may occur.

It will be convenient to discuss labor and capital resources separately. . . . In this section we shall first consider differences in the kinds and quantities of labor resources owned by different individuals. Next, differences in capital resources owned will be discussed. Finally, we shall examine the effects on income distribution of certain interferences with the price mechanism.

■ *Differences in Labor Resources Owned*

The labor classification of resources is composed of many different kinds and qualities of labor. These have one common characteristic — they are human. Any single kind of labor is a combination or complex of both inherited and acquired characteristics. The acquired part of a man's labor power is sometimes referred to as human capital. We shall make no attempt to separate inherited and acquired characteristics.

Labor can be subclassified horizontally and vertically into many largely separate resource groups. Vertical subclassification involves grading workers according to skill levels from the lowest kind of undifferentiated manual labor to the highest professional levels. Horizontal subclassification divides

---

[2] The term *individual* will be used throughout the rest of the chapter to refer to a spending unit, regardless of its size or composition.

workers of a certain skill level into the various occupations requiring that particular degree of skill. An example would be the division of skilled construction workers into groups — carpenters, bricklayers, plumbers, and the like. Vertical mobility of labor refers to the possibility of moving upward through vertical skill levels. Horizontal mobility means the ability to move sideways among groups at a particular skill level.

Horizontal Differences in Labor Resources. At any specific horizontal level individuals may receive different incomes because of differences in the demand and supply conditions for the kinds of labor they own. A large demand for a certain kind of labor relative to the supply of it available will make its marginal revenue product and its price high. On the same skill level a small demand for another kind of labor relative to the supply available will make its marginal revenue product and its price low. The difference in prices tends to cause differences in income for owners of the kinds of labor concerned.

Suppose, for example, that bricklayers and carpenters initially earn approximately equal incomes. A shift in consumer tastes occurs from wood to brick construction in residential units. The incomes of bricklayers will increase, while those of carpenters will decrease, because of the altered conditions of demand. Over a long period of time horizontal mobility between the two groups tends to decrease the income differences thus arising, and welfare will be increased in the process.

Quantitative differences in the amount of work performed by individuals owning the same kind of labor resource may lead to income differences. Some occupations afford considerable leeway for individual choice of the number of hours to be worked per week or month. Examples include independent professional men such as physicians, lawyers, and certified public accountants, along with independent proprietors such as farmers, plumbing contractors, and garage owners. In other occupations hours of work are beyond the control of the individual. Yet in different employments of the same resource differences in age, physical endurance, institutional restriction, custom, and so on can lead to differences in hours worked and to income differences among owners of the resource.

Within a particular labor resource group qualitative differences or differences in the abilities of the owners of the resource often create income differences. Wide variations occur in public evaluation of different dentists, or physicians, or lawyers, or automobile mechanics. Consequently, within any one group variations in prices paid for services and variations in the quantities of services sold to the public will lead to income differences. Usually a correlation exists between the ages of the members of a resource group and their incomes. Quality tends to improve with accumulated experience up to a point. Data reported by Friedman and Kuznets suggest, for example, that the incomes of physicians tend to be highest between the tenth and twenty-fifth years of practice, and the incomes of lawyers tend to be highest between the twentieth and thirty-fifth years of practice.[3]

Vertical Differences in Labor Resources. The different vertical strata themselves represent differences in labor resources owned and give rise to major labor income differences. Entry into high-level occupations, such as the professions or the ranks of business executives, is much more difficult than is entry into manual occupations. The relative scarcity of labor at top levels results from two basic factors: (1) individuals with the physical and mental characteristics necessary for the performance of high-level work are limited in number; and (2) given the necessary physical and mental characteristics, many lack opportunities for training and the necessary social and cultural environment for movement into high-level positions. Thus, limited vertical mobility keeps resource supplies low relative to demands for them at the top levels; and it keeps resource supplies abundant relative to demands for them at the low levels.

Differences in labor resources owned because of differences in innate physical and mental characteristics of individuals are accidents of birth. The individual has nothing to do with choosing them. Nevertheless, they account partly for restricted vertical mobility and for income differences. The opportunities of moving toward top positions and relatively large incomes are considerably enhanced by the inheritance of a strong physical constitution and a superior intellect; however, these by no means insure that individuals so endowed will make the most of their opportunities.

Opportunities for training are more widely available to individuals born into wealthy families than

[3] Milton Friedman and Simon Kuznets, *Income from Independent Professional Practice* (New York: National Bureau of Economic Research, 1945), pp. 237–260.

to those born into families in lower-income groups. Some of the higher-paying professions require long and expensive university training programs — often beyond the reach of the latter groups. The medical profession is a case in point. However, we often see individuals who have had the initial ability, drive, and determination necessary to overcome economic obstacles thrown in the way of vertical mobility.

Differences in social inheritance constitute another cause of difference in labor resources owned. These are closely correlated with differences in material inheritance. Frequently, individuals born "on the wrong side of the tracks" face family and community attitudes that sharply curtail their opportunities and their desires for vertical mobility. Others, more fortunately situated, acquire the training necessary to be highly productive and to obtain large incomes because it is expected of them by the social group in which they move. The social position alone, apart from the training induced by it, may be quite effective in facilitating vertical mobility.

When vertical mobility can occur but is blocked, income differences persist and welfare is below its potential maximum. If those who are denied access to higher value of marginal product jobs and occupations were able to attain these, the result would be higher real net national product, as well as greater equality in income distribution.

■ Differences in Capital Resources Owned

In addition to inequalities in labor incomes large differences occur in individual incomes from differences in capital ownership. Different individuals own varying quantities of capital — corporation or other business assets, farmland, oil wells, and property of various other types. We shall examine the fundamental causes of inequalities in capital holdings.

Material Inheritance. Differences in the amounts of capital inherited or received as gifts by different individuals create large differences in incomes. The institution of private property on which private enterprise rests usually is coupled with inheritance laws allowing large holdings of accumulated property rights to be passed from generation to generation. The individual fortunate enough to have a wealthy father inherits large capital holdings; his resources contribute much to the productive process; and he is rewarded accordingly. The son of a Southern sharecropper — who may be of equal innate intelligence with the son of a wealthy father, but inherits no capital — contributes less to the productive process and receives a correspondingly lower income.

Fortuitous Circumstances.   Chance, luck, or other fortuitous circumstances beyond the control of individuals constitute a further cause of differences in capital holdings. The discovery of oil, uranium, or gold on an otherwise undistinguished piece of land brings about a large appreciation in its value or its ability to yield income to its owner. Unforeseen shifts in consumer demand increase the values of certain capital holdings, while decreasing the values of others. National emergencies, such as war, lead to changes in valuations of particular kinds of property, and hence to differential incomes from capital. Fortuitous circumstances can work in reverse also, but even so, their effects operate to create differences in the ownership of capital.

Propensities to Accumulate.   Differing psychological propensities to accumulate and differing abilities to accumulate lead to differences in capital ownership among individuals. On the psychological side a number of factors influence the will to accumulate. Stories circulate of individuals determined to make a fortune before they reach a certain age. Accumulation sometimes occurs for purposes of security and luxury in later life. It sometimes occurs from the desire to make one's children secure. The power and the prestige accompanying wealth provide the motivating force in some cases. To others, accumulation and manipulation of capital holdings is a gigantic game — the activity involved is fascinating of itself. Whatever the motives, some individuals have such propensities and others do not. In some instances the will to accumulate may be negative, and the opposite of accumulation occurs.

The ability of an individual to accumulate depends largely on his original holdings of both labor and capital resources. The higher the original income, the easier saving and accumulation tend to be. The individual possessing much in the way of labor resources initially is likely to accumulate capital with his income from labor — he invests in stocks and bonds, real estate, a cattle ranch, or other property. Or the individual possessing substantial quantities of capital initially — and the ability to manage it — receives an income sufficient to allow saving and investment in additional capital. In the process of accumulation labor and capital resources of an individual augment each other in providing the in-

come from which further accumulation can be accomplished. . . .

A Greater Measure of Equality

For various reasons — economic, ethical, and social — many people favor some mitigation of income differences. The causes of differences should furnish the clues for measures leading toward their mitigation — if movement toward greater equality is thought by society to be desirable. Thus, equalizing measures may be (and are) attempted via the price system, or they may be (and are) attempted through redistribution of resources among resource owners. We shall consider each of these in turn.

Via Administered Prices.   Equalizing measures attempted via administered prices are likely to miss their mark except in monopsonistic cases. Where competitive and monopolistic conditions prevail in product markets, and where competitive conditions prevail in the purchase of a given resource, the equilibrium price of the resource tends to be equal to its value of marginal product or its marginal revenue product, as the case may be. Additionally, the resource tends to be so allocated that its price is the same in its alternative employments. Successful administered price increases are likely to result in unemployment and malallocation of the resource, and these in turn contribute toward greater rather than smaller income differences. As we have observed before, administered resource prices in monopsony cases can offset monopsonistic exploitation of a resource by increasing both its price and its level of employment.

■ *Via Redistribution of Resources*

The major part of any movement toward greater income equality must consist of redistribution of resources among resource owners, since this is the major cause of income differences. Redistributive measures can take two forms: (1) redistribution of labor resources and (2) redistribution of capital resources.

Labor Resources.   Labor-resource ownership can be redistributed through measures designed to increase vertical mobility. Greater vertical mobility will increase labor supplies in the higher vocational levels and decrease labor supplies in the lower levels. Greater supplies at the higher levels will decrease values of marginal product or marginal revenue products, and will reduce the top incomes. Smaller supplies at the lower levels will increase values of marginal product or marginal revenue products, thereby increasing incomes at the lower occupational levels. The transfers from lower to higher occupations will mitigate income differences and will increase net national product in the process.

At least three methods of increasing vertical mobility can be suggested. First, greater equality in educational and training opportunities can be provided. Second, to the extent that differences in capital ownership are reduced, greater equality in economic opportunities for development of high-grade labor resources will tend to occur. Third, measures may be taken to reduce the barriers to entry established by groups and associations of resource owners in many skilled and semiskilled occupations.[4]

Measures to increase horizontal mobility also can serve to decrease income differences. These include the operation of employment exchanges, perhaps some subsidization of movement, vocational guidance, adult education and retraining programs, and other measures of a similar nature. The argument is really for a better allocation of labor resources, both among alternative jobs within a given labor resource category and among the labor resource categories themselves. Greater horizontal mobility, as well as greater vertical mobility, will increase net national product at the same time that it decreases income differences.

Capital Resources. Policy measures to redistribute capital resources meet considerable opposition in a private enterprise economy. Many advocates of greater income equality will protest measures designed to redistribute capital ownership — and these measures are the ones that will contribute most toward such an objective. The opposition centers around the rights of private property ownership and stems from a strong belief that the right to own property includes the right to accumulate it and to pass it on to one's heirs.

Nevertheless, if income differences are to be mitigated, some means of providing greater equality in capital holdings among individuals must be employed. The economy's system of taxation may move in this direction. In the United States, for example, the personal income tax, the capital gains tax, and

estate and gift taxes, both federal and state, already operate in an equalizing manner.

The personal income tax by its progressive nature serves to reduce income differences directly, and in so doing, it reduces differences in abilities to accumulate capital. But the personal income tax alone cannot be expected to eliminate income differences without seriously impairing incentives for efficient employment of resources and for reallocation of resources from less-productive to more-productive employments.

The capital gains tax constitutes either a loophole for escaping a part of the personal income tax or a plug for a loophole in the personal income tax, depending on one's definition of income. The capital gains tax is applied to realized appreciation and depreciation in the value of capital assets. Those who can convert a part of their income from capital resources into the form of capital gains have that part of their remuneration taxed as capital gains at a rate ordinarily below the personal income tax rate. For them the capital gains tax provides a loophole through which personal income taxes can be escaped. Yet if certain capital gains would escape taxation altogether under the personal income tax, but are covered by the capital gains tax, the latter can be considered as a supplement to the personal income tax. In either case the capital gains tax allows some remuneration from capital resources to be taxed at rates below the personal income tax rates, and, if differences in opportunities to accumulate capital are to be mitigated, this tax must be revised to prevent individuals from taking advantage of its lower rates.

Estate and gift taxes will play the major roles in any tax system designed to reduce differences in capital ownership. The estate taxes in such a system would border on the confiscatory side, above some maximum amount, in order to prevent the transmission of accumulated capital resources from generation to generation. Gift taxes would operate largely to plug estate tax loopholes. They would be designed to prevent transmission of estates by means of gifts from the original owner to his heirs prior to the death of the original owner.

Redistribution and the Price System. Redistribution of labor resource and capital resource holdings can be accomplished within the framework of the price system and the private enterprise economic system if movement toward greater income equality is thought by society to be desirable. Redistribution measures, such as those sketched above, need not

---

[4] An example of such a barrier is provided by the professional association that controls the licensing standards which prospective entrants must meet in order to practice the profession.

seriously affect the operation of the price mechanism. In fact the price mechanism can act as a positive force assisting the measures to reach desired objectives. Some of the fundamental measures — educational opportunities, progressive income taxes, gift and estate taxes — are already in existence, although their effectiveness could be greatly increased. Redistribution measures can be thought of as rules of the free enterprise game — along with a stable monetary system, monopoly control measures, and other rules of economic conduct.

Summary

Individual claims to net national product depend on individual incomes; thus, the theory of product distribution is really the theory of income distribution. Marginal productivity theory provides the generally accepted principles of income determination and income distribution. Resource owners tend to be remunerated according to the marginal revenue products of the resources they own, except in cases where resources are purchased monopsonistically.

Incomes are unequally distributed among spending units in the United States. Income differences stem from three basic sources: (1) differences in labor resources owned, (2) differences in capital resources owned, and (3) restrictions placed on the operation of the price mechanism. With regard to labor resources, different individuals own different kinds of labor at the same general skill level. We call

these horizontal differences in labor resources. Different individuals also own different kinds of labor graded vertically from undifferentiated manual labor to top-level professions. Differences in capital resources owned result from differences in material inheritance, fortuitous circumstances, and differences in propensities to accumulate.

Administered prices for a given resource often lead to unemployment or malallocation of some units of the resource and, hence, to differences in incomes among owners of the resource. The case of monopsony provides an exception. Under monopsony administered resource prices can offset monopsonistic exploitation of the resources involved.

Attacks on income differences, if society desires to mitigate those differences, should be made by way of redistribution of resources among resource owners. Attacks made by way of administered prices are not likely to accomplish this task. Redistribution of labor resources can be accomplished through measures designed to increase both horizontal and vertical mobility. These will in turn increase net national product.

The tax system offers a means of effecting redistribution of capital resources. Estate and gift taxes will bear the major burden of effective redistribution and may be supplemented by personal income and capital gains taxes.

Redistribution of resources can be accomplished within the framework of the price system and the private enterprise economy.

THE ECONOMICS OF THE NEW UNEMPLOYMENT

Martin Feldstein

This selection provides a recent example of the neoclassical economic analysis of underemployment. While the neoclassical analysis of unemployment was dominated in the 1960s by a focus on "skills," orthodox economists have more recently shifted their

Source: Reprinted with permission of Martin Feldstein from *The Public Interest*, No. 33, Fall 1973. Copyright © 1973 by National Affairs, Inc.

focus to the operations of the labor market. Feldstein's comments reflect this shift. The policy implications of his arguments seem clear: All we can hope for is to improve the efficiency of the labor market. Because this analytic perspective does not examine the structure of demand for labor — the actual structure and composition of jobs themselves — it provides no basis for seeking to change that job structure.

This selection includes the bulk of a longer article

that appeared in *The Public Interest*. Another long section of that article dealt with the problems of unemployment among youth.

Feldstein teaches economics at Harvard University and has written widely on the economics of employment, health care, and public finance.

Unemployment among mature workers reflects several distinct problems. Identifying these separate aspects suggests a mix of possible policies for lowering the unemployment rate. This section will discuss four reasons why the adult unemployment rate is higher than it should be. Several possible policies will be discussed briefly.

Some unemployment is, of course, the inevitable consequence of a healthy and dynamic economy. The changing mix of output and the process of technological advance displace workers who generally become temporarily unemployed. Women often return to the labor force as their children grow older; in 1971, reentrants accounted for 40 per cent of the unemployment among women 20 years old and over. Families occasionally migrate to new areas in order to find better employment opportunities and then spend time searching for work. All of these sources of unemployment produce important gains for the economy and often for the unemployed themselves. It is clear that they should not be discouraged. In particular, it is important to avoid the temptation — to which other countries have sometimes succumbed — to prevent temporary unemployment by permanent subsidies for unwanted output and inefficient technology.

Although some unemployment among adults is appropriate, the actual unemployment rates among experienced men clearly represent an undesirable and unnecessary waste of resources. In the post-War period, the unemployment rate among males aged 20 and over averaged 3.5 per cent. In 1971, it was an unfortunate 4.4 per cent. As already noted, the rate has generally been higher among women than men. In 1971, it was 5.7 per cent. The combined unemployment rate for adults (persons aged 20 and over) was 4.9 per cent. These rates, and the U.S. post-War experience in general, are much higher than the unemployment rates experienced in most other industrial nations. Even Britain, which unlike some other European countries does not maintain full employment by temporary imports and exports of foreign laborers, achieved an average adult unemployment rate below 2.5 per cent in the 1960's. What

could be done in the United States to achieve a comparable performance?

Although better management of aggregate demand has a more important role to play in lowering the adult unemployment rate than in improving the teenage employment situation, macroeconomic policies cannot do the job alone . . . .

It is now time to consider the more specific reasons why a variety of policies are needed to achieve a more desirable level of unemployment among adult workers. To do so, it is useful to distinguish and analyze the implications of four different sources of adult unemployment: (1) the cyclical and seasonal volatility of the demand for labor; (2) the weak labor force attachment of some groups of workers; (3) the particular difficulty in finding permanent employment for persons with very low skills or other employment disabilities; and (4) the average of several months of unemployment among job losers.

Cyclical and Seasonal Variation in Demand

The American unemployment rate is not only higher than the rates observed in foreign countries but also much more cyclically volatile. During the 1960's, the total U.S. unemployment rate varied from 3.5 per cent to 6.7 per cent. The cyclical variation in unemployment — the gap between peak and trough — was 3.2 per cent. The unemployment rate was nearly twice as high in the worst year as in the best. During the same decade, the corresponding British unemployment rate (adjusted to U.S. definitions) varied from 2.1 to 3.4 per cent. The cyclical variation was only 1.3 per cent, substantially less than half of the U.S. gap. Despite the much lower rate in the best year, the cyclical swing only increased the British rate by some 60 per cent.

It would be wrong to infer from these data that Britain's less volatile unemployment rate is due to a more stable growth of demand and production. A comparison of American and British experience shows instead that changes in aggregate demand have a substantially smaller impact on employment in Britain than they do in the United States. More specifically, I have examined statistically the relation between annual changes in the unemployment rate and the corresponding changes in industrial production in the two countries. The results show that a one per cent change in industrial production has about twice as big an effect on the unemployment rate in the United States as it does in Britain. Moreover, while nearly all of the year-to-year variation in the U.S. unemployment rate can be explained by fluctuations in industrial production, the association between unemployment and industrial production is much weaker in Britain. . . .

A variety of special schemes might be developed in the United States to encourage firms to reduce the sensitivity of employment to changes in aggregate demand: required minimum notice before employees are laid off, large compulsory severance payments, a guaranteed annual wage, substantial tax penalties (or rewards) for volatile (or stable) employment, and the like. Similar policies have already been adopted by some European countries; however, such actions can only lower the volatility of unemployment by reducing the efficiency of the labor market and therefore lowering real wages. There is no reason for the government to impose a lower wage and correspondingly greater employment security than the employees themselves actually want. Collective bargaining agreements can achieve any desired degree of employment security through the same techniques of minimum notice, supplementary unemployment benefits, and so on. The outcome of collective bargaining, moreover, can reflect the employees' preferences and the real opportunity costs of lost earnings. The government should only provide inducements to disguised unemployment to the extent that these are considered a more efficient form of deficit spending or that they provide tangible benefits to persons other than the individual employees and employers. It should go without saying that the government should also avoid policies that artificially stimulate the responsiveness of unemployment to changes in aggregate demand. . . .

Seasonal variation in employment demand raises quite different issues from the cyclical variation that has been discussed until now. Seasonal unemployment is clearly not involuntary. An individual who accepts a job with seasonal fluctuations knows that he will be laid off or at least that there will be a significantly higher probability of being laid off. The total effect of seasonal variations in unemployment is substantial. During the twelve months from June 1971 through May 1972, the seasonally adjusted unemployment rate remained nearly constant, varying only between 5.2 and 5.5 per cent. In the same period, the seasonally unadjusted rate varied from a low of 4.5 per cent to a high of 6.3 per cent. If seasonal unemployment could be avoided com-

pletely, the average unemployment rate would fall by more than 0.75 per cent. While some seasonal unemployment may be technically necessary, other seasonal unemployment could no doubt be eliminated by changes in production methods, increased holdings of inventories, the integration of firms with complementary seasonal demands, and other means. Additional reductions in seasonal unemployment could be achieved if workers who are seasonally laid off would make the transition to new jobs with less time out of work. If these improvements could eliminate half the current seasonal unemployment, more than 300,000 man-years of unemployment could be avoided every year. It should be emphasized, however, that some amount of seasonal unemployment is desirable. Even if public policies could be designed to eliminate seasonal unemployment completely, this would only be achieved at substantial real economic costs. The proper aim of public policy should be to avoid distorting the natural pattern of seasonal unemployment that would reflect both the preferences of employees and the attempts of employers to produce at minimum cost . . . .

Weak Labor Force Attachment

Unemployment caused by weak labor force attachment is generally a smaller but more serious problem among adults than among young workers. While some of the unemployed adults who are not seeking permanent employment are still students or are mothers with young children, the social problems are associated with the group with low skills and little education. These adults suffer from the same limited opportunities as some of the young workers described in the last section. Because they have low skills, little education, and generally bad work habits, they never enter the mainstream of employment opportunities. The only jobs open to them are the dead-end jobs with low pay and no future.

High unemployment among the men and women in this "secondary labor market" reflects their rejection of the jobs that are available.[1] Many of those with very limited job opportunities prefer to remain unemployed rather than accept what they consider undesirable jobs. Many others who take these jobs soon quit.

[1] See P. Doeringer and M. Piore, *Internal Labor Markets and Manpower Analysis* (Lexington, Mass., 1971), Chapter 9, for an extensive discussion of the characteristics of the secondary labor market.

Boston's experience with trying to secure employment for a large group of such low-skill workers dramatically illustrates that the problem is not providing jobs but making these jobs acceptable to the unemployed. During the eight months beginning in September 1966, Boston's ABCD program referred some 15,000 disadvantaged workers to jobs. Seventy per cent were actually offered jobs. Nearly half of the job offers — 45 per cent — were rejected. Of those who did accept work, less than half remained on the job for one month. A very high proportion of these separations were voluntary. Even among those over age 25 who were being paid more than $1.75 per hour in 1967, the separation rate in the first month was 33 per cent.

What can be done to reduce unemployment among low-skilled adult workers? It is clear that the problem cannot be solved by increasing aggregate demand in order to create more jobs. There is no evidence of a shortage of jobs for this group. The Boston experience shows that jobs can be found but that they will not be accepted.[2] *Lowering the rate of unemployment requires steps to bring the characteristics of the actual jobs and the standards of the acceptable jobs closer together.*

It is sometimes suggested that expansionary macroeconomic policy can play an important role by improving the quality of the jobs available to the least able workers. Those who support this view argue that the better jobs and higher pay that become available in a tighter labor market will reduce the voluntary unemployment and non-participation among this group. There is, unfortunately, insufficient data with which to evaluate this proposition. The aggregate unemployment statistics by age, sex, and race do not provide enough detail to identify the low-skilled workers. Although such workers are a disproportionately large fraction of non-white males, it is impossible to say how much of the fall in unemployment for this group during any cyclical tightening is actually due to a reduction in voluntary unemployment among those who are able to find better jobs.

The best available evidence — the statistics on labor force participation rates — indicate a pessimis-

tic conclusion. Since 1948, the labor force participation rates of non-white adult males have dropped dramatically: from 97.2 per cent to 92.0 per cent among 35 to 44 year olds, and from 94.7 per cent to 86.9 per cent among 45 to 54 year olds. (Among white males in those age groups the changes were extremely small: from 98.0 per cent to 97.0 per cent and from 95.9 per cent to 94.7 per cent.) This nearly threefold increase in voluntary withdrawal from the labor force occurred during a 25-year period in which wage rates rose nearly 50 per cent. This is clearly contrary to the notion that higher wage rates would reduce voluntary non-employment. Much of the decrease in labor force participation occurred at the same time as labor markets were tightening. From 1961 through 1969, while the overall unemployment rate was falling from 6.7 per cent to 3.5 per cent, non-white adult male labor force participation rates also continued to fall: from 94.8 per cent to 92.7 per cent among 35 to 44 year olds and from 92.3 to 89.5 per cent among 45 to 54 year olds.

Similar conclusions are implied by the fall in the labor force participation rates of non-white adult males living in urban poverty neighborhoods during the period from 1967 through 1969, when the unemployment rate for that group was falling sharply. In 1967, with an unemployment rate of 5.7 per cent among non-white adult males in urban poverty areas, 19.6 per cent of that group were neither employed nor seeking work. By 1969, their unemployment rate had fallen to 4.3 per cent, but despite the tightening of the labor market, non-participants rose to 21.4 per cent of that population group.

The evidence on non-participation rates contains two lessons. It is a warning that macroeconomic expansion and tighter labor markets are unlikely to bring a significant reduction in the voluntary unemployment that characterizes low-skill groups. It is also a reminder that the officially defined unemployment rate is the tip of the iceberg. For these low-skill groups, withdrawal from the labor force is much more common than official unemployment.

Manpower Programs and Voluntary Non-Employment

Recognition of these limits of expansionary macroeconomic policies has encouraged the creation of several major manpower programs during the past decade. All these programs share the common phi-

[2] The special problem of those with such severe employment handicaps that they cannot earn the minimum wage will be discussed below. See P. Doeringer, *Programs to Employ the Disadvantaged* (Englewood Cliffs, New Jersey, 1969), for a more detailed description of this experience.

losophy that the best way to reduce non-employment in the groups designated as disadvantaged is to provide training that can improve the quality of jobs open to them. During the nine years from 1963 through 1971, there were more than six million new enrollments in federal manpower programs. The total federal cost of these programs from 1963 through 1971 was nearly $7 billion; in 1971, the federal obligation was $1.5 billion.

Despite 10 years of experience with these large programs, there has been no clear and definitive evaluation of their impact. We do not know whether unemployment rates are lower and participation rates higher for those who have enrolled in a manpower program than for those with the same characteristics of age, sex, education, etc., who have not. There have apparently been no controlled experiments to compare the effects of institutional training under the MDTA program with on-the-job training in the JOBS program. The isolated evaluations of particular local experiences or the results within individual firms have generally suggested that manpower programs have positive but small effects. The interpretation of these evaluations is clouded, however, by a lack of adequate controls and by the problem of self-selecting trainees. The clearest successes have been obtained by large firms that have combined expensive periods of on-the-job training with opportunities for further employment and advancement.[3]

Among adults who have been out of school for several years or more, the handicap of low skills is exacerbated by the problem of bad employment habits. Absenteeism, frequent lateness, petty thefts, and high quit rates are characteristic of workers in the secondary labor markets. It is difficult for them to break these habits and conform to the discipline of mainstream employment. The possibility of preventing these problems by means of better experience and training for young workers makes the policies discussed earlier all the more important.

Both macroeconomic policies and manpower programs seek to reduce non-employment by making the available work more attractive. It is important not

[3] See Robert Hall, "Prospects for Shifting the Phillips Curve Through Manpower Policy," *Brookings Papers on Economic Activity* (1971), for a discussion of this evidence and a generally pessimistic view of the potential of manpower programs. Peter Doeringer provides several case studies in *Programs to Employ the Disadvantaged* (1969).

to lose sight of the fact that the extent of voluntary non-employment also depends on the attractiveness of not working. Today's welfare rules are a notorious deterrent to work for those who are receiving welfare. Moreover, the rapid rise during the last decade in the value of public assistance available to a family with little or no earnings — including cash payments, Medicaid, food stamps, and housing subsidies — has substantially increased the attractiveness of non-employment or intermittent employment for those with low skills. The increased levels of unemployment compensation also encourage intermittent work, especially among two-earner families.

There is also the complex problem of unreported earnings among low-income families. Some of this derives from criminal activities or from lawful services performed for illegal employers. But cash payments designed to avoid taxes and to prevent reductions in unemployment compensation or welfare benefits are also important. For casual workers in the secondary labor market, cash payments can avoid federal income taxes at a minimum marginal rate of 14 per cent, plus combined employer and employee social security taxes in excess of 10 per cent, plus state income, unemployment compensation, and workmen's compensation taxes. These taxes may easily total more than 30 per cent of the worker's gross pay. By evading taxes and receiving payment in cash, the effective net wage can be increased by nearly 50 per cent. This provides a substantial incentive to both employers and employees in situations where record-keeping practices can be lax to share the potential gains of non-reporting. The higher wages in such casual labor markets are a further inducement to intermittent employment.

The most effective way to achieve a substantial reduction in non-employment among low-skilled groups is to combine improved manpower programs with a reexamination and redesign of the current adverse incentives.

The Current Unemployables

In addition to those who are cyclically unemployed or voluntarily out of work, there is a substantial residue of unemployables who would be unable to find steady employment even in a very tight labor market. Permanent physical disability, subnormal intelligence, or psychological problems severely limit the productivity of these men and women. The problem is most serious among those with both a physical impairment and limited education. Law and custom prevent firms from lowering wages to the levels at which it would pay to hire handicapped individuals.

Although vocational rehabilitation could improve the prospects for some of them, in many cases — especially among those who are older and less educated — the costs of additional training would exceed the benefits. *Two forms of job creation for these permanently disadvantaged workers have been suggested: subsidies to firms and direct permanent public employment. A third option, integrating the minimum wage law with general income maintenance, is also possible.*

Wage subsidies to private firms are designed to fill the gap between the productivity of these very low-skilled workers and the minimum wage. The primary objection to such a policy is that much of the subsidy would be paid for hiring workers who would have been hired anyway. Although this problem might be reduced by a careful procedure of certifying eligible handicapped workers, such a process would inevitably involve a large number of arbitrary individual decisions. The task would be made more difficult by the need to specify different subsidies for different degrees of occupational handicap. The scope for abuse, however, would be very much limited if the total wage (including the subsidy) were limited to the legal minimum wage in that type of employment and if the handicapped individual could take his wage subsidy to any employer. Since most workers can earn more than the minimum wage, there would be no incentive to seek an inappropriate wage subsidy. Even if low-skill workers in general were subsidized excessively, there would be no undue subsidy to employers if workers could take these subsidies to any firm. Competition among firms for these subsidies would pass the advantage of the subsidy back to the low-income workers themselves. The most serious problem with the subsidy plan would then be that substantial government funds would go to raising the wages of very-low-paid employees rather than to reducing unemployment.[4] A system of wage subsidies to close the gap between the productivity of handicapped

workers and the minimum wage is therefore quite appealing. It would of course be appropriate to permit state and local governments to compete with private firms in hiring workers with wage subsidies.

Permanent public employment for those who are currently unemployable in the private sector is advocated by those who doubt the potential efficacy or cost-effectiveness of private wage subsidies. A further advantage claimed for public employment is that the government, unlike private employers, could give primacy to job creation and make the production of a useful product a secondary consideration. Such a philosophy currently guides the program of sheltered workshops for the blind and for others with severe physical or mental impairments. Should it, however, be extended to those with less obvious occupational handicaps? The difficulty with a program of public employment is indicated by the question posed by Charles Schultze and his colleagues:

> What would be the appropriate size of a public employment program? The answer depends on the answers to two other questions: How many potential enrollees are there, and what proportion of them would actually enroll? . . . Two alternative actions might be taken to determine the "proper" size of a public employment program. One would be to guarantee a job to everyone applying, and find out how many do apply. A more practical procedure would be to start at a relatively low level and, if the jobs offered at that level were quickly snapped up, to offer more until some acceptable degree of saturation is reached.[5]

The number of enrollees would, of course, depend on the rate of pay and the conditions of work. If the pay were not limited to the minimum wage, workers would be drawn away from productive private employment into these unproductive public positions. Even if these special public employees were only paid the minimum wage for manufacturing employees, workers who are currently employed in private jobs in agriculture and services would find public employment more advantageous. If the managers of the public employment program consider any useful

---

[4] A second objection to the use of wage subsidies is that for some workers no feasible subsidy would be large enough to induce an employer to hire them if managers fear that, because of their unreliability, production lines would be interrupted, machinery destroyed, and so on. This is unlikely to be a very serious problem. Although such unreliability may make some people unemployable

at any wage in some firms and occupations, there are clearly other jobs in which they could be profitably employed at a sufficiently low net wage.

[5] C. Schultze, E. Fried, A. Rivlin, and N. Teeters, *Setting National Priorities; The 1973 Budget* (Washington, Brookings Institution, 1972), pp. 200–201.

output to be of secondary importance, public employment is likely to be less productive and therefore more costly to the nation than private wage subsidies. Moreover, if the case for subsidized job creation rather than direct income support is based on the value to the individual of a sense of accomplishment, it is important that the employee be involved in useful production. There seems little reason to support a program of public employment with little concern for production unless a program of private wage subsidies has been tried and rejected.

An alternative to the development of a formal wage subsidy program is to integrate the minimum wage law and the system of income maintenance. With a negative income tax, such an integration could be accomplished simply if the minimum wage were interpreted as applying to the sum of the employee's market wage and the income maintenance payment converted to an hourly basis. The rules would have to take into account the problems of families with more than one earner, of varying wage rates, and of temporary unemployment, but this could be done without altering the basic notion of integrating income maintenance and the minimum wage. Such an integration would strengthen the income maintenance provisions for those who would otherwise be involuntarily unemployed while avoiding the cumbersome administrative problems of direct wage subsidies.

Duration of Unemployment

A worker who is laid off often does not accept the first job offer in his own line of work but investigates several job possibilities over a period of weeks before accepting new employment. Part of this process of searching is information gathering. The worker who has not recently been unemployed generally does not know what wage and working conditions his own skills and experience will command in the market. He spends time locating relevant jobs and learning about them. Part of the search also consists of delaying in the expectation that the next job offer may be better. The greater the individual's uncertainty and the greater the variance of wage rates and working conditions in his relevant market, the longer he will tend to search.

Not all unemployment can be interpreted as conscious or unconscious search. Some skilled workers and union members know just what the local market wage is in their occupation and prefer to wait until

such work becomes available rather than accept alternative work at lower pay. Some workers are waiting to be rehired into the same job from which they were temporarily laid off because of a seasonal or cyclical fall in demand or because of scheduling problems. Some workers, especially those with severe handicaps, are not able to find any employment. At the other extreme, some of those who report themselves as unemployed and looking for work are actually temporarily out of the labor force and not interested in finding employment.

The average duration of unemployment during the post-War period has been about three months. This varies cyclically: In 1971, it was 11 weeks; in 1969, it briefly dropped below eight weeks, and in 1961, it rose to over 16 weeks. These mean durations reflect a very skewed distribution. Although the mean in 1971 was 11 weeks, more than two thirds of the unemployed had durations of less than 11 weeks and 45 per cent were out of work for less than five weeks.

Any reduction in the mean duration of unemployment would lower the average unemployment rate. *A fall of one month in the average duration of unemployment would lower the unemployment rate from 4.5 per cent to less than 3.0 per cent. Even a two-week reduction would reduce the unemployment rate by 0.75 per cent.* Those who stress the importance of search activity suggest that the duration of unemployment could be reduced by improving the flow of job market information. The computerized "job banks" recently developed by the Department of Labor are a primary example of how this might be done.

The duration of unemployment also depends on the cost to the unemployed of remaining out of work. Our current system of unemployment compensation substantially reduces — indeed often almost completely eliminates — the cost of temporary unemployment. Because unemployment compensation affects not only the duration of job search by the unemployed, but also the cyclical and seasonal variation in labor demand and the job attachment of many low-skill workers, it will be dealt with more generally in the next section.

The Effects of Unemployment Compensation

For more than 30 years, unemployment compensation has provided valuable support for millions of unemployed workers and has been an important source of security to millions more who are employed. It is important to reexamine and strengthen this system by adapting it to the changing nature of unemployment.

All of the basic features of our current unemployment system were designed and adopted in the depths of the Depression. The modern Keynesian principles of income determination were neither understood nor accepted. Now we are all Keynesians. We have come to accept the government's general responsibility for maintaining a high level of demand through variations in spending, taxation, and monetary policy. The structure of unemployment has changed accordingly. The large pool of long-term unemployed workers has been replaced by a much smaller relative number whose durations of unemployment are also much shorter. Almost every unemployed person can now find a job in a very short time. But despite the changing nature of unemployment, the system of unemployment compensation continues essentially in its original form.

Under the economic conditions that have prevailed in the post-War period, our current system of unemployment compensation is likely to have increased the average rate of unemployment. The usual presumption, that unemployment compensation reduces unemployment because it automatically increases government spending when unemployment rises, is really irrelevant. The same fiscal stimulus would now be provided through other expenditure increases or tax cuts by a government committed to maintaining aggregate demand. The primary effect on aggregate unemployment of our current system of unemployment compensation is not its contribution to aggregate demand but its adverse impact on the incentives of employers and employees. As a result, unemployment compensation is likely to increase nearly all sources of adult unemployment: seasonal and cyclical variations in the demand for labor, weak labor force attachment, and unnecessarily long durations of unemployment.

Our current system of unemployment has two distinct but related bad incentive effects. First, for those who are already unemployed it greatly reduces and often almost eliminates the cost of increasing the period of unemployment. Second, and more generally, for all types of unsteady work — seasonal, cyclical, and casual — it raises the net wage to the employee relative to the cost to the employer. The first of these effects provides an incentive to inappropriately long durations of unemployment. The

second provides both employers and employees with the incentive to organize production in a way that increases the level of unemployment by making the seasonal and cyclical variation in unemployment too large and by making casual and temporary jobs too common. Both of these disincentive effects require further explanation.

A detailed example can be very helpful. Consider a worker in Massachusetts in 1971 with a wife and two children. He earns $500 per month or $6000 per year if he experiences no unemployment. She earns $350 per month or $4200 per year if she experiences no unemployment. If he is unemployed for one month, he loses $500 in gross earnings but less than $100 in net income. How does this occur? A reduction of $500 in annual earnings reduces his federal income tax by $83, his Social Security payroll tax by $26, and his Massachusetts income tax by $25. The total reduction in taxes is $134. Unemployment compensation consists of 50 per cent of his wage plus dependents' allowances of $6 per week for each child. Total unemployment compensation is therefore $302. This payment is not part of taxable income. His net income therefore falls from $366 for the month if he is employed (i.e., his $500 gross earnings less $134 in taxes) to the $302 paid as unemployment compensation. *The combination of taxes and unemployment compensation imposes an effective marginal tax rate of 87 per cent* — i.e., the man's net earnings fall by only 13 per cent of his gross pay ($64) when he is unemployed for a month. The same very high marginal rate continues for several more months. If he returns to work after one month, his annual net income is only $128 higher than if he returns after three months. Moreover, part of this increase in income would be offset by the cost of transportation to work and other expenses associated with employment.

If the man does not become unemployed but his wife loses her job, the implied marginal rate may be even higher. If she is unemployed for three months, her gross earnings fall by $1050 but the family's net income may fall by only $72. The fall in earnings reduces taxes by $297 while the unemployment compensation provides $525 in regular benefits and an additional $156 in dependent's benefits.[6] *The effective marginal tax rate is over 93 per*

---

[6] In Massachusetts the wife may collect dependents' benefits when her husband is still employed if she has previously listed the children as income tax dependents.

cent. If the family has three children instead of two, the family's net income is actually higher if the woman is unemployed for three months than if she works for that period.

These astounding figures are not very sensitive to the specific details of the example. Extremely high effective marginal rates would also be implied if the man were not married, or if he were married but his wife did not work, or if his income were 30 per cent higher or lower. For example, a single man with earnings of $500 per month faces a 78 per cent marginal rate. If he is married with two children and his wife does *not* work, his marginal rate is 84 per cent. With monthly earnings of $650, the unemployed married man with two children has an effective marginal rate of 83 per cent; if his monthly income is $350, the marginal rate is 87 per cent. In every case, a middle-income or lower-income individual loses almost no net income if he is unemployed for a short time. Only as incomes rise substantially does the net income loss become significant. For a married man with two children and monthly earnings of $900, the effective marginal rate when he becomes unemployed is 63 per cent; with monthly earnings of $1500 the marginal rate falls to 49 per cent.

In some industries the cost of unemployment is reduced further or even made negative by the supplementary unemployment benefits paid by employers under collective bargaining agreements. The effect of these is particularly important because it continues to apply on an earnings-related basis even above the level at which the state unemployment compensation plans reach their maximum.

Incentives to Prolonged Unemployment

How do people respond to these very high rates of marginal net unemployment compensation? The response of course varies among individuals and differs according to specific circumstance. But the overall effect is almost certainly to increase the duration of the typical spell of unemployment and to increase the frequency with which individuals lose jobs and become unemployed.

Consider first the duration of unemployment. As we have seen, a man who normally earns $500 per month will lose only about $75 of additional net income if he remains out of work for two months instead of one month. Each additional week of unemployment costs him less than $20, substantially

less if there are costs for traveling to work, union dues, and other expenses connected with employment. The unemployed person who does not expect to be recalled by his previous employer can expect to find a better job by searching and waiting for a longer time. Because the cost of additional waiting time and searching time is so very low, the unemployed worker is encouraged to wait until there is almost no chance of a better job. For example, since finding a job that pays as little as five per cent more means an increase in net income of approximately $200 per year, even an additional 10 weeks of unemployment would pay for itself within a year. It is clear that an individual who is actively searching for a better job in this way is neither loafing nor cheating. He is engaged in trying to increase his long-run income. *His search is economically rational from his personal point of view but inefficiently long for the economy as a whole.* The unemployed individual loses valuable productive time in order to achieve a slight gain in future income because taxpayers provide a $1000 subsidy during his 10 weeks of increased search.

Not all the increased duration of unemployment is due to the search for a better job. When the return to work adds less than $20 to the week's net income, there is certain to be a strong temptation to use some time for doing repairs and other tasks at home or simply taking a short period of additional vacation. Some who are waiting to be recalled to a previous job may also engage in casual work for unreported income. All of these temptations are likely to be even stronger when there is another person in the family who is employed. Glaring evidence of this type of voluntary unemployment is found in the "inverse seniority" provisions that are now part of the employer-employee agreements in several industries; these provisions give workers with more seniority the privilege of being laid off *earlier* than other workers and rehired *later*.

There are, of course, rules in our unemployment compensation system designed to limit the extent to which individuals voluntarily extend their duration of unemployment. A worker who is deemed unavailable for work or who refuses suitable employment may be disqualified from receiving benefits. Although this may prevent flagrant abuses and deter some from any voluntary unemployment, it is commonly observed that many who could find employment in their own line of work are able to continue receiving unemployment benefits. The state Employment Service is limited in its ability to find suitable jobs for unemployed workers because it is only notified of a fraction of all openings. Moreover, it is not at all difficult for a worker who is interviewed by a prospective employer to avoid being offered a job if he prefers to remain unemployed.

Incentives to More Unstable Employment

Longer durations of unemployment are only the first of the bad incentive effects identified above. The more general effect of unemployment compensation is to increase the seasonal and cyclical fluctuations in the demand for labor and the relative number of short-lived, casual jobs. It does this by raising the employee's net wage for such unstable jobs relative to the cost to employers. This distortion in the cost of unstable employment influences the patterns of production and consumption in the economy. *Because the price of unstable labor has been artificially subsidized, employers organize production in a way that makes too much use of unstable employment.* Similarly, the economy as a whole consumes relatively too much of the goods that are produced in this way.

A worker who accepts a seasonal job knows that he will be laid off (or will have a much greater risk of being laid off) when the season ends. Similarly, a worker in a casual or temporary job or in a highly cyclical industry knows that he is much more likely to be laid off than a worker with a regular job in an industry that is not cyclically sensitive. If there were no unemployment compensation, workers could be induced to accept such unstable jobs only if the wage rate were sufficiently higher in those jobs than in the more stable positions in which they could find alternative work. The pay differentials among jobs would reflect the chances of being laid off and the expected duration of unemployment after being laid off. The higher cost of labor in unstable jobs would induce employers to reduce the instability of employment by greater smoothing of production through increased variation in inventories and delivery lags, by additional development of off-season work, by incurring costs to improve scheduling, by less cyclical sensitivity of employment to changes in production, by the introduction of new techniques of production (e.g., new methods of outdoor work in bad weather to reduce seasonal layoffs), and so on. The higher wages in unstable employment would also increase the prices of the output produced by

such firms and industries. The higher prices of these goods and services would reduce the demand for them. This would further reduce the amount of unstable employment in the economy.

In the absence of unemployment compensation, the amount of unstable employment would reflect the employees' balancing of higher wages and employment stability, the employers' attempts to produce at minimum cost, and the consumers' choice among goods and services at prices that reflect their cost of production. The effect of unemployment compensation is to offset the market forces that would otherwise prevent an excessive amount of unstable employment. Because unemployment compensation provides a subsidy to workers in unstable employment, it reduces the wage differential required to attract workers to seasonal, cyclical, and temporary jobs. Because employers pay a relatively small premium for their unstable employment, there is little incentive to reduce this instability. Finally, the prices of these goods and services do not reflect the higher social cost of production with unstable employment. The taxpayers subsidize the consumption of those goods whose production creates the most unstable employment.[7]

Imperfections in Financing

To what extent are these harmful incentives offset by the current method of financing unemployment compensation through an experience-rated employer tax? Employers contribute to the state unemployment compensation fund on the basis of the unemployment experience of their own previous employees. Within limits, the more benefits that those former employees draw, the higher is the employer's own tax rate. The theory of experience rating is clear. If an employer paid the *full* cost of the unemployment benefits that his former employees received, unemployment compensation would provide no incentive to an excess use of unstable employment. Although money wages would not be substantially higher for such jobs, the total cost to the employer would be.

In practice, however, experience rating is a very

[7] In describing the harmful effects of unemployment compensation, I do not wish to imply that these outweigh the benefits of the program. Unemployment compensation provides valuable support and security to millions of workers. The problem, however, is to redesign the system to preserve the advantages while reducing the harmful incentives.

imperfect check on the disincentive effects of un-employment compensation. There are three reasons for this. First, the extent of experience rating is limited by a maximum rate of employer contribution. The maximum rate applies when its reserve ratio is below some low level, generally five per cent or less. In the long run, any firm in which average annual benefits generally exceed average annual contributions will pay the maximum rate of the tax. A firm in a seasonal industry that lays off 20 per cent of its average labor force for two months each year will pay the maximum rate if the average wage of those laid off is equal to or greater than $500 per month. More generally, using the three-month mean unemployment duration and assuming that those who become unemployed had earned an average of $500 per month, any firm in which an average of 11 per cent of the average labor force become unemployed each year will pay the maximum. A study of experience in Massachusetts found that in 1959 the maximum tax rate was paid by 31 per cent of construction employers, 40 per cent of apparel manufacturers, and 26 per cent of leather manufacturers. For any firm that already pays the maximum rate, there is no cost for additional unemployment and no gain from a small reduction in unemployment.

The second reason that the current method of experience rating has only a limited deterrent effect is that the relation between current layoffs and contributions is often quite weak. This is partly because the unemployment tax reflects the firm's entire experience since the beginning of the unemployment compensation system. A firm that has paid contributions in excess of benefits for a long time will have a very high reserve ratio and a contribution rate that will not respond to a change in the layoff rate for a long time. The weak link between layoffs and the contribution rate is also due to the way in which the system pools all workers in the firm. A firm in which most employees are not subject to seasonal or cyclical variations can have high layoff rates for certain jobs and in certain product lines without increasing its contribution rate.

Even if there were neither a maximum rate nor a · minimum rate and the contribution rate responded quickly and continuously to changes in the unemployment rate, there would still be a strong incentive to excessive unemployment. This occurs primarily because a worker who is temporarily unemployed avoids income tax and social security payroll tax at his maximum marginal rate on the lost earnings while paying no tax on the unemployment compensation. Since the marginal rate for even relatively low-income families can be over 30 per cent when federal, state, and payroll taxes are combined, the tax effect is quite substantial. In the example discussed above, a married man with a working wife and two children whose wage rate is $500 per month would receive only an extra $64 of net income by reducing his unemployment from two months to one month; if his unemployment benefits were taxed in the same way as other earnings, he would receive more than twice as much, $154. The $90 differential represents a current subsidy out of general tax revenues in addition to the unemployment compensation.

In summary, it is clear that our current unemployment compensation system provides incentives to employers and employees to behave in ways that increase the rate of unemployment in our economy. Although there have been no careful studies to assess the magnitude of these incentive effects, there is a variety of statistical evidence to support the common observation that these effects are economically important. It has been shown that the number of weeks of unemployment per year declines sharply as the wage rate increases. Moreover, mean durations of unemployment appear to be longer in states with more ample unemployment benefits. The very existence of the "inverse seniority" provisions shows that some workers value the opportunity to become unemployed.

The Lessons of the British Experience

The recent British experience is particularly interesting. Until 1966, unemployment insurance in Britain paid a relatively low flat-rate benefit that was not related to the unemployed person's previous earnings. There was also an additional flat-rate dependents' allowance. The "earnings-related supplement," first payable in September 1966, provided for an additional payment equal to one third of the claimant's previous average weekly earnings between £9 and £30. The maximum supplement was therefore £7. The total benefit is subject to a maximum of 85 per cent of the average weekly earnings. The effect of the earnings-related supplement was, in effect, to convert the British system from one with very low relative unemployment benefits for all but the lowest wage group to a benefit structure more similar to that in the United States.

In October 1966, one month after the change in unemployment insurance, British unemployment began rising dramatically. The number of registered unemployed rose from 340,000 in September to 436,000 in October and 543,000 in November. The registered unemployment rate for males rose from 1.6 per cent in August to 3.3 per cent in January. It is, of course, difficult to know how much of this increase should be attributed to the change in unemployment compensation. Other macroeconomic and tax policies occurred at approximately the same time. It is noteworthy, however, that unemployment rates had been above three per cent only once before in the post-War period (during an unusually bad winter) and that such a rapid rise in the rate of unemployment had not been seen before. Moreover, the male unemployment rate has remained over three per cent ever since. The previous relation between the unemployment rate and the vacancy rate ceased to hold after 1966. An examination of the occupational composition of unemployment shows that the proportional rise in unemployment was greatest among skilled married workers and least among the lower-paid unskilled workers (who would benefit less from the earnings-related supplement). The increase among professional, technical, and administrative occupations was also greater than would be expected on the basis of recessions in the recent past. A survey of unemployed workers designed to evaluate the effect of the earnings-related supplement found a significant effect: An increase of £1 per week in the level of unemployment benefits tended to increase the length of unemployment by almost half a week. Although there are problems in interpreting each piece of data on the British experience, the evidence as a whole clearly indicates that the new method of earnings-related unemployment compensation has raised the level of unemployment.

There is little room for doubt about the qualitative conclusion that our current system of unemployment compensation increases the rate and duration of unemployment. Although the magnitude of this effect is unknown, it should be emphasized that rather small changes in the duration of unemployment, the cyclical and seasonal fluctuation in labor demand, and the frequency of temporary jobs can have a very important impact on the overall rate of unemployment. A reduction of two weeks in the current average duration of three months would by itself lower the overall rate of unemployment by 0.75

per cent. If one third of the seasonal unemployment were avoided, the overall unemployment rate would fall by an additional 0.25 per cent. If the cyclical variation in labor demand were also reduced by 20 per cent,[8] this would reduce unemployment by another 0.25 per cent. A decrease in the number of casual temporary jobs would have a further impact. Although each of these changes is small, the total effect is a fall in the unemployment rate of more than 1.25 per cent. These numbers should not be interpreted as specific estimates of the extent to which our current system of unemployment compensation raises the unemployment rate. They should be viewed as illustrations of the powerful cumulative effect of small changes in the several sources of adult unemployment. It is quite possible, however, that the disincentive effects of our current system are responsible for at least this much increased unemployment.

Improving the Current System

The challenge at this time is to restructure the unemployment compensation system in a way that strengthens its good features while reducing the harmful disincentive effects. The virtue of our system is that it permits the family of a lower-income or middle-income worker who is temporarily unemployed to maintain approximately its previous level of spending. Although the fall in net income is relatively greater among higher-income workers, almost all insured families are protected against a substantial change in net income. The disadvantage of our current system is that it raises the rate of unemployment and imposes a loss of economic welfare. This welfare loss occurs because the unemployment compensation system encourages each individual employee to act in a way that is in conflict with the interests of all employees as a group. More specifically, although most of the cost of the unemployment benefits and the reduced federal and state tax collections falls ultimately on employees as a whole,[9] each individual employee is induced to behave in ways that increase this cost. It is rational for the

---

[8] Recall that the post-War cyclical variation in British unemployment is substantially less than half the American experience.

[9] The fact that the tax is nominally paid by employers is irrelevant. The variable rate makes the incidence issue more complex, but the statement in the text is essentially correct.

unemployed individual to delay returning to work and for the job seeker to give less than the correct weight to the risk of future unemployment. For the group as a whole, however, such behavior incurs costs that far outweigh the benefits. This is the essence of the loss of economic welfare.

What could be done to reduce the harmful disincentives without losing the valuable features of unemployment compensation? Some gains could be achieved by removing the ceiling on the employer's rate of contribution and by lowering the minimum rate to zero. Employers would then pay the full price of the unemployment insurance benefits. The change in the rates of contribution would encourage employers to stabilize production and employment. It would also tend to increase prices for goods produced in firms with unstable employment. This would have the effect of shifting production to firms and industries with more stable employment.

Further improvement could be achieved if unemployment insurance benefits were taxed in the same way as other earnings. This would eliminate the anomalous situations in which a family's net income is actually reduced when an unemployed member returns to work. More generally, it would significantly reduce the very high implicit marginal tax rates that an unemployed person faces when he considers returning to work. It would also end the distorting situation in which, for the same total cost to the employer, a worker with some unemployment during the year receives more net income than a fully employed worker. Since the lowest-income families pay no income tax, the taxation of unemployment benefits would not be a burden to the poor. Even at higher incomes, the total effect on family income of taxing benefits would be small even though the marginal effect is sizable. In any case, the current system is inequitable in imposing a higher tax on an employed person than a person *with the same net income* and family circumstances who does not work steadily throughout the entire year.

THE DUAL LABOR MARKET: THEORY AND IMPLICATIONS

Michael J. Piore

Piore discusses the importance of understanding segmentations in the labor market. Although not intended as part of the more general radical analysis, Piore's selection clearly illustrates some of the important economic forces postulated by that analysis as determinants of labor market stratification. Like more radical writers, Piore argues that the stratifications pose almost insurmountable barriers to individual movements between sectors. He differs with orthodox analysis in arguing that workers' income and status do not reflect their productivity in uniform ways throughout the economy; at least in the "secondary" market, incomes bear little relationship to productivity.

Source: Reprinted from Michael J. Piore, "Jobs and Training," in Beer, Barringer, eds., *The State and the Poor,* by permission of the publisher. Copyright © 1970 by Winthrop Publishers, Inc.

The selection comes from a longer paper originally written for a faculty seminar sponsored by the Kennedy School of Government at Harvard University. The papers were later reprinted in a book edited by Beer and Barringer, *The State and the Poor.* The rest of Piore's essay applies his general comments here to some local labor markets in Massachusetts.

Piore is an associate professor of economics at Massachusetts Institute of Technology. With Peter Doeringer, he has written *Internal Labor Markets and Manpower Analysis.*

The central tenet of the analysis [in Piore's paper] is that the role of employment and of the disposition of manpower in the perpetuation of poverty is best understood in terms of a dual labor market. One sector of that market, which I have termed elsewhere the primary market,[1] offers jobs which possess several of the following traits: high wages, good working conditions, employment stability and job security, equity and due process in the administration of work rules, and chances for advancement. The other, or secondary sector, has jobs which, relative to those in the primary sector, are decidedly less attractive. They tend to involve low wages, poor working conditions, considerable variability in employment, harsh and often arbitrary discipline, and little opportunity to advance. The poor are confined to the secondary labor market. The elimination of poverty requires that they gain access to primary employment.

The factors which generate the dual market structure and confine the poor to the secondary sector are complex. At some injustice to that complexity, they may be summarized as follows: First, the most important characteristic distinguishing jobs in the primary sector from those in the secondary sector appears to be the behavioral requirements which they impose upon the work force, particularly that of employment stability. Insofar as secondary workers are barred from primary jobs by real qualifications, it is generally their inability to show up for work regularly and on time. Secondary employers are far more tolerant of lateness and absenteeism, and many secondary jobs are of such short duration that these do not matter. Work skills, which receive considerable emphasis in most discussions of poverty and employment, do not appear a major barrier to primary employment (although, because regularity and punctuality are important to successful learning in school and on the job, such behavioral traits tend to be highly correlated with skills).

Second, certain workers who possess the behavioral traits required to operate efficiently in primary jobs are trapped in the secondary market because their superficial characteristics resemble those of secondary workers. This occurs because employment decisions are generally made on the basis of a few readily (and hence inexpensively) assessed traits such as race, demeanor, accent, educational attainment, test scores, and the like. Such traits tend to be statistically correlated with job performance but not necessarily (and probably not usually) causally

related to it. Hence, a number of candidates who are rejected because they do not possess these traits are actually qualified for the job. Exclusion on this basis may be termed *statistical discrimination*. In addition to statistical discrimination, workers are also excluded from primary employment by discrimination *pure and simple*.

Discrimination of any kind enlarges the captive labor force in the secondary sector, and thus lowers the wages which secondary employers must pay to fill their jobs. This gives to such employers an economic stake in its perpetuation. Since it limits the supply of labor in the primary sector and raises the wages of workers who have access to jobs there, primary workers also have a stake in discrimination. Discrimination pure and simple is not generally of economic value to primary employers since it forces them to pay higher wages without obtaining corresponding economic gains. In statistical discrimination, however, the higher wages are compensated by the reduced cost of screening job candidates, and the interest of secondary employers and primary workers in such discrimination is shared by primary employers as well.

Third, the distinction between primary and secondary jobs is not, apparently, technologically determinate. A portion — perhaps a substantial proportion — of the work in the economy can be organized for either stable or unstable workers. Work normally performed in the primary sector is sometimes shifted to the secondary sector through subcontracting, temporary help services, recycling of new employees through probationary periods and the like. Nor is the primary-secondary distinction necessarily associated with a given enterprise. Some enterprises, most of whose jobs possess the character of primary employment and are filled with stable, committed workers, have subsections or departments with inferior job opportunities accommodated to an unstable work force. Secondary employers generally have a few, and some have a large number, of primary jobs. Nonetheless, despite a certain degree of elasticity in the distribution of work between the primary and secondary sectors, shifts in the distribution generally involve changes in the techniques of production and management and in the institutional structure and procedures of the enterprises in which the work is performed. The investment necessary to effect these changes acts to strengthen resistance to anti-poverty efforts.

Fourth, the behavioral traits associated with the

[1] See Michael J. Piore, "Public and Private Responsibilities in On-The-Job Training of Disadvantaged Workers," Massachusetts Institute of Technology, Department of Economics Working Paper No. 23, June 1968.

secondary sector are reinforced by the process of working in secondary jobs and living among others whose life-style is accommodated to that type of employment. Hence, even individuals who are forced into the secondary sector initially by discrimination tend, over time, to develop the traits predominant among secondary workers. Thus, for example, by working in a world where employment is intermittent and erratic, one tends to lose habits of regularity and punctuality. Similarly, when reward and punishment in the work place are continually based upon personal relationships between worker and supervisor, workers forget how to operate within the impersonal, institutional grievance procedures of the primary sector and when they do gain access to primary jobs, are frustrated by the failure of the system to respond on a personal basis and their own inability to make it respond on an institutional basis.

Finally, income sources alternative to employment among the poor, especially public assistance and illicit activity, tend to be more compatible with secondary than with primary employment. The public assistance system discourages full-time work, and forces those on welfare into jobs which are either part time or which pay income in cash which will not be reported to the social worker or can be quickly dropped or delayed when the social worker discovers them or seems in danger of doing so. The relationship between social worker and client builds upon the personal relationship which operates in the secondary sector rather than the institutional mechanisms which tend to operate in the primary sector. Illegitimate activity also tends to follow the intermittent work pattern prevalent in secondary employment, and the attractions of such activity, as well as life patterns and role models it presents to those not themselves involved but associating with people who are, foster behavioral traits antagonistic to primary employment.

The central implications of the dual market interpretations of poverty are that the poor do participate in the economy; that it is the manner of their participation, not the question of participation per se, which constitutes the manpower problem of the poor; and that their current mode of participation is ultimately a response to a series of pressures — economic, social, and technical — playing upon individuals and labor market institutions. This suggests that a distinction can be drawn between policies designed to alleviate the pressure which generate the dual market structure in the first place, and those which attempt to attack the problem by moving individuals from secondary to primary employment directly. The latter policies operate against the prevailing pressures but leave the forces which generate them intact. The next section of the paper draws heavily upon this distinction. The thrust of the argument in that section is that, in concentrating upon training, counseling, and placement services for the poor, manpower policy has overemphasized direct approaches and that more weight should be placed upon policies which affect the environment in which employment decisions are made and the pressures which it generates. Among such policies, we include anti-discrimination policy, occupational licensing reform, the structure of public assistance, and the legal distinctions between legitimate and illegitimate activity. [Ed.: This section has not been included.]

A further implication to be drawn from the analysis of the dual labor market is that, because the poor do participate in the economy, there are certain groups interested in that participation and the way in which it occurs. Policies directed at the movement of the poor out of the secondary market and into primary employment work against the interests of these groups and, for that reason, are in danger of being subverted by them. This is one of the major reasons for concentrating upon indirect approaches, for these are not susceptible to the same kind of subversion and in fact, because they alleviate the pressures generating the dual market structure, they reduce the resistance to policies that move directly against that structure. The dangers to which existing institutions subject programs designed to move the poor directly out of the secondary market are twofold: The new institutions created by these programs can be rejected by the prevailing economic system and isolated off to one side. A program, for example, would then recruit workers into training which provides skills little utilized in either the secondary or the primary market. Alternatively, the new institutions may be captured by the prevailing economic system and used to facilitate its operation. Examples of programs subverted in this way are the neighborhood employment offices which recruit secondary workers for secondary jobs, and training provided in primary employment to workers who would have gotten it anyway in establishments that otherwise would have financed it themselves. The central problem in the design of direct approaches to manpower programs is to organize them in such a way that they can resist this twofold threat of rejection, on the one hand, and capture, on the other. . . .

While these conclusions follow directly from the dual market interpretation of the poverty problem, they are not uniquely dependent upon it. The dual labor market is one of a class of theoretical constructs which views poverty in the United States in terms of a dichotomy in the economic and social structure. Such a dichotomy is implicit in the concept of a "culture of poverty" and in the expression of public policy goals associated with poverty in terms of an income cut off. Most such views of poverty entertain the idea that the dichotomy is a product of forces endogenous to the economy (or, more broadly, the society as a whole).[2] It follows that attempts to eliminate poverty will tend to run counter to the natural operation of the economy; that they will be resisted by existing institutions and are in jeopardy of rejection. To say all this is perhaps to say little more than that, if poverty were easy to eliminate, it wouldn't be around in the first place. But it does, at least, point to the task of equipping the institution which works with the poor to withstand the rejection pressures as a central problem in the program design.

What the dual labor market interpretation implies which is not implicit in dichotomous interpretations in general is that the poor are not only separated from the nonpoor in the negative sense of exclusion from activities and institutions to which the non-poor have access, they are also separated from the nonpoor in the positive sense that they have economic value where they are and hence that there are groups interested, not only in resisting the elimination of poverty, but in actively seeking its perpetuation. It is this which makes new institutions created to work with the poor in the labor market subject to the threat of capture as well as the threat of rejection.

The major alternative to the dual labor market interpretation as a foundation for manpower policy is one that associates poverty with either the inability to find work or with full-time work at low wages. This interpretation of poverty would emphasize the high incidence of unemployment among the poor and

their relatively low rates of labor force participation, on the one hand, and the number of people employed full time, full year at low-paying jobs, on the other. It should be noted that many upon whom this interpretation focuses attention, but the dual labor market emphasis ignores, are incapable of productive employment in any realistic sense and, hence, their poverty is beyond reach of manpower policy. This group includes, for example, large numbers of aged; people with serious physical handicaps; major mental and emotional disorders; and small children in families headed by these individuals. A small proportion of the people in these groups can be helped to work: there is a series of programs designed to do this; we did not investigate them. The dual market interpretation implies that much of the remainder of what appears statistically to be an unemployment problem results from the attempt to classify and interpret the experience of the secondary market in a set of statistical categories derived from a model of the primary labor market. Thus, for example, measured unemployment and labor force participation rates in poor neighborhoods are distorted by numbers of individuals who are frictionally unemployed because of the instability of jobs, unwilling to work continuous five-day weeks, working illegal or quasi-illegal jobs, supported by family members not classified as such by the survey, and the like. The second group of poor which the dual labor market interpretation tends to slight (the full-time, full-year, but low-wage workers) could not be separately identified for Massachusetts. This number is large nationally, but, we would like to argue, probably concentrated in the South and in rural areas.

The dual labor market provides quite a convincing interpretation of the realities of the black urban ghetto labor markets. The combination of high measured unemployment rates and bitter complaints of narrow employment opportunity, on the one hand, with high turnover rates and persistent employer complaints of labor shortage cannot be reconciled with a conventional unemployment interpretation but are readily comprehended with a two-sector model in which the sectors are distinguished by the relative stability of jobs and workers. Such a model is also consistent with autobiographical and sociological descriptions of urban ghetto life. In Massachusetts, it certainly constitutes an accurate diagnosis of black and Puerto Rican poverty in the city of Boston. How far beyond these ghetto communities the applicability of the model extends is a moot question. Some at-

[2] The alternative to this view is one in which poverty is defined in relation to a continuum: there is no great chasm to bridge and a marginal movement of individuals within the existing system will meet the public policy objective.

tempt to assess its limits was made for the present study. Within Boston, it was generally felt by those working in manpower programs that the model is somewhat less applicable to the white ethnic poor than to the black poor. It appears that a larger proportion of the white ethnic poor are simply locked into low-wage jobs which do not possess the combination of debilitating characteristics typical of low-paying black employment. On the other hand, many of these ethnic white workers do not think of themselves as poor and resent efforts to treat them as such.

THE CHARACTERISTICS OF MARGINAL INDUSTRIES

Barry Bluestone

This excerpt describes the economic characteristics of jobs in the secondary labor market. It makes clear that the economic determinants of such low-wage jobs are deeply rooted, and that one cannot expect sudden changes in the basic structure of employment available to disadvantaged workers. Although the data came from the 1960s, more recent data would portray much the same picture.

This reprinted portion is from the second half of an article called "Lower-Income Workers and Marginal Industries" from Louis Ferman *et al.*, eds., *Poverty in America.*

Bluestone teaches economics at Boston College.

A "character" sketch . . . applied to low-wage industries permits some insight into the dynamics of the low-wage sector of the economy. While it may not allow a perfect understanding of all low-wage jobs, it does unveil the economic and social forces conducive to the persistence of poverty employment within the confines of a materially affluent society.

Growth Rate of Average Hourly Earnings

Delehanty and Evans report that between 1958 and 1963, the gain in average hourly earnings in all manufacturing was 17 percent, while the gain in

Source: Barry Bluestone, "Lower-Income Workers and Marginal Industries," in Louis Ferman *et al.*, eds., *Poverty in America.* Copyright © by The University of Michigan 1965, 1968. All rights reserved. Published in the United States of America by The University of Michigan Press. United Kingdom agent: The Cresset Press.

low-wage industries was limited to 13.6.[1] Over a longer period, 1953 to 1963, the median increase for low-wage two-digit industries was only 30 percent while the median in other manufacturing industry exceeded 45. The differential in wage growth rates is also reflected in the relative changes in wages in broader employment categories. Between 1947 and 1966, wages in non-durable goods and retail trade rose less rapidly than wages in all manufacturing, and overall, low-wage industries within manufacturing produced the smallest gains both relatively and absolutely.

Rather than closing, the earnings gap between low-wage industries and most high-wage industries appears to be growing. Relative to the average worker in society, the working poor wage-earner is more poor today than he was 20 years ago, and although some workers in low-wage industries have escaped absolute poverty in the sense that they have broken through the artificial $3,000 threshold, their income position, relatively speaking, has deteriorated. Small decreases in the percentage of low-wage employment among industries in recent years . . . reflect a minor reduction in absolute working poverty, but camouflage the fact that wage increases have not been spread throughout the industry. Rather, wage dispersion within the low-wage industries has been reduced, possibly due to upward pressure on lowest

[1] George E. Delehanty and Robert Evans, Jr., "Low-Wage Employment: An Inventory and an Assessment," Northwestern University, mimeo, no date, p. 9.

wages because of broader coverage of minimum wage laws.

Demand for Labor in Low-Wage Industry

All things equal, industries with increasing demand for labor are generally expected to have wages increasing at a faster pace than those where labor demand has slackened. Yet in this regard, empirical evidence on low-wage industry appears equivocal. While a number of low-wage industries have had steadily declining employment consistent with slow rather than rapid wage advance, other low-wage industries have had relatively high employment growth rates.

Lumber and wood products, textile mill products, leather and leather goods, laundries and cleaning services, and footwear are prime examples of the declining low-wage industry. On the other hand, apparel and related products, furniture and textiles, and above all, retail trade, contradict the expectation as all of these have had healthy advances in employment without eliminating their poverty wage scales. A number of industries have had large decreases in employment yet have not fallen prey to low wages. Over the last two decades both mining and primary metal industries have had absolute decreases in nonsupervisory production personnel yet have managed to keep wages at a high level. Indeed primary metal industries have increased wages at a rate in excess of the average for all manufacturing firms. Obviously all things have not been equal in the economy, and hence other factors must be called upon to explain the dimensions of low-wage industry.

Productivity of Low-Wage Industries

When the productivity of a firm increases, presumably wages can be raised, profits can be increased, prices can be lowered, or a combination of the three can occur. In oligopolistic industries, productivity has been rising fairly steadily and the result, at least in part, has been expanding wages and profit margins, often at the same, or higher, growth rate as the productivity rate. When low-wage manufacturing industries are investigated, they are found, on the average, to possess productivity growth rates consistent with the gains in the rest of manufacturing. Using the ratio of the Federal Reserve Board's "Production Index" divided by total employment as a measure of productivity for the years 1958–1963, Delehanty and Evans found a 26 percent median increase in productivity for low-wage two-digit manufacturing classifications. For the remaining manufacturing sectors, the median increase was slightly *less,* 25 percent. Nevertheless, absolute productivity in the low-wage sectors was found to be well below that in non-low-wage industries. The value-added per production worker man/hour in the low-wage sectors was only $3.63 while in other manufacturing industry the median was more than double, $8.17.[2]

The low absolute productivity of labor in low-wage industry, no matter whether the cause is too little complementary capital or inefficient management, partly explains the low level of wages in the poverty industries. But the productivity gains in low-wage industry are not reflected in the relative wage rate changes in low-wage industry. Rather than contributing to higher wages, productivity increases are either being absorbed into broader profit margins or otherwise into lower prices due to raging competition. Productivity, then, cannot alone explain the plight of the low-wage industry and its poverty-stricken workforce.

Profits

Periodically, it is suggested that poverty wages are the result of employee exploitation by profit-grubbing monopolistic firms. Indeed, firms maintaining influence in labor markets can artificially reduce wages below the return due to workers based on their productivity and thereby accrue higher money profits for the company. In some low-wage industries where the local labor market is at the mercy of a company town, no doubt exploitation of this kind is practiced. Yet in general, the evidence points to low-profit margins in the bulk of low-wage industry.

Using Stigler's study of capital and the return on capital in manufacturing, Delehanty and Evans computed the median rates of return (profit margins) over the years 1948 to 1957 for both all manufacturing and an isolated set of low-wage industries. The median for the former was 7.33 percent while for low-wage industry the median was limited to 5.75 percent, a considerably smaller profit margin.[3] More recent data from the Federal Trade and the Securities and Exchange Commissions gave comparable results, although they showed a declining relative

[2] *Ibid.,* p. 11.
[3] *Ibid.,* p. 13.

and absolute gap in the profit margin between all manufacturing and the low-wage sector.[4] Some wage exploitation may be occurring in a few specific industries; nevertheless, the low-profit margins recorded here and reported in addition by Gus Tyler[5] of the International Ladies' Garment Workers Union lead us to believe that individual low-wage industries, by and large, have had little success in attempting wage exploitation. The working poor are being exploited by the economy as a whole rather than by the individual firms employing them.

Concentration and Competition

The degree of market concentration in an industry or conversely market competition determines the ability of a firm to administer prices rather than be forced through economic pressure to submit to the ensuing set of market prices. When product market competition is fierce, because of a plethora of small firms competing where none can control the market, productivity increases tend to resolve into lower commodity prices rather than higher profit margins or higher wages. In contrast to mammoth oligopolistic industries which can set prices without fear of open price conflict, many relatively small firms which produce the same commodity cannot match the wages of the titans. Wage increases in manufacturing giants can be passed along at rates equal to productivity, while the competitive firm is often forced to lower prices rather than increase profits or wages. In some cases, the oligopolistic firm may be forced to raise wages even above productivity gains, paying for this by cutting into monopoly profits or by boosting the price of their products. The highly competitive firm is rarely in such a position.

Data from Kaysen and from Delehanty and Evans point to the much lower concentration ratios in the low-wage industries.[6, 7] For instance, the latter found that of the 1,132 five-digit product classes in all manufacturing, 23 percent were such that the four largest producers for each product made 60 percent or more of the total output. Prime examples are the industrial titans of automobile, steel, rubber, and aluminum. Among low-wage industry, however, only 9 percent of the product classes were produced in highly concentrated industries. Clearly the degree of competitiveness among the low-wage industries is greater than that for the rest of manufacturing, and the same generally holds, probably even to a greater extent, for retail trade and services, both low-wage sectors.

This analysis appears to account for the disparity between productivity and wage gains in the low-wage sector versus the better paying industries. While productivity in low-wage industries has kept pace with or in some cases has exceeded the rest of industry, wages and profits have not risen as quickly because of the raging price competition in the low-wage sector not present in the rest of the economy.

Nonetheless, a highly concentrated industry per se does not guarantee a higher wage scale, for there is nothing inherent in the size of a firm or in the absence of product market competition which accounts for better wages. Rather, oligopoly provides what might be called a "permissive economic environment" within which other forces can more easily work for higher wages.[8] Needless to say, such an economic climate is nonexistent for the frail, competitive, often low-wage, firm. A permissive economic environment entails capital-intensive production possibilities, the ability to set prices based on product demand conditions, high public visibility, low firm entry, and the opportunity for strong unionism.

Utilization of Capital

Where each worker has a great deal of machinery at his command, output per man will be large and the wage bill correspondingly will be a small fraction of the total costs incurred by the producer. Such wages will have a tendency to be higher than where production is labor-intensive. Furthermore, resistance to wage increases will be less in the capital-intensive industry since wages make up a small part of operating costs.

Data on manufacturing production functions in the United States give adequate evidence to support the hypothesis that low-wage industries in general

[4] *Ibid.*, p. 14.

[5] Gus Tyler, "Marginal Industries, Low Wages, and High Risks," *Dissent*, Summer 1961, pp. 321–325.

[6] Carl Kaysen and Donald F. Turner, *Antitrust Policy: An Economic and Legal Analysis*, Harvard University Press, Cambridge, 1959. (See appendices.)

[7] Delehanty and Evans, *op. cit.*, pp. 19–20.

[8] Harold M. Levinson, "Unionism, Concentration, and Wage Changes: Toward a Unified Theory," *Determining Forces in Collective Wage Bargaining*, John Wiley and Sons, New York, 1967.

are less capital-intensive than more lucrative industries.[9] In four of six low-wage manufacturing industry classifications the extent of capital available was significantly related to the wage level.[10] In most cases, the correlation was also significant between the size of the firm and the amount of capital per worker. In both cases the same results certainly must extend to retail trade and services.

Part of the low-wage pattern found in labor-intensive firms is no doubt due to unexploited economies of scale and to the fact that small wage increases, let alone large, add considerably to total operating costs of small firms which are weak in capital. Hence, the lack of capital in the low-wage firm accounts for some of the growing gap in relative incomes between the average worker and the working poor.

Product Demand

Although there is little data on the demand for different products, it is plausible to posit that the demand for many low-wage industry commodities is quite elastic due to product substitutes and foreign competition. Only recently is foreign competition in the heavy goods industry beginning to dent domestic sales and prices in the high-wage sector. In textiles, miscellaneous manufacturing, watches and clocks and apparel, foreign competition has been fierce and in some cases has not completely destroyed a comparatively inefficient domestic industry only because of restrictive tariffs.

To the extent that a product has inelastic demand, wages can be raised at the expense of higher prices, as in the automobile industry. But where demand is highly elastic, a small increase in price reduces the demand precipitously. When cigar prices rise, smokers switch to pipes and cigarettes; when domestic textile prices rise, fashions turn to imported fabrics. Consequently, the low-wage firm has little recourse to a price increase as a means of boosting wages or profit margins for that matter. If the firm faces an elastic demand, it runs itself out of the market when it raises prices too high. The choice for workers in this industry becomes not low wages or high wages, but low wages or no wages.

In the bituminous coal industry for example, the choice was against paying low wages to a multitude of coal-miners. Instead, the industry was mechanized; prices remained competitive but a great part of the workforce was eliminated. Many were thrown out of lifelong work, but those who survived the cut received an adequate wage for their continuing toil.

Public Visibility

When General Motors Corporation announces net profits in excess of 20 percent per year, employs over 400,000 workers, and controls prices in a $20 billion-plus industry, the nation cannot help but take notice. The same holds for other major industries in the country. But the near invisible low-wage sector of the economy escapes the constant public scrutiny to which the industrial giants are subjected. A large firm can hardly escape paying relatively high wages even if there is little internal pressure from its workforce. The small "invisible" firm, on the other hand, often avoids the sharp eye of the government inspector and the acute sensitivities of an aroused public opinion. Consequently, low wages and poor working conditions have a much better chance of survival in the industries of the working poor. Similarly, laws are so drawn as to exclude many workers in the low-wage sector. As late as 1963, for instance, maximum wage laws excluded from coverage over one and one-half million restaurant workers, 489,000 hotel and motel employees, over a half million laundry workers, 700,000 hospital workers, over three million retail clerks, and, in addition, millions of farmers and thousands of loggers and agricultural processing workers.[11] Ironically, the minimum wage law covers *all* auto, steel, rubber, and aluminum workers where the average wage is over twice the minimum and literally no one earns below one and a half times the legal minimum wage.

Unionization

Although low-wage industry is not as highly unionized as high-wage manufacturing, it is not totally unorganized. Unions exist in many low-wage industries, but they are beset by a number of nearly insurmountable hurdles brought on by the character-

[9] George H. Hildebrand and Ta-Chung Liu, *Manufacturing Production Functions in the United States, 1957.* (As used in Delehanty and Evans.)
[10] Delehanty and Evans, p. 23.

[11] AFL-CIO, "The Low-Paid Worker," *American Federationist*, August, 1964.

istics of most low-wage industry. The same barriers account for the sectors of low-wage industry devoid of unionization.

There is nothing inherent in the nature of oligopolistic industrial giants which explains, not their ability, but their actual granting of higher wages. If we are to fully understand the causes of high wages and, consequently, those of low wages and working-poor jobs, it is necessary to include the all-important dimension of unionization.

A number of studies over the past few years have shown that greater rates of wage increases have been strongly associated with (1) a relatively high degree of oligopoly, (2) high profit rates, and (3) strong unions.[12] Yet these forces do not act independently, but rather bear systematic relation to each other. High product market concentration and high profits provide the footing for a "permissive economic environment" in which strong unions can reap economic and social rewards for their members. Where an industry is inhabited by a few massive price-setting, highly mechanized, non-competitive, publicly visible, and highly profitable firms, entry of new firms is highly improbable and, indeed, quite rare. The needed initial resources are too vast to be accumulated by a newcomer. Consequently, unions, once they have become established, are relatively secure and free from the competition forced on them by an unorganized sector in the industry. Free to press for higher wages without fear of eliminating jobs by pricing their firm's product above unorganized competition, the union can demand their share of productivity and productivity gains, which in a capital-intensive industry are usually relatively high. With the industry held up to the inspection of both government and the public, the industry is doubly careful to refrain from "inappropriate" activities vis-à-vis their employees and their union. The high profits of the titans of industry present a choice target for union wage demands when bargaining sessions open.

In some high-wage industries, the product market nevertheless fails to be characterized by oligopolistic, highly profitable firms. High wages in these industries can usually be explained by the ability of

the market to self-regulate entry or for unions to tightly control firm entry themselves. This is usually due to the "spatial" characteristics of the industry. The coal industry located in Appalachia is controlled in this way by the United Mine Workers. The Teamsters Union, which operates in a highly competitive industry, nevertheless reaps high wages for its members since it is able to control entry through over-the-road spatial agreements.

Consequently, we can conclude that most industries which are capital intensive, highly profitable, and free from raging competition have the *ability* to raise wages with relatively less pain and effort than other industry. Furthermore, it is precisely this economic environment which provides the most suitable conditions for strong unions. They can tackle the ability of their industries to pay high wages and turn it, through collective bargaining and the threat of collective action, into real wage advances for their members. In other industries where unions can control entry and organize the whole market, high wages are also possible, although sometimes, as in the bituminous coal case, at the expense of eliminating many jobs.

In the low-wage sector, we have found nearly the opposite conditions. And, indeed, to a great extent, the low-wage industries represent the end result of a "repressive economic environment." Absolute productivity is well below that of all industry; less capital is utilized in production; profit rates are smaller, and most importantly, competition flourishes. The ability of many low-wage industries to pay adequate wages without drastically cutting employment is seriously open to question. Furthermore, the repressive environment decidedly stymies union organization and the pressure of unions for higher wages. Where an industry is so established that entry is free and open to new, unorganized firms, we can expect weak unions and most probably low wages. Where industries are marked by easy entry, fierce national and international competition, highly elastic product demand, low profits, and low productivity, we can almost be assured of two things: if a union exists at all, it is bound to be weak and ineffective, and there will surely be large numbers of working poor. Such is the case in textiles, apparel and related products, cigar manufacturing, fertilizer manufacture, and so forth. Many of the same characteristics are found in agriculture and the retail and service trades.

The same characteristics do not always apply to

[12] See Arthur Ross and William Goldner, "Forces Affecting Interindustry Wage Structure," *Quarterly Journal of Economics*, Vol. 64, No. 2, May 1950, pp. 254–305; William G. Bowen, *Wage Behavior in the Postwar Period*, Princeton, 1960; Harold M. Levinson, *op. cit.*

all industries which pay low wages and employ America's working poor. Some fail to pay higher wages because of foreign competition, watches and clocks for instance. Some, such as nursing care and retail trade, fail primarily because of low advances in productivity. Others fail for the most part due to one or more of these factors plus elastic demand for the product, e.g., cigar manufacturing.[13] Most fail, however, because of the competitiveness of their product markets.

It is interesting to note that precisely where the market approaches its theoretical best — in the firms furthest from monopoly and closest to laissez faire — the market cannot supply jobs adequate enough to feed a man's family satisfactorily. In part, this arises because of the fact that the marginal industry exists in an economy alongside of oligopolies. As Gus Tyler has put it most eloquently:

> Just as small industry must lose out to oligopoly in the struggle for the market, so too, must the worker in the competitive, mobile, low-profit

[13] Note that no working poor are in the cigarette industry although over one-half of all cigar workers are paid low wages. This is mostly due to the fact that cigarette manufacture is capital-intensive, oligopolistic, highly profitable, strongly unionized, and faces an inelastic market for its product. In the cigar industry the conditions are reversed.

trades lose his standing relative to the worker in the mechanized, immobile, high-profit industries.

The 25 percent profit return on original investment not uncommon in steel and autos as contrasted with the 1 percent profit in garments does not derive from an inherent virtue of metal over fabrics, but from the monopoly character of the former and the competitive character of the latter. The workers in the latter industries suffer although many of them possess skills as great or even greater than those required in the basic industries.[14]

The inadequate incomes of most of the working poor are not of their own making. If we are to blame them for anything it must be for not having the good fortune to complete an education topped off by a college degree. Rather we must blame the economic system which in too many instances provides less than an adequate job for those of adequate talents. In dealing with the working poor it is not enough to deal with the problems of individuals — too little schooling, not enough training, inadequate housing and filthy neighborhoods, no hope, and no potential power. We must also find solutions to an economic system which continues to propel a poverty-wage sector right into the decade of the '70s.

[14] Tyler, op. cit., pp. 323–324.

INSTITUTIONS ON THE PERIPHERY

Bennett Harrison

The secondary labor market does not exist by itself. In this selection Harrison argues that three other institutions feed into, complement, and reinforce the secondary labor market — the welfare economy, the training sector, and the "irregular economy."

Source: "Institutions on the Periphery," by Bennett Harrison, from "Employment, Unemployment and the Structure of the Urban Labor Market," from the *Wharton Quarterly*, Spring 1972. Copyright © 1972 by the Trustees of the University of Pennsylvania. Reprinted with permission.

Harrison teaches urban planning and economics at the Massachusetts Institute of Technology.

. . . There appear to be at least four kinds of labor-time-consuming and remunerative activities in urban economies which display remarkably similar characteristics. Mobility among these "segments" seems to take place regularly and easily, while (by contrast) workers in these segments are able to move into the core of the economy only very infrequently. These commonalities and contrasts lead us to group the four segments into a single stratum: the "periphery."

The first and certainly the most important of these peripheral segments is the "secondary labor market." Research — much of it concerned with the study of ghetto labor markets — has disclosed the existence of a class of jobs which contrast sharply with those in the primary labor market along each of the three dimensions we have discussed: productivity, earnings, and stability.[1] Secondary workers tend to display relatively low average and marginal productivity. While this is partly explained by human capital deficiencies, an at least equally important factor is the absence of economic power in this part of the economy. With little or no oligopolistic power, and with small absolute and relative profits, secondary firms tend to use more antiquated capital, which of course tends to diminish productivity. Finally, the jobs themselves often do not *require* skills of any great consequence, involving instead the kind of routine unskilled tasks which attract (and at the same time reinforce the life styles of) casual laborers.

Workers in the secondary labor market receive, and firms in this stratum of the economy pay, very low wages. During the period of July, 1968 through June, 1969, 37% of the black and 51% of the Puerto Rican male household heads living in Harlem and working at least 35 hours a week, 50 weeks a year averaged less than $100 per week in earnings. Nationally, in 1966, 86.3% of all employees working in nursing homes and related facilities earned less than $1.60 per hour, the legal minimum wage. For employees of laundry and cleaning services, fertilizer manufacturers, eating and drinking places, gasoline service stations, and retail food stores, the 1966 percentages were 75.4%, 41.7%, 79.4%, 66.7%, and 47.6% respectively. Low productivity contributes to the explanation of these low wages, but so does the lack of market power among peripheral employers.

Moreover, dual labor market theorists believe that these factors are interdependent; the marginal

---

[1] It is important to observe that this contract between the primary and secondary labor markets takes place in the dimension of jobs, i.e., specific industry-occupation combinations, and not in the simple dimensions of either industry alone or occupation alone. David Gordon has theorized — and Howard Wachtel and David Taylor have demonstrated empirically — that wages, tenure and productivity vary across industries (within occupations) and across occupations (within industries).

The Structure of Urban Labor Markets

firm, by paying low wages and by not providing its workers with adequate complementary capital, discourages its labor force from taking those actions or developing those attitudes which would lead to increased productivity which, if capitalized, could increase the firm's capacity to pay higher wages. The lack of economic power which characterizes peripheral firms (as reflected, for example, in the relatively high elasticity of their output demand curves) also makes it impossible for them to raise wages and other input costs without eroding profit margins, often to the shut-down point. Finally, the low wages found in the secondary labor market are partly the result of the relative simplicity of the technologies in secondary industries; since skill requirements are minimal, the opportunity cost of secondary labor is low, given the large pool of readily available substitutable workers out "on the street."

While the primary labor market is characterized by a mutual employer-employee "taste" for stability, both firms and workers in the secondary labor market seem to benefit from *unstable* work-force behavior. That secondary labor is significantly more unstable than primary labor (or, to be more precise, that it is possible to identify distinct stability thresholds in the labor force) has been demonstrated by

Robert Hall and Edward Kalachek in studies of national and urban samples, respectively.

Secondary employers have several reasons for placing a low value on turnover, in sharp contrast to their fellows in the primary labor market. They can as a rule neither afford nor do their technologies require them to invest heavily in "specific training." Instead, they tend to rely on the "general training" (e.g., literacy, basic arithmetic) provided socially through the school system. With minimal investment in their current labor force, and given the ready availability of substitute labor outside the firm, such employers are at the very least indifferent to the rate of turnover. Moreover, these firms lack the size and wealth necessary for the development of internal labor markets. Nor have they any reason to want to develop such institutions; since their skill requirements are minimal, they are unlikely to encounter periods where the labor they need is scarce and therefore expensive to recruit through conventional ("external") labor markets.

Finally, everything we've hypothesized about the technology of secondary industries implies that the typical job is easily and quickly learned, so that learning curves probably have both low asymptotes and steep slopes. To keep a worker employed for an extended period usually requires the granting of raises in pay and various employee benefits. Moreover, there is a definite correlation between labor force stability and the probability of that force being organized. It follows that employers who already have little to lose (in terms of foregone output) by discouraging long tenure of specific workers will have still other reasons for discounting stability.

Workers, for their part, seem similarly to have a rational preference for instability in the secondary labor market. The jobs are boring, and don't pay well. Employers seem not to mind — and perhaps even to encourage — casual attitudes toward work. The penalties for poor industrial discipline are generally not severe. Doeringer's studies of anti-poverty programs in Boston led him to conclude about the job placement system for ghetto workers that it was seldom able to refer its clients to jobs paying more than they were earning before — "only $2.00 an hour or less." This lack of upward mobility in the placement system contributes to the poor work habits and weak job attachment of the "hard-to-employ":

The availability of alternative low-wage job opportunities and the unattractiveness of such low-wage work interact to discourage the formation of strong ties to particular employers.[2]

That low wages are the principal motivating factor seems to be confirmed by the finding that, "for wage rates higher than the 'prevailing' ghetto wage, disadvantaged workers are more likely to be stable employees than other workers." These relationships between tenure and wage rates were found to be at best only weakly related to the educational attainment of the workers. And, of course, this entirely rational instability frustrates union organization so that there is no pressure for change, e.g., improvement in wages and working conditions — pressure which has been institutionalized in the core of the economy.

Thus, where primary employers and employees interact in an institutional setting characterized by high productivity, non-poverty level wages and high work-force stability, the firms (or divisions of firms) and work forces in the secondary labor market tend to organize themselves into production systems displaying low productivity, poverty level wages and low stability (high turnover).

The second segment of the periphery might be called the "welfare sector." The Manpower Administration of the U.S. Department of Labor recognizes that:

> Another possible alternative to low-wage, irregular jobs for some slum residents, especially women with children but no husbands to help in family support, is public assistance. The division of the poor between those with jobs and those depending on welfare is by no means stable or clear cut. Women may receive assistance in some months of the year and work in other months, or they may be on welfare and at the same time work openly or covertly.[3]

Recipients of AFDC (Aid to Families With Dependent Children) have been widely regarded as caught in a chronic, static condition of dependency, handed down from one generation to the next. Welfare has been viewed as an alternative to work, increasingly unrelated to such economic

[2] Peter B. Doeringer, "Ghetto Labor Markets — Problems and Programs," Program on Regional and Urban Economics, Discussion Paper No. 35, Harvard University, May 1968, pp. 10–11.

[3] U.S. Department of Labor, *1971 Manpower Report of the President* (Washington, D.C.: U.S. Government Printing Office, 1971), p. 97.

factors as the general level of unemployment or the participation of women in the labor force . . . But there are also many families whose members are on welfare rolls for very short periods of time and never sever their connection with the labor force, even when they are on welfare.[4]

There is substantial evidence that many people on welfare display much the same kind of turnover found in the secondary labor market. In 1966, for example, about 45,000 new families were added to the AFDC rolls each month, 41,000 left, and a third of the "new" additions had in fact been on welfare before, had dropped off, and were now enrolling again. A study of the Philadelphia AFDC caseload in 1962 showed that only 13% of the mothers had no history of work. Most remarkable of all, of those who did have a work history, "40% had been employed in skilled or semi-skilled jobs." In a study of the Harlem economy, Thomas Vietorisz and I found that 6.7% of the full-time employed and 11.8% of the part-time employed workers in 1966 were in families which received welfare that year.[5]

Just as the "welfare economy" shares the peripheral characteristic of instability, so it is that the typical "rate" of welfare income in the U.S. is extremely low — the conventional wisdom about welfare and Cadillacs notwithstanding. In 1966, of the 3.1 million people who received public assistance, only 304,000 (less than 10%) were in families (cases) receiving more than $2,000 during the entire year; only 834,000 (a quarter of the total) received more than $1,000. This little-known fact about the *magnitude* of the average welfare payment obtains in even the wealthiest urban areas. In New York, for example, the average weekly welfare allowance in 1967 for a family of four was only $63.22 (during the same year, manufacturing workers in the city averaged $106.60 per week). Even the poorest-paying industry in the city — rubber and miscellaneous plastics (SIC 30) — paid an average wage of $87.20, almost $25 a week above the welfare "rate."

Workers' willingness to accept jobs paying less than (say) $1.30–1.60 per hour appears to depend upon the availability of supplemental forms of income — such as welfare. If workers refused to take such low-paying jobs, many firms would — according to Barry Bluestone — face bankruptcy, and many "labor-intensive" goods and services would — in Herbert Gans' view — go unproduced. It is in this sense that the welfare system may be said to constitute a public subsidy for low-wage "secondary" employers.

The third peripheral segment in our model of urban labor markets might be called the "training sector." The Johnson Administration is "on record" as having recognized that "a man may enroll in one of the training programs which pay stipends, in order to get funds to tide him over a lean period." And *New York Times* writer John Herbers concludes that:

> a good many of the manpower training programs are tending to become more of a holding action to keep people out of the unemployed columns than a means of putting them permanently into the work force. There are reports of men going out of one training program into another.[6]

In fact, at least one official program (STEP) is designed explicitly for the purpose of providing "further training" for those program graduates unable to find work.

The training programs of the federal government have thus taken on the basic attributes of the peripheral stratum of the economy: low "wages" and low stability. Cumulative figures from 1968 through January, 1970 (i.e. prior to the recession) show that, of 84,703 actual contract hires in the National Alliance of Businessmen's Job Opportunities in the Business Sector program, 50,225 quit or were laid off. The high implicit quit rate is not surprising; jobs in the NAB-JOBS program paid low wages, the core employers participating in the program often segregated their "hard-core" workers from the "mainstream" force, and layoffs were highly probable. In fact, one steel firm reported to an investigating Congressional committee that, since layoffs are "an inherent part of the American economy," it used part of the Manpower Administration subsidies "in coun-

[4] U.S. Department of Labor, *1968 Manpower Report of the President* (Washington, D.C.: U.S. Government Printing Office, 1968), p. 96.

[5] Thomas Vietorisz and Bennett Harrison, *The Economic Development of Harlem* (New York: Praeger Publishers, 1970), Chapter 1.

[6] Quoted in Bennett Harrison, "National Manpower Policy and Public Service Employment," *New Generation,* Winter 1971, p. 4.

seling for anticipated layoffs. Many of the trainees at this firm since have been laid off."

Of the several components of the relatively new Public Service Careers Program, only the New Careerists receive a training stipend, which averaged $2,819 per trainee in 1968. The Department of Labor recently reported that 40% of the New Careerists leave the program within the first six months of training. Again we see the combination of low earnings and high turnover which are the identifying characteristics of the peripheral economy.

Sar Levitan and Robert Taggart, III, describe the government's principal program for young dropouts, the Neighborhood Youth Corps:

> Almost all are entry level positions requiring few skills. Men are usually assigned to maintenance and custodial work, while women typically work in clerical or health positions. Most (jobs) pay near the minimum wage ($1.60/hour), with extra stipends for household heads with dependents. . . . Stripped of their titles, almost all the jobs were menial and unattractive. . . . A comprehensive follow-up of enrollees leaving the program between January and September 1966 found that 40 weeks after termination, less than two-fifths were employed (and) more than a fourth were not in the labor force. . . .[7]

Similar descriptions can be found in the literature on the Work Incentive Program, the Job Corps, and other government training programs.

There is a fourth source of income available to urban (and especially to ghetto) dwellers, the existence of which further confounds the conventional neo-classical analysis of labor supply (according to which potential workers trade off hours of homogeneous "work" against hours of homogeneous "leisure" against the datum of an average hourly wage rate). Louis Ferman has named the sector in which this income is "earned" the "irregular economy":

> A man may have his own type of "hustle" — an easy way to earn money, sometimes legitimate, sometimes partly not, that puts him in a quasi-entrepreneurial role.[8]

While all irregular activity is not illegal, it is the latter type of "work" which is undoubtedly the most

controversial — and the most lucrative (although the high risk associated with narcotics distribution, grand theft and other serious criminal activities probably induces the same kind of discontinuous work patterns found elsewhere in the periphery of the economy, with the result that annual income is still relatively low for all but a very few professional criminals).

Stanley Friedlander's interviews in Harlem have led him to conclude that perhaps two-fifths of all adults in that ghetto had some illegal income in 1966, and that 20% appeared to exist entirely on money derived from illegal sources (it is, for obvious reasons, not possible to quantify this illegal income). Friedlander also found that the unemployment rates in 16 cities in 1966 correlated negatively with the crime rates in these cities, suggesting that, "the larger the sources of illegal income, the fewer the people in the slums who persist in looking for legitimate jobs (or the greater the numbers who report themselves as employed when they are not, in order to explain their style of life to the enumerators)." This makes it clear why conventional labor-leisure constructs cannot serve as useful models of the real time-allocation decision process in the inner city.

Intersectoral Mobility

An elaborate mythology has developed in America according to which generations of immigrants were allegedly able to lift themselves out of poverty through education, training, and the development of public job placement institutions. It is therefore important to examine the extent to which upward mobility from the periphery to the core of the economy is facilitated (or hindered) by the school and job placement systems to which peripheral workers and their children have access.

I have already reviewed or referred to the research (including my own) which indicates that the public education system does not (by itself, at any rate) promote the kind of intersectoral mobility for the peripheral worker which he or she has been led to expect.

Similarly, public job placement systems — some of them developed explicitly for the purpose of "helping the poor" in the periphery of the economy — have been unable to make significant contributions to intersectoral mobility. Earl Main has studied the institutional training programs financed under the Manpower Development and Training Act. He con-

---

[7] Sar A. Levitan and Robert Taggart, III, *Employment of Black Youth in Urban Ghettos* (New York: Twentieth Century Fund, 1971), p. 101.

[8] *1968 Manpower Report,* p. 94.

cludes that the placement function has succeeded in helping the disadvantaged to find new jobs, but not in increasing their wage incomes. Doeringer's study of the poverty program in Boston came to a similar conclusion.

A recent study of manpower training programs in four cities showed that "graduates" averaged only $3,000 per year in post-training wages. The Olympus Corporation researchers who conducted the study attributed much of this outcome to the Federal "requirement that training be offered only in occupations where there is a 'reasonable expectation of employment.' To meet this requirement while keeping per capita training costs low, MDTA administrators have chosen to train for jobs where openings occur because of high turnover, whether or not they are characterized by high demand." [9] Together, these results imply that government placement programs simply *recirculate* the poor among a class of employers who tend to pay low wages. In other words, public programs designed to promote mobility in fact serve as a recruiting instrument for employers in the secondary labor market!

This interpretation is argued most forcefully by Stephan Michelson, who addresses himself to the U.S. Training and Employment Service, the government's principal placement institution.

> With local budgets often being a function of placements, local offices are discouraged from sending Negroes for jobs from which they will be automatically excluded. Thus, U.S. [T.] E.S. tacitly aids the job discrimination which, with a different administrative procedure, it could confront.[10]

Recently, the Urban Coalition published a penetrating evaluation of USTES, which supports the hypotheses presented above about the *de facto* role of government job placement programs.

The Employment Service today is an inflexible bureaucracy, absorbed in its own paper work, with a staff that is either incapable of or disinterested in committing the resources necessary to make the chronically unemployed self-supporting. The inability of the ES to provide meaningful assistance results in more individuals dropping out of the labor force, thereby contributing to the very problems the manpower programs were designed to solve. In 1970, despite a growing national work force and increased unemployment, only 11.5% of the work force sought out the service of the ES' 2200 local offices. Those who actually received job placements as a result of ES assistance represented 5.3% of the work force.

The jobs listed with the Service have decreased over the past five years and, for the most part, represent only the lowest levels of the economy. Almost half are considered unfillable by ES administrators because of low salaries, excessive job requirements or untenable working conditions. For their part, employers view the ES as the placement agency of last resort. Major employers, including state and local governments, conduct their own recruiting or rely on public advertising.[11]

More explicitly,

> The chief weakness of the ES with regard to minorities is that it mirrors the attitudes of employers in the community. The ES could provide a model of vigilance and aggressiveness toward affirmative action for equal employment opportunity. Instead, it is frequently a passive accessory to discriminatory employment practices; it is widely viewed in that light by the minority community.[12]

Findings such as these lead to the conclusion that the Employment Service does indeed serve essentially as a placement service for the secondary labor market.

[9] "Manpower Programs in Four Cities," *Manpower*, January 1972, p. 12.

[10] Stephan Michelson, *Incomes of Racial Minorities* (Washington, D.C.: The Brookings Institution, 1968, unpublished manuscript), pp. 8–23.

[11] Lawyers' Committee for Civil Rights Under Law and the National Urban Coalition, *Falling Down on the Job: The United States Employment Service and the Disadvantaged* (Washington, D.C.: The National Urban Coalition, April 1971), p. 111.

[12] *Ibid.*, p. 60.

A THEORY OF LABOR MARKET SEGMENTATION

Michael Reich, David M. Gordon, and Richard C. Edwards

Most orthodox economists see divisions in the labor market as falling from the sky, as having been inherited from some mystical historical sources. In this selection, the authors argue that fundamental divisions in the labor market, including the split between the primary and the secondary labor market, arose from within the economy, that political and economic forces within American capitalism have given rise to and perpetuated segmented labor markets.

The authors teach economics at the University of California at Berkeley, the New School for Social Research, and the University of Massachusetts at Amherst respectively.

A growing body of empirical research has documented persistent divisions among American workers: divisions by race, sex, educational credentials, industry grouping, and so forth (F. B. Weisskoff, B. Bluestone, S. Bowles and H. Gintis, D. Gordon, 1971 and 1972, B. Harrison, M. Reich, H. Wachtel and C. Betsey, and H. Zellner). These groups seem to operate in different *labor markets*, with different working conditions, different promotional opportunities, different wages, and different market institutions.

These continuing labor market divisions pose anomalies for neoclassical economists. Orthodox theory assumes that profit-maximizing employers evaluate workers in terms of their *individual* characteristics and predicts that labor market differences among groups will decline over time because of competitive mechanisms (K. Arrow). But by most measures, the labor market differences among groups have not been disappearing (R. Edwards, M. Reich, and T. Weisskopf, chs. 5, 7, 8). The continuing importance of *groups* in the labor market thus is neither explained nor predicted by orthodox theory.

Source: American Economic Review, LXIII, 2, May 1973. Reprinted with permission of the authors and the American Economic Association.

This research was supported by a grant from the Manpower Administration, U.S. Department of Labor. Needless to say, we alone are responsible for the views expressed in this paper.

Why is the labor force in general still so fragmented? Why are group characteristics repeatedly so important in the labor market? In this paper, we summarize an emerging radical theory of labor market segmentation; we develop the full arguments in Gordon, Edwards, and Reich. The theory argues that political and economic forces within American capitalism have given rise to and perpetuated segmented labor markets, and that it is incorrect to view the sources of segmented markets as exogenous to the economic system.

Present Labor Market Segmentation

We define labor market segmentation as the historical process whereby political-economic forces encourage the division of the labor market into separate submarkets, or segments, distinguished by different labor market characteristics and behavioral rules. Segmented labor markets are thus the outcome of a segmentation process. Segments may cut horizontally across the occupational hierarchy as well as vertically. We suggest that present labor market conditions can most usefully be understood as the outcome of four segmentation processes.

■ Segmentation into Primary and Secondary Markets

The primary and secondary segments, to use the terminology of dual labor market theory, are differentiated mainly by stability characteristics. Primary jobs require and develop stable working habits; skills are often acquired on the job; wages are relatively high; and job ladders exist. Secondary jobs do not require and often discourage stable working habits; wages are low; turnover is high; and job ladders are few. Secondary jobs are mainly (though not exclusively) filled by minority workers, women, and youth.

■ Segmentation Within the Primary Sector

Within the primary sector we see a segmentation between what we call "subordinate" and "independent" primary jobs. Subordinate primary jobs are routinized and encourage personality characteristics of dependability, discipline, responsiveness to rules and authority, and acceptance of a firm's goals. Both factory and office jobs are present in this segment. In contrast, independent primary jobs encourage and require creative, problem-solving, self-initiating characteristics and often have professional standards for work. Voluntary turnover is high and individual motivation and achievement are highly rewarded.

▪ Segmentation by Race

While minority workers are present in secondary, subordinate primary and independent primary segments they often face distinct segments within those submarkets. Certain jobs are "race-typed," segregated by prejudice and by labor market institutions. Geographic separation plays an important role in maintaining divisions between race segments.

▪ Segmentation by Sex

Certain jobs have generally been restricted to men; others to women. Wages in the female segment are usually lower than in comparable male jobs; female jobs often require and encourage a "serving mentality" — an orientation toward providing services to other people and particularly to men. These characteristics are encouraged by family and schooling institutions.

The Historical Origins of Labor Market Segmentation

The present divisions of the labor market are best understood from an historical analysis of their origins. We argue that segmentation arose during the transition from competitive to monopoly capitalism. Our historical analysis focuses on the era of monopoly capitalism, from roughly 1890 to the present, with special emphasis on the earlier transitional years.

During the preceding period of competitive capitalism, labor market developments pointed toward the progressive *homogenization* of the labor force, not toward segmentation. The factory system eliminated many skilled craft occupations, creating large pools of semiskilled jobs (N. Ware). Production for a mass market and increased mechanization forged standardized work requirements. Large establishments drew greater numbers of workers into common working environments.

The increasingly homogeneous and proletarian character of the work force generated tensions which were manifest in the tremendous upsurge in labor conflict that accompanied the emergence of monopoly capitalism: in railroads dating back to 1877, in steel before 1901 and again in 1919, in coal mining during and after the First World War, in textile mills throughout this period, and in countless other plants and industries around the country. The success of the Industrial Workers of the World (*IWW*), the emergence of a strong Socialist party, the general (as opposed to industry-specific) strikes in Seattle and New Orleans, the mass labor revolts in 1919 and 1920, and the increasingly national character of the labor movement throughout this period indicated a widespread and growing opposition to capitalist hegemony in general. More and more, strikes begun "simply" over wage issues often escalated to much more general issues (J. Brecher, J. Commons).

At the same time that the work force was becoming more homogeneous, those oligopolistic corporations that still dominate the economy today began to emerge and to consolidate their power. The captains of the new monopoly capitalist era, now released from short-run competitive pressures and in search of long-run stability, turned to the capture of strategic *control* over product and factor markets. Their new concerns were the creation and exploitation of monopolistic control, rather than the allocational calculus of short-run profit-maximization. (For examples see A. Chandler, B. Emmet and J. Jeuck, R. Hidy and M. Hidy, and A. Nevins.)

The new needs of monopoly capitalism for control were threatened by the consequences of homogenization and proletarianization of the work force. Evidence abounds that large corporations were painfully aware of the potentially revolutionary character of these movements. As Commons notes, the employers' "mass offensive" on unions between 1903 and 1908 was more of an ideological crusade than a matter of specific demands. The simultaneous formation of the National Civic Federation (*NCF*), a group dominated by large "progressive" capitalists, was another explicit manifestation of the fundamental crises facing the capitalist class (J. Weinstein). The historical analysis which follows suggests that to meet this threat employers actively and consciously fostered labor market segmentation in order to "divide and conquer" the labor force. Moreover, the efforts of monopolistic corporations to gain greater control of their product markets led to a dichotomization of the industrial structure which had the indirect and unintended, though not undesired, effect of reinforcing their conscious strategies. Thus labor market segmentation arose both from conscious strategies and systemic forces.[1]

■ Conscious Efforts

Monopoly capitalist corporations devised deliberate strategies to resolve the contradictions between the increased proletarianization of the work force and the growth and consolidation of concentrated corporate power. The central thrust of the new strategies was to break down the increasingly unified worker interests that grew out of the proletarianization of work and the concentration of workers in urban areas. As exhibited in several aspects of these large firms' operations, this effort aimed to divide the labor force into various segments so that the actual experiences of workers were different and the basis of their common opposition to capitalists undermined.[2]

The first element in the new strategy involved the internal relations of the firm. The tremendous growth in the size of monopoly capitalist work forces, along with the demise of craft-governed production, necessitated a change in the authority relations upon which control in the firm rested (R. Edwards). Efforts toward change in this area included Taylorism and Scientific Management, the establishment of personnel departments, experimentation with different organizational structures, the use of industrial psychologists, "human relations experts" and others to devise appropriate "motivating" incentives, and so forth (L. Baritz, A. Chandler, S. Marglin and F. Miller and M. Coghill). From this effort emerged the intensification of hierarchical control, particularly the "bureaucratic form" of modern corporations. In the steel industry, for example,

a whole new system of stratified jobs was introduced shortly after the formation of U.S. Steel (K. Stone). The effect of bureaucratization was to establish a rigidly graded hierarchy of jobs and power by which "top-down" authority could be exercised.

The restructuring of the internal relations of the firm furthered labor market segmentation through the creation of segmented "internal labor markets." Job ladders were created, with definite "entry-level" jobs and patterns of promotion. White-collar workers entered the firm's work force and were promoted within it in different ways from the blue-collar production force. Workers not having the qualifications for particular entry-level jobs were excluded from access to that entire job ladder. In response, unions often sought to gain freedom from the arbitrary discretionary power of supervisors by demanding a seniority criterion for promotion. In such cases, the union essentially took over the management of the internal labor markets: they agreed to allocate workers and discipline recalcitrants, helping legitimize the internal market in return for a degree of control over its operation (P. Doeringer and M. Piore).

One such effort at internal control eventually resulted in segmentation by industry. Firms had initially attempted to raise the cost to workers of leaving individual companies (but not the cost of entering) by restricting certain benefits to continued employment in that company. Part of this strategy was "welfare capitalism" which emerged from the NCF in particular, and achieved most pronounced form in the advanced industries. At Ford, for example, education for the workers' children, credit, and other benefits were dependent on the workers' continued employment by the firm and therefore tied the worker more securely to the firm. For these workers, the loss of one's job meant a complete disruption in all aspects of the family's life. Likewise, seniority benefits were lost when workers switched companies (Weinstein). As industrial unions gained power, they transformed some of these firm-specific benefits to industry-wide privileges. The net effect was an intensification not only of internal segmentation, but also of segmentation by industry, which, as we discuss in the next section, had other origins as well.

At the same time that firms were segmenting their internal labor markets, similar efforts were under way with respect to the firm's external relations. Employers quite consciously exploited race, ethnic, and sex antagonisms in order to undercut

---

[1] We have paid more attention in this brief summary to employers' conscious efforts because the other papers presented in this session provide a complementary emphasis on systemic forces. We fully develop both explanations in Gordon, Edwards, and Reich.

[2] These efforts were "conscious" in the following sense. Capitalists faced immediate problems and events and devised strategies to meet them. Successful strategies survived and were copied. These efforts were not "conscious" in the sense that those who undertook them understood fully the historical forces acting upon them or all the ramifications of their policies. As we argue in the text, in certain cases capitalists acted out of a broader class consciousness.

unionism and break strikes. In numerous instances during the consolidation of monopoly capitalism, employers manipulated the mechanisms of labor supply in order to import blacks as strikebreakers, and racial hostility was stirred up to deflect class conflicts into race conflicts. For example, during the steel strike of 1919, one of the critical points in U.S. history, some 30,000 to 40,000 blacks were imported as strikebreakers in a matter of a few weeks. Employers also often transformed jobs into "female jobs" in order to render those jobs less susceptible to unionization (Brecher, D. Brody, Commons).

Employers also consciously manipulated ethnic antagonisms to achieve segmentation. Employers often hired groups from rival nationalities in the same plant or in different plants. During labor unrest the companies sent spies and rumor mongers to each camp, stirring up fears, hatred, and antagonisms of other groups. The strategy was most successful when many immigrant groups had little command of English (Brecher, Brody).

The manipulation of ethnic differences was, however, subject to two grave limitations as a tool in the strategy of "divide and conquer." First, increasing English literacy among immigrants allowed them to communicate more directly with each other; second, mass immigration ended in 1924. Corporations then looked to other segmentations of more lasting significance.

Employers also tried to weaken the union movement by favoring the conservative "business-oriented" craft unions against the newer "social-oriented" industrial unions. An ideology of corporate liberalism toward labor was articulated around the turn of the century in the NCF. Corporate liberalism recognized the potential gains of legitimizing some unions but not others; the NCF worked jointly with the craft-dominated American Federation of Labor to undermine the more militant industrial unions, the Socialist party, and the IWW (Weinstein).

As the period progressed, employers also turned to a relatively new divisive means, the use of educational "credentials." For the first time, educational credentials were used to *regularize* skill requirements for jobs. Employers played an active role in molding educational institutions to serve these channeling functions. The new requirements helped maintain the somewhat artificial distinctions between factory workers and those in routinized office jobs and helped generate some strong divisions within the office between semiskilled white-collar workers and their more highly skilled office mates (Bowles, Bowles and Gintis, Cohen and Lazerson and Edwards).

Systemic Forces

The rise of giant corporations and the emergence of a monopolistic core in the economy sharply accentuated some systemic market forces that stimulated and reinforced segmentation. As different firms and industries grew at different rates, a dichotomization of industrial structure developed (R. Averitt, T. Vietorisz and B. Harrison, and J. O'Connor). The larger, more capital-intensive firms were generally sheltered by barriers to entry, enjoyed technological, market power, and financial economies of scale and generated higher rates of profit and growth than their smaller, labor-intensive competitive counterparts. However, it did not turn out that the monopolistic core firms were wholly to swallow up the competitive periphery firms.

Given their large capital investments, the large monopolistic corporations required stable market demand and stable planning horizons in order to insure that their investments would not go unutilized (J. K. Galbraith). Where demand was cyclical, seasonal, or otherwise unstable, production within the monopolistic environment became increasingly unsuitable. More and more, production of certain products was subcontracted or "exported" to small, more competitive and less capital-intensive firms on the industrial periphery.

Along with the dualism in the industrial structure, there developed a corresponding dualism of working environments, wages, and mobility patterns. Monopoly corporations, with more stable production and sales, developed job structures and internal relations reflecting that stability. For example, the bureaucratization of work rewarded and elicited stable work habits in employees. In peripheral firms, where product demand was unstable, jobs and workers tended to be marked also by instability. The result was the dichotomization of the urban labor market into "primary" and "secondary" sectors, as the dual labor market theory has proposed (Gordon, 1972, Piore).

In addition, certain systemic forces intensified segmentation within corporations in the primary sector. As Piore has argued, the evolution of technology within primary work places tended to promote distinctions between jobs requiring general and specific skills. As new technologies emerged which replicated these differential skill requirements, employers found that they could most easily train for particular jobs those workers who had already developed those different kinds of skills. As highly tehnical jobs evolved in which the application of generalized, problem-solving techniques were required, for instance, employers found that they could get the most out of those who had already developed those traits. Initial differences in productive capacities were inevitably reinforced.

The Social Functions of Labor Market Segmentation

As the preceding historical analysis has argued, labor market segmentation is intimately related to the dynamics of monopoly capitalism. Understanding its origins, we are now in a position to assess its social importance.

Labor market segmentation arose and is perpetuated because it is *functional* — that is, it facilitates the operation of capitalist institutions. Segmentation is functional primarily because it helps reproduce capitalist hegemony. First, as the historical analysis makes quite clear, segmentation divides workers and forestalls potential movements uniting all workers against employers. (For an interesting analysis, see C. Kerr and A. Siegel). Second, segmentation establishes "fire trails" across vertical job ladders and, to the extent that workers perceive separate segments with different criteria for access, workers limit their own aspirations for mobility. Less pressure is then placed on other social institutions — the schools and the family, for example — that reproduce the class structure. Third, division of workers into segments legitimizes inequalities in authority and control between superiors and subordinates. For example, institutional sexism and racism reinforce the industrial authority of white male foremen.

■ *Political Implications*

One of the principal barriers to united anticapitalist opposition among workers has been the evolution and persistence of labor market segmentation. This segmentation underlies the current state of variegation in class consciousness among different groups of workers. A better understanding of the endogenous sources of uneven levels of consciousness helps to explain the difficulties involved in overcoming divisions among workers. Nonetheless, if we more clearly understand the sources of our divisions, we may be able to see more clearly how to overcome them.

REFERENCES

K. Arrow, "Some Models of Racial Discrimination in the Labor Force," in A. Pascal, ed., *The American Economy in Black and White,* Santa Monica 1971.

R. Averitt, *The Dual Economy,* New York 1967.

L. Baritz, *Servants of Power,* Middletown, Conn. 1964.

B. Bluestone, "Institutional and Industrial Determinants of Wage Differentials," mimeo, Boston College 1971.

S. Bowles, "Understanding Unequal Economic Opportunity," *Amer. Econ. Rev., Proc.,* May 1973.

———— and H. Gintis, "IQ in the U.S. Social Structure," *Social Policy,* Jan.–Feb. 1973.

J. Brecher, *Strike!,* San Francisco 1972.

D. Brody, *Steelworkers: The Non-Union Era,* New York 1965.

A. Chandler, *Strategy and Structure,* New York 1966.

D. Cohen and M. Lazerson, "Education and the Industrial Order," *Socialist Revolution,* Mar.–Apr. 1972.

J. Commons, *History of Labor in the United States,* New York 1935.

P. Doeringer and M. Piore, *Internal Labor Markets and Manpower Analysis,* Lexington, Mass. 1972.

R. Edwards, "Alienation and Inequality: Capitalist Relations of Production in Bureaucratic Enterprises," unpublished Ph.D. dissertation, Harvard Univ. 1972.

————, M. Reich, and T. Weisskopf, *The Capitalist System,* Englewood Cliffs 1977.

R. Edwards, M. Reich, and D. Gordon, eds. *Labor Market Segmentation,* Lexington, Mass. 1975.

B. Emmet and J. Jeuck, *Catalogues and Counters,* Chicago 1950.

J. K. Galbraith, *The New Industrial State,* Boston 1967.

D. Gordon, "Class, Productivity, and the Ghetto: A Study of Labor Market Stratification," unpublished Ph.D. dissertation, Harvard Univ. 1971.

————, *Theories of Poverty and Underemployment,* Lexington, Mass. 1972.

D. Gordon, R. C. Edwards, and M. Reich, "Labor Market Segmentation in American Capitalism," forthcoming, 1977 or 1978.

B. Harrison, *Education, Training and the Urban Ghetto*, Baltimore 1972.

R. Hidy and M. Hidy, *Pioneering in Big Business 1882–1911*, New York 1955.

C. Kerr and A. Siegel, "The Interindustry Propensity to Strike," in A. Flanders, ed., *Collective Bargaining*, Baltimore 1969.

S. Marglin, "What Do Bosses Do?", *Review of Radical Pol. Econom.* Summer 1974.

F. Miller and M. Coghill, *The Historical Sources of Personnel Work*, Ithaca 1961.

A. Nevins, *Ford: The Times, The Man, The Company*, New York 1954.

J. O'Connor, *Fiscal Crisis of the State*, New York 1973.

M. Piore, "Notes for Theory of Labor Market Stratification," in Edwards *et al.*, eds., *Labor Market Segmentation.*

M. Reich, "The Economics of Racism," in D. Gordon, ed., *Problems in Political Economy*, Lexington, Mass. 1977.

K. Stone, "Labor Management and the Origin of Job Structures in the Steel Industry," in Edwards *et al.*, eds., *Labor Market Segmentation.*

T. Vietorisz and B. Harrison, "Labor Market Segmentation: Positive Feedback and Divergent Development," *Amer. Econ. Rev., Proc.*, May 1973.

H. Wachtel and C. Betsey, "Low Wage Workers and the Dual Labor Market," *Rev. Econ., Stat.*, 1974.

N. Ware, *The Industrial Worker, 1840–1860*, Chicago 1964.

J. Weinstein, *The Corporate Ideal in the Liberal State*, Boston 1967.

F. B. Weisskoff, "Women's Place in the Labor Market," *Amer. Econ. Rev., Proc.*, May 1972, 62, 161–166.

H. Zellner, "Discrimination Against Women, Occupational Segregation, and the Relative Wage," *Amer. Econ. Rev., Proc.*, May 1972.

THE USES AND LIMITS OF MANPOWER POLICY

Lloyd Ulman

Manpower Policy was the favored instrument for the liberal attack on underemployment. Its admitted failures during the 1960s have led to criticism and reevaluation of the potential for manpower policy among its proponents. In this selection, a leading labor economist and a liberal advocate of manpower policy responds to the critics and seeks to outline a more modest set of purposes and expectations for the continued application of manpower tools.

The selection comes from a longer article (with the same title) that appeared in a collection of essays, published by *The Public Interest,* evaluating Great Society programs.

Lloyd Ulman teaches economics at the University of California at Berkeley, directs its Institute for Industrial Relations, and has written many books and articles on manpower problems.

The Sympathetic Critics

Although the war on poverty broadened, redirected, and complicated the administration of manpower policy, it left intact, and indeed strengthened, its emphasis on unemployment and the unemployed . . . But in neither its modified nor its pre-war on poverty form has the policy escaped criticism. And the criticism has emanated from sympathetic as well as skeptical quarters.

The sympathetic critics themselves are in two camps, one housing those who believe in a grand policy aimed primarily at the macroeconomic targets

Source: Reprinted with permission of Lloyd Ulman from *The Public Interest*, No. 34, Winter 1974. Copyright © 1974 by National Affairs Inc.

originally specified by the Swedes, and the other characterized by the belief that the policy should be directed and restricted to such high-unemployment groups as non-white minorities, women, young people in their late teens, and the aged unemployed. Both groups agree on the desirability of improving administration and efficiency through some "decategorization" and "decentralization" — i.e., reducing the number and halting the proliferation of specifically legislated and separately administered programs, and granting local authorities more discretion in determining the mix of the manpower programs in their respective communities. Both groups call for at least a partial return to "creaming," or selecting the more promising or better qualified applicants for training. This practice was largely abandoned during the war on poverty in favor of concentrating on the most disadvantaged individuals in the disadvantaged groups. But the latter practice tended to produce more trainee dropouts and, even in cases where the training was completed, to result in the displacement in dead-end jobs of the unskilled people who did not go through the public manpower programs by those who did.

However, the trade-off-oriented critics want the policy directed to job bottlenecks as well as to disadvantaged people; they would extend "creaming" to cover admission of employed people as well as the unemployed, so that, as the more advantaged trainees move up the ladder to the unoccupied rungs, their places at the bottom could be filled by more marginal workers. By the same token, they would have the policy devote more resources to subsidizing private employers to provide training for their own skill requirements. On the other hand, less ambitious critics — including observers with greater familiarity with the actual operation of the American programs — feel that subsidy funds have already supported training that would have been provided by employers in the absence of such support.

Finally, the big-policy buffs believe that the American policy is carried out on too small a scale to be effective, and that substantial enlargement would yield significant results. They are undeterred by the record of growth — with training enrollments rising from 34,000 in 1963 to 1.4 million in 1971, as federal obligations climbed from $56 million to $1.5 billion for training, and from under $300 million in 1961 to $4.8 billion in 1972 on the whole array of programs. They would place this in

perspective by pointing out that the tax cut of 1964 released some $14 billion, or noting that manpower programs cost only about a third of one per cent of GNP in the United States compared to 1.5 per cent in Sweden. The more cautious critics point out that the Manpower Development and Training Program's efforts in the past to train for skill shortages have not been very successful. Moreover, they fear that a magnification of such efforts under a large-scale, demand-oriented policy would more likely than not result in the planners' nightmare, i.e., the attempt to forecast trends and changes in occupational demand.

The Skeptics

To the skeptics, the growth of manpower policy means simply that an ugly duckling has been turning into an ugly duck. Their skepticism about even the potential effectiveness of manpower policy derives primarily from their views of the nature of post-War unemployment and poverty, although not all who share these views in fact reject all labor market policies. Their analyses lead them to reject the structuralist diagnosis, at least to the extent to which active labor market policy is indicated as a prescription. On the other hand, these analyses differ among themselves in various important respects, so that different skeptics find different reasons for their skepticism. We might distinguish at the outset two main sources of skepticism. The first is the view that much of the unemployment at which manpower policies are aimed has been voluntary and socially useful in nature. The second is the view that such unemployment is socially undesirable and is caused by various barriers to mobility, but that the barriers in question will not yield to the application of manpower policy.

The argument that much contemporary unemployment is voluntary, and that it might be socially useful, is related to the inability of the manpower administrators in the early 1960's to find long-time unemployed married men in large numbers. Instead, unemployment was found to be concentrated increasingly among women, the young, and the non-white, and to be predominantly characterized by short duration and high (and for some groups, increasing) incidence, including high quit rates. (Indeed, the high levels of unemployment that have prevailed in the United States, relative to other industrialized countries such as the United Kingdom and Sweden, have been traced to relatively high quit and layoff rates, which have helped to make the trade-off between inflation and unemployment more adverse on this side of the Atlantic.) There are two main reasons for holding that such unemployment is voluntary in nature and that it does not constitute as serious a social problem as unemployment of middle-aged family men. In the first place, it is pointed out that married women and teenagers may become unemployed more readily than married men because they have more useful alternatives to paid work, either at home or in educational institutions. As the representation of such secondary groups in the labor force increases, the proportion of total unemployment motivated by such relatively productive alternatives likewise rises.

In the second place, it is maintained that, as individual and family incomes and assets increase, individuals find it profitable to spend more and more time in job search activity, taking more time between jobs (or before accepting a first job) and possibly quitting one's job more readily in order to get a better one. Training programs are inappropriate solutions under such conditions. Lack of skill is not the problem, for there really is no problem at all. In fact, to the extent that such programs lure employed or voluntarily unemployed people out of the labor force into the programs (either as trainees or as instructors), they might even be a counterproductive source of inflationary bottlenecks. But it will be recalled that a case might be made for improving the quality of information about the labor markets; this would reduce the costs of search to employers and employees and hence would presumably lower the duration of both unemployment and job vacancies. Actually, efforts are being made to improve the Employment Service by establishing "job banks" and by planning for their conversion into a computerized system of job-matching. But such efforts also could be counterproductive, since they could induce workers to quit their jobs and look around more frequently. What is gained on the swings (lower duration) is lost on the roundabout (higher incidence).

The second body of skeptical opinion emanates from an analysis that posits the same characteristics of unemployment as the first: short duration and rapid turnover. It differs from the first, however, in maintaining that such unemployment is essentially structural rather than frictional in nature, resulting not from the purposeful pursuit of superior opportunity but rather from frustration and apathy induced by the existence of barriers to opportunity.

But manpower policies are rejected as a corrective device since, it is maintained, the barriers are not caused by lack of education or information. One cause of immobility is discrimination based on color and sex, which has the effect of reducing the economic value of education to those discriminated against. Thus individuals with identical educational attainment can earn significantly different incomes. Lower rates of return on education in turn might well discourage investment in education by individuals in the groups concerned, who thus might indeed suffer from an educational deficiency. But compensatory training could not improve the situation substantially as long as discrimination remains to depress the return on training.

Discrimination, however, is not always regarded as a sufficiently powerful influence to create important or lasting barriers to mobility and opportunity all by itself. According to the neo-classical economists, the least bigoted employers in the dominant groups would be willing to hire discriminated-against labor at lower rates of pay, and thus enjoy and exploit a competitive advantage over their more bigoted rivals and drive them out of business. Hence discrimination is usually regarded as working in concert with other barriers to mobility. The latter, according to the "dual labor market" theory, have the effect of dividing the work force into two groups, one employed in sheltered markets — characterized by systems of internal training and promotion, great job security, and high wages — and the other crowded into "secondary" markets with low-wage, dead-end, short-term jobs. Since the number of entry-level jobs in the preferred sector is small relative to the supply of potential applicants from the secondary sector, employers might resort to racial or sex discrimination as a cheap means of screening some applicants out (just as they might use educational credentials as a cheap way of screening others in).

The theory is rather vague in its attempt to specify factors which make for "primary" internal markets in some industries and not in others, but technological considerations are supposed to play an important role. In this sense, this market segmentation approach is in the tradition of the early structuralists. But the newest structuralists part company with the oldest in at least one important respect. They regard unemployment as a quit-and-layoff phenomenon in secondary markets rather than as a displacement phenomenon; to them the main problem is not lack of job openings but low wages and dead-end jobs which induce frequent quitting as a symptom of poor morale. Training would not yield a satisfactory answer to a problem characterized by lack of motivation. Instead they have emphasized affirmative action measures to compel "primary" employers to abandon screening by color or sex; and they have advocated the negative income tax or similar transfer policies that would have the effect of supplementing the depressed incomes earned in the secondary sectors. On the other hand, advocacy of income redistribution in this context might be regarded as in the tradition of the Triple Revolutionaries who first insisted that income be divorced from work.

The Question of Efficiency

In the light of the administrative misadventures of manpower policy and of the strong *a priori* criticism reviewed above, one might have been led to predict a dismal performance on the part of the manpower programs. It certainly is true that the developments which inspired the policy persisted long after the policy's introduction and expansion had occurred. Manpower policies did not reverse the rise in unemployment among women and youth, nor did they prevent the nation's inflation-unemployment dilemma from deepening. Big-policy advocates, as we have noted, would object that active labor market measures have not been deployed on a sufficiently large scale to affect large-scale economic developments. However, in Sweden, where the policy has been developed on a scale that is quite large by United States standards, it has not been able to prevent adverse movements in the Swedish Phillips Curve.

In an attempt to determine whether some of the programs actually introduced in this country have been effective and hold promise for the future, numerous benefit-cost studies have been made. With benefits measured as some type of post-training differential in incomes, most of the studies of MDTA programs indicated very high rates of return. There is some indication that on-the-job-training programs, which cost less than institutional training, have yielded higher rates of return than the latter. It was also found that training exerted a greater impact on the most disadvantaged individuals — those with the lowest levels of education or of pre-training earnings or with the worst records of unemployment. For

the Neighborhood Youth Corps programs, which offered more subsidy than training, results were rather mixed and did not unequivocally indicate a record of overall effectiveness either in increasing the earnings of enrollees or in reducing high-school dropout rates. Studies of the effectiveness of the Job Corps (an expensive residential training and rehabilitation program for underprivileged school dropouts with bad work experience) yielded mixed results. A rather rough study of JOBS (or Job Opportunities in the Business Sector, under which training programs were carried on by private employers, with or without subsidy) indicated large apparent increases in earnings between 1966 and 1968. The Work Incentive Program, designed to provide training and placement in public employment to welfare recipients, was misnamed, because the welfare system's eligibility requirements have constituted a notorious disincentive for recipients to strive for gainful employment. Predictably, its record of completions and placements was very poor.

Critics of labor market policy have included critics of the research on policy effectiveness. Since some of them are proponents of human capital analysis, which relies heavily on empirical benefit-cost research, it might appear that they were gently hoist with their own petard. They claim, however, that these studies did not yield accurate assessments of benefits. Perhaps the criticism most strongly advanced is that most of the studies were characterized by the absence of adequate reference or "control" groups (or of any at all). This is an important consideration; however, the difficulty in obtaining a control group which is the identical twin of the target group in every relevant respect save that of completion of the program in question is so great as to raise a serious question of operationality. Even among people alike in respect to education, age, sex, and color, there are motivational and other differences between those who sought admission to the program and those who did not, between those admitted and those who were not, between those who completed the course and those who dropped out. Another criticism of most studies is that they assumed that the income differentials observed a short time after completion of the course (the benefits involved) would persist over a 10-year period. In at least some instances, however, it is more reasonable to believe that the magnitude of such benefits would dwindle over time, since the higher earnings of the trainees reflect more aggressive placement efforts on their behalf as well as the acquisition of skills. A third line of criticism is that some programs train and place people in high-turnover, unskilled occupations, raising the possibility that the trainees might merely be displacing previous job applicants. Related to this is the observation that, even where earnings were significantly raised by the programs, they remained below poverty levels, so that manpower training cannot be regarded as a substitute for direct income redistribution. Finally, some of the studies were made when the administrators were still "creaming" the pool of applicants for the most able and qualified individuals; moreover, the instructors themselves might have been the cream of their own crop. Hence attempts to expand the programs could run into diminishing returns.

Proponents of manpower policy have also criticized the evaluations. They object to inclusion of support payments to trainees, which are transfer payments, among costs properly chargeable to manpower programs. This implies agreement with the assertion that manpower development cannot be regarded as a substitute for direct income supplementation. However, the proponents of course believe that manpower development is worthy in its own right. This view is implicit in another caveat — that it might be desirable to retain a program which yields significant benefits in the form of increased earning power even if its costs, which are borne by the public, exceed those benefits which accrue to the disadvantaged groups. By the same reasoning, they would reject the position that direct income transfers are preferable to manpower development programs because the cost of the latter is greater; they would hold that such cost differentials are overwhelmed by the extra social benefit derived from improving the employability of people. Also, as a counterpoint to the diminishing returns argument, it might be maintained that costs in the early period covered by the studies reflected the administrative growing pains referred to above, and that costly duplication and overlapping could be reduced as the manpower programs develop in the future.

A Place for Manpower Policy

Although favorable (as well as unfavorable) results yielded by benefit-cost studies must be interpreted with great caution, they might also justify reexamination of the analyses which imply that all manpower policies would be largely ineffective. In fact,

some interesting current research challenges the hypothesis that much of the unemployment, especially around cyclical peaks and among disadvantaged groups at such times, is either voluntary or frictional in nature. While awaiting publication and evaluation of this new work, we might give some thought to an old finding. In 1955, when unemployment averaged 4.4 per cent, 55.5 per cent of those who changed jobs (or 4.6 out of 8.2 million people) experienced no unemployment at all. (Another survey of the labor force, in 1961, revealed that 60 per cent of the people who made only one job change that year had experienced no unemployment, that 80 per cent of those who changed jobs once in order to improve their status did so without incurring unemployment, and that among male job changers 40 per cent of those without unemployment landed a higher-paying job, as compared with only 26 per cent of those who experienced some unemployment between jobs. In 1961, however, the unemployment rate average was 6.7 per cent.) This casts some doubt on the assumption that job search is carried on most efficiently when the individual is not working and hence on the conclusion that unemployment is mainly voluntary. If unemployment is indeed involuntary, it does not follow that diversion of unemployed (and underemployed) individuals from the labor force into training programs would generate inflationary pressure on wages.

Nor does it follow that training programs need be ineffective in situations where barriers to mobility are thrown up by discrimination or even by a shortage of good jobs. Recourse to educational credentials as a cheap screening device (provided at public expense) by high-wage employers in protected labor markets suggests that at least some of the qualified applicants may be educated beyond purely economic requirements. If so, even relatively short compensatory training courses might bring those with educational deficiencies up to entry levels. Moreover, the social pressure on employers to hire duly certified graduates of public training programs could constitute a salutary dose of compensatory credentialing. Certainly, the criticism that benefit-cost studies are likely to overstate the payoff to training per se, because they do not take into account the effectiveness of aggressive placement efforts, is wide of the mark.

It is true, of course, that merely lengthening a queue of qualified job seekers does not increase the number of jobs which they are qualified to hold.

However, the number of good jobs annually available is greater than suggested by the dual market theory. The latter suggests, as a stereotype, two compartmentalized sectors; in the high-wage internal labor markets, all are protected by non-academic tenure, and turnover is negligible; in the unprotected, low-wage sector, quits and firings are the order of the day. In fact, all the theory really requires is that turnover in the good-job sector be significantly lower than in the bad-job sector; and in this respect it can claim anticipatory confirmation in long-standing findings that high-wage industries tend to have lower quit rates than low-wage industries (even after allowance for differences in skill levels).

However, the *absolute* levels of separations — including layoffs, discharges, and retirements, as well as quits — are quite high even in industries whose relative quit rates are low, and whose wages are relatively high. Thus in 1967 petroleum and coal products ranked first among 29 industrial categories in average hourly earnings, and last in separations of production workers, but the latter still averaged 2.2 per cent a month. This means that in a year of high employment (unemployment was 3.8 per cent in 1967) this industry had to hire about 125 persons to keep an average of 100 on the job. Figuring this way, the eight highest-paying industries in 1967 (the lowest wage was six per cent above the average for all manufacturing) turned over about three million production employees (out of a combined work force of about six million). Of course, if the ranks of qualified and credentialed job applicants were swelled by an expanded manpower development system, quit rates could be expected to fall. And if the overall unemployment rate were allowed to rise, fewer vacancies would be created on a replacement basis.

Nevertheless, the order of magnitude suggests that some potentialities for upward mobility exist, even within protected sectors. Some elbow room exists for labor market policies. It would permit the latter to contribute to a reduction in the spread of unemployment between the disadvantaged groups and the rest, and to a reduction in the concentration of employment of the disadvantaged in the secondary sectors, although the major problems in lowering the barriers to mobility would remain.

Although spreading the misery more evenly would serve the cause of distributive equity, that cause could better be served if there was happiness to spread around instead of misery. This could occur if the major barriers to mobility are greatly reduced *and* if, as they are being reduced, the total number of good jobs grows rapidly enough to absorb the unemployed and the underemployed. Experience has taught that the economy has tended to produce such a happy outcome when operating close to capacity or approaching that neighborhood. At such times, the maintenance of high and rising levels of demand acts like a giant suction pump as the relatively great growth in employment in the high-wage sectors forces wages up more rapidly elsewhere and results in a reduction of unemployment, both recorded and "hidden," which is especially great in the high-unemployment groups. Thus more jobs are created in the protected sectors, while more jobs elsewhere have their wages raised.

The trouble with this story, however, is that it does not end at this point. The process is invariably accompanied by inflation, which tends to perpetuate itself, and even accelerate, as unions in the protected sectors seek to make up ground lost while their employers have been raising prices to lift profit margins from pre-expansion levels. To counter these inflationary pressures, demand is then deflated, the suction is turned off, and wage and unemployment differentials widen again. This is the unhappy sequel which manpower policy was originally designed to prevent; and if it could reduce inflationary tendencies at high levels of employment, it could also indirectly reduce barriers to economic opportunity and equality — including barriers which might not have originated in lack of skill or information at all.

Moderate Expectations

Few believe that manpower policy could satisfactorily perform either of these tasks unaided, even if it were scaled up to Swedish proportions. It is highly doubtful whether it alone could increase mobility and otherwise improve the trade-off sufficiently to induce employers to resist cost push, and to prevent them from "administering" price increases when they are still operating well below capacity. It is highly doubtful whether it alone could level barriers to mobility sufficiently to effect a satisfactory redistribution of employment, unemployment, and income, or to significantly reduce poverty levels. That is why most observers, proponents of the policy as well as critics, now agree that manpower policy cannot be regarded as an alternative to direct wage and price restraint, to efficient enforcement of anti-discrimination legislation, and to direct income transfers to the poor. The proponents would agree that these other policies would be necessary as a complement to manpower policy.

But they might also maintain that manpower policy complements the other policies, too. It could increase the efficiency of wage-price restraint (which certainly could use all the help it can get) by removing inflationary bottlenecks, which often fuel union demands for more widespread wage increases in order to maintain or restore traditional relationships. It could help anti-discrimination policy by compensating for deficiencies in worker training and education that might have resulted from past discrimination. However, with respect to anti-discrimination policy, and even more with respect to direct income redistribution, political complementarity is of greater importance than technical complementarity. The day may come when the egalitarian spirit of the American public might drive it to embrace policies that would divorce income from work as a general principle. But as the Presidential election of 1972 made plain, that day is not at hand. (Nor is the era of consumer satiety, on which the divorce was originally predicated, about to dawn.) The so-called work ethic still dominates, and it is held strongly not only by the white tax-paying middle classes but by the underprivileged and the poor themselves, who want intensely to enhance their sense of worth along with their incomes. Policies designed to help the individual achieve these two objectives range from counseling-training-placement through public employment to wage subsidies or supplements. The exact mix will vary in response to changing needs and the relative efficiency of the different approaches. But some programs to improve and equalize work opportunity must be offered, if only as a condition for the provision of separate income supplementation for those among the poor for whom income must truly be divorced from work.

If the existence of a battery of manpower development policies is essential to the development of more thoroughgoing and effective policies of income supplementation, the latter are also conducive to the efficiency of the former. In the first place, a more effective division of labor between the two types of policy would be feasible, so that the training and information programs could concentrate more exclusively on their more narrowly defined functions. In the second place, the training programs, even if concentrated on the groups with the greatest problems of unemployment and deprivation, would be able to select the more promising individuals in those groups for training or placement. This would minimize the "displacement" problem. Such "creaming" of the more trainable individuals, in turn, would permit training — even when conducted in educational institutions — to be geared more closely to ladder-job openings, whether in the private sector or in public service.

Manpower policies with these attributes could avoid much of the administrative inefficiency which has been experienced to date, including the wasteful overlapping and duplication of activities. "Decategorization" and decentralization through revenue sharing have been officially proposed as a means to the same ends. A concluding note of caution, however, should be clearly sounded. Revenue sharing is unavoidably susceptible to the diversion of federally-generated resources away from activities designed to increase the economic potential of the disadvantaged, and in the direction of more well-to-do groups with superior economic and political power in the local community — whether through public works, lower taxes, or negotiated wage increases. From the viewpoint of manpower policy, revenue sharing is not an efficient instrument. Efforts to promote local autonomy and flexibility cannot dispense with federal guidance and direction to the degree required to secure an acceptable level of efficiency in policies designated to further the agreed-upon objectives of manpower policy. For it is at levels of government farther removed from local grass roots that such worthy interests of economically weak minorities can be more decently and efficiently promoted.

PUTTING-ON THE POVERTY PROGRAM

David Wellman

Wellman's classic description of a program for "disadvantaged" youth illustrates the futility of one of the principal liberal policies intended to solve ghetto employment problems. Programs cannot simply "motivate" young ghetto workers to accept and stay with jobs unless the basic structure of employment opportunities available to them is changed. As the chapter introduction also argued, their perceptions of the job market described in this selection are much too accurate for them to change those attitudes until the job market itself changes. The selection has been excerpted from a longer piece of the same title, which first appeared in an underground magazine at the University of California at Berkeley called *Steps*. The article was later reprinted by the Radical Education Project, and a different version of the same piece once appeared in *Trans-action* magazine.

Trained as a sociologist, Wellman has written widely on the problems of cities and the poor.

"I guess these kids just don't want jobs. They're unwilling to try and help themselves. The clothes they wear are loud; they won't talk decent English; they're boisterous; and they constantly fool around. They refuse to take this program seriously."

"But isn't there a job shortage in Oakland?" I asked. "Does it really matter how they act?"

"There's plenty of jobs. They're just not interested."

It was the summer of 1966. The man with whom I was speaking was a counsellor for the Youth Opportunities Center in West Oakland. At the time, he was working on a federally sponsored program known as TIDE. I was observing the program for some graduate research that I was conducting. The purpose of TIDE was to help lower class youth become employable on the job market. The program ran for four weeks. I observed two four-week sessions. Youth from the ages of 16 to 22 were selected by local poverty program workers in the Bay Area. To make the program attractive for unemployed

Source: David Wellman, "Putting-On the Poverty Program," originally from *Steps,* reprinted with permission from Radical Education Project.

ghetto youth, the government paid participants five dollars a day. Two groups were involved: twenty-five young men and twenty-five young women. These groups met separately, only coming together periodically on common projects. I worked exclusively with the male group.

The young men who participated in the program had a distinctive style. They were "cool." Their hair was characteristically "processed" in one form or another. All sported a kind of sun glasses which they called "pimp's glasses." (These are very lightly tinted glasses, with small frames, which look like "granny glasses.") Their clothes, while usually inexpensive, were "loud" and ingeniously altered to express style and individuality. They spoke in a "hip" vernacular. Their vocabulary was small, yet very expressive. These young men are part of a "cool world" in the ghetto. They represent a distinctively black, working-class culture.

To most liberals these men are "culturally deprived" or "social drop-outs." Most of them had flunked out of or been kicked out of school. Few had any intention of getting a high school degree. They had long and serious arrest and prison records. They seemed uninterested in "making it" in terms of majority social values and norms. They were skeptical, critical, and hostile toward both the TIDE program [and] white society in general.

The TIDE workers were liberals: sincere, well-meaning people. Those things which, for the young men, defined their own special culture were, for the TIDE workers, symptoms of cultural deprivation. They assumed that if the young men would only act a little less "cool" and learn to smooth over some of their unfortunate encounters with white authorities, they too could become full-fledged working members of society and find their place in the sun. The men were told that the aim of the program was to help them get jobs. TIDE would not train them for jobs. Instead it would train them to *apply* for jobs. They were going to learn how to take tests, how to make a good impression during a job interview, how to speak well, and how to fill out an application form properly. To accomplish these things, they would play games like dominoes to ease the pain associated with numbers and arithmetic; they would conduct mock interviews, take mock tests, meet with management representatives, and go on tours of places where employment was a good possibility for them. They were told to consider the TIDE program as a "job." That is, they were to be at the YOC office on time, dressed as if they were at a job, and be docked if they were late or made trouble. If they took the program seriously and did well, they were told, they stood a pretty good chance of getting a job at the end of four weeks. The unexpressed aim of TIDE then, was to prepare Negro youth for white society. Public government would serve as an employment agency for white, private enterprise.

It was obvious from the outset that the program was aimed at changing the youth by making them more acceptable to employers. Their grammar and pronunciation were constantly corrected. They were subtly told that their appearance would have to be altered for them to get a job. "Don't you think you could shine your shoes?" "Haven't you got trousers that are pressed better?" "It's not a good idea to wear tee-shirts and jeans to a job interview." Promptness, a virtue few of them possessed, was lauded. The penalty for tardiness was being put on a "clean-up committee" or being docked.

For the liberal white TIDE workers the program became a four-week exercise in futility. They seemed to feel that they weren't asking very much of the men. All they really asked was that they learn to make a good impression on white society. This "simply" entailed dressing a little better, increasing one's vocabulary, learning the art of taking tests, and broadly speaking, accepting the "rules of the game." This was "all" they demanded. And yet the men were uncooperative. They fooled around, often refused to take the program seriously, and insisted upon having a "good time." The only conclusion TIDE workers could arrive at was "they just don't want jobs."

What belies this proposition is the seriousness with which most of the men took *actual and distinct job possibilities.* For example, when told there was a job at such-and-such a factory and that a particular test was required, the men studied hard and earnestly applied for the job. The TIDE program *itself*, however, seemed to be viewed as only distantly related to getting a job. The men wanted jobs, but indicated that they felt their inability to take tests and fill out forms was not the problem. They talked about the shortage of jobs available to people without skills. They would pump the YOC people daily about job openings. Their desire for work was obviously not the problem.

Yet, one could hardly deny that the young men fooled around and refused to meet the program on its own terms. If ambition was not the problem, how then do we understand the fact that the men rarely took TIDE seriously?

To one way of thinking, TIDE really didn't demand much of the men. It simply asked that they change certain outward appearances. From the perspective of the men, however, the program seemed to demand a great deal. It asked that they change their manner of speech and dress. It asked that they ignore their lack of skills and society's lack of jobs. It asked that they act as if their arrest records were of consequence in obtaining a job. It asked, most importantly, that they pretend *they,* and not society, bore the responsibility for unemployment. TIDE didn't demand much of the men: only that they become white.

What took place during the four-week program, then, was a daily struggle between white, middle-class ideals of conduct and behavior, and the mores and folkways of the black community. The men were handling TIDE in the same manner that the black community has *always* treated white invasions and threats to its self-respect. They were using subtle forms of subversion and deception.

Confronted by a hostile society and lacking the social tools necessary for material well-being, members of the Negro community have devised ingenious mechanisms for coping with this hostility and simultaneously maintaining their self-respect and human dignity. Historians and sociologists alike have pointed to subtle forms of slave subversion, the content and ritual of Negro spirituals, and recently to the meaning of the Blues as means by which the black man in America has struggled to preserve his integrity as a human being. Many of these devices have persisted until today. They are currently to be found within the structure and culture of the black community. Some of the devices are new. They reflect new forms of struggle with current problems.

"Putting someone on" ("putting the 'hype' on someone," or "running a 'game' on a cat") seems to be an important device used by Negroes to maintain their personal integrity. "Putting someone on" is used as much in relations with black people as it is in relations with members of the white community. In both instances it allows one to maintain personal integrity in the face of a hostile or threatening situation. To "put someone on" is to publicly lead him to believe that one is "going along with" what he has to offer or say, while at the same time privately rejecting the offer, and subtly subverting it. "Putting someone on" may or may not be malicious, but this is not a defining characteristic. "Putting someone on" fails if the other person catches on: he is no longer "put-on." This allows the individual who is "putting someone on" to take pride in the feeling that he has "put something over on" the other person, often at his expense. It thereby allows each party to feel that it has been "successful." "Putting someone on" is to be contrasted with "putting someone down." This is an active and public process involving both defiance and confrontation.

TIDE was evidently interpreted by the men as a threat to their self-respect, as being defeating, useless, and humiliating. They responded to it in much the same way as they would to people inside and outside the ghetto who seemed to threaten their concept of dignity. Sometimes TIDE was "put on." Sometimes it was "put down." It was only taken seriously when it met the needs of the men. And then, only on *their* terms — without a loss of human dignity.

Putting-on the YOC

There was almost no open defiance or hostility toward those in charge of TIDE. It seemed as if the men were going along with the program. Two things, however, first led me to believe that if the men "accepted" the program, they did so only on their *own* terms.

They all appeared to have a "tuning out" mechanism. They just didn't "hear" certain things. For example, one young man was a constant joker and spoke incessantly. It mattered little to him whether or not someone else was speaking or if the group was supposed to be working on something. When he was told to "knock it off" (which was always) he simply never "heard" the command. On the other hand, when he was involved with the program and interested, he could hear just fine and responded to speakers quite adequately. "Tuning out" was, moreover, often a collective phenomenon. For instance,

there was a radio in the room where the men worked. They would play it during lunch and coffee breaks. When the instructor would enter and tell them that work was to begin, they all seemed to be on a wave length frequency that differed from their instructor's. He would tell them that time was up, but they would continue listening and dancing to the music as if there were no one else in the room. However, without so much as acknowledging the instructor and without a word to each other or to him, when *they* were finished listening the radio went off and the session began.

This "tuning out" mechanism was frequently in operation. Conversations began and ended without any response to instructors. Men would embark on "projects" of their own during a class: looking out the window and talking to people on the street; fighting with each other; or reading comic books. During each of these "projects" they seemed "deaf" to the teacher. It is important to note that this "deafness" was *systematic*. When they were interested or wanted to participate in the program, the men were no longer "deaf." They "tuned out" and "turned on" when *they* saw fit and at no other time. In this respect, there was little authority or control that instructors could exert over the young men: authority was undercut by deafness. The men were "going along with" the program — in a way. They weren't challenging it. But they were undermining its purpose: putting it on.

The second technique which I found the men using as a means of selectively accepting the program was "playing stupid." When they wanted to they could be incredibly "stupid." A major part of the program, for instance, was devoted to teaching them how to fill out employment applications properly. They were given lengthy lectures on the importance of neatness and lettering on these forms. They were expected to fill out such forms at least two or three times a week. After having filled them out a number of times, some of the men suddenly didn't know their mother's name, the school they last attended or their telephone numbers.

This "forgetfulness" or "stupidity" was sometimes duplicated during mock job interviews, which were conducted almost daily. Five or more of the men would serve as "employers" and interview their fellow trainees for an imaginary job. The "interviewers" usually took their job seriously. But after it became apparent that the interview was a game, many of the interviewees developed into hopelessly incapable job applicants. They didn't have social security numbers, they could not remember their last job, they didn't know what school they had gone to, and they didn't know if they really wanted the "job." To the absolute frustration of the interviewers and instructors alike, the "prospective workers" simply behaved like incompetents. Interestingly enough, when the instructor told them one morning that this time the interview was "for real" and that those who did well would actually be sent out on a job interview with a "real" firm, the "stupid" and "incompetent" transformed literally overnight into model job applicants.

The responses to learning how to take tests for jobs and how to pass a driver's test were similar to the responses to mock interviews and filling out practice applications. The YOC used many of the tests that various government agencies gave to prospective workers. These included preference tests, intelligence tests, and aptitude tests. The men were required to take these tests almost daily. Some of the tests were boring and easy to catch on to. For example, the examiner would read off a number and those being tested would have to circle that number on an answer sheet. The first few times they took these tests most of the men worked hard to master them. After they had gotten the knack of it, however, and found themselves still without jobs and taking the same tests, their response changed radically. Some of them no longer "knew" how to do the test. Others found it necessary to "cheat" by looking over someone else's shoulder. Still others flunked tests they had passed the day before. Yet when they were informed of job possibilities that existed at the Naval Ship Yard or with the Post Office, they insisted on giving and taking the test themselves. In one instance, some of them read up on which tests were relevant for a particular job and then practiced that test for several hours by themselves. Their "stupidity" was a put-on. It was a way of ridiculing the tests and subverting the ritual of humiliating "practice" without openly challenging the program or its workers.

These two mechanisms for dealing with the TIDE program were used differently and at different times by many TIDE participants. Some men "tuned out" and "played stupid" more consistently than others. These men were usually less interested than others in being acceptable to white society. Overall, however, there was little variation in behavior. "Stupidity" occurred when jobs were unavailable.

"Tuning out" and "playing stupid" were only two of the many ways in which the TIDE program was regularly "put-on." TIDE was supposed to be viewed as a "job" by those participating in it. As anyone who has been employed recently knows, any good job includes as part of the normal routine a number of legitimate "breaks" for coffee, lunch, and so on. The young men "employed" by TIDE were rather well acquainted with this ritual, and were very insistent that it be included as part of their job too. Since they were given a voice in deciding the content of the program, "breaks" were made a must for their daily routine. And no matter what the activity, or who was addressing them, "breaks" were religiously adhered to by the men. The program started at 9:30 a.m. They decided their first break would be for coffee at 10:30. This break was to last until 11:00. And while "work" was absolutely not allowed to proceed a minute past 10:30, it was usually 11:15 or so before they actually got back to business, just before their lunch break. Lunch began exactly at 12:00. Theoretically, work resumed at 1:00. This usually meant 1:15, since they had to listen to "one more" song on the radio before work could begin. The next break did not come until 2:30 p.m. The afternoon break was to last until 3:00. However, since they were finished at 3:30, and because it took another 10 minutes to get them back to work, the men could often talk their way out of the remaining business scheduled between 3:00 and 3:30. Considering they were being paid five dollars a day for five hours of work, they didn't have a bad "hustle." Of the five hours considered as "work," almost half were regularly devoted to "breaks."

"Games" were another important part of the TIDE program subverted by the "put-on." Early in the program the instructor told the men he thought it might be helpful for them to master math and language by playing games — dominoes, scrabble, and various card games. The men considered this a fine idea. But what their instructor had intended for a pastime during the breaks, involving at most an hour a day, the men rapidly turned into a major part of their instruction. They set aside 45 minutes in the morning and 45 minutes in the afternoon for games. But since they participated in these games during their breaks as well, "games" soon became a stumbling block to getting sessions back in order after "breaks." The instructor would say: "Okay, let's get back to work." To which the men would sometimes reply: "But we're already working on our math —

we're playing dominoes and you said that would help us with our math." While usually said in half-seriousness, it was a difficult concept for the instructor to answer and overcome. According to *his* definition, they *were* working on their "math." With his authority undercut in this way, he had no alternative but to allow them to continue for a few minutes more. When he again called for order, the men would demand to be allowed to "finish" their game. Since finishing a game was a vaguely defined notion at best, they would usually get their way. More and more time, then, was whittled away from the substantive aspects of the program.

It finally got to a point where the instructor decided that "games" would only be a formal part of the program on certain days. The idea of using games to master certain useful techniques had been used by the men to undercut and subvert the overall program and the instructor knew it—though could *not* admit it. He therefore had to curtail the abuse. The games "put-on" had been found out, and so had failed. The men could no longer use games as a "put-on." But games were trimmed from the program only at the expense of constant struggle between the men and their instructor. Games became a constant and unresolved issue. On the days when games were not formally part of the program, the men would continue to play them during breaks. In this way, games would usually extend into the formal sessions anyway. And on days when they *were* part of the program, games encroached upon the rest of the session as before.

To familiarize the men with the kinds of jobs potentially available to them when they had finished the TIDE program, their instructors took them on excursions to various work situations. The instructor presented them with different opportunities for such trips, and they were to decide which they would take. The criteria the men used for choosing trips are significant. They were most interested in excursions involving an entire day. It hardly seemed to matter what *sort* of company they visited, so long as it took all day. They would only agree to half-day trips if there were no other alternative, or if there were some possibility that the company would give away "free samples." So, for example, even though it was pointed out to them that the Coca-Cola Company was not hiring, they wanted to go there. They knew they could get free cokes. They also wanted to go to many candy and cookie factories for much the same reason. In contrast, they turned down a

trip to a local steel mill which they knew was hiring. The fact that it was hiring had become irrelevant for them. TIDE was not designed to get them an interview. Its purpose was to show them what sorts of jobs might be available. Given the circumstances, they reasoned, why not see what was enjoyable as well as available.

It was obvious that the men used trips like these to get away from the dull, daily routine in the YOC office. The trip to a steel mill, though previously rejected in favor of more enjoyable possibilities, was soon considered a good idea after all when the other alternatives fell through. If they didn't go to the steel mill, they would have to work in the office.

Their behavior on the trips themselves provides still another indication of the way the men used these excursions for their own ends. They were not very interested in the company conducting the tour. They seemed more interested in the bus ride out there, the possibility of a free lunch, or just fooling around. This apparently "frivolous" interest might seem a product of the kind of tours they chose: tours of bottling plants, of Fort Ord, and of cookie factories. Interestingly enough, however, their behavior altered only slightly when they visited more promising job possibilities, such as the Alameda Naval Air Station, the Oakland Naval Supply Station, and various container factories.

The trip to the Naval Air Station, for example, was an all-day trip. But the men spent most of their time putting "the make" on a cute young WAVE who was their guide for the day. She had a very difficult time keeping her "cool." They were quite adept at the game of provoking her, and played it the entire day.

To some extent, this behavior can be accounted for by the fact that the tour did not focus on potential job situations. Instead, it focused on the "interesting sights" of the base. Nevertheless, when they toured possible job situations, such as the warehouses and loading docks, their behavior scarcely changed. They were much more interested in visiting the air control tower, the aircraft carriers, and the mess hall than they were in seeing what work they might eventually do. Apparently the tour was viewed as an outing, or a "good time," and not as a job seeking situation. TIDE had told them it would not get jobs for them. It would show them how to apply for jobs. Since they were not there to apply for a job, they wanted at least to enjoy themselves. When the tour got boring or they got tired, they even refused to see the sights. They insisted on sleeping in the buses or listening to their transistor radios on the lawn. One thing the tour did produce, however, was a great deal of discussion about the war in Vietnam. Almost none of the men were interested in serving in the armed forces. Some of them would yell at passing sailors through the bus windows: "Vietnam, Baby!" or "Have a good time in Vietnam, man!"

The trip to the Oakland Naval Supply Station was similarly received. It was less interesting, however, and there was no pretty young lady guide to take them through the base. Although there were more potential jobs at this location, again the spirit of an outing prevailed.

The men cleverly manipulated this tour to meet their own needs and interests. While they were being shown the assembly line that packaged material, where they might possibly work, they drifted instead into the more interesting control room (replete with computers and television cameras) where they hardly had the qualifications to work. When they were taken on a tour of the warehouses, where again they might possibly work, they fell to the sides and spoke with friends who were already working there. The relationship between touring a possible work situation and actually being offered a job there was far too oblique to be of interest. They transformed the experience, therefore, into one which more adequately satisfied their interests and enthusiasms.

It might seem that what I have described so far indicates that these men "went along with" the program, but were in fact reluctant to get a job. I would, on the contrary, regard their behavior as a "putting-on" of the YOC. Each of the above examples shows the men accepting the program, *on their own terms,* and inverting it to meet their own needs, *while at the same time* leading those in charge to think that the explicit aims of the program were being carried out. In this respect, each example is a classic "put-on." And when the men were not "putting-on" the YOC, they were "putting-down" the people and assumptions associated with it.

Putting-down the YOC

"Putting something down" is almost the reverse of "putting someone on." It is a more active and public process. It involves, among other things, confrontation and defiance. When someone is "put-down" he knows it. The success of a "put-down" depends on

his knowing it, whereas a "put-on" is only successful when its victim is unaware of what is happening. There were many aspects of the TIDE program which were actively "put-down" by the young men involved.

Among the most glaring "put-downs" were those aimed at the kinds of jobs for which the men were learning to apply. These jobs usually involved unskilled labor: post office work, warehouse and longshore jobs, truck driving, and assembly-line work. Some work was also to be had in the service industry, while some was outright menial labor: chauffers, janitors, bus boys, and so on. The reaction of most of the men to this limited prospect was best expressed by a question asked of the instructor by one young man:

"How about some tests for IBM?" he inquired with a straight face.

The room was in an uproar. They thought that was a great question. Many of them were hysterical with laughter. They seemed to feel they had really put this cat down hard. His response was typically bureaucratic, yet very disarming.

"Say, that's a good suggestion. Why don't you put it in the suggestion box?"

They didn't seem able to cope with that retort and so things got somewhat back to normal.

However, when employers came to the TIDE sessions to show the men how an interview should be conducted, they were treated in similar fashion. These employers usually represented companies which hired men for unskilled labor. They came to illustrate good interview technique. They did *not* come to interview men for real jobs. Their visits were sort of helpful-hints-for-successful-interviews sessions. One of the more socially mobile men was usually chosen to play the role of job applicant. The entire interview situation was played through. Some employers even went so far as to have the "applicant" go outside and knock on the door to begin the interview. The men thought this was both odd and funny, commenting to the employer:

"Man, you've already seen the cat. How come you making him walk out and *then* walk back in?"

The employer responded with a look of incredulity: "But that's how you get a job. You have to sell yourself from the moment you walk in that door."

The men seemed unimpressed and continued to crack jokes among themselves about the scene. The interview continued. The employer would put on a real act, beginning the interview with all the usual small talk he'd normally use to draw people out and put them at ease.

"I see from your application that you played football in high school."

"Yeah."

"Did you like it?"

"Yeah."

"Football really makes men and teaches you teamwork."

At about this point the men would get impatient.

"Man, the cat's here to get a job, not talk about football!"

"When are you going to tell him about the job?"

A wise-cracker chimed in: "Maybe he's interviewing him for a job with the Oakland Raiders."

The point of all this was usually well taken by the employer, and he would begin to ask questions more germane to the particular job. He would ask about the "applicant's" job experience, his draft status, school record, interests, skills and so on. The young man being interviewed usually took the questions seriously and answered frankly. But after awhile, the rest of the group would tire of playing this game and begin to ask (unrecognized, from the floor) about the specifics of a "real" job.

"Say man, how much does this job pay?"

"What kind of experience do you need?"

"What if you got a record?"

"How many days off do you get?"

The employer would politely remind them that this wasn't a "real" interview. But this would only satisfy the young men for a short while, and they would soon resume their questions. It didn't take long to rattle the interviewer completely. Sometimes the instructor would intervene and tell the men that the gentleman was there to help them, and would request that they treat him more gently. Again, this would stifle revolt for only a short while. Then, in a mood of outright defiance, they might begin playing dominoes while the interview went on. If this didn't evoke an irritated response, they might begin to play the game rather enthusiastically by loudly slapping down the dominoes each time they scored a point. In one instance, several of the men began slapping the tables rhythmically with dominoes, during the interview. That got the response they were looking for.

"Look!" said the employer, who had completely lost control of the situation. "If you're not interested in learning how to sell yourself why don't you just leave the room so that others who are interested can benefit from this?"

"Oh no!" was the response of the ringleaders, "We work here. If you don't dig us, then *you* leave!"

It wasn't too much later that he did.

Sometimes during these interviews the very nature of the work being considered was "put down." During an "interview" for a truck driving job, some of the men began to ask the employer about salesman jobs. Others asked him about executive staff positions. They weren't very interested in talking about a job driving a truck. They continually interrupted the interview with "irrelevant" questions about the role of an executive. They wanted to know how much executives were paid and what they did to get their jobs. At one point the employer himself was asked point-blank how much he was paid, what his experience was, and what he did. To some extent they had turned the tables and were enjoying the opportunity to interview the interviewer. He finally told them, in fact:

"I'm here to *do* the interviewing, not to *be* interviewed."

In spite of this they managed to return to interviewing him. And when they weren't doing that, they were asking him about the qualifications necessary for other, more skilled jobs. In most such situations it became quite clear that they were not interested in the kinds of jobs most employers had to offer—not interested enough, that is, to participate seriously in a mock interview for an imaginary job.

The young TIDE participants were remarkably unimpressed, moreover, by the status of an employer. Regardless of his rank, the men treated their visitors as they would their peers. Sometimes visiting employers were treated more harshly and with genuine, open defiance. On one tour of a factory the men were escorted by the vice-president in charge of hiring. To some people this might have been considered an honor, and the man would have been treated with an extra ounce of deference. To the TIDE participants, however, he was just another guide. And after informing the men of the large number of unskilled positions available, he was asked about hiring some of them, on the spot. He responded by saying that this was just a tour and that he was in no position to hire anyone immediately. Some of the men were noticeably irritated at this answer. One looked at him and said:

"Then you're just wasting our time, aren't you?"

Although shaken, the executive persisted, telling the men about technical operations at the plant. Throughout his talk he referred to his audience as "boys."

"Now, when you boys come to apply for a job you will need proof of a high school education."

"If you boys want to work here you will need to join the union."

This constant reference to "boys" was obviously bothering the men. Each time the word would crop up, they squirmed in their seats, snickered, or whispered angrily to each other. The vice-president seemed unaware of the hostility he aroused. But finally, one of the bolder men spoke up firmly.

"We are young mens!, not boys."

The speaker blushed nervously and apologized. He made a brave attempt to avoid repeating the phrase. Habit, however, was victorious and the word slipped in again and again. Each time he said "you boys" he was corrected, aloud, and with increasing hostility. For a while it seemed as though the young men were more interested in catching him saying "you boys" than in anything else he said. . . .

Throughout the entire TIDE program the young men had been "putting-down" people and projects. The men used the context of a government training program as a protective device which enabled them to "put down" institutions and individuals otherwise impervious to attack. TIDE provided insulation for them. And it offered an opportunity for meeting with people otherwise unavailable to them. In addition, the men rapidly developed a high degree of group consciousness upon which they could fall back for protection and inspiration. Armed in this manner, they then went out to "get" or "put down" normally inaccessible institutions. When consulted about whom they wanted to come and speak to them (which the men seemed to interpret as "come be put down by them"), they called for the police, a city councilman, state assemblymen, businessmen, and officials of the poverty program. Almost all these people were "put down" in one way or another when they appeared at the YOC. The TIDE people were anxious to have these visitors. TIDE workers thought it was a good idea for the young men to meet with community leaders and officials, in order to show them that these leaders were interested in their problems and would help if the men would show a little initiative. The men "showed initiative" by inviting important people to speak with them: to be "put down"

by them. They "put on" the YOC in order to "put down" this array of visitors. The "put-downs," then, were also a "put-on" of the YOC. By using the program as a cover for airing their grievances, the men were, in effect, altering TIDE to meet their needs.

As the program was conceived by the government, TIDE did not meet the needs of the young men. Indeed, it wasn't meant to. The Great Society was trying to run a game on black youth. It wanted them to cease being what they were. It wanted to lead them into white middle-class America. It tried to trick them by leading them to believe that America was interested in getting them jobs.

But there aren't many jobs in America for young men who have arrest records, who lack skills, and who are black. There aren't jobs for black youth who refuse to accept white America's definition of self-respect and integrity. The young men knew that. TIDE knew it too. The very jobs over which TIDE had some control (that is, government jobs) are rarely filled by people with the backgrounds of ghetto youth. But TIDE didn't train the youth to work. It attempted to train them to pretend that there was no problem.

The men saw through it. They diagnosed it as a sham. They rejected its invitation into white America.

When a "put-on" is detected, it fails.

TIDE was more than a "put-on" of black youth. It was also an attempt to persuade the youth to "put on" potential employers. By training men to speak well, dress well, fill out application forms properly, and to take tests easily, TIDE evidently sought to "fool" employers into hiring these young men. But this was never made explicit to the men. Why, then, didn't TIDE workers just come right out and say it: "Look men. What we're suggesting is that you put on your employers; make them believe you're someone you're not."

The suggestion is absurd. The reasons for its absurdity are revealing.

It wouldn't work. This "new" approach would really not be new. It would only assert more openly that black culture is not acceptable to white society. It would still be asking the men to pretend they were someone else. It would still imply that there is something wrong with who they are. Finally, it would assume that there is work for those who want it. The young men knew there wasn't.

It could never happen. To suggest that the young men had to "put on" employers in order to win jobs implies that the employers have some responsibility for unemployment and racial exclusion. But the TIDE program, indeed much of the Great Society, assumes that the door to happiness — to America — is open if people will seek to enter on middle-class terms. "Teaching" the TIDE participants to "put on" the interviewer runs counter to the assumptions which are held dear by the poverty program and the nation. It would be impossible for government representatives even to entertain such a step.

Our hypothetical proposition would also threaten the morale of the TIDE workers. I'm sure that most of them were well-intentioned, good, liberal people. They are also human beings. And as human beings they must strive for personal integrity in their work situation. Their job is not an enviable one. Facing fantastic barriers, they must try to get work for people. Their success is limited. But for them to recognize that society bears most of the responsibility for inequality would be to render their work worthless. To ask them to admit that their work is a "put-on" is to threaten their concept of self-worth. The institutional framework of the TIDE worker, like that of most welfare workers, therefore calls

forth an orientation which holds the client, and not society, responsible for his situation.

The TIDE worker, then, would never consider asking the men to "put on" employers. Faced with defeat and frustration, as they were, they responded predictably: "they just don't want jobs." Ironically enough, the institutional requirements of northern liberalism have called forth a response very similar to the familiar line of southern racism. Wasn't it the "old fashioned" southern bigot who used to say: "Negroes don't have jobs because they are lazy and shiftless"? There is a difference to be sure. The southerner felt that black people are inherently shiftless and lazy. Thus, they are destined to be without jobs of consequence. Most modern liberals seem to view black people as temporarily hindered by psychological and cultural impediments. Inequities in the employment and opportunity structure of America, they seem to suggest, are minor in comparison with the deficiencies of black people themselves. What black people need, according to the liberals, is cultural enrichment and the ability to "sell themselves" to white society. In the end, northern liberals and southern racists agree: the problem is mainly with Negroes.

TAKING PUBLIC EMPLOYMENT SERIOUSLY

Barry Bluestone and Bennett Harrison

As the 1960s gave way to the 1970s, more and more liberals began turning from a policy emphasis on training programs to a policy emphasis on public employment. By 1976, almost all liberal Democrats in Congress had united behind the "Full Employment and Balanced Growth Act," submitted to both the Senate and the House. H.R. 50, the bill referred to in this selection, was the forerunner of that bill. In this critique of H.R. 50, Bluestone and Harrison clearly develop some of the critical differences between liberal and

radical approaches to medium-run employment problems. H.R. 50 is essentially a gesture, Bluestone and Harrison argue, because it fails to take basic political economic forces into account. "The goals of the Bill deserve the support of progressive elements in society," they conclude, "but neither H.R. 50 nor its successors go far enough to provide any hope of their implementation.

Bluestone teaches economics at Boston College. Harrison teaches urban studies and economics at the Massachusetts Institute of Technology.

Source: This paper, originally entitled "A critique of H.R. 50," was presented as testimony at public hearings in Boston on full-employment policies staged by the House Committee on Education and Labor in late 1975.

The Equal Opportunity and Full Employment Act (H.R. 50) was first introduced to the 94th Congress. H.R. 50 is a bill "to establish a national policy and nationwide machinery for guaranteeing to all adult Americans able and willing to work the availability of equal opportunities for useful and rewarding employment." This critique of H.R. 50 will contain five parts. Part I consists of an *interpretation* of the act. Part II contains an *economic* critique; Part III, a *political* critique. In Part IV we suggest some specific machinery for implementing the kind of *comprehensive economic development* program needed to "deliver" on the promises being made in H.R. 50. Part V will summarize our remarks.

I. An Interpretation of H.R. 50

At a fundamental level, H.R. 50 can be thought of as a statement of political commitment to a full employment economy tied to a massive planning effort directed at fulfilling this commitment. It commits the federal government to guaranteeing a job in the private or public sector to anyone "willing and able" to work. It would do this, according to the bill, by indepth *micro* planning of the economy so as to maximize employment in the regular private and public sectors and by providing a new public sector job *reservoir* for those who *temporarily* cannot find employment in the regular economy. In this way, according to the Bill's sponsors, we would no longer waste human resources and we would begin to produce desired public services and public works.

The Employment Act of 1946 made it the federal government's responsibility to use fiscal and monetary *macroeconomic* policies to provide for full employment, stable prices, and a favorable balance of payments. H.R. 50 goes well beyond the 1946 Act, stipulating that full employment takes precedence over all other goals and envisioning the need for *microeconomic* planning for this purpose. In addition to macroeconomic policy, the present bill calls for the annual Presidential promulgation of a "Full Employment and National Purposes Budget," and establishes local planning councils to develop local work projects, à la the Canadian Local Initiatives Program. Priority target sectors are identified, e.g., housing, health, and mass transit.

To carry out the Bill's purpose, a Job Guarantee Office (JGO) would be created which would have three methods of placing jobseekers: (1) Through the current employment service (to be renamed the United States Full Employment Service); (2) Through the placement of workers in public service jobs planned at the local level; and (3) Through

placement in a standby Job Corps where jobseekers would be registered and compensated.

A new agency called the National Institute for Full Employment would carry out a massive research effort on a whole range of issues related to employment, labor markets, and planning. Executive agencies (mainly the Office of Management and Budget?) would forecast expected private employment growth and compute the employment impacts of alternative federal budgets and the plans of the local councils.

Thus, the Bill calls for a political commitment to full employment as a first priority item of government policy, and for a massive research and planning effort to analyze and forecast expected private employment and the employment impacts of alternative federal budgets. It encourages local councils to propose new work projects. These provisions constitute a major step forward in American statecraft, and we applaud them. There is no question that we *do* now have the technical capacity to prepare such "Full Employment and National Purpose Budgets." The U.S. Bureau of Labor Statistics has already begun to promulgate the tools. Presidents (and Congresspeople) *can* estimate the industry-occupation (and even to some extent the locational) impacts of alternative federal budgets. They could then "fold in" the proposals from the local planning councils and projections of normal private and nonfederal public growth, totaling up the employment forecast (by type and location of job). These totals would then be compared with a forecast of the future size of the labor force to arrive at a prediction of the unemployment rate. If that is too high, the budget can be juggled, allocations to the local planning councils can be increased, etc. *More rational use of the federal budget as an economic development/job creation instrument is now feasible,* and H.R. 50 is most farsighted by recognizing this fact and requiring the President to use the budget in that manner.

But H.R. 50 is, in our opinion, very weak about the crucial matter of implementation. Specifically, how will the President and Congress be able to *act* on the plans generated by the research? How will the local councils acquire the *capital* with which to create jobs? Is this an *enterprise* development bill or a blown-up public service employment bill? If existing governments or private employers are to be eligible prime sponsors, how will we deal with the "maintenance of effort" problem?

In sum, while the political commitment to a job as a right of citizenship is a great and statesman-like step forward in the development of American government, H.R. 50 still begs the crucial question of how the public sector can actually *create* new jobs.

II. An Economic Critique

At one level, the Bill can be seen as simply reworking the present programs that are used to insure work or compensation for all those "willing and able to work." The three methods of placing jobseekers through the Job Guarantee Office (JGO) have analogues in the present system. The U.S. Full Employment Service would presumably work similarly to the present U.S. Employment Service placing workers in private sector jobs. The newly created public and private sector "reservoir" of jobs involves a reworking of Public Employment Program (PEP) and Public Service Employment (PSE) type programs — probably on a much larger scale and with greater planning of work activities. Finally the standby Job Corps looks much like a simple reworking of the Unemployment Insurance Benefit program already on the books, with provision for no time limit on how long one could collect benefits. If this is what is envisioned, all well and good. But we should not see this as a panacea for economic problems. At best it shifts the blame for unemployment for the victim to the government.

A much more important problem is that H.R. 50 is basically written with *short-term cyclical* unemployment in mind. That is, the Bill seems to envision an economy which has fluctuating employment in the private sector but no tendency toward long-run rising structural unemployment. In this vein, H.R. 50 would provide temporary jobs on public service and works projects whenever a gap arose between the number of jobs in the private sector and the total number of jobseekers. As the economy "normally" moved to full employment in the private sector, the government would be able to reduce the number of public "reservoir" jobs until the next private sector recession.

This is becoming a rather naive view of the American economy. Increasingly the economy is facing more and more structural underemployment with large numbers of workers no longer qualified for decent jobs at decent remuneration in the private sector, as much because of the proliferation of "secondary labor market" jobs as because of the technical insophistication of these workers. Even when the economy picks up after a recession, many of these workers are not rehired. This kind of thing is implicit in the notion of a rising "full employment" unemployment rate. At one time, 3 percent unemployment was considered "full employment." Under Kennedy, 4% was an interim full employment target. Then it rose to 5% and many now in the Ford Administration think of 6–7.5% as relative full employment. This leaves upwards of 5 million people unemployed (official accounting procedures) at "full employment." If this is true, then the job of the JGO becomes much more difficult and complex than envisioned in H.R. 50. The real problem is what should be done as the "reserve army of unemployed" in the private sector grows over time. Of course, the magnitude of the task is even more immense if we consider *underemployment*, as measured by one or another "subemployment" index.

According to the Bill, this situation would have to be dealt with by expanding the public sector over time as the private sector shrunk. But here the Bill lets us down altogether. *The main problem with H.R. 50 is that it creates job slots, but fails to provide all of the complementary inputs required for productive work.* All economists — traditionalists and radicals alike — realize that for labor to be productive, it must have capital and raw materials to work with. Without plant and machinery and without raw materials, labor's productivity is miniscule. This is the primary reason why many public service employment programs often *do* contain a degree of make-work. With the exception of some WPA and CCC projects in the 1930s, most public service employment programs fail to appropriate any funds for capital equipment. The PEP program only supplied funds for wages and administrative overhead. Without provision for capital equipment, many of the jobs created will have extremely low productivity. Thus the conservatives will, in effect, see a self-fulfilling prophesy, with public service jobs being little more than disguised welfare.

Nowhere in H.R. 50 is attention paid to "capitalizing" jobs in the work "reservoir." This is particularly perplexing because the Bill explicitly calls for reservoir projects including construction and maintenance of public buildings and other projects which require extensive amounts of equipment. Even public service jobs in welfare, education, health, and environmental protection require complementary inputs of transportation, books, typewriters, etc. Capitalizing these public service jobs is obviously necessary.

Presumably the authors of the Bill evaded this question because inclusion of "capitalization" would smack of "public enterprise" and "socialism." But without capital, the program is unworkable. Some local governments are presently trying to combine CETA wage subsidies with the community Development Block Grants from HUD and EDA's Public Works grants and loans. But the dollar amounts are *far* too small and local governments are *not* for the most part competent to "package" such resources, due to the fragmentation of agencies within state and local government. Moreover, the Bill ignores the very serious "maintenance of effort" problem, where local prime sponsors use part of the federal grant to finance activities they would have undertaken anyway, in the absence of the grant. The result is that net (actual) job creation falls short of the expected job-creation for a given federal expenditure. The problem is real; how would H.R. 50's designers deal with it?

Along with the problem of "capitalization" and the implicit "cyclical" perspective on unemployment, H.R. 50 fails to deal with the central issue of local and regional economic development. The main reason why unemployment is so pervasive and persistent in a growing number of areas in the U.S. is that economic development has slowed down to a crawl. Beyond a lack of explicit planning for development, there is little capital inflow into large areas of the country and, in some cases, a good-sized capital outflow. In some cases, the outflow is from one region to another within the nation's boundaries. Increasingly, however, the flow is to other countries via the multinational corporations (especially the banks). Economic development of depressed areas then requires (1) planning, (2) job slots, and (3) capital. H.R. 50 provides for the first two, but fails once again on number three.

Economic development is more than a problem of just keeping capital around in order to provide meaningful jobs in what otherwise would be depressed areas. True planning and development requires the ability to boost certain industries at the expense of others. If we make a commitment to mass transit as part of a local, regional, or national development scheme, this necessarily means expanding parts of the transportation industry at the expense of other sectors of the economy. There is no escaping this conclusion: public planning requires actions that will unquestionably injure some private corporations, by reallocating capital from those sectors whose outputs

Congress believes to be excessive to those whose outputs it believes to be underdeveloped.

The opponents of H.R. 50 are bound to bring up the spectre of runaway inflation caused by wage-price spirals. With a full employment economy, the federal government will be in direct competition for labor with the private sector. From the perspective of the private sector, there will be a massive "shortage" of labor and the bidding process will push up labor costs and inevitably prices. Given built-in cost-of-living protection, such labor shortages will lead inevitably to the price spiral and there will be nothing to turn it around.

The truth of the matter, as we see it, is that the above argument is not far off the mark, given no government intervention or limited intervention in the setting of wages and prices. "Full" employment in the face of no controls always leads to inflation as firms attempt to keep their profits up. Thus, without some form of far-reaching incomes policy, H.R. 50 *will* be highly inflationary. And once we begin to talk about an incomes policy, we must think carefully about what political mechanisms can be developed to set "fair" prices, wages, and profits. The point to remember is that a "full employment" policy as outlined in H.R. 50 is tantamount to a high level minimum wage law which pushes up labor costs in both the private and public sector. The public jobs "reservoir" ensures a decent minimum wage while the standby Job Corps provides a mechanism to compensate those workers who become disemployed because of higher wages. This is all well and good, but it must be realized that to the extent that H.R. 50 provides an alternative to poverty wage jobs in the "secondary labor market," there will be a substantial *disemployment* effect which will rapidly expand the need for the public jobs "reservoir" and expand the standby Job Corps.

Another shortcoming of the Bill is that it fails to deal with some specific short-run employment problems. A key one is the question of plant closings. Recently we have seen whole industries lay off up to one-third of their employees with little prior notification. The result has been wholesale disruption of families, communities, and even regions. Without some control over the procedure by which major employers can dislocate workers, it will fall completely to the public sector to take care of those who lose their jobs. There will be even less concern among private employers when contemplating closing down part of their operations in any particular region or locality, should H.R. 50 be passed in its present version. The "insurance" of public service jobs and a commitment to full employment may thus lead to even greater "reckless driving" on behalf of individual employers, unless some mechanism such as "experience rating" in unemployment compensation is used in the overall full employment program. We believe that at least some portion of the public job "reservoir" funding and standby Job Corps should come from business through employment experience-rated taxes. In addition, H.R. 50 or some other piece of legislation should deal with mechanisms to curtail the unregulated right of employers to discharge huge numbers of workers whenever they feel this is necessary to maintain profits. Again, it seems that a government-guaranteed "right to a job" cannot be seriously enforced without radically altering the traditional "right to dispose of private property." H.R. 50 is very naive on this fundamental conflict.

Finally, one last point. Section 6 of H.R. 50 refers to the compensation of Job Corps members. It mentions only the payment of a "monthly sum" appropriate to the skill level of the individual Corps members. Clearly we should be moving in the direction of defining adequate compensation in terms of compensation plus other "fringe" benefits necessary to ensure a decent standard of living. Jobs in the public employment "reservoir" and the Standby Job Corps should offer pension rights, medical insurance, and possibly life and disability insurance, as well as wage-equivalent grants. This would at least ease the present problem under Unemployment Compensation (UIB), where an unemployed worker loses not only part of his or her earnings, but company-paid medical insurance and other benefits as well. (Of course, some form of national health insurance would largely eliminate this problem).

III. A Political Critique

Beyond the economic critique, there are a number of political issues that must be considered, having to do with the *style* of the Bill. In its creation of new agency titles and the endless shopping list of "good things to do," especially given the absence of a capitalization plan, H.R. 50 sounds absolutely utopian. In order to make the Bill less utopian, a great deal must be added to each section of the Act, spelling out in detail how the program would work. This detail would have to take into account all of the economic critiques outlined above and specifically deal with the question of "capitalization."

In addition, the Bill must be "costed out" to suggest just how much would have to be spent where — and where considerable savings could actually be made (the mention of $15 billion in the emergency appropriation is a bit irresponsible, since none of the technical forecasts mandated by the Bill were in fact computed to arrive at that — or any other — figure). On the optimistic side, it is conceivable that large amounts of welfare expenditures could be transferred into the work programs, although we strongly oppose financing a patently experimental program at the short-term expense of welfare recipients. On the other hand, capital-spending may require large new outlays in line with the economic development and full-employment goals envisioned in the Bill.

Equally important on the financing side is how the funds will be *raised* for the purposes of fulfilling H.R. 50. Will they come out of the already inequitable income tax structure? Will there be new taxes on private corporations? Will the government begin to go into production and use the revenues from sales to pay for certain work projects? Will the government capitalize cooperatives or private firms with equity and use any dividends to pay for the program? All of these are questions that must be further investigated. Others are actively discussing them; why not the authors of H.R. 50?

The most important issue raised by H.R. 50 has to do with *planning*. In order to avoid the great potential for undemocratic control, the Bill calls for local planning councils to develop plans for the public jobs reservoir and to oversee the local and regional operation of the JGO. While decentralized planning protects against autocratic rule, it nevertheless creates an immense problem of coordination. In effect there is always some trade-off between efficiency in planning and democratic decision-making. Somehow a mechanism must be developed so that planning can be coordinated with a minimum amount of autocratic control. At present the House Bill is unclear on the relative strength of the national Job Guarantee Office and the hundreds of individual local planning councils. The relationship between the two must be thought out carefully.

IV. Toward an Economic Development System to Implement the Job Guarantee

To create jobs, it is necessary to create enterprises and projects that use labor — along with capital — to produce goods and services. The supply of capital available for building such enterprises — for expanding the productive capacity of the economy — needs to be increased. Eliminating the tax incentives on foreign investment (e.g. elements of the Bank Holding Act of 1969, the DISC program, etc.), seriously repealing many unproductive national and state business tax incentives, and similar policies are needed.

Then, we need mechanisms for reallocating more of the capital that *is* available for domestic investment from the overdeveloped parts of the private sector to the public sector. These would be used to finance the high-priority budget areas, and as a fund for "fueling" those local jobs councils which are really the heart of H.R. 50's "delivery system." AFL-CIO Secretary-Treasurer Lane Kirkland has proposed a national economic development bank, which would be funded mainly by the requirement that all private banks — as a condition of retaining (or getting) federal charters — subscribe to the development bank. This is a concrete, nitty-gritty proposal for reallocating capital from the private to the public sector. Kirkland lists new enterprise development, emergency aid to ailing businesses, and the guarantee of state and municipal bonds as top priorities for the national development bank. Other people (including the authors) are currently working on similar models, especially as devices for promoting low-income community economic development.

If the private sector chronically underinvests in those parts of the economy where it is especially difficult to make a "competitive profit" — or chooses to disinvest in an activity (or region) because there's more money to be made elsewhere (say, in Taiwan) — then useful jobs are not being created — or are actually being destroyed. The remedy is, in our opinion, a great increase in *enterprise development,* whether publicly-owned (as in the case of municipal or county electric utilities), organized as neighborhood-based cooperatives, or simply locally-controlled private businesses. One important potential "side-effect" of publicly-financed (but deliberately-decentralized) program to expand the number of enterprises in the American economy is the brake this might place on the power of "oligopolistic" firms to use their market power to raise (or otherwise maintain high) prices. We strongly believe that monopoly cannot be defeated by anti-trust laws. It must be confronted directly, in the marketplace, by *competition.* Thus, for example, Illinois Senator Adlai Stevenson's proposed Public Oil Corp. would directly compete with (e.g.) EXXON, thereby helping to reveal to the public the *true* cost of "mining" and processing petroleum.

In sum, we believe that the creation of "full employment" requires providing the institutions contemplated in H.R. 50 with *capital* and the *power* to create new enterprises. Increased savings, reallocation of capital from the private to the public sector, and encouragement of the widespread development of new public and private (but *locally-owned*) enterprises are the main elements of the sort of program that is needed. H.R. 50 needs to incorporate them.

V. Summary

In sum, H.R. 50 speaks to the best of humanitarian motives and presents the first beginnings of a comprehensive program to assure a decent standard of living through full employment for all. What it fails to do is to come to grips with three fundamental issues:

1. The issue of long-run relatively high levels of structural unemployment created by increased disemployment in the private sector.
2. The issue of "capitalizing" public sector employment, in particular, and enterprise/project development, in general.
3. The issue of providing the proper balance between local democratic control of the economic planning mechanism and coordinated public planning.

The goals of the Bill deserve the support of progressive elements in society — but equally require that we begin to understand the types of changes mandated by the changing structure of the American economy. Specifically, a "full employment" bill needs not only to identify the kinds of jobs (in the kinds of sectors) that are "needed" (according to some people's value judgments), but must also mandate concrete legal processes for acquiring and allocating capital with which to create the enterprises or projects in which these jobs will be "embedded."

WORKING IN CHINA

Charles Bettelheim

Many traditional arguments about employment problems focus on the inevitability of jobs such as those that we experience in our own society. "It would be nice if there weren't such specialization and hierarchy," we hear, "but there must be." "It would be wonderful if inequality weren't inevitable," they tell us, "but it is." We must preserve capitalism, as Arthur Okun argues in the selection in Chapter 1, to maintain incentives for work effort and productive contribution.

The following selection helps us dare to project a different kind of working experience. Charles Bettelheim describes some of the changes in work that the Chinese are effecting in their march along the socialist path. They call into question many of our inherited notions about technology and job structure. They present a vision of a wholly different set of "employment problems" — the problem of designing machines and job structures that, as Comrade Li puts it in this selection, "enables the workers to give full expression to their initiative."

This selection comes from a short book by Bettelheim, *Cultural Revolution and Industrial Organization in China,* in which he reports on some of the major changes taking place in China as a result of the Cultural Revolution of the 1960s.

Bettelheim is a leading French Marxist economist and has written many books on problems of the transition to socialism.

The General Knitwear Factory in Peking was built in 1952 and is located in the center of the city. In 1971 it employed 3,400 people, 60 percent of whom were women. Production is diversified and ranges from weaving (cotton and synthetic fabrics) to finished goods (sweaters, jackets, etc.). Total annual output is on the order of 20 million items. The factory produces for the domestic market as well as for export to Southeast Asia, the Middle East, Africa, and Eastern Europe.

The three principal shops are devoted to weaving, bleaching, and sewing. There are also auxiliary shops,

Source: From Charles Bettelheim, *Cultural Revolution and Industrial Organization in China.* Copyright © 1974 by Monthly Review Press. Reprinted by permission of Monthly Review Press.

including a shop for general mechanical work, where machinery is repaired or modified. The factory includes a child-care center where children can be boarded for as long as a week, and a canteen which serves three meals a day. Two women workers and the vice-chairman of the revolutionary committee gave the following account of the workers' living and working conditions in this factory:

"We pay particular attention to working conditions and are guided in this by the Chinese Communist Party. We are concerned with the welfare of the workers and the preservation of human initiative. In the old society things were very different. The capitalists did not care about such matters.

"The shops have air conditioners that maintain an even temperature. Elaborate safeguards protect the workers against injury from their machines. These protective devices are occasionally disregarded and a few accidents have occurred, but they are very rare. A few installations are not safe and must be replaced. Some shops, such as the one containing the dryers, are excessively hot; the workers in that area receive a special allowance, eat more meat, and rest more frequently. What matters, however, is to reduce the heat. A high temperature around the dryers is inevitable, but every effort is made to minimize its effects on the surrounding areas. You have seen wagons that carry ice; this is one of the ways in which we try to reduce the heat. Bathing facilities are also available to the workers.

"In the sewing shops we work eight hours a day and take half an hour for a meal. There are two additional fifteen-minute breaks for physical exercises designed to prevent work-related disabilities. These are at the same time military exercises, for we must all be prepared in case of an imperialist invasion.

"Our factory has an infirmary, and in every shop there are barefoot doctors.[1] All doctors attached to

[1] In addition to the doctors trained in medical schools, China has over a million doctors who received rapid training (often after an initial practice such as nursing). These "barefoot doctors" continue to participate in production while devoting a portion of their time to preven-

the infirmary are required to make daily rounds of the shops. This reduces the need for a worker to consult a doctor elsewhere. If sick workers cannot be properly treated in the factory, they are immediately sent to a hospital. A hospital is located right across from the factory, and there is another one in this district. There is no charge for consultation and medication. The workers get their regular pay while out sick.

"Of course, we do not claim that we have done enough to improve working conditions. We must make even greater efforts, for there are always new problems to be solved. The world changes all the time and new contradictions keep cropping up.

"Women get an extra day off each month. Those who are seven months pregnant work seven hours per day instead of eight. When their work is particularly difficult, as in the case of pedal-operated sewing machines, pregnant women do this work only during the first six months of pregnancy, and are then given different jobs. In case of special difficulties, the doctor may recommend a change of work. After a normal confinement, a woman receives a fifty-six-day paid maternity leave. In case of a more difficult confinement, this leave is increased to seventy days. Until her child is one year old, a breast-feeding mother gets two additional thirty-minute breaks a day to nurse her baby; this is reduced to a single thirty-minute period a day during the next six months. Breast feeding is discontinued when the child reaches the age of eighteen months. Between the ages of eighteen months and seven years, children remain full time in the nursery, and stay with their families only once a week; but mothers who do not want to leave them there full time may leave them in the nursery for the afternoon or for the day. In any case, there is enough room for all the children. We don't know the exact number of babies between the ages of fifty-six days and three years. The children between the ages of three years and seven years — those who have not reached school age — number slightly over two hundred.

_____

tive medicine and ordinary medical care. The term "bare-foot doctors" derives from the fact that in southern China, where rice constitutes the chief crop, the peasants customarily work barefoot in the rice fields. When bare-foot doctors cannot easily handle cases, they direct the patient to a specialized center where more skilled treatment is available. This is an example of the manner in which the Chinese masses themselves deal with the solution of their problems.

"Factory pay averages 54 yuan per month, ranging from a high of 102 to a low of 30. Minimum living expenses per person and per month come to about 12 yuan. In cases where all the members of the factory worker's family do not earn 12 yuan, an allowance is provided. Retired workers receive 60 percent of their pay." . . .

The Cultural Revolution saw the emergence of new mass organizations which, aided and guided by the Central Committee, were gradually modified and unified. At the General Knitwear Factory in 1971 these organizations consisted of the workers' management teams, the Red Guards, and the revolutionary committees, all of which came into existence following the dissolution of the factory party committee. Similar organizations, not always bearing the same names, have been formed or are being formed in many other Chinese factories. The General Knitwear Factory is a model factory in terms of the new management relations.

The Workers' Management Teams

Li Chou-hsia, a woman worker and member of the Peking factory's revolutionary committee, described the workers' management teams and their functions. During the Cultural Revolution, she explained, the masses not only rejected the revisionist line, but were also strengthened in struggle; steeped in the study and application of Mao Tse-tung Thought, they demanded participation in management, in keeping with the Anshan Constitution.

Li Chou-hsia explained it as follows:

"Now that these teams exist, the emphasis is no longer only on mutual aid and comradeship but also on helping party members. In the old days a party member was regarded only as a moving force and not as a possible target of the revolution as well. In fact, there are living ideas among the masses, and it is necessary to organize discussions with the party members so that they may benefit ideologically from contact with the workers. The comrades used to be reluctant to help party members, but the workers' management teams have changed this situation. The masses now take the initiative in going to the party members to further the ideological revolutionization of the party."

This ideological revolutionizing activity among party members — due to the initiative of the masses and to intervention by the workers' management teams — is of decisive importance. It aims at a radical transformation of practice and ideas by ridding them of bourgeois ideological influences. It helps shatter the myth that party members are custodians of Marxism-Leninism and proletarian ideology, who stand above the masses and may criticize them while remaining exempt from their criticism.

The Cultural Revolution has helped shatter this myth. In principle, only cadres and functionaries may be subjected to public criticism. The ideological revolutionization of ordinary workers is pursued primarily through the collective study of Marxism-Leninism, and in private and family discussions. Ideological revolutionizing activity is therefore no longer the political concern of the cadres alone. As a member of the revolutionary committee put it, "Today everybody is involved in political work." The extension of this political activity is making it increasingly difficult for cadres to place themselves above the workers, and is steadily reducing the possibilities for the growth of capitalist tendencies.

The workers' management teams are called on to assist management: to make suggestions in all five areas of their concern, discuss them in the shops and among the work teams, stimulate workers' initiative and coordinate their ideas, aid the revolutionary committee, and formulate criticism. They act as intermediaries between management and workers, encouraging the workers to discuss the proposals and decisions of management, and informing management of the workers' opinions. They thus establish links "from the top down and from the base up." Criticism from the rank and file is considered the most important. It helps management correct its style of work, and makes it possible to check on the cadres, their decisions, and the manner in which these are implemented. All these activities are inspired by collective expressions of opinion.

The workers' management teams are also concerned with relations between the workers of their own factory and those of other factories. There are numerous contacts between the teams of various production units. At the General Knitwear Factory, the teams deal with problems involving the upgrading of product quality. There is no department of quality control. The system is one of self-control and each work team controls its own work. The workers make every effort to find collective solutions to whatever problems come up.

The workers' management teams are also involved in planning factory output. The workers are repeat-edly consulted before a plan is formally adopted. The planning project is scrutinized concretely in terms of how it will affect each shop and each work team. The workers divide into small groups for this purpose, which enables them to express themselves fully on the plan's significance, its implications for each worker, and on possible improvements in terms of production, quality, product diversification, etc. This results in numerous exchanges between workers and managerial bodies, with the workers' management teams acting as go-betweens. The overall plan is thus scrutinized repeatedly, and its final adoption is the outcome of a common effort by the various work teams and shops. The same method of multiple exchanges "from the top down and from the base up" has been adopted between the factories and various specialized agencies . . . .

Working closely with the workers and the three-in-one teams (cadres, technicians, workers), the workers' management teams make a thorough review of possible innovations and modifications that could help reduce investment costs. In the General Knitwear Factory, as well as in many other Chinese factories, investment estimates initially projected for the plan are frequently lowered following examination by the workshops concerned and by the general machine shop. (Almost all Chinese factories have a shop for general mechanical work which plays a very important role. It repairs and modifies materials, and achieves innovations within the factory itself. In rural districts, the general machine shop is always among the first to be established; it keeps in constant touch with local factories.)

The notion of "relying on one's own strength" has a profound effect on the attitude toward the requirements of accumulation. "In keeping with Chairman Mao's teachings," a member of the revolutionary committee explained, "a three-in-one team has been organized in our factory for the purpose of achieving a technical revolution. This is a specialized team, but a campaign is under way to enlist mass participation in this effort. We must not rely exclusively on this specialized team which, at any rate, consists of few people.

"The objectives of this technical revolution are suggested by the various shops and are designed to upgrade quality, increase productivity, ensure safe working conditions, and reduce work tensions. These are generally the areas in which technical innovations are achieved. This approach may result in the development of new raw materials, new techniques, new technologies, new installations, and new methods.

"Certain changes enable us also to improve quality and make labor less burdensome. In the dyeing and printing shop, for instance, everything used to be done by hand. This shop is being upgraded, but we still lack a number of machines. Those you saw this morning, which can dye and print an entire roll of jersey, were made with the help of old machines we received from another factory. The experts and specialists had always claimed that this type of machine could not possibly dye and print jersey in two colors. The workers said: 'Why can't it be done? Let's try it!' After the Cultural Revolution, they proposed the attempt be made, and after a few trials it turned out to be quite practical to print in two colors. Nevertheless, we still have problems.

"The sewing shop has machines that make it possible to cut out sleeves and sew them onto jackets in a single operation. Each machine requires but one operator, and this new technique represents progress. But the work is very hard — the worker must simultaneously hold the cloth with her hands and operate the foot pedals, and give her full attention to this job eight hours a day. Some women workers said that this improved technique is not really an improvement because the women who operate these machines get no rest at all. A few of these machines were set aside, and we studied the problem with the operators. We succeeded in modifying the machines by eliminating the pedals.

"There were other problems. It was necessary, for instance, to cut the threads between the pieces to separate them. Here too we solved the problem through innovation — the pieces are now made and overlapped automatically, and the worker has only to position the cloth and hold it in place by hand. If this machine were in general use, the length of apprenticeship — six months in the case of the old foot-operated machines — and labor intensity could be considerably reduced.

"We are always looking for new improvements and new ways to reduce waste. These technical innovations are an important means of developing industry. Our approach requires big machines which we will develop in due time. It is well worth taking two or even five years to develop a good machine. What matters most is for the workers themselves to take the initiative in determining the need for innovation, for the working class must liberate itself."

Both in the General Knitwear Factory and in numerous other Chinese factories, the innovations achieved through mass initiative are sometimes of a high technical order. They are often created locally, but a Chinese factory is not a closed world and innovations are widely circulated among factories under the impetus of the workers' management teams.

The teams report their activities at meetings and discussions attended by all the workers of the shop or by all work teams concerned, listen to criticism, and see to it that the workers' ideas are given full consideration. The procedure is the same as that followed in the elaboration of the plan. When there are too many workers in a shop for discussion purposes, they break up into small groups where they can all express their opinions. A member of the revolutionary committee stressed the fact that no decision is made at any level without prior consultation with the workers. He added: "If the leading cadres were permitted to make their own decisions, even the new cadres might eventually follow the old road."

Members of the workers' management teams attend the meetings of the party committee cells at the appropriate level — work team, shop, factory. (The party also holds separate meetings at which its particular problems are discussed.) These meetings are held in the factory. The workers' management teams have their own meetings: once a month on the factory level, every two weeks on the shop level, every day on the work level. The daily meetings deal with problems that come up during the day, and a balance sheet is drawn up every evening. The problems may touch on relations with the cadres, on political questions, or on everyday life (housing, relocation, personal and family matters, etc.). Factory or shop managers do not attend these meetings, which further workers' initiative and prevents the workers' management teams from getting caught up in an administrative web.

The workers' management teams organize the study of the basic works of Marx, Lenin, and Mao Tse-tung. In their role of acting as a control and stimulating initiative, they help the party committee and the revolutionary committee resolve political and ideological questions. Since these committees are mass groupings, they must follow the leadership of the party, which plays a decisive role in determining their ideological orientation. Problems that arise between the party and the workers' management teams are settled through discussion — party leadership is *political,* not administrative. The leadership of the party committee or cell is exercised jointly with the workers' management teams in common meetings where those affected by the decisions can participate in the discussions; decisions made without full consultation with the masses may well be inadequate. Decisions made at the shop or work team levels, however, are not transmitted by the workers' management team representatives but by the party cell secretaries or by the representatives of the administrative management team in each shop.

"The extension of workers' management team activity," explained Comrade Li, "entails several advantages: it enables the workers to give full expression to their initiative, apply their intelligence and wisdom, gain experience in collective management of a socialist enterprise, and develop lower-echelon cadres. Vice-chairman Lin Piao has said that ours are mass policies, democratic policies. Management, therefore, is not the exclusive concern of a handful of people, but must involve everyone. The activities of the workers' management teams accurately reflect the need to implement this slogan. Everybody is involved in political and ideological work." . . .

Intellectual Labor and Manual Labor

The division between manual labor and intellectual labor in a capitalist factory is reflected in the distinction between the immediate production work assigned to the workers and the tasks of the engineers and technicians who supervise production processes and make decisions regarding changes in work procedures, the utilization of machines, technical rules, etc. When this division is maintained or grows sharper, as is the case in capitalist factories, it places the immediate producers in a subordinate position with respect to the engineers and technicians. The transformations that occurred during the Cultural Revolution signify that a struggle is being waged in China to eliminate this aspect of the division of labor as well.

One of the outcomes of this struggle has been the formulation of what the Chinese call three-in-one combination teams, teams charged with technical questions and consisting of workers, technicians, and cadres. According to a formulation widely used in China, the workers are the backbone of these teams, their leading force. The three-in-one teams take charge of the technical transformation of the factories, technical renovation, innovations and changes in technical regulations, and the struggle against the "unreasonable rules" that existed in these areas. Because of these "unreasonable rules," only engineers and technicians had the privilege of modifying machines.

The activities of the three-in-one teams, political and ideological education, and the integration of the engineers in manual labor, are gradually obliterating the separation between engineers and technicians on the one hand and workers on the other, as well as the domination of the workers by the technicians and engineers. This trend is reinforced by the profound transformation of the system of education, a complex task which is far from complete, requiring both time and experimentation in the resolution of problems.

Close links have been established between education and production work. The new technicians and engineers come straight from production; after completing the general course they spend two or three years as workers, peasants, or members of the People's Liberation Army (soldiers are also directly involved in production). Their fellow workers then select those who are to continue their studies (with their consent, of course); the choice is based on the candidate's overall practice and not only on intellectual criteria. The basic criterion is willingness to serve the people — to acquire knowledge not for personal advantage but for use in the service of the people. Admission to the university involves three steps: an individual request for admission, the designation of fellow workers, and a determination of the course of work in terms of the student's capacity and the needs of his or her production unit. Students keep in close touch with their workplace.

The old forms of the division of labor are obviously still far from completely shattered. Certain kinds of work are more attractive than others, but the less appealing jobs are increasingly being integrated into collective tasks which enable each individual to play a clearly useful and active role. Workers also have numerous possibilities for learning new skills, not only through the engineering schools, but also because of the reorganization of the production processes and the various ways in which the factory itself provides professional training opportunities. The effort to make work less fragmentary by modifying its conditions and enabling each worker to master part of the production process is also very important. The assembly line must not dominate the worker; increasingly, it is the worker who is setting its pace.

The process of revolutionizing the mode of work is of necessity a long one — but it has been partially initiated through recognition of the fact that specific forms of the division of labor do not result from an abstract development of the productive forces, but that a work mode results from a transformation of the relations of production by past or present class struggles.

The transformations designed to eliminate the division between manual labor and intellectual labor are of decisive importance in achieving progress along the road to socialism. Generally speaking, they signify that one of the most profound characteristics of all class societies — the social separation between theory and practice — is in the process of being eliminated. In the capitalist mode of production this separation manifests itself concretely in the accumulation of both scientific and technical theoretical knowledge, and "practical" knowledge. The former assumes the form of sciences and technologies supposedly represented exclusively by scientists, engineers, and technicians; "practical" knowledge is reduced to mere routine or simple tricks of the trade.

Although the sciences and techniques have assumed an *apparently* autonomous guise which has given a considerable impulse to the development in knowledge, their growing separation from the practice of material production nevertheless produces contradictory social effects: it tends to deprive the immediate producers of knowledge that could enrich their practice of production and enable them to transform it themselves. Concurrently, this separation deprives the engineers, and especially the scientists, of useful practical types of knowledge. The social affirmation of the primacy of practice thus has considerable implications in China; it profoundly affects the reproduction of scientific and technical knowledge, the apparent autonomy of which can thus be torn up by the roots.

One of the effects of the separation between the sciences and techniques and the practice of production, contrary to what one might think, is the conservative character of technique. The illusion of the primacy of theory tends to arouse enormous social resistance to technical changes suggested by workers, especially when these changes contradict the ideas sanctioned by scientists and technicians. The Cultural Revolution in China has shown how thousands of innovations had previously been blocked by technicians who viewed them as inconsistent with the scientific and technical concepts they had been

taught. The notion of the primacy of theory, which reflects bourgeois concepts and the capitalist division of labor, thus tends to render "unacceptable" any production method or technical change that is considered "technically invalid," thereby fostering theoretical conservatism.

In China today the relation between abstract knowledge in its theoretical form and the practice of production is being increasingly modified; problems are no longer "settled" through appeal to theory alone. There is concrete evidence to show that when the primacy of practice is socially acknowledged, a whole range of transformations that cannot as yet be synthesized theoretically can nevertheless be incorporated into practice; this accelerates technical change and gives rise to a new type of technical development. (In the altogether different domain of medicine, for example, the use of acupuncture is a striking example of how practice can take a "lead" over theory.) The three-in-one teams directed by the workers provide a concrete social basis for this kind of development of technique and industrial production. These teams have made it possible to achieve a considerable number of technical innovations which bear not only on the production of new machinery, but also on the transformation of existing machines. Machines are no longer viewed as immutable objects, but as subject to modification by the workers themselves.

The innovations and technical renovations impelled by the three-in-one teams often produce as much as a threefold increase in the productive capacity of old machines. This affects the economic potential, since it makes possible a rapid growth in the productive capacity of the existing machines, and a development of the productive forces that requires minimal prior accumulation.

In addition to affecting the transformation of technique, the three-in-one teams are also transforming the relations of the workers to their means of production. The expanding activities of the three-in-one teams are occurring in a context of class struggle. Technology is never neutral; it is never above or beside the class struggle. The class struggle, and the changes it imposes on the production process and production relations, ultimately determines the specific character of the productive forces and of their development. The socialist transformation of the production processes thus fosters the progressive obliteration of the social *separation* between scientific and technical activities and directly productive activities. This transformation also presupposes that — contrary to the practice of capitalist countries — the achievement of innovations is not subordinated to the possibility of selling new products or new services yielding increasing profits. China has eliminated this subordination and thus cleared the way for a vast expansion of innovation and renovation, of technical changes many of which result not in the construction of new machines or new factories but in the transformation and perfecting of existing machines or factories.

Socially, scientific and technical activities are being integrated into the activities of the associated workers; the capitalist division of labor separates these activities. This integration signifies that the conception of new techniques or new work processes no longer falls within the competence of a minority of specialists alone, but can be mastered by the great majority of workers, whose capabilities can thereby be fully mobilized.

BIBLIOGRAPHY

I. IMPRESSIONS, DEFINITIONS, AND MAGNITUDES

A. Impressions

Elliot Liebow. *Tally's Corner.* Boston: Little, Brown, 1967.
Studs Terkel. *Working.* New York: Pantheon, 1974.

B. Definitions

Stanley Moses. "Labor Supply Concepts: The Political Economy of Conceptual Change," *Annals* of the American Academy of Political and Social Science, March 1975.
Thomas Vietorisz, Robert Mier, and Jean Giblin. "Subemployment: Exclusion and Inadequacy Indexes," *Monthly Labor Review,* May 1975.

C. Magnitudes

Report of the National Advisory Commission on Civil Disorders. New York: Bantam, 1968. Useful summary from sixties' perspective.
Thomas Vietorisz, Robert Mier, and Bennett Harrison. "Full Employment at Living Wages," *Annals* of the American Academy of Political and Social Science, March 1975.
Frank Furstenberg. "Counting the Jobless: The Impact of Job Rationing on the Measurement of Unemployment," *Annals* of the American Academy of Political and Social Science, March 1975.
Herman Miller. "Measuring Subemployment in Poverty Areas of Large United States Cities," *Monthly Labor Review,* October 1973.
Manpower Report of the President. Washington, D.C.: U.S. Government Printing Office. The most recent edition provides useful data in its appendices.

II. THEORIES OF EMPLOYMENT AND INCOME

A. Orthodox Economic Perspectives

Albert Rees. *The Economics of Work and Pay.* New York: Harper & Row, 1973. Chapter 4.

K. W. Rothschild. *The Theory of Wages.* New York: Kelly, 1974. Chapters 2–5.

B. Radical Perspectives

Karl Marx. "The Labor Theory of Value and the Theory of Exploitation," in Robert Freedman, ed., *Marx on Economics.* New York: Harcourt Brace, 1969. Pp. 29–105.

Samuel Bowles and Herbert Gintis. *Schooling in Capitalist America.* New York: Basic Books, 1975. Chapters 3–5.

Harry Braverman. *Labor and Monopoly Capital.* New York: Monthly Review Press, 1974.

III. PERSPECTIVES ON EMPLOYMENT PROBLEMS

A. Liberal and Conservative Views

Robert Hall. "Why Is There So Much Unemployment at Full Employment?", *Brookings Papers on Economic Activity, 1970,* Number 1.

Martin Feldstein. *Lowering the Permanent Rate of Unemployment,* U.S. Congress, Joint Economic Committee, 1974.

Peter Doeringer and Michael Piore. *Internal Labor Markets and Manpower Analysis.* Lexington, Mass.: D. C. Heath, 1971.

B. Radical Perspectives

David M. Gordon. *Theories of Poverty and Underemployment.* Lexington, Mass.: D. C. Heath, 1973.

Bennett Harrison. *Education, Training, and the Urban Ghetto.* Baltimore: Johns Hopkins Press, 1972.

IV. POLICY PERSPECTIVES

A. General

Sar A. Levitan and Garth L. Mangum. *Federal Training and Work Programs in the Sixties.* Ann Arbor: Institute of Labor and Industrial Relations, 1969.

David M. Gordon. *Theories of Poverty and Underemployment.* Lexington, Mass.: D. C. Heath, 1973. Chapter 6.

B. Training Programs

Peter B. Doeringer, ed. *Programs to Employ the Disadvantaged.* New York: Prentice-Hall, 1969. Case studies.

Jules B. Cohn. *The Conscience of the Corporations: Business and Urban Affairs.* Baltimore: Johns Hopkins Press, 1971. Critical review of "socially oriented" corporate programs.

Barry Bluestone. "Economic Theory, Economic Reality, and the Fate of the Poor," in H. Sheppard *et al.,* eds., *The Political Economy of Public Service Employment.* Lexington, Mass.: D. C. Heath, 1972. Radical perspective.

C. Ghetto Economic Development

John F. Kain and Joseph J. Persky. "Alternatives to the Gilded Ghetto," *The Public Interest,* Winter 1969. Argue for ghetto dispersal.

Bennett Harrison. *Urban Economic Development: Suburbanization, Minority Opportunity, and the Condition of the Central City.* Washington, D.C.: Urban Institute, 1974. Argues for ghetto development.

Matthew Edel. "Development vs. Dispersal: Approaches to Ghetto Poverty," in Edel and J. Rothenberg, eds., *Readings in Urban Economics.* New York: Macmillan, 1972. Compares the two approaches.

D. Public Employment

Harold Sheppard *et al.,* eds. *The Political Economy of Public Service Employment.* Lexington, Mass.: D. C. Heath, 1972. Includes many different perspectives.

RACE

*I'm not going to lower my pride to be no type of porter. And I'll always be like
that. Long as I live. I rather starve than be somebody's porter. Just like they
said, when you take a man's pride, Jim, you might rather take the man, too. . . .
Even if the job was a hundred fifty dollars. I'm not going to be nobody's porter.*

— a 19-year-old black high school graduate[1]

Throughout the 1960s and early 1970s, the press called it the "hidden issue."
People talked about the "urban crisis" or "crime in the streets," about the
"welfare problem" or "urban unrest." Hidden beneath those issues and slogans,
however, lay a different problem altogether. Many people were really talking
about "race" — about the special problems of blacks and other minority groups
in American cities.[2]

People rarely dared to talk openly about the issue of race for several important reasons. Our democratic ideology created strong pressure against racist
attitudes, against scorning people because of their skin color. And in their militant protests of the 1960s, blacks also dramatized this ideological imperative,
forcefully claiming that America had been denying them the rights that they deserved as citizens of a democratic society. Together, these two pressures made
it difficult for people to talk openly about what they saw in the cities.

What they saw was that many of our most severe problems were concen-

---

[1] Quoted in Herb Goro, *The Block* (New York: Random House, 1970), p. 156.

[2] The issue was hidden in the first edition of this reader as well, woven through other
chapters but never isolated by itself. So I have added this separate chapter to this
second edition more clearly to focus on race as a separate "urban problem."

In the first paragraphs of this introduction, I refer to "blacks and other minority
groups." In American cities today, those "other minority groups" suffering disadvantages
mainly include chicanos and Puerto Ricans. In the body of the introduction, I stop referring to those other groups and focus on blacks alone. Despite that excision, which I
make for simplicity of exposition, I believe that many problems confronting chicanos and
Puerto Ricans are similar to those facing blacks and that the different analytic perspectives summarized here apply equally to those other groups. I apologize to any members
of those "other minority groups" who may feel that their own problems are slighted here.

Finally, I should note that many of the analytic differences isolated here also apply to
the problem of discrimination by sex — to the problems confronted by women in our
society. I have not treated sexism as a separate problem in this book because it is not an
especially "urban" problem and has not been associated with the "urban crisis."

trated among blacks and other minority groups like chicanos and Puerto Ricans. Those minority groups suffered the worst employment problems, lived in the worst housing, were most frequently both the victims and the agents of urban crime . . . the list went on. Those minority groups were also making the most noise about their conditions, refusing to wait patiently for their promised assimilation. For many Americans, the "urban crisis" would never have existed if blacks and other minorities had been willing to "accept" their conditions of deprivation more patiently.

However buried below the surface, the same questions flickered through most conversations about our cities. Why is race so important? Why are blacks and other minorities in the worst shape? Why have they not been assimilated into our society like other ethnic minorities before them? Is it all white America's fault, the consequences of several centuries' oppression and discrimination? Or — and this question was usually whispered — is there something intrinsically wrong with blacks and other minorities as racial groups?

Because these questions were rarely uttered, they rarely received the direct analytic attention that they deserved. This chapter tries to bring them out into the open, taking them seriously and exploring them seriously. This introduction first defines the problem of race, then compares liberal and conservative positions with the radical analysis. A final short section introduces the readings in this chapter.

Definitions and Magnitudes

The first way to define the problem of race is the simplest. Blacks experience worse living and working conditions than whites do. Since World War II, for instance, (median) black families have earned only about three-fifths as much as (median) white families. Blacks have been about twice as likely to suffer unemployment.[3] Although estimates vary, blacks appear to pay significantly higher rents for comparable housing than whites do and/or to live in worse housing than whites of comparable incomes do.[4]

Given those clear racial disadvantages, there are two common frameworks within which racial problems are further defined.

One framework focuses on *equality of opportunity*. From this perspective, blacks suffer problems because they are not given the same opportunities to succeed as are whites in comparable circumstances. Black children are forced to study in worse schools, for instance, and black high school graduates are often channeled toward low-status jobs more than white high school graduates are. This focus on equality of opportunity tends to emphasize the simple act of discrimination as the source of racial disadvantage: blacks are denied equal opportunities because whites *discriminate* against them. If this were true, then a campaign to end discriminatory actions themselves would presumably play a major role in improving the situations of blacks.[5]

---

[3] For more complete data, see the selection by Jhabvala and the Editor's Supplement in this chapter.

[4] See John Kain and John Quigley, *Racial Discrimination in Housing* (New York: National Bureau of Economic Research, 1974), pp. 63ff, for discussion of the evidence and problems of measurement.

[5] To try to measure this kind of discrimination, many social scientists try to control for all the kinds of characteristics that might affect an individual's employment or income and then look at how much of the differences between white and black status is *not*

A second framework focuses on *equality of outcome.* This perspective goes a little beyond the first focus on discrimination. It suggests that, since the history of racial oppression in this country has had deep and complicated effects, we can never isolate one or two decisive acts of discrimination. We should look at the whole pattern of economic outcomes by race. Public policy should focus, from this perspective, on creating movement toward more and more equal outcomes. Rather than emphasizing acts of discrimination that may deny blacks (or other minorities) equal opportunities, this perspective focuses on the rights of blacks to attain equal standing with whites of comparable backgrounds. Despite many antidiscrimination programs during the 1960s, for instance, blacks still suffer equivalent disadvantages during the 1970s. This suggests to many that simple antidiscrimination measures are not enough to solve racial problems, that more significant steps should be taken to create more substantial movement toward equal outcomes.

These two frameworks suggest a third major definitional concern. People would pay less attention to the problems of race if it seemed obvious that these problems were going away. Many other ethnic groups have come to the United States in its history, and many of those groups have overcome initial disadvantages. The disadvantages of blacks have stubbornly *persisted.* This persistence suggests the need for more careful analytic attention and more dramatic policy steps.[6] If patterns of racial disadvantage have changed so little over time, there must be some fundamental causes of that disadvantage.

These definitions merely serve to reiterate the same initial questions: Racial problems persist in the United States. Why?

Conservative and Liberal Views

The conservative and liberal perspectives on racial problems begin from some common analytic foundations. When conservatives and liberals begin to consider policy questions, their prescriptions become increasingly divergent. Since several of the reading selections clearly summarize these perspectives, this introduction can be brief.

Beginning from orthodox economic analysis, both conservatives and liberals argue that competition under capitalism makes racial discrimination unlikely. Capitalists must maximize their profits. In order to maximize profits, they must hire the most productive workers. Since race, as an ascriptive characteristic, has nothing to do with productivity, capitalists will be forced to ignore it. They might like to indulge in their discriminatory prejudices, but the pressures of economic competition will not afford them the luxury. "In a free market," as Milton Friedman puts it in the selection in this chapter, "[those pressures] will tend to drive him out."[7]

Flowing from this logical foundation, both conservatives and liberals tend to assume that the factors helping create and perpetuate racism come from *out-*

---

explained by those variables. The assumption is that the differences *not* explained, for instance, by years of schooling, are explained by discrimination — by inequality of opportunity. For an example of this kind of analysis, see Otis Dudley Duncan, "Inheritance of Poverty or Inheritance of Race," in Daniel P. Moynihan, ed., *On Understanding Poverty* (New York: Basic Books, 1969).

[6] See the Editor's Supplement in this chapter.

[7] Although this part of the analysis is more typically advanced by conservatives than by liberals, the basic economic premise is common to both groups.

side the economic system. Since the logic of the market system works against racism, they argue, then the persistence of racism must come from somewhere else. Conventionally, they attribute the *origins* of racism to precapitalist cultures and ascribe its *persistence* to dogged psychological prejudice.[8]

Finally, both conservatives and liberals agree that policy measures designed to combat racism should tamper as little as possible with underlying economic mechanisms. Since they see our economy as a market system and since they argue that market pressures tend to erode racial discrimination, they argue that antidiscriminatory policies should not compromise the market itself. They are willing to relax this axiom somewhat in certain circumstances to varying degrees, of course, but it remains a major building block of their analyses nonetheless.

These initial axioms would suggest that racism ought to have been declining. It has not been, at least for a very long time. So both conservatives and liberals are immediately confronted with an obvious question: Why has racism persisted? Their answers differ substantially in emphasis.

Conservatives have recently focused on two possible explanations of persistence. It may possibly be true, first of all, that blacks suffer economic disadvantages because they, as a racial group, have lower IQ's than whites do. This could explain, in their view, why blacks continue to appear to employers to have lower productivities than white employees do.[9] Second, blacks may persistently suffer disadvantage because they have failed to take advantage of available opportunities to improve themselves; earlier ethnic groups climbed the socioeconomic ladder through hard work and patience, according to this view, and blacks have simply failed to emulate their example.[10] Both these explanations have a common effect. They tend to "blame the victims" for their problems, averting our gaze from more structural social forces.[11]

Liberal analyses have largely focused on more structural forces. Liberals tend to view racial problems in terms of "vicious circles." Once a problem starts, they argue, it may get reproduced. For instance, employers may not hire blacks because they think that blacks, as a group, tend to stay on the job for less time than whites do; if they value stable employees, they may save themselves some hiring and screening costs if they stay away from blacks.[12] To pick a second example, liberals have analyzed the results of different schooling programs and argue that black disadvantages are reinforced if blacks study in segregated schools — even if those schools are equally endowed; busing programs creating more integrated schools, in this view, would help insure that blacks were exposed to the kinds of social and cultural values that have helped

[8] For example, Gary Becker begins his analysis in *The Economics of Discrimination* (Chicago: University of Chicago Press, 1957) by *assuming* that employers have a distaste for associating with blacks. He never examines or explains where that "distaste" comes from.

[9] See Arthur R. Jensen, "How Much Can We Boost IQ and Scholastic Achievement?", *Harvard Educational Review,* Winter 1969; and Richard J. Herrnstein, "IQ," *The Atlantic Monthly,* September 1971.

[10] See Edward Banfield, *The Unheavenly City Revisited* (Boston: Little, Brown, 1974), Chapter 4; and Thomas Sowell, *Race and Economics* (New York: McKay, 1975).

[11] For an elaboration of this view of conservative perspectives, see William Ryan, *Blaming the Victim* (New York: Pantheon, 1968).

[12] This kind of discrimination has been called "statistical discrimination" because it is based on the law of averages rather than on personal prejudice. See, for instance, Joseph Stiglitz in G. Von Furstenberg *et al.,* eds., *Patterns of Racial Discrimination, Vol. II: Employment* (Lexington, Mass.: D. C. Heath, 1974).

whites get ahead.[13] Both of these examples illustrate the liberal tendency to avoid blaming individual victims for their problems.

These different analytic emphases explain some of the differences between conservative and liberal policy orientations.

Conservatives urge a policy of doing little or nothing to overcome racial problems. They are especially concerned that the "free market" not be adulterated. And they argue that the government has no right to be dictating racial solutions to free citizens in a democratic society. As a result, they oppose busing programs to achieve integrated schools — this kind of busing imposes integration on freely constituted residential neighborhoods — and they oppose compulsory antidiscriminatory hiring policies, which would compromise employers' ability to follow the profit-maximizing grail. As Edward Banfield suggests in his general selection in Chapter 1 of this book, conservatives argue that antidiscriminatory programs may do more harm than good.[14]

Liberals typically urge us to do something, almost anything, to begin some movement toward less discrimination and more equal outcomes. They urge us to spend money — as they always have — to try to improve the quality of the schools and neighborhoods in which blacks first face society. And they argue that some compulsory government programs, like busing and hiring policies, are required to break through the vicious circles in which social structures have trapped us for so many years. There are risks to some of these government initiatives, liberals agree, but they argue that we cannot afford to stand still.

The Radical View

Radicals begin their analyses of racism from a fundamentally different perspective than conservatives and liberals do. They build from a different foundation and, having established that basis for discussion, interpret concrete circumstances in substantially different ways from either conservatives or liberals.

Radicals begin with an exploration of the relationships between capitalism and racism.

They argue, first, that the original development of capitalism played a central role in the original appearance of racist attitudes. Early capitalist merchants found the slave trade profitable, they suggest, and encouraged racist attitudes to help justify their traffic in human beings.[15]

The radical perspective also suggests that the continuing development of capitalism has reinforced and exacerbated racial problems in many ways. Capitalists have often used black workers as strike breakers, intensifying conflicts between white and black workers. Speculators have often encouraged "block-busting" to make quick and easy real estate profits. In general, capitalists have often encouraged racial problems as one way, among many, of keeping workers divided among themselves.[16]

These two premises conflict sharply with the orthodox economic analysis. Whereas that perspective suggests that racism has *external* origins, the radical arguments points at *internal* sources.

[13] See, for instance, David K. Cohen, Thomas F. Pettigrew, and Robert T. Riley, "Race and the Outcomes of Schooling," in Frederick Mosteller and Daniel P. Moynihan, eds., *On Equality of Educational Opportunity* (New York: Vintage Books, 1972).

[14] See Thomas Sowell, *Race and Economics* (New York: David McKay, 1975), and Nathan Glazer, *Affirmative Discrimination* (New York: Basic Books, 1976).

[15] See, for instance, Eric Williams, *Capitalism and Slavery* (New York: Putnam, 1966).

[16] See R. C. Edwards *et al.*, eds., *Labor Market Segmentation* (Lexington, Mass.: D. C. Heath, 1975).

What about the forces of competition, which, in the orthodox view, would tend to erode racism under capitalism? Radicals respond by arguing that two characteristics of capitalist economies tend internally to generate forces reproducing racial problems.

First, radicals argue that capitalism tends to develop *unevenly* at various times.[17] Criteria of profitability tend to reinforce differences between groups or regions as often as they tend to equalize them. For instance, corporations have recently been moving manufacturing investment out of the Northeastern and Middle Western regions of the United States. That has amounted to an abandonment of older central cities in which many poor people live, including many blacks. The external emigration of capital tends to reinforce the poverty of those central-city residents.

Second, radicals argue that capitalists must respect their *common class interests* as much as they must pursue their individual concerns with firm profitability. It might be against their individual interests to discriminate against individual black employees, over the long run, but it may be in their collective class interest to use racial divisions to keep workers divided along racial lines. If they began to erode those racial divisions through individual hiring decisions, they might quickly find themselves with a more and more unified and potentially powerful working class.[18]

In general, these arguments suggest that racial divisions serve a useful function for capitalists. Like divisions among workers by sex, these racial divisions reduce workers' potential bargaining power. In his selection in this chapter, Michael Reich summarizes some interesting empirical evidence that supports this general view.

These analytic foundations provide the basis for the radical response to conservative and liberal perspectives.

Radicals respond to the conservative position in fairly simple ways. They suggest that the conservative position fails to take account of the underlying economic structures that limit, or determine individual actions. Taking these structures into account, we would pay much less attention to the factors that conservatives mention. Regardless of the average IQ's of different groups, for instance, radicals argue that cognitive intelligence plays a surprisingly limited role in determining individuals' economic success; ascribing failure to IQ fails to take account of the much more important forces (in this view) that affect economic outcomes.[19] To blame individuals for failing to take advantage of their opportunities suffers many of the same problems, in the radical view. Earlier ethnic groups may have been able to climb the socioeconomic ladder, as the conservatives suggest, but the structure of that ladder has since changed. The labor market has become much more segmented, radicals argue, and individual effort provides much less certain access to promising job ladders.[20]

The radical response to the liberal argument is somewhat different. Liberals

[17] This point is developed by John Gurley, "Maoist Economic Development," *Review of Radical Political Economics,* Winter 1970.

[18] For a further development of this point, see David M. Gordon, "Capitalist Efficiency and Socialist Efficiency," *Monthly Review,* July–August 1976.

[19] See Samuel Bowles and Herbert Gintis, *Schooling in Capitalist America* (New York: Basic Books, 1976), Chapter 4.

[20] See M. Reich, D. Gordon, and R. Edwards, "A Theory of Labor Market Segmentation," in Chapter 2 of this book; and Edwards *et al.,* eds., *Labor Market Segmentation.*

also take account of structural sources of racial problems, but radicals suggest that the liberal analysis does not probe deeply enough. Liberals treat the structural sources of racial disadvantage as "accidents," as vestiges of some earlier era. However difficult it may be to break through those vicious circles initially, liberals nonetheless expect that economic forces will not impede our progress once a "breakthrough" is achieved. Radicals suggest a different perspective. In concluding that racism serves important structural economic functions, radicals argue that no single "breakthrough" will be enough to sustain movement toward more equal outcomes. Economic forces will continue to impede progress; until the underlying structural sources of racism are excised, radicals argue, progress will continue to be insignificant.

These criticisms of the conservative and liberal positions carry over to the radical attack on conservative and liberal policy positions.

Radicals argue that we cannot possibly do "nothing," as the conservatives would have it, because we, as members of a social system, have a democratic obligation to transform those features of a social system that oppress individual members of particular groups. Radicals also argue that liberal policy prescriptions are insufficient. In this case, two elements of that policy critique seem most important. First, radicals argue that liberal programs are not fundamental enough because they do not attack the sources of racism in the underlying economic system itself. Second, radicals argue that many liberal antidiscriminatory policies end up dividing whites and blacks rather than uniting them in common programs. For instance, liberal recommendations for antidiscriminatory hiring policies do not, as a rule, *also* recommend changing the underlying shape of the job structure. As a result, liberals end up recommending that some whites should give up jobs in favor of some blacks in order to help equalize the job prospects of blacks. These whites necessarily resent those recommendations. Instead, radicals argue, we should change the structure of jobs so that both blacks and whites are able to improve their working and living standards.[21] Because liberals do not dare to tackle the more basic question of the shape of the job structure itself, radicals argue, their programs force us to fight with each other.

In general, these different elements of the radical analysis converge in two main points. First, radicals argue that, since the economic system helps reinforce racism, we must change the economic system in order to begin fundamentally to eliminate racism. Second, radicals argue that, since the economic system tends to pit blacks against whites and to profit from those divisions, we should struggle to overcome those divisions through programs that unite blacks and whites in order to strengthen our struggles against the system as a whole.

Readings

The first group of readings provides some Impressions, Definitions, and Magnitudes. The first selection tells the story of a black teenager facing the world in which so many other blacks have suffered disadvantage — the world of work. The second selection, by Firdaus Jhabvala, summarizes the different dimensions of disadvantage that blacks experience. An Editor's Supplement focuses

[21] It is not utopian to talk about changing the structure of jobs. There is nothing eternally necessary about our present structures. For more on this argument, see Gordon, "Capitalist Efficiency and Socialist Efficiency."

on the particular problem of persistence, summarizing some data which appear to show that despite many government programs, the gap between blacks and whites has not decreased for many years.

The second group of readings presents aspects of different analytic perspectives. The selection by Milton Friedman reflects the general conservative point of view; although somewhat more out-of-date than other selections, it nonetheless represents the prevailing conservative reaction to various antidiscriminatory measures. The selection by Barbara R. Bergmann represents the liberal perspective. While admitting that racial problems are serious and demand our attention, the selection argues that they can be substantially improved without our needing to change the underlying economic system. The third selection, by Robert Cherry, summarizes the conservative and liberal views and contrasts them with the radical view, arguing that the radical view more closely represents reality. He draws heavily on the work of Michael Reich, author of the fourth selection in this group, who presents empirical evidence supporting the view that racism is in the interests of neither white nor black workers because it weakens their bargaining with employers. In the final analytic selection, Harold M. Baron and Bennett Hymer focus on the specific mechanisms in large cities that tend to perpetuate racial divisions.

A final piece summarizes some of the most important policy differences among these perspectives. Firdaus Jhabvala criticizes various reformist solutions to racial discrimination and argues the need for a systematic attack on the economic roots of racism.

LOOKING FOR A JOB

George Goodman, Jr.

This short selection describes the problems that a young black man faces in looking for a job. Many different problems intersect — racism, social environment, employers' and employees' attitudes. In this case, at least, lack of skills does not seem to be a problem. Above all, as Freddy Rivers himself observes, the most important problem is the most basic — he needs "a real job that pays you enough to live."

George Goodman, Jr., is a reporter for *The New York Times,* where this article first appeared.

On hot days, Freddy Rivers, a 21-year-old black in search of a job paying more than "chump change," stands on the steps of a crumbling stoop with twisted railing.

He lives three flights up with his mother, a domestic who labors six days a week as the chief breadwinner for a fatherless family of six.

In $40 platform shoes, tight-fitting pants and a red sweater with leather patchwork trim, Freddy is flashy but broke. He is compact and muscular — 140 pounds on a 5-foot 8-inch frame that looks like a dancer's.

He stands there watching the endless meandering of glassy-eyed prostitutes, dope fiends, winos and hustlers with varying specialties. Occasionally, he sips from a half-pint bottle of cheap wine in a brown paper bag. Sometimes he smokes marijuana and talks with Bumpy, a school chum from days past.

"To walk down these streets, standing tall, you got to be ready to rumble," Freddy said. "You've got to be ready to fight for your self-respect or else they will think you're a punk."

Outside Harlem, Freddy walks with less self-assurance, hunting for a job in a market where jobs are hard to find, even for whites.

Freddy's job difficulties are typical of those faced by several thousand black and Puerto Rican young people who make up what one labor expert describes as "the subemployment index." According to Herbert Hill, national labor director of the Na-

tional Association for the Advancement of Colored People, these youths represent a generation of slum-area youths, many of whom are "forced by society into an existence of social banditry as a means of livelihood."

Mr. Hill said the great majority of the blacks in 25 of the country's largest urban slum areas were caught in a severe, long-term economic depression.

"Despite improvement for a thin strata of middle-class blacks," Mr. Hill said, "the status of blacks and Puerto Ricans like those in New York City slums is worse than it has been at any time since the end of the Second World War."

"The average Negro family needs an additional wage earner to earn substantially more than one half the income of a comparable white family," he added.

Heroin "is the big thing today," said Mrs. Rivers, sitting in her family's $115-a-month, carefully furnished five-room apartment. She said she had "burned up more than one stove in the kitchen, trying to keep the family warm."

"I have begged the landlord unsuccessfully for the last five years to give the rooms a fresh painting," she said. "Freddy, my baby, is doing the painting now. God bless that boy."

Recalls Sleeping in Park

"I have worked in other peoples' houses six days a week, sometimes from 6 A.M. to 12 midnight," she went on. "I can't know everything my kids are doing, but I hope the Lord is watching out."

"When I came here from Savannah, Ga., in 1945," Mrs. Rivers went on, "Freddy's daddy and me used to bike-ride and go dancing at the Dawn Casino. We used to have nice night spots, as nice as any of the best in the city. We liked to drink beer and sometimes, in the summer, we slept all night in Morningside Park." She noted it would not be wise to do so today.

Early Rivers, whom she divorced before his recent death, "never did much for the kids," Mrs. Rivers said. But Freddy, sitting on the window sill, waving and calling to friends in the street, stood up to proclaim: "At least he headed me in the right direction looking for work."

Freddy said school has always been a problem for him, particularly reading.

"I had one old-time black dude as a teacher who really tried to help me," he said. "He was a proper kind of man from the old school, but except for him most of my teachers were jiving, working for the money."

When he was 16, Freddy said, he saw his first glassine bag of heroin. He said a friend convinced him to snort, "and I got a most beautiful high."

Three years later, he said, he was arrested for possession of 20 half-ounces that someone had given him to sell at $45 a bag. "My customer was a middle-aged white man, and I was scared," Freddy said. The first sale was successful, but within weeks, Freddy was arrested.

"It was moms," he said, who came through with a $1,000 fine that saved him from five months in jail.

"After that, I couldn't juggle with heroin any more," he said. "But I got suspended from school because of the bust."

Freddy enrolled in a Manpower Development Training Program in Brooklyn, where he learned metal-working and welding. His certificate shows high marks in the program.

With his mother out of the room, Freddy told of another involvement with the police — a drugstore robbery attempt. He was shot in the leg and spent three days in the prison hospital on Rikers Island.

Failed at 5 Jobs

"I was released after the trial because they couldn't find a roscoe [gun]," he said.

With more difficulty, Freddy talked about how he had "chumped" (failed) through five jobs as a metal worker. He said he was either given tasks requiring more training than he had received or had poor relations with employers who "had hangups either because they thought I was too young or else because I was black. You can tell a racist dude right away."

Salvatore Larga, Freddy's teacher in the manpower-development program, said he could not understand why Freddy had had difficulty, "unless they were trying to hinder him rather than help."

"This boy," Mr. Larga said, "has a real talent for becoming a fine metal worker."

One employer said that he "might have made it with Fred, but he came into the shop when we were having all kinds of problems."

"He was a little immature," said the employer, who asked not to be identified. "But he had a tough foreman, too. Fred had a temper, but I liked him. Unfortunately, we are in business for money."

At another job, Freddy said, he made a mistake while using a metal-bending machine — a mistake he was ashamed of and tried to hide. When it was noted, he said, he was discharged.

Mrs. Shirley Carlisle, a counselor at the Vocational Foundation, 353 Park Avenue near 52nd Street, where Freddy and 3,000 other young people go for morale-boosting:

"There are two sides to the problem of attitudes — employers and employees," she said. "The kids know that employers view them with low esteem. They sometimes react to racism by missing work or coming late. An appearance of self-assertion — a need for recognition — by young people is often misinterpreted to mean militancy or hostility."

"I have high hopes for Freddy," she said. "I see him sitting on the fence right now, but I know he believes in himself, and I know he has a strong degree of personal strength. What he needs is a real opportunity."

James McNamara, director of the city's Manpower and Career Development Agency, said racism was the problem at the heart of all the others, particularly in cases like Freddy's. He said that among 3,386 journeymen members of Local 28, whose members — "the cream of the building tradesmen" — earn as much as $350 a week, only 44 are black or Puerto Rican.

"It's not just disgraceful," he said, "but it's the basis of a lawsuit being prepared by the U.S. District Attorney."

"The 44 figure is right," said Mr. Hill, the N.A.A.C.P. official. "But it includes all nonwhite minorities. Actually, there are only 20 blacks in the union, and the N.A.A.C.P. has fought for 20 years against Local 28 in numerous lawsuits. Twenty black men is what we have to show for it."

Whether a lawsuit will help Freddy Rivers is not clear. He has a criminal record, which barred him from the Marine Corps when he tried to enlist, and it will continue to be a stumbling block to employment.

"Right now," Freddy said, "what I want is a job — a real job that pays you enough money to live."

THE ECONOMIC SITUATION OF BLACK PEOPLE

Firdaus Jhabvala

This selection summarizes many different indicators of racial inequalities in the United States. Whatever the index, as Jhabvala shows, equality will be a long time coming in this country. At the time of writing, the most recent data to which the author had access covered 1973; if anything, more recent data strengthen his case. The selection, drawn from a longer manuscript, is being published for the first time in this book.

Jhabvala formerly taught economics at Lincoln University and now teaches and does economic research at the Technological Institute of Villahermosa in Tabasco, Mexico.

How do we measure the economic status of black people? Our response to this question depends in part upon objective economic facts and in part on our subjective concern. Both objective facts and subjective views tend to change. Before reviewing the facts, it is important to note some of the changes in concern.

In 1960, before the rebellions of the sixties, the President's Commission on National Goals published its report.[1] It did not pay much attention to the problems of black people. Only six pages are devoted to "The Race Problem" in a 372-page report. The report argues that racial prejudice is "ancient." Its principal concern is that the life expectancy at birth of blacks is about seven years less than that of whites due, perhaps, to "the design of negligence." The report adds that "A tremendous economic loss is involved. The working years of a colored person are roughly 12 to 15 percent less than they should be. In terms of the production of goods and services, the growth of the economy, that is a waste we cannot afford."[2] The report says that the economic loss from such actions runs to billions a year, the loss in

human satisfactions is beyond calculation and the political consequences are desperately bad. But the report does not take those consequences seriously enough to explain inequalities or propose solutions.

By 1968, times had changed. With riots occurring in black ghettoes around the country, the Kerner Commission was appointed to study civil disorders. Their report concluded that "white racism is essentially responsible for the explosive mixture which has been accumulating in our cities since the end of World War II."[3] The Commission advocated national reforms in employment, education, the welfare system and housing at the national level together with community programs. The purpose of these programs was to eliminate the possibility of civil disorders. Obviously, the Commission would not have been created if the disorders had not existed. Lyndon Johnson stated that the conditions that breed despair and violence should be attacked "not because we are frightened by conflict, but because we are fired by conscience."[4] But the timing and urgency of the Kerner Commission Report suggest otherwise. The disorders convinced the power structure to take black demands more seriously.

Did the economic situation of black people get significantly better after the "war on poverty" and other programs erected in response to the turbulence? Now that the turbulence is perceived as having passed, several spokesmen have argued that the economic position of black people has improved to the point where a period of tranquility would help middle-class blacks provide effective leadership to the black community. What is needed from the white power structure is a period of benign neglect. Some authors have argued that the majority of blacks are in the middle class, and that the rest will follow. What do the facts say? Have the facts changed, or have whites simply relaxed because times are more quiet?

Source: Extract from "Black People and the American Economic System," an unpublished manuscript. Reprinted with permission of the author.

[1] President's Commission on National Goals, *Goals for Americans,* Prentice-Hall, 1960.

[2] *Ibid.,* p. 43.

[3] National Advisory Commission on Civil Disorders, *Report,* Bantam, 1968, p. 203.

[4] "Address to the Nation," July 27, 1967.

Income

One yardstick used to measure the economic situation of black people is the relationship between the income of black people and that of white people. The earliest numbers that I could find, drawn from a reasonably large survey, are from a study made by the Department of Labor in 1919. The average annual income of the 741 black families in all 12 localities examined was $1,139.49. The average for the 12,096 white families in the 92 localities studied was $1,513.29.[5] The resulting ratio of the two figures is .75.

After suffering serious economic setbacks all through the 1930's, the black position improved substantially during the latter half of World War II. By 1945, the median income of nonwhite families was listed as $1,538 and that of white families $2,718.[6] The ratio is .57. The inflation of 1946 boosted these figures to $1,834 and $3,094 respectively.[7] The ratio of the two figures is .59. During the fifties, the ratio of median nonwhite to median white incomes varied between .51 and .57.[8] Figures for black people are not available. However, later figures indicate that the ratio for black people was probably about two percentage points below that for nonwhites. Thus, the fifties eroded the gains made by blacks during World War II and the relative position of black people declined again.

During the latter half of the sixties, a small rise in the ratio between median incomes of black and white families became apparent. A peak of .61 was reached in 1969 and 1970. Since then, a small and steady decline has reversed the ratio back to .58 in 1973.[9] Do these figures convey a picture of economic progress during the post-War period, or even during this century? No. Nevertheless, even these figures overstate the income received by black people in at least the following four ways.

[5] U.S. Department of Labor, *Monthly Labor Review,* December 1919, p. 39. The one possible defect of this study is that it excluded families in which total earnings were less than 75 per cent of total income.

[6] U.S. Bureau of the Census, *Current Population Reports,* Series P-60, Number 2, March 1948, p. 11.

[7] U.S. Bureau of the Census, *Current Population Reports,* Series P-60, Number 1, January 1948, p. 10.

[8] U.S. Bureau of the Census, "Social and Economic Status of the Black Population in the United States 1973," *Current Population Reports,* Series P-23, Number 48, July 1974, p. 17. (This study will hereinafter be cited as "Black Status 1973.")

[9] *Ibid.,* p. 17.

First, the 1973 ratio of median incomes of black and white families is lower than that of 1946. Further, even if the South is excluded, the 1973 ratio is .60 — 15 percentage points below the figure given earlier for 1919. If we recall that the median ratio improved seven percentage points from 1964 to 1969 and if we attribute this to the Civil Rights Movement, it would take double the effort of the Civil Rights Movement to recover relative black economic losses since 1919.

Second, a comparison of the white and nonwhite distributions of income in 1945 with those of 1973 indicates that the two sets of distributions are comparable. While 11.5% of white families and 33.5% of nonwhite families earned under $1,000 in 1945, 13% of white and 34% of black families earned under $5,000 in 1973. While 19.2% of white and 48.8% of nonwhite families earned under $1,500 in 1945, 22% of white and 48% of black families earned under $7,000 in 1973. Likewise, while 31.1% of white and 63.2% of nonwhite families earned under $2,000 in 1945, 37% of white and 65% of black families earned under $10,000 in 1973. Thus, the two distributions are similar in both years. Therefore, the economic position of black people relative to that of white people has remained frozen in the post-War period.[10]

Third, black families are significantly larger. In 1970, the average size of the black family was 4.3; that of the white family was 3.5.[11] Thus, the average black family was about 23% larger in size. In making comparisons between black and white *people,* we must deflate the incomes of black families 23%. Thus, the average income of the median black family member would be only about 47% of his or her white counterpart's income.

Finally, several concepts and methods used to collect and present the data give a rosier picture than the true situation. Income data for unrelated individuals are not presented in the latest annual statistics of black people. However, 840,000 blacks and 4.1 million whites are listed as low-income un-

[10] The 1945 distributions are taken from *Current Population Reports,* Series P-60, Number 2, *op. cit.,* p. 11. The 1973 distributions are taken from "Black Status 1973," *op. cit.,* p. 19.

[11] U.S. Bureau of the Census, "Social and Economic Status of the Black Population in the United States 1971," *Current Population Reports,* Series P-23, Number 42, July 1972, p. 44. (This study will hereinafter be cited as "Black Status 1971.")

related individuals in 1970.[12] Ashenfelter has noted that part of the increase in income of black people in the mid-sixties is probably statistical and not real.[13] Likewise, large numbers of blacks go uncounted. For example, in the 1960 Census, it was estimated that while 2.8% of the white population were not enumerated, 10.9% of the nonwhite population were left out.[14] Since the 1970 Census was conducted largely by mail,[15] the inclusion of poor people without addresses is unlikely in the census. Since blacks predominate proportionately more among the poor, statistics tend to undercount poor blacks and thus overstate the position of all blacks.

My conclusion from examining income statistics is that the relative economic position of black people in the long run has stayed the same. Government data simply do not support the rhetoric of economic improvement. The black person standing in the middle of blacks earns about half as much as the white person in a similar position. This has been true for a long, long time.

If there is a recent change in the economic position of black people, it is downwards both relatively and absolutely. The percentage of black families earning less than $5,000 (in 1973 dollars) rose from 32% in 1969 to 34% in 1973. Over the same period, the median real income of black families *fell* $11 while that of white families rose $726.[16] In fact, in 1973, the median income of black families was only $306 ahead of that of white families in 1946 if the former is adjusted for inflation.[17] This minute difference evaporates when we consider the increased taxes upon present-day blacks. Thus, blacks are receiving less income today than did whites almost thirty years ago.

Why are blacks so far behind whites and not catching up? One important reason is the plight of the black worker: his/her occupation and the extent of unemployment in the black community.

Occupation and Employment

Black people are mostly engaged in lower-paying occupations. They are underrepresented among white-collar and farm workers, proportionally represented among blue-collar workers, and overrepresented among service workers. Within each broad group, they are underrepresented in the upper levels. Thus, in 1973, within the white-collar group, they comprised only 1.4% of engineers but 8.0% of clerical workers. Blacks formed 3.1% of farmers but 12.3% of farm laborers and supervisors. In the blue-collar groups, 6.3% of craft and kindred workers but 19% of nonfarm laborers were black. And among service workers, blacks formed 37.6% of the more low-paid private household workers and 16.6% of the marginally better-paid non-private household workers.[18]

Within occupations, blacks are underrepresented in higher-paying industries. For example, in a survey of nine industries with high average hourly earnings in 1970, only 3% of blacks held higher-paid jobs, although 20% of all jobs were in this category.[19] Likewise, the federal government reflects private employment practices. Thus, in May 1973, blacks formed 21.9% of the GS-1 to GS-4 group and 2.5% of the GS-16 to GS-18 group. Blacks comprised 34.3% of the WS-1 to WS-6 Regular Supervisory group and 0.3% of the WS-16 to WS-19 group.[20]

In fact, blacks have still not caught up with whites before the Great Depression in terms of occupations. For instance, a comparison of the black labor force in 1973 with the national labor force of 1920 reveals that there were relatively more blacks working as service workers and nonfarm laborers in 1973 than there were unskilled workers in the national labor force of 1920.[21]

Another way to measure occupational inequalities between blacks and white is to look at unem-

---

12 "Black Status 1971," *op. cit.*, p. 47.

13 Orley Ashenfelter, "Changes in Labor Market Discrimination Over Time," *Journal of Human Resources,* Fall 1970.

14 National Academy of Sciences, "America's Uncounted People," *Report of the Advisory Committee on Problems of Census Enumeration,* Washington, D.C., 1972, p. 28. Estimates also show fewer nonwhites (30%) being subsequently found in households than whites (70%). *Ibid.,* p. 29.

15 "Black Status 1973," *op. cit.*, p. 140.

16 *Ibid.,* p. 19.

17 The 1973 income of black families is adjusted for inflation according to the Consumer Price Index.

18 "Black Status 1973," *op. cit.*, p. 56, provides all the data in this paragraph.

19 "Black Status 1971," *op. cit.*, p. 70.

20 "Black Status 1973," *op. cit.*, p. 58.

21 The 1973 distribution for blacks is taken from "Black Status 1973," *op. cit.*, p. 56, and the 1920 distribution of occupations from U.S. Department of Labor, *Monthly Labor Review,* June 1938, p. 1391.

ployment rates. Since World War II, the unemployment rate for blacks has been about twice the rate for whites. The lowest ratio listed between the unemployment rates for blacks and whites is 1.6 in 1949. The highest is 2.3 in 1956.[22] Currently, the ratio is 2.0. In December 1974, 12.8% of the nonwhite labor force was reported unemployed, whereas the unemployment rate for whites was given as 6.4%.[23] The nonwhite figure is the highest at least since 1948.[24]

Blacks are likely to be unemployed longer than whites. In 1972, of those unemployed, 41% of the nonwhites were unemployed 15 weeks or more. The figure for whites was 33%. Blacks have more spells of unemployment. In 1972, 20% of the nonwhite labor force had more than two spells of unemployment. The figure for whites was 16%. The precarious situation of the black labor force is also evinced in the number of blacks taking turns being unemployed: 22% of the black labor force was unemployed at some time during 1972. The corresponding figure for the white labor force was 15.%[25]

The conclusion is that blacks are in low-paying occupations, are twice as likely to be unemployed, for longer periods of time, and more often. That is, blacks generally have awful jobs when they chance to have them. Why do blacks tend to have the inferior jobs of this society and figure prominently among the unemployed? The answer most often provided is that they lack the educational skills needed to secure society's good jobs. Is this true?

Education

The difference between blacks and whites as measured by the median years of schooling has been narrowing. In 1890, the difference was 6.5 years. In 1970, it was only 0.5 years.[26] This statistic is often suggested as an indicator of diminishing inequality in education. Are educational inequalities disappearing? No. Other factors, such as the kinds of colleges people graduate from, are more relevant in-

dices of contemporary educational inequality. These factors, rather than high school education, determine who goes into higher-paying occupations. The idea of what constitutes a good education has changed over time. Therefore, schooling statistics are obsolete and misleading when considering how many blacks receive a good education. These statistics are more relevant as indices of basic verbal and quantitative skills — reading, writing and arithmetic.

In 1970, 44.4% of all black college students attended predominantly black colleges.[27] Perhaps 30% of black college students attended two-year colleges in October 1971.[28] The educational standing of a college depends largely upon the money it can command. These colleges have puny endowments and are often at the mercy of local legislators for their very survival. Therefore, they are the weakest colleges in the land, at the bottom of the heap. Since junior colleges and black colleges provide an inferior curriculum, facilities and environment — these are the very colleges with high drop-out rates. For example, Monroe claims that "Many of the larger community colleges would be fortunate to have 30 per cent of the freshman class return for the second year. Fifty per cent returnees is a high figure." [29] Figures for black students in these colleges are even lower. Thus, the inevitable result is that far fewer blacks complete college. In fact, in 1971, fewer blacks, 25 to 34 years old, both absolutely and relative to whites, had completed four years of college than whites, when compared with 1960. Naturally, the percentage gap widened from 7.4 in 1960 to 10.9 in 1971.[30]

When blacks do complete college, they tend to be concentrated in low-paying fields. Often entry into high-paying areas is impossible because the college attended does not provide the necessary training. Black students often find themselves in such colleges because they have been tracked into the vocations while in high school. The result of these processes is that large numbers of educated blacks go into fields such as education, usually not high-paying. All these factors make education less

[22] "Black Status 1971," op. cit., p. 52.

[23] U.S. Department of Labor, *Monthly Business Statistics,* January 10, 1975, p. 4.

[24] U.S. Department of Labor, *Handbook of Labor Statistics,* 1974, Bureau of Labor Statistics Bulletin 182, p. 143.

[25] "Black Status 1973," op. cit., p. 62.

[26] Cited in M. Reich, "Racial Discrimination and the White Distribution of Income," Ph.D. dissertation, Harvard University, 1973.

[27] "Black Status 1971," op. cit., p. 88.

[28] U.S. Bureau of the Census, "Social and Economic Characteristics of Students, October 1971," *Current Population Reports,* Series P-20, Number 241, October 1972, p. 2.

[29] Charles Monroe, *Profile of the Community College,* Jossey-Bass 1972, p. 208.

[30] "Black Status 1971," op. cit., p. 84.

useful to blacks in terms of increased income. The more blacks are educated, the less they earn proportionately.[31] This means that there is more inequality among the elite than the hoi polloi. The result of persistent inequality in higher education is that blacks continue to be channeled into low-paying occupations. The inequality in higher education is undoubtedly due largely to the schools that blacks graduate from.

The schools attended by blacks suffer from all the problems of being located in ghetto neighborhoods. On balance, these schools are not as well funded as others. Learning in the ghetto is mostly outside the classroom. This shows up in at least four statistics: the number of years that black students are behind the most common grade level for their age, drop-out rates, young people who are not high school graduates, or the employment of young high school graduates.

First, in 1971, 14.3% of male Negroes, 14 to 17 years old, were two or more years below the modal grade. The corresponding percentage for white males was 5.4. Figures for females were 9.7 and 3.1% respectively for the two groups.[32] Second, in 1971, 11.6% of black males and 10.5% of black females were high school dropouts among persons 14 to 19 years old. The percentages for white males and females were 6.9 and 7.8 respectively.[33] In 1970, with more jobs available, the differences were even wider. Third, in 1970, 57% of the black males 16 to 21 years old not attending school were not high school graduates. The figure for whites is 38%. Finally, among high school graduates in this last age group, the unemployment rate for blacks was 28%. The rate for whites was 16%.[34] Why do blacks fare so badly in education?

The immediate answer to this question is that they live in poor neighborhoods. How do we know this? If we look at indices of housing and health, we see the yawning gaps between blacks and whites.

Housing

Where do black people live? Mostly in central cities. In 1960, 56% of all black housing units occupied year-round were in central cities. By 1970, this per-

centage had risen to over 61. Meanwhile, housing for whites in central cities fell from 34% of all housing for whites in 1960 to 31% in 1970.[35] Thus, the percentage of blacks in the central cities keeps rising.

Within the central cities, blacks are heavily concentrated in low-income areas. In 1970, in each of the 24 cities with the highest concentrations of black people, blacks formed at least 50% of the population in low-income areas. In the nation's capital, they comprised 93% of the residents of low-income areas. Thus, in the cities, blacks comprise the bulk of the poor.[36]

What kind of housing do black people have? One index of the quality of housing is the availability of complete plumbing facilities. In 1970, while 5% of white housing lacked some or all plumbing facilities, 17% of Negro housing was this way.[37] In 1970, the median value of Negro housing was $10,700; for houses occupied by whites, it was $17,400.[38] The degree of overcrowding or serious overcrowding (defined as more than 1 and more than 1.5 persons per room respectively) of Negroes varies from 2.5 to 8 times as much as that for non-Negroes.[39]

Households of black people are less likely to have appliances. For instance, in 1970, while only 3% of Negro households had dishwashers, 49% of white households did.[40] Moreover, in 1970, blacks were less likely (42%) than white (65%) to own the houses they resided in.[41] All the problems of residence are exacerbated by the diminished mobility of black people. For example, in 1970, while 15% of white households had no automobile, 43% of black households did not have an automobile.[42] The conclusion is that black people are likely to be more crowded into more dilapidated houses which they are less likely to own, located in worse neighborhoods from which they are less able to move than white people.

The kind of neighborhood in which black people live affects them in several ways. The dehumanizing qualities of such neighborhoods — especially fear and humiliation — are reflected in what appears to the middle-class observer as pathological behavior.

[31] Herman Miller, *Income Distribution in the United States*, U.S. Bureau of the Census, 1966, p. 165.

[32] "Black Status 1971," *op. cit.*, p. 80.

[33] *Ibid.*, p. 81.

[34] *Ibid.*, p. 82.

[35] "Black Status 1973," *op. cit.*, p. 109.

[36] *Ibid.*, p. 131.

[37] "Black Status 1971," *op. cit.*, p. 94.

[38] *Ibid.*, p. 95.

[39] *Ibid.*, p. 96.

[40] *Ibid.*, p. 97.

[41] *Ibid.*, p. 92.

[42] *Ibid.*, p. 97.

In truth, it is the best response of an experienced individual to a hostile environment. In such an atmosphere, the rearing of children in accordance with the laws of an alien, white society becomes impossible. The shattered lives of most ghetto teenagers bear testimony to this fact. In order to "succeed," these teenagers will have to accept and absorb the values and mores of the white world outside and develop patterns of speech, dress, thought, and mannerisms which are foreign to them. If all this works out, then they must hope that their employer does not regard the color of their skin as a significant variable.

The fact of widespread segregation in housing patterns together with laws that favor ghetto landlords and merchants forces black people to pay more rent and other expenses than others. For example, the Kerner Commission felt that blacks paid a color tax of at least 10% in order to secure housing.[43] This continuous drain on their meager resources prevents ghetto people from getting a dollar's worth for a dollar spent. Dilapidated neighborhoods are a menace to mind and body. It is hard to develop as a human being to one's full potential in these neighborhoods. The overall effect of ghetto housing is to add another burden upon the shoulders of poor black people.

Health

Another reflection of the awful neighborhoods in which black people live is the health of these communities. When we consider the health indices of black people, a familiar scene emerges: these are usually twenty or more years behind those of white people. Thus infant mortality under 28 days, from 28 days to eleven months, and under one year, were all higher for nonwhite babies in 1972 than the corresponding rates for white babies in 1950.[44] The expectation of life at birth for nonwhite males in 1971 was actually less than it was in 1959–61. Over this period, the difference in life expectancy at birth between white and nonwhite males widened from 6.1 years to 7.1 years.[45] The nonwhite figure is lower than that for white males in 1940.[46] The median

weight of the nonwhite baby is seven ounces less than that of the white baby.[47] The number of visits to the physician and dentist by nonwhites are significantly less than by whites for similar income levels. When they do visit physicians, nonwhites are much more likely to use hospital clinics than whites.[48] In general, while the physical indices of well-being of white people are near those of the Scandinavian countries, these same indices for black people are closer to those of a "developing" country.

An increasing body of literature links several forms of birth defects to the amount and quality of nutrition received by the mother. This is correlated with family income which black people do not have enough of. Thus, the health of black children is seriously affected by the economic position of black families. Among others, Hurley establishes a causal relationship between poverty and mental retardation.[49] Similarly, nonwhites are the victims of physical crime more often mostly because they live in more dilapidated neighborhoods. The tough situation faced by nonwhites can be seen in the following statistics: in 1971, homicide accounted for 81.6 deaths per 100,000 of the nonwhite male population. The corresponding figure for white males was 7.9. Similarly, death by all causes for nonwhite males actually rose from 1,238.2 per 100,000 of population in 1965 to 1,257.7 in 1971. In the same years, the rate for white males fell from 909.3 to 874.9. In fact, in 1971, of the several causes of death, nonwhites had higher death rates than whites in every category listed except Arteriosclerosis and Suicide.[50]

Indifferent and hostile lawmen, poor medical treatment, inadequate food of quality, and unprotected neighborhoods all make nonwhites more susceptible to death. In such a situation, life creates fear and alienation from one's surroundings which themselves become contributing factors to the deterioration of life in the neighborhood. Like the other factors examined in this section, the housing and health of black people contribute to trapping them in poverty.

[43] National Advisory Commission on Civil Disorders, *Report, op. cit.,* p. 471.

[44] "Black Status 1973," *op. cit.,* p. 16.

[45] *Ibid.,* p. 113.

[46] U.S. Bureau of the Census, *Statistical Abstract of the United States,* 1972, p. 55.

[47] *Ibid.,* p. 51.

[48] Harold Vatter and Thomas Palm, eds., *The Economics of Black America,* Harcourt Brace Jovanovich, 1972, pp. 171–173.

[49] Rodger Hurley, *Poverty and Mental Retardation,* Vintage Books, 1969.

[50] "Black Status 1973," *op. cit.,* p. 115.

The Vicious Cycle

Black people have lower incomes than whites. This is the result of low-paying occupations and worse employment conditions than those of white people. In turn, this is because blacks do not graduate from respectable educational institutions. They do not enter respectable educational institutions because they come from inferior schools. But these schools are located in awful neighborhoods. Black people live in awful neighborhoods because they do not have the income to move to better ones. In other words, blacks are caught in a vicious cycle reinforced over and over again by a lack of income. All these factors — income, employment, occupation, education, housing, health — are influenced by capital. In a capitalist society, groups without capital are deprived of all the things that capital can procure. The goal of a capitalist society is to accumulate capital. How much capital do blacks own?

Wealth

Terrel lists the average net wealth of black families in 1967 as $3,779 and that of white families as $20,153. The resulting ratio is 18.8%.[51] Even this figure overstates the black position, since a relatively larger fraction of the assets of blacks are nonfinancial. Becker guessed that total black ownership of capital was about 1/150 of that of white ownership.[52] Soltow has projected the growth of the average wealth of whites and nonwhites. His conclusion is that "The nonwhite level in 1962 was still behind that of whites in 1870. Equation values at age 50 for these levels were $1,180 and $3,080 . . . . it would be near the year 2000 before nonwhites would have the level of whites at the end of the Civil War. The reader may think this is preposterous. Recall that the nonwhite mark today is still not that of whites 93 years ago."[53]

If the existing distribution of wealth remained the same, blacks would be continually deprived of the earnings of wealth. How much would black peo-

ple earn if there were no racism and the current distribution of wealth? If blacks could magically attain the status of white people in all economic matters, but owned only 20% of the wealth per capita of whites, the maximum ratio of average black to white incomes would be about 78%.

I derive this figure assuming that 10% of the earning population is black and 90% white, and that three-fourths of output accrues to wage and salary earners and a fourth to property owners. Then, of every $100 of income, $75 would go to wage earners. Black people, sharing equally here, would receive 10% of $75 or $7.50. Of the remaining $25 received by property owners, black people would receive only 2% or $0.50. Their total income from both sources would be $8. White people would receive the remaining $92. Of every 100 people, 10 would be black. Therefore, the income per capita of these 10 black people would be $8/10 or $0.80. Similarly, the income per capita of the white people would be $92/90 or $1.02. Therefore, the ratio of average black/white incomes would be 0.80/1.02 or 78%. Thus, under racially utopian but economically capitalist conditions, the maximum that black people would earn would be less than four-fifths of average white incomes.

Under capitalism, those who own capital call the tune. Black people own less than 2% of the capital of the U.S. Therefore, they have less than 2% of the "system." Of course, this is an extremely marginal share. Black people are marginal to the capitalist system. All the data I have presented in this section back up this statement.

Summary

In this section, I have presented the economic situation of black people. An approximate summary balance sheet of the distance in time that blacks as a group are behind whites is:

Index	Approximate Time That Blacks Are Behind Whites
Income	30 years
Employment	50 years or more
Education	over 20 years
Housing	20 to 30 years
Health	from 20 to 30 years
Wealth	over 100 years

[51] H. S. Terrel, "Wealth Accumulation of Black and White Families: The Empirical Evidence," *Journal of Finance,* May 1971.

[52] Gary Becker, *The Economics of Discrimination,* Univ. of Chicago Press, 1957, p. 20.

[53] Lee Soltow, "A Century of Personal Wealth Accumulation," in Vatter and Palm, eds., *The Economics of Black America, op. cit.,* p. 84.

This does not imply that blacks are catching up. The time lag between blacks and whites has remained the same at least since World War II and probably earlier. The gap could become wide as in the last few years. Comparisons of blacks over time neglect the dynamic aspects of social change. Such studies reveal their segregationist bias when they say: "Look how far blacks have come since slavery or 1948. Don't ask about the white position during the same time." However, the relevant economic comparisons for black people are with white people. Today's blacks do not live among the blacks of 1948 or the Civil War. They live among whites. This is why I make relevant comparisons between blacks and whites over time. Other comparisons are largely irrelevant.

HAS DISCRIMINATION DECLINED?

Editor's Supplement

Many conservatives and liberals argue that racial conditions are improving all the time. Counseling patience, they suggest that discrimination against blacks is declining. Although they admit that discrimination has wrought deep differentials between blacks and whites, they see the silver lining of improvement in all the dreary statistics. "The movement of the Negro up the class scale," in Edward Banfield's words, "appears as inexorable as that of all other groups." [1]

Has discrimination declined?

Discrimination refers to a relative condition. It does not focus on the absolute conditions that blacks experience. Rather, it compares their experiences with some group that does not suffer discrimination. In the United States, this usually involves comparisons between blacks and whites.

There are many ways of comparing the economic conditions of blacks and whites. One of the simplest and most comprehensive involves comparing outcomes in the economy. If blacks earn less than whites, on average, this means that they are suffering the results of either present or past discrimination. If those inequalities persist over time, that means that — no matter how much discrimination may "appear" to have diminished — blacks continue to experience the same unequal outcomes as before.

This kind of comparison can be pursued for several different indices of economic outcome: median incomes, unemployment rates, and incidence of poverty. In Table 1, the three columns present trends in these basic comparisons over time. Column 1 traces the ratio of black median family income to white median family income. Column 2 charts the ratio of the black unemployment rate to the white unemployment rate. And Column 3 records the ratio of the percentage of blacks who are poor to the percentage of whites who are poor. One might infer that "discrimination was declining" if (a) the ratio of median incomes increased in Column 1, indicating that median black incomes were rising relative to whites; and/or (b) that the ratio of unemployment rates in Column 2 declined, indicating that average black unemployment rates were falling relative to white rates; and/or (c) that the ratio of poverty incidence in Column 3 decreased, indicating that the incidence of poverty among blacks was declining relative to that among whites.

By and large, it appears that none of these indices confirms impressions that discrimination is declining to any great degree. Blacks' median incomes have slightly increased, relative to white median incomes; relative unemployment rates have remained roughly constant; and relative poverty incidence has, if anything, increased.

These are aggregate figures. We have reason to think that some of these variables might change over the business cycle. For instance, it is com-

[1] Edward Banfield, *The Unheavenly City Revisited* (Boston: Little, Brown, 1974), p. 96.

TABLE 1. Racial Inequality Over Time, 1950–1973

Year	1 Black Income White Income	2 Black Unemployment White Unemployment	3 Black Poverty White Poverty
1950	.54	1.8	n.a.
1951	.53	1.7	n.a.
1952	.57	1.9	n.a.
1953	.56	1.7	n.a.
1954	.56	2.0	n.a.
1955	.55	2.2	n.a.
1956	.53	2.3	n.a.
1957	.54	2.1	n.a.
1958	.51	2.1	n.a.
1959	.54	2.2	2.9
1960	.55	2.1	3.1
1961	.53	2.1	3.2
1962	.53	2.2	3.4
1963	.53	2.2	3.3
1964	.56	2.1	3.3
1965	.55	2.0	3.5
1966	.60	2.2	3.5
1967	.62	2.2	3.4
1968	.63	2.1	3.4
1969	.63	2.1	3.3
1970	.64	2.0	3.2
1971	.63	1.8	3.1
1972	.62	2.0	3.5
1973	.60	2.1	3.5
1974	.62	2.0	3.3

Col. 1: Median Black Family Income/Median White Family Income
Col. 2: % of Black Labor Force Unemployed/% of White Labor Force Unemployed
Col. 3: % of Black Population Living in Poverty/% of White Population Living in Poverty

Sources: Cols. 1 and 3 from U.S. Bureau of the Census, "The Social and Economic Status of the Black Population in the U.S., 1974," *Current Population Reports,* Series P-23, Number 54, July 1975, pp. 25 and 42 respectively.

Col. 2 from *Manpower Report of the President,* 1974 (Washington D.C.: U.S. Government Printing Office, 1975), p. 230.

monly said that blacks are "last hired, first fired." During boom periods, this would mean that many more blacks were being "last hired" than usual. This would mean, in turn, that the suddenly increasing demand for black labor would be pushing their median incomes up relative to white workers. Indeed, as Column 1 shows, this index of relative incomes rose rapidly during the boom years of the mid-1960s.

There are statistical techniques with which one can control for these variations over the business cycle. Controlling for the effect of the cycle, one might get an even more accurate measure of the underlying changes in "discrimination" over time. Several recent attempts to perform this statistical analysis seem to come to the same conclusion.[2] Reviewing both the data and those studies, economist

[2] See, for instance, Orley Ashenfelter, "Changes in Labor Market Discrimination Over Time," *Journal of Human Resources,* Fall 1970; and Michael Reich, "Racism and the White Distribution of Income," Ph.D. dissertation, Harvard University, 1973, Chapter 2.

Lester Thurow concluded in 1975: "Nothing has changed in the past 30 years. No progress has been made." [3]

Some reach different conclusions. It is possible to look at the experiences of particular groups of blacks and sustain more favorable impressions. Blacks graduating from college, for instance, seem to be faring much better, relative to whites, than they did be-

[3] Quoted in *The New York Times,* November 30, 1975.

fore. [4] Middle-class blacks considerably improved their circumstances during the 1960's. [5]

But the aggregate data return to shadow those more partial results. Blacks as a group appear to experience as much inequality today, in the end, as they did at the end of World War II. Has discrimination been declining? These data suggest that it has not.

[4] See some summary data in Richard Freeman, "Changes in the Labor Market for Black Americans, 1948/1972," *Brookings Papers in Economic Activity,* 1973, Number 1.

[5] For some of these favorable conclusions, see Thomas Sowell, *Race and Economics* (New York: McKay, 1975).

DISCRIMINATION AND THE FREE MARKET

Milton Friedman

Friedman develops here the core of the conservative approach to racial discrimination. He makes two main points. First, the free market creates pressures that chip away at discrimination. Second, the government should not impose compulsory antidiscriminatory policies upon the free market.

This selection comes from Friedman's classic book, *Capitalism and Freedom.*

Friedman is one of the most eminent economists in the United States. He teaches at the University of Chicago, has written numerous books and articles, and writes a regular column for *Newsweek.*

It is a striking historical fact that the development of capitalism has been accompanied by a major reduction in the extent to which particular religious, racial, or social groups have operated under special handicaps in respect of their economic activities; have, as the saying goes, been discriminated against. The substitution of contract arrangements for status ar-

rangements was the first step toward the freeing of the serfs in the Middle Ages. The preservation of Jews through the Middle Ages was possible because of the existence of a market sector in which they could operate and maintain themselves despite official persecution. Puritans and Quakers were able to migrate to the New World because they could accumulate the funds to do so in the market despite disabilities imposed on them in other aspects of their life. The Southern states after the Civil War took many measures to impose legal restrictions on Negroes. One measure which was never taken on any scale was the establishment of barriers to the ownership of either real or personal property. The failure to impose such barriers clearly did not reflect any special concern to avoid restrictions on Negroes. It reflected rather, a basic belief in private property which was so strong that it overrode the desire to discriminate against Negroes. The maintenance of the general rules of private property and of capitalism have been a major source of opportunity for Negroes and have permitted them to make greater progress than they otherwise could have made. To take a more general example, the preserves of discrimination in any society are the areas that are most monopolistic in character, whereas discrimination against groups of particular color or religion is least in those areas where there is the greatest freedom of competition.

As pointed out in chapter 1 [of Friedman's book], one of the paradoxes of experience is that, in spite of this historical evidence, it is precisely the minority groups that have frequently furnished the most vocal and most numerous advocates of fundamental alterations in a capitalist society. They have tended to attribute to capitalism the residual restrictions they experience rather than to recognize that the free market has been the major factor enabling these restrictions to be as small as they are.

We have already seen how a free market separates economic efficiency from irrelevant characteristics. As noted in chapter 1, the purchaser of bread does not know whether it was made from wheat grown by a white man or a Negro, by a Christian or a Jew. In consequence, the producer of wheat is in a position to use resources as effectively as he can, regardless of what the attitudes of the community may be toward the color, the religion, or other characteristics of the people he hires. Furthermore, and perhaps more important, there is an economic incentive in a free market to separate economic efficiency from other characteristics of the individual. A businessman or an entrepreneur who expresses preferences in his business activities that are not related to productive efficiency is at a disadvantage compared to other individuals who do not. Such an individual is in effect imposing higher costs on himself than are other individuals who do not have such preferences. Hence, in a free market they will tend to drive him out.

This same phenomenon is of much wider scope. It is often taken for granted that the person who discriminates against others because of their race, religion, color, or whatever, incurs no costs by doing so but simply imposes costs on others. This view is on a par with the very similar fallacy that a country does not hurt itself by imposing tariffs on the products of other countries.[1] Both are equally wrong. The man who objects to buying from or working

alongside a Negro, for example, thereby limits his range of choice. He will generally have to pay a higher price for what he buys or receive a lower return for his work. Or, put the other way, those of us who regard color of skin or religion as irrelevant can buy some things more cheaply as a result.

As these comments perhaps suggest, there are real problems in defining and interpreting discrimination. The man who exercises discrimination pays a price for doing so. He is, as it were, "buying" what he regards as a "product." It is hard to see that discrimination can have any meaning other than a "taste" of others that one does not share. We do not regard it as "discrimination" — or at least not in the same invidious sense — if an individual is willing to pay a higher price to listen to one singer than to another, although we do if he is willing to pay a higher price to have services rendered to him by a person of one color than by a person of another. The difference between the two cases is that in the one case we share the taste, and in the other case we do not. Is there any difference in principle between the taste that leads a householder to prefer an attractive servant to an ugly one and the taste that leads another to prefer a Negro to a white or a white to a Negro, except that we sympathize and agree with the one taste and may not with the other? I do not mean to say that all tastes are equally good. On the contrary, I believe strongly that the color of a man's skin or the religion of his parents is, by itself, no reason to treat him differently; that a man should be judged by what he is and what he does and not by these external characteristics. I deplore what seem to me the prejudice and narrowness of outlook of those whose tastes differ from mine in this respect and I think the less of them for it. But in a society based on free discussion, the appropriate recourse is for me to seek to persuade them that their tastes are bad and that they should change their views and their behavior, not to use coercive power to enforce my tastes and my attitudes on others.

Fair Employment Practices Legislation

Fair employment practice commissions that have the task of preventing "discrimination" in employment by reason of race, color, or religion have been established in a number of states. Such legislation clearly involves interference with the freedom of individuals to enter into voluntary contracts with one another.

---

[1] In a brilliant and penetrating analysis of some economic issues involved in discrimination, Gary Becker demonstrates that the problem of discrimination is almost identical in its logical structure with that of foreign trade and tariffs. See G. S. Becker, *The Economics of Discrimination* (Chicago: University of Chicago Press, 1957).

It subjects any such contract to approval or disapproval by the state. Thus it is directly an interference with freedom of the kind that we would object to in most other contexts. Moreover, as is true with most other interferences with freedom, the individuals subjected to the law may well not be those whose actions even the proponents of the law wish to control.

For example, consider a situation in which there are grocery stores serving a neighborhood inhabited by people who have a strong aversion to being waited on by Negro clerks. Suppose one of the grocery stores has a vacancy for a clerk and the first applicant qualified in other respects happens to be a Negro. Let us suppose that as a result of the law the store is required to hire him. The effect of this action will be to reduce the business done by this store and to impose losses on the owner. If the preference of the community is strong enough, it may even cause the store to close. When the owner of the store hires white clerks in preference to Negroes in the absence of the law, he may not be expressing any preference or prejudice or taste of his own. He may simply be transmitting the tastes of the community. He is, as it were, producing the services for the consumers that the consumers are willing to pay for. Nonetheless, he is harmed, and indeed may be the only one harmed appreciably, by a law which prohibits him from engaging in this activity, that is, prohibits him from pandering to the tastes of the community for having a white rather than a Negro clerk. The consumers, whose preferences the law is intended to curb, will be affected substantially only to the extent that the number of stores is limited and hence they must pay higher prices because one store has gone out of business. This analysis can be generalized. In a very large fraction of cases, employers are transmitting the preference of either their customers or their other employees when they adopt employment policies that treat factors irrelevant to technical physical productivity as relevant to employment. Indeed, employers typically have an incentive, as noted earlier, to try to find ways of getting around the preferences of their consumers or of their employees if such preferences impose higher costs upon them.

The proponents of FEPC argue that interference with the freedom of individuals to enter into contracts with one another with respect to employment is justified because the individual who refuses to hire a Negro instead of a white, when both are equally qualified in terms of physical productive capacity, is harming others, namely, the particular color or religious group whose employment opportunity is limited in the process. This argument involves a serious confusion between two very different kinds of harm. One kind is the positive harm that one individual does another by physical force, or by forcing him to enter into a contract without his consent. An obvious example is the man who hits another over the head with a blackjack. A less obvious example is stream pollution discussed in chapter 2. The second kind is the negative harm that occurs when two individuals are unable to find mutually acceptable contracts, as when I am unwilling to buy something that someone wants to sell me and therefore make him worse off than he would be if I bought the item. If the community at large has a preference for blues singers rather than for opera singers, they are certainly increasing the economic well-being of the first relative to the second. If a potential blues singer can find employment and a potential opera singer cannot, this simply means that the blues singer is rendering services which the community regards as worth paying for whereas the potential opera singer is not. The potential opera singer is "harmed" by the community's taste. He would be better off and the blues singer "harmed" if the tastes were the reverse. Clearly, this kind of harm does not involve any involuntary exchange or an imposition of costs or granting of benefits to third parties. There is a strong case for using government to prevent one person from imposing positive harm, which is to say, to prevent coercion. There is no case whatsoever for using government to avoid the negative kind of "harm." On the contrary, such government intervention reduces freedom and limits voluntary co-operation.

FEPC legislation involves the acceptance of a principle that proponents would find abhorrent in almost every other application. If it is appropriate for the state to say that individuals may not discriminate in employment because of color or race or religion, then it is equally appropriate for the state, provided a majority can be found to vote that way, to say that individuals must discriminate in employment on the basis of color, race or religion. The Hitler Nuremberg laws and the laws in the Southern states imposing special disabilities upon Negroes are both examples of laws similar in principle to FEPC. Opponents of such laws who are in favor of FEPC cannot argue that there is anything wrong with them in principle, that they involve a kind of state action that ought not to be permitted. They can only argue that the particular criteria used are irrelevant. They can only seek to persuade other men that they should use other criteria instead of these.

If one takes a broad sweep of history and looks at the kind of things that the majority will be persuaded of if each individual case is to be decided on its merits rather than as part of a general principle, there can be little doubt that the effect of a widespread acceptance of the appropriateness of government action in this area would be extremely undesirable, even from the point of view of those who at the moment favor FEPC. If, at the moment, the proponents of FEPC are in a position to make their views effective, it is only because of a constitutional and federal situation in which a regional majority in one part of the country may be in a position to impose its views on a majority in another part of the country.

As a general rule, any minority that counts on specific majority action to defend its interests is short-sighted in the extreme. Acceptance of a general self-denying ordinance applying to a class of cases may inhibit specific majorities from exploiting specific minorities. In the absence of such a self-denying ordinance, majorities can surely be counted on to use their power to give effect to their preferences, or if you will, prejudices, not to protect minorities from the prejudices of majorities.

To put the matter in another and perhaps more striking way, consider an individual who believes that the present pattern of tastes is undesirable and who believes that Negroes have less opportunity than he would like to see them have. Suppose he puts his beliefs into practice by always choosing the Negro applicant for a job whenever there are a number of applicants more or less equally qualified in other respects. Under present circumstances should he be prevented from doing so? Clearly the logic of the FEPC is that he should be.

The counterpart to fair employment in the area where these principles have perhaps been worked out more than any other, namely, the area of speech, is "fair speech" rather than free speech. In this respect the position of the American Civil Liberties Union seems utterly contradictory. It favors both free speech and fair employment laws. One way to state the justification for free speech is that we do not believe that it is desirable that momentary majorities decide what at any moment shall be regarded as appropriate speech. We want a free market in

ideas, so that ideas get a chance to win majority or near-unanimous acceptance, even if initially held only by a few. Precisely the same considerations apply to employment or more generally to the market for goods and services. Is it any more desirable that momentary majorities decide what characteristics are relevant to employment than what speech is appropriate? Indeed, can a free market in ideas long be maintained if a free market in goods and services is destroyed? The ACLU will fight to the death to protect the right of a racist to preach on a street corner the doctrine of racial segregation. But it will favor putting him in jail if he acts on his principles by refusing to hire a Negro for a particular job.

As already stressed, the appropriate recourse of those of us who believe that a particular criterion such as color is irrelevant is to persuade our fellows to be of like mind, not to use the coercive power of the state to force them to act in accordance with our principles. Of all groups, the ACLU should be the first both to recognize and proclaim that this is so. . . .

Segregation in Schooling

Segregation in schooling raises a particular problem not covered by the previous comments for one reason only. The reason is that schooling is, under present circumstances, primarily operated and administered by government. This means that government must make an explicit decision. It must either enforce segregation or enforce integration. Both seem to me bad solutions. Those of us who believe that color of skin is an irrelevant characteristic and that it is desirable for all to recognize this, yet who also believe in individual freedom, are therefore faced with a dilemma. If one must choose between the evils of enforced segregation or enforced integration, I myself would find it impossible not to choose integration.

The preceding chapter, written initially without any regard at all to the problem of segregation or integration, gives the appropriate solution that permits the avoidance of both evils — a nice illustration of how arrangements designed to enhance freedom in general cope with problems of freedom in particular. The appropriate solution is to eliminate government operation of the schools and permit parents to choose the kind of school they want their children to attend. In addition, of course, we should all of us, insofar as we possibly can, try by behavior and speech to foster the growth of attitudes and opinions that would lead mixed schools to become the rule and segregated schools the rare exception.

If a proposal like . . . [educational vouchers] were adopted, it would permit a variety of schools to develop, some all white, some all Negro, some mixed. It would permit the transition from one collection of schools to another — hopefully to mixed schools — to be gradual as community attitudes changed. It would avoid the harsh political conflict that has been doing so much to raise social tensions and disrupt the community. It would in this special area, as the market does in general, permit co-operation without conformity.

The state of Virginia has adopted a plan having many features in common with that outlined in the preceding chapter. Though adopted for the purpose of avoiding compulsory integration, I predict that the ultimate effects of the law will be very different — after all, the difference between result and intention is one of the primary justifications of a free society; it is desirable to let men follow the bent of their own interests because there is no way of predicting where they will come out. Indeed, even in the early stages there have been surprises. I have been told that one of the first requests for a voucher to finance a change of school was by a parent transferring a child from a segregated to an integrated school. The transfer was requested not for this purpose but simply because the integrated school happened to be the better school educationally. Looking further ahead, if the voucher system is not abolished, Virginia will provide an experiment to test the conclusions of the preceding chapter. If those conclusions are right, we should see a flowering of the schools available in Virginia, with an increase in their diversity, a substantial if not spectacular rise in the quality of the leading schools, and a later rise in the quality of the rest under the impetus of the leaders.

On the other side of the picture, we should not be so naïve as to suppose that deep-seated values and beliefs can be uprooted in short measure by law. I live in Chicago. Chicago has no law compelling segregation. Its laws require integration. Yet in fact the public schools of Chicago are probably as thoroughly segregated as the schools of most Southern cities. There is almost no doubt at all that if the Virginia system were introduced in Chicago, the result would be an appreciable decrease in segregation, and a great widening in the opportunities available to the ablest and most ambitious Negro youth.

CAN DISCRIMINATION BE ENDED UNDER CAPITALISM?

Barbara R. Bergmann

This selection illustrates a liberal approach to the problem of racial discrimination. Bergmann agrees with Milton Friedman that, as she puts it here, "the essential nature of capitalism is such as to discourage rather than encourage discrimination." But, unlike Friedman, she argues that strong government measures will do even more to "discourage" it. With an optimism about government intervention that is characteristic of liberals, she feels that "there is good reason to hope" that improvements in black status "may accelerate."

This article was originally written in 1971. Bergmann cannot be held responsible, therefore, for more recent data indicating that blacks have suffered some setbacks during the current economic crisis.

Bergmann teaches economics at the University of Maryland. Author of many articles, she has been one of the leading scholars within the economics profession on the problems of minorities — both blacks and women.

Source: From *Modern Political Economy: Radical and Orthodox Views on Crucial Issues,* James Weaver, ed., Allyn & Bacon, 1973, pp. 312–317. Reprinted with permission of the author.

The affliction of American society by the evils of discrimination, poverty, crime, wars, pollution, and alienation have led an indeterminate number of people to a belief that "the system" that is responsible for such evils must be radically altered. Since a chief feature in almost anybody's view of "the system" is our capitalist economy, there is a tendency to declare the capitalist nature of our economic setup to be the chief culprit in creating these evils and perpetuating them. While it is tempting to reason in this way, particularly if one enjoys believing that all evils arise out of a single source, I believe such reasoning to be mistaken. In particular, I believe that racial discrimination can be reduced drastically in the absence of a revolution or even an evolution that would overthrow capitalism. I must confess that this belief is far from certitude. No really serious student of racial affairs pretends to a clear view of the future of racial discrimination in the United States. Anyone who does is a propagandist. Only tendencies can be discerned, and those only dimly.

Our first task is to explore the connection between racial discrimination and capitalism. Is the nature of capitalism such that racial discrimination is natural to it? Is racial discrimination beneficial to the continued existence of capitalism and to the prosperity of the capitalists? Or is racial discrimination inimical to capitalism and capitalism inimical to racial discrimination? To put the matter succinctly, is racial discrimination meat and drink to capitalism, or is it poison?

I shall argue that the essential nature of capitalism is such as to discourage rather than encourage discrimination, which I believe persists among us for noneconomic reasons. Arguing that capitalism and racial discrimination are inimical to each other is not sufficient, however, to establish that racism can be cured without a revolution. If capitalism *is* inimical to racism, then its persistence in the United States for so long and in so virulent a form would argue that the underlying disposition toward it in our society is a strong one. Thus it might be true that to get rid of it a cataclysmic event such as the overthrow of capitalism might be necessary. However, there is evidence that after decades of no progress, we are now moving ahead and that even more rapid progress is possible and probable. This part of the argument is on somewhat slighter ground than the argument about the capitalism-racism connection, and the reader will have to draw his or her own conclusions as to whether the degree of progress on this problem (and others) will be such as to justify maintaining an economic system which in major outline is like the present one.

Discrimination and Capitalism

Marx tells us that the emergence of capitalism meant that the "cash nexus" became the relationship *par excellence* between man and man. In precapitalist societies the right to buy or sell was often restricted according to the social class or location one was born into; much property was inalienable, elaborate restrictions hedged each transaction. Under pure capitalism, all that is necessary for transactions to take place is the desire of the parties and the wherewithal on the part of the buyer. For example, the notion that certain people should be debarred from certain types of work unless they are members of certain families, while a commonplace in village India, is completely alien to the ideology of capitalism. The questions "How is this man related to me socially?" "Do I like him?" "Is his face black or white?" are not the questions *homo oeconomicus* of capitalism is supposed to ask himself when he is contemplating a sale or a purchase.

The economy of the United States is not, of course, pure *laissez-faire* capitalism, and Americans do sometimes give jobs to their dumb nephews, give discounts to their friends, and refuse to buy from and sell to black people when it might be in their financial interest to do otherwise. The point to understand here is that such behavior is anomalous from the point of view of the capitalist ideology, and is a deviation from normal capitalist practice. The normal practice is that each man buys as cheap as he can and sells as dear as he can, without regard to the identity of those he trades with.

Let us look more closely at the effects of racial discrimination on the financial welfare of those private citizens who practice it. Practicing racial discrimination usually means excluding blacks from the possibility of making certain transactions. "I won't hire you for this job because you are black," "I will not rent this apartment to you or sell you this house because you are black," "You cannot eat a sandwich at my soda fountain because you are black." This kind of behavior undoubtedly injures the black people against whom it is directed. *But it also causes financial losses to the discriminator.* The reason is that the discriminator is trifling with the law of supply and demand, the most sacred law in the capitalist canon. When he refuses to hire blacks he artificially reduces the supply of labor to himself, raising the price he must pay to the white labor he does hire, and therefore hurting himself financially. When he refuses to sell his product or his house to blacks he artificially reduces the demand for them, thus reducing the price he extracts from the white customers he does deal with.

I do not want to give the impression that the losses to the discriminator are large and unmixed with gains. Certainly, the losses to the discriminator must be very small as compared to the losses of the discriminated-against. Moreover, when the discriminator refuses to hire blacks he may be forcing them to overcrowd those occupations considered "fitting" for blacks, and thus his actions may have the effect of lowering the wage in those occupations. Thus what the discriminator loses by refusing to hire blacks as machine operatives he may make up to some degree by the low wage for which he can hire a janitor. Nevertheless, the proper conclusion seems to be that no important financial gains accrue to discrimination; in all probability discriminators suffer losses because of their discriminatory conduct.

Of course, some people do gain from discrimination. First and foremost are those who have no qualms about buying or selling to blacks. These include employers in industries (such as laundries) that have lots of jobs considered "fit" for blacks. They include slumlords who rent apartments to the blacks who are excluded by discriminators from other apartments. They also include those few black businessmen who can monopolize a segregated black clientele. And, of course, they include those white workers who are protected in some occupations from the competition of black workers. I have elsewhere made estimates of the wage rate gains accruing to white workers from this source. I found them to be on the order of 10 per cent for white workers with less than an elementary education and trivial for all other white workers.[1]

One interesting thing about this list of the financial beneficiaries of discrimination is that the beneficiaries of discrimination are in general different people from the actual discriminators. While there is some overlap (the slumlord may own some property on the white side of the tracks), it is probably cor-

rect to say that the discriminators and the beneficiaries of discrimination are for the most part different. Undoubtedly, some of the beneficiaries cheer on the discriminators from the sidelines, but the cheerleaders are not part of the playing team in this game, for the most part.

The second interesting thing is that the financial gains we have been able to discover from discrimination are not large. Few if any businessmen are making a very lucrative business out of discrimination, least of all the ones who are most guilty of conducting the exclusionary policy on which our whole racial system is based. Some radicals claim that the real economic benefit from discrimination is that it gives discriminatory bosses the power to threaten their white workers with the hungry blacks who will be glad to take their jobs unless the white workers continue to knuckle under at low wages. While such a threat may be effective in isolated instances, it can hardly be considered as an important factor in labor relations in the United States of today.

Why Racial Discrimination?

If economic incentives on discriminators under capitalism discourage discrimination rather than encourage it, how can it persist? The answer, of course, is that economic forces are far from the whole story in racial matters and are probably a minor part of the story. Human beings seem to have the tendency to set up hierarchical relationships, and to live in social systems in which A is treated with more respect than B for reasons X, Y, and Z. The reasons for looking down on a person can be the presence of calluses on the hands, the absence of a penis, the presence or absence of a cross around the neck, the presence of a pigment in the skin. This tendency has displayed itself in the United States under capitalism, but it has also displayed itself under other flags, under other economic systems, and in other eras. The division of labor, so lauded by economists since the time of Adam Smith, seems to be a powerful force in pushing one part of the population to think itself as superior to the other part. The division of labor is hardly a fault attributable to capitalism, although noncapitalist economies may be better able to reduce it if they desire to do so.

I would expect a given degree of racial prejudice in the population to express itself in economic terms more virulently under a socialist system such as that of the Soviet Union than under a capitalist system.

[1] "The Effect on White Incomes of Discrimination in Employment," *Journal of Political Economy*, March–April 1971.

Under capitalism, the desire to hold down people of the wrong race (or sex, or religion) may be moderated by the incentive to make money out of buying from them and selling to them. In a socialist economy such a moderating force may be entirely absent, since individual managers are typically given little or no personal financial incentive to make any purchase or sale. One might believe that a noncapitalist government would be more willing and more able to reduce the degree of racial prejudice in the country's population; unfortunately, we have the counterexample of the government of the Soviet Union in fanning the anti-Semitic feelings of the population.

Is Racial Discrimination Lessening in the U.S.?

In the post-World War II period we have annual data on nonwhite and white median incomes. Between 1947 and 1965 the ratio of nonwhite to white median incomes fluctuated between .51 and .57. During this nineteen-year period, its fluctuations seem random; they have little connection with fluctuations in the unemployment rate or any other likely variable. In 1965, the ratio was .55. Then in 1966 it climbed to an unprecedented .60 and it climbed again in 1967 and 1968 to .62 and .63, a 15 per cent increase in four years.[2] Now it is certainly possible to make too much out of a three-year rise in this ratio, and we will certainly want to watch it closely during the current recession. Nevertheless, I would like cautiously to suggest that this movement in the ratio represents the first fruit of the agitation of the 1960s in favor of a better deal for black citizens.

Some evidence that is to me even more persuasive is the improvement over the period 1960–1969 in the occupational distribution of black men. In that period, black men over twenty-five increased their participation in professional and technical occupation by 107 per cent. In 1960 black men had 72 per cent

of the jobs in such fields that one might have expected them to hold judging from their educational achievement. In 1969, this percentage had risen to 82 per cent. In managerial occupations, participation of black men increased by 117 per cent over this period, with the ratio of actual jobs to expected jobs rising from 27 per cent in 1960 to 36 per cent. Jobs as craftsmen for black men increased 52 per cent over the period and sales jobs by 42 per cent.

An interesting event of the 1960s from our point of view was the desegregation of public accommodations under federal law with remarkably little fuss, showing everyone that changes staunchly resisted in advance can be quite calmly accepted if the force is there to push them. These days even the most hardened racists probably think nothing about sharing restaurants with Negroes. On a much more limited scale, white workers are more or less cheerfully sharing work places with Negroes, although most of those who now do so would have abhorred the idea ten years ago.

Only continued agitation for fair-employment practices and improved enforcement of laws against discrimination will insure the continuance of this trend. However, I think there is good reason to hope that it may accelerate. That hope is based on the nature of the capitalist system. It is good business to sell to blacks and good business to hire them. As time goes on, it will become more and more *respectable* to hire and sell to them with fewer and fewer restrictions. As this happens, good business sense will insure that these opportunities are taken advantage of. Those black men and women modeling clothes in the recent Sears catalogs may have been put there because of threats of boycott. They will probably stay there because it is good business to keep them there.

Finally, capitalists are vitally concerned with the preservation of the system in something like its present form and will give ground if they think they have to. If capitalists are convinced that racial injustice is helping to create resentments which endanger the system, they are sufficiently flexible to do their part to end it. It is up to all of us to keep the pressure on them to see that they do.

[2] *Consumer Income: Income in 1968 of Families and Persons in the United States* (Washington, D.C.: U.S. Bureau of the Census, 1969).

ECONOMIC THEORIES OF RACISM

Robert Cherry

This essay surveys alternative economic theories of racism, contrasting conservative, liberal, and radical views. The author focuses on the analytic bases of those differing models, their policy implications, and their consistency with empirical evidence. He also reviews the history of the different approaches to racism, arguing that we can best understand some of the implications of each model by studying the historical context in which it arose.

Cherry's essay was written especially for this second edition. The author has been teaching economics at Montclair State College in New Jersey.

In recent years economists have "discovered" the existence of racial discrimination in the United States. Starting in the late 1950s, but especially in the last eight years, they have proposed numerous explanations of the dynamics of racial discrimination in the labor market. This survey article will outline the basic properties and policy implications of various conservative, liberal, and radical models of labor market discrimination. Some of the historical circumstances that influenced the development of these theories will also be discussed. This article concludes with a summary of the most important findings and an attempt to apply these results to the current U.S. situation.

Conservative Theories of Racial Discrimination

■ General Attitudes

Conservative theories claim racial discrimination is not very significant and is progressively decreasing. As Milton Friedman writes,

It is a striking historical fact that the development of capitalism has been accompanied by a major reduction in the extent to which particular religious, racial, or social groups have ... been dis-

Source: Robert Cherry, an essay written for this book. The author wishes to acknowledge the help of William Tabb and especially David Gordon for their invaluable criticisms and suggestions.

criminated against. The substitution of contract arrangements for status arrangements was the first step towards the freeing of the serfs in the Middle Ages.... The maintenance of the general rules of private property and of capitalism have been a major source of opportunity for Negroes.[1]

While most members of society perceive discrimination in employment as something reprehensible — to be legislated against — conservative theories often consider it no different from a consumer who discriminates against apples by buying pears. Friedman continues:

It is hard to see that discrimination can have any meaning other than a "taste" of others that one doesn't share. We do not regard it as "discrimination" ... if an individual is willing to pay to listen to one singer [rather] than another.... Is there any difference in principle between the taste that leads a householder to prefer an attractive servant to an ugly one and the taste that leads another to prefer a white to a Negro.... The appropriate recourse is for me to seek to persuade them that their tastes are bad and that they should change their views and their behavior, not to use coercive power to enforce my tastes and my attitudes on others.[2]

■ Analytical Framework

The key assumption of the conservative analysis is that racism is not profitable to capitalists. In order to support this assumption, Gary Becker developed a model of discrimination.[3]

His model is based on the traditional economic assumption that capitalists *react* to market conditions. In the labor market this implies that capitalists react to the various offers to work of individual workers. These offers — how many would be willing to work at various wage levels — are determined

[1] Milton Friedman, *Capitalism and Freedom* (1962), 110.
[2] *Ibid.*, 111.
[3] Gary Becker, *The Economics of Discrimination* (1957).

solely by workers themselves. Capitalists are free to determine only how many to hire at each of the worker's wage offers. Hence, the only form that discrimination takes, according to this assumption, is *employment* discrimination. An employer who has an aversion to contact with black workers is said to have a "taste" or "preference" for discrimination. The employer, who has this "taste," chooses to hire a white worker less qualified than a black worker in order to limit his/her contact with blacks. In this case, the employer would be willing to pay a price (loss of efficiency and, hence, profits) for his/her taste. The stronger his/her taste for discrimination, the more profits he/she would be willing to lose in order to limit contact with black workers.[4]

■ *Extensions of Becker's Model*

The simplest extensions of Becker's model take the preferences of white workers, instead of capitalists, as the primary motivating force for discrimination. The most well-known model to incorporate the psychological preferences of white workers is the crowding model of Barbara Bergmann.[5] In this model the capitalists take as given the preferences of white workers to work with other white workers. In this case the capitalist realizes that white workers would have to be paid a premium (higher wages) to work in an integrated work place. This potentially increased cost discourages capitalists from hiring blacks. Instead, the capitalists choose white workers and, where necessary, increased capital equipment to compensate for the labor shortage created, rather than an integrated work force. In turn, capitalists who hire predominantly unskilled labor hire only

black workers. So black workers are crowded into low wage labor-intensive production while white workers are crowded into high wage capital-intensive production. Finally, these two groups tend to be "noncompeting."

It has also been proposed that the preferences of white *consumers* forces owners to discriminate. According to Friedman,

> ... consider a situation in which there are grocery stores serving a neighborhood inhabited by people who have a strong aversion to being waited on by Negro clerks. Suppose one of the grocery stores has a vacancy for a clerk and the first applicant qualified in other respects happens to be a Negro. Let us suppose that as a result of the law the store is required to hire him. The effect of this action will be to reduce the business done by this store. ... When the owner of the store hires white clerks in preference to Negroes in the absence of the law, he may not be expressing any preference or prejudice or taste of his own. He may simply be transmitting the tastes of the community.[6]

The general properties of these three conservative models are:

1. Capitalists have no control over the supply decisions of workers. Capitalists do not shape or influence the attitudes of white workers.
2. Discrimination is not based upon the attempt of capitalists to maximize profits. Capitalists are either psychologically motivated or agents of the psychological motivation of white workers or consumers.
3. Psychological factors are the principal motivating forces of discrimination.

■ *Economic Effects of Racial Discrimination*

In all of the various conservative models the principal monetary beneficiaries of discrimination are white workers. These models do have minor differences, however, with respect to the economic effects of discrimination on capitalists' income.

In Becker's model capitalists lose financially from discrimination, since discrimination restricts labor supply, lowering the unit labor productivity of the firm. This lower productivity leads to higher unit labor cost and lower profits.

---

[4] An alternative formulation is attempted by R. Franklin and M. Tanzer, "Traditional Microeconomic Analysis of Racial Discrimination," in D. Mermelstein, *Economics: Mainstream Readings and Radical Critique* (1970). They argue that the aversion to blacks among white workers, owners, and/or consumers affects hiring decisions according to how personalized the production process is.

"Capital-intensive modes of production generally separate the product and/or service from the worker. Moreover, the technical conditions of production ... tend to require a minimum of personal interaction on equal terms or interaction on terms in which the Negro has jobs vested with authority over whites. Therefore, the employer in capital-intensive operations has less reason to be concerned with product-color connection." (p. 122)

[5] Barbara Bergmann, "The Effect on White Income of Discrimination in Employment," *Journal of Political Economy* 79 (March–April 1971).

[6] Friedman, 112.

In Bergmann's model the losses to the capitalists from discrimination are slight. Bergmann claims that capitalists are able to compensate for changes in the available labor force by adjusting their capital investment decisions. Also, it is mostly in the unskilled categories, where workers are relatively interchangeable without losses in efficiency, that discrimination is most prevalent.

Friedman's model implies that capitalists are indifferent to the preferences of consumers. The owner would earn the same "normal" profits whether the consumer wishes to purchase apples, oranges, white service help, or black service help!

Liberal Theories of Racial Discrimination

▪ General Attitudes

Liberals tend to see racial discrimination as an unintended outgrowth of structural and institutional mechanisms. To them, racial discrimination is caused neither by individual pathologies, as claimed by the conservatives, nor by conscious profiteering, as claimed by the radicals. Liberals, therefore, believe that (conservative) policies to change individual values are ineffective, while (radical) policies to eliminate private ownership are unnecessary. Instead, liberals propose governmental actions to correct the structural and institutional mechanisms that cause racial discrimination to persist.

▪ Analytical Framework

The key assumption of the liberal analysis is the presence of structural and/or institutional mechanisms. The two factors most often cited by liberals are: (1) the structure of the alleged black subculture and (2) the structure of hiring practices.

Michael Piore has formulated a model that emphasizes the role of the black subculture in perpetuating the inferior occupational position of black workers. First, Piore argues that many blacks are excluded from primary jobs because they lack the necessary behavioral requirements, such as reporting for work punctually and daily. This *causes* employers in the secondary work force to adjust job specifications to the inferior work habits of these workers. Furthermore, according to Piore,

> [T]he behavioral traits associated with the secondary sector are reinforced by the process of working in secondary jobs and living among others whose life-style is accommodated to that type of employment. Hence even individuals [with the "proper" work habits] who are forced into the secondary sector ... tend, over time, to develop the traits predominant among secondary workers. Thus, for example, by working in a world where employment is intermittent and erratic, one tends to lose habits of regularity and punctuality.[7]

Third, the environment of the black subculture, where illegal activities are an important alternative source of income, reinforce antisocial tendencies within the black population. Finally, government welfare programs instill dependency and antiwork traits within the black population.

This argument implies that *current* employment decisions reflect legitimate concerns for productivity and not racial discrimination per se. This "vicious cycle of poverty" thesis locates the source of the problem in the black subculture, reinforced by institutional (welfare) factors.

Other liberals have claimed that discrimination perpetuates segmentation of black workers into the secondary sector through the use of superficial characteristics and measures in the hiring process. Employers, attempting to minimize their hiring costs, often refer to a few readily and hence inexpensively assessed traits which unintentionally discriminate against blacks. Statistical discrimination, as this process has been labeled, seems to have been first formulated by Melvin Reder but has been also used by Piore and in the feedback mechanism of Franklin and Tanzer. According to the feedback mechanism:

> The possession of low-paying occupations [by many blacks] is confused in the mind of the populace with belonging to an "inferior" race. ... As a result whites making [hiring] decisions qua individuals tend to (a) underestimate the Negro's actual and/or potential ability and/or (b) dislike Negroes because they are judged to have an inferior style of life.[8]

▪ Economic Effects of Racial Discrimination

Liberal models, which posit the "vicious cycle of poverty" thesis, imply that *present* discrimination has

---

[7] Michael Piore, "The Dual Labor Market: Theory and Implications." [See Chapter 2 of this book.] Models of K. Arrow and J. Stiglitz also emphasize the role of inferior work habits. For a discussion of these models see Stanley Masters, *Black-White Income Differentials* (1975), pp. 9–10.

[8] Franklin and Tanzer, 123–24.

little or no effect on income distribution. In the statistical discrimination model, white workers gain by having a more favorable access to jobs in the primary sector. Capitalists in the secondary sector gain by having an increased supply of workers available, while those in the primary sector are able to offset the higher wages by the reduced cost of screening job candidates. In this model, while the source of discrimination is inadvertent — since it does provide an economic benefit to white workers and somewhat to capitalists — there develop "groups interested, not only in resisting the elimination of poverty, but in actively seeking its perpetuation."[9]

General Agreement of Liberal and Conservative Theories

The preceding sections have identified the differences between the liberal and conservative theories of racial discrimination. These differences, however, are less significant than their points of agreement.

First, since both groups of models reject the claim that capitalists *as a group* gain financially from racial discrimination, they also reject measures which would change private property rights as methods of diminishing discrimination. Therefore, their proposals only differ as to the necessity (and methods) of strengthening and/or redirecting the competitive market mechanisms.

Second, both models assume that capitalists hire workers according to marginal productivity calculations. They differ only as to the factor(s) used to discount black productivity. In Becker's model, capitalists discount black productivity because of their aversion to blacks. In the statistical discrimination model, black productivity is discounted because of the use of superficial measures. In the "vicious cycle of poverty" model, black productivity, as measured by educational attainment, is discounted because of the lack of stable work habits.

Third, both liberal models discussed agree with the conservative models that the primary cause of low wages/high unemployment among blacks is due to *personal* defects.[10] They both draw upon racial

theories developed in psychology and sociology. While the conservatives tend to draw on genetic theories of inferiority, liberals tend to use cultural theories of inferiority. These ideas are widely and uncritically disseminated in introductory economics courses.[11] It is not surprising, therefore, that the most influential urban book, Edward Banfield's *The Unheavenly City Revisited,* gives equal weight to Friedman's and Piore's theories of black poverty.[12]

Radical Theories of Racial Discrimination

■ *General Attitudes*

The radical outlook is in fundamental opposition to that of the liberal and conservative outlooks.

1. Conservative and liberals (C/L) claim that racism is not a fundamental aspect of capitalism. Radicals (R) disagree.
2. C/L claim that racism has an inconsequential, if not negative, effect on capitalists' income. R claim that racism is profitable to capitalists.
3. C/L claim that racism is psychologically or structurally motivated. R claim that racism is economically motivated.
4. C/L tend to see white and black workers crowded into "noncompeting" groups. R emphasize the effects of racism on the divisive competition between white and black workers.
5. C/L take the preferences of white workers as given. R emphasize the ability of capitalists to shape and influence these preferences.

Radicals claim that the history of the United States is interwoven with racism. Westward expansion, slavery, anti-immigration policies, American imperialism, and nativist populism (states' rights movements) have all been fundamentally influenced by American racial attitudes.

---

[9] Piore.

[10] Piore claims that these superficial (racial) measures are persistently used because they "tend to be statistically correlated with job performance." This means that the *average* black applicant is less productive than the *average* white applicant.

[11] For example, Paul Samuelson, drawing on the Coleman Report, states: "Finally, if a black child comes from a home where no father is present, where no books line the shelves, and where the mother is hard pressed to care for many children on a limited relief check, then, at the age of six, the beginning student is already under a handicap with respect to learning performance and educational achievement." He then goes on to indicate that Jensen's genetic inferior thesis is the contending explanation. Paul Samuelson, *Economics,* 9th ed. (1974), 791, 792n.

[12] Edward Banfield, *The Unheavenly City Revisited* (1974), 122–26.

Moreover, all these activities, building upon and exploiting racist notions, were significantly profitable to the capitalist class. Westward expansion enabled capitalists to capture economic rents on natural resources at a minimum cost. Slavery benefited Northern shipping interests as much as it did Southern planters. Anti-immigration attitudes enabled capitalists to rationalize repressive actions against militant workers' organizations, whether or not they were dominated by immigrant workers.[13] Racist attitudes toward Latin Americans facilitated U.S. imperialist adventures into Puerto Rico, Central America, and South America, enabling U.S. capitalists to exploit labor and natural resources. Southern nativist attitudes enabled capitalists to obtain a nonunionized black and white cheap labor force in the Southern states.

Radicals also believe that white workers have lost from discrimination. If black workers were isolated and segmented from white workers, as nonradical theories assume, then the white working class would gain financially from racial discrimination. Radicals, however, claim that black and white workers are highly interchangeable. In this case it is possible for capitalists to use black workers as a threat to white workers, causing the latter to mute their demands. More importantly, in an integrated work force, racism leads each group of workers to compete against each other instead of presenting a united force against the capitalist. In this divided situation the capitalist lowers the wages of both black and white workers.

Finally, if the capitalist class benefits from racism, and especially from the development of racist attitudes among white workers, it stands to reason that they would consciously promote these attitudes through corporate foundations, the national media, and national news services. In recent years it could be argued that all these information sources promoted the racist ideas of cultural inferiority (e.g., Moynihan, Banfield) and genetic inferiority (e.g., Jensen, Shockley) totally out of proportion to their scientific merits, as well as the most outspoken anti-white forces in the black separatist movement (e.g., Stokely Carmichael, Roy Innis), in order to subvert the progressive changes brought about through the civil rights movement of the 1960s.

[13] See Thomas Gossett, *Race: The History of an Idea* (1965) and Phillip Foner, *The History of American Labor Movement,* Vol. 4.

▪ Analytical Framework

The first key assumption of the radical analysis is that the notion of "noncompeting" groups of black and white workers can no longer be supported empirically. In 1930, 81 percent of all black female workers were employed as either household domestics or agricultural laborers. These are the kinds of data that lend support to the "noncompeting" group view of blacks as an isolated marginal work force. These notions, however, no longer find support in occupational data. The 1970 Occupational Census shows that minority workers are now overrepresented in the *industrial* blue-collar work force. Black workers now represent a significant percentage of workers in auto, steel, machinery, transportation, etc.[14]

Once competition between white and black workers is incorporated into the analysis, it is possible to formalize a model of discrimination in which capitalists gain and white workers lose. One such model is Michael Reich's model of discrimination.[15] According to this radical formulation, racism enables the capitalists to restrict the opportunities of black workers and to use harsher tactics in repressing collective activities of black workers. For these reasons racism leads black workers to be "willing" to offer their labor services at a reduced rate. Therefore, in Reich's model, racism principally takes the form of *wage* discrimination rather than *employment* discrimination. Whereas Becker claims that racism leads capitalists to decrease their employment of black workers, Reich claims that it enables them to employ black workers at a lower wage rate.

Second, these racist wage differentials enable the capitalists to reduce the wage demands of white workers as well. Reich hypothesizes that the greater the extent of racism, the more unequal the distribution of income within the *white* population. That is, as racism increases, white workers receive a smaller share of income going to the white population while capitalists receive an increasing share.

▪ Variations of Reich's Model

Models of discrimination formulated by Morris Silver and by William Tabb emphasize different as-

[14] See Robert Cherry, "Class Struggle and the Nature of the Working Class," *Review of Radical Political Economy* 5 (Summer 1973) 47–86, especially Section V.

[15] Michael Reich, "The Economics of Racism," this book; and Reich, "Racial Discrimination and the White Distribution of Income," Ph.D. dissertation, Harvard University, 1973.

pects of the radical model. Silver emphasizes the effect that racism has on the cost to white workers (W) of collusion with black workers (N).

[I]f being associated with N workers in joint actions involves a psychic cost to W workers, the monetary equivalent of this cost must be added to the other costs of collusion. Higher costs of collusion lessen the extent or effectiveness of joint action and since it seems reasonable to suppose that the types of joint worker action harming employers (e.g., direct economic actions against employers, preventing the passage of "right to work" laws . . .) are more important than those benefitting them . . . the wages of both groups of workers (W and N) would be reduced while profits would be increased. . . . Far from being indifferent to the existence of discriminatory attitudes on the part of workers, the capitalist gains from them and may find it profitable to invest in their creation.[16]

Tabb emphasizes that capitalists, by promoting among white workers ideas of racial superiority, are able to create a more docile white work force. This docility on the part of white workers, together with their isolation from black workers, enables capitalists to trade-off short-term costs (higher wages) for greater long-term profits. Tabb claims that racial harmony may seem to be costly to white workers but this is only shortsightedness. For if white workers reject the short-term minor benefits and instead build a multiracial movement they can win much more in the long run.[17]

■ Alternative Radical Models

Another group of models, which are generally considered radical models, claim, just as the previous radical models do, that capitalism intensified and manipulated racial attitudes for profit-seeking reasons. They add, however, that once U.S. capitalism passed its competitive stage, the profitable use of racism diminished for the capitalist class. Under monopoly capitalism, according to these models, ideological and psychological factors rather than economic ones explain the persistence of racism. This thesis — which claims that ideologies, originally

based on economic factors, can develop an independent life when these economic factors disappear — is most identified with the work of historian Eugene Genovese. In economics the clearest example is the work of Harold Baron.

Baron argues that noneconomic factors are the primary explanation of discrimination:

Once White nationalism . . . [was] . . . grounded in a whole range of institutional and ideological forms, the special economic surplus extraction [profiteering] features of racial controls could drop to secondary importance and yet the overall system of racial subordination would remain intact. This process did occur in the twentieth century. . . . The maintenance needs of White quasinationalism included those symbolic and social relations that bolster the coherence and consensus that make it a viable entity. . . . Appeals to racism become an important solidarity mechanism.[18]

This emphasis on noneconomic factors is also apparent in the model of Paul Baran and Paul Sweezy. They argue:

[I]n its monopoly phase . . . there took place a proliferation of social strata and status groupings. . . . In such a social structure individuals tend to see and define themselves in terms of the "status hierarchy" and to be motivated by ambitions to move up and fears of moving down. These ambitions and fears are of course exaggerated, intensified, played upon by the corporate sales apparatus [advertising]. . . . The net result of all this is that each status group has a deep-rooted psychological need to compensate for feelings of inferiority and contempt for those below. It thus happens that a special pariah group acts as a kind of lightning rod for the frustrations and hostilities of all the higher groups, the more so the nearer they are to the bottom.[19]

According to these authors, the American oligarchy desired to eliminate racial discrimination.[20] However, racist ideas were so deeply rooted among white workers that the genuine attempts of the ruling oli-

[16] Morris Silver, "Employee Taste for Discrimination, Wages and Profits," in Mermelstein, 128.
[17] William Tabb, "Capitalism, Colonialism, and Racism," Review of Radical Political Economy 3 (Summer 1971), 90–106.

[18] Harold Baron, "Racial Domination in Advanced Capitalism: A Theory of Nationalism and Divisions in the Labor Market," in R. C. Edwards, et al., eds., Labor Market Segmentation (1975).
[19] Paul Baran and Paul Sweezy, Monopoly Capital (1966), 265.
[20] Ibid., cf. 270–71.

garchy — Kennedy administration and Warren Supreme Court — to diminish racial discrimination were ineffective.[21]

▪ Economic Effects of Racial Discrimination

The radical models of Reich, Silver, and Tabb have the same economic outcomes. Capitalists financially gain while white workers lose from racial discrimination.[22]

The alternative models of Baron, of Baran and Sweezy, and of Franklin and Resnik do not believe that the economic gains from racism form a consistent long-term pattern. From their points of view the long-term persistence of racism must be caused by factors other than financial rewards. All three models do seem to indicate, however, that in the current period the short-term economic rewards from discrimination are going primarily to white workers. Both Baran and Sweezy and Franklin and Resnik, when listing the private interests that benefit from discrimination, include some that benefit the capitalist class and some that hurt them.[23] However, when each model *synthesizes* these conflicting interests, they indicate that racial discrimination is not in the current economic interest of the capitalist class.

Baron's model is the only one of these alternative models indicating that, on net, the capitalists gain financially from discrimination. In Baron's model, racial discrimination, though not motivated by economic factors, enables capitalists to decrease the cost of the business cycle by using black workers as a reserve army. When the economy contracts, capitalists can more easily lay off excess workers, since a racist society is more willing to accept higher unemployment if the unemployed are disproportionately black. Also, when the economy expands, there is a ready labor supply that can be hired at the existing wage rate. In this way the higher costs of a privileged white labor force are more than compensated for by the presence of a reserve army of workers. According to Baron, however, "The gains from discrimination are at most 1–2 percent of total national wages."[24] Baron is quick to point out that this meager sum is inconsequential and not a determin-

ing factor in explaining capitalists' actions. Indeed, the attitude of this entire group of alternative radical models could be summed up by Baron:

> [Profits] hardly seem to be significant enough magnitude for corporate leadership to calculate it is sufficient grounds for maintaining the racial system with all its potential for social disruption and the large costs for repression and welfare controls.[25]

Policy Proposals and Empirical Evidence

▪ Policy Proposals

The conservative models of Friedman, Becker, and Bergmann all imply a laissez-faire approach to discrimination. Friedman's thesis defines discrimination as a matter of consumer choice; since there is nothing reprehensible about consumer choice, we do not need to legislate against discrimination. Becker's thesis that discrimination entails a cost to the capitalists implies that competitive market forces would drive the more racist firms out of business. Accordingly, Becker and Bergmann foresee the gradual elimination of racial discrimination through the natural workings of the free market. The only government actions that either author would support would be those that strengthen free market forces, such as legislating against discriminatory union practices and antitrust legislation.

All the liberal models lead to some form of recommended government intervention. Those that emphasize the "vicious cycle of poverty" thesis propose special educational programs, such as Head Start (to compensate for the dysfunctional black subculture), and changes in the welfare system, such as the negative income tax, which would reinforce rather than discourage work incentives. Those that emphasize statistical discrimination propose government affirmative action programs (and even quotas in nonprofessional employment) to guarantee that qualified black workers are not rejected on superficial generalizations.

The radical models of Reich, Silver, and Tabb propose the formation of multiracial working class organizations to fight discrimination. They claim that discrimination is encouraged by the capitalist class, who seek to divide black and white workers in order

---

[21] See also the book by Raymond Franklin and Solomon Resnik, *The Political Economy of Racism* (1973), 31.

[22] See Reich, this book, for a clear statement of this view.

[23] Baran and Sweezy, 263–64; Franklin and Resnik, 22.

[24] Baron, 53.

[25] *Op. cit.*

to decrease the wages of all workers. Therefore, multiracial unity is in the economic interest of all workers.

The alternative radical models of Baron, of Baran and Sweezy, and of Franklin and Resnik all emphasize the positive role of a black separatist movement and the inability of blacks to ally with white industrial workers. According to Baron, white antiracist groups

> are forced to deal with the reality of Black nationalism as more than just a cultural expression. . . . Until antiracist White forces learn how to master some of the contradictions within the White quasi-nation . . . they will not present themselves as a very attractive group for Blacks to ally with.[26]

According to Baran and Sweezy, blacks can gain some token progress through alliances with progressive capitalists. For genuine progress, however, blacks in the United States must ally themselves with black liberation movements in Asia and Africa and *hope* for the collapse of capitalism.[27]

Franklin and Resnik foresee the collapse of at least the Democratic Party and propose that blacks, who are progressively gaining political control of urban centers, should try to form alliances with white professionals: "Teachers, lawyers, and union leaders [who] may be propelled to seek a 'radical' departure from the Party's present state of drift." [28]

▪ Empirical Evidence

The two major implications of the conservative analysis are:

1. Competitive industries are less discriminatory than monopolistic industries.
2. Competitive pressures should lead to reductions in labor market discrimination over time.

Becker attempts to support the first contention using arbitrarily aggregated black male industrial employment figures.[29] A more careful and rigorous evaluation of these data shows that there exists no correlation between the degree of competition in an industry and its racial hiring practices.[30]

Stanley Masters finds that empirical evidence completely contradicts the second contention. According to Masters:

> Although the evidence is rather limited, there does not appear to have been any significant decrease in labor-market discrimination in the century following the Civil War.[31]

Masters bases his conclusions on (a) Fogel and Engerman, who maintain that "the gap between wage payments to blacks and whites in comparable occupations increased steadily from the immediate post Civil War decades down to the eve of World War II";[32] (b) the Occupational Index of Dale Heistand, which shows that, except for World War II, there was no change in the occupational position of black relative to white males; and (3) Gwartney's results, which show that the meager 0.3 percent per year improvement in the black-white national income ratio over the period 1948–64, found by Rasmussen, disappears once an adjustment is made for blacks living outside the South (e.g., regional black-white income ratios did not change).[33]

The radical model emphasizes the economic cost of discrimination to white workers and the economic benefit to the capitalist class. Since radicals emphasize *wage* discrimination, the measure of discrimination used is racial wage differentials. Using this measure, Reich tested various models with data from the forty-eight largest U.S. cities. In each model he found that the level of discrimination adversely affected white workers' income and years of schooling, as well as the degree of unionization and welfare payments. On the other hand, the level of dis-

---

[26] Ibid., 66.

[27] Baran and Sweezy, 280. Elsewhere they state, "If we confine our attentions to the inner dynamics of advanced monopoly capitalism, it is hard to avoid the conclusion that the prospect of effective revolutionary action to overthrow the system is slim." (364) Their main hope is that the increasing "psychic disorders" created by monopoly capitalism may lead Negroes and youth to revolutionary action (cf. 364–65).

[28] Franklin and Resnik, 271. They are, however, extremely pessimistic that such an alliance will materialize (cf. 273).

[29] Becker, 44–46.

[30] Franklin and Tanzer, cf. 119–21.

[31] Masters, 46.

[32] Robert Fogel and Stanley Engerman, *Time on the Cross* (1974), 261.

[33] James Gwartney, "Changes in the Nonwhite/White Income Ratio, 1937–67," *American Economics Review* 60 (December 1970); David Rasmussen, "A Note on the Relative Income of Nonwhite Men, 1948–1964," *The Quarterly Journal of Economics* 84 (February 1970).

crimination positively correlated with capitalists' income.[34]

Masters attempts to test the liberal hypothesis that government antiracist legislation should lead to a continuous improvement in the relative position of blacks.[35] He finds that the relative improvement of blacks during the pre-Civil Rights Act period (1948–63) was only 0.05 percent per year, while since then it has been 1.12 percent per year. For these results to support the liberal thesis, Masters assumes that the Civil Rights Act was responsible for the changes in labor market practices. Radicals would argue that it was the multiracial working class militant unity which forced the Civil Rights Act to be enacted and forced it to be implemented. Masters offers no test that would show which of these underlying mechanisms is responsible for his results. Therefore, his results are compatible with both the liberal and radical theories of discrimination.[36] Implicitly aware of this, Masters concludes his study with these remarks:

> If future events should contradict Myrdal's [liberal] optimism, and if the values and analysis presented earlier are accepted, then increased attention should be devoted to examining the radical perspective and its policy implications.[37]

Historical Evaluation of Theories of Racial Discrimination

The preceding sections have enabled us to identify the key conceptual differences between, and the relative empirical support for, each of the various models of racial discrimination. There are still, however, a number of important questions left unanswered.

1. Suppose we assume that Reich's finding that white workers financially lose from racism is correct and that the contention of others that white workers have psychologically motivated racist attitudes is also correct. It still remains to be answered whether or not the subjective attitudes of white workers can be overcome so

that multiracial working class unity is a viable strategy for fighting racism.
2. Do government actions cause a decrease in racist attitudes and practices, as liberals claim, or does multiracial working-class unity force a government *reaction*, as radicals claim?
3. Why was the conservative theory of racial discrimination developed and favorably received if it so miserably reflected reality?

A very brief examination of the history of racism, especially during this century, can help to begin the task of answering these questions.

During the 1890s a multiracial Southern Populist movement developed among poor whites and blacks. This movement won state elections in Georgia and came close in Louisiana. It led to the successful organizing of coal miners in Alabama and a general strike in New Orleans in support of *black* dockworkers.[38]

This movement was reversed when racist Social Darwinist myths of black inferiority convinced many whites to reject interracial unity. The rejection of this unity paved the way for the successful institution of Jim Crow laws, segregated unions, and the disenfranchisement of black voters. The racial disunity that these actions created hurt poor Southern white workers by destroying the Southern Populist movement, weakening the union organizing drives, and disenfranchising many white voters.[39]

In the North, the last quarter of the nineteenth century saw the rapid rise of militant trade unionism. But, as in the South, the acceptance of racist myths intensified working-class disunity. Labor militancy was increasingly blamed on the criminal antidemocratic tendencies of Slavic and Italian immigrants. A new ideology, which claimed that these immigrants were of a different and inferior racial stock (non-Teutonic) than earlier immigrants, was popularized and accepted by many "native" workers.[40] The wide acceptance of these ideas enabled

---

[34] See Reich's article for more detailed explanation of his models tested and findings.

[35] Masters, cf. 140–49.

[36] Unfortunately, Masters uses the Baran and Sweezy model for predictive purposes, which adversely affects his evaluation of the radical model (p. 141).

[37] *Ibid.*, 184.

[38] See C. Vann Woodward, *Origins of the New South, 1877–1913* (1951); C. Vann Woodward, *The Strange Career of Jim Crow* (1966).

[39] Historical accounts usually imply that Jim Crow laws were instituted at the end of Reconstruction (1876). Not one Southern state had Jim Crow laws before the 1890s.

[40] For a good account of the development of these racist ideas and the Eugenics Movement which resulted, see Mark Haller, *Eugenics* (1963) and John Higham, *Strangers in the Land* (1972).

capitalists to use the most brutal actions possible against both immigrant and "native" worker strikes.[41] Samuel Gompers's promotion of segregated unions enabled capitalists to use immigrant workers, as well as blacks, as strikebreakers. Moreover, these ideas were used by Gompers to convince white native workers that they had more to gain by allying with capitalists to restrict immigration than to ally with immigrants to win more for all workers. During the twenty-five years that Gompers led the trade union movement, the effect of these racial and ethnic divisions, which his policies promoted, led to the weakening of the entire labor movement. When racist immigration restrictions were finally enacted in 1924, it was a hollow victory for labor.[42] The post-World War I period saw the largest drop in union membership ever and the rise of the company association movement.

In the 1930s a totally different labor movement developed. A number of mass organizing activities fundamentally weakened the forces of racism in the South. In 1931, a case involving nine Negro youths convicted of raping two white women in Mississippi — the Scottsboro trials — became the focus of a nationwide protest against the lack of legal rights for Southern blacks.[43] The organizing activities of the United Mine Workers in Alabama and the Textile Workers' Union in North Carolina, with the stress in both efforts on developing multiracial unity, helped the organization of multiracial Unemployment Councils and Sharecroppers' Unions in the South.[44] By

1937 Gallup Polls indicated that 65 percent of Southerners were in favor of Federal Anti-Lynching legislation.[45] Not only did this lead to the decimation of the Klan but forced it to spend all its remaining energies on stopping unions rather than on preserving white racial supremacy.[46]

In the North, multiracial unity also developed. In 1919 an attempt to unionize the steel industry failed. An industrywide strike of 365,000 workers, lasting fifteen weeks, was defeated when ethnic divisions and the use of 40,000 black strikebreakers weakened the strike's effectiveness. Learning from these mistakes, the Steel Workers' Organizing Committee, during the 1936 organizing drive, placed special emphasis on overcoming the racist attitudes of many steelworkers and encouraging blacks to join the union.[47] The National Negro Congress, founded in 1936, had as its major purpose the development of multiracial working-class unity as the principal means for black advancement. It was instrumental in the successful struggles for unionization in many industries where blacks were a significant part of the work force.

The crucial role played by multiracial unity is best exemplified by the organizing efforts in the auto industry. Whereas General Motors and Chrysler were successfully unionized in 1937, Ford was not unionized until 1941.[48] According to Howe and Widick, this was due to the systematic effort of Henry Ford to create racial divisiveness within his work force. On the one hand, Ford, through the Dearborn Press and other media, was able to foment racist ideas in the minds of white workers. On the other hand, Ford, through his support of black colleges and the doling of patronage, was able to win the support of black leaders in Detroit.[49] As a result, these leaders actively supported Henry Ford against the UAW.

---

[41] Sterilization laws were passed in twenty-five states between 1907 and 1930 based on the Eugenics Movement's recommendations. Feeblemindedness and criminality were sufficient reasons for sterilization. Other, more traditional examples of the brutality were the Palmer Raids, the Sacco-Venzetti frame-up, and the police attacks on IWW organizers.

[42] Between 1896 and 1917 immigration restriction laws passed different bodies of Congress thirty-one times, and were vetoed by four different presidents. In 1917 a literary requirement was finally enacted. Henry Fairchild, "Literacy Test," *Quarterly Journal of Economics* 31 (1917), 447–51.

[43] The Scottsboro case was rejected initially by the NAACP, and later they refused to join the International Lawyers' Defense (ILD) because of the tactics (mass protests rather than a no-publicity legal approach) employed. See Hugh Murray, "The NAACP Versus the Communist Party . . . ," in Bernard Sternsher, ed., *The Negro in Depression and War* (1969), 267–80.

[44] See John Williams, "Struggles of the Thirties in the South," and Erwin Hoffman, "The Genesis of the

Modern Movement," both in Sternsher, 166–80 and 193–215 respectively. Also, see Horace Cayton, *Black Workers and the New Unions* (1939), and Hosea Judson, *Black Worker in the Deep South* (1973).

[45] Robert Zangrando, "The NAACP and a Federal Anti-Lynching Bill," in Sternsher, 189.

[46] David Chalmers, *Hooded Americanism* (1965), 316; Stetson Kennedy, *Southern Exposure* (1946).

[47] See Cayton, 90–220.

[48] This does not mean that the unionizing of General Motors was easy. It required a forty-four-day sit-down strike in the Flint Plant, January–February 1937.

[49] Irving Howe and B. J. Widick, *Walter Reuther* (1949), Ch. 10.

Since Ford had concentrated his entire employment of black workers in the key River Rouge Plant, where they totaled 12 percent of the work force, a continued alliance between black workers and management would defeat any organizing effort.[50] The National Negro Congress, however, was able to mobilize support for the UAW within the NAACP and Urban League, which, in turn, enabled the UAW to circumvent the Negro establishment in Detroit. By 1941 enough black workers supported the UAW for the organizing drive to be successful.

This brief sketch of labor history supports the radical claim that multiracial unity is in the economic interest of all workers. It also shows that a multiracial working-class movement can be built. Moreover, the development of this antiracist consciousness among large sections of the white working class was not due to liberal actions. During this period liberal forces were largely inactive. For example, despite mass multiracial sentiment Roosevelt refused to support federal antilynching legislation publicly or to pardon the Scottsboro defendants; the NAACP was completely ineffectual in its attempts to rely on liberal support; and the corporate foundations were still supporting research into genetic inferiority theories.[51]

By the beginning of the Second World War, the success of the multiracial mass working-class movements created the following environment:

1. The unionizing efforts were convincing many that racism was fundamentally economic in nature, with white workers losing and capitalists gaining.
2. Theories of black genetic inferiority were losing not only their wide acceptance but their respectability as well.
3. The lack of legal concessions was weakening the effectiveness of liberal channels of antiracist protest — legal lobbying of the NAACP on behalf of the black people. Instead, many

blacks were increasingly sympathizing with more radical anticapitalist organizations.[52]

It is only at this point that the liberal response to racism begins. Moreover, if we look more closely at the liberal actions, we will find that they were not only reactions to an already formed mass antiracist sentiment but also a conscious attempt to counter and redirect the *radical* aspects of this sentiment.

The first and most influential response of the liberals was the well-known study by Gunnar Myrdal, *An American Dilemma,* funded by the Carnegie Corporation.[53] This report attacked racism and theories of black genetic inferiority. This, we have argued, was only a reaction to an already formed mass antiracist sentiment. The other major aspects of the report, however, were attempts to counter the other two aspects of the antiracist sentiment listed above. Myrdal continuously attempted to convince readers that racism was not financially motivated. Instead, Myrdal developed a model that viewed racism as part of sociopsychological process. This process is almost identical with the feedback mechanism of Franklin and Tanzer. Another major objective was to convince readers that the NAACP was the most effective channel for antiracist protests.

The Myrdal Report's assault on economic explanations of racial discrimination created a favorable intellectual climate for Gordon Allport's influential study, *The Nature of Prejudice.*[54] This work developed the thesis that racist attitudes were purely psychologically motivated. In support of this thesis Allport analyzed numerous and often obscure examples of *nonmarketplace* discrimination while ignoring all examples of *labor market* discrimination.

At the same time that these liberal theories were being widely circulated, a number of important liberal initiated actions occurred — desegregation of the Armed Forces, the 1948 Democratic Party plat-

---

[50] Gunnar Myrdal, *An American Dilemma* (1944), 1119–21.

[51] The Carnegie Foundation, through its funding of the Eugenics Records Office, in 1903, was the initial financier of the Eugenics Movement. Even as late as 1936 it was funding research generally supportive of eugenical measures. See Association for the Investigation of Eugenical Sterilization (Abraham Myerson *et al.*), *Eugenical Sterilization* (1936).

[52] See Report of the *National Advisory Commission on Civil Disorders* (1968), 222, for a brief account of the black revolt against the policies of the NAACP; and St. Clair Drake, *Black Metropolis* (1945) for an account of the popularity of the Communist Party among Chicago blacks (734–40).

[53] The Carnegie Foundation, beginning in 1938, enlisted the services of Myrdal and over twenty leading academicians to prepare this and numerous supplementary works.

[54] Gordon Allport, *The Nature of Prejudice* (1954).

form,[55] and the 1954 Supreme Court school desegregation ruling. These actions were directly related to the Myrdal-Allport outlook. First, none of them attacked labor market discrimination. For example, the Fair Employment Commission, which Roosevelt reluctantly created in 1941, in direct response to mass protests, never led to any legislative proposals and was conveniently forgotten after the war.[56] Second, a major effect of these actions was to win many antiracist forces to a liberal (legislative and legal) strategy, rather than continuing a labor-market oriented strategy. For example, at the same time that these liberal legalist actions were being initiated, liberal forces, aided by the anticommunist Cold War hysteria, subverted attempts to expand union organizing activities in the South.[57]

By the mid-1950s the liberal response had convinced many, especially intellectuals, that racist attitudes were psychologically motivated and could be most effectively changed through liberal actions. The defeat of radical antiracist ideas was a necessary precondition for the favorable acceptance of Becker's ideas. Becker's theory can be viewed as a logical extension of Allport's thesis — an attempt to apply the psychological model to explain labor market discrimination.

The reemergence of anti-racist militancy in the

1960s — sit-ins and freedom rides — rekindled the mass antiracist sentiment developed during the 1930s. Again, the liberal response was to redirect this sentiment toward *noneconomic* demands to be gained through legalistic and legislative actions. This time the multiracial antiracist movement could not be constrained by the liberal boundaries. Ghetto rebellions and campus protests continued, forcing some economic reforms. As before, the entire working class gained from these reforms.

The white working class benefited by the massive expansion of social services (health, education, etc.) that the antiracist movement won.[58] Middle-class professionals benefited from the expansion of professional jobs in the expanding social service industry. All benefited from the renewed commitment to full employment stimulated by antiracist protests. In addition, the antiracist movement opened the way for other oppressed groups to protest against their unfair treatment. As James Q. Wilson reluctantly admitted:

> The nonpolitical strategies developed by the Negro for gaining bargaining power — sit-ins, the protest march, and passive resistance — have already [1965] been adopted by whites.... Physically obstructing the operation of an organization — often illegally — has, in the 1960s, become a commonplace method for attempting to change the behavior of that organization. This "spillover" of civil rights tactics into other areas of social conflict has probably been one of the most important consequences of increased Negro militancy.[59]

Once again liberals reacted in another attempt to redefine the movement's objectives. To stop the movement for direct economic reform, liberals, through the use of "culture of poverty" arguments, began to attack the *legitimacy* of direct economic reforms. The "culture of poverty" thesis claimed that *past* discrimination had so brutalized the black population as to make their *present* culture dysfunc-

---

[55] The antiracist platform of the Democratic Party has always been considered a courageous principled stand. However, in light of the mass antiracist sentiment then present, it may have been a *pragmatic necessary* action to forestall mass defections of urban workers to the Henry Wallace ticket. Remember, Truman was expected to lose before this platform was adopted, and despite the bolting of the Southern wing of the Democratic Party he *gained* strength to win.

[56] Ralph Dalfiume, "The 'Forgotten Years' of Negro Revolution," in Sternsher, 298–311, documents the largely ineffective protest made by black Americans against unfair labor practices in defense plants and training programs. The symbolic Commission resulted, when Roosevelt was forced to respond to the threatened March on Washington, led by A. Phillip Randolph.

[57] Radical forces within the CIO successfully fought for the adoption, in 1946, of a mass campaign to organize in the South. However, the liberal leadership of the CIO (Phillip Murray–Walter Reuther) refused to allow radical participation in the project, though they were the most experienced and successful trade union organizers in the South. This organizing drive, which would have benefited all workers by eliminating cheap Southern labor, was quickly abandoned by the liberal trade union leaders.

[58] For example, the antiracist struggle for open admissions in New York City, enabled Italian and Irish working-class students, who had also been discriminated against, to attend the city universities in large numbers for the first time.

[59] James Q. Wilson, "The Negro in Politics," *Daedalus* 94 (Fall 1965), 973.

tional.[60] It is this culture and not present-day marketplace discrimination that explained the inferior economic status of black Americans. Hence, according to this thesis, it would be a *mistake* to try to improve the economic position of blacks through direct economic reforms.

Conclusions

■ Summary of Findings

When comparing the various theories of discrimination, we found:

1. The underlying explanation of discrimination according to:
   — conservatives was psychological motivation;
   — liberals was institutional and structural mechanisms;
   — radicals was profiteering.
2. The key purpose of these theories is to determine which groups financially benefit and which groups lose from racism. Only the radical model claimed that capitalists gained and white workers lost from discrimination.
3. Only the radical and liberal models found any empirical support.
4. The conservative model, having no empirical support, must derive its acceptance from ideological preconceptions.
5. A new emphasis was injected into radical thought when economic factors were replaced by psychological factors. These alternative models became racially based instead of class-based.

When comparing the policy implications of the various models, we found that the conservative models rely on education to eliminate racist practices; the liberal models rely on the government; and the radical models rely on the working class.

From the historical section, the emergence of successful multiracial protest movements showed that:

1. A multiracial antiracist movement is possible.

---

[60] One theory of why liberal academicians responded this way is found in William Ryan, *Blaming the Victim* (1969), 3–30.

2. This type of movement was crucial for winning economic gains for the entire working class.
3. Liberal policies were reactions to mass pressure rather than to leadership measures.
4. Liberal reactions attempted to redefine rather than advance already formed mass antiracist sentiments.
5. The intellectual and political climate of the 1950s explains the wide acceptance of Becker's theory, which was an application of Allport's psychological explanation of racial discrimination to the labor market.

■ Implications for Today

The 1970s are witnessing the most difficult economic crisis for capitalism since the Great Depression. One approach to stem the long-term downturn (since 1965) in corporate profit rates and labor productivity increases has been to lower workers' standard of living.[61] Racism has created so much divisiveness and diversion within the working class that it is one of the principal reasons for the lack of militant response on the part of workers. Antibusing and antiimmigration actions have increasingly diverted the hostilities of the white working class. Racist attitudes weakened the response to government cutbacks in essential services, which affected broad sections of the population through the loss of services and/or jobs. Most students reading this article have been hurt by racism since racist ideas have justified cutbacks in teaching, paramedical, and social service jobs.

Furthermore, the unstable international situation seems to be creating the conditions for another global conflict. Influential spokesmen, such as George Meany, George Wallace, and John Roche (*TV Guide*), have begun arguing for the need to stop the spread of communism militarily. Historically, fascist movements, based on racist ideas, have often been instrumental in convincing sections of the population of the necessity of war.

The 1930s shows that these setbacks and dangers can be defeated. It is up to us to apply those lessons and act.

---

[61] For various explanations of the crisis, see David Mermelstein, *The Economic Crisis Reader* (1975).

THE ECONOMICS OF RACISM

Michael Reich

This short essay summarizes some of the differences in orthodox and radical analyses of the economics of racism. Reich suggests some statistical tests of the two models and summarizes some important empirical evidence supporting the radical view. He concludes that racism serves a critical economic function by weakening the strength of the working class and promoting competition and class divisions among its members.

Written originally for this book of readings, the essay draws on the author's doctoral dissertation in economics at Harvard University, "Racism and the White Distribution of Income."

Reich teaches economics at the University of California at Berkeley.

In the late 1950s and early 1960s it seemed to many Americans that the elimination of racism in the United States was finally being achieved, and without requiring a radical restructuring of the society. The civil rights movement was growing in strength, desegregation orders were being issued, and hundreds of thousands of blacks were moving to Northern cities where discrimination was supposedly less severe than in the South. Government reports seemed to validate the optimism: for example, by 1969 the gap between blacks and whites in median years of schooling for males aged 25 to 29 years old was only one fourth the gap that had existed in 1960.[1]

But by 1970 the optimism of earlier decades had vanished. Despite new civil rights laws, elaborate White House conferences, special ghetto manpower programs, the War on Poverty, and stepped-up tokenist hiring, racism and the economic exploitation of blacks has not lessened. During the past twenty-five years the absolute male black-white income gap has more than doubled, while there has been virtually no permanent improvement in the relative economic position of blacks in America. Median black incomes have been fluctuating at a level between 47 percent and 62 percent of median white incomes, the ratio rising during economic expansions and falling to previous low levels during recessions.[2] Segregation in schools and neighborhoods has been steadily increasing in almost all cities, and the atmosphere of distrust between blacks and whites has intensified. Racism, instead of disappearing, seems to be on the increase.

Racism has been as persistent in the United States in the twentieth century as it was in previous centuries. The industrialization of the economy led to the transformation of the black worker's economic role from one of agricultural sharecropper and household servant to one of urban industrial operative and service worker, but it did not result in substantial relative improvement for blacks. Quantitative comparisons using Census data of occupational distributions by race show that the occupational status of black males is virtually the same today as it was in 1910 (the earliest year for which racial data are available).[3]

Source: Michael Reich, an essay written for this book. The author wishes to acknowledge the help of Samuel Bowles, who encouraged him to work on this problem and has provided critical guidance at every stage.

[1] "The Social and Economic Status of Negroes in the United States, 1969," Bureau of Labor Statistics Report No. 375 (October 1967), p. 50.

[2] The data refer to male incomes, and are published annually by the U.S. Census Bureau in its P-60 Series, "Income of Families and Persons...." Using data for the years 1948 to 1964, Rasmussen found that, after controlling for the effects of the business cycle, the average increase in the racial ratio of median incomes was only .3 percent per year, or 5 percent over the 16 years. See David Rasmussen, "A Note on the Relative Income of Nonwhite Men, 1948–64," *Quarterly Journal of Economics*, February 1970. Thurow, using a slightly different technique, estimated that no relative increase in black incomes would occur after unemployment was reduced to 3 percent. See L. Thurow, *Poverty and Discrimination* (Washington, D.C.: Brookings Institution, 1969), pp. 58–61. And Batchelder found that stability in the ratio over time despite migration of blacks from the South to the North; within regions in the North the ratio declined. Alan Batchelder, "Decline in the Relative Income of Negro Men," *Quarterly Journal of Economics* (November 1964).

[3] Since income data by race are not available before 1940, a relative index must be based on racial occupa-

This paper presents a radical analysis of racism and its historical persistence in America, focusing on the effects of racism on whites. The paper contrasts the conventional approach of neoclassical economic analysis — with its optimistic conclusions concerning the possibility of eliminating racism — with a radical approach — which argues that racism is deeply rooted in the current economic institutions of America, and is likely to survive as long as they do. A statistical model and empirical evidence are presented which support the radical approach and cast doubt on the conventional approach. The specific mechanisms by which racism operates among whites are also discussed briefly.

The Pervasiveness of Racism

When conventional economists attempt to analyze racism, they usually begin by trying to separate various forms of racial discrimination. For example, they define "pure wage discrimination" as the racial difference in wages paid to equivalent workers, i.e., those with similar years and quality of schooling, skill training, previous employment experience and seniority, age, health, job attitudes, and a host of other factors. They presume that they can analyze the sources of "pure wage discrimination" without simultaneously analyzing the extent to which discrimination also affects the factors they hold constant.

But such a technique distorts reality. The various forms of discrimination are not separable in real life. Employers' hiring and promotion practices, resource allocation in city schools, the structure of transportation systems, residential segregation and housing quality, availability of decent health care, behavior of policemen and judges, foremen's prejudices, images of blacks presented in the media and the schools, price gouging in ghetto stores — these and the other forms of social and economic discrimination interact strongly with each other in determining the occupational status and annual income, and welfare, of black people. The processes are not simply additive, but are mutually reinforcing. Often,

a decrease in one narrow form of discrimination is accompanied by an increase in another form. Since all aspects of racism interact, an analysis of racism should incorporate all of its aspects in a unified manner.

No single quantitative index could adequately measure racism in all its social, cultural, psychological, and economic dimensions. But, while racism is far more than a narrow economic phenomenon, it does have very definite economic consequences: blacks have far lower incomes than whites. The ratio of median black to median white incomes thus provides a rough, but useful, quantitative index of the economic consequences of racism for blacks as it reflects the operation of racism in the schools, in residential location, in health care — as well as in the labor market itself. We shall use this index statistically to analyze the causes of racism's persistence in the United States. While this approach overemphasizes the economic aspects of racism, it is nevertheless an improvement over the narrower approach taken by conventional economists.

Competing Explanations of Racism

How is the historical persistence of racism in the United States to be explained? The most prominent analysis of discrimination among economists was formulated in 1957 by Gary Becker in his book *The Economics of Discrimination*.[4] Racism, according to Becker, is fundamentally a problem of tastes and attitudes. Whites are defined to have a "taste for discrimination" if they are willing to forfeit income in order to be associated with other whites instead of blacks. Since white employers and employees prefer not to associate with blacks, they require a monetary compensation for the psychic cost of such association. In Becker's principal model white employers have a taste for discrimination; marginal productivity analysis is invoked to show that white employers hire fewer black workers than efficiency criteria would dictate — as a result, white employers lose (in monetary terms) while white workers gain from discrimination against blacks.

Becker does not try to explain the source of white tastes for discrimination. For him, these attitudes are determined outside of the economic system. (Racism could presumably be ended simply by changing these attitudes, perhaps by appeal to

tional data. Hiestand has computed such an index: he finds at most a 5 percent increase in blacks' status between 1910 and 1960; most of this improvement occurred during the labor shortages of the 1940s. See D. Hiestand, *Economic Growth and Employment Opportunities for Minorities* (New York: Columbia University Press, 1964), p. 53.

[4] University of Chicago Press.

whites on moral grounds.) According to Becker's analysis, employers would find the ending of racism to be in their economic self-interest, but white workers would not. The persistence of racism is thus implicitly laid at the door of white workers. Becker suggests that long-run market forces will lead to the end of discrimination anyway — less discriminatory employers, with no "psychic costs" to enter in their accounts, will be able to operate at lower costs by hiring equivalent black workers at lower wages, thus driving the more discriminatory employers out of business.[5]

The radical approach to racism argued in this paper is entirely different. Racism is viewed as rooted in the economic system and not in "exogenously determined" attitudes. Historically, the American Empire was founded on the racist extermination of American Indians, was financed in large part by profits from slavery, and was extended by a string of interventions, beginning with the Mexican War of the 1840s, which have been at least partially justified by white supremacist ideology.

Today, transferring the locus of whites' perceptions of the source of many of their problems from capitalism and toward blacks, racism continues to serve the needs of the capitalist system. Although an individual employer might gain by refusing to discriminate and agreeing to hire blacks at above the going black wage rate, it is not true that the capitalist class as a whole would profit if racism were eliminated and labor were more efficiently allocated without regard to skin color. I will show below that the divisiveness of racism weakens workers' strength when bargaining with employers; the economic consequences of racism are not only lower incomes for blacks, but also higher incomes for the capitalist class coupled with lower incomes for white workers. Although capitalists may not have conspired consciously to create racism, and although capitalists may not be its principal perpetuators, nevertheless racism does support the continued well-being of the American capitalist system.

Capitalist society in turn encourages the persistence of racism. Whatever the origins of racism, it is likely to take root firmly in a society which breeds an individualistic and competitive ethos, status fears among marginal groups, and the need for visible scapegoats on which to blame the alienating quality of life in America — such a society is unlikely magnanimously to eliminate racism even though historically racism may not have been created by capitalism.

Racism cannot be eliminated just by moral suasion; nor will it gradually disappear because of market forces. Racism has become institutionalized and will persist under capitalism. Its elimination will require more than a change of attitudes; a change in institutions is necessary.

We have, then, two alternative approaches to the analysis of racism. The first suggests that capitalists lose and white workers gain from racism. The second predicts the opposite — that capitalists gain while workers lose. The first says that racist "tastes for discrimination" are formed independently of the economic system; the second argues that racism is symbiotic with capitalistic economic institutions.

The two approaches reflect the theoretical paradigms of society from which each was developed. Becker follows the paradigm of neoclassical economics in taking "tastes" as exogenously determined and fixed, and then letting the market mechanism determine outcomes. The radical approach follows the Marxian paradigm in arguing that racial attitudes and racist institutions must be seen as part of a larger social system, in placing emphasis on conflict between classes and the use of power to determine the outcomes of such conflicts. The test as to which explanation of racism is superior is, in some ways, an illustrative test of the relative explanatory power of these competing social paradigms.

The very persistence of racism in the United States lends support to the radical approach. So do repeated instances of employers using blacks as strikebreakers, as in the massive steel strike of 1919, and employer-instigated exacerbation of racial antagonisms during that strike and many others.[6] How-

[5] Some economists writing on discrimination reject Becker's "tastes" approach, but accept the marginal productivity method of analysis. See, for example, L. Thurow, *op. cit.* The main substantive difference in their conclusions is that for Thurow, the entire white "community" gains from racism; therefore, racism will be a little harder to uproot. See also A. Krueger, "The Economics of Discrimination," *Journal of Political Economy,* October 1963.

[6] See, for example, David Brody, *Steelworkers in America: The Nonunion Era* (Cambridge: Harvard University Press, 1960); Herbert Gutman, "The Negro and the United Mineworkers," in J. Jacobson, ed., *The Negro and the American Labor Movement* (Garden City, N.Y.: Anchor, 1968); S. Spero and A. Harris, *The Black Worker* (New York: Atheneum, 1968), *passim.*

ever, the particular virulence of racism among many blue- and white-collar workers and their families seems to refute the radical approach to support Becker.

The Empirical Evidence

Which of the two models better explains reality? We have already mentioned that the radical approach predicts that capitalists gain and workers lose from racism, while the conventional Beckerian approach predicts precisely the opposite. In the latter approach racism has an equalizing effect on the white income distribution, while in the former racism has an unequalizing effect. The statistical relationship between the extent of racism and the degree of inequality among whites provides a simple, yet clear test of the two approaches. This section describes that test and its results.

First we shall need a measure of racism. The index we use, for reasons already mentioned, is the ratio of black median family income to white median family income (B/W). A low numerical value for this ratio indicates a high degree of racism. We have calculated values of this racism index, using data from the 1960 Census, for each of the largest forty-eight standard metropolitan statistical areas (SMSA's). It turns out there is a great deal of variation from SMSA to SMSA in the B/W index of racism, even within the North; Southern SMSA's generally demonstrated a greater degree of racism. The statistical technique we shall use exploits this variation.

We shall also need measures of inequality among whites. Two convenient measures are (1) S_1, the percentage share of all white income which is received by the top 1 percent of white families, and (2) G_w, the Gini coefficient of white incomes, a measure that captures inequality within as well as between social classes.[7]

Both of these inequality measures vary considerably among the SMSA's; there is also a substantial amount of variation in these variables within the

subsample of Northern SMSA's. Therefore, it is interesting to examine whether the pattern of variation of the inequality and racism variables can be explained by causal hypotheses. This is our first statistical test.

A systematic relationship across SMSA's between racism and white inequality does exist and is highly significant: the correlation coefficient is −.47.[8] The negative sign of the correlation coefficient indicates that where racism is greater, income inequality *among whites* is also greater. This result is consistent with the radical model and is inconsistent with the predictions of Becker's model.

This evidence, however, should not be accepted too quickly. The correlations reported may not reflect actual causality, since other independent forces may be simultaneously influencing both variables in the same way. As is the case with many other statistical analyses, the model must be expanded to control for such other factors. We know from previous inter-SMSA income distribution studies that the most important additional factors that should be introduced into our model are (1) the industrial and occupational structure of the SMSA's; (2) the region in which the SMSA's are located; (3) the average income of the SMSA's; and (4) the proportion of the SMSA population that is black. These factors were introduced into the model by the technique of multiple regression analysis. Separate equations were estimated with G_w and S_1 as measures of white inequality.

In all the equations the statistical results were strikingly uniform: racism was a significantly unequalizing force on the white income distribution, even when other factors were held constant. A 1 percent increase in the ratio of black to white median incomes (i.e., a 1 percent decrease in racism) was associated with a .2 percent decrease in white inequality, as measured by the Gini coefficient. The corresponding effect on S_1 was two-and-a-half times as large, indicating that most of the inequality among whites generated by racism was associated with increased income for the richest 1 percent of white families. Further statistical investigation revealed that increases in racism had an insignificant

---

[7] The Gini coefficient varies between 0 and 1, with 0 indicating perfect equality, and 1 indicating perfect inequality. For a more complete exposition, see H. Miller, *Income Distribution in the United States* (Washington, D.C.: Government Printing Office, 1966). Data for the computation of G_w and S_1 for 48 SMSA's were taken from the 1960 Census. A full description of the computational techniques used is available in my dissertation.

[8] The correlation coefficient reported in the text is between G_w and B/W. The equivalent correlation between S_1 and B/W is $r = -.55$. A similar calculation by S. Bowles, across states instead of SMSA's, resulted in an $r = -.58$.

effect on the share received by the poorest whites, and resulted in a small decrease in the income share of whites in the middle-income brackets.[9]

The Mechanisms of the Radical Model

Within the radical model, we can specify a number of mechanisms which further explain the statistical finding that racism increases inequality among whites. We shall consider two mechanisms here: (1) total wages of white labor are reduced by racial antagonisms, in part because union growth and labor militancy are inhibited; and (2) the supply of public services, especially in education, available to low- and middle-income whites is reduced as a result of racial antagonisms.

Wages of white labor are lessened by racism because the fear of a cheaper and underemployed black labor supply in the area is invoked by employers when labor presents its wage demands. Racial antagonisms on the shop floor deflect attention from labor grievances related to working conditions, permitting employers to cut costs. Racial divisions among labor prevent the development of united worker organizations both within the workplace and in the labor movement as a whole. As a result, union strength and union militancy will be less, the greater the extent of racism. A historical example of this process is the already mentioned use of racial and ethnic divisions to destroy the solidarity of the 1919 steel strikers. By contrast, during the 1890s, black-white class solidarity greatly aided mine-workers in building militant unions among workers in Alabama, West Virginia, Illinois, and other coalfield areas.[10]

The above argument and examples contradict the common belief that an exclusionary racial policy will strengthen rather than weaken the bargaining power of unions. But racial exclusion increases bargaining power only when entry into an occupation or industry can be effectively limited. Industrial-type unions are much less able to restrict entry than craft unions or organizations such as the American Medical Association. This is not to deny that much of organized labor is egregiously racist.[11] But it is im-

portant to distinguish actual discrimination practice from the objective economic self-interest of union members.

The second mechanism we shall consider concerns the allocation of expenditures for public services. The most important of these services is education. Racial antagonisms dilute both the desire and the ability of poor white parents to improve educational opportunities for their children. Antagonism between blacks and poor whites drives wedges between the two groups and reduces their ability to join in a united political movement pressing for improved and more equal education. Moreover, many poor whites recognize that however inferior their own schools, black schools are even worse. This provides some degree of satisfaction and identification with the status quo, reducing the desire of poor whites to press politically for better schools in their neighborhoods. Ghettos tend to be located near poor white neighborhoods more often than near rich white neighborhoods; racism thus reduces the potential tax base of school districts containing poor whites. Also, pressure by teachers' groups to improve all poor schools is reduced by racial antagonisms between predominantly white teaching staffs and black children and parents.[12]

The statistical validity of the above mechanisms can be tested in a causal model. The effect of racism on unionism is tested by estimating an equation in which the percentage of the SMSA labor force which is unionized is the dependent variable, with racism and the structural variables (such as the SMSA industrial structure) as the independent variables. The schooling mechanism is tested by estimating a similar equation in which the dependent variable is inequality in years of schooling completed among white males aged 25 to 29 years old.[13]

Once again, the results of this statistical test strongly confirm the hypotheses of the radical model. The racism variable is statistically significant in all the equations and has the predicted sign: a greater degree of racism results in lower unionization rates

[9] A more rigorous presentation of these variables and the statistical results is available in my dissertation.

[10] See footnote 6.

[11] See Herbert Hill, "The Racial Practices of Organized Labor," in J. Jacobson, ed., *The Negro and the American Labor Movement* (Garden City, N.Y.: Anchor paperback, 1968).

[12] In a similar fashion, racial antagonisms reduce the political pressure on governmental agencies to provide other public services which would have a pro-poor distributional impact. The two principal items in this category are public health services and welfare payments in the Aid to Families with Dependent Children program.

[13] These dependent variables do not perfectly represent the phenomena described, but serve as reasonable proxy variables for these purposes.

and greater amounts of schooling inequality among whites. This empirical evidence again suggests that racism is in the economic interests of capitalists and other rich whites and against the economic interests of poor whites and white workers.

However, a full assessment of the importance of racism for capitalism would probably conclude that the primary significance of racism is not strictly economic. The simple economics of racism does not explain why many workers seem to be so vehemently racist, when racism is not in their economic self-interest. In extra-economic ways, racism helps to legitimize inequality, alienation, and powerlessness — legitimization which is necessary for the stability of the capitalist system as a whole. For example, many whites believe that welfare payments to blacks are a far more important factor in their high taxes than is military spending. Through racism, poor whites come to believe that their poverty is caused by blacks who are willing to take away their jobs, and at lower wages, thus concealing the fact that a substantial amount of income inequality is inevitable in a capitalist society.

Racism also provides some psychological benefits to poor and working-class whites. For example, the opportunity to participate in another's oppression may compensate for one's own misery. The parallel here is to the subjugation of women in the family: after a day of alienating labor, the tired husband can compensate by oppressing his wife. Furthermore, not being at the bottom of the heap is some solace for an unsatisfying life; this argument was successfully used by the Southern oligarchy against poor whites allied with blacks in the inter-racial Populist movement of the late nineteenth century.

In general, blacks as a group provide a convenient and visible scapegoat for problems that actually derive from the institutions of capitalism. As long as building a real alternative to capitalism does not seem feasible to most whites, we can expect that identifiable and vulnerable scapegoats will always prove functional to the status quo. These extra-economic factors thus neatly dovetail with the economic aspects of racism discussed in the main body of this paper in their mutual service to the perpetuation of capitalism.

RACIAL DUALISM IN AN URBAN LABOR MARKET

Harold M. Baron and Bennett Hymer

This selection discusses the institutional "specification" of labor market segmentation by race in a local community. It illustrates the radical argument that basic economic institutions have effected important separations among sectors in the economy. The authors further elaborate the mechanisms underpinning racism.

The selection comes from a long article called "The Negro Worker in the Chicago Labor Market." A section on "De Facto Barriers" has been deleted from this discussion; it details the effect of extra-labor market insti-

tutions on the preservation of the dual labor market structure.

At the time that they wrote this essay, the authors were both members of the Research Department of the Chicago Urban League.

The types of disparities between white and Negro workers which were described in the first part of the paper have been permanent features of the Chicago labor market since World War I. Prior to the war Chicago had only a small Negro population, largely employed in menial- and personal-service-type occupations. During a tight wartime labor market, aggravated by the cessation of European immigration,

Source: From *The Negro and the American Labor Movement,* copyright © 1968 by Julius Jacobson, editor. Reprinted by permission of Doubleday & Company, Inc.

many employers began to recruit Negro labor from the South to fill manpower shortages. It was at this point of time that Negroes formed a sizable and distinct ethnic group in the Chicago labor force.

For the majority of Negroes coming to Chicago from the South, their point of entry into the labor market was at the bottom of the occupational hierarchy. Both rural work backgrounds and the emergence of discriminatory policies prevented their movement into higher-skilled and better-paying occupations. Soon after, the racial occupation lines that were emerging became permanently frozen.

Since 1920 there has been only a small change in the status of the Negro worker relative to that of the white worker. While both groups have improved their employment conditions — higher wages, more leisure — Negroes have not been able to catch up and close the gaps in income, occupation, and training. A comparison between Negro and white immigrants to the city further illustrates the inability of the Negro worker to eliminate these disparities. White immigrants in one or two generations were able to disperse throughout society and the economy of the Northern city. Negroes, on the other hand, one hundred years after emancipation and following almost three generations of intensive migration to the North, are still confined to certain sectors of the labor market.

A constantly increasing proportion of the Negro population in Chicago has been born and reared in the North. If Negroes operated only under the same handicaps that European immigrants did, we would expect to find a closing of the gap as the percentage of second and third generations of Northern Negroes increased. Instead, we find that the disparities have become fixed features of the overall socioeconomic structure. Neither urbanization nor substantial increases in the level of Negro educational attainment have eradicated the disparities in income and occupations between whites and Negroes. In other words, just as the large city has confined Negroes to residential ghettos and segregated schools, so has it locked them into definite (and inferior) sectors of the labor market.

To date, no satisfactory explanation has been offered for the perpetuation of Negroes' second-class status in the Northern city. Instead, comprehension of the Negro worker's position in the Northern labor market has been obscured by the myths inherited from America's racial history. In accounting for the Negro's status in the Northern city, Amer-icans have substituted a continuation of Southern economic folklore for fact. Explanations tend to be deduction from myths instead of cold analysis of the urban status quo. . . .

The racial folklore of the Negro worker's experience in the Northern labor market can now be replaced with a more sophisticated analysis. By utilizing recent findings in the study of Northern race relations and urban labor markets, the disparities between white and Negro workers can be related to institutional factors within the large urban labor market — the existence of barriers that divide the labor market into distinct compartments based upon race.

For expository purposes a blueprint of the typical Northern labor market will be drawn. Although the main point of reference is Chicago, the model is highly applicable to other urban labor markets having a sizable Negro labor force. Basically, the blueprint consists of three generalizations describing the way in which the Chicago labor market generates differences based upon race. These generalizations are:

1. The labor market is divided into two racial components — a sector for the deployment of white labor and a sector for the deployment of Negro labor. Each sector has its own separate institutions and mechanisms for the recruitment, training, and allocation of jobs and workers. Firms are cognizant of this division and have different perceptions of the two labor forces when they shop for labor.

2. The Negro labor force has served as a pool of surplus labor used to fill shortages of white labor that occur during war years or periods of rapid economic growth. A large segment of the Negro labor force has been frozen into positions that are regarded as traditionally Negro jobs. These jobs are usually marginal and low paying; they require little skill or formal training; they often involve physical hazards; they frequently offer only seasonal or cyclical employment; and they are frequently in stagnant or declining industries.

3. Northern *de facto* segregation, in general, is maintained by a complex of interrelated and mutually supportive institutions whose combined effect is greater than the sum of the effects of each institution considered singularly. The racial distinctions and differentiations

created in any one institutional area operate as effective barriers supporting the segregation and status differentiation that occurs in other institutions. The division of the labor market into a Negro sector and a white sector is made more effective by the existence of the barriers in non-labor-market institutions. These barriers feed back to limit the Negro worker's access in many areas of the labor market.

Racial Dualism in the Urban Labor Market

The racially dual labor markets found in Northern cities have their origins in the earlier system of Southern slavery and rural peonage.[1] However, if the Negro's subordinate position in the North were merely a historical atavism from his Southern past, it would be expected that race would lose its significance as a social and economic category with the passage of time. Instead, we find that the Negro's second-class status has been effectively institutionalized in the Northern city — far removed from Southern rural conditions.

The marked and systematic disparities that exist between whites and Negroes in regard to income, employment, occupation, and labor-force participation offer *prima facie* evidence that a dual racial labor market exists. The two distinct and enduring patterns of employment characteristics that have been described cannot be explained in terms of a single homogeneous market. The description of these disparities, however, documents the dualism at only a general level of observation.

In more specific terms, a racially dual labor market means that there exists a primary metropolitan labor market in which firms recruit white workers and in which white workers look for jobs; side by side with the major market, there exists a smaller labor sector in which Negroes are recruited and in which Negroes look for employment.[2] For each sector there are separate demand and supply forces determining the allocation of jobs to workers and

workers to jobs. Over time, this dualism is characterized by a transfer of jobs from the white sector to the Negro sector as the economy develops and as the Negro labor force expands in absolute and relative numbers.[3]

To understand the perpetuation of the Negro's second-class status, it is necessary to examine the mechanisms by which the labor market and in a broader sense the general socioeconomic structure have distributed jobs between whites and Negroes. The conception of a division of the labor market along racial lines in a city such as Chicago is an important factor in understanding how racial differences have been systematically maintained.

The racial divisions in the Chicago labor market are visible in many dimensions — by industry, by occupation, by geographic area, by firms, and by departments within firms. In general, Negro workers tend to be hired by certain industries and by particular firms within those industries. Some firms have absolute racial barriers in hiring, with Negroes being completely excluded. Within all industries and even in government employment there is unmistakable evidence of occupational ceilings for Negroes. Within single establishments that hire both whites and nonwhites, Negro workers are usually placed in particular job classifications and production units. A good rule of thumb is that the lower the pay or the more disagreeable and dirty the job, the greater the chance of finding a high proportion of Negroes.

Racial concentration by industry in Chicago is shown in the fact that 20 percent of employed Negro males work for federal, state, or local government as compared to only 6 percent of employed white males. Six percent of Negro males are in the primary metal industry as compared to 3 percent of white males. At the other extreme, 1.5 percent of white males are in the banking and finance industry as compared to only 0.2 percent of Negro males. The existence of limited entry for Negroes can also be found in manufacturing — for example, 6 percent of all white men are employed in the nonelectrical machinery industry while only 2 percent of all Negro men are in that field.

While an examination of broad industrial classifi-

---

[1] Both these systems can be considered as forms of social and economic segregation, which made possible the exploitation of the Negro labor force by the Southern landed ruling class. The division of the labor force also enabled many Southern manufacturers to practice wage discrimination, i.e., to pay Negroes less than whites for similar work and to pay Southern whites lower wages than Northern whites.

[2] In the Chicago area Negro workers comprise one seventh of the total labor force.

[3] It should be noted that the generalization concerning the dual labor market is made at a high level of abstraction and that there are obvious exceptions at the level of particulars. The need here is to comprehend the process, and comprehension requires some degree of abstraction.

cations indicates certain tendencies toward racial dualism in the labor market, the pattern becomes much more distinct when individual firms and occupations within an industry are considered. A recent survey based on a sample of firms from the membership of the Chicago Association of Commerce and Industry makes this point strongly by showing the percentage of firms in the Chicago labor market that do not employ nonwhites. Seven out of every ten small firms, one out of every five medium-sized firms, and one out of every thirteen large firms do not hire nonwhites. Construction, transportation and utilities, and finance and insurance are the *most segregated* industries. Those small firms that employ any nonwhites tend to have labor forces with a very high proportion of nonwhite workers. While nonwhites account for 10.4 percent of total employment by small firms, they are confined to 30.9 percent of the universe of small firms.

Employment of some nonwhites by a firm does not necessarily mean that it has an integrated work force. Within a firm, racial segregation can take place on the basis of production units, branch operation, or occupational classification. Table 1 offers conclusive proof of this point. For each major occupation it shows the percentage of employees working for firms that have no nonwhites in that particular occupational classification. It stands out clearly that within individual firms, four occupations — professional, managerial, sales, and craftsmen — tend to exclude nonwhites. In the case of professionals and managers Table 1 understates the segregation of Negroes, as a high proportion of the nonwhites in these classifications are Orientals.

TABLE 1. Proportion of Employment Segregation by Occupational Groups and Color

Occupation	Percent Segregated (nonwhite)
Professional	43.3%
Manager	75.1
Clerical Workers	27.3
Sales Workers	54.7
Craftsmen, Skilled	66.2
Semiskilled	11.5
Service Workers	8.0
Laborers	11.0

Source: Chicago Association of Commerce and Industry, *Manpower Survey, 1964,* p. 16, Table 11.

In some firms that are integrated by occupation, departments within that occupational group may be divided along racial lines. Negroes are especially segregated into hot, dirty departments like foundries and heat-treating shops. Sometimes within the same operation there will be occupational segregation in which the laborers are Negro and the machine operators are white, or in other cases the machine operators are Negro and the higher-paid mechanics are white. A plant might have an integrated semiskilled work force, but it will almost invariably have segregation of its craftsmen and lower-level supervisory employees, even though most of these jobs are filled by within plant recruitment. In general, the lower the position on the occupational scale, the greater the chance that there will be integration for a particular job classification. . . .

In response to this segregated job pattern in the total labor market, Negroes and whites have developed separate patterns of job seeking. Whites do not seek employment with firms that they identify as being totally in the Negro labor market, nor do they seek jobs that they identify as being Negro jobs. In firms which have integration among their unskilled or semiskilled workers, it is the whites in these categories who operate with the expectation that they will be chosen for on-the-job training or considered for promotion.

Negroes, on the other hand, shop in what they consider to be the Negro labor market. Firms are identified as employing Negroes, e.g., in Chicago certain mail-order houses and the Post Office; or jobs, such as laborer or foundry work, are identified as being Negro jobs. The Negro job seeker expects automatic rebuff outside the identified Negro labor market, and he accordingly limits his shopping to the places where he feels that he has some chance of success. Not surprisingly, most jobs in the white labor market are never sought by Negroes.

These segregated job-seeking patterns are reinforced by several practices. Many firms fill vacancies by word of mouth to friends and relatives of employees, thus recruiting from the same racial groups as their present labor force. Labor-market intermediaries — the Illinois State Employment Service, some five hundred private employment agencies, and vocational counselors — tend to operate on the basis of the dual labor market. Negro youngsters in school are encouraged to seek careers in occupations that are traditionally Negro jobs. Nonwhite job seekers are counseled to apply for positions within the

Negro labor market. Both public and private employment services, in spite of legal prohibitions, tend to respect the racial lines of the labor market in their referrals.

Surplus Labor Supply

The concept of dualism is a convenient way of describing a major feature of Northern race relations in the area of employment — the segregation and division of the white and Negro labor forces. To understand further the operation of urban labor markets where there is a sizable Negro labor force, it is necessary to describe the processes of how Negroes advance occupationally and how certain jobs are either kept from or allocated only to the Negro labor force.

Our second generalization, i.e., the surplus labor pool, shows that the Negro labor force has served as an excess supply of labor utilized for jobs that whites have recently vacated, or for jobs where there are shortages of white labor, or for jobs that have become traditionally Negro jobs. According to this generalization, the Negro labor force can be broken down into three distinct groups:

1. A Negro *service sector* selling goods and services to the Negro community.
2. A *standard sector* regularly employed by major white-controlled firms or institutions, including government.
3. A *surplus labor factor* that is without work or tenuously employed in low-paying, marginal jobs.

By the Negro service sector we refer to Negroes self-employed or employed by firms, either white or Negro owned, which service the Negro community. In the case of professional services, such as medical or legal, the persons within this sector are usually well paid. At the other extreme are small neighborhood retail establishments providing only a subsistence income to their proprietors. In general, the size of the service sector is dependent upon the amount of money that Negroes have available for consumption expenditures.

By the standard sector of the Negro labor force we refer to workers regularly employed in firms and institutions that supply goods and services to the total economy. Annual earnings in this sector are

well above the subsistence level and in many cases are comparable to those for whites. Jobs in this sector are either with major employers or with firms that are competitive with the major companies. Within this standard sector Negro workers are often segregated by firm and within firms by job classification or production unit. The size of this sector is generally determined by the extent to which past or present labor shortages have allowed the entry of Negro workers into areas where previously just whites were hired. Currently, approximately half the Negro labor force is in this category.

The surplus sector of the Negro labor jobs consists of workers occupied in traditional Negro jobs outside the standard sector and workers who are unemployed or are out of the labor force, or are in marginal jobs. Workers in the surplus sector who have jobs occupy positions that are at the very bottom of the occupational ladder. These jobs are low paying, involve dirty and unsafe work, are often of short duration, and have little advancement potential. Many of these jobs are assigned to the Negro labor force only as the white labor force advances into higher occupations. Traditional Negro jobs like bootblacks, car washers, busboys, washroom attendants, porters, and servants are positions that through custom have gradually formed an area of employment exclusively for Negroes, or other minority groups, regardless of employment conditions elsewhere in the labor market.

Table 2 provides estimates for each of these sectors of the Negro labor force for 1959. Because earlier data were not available, changes in the relative and absolute sizes of each sector cannot be measured.

Many workers in the surplus sector are dependent upon some form of public aid for their incomes. In Chicago approximately one fourth of all Negroes receive some form of public assistance. All persons in this sector have low incomes, close to or at a sub-

TABLE 2.   Estimates of the Sectors of the Negro Labor Supply in Chicago Metropolitan Area by Sex, 1959

	Male	Female
Standard Sector	125,000	57,000
Negro Service Sector	20,000	15,000
Surplus Sector	80,000	53,000
Total	225,000	125,000

sistence level, that cover only the basic necessities. For all members of this sector, both those with and those without work, the level of subsistence income is primarily established outside the labor market by the political determination of welfare payments. The level of welfare payments serves as an effective minimum income. The size of this sector has generally been dependent upon the degree of unemployment in the general labor market and, in earlier years, upon the amount of white immigration.

The concept of the surplus labor supply can also be viewed as a dynamic process occurring over time. Usually some Negro workers are moving from the surplus sector into the standard sector. This movement is often accelerated in periods of rapid economic growth when tight labor markets help break down many discriminatory barriers. Many firms will begin to shop in the Negro labor market when they are confronted by a shortage of white labor. In Illinois these positions are often in declining industries that are losing their labor force to the growth industries.[4] Sometimes this movement reverses itself. For example, many Negroes in the Chicago meat-packing industry were forced back into the surplus sector when displaced from their jobs at the time the packinghouses left Chicago. But usually the break-throughs in employment that occur are irreversible partly because of social custom, and partly because of seniority and other forms of job security.

In the last twenty-five years the number of Negro workers who have left the Negro surplus labor sector has increased considerably. However, the Negro labor force is still growing today, primarily through the entry of indigenous teen-agers and secondarily through the migration of Southerners. In the face of this growing labor force the expansion in employment opportunities for Negroes has not been sufficient either to have eliminated or to have reduced substantially the size of the surplus labor pool. Negro teen-agers are frequently trapped in the surplus labor sector because of the inadequate preparation they receive in inferior, segregated schools like those in Chicago. Negro workers displaced from Southern agriculture are even worse off as the gap between the requirements necessary for industrial employment and unskilled Southern rural labor has widened over time.

The concepts of the dual labor market and the surplus labor supply can be more closely related by considering their more general usage. Social scientists who specialize in the study of underdeveloped countries point out that these economies are usually composed of two clearly identifiable sectors: an advanced industrialized sector using modern technology and skilled labor, and a subsistence peasant sector, using very little machinery and containing a large unskilled labor force that has high rates of unemployment and underemployment. We find a parallel in the urban labor market that we have been examining. Here, there is a white labor force which, for the most part, uses modern technology and contains a large percentage of skilled and highly skilled workers; then there is a Negro labor force which, to a large extent, is unskilled and employed in jobs either located in declining industries or providing only marginal types of employment. In fact, the surplus sector of the Negro labor force forms a type of urban peasantry comparable in certain aspects to the subsistence sector in underdeveloped economies. Since this supply of labor is outside the general economy and workers in it live at a subsistence income, they can easily be attracted into regular employment in large numbers without forcing wages to rise.

That racial dualism exists in most urban labor markets and that the Negro labor force has served as a surplus labor pool may explain why unemployment rates in the U.S. have been above those tolerated by workers in the Western European countries.[5] In the U.S. the unemployment rate for Negroes is almost always double that for whites, if not higher, and a much greater proportion of the Negro labor force is concentrated in undesirable jobs. An equitable distribution of unemployment would probably raise the white unemployment rate by at least 1 percent. In this context, dualism can be considered as a way of minimizing the potential economic and social grievances resulting from unemployment and other forms of economic injustice. Given the tendency of the economy over the last eight years to function at levels where unemployment seldom falls below 5 percent, white workers are only protecting

---

[4] Dale Hiestand, *Economic Growth and Employment Opportunities for Minorities* (New York: Columbia University Press, 1964), 87.

[5] Joseph W. Garbarino, "Income Policy and Income Behavior," and Murray Edelman and R. W. Fleming, "Unemployment and Wage — Price Policies" in Arthur Ross, ed., *Employment Policy and the Labor Market* (Berkeley: University of California, 1965).

a narrow economic interest by excluding Negroes from many occupations. Because of a lack of political and social power, the Negro labor force has not been able to impose its own political constraint concerning the level of unemployment it will tolerate. One impact of the current civil rights movement may be to reduce the permissible rate of Negro unemployment. . . .

Conclusion

Segregation in the Northern labor market has been as efficient a mechanism for subjugating Negroes to second-class status as segregation in housing and education. In Chicago the process of allocating jobs to white workers is so effectively separated from the process of allocating jobs to Negro workers that year after year the differentials between white and Negro workers are maintained. At the same time, a large segment of the Negro labor force is relegated to the role of an urban peasantry destined to live off welfare payments and white paternalism. The Negro labor force, unlike those of other large ethnic groups, has not been allowed to assimilate into the metropolitan labor market. One hundred years after emancipation and forty-five years after urbanization, Negroes in Chicago are still systematically restricted in both the skills they may acquire and the extent to which they can utilize any given level of skills.

Racial dualism in the urban labor market is a structural phenomenon. While this does not necessarily mean that the social and economic order depends on segregation, it does tell us that our basic social and economic institutions have to be revamped in order to achieve equality. A dual structure based upon race is not merely a slight deviation from some acceptable norm as to how the labor market should function, but an essential feature of urban labor markets and American race relations.

Several implications immediately follow from this conclusion. (1) Programs and policies to eliminate segregation in the labor market have to be more extensive than those that now exist. Changes on the demand side — the removal of discriminatory barriers in hiring — can have only limited impact so long as conditions on the supply side remain stationary: inferior Negro public schools, housing segregation. (2) So long as current programing is continued under the same institutional assumptions — that the labor market is not divided racially — Negroes can make advancements only during periods of exceptional economic growth. Current programs are still applicable only in situations where the labor market is tight. And (3) the current pattern of racial disparities will perpetuate itself so long as only the market mechanism is relied upon as a corrective device and so long as supportive institutions that help shape the supply of labor continue their racist policies. Individual decision-making units in the labor market — the large firm or union — cannot by themselves produce changes in the institutional framework. At most, their policies can result in marginal adjustments. Concerted action and long-range planning by all important groups — employers, unions, placement agencies, and government — are necessary to produce the structural changes for the erosion of the dual structure. The labor market, if allowed to operate only through its own internal forces, does not generate sufficient economic or social pressure to eliminate racial disparities.

Recent events in the labor market can be evaluated against this background. So far the main institutional impact of the civil rights movement in Chicago has been in the area of employment, as both school and housing segregation have remained the same or even increased since Birmingham. On the demand side of the labor market, there has been a partial lowering of discriminatory barriers as firms seek to comply with new laws and federal executive orders. An even greater lowering of barriers has been brought about by the labor shortages created by the present five-year-long economic boom.

In most major firms absolute racial restrictions have been removed. The biggest changes have been in those firms which are U.S. government contractors and therefore subject to review under the President's Equal Employment Opportunity Program. A few Negroes are now moving into professional and managerial positions for which, regardless of qualifications, they never would have been considered a few years ago. In some firms a fair number of female clerical workers are being hired.

However, these breakthroughs into new job classifications usually involve only a handful of Negro employees. They provide a symbolic token that the firm no longer discriminates absolutely. Most firms are pursuing only cautious programs of integration designed to be easily observable so as to satisfy government enforcement officers and civil rights groups. The current interest of many firms in race relations and the expensive rituals undertaken to indicate this interest still have not produced a major alteration in the employment structure. The openings in the better jobs are still minimal. The National Industrial Conference Board reports on a survey of forty companies: "Negroes, generally, still are being hired for low-paying, low-status jobs. The number of [Negroes] being employed in nontraditional Negro jobs is very small." The NICB further states: "There is a gap between policy and practice in the area of Negro employment. Few of the companies studied are doing as well as they want to do or so well as their top officers think they are doing." [6]

[6] "Chief Executives View Negro Employment," *The Conference Board Record* (May 1965), 32.

The current status of the Negro worker in the Chicago labor market may be characterized by the statement that although some discriminatory barriers on the demand side have been slightly lowered, most on the supply side still remain. Regarding the employment of semiskilled and unskilled workers by firms subject to compliance with the President's Equal Employment Opportunity Program, one close observer of discrimination in Chicago comments: "In the past, personnel men used to discriminate against nine out of ten Negro applicants; today they only discriminate against eight out of ten."

A CRITIQUE OF REFORMIST SOLUTIONS TO DISCRIMINATION

Firdaus Jhabvala

Building upon the radical analysis of racial discrimination developed in the previous selections, Jhabvala reviews some common reformist proposals to improve the situation of blacks (and other minority groups).

Criticizing several different policies in turn, Jhabvala concludes that all of them are inadequate for addressing the problems of black people. "People who desire meaningful change in the relations between black people and the American economic system," Jhabvala concludes, "need to work harder to replace capitalist institutions."

Like the second selection in this chapter, this piece comes from a longer manuscript; the selection is also published for the first time in this book.

Jhabvala formerly taught economics at Lincoln University and now teaches and does economic research at the Technological Institute of Villahermosa in Tabasco, Mexico.

The radical analysis recommends the replacement of capitalist relationships as a necessary ingredient in

Source: Extract from "Black People and the American Economic System," an unpublished manuscript. Reprinted with permission of the author.

ending the disadvantages of color. In this section, I analyze those programs accepted as bona fide attempts to solve the problems of black people. I first discuss federal programs in manpower training and welfare compensation. Then, I deal with the encouragement of black capitalism. This is followed by a discussion of ghetto economic development and whether the ghetto should be gilded or dispersed. All these solutions presuppose an expanding capitalist economy that can spare something for black people after taking care of profit requirements. At the present time, this requirement does not exist. Finally, reparation schemes are examined. These are based largely upon the accumulation of political power by black people, or at least a fundamental change in the power relationships that affect black people. They are therefore qualitatively different from the other solutions.

Manpower Training

Thurow, Tobin, and several other economists have advocated manpower training programs as a vital micro supplement to a macro policy of tight labor markets.[1] Proponents of these programs accept that a tight labor market is essential for the poor to secure reasonable amounts of employment. The theory is that a tight labor market forces employers to move further down the queue in order to fill up their labor force. If, at the same time, semiskilled labor is provided, then blacks and other disadvantaged groups will reap large benefits, since they would be hired proportionately more than their number in the labor force.

About a dozen different manpower programs have been erected in recent years, mostly to provide better employment opportunities at the bottom of the labor force. Different programs provide training on and off the job; part-time and full-time; to students and nonstudents; for students in school and out of school; straight public employment; and placement after training. Federal obligations for work and training amounted to $2.753 billion in fiscal 1973 and created 927,400 enrollment opportunities.[2] Not counting those in school in the Neighborhood Youth Corps, enrollees totalled 915,000[3] and perhaps half a million of them secured jobs in 1973 — one for every eight people officially unemployed in 1973.

Two basic problems plague manpower programs. First, the programs are pitifully inadequate to affect unemployment significantly. In fiscal 1973, the largest work program funded federally was the Public Employment Program with federal obligations of $1.239 billion and 178,000 enrollees, or 4 percent of the unemployed in 1973.[4] This program cost $7,000 to put one person to work. It would therefore cost about $42 billion to employ today's unemployed force of about 6 million. All federal obligations under work and training programs amounted to $2.753 billion in 1973, perhaps 7 percent of what is needed to employ the unemployed. The size of manpower programs therefore reveal them as token programs.

The second problem is that work and training programs are not geared to serve the unemployed. A study of the participants in three of these programs notes that they often viewed their jobs as repressive and stifling. "What is striking is the num-

ber of these grievances that occurred on the program job."[5] "In fact, the program job increased the original grievance rate to the point that it approximates that of the casual sometime worked group."[6] The study noted that there was no lack of desire for income among participants. There was no difference between stayers and leavers in personal efficacy ("Where there's a will there's a way."). In fact, when the program does not lead to a desirable job, the efficacious person tends to drop out. People stayed if the pay, job satisfaction, and chance to get ahead were reasonable.[7] Large numbers of enrollees drop out of these programs — for example, over a third in the case of Manpower Development and Training Act (MDTA) programs.[8] Fewer find employment — about one-half in the case of MDTA programs.[9] Thus, manpower programs hardly serve the unemployed who are in these programs.

If manpower programs are token programs and irrelevant to the needs of most unemployed people, whom do these programs serve? The programs fulfill an essential role through appeasing the bottom of the labor force. An illusion of upward mobility is sought to be created and sustained. Thereby, the responsibility for being unemployed is placed squarely upon the unemployed. If the government will even pay to retrain them, then they have no cause to be unemployed. Thus, manpower programs help "cool-out" the unemployed just as two-year colleges cool-out students.

Apart from nurturing the myth of governmental interest in the unemployed, these programs subsidize corporations which are supposed to train and employ the "hard-core" unemployed. Corporations employ these people only when labor is very scarce, as in the latter half of World War I when unemployment was less than one million. What has been happening is that pockets of employment open up and close down periodically.[10] When a pocket of employment opens up, there is a rush to be retrained and to secure what are perceived as permanently favorable jobs. Manpower training assists the un-

[1] See, for instance, Lester Thurow, *Poverty and Discrimination,* Brookings, 1969.

[2] U.S. Department of Labor, *Handbook of Labor Statistics, 1974,* Bureau of Labor Statistics Bulletin No. 182, p. 139. (This source will hereinafter be cited as *Labor Handbook 1974.*)

[3] *Ibid.,* p. 142.

[4] *Ibid.,* pp. 139, 142, and 144.

[5] U.S. Department of Labor, "Work Attitudes of Disadvantaged Black Men," Report No. 401, 1972, p. 7.

[6] *Ibid.,* p. 8.

[7] *Ibid.,* p. 23.

[8] *Labor Handbook 1974, op. cit.,* p. 143.

[9] *Loc. cit.*

[10] For example, according to *ibid.,* p. 165, 15.4 percent of the labor force was unemployed in 1972 at some time during the year.

employed in this rush. However, simultaneously, in another pocket of the economy, workers are being laid off. They join the unemployed and attempt to retrain to secure jobs. Thus, manpower programs do not affect the size of the employed labor force. They merely retrain people already trained in skills not currently in demand. Therefore, these programs merely offset the cost to employers of retraining the unemployed. This conclusion is substantiated by the data that show no relationship between manpower programs and unemployment, which has steadily risen since the end of World War II, from a low of 1.8 million in 1953 to over 6 million in December 1974.[11]

Manpower programs do not alter the structure of industrial organization; rather, they attempt to serve it. At best, they provide job trainees with temporary, tenuous, dead-end jobs in the secondary sector. Meanwhile, the pool of unemployeds does not not become smaller.[12] Manpower programs are therefore irrelevant to the basic problem which is that the normal functioning of the capitalist system creates a class of "hard-core" unemployed people. To convert the unemployed into a responsible, skilled, mobile labor force is to undo the handiwork of the capitalist system carried out during the entire life of the individual.

Welfare Recipients

Welfare recipients are often portrayed as unwed mothers, predominantly black, procreating as fast as the government assists them. Of course, this is far from the reality of welfare. Five facts stand out: First, the amount of money received by these recipients is paltry. Second, the welfare system is expanding because the condition of the poor is getting worse. Third, welfare payments constitute an im-

portant tool in regulating the pressure of the poor upon the ruling class; that is, welfare payments are increased when the poor contemplate rebellious behavior and are diminished at other times. Fourth, welfare payments are a means to keep the pool of cheap labor large enough so that unorganized labor stays cheap. Fifth, the welfare system is heavily biased against black people.

Payments to welfare recipients cannot be great because the government is a committee to manage the collective affairs of capitalists, not welfare recipients. The state tends to pacify the poor so that they do not revolt rather than care for their welfare. The prevailing ethic is that social welfare is a right to be earned by the individual through hard work and thrift. One gets what one pays for, just as in health, education, or housing. It does not matter that health is a good that a one-year-old cannot pay for. That is just too bad. The result of such thought is that very little is received by people in state-defined poverty.

In fiscal 1974, social welfare expenditures under public law amounted to $242.3 billion. Of this amount, Public Assistance programs spent $25.4 billion or about one-tenth of the total. Even this overstates the amount of welfare payments, popularly identified as Aid to Families with Dependent Children (AFDC), which is one of seven federal programs called Public Assistance. Of these, the one growing the fastest constitutes Vendor Medical Payments, which amounted to $11.2 billion in fiscal 1974.[13] In contrast, federal payments for AFDC amounted to $7.2 billion in 1973.[14] Welfare recipients receive little in comparison with other recipients of public social welfare.

Another indicator of governmental generosity toward welfare recipients is that Public Assistance expenditures have not been rising rapidly in the long run. For example, while 3.4 percent of GNP was allocated to federal Public Assistance programs in 1940, the figure was only 1.1 percent in 1973.[15] Likewise, from 1950 to 1970, Public Assistance expenditures failed to keep up with all social welfare expenditures and rose only half as fast as Social Insurance expenditures.[16] Expenditures for welfare

---

[11] *Ibid.*, p. 144; and U.S. Department of Commerce, *Monthly Business Statistics*, January 10, 1975, p. 4.

[12] There is much evidence that ghetto people take turns being unemployed. Thus, Doeringer *et al.* report: "Although 85 per cent of those entering ABCD's employment centers are unemployed when they apply, almost all have had quite recent work experience. Youths in the process of moving from school to work are virtually the only ones without a record of past employment." Peter Doeringer *et al.*, *Low-Income Labor Markets and Urban Manpower Programs: A Critical Assessment*, U.S. Department of Labor Research Findings Monograph, No. 12, 1972.

[13] These three numbers come from Alfred Skolnik and Sophie Dales, "Social Welfare Expenditures, Fiscal Year 1974," *Social Security Bulletin*, January 1975, p. 6.

[14] *Social Security Bulletin*, December 1974, pp. 68–69.

[15] *Ibid.*, p. 74.

[16] Skolnik and Dales, *op. cit.*, p. 6.

recipients are therefore not rising faster than other social welfare expenditures.

If welfare expenditures are neither large nor rising fast, the average benefit received through AFDC must be both smaller and rising less rapidly than through other social programs. This is precisely the case. In 1973, the average monthly benefit per family in AFDC was $195.21. It was $225.50 for families of disabled workers.[17] Similarly, the rise in average benefits under AFDC has been slower than under Old Age, Survivorship, Disability and Health Insurance. From 1961 to 1973, during the "welfare explosion," average monthly benefits under AFDC rose only 70 percent while more than doubling under the other programs just listed.[18] Welfare payments are not generous. Rather, more people have been forced onto welfare as the economic position of the lower half of the population has deteriorated absolutely. The result is that, while in 1961, AFDC payments were made to 916,000 families including 3.6 million recipients, by 1973 the numbers had risen to 3.156 million families and 10.8 million recipients.[19]

Piven and Cloward argue that the deteriorating position of the poor is the reason for the expansion of welfare rolls.[20] They say that while black teenage unemployment rates used to be 7 percent in World War II, they are near 40 percent now. Similarly, I have noted that the number of poor blacks actually increased 1970 to 1972, that real incomes of workers today are clearly less than in 1965, and that since 1954 over 2.7 million workers have been unemployed each year.[21] It is therefore logical that welfare rolls should expand.

The Social Security program reflects all the biases of the government in the provision of economic security. Wages are the only kind of income taxed. In 1975, only the first $14,100 of income is taxed at a flat rate of 5.85 percent. Therefore, those earning more than the ceiling pay a lower effective rate. Blacks are heavily represented in this group. Individuals are restricted as to the amount they can earn from labor while receiving benefits. Black people are less likely to work each quarter and therefore less likely to qualify for credit to be fully insured. The lower expectation of life for black people means that they are less likely to be around to collect payments even if they do have regular jobs that add up to a long record of payments for social security. Spotty employment records, the noncoverage of occupations in which blacks predominate, and the lower life expectancy of blacks all result in lower percentages of the black poor receiving social security income when compared with poor whites. Because of these and other factors, dependence on public assistance income by blacks is more than twice as great as that of whites.[22] Thus, social programs tend to be two-tiered: the upper tier, social insurance, predominantly serves white workers; blacks tend to be served by the lower tier, AFDC.

Piven and Cloward believe that two principal inferences can be drawn about relief programs: (1) they aim to moderate or prevent disorders by the very poor; and (2) they attempt to maintain a low wage labor pool. Thus, if the poor are not creating disorders and disruptions, they will be shaken off the welfare rolls so that (2) above may be better served. When they are creating disruptions, welfare rolls expand, satisfying (1) above. Piven and Cloward explain the welfare explosion of the late sixties stressing the urban upheavals of the mid-sixties. However, urban upheavals or tranquillity apart, the number of black poor actually increased from 1970 to 1972, and this trend has probably accelerated in the last three years of economic dislocation. Welfare rolls expand simply because of rising poverty in America, especially at the bottom. In conclusion, welfare payments at best provide a thin cosmetic covering for America's sores and cannot be counted upon to help black people. Welfare payments just cannot arrest the continuous exploitation of black people by capitalist institutions.

Black Capitalism

One of the doors pointed out to blacks in order to advance is labeled black capitalism. Four facts stand out in considering the relative merits of black capi-

[17] *Social Security Bulletin,* January 1975, pp. 63 and 50.

[18] *Ibid.,* pp. 63 and 51.

[19] *Social Security Bulletin,* December 1974, pp. 68–69.

[20] Frances Fox Piven and Richard Cloward, *Regulating the Poor,* Pantheon, 1971.

[21] *Labor Handbook 1974, op. cit.,* p. 144.

[22] U.S. Bureau of the Census, "The Social and Economic Status of the Black Population in the United States, 1971," *Current Population Reports,* Series P-23, Number 42, July 1972, p. 47. (Hereinunder cited as "Black Status 1971.")

talism as a means to uplift black people. First, the present state of black capitalism is pitiful. Second, as a consequence, black firms are appendages to white-dominated firms. Third, the future of all capitalism, but especially American capitalism, is increasingly bleak. Fourth, capitalism is the mechanism most used to exploit blacks, not to help them.

There are very few black firms. Black businesses comprised 2.2 percent of all firms in 1969. Other minorities owned almost as many firms (2.1 percent) and grossed receipts more than one-third as much greater than black businesses, which amounted to only 0.3% of that of all firms.[23] The scale of operation of black businesses is even smaller. Over three-fourths of all black-owned firms in 1969 had no paid employees; 95 percent of these firms were sole proprietorships.[24] Present-day black capitalism consists of very few firms, mostly sole proprietorships employing only the owner. The position of these firms in the economy is at best marginal and tenuous. In the best of times, black capitalists can hardly provide employment to themselves, let alone employing the mass of unemployed blacks. When bad times strike, their firms fold.

The ten most important industry groups of black-owned firms ranked by receipts[25] demonstrates the character of these businesses. Eight of these industries are either service industries (wholesale trade, eating and drinking places, personal services, trucking and warehousing, insurance carrier) or retail outlets for other firms (automotive dealers and gasoline filling stations, food stores, and miscellaneous retail stores). Much of the business of the last two (special trade contractors, and general building contractors) fall into the category of a service or retail outlet or both. It is plain from this list that black firms are appendages to white firms. Therefore, black capitalism, as it exists, is an extremely shaky proposition.

Blacks are urged to become competitive capitalists in an era dominated by monopoly capitalism. Blacks are urged to support the advanced capitalism of the U.S. when it is in a stage of stagnation and decay. There was a time when a belligerent person could become a big capitalist during his life. But blacks

were shackled to slavery or peonage during the hey-day of American capitalism. At present, black capitalists would do extremely well merely to hold on to their minuscule amounts of capital. Given that even several large corporations face hard times, black capitalism is the easiest way for blacks to lose whatever they have.

In America, the two words *black* and *capitalism* have diametrically opposite connotations. Thus, *black* implies a group of people mostly poor, mostly not in possession of capital and mostly at the exploited end of capitalism. *Capitalism* involves an individual ethos, smacks of wealth and the ability to appropriate output from others, notably but certainly not exclusively from blacks. Capitalist exploitation of most black people will not be lessened even if the color of the exploiter is different. Black capitalism can at best move a handful of blacks into the capitalist class. The mass of black people will remain unaffected, and inequities among blacks will increase as average figures are elevated by a few extremely rich blacks. In this way, black capitalism is a divisive philosophy designed to lure away some blacks toward capitalism, their primary exploiter. Thus, it is hoped that the possibility of a solution for blacks as a group would be destroyed. Such a solution demands the unity of black people against capitalism.

Ghetto Economic Development

Black capitalism has several drawbacks. Therefore, some people argue that blacks should seek communal economic advances through economic organizations such as CDC's (Community Development Corporations). These corporations would receive financial support from the federal government. Proponents of CDC's, such as Vietorisz and Harrison,[26] argue for both the financial and social benefits of CDC's that accrue to ghetto residents. Most plans provide for shares in CDC's to be divided among ghetto residents or for them to subscribe to these shares. Growth of the CDC is visualized through its retention of profits and by the subscription of new shares by ghetto dwellers out of savings.

The basic problem with CDC's is that they are politically infeasible. The federal government will

[23] U.S. Bureau of the Census, *Statistical Abstract of the United States,* 1973, p. 474.

[24] U.S. Bureau of the Census, *Statistical Abstract of the United States,* 1972, p. 471.

[25] "Black Status 1971," *op. cit.,* p. 76.

[26] Thomas Vietorisz and Bennett Harrison, "Ghetto Development, Community Corporations and Public Policy," *Review of Black Political Economy,* Fall 1971.

certainly resist successfully attempts to subsidize community-oriented black organizations with a significant economic muscle. Further, CDC proponents overestimate the chance of the black community's controlling the ghetto infrastructure. Thus, Vietorisz and Harrison maintain that a "social and political program of ghetto development might, apart from the coordinated planning of enterprises, contain some of the following elements:

1. Management of local branch stores of national chains by CDC;
2. Public housing, administered and owned by a combination of tenants and community housing groups;
3. Election of autonomous local school boards with powers comparable to those of middle-class suburban residential communities;
4. Majority representation on the boards of directors of local hospitals and other public health facilities;
5. Autonomous local institutions responsible to the community at large for administering manpower training and recruitment services as well as unemployment, welfare, and other transfer operations; and
6. Community control of police, elected civilian review board in each precinct, with powers to investigate, subpoena, and initiate proceedings for the removal of policemen convicted of brutality against the residents of the community." [27]

Any of these elements would yield substantial control in an important area of the ghetto. Black people would replace white-dominated institutions with institutions of their own. That involves a change in power relationships in favor of black people through the extraction of concessions. However, concessions will be forthcoming only when the system's rulers feel threatened. They will not feel threatened by something they support, such as black capitalism. But why should they support something that has the trappings of black socialism? Even if social ownership of ghetto capital was secured, the CDC would still have to deal with white-owned enterprise outside the ghetto. It would be funded by the federal government. He who pays calls the tune, at least under capitalism. The CDC would therefore be dependent upon the federal govern-

ment to an extent that would make the pursuit of ghetto goals impossible. The money for the CDC, if all goes well, will come out of the pockets of taxpayers. The suppliers of the CDC, white-dominated corporations, will clean up. As in urban renewal, income will be transferred from the taxpayer to the corporation leaving behind a bewildered and bitter black community at odds with an angered taxpayer who believes that "enough has been done for these people."

An additional problem is that the ghetto has been depleted to the point where it has little if any surplus to reinvest. For instance, in some preliminary calculations of Harlem, Zweig[28] estimated that "Harlem residents own at most $350 million of land and structures in Harlem, the majority in residential buildings. This capital stock generates at most $22 million annually for further investment." If anything, Zweig's estimates are liberal and overstate the figures involved. For instance, the $22 million figure quoted does not include any corporate pay-out (or dividends), which would decrease the amount available for new investment.

The ghetto is unable to produce a large surplus simply because it has been decapitalized through the inequities faced by blacks. Ghetto infrastructure was not erected to benefit ghetto residents. It was erected to maintain law and order or in response to the struggles of black people. The infrastructure is less suited to ghetto development because that has never been its purpose. Much like a poor country, the infrastructure assists the quick and intensive exploitation of the resources of the country without improving the living standard of the mass of the people. Ghetto schools, public transportation, the police, and public housing all demonstrate that ghetto infrastructure is basically unsuited to economic development in its present form. Vigilant community control over ghetto institutions will certainly improve their performance temporarily. However, it is in the nature of the beast to revert to its old habits of oppressing rather than assisting the ghetto community.

Ghetto Dispersal versus Ghetto Gilding

One of the strategies often advanced to improve the ghetto is to eliminate it. How? By dispersing the

[27] *Ibid.*, pp. 34–35.

[28] Michael Zweig, "The Dialectics of Black Capitalism," *Review of Black Political Economy*, Spring 1972 and Fall 1972.

ghetto in little digestible pieces into white suburbia and thereby absorb it into the mainstream of American life. Then, personal racism would be broken down, ghetto children would be better educated, jobs would be more accessible, safety more ensured, etc. Thus, the ghetto would be swallowed up and join affluent middle America. The Kerner Report suggested this idea to further integration, as do Kain and Persky.[29]

Several problems arise with such a strategy. First, it assumes that institutional racism will cease to exist. My analysis suggests that employers would still manipulate blacks in the labor market; the state would still ignore the interests of blacks, blacks would still go to predominantly black and community colleges, etc., and at the end of the day return to their dispersed ghetto. At best, one institutional barrier would be eliminated — housing. All the other institutional obstacles faced by blacks would be untouched.

Second, the political influence of the ghetto as a community would be even less than now. Further, sending blacks to suburbia would provide each suburb with a small dilapidated section where blacks would live. Several cities in poor countries are in fact organized this way. However, the geographical proximity of the ruling and ruled classes does not alter the different institutional mechanisms used by the two groups. Oppression is not a geographical concept.

Third, sponsors of ghetto dispersal ideas fail to explain why the federal government would invest the large amount of money needed to disperse the ghetto. Moreover, even if this occurred, the terms of trade within capitalism do not favor black people. Thus, if black people were given new possessions, capitalist predators would soon denude them of these possessions.

Fourth, even if blacks can and want to be moved towards whites, will white society accept such a move? The hue and cry over public housing projects is certain to accompany any proposal to put ghetto people next door. Similarly, busing runs into the opposition of the whites among whose children black children are sought to be dispersed. It is especially hard to integrate the poor when the ruling elite is virtually lily-white.

Because of all these reasons, the ghetto cannot be dispersed while major capitalist institutions remain intact. Therefore, at best, the dispersal of existing ghettos will create new minighettos in the suburbs. Dispersing the sores of capitalism may move them around so that they do not appear so large and concentrated. But such a strategy will not eliminate the sores. Ideas to disperse the ghetto ignore the historical context within which ghettos have been formed. This context involves both capitalism and racism, which have an important stake in the ghetto and will resist attempts to dismantle the ghetto.

A second strategy to improve conditions in the ghetto advocates the provision and subsidization of adequate services in the ghetto. This would increase the income of ghetto residents, make life more bearable for them, and probably persuade them not to revolt. The Kerner Report accepted ghetto gilding as a holding action preceding its dispersal. However, why should the outside world which profits from the ghetto put money into it? The whole idea is to profit from the ghetto through low wages paid to its residents and high prices charged it for inadequate services. Under capitalism, the idea is to drain the ghetto, and pump money into it. Even if ghetto gilding got under way, nothing would prevent the further migration of poor blacks into the gilded ghetto. In turn, the gilded ghetto would become an even more attractive place for parasites feeding off it. The drain out of the ghetto would certainly increase, necessitating still more money to be spent on gilding projects. Successful gilding would at best lead to the geographical division of the races. The problems of black people would be just as imposing once they stepped out of their gilded ghetto — gilded for them by the white world outside.

Reparations

Partly as the result of the total inadequacy of the other solutions, and partly as the result of rising consciousness among blacks of their oppression, one of the most frequent recent demands made by blacks has been for reparations. Monetary terms cannot approximate the pain of past injustice or the money needed to rectify these injustices. This is not because such calculations cannot be made but because "it is sheer madness to work at such theoretical manipulations in a society where leaders cannot even commit themselves to feeding the hungry let alone entertain thoughts of class justice."[30]

---

[29] See John Kain and Joseph Persky, "Alternatives to the Gilded Ghetto," *The Public Interest,* Winter 1969.

[30] Jim Marketti, "Black Equity in the Slave Industry," *Review of Black Political Economy,* Winter 1972, p. 43.

Still, the Republic of New Africa[31] has demanded $400 billion and five southern states, and the Black Manifesto[32] calls for the payment of $500 million by the churches and synagogues of white America to be disbursed in specific ways as a first installment in a reparations program. Marketti estimated the present-day value of black equity in the slave industry between $48 billion and $995 billion. The wide range is primarily due to the different rates of interest that may be used to compound the value of black equity in the slave industry. In response to a *New York Times* editorial, Richard America[33] demanded that by some foreseeable date (such as 1990) black people have ownership, control and the means of managing approximately 10 percent of corporate America. Browne[34] maintains that the development of a minimal reparational formula should include at least: (1) a payment for slave labor prior to 1863; (2) a payment for underpayment of black people since 1863; and (3) a payment to compensate for the black man's being denied the opportunity to acquire a share of America's land and natural resources when they were widely available to white settlers. Richard America[35] would have liked to see the then-expected $20 to $30 billion saved by the ending of the Viet Nam War appropriated to redistributive programs. Even though this peace dividend was not available, he would have liked to see the amount spent and perhaps more. However, nothing like this amount has been spent for redistributive purposes or reparations.

The diversity of methods of compensation reflect the varying views of a heterogeneous community whose overwhelming similarities are those of perceived color and real oppression. Several possible ways have been suggested to execute a reparations program. Browne suggests six. Bittker[36] has ar-

gued most persuasively for such a scheme. Would white America buy such a scheme? Perhaps. Reasons would be advanced for extending or reiterating control over the black community through an economic bounty. Also, it is highly likely that the provision of funds in large amounts would be used to divide the black community — to isolate those not considered desirable by the federal government. Conservative pressure to "get your money's worth" is never lacking. An excuse to evade such a program is that once a commitment to a reparations program is made, other concessions will be demanded. A hefty reparations program would also constitute an open admission of a racist system. Thus far, all that rich, white America accepts is that "prejudice" exists, mostly in the South, which must be combated by laws which uphold the American heritage. To fault the heritage itself would require a revolutionary change of heart and mind not just among the system's rulers but more importantly the mass of white workers.

In the long run, neither racism nor capitalism work to the advantage of white workers. However, the current situation is that white workers generally support both racism and capitalism. Racial divisions among workers hurt all workers. The solutions I have examined in this section have not eliminated the inequities faced by blacks. Even the various reparations programs would need strong political support. A sizable part of the white population will have to support these demands or at least not be hostile to them. This is why I advocate renewed attempts to approach white workers with the truth about capitalism and racism.

Summary

I have suggested that the replacement of capitalist relationships by more humane ones is obviously necessary to improve the black situation. Blacks are hurt most by capitalist institutions, operating normally, pauperizing the poor. A change in the black situation will occur when blacks show more political strength. Such a change will come about when white workers are approached with the truth about capitalism. Their emotions are invested in the system. Their life-style is framed by the system. This life-style oppresses blacks. But it is not the average redneck who gains from racism; the big boys do. If the similarities of work, powerlessness, and the consequent

[31] Republic of New Africa, "We Want Georgia, South Carolina, Louisiana, Mississippi, and Alabama — Right Away," *Esquire,* January 1969.

[32] "The Black Manifesto," *Review of Black Political Economy,* Spring/Summer 1970.

[33] Richard America, Jr., "What Do You People Want?" *Review of Black Political Economy,* Spring/Summer 1970.

[34] Robert S. Browne, "The Economic Basis for Reparations to Black America," *Review of Black Political Economy,* Winter 1972.

[35] Richard America, Jr., "A New Rationale for Income Redistribution," *Review of Black Political Economy,* Winter 1972.

[36] Boris Bittker, *The Case for Black Reparations,* Vintage, 1973.

alienation were emphasized, and the dissimilarities of race were deemphasized, an interracial movement of workers could be established. This would prevent capitalists from manipulating workers through race.

But capitalists would still be able to divide and control working people in other ways. They would have to be hobbled in many ways before major concessions could be extracted by the poor and maintained. It will be impossible for blacks to eliminate racism while simultaneously turning a deaf ear to other oppressed groups such as women or most Third World peoples. Obnoxious phenomena tend to go together and one struggles against them because they are obnoxious and not because a particular phenomenon affects one personally.

Capitalism is already contracting in much of the world. In the poorer parts of the capitalist world, movements continually challenge the hegemony of leaders who serve U.S. corporate interests. In several of these places, nationalist movements restrict the operations of U.S. corporations. Other countries, such as China and Cuba, are openly hostile to the capitalist world. The richer capitalist countries also challenge U.S. hegemony in the capitalist world. The result of all this is that capitalism is becoming increasingly unprofitable and anachronistic, dragging on past its time. As the leading capitalist country, the U.S. suffers a serious loss of power. This can be seen in the worsening terms of trade between the U.S. and the rest of the world, or the decline of the dollar. In turn, this diminishes the American ability to impose force upon the insubordinate members of the capitalist world. The consequent loss of power ensures that the domestic standard of living will continue to decline.

This decline in living standards is a reflection of the maturation, stagnation, and decay of U.S. capitalism. Those who benefit from American capitalism must not be permitted to attribute this decline to anyone but themselves. The basis of capitalism is greed. As capitalism does not expand, the greedy cannot be induced to undertake economic activity. This is the source of the problems faced by the American worker today. We must not permit racist appeals to deflect popular attention from the source of its problems. Hence, "issues" such as busing are deliberate ploys to incite racist feelings in working-class whites, at least partly in the expectation that they will overlook their economic woes. While such strategies may continue to divide working people along racial lines, U.S. capitalism is weakening. This holds hopes for its eventual replacement by a more humane system in which race would be irrelevant in determining access to societal institutions.

Such a result would destroy the power of the capitalist class in the U.S., which is doing all it can to prevent it from happening. It is trying to hold together the same institutions that give it power and that oppress black people. If the capitalist class succeeds, black people will continue to fail to advance. People who desire meaningful change in the relations between black people and the American economic system need to work harder to replace capitalist institutions.

BIBLIOGRAPHY

I. IMPRESSIONS, DEFINITIONS, AND MAGNITUDES

A. Impressions

Herb Goro. *The Block.* New York: Random House, 1970.
Malcolm X. *Autobiography.* New York: Grove Press, 1966.
Eldridge Cleaver. *Soul on Ice.* New York: Random House, 1968.

B. Definitions and Magnitudes

Andrew F. Brimmer. "Economic Situation of Blacks in the United States," Statement before the Joint Economic Committee of the U.S. Congress, February 23, 1972.

U.S. Bureau of the Census. "The Social and Economic Status of the Black Population of the United States, 1974," *Current Population Reports,* Series P-23,
Number 54, July 1975.

Michael Flax. *Blacks and Whites: An Experiment in Social Indicators.* Washington,
D.C.: Urban Institute, 1971.

II. THEORIES OF DISCRIMINATION

A. Orthodox Economic Perspectives

Thomas Sowell. *Race and Economics.* New York: McKay, 1975.

Gary Becker. *The Economics of Discrimination.* Chicago: University of Chicago
Press, 1957.

Lester Thurow. *Poverty and Discrimination.* Washington, D.C.: Brookings Institution, 1969.

Anthony Pascal, ed. *Racial Discrimination in Economic Life.* Lexington, Mass.:
D. C. Heath, 1972.

George Von Furstenberg *et al.,* eds. *Patterns of Racial Discrimination.* Lexington,
Mass.: D. C. Heath, 1974.

B. Radical Economic Perspectives

William Tabb. *The Political Economy of the Black Ghetto.* New York: Norton, 1970.

Harold M. Baron. "Racial Domination in Advanced Capitalism: A Theory of Nationalism and Divisions in the Labor Market," in R. C. Edwards *et al.,* eds.,
Labor Market Segmentation. Lexington, Mass.: D. C. Heath, 1975.

Michael Reich, "Racism and the White Distribution of Income," Ph.D. dissertation,
Harvard University, 1973.

Raymond Franklin and Solomon Resnik. *The Political Economy of Racism.* New
York: Holt, Rinehart and Winston, 1973.

Daniel Fusfeld. *The Basic Economics of the Urban Racial Crisis.* New York: Holt,
Rinehart and Winston, 1973.

C. Empirical Analyses

Stanley Masters. *Black-White Income Differentials.* Madison: University of Wisconsin Press, 1975.

Barry Chiswick. "Racial Discrimination in the Labor Market: A Test of Alternative
Hypotheses," *Journal of Political Economy,* November 1973.

Albert Wohlstetter and Sinclair Coleman. "Race Differences in Income,"·in Anthony Pascal, ed., *Racial Discrimination in Economic Life.* Lexington, Mass.:
D. C. Heath, 1972.

III. POLICY PERSPECTIVES

A. General

William Tabb. "Race Relations Models and Social Change." *Social Problems,*
Spring 1971.

Robert S. Browne. "Toward an Overall Assessment of our Alternatives," *Review of
Black Political Economy,* Spring/Summer 1970.

Barbara Bergmann. "Reducing the Pervasiveness of Discrimination," in Eli Ginzberg, ed., *Manpower Goals for America.* Forthcoming.

Marcus Alexis *et al.* "An Economic Bill of Rights," *Review of Black Political Economy,* 1973, III, 1.

B. Black Capitalism

Barry Bluestone. "The Political Economy of Black Capitalism," *Review of Radical Political Economics,* Summer 1969.

Andrew Brimmer. "The Economic Potential of Black Capitalism," *American Economic Review,* May 1970.

Charles Tate. "Brimmer on Black Capitalism: An Analysis." *Review of Black Political Economy,* Spring/Summer 1970.

E. Ofari. *The Myth of Black Capitalism.* New York: Monthly Review Press, 1970.

C. Integration

John Kain and Joseph Persky. "Alternatives to the Gilded Ghetto," *The Public Interest,* Winter 1969.

U.S. Commission on Civil Rights. "Racism in America and How to Combat It," *Clearing House Publication,* Urban Series No. 1, January 1970.

D. Ghetto Economic Development

Thomas Vietorisz and Bennett Harrison. "Ghetto Development, Community Corporations and Public Policy. *Review of Black Political Economy,* Fall 1971.

Bennett Harrison. "Ghetto Economic Development: A Survey," *Journal of Economic Literature,* March 1974.

Thaddeus Spratlen. "Ghetto Economic Development: Content and Character of the Literature," *Review of Black Political Economy,* Summer 1971.

E. Reparations and Black Nationalism

Richard America, Jr. "What Do You People Want?", *Review of Black Political Economy,* Spring/Summer 1970.

"The Black Manifesto." *Review of Black Political Economy,* Spring/Summer 1970.

EDUCATION

We Americans have suffered such losses of humane communality that we cannot allow ourselves to see the waste of life that stares us in the face. Our very sense of crisis is often nothing more than a refined technique of avoidance. Thus we have a "problem of the schools," and talk to each other solemnly about improved facilities, better methods of instruction, more supervision, ignoring all the while the painful truth that what children need most is for the lives of their elders to make sense.

We are our children's problem. . . .

— George Dennison[1]

The most deadly of all possible sins is the mutilation of a child's spirit.

— Erik Erikson[2]

There can be little question that we have been experiencing a crisis in our schools. Throughout the country students and parents have been attacking the educational systems. Public funds for education have been cut. Some school systems are facing bankruptcy. Many have been losing faith in the omnipotence of education. The cries of sickness have indeed been so urgent, as conservative critic Irving Kristol notes, "that one is astonished to learn . . . the patient has survived." [3]

The crisis of the classroom came from two main sources. The first was mainly political. Throughout the 1960s different movements struggled for equality and liberation. Blacks, women, and youth all tried to change the institutions that they felt had been oppressing them. The schools were one of the major targets. Schools channeled minority groups into inferior social positions, the movements charged, and brainwashed them to accept those positions. "We would point out," as Jonathan Kozol summarized the terms of protest, "that schools contained and silenced, muted and anesthetized our children." [4]

---

[1] From an article in "Annual Education Review," *The New York Times,* January 12, 1970, p. 52.

[2] Quoted in Charles Silberman, *Crisis in the Classroom* (New York: Random House 1970), p. 10.

[3] From an article in "Annual Education Review," *The New York Times,* January 8, 1973, p. 55.

[4] Jonathan Kozol, *The New York Times,* "Op Ed Page," April 1, 1971.

Second, academics began to question the traditional view that schools could improve opportunities for the disadvantaged. "Education has always seemed," as Godfrey Hodgson wrote, "one of the most acceptable ways of using the national wealth to provide opportunities for the poor without offending the comfortable." [5] In the late 1960s and early 1970s, however, many social scientists began to find evidence that cast doubt on this conventional view. While one could not always decide from all this evidence what the role of the schools really was, it seemed clear that schools did not perform as most Americans had always thought they did.

If everyone could agree that there was a crisis, few could agree on its resolution. In the early 1960s, educational disputes revolved around simple programmatic problems: how large should ghetto classrooms be? How many extra dollars should we pour into slum schools? Now much more troublesome debates unfold. What are the basic functions of schools in our society? If we dislike the way that they perform, is there anything that we can do about them?

Not surprisingly, the answers to these basic questions tend to reflect the general orientations of those who dare to answer. Viewing problems through the conservative, liberal, and radical perspectives, we can appreciate how fundamental the crisis of our classrooms has now become.

In this introduction to the readings, there are four sections. First, I discuss the several ways in which we define and measure the failures of central-city schools. Second, I briefly outline the conservative and liberal perspectives on those problems. Third, I discuss at greater length the structure of the radical analysis of those problems. Finally, I summarize the purpose and contents of the readings.

Dimensions of Failure in Ghetto Schools

We now recognize four different levels on which ghetto schools in central cities have been failing.

First, students in ghetto schools do not continue as far in school as students do in most other schools; we have faulted ghetto schools for failing to stimulate them. (Some critics have obviously blamed the students for their lack of motivation.) This was the first level of failure that we began to measure. James B. Conant popularized the use of "dropout" rates as an index of this problem, comparing the varying percentages of students who graduate from different high schools.[6] Although it is still true that fewer students graduate from high school in predominantly black central-city systems than in white suburban systems, this difference in the number of years of schooling completed by blacks and whites has been narrowing rapidly in recent years.[7] Now it begins to appear that "truancy rates" constitute a better measure of the quantity of schooling that different students receive. It seems to have become more and more routine for students to graduate rather automatically from central-city schools, as long as they appear occasionally in class. Although larger numbers of students are nominally completing high school, they are tending to spend fewer and fewer

[5] Godfrey Hodgson, "Do Schools Make A Difference?" *The Atlantic,* February 1973, p. 16.

[6] James B. Conant, *Slums and Suburbs* (New York: McGraw-Hill, 1961).

[7] U.S. Bureau of the Census, *The Social and Economic Status of Negroes in the United States, 1974,* Current Population Reports, Series P-23, No. 54, p. 97.

days in school each year. Truancy rates appear to have been rising in many ghetto schools.

Second, among students receiving a constant quantity of schooling — among those graduating from high school, for instance — black students in ghetto schools seem to learn "less" in school. Traditionally, scholars have used standardized achievement test scores to measure the quantity of schooling at different levels, even though achievement test scores represent somewhat imperfect measures of quality. Using achievement test scores from over 600,000 American students, the federally sponsored survey, *Equality of Educational Opportunity* (widely known as the Coleman Report after its principal author), reported that black students had lower achievement scores than white students had at every grade level, that only a portion of this difference could be explained by the poorer socioeconomic backgrounds of black students, and that the gaps in achievement scores tended to grow larger at higher educational levels. The report concluded from these separate results that white students received much higher quality education while in school than did black students.[8]

Third, we count these first two failures doubly. We have come to hope that schools in ghetto areas would compensate for the impoverished family and social background of many ghetto students, making up for their disadvantages in readiness to learn when they begin school. By the standards of the Coleman Report, this goal would require that ghetto schools narrow the educational gap between blacks and whites as they proceed through school. In fact, as noted above, the gap between achievement scores of blacks and whites widens.

Fourth, ghetto schools suffer failures of commission as well as of omission. Plainly and simply, the schools seem to destroy many students who pass through their doors. With their authoritarianism, their arbitrary bureaucratic practices, their preoccupation with order and compliance, the schools seem to create confusion, alienation, and rebellion where little existed before. From the lowest grades, teachers enforce rules and rule with enforcers. The facilities sometimes look more like prisons than learning institutions. Ghetto schools, as Jonathan Kozol wrote, often bring "death at an early age."[9]

People who believe in numbers sometimes distrust those kinds of qualitative generalizations. So here are some statistics: Detailed studies have shown that the highest rates of school vandalism "occur in schools with obsolete facilities and equipment, low staff morale and high dissatisfaction and boredom among the pupils."[10] And vandalism, without doubt, is highest in ghetto schools. It has been rising rapidly. In Philadelphia, for instance, there was a 600 percent increase in assaults in the school over a five-year period in the 1960s. "The message is inescapable," the Urban Education Task Force concluded. "It is a large vote of no confidence in the schools by a growing number of pupils."[11]

Conservative and Liberal Views

Throughout the early 1960s, most observers shared a surprisingly common view of the American educational system and its problems. Everyone seemed to

---

[8] James S. Coleman *et al.*, *Equality of Educational Opportunity* (Washington, D.C.: U.S. Government Printing Office, 1966), p. 21.

[9] Jonathan Kozol, *Death at an Early Age* (Boston: Houghton Mifflin, 1967).

[10] Quoted in Urban Education Task Force, *Report* (New York: Praeger, 1970), p. 175.

[11] Data from *ibid.*, p. 179. Quote from *ibid.*, p. 181.

agree on the role of the schools in America. Most people seemed to agree on their problems. This consensus produced some experimental educational policies in the early 1960s. The experiments seemed to fail. The consensus began to crumble. As people began to respond to the new uncertainties, conservatives and liberals responded in characteristically different ways. Their specific reactions reflected their more general inclinations.

The original consensus had built upon a general economic analysis of the role of education in our economic system. This analysis begins from a set of four related assumptions about education in an advanced society like the United States. The assumptions derive from the perspectives' common views of the functioning of the economic market place.

First, the analysis assumes that the principal utility of educational achievement derives from education's influence on economic productivity.[12] Economists call it "returns to education," or, more mechanistically, "returns to investments in human capital."[13] They presume that more education will increase the level of an individual's general skills, thus increasing his "marginal productivity," and will consequently increase the amount of money he can expect to earn in his lifetime. Since additional years of education are clearly associated with higher individual earnings on the average in the United States, economists argue that increased education for those who are poor can play a significant role in lifting them out of poverty.[14] And because "adult education, training and retraining are difficult, slow and costly processes," as James Tobin acknowledges, "our main hope must be in the education of our children."[15]

Second, the analysis assumes that cognitive achievement tests accurately reflect the skill dimension through which education effects increased productivity. Those with more education are more productive, it presumes, especially because they have learned how to read and reason more skillfully. This assumption has been mirrored in the Coleman Report, which used achievement test scores as the best available measure of educational outcomes. The assumption has acquired even more importance in a new strain of economic analysis — the analysis of educational production functions. From this new perspective, economists are trying to understand how to allocate resources in education most efficiently. Toward that end, they are studying how much various inputs contribute to outputs in education: do teachers with master's degrees contribute much more than teachers with bachelor's degrees to one unit of output; do extra library facilities add substantially to the reading scores of students; or does the educational level of a child's parents fundamentally determine the child's educational success? In all such cases, analysts have used standardized achievement test scores as the appropriate measure of educational output, and have studied the statistical determinants of variations in test scores among schools and among individual students.[16]

[12] For a useful general source, see Mark Blaug, ed., *The Economics of Education* (London: Penguin, 1968).

[13] See Gary Becker, *Human Capital* (New York: NBER, 1964).

[14] For evidence for the country as a whole, see Herman Miller, *Rich Man, Poor Man* (New York: Crowell, 1964).

[15] Tobin, "Raising the Incomes of the Poor," in Kermit Gordon, ed., *Agenda for the Nation* (Washington, D.C.: Brookings Institution, 1968), p. 91.

[16] Samuel Bowles provides a useful summary of this strain of analysis and its limitations in "Towards an Educational Production Function," in W. Lee Hansen, ed., *Education, Income and Human Capital* (New York: National Bureau of Economic Research, 1970).

Third, the analysis assumes that the role of education in a democratic society has been and can be that of guaranteeing equality of economic opportunity. As John H. Fischer has written:

> The dependence of democracy on popular education has been a continuing theme in our history. But it was not until the end of World War II that the country began seriously to consider the full implications of that relationship, and later still that it officially acknowledged the corollary proposition that to limit a man's education is to limit his freedom.[17]

Education had been the route through which other disadvantaged groups had achieved social mobility, many observed, so it could also provide equality of opportunity for presently disadvantaged groups. If the rest of society somehow conspired to produce inequalities in the social and economic structure, then schools would counter those pressures by keeping open the yellow brick road.

Fourth, the analysis also assumed that education has played an essential role in increasing opportunities for social and economic mobility over time. This involves a set of three related assumptions: first, that the income distribution has become more equal over time; second, that the amount of intergenerational mobility within that distribution has increased; and third, that increasing intergenerational mobility in the acquisition of education has played an important causal role in effecting the first two phenomena.[18]

Together, these four principal assumptions about education produced a single coherent perspective on educational objectives: that to improve the productivity of the low-skilled and the poor — in order to equalize their economic opportunities — we must improve their education; that to improve their education in that sense, we must raise their level of cognitive achievement by improving their abilities to read and reason; that the schools can effect this increasing equality of opportunity because they have played that role historically; and that, in general, it is becoming easier for the schools to fulfill this equalizing function because our society is continuing to become more educationally mobile (and simultaneously more meritocratic) over time.

What explains the failures of those earlier experiments within this general analytic framework?

Conservatives offered three kinds of explanations. First, they wondered whether an unequal distribution of IQ might not explain the failure of schools to produce more equality; "a point must soon be reached below which the dropout rate cannot be reduced," Edward Banfield concluded, "for there will be *some* number of students who are simply not capable of doing high school work"[19] Second, they proposed that certain intrinsic elements of lower-class culture made it unlikely that lower-class students would be able to take advantage of educational opportunities; "the lower-class person cannot as a rule be given much training," Banfield wrote, "because he will not accept it."[20] Third, con-

---

[17] "Race and Reconciliation: The Role of the Schools," *Dædalus,* Vol. II of *The Negro American,* Winter 1966, p. 24.

[18] For a brief discussion of the interrelations among the hypothesized trends, see Peter Blau and Otis Dudley Duncan, *The American Occupational Structure* (New York: Wiley, 1968), pp. 112–13.

[19] Edward Banfield, *The Unheavenly City* (Boston: Little, Brown, 1970), p. 134. Emphasis in the original.

[20] *Ibid.,* p. 139.

servatives argued that the educational system was inefficient in achieving its designated economic functions because the public school system was a monopoly without competition among schools; in this view, there was nothing to prevent some schools from becoming more and more rotten.

Liberals, on the defensive because of the earlier appearances of reform failure, offered several responses to those failures.

A first set of responses was methodological. Liberals wondered whether some conservatives had been too quick to conclude failure before all the returns were in.[21] And many liberals argued that the severity of our educational problems required pursuing reformist policies even if those policies had less impact than originally expected. "With better schools we can only make a small difference," as one liberal school administrator put it. "But it is worth that investment." [22]

Another set of responses was more substantive. The famous Coleman Report on inequalities in educational achievement had reached two interesting conclusions upon which liberals seized. One result of their study suggested, as Mosteller and Moynihan summarized the report, that "racial integration where minority group students were not a majority seemingly improved the level of achievement for them, without lowering it for others." [23] This result suggested that minority students might benefit from programs that would expose them to more white students in school. Another result suggested that students who felt that they had more "control" of their environment did relatively better in school than those who did not.[24] This result suggested to many liberals that they should pursue measures that would develop an emergent sense of control among ghetto students, providing them with more and more incentive to structure their own lives.

In general, most liberals argued that educational reform had not yet been given a chance. "I say liberalism hasn't been tried," as Thomas Pettigrew, a liberal proponent of busing, put it.[25]

These analytic responses framed the kinds of policy recommendations that conservatives and liberals were making.

On the one hand, conservatives argued that there were few policy measures that could have any effect. If IQ and lower-class culture were impeding the impact of schooling reforms, then little could be done to overcome these problems. If the schools' monopolistic inefficiencies were the problem, one change might help. Allow students and their families to choose among schools, as Milton Friedman suggested, providing them with "educational vouchers" to pay for their education at the school of their choice. To ensure equal access to good

[21] As John Kain and Eric Hanushek conclude: "We contend that the [Coleman] Report's analysis does not provide reasonable tests of the hypotheses attributed to it. In fact, the 'findings' could have been the result of the analytic methods combined with systematic errors of measurement rather than any underlying behavioral relationship." From Kain and Hanushek, "On the Value of *Equality of Educational Opportunity* as a Guide to Public Policy," in F. Mosteller and D. P. Moynihan, eds., On *Equality of Educational Opportunity* (New York: Vintage, 1972), p. 137.

[22] Quoted in Godfrey Hodgson, "Do Schools Make A Difference?," p. 45.

[23] Frederick Mosteller and Daniel P. Moynihan, "A Pathbreaking Report — Further Studies of the Coleman Report," in Mosteller and Moynihan, eds., On *Equality of Educational Opportunity*, p. 24.

[24] *Cf.* James S. Coleman, "The Evaluation of *Equality of Educational Opportunity*," in *ibid.*

[25] Quoted in Hodgson, "Do Schools Make A Difference?," p. 40.

schools, the government could provide special subsidies to the children of poorer families. The superior schools would flourish, while the inferior schools would be forced either to improve or to close their doors for lack of revenues.[26]

With that last exception, conservatives generally argue, in Daniel P. Moynihan's words, that we should "leave well enough alone." [27]

Liberal policy recommendations flow from their own analyses of failure. We should continue to experiment, at the least, because we have not yet fully tested different kinds of potential reforms. Reflecting their more substantive conclusions, liberals argue that improved schooling achievement could be effected for ghetto students by moving in either of two directions. Some argue that greater integration is necessary and that some kinds of busing programs are required to achieve this integration. Others argue that ghetto students could acquire a greater sense of control through programs of greater "community control" over the schools or through various kinds of "open classroom" programs encouraging ghetto children to work on their own.[28]

Through whichever policies, liberals have learned, the road toward educational reform will not be smooth. But they insist that it is necessary to keep on trucking. As Charles Silberman has written: "Students, parents, teachers, administrators, school board members, college professors, taxpayers — all will have to act, which means that all will have to make difficult decisions; the road to reform is always uphill." [29]

The Radical View

A radical analysis of education argues that the role of education in capitalist societies is determined by the structure of basic "system-defining" capitalist institutions. As Chapter 1 noted, these basic institutions help preserve class divisions in society and help stabilize patterns of production and distribution. Within that context, education tends to serve two primary functions in capitalist societies: first, to instill in individuals both the ideology and the set of individual personality traits upon which the capitalist mode of production depends; and second, to help preserve or create economic and social class divisions.[30]

According to this analysis, the current "failures" of ghetto schools reflect education's success at its appointed roles; in this view, the schools are not failing at but are in fact fulfilling their objectives. I have outlined this argument in three stages. First, I amplify the radical analysis of the function of education in the United States by summarizing the kinds of evidence that radicals cite to refute basic liberal and conservative assumptions about education. Second, with that evidence in hand, I briefly outline the argument that current problems in ghetto schools derive from the functions of education in capitalist societies. And third, given that argument, I discuss the kinds of circumstances in which ghetto education could "improve" and argue that these circumstances are pre-

[26] Milton Friedman, "Government and Education," in *Capitalism and Freedom* (Chicago: University of Chicago Press, 1962).

[27] Daniel P. Moynihan, "Equalizing Education: In Whose Benefit?" *The Public Interest*, Fall 1972, p. 86.

[28] For a summary of some of these positions, see Silberman, *Crisis in the Classroom.*

[29] *Ibid.*, p. 524.

[30] Almost all the following is based upon and fully developed in Samuel Bowles and Herbert Gintis, *Schooling in Capitalist America* (New York: Basic Books, 1976).

cluded unless basic capitalist institutions change enough to permit radical changes in the functions of schools.

As the previous section suggested, the liberal and conservative analysis of education built from four principal assumptions. In summarizing the radical critique of those assumptions, I first quote the assumption from the previous section and then summarize the arguments and evidence against it.

1. "...to improve the productivity of the low-skilled and the poor — in order to equalize their economic opportunities — we must improve their education."

This assumption implies that anyone can increase his/her income by increasing his/her education, or, in other words, that variations in income correspond to variations in educational attainment for everyone in the economy. The radical analysis counters that the pattern of class stratification in the United States constrains the potential of education for increasing individuals' income. For blacks, for instance, the strength of class barriers in the labor market is so great that the income of blacks does not vary significantly with their educational levels. To the extent that this is true, then, one cannot assume that increasing educational attainment among blacks will necessarily increase their incomes. It has not in the past.

Statistical evidence seems to support this argument. In the United States, blacks do not appear significantly to increase their earning power unless they graduate from college; between the ninth and fifteenth grades of school, income does not vary significantly with educational attainment. In addition, there is some evidence that returns to education vary by class as well as race.[31] Because blacks and some lower-class whites seem to realize this, their incentives about education inevitably differ drastically from those of many whites.[32]

2. "...to improve their education in that sense, we must raise their level of cognitive achievement by improving their abilities to read and reason."

Radicals argue that education does not increase individuals' productivity by improving their cognitive abilities. Rather, it produces a set of personality traits compatible with capitalist modes of production. It screens potential workers through a sieve, sorting them according to their capacities to work persistently, to respond to incentives like wages, to conform to work requirements, and to defer gratification.[33] Ivar Berg has presented extensive evidence on this point, showing that education bears little relationship in the United States to determinants of productivity on the job except through its effects on personality.[34] Gintis summarizes varieties of evidence that educational attainment varies principally with those kinds of personality characteristics.[35] The implication is clear — if we want to improve the economic opportunity of our disadvantaged citizens, we should teach them to acquiesce, conform, and defer. We cannot expect that an improvement in their reading abilities will have any effect on their economic status.

---

[31] See the Editor's Supplement in this chapter for some of this evidence.

[32] This comment should not imply, of course, that these groups should not continue in school. It simply means that they may choose not to continue in school if schooling is justified solely on economic grounds.

[33] On these general points, see Bowles and Gintis, *Schooling in Capitalist America*, Chapters 4–5.

[34] *Education and Jobs: The Great Training Robbery* (New York: Praeger, 1969).

[35] "Education, Technology, and the Characteristics of Workers' Productivity," *American Economic Review,* May 1971. See also Bowles and Gintis, *Schooling in Capitalist America*

3. "... the schools can effect this increasing equality of opportunity because they have played that role historically."

Radicals argue that schools have not functioned to improve equality of opportunity, but rather that they have functioned to preserve class stratifications. "Curriculum has always been used to assign social rank," as Ivan Illich puts it.[36] There are many pieces of evidence that the entire structure of social and economic institutions in the United States reinforces this educational role. First, it has been shown that the socioeconomic class of parents bears a consistently positive relationship to the quality of schools available for their children; children from higher classes are afforded higher class rank through the distributive process of schooling.[37] Second, it has been effectively demonstrated that both cognitive achievement and "productive" personality traits vary directly with the quality of school resources; the better the resources, the more productive the schooling for its students.[38] Finally, we have plentiful evidence that the effects of government finance of education tend to reinforce this class inequality of resources among localities.[39] None of this evidence should be regarded as the unfortunate residue of a more hierarchical past. The schools, like other public institutions today, tend disproportionately to benefit the more advantaged classes.

4. "... in general, it is becoming easier for the schools to fulfill this equalizing function because our society is continuing to become more educationally mobile (and simultaneously more meritocratic) over time."

Radicals argue that educational mobility has not been increasing over time in this country. Rather, they argue that the schools have become increasingly important in the distribution of class status over time, and that they have therefore tended to militate increasingly against social mobility. Illich makes the argument through an analogy with the historical role of religion:

> School has become the world religion of a modernized proletariat, and makes futile promises of salvation to the poor of the technological age. The nation-state has adopted it, drafting all citizens into a graded curriculum leading to sequential diplomas not unlike the initiation rituals and hieratic promotions of former times. The modern state has assumed the duty to enforce the judgment of its educators through well-meant truant officers and job requirements, much as did the Spanish kings who enforced the judgments of their theologians through the conquistadors and inquisition.[40]

As other chapters have shown, equality has not been increasing in this country.[41] The Editor's Supplement among the readings in this chapter summarizes some evidence that intergenerational educational mobility has not been increasing either. There seems little reason to assume, given that evidence, that the schools' potential for equalizing economic opportunity is increasing.

---

[36] Why We Must Abolish Schooling," *New York Review of Books,* July 2, 1970, p. 12.

[37] See Bowles and Gintis, *Schooling in Capitalist America,* Chapter 4; and Christopher Jencks *et al., Inequality: A Reassessment of the Effect of Family and Schooling in America* (New York: Basic Books, 1972).

[38] See Bowles and Gintis, *Schooling in Capitalist America.*

[39] Stephan Michelson, "The Political Economy of Public School Finance," in Martin Carnoy, ed., *Schooling for Corporate America* (New York: McKay, 1975).

[40] Illich, "Why We Must Abolish Schooling," p. 11.

[41] See the Editor's Supplement on "Trends in Poverty" in Chapter 5.

Given these pieces of the radical argument, the radical explanation for ghetto educational problems flows quite directly. Educational institutions in the ghetto help reinforce the lower-class status of ghetto blacks. Schools in the ghetto help channel ghetto blacks into the secondary labor market and to prepare them psychologically to accept lower-class status. It seems clear by now that many young blacks understand these facts about their schools, learning from their elders' experience in the world that their schools offer them nothing worth acquiring. They understand that they have little control over their own fates, because race so thoroughly determines individual outcomes in society regardless of individual characteristics.[42] And for valid historical reasons, they are unlikely to accept their indoctrinations toward lower-class status. The circumstances do not induce them to be patient with the schools. Indeed, they are likely to become particularly impatient. And with their impatience in school, they are likely neither to develop skills nor to acquire the personality characteristics through which education can bring them rewards in the larger society. The response of the schools is to try even harder to fulfill their roles, by becoming more authoritarian and demanding of those personality characteristics.

There appear to be only three ways this constellation of circumstances could change enough for ghetto schools to improve and for blacks to "apply" themselves more traditionally to their educational advancement.

First, if the class structure of the economy changed enough so that blacks could realize equal returns with whites for additional years of education or additional educational achievements, then they might apply themselves more consistently. Both their schools and their educations would probably improve as a result. Second, the economy could begin to reward different sets of characteristics, demanding creativity in its workers rather than conformity, or originality rather than docility. The schools would inevitably change, tending to emphasize those characteristics. They would loosen their structures and relax their expectations. Students would probably respond to this newer freedom by developing their creativity and originality. Third, the schools could seek an independence of the more basic institutions. They could try to ignore the demands of the economy for certain kinds of personalities and could establish for themselves independent sets of objectives. They could try to respect and respond to the present lives of children.

None of these three possibilities seems to me at all likely. The first would require a restructuring of all our social institutions, for — as Chapters 2 and 3 on employment and race argued more extensively — racism pervades our society and serves almost indispensable functions in the stabilization of the capitalist system. We cannot easily replace those functions with some other stabilizing phenomenon adequately enough to ensure equal opportunities in the economy for members of minority groups. The second would require a fundamental change in both the process and objectives of economic production in this country. Conforming, deferring, persevering workers seem absolutely necessary to the preservation of profits for owners of capital. Independent, creative workers would not fit well with the ways in which production is managed. The third would require of the schools an independence of society that they have never achieved. Were the schools to achieve this independence — through the pursuit of different objectives — the economy would have to find different mechanisms for the development of suitable personality structures among its workers. It

42 See the Editor's Introduction in Chapter 3.

seems impossible to anticipate both the shape of those mechanisms and their impact on the schools.[43]

In short, ghetto schools will continue to "fail" in liberal terms (but succeed in the "system's" terms) unless basic economic institutions stop placing demands on educational institutions, or unless some other institutions arise to satisfy those demands.

The Readings

The first three selections provide some basic Impressions, Definitions, and Magnitudes of ghetto education problems. Janet Sideman's short piece describes the experience of one intelligent, expressive, and energetic black student in a ghetto school. His story highlights both the ways in which schools try to channel those students and the ways in which students react to the schools. The brief selection from the Coleman Report and the Editor's Supplement provide evidence about different dimensions of inequality in American schools, relating the failures of ghetto schools to the general pattern of educational inequalities in education.

The second group of readings summarizes many of the analytic arguments developed by each of the three perspectives. Lester C. Thurow summarizes the economic analysis upon which the general conservative and liberal view of schooling formerly built. Frederick Mosteller and Daniel P. Moynihan review various conclusions about the programs and analyses of the 1960s, concluding in somewhat conservative fashion that too much had been expected and that, perhaps, we should lower our sights. Samuel Bowles presents a general exposition of the radical view. Bennett Harrison provides some more graphic empirical evidence that education does not enhance the economic opportunities either of ghetto residents or of minority people living outside the ghettos — suggesting that something more fundamental than the simple failures of ghetto schools is at stake.

The final selection by Bowles and Herbert Gintis provides a counterpoint to the preceding selections. Bowles and Gintis argue that schooling could serve more progressive functions in the United States if a socialist movement were to take root. They explore the potential ties between schooling and a socialist movement, arguing that learning can, in the proper social context, help us develop as better and more productive people.

[43] All these points are further developed in Bowles and Gintis, *Schooling in Capitalist America.*

DEATH OF A DROPOUT

Janet Sideman

This story provides a tragic glimpse of the reality of ghetto schools. It illustrates both the responses of those schools to problem students and the classic dimensions of student rebellion against the schools and their economic functions.

The selection originally appeared in *The New Republic.*

In early May [1967], newspapers reported that Clarence Brooker, age 19, Negro, was accidentally killed by a policeman in the Northeast section of Washington, D.C. A policeman was patrolling his regular beat, when he saw a group of boys milling about the street. Complaints from shopkeepers had already been received about them. The policeman stopped in front of the group and one of the boys, Clarence Brooker, dropped a bag of cookies onto the sidewalk. The bag broke, the crushed cookies were strewn over the street, the policeman attempted to arrest Brooker for disorderly conduct. There was a struggle and a chase, two shots were fired, and the boy was finally apprehended. It is unclear where he died, but the policeman was surprised that Clarence Brooker was dead at all. No one had realized that he had a bullet in his back, since there was no external bleeding. An investigation was demanded and the case is now before a grand jury. Among other items of interest mentioned in the reporting was that Clarence Brooker, besides having a police record, was also a high school dropout — one of many. (The dropout rate in the District's senior high schools last year was 12.3 percent.)

About two years ago I taught eleventh grade English in a Northeast Washington high school that had a special program for dropouts. Clarence Brooker was one of my students. The program had an all Negro enrollment. Most of the students lived in the Northeast ghetto section.

On the opening day of school I was informed that, although books had been ordered, they had not

Source: Janet Sideman, "Death of a Dropout," from the June 3, 1967, issue of *The New Republic.* Reprinted by permission of *The New Republic.* Copyright © 1967, Harrison-Blaine of New Jersey, Inc.

yet arrived, and I should not count on them arriving at all. When I met the class, I asked them to write about something they enjoyed doing or that interested them. I mentioned that we would have no books for a while, but if I knew what they liked, I could base class work on this. They kept asking when the books would come. I said I didn't know, but you didn't have to carry a book to school in order to learn.

The students began writing, and after about 15 minutes, some began handing their papers in. The girls returned to their desks and sat, staring into space. The boys were more restless, and some got up and left the room. Browsing through the papers, I remarked that no one had crossed anything out or erased. You expect changes in written work. All the compositions were about half a page and in beautiful "penmanship." The letters were even, perfectly formed and slanted from left to right. The right-hand margins were as straight as a ruler. The compositions could be "classified" (using the professional jargon) as those that "demonstrated skills had not been learned" and those that were "literate." Here is an example of the former:

"Well I like everyone in the class. I have no pick. I am new here but that don't mean that I take of myself. The reason I here is because I drop out of school but I well like it here. The thing that interest me most is getting of school and having my diploma so I can say that I lest finish school without having to shy."

The other group wrote pieces something like this:

"My name is .... My address is .... I like school a little. My favorite subjects are English and Math. My favorite sports are softball and football. I would like to finish school and become a clerk-typist. I came here because I know how hard it is to get a good job without a high school diploma. And I wouldn't want to be referred to as a dropout. I don't think it's going to be hard to finish school because I'm beginning to like going here."

Clarence Brooker was one of the first to finish, and after he brought the paper to my desk, he wandered from the room, returned, and roamed up and

217

down the aisles, looking to see what the others were writing.

He had wide shoulders and was very muscular, which made him seem taller than he was. The photo of him in the newspapers gave the impression that he looked dull and impassive, but he had a very expressive face. His handwriting was clear, almost feminine because he paid such attention to details. The Os and As were perfect circles, the loops of the Ys and Gs were of equal length. His name was written in the upper right-hand corner, the date beneath it of equal length. "English XI" was in the left-hand corner, "Composition" in the middle.

"My interest is girls, booze and money, but the reason I came back is because I want my diploma. My diploma will help me very much in the future.

"My plan in the near future is to join the Air Force, and in order to join, I have to have my diploma.

"After I finish my service career, my other three interests will go into effect."

So from the English teacher's viewpoint Clarence was way ahead of the game — he was literate. That is, he conjugated verbs properly, he knew when to begin a new paragraph, he even had a good "clincher sentence," and the textbook tells us this is one of the most difficult problems in writing a composition. He had followed the assignment, he told me what interested him. He even had a bit of originality left in him. One of the better students in the class. So why had he dropped out? Because school had no relation to his life.

Dropouts are like nonchurchgoers; both might feel guilty or worried, but they soon discover their everyday lives are not altered by nonattendance. They can sleep late. There are no immediate consequences, and the future? Well, that is a long way off. Who knows if it was the air force that brought Clarence Brooker back? Anyway he carried an additional burden. He had more energy than was good for him and he didn't know what to do with it. That's the last thing you want from the congregation. They're only required to know when to rise, when to kneel, and to wait patiently while the organist finds the right page.

A few days later I requested another piece of writing. I began the sermon by asking the class to try to put their feelings into words. If they were interested in something, they should try to examine why. My words were stilted, but 30 wary faces do not make you very relaxed. "You have a language as a means of guiding and controlling your lives, so you can express ideas and understand situations. Do you think you would be able to have thoughts without a language?" I concluded. The girls dutifully began writing their names and the date at the top of the blue-lined paper. Clarence Brooker and some boys around him started laughing and yawning. What was the trouble? Clarence answered for them. They were bored. They knew what interested them, but I would never let them write about it. Yes I would, what was it?

"Sex," Clarence answered.

"You can write about it, but since I want you to put feelings into words, you might think I was trying to pry into your private lives, and that is not what I intended. Maybe you would feel freer with something less personal." He insisted that was what they really wanted to write about, and I agreed. Could they use a dictionary? Of course, that's what it was there for. Clarence had a perpetual grin on his face and after some writing would mutter something to those around him. The dictionary was passed from desk to desk. Snickers went around the room, pounding on desks, glances to see who would begin first.

"The point of this is to use words not noise."

I was uneasy, maybe I had overstimulated them. Teachers are always warned about this. The boys had been discipline problems before, the girls were pregnant or already mothers. It is important that limitations be set. Clarence was one of the first to finish, and waved his paper in the air as he brought it up. The bell rang while he was grabbing a pen away from one of the boys who had not yet finished. But nothing was produced that was stimulating, let alone overstimulating. The majority of the papers were definitions from the dictionary, with some moralizing attached.

"Sex is a division into male and female, relating to reproductive organs. Sex should mainly be active among adults who are married, but it doesn't always happen that way."

Here is the one Clarence Brooker wrote:

"Sex is, or shall I say, can be a form of both pleasure and relaxation. To me, sex is a *need* that has to be fulfilled by a member of the opposite sex. Some people use sex as a plaything, but sex should be regarded as being essential to life.

"Birth control pills should be abolished and so should abortions. Women getting rid of children should be sentenced to jail because it's a form of murder."

Grammatically correct, and the most original within the framework of the class, but not radically different. One newspaper article reported that Clarence committed rape and other sexual offenses, but his composition gives no hint of that. It is quite respectable today to consider sex a *need,* and many people agree with Clarence's view of birth control.

The next day the students wanted to hear the compositions and I read a few. They were very disappointed. I asked them if they could explain why, since they obviously had strong feelings about things, they could not express them in writing. The listlessness had begun, the wandering in and out, the slamming of the door, tapping feet. Their explanation was that they shouldn't be doing any writing or discussing at all.

"We want to get down to work." What was the definition of work in 11th grade English? Spelling, grammar, nouns, tests. And when are we going to get books?

I went to the central English department to see if I could get a book used by other D.C. schools. There happened to be one lying around, with Eleventh Grade English on it in capital letters.

"With this type of student, your classwork must have intensive structure," I was told. "Since it is lacking in the homes, the schools must provide it."

A lesson from the book was mimeographed. The sheets were passed out, heads were bent, *Adverbs* written in the center of the lined paper, numbers one to 20 to the right of the red vertical margin line. Correct the following sentences. (1) The parts of this camp stove fit together very simple. . . .

It was very peaceful. All the pens were moving in unison, a studious classroom scene. Then Clarence Brooker was finished. If we had had books, I could have told him to begin the next lesson. He left the room, returned, wandered about. I told him I would correct his paper with him. Wasn't I going to grade it? I wrote an A in red ink. Wasn't I going to enter it in the record book? It was entered. Most of the students had done well. What was interesting was that students who could barely construct a sentence in a composition were able to recognize the incorrect use of an adverb in an isolated sentence. A student told me he was unable to pass the written part of the Civil Service Exam, would I give him additional work in grammar? I showed him one of his tests, where he was able to "correct the following verb

forms," and substitute "I am" for "I is." Yet he always said "I is" and always wrote it in compositions. I never was able to convince him that the solution was not in additional exercises.

If the students could have defined what education meant to them, they would not have used words like understanding, ideas, or thought, for only words that could be attached to "things" had any meaning to them. They must have work. Work comes from a book and can be numbered and titled. A grade can be set down on paper and you can amass a collection of these papers to prove that you have been to school.

But what do you do with someone like Clarence Brooker, who is smart, who has this energy? He wanted work, but he wouldn't wait patiently when he finished, and he refused any other alternative. The class had been in session two weeks, and I decided to keep on mimeographing lessons for a while. I wasn't getting to know the class too well because Clarence was occupying most of my time. The wandering had developed into explosive noises. He wrote on other students' papers, he mimicked them. I spoke to him many times. Yes, he really wanted his diploma, he really did want to join the air force. He was very nice, his eyes responded to what I was saying. From a distance you would have thought we were having a conversation. You do very well in your work, maybe it's time for you to begin something new. Yes ma'am. Bring a book, any book, to class. Yes ma'am. He never did. Bring a book from the school library. Yes ma'am. He never went, he just wandered around the halls.

I asked another teacher if he had any "behavior problems."

"I never let them start," he answered. "From the first day, if there's any trouble, out they go. That's the only way to treat these kids. If you don't show them who's boss, they'll walk right over you. Besides, it's not fair to the rest of the class."

The school social worker said, "These children need authority because they don't get it on the outside. If the teacher doesn't show he is in control, it becomes very frightening for them."

I asked the principal if Clarence could be transferred to another class with a male teacher.

"We can't do it. He has to have eleventh grade English to graduate. Just drop him if he disrupts the class."

His classmates didn't have much sympathy with Clarence either. A girl spoke to me about him after class. "I know I shouldn't tell you how to run things, but you shouldn't let that boy in the class. We can't get any work done."

"But don't you think it's important that we try and see if we can't work something out with students like that?"

"I don't know about that. All I know is he's keeping me from learning."

So I hadn't followed the rules. I hadn't asserted my authority as teacher. If I could not make Clarence sit still, he had to be dropped. I had done neither, therefore he was walking all over me, which was to be expected.

"You really want to join the air force?"

"Yes."

"And you need a high school diploma to do that?"

"Yes."

"Then as a favor to me, I want you to think about something. Will you explain to yourself how you can want something badly, and yet, at the same time, do something that you know will give you the very opposite of what you want?"

"I'll try to stick it out," he answered. I had not got through at all. He didn't appear for the next few days, then came in late, left, then banged on the door glass until I started to go toward him. It dragged on for a few more days, then he was dropped. The policeman stationed in the building was instructed not to let him enter. I looked up his record to see what his other classes were and discovered that his other teachers had dropped him weeks before.

When I discussed this with other teachers and friends, I was advised not to take it personally. I didn't, and that's what made it so disquieting. I would have felt better if Clarence had been personally hostile, for that would have meant he had formed some opinion, passed some judgment.

Perhaps it is useless to investigate who was to blame for putting Clarence Brooker and hundreds of other dropouts on the street. The Negro child's education must be structured, it must be consistent. So he is taught to identify abstractions with visual things on the assumption that abstractions are too much for him to handle. He then becomes dependent on material symbols and equipment, and then in the cruelest inconsistency of all, is provided with schools that have substandard equipment, and little or no material to satisfy this dependency. His private life is full of tension and conflict, so he is given work where tension and conflict are eliminated and he never learns to cope with them.

He faces inequality, therefore he is taught conformity, which is mistaken for equality. He never conceives of a class as a miniature community, where people of different character and ability have to live together. And he never experiences equality, since he must have authority, which by its very definition means that someone is above him.

Well, one May evening Clarence Brooker, who was too smart for his own good and couldn't stick it out, dropped a bag of cookies in front of a policeman and was shot. Did he know why he dropped it? The policeman symbolized authority? But this authority wasn't going to be walked over, he carried a gun to prove it. If he were not a dropout, would Clarence be alive today? Who can say? He got an A on his adverbs. He knew that the parts of this camp stove fit together very simply.

SEGREGATION AND ACHIEVEMENT IN THE PUBLIC SCHOOLS

James S. Coleman and Others

In 1966, the federal government published the results of a mammoth survey of students and schools in the United States, *Equality of Educational Opportunity*. The survey was intended to measure the extent of educational inequality in this country, and its results have become standard sources for analysis of achievement in the schools. This very brief excerpt from the report sketches one dimension of inequality in American schools — the large gaps in achievement scores between predominantly white and black schools. The Editor's Supplement following this excerpt summarizes evidence of other dimensions of inequality.

The leading author of the report, James S. Coleman, teaches sociology at Johns Hopkins University.

Segregation in the Public Schools

The great majority of American children attend schools that are largely segregated — that is, where almost all of their fellow students are of the same racial background as they are. Among minority groups, Negroes are by far the most segregated. Taking all groups, however, white children are most segregated. Almost 80 percent of all white pupils in 1st grade and 12th grade attend schools that are from 90 to 100 percent white. And 97 percent at grade 1, and 99 percent at grade 12, attend schools that are 50 percent or more white.

For Negro pupils, segregation is more nearly complete in the South (as it is for whites also), but it is extensive also in all the other regions where the Negro population is concentrated: the urban North, Midwest, and West.

More than 65 percent of all Negro pupils in the first grade attend schools that are between 90 and 100 percent Negro. And 87 percent at grade 1, and 66 percent at grade 12, attend schools that are 50 percent or more Negro. In the South most students attend schools that are 100 percent white or Negro.

Source: James S. Coleman *et al.*, "Segregation and Achievement in the Public Schools" from *Equality of Educational Opportunity* (Washington, D.C.: U.S. Government Printing Office, 1966).

The same pattern of segregation holds, though not quite so strongly, for the teachers of Negro and white students. For the Nation as a whole, the average Negro elementary pupil attends a school in which 65 percent of the teachers are Negro; the average white elementary pupil attends a school in which 97 percent of the teachers are white. White teachers are more predominant at the secondary level, where the corresponding figures are 59 and 97 percent. The racial matching of teachers is most pronounced in the South, where by tradition it has been complete. On a nationwide basis, in cases where the races of pupils and teachers are not matched, the trend is all in one direction: white teachers teach Negro children but Negro teachers seldom teach white children; just as, in the schools, integration consists primarily of a minority of Negro pupils in predominantly white schools but almost never of a few whites in largely Negro schools.

In its desegregation decision of 1954, the Supreme Court held that separate schools for Negro and white children are inherently unequal. This survey finds that, when measured by that yardstick, American public education remains largely unequal in most regions of the country, including all those where Negroes form any significant proportion of the population. . . .

Achievement in the Public Schools

The schools bear many responsibilities. Among the most important is the teaching of certain intellectual skills such as reading, writing, calculating, and problem solving. One way of assessing the educational opportunity offered by the schools is to measure how well they perform this task. Standard achievement tests are available to measure these skills, and several such tests were administered in this survey to pupils at grades 1, 3, 6, 9, and 12.

These tests do not measure intelligence, nor attitudes, nor qualities of character. Furthermore, they are not, nor are they intended to be, "culture free."

TABLE 1. Nationwide Median Test Scores for 1st- and 12th-Grade Pupils, Fall 1965

| Test | Racial or ethnic group | | | | | |
	Puerto Ricans	Indian Americans	Mexican-Americans	Oriental Americans	Negro	Majority
1st grade:						
Nonverbal	45.8	53.0	50.1	56.6	43.4	54.1
Verbal	44.9	47.8	46.5	51.6	45.4	53.2
12th grade:						
Nonverbal	43.3	47.1	45.0	51.6	40.9	52.0
Verbal	43.1	43.7	43.8	49.6	40.9	52.1
Reading	42.6	44.3	44.2	48.8	40.9	51.9
Mathematics	43.7	45.9	45.5	51.3	42.2	51.8
General information	41.7	44.7	43.3	51.3	41.8	51.8
Average of the 5 tests	43.1	45.1	44.4	50.1	41.1	52.0

Quite the reverse: they are culture bound. What they measure are the skills which are among the most important in our society for getting a good job and moving up to a better one, and for full participation in an increasingly technical world. Consequently, a pupil's test results at the end of public school provide a good measure of the range of opportunities open to him as he finishes school — a wide range of choice of jobs or colleges if these skills are very high; a very narrow range that includes only the most menial jobs if these skills are very low.

Table 1 gives an overall illustration of the test results for the various groups by tabulating nationwide median scores (the score which divides the group in half) for 1st-grade and 12th-grade pupils on the tests used in those grades. For example, half of the white 12th-grade pupils had scores above 52 on the nonverbal test and half had scores below 52. (Scores on each test at each grade level were standardized so that the average over the national sample equaled 50 and the standard deviation equaled 10. This means that for all pupils in the Nation, about 16 percent would score below 40 and about 16 percent above 60).

With some exceptions — notably Oriental Americans — the average minority pupil scores distinctly lower on these tests at every level than the average white pupil. The minority pupils' scores are as much as one standard deviation below the majority pupils' scores in the 1st grade. At the 12th grade, results of tests in the same verbal and nonverbal skills show that, in every case, the minority scores are farther

below the majority than are the 1st-graders. For some groups, the relative decline is negligible; for others, it is large.

Furthermore, a constant difference in standard deviations over the various grades represents an increasing difference in grade level gap. For example, Negroes in the metropolitan Northeast are about 1.1 standard deviations below whites in the same region at grades 6, 9, and 12. But at grade 6 this represents 1.6 years behind; at grade 9, 2.4 years; and at grade 12, 3.3 years. Thus, by this measure, the deficiency in achievement is progressively greater for the minority pupils at progressively higher grade levels.

For most minority groups, then, and most particularly the Negro, schools provide little opportunity for them to overcome this initial deficiency; in fact they fall farther behind the white majority in the development of several skills which are critical to making a living and participating fully in modern society. Whatever may be the combination of non-school factors — poverty, community attitudes, low educational level of parents — which put minority children at a disadvantage in verbal and nonverbal skills when they enter the first grade, the fact is the schools have not overcome it.

Some points should be borne in mind in reading the table. First, the differences shown should not obscure the fact that some minority children perform better than many white children. A difference of one standard deviation in median scores means that about 84 percent of the children in the lower group are below the median of the majority students — but 50 percent of the white children are themselves below that median as well.

A second point of qualification concerns regional differences. By grade 12, both white and Negro students in the South score below their counterparts — white and Negro — in the North. In addition, Southern Negroes score farther below Southern whites than Northern Negroes score below Northern whites. The consequences of this pattern can be illustrated by the fact that the 12th-grade Negro in the nonmetropolitan South is 0.8 standard deviation below — or, in terms of years, 1.9 years behind — the Ne-

gro in the metropolitan Northeast, though at grade 1 there is no such regional difference.

Finally, the test scores at grade 12 obviously do not take account of those pupils who have left school before reaching the senior year. In the metropolitan North and West, 20 percent of the Negroes of ages 16 and 17 are not enrolled in school — a higher dropout percentage than in either the metropolitan or nonmetropolitan South. If it is the case that some or many of the Northern dropouts performed poorly when they were in school, the Negro achievement in the North may be artificially elevated because some of those who achieved more poorly have left school.

CLASS, RACE, AND EDUCATION

Editor's Supplement

The preceding selection from the Coleman Report highlights one aspect of educational inequality in this country: the disparity in achievement scores among schools with different racial compositions in different geographic areas. This brief supplement will summarize some scattered pieces of evidence on other elements of educational inequality. Four dimensions of inequality seem especially important: years of schooling, quality of schooling, returns to schooling, and intergenerational equality.

Years of Schooling

The level attained in school varies widely in this country by class and race, although racial inequalities have diminished substantially in very recent years.

In general, although the absolute level of educational attainment has increased considerably in the last century in the United States, the distribution of attainment has not become more equal. Roughly 20 percent of those born between 1890 and 1894 graduated from high school, 40 percent of those born

between 1910 and 1914, and 60 percent of those born between 1930 and 1934.[1] Despite this rapid increase in numbers of high school graduates, however, inequalities in educational achievement have not diminished. One measures educational inequalities in the same way that one measures income inequalities. In the U.S. income distribution, it has been true since World War II that the poorest 20 percent of families have received roughly 5 percent of total income received by individuals.[2] With education, one can measure the shares of different groups in total years of schooling attained by the population. If the distribution of educational attainment had become noticeably more equal over time, the most poorly educated group would have increased its share of total years of schooling. By this standard, the distribution has hardly changed at all in the first part of this century. The most poorly

[1] Christopher Jencks and David Riesman, *The Academic Revolution* (Garden City, N.Y.: Doubleday, 1968), p. 77.
[2] See the Editor's Supplement in Chapter 5, "Poverty and Welfare," in this book.

educated third of the male population born between 1910 and 1914 received 20 percent of total years of schooling, while the most poorly educated third born between 1930 and 1934 received 22 percent.[3]

By some other standards, inequalities in years of schooling attained have decreased somewhat. One can measure the amount of inequality in years of schooling by measures of the dispersion of educational attainment. One index of this dispersion is called the "Coefficient of Variation"; the lower the index, the more equal is the distribution of years of schooling. This index was 0.30 for all individuals born between 1915 and 1924. For individuals born between 1940 and 1944, it had declined to 0.23, almost a 25 percent decline.[4]

Years of schooling vary substantially by socioeconomic class. Those who come from more affluent backgrounds are destined to spend much more time in school than are those from less affluent families. According to Bowles and Gintis, for instance, a child whose family comes from the 90th percentile of families may expect, on average, five more years of schooling than a child from the lowest decile may.[5] Even among those who graduated from high school in the 1960s, to pick another example, children of families earning more than $15,000 were more than six times as likely to attend college as were those from families earning less than $3,000.[6]

These inequalities in schooling attainment by class background do not reflect differences in ability. If one controls for students' IQ's, the results remain the same. Bowles and Gintis state the conclusion precisely:

> The data indicate that an individual in the ninetieth percentile in social class background is likely to receive five more years of education than an individual in the tenth percentile; they also indicate that he is likely to receive 4.25 more years schooling than an individual from the tenth percentile with the same IQ.[7]

Blacks leave school at lower levels than whites do, although the gap between blacks and whites has closed rapidly in recent years.[8] In 1960, for instance, 42 percent of nonwhite males between twenty and twenty-four years old had completed at least four years of high school, while 66 percent of their white peers had reached the same level. By 1974, fully 72 percent of black males in that age range had graduated from high school, while 85 percent of white males of the same age had completed at least twelve years.[9] The median educational level of blacks between twenty-five and twenty-nine had climbed to 12.6 years by 1974; the median level for whites of the same age was 12.9 years.

To a certain extent, however, racial inequalities have simply been displaced onto a higher level of schooling. In 1960, 4.1 percent of blacks from twenty-five to thirty-four years of age had completed college compared to 11.9 percent of whites from that age cohort, a percentage point difference of 7.8 points.[10] By 1974, the percentage of black college graduates in that age cohort had increased to only 8.1 percent and they were now 13.0 percentage points behind their white peers.[11]

Quality of Schooling

The most prevalent measure of educational quality relies on comparisons of achievement test scores among students at a given grade level. The preceding selection from the Coleman Report provides evidence on variations in achievement level by race. Class differences also appear significant. Based on a variety of data, Jencks and colleagues conclude that variations in family background explain more than one-third of total variations in cognitive achievement.[12] In another set of comparisons relying on data from the Coleman Report, Larry Seidman found that average sixth-grade achievement scores among upper-class white students were 43 percent higher than those for lower-class white students; that upper-class blacks scored 29 percent higher than lower-class blacks; and that lower-class whites scored only 19 percent above lower-class blacks.[13]

---

[3] Jencks and Riesman, *Academic Revolution.*

[4] Christopher Jencks *et al., Inequality* (New York: Basic Books, 1972), p. 21.

[5] Samuel Bowles and Herbert Gintis, *Schooling in Capitalist America* (New York: Basic Books, 1976), p. 30.

[6] Cited, *ibid.*, p. 31.

[7] *Ibid.*, p. 32. (Emphasis added.)

[8] See the Editor's Introduction to this chapter for some additional comments on this tendency.

[9] These data come from U.S. Bureau of the Census, "The Social and Economic Status of the Black Population in the United States, 1974," *Current Population Reports*, Series P-23, No. 54, July 1975, p. 97.

[10] *Loc. cit.*

[11] *Loc. cit.*

[12] Jencks *et al., Inequality*, p. 76.

[13] From an unpublished paper, Harvard College, 1968.

Returns to Schooling

Another quite different measure of educational quality relies on estimated monetary returns to years of schooling. Whatever the relationship between an additional year of schooling and additional income — whether it can be adduced to increased productivity or to the effects of a "screening process" — monetary returns to additional years of education represent one kind of reward available in society to those who continue in school. If the rewards are unequal, then those who receive fewer rewards have much less economic incentive to continue their education.

Evidence has accumulated that the monetary returns to education vary substantially between blacks and whites. Many analysts have found either of two principal results in different studies: first, that additional years of schooling are associated with statistically significant increases in monetary returns for whites but are not associated with returns for blacks (at least for certain schooling increments, especially grades nine through eleven); or second, that the returns associated with increased schooling are much larger for whites than for blacks.[14] Randall Weiss found, for example, that an extra year of schooling (between grades one and twelve) was associated with $457.78 extra annual income among white males between thirty-six and forty-five and with only $123.67 extra annual income among black males in the same group (controlling for age, marital status, and veteran status). Among blacks in other age groups, Weiss found no statistically significant association between income and education, even for the youngest group of blacks (between twenty-six and thirty-five).[15]

There is also strong evidence that economic returns to school vary substantially by economic class. Jencks *et al.* find, for instance, that fully one-fifth of the income advantages gained by people from "high-status" families is due to the fact that they achieve higher occupations than do people from lower-status families who went as far in school.[16] If one could add together the advantages that higher-class students have in (a) going farther in school because of their class background (controlling for IQ); (b) going to better-quality schools because of their class background (controlling for IQ); and (c) earning higher economic returns to that schooling (controlling for IQ), Jencks *et al.* estimate that one could explain "40 or 50 per cent of the total gap" between workers from higher and lower status families.[17]

Intergenerational Equality

We tend to assume that the American educational system, if at one moment its resources and returns may not be equally distributed, at least helps promote increasing intergenerational equality. This implies that the children of the least-educated will have an increasingly good chance of moving up in the educational distribution over time, that they are increasingly less certain to become the least-educated of their own generation.

Some evidence has become available on this measure of equality, and it seems to belie our conventional assumptions. It does not appear that the American educational system has been promoting intergenerational equality. Jencks and Riesman report, for instance, that the percentage of the best-educated sixth in the male population who were born into that sixth (by virtue of their fathers' educations) had increased slightly between someone of like description born in 1897–1906 and one born in 1927–1936.[18] And William Spady finds much the same general result.[19] In relative terms, Spady shows that the educational gaps between children with fathers of varying educational attainment have remained fairly constant over a period of forty years.

Perhaps more important, the relationship between education and income equality is probably breaking down somewhat. Over the first two-thirds of this century, inequalities in educational attainment, as we saw above, have been declining slightly. But this increasing equality of years of schooling achieved has *not* been accompanied by corresponding declines in

[14] See Giora Hanoch, "An Economic Analysis of Earnings and Schoolings," *Journal for Human Resources*, Summer 1967; and Bennett Harrison, the selection in this chapter.

[15] Randall Weiss, "The Effect of Education on the Earnings of Blacks and Whites," *Review of Economics and Statistics*, May 1970, p. 54. For an argument that returns to education for blacks have been improving in recent years, see Finish Welch, "Black-White Differences in Returns to Schooling," *American Economic Review*, December 1973.

[16] Jencks *et al.*, *Inequality*, p. 215.

[17] *Ibid.*, p. 216.

[18] These data are summarized in Bowles and Gintis, *Schooling in Capitalist America*, p. 34.

[19] *Ibid.*, p. 35. See also Editor's Supplement in Chapter 3.

the inequality of income. In the period since World War II, for instance, inequality in education declined by nearly one-third, but inequality in income remained virtually constant (or may even have increased somewhat). The same results hold for the comparison between races. Black schooling attainment has been catching up to white school attainment with great rapidity since World War II.

But the income gap between blacks and whites has hardly declined at all. As Bowles and Gintis conclude, "where there is a discernible trend toward a more equal educational system . . . the impact on the structure of economic opportunity is minimal at best." [20]

[20] *Ibid.*, pp. 35–36, for quote and review of data.

EDUCATION AND ECONOMIC EQUALITY

Lester C. Thurow

This selection summarizes the economic arguments that have traditionally justified heavy reliance on improving educational opportunities to increase economic equality. Thurow responds with a brief critique of those economic models.

This selection is an excerpt from a longer article (with the same title) that originally appeared in *The Public Interest.*

Thurow teaches economics at the Massachusetts Institute of Technology and has written widely about the problems of poverty, education, and the labor market.

However much they may differ on other matters, the left, the center, and the right all affirm the central importance of education as a means of solving our social problems, especially poverty. To be sure, they see the education system in starkly contrasting terms. The left argues that the inferior education of the poor and of the minorities reflects a discriminatory effort to prevent them from competing with better-educated groups, to force them into menial, low-income jobs. The right argues that the poor are poor because they have failed to work hard and get the education which is open to them. Moderates usually subscribe to some mixture of these arguments: The poor are poor because they have gotten bad educations, partly as a result of inadequately funded and

therefore inferior school systems, but partly also as a result of sociological factors (e.g., disrupted families) that prevent poor children from absorbing the education that is available. Yet despite these differences, people at all points of the political spectrum agree that, if they were running the country, education policy would be the cornerstone of their effort to improve the condition of the poor and the minorities: If the poor or the minorities were better educated, they could get better jobs and higher income. This idea has had a profound influence on public policy in the last decade.

This acceptance of the efficacy of education is itself derived from a belief in the standard economic theory of the labor market. According to this theory, the labor market exists to match labor demand with labor supply. At any given time, the pattern of matching and mismatching gives off various signals: Businesses are "told" to raise wages or redesign jobs in skill-shortage sectors, or to lower wages in skill-surplus sectors; individuals are "told" to acquire skills in high-wage sectors and are discouraged from seeking skills and jobs in sectors where wages are low and skills are in surplus. Each skill market is "cleared," in the short run, by increases or reductions in wages, and by a combination of wage changes, skill changes, and production-technique changes over the long run. The result, according to the theory, is that each person in the labor market is paid at the level of his marginal productivity. If he adds $3,000 to total economic output, he is paid $3,000; if he adds $8,000, he is paid $8,000.

This theory posits *wage competition* as the driving force of the labor market. It assumes that people come into the labor market with a definite, pre-existing set of skills (or lack of skills), and that they then compete against one another on the basis of wages. According to this theory, education is crucial because it creates the skills which people bring into the market. This implies that any increase in the educational level of low-income workers will have three powerful — and beneficial — effects. First, an educational program that transforms a low-skill person into a high-skill person raises his productivity and therefore his earnings. Second, it reduces the total supply of low-skill workers, which leads in turn to an increase in *their* wages. Third, it increases the supply of high-skill workers, and this lowers their wages. The net result is that total output rises (because of the increase in productivity among formerly uneducated workers), the distribution of earnings becomes more equal, and each individual is still rewarded according to merit. What could be more ideal?

Empirical studies seemingly have confirmed this theory. The economic literature on "human capital" is full of articles that estimate the economic rate of return for different levels of education; while the results differ slightly depending on the data and methods used, most studies find a rate of return on higher education slightly above 10 per cent per year for white males. This rate of return, as it happens, is approximately the same as that of investments in "physical capital" (e.g., new machines). From these findings, two conclusions seem to follow. First, educational investment produces just as much additional output as physical investments in plant and capital; and second, education is a powerful tool for altering the distribution of income in society. Such calculations are in common use in discussions of public education policy, and they form a major justification for heavy public investment in education.

Yet, despite this seeming confirmation, there is reason to doubt the validity of this view of the labor market and the importance of the economic role it assigns to education. As we shall see, a large body of evidence indicates that the American labor market is characterized less by wage competition than by *job competition*. That is to say, instead of people looking for jobs, there are jobs looking for people — for "suitable" people. In a labor market based on job competition, the function of education is not to confer skill and therefore increased productivity and higher wages on the worker; it is rather to certify his "trainability" and to confer upon him a certain status by virtue of this certification. Jobs and higher incomes are then distributed on the basis of this certified status. To the extent that job competition rather than wage competition prevails in the American economy, our long-standing beliefs about both the economic benefits of education and the efficacy of education as a social policy which makes for greater equality may have to be altered.

Defects of the "Wage Competition" Theory

While it is possible to raise a number of theoretical objections against the "human capital" calculations which seem to confirm the wage competition theory, it is more instructive to see if in our actual post-war experience, existing educational programs have had the effects that the wage competition theory would predict. In fact, there are a number of important discrepancies. The first arises from the fact that, in the real world, the distributions of education and IQ are more equal than the distribution of income, as Figure 1 indicates. The usual explanation for this disparity is that income is disproportionately affected by the *combination* of education and intelligence. This would explain the wider *dispersion* of income than of education or intelligence — but it cannot explain the markedly different *shapes* of the distributions. Clearly, other factors are at work.

A second discrepancy is revealed by the fact that, while the distribution of education has moved in the direction of greater equality over the post-war period, the distribution of income has not. In 1950, the bottom fifth of the white male population had 8.6 per cent of the total number of years of education, while the top fifth had 31.1 per cent (See Table 1). By 1970, the share of the bottom fifth had risen to 10.7 per cent and that of the top fifth had dropped to 29.3 per cent. According to the wage competition theory, this should have led to a more equal distribution of earnings, whereas in fact the distribution of income among white males has become more *un*equal, as Table 2 indicates. From 1949 to 1969, the share of total income going to the lowest fifth has dropped from 3.2 per cent to 2.6 per cent while the share going to the highest fifth rose from 44.8 per cent to 46.3 per cent. Empirically, education has not

FIGURE 1. Distribution of Income, Education, and Intelligence (IQ) of Males Twenty-five Years of Age and Over in 1965.

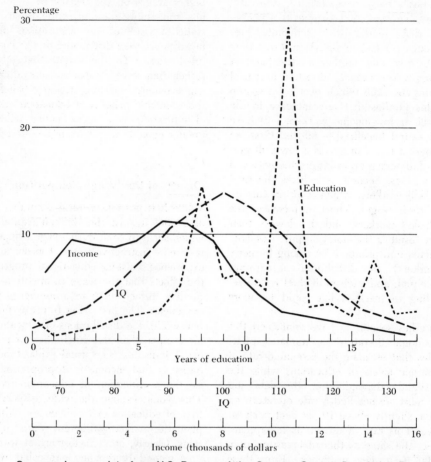

Sources: Income data from U.S. Bureau of the Census, *Current Population Reports,* Series P-60, No. 51 "Income in 1965 of Families and Persons in the United States" (1967), p. 34; education data estimated from U.S. Bureau of the Census, *Statistical Abstract of the United States: 1967,* p. 113; IQ data from David Wechsler, *Wechsler Adult Intelligence Scale Manual* (Psychological Corp., 1955), p. 20.

TABLE 1. Distribution of Education Among Adult White Males

	Percentage Share of Years of Educational Attainment	
	1950	1970
Lowest Fifth	8.6	10.7
Second Fifth	16.4	16.4
Middle Fifth	19.0	21.3
Fourth Fifth	24.9	22.3
Highest Fifth	31.1	29.3

TABLE 2. Distribution of Income Among Adult White Males

	Percentage Shares of Total Money Income	
	1949	1969
Lowest Fifth	3.2	2.6
Second Fifth	10.9	9.4
Middle Fifth	17.5	16.7
Fourth Fifth	23.7	25.0
Highest Fifth	44.8	46.3

been having the equalizing impact that the rate-of-return calculations would have led one to expect.

Black/white income gaps reveal the same discrepancies. From 1952 to 1968, the mean education of black male workers rose from 67 per cent to 87 per cent of that of white male workers—yet median wage and salary incomes rose only from 58 per cent to 66 per cent. Most of this increase, moreover, can be traced to black emigration from the South, with its lower relative incomes for blacks. As a result, education does not seem to have equalized black and white incomes in the manner that the rate-of-return calculations would indicate.

Similarly, a more rapid rate of growth of education should have led to a more rapid growth of the economy. In the early 1950's, the college-educated labor force was growing at a rate of 3 per cent per year. In the late 1960's, it was growing at a 6 per cent rate. Yet there does not seem to be any evidence that the rate of growth of productivity of the economy as a whole has accelerated correspondingly. If anything, the opposite has happened. Productivity today may be increasing more slowly than its historic rate of growth of 2.9 per cent per year.

Moreover, the entire theory assumes a labor market where wage competition is the most important short-run method for equilibrating the supplies and demands for different types of labor. Yet the real world reveals very sluggish wage adjustments in most sectors of the economy. Not only is there considerable variance in wages for different individuals with the same skills; there is also little tendency for the existence of unemployment to lower wages. There may be many unemployed airline pilots or engineers today, but their joblessness does not lead to lower wages for those lucky enough to remain employed. In fact, wage competition simply is not the all-pervasive force that economic theory supposes it to be.

Perhaps the most devastating problem with the simple wage competition view is that it cannot explain the existence of unemployment. When the demand for labor falls, wages are supposed to fall until enough jobs have been generated to keep everyone fully employed at the new lower wages. Yet the real world is full of unemployed workers whose presence does not seem to have led to falling wages for those who are employed.

The absence of wage competition is also indicated by employers' lack of interest in relative wage differentials when designing new plants. In the several cases investigated by Piore and Doeringer, plant designers typically did not take account of (or even know) the relative prices of different types of labor when designing new plants. They could not economize on expensive skills, since they did not know which skills were expensive and which cheap. They simply used an average wage rate in making their calculations.

Now there are plausible *ad hoc* explanations for all of these aberrant observations — but the necessity for so many *ad hoc* explanations is itself suspicious. Our experience with large investments in higher education entitles us to have doubts about the value of education as a means of altering the distribution of income. In the post-war years, this experience has not been encouraging. Large investments have been made. What little has happened to the postwar distribution of adult white male incomes has been contrary to expectation. Before further investments are made for such purposes, we should first get clear on why past investments have not had the expected and desired results.

MODEST SATISFACTION IS NO VICE

Frederick Mosteller and Daniel P. Moynihan

In this selection, Mosteller and Moynihan carefully review the results of all the experiments and all the studies on educational reform in the 1960s. Their conclusions summarize the state of the conservative/liberal conventional wisdom in the early 1970s. Failing to question the larger relationship between education and the economy — which is addressed in the following selection by Bowles — they reach two main conclusions. First, there is little, based on our analyses, that we know for certain would improve the performance of the schools in achieving some objectives we have set for them. Second, what we have is not so bad after all: "It truly is not sinful," they conclude, "to take modest satisfaction in our progress."

This selection represents a major portion of the introductory essay to the book edited by Mosteller and Moynihan, *On Equality of Educational Opportunity*, which reviews the educational studies of the previous decade.

Mosteller teaches statistics at Harvard University and has written many standard statistical texts. Moynihan has been a professor at Harvard University, has held many major government positions, has written widely on poverty and general social issues, and is now a U.S. senator from New York.

No single program can be expected to close the gap in educational achievement between the disadvantaged minorities and the white group. Furthermore, we do not know what school programs might offer the largest improvements for the cost involved. We must also recognize that strengthened educational achievement may not be the most important social reform needed. Indeed, higher income and better occupational chances probably are more immediate targets of reform groups, with educational achievement regarded as part of the means toward such change, as well as having value in itself. Consequently, we mention here a few key recommendations . . . .

1. *Educational goals. Both nationally and locally, we should reappraise the aims, goals, and measures*

of success in education. We should adopt equality of educational opportunity, defined for the moment as equality of educational achievement for the several ethnic/racial groups, as a national goal.

Equality of educational opportunity has had a changing meaning over the years, and it will continue to change. It is essential both to understand *and to accept* this fact. We must also accept a future where people hold sharply divergent views as to just what the term implies. The tensions, touched upon earlier, between the ideals of liberty and equality in American life will almost certainly persist, so that we must not expect that any final understanding of the term will ever be achieved. Nor need it be. But clearly a good deal more systematic thought could be addressed to this subject. In addition, it is possible to hope that at least some persons who now employ the same term to refer to widely differing conceptions of social equity will learn to perceive, and to accept, these differences.

We recommend further that thought be given to the goals and needs of education in the nation. This thought needs to challenge platitudes (and avoidances) about making the most of oneself in every possible way. It must recognize the limitations imposed by the twenty-four-hour day, as well as by the personal weaknesses and strengths each of us has. Perhaps most especially in the period immediately ahead, it will be necessary for all involved in education — researchers not least — to bear ever in mind the dictum that tastes differ. . . .

2. *Long-range research programs. We recommend that the nation launch a vigorous program in educational research for the purpose of improving national, state, and local educational policy.*

The economist Boulding says "I am struck . . . with the relatively meager resource which is devoted to the problem of human learning, in spite of the fact that this is the core of virtually all developmental processes." [1] The nation needs to mount a sub-

[1] Kenneth Boulding, *The Impact of the Social Sciences*, New Brunswick, N.J.: Rutgers University Press, 1966, pp. 106–7.

stantial program of educational research which has the definite intent of informing policy. The program should be long-range, but flexible. It needs to be evolutionary rather than revolutionary. (But see recommendation 5.) It needs to take account of the very long cycle time of education. It should prepare the nation to accept the idea of controlled field investigations on a large scale that actually involve randomization at some level — the school or the school district. As Campbell [2] says, "We need to develop the political postures and ideologies that make randomization at these levels possible." Some of the ideas required here are discussed further in the Gilbert and Mosteller chapter.

What sorts of future studies are needed? Dyer mentions several in his chapter. We have recommended long-range planning, but let us add some obvious needs.

Planned-in-advance appraisals of year-long preschool programs are conspicuously missing. Such appraisals cannot be carried out properly unless well planned. The programs and the appraisal should be designed to concentrate upon some *few* specific school gains — whether cognitive gains, social gains, or athletic gains — rather than the whole child. It is not that the whole child isn't important, it is just that we would prefer to find out how to teach *something* to poor children rather than continue to learn that we fail at teaching *everything*. It should be anticipated that the first attempts at appraisal may not be well done. We mustn't be too upset when first-time programs appraised for the first time don't give satisfactory results. We have to learn to teach and to appraise. Feedback should help.

The summer-loss effect for lower-class students should certainly be followed up and either verified or put to bed. If it holds then active steps should be taken to compensate for it.

The problems of tracking and ability grouping have not been much discussed in this chapter. Furthermore, years of research on these problems have not reached stable conclusions. If a student gets into a slow track, he will not be able to catch up with people in faster groups because the pace of the track is slower. On the other hand, maybe he couldn't have kept up anyway. Since the evidence on tracking goes both ways, and since the intellectual and ideological

arguments do the same, society may not wish to pay for more evidence on this point, but may prefer to decide on the basis of its own value system to what extent it regards tracking as acceptable. Although both teachers and educational administrators have discussed the arguments for and against tracking and ability grouping until they are weary, parents need to be made aware of these arguments and of the available choices.

One rather basic study should try to find out how teachers and students actually use their time and the effect of this time on various sorts of achievement. To what extent is the teacher actually teaching a group or an individual? To what extent is he keeping order, filling out forms, or working on supplementary school activities? Philip W. Jackson's opening chapter in *Life in Classrooms* [3] illuminates the problem of what is required of a teacher just to keep the class going without teaching them anything. We realize that time budgets have been researched in the past, but we need them studied from the point of view of differential achievement.

To what extent are students working on cognitive material inside and outside the class? We speak here of actual attention, not physical presence in a room or being near a book.

We have discussed the whole problem of education largely from the rather simple point of view of gross results of cognitive tests given to masses of students. We must not forget that in the end learning is an individual accomplishment. No matter how many teachers, friends, computing machines, and relatives surround a student, he himself finally has to learn to spell and memorize the multiplication tables. And as for the famous institution of higher learning composed of Mark Hopkins on one end of a log and a student on the other, Socrates himself could do no good if the student paid no attention to him or the subject. And so we must find out about attention and motivation, much more difficult problems than those of time budgets or achievement. For example, it is said that few Americans read books compared with Europeans. If this is true, have they been turned off by reading in school? Not turned on by it? Or have they better things to do?

The compensatory programs, begun on a massive national scale during the 1960s, pose a set of problems worth noting. A sequence was followed that

[2] Donald T. Campbell, "Reforms as Experiments," *American Psychologist,* Vol. 24, No. 4, April 1969, p. 425.

[3] Philip W. Jackson, *Life in Classrooms,* New York: Holt, Rinehart and Winston, Inc., 1968.

seems guaranteed to produce confusion, if not bit-terness. First, the programs were launched on a crash basis across a continent. Inevitably, the activi-ties that followed varied enormously from one place to another. They were subsumed under a standard heading, however, and it was promptly reported that they were succeeding beautifully. This, as we have argued, is something no one can know so soon. Thereupon, more sophisticated evaluations began, and alas, it typically turned out that there had been no success at all, or at best, little. Again, as we have argued, this is almost the preordained conclusion to be had from the kind of survey made. This is fol-lowed by allegations of methodological inadequacy in the surveys, also by assertions that the real aims of the program were not those purportedly tested. Before long a bright and promising enterprise has been reduced to a dismal squabble.

There *is* an alternative. It is absurd to reject the possibility of compensatory educational programs' doing what they set out to do. However, it is equally absurd to suppose that this achievement can be established in the time perspectives that have so far been imposed upon them. It takes a long time for a child to grow up, and perhaps an even longer time to learn what has strengthened or weakened his edu-cation. We simply must submit to the discipline of the growth process. Simultaneously, it is surely just as important to be clear at the outset that a variety of goals — not just cognitive achievement — are ap-propriate to all forms of education, compensatory education included, and that just as we ought to seek to achieve such goals, we ought also to try to assess that achievement.

3. *Periodic assessment. At regular intervals, the nation should measure the state of the schools, its students and teachers, with a view to appraising progress toward its goals.*

Drawing upon the experiences of the EEOR, there should be a regular assessment of schools on a national level, designed to monitor the progress toward equality of educational achievement and other goals, and to help guide us in our further work. This overall monitoring would be carried out inde-pendently of the experimental and developmental programs. The survey should be taken at regular time intervals, about every five years.

For the moment it is enough to be clear that the social science critique of widely held social beliefs is not something that is wisely left to random and in-termittent initiatives, whether by government, foun-

dations, or individual researchers. Once begun, a kind of collective commitment to keep at the task is neces-sary if the new truths are not to cause more mischief than the old myths. Ultimately one might expect such periodic assessments of schools to be part of a general system of social indicators, but there is no need to wait and we should not wait for that development.

The National Assessment of Educational Progress of the Education Commission of the States gives us the first appraisal of what this country's schoolchil-dren and young adults know and can do. The assess-ment includes ten subjects: citizenship, science, writ-ing, literature, mathematics, reading, music, art, social studies, and career and occupational develop-ment. The Commission plans to appraise and reap-praise each subject, some every three and some every six years. Since the subjects, such as writing, are so broad, they are broken into ten to fourteen parts, and individuals respond to one or a few parts. The assessment does not report at the level of individ-uals, schools, school districts, or states, but at the level of four regions of the country and the country as a whole.

Insofar as possible, the reports of the assessments offer factual results and avoid discussing policy im-plications. Naturally, others should and will use the results for policy.

As first results appear, policy-makers have age, re-gion of country, community size, sex, and race as background variables, together with the absolute and comparative performance for the questions and tasks studied. When the resurveys begin to appear, assessments of change in amounts and kinds of knowl-edge and skill will become possible for the first time.

Once the goals discussed in recommendation 1 have been established, individual school districts may well wish to monitor the extent to which their individually chosen goals have been achieved.

4. *Employment and income programs. We recom-mend increased family-income and employment-training programs, together with plans for the evaluation of their long-run effects on education.*

Recognizing that what can be done at school is conditioned by the situation in the home, we believe that employment and income strategies designed to strengthen the home environment of the child and his family have over the long run a chance to pro-duce a great additional component to educational achievement of a child. This belief is not a proven fact, and it would be valuable to try to determine the contributions these social developments make. This will be difficult because we have no more apparatus for appraising the contributions of various social reforms and choosing among or strengthening them than we have for school improvements.

5. *New kinds of schools. We recommend that new kinds of schools be developed and evaluated, and that in existing schools new sorts of educational policies substantially different from those of the past be tried in a research and development manner.*

Returning to schools as a source to consider changing, we recommend that there be explorations of new methods of handling schools and that new types of schools be developed and evaluated. Here, as opposed to the situation in recommendation 2, revolutionary ideas can be most valuable. The caveat as always is not to get locked into an idea. We are not searching for *the* one good way to educate people, only for better ways and for a variety of ways that will serve the individual and the nation well. . . . For a small fraction of the costs of national compensatory educational programs, it is probably possible for the nation to purchase the entire daytime program time of the equivalent of a national commercial television network (say from dawn to 7 P.M. weekdays and until noon on Saturday). Included in the price would be funds to create programs all through the week. We could have a national school of the air, indeed several of them, if this idea proved to have merit. Naturally there are political problems, but these could probably be solved. (There is political danger in just one large school.) The real question is, would such a school of the air do much for education in this country? We know that when such courses have been tied in with credit courses in secondary schools and in colleges and in industry, many students have learned enough to pass national examinations in the subject. The preschool program *Sesame Street* is being well received. Would we want such a national school to be primarily preschool, elementary school, secondary school, junior college, four-year college, or adult education? Or should there be a mix? Surely such a possibility should be considered with great care. Young people already spend as much of their time watching TV as on anything else, perhaps 1000 hours a year. Presumably what could be done with lectures and color tape could be done with such a school of the air. Naturally, problem sections and laboratory work would have to supplement such a school program. We are not proposing this as a labor-saving device but as a procedure for

offering a high-quality supplement to present educational procedures.

Urie Bronfenbrenner[4] has just completed a comparative study of elementary education in Russia and in the United States. He finds that the Soviet children understand better than ours how to share and cooperate to reach a common goal. He finds that our children have more individual initiative and resourcefulness, theirs more conformity. He finds too that adults there spend more time with children than we do in this country now, although he points out that in earlier periods we did the same. Now our leisure as well as our working hours are stratified by age group. May it not be to our advantage to explore further this work of Bronfenbrenner's with a view to finding out whether some features of Soviet education could profitably be adapted to our system, just as they are finding it worthwhile to adapt some of our capitalistic production methods to their economic system?

6. *Optimism. We recommend that the electorate maintain persistent pressure on its government agencies, school boards, legislatures, and executives to set specific targets, develop and revise programs, and report on progress toward local, state, and national goals in education with an attitude that optimistically expects gains, but, knowing their rarity, appreciates them when they occur.*

Much of our discussion has focused on the touchy problem of the effect of modest changes in facilities, teachers, or curricula on academic achievement. Let us look at the matter differently. The third-best American dream, third after "Anyone Can Be President" and "Anyone Can Make a Million Dollars," is "Anyone Can Go To College." Through the years we have grown to think that more and more members of our population should go. Taubman and Wales[5] find that the average ability level of high-school graduates who enter college was as high in the '60's as at any time since the '30s. By 1970, we have managed to put about 80 percent of seventeen-year-olds through the 12th grade. We send about 50 percent of the eighteen- to twenty-one-year-olds to college,

[4] Urie Bronfenbrenner, *Two Worlds of Childhood, U.S. and U.S.S.R.*, New York: Russell Sage Foundation, 1970.

[5] Paul Taubman and Terence J. Wales, "Mental Ability and Higher Educational Attainment Since 1910," National Bureau of Economic Research, Discussion Paper No. 139, October, 1969.

and nearly half of those attending four-year colleges complete the degree.[6]

How does this compare with the rest of the world? It is hard to get comparable figures, but the data in Table 3 bear on the point.

Table 3 shows that we are sending 1.5 to 3 times as many to colleges and universities as other industrialized countries. (The figure 23.9 percent here differs from the 50 percent mentioned earlier because of the different age group used as a base.) Thus for substantial parts of our population we have learned how to provide access to the educational process reasonably well.

TABLE 3.   Percentage of Age Group 20–24 Years Enrolled in Higher Education in Twelve Countries

Country	1965 (percent)
Austria	7.5
Canada	8.6 [c]
France	14.1 [a]
Germany	8.9
Italy	7.7
Japan	14.6 [c]
Netherlands	14.3
Norway	7.8
Sweden	11.1 [d]
United Kingdom	8.5
USSR	11.8 [b]
USA	23.9 [c]

[a] Universities only.

[b] Includes evening and correspondence students.

[c] Age group 18–24 years (Canada, USA, Japan).

[d] Universities and degree-granting institutions only.

Sources: "Access to higher education in Europe," UNESCO Conference Report, Vienna, November 20–25, 1967, published by UNESCO, Paris, 1968.

Development of Secondary Education, Organization for Economic Cooperation and Development, Paris, 1969.

It is easy to ask the inevitable question whether sending so many young people to college, and especially colleges as now taught, is a wise social goal. It is a question well worth discussing at some other place and time, one worthy of many a book. But answering it would deflect us from our main point. Society still sets these goals for itself. It has been

[6] Abbott L. Ferriss, *Indicators of Trends in American Education,* New York: Russell Sage Foundation, 1969, pp. 52, 105, 115.

willing to pay the bills to achieve this dream and in spite of violent debate there is little sign of interest slackening. Thus in the midst of all our discussion of how little we know about the educational process, we should reflect that we have through a great variety of types of colleges and universities been able to come close to satisfying the third dream.

The middle third of the twentieth century in the United States was, for all its ambiguities, a period of extraordinary social idealism and not less extraordinary social progress. There were no two areas of social policy in which progress toward a social ideal largely conceived and widely propounded was more conspicuous than those of equality of educational opportunity and equality of the races. The nation entered this period bound to the mores of caste and class. The white race was dominant. Negro Americans, Mexican Americans, Indian Americans, Oriental Americans, were all somehow subordinate, somehow something less than fully American. (Puerto Ricans had barely touched the national consciousness.) Education beyond a fairly rudimentary point was largely determined by social status. In a bare third of a century these circumstances have been extensively changed. *Changed!* Not merely a sequence of events drifting in one direction or another. To the contrary, events have been bent to the national will. Things declared to be desirable have been attained through sustained and systematic effort.

It is a paradoxical quality of such achievements that they are typically accompanied by intense feelings of dissatisfaction and disappointment on the part of those principally involved. It would have to be said that the nation ended this period (for there was a kind of ending in the late 1960's) with racial tensions higher than at any time in our history, and with dissatisfaction with the educational system approaching the point of crisis. These developments are not to be undone, and their aftermath will be with us for years to come. We see no way to avoid this, but, that being the case, we do recommend that some attention be paid to our national achievements, even as dissatisfaction mounts with respect to newer goals as yet unachieved. For this is the point. To a striking degree, things thought to be desirable in the area of racial equality, and even more so in the area of educational opportunity, have been achieved.

Especially in the period after World War II, Negroes made pronounced gains on whites in the areas of income, occupation, and education. During this period the income gap between young blacks and young whites narrowed. The education gap closed sharply. In 1940, only 12 percent of nonwhites twenty-five to twenty-nine years old had graduated from high school. By 1965 half had done so. High-school graduations became normal for all groups, while in the years immediately following, the number of black students in colleges doubled. Clearly some gaps are narrowing.

The statistics are familiar; the lesson to be drawn from them is not. The United States made extraordinary efforts to achieve certain social goals during this period, and given the way the goals were at first defined, they were substantially achieved. Especially with regard to educational goals, this involved large public expenditures, and these expenditures were forthcoming. Thus between 1955 and 1968 educational expenditures for operating purposes in higher education increased *five times,* from $4 billion per year to $20 billion. The proportion of the gross national product devoted to higher education more than doubled during this same period. As the nation entered the 1970s, it was commonly forecast that upwards of two thirds of young persons would be attending college by the 1980s.

As the 1970s began, the issues of education and race in the United States commenced to enter a new phase, involving new and yet more difficult issues. For most purposes it is accurate to state that these issues first appeared in connection with the continued existence in the eleven states of the South (Alabama, Arkansas, Florida, Georgia, Louisiana, Mississippi, North Carolina, South Carolina, Tennessee, Texas, Virginia) of a legally established dual school system which separated students on the basis of "race." In 1954 the Supreme Court declared that separate education was "inherently unequal," and in 1955 the Court issued its mandate for "all deliberate speed" in according all children equal protection of the laws. Litigation had only begun. Some black children were placed in previously all-white schools, and later the courts insisted that all students be given "freedom of choice," that is to say be allowed to attend any school of their choosing within their school system. The rules were changed, but the results were not. For practical purposes a dual school system persisted in the South. In the 1960s a combination of civil-rights statutes and the beginning of large-scale federal aid to elementary and secondary education gave the executive branch of the national government its first real leverage with respect to the dual school system in the South. Steadily pressure mounted.

The courts continued to play an active role. In 1968 the Supreme Court held, in *Green v. New Kent County Board of Education,* that freedom of choice is an acceptable desegregation device only if it is effective in accomplishing desegregation. By this point the courts were, in effect, insisting on a mixture of races as a measure of compliance with earlier rulings. In 1969, in *Alexander v. Holmes County Board of Education,* the Court further determined that the time for "all deliberate speed has passed" and positive desegregation must take place immediately.

> Under explicit holding of this Court the obligation of every school system is to terminate dual school systems at once and to operate now and hereafter only unitary school systems.

A combination of court rulings, program leverage, and executive initiative led to rapid changes thereafter. In the spring of 1970 the dual school system of the South was still essentially intact. In the fall of 1970 it was almost entirely disestablished. A statement issued October 22, 1970, by the Secretary of Health, Education, and Welfare recounts this transformation.

> Of the approximately 2,700 school districts in the Southern States more than 97 percent — or all but 76 districts — have desegregated pursuant to voluntary plans and court orders.
>
> Of the 3.1 million black children in these States, 27.4 percent — or 825,024 — live in districts that desegregated prior to this year; an additional 63.0 percent (or more than 1.89 million) live in the more than 600 districts desegregating by voluntary plan and court order this fall. 9.6 percent — or 288,485 — live in the 76 districts still not listed in compliance.
>
> Of the 7.4 million white students in these States, 48.3 percent — or 3,570,163 — live in districts that desegregated prior to this fall; 42.2 percent — or 3,134,358 — live in the more than 600 districts desegregating this fall. 9.5 percent — or 705,576 — live in the 76 districts not yet in compliance.
>
> Of the 76 districts not yet in compliance, 59 are currently in litigation, and the remaining 17 are either involved in negotiations or subject to administrative proceedings by HEW or litigation.

In the fall of 1967, 4.3 percent of the South's black children were in *school systems* that had desegregated under [then] current law. In the fall of 1968, this percentage rose to 6.1 percent; it reached 27.2 percent; and in 1970, the percentage reached 90.5 as noted above.

With regard to the number of minority children presently attending desegregated *schools*, the figures are presently being ascertained. During the last three years, HEW has arbitrary defined "desegregated schools" as those schools which are 50 percent or more white. Under this standard, in the fall of 1967, 13.9 percent of the black children in the South attended such schools. In 1968, this percentage rose to 18.4; and in the fall of 1969 it rose to an estimated 28.9 percent. The National Schools Survey, the government's method for determining school enrollment by race and ethnic group, was conducted throughout the Nation this fall, and virtually every school district in the country was required to complete survey forms by October 15. These survey forms are now arriving at HEW, and the results will be compiled by this winter.

The percentage of black children attending majority white schools is not, of course, the only measure of successful desegregation. About 35 percent of the black children in the South live in school districts where minority children constitute 50 percent or more of the school enrollment. In such districts, most of which have desegregated for the first time this fall, defining "desegregation" only by the fact that black children attend majority white schools misses the point.

Indeed, the desegregation of schools in such districts eliminates majority white schools.

Now the new phase was to begin. Stated simply, the end of the dual school system did not necessarily mean the end of all-white or all-black schools. Patterns of residential separation of blacks and whites led to schools of corresponding composition. The issue was the persistence or elimination of racial identity of schools, quite apart from the existence of a dual school system.

The final results of the 1970 National Schools Survey carried out by the Department of HEW suggested both the extent and the limits of the effects to be had from the desegregation efforts of the 1950s and 1960s. The Department was justified in claiming that "unprecedented progress has been made in school desegregation since 1968." During that short time the number of black children in all-black schools in the South dropped from 68 percent to 14 percent! The proportion of black students attending majority white schools in the South rose from 18.4 percent in 1968 to 39.0 percent in 1970. In the thirty-two Northern and Western states (excluding, that is, the South and the six Border States and the District of Columbia), there was virtually no change during this period. In 1968, 27.6 percent of Negro pupils were in majority white schools; in 1970, the proportion was 27.7 percent. Thus, at the outset of the new decade, the schools of the Old South were, at least statistically, more racially integrated than those of the North and West.

In the fall of 1970 the Supreme Court heard arguments in which the school boards of Charlotte, North Carolina, and Mobile, Alabama, contended that they were obligated under the Constitution merely to draw nonracially motivated attendance areas, just as school districts outside the South are generally permitted to do. Attorneys for the plaintiffs, as well as the United States as *amicus curiae*, asserted that a school district which, over the years, has taken steps to segregate children, has a legal obligation to take affirmative steps to undo the results of that segregation. In a word, busing.

In one form or another, this new set of issues is bound to trouble the 1970s. Will the courts require that the schools of the South integrate in the future because they have segregated in the past, while allowing Northern and Western schools to segregate on grounds that they had been integrated in the past — or at least that they had never tried to prevent integration? The point here is that residential patterns resulting from a cumulation of individual acts are nonetheless held to reflect a certain kind of social will, which may or may not be in accordance with fundamental law. Certainly the experience of urban areas outside the South has not been one of rapid or easy racial mixture. The contrary appears to be the case. But is this unconstitutional? At the outset of the 1970s no one knew. Was it desirable? Here again views, on the part both of blacks and whites, differed. In a city such as New York, for example, the demand was increasingly heard from black parents that the teachers and administrators dealing with their children also be black. This was a demand, in effect, for the creation of situations which in the South civil-rights attorneys were asserting to be unconstitutional. In the elections of 1970 in California, a black school administrator was elected Superintendent of Public Instruction, but a white judge who had ordered large-scale busing in Los Angeles County was defeated. Nothing any longer was simple.

Large efforts at social change are rarely carried out with ease and precision. As the 1970 school year proceeded, charges of fraud and bureaucratic bungling were heard from civil-rights groups. (See Jack Rosenthal, "Rights Groups Call School Plan a Fraud." *The New York Times,* November 28, 1970.) It is important to note that a considerable shift had occurred. Where previously these groups had charged that little or no school desegregation was taking place, they now tended to argue that the new unitary school systems continued to discriminate against blacks in various ways, that blacks still did not receive "quality" education, and that special federal funds were not being used for educational purposes. Clearly, a major social change had in fact occurred by the fall of 1970. That other problems remained, or that new ones had been created, is normal enough. We have a long way to go, but we are advancing.

It is simply extraordinary that so much has been done, and — again — scarcely to be remarked that it has not been done flawlessly. The difficulties of the EEOR can be better appreciated in this time-expenditure perspective. Education research scarcely existed as a Federal activity prior to the 1960s. Then in the span of a year — 1964 to 1965 — the Office of Education funds for this purpose doubled from $19 million to $37 million. The next year they tripled, to $100 million. Indeed, over 80 percent of Federal monies appropriated by 1969 for educational research and development were forthcoming in the years 1965–69. It is hardly to be wondered that the EEOR raised more questions than it answered. The Federal government had only that moment begun seriously attending to such questions. But — again — *it had begun*. Further, for all the disappointments and miscalculations of the period, public support for educational expenditure remained high. During the 1960s, for example, public willingness to see more funds expended in such areas as defense and space exploration dropped off considerably, even sharply. But at the end of the decade, as at the outset, opinion surveys recorded nearly two thirds of the public willing to spend *more* money on education.

No small achievement! In truth, a splendid one. More the reason, as even more difficult goals are set for the future, to pause and take note of what has been accomplished. It truly is not sinful to take modest satisfaction in our progress.

Needs and Hopes

What is needed is innovation, experiment, effort, measurement, analysis. What may be hoped for is a process by which the great gaps separating the educational achievement of different ethnic/racial groups begin to narrow. It may be hoped that before the century is out the great gaps will have disappeared. It may also happen that in the process a general theory of education will have evolved, been tested, replicated, and accepted. Just possibly. The creation of this new myth would be a great intellectual achievement, its critique the challenge of the twenty-first century. For the moment, we should strive for equalization. That would be a great social achievement, one the society needs, and one it will probably support with funds, patience, and good sense.

UNEQUAL EDUCATION AND THE SOCIAL DIVISION OF LABOR

Samuel Bowles

This long essay lays out most of the central elements of the radical analysis of educational problems. It argues that the apparent "failures" of schools actually reflect their successes; that is, their successful fulfillment of some of their important functions in reproducing the inequalities and hierarchies of the social division of labor in capitalist societies. Bowles develops this argument historically, statistically, and functionally.

Bowles's article originally appeared in 1971. Since then, his analysis has been further developed, revised, and refined by him and Herbert Gintis in their book *Schooling in Capitalist America* (New York: Basic Books, 1976). Many more recent data sources and analyses are used in the book. Students interested in the argument developed here should explore it further in the book. (This article, rather than the more recent book, has been selected for this volume because it proved to be difficult to excerpt the book without splintering its argument.)

Bowles teaches economics at the University of Massachusetts in Amherst and has written widely on the economics of education.

The ideological defense of modern capitalist society rests heavily on the assertion that the equalizing effects of education can counter the disequalizing forces inherent in the free-market system.* That educational systems in capitalist societies have been highly unequal is generally admitted and widely condemned. Yet educational inequalities are taken as passing phenomena, holdovers from an earlier, less enlightened era, which are rapidly being eliminated.

The record of educational history in the United States, and scrutiny of the present state of our col-

Source: Samuel Bowles, "Unequal Education and the Social Division of Labor," from *The Review of Radical Political Economics*, Vol. 3, No. 4, Fall–Winter 1971, pp. 38–66. Copyright © 1971 by Union for Radical Political Economics. Reprinted with permission.

* Many of the ideas in this essay have been worked out jointly with Herbert Gintis and other members of the Harvard seminar of the Union for Radical Political Economics. I am grateful to them and to Janice Weiss and Christopher Jencks for their help.

leges and schools, lend little support to this comforting optimism. Rather, the available data suggest an alternative interpretation. In what follows I argue (1) that schools have evolved in the United States not as part of a pursuit of equality, but rather to meet the needs of capitalist employers for a disciplined and skilled labor force, and to provide a mechanism for social control in the interests of political stability; (2) that as the economic importance of skilled and well-educated labor has grown, inequalities in the school system have become increasingly important in reproducing the class structure from one generation to the next; (3) that the U.S. school system is pervaded by class inequalities, which have shown little sign of diminishing over the last half century; and (4) that the evidently unequal control over school boards and other decision-making bodies in education does not provide a sufficient explanation of the persistence and pervasiveness of inequalities in the school system. Although the unequal distribution of political power serves to maintain inequalities in education, the origins of these inequalities are to be found outside the political sphere, in the class structure itself and in the class subcultures typical of capitalist societies. Thus, unequal education has its roots in the very class structure which it serves to legitimize and reproduce. Inequalities in education are part of the web of capitalist society, and are likely to persist as long as capitalism survives.

The Evolution of Capitalism and the Rise of Mass Education

In colonial America, and in most pre-capitalist societies of the past, the basic productive unit was the family. For the vast majority of male adults, work was self-directed, and was performed without direct supervision. Though constrained by poverty, ill health, the low level of technological development, and occasional interferences by the political authorities, a man had considerable leeway in choosing his working hours, what to produce, and how to produce it. While great inequalities in wealth, political power, and other aspects of status normally existed, differences in the degree of autonomy in work were relatively minor, particularly when compared with what was to come.

Transmitting the necessary productive skills to the children as they grew up proved to be a simple task, not because the work was devoid of skill, but because the quite substantial skills required were virtually unchanging from generation to generation, and because the transition to the world of work did not require that the child adapt to a wholly new set of social relationships. The child learned the concrete skills and adapted to the social relations of production through learning by doing within the family. Preparation for life in the larger community was facilitated by the child's experience with the extended family, which shaded off without distinct boundaries, through uncles and fourth cousins, into the community. Children learned early how to deal with complex relationships among adults other than their parents, and children other than their brothers and sisters.[1]

Children were not required to learn a complex set of political principles or ideologies, as political participation was limited and political authority unchallenged, at least in normal times. The only major socializing institution outside the family was the church, which sought to inculcate the accepted spiritual values and attitudes. In addition, a small number of children learned craft skills outside the family, as apprentices. The role of schools tended to be narrowly vocational, restricted to preparation of children for a career in the church or the still inconsequential state bureaucracy.[2] The curriculum of the few universities reflected the aristocratic penchant for conspicuous intellectual consumption.[3]

The extension of capitalist production, and particularly the factory system, undermined the role of the family as the major unit of both socialization and production. Small peasant farmers were driven off the land or competed out of business. Cottage industry was destroyed. Ownership of the means of production became heavily concentrated in the hands of landlords and capitalists. Workers relinquished control over their labor in return for wages or salaries. Increasingly, production was carried on in large organizations in which a small management group directed the work activities of the entire labor force. The social relations of production — the authority structure, the prescribed types of behavior and response characteristic of the work place — became increasingly distinct from those of the family.

The divorce of the worker from control over production — from control over his own labor — is particularly important in understanding the role of schooling in capitalist societies. The resulting social division of labor — between controllers and controlled — is a crucial aspect of the class structure of capitalist societies, and will be seen to be an important barrier to the achievement of social-class equality in schooling.

Rapid economic change in the capitalist period led to frequent shifts of the occupational distribution of the labor force, and constant changes in the skill requirements for jobs. The productive skills of the father were no longer adequate for the needs of the son during his lifetime. Skill training within the family became increasingly inappropriate. . . .

While undermining the main institutions of socialization, the development of the capitalist system created at the same time an environment — both social and intellectual — which would ultimately challenge the political order. Workers were thrown together in oppressive factories, and the isolation which had helped to maintain quiescence in earlier, widely dispersed peasant populations was broken down.[4]

---

[1] This account draws upon two important historical studies: P. Aries, *Centuries of Childhood* (New York: Vintage, 1965); and B. Bailyn, *Education in the Forming of American Society* (Chapel Hill: University of North Carolina Press, 1960). Also illuminating are anthropological studies of education in contemporary pre-capitalist societies. See, for example, J. Kenyatta, *Facing Mount Kenya* (New York: Vintage Books, 1962), pp. 95–124. See also Edmund S. Morgan, *The Puritan Family: Religion and Domestic Relations in Seventeenth Century New England* (New York: Harper and Row, 1966).

[2] Aries, *Centuries of Childhood.* In a number of places, e.g., Scotland and Massachusetts, schools stressed literacy so as to make the Bible more widely accessible. See C. Cipolla, *Literacy and Economic Development* (Baltimore: Penguin Books, 1969); and Morgan, *Puritan Fam-*

ily, chap. 4. Morgan quotes a Massachusetts law of 1647 which provided for the establishment of reading schools because it was "one chief project of that old deluder, Satan, to keep men from knowledge of the Scriptures."

[3] H. F. Kearney, *Scholars and Gentlemen: Universities and Society in Pre-Industrial Britain* (Ithaca, N.Y.: Cornell University Press, 1971).

[4] F. Engels and K. Marx, *The Communist Manifesto* (London, England: G. Allen and Unwin, 1951); K. Marx,

With an increasing number of families uprooted from the land, the workers' search for a living resulted in large-scale labor migrations. Transient, even foreign, elements came to constitute a major segment of the population, and began to pose seemingly insurmountable problems of assimilation, integration, and control.[5] Inequalities of wealth became more apparent, and were less easily justified and less readily accepted. The simple legitimizing ideologies of the earlier period — the divine right of kings and the divine origin of social rank, for example — fell under the capitalist attack on the royalty and the traditional landed interests. The general broadening of the electorate — first sought by the capitalist class in the struggle against the entrenched interests of the pre-capitalist period — threatened soon to become an instrument for the growing power of the working class. Having risen to political power, the capitalist class sought a mechanism to ensure social control and political stability.[6]

An institutional crisis was at hand. The outcome, in virtually all capitalist countries, was the rise of mass education. In the United States, the many advantages of schooling as a socialization process were quickly perceived. The early proponents of the rapid expansion of schooling argued that education could perform many of the socialization functions that earlier had been centered in the family and, to a lesser extent, in the church.[7] An ideal preparation for factory work was found in the social relations of the school: specifically, in its emphasis on discipline, punctuality, acceptance of authority outside the family, and individual accountability for one's work.[8]

The social relations of the school would replicate the social relations of the work place, and thus help young people adapt to the social division of labor. Schools would further lead people to accept the authority of the state and its agents — the teachers — at a young age, in part by fostering the illusion of the benevolence of the government in its relations with citizens.[9] Moreover, because schooling would ostensibly be open to all, one's position in the social division of labor could be portrayed as the result not of birth, but of one's own efforts and talents.[10] And if the children's everyday experiences with the structure of schooling were insufficient to inculcate the correct views and attitudes, the curriculum itself would be made to embody the bourgeois ideology.[11]

---

the most intelligent, best educated and the most moral for support. The ignorant and uneducated I have generally found the most turbulent and troublesome, acting under the excited passion and jealousy." Quoted in Michael B. Katz, *The Irony of Early School Reform* (Cambridge, Mass.: Harvard University Press, 1968), p. 88.

[9] In 1846 the annual report of the Lowell, Mass., School Committee concluded that universal education was "the surest safety against internal commotions" (*1846 School Committee Annual Report*, pp. 17–18). It seems more than coincidental that, in England, public support for elementary education — a concept which had been widely discussed and urged for at least half a century — was legislated almost immediately after the enfranchisement of the working class by the electoral reform of 1867. See Simon, *Studies in the History of Education, 1780–1870*. Mass public education in Rhode Island came quickly on the heels of an armed insurrection and a broadening of the franchise. See F. T. Carlton, *Economic Influences upon Educational Progress in the United States, 1820–1850* (New York: Teachers College Press, 1966).

[10] Describing the expansion of education in the nineteenth century, Katz concludes: "... a middle class attempt to secure advantage for their children as technological change heightened the importance of formal education assured the success and acceptance of universal elaborate graded school systems. The same result emerged from the fear of a growing, unschooled proletariat. Education substituted for deference as a source of social cement and social order in a society stratified by class rather than by rank." (M. B. Katz, "From Voluntarism to Bureaucracy in U.S. Education," mimeograph, 1970.)

[11] An American economist, writing just prior to the "common school revival," had this to say: "Education universally extended throughout the community will tend to disabuse the working class of people in respect of a notion that has crept into the minds of our mechanics and is gradually prevailing, that manual labor is at present very inadequately rewarded, owing to combinations of the rich against the poor; that mere mental labor is comparatively worthless; that property or wealth ought

---

The 18th Brumaire of Louis Bonaparte (New York: International Publishers, 1935).

[5] See, for example, S. Thernstrom, *Poverty and Progress: Social Mobility in the 19th Century City* (Cambridge: Harvard University Press, 1964).

[6] B. Simon, *Studies in the History of Education, 1780–1870*, vol. 1 (London, England: Lawrence and Wishant, 1960).

[7] Bailyn, *Education in the Forming of American Society*.

[8] A manufacturer, writing to the Massachusetts State Board of Education from Lowell in 1841 commented: "I have never considered mere knowledge ... as the only advantage derived from a good Common School education. ... (Workers with more education possess) a higher and better state of morals, are more orderly and respectful in their deportment, and more ready to comply with the wholesome and necessary regulations of an establishment. ... In times of agitation, on account of some change in regulations or wages, I have always looked to

Where pre-capitalist social institutions, particularly the church, remained strong or threatened the capitalist hegemony, schools sometimes served as a modernizing counter-institution.[12]

The movement for public elementary and secondary education in the United States originated in the nineteenth century in states dominated by the burgeoning industrial capitalist class, most notably in Massachusetts. It spread rapidly to all parts of the country except the South.[13] In Massachusetts the extension of elementary education was in large measure a response to industrialization, and to the need for social control of the Irish and other non-Yankee workers recruited to work in the mills.[14] The fact that some working people's movements had demanded free instruction should not obscure the basically coercive nature of the extension of schooling. In many parts of the country, schools were literally imposed upon the workers.[15]

---

not to be accumulated or transmitted; that to take interest on money let or profit on capital employed is unjust.... The mistaken and ignorant people who entertain these fallacies as truths will learn, when they have the opportunity of learning, that the institution of political society originated in the protection of property." (Thomas Cooper, *Elements of Political Economy* [1828], quoted in Carlton, *Economic Influences upon Educational Progress in the United States, 1820–1850*, pp. 33–34.

Political economy was made a required subject in Massachusetts high schools in 1857, along with moral science and civic polity. Cooper's advice was widely but not universally followed elsewhere. Friedrich Engels, commenting on the tardy growth of mass education in early nineteenth-century England, remarked: "So shortsighted, so stupidly narrow-minded is the English bourgeoisie in its egotism, that it does not even take the trouble to impress upon the workers the morality of the day, which the bourgeoisie has patched together in its own interest for its own protection." (Engels, *The Condition of the Working Class in England* (Stanford, Calif.: Stanford University Press, 1968).

[12] See Thernstrom, *Poverty and Progress*. Marx said this about mid-nineteenth-century France: "The modern and the traditional consciousness of the French peasant contended for mastery... in the form of an incessant struggle between the schoolmasters and the priests." (Marx, *The 18th Brumaire of Louis Bonaparte*, p. 125.)

[13] Janice Weiss and I are currently studying the rapid expansion of southern elementary and secondary schooling which followed the demise of slavery and the establishment of capitalist economic institutions in the South.

[14] Based on the preliminary results of a statistical analysis of education in nineteenth-century Massachusetts being conducted jointly with Alexander Field.

[15] Katz, *Irony of Early School Reform* and "From Voluntarism to Bureaucracy in U.S. Education."

The evolution of the economy in the nineteenth century gave rise to new socialization needs and continued to spur the growth of education. Agriculture continued to lose ground to manufacturing; simple manufacturing gave way to production involving complex interrelated processes; an increasing fraction of the labor force was employed in producing services rather than goods. Employers in the most rapidly growing sectors of the economy began to require more than obedience and punctuality in their workers; a change in motivational outlook was required. The new structure of production provided little built-in motivation. There were fewer jobs such as farming and piece-rate work in manufacturing in which material reward was tied directly to effort. As work roles became more complicated and interrelated, the evaluation of the individual worker's performance became increasingly difficult. Employers began to look for workers who had internalized the production-related values of the firm's managers.

The continued expansion of education was pressed by many who saw schooling as a means of producing these new forms of motivation and discipline. Others, frightened by the growing labor militancy after the Civil War, found new urgency in the social-control arguments popular among the proponents of education in the antebellum period.

A system of class stratification developed within this rapidly expanding educational system. Children of the social elite normally attended private schools. Because working-class children tended to leave school early, the class composition of the public high schools was distinctly more elite than the public primary schools.[16] And as a university education ceased to be merely training for teaching or the divinity and became important in gaining access to the pinnacles of the business world, upper-class families used their money and influence to get their children into the best universities, often at the expense of the children of less elite families.

Around the turn of the present century, large numbers of working-class and particularly immigrant children began attending high schools. At the same time, a system of class stratification developed within secondary education.[17] The older democratic ideol-

---

[16] Katz, *Irony of Early School Reform.*

[17] Sol Cohen describes this process in "The Industrial Education Movement, 1906–1917," *American Quarterly* 20, no. 1 (Spring 1968): 95–110. Typical of the arguments then given for vocational education is the following, by the superintendent of schools in Cleveland: "It

ogy of the common school — that the same curriculum should be offered to all children — gave way to the "progressive" insistence that education should be tailored to the "needs of the child." [18] In the interests of providing an education relevant to the later life of the students, vocational schools and tracks were developed for the children of working families. The academic curriculum was preserved for those who would later have the opportunity to make use of book learning, either in college or in white-collar employment. This and other educational reforms of the progressive education movement reflected an implicit assumption of the immutability of the class structure.

The frankness with which students were channeled into curriculum tracks, on the basis of their social-class background, raised serious doubts concerning the "openness" of the social-class structure. The relation between social class and a child's chances of promotion or tracking assignments was disguised — though not mitigated much — by another "progressive" reform: "objective" educational testing. Particularly after World War I, the capitulation of the schools to business values and concepts of efficiency led to the increased use of intelligence and scholastic achievement testing as an ostensibly unbiased means of measuring the product of school-

---

is obvious that the educational needs of children in a district where the streets are well paved and clean, where the homes are spacious and surrounded by lawns and trees, where the language of the child's playfellows is pure, and where life in general is permeated with the spirit and ideals of America — it is obvious that the educational needs of such a child are radically different from those of the child who lives in a foreign and tenement section." (William H. Elson and Frank P. Bachman, "Different Course for Elementary School," *Educational Review* 39 (April 1910): 361–63.

See also L. Cremin, *The Transformation of the School; Progressivism in American Education, 1876–1957* (New York: Alfred A. Knopf, 1961), chap. 2, and David Cohen and Marvin Lazerson, "Education and the Industrial Order," mimeograph, 1970.

[18] The superintendent of the Boston schools summed up the change in 1908: "Until very recently (the schools) have offered equal opportunity for all to receive *one kind* of education, but what will make them democratic is to provide opportunity for all to receive such education as will fit them *equally well* for their particular work." (Boston, *Documents of the School Committee, 1908,* no. 7, p. 53, quoted in Cohen and Lazerson, "Education and the Industrial Order.")

ing and classifying students.[19] The complementary growth of the guidance counseling profession allowed much of the channeling to proceed from the students' own well-counseled choices, thus adding an apparent element of voluntarism to the system.

The legacy of the progressive education movement, like the earlier reforms of the mid-nineteenth century, was a strengthened system of class stratification within schooling which continues to play an important role in the reproduction and legitimation of the social division of labor.

The class stratification of education during this period had proceeded hand in hand with the stratification of the labor force. As large bureaucratic corporations and public agencies employed an increasing fraction of all workers, a complicated segmentation of the labor force evolved, reflecting the hierarchical structure of the social relations of production. A large middle group of employees developed, comprising clerical, sales, bookkeeping, and low-level supervisory workers.[20] People holding these occupations ordinarily had a modicum of control over their own work; in some cases they directed the work of others, while themselves under the direction of higher management. The social division of labor had become a finely articulated system of work relations dominated at the top by a small group with control over work processes and a high degree of personal autonomy in their work activities, and proceeding by finely differentiated stages down the chain of bureaucratic command to workers who labored more as extensions of the machinery than as autonomous human beings.

One's status, income, and personal autonomy came to depend in great measure on one's place in the work hierarchy. And in turn, positions in the social division of labor came to be associated with educational credentials reflecting the number of years of schooling and the quality of education received. The increasing importance of schooling as a mechanism for allocating children to positions in the class structure played a major part in legitimizing the structure

---

[19] R. Callahan, *Education and the Cult of Efficiency* (Chicago: University of Chicago Press, 1962). Cohen and Lazerson, "Education and the Industrial Order," and Cremin, *Transformation of the School.*

[20] See M. Reich, "The Evolution of the U.S. Labor Force," in *The Capitalist System* (eds.), R. Edwards, M. Reich, and T. Weisskopf (Englewood Cliffs, N.J.: Prentice-Hall, Inc., 1972).

itself.[21] But at the same time, it undermined the simple processes which in the past had preserved the position and privilege of the upper-class families from generation to generation. In short, it undermined the processes serving to reproduce the social division of labor.

In pre-capitalist societies, direct inheritance of occupational position is common. Even in the early capitalist economy, prior to the segmentation of the labor force on the basis of differential skills and education, the class structure was reproduced generation after generation simply through the inheritance of physical capital by the offspring of the capitalist class. Now that the social division of labor is differentiated by types of competence and educational credentials as well as by ownership of capital, the problem of inheritance is not nearly so simple. The crucial complication arises because education and skills are embedded in human beings; unlike physical capital, these assets cannot be passed on to one's children at death. In an advanced capitalist society in which education and skills play an important role in the hierarchy of production, then, the absence of confiscatory inheritance laws is not enough to reproduce the social division of labor from generation to generation. Skills and educational credentials must somehow be passed on within the family. It is a fundamental theme of this essay that schools play an important part in reproducing and legitimizing this modern form of class structure.

Class Inequalities in U.S. Schools

Unequal schooling reproduces the social division of labor. Children whose parents occupy positions at the top of the occupational hierarchy receive more years of schooling than working-class children. Both the amount and the content of their education greatly facilitates their movement into positions similar to those of their parents.

Because of the relative ease of measurement, inequalities in years of schooling are particularly evident. If we define social-class standing by the income, occupation, and educational level of the parents, a child from the 90th percentile in the class distribution may expect on the average to achieve

[21] The role of schooling in legitimizing the class structure is spelled out in S. Bowles, "Contradictions in U.S. Higher Education," *Review of Radical Political Economics* (Spring 1974).

TABLE 1. Percentage of Male Children Aged 16–17 Enrolled in Public School, and Percentage at Less than the Modal Grade Level, by Parent's Education and Income, 1960 [a]

Parent's Education	Enrolled in Public School	Below Modal Level
Less than 8 years		
Family income:		
less than $3,000	66.1	47.4
$3,000–4,999	71.3	35.7
$5,000–6,999	75.5	28.3
$7,000 and over	77.1	21.8
8–11 years		
Family income:		
less than $3,000	78.6	25.0
$3,000–4,999	82.9	20.9
$5,000–6,999	84.9	16.9
$7,000 and over	86.1	13.0
12 years or more		
Family income:		
less than $3,000	89.5	13.4
$3,000–4,999	90.7	12.4
$5,000–6,999	92.1	9.7
$7,000 and over	94.2	6.9

[a] According to Census definitions, for 16-year-olds 9th grade or less and for 17-year-olds 10th grade or less define as below the modal level. Father's education is indicated if father is present; otherwise mother's education is indicated.

Source: U.S. Bureau of the Census, *Census of Population, 1960,* vol. PC-(2)5a, Table 5.

over four and a half more years of schooling than a child from the 10th percentile.[22] As can be seen in Table 1, social-class inequalities in the number of years of schooling received arise in part because a disproportionate number of children from poorer families do not complete high school.[23] Table 2 in-

[22] The data for this calculation to white males who were aged 25–34 in 1962. See S. Bowles, "Schooling and Inequality from Generation to Generation" (Paper presented at the Far Eastern Meetings of the Econometric Society, Tokyo, 1970).

[23] Table 1 understates the degree of social-class inequality in school attendance because a substantial portion of upper-income children not enrolled in public schools attend private schools. Private schools provide a parallel educational system for the upper class. I have not given much attention to these institutions as they are not quantitatively very significant in the total picture. Moreover, to deal extensively with them might detract attention from the task of explaining class inequalities in the ostensibly egalitarian portion of our school system.

TABLE 2. College Attendance in 1967 among High School Graduates, by Family Income [a]

Family Income[b]	Percent Who Did Not Attend College
less than $3,000	80.2
$3,000–3,999	67.7
$4,000–5,999	63.7
$6,000–7,499	58.9
$7,500–9,999	49.0
$10,000–14,999	38.7
$15,000 and over	13.3

[a] Refers to individuals who were high school seniors in October 1965 and who subsequently graduated from high school. 53.1 percent of all such students did not attend college.

[b] Family income for 12 months preceding October 1965.

Source: U.S. Bureau of the Census, *Current Population Report*, Series P-20, no. 185, 11 July 1969, p. 6. College attendance refers to both two- and four-year institutions.

TABLE 3. Inequalities in Elementary School Resources: Percent Difference in Resource Availability Associated with a One Percent Difference in Mean Neighborhood Family Income

Resource	Within Cities 1	Between Cities 2
Current real education expenditure per student	n.a.	.73 [b]
Average real elementary schoolteacher salary	.20 [a]	.69 [b]
Teacher-student ratio	.24 [a]	n.a.
Real expenditure per pupil on teacher salary	.43 [a]	n.a.
Verbal ability of teacher	.11 [a]	1.20 [a]

Sources: [a] John D. Owen, "The Distribution of Educational Resources in Large American Cities," *Journal of Human Resources* 7, no. 1 (Winter 1972): 26–38.

[b] John D. Owen, "Towards a Public Employment Wage Theory: Some Econometric Evidence on Teacher Quality," *Industrial Labor Relations Review* 25, no. 2 (January 1972): 213–222.

dicates that these inequalities are exacerbated by social-class inequalities in college attendance among those children who did graduate from high school: even among those who had graduated from high school, children of families earning less than $3,000 per year were over six times as likely *not* to attend college as were the children of families earning over $15,000.[24]

Because schooling, especially at the college level, is heavily subsidized by the general taxpayer, those children who attend school longer have access for this reason alone to a far larger amount of public resources than those who are forced out of school or who drop out early.[25] But social-class inequalities in public expenditure on education are far more severe than the degree of inequality in years of schooling would suggest. In the first place, per-student public expenditure in four-year colleges greatly exceeds that in elementary schools; those who stay in school longer receive an increasingly large *annual* public subsidy.[26] Second, even at the elementary level,

schools attended by children of the poor tend to be less well endowed with equipment, books, teachers, and other inputs into the educational process. Evidence on the relationship between the level of school inputs and the income of the neighborhoods that the schools serve is presented in Table 3.[27] The data in this table indicate that both school expenditures and more direct measures of school quality vary directly with the income levels of the communities in which the school is located.

Inequalities in schooling are not simply a matter of differences in years of schooling attained or in resources devoted to each student per year of schooling. Differences in the internal structure of schools themselves and in the content of schooling reflect the differences in the social-class compositions of the student bodies. The social relations of the educational process ordinarily mirror the social relations of the work roles into which most students are likely to move. Differences in rules, expected modes of behavior, and opportunities for choice are most glaring

[24] For recent evidence on these points, see U.S. Bureau of the Census, *Current Population Reports* (Series P-20), nos. 183 and 185.

[25] W. L. Hansen and B. Weisbrod, "The Distribution of Costs and Direct Benefits of Public Higher Education: the Case of California," *Journal of Human Resources* 5, no. 3 (Summer 1970), 361–370.

[26] In the school year 1969–70, per-pupil expenditures of federal, state, and local funds were $1,490 for colleges

and universities and $747 for primary and secondary schools. U.S. Office of Education, *Digest of Educational Statistics, 1969* (Washington, D.C.: Government Printing Office, 1969).

[27] See also P. C. Sexton, *Education and Income* (New York: Viking Press, 1961).

when we compare levels of schooling. Note the wide range of choice over curriculum, life style, and allocation of time afforded to college students, compared with the obedience and respect for authority expected in high school. Differentiation occurs also within each level of schooling. One needs only to compare the social relations of a junior college with those of an elite four-year college,[28] or those of a working-class high school with those of a wealthy suburban high school, for verification of this point.[29]

The various socialization patterns in schools attended by students of different social classes do not arise by accident. Rather, they stem from the fact that the educational objectives and expectations of both parents and teachers, and the responsiveness of students to various patterns of teaching and control, differ for students of different social classes.[30] Further, class inequalities in school socialization patterns are reinforced by the inequalities in financial resources documented above. The paucity of financial support for the education of children from working-class families not only leaves more resources to be devoted to the children of those with commanding roles in the economy; it forces upon the teachers and school administrators in the working-class schools a type of social relations which fairly closely mirrors that of the factory. Thus, financial considerations in poorly supported working-class schools militate against small intimate classes, against a multiplicity of elective courses and specialized teachers (except disciplinary personnel), and preclude the amounts of free time for the teachers and free space required for a more open, flexible educational environment. The lack of financial support all but requires that students be treated as raw materials on a production line; it places a high premium on obedience and punctuality; there are few opportunities for independent, creative work or individualized attention by

teachers. The well-financed schools attended by the children of the rich can offer much greater opportunities for the development of the capacity for sustained independent work and the other characteristics required for adequate job performance in the upper levels of the occupational hierarchy.

Much of the inequality in American education exists between schools, but even within a given school different children receive different educations. Class stratification within schools is achieved through tracking, differential participation in extracurricular activities, and in the attitudes of teachers and guidance personnel who expect working-class children to do poorly, to terminate schooling early, and to end up in jobs similar to those of their parents.[31]

Not surprisingly, the results of schooling differ greatly for children of different social classes. The differing educational objectives implicit in the social relations of schools attended by children of different social classes has already been mentioned. Less important but more easily measured are differences in scholastic achievement. If we measure the output of schooling by scores on nationally standardized achievement tests, children whose parents were themselves highly educated outperform children of parents with less education by a wide margin. A recent study revealed, for example, that among white high school seniors, those whose parents were in the top education decile were on the average well over three grade levels ahead of those whose parents were in the bottom decile.[32] Although a good part of this discrepancy is the result of unequal treatment in school and unequal educational resources, much of it is related to differences in the early socialization and home environment of the children.

Given the great social-class differences in scholastic achievement, class inequalities in college attendance are to be expected. Thus one might be

[28] See J. Binstock, *"Survival in the American College Industry"* mimeograph, 1971.

[29] E. Z. Friedenberg, *Coming of Age in America* (New York: Random House, 1965). It is consistent with this pattern that the play-oriented, child-centered pedagogy of the progressive movement found little acceptance outside of private schools and public schools in wealthy communities. See Cohen and Lazerson, "Education and the Industrial Order."

[30] That working-class parents seem to favor more authoritarian educational methods is perhaps a reflection of their own experiences which have demonstrated that submission to authority is an essential ingredient in one's ability to get and hold a steady, well-paying job.

[31] See, for example, S. B. Hollingshead, *Elmtown's Youth* (New York: John Wiley, 1949); W. L. Warner and P. S. Lunt, *The Social Life of a Modern Community* (New Haven: Yale University Press, 1941); R. Rosenthal and L. Jacobson, *Pygmalion in the Classroom* (New York: Holt, Rinehart, and Winston, 1968); and W. E. Schafer, C. Olexa, and K. Polk, "Programmed for Social Class: Tracking in High School," *Transaction* 7, no. 12 (October 1970), pp. 39–46.

[32] Calculation based on data in James S. Coleman *et al. Equality of Educational Opportunity*, vol. 2 (Washington, D.C.: U.S. Office of Education, 1966), and methods described in Bowles, "Schooling and Inequality from Generation to Generation."

TABLE 4. Probability of College Entry for a Male Who Has Reached Grade 11

		Socioeconomic Quartiles[a]			
		Low 1	2	3	High 4
	Low 1	.06	.12	.13	.26
	2	.13	.15	.29	.36
Ability Quartiles[a]	3	.25	.34	.45	.65
	High 4	.48	.70	.73	.87

[a] The socioeconomic index is a composite measure including family income, father's occupation and education, mother's education, etc. The ability scale is a composite of tests measuring general academic aptitude.

Source: Based on a large sample of U.S. high school students as reported in John C. Flannagan and William W. Cooley, *Project TALENT, One-Year Follow-Up Studies,* Cooperative Research Project No. 2333, School of Education, University of Pittsburgh, 1966.

tempted to argue that the data in Table 1 are simply a reflection of unequal scholastic achievement in high school and do not reflect any *additional* social-class inequalities peculiar to the process of college admission. This view, so comforting to the admissions personnel in our elite universities, is unsupported by the available data, some of which is presented in Table 4. Access to a college education is highly unequal, even for children of the same measured "academic ability."

The social-class inequalities in our school system and the role they play in the reproduction of the social division of labor are too evident to be denied. Defenders of the educational system are forced back on the assertion that things are getting better, that inequalities of the past were far worse. And, indeed, some of the inequalities of the past have undoubtedly been mitigated. Yet, new inequalities have apparently developed to take their place, for the available historical evidence lends little support to the idea that our schools are on the road to equality of educational opportunity. For example, data from a recent U.S. Census survey reported in Table 5 indicate that graduation from college has become increasingly dependent on one's class background. This is true despite the fact that the probability of high school graduation is becoming increasingly equal across social classes. On balance, the available data suggest that the number of years of schooling attained by a child depends upon the social-class standing of his father at least as much in the recent period as it did fifty years ago.[33]

The argument that our "egalitarian" education compensates for inequalities generated elsewhere in the capitalist system is so patently fallacious that few persist in maintaining it. But the discrepancy between the ideology and the reality of the U.S. school system is far greater than would appear from a passing glance at the above data. In the first place, if education is to compensate for the social-class immobility caused by the inheritance of wealth and privilege, education must be structured so as to yield a negative correlation between social-class background of the child and the quantity and quality of his schooling. Thus the assertion that education compensates for inequalities in inherited wealth and privilege is falsified not so much by the extent of the social-class inequalities in the school system as by their very existence, or, more correctly, by the absence of compensatory inequalities.

Moreover, if we turn from the problem of intergenerational immobility to the problem of inequality of income at a given moment, a similar argument applies. In a capitalist economy, the increasing importance of schooling in the economy exercises a disequalizing tendency on the distribution of income even in the absence of social-class inequalities in quality and quantity of schooling. To see why this is so, consider a simple capitalist economy in which only two factors are used in production: uneducated and undifferentiated labor, and capital, the ownership of which is unequally distributed among the population. The only source of income inequality in this society is the unequal distribution of capital. As the labor force becomes differentiated by type of skill or schooling, inequalities in labor earnings contribute to total income inequality, augmenting the inequalities inherent in the concentration of capital. This will be the case even if education and skills are

[33] See P. M. Blau and O. D. Duncan, *The American Occupational Structure* (New York: Wiley, 1967). More recent data do not contradict the evidence of no trend toward equality. A 1967 Census survey, the most recent available, shows that among high school graduates in 1965, the probability of college attendance for those whose parents had attended college has continued to rise relative to the probability of college attendance for those whose parents had attended less than eight years of school. See U.S. Bureau of the Census, *Current Population Reports* (Series P-20), no. 185, 11 July 1969.

TABLE 5. Among Sons Who had Reached High School, Percentage Who Graduated from College, by Son's Age and Father's Level of Education

Son's Age in 1962	Likely Dates of College Graduation[a]	Less than 8 Years	Father's Education					
			Some High School		High School Graduate		Some College or More	
			Percent Graduating	Ratio to < 8	Percent Graduating	Ratio to < 8	Percent Graduating	Ratio to < 8
25–34	1950–59	7.6	17.4	2.29	25.6	3.37	51.9	6.83
35–44	1940–49	8.6	11.9	1.38	25.3	2.94	53.9	6.27
45–54	1930–39	7.7	9.8	1.27	15.1	1.96	36.9	4.79
55–64	1920–29	8.9	9.8	1.10	19.2	2.16	29.8	3.35

[a] Assuming college graduation at age 22.

Source: Based on U.S. Census data as reported in William G. Spady, "Educational Mobility and Access: Growth and Paradoxes," *American Journal of Sociology* 73, no. 3 (November 1967): 273–86.

distributed randomly among the population. The disequalizing tendency will of course be intensified if the owners of capital also acquire a disproportionate amount of those types of education and training which confer access to high-paying jobs.[34] A sub-

[34] A simple statistical model will elucidate the main relationships involved.

Let y (individual or family income) be the sum of w (earnings from labor, including embodied education and skills, L) and k (earnings from capital, K), related according to the equation $y = w + k = aK^A L^B$. The coefficients A and B represent the relative importance of capital and labor as sources of income. The variance of the logarithm of income (a common measure of inequality) can then be represented by the following expression:

$$\text{var} \log y = A^2 \text{var} \log K + B^2 \text{var} \log L$$
$$+ 2AB \text{ covar } (\log L, \log K).$$

The first term on the right represents the contribution of inequalities in capital ownership to total inequality, the second measures that part of the total income inequality due to inequalities of education and skills embodied in labor, and the third represents the contribution to income inequality of social class inequalities in the supply of skills and schooling. Prior to the educational differentiation of the labor force, the variance of labor was zero. All workers were effectively equal. The variance of the logarithm of income would then be due entirely to capital inequality and would be exactly equal to $A^2 \text{var} \log K$. The rise of education as a source of income and labor differentiation will increase the variance of the logarithm of embodied labor unless all workers receive identical education and training. This is true even if the third term is zero, indicating no social class inequalities in the provision of skills and education.

To assert the conventional faith in the egalitarian influence of the rising economic importance of education, one would have to argue that the rise of education is likely to be associated with either (1) a fall in A, the

stantial negative correlation between the ownership of capital and the quality and quantity of schooling received would have been required merely to neutralize the disequalizing effect of the rise of schooling as an economic phenomenon. And while some research has minimized the importance of social-class biases in schooling,[35] nobody has yet suggested that class and schooling were inversely related!

Class Culture and Class Power

The pervasive and persistent inequalities in American education would seem to refute an interpretation of education that asserts its egalitarian functions. But the facts of inequality do not by themselves suggest an alternate explanation. Indeed, they pose serious problems of interpretation. If the costs of education borne by students and their families were very high, or if nepotism were rampant, or if formal segregation of pupils by social class were practiced, or if educational decisions were made by a select few whom we might call the power elite, it would not be difficult to explain the continued inequalities in U.S. education. The problem of interpretation, how-

relative importance of capital as a source of earnings; (2) a decrease in the size of the covariance of the logarithms of capital and labor; (3) a decrease in the inequality of capital ownership; or (4) an increase in equality in the supply of education. While each is possible, I see no compelling reason why education should produce these results.

[35] See, for example, Robert Hauser, "Educational Stratification in the United States," *Sociological Inquiry,* 40.

ever, is to reconcile the above empirical findings with the facts of our society as we perceive them: public and virtually tuition-free education at all levels, few legal instruments for the direct implementation of class segregation, a limited role for "contacts" or nepotism in the achievement of high status or income, a commitment (at the rhetorical level at least) to equality of educational opportunity, and a system of control of education which, if not particularly democratic, extends far beyond anything resembling a power elite. The attempt to reconcile these apparently discrepant facts leads to a consideration of the social division of labor, the associated class cultures, and the exercise of class power.

I will argue that the social division of labor — based on the hierarchical structure of production — gives rise to distinct class subcultures. The values, personality traits, and expectations characteristic of each subculture are transmitted from generation to generation through class differences in family socialization and complementary differences in the type and amount of schooling ordinarily attained by children of various class positions. These class differences in schooling are maintained in large measure through the capacity of the upper class to control the basic principles of school finance, pupil evaluation, and educational objectives. This outline, and what follows, is put forward as an interpretation, consistent where testable with the available data, though lacking as yet in firm empirical support for some important links in the argument.

The social relations of production characteristic of advanced capitalist societies (and many socialist societies) are most clearly illustrated in the bureaucracy and hierarchy of the modern corporation.[36] Occupational roles in the capitalist economy may be grouped according to the degree of independence and control exercised by the person holding the job. Some evidence exists that the personality attributes associated with the adequate performance of jobs in occupational categories defined in this broad way differ considerably, some apparently requiring independence and internal discipline, and others emphasizing such traits as obedience, predictability, and willingness to subject oneself to external controls.[37]

These personality attributes are developed primarily at a young age, both in the family and, to a lesser extent, in secondary socializing institutions such as schools.[38] Because people tend to marry within their own class (in part because spouses often meet in our class-segregated schools), both parents are likely to have a similar set of these fundamental personality traits. Thus, children of parents occupying a given position in the occupational hierarchy grow up in homes where child-rearing methods and perhaps even the physical surroundings tend to develop personality characteristics appropriate to adequate job performance in the occupational roles of the parents.[39] The children of managers and professionals are taught self-reliance within a broad set of constraints;[40] the children of production-line workers are taught obedience.

---

[36] Max Weber referred to bureaucracy as the "most rational offspring" of discipline, and remarked: ". . . military discipline is the ideal model for the modern capitalist factory. . . ." See "The Meaning of Discipline," reprinted in H. H. Gerth and C. W. Mills, eds., *From Max Weber: Essays in Sociology* (New York: Oxford University Press, 1958), p. 261.

[37] For a survey of the literature see J. P. Robinson, R. Athanasiou, and K. Head, "Measures of Occupational Attitudes and Occupational Characteristics" (Survey Research Center, University of Michigan, February 1969).

[38] See, for example, Benjamin Bloom, *Stability and Change in Human Characteristics* (New York: Wiley, 1964).

[39] Note, for example, the class differences in child rearing with respect to the importance of obedience. See M. Kohn, "Social Class and Parental Values," in *The Family*, ed. R. Coser (New York: St. Martin's Press, 1964); and L. Dolger and J. Ginandes, "Children's Attitudes towards Disciplines as Related to Socioeconomic Status," *Journal of Experimental Education* 15, no. 2 (December 1946): 161–165. See also the study of differences in child-rearing practices in families headed by bureaucrats as opposed to entrepreneurs by D. Miller and G. Swanson, *The Changing American Parent* (New York: Wiley, 1958). Also, E. E. Maccoby, P. K. Gibbs, et al., "Methods of Child-Rearing in Two Social Classes," in *Readings in Child Development*, ed. W. E. Martin and C. B. Stendler (New York: Harcourt Brace, 1954). While the existence of class differences in child rearing is supported by most of the available data (but see H. Lewis, "Child-Rearing Among Low-Income Families," in *Poverty in America*, ed. L. Ferman et al. (Ann Arbor, Michigan: University of Michigan Press, 1965)), the stability of these differences over time has been questioned by U. Bronfenbrenner, "Socialization and Social Class through Time and Space," in *Education and Society*, ed. W. W. Kallenbach and H. M. Hodges (Columbus, Ohio: C. E. Merrill, 1963).

[40] See M. Winterbottom, "The Sources of Achievement Motivation in Mothers' Attitudes toward Independence Training," in *The Achievement Motive*, ed. D. C. McClelland et al. (New York: Appleton-Century-Crofts,

Although this relation between parents' class position and child's personality attributes operates primarily in the home, it is reinforced by schools and other social institutions. Thus, to take an example introduced earlier, the authoritarian social relations of working-class high schools complement the discipline-oriented early socialization patterns experienced by working-class children. The relatively greater freedom of wealthy suburban schools extends and formalizes the early independence training characteristic of upper-class families.

Schools reinforce other aspects of family socialization as well. The aspirations and expectations of students and parents concerning both the type and the amount of schooling are strongly related to social class.[41] The expectations of teachers, guidance counselors, and school administrators ordinarily reinforce those of the students and parents. Schools often encourage students to develop aspirations and expectations typical of their social class, even if the child tends to have "deviant" aspirations.

It is true that to some extent schools introduce common elements of socialization for all students regardless of social class. Discipline, respect for property, competition, and punctuality are part of the implicit curriculum of virtually all schools. Yet, given the existing institutional arrangements, the ability of a school to change a child's personality, values, and expectations is severely limited. The responsiveness of children to different types of schooling seems to depend importantly upon the types of personality traits, values, and expectations developed through the family. Furthermore, children spend a small amount of time in school — less than one-quarter of their waking hours over the course of a year. Thus schools are probably more effective when they attempt to complement and reinforce rather than to oppose the socialization processes of the home and neighborhood. It is not surprising, then, that social-class differences in scholastic achievement and other measures of school success are far greater than

would be accounted for by differences in the measured school financial resources and other inputs (quality and quantity of teachers, etc.) alone.[42]

In this interpretation class differences in the total effect of schooling are primarily the result of differences in what I have called class subculture. The educational system serves less to change the results of the primary socialization in the home than to ratify them and render them in adult form. The complementary relationship between family socialization and schools serves to reproduce patterns of class culture from generation to generation.

The operation of the labor market translates differences in class culture into income inequalities and occupational hierarchies. The personality traits, values, and expectations characteristic of different class cultures play a major role in determining an individual's success in gaining a high income or prestigious occupation. The apparent contribution of schooling to occupational success and higher income seems to be explained primarily by the personality characteristics of those who have higher educational attainments.[43] Although the rewards to intellectual capacities are quite limited in the labor market (except for a small number of high-level jobs), mental abilities are important in getting ahead in school. Grades, the probability of continuing to higher levels of schooling, and a host of other school success variables are positively correlated with "objective" measures of intellectual capacities. Partly for this reason, one's experience in school reinforces the belief that promotion and rewards are distributed fairly. The close relationship between educational attainments and later occupational success thus provides a meritocratic appearance to mask the mechanisms that reproduce the class system from generation to generation.

1953); and M. Kohn, "Social Class and Parent-Child Relationships: An Interpretation," *American Journal of Sociology* 68, no. 4 (January 1963), 471–480.

[41] See, for example, S. M. Lipset and R. Bendix, *Social Mobility in Industrial Society* (Berkeley, Calif.: University of California Press, 1959); and T. Iwand and J. Stoyle, "Social Rigidity: Income and Occupational Choice in Rural Pennsylvania," *Economic and Business Bulletin* 22 (Spring–Summer 1970): 25–30.

[42] S. Bowles, "Toward an Educational Production Function," in *Education, Income, and Human Capital*, ed. W. L. Hansen (New York: National Bureau of Economic Research, 1970).

[43] This view is elaborated in H. Gintis, "Education, Technology, and Worker Productivity," *American Economic Association Proceedings* 61, no. 2 (May 1971): 266–279. For other studies stressing the noncognitive dimensions of the schooling experience, see T. Parsons, "The School Class as a Social System: Some of Its Functions in American Society," *Harvard Educational Review* 29, no. 2 (Fall 1959): 297–313, and R. Dreeben *On What Is Learned in School* (Reading, Mass.: Addison-Wesley, 1968).

So far, the perpetuation of inequality through the schooling system has been represented as an almost automatic, self-enforcing mechanism, operating only through the medium of class culture. An important further dimension of the interpretation is added if we note that positions of control in the productive hierarchy tend to be associated with positions of political influence. Given the disproportionate share of political power held by the upper class and their capacity to determine the accepted patterns of behavior and procedures, to define the national interest, and in general to control the ideological and institutional context in which educational decisions are made, it is not surprising to find that resources are allocated unequally among school tracks, between schools serving different classes, and between levels of schooling. The same configuration of power results in curricula, methods of instruction, and criteria of selection and promotion that confer benefits disproportionately on the children of the upper class.

It is not asserted here that the upper class controls the main decision-making bodies in education, although a good case could probably be made that this is so. The power of the upper class is, hypothesized as existing in its capacity to define and maintain a set of rules of operation or decision criteria — "rules of the game" — which, though often seemingly innocuous and sometimes even egalitarian in their ostensible intent, have the effect of maintaining the unequal system.

The operation of two prominent examples of these rules of the game will serve to illustrate the point. The first important principle is that excellence in schooling should be rewarded. Given the capacity of the upper class to define excellence in terms on which upper-class children tend to excel (e.g., scholastic achievement), adherence to this principle yields inegalitarian outcomes (e.g., unequal access to higher education) while maintaining the appearance of fair treatment.[44] Thus the principle of re-

warding excellence serves to legitimize the unequal consequences of schooling by associating success with competence. At the same time, the institution of objectively administered tests of performance serves to allow a limited amount of upward mobility among exceptional children of the lower class, thus providing further legitimation of the operations of the social system by giving some credence to the myth of widespread mobility.

The second example is the principle that elementary and secondary schooling should be financed in very large measure from local revenues. This principle is supported on the grounds that it is necessary to preserve political liberty. Given the degree of residential segregation by income level, the effect of this principle is to produce an unequal distribution of school resources among children of different classes. Towns with a large tax base can spend large sums for the education of their disproportionately upper-class children, without suffering a higher-than-average tax rate.[45] Because the main resource inequalities in schooling thus exist between, rather than within, school districts,[46] and because no effective mechanism exists for redistribution of school funds among school districts, poor families lack a viable political strategy for correcting the inequality.[47]

The above rules of the game — rewarding "excellence" and financing schools locally — illustrate the complementarity between the political and economic power of the upper class. In each case, adherence to the rule has the effect of generating unequal consequences via a mechanism that operates largely outside the political system. As long as

---

[44] Those who would defend the "reward excellence" principle on the grounds of efficient selection to ensure the most efficient use of educational resources might ask themselves: Why should colleges admit those with the highest college entrance examinatioin board scores? Why not the lowest, or the middle? According to conventional standards of efficiency, the rational social objective of the college is to render the greatest *increment* in individual capacities ("value added," to the economist), not to produce the most illustrious graduating class ("gross out-

put"). Yet if incremental gain is the objective, it is far from obvious that choosing from the top is the best policy.

[45] Some dimensions of this problem are discussed in S. Weiss, "Existing Disparities in Public School Finance and Proposals for Reform" (Research Report to the Federal Reserve Bank of Boston, no. 46, February 1970).

[46] Recall that Owen, whose data appear in Table 3, found that the relationship of various measures of teacher quality to the family income level of the area served by the schools was considerably higher between cities than within cities.

[47] In 1969, federal funds constituted only 7 percent of the total financing of public elementary and secondary schooling. Moreover, current distribution formulas concerning state and federal expenditures are only mildly egalitarian in their impact. See K. A. Simon and W. V. Grant, *Digest of Educational Statistics, 1969* (Washington, D.C.: Department of Health, Education and Welfare, 1969).

one adheres to the "reward excellence" principle, the responsibility for unequal results in schooling appears to lie outside the upper class, often in some fault of the poor — such as their class culture, which is viewed as lying beyond the reach of political action or criticism. Likewise, as long as the local financing of schools is maintained, the achievement of equality of resources among children of different social classes requires the class integration of school districts, an objective for which there are no effective political instruments as long as we allow a market in residential properties and an unequal distribution of income.

Thus, the consequences of an unequal distribution of political power among classes appear to complement the results of class culture in maintaining an educational system that has been capable of transmitting status from generation to generation, and capable in addition of political survival in the formally democratic and egalitarian environment of the contemporary United States.

The role of the schools in reproducing and legitimizing the social division of labor has recently been challenged by popular egalitarian movements. At the same time, the educational system is showing signs of internal structural weakness.[48] These two developments suggest that fundamental change in the schooling process may soon be possible. Analysis of both the potential and the limits of educational change will be facilitated by drawing together and extending the strands of our argument.

The Limits of Educational Reform

If the above attempt to identify the roots of inequality in American education is convincing, it has done more than reconcile apparent discrepancies between the democratic forms and unequal content of that education. For it is precisely the sources of educational inequality which we must understand in order to develop successful political strategies in the pursuit of educational equality.

I have argued that the structure of education reflects the social relations of production. For at least the past 150 years, expansion of education and changes in the forms of schooling have been responses to needs generated by the economic system. The sources of present inequality in American edu-

cation were found in the mutual reinforcement of class subcultures and social-class biases in the operations of the school system itself. The analysis strongly suggests that educational inequalities are rooted in the basic institutions of our economy. Reconsideration of some of the basic mechanisms of educational inequality lends support to this proposition. First, the principle of rewarding academic excellence in educational promotion and selection serves not only to legitimize the process by which the social division of labor is reproduced. It is also a basic part of the process that socializes young people to work for external rewards and encourages them to develop motivational structures fit for the alienating work of the capitalist economy. Selecting students from the bottom or the middle of the achievement scale for promotion to higher levels of schooling would go a long way toward equalizing education, but it would also jeopardize the schools' capacity to train productive and well-adjusted workers.[49] Second, the way in which local financing of schools operates to maintain educational inequality is also rooted in the capitalist economy, in this case in the existence of an unequal distribution of income, free markets in residential property, and the narrow limits of state power. It seems unwise to emphasize this aspect of the long-run problem of equality in education, however, for the inequalities in school resources resulting from the localization of finance may not be of crucial importance in maintaining inequalities in the effects of education. Moreover, a significant undermining of the principle of local finance may already be underway in response to pressures from the poorer states and school districts.

Of greater importance in the perpetuation of educational inequality are differential class subcultures. These class-based differences in personality, values, and expectations, I have argued, represent an adaptation to the different requirements of adequate work performance at various levels in the hierarchical social relations of production. Class subcultures, then, stem from the everyday experiences of workers in the structure of production characteristic of capitalist societies.

It should be clear by this point that educational equality cannot be achieved through changes in the school system alone. Nonetheless, attempts at educa-

---

[48] See S. Bowles, "Contradictions in U.S. Higher Education," *op. cit.*

[49] Consider what would happen to the internal discipline of schools if the students' objective were to end up at the bottom of the grade distribution!

tional reform may move us closer to that objective if, in their failure, they lay bare the unequal nature of our school system and destroy the illusion of unimpeded mobility through education. Successful educational reforms — reducing racial or class disparities in schooling, for example — may also serve the cause of equality of education, for it seems likely that equalizing access to schooling will challenge the system either to make good its promise of rewarding educational attainment or to find ways of coping with a mass disillusionment with the great panacea.[50]

[50] The failure of the educational programs of the War on Poverty to raise significantly the incomes of the poor is documented in T. I. Ribich, *Education and Poverty* (Washington, D.C.: The Brookings Institution, 1968). In the case of blacks, dramatic increases in the level of schooling relative to whites have scarcely affected the incomes of blacks relative to whites. See R. Weiss, "The Effects of Education on the Earnings of Blacks and Whites," *Review of Economics and Statistics* 52, no. 2 (May 1970): 150–59. It is no wonder that Booker T. Washington's plea that blacks should educate themselves before demanding equality has lost most of its once widespread support.

Yet, if the record of the last 150 years of educational reforms is any guide, we should not expect radical change in education to result from the efforts of those confining their attention to the schools. The political victories of past reform movements have apparently resulted in little if any effective equalization. My interpretation of the educational consequences of class culture and class power suggests that these educational reform movements failed because they sought to eliminate educational inequalities without challenging the basic institutions of capitalism.

Efforts to equalize education through changes in government policy will at best scratch the surface of inequality. For much of the inequality in American education has its origin outside the limited sphere of state power, in the hierarchy of work relations and the associated differences in class culture. As long as jobs are defined so that some have power over many and others have power over none — as long as the social division of labor persists — educational inequality will be built into society in the United States.

EDUCATION AND UNDEREMPLOYMENT IN THE URBAN GHETTO

Bennett Harrison

One of the important strands of the radical analysis of education is that the economic utility of education is constrained by the class structure of the economy. In the United States, radicals have observed, some groups are not able to improve their economic opportunities almost regardless of their education. Most of these observations have been based on an analysis of national data. Harrison summarizes some evidence based on local ghetto samples, a more relevant population base. His conclusions are striking confirmation of the general argument.

Source: Bennett Harrison, "Education and Underemployment in the Urban Ghetto," *American Economic Review,* December 1972. Reprinted with permission of the author and the American Economic Association.

The essay, written originally for the first edition of this book, draws on material elaborated in the author's book, *Education, Training, and the Urban Ghetto* (Baltimore: Johns Hopkins Press, 1972). A revised version of this essay appeared in *The American Economic Review,* December 1972. Some of those revisions for *The American Economic Review* have been incorporated into this version with the permission of the author and the *AER.*

Harrison is now associate professor of economics and urban studies at the Massachusetts Institute of Technology. He has written several books and many articles on the problems of ghetto poverty and public employment.

TABLE 1. Income, Unemployment, and Subemployment in Ten Urban Ghettos

Ghetto and City	Unemployment Rate Ghetto[a]	Unemployment Rate SMSA	Ghetto Subemployment Rate[a]	Median Individual Weekly Wage[a]	Median Annual Family Income[a]	BLS Lower Level Family Budget[b]
Roxbury (Boston)	6.5	2.9 [a]	24.2	$74	$4224	$6251
Central Harlem (New York City)	8.3		28.6	73	3566	
East Harlem (New York City)	9.1	3.7 [a]	33.1	67	3641	6021
Bedford-Stuyvesant (New York City)	6.3		27.6	73	4736	
North Philadelphia	9.1	3.7 [a]	34.2	65	3392	5898
North Side (St. Louis)	12.5	4.4 [a]	38.9	66	3544	6002
Slums of San Antonio	7.8	4.2 [b]	47.4	55	2876	n.a.
Mission-Fillmore (San Francisco)	11.4	5.4 [a]	24.6	74	4200	6571
Salt River Bed (Phoenix)	12.5	3.3 [b]	41.7	57	2520	n.a.
Slums of New Orleans	9.5	3.3 [b]	45.3	58	3045	n.a.

[a] November 1966

[b] March 1967

Source: Computations from unpublished 1966 UES data files and BLS worksheets.

There are at least seven million men and women in America who are labor force participants and yet who are poor.* In the congested ghetto areas of our central cities, even the *most* stable families — those with both parents present and with the male head working full time — are unable to earn more than about $100 a week in the marketplace.[1] Individual ghetto male family heads earn considerably less than

* All figures in this paper represent calculations from unpublished microdata files, including the Office of Economic Opportunity's 1966 and 1967 *Surveys of Economic Opportunity* (hereafter SEO) and the U.S. Department of Labor's 1966 *Urban Employment Survey* (hereafter UES). This was the most recent microdata available for use by independent researchers at the time of this research.

I would like to acknowledge receipt of dissertation fellowships from the Office of Economic Research, Economic Development Administration, U.S. Department of Commerce; and from the Manpower Administration, U.S. Department of Labor. Additional support was provided by the Bureau of Business and Economic Research of the University of Maryland, and by the University's Computer Science Center. Constructive criticism of earlier drafts and materials was contributed by Barbara Bergmann, Norman Glickman, Lawrence Klein, Stephan Michelson, William Milligan, Mancur Olson, Thomas

$100 — when they work. But ghetto residents are able to find work far less often than those living outside the slums. Still others are involuntarily part-time employed — looking for full-time work but unable to find it.

Data from the 1966 Urban Employment Survey (UES) document these conclusions. In general, as the figures in Table 1 illustrate, the jobs to which ghetto workers have access were found to be of poor quality and paid wages which were substandard by a number of widely accepted benchmarks. Occupation by occupation, the median wage rates of ghetto workers averaged only 40–60 percent of the

Vietorisz, and several anonymous referees. Marianne Russek provided programming assistance. Elisabeth McDonnell supplied the diagrams.

[1] On the labor force participation of low-income persons, see Harold L. Sheppard, *The Nature of the Job Problem and the Role of New Public Service Employment* (Kalamazoo, Mich.: W. E. Upjohn Institute, January 1969). According to my calculations from the 1966 UES data files, median weekly family earnings in ten urban ghettos were highest in male-headed households in Central Harlem; a 95 percent confidence interval for this $103/week median is $85–120.

1966 annual average wage rates in the corresponding metropolitan area. Given the extent of low-wage work in the slums, it is perhaps not too surprising that so many ghetto men leave (or do not form) families so that mother and children will be eligible for welfare — what amounts to a desperately needed second income. Broken homes in the ghetto may sometimes represent a rational response to the need for multiple incomes. Yet the median incomes of female-headed UES households (including welfare receipts), added to the median individual incomes of "unattached" adult males, still sum to less than $4,000. In 1966, ghetto families with both parents present received only about $3,500 in gross income. As the data in Table 1 indicate, this is some $2,500 below the benchmark established by the Department of Labor as a minimum family budget just adequate to sustain an urban family of four in a cheap, rented apartment, with an eight-year-old automobile, and subsisting on a diet consisting largely of dried beans.[2]

In conducting the 1966 UES, the Department of Labor's survey researchers recognized the inability of the conventional measure of unemployment to capture the full force of labor market failure in the ghetto.[3] As the first step toward a remedy, a new index number called the "subemployment rate" was constructed, consisting of the sum of those who are actually unemployed, those working part-time but

seeking full-time work, heads of households under 65 years of age earning less than $60 a week full-time, nonheads under 65 years of age earning less than $56 a week full-time, half the number of male nonparticipants aged 20–64 (on the grounds that they have given up looking not because they do not want to work but because of the "conviction — whether right or wrong — that they can't find a job"), and half of the "unfound males."[4]

Among the ten ghettos surveyed by the Department of Labor in 1966 and listed in Table 1, the highest subemployment rate was found in the predominantly Mexican-American slum areas of San Antonio; nearly one out of every two ghetto residents was unemployed or underemployed. The lowest subemployment rate in the sample was 24.2 percent in Boston's Roxbury–South End neighborhoods. Clearly, the problem of underemployment reflected in this indicator lies at the very core of the "urban crisis." Why is underemployment so high?

Education and the Elmination of Poverty

Neoclassical theories of unemployment and poverty are oriented almost entirely toward the "supply side."[5] Recent research efforts (including my own) indicate, however, that investments in the human capital of minority workers have *not* significantly contributed to eliminating poverty.[6] This suggests a

[2] See U.S. Bureau of Labor Statistics, "Three Standards of Living for an Urban Family of Four Persons: Spring 1967," *Bulletin* 1570-5 (Washington, D.C.: U.S. Government Printing Office, 1967). For comparative purposes, it should be noted that the income estimates in Table 1 refer to the year preceding November 1966, while the BLS budgets refer to March 1967. For an extended discussion of the relevance of the BLS cross-section urban budgets as normative benchmarks against which to judge various income distributions, see Thomas Vietorisz and Bennett Harrison, "Ghetto Development, Community Corporations, and Public Policy," *Review of Black Political Economy,* Fall 1971, pp. 28–43.

[3] "The traditional unemployment measure counts as working the person who is working only part-time, although he is trying to find full-time work; gives no consideration to the amount of earnings; omits those who are not "actively looking for work'— even though the reason for this is their conviction (whether right or wrong) that they can't find a job, at least one they want; and omits the "undercount" factor — those who are known to be present in the community but who do not show up at all under the present survey methods." U.S. Department of Labor, "A Sharper Look at Unemployment in U.S. Cities and Slums" (Washington: U.S. Government Printing Office, 1967), p. 5.

[4] Highly imperfect and even arbitrary in its weights (if not in its definitions), the index nevertheless represents an extremely important first step toward the measurement of *underemployment* in the United States. Indeed, in all countries — rich and poor alike — the study and the reporting of underemployment as a measure of the *quality* of working life is bound to become increasingly important to the formation of public policy.

[5] The originators of the antipoverty program decided that "poverty was to be eliminated by raising everyones marginal product to the level where [they] would be able to earn acceptable income. Education and training programs were to be the principal means for raising marginal products.... Increasing workers' human capital could eliminate poverty." Lester Thurow, "Raising Incomes Through Manpower Training Programs," in Anthony Pascal, ed., *Contributions to the Analysis of Urban Problems* (Santa Monica: The RAND Corporation, August, 1968), p. 3868.

[6] See, for example, the following: Ivar Berg, *Education and Jobs: The Great Training Robbery* (Praeger, 1970); Stephan Michelson, "Incomes of Racial Minorities" (Washington, D.C.: The Brookings Institution, 1968), unpublished manuscript; and Randall D. Weiss, "The Effect of Education on the Earnings of Blacks and Whites," *Review of Economics and Statistics,* May 1970.

need for revision of the current orthodoxy which asserts that poverty is a function of inadequate education and training. My own contribution to this critical literature has focused on the residents of eighteen central-city ghettos across the country.

Formal education is widely thought to be the principal instrument by which past generations of ghetto dwellers climbed out of the urban slums and into the American middle class.[7] Apparently, many take it for granted that the formula will work again — is working now — for the newest inhabitants of the urban ghettos. Public education, it is frequently argued, may in the last analysis be the most effective antipoverty instrument of all.[8] Under reasonable assumptions about the mix of academic, technical, and institutional ("sheepskin") prerequisites for skilled or at least semiskilled employment, we should expect to find that ghetto workers, like others, realize a meaningful return to the decision to remain in school. Certainly this has been the usual conclusion of studies on national samples,[9] and on suburbanites of both races in at least one American city.[10]

None of these studies has explicitly examined the human capital of *ghetto* residents, however. The poverty areas of our central cities, and the more compact "hardcore" ghetto communities within them, contain families of many races and ethnic origins: Blacks, Puerto Ricans, Chicanos, some American Indians, and substantial numbers of poor whites. There is new evidence that ghetto workers — and Blacks in particular — *are* investing in themselves through the mechanism of public education. In fact, Blacks in the urban slums have achieved levels of schooling comparable to those of whites in the same neighborhoods, as shown by the overlapping confidence intervals between the two portions of Table 2, which is constructed from 1966 UES materials. Moreover, ghetto Blacks seem to have achieved about the national nonwhite average for years of school completed.[11] In fact, the gap between the national average school completion rates of young whites and blacks has itself nearly disappeared. By 1970, the interracial difference in median years of schooling for persons under 35 years of age was only .4. [12]

[7] See, for example, U.S. Commission on Civil Rights, *A Time to Listen . . . A Time to Act* (Washington, D.C.: U.S. Government Printing Office, 1967); Philip Hauser, "Demographic Factors in the Integration of the Negro," *Dædalus,* Fall, 1965, pp. 867–870; and Everett Hughes, "Anomalies and Projections," *ibid.,* p. 1134.

[8] In studying the "vicious circle of the 'Three E's', Education, Employment, and Environment" (sic), participants in a recent New Jersey conference on urban problems concluded: "After much research and study of the problem, it is now plain that the real place to begin to break through is in the area of education, because without correcting this problem first, the other two will . . . defy effective solution at all." David N. Alloway and Francesco Cordasco, *The Agony of the Cities* (Upper Montclair, N.J.: Montclair State College, 1969), p. 23. Philip Hauser firmly believes that "the Negro's major handicap in his efforts to advance in America . . . is undoubtedly to be found in his limited education and skills," Hauser, *op. cit.,* pp. 867–868.

[9] Studies which attribute an important income effect to education include Lowell Gallaway, "The Negro and Poverty," *Journal of Business,* January 1967, pp. 27–35; W. Lee Hansen, "Total and Private Rates of Return on Investment in Schooling," *Journal of Political Economy,* April 1963, pp. 128–140; H. S. Houthakker, "Education and Income," *Review of Economics and Statistics,* February 1959, pp. 24–28; Elizabeth Waldman, "Educational Attainment of Workers," *Monthly Labor Review,* February 1969, pp. 14–22; and Herman P. Miller, "Annual and Lifetime Income in Relation to Education," *American Economic Review,* December 1960, pp. 962–986. A significant inverse relationship between education and un-

employment is reported in Harry J. Gilman, "Economic Discrimination and Unemployment," *American Economic Review,* December 1965, pp. 1077–1096; and Jeffrey K. Hadden and Edgar F. Borgatta, *American Cities: Their Social Characteristics* (Chicago: Rand McNally, 1965), pp. 138–140.

[10] Werner Z. Hirsch and Elbert W. Segelhorst, "Incremental Income Benefits of Public Education," *Review of Economics and Statistics,* November 1965, pp. 392–399. This is a study of a St. Louis suburb.

[11] A third of the nonwhite workers living in the poverty areas of the nation's twelve largest cities in March 1966, had completed at least twelve years of school, according to my calculations from the 1966 SEO tapes. About 38 percent of the Blacks living in the ten UES areas (identified in Table 2) had attained at least that level of schooling by November 1966. For the nation as a whole in 1966, only about 28 percent of the nonwhites aged 25 or more were high school graduates. While no 1966 national statistics on the educational attainment of younger Blacks have been published, Table 2 shows that, at least in the ghetto, younger Blacks do better than the racial average; they *are* staying in school longer. Nationally, the rate of high school completion for Black adults aged 20 and over is therefore probably somewhat greater than 28 percent. It is the similarity of these national and ghetto estimates which is reported in the text.

[12] U.S. Bureau of the Census, "The Social and Economic Status of Negroes in the United States, 1970," *Current Population Reports,* Series P-23, No. 38 (Washington, D.C.: U.S. Government Printing Office, 1971), Table 65.

TABLE 2.   Educational Attainment of Negro and White Ghetto Residents, November, 1966

Ghetto	All Persons Age 20 and Over			Persons Age 20–24 Only		
	Sample Size	Median Years Completed [a]	Percent With 12 Or More Years	Sample Size	Median Years Completed [a]	Percent With 12 Or More Years
Negroes						
Roxbury (Boston)	1897	11.5 ± 0.2	45.4	282	12.2 ± 0.3	57.1
Central Harlem (New York City)	2501	11.4 ± 0.2	45.2	214	12.3 ± 0.4	69.2
East Harlem (New York City)	689	10.7 ± 0.4	38.0	85	11.7 ± 0.7	47.1
Bedford-Stuyvesant (New York City)	2711	11.7 ± 0.2	47.3	338	12.3 ± 0.3	64.5
North Philadelphia	2414	10.5 ± 0.2	33.8	271	12.1 ± 1.0	53.5
North Side (St. Louis)	2791	9.7 ± 0.2	29.7	280	12.1 ± 0.4	52.9
Slums of San Antonio	320	11.1 ± 0.6	43.4	31	12.7 ± 0.8	80.6
Mission-Fillmore (San Francisco)	720	12.1 ± 0.3	52.5	113	12.5 ± 0.4	71.7
Salt River Bed (Phoenix)	661	9.0 ± 0.4	23.6	53	11.9 ± 0.9	49.1
Slums of New Orleans	2047	8.8 ± 0.2	23.1	266	11.9 ± 0.5	49.2
Whites [b]						
Roxbury (Boston)	858	11.1 ± 0.3	42.8	85	12.3 ± 0.8	61.2
Central Harlem (New York City)	139	10.8 ± 1.0	46.0	17	12.4 ± 2.4	76.5
East Harlem (New York City)	796	10.3 ± 0.4	38.3	91	12.4 ± 0.6	67.0
Bedford-Stuyvesant (New York City)	196	11.4 ± 0.7	46.4	9	11.2 ± 1.6	44.4
North Philadelphia	199	11.7 ± 0.9	48.2	17	12.3 ± 0.9	64.7
North Side (St. Louis)	226	8.8 ± 0.7	27.0	14	12.2 ± 1.4	57.1
Slums of San Antonio	157	11.5 ± 0.8	47.8	15	12.0 ± 2.6	53.3
Mission-Fillmore (San Francisco)	881	12.1 ± 0.3	54.3	123	12.9 ± 0.6	79.7
Salt River Bed (Phoenix)	570	9.2 ± 0.4	28.4	41	12.1 ± 1.0	53.7
Slums of New Orleans	593	9.4 ± 0.4	35.2	55	12.3 ± 1.1	63.6

[a] 95 percent confidence intervals shown
[b] Excludes Mexican-Americans, Puerto Ricans, and other Spanish-surnamed persons
Source: Computations from unpublished 1966 UES data files

Data on institutional training in the ghetto areas of New York City are displayed in Table 3, together with comparative figures for nonghetto Detroit. In every case, the incidence of program completion among ghetto dwellers during fiscal year 1969 was lower than for workers residing in the nonghetto control area. *Within* the ghetto, however, Black men compared quite favorably with their white neighbors in terms of the incidence of completion of training programs.

Have ghetto dwellers been able to translate this acquired human capital into improved economic status? Are the interracial differences in the marginal efficiency of human capital as significant *within* the ghetto as they are in the nation as a whole? Has ghetto underemployment been relieved by increased education and training? These are the specific questions to which we now turn our attention.

From my own independent thesis research, it now seems clear that Black workers in the urban slums have not been able to translate their additional schooling into more than token increases in earnings or reductions in the chances of being unemployed. Indeed, in a substantial number of cases I was unable to find statistically significant evidence of *any* income or employment effect at all, in models which controlled for age, race, sex, industry in which the worker is employed, city in which the worker lives, and participation by the worker in any of five different training programs.[13]

[13] The models employed in this study make no attempt to control for possible variations in educational returns attributable to differences in the *quality* of education. In this, I am following the precedent set by Gary Becker, in *The Economics of Discrimination* (Chicago: University of Chicago Press, 1957) who assumed that

TABLE 3. Proportion of Labor Force Having Completed In-School Vocational Training or Institutional Training, By Race, Sex, and Residence July 1968–June 1969
(in percent)

	Whites		Blacks	
	Men	Women	Men	Women
Completed in-school vocational training				
New York City ghettos[a]	5	15	11	12
Detroit nonghetto[b]	16	28	16	22
Completed institutional training				
New York City ghettos[a]	22	20	24	17
Detroit nonghetto[b]	41	34	36	20

[a] N = 2,651 individuals aged 16–54 and out of school. Sample areas include Harlem, Bedford-Stuyvesant, and the South Bronx.

[b] N = 3,899 individuals aged 16–54 and out of school.

Source: David M. Gordon, "Class, Productivity, and the Ghetto," Ph.D. dissertation, Harvard, 1971, Appendix C, based upon 1969 UES.

■ *Central-City Poverty Areas in Twelve SMSA's*

White workers in these geographically extensive low-income areas[14] earn on the average well over twice as much per extra year of schooling as Blacks. The Black payoff varies very much more than the white payoff — from city to city, from one industry to another, across the sexes, and by age. For Black Houston women working in personal services, increased education actually *reduces* expected weekly earnings. And the older the woman, the greater the deficit. In one model, designed to isolate the effects of passage of important institutional milestones, the weekly wage of white high school graduates in the twelve sets of poverty areas is nearly $25 higher than that of whites who never entered high school. For Blacks, the difference is only $8.83 (see Figure 1). High school, therefore, has *three times* as high a marginal payoff for ghetto whites as for ghetto Blacks.[15] On the assumptions of a forty-year working life, a rectangular lifetime earnings distribution,[16] and a 6 percent rate of time preference, the present value of the lifetime return to completion of high school is nearly $19,000 for whites but only $6,000 for Blacks. Clearly, education has a very high opportunity cost for Blacks living in the urban ghetto. There are any number of "largely illegal" activities out "on the street" that are capable of returning at least $6,000 in a single year.[17]

For whites, the risk of unemployment falls with years of school completed. Over the interval 9 to 12 years inclusive, the expectation of joblessness falls by 4.0 percent (see Figure 2). The average payoff per year of school completed over the entire

whites and Negroes of equivalent age and sex were equally productive at the margin. It may be argued that the exclusion of quality controls in no way vitiates the results described in the text. Following Weiss (*op. cit.*), I shall assume that the "quality of schooling, grades, individual ability and motivation, and *parents'* income, education, and occupation [are] probably . . . correlated positively with years of school [such that] estimates of the increase in earnings associated with an additional year of school will [in the absence of controls for the above factors] be biased upward." In other words, my estimates of the marginal returns to education are, if anything, *overstated*.

[14] From the 61,517 persons aged 14 or more who are described in the March, 1966, SEO, I selected for analysis those 11,454 persons living in the nation's twelve largest SMSA's: Baltimore, Chicago, Cleveland, Detroit, Houston, Los Angeles, New York, Philadelphia, Pittsburgh, St. Louis, San Francisco, and Washington, D.C. These are the only areas that are individually identifiable on the current edition of the SEO tapes. For technical documentation on the definition of "poverty area" as employed in the SEO, see J. R. Wetzel and Susan B. Hol-

land, "Poverty Areas of Our Major Cities," *Monthly Labor Review,* October 1966, pp. 1105–1110.

In order to permit comparisons among wage rates in the twelve different cities, it was necessary to construct a cross-section inter-city deflator. The "fixed market bundle" data for such an index was obtained from the BLS Lower Level Family Income Schedule for March 1967. (See U.S. Bureau of Labor Statistics, "Three Standards of Living," *op. cit.*)

[15] This is, of course, the mean size of the "payoff gap." At the .05 level, the difference *may* be anywhere from one to sixteen times, since 95 percent confidence intervals about the regression coefficients are $16–$32 for whites and $2–$14 for nonwhites.

[16] This is, of course, a most unrealistic assumption. But it is also an inexpensive one, and it facilitates computation. Actually, we need only require that blacks and whites in the ghetto have reasonably *similar* lifetime earnings distributions — whatever their specific shape. On different assumptions, the present values will of course be different.

[17] The preceding discussion is based upon comparative returns during a single survey week. Since nonwhites experience substantially higher annual unemployment rates than whites, the annual earnings "gap" is undoubtedly larger than that reported in the text.

FIGURE 1. Incremental Weekly Earnings Associated with Education–Central City Poverty Areas in Twelve SMSAs: March 1966

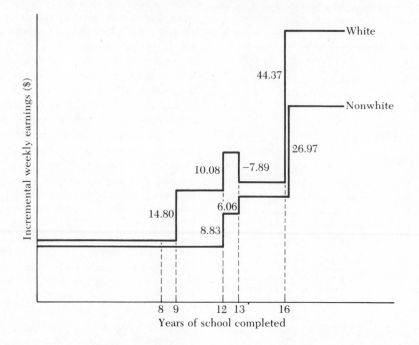

range tested (0–18 years) is a 0.6 percent reduction (as indicated by a less-than-satisfactory simple linear model). Among all twelve cities, fifteen industries, sex, and age, this payoff varies (for whites) by no more than 0.4 percent. For Blacks, on the other hand, the average effect of education on unemployment, as well as the effect over the 9 to 12 interval, is zero. A white college graduate from the slums can expect to be involuntarily out of work nearly three weeks less per year than a white high school dropout who also lives in one of the urban ghettos in the sample. But the Black college graduate faces only a 0.7 percent lower risk of unemployment as the high school dropout and that effect is attributable to the high school, not the college diploma (8.3 percent of the nonwhite ghetto sample completed at least some college). There is, however, more intercity and interindustry variation around the Black average "slope." Interaction models indicate that this slope attains a maximum payoff of −1.8 percent for twenty-year-old St. Louis women employed in personal services. Obviously, the demand for unskilled Black workers varies substantially from one city to another, far more so than is the case for white workers from the ghetto. I interpret this to

be yet another indirect manifestation of the presence of racial discrimination.

Additional researches into the structure of occupational status[18] lead to the conclusion that education facilitates the entry of both white and Black ghetto workers into new occupations, and (at least for whites) leads to greater interoccupational mobility. Moreover, by national standards, these variations represent a "move up" into higher status positions. But this finding only confirms that the effects of racial discrimination pervade even these poorest neighborhoods in the urban economy, for, even though they share many similar problems associated with their common environment, ghetto residents diverge significantly by race insofar as their labor force status is concerned. Education may help members of both races to move into what are considered nationally to be more prestigious positions. But, once

[18] These status calculations employ an ordinal prestige scale for detailed occupational categories, developed by the National Opinion Research Center and Professor Otis Dudley Duncan. See Duncan, "A Socioeconomic Index for All Occupations," in Albert J. Reiss, Jr., ed., *Occupations and Social Status* (Glencoe, Ill.: The Free Press, 1961).

there, the nonwhites find themselves underemployed again: receiving earnings that are hardly above the levels enjoyed in the previous position, and facing the same expectations of underemployment as before. For ghetto whites, on the other hand, the occupational mobility facilitated by education is translated into substantially higher earnings and significantly lower risks of joblessness. The contrast is dramatic.

Probably the most dramatic of these findings concerns the virtual absence for Blacks of any relationship between education and unemployment, after the effects of age, sex, industry, city, training experience and full-time/part-time status have been removed. In an earlier study of the Harlem economy,[19] it was found that when we stratified both unemployment and labor force participation rates by age, sex and years of school completed, the resulting tables displayed a surprising absence of the expected inverse relationship between education and unemployment, or the expected direct relationship between education and labor force participation. In fact, many of the cells showed precisely the opposite

[19] Thomas Vietorisz and Bennett Harrison, *The Economic Development of Harlem* (New York: Praeger, 1970).

effects. From this, we hazarded a tentative explanation, for which I now feel considerably more confidence after completing my thesis research on seventeen additional ghetto areas. Perhaps education increases the expectations and standards of ghetto workers which, when unmet by discriminating or otherwise exploitative employers, leads to frustration. This in turn may reduce the job attachment of the worker. If presently employed, he or she may display greater absenteeism, more frequent recalcitrance when given orders by foremen, or less patience with what is perceived as racist behavior on the part of coworkers.[20] If the ghetto worker is not

[20] Harold Sheppard's famous studies of "workers with the blues" have shown that "the greater a person's education achievements, as measured by years of school, the greater are his life and job aspirations," and the greater his discontent if he fails to achieve those goals. (See Harold L. Sheppard, "Discontented Blue-Collar Workers," *Monthly Labor Review*, April 1971, p. 28.)

In their study of Boston Labor market institutions, Doeringer and his colleagues found that ghetto jobseekers were systematically placed in jobs they had just left. This lack of upward mobility in the placement system probably contributes to the poor work habits (such as tardiness and high quit rates) which then frighten off other and perhaps genuinely concerned businessmen. Doeringer hypothesizes that "the availability of alterna-

FIGURE 2. Incremental Unemployment Rates Associated with Education– Central City Poverty Areas in Twelve SMSAs: March 1966

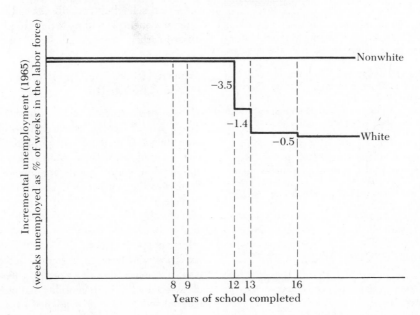

presently employed, then — although he is indeed searching for work — the change in his standards or expectations may lead him to increase his reservation wage. If the offered positions do not meet his standards, then he will reject the job and search further, or turn to other income generating activities such as public welfare or "the hustle." [21] In this way, he may remain unemployed for a relatively long period of time.

▪ Ten Racial Ghettos in Eight SMSA's

The earnings variable used with this sample[22] is hourly, rather than weekly, earnings, and the unemployment variable refers to the survey week rather than — as with the earlier sample — the previous year. In the ten urban ghettos studied, education has only a limited impact upon hourly earnings, and practically no effect at all upon the conditional probability of unemployment in any given week. Because of the relatively greater homogeneity of the population within each of these geographically rather compact areas, the regression results were not very sensitive to race.[23]

A number of different earnings models yielded estimated returns of from 3 to 9 cents per hour for each additional year of schooling and — over the interval 9 to 12 years inclusive — an average return of 15 cents. Workers with at least some college received, on the average, only 20 cents more per hour

than high school graduates who went directly to work and did not go to college. One model was designed to test for the existence of an upper limit to hourly wages and salaries in the ghetto, irrespective of education, i.e., the upper asymptote $e\alpha$ in the function $w = e\alpha - \beta E^{-1}$. Such limits were indeed found, ranging from a low of $1.56 per hour in San Antonio's chicano *barrios* to a high of $2.04 per hour in the Bedford-Stuyvesant ghetto of New York City. *No* amount of education would lead us to expect a Bedford-Stuyvesant worker of having an hourly wage of more than $2.04. That is the meaning of such a finding. All ten asymptotes were statistically significant.

When the UES data are pooled, increased schooling appears to reduce the probability of unemployment very slightly in the ghettos of New York, Philadelphia, St. Louis, and San Antonio. For the ten individual ghetto models, however, this effect was discovered only for the Salt River Bed section of Phoenix. The discrepancy appears to lie in the fact that, while each individual UES ghetto is relatively homogeneous with respect to race, the pooled sample contains many different minority groups. My pooled regression model did not attempt to capture this source of variation; had it done so, the results would undoubtedly have been far more consistent. In other words, for any given urban ghetto area, unemployment is *not* (with the single exception of the Phoenix slums) affected by increased schooling. In fact, the *individual* San Antonio model indicates that increased schooling actually *raises* the probability of unemployment, a finding whose implications we discussed earlier.

Minority Economic Opportunity Outside the Ghetto

It has been suggested that a sample of ghetto residents is inherently biased, since those for whom education *has* paid off will presumably have moved out, leaving us with a sample skewed toward the "failure." A very recent (and decidedly unofficial) finding of the Bureau of Labor Statistics' Urban Employment Survey Group provides us with some remarkable direct evidence that the ghetto samples are probably *not* biased — at least not because of selective outmigration. Of 7,200 ghetto families in six cities who were to be reinterviewed by the BLS over a twelve-month period in 1968–69 (a period of exceptionally high mobility nationally), only 900 had moved from one residence to another. And of

tive low wage job opportunities and the unattractiveness of such low wage work interact to discourage the formation of strong ties to particular employers ... for wage rates higher than the 'prevailing' ghetto wage, disadvantaged workers are more likely to be stable employees than other workers." Peter B. Doeringer, "Ghetto Labor Markets: Problems and Programs," Program on Regional and Urban Economics, Discussion Paper No. 35, Harvard University, 1968, pp. 10–11.

[21] The functional similarities and complementarities between these "irregular" activities and the low-wage jobs which make up what some economists call the "secondary labor market" are explored in Daniel Fusfeld, "The Basic Economics of the Urban and Racial Crisis," *Review of Black Political Economy*, Spring–Summer 1970, pp. 58–83, and Bennett Harrison, *Education, Training and the Urban Ghetto* (Baltimore: Johns Hopkins University Press, 1972), Chapter 5.

[22] The UES areas in this sample are identified in Table 1. Usable records on 37,330 individuals, aged 14 and over were available. The wage data were again adjusted to control for intercity variations in the cost of living.

[23] Nearly 85 percent of the sample is nonwhite, i.e., Puerto Rican, Mexican-American, Indian, Asian, Negro, and other nonwhites.

these 900 families, only 60 had moved *out* of the ghetto; all of the rest were either intraghetto moves (750) or involuntary relocations, for example, to jail or into the armed forces (90). In other words, the rate of outmigration from the urban ghetto, only two years after the date of the surveys we are analyzing, was less than 1 percent.

This same question about selective out-migration motivated the extension of my researches to urban workers living *outside* the ghettos, (*a*) in nonpoverty central-city neighborhoods, and (*b*) in suburban communities.[24] The results of these studies seem to validate the earlier findings. More important, they cast considerable doubt on the accuracy of some of our most cherished assumptions about the intrametropolitan spatial distribution of poverty and discrimination.

In terms of average economic opportunity, Figures 3 through 5 show that — for weekly earnings, annual unemployment, and occupational status among males — the white levels improve monotonically with "distance" from the core, while Black opportunity increases somewhat with the "move" from the ghetto to the nonpoverty central city, but falls again with the further "move" out to the suburban ring. (When 95 percent confidence intervals are constructed around these means or medians, comparisons remain just as dramatic as in these figures.) For whites, employment opportunity definitely rises (or at least does not fall) as we move from the innermost to the outermost sample areas. For Blacks, however, the three descriptors of employment opportunity show relatively little sensitivity to intrametropolitan residential location. Black earnings are

[24] The source of these data is, again, the 1966 SEO.

FIGURE 3. Median Male Earnings — by Intrametropolitan Location

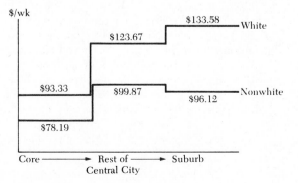

FIGURE 4. Mean Male Unemployment Rates — by Intrametropolitan Location

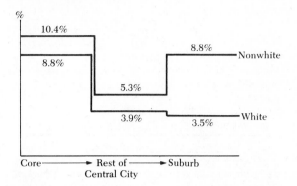

FIGURE 5. Median Male Occupational Status — by Intrametropolitan Location

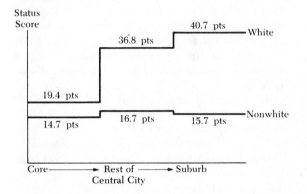

significantly higher outside the ghetto than inside, but, once "outside," there is no significant difference between the median levels associated with central-city as against suburban residence. Black unemployment rates in the ghetto and in the suburbs are not statistically different from one another, and may be only slightly lower in the nonpoverty central city. Finally, the indicator of occupational status for Black men is *totally* insensitive to residential location.

Nor are the marginal returns to Black education significantly greater in the suburbs than in the ghetto. In Table 4, the only statistically significant difference for Blacks is between the returns to college completion for central-city residents who live (*a*) inside and (*b*) outside the ghetto. To summarize the more extensive thesis results for whites and Blacks, education is associated with increased mobility into what are nationally considered to be higher status occupations. For whites, this promise is realized; as education increases, whites move into new occupations where they receive higher earnings and

TABLE 4. Partial Regression Results from Multivariate Models by Race and Location of Residence: March, 1966

Region	Whites			Nonwhites		
	Incremental Return to H.S.	Incremental Return to College	Cumulative Effect *	Incremental Return to H.S.	Incremental Return to College	Cumulative Effect *
Central-City Poverty Areas	$24.88	$36.48	$61.36	$8.83	$33.03	$41.86
Rest of Central City	9.16	51.62	76.30	0 †	53.50	53.50
Suburban Ring	32.80	65.32	98.12	0 ‡	38.87	38.87

* Sum of all individual "steps" in the step-function regression models.
† 79% of the observations in this cell displayed maximal schooling of ≤ 12 years.
‡ 85% of the observations in this cell displayed maximal schooling of ≤ 12 years.
Source: Author's calculations from the 1966 *Survey of Economic Opportunity.*

face lower expectations of unemployment. Moreover, these marginal improvements in white employment status are greater in the nonpoverty areas of the central city than in the poverty areas, and greater still in the suburbs. For Blacks, however, the promise is *not* realized; as their education increases, Blacks move into new occupations, but their earnings are hardly affected at all by anything short of a college degree, and there is no effect whatever on their chances of finding themselves without a job over the course of the year. Moreover, the cumulative effects do not differ from one sample region to another; e.g., there is no significant difference (at the 95 percent level) among the entries in the last column of Table 4.

Thus, it appears that urban Blacks are severely constrained in their search for decent employment, regardless of where in the metropolis they reside. There is no evidence to support the widespread belief that, through education, unskilled or semiskilled Black workers presently living in the ghetto can be "suburbanized": relocated to the metropolitan ring, where their economic opportunities are assumed to be substantially greater. This belief is reflected in a widely quoted policy recommendation made by Professor John F. Kain. Government programs, says Kain, "should emphasize the strengthening of the Negro's ability to break out of the ghetto [by] education and job training and the expansion of suburban housing opportunities." [25] But my findings suggest

that there is probably little to be gained from policies designed to rearrange the intrametropolitan spatial configuration of minority residences. In *no* part of the American city does the labor market "work" adequately for nonwhites. In particular, there is no evidence to support the assertion that Black economic opportunity in the suburbs is greater than in the ghetto. Taken together with the increasing resistance of middle-class white Americans to all forms of social protest and particularly to integration — a resistance which implies that the social costs of enforced integration would be extremely high — one cannot react to these materials with anything other than the deepest pessimism about the potential effectiveness of policies for "suburbanizing" Blacks who presently live in the urban ghetto. The costs of such policies would probably be very great, and the expected benefits now seem to be very small, at least in terms of short-run employment opportunity.

Conclusion

Do these findings suggest that public investment in ghetto schools should be cut back? I believe not. In Michelson's words: "Equal education should be a goal in itself, not diminished for its failure to produce income for nonwhites." [26] Continued education should be an important objective of all those concerned with improvement in the lives of ghetto residents. Certainly any final judgment should be withheld pending the availability of true longitudi-

[25] John F. Kain, "The Big Cities' Big Problem," *Challenge,* September/October, 1966, reprinted in Louis A. Ferman *et al.,* eds., *Negroes and Jobs* (Ann Arbor: University of Michigan, 1968).

[26] Michelson, "Incomes of Racial Minorities," *op. cit.,* pp. 8–28.

nal data (indeed, Finish Welch has discovered evidence that Black-white income differences may be shrinking over time, although not necessarily in the ghetto).[27]

Nevertheless, as a short-run antipoverty policy instrument, education without a supply of jobs which utilize and reward the capabilities of ghetto workers is unlikely to have much impact. The prevalence of ghetto unemployment, involuntary part-time employment, and substandard wages, in conjunction with these new findings on nonwhite educational attainment and the recent studies of the relatively modest technical skills required for the "average" performance of an extremely broad range of "typically urban" jobs,[28] strongly suggests that existing urban labor markets under-utilize ghetto workers and do not permit these individuals to realize their potential productivities. If this interpretation is correct, then the remedy must be sought in opening up *new* urban job markets to the ghetto poor, markets whose jobs are physically accessible to ghetto residents, whose availability is made known to them, and whose entry level wages and promotional pos-

sibilities will in fact lead to a significant improvement in their levels of living.[29]

In other words the findings reported in this paper seem to call rather convincingly for a change in emphasis away from concentration on the alleged defects of the ghetto poor themselves toward the investigation of defects in the market system which constrains the poor from realizing their potential. Without a direct transformation and augmentation of the demand for their labor, significant improvement in the economic situation of ghetto dwellers is unlikely.[30] Attempts to change the worker himself — whether to remedy his personal "defects" or to move him to a "better" environment — have not worked up until now, and the several new microdata sources explored in this study provide little if any evidence to support the belief that such attempts will be sufficient in the future.

[27] Finis Welch, "Black-White Differences in Returns to Schooling," *American Economic Review,* December 1973.

[28] See Ivar Berg, *Education and Jobs: The Great Training Robbery* (New York: Praeger, 1970); and Harrison, *Education, Training and the Urban Ghetto, op. cit.,* Chapter 1.

[29] Federally supported and widely publicized attempts to open up existing urban labor markets to minorities have not been particularly successful. For a detailed review of evidence on such programs, see Harrison, *Education, Training and the Urban Ghetto,* Chapters 1 and 6.

[30] This conclusion constitutes one of the strongest arguments for a program of public service jobs for the disadvantaged. See Bennett Harrison, "Public Employment and Urban Poverty," Urban Institute Paper No. 113–43, Washington, June 1971; and Harold L. Sheppard, *The Nature of the Job Problem and the Role of New Public Service Employment* (Kalamazoo, Mich.: Upjohn Institute, 1969).

SCHOOLING FOR A SOCIALIST AMERICA

Samuel Bowles and Herbert Gintis

Many of the selections in this chapter argue that educational problems reflect the basic dynamics and structure of our economic system. They suggest that those problems will persist as long as capitalism continues to dominate our economic lives.

Source: From Chapter 11, "Education, Socialism, and Revolution," from *Schooling in Capitalist America: Educational Reform and the Contradictions of Economic Life* by Samuel Bowles and Herbert Gintis, © 1976 by Basic Books, Inc., Publishers, New York.

In this selection, Bowles and Gintis apply the logic of that argument to the further question — what would it take to develop a different kind of schooling? They sketch the kind of socialist directions that this country might take *and* the role that a truly liberatory educational process might play in supporting that movement.

This selection comes from the concluding chapter of their recent book, *Schooling in Capitalist America.* Throughout the rest of their book, they rigorously develop the arguments and premises upon which this selection rests.

Both authors teach economics at the University of Massachusetts in Amherst. They have written widely, not only on education but also more generally on radical political economics.

> The tradition of all the dead generations weighs like a nightmare on the brain of the living. And just when they seem engaged in revolutionizing themselves and things, in creating something that has never yet existed, precisely in such periods of revolutionary crisis they anxiously conjure up the spirits of the past to their service and borrow from them names, battle cries and costumes, in order to present the new scene of world history in this time-honored disguise and this borrowed language.
>
> — Karl Marx,
> *The Eighteenth Brumaire*
> *of Louis Napoleon* (1852)

Venereal disease ravaged the population of prerevolutionary China, attacking one in ten in urban areas. The colonial administration in the British-held ports was concerned indeed, and went to great lengths to battle the dread disease. In 1920, the wife of a High Court judge, as part of a concerted effort, collected the names of all 900 brothels owners in Shanghai. They were invited to a grand ball where they would be given paper carnations and Christian Bibles; one hundred eighty, chosen at random, would be "invited to close their establishments. Only twenty of the flourishing businessmen showed up, and none saw fit to restrict their activities. In Shanghai alone 150,-000 prostitutes were working. Their number was continually swelled by the poverty and famine to which prostitution was a welcome alternative. It was not surprising that the colonial administration, despite its good will, made no headway. Venereal disease was simply a fact of life. Yet after the revolution, progress was so rapid that, in 1969, Dr. Joshua Horn could say: "Active venereal disease has been completely eradicated from most areas and completely controlled throughout China." [1] The British administration should not have been so pessimistic. Often the best social policy is a revolutionary policy. But how could they have suspected that?

Education and venereal disease are social problems of a different order. But our analysis of the dynamics of liberal educational reform and the weakness of its successes urges upon us a correspond-

[1] Joshua Horn, *Away with All Pests* (New York: Monthly Review Press, 1969), p. 86.

ingly radical alternative. What we demand of U.S. schools is perfectly straightforward. We envision an educational system which, in the process of reproducing society, vigorously promotes personal development and social equality. What we have shown in this book is equally straightforward: The major characterics of the educational system in the United States today flow directly from its role in producing a work force able and willing to staff occupational positions in the capitalist system. We conclude that the creation of an equal and liberating school system requires a revolutionary transformation of economic life.

The most critical aspect of U.S. capitalism is that a few people own and control the bulk of productive resources, while most — aside from personal possessions — own only their labor power. The U.S. economy exhibits the most extensive and complete wage-labor system in the history of civilization. This system, which emerged historically as a progressive force in the service of economic productivity and the ethos of individuality and personal freedom, has long become repressive and anachronistic, an obstacle to further human progress. The many must daily acquiesce to domination by the few, giving rise to the systemic perpetuation of extensive inequalities — not only between capital and wage labor, but among working people as well. The stability and security of these economic power relationships require the creation and reinforcement of distinctions based on sex, race, ethnic origin, social class, and hierarchical status.

The educational system, basically, neither adds to nor subtracts from the degree of inequality and repression originating in the economic sphere. Rather, it reproduces and legitimates a preexisting pattern in the process of training and stratifying the work force. How does this occur? The heart of the process is to be found not in the content of the educational encounter — or the process of information transfer — but in the form: the social relations of the educational encounter. These correspond closely to the social relations of dominance, subordination, and motivation in the economic sphere. Through the educational encounter, individuals are induced to accept the degree of powerlessness with which they will be faced as mature workers.

The central prerequisite for personal development — be it physical, emotional, aesthetic, cognitive, or spiritual — lies in the capacity to control the conditions of one's life. Thus a society can foster personal development roughly to the extent that it allows and requires personal interaction along the lines of equal, unified, participatory, and democratic cooperation and struggle. Needless to say, these very conditions are those most conducive to social and economic equality. The U.S. educational system, in the present nexus of economic power relationships, cannot foster such patterns of personal development and social equality. To reproduce the labor force, the schools are destined to legitimate inequality, limit personal development to forms compatible with submission to arbitrary authority, and aid in the process whereby youth are resigned to their fate.

Hence we believe — indeed, it follows logically from our analysis — that an equal and liberating educational system can only emerge from a broad-based movement dedicated to the transformation of economic life. Such a movement is socialist in the sense that private ownership of essential productive resources must be abolished, and control over the production process must be placed in the hands of working people.

The goals of such a revolutionary socialism go beyond the achievement of the Soviet Union and countries of Eastern Europe. These countries have abolished private ownership of the means of production, while replicating the relationships of economic control, dominance, and subordination characteristic of capitalism. While the abolition of private property in the means of production has been associated with a significant reduction in economic inequality, it has failed to address the other problems with which we have dealt in this book. The socialism to which we aspire goes beyond the legal question of property to the concrete social question of economic democracy as a set of egalitarian and participatory power relationships. While we may learn much about the process of building a socialist society from the experiences of the Soviet, Cuban, Chinese, and other socialist peoples — and indeed, may find some aspects of their work downright inspiring — there is no foreign model for the economic transformation we seek. Socialism in the United States will be a distinctly American product growing out of our history, culture, and struggle for a better life.

What would socialism in the United States look like? [2] Socialism is not an event; it is a process. So-

---

[2] For an extensive bibliography addressed to this question, see James Campen, *Socialist Alternatives for America: A Bibliography,* Union for Radical Political Economics, Spring 1974.

cialism is a system of economic and political democracy in which individuals have the right and obligation to structure their work lives through direct participatory control. Our vision of socialism does not require as a precondition that we all be altruistic, selfless people. Rather, the social and economic conditions of socialism will facilitate the full development of human capacities. These capacities are for cooperative, democratic, equal, and participatory human relationships; for cultural, emotional, and sensual fulfillment. We can ascribe to a prospective U.S. socialism no fixed form, nor is socialism a solution to all the problems we have discussed here. Socialism directly solves many social problems, but, in many respects, it is merely a more auspicious arena in which to carry on the struggle for personal and social growth. Its form will be determined by practical activity more than abstract theorizing. Nevertheless, some reasonable aspects of socialism in the United States of direct relevance to the transformation of education can be suggested.

The core of a socialist society is the development of an alternative to the wage-labor system. This involves the progressive democratization of the workplace, thus freeing the educational system to foster a more felicitous pattern of human development and social interaction. The ironclad relationship between the division of labor and the division of social product must also be broken: Individuals must possess, as a basic social right, an adequate income and equal access to food, shelter, medical care, and social services independent of their economic position. Conversely, with the whip of material necessity no longer forcing participation in economic life, a more balanced pattern of material, symbolic, and collective incentives can, indeed must be developed. Essential in this respect is the legal obligation of all to share equitably in performing those socially necessary jobs which are, on balance, personally unrewarding and would not be voluntarily filled. An educational system thus freed from the legitimation of privilege could turn its energies toward rendering the development of work skills a pleasant and desirable complement to an individual's life plans.

The object of these changes in the social division of labor is not abstract equality, but the elimination of relationships of dominance and subordinacy in the economic sphere. There will certainly always be individual differences in ability, talent, creativity, and initiative, and all should be encouraged to develop these capacities to their fullest. But in a socialist system, they need not translate into power and subordinacy in control of economic resources. For similar reasons, historical patterns of racial, sexual, and ethnic discriminations must be actively redressed as socially divisive and unjust. What is now called household work will also be deemed, at least in part, socially necessary labor. This work, whether done in collective units or individual homes, must be equitably shared by all individuals.

Another central goal of socialism in the United States must be the progressive democratization of political life. From production planning, the organization of social services, and the determination of consumption needs at the local level right up to national economic planning and other aspects of national policy, decisions will be made in bodies consisting of or delegated by those affected by the result. We envisage a significant role for the national government: assuring regional economic equality; integrating and rationalizing local production, service and consumption plans; and directly implementing other social and economic policies which are infeasible at the local level. The egalitarian and democratic nature of economic life should vastly increase the responsiveness and flexibility of governmental institutions. While mediating disputes between groups and regions will remain a central political function, economic equality will eliminate the need of the state to pander to interests and powers of a small minority who control production. Though political activity will not be a major preoccupation of most, the process of participation in work and community should dramatically increase the political sophistication, participation, and knowledgeability of citizens. Indeed, we venture to suggest that all of the glaring inadequacies of political democracy in the United States are attributable to the private ownership of the means of production and the lack of a real economic democracy.[3]

It is a tenet of liberal thought that social equality can be purchased only at the expense of economic

efficiency. Yet the evidence is less than persuasive. Democratic social relationships in production lead to highly motivated and productive workers, who will turn their creative powers toward the improvement of work and the satisfaction of consumer needs rather than profit. Moreover, democratic control of work can reorient technology toward the elimination of brutalizing jobs, toward a progressive expansion of the opportunity of attaining skills through on-the-job and recurrent education, and toward a breakdown of the division between mental and physical labor. The elimination of racial and sexual discriminations would liberate a vast pool of relatively untapped talents, abilities, and human resources for productive purposes. Comprehensive and rational economic planning leads to heightened efficiency through elimination of wasteful competition and redundancy in the provision of services (e.g., insurance, banking, and finance), the elimination of unemployment, rational programs of research and development, and a balanced policy of resource development with environmental stability.

The increased efficiency of socialist economic life should quickly reduce the workweek devoted to the production of social necessities, thus freeing individuals for creative leisure and more informal production. Indeed, this aspect of individual development in U.S. socialism will represent one of its most central successes — a veritable new stage in the history of humankind. Under capitalism, a true dedication to the fostering of individual capacities for creative leisure and craft production is incompatible with generating a properly subservient labor force. We expect the creative production and consumption of social amenities to form an ever-increasing portion of economic activity in socialist society. Thus, there must be a stress on the development of a vital craft and artistic sector in production as a voluntary supplement to socially necessary work. It can be organized on a master-apprentice or group-control line and open to all individuals. Far from being a neglected afterthought in socialist society, this sector will be a major instrument in channeling the creative energies unleashed by liberated education and unalienated work toward socially beneficial ends.

To those of us who envision economic equality and a social system dedicated to fostering personal growth, democratic and participatory socialism is clearly desirable. But is such a system of economic democracy feasible? The conventional wisdom in

[3] For an expansion of this theme, see William R. Torbert, *Being for the Most Part Puppets* (Cambridge, Massachusetts: Schenkman, 1973); Sidney Verba and Norman Nie, *Participation in America* (New York: Harper and Row, 1972); Carole Pateman, *Participation and Democratic Theory* (Cambridge, England: Cambridge University Press, 1970); and Peter Bachrach, *The Theory of Democratic Elitism: A Critique* (Boston: Little, Brown and Company, 1967).

academic social science supports a negative reply. Yet in this book we have shown that the cynicism bred by modern mainstream economics, sociology, and political science is based on a series of myths: that inequality is due to unequal abilities; that hierarchical authority is necessitated by modern technology; that capitalism is already meritocratic; and that the existing situation corresponds to people's needs and is the product of their wills.

Just as the philosophers of ancient Greece could not conceive of society without master and slave and the Scholastics of medieval times without lord and serf, so, today, many cannot conceive of society without a controlling managerial hierarchy and a subservient working class. Yet neither technology nor human nature bar the way to democratic socialism as the next stage in the process of civilization. Unalienated work and an equal distribution of its products is neither romantic nostalgia nor postindustrial Luddism. The means of achieving social justice and of rendering work personally meaningful and compatible with healthy personal development are as American as apple pie: democracy and equality.

What is the role of education in this process? In the context of U.S. capitalism, a socialist education is a revolutionary education. Our objective for U.S. schools and colleges here and now is not that they should become the embryo of the good society but that struggles around these institutions, and the educational process itself, should contribute to the development of a revolutionary, democratic socialist movement. An ideal education for a socialist society may, in some respects, be irrelevant to the task of bringing that society into existence. This danger is not intrinsically great, however, for the struggle to liberate education and the struggle to democratize economic life are inextricably related. The social relations of education can be altered through genuine struggle for a democratic and participatory classroom, and for a reorganization of power in education. The process of creating a socialist educational system for the United States, if successful, renders the contradictions among administrators, teachers, and students nonantagonistic in the sense that the day-to-day outcomes of their struggles may be the positive, healthy development of both structures and individuals beneficial to all parties concerned. The experience of struggle and control promotes personal growth, forges solidarity, and prepares the student for a future of political activity in factory and office.

The consciousness nurtured in such an integrated educational encounter is one of self-worth, cooperation, and an implacable hostility to arbitrary authority.

Even following a successful transformation of formal power relationships in the economic sphere, education will be part of the struggle for democratization of substantive social relationships. The educational system will be set the task of preparing youth for a society which, while geared toward the progressive realization of revolutionary goals, still bears the technological and cultural heritage of the present system. In this setting, the social relations of education will themselves be transitional in nature. For instance, the elimination of boring, unhealthy, fragmented, uncreative, constraining, and otherwise alienated but socially necessary labor requires an extended process of technological and organizational change in a transitional phase. The shift to automated, decentralized, and worker-controlled technologies requires the continuous supervision and cooperation of the workers themselves. Any form this takes in a transitional society will include a constant struggle among three groups whose ultimate interests may converge, but whose daily concerns remain distinct: managers concerned with the development of the enterprise, technicians concerned with the scientific rationality of production, and workers concerned with the impact of innovation and management on job satisfaction and material welfare. The present educational system does not develop in an individual the capacities of cooperation, struggle, autonomy, and judgment appropriate to this task. The need for developing innovative educational forms is here paramount.

Revolutionary Education

We must force the frozen circumstances to dance by singing to them their own melody.

— Karl Marx

A revolutionary education must be guided by a revolutionary educational philosophy. In this section, we tentatively suggest what such a philosophy might look like. We have been motivated by several concerns. First, educational goals must recognize the correspondence between the social relationships of economic life and those of the educational encounter. Work and personal development are intimately related not only in capitalist, but in any conceivable society. Second, we want to embrace the élan of the contemporary egalitarian and antiauthoritarian critique of U.S. education while avoiding the pitfalls described in the previous chapter.

Hence, we shall develop a dialectical humanism, largely inspired by the Marxist concept of personal development through the dialectical interaction between individuals and their environments. In this approach, the educational system is judged by the way it resolves the basic contradiction between the reproduction needs of the community and the self-actualizing needs of students and, more narrowly, its inevitable reflection in the contradiction between teacher and student.

The development of simple forms of life, from birth to death, is governed by the unfolding of genetic potential. The organism's natural and social environment can promote, retard, or even end this unfolding but has little effect on the forms that it may assume. Complex forms of life, in contrast, exhibit learned components of behavior. That is, the organism's path of maturation depends on its particular interaction with its environment. The higher on the evolutionary ladder, the greater the tendency for the individual organism to be the product of its social experience and less of its genetic unfolding. In the case of human beings, the staggering variety of past and present patterns of social interaction attests to the importance of learned components of behavior.

The primacy of social experience in human maturation implies a basic contradiction to which all educational theory must relate: the contradiction between individual and community. Among the manifold potential paths of individual development, only certain ones are compatible with the reproduction of the community. At each point in one's personal development, the individual acts on the basis of interest, inclinations, and personal codes. The final result of this is submission to the requirements of social life or, failing this, the destruction of either individual or community as constituted. The contradiction is an inescapable aspect of modern life whether the community is slave or "free," class or classless, democratic or totalitarian, purgatory or utopia.

Of course, this contradiction has its realm of freedom as well as its realm of necessity: the poles of the individual/community dichotomy depend on one another for the very existence of each. Personal development is inconceivable outside a structured social context, and no community can transcend the individuals participating in its reproduction. Or more pointedly, we have the potential to choose paths of personal development more conducive to our needs by reorganizing the institutions which frame our social experience toward forms we embrace but within which we struggle for autonomy and solidarity, individuality and acceptance, free space and social security.

The contradiction between individual and community is mediated by formal and informal institutions — kinship and peer group, rites of passage, churches and armies, guild and factories, town meetings, prisons and asylums. In American society, one of these institutions is the school. The essence of the school (or of its social surrogate) lies in its counter-position to the student, who is taken with manifest needs and interests and turned against his or her will into a product of society.

Schools cannot be considered repressive merely because they induce children to undergo experiences they would not choose on their own, or because they impose forms of regimentation which stifle immediate spontaneity. Schools, or any other institution that mediates the passage to full adult social participation, are intrinsically constraining. Schools which deny this role, or claim compatibility with a society in which this role is unnecessary, are hypocritical and misleading. Worse, they are positively harmful. They thereby forfeit their roles as historical agents. To wish away this contradiction between individual and community is quickly to be pushed aside in the historical struggle for human liberation.

Nor would this stance be desirable were it possible. Human development is not the simple "unfolding of innate humanity." Human potential is realized only through the confrontation of genetic constitution and social experience. Dogma consists precisely in suppressing one pole of a contradiction.[4] The dogma of repressive education is the dogma of necessity which denies freedom. But we must avoid the alternative dogma of freedom which denies necessity. Indeed freedom and individuality arise only through a confrontation with necessity, and personal powers develop only when pitted against a recalcitrant reality. Accordingly, most individuals seek environments which they not only draw on and interact with, but also react against in furthering the development of their personal powers, Independence,

---

[4] Mao Tse-tung, "On Contradiction," in *Selected Works of Mao Tse-tung*, Vol. I (Peking, 1951).

creativity, individuality, and physical prowess, are, in this sense, developed in institutionalized settings, as are docility, subservience, conformity, and weakness. Differences must not lie in the presence or absence of authority but in the type of authority relations governing activity.

If authority alone were the culprit, the cure would be its abolition — a quick and painless excision — as advocated, for example, by Theodore Roszak:

> . . . to teach in freedom, in complete freedom, in response to the native inclination of the student; to be a teacher only when and where and insofar as the student authorizes us to be.[5]

But to assert authority as the culprit is to suppress the inevitable contradiction between individual and community. Too often, this is done and, frequently, by the most sensitive and poignant interpreters of youth's predicament. Thus, Peter Marin can write:

> [In education] the individual is central; the individual in the deepest sense, *is* the culture, not the institution. His culture resides in him, in experience and memory, and what is needed is an education that has at its base the sanctity of the individual's experience and leaves it intact.[6]

Of course, education can recognize the sanctity of the individual's experience, but it cannot leave it intact.

The teacher is delegated by society to mediate the passage to adulthood, and his or her obligation is dispatched only when society's trip is successfully laid on its new members. The student, on the other hand, seeks the power — within the constraints placed on him or her by society and its coercive instruments — to use the educational encounter toward personal ends. This contradiction is pervasive and inevitable, independent from the wills of the individuals involved, and independent as well from the formality or informality of the teacher-student relationship. It stands above whatever warmth and personal regard these adversaries have for one another as human beings. By denying the necessary conflict between teacher and student, the radical teacher is suppressing a most manifest, and personally destructive contradiction: that his or her personal interests, goals, and ideals often involve the negation of his or her social role. Personally expedient, perhaps, but socially irrelevant. Society cannot be suppressed as easily as the consciousness of contradictions in our lives. The majority of individuals with senses tuned to the realities of everyday life will take pleas for a release from the bonds of authority for what they are: poetic fancy. The creators of valid educational values must begin by affirming this contradiction and proceed to ask whether its process of resolution, reappearance, and reresolution in the educational encounter promotes or retards our personal development, cultivates or stunts our potential for equal and cooperative relationships, fosters or hinders the growth of our capacities to control the conditions of our lives.

The immediate implication is that education need distort human development only to the extent demanded by the repressiveness of the social relationships of adult life. The educator must represent society in mediating the contradiction between individual and community in order to fulfill his or her institutional role. Or unwilling, he or she must make war on social institutions and, by opposing them, change them. Even within the individual classroom, the dissident teacher can become an effective subversive through teaching the truth about society; through inspiring a sense of collective power and mutual respect; through demonstrating that alternatives superior to capitalism exist; through fighting racist, sexist, and other ideologies of privilege through criticizing and providing alternatives to a culture that, in Woody Guthrie's words:

> . . . makes you feel you're not any good . . . just born to lose, bound to lose . . . because you're too old or too young or too fat or too thin or too ugly or too this or too that, that runs you down, that pokes fun at you on account of your bad luck or your hard traveling. . . .

But institutional change in education, unless itself random and chaotic, is the culmination of the coordinated activity of social classes. The politics of a revolutionary education like its philosophy are grounded in dialectics. They must proceed from a commitment to a revolutionary transformation of our entire society.

---

[5] Theodore Roszak, "Educating Contra Naturam," in Ronald Gross and Paul Osterman, eds., *High School* (New York: Clarion, 1971), pp. 64–65.

[6] Peter Marin, "The Open Truth and Fiery Vehemence of Youth," in Gross and Osterman (1971), *op. cit.*, p. 44.

BIBLIOGRAPHY

I. IMPRESSIONS, DEFINITIONS, AND MAGNITUDES

A. Impressions

Herbert Kohl. *36 Children.* New York: New American Library, 1967.
James Herndon. *The Way It Spozed to Be.* New York: Simon & Schuster, 1968.
George Dennison. *The Lives of Children.* New York: Random House, 1969.

B. Definitions and Magnitudes

James S. Coleman *et al. Equality of Educational Opportunity.* Washington, D.C.: U.S. Government Printing Office, 1967.
U.S. Civil Rights Commission. *Racial Isolation in the Public Schools.* Washington, D.C.: U.S. Government Printing Office, 1967.
Charles Silberman. *Crisis in the Classroom.* New York: Random House, 1970.

II. ECONOMIC PERSPECTIVES ON EDUCATION

A. Orthodox Economic Perspectives

Mark Blaug, ed. *An Introduction to the Economics of Education.* London: Penguin, 1972.
Gary Becker. *Human Capital,* 2nd ed. New York: National Bureau of Economic Research, 1974.
Jacob Mincer. *Schooling, Experience and Earnings.* New York: National Bureau of Economic Research, 1974.

B. Radical Political Economic Perspectives

Christopher Jencks *et al. Inequality.* New York: Basic Books, 1972.
Samuel Bowles and Herbert Gintis. *Schooling in Capitalist America.* New York: Basic Books, 1976.

C. Empirical Studies

Frederick Mosteller and Daniel P. Moynihan, eds. *On Equality of Educational Opportunity.* New York: Vintage, 1972.

III. POLICY PERSPECTIVES

A. Integration and Busing

U.S. Civil Rights Commission, *Racial Isolation in the Public Schools.* Washington, D.C.: U.S. Government Printing Office, 1967. Makes strong argument for integration.
David Armor. "The Evidence on Busing." *The Public Interest,* Summer 1972. Says evidence does not support busing.
Thomas Pettigrew *et al.* "Reply to Armor." *The Public Interest,* Winter 1973. Sharp reply on evidence and policy.

B.   Community Control and Compensatory Education

Henry M. Levin, ed. *Community Control of Schools.* Washington, D.C.: Brookings Institution, 1969. Collection of essays.

C.   Free Schools

Jonathan Kozol. *Free Schools.* New York: Bantam, 1972. Skeptical.
Allen Graubard. *Free the Children.* New York: Vintage, 1973. A careful review of the experience.

POVERTY AND WELFARE

EDITOR'S
INTRODUCTION   *While income and wealth taxation may help a bit to dry up these well-springs of material inequalities, the real attack on them comes from civil rights groups, anti-poverty campaigns, anti-monopoly drives, etc., all working within the context of capitalism; from socialists who call for the nationalization of means of production; and from Maoists, hippies, and others who are rebelling against the capitalist mentality with its heavy emphasis on selfishness and material rewards. It might well be that this last movement poses the ultimate threat to material inequalities — the hippies rather than the Internal Revenue Service.*

—John G. Gurley[1]

Michael Harrington published *The Other America* in 1962. He charged that "the America of poverty is hidden today in a way that it never was before. Its millions are socially invisible to the rest of us." [2] By 1970, the charge could no longer be made. The poor had been detected, inspected, and injected many times. A War on Poverty had been declared. Commissions had studied the problem from nearly every angle. The poor themselves had organized to demand a larger slice of the pie. To most observers of American politics, it seemed that provision of an adequate income to the poor, as they often put it, "was an idea whose time had come."

But it never came. President Nixon's Family Assistance Plan sank in the quicksands of party politics. George McGovern's income maintenance proposals were emasculated by the pressures of the 1972 presidential campaign. By the middle years of the decade, in serious recession and economic crisis, we were all becoming poorer. Pressure for income redistribution had dissipated. A movement had died. Scholars were writing its histories.

One cannot understand the political life cycle of the poverty movement without understanding the relationship between the causes of the problem and its potential solutions. In this chapter I try to sort through the different perspectives

[1] John G. Gurley, "Federal Tax Policy: A Review Article," *National Tax Journal*, September 1967.

[2] (London: Penguin, 1962), p. 10.

on the poverty problem to provide that kind of background. In the first section, I present several definitions of poverty and some estimates of the magnitude of poverty according to each definition. In the second section I briefly sketch the liberal and conservative views of poverty and potential solutions to the problem. The third section outlines the radical perspective. The final section briefly introduces the purposes and contents of the readings.

Definitions and Magnitudes

Any society effectively establishes its own definitions of poverty — its own definitions, that is, of the income level below which families cannot provide themselves an adequate standard of living. There is no eternally fixed poverty standard applicable to all social circumstances. Even within one society at a given moment, different people will suggest different definitions of poverty.

Each definition typically reflects preferences about the shape of that society's distribution of income (or consumption). An income distribution expresses the proportions of families that earn varying levels of income during a specific period of time, like a year. In 1974 in the United States, for instance, 5.4 percent of American families earned less than $3,000, 7.8 percent earned between $3,000 and $4,999, 8.8 percent earned between $5,000 and $6,999, and so on.[3]

In a market economy, in which people earn income as payments for owned factors of production, the market income distribution represents the outcome of a complicated market process: potential earners acquire skills, shop for jobs, learn more skills on the job, receive income from property, win lotteries. . . . All these activities result in a family's final market income. Given that final *market* income distribution, a society can also express and manifest its preferences about the final shape of the distribution "take-home" income. People might decide, for instance, that no family should be forced to live on as little income as they are able to earn through the market; they might want to transfer some money, through the government, away from the more affluent toward the relatively poor.

In a market economy, these implicit and explicit preferences about changes from the market distribution of income to the final distribution of income provide the best guide to a society's definitions of poverty. Three kinds of definitions of poverty seem most common in the United States. One involves an explicit definition of "absolute poverty." The second involves an explicit definition of "relative poverty." The third involves a definition implicit in the kinds of programs that the government has traditionally established to ameliorate poverty.

An *absolute poverty* definition specifies a "minimum subsistence income" — an income level below which the society feels that families should not be forced to live. It might represent the smallest income necessary to prevent families from starving, or it might allow slightly more comfortable subsistence.

Two different absolute poverty definitions have been proposed and debated in recent years.

The first was first developed and codified by the U.S. Government. Formulated by the U.S. Social Security Administration (and therefore known as the SSA definition), this standard begins with the Department of Agriculture's esti-

---

[3] U.S. Bureau of the Census, "Money Income and Poverty Status of Families and Persons in the United States, 1974 (Advance Report)," *Current Population Reports,* Series P-60, Number 99, July 1975.

mates of the cost of food for a "nutritionally adequate family diet" — the least expensive food items necessary to maintain a family in relatively decent health. That dollar amount is then multiplied by three, relying on studies during the 1950s which showed that low-income families spent one-third of their incomes on basic food necessities. By 1974, according to this standard, a family of four was considered poor if its annual income fell below $5008.[4] By this definition, roughly 24 million Americans lived in poor families in 1974, or nearly 12 percent of the population.[5]

Although this SSA definition of absolute poverty has been used by the federal government for its official estimates for over a decade now, the SSA definition has been sharply criticized. Two main kinds of criticisms have been leveled against the definition. One argues that the SSA standard itself ought to have been adjusted to take account of changes in the relationship between food costs and other costs.[6] The second and more important criticism suggests that the SSA standard establishes much too low a level of poverty, that the SSA poverty threshold is hardly an adequate basis for subsistence.[7]

Instead, many have argued that we should rely on another absolute definition of poverty. The U.S. Bureau of Labor Statistics has defined a budget standard that it calls "lower than moderate." Although higher than the SSA standard, it provides a spare existence indeed. For instance, each adult in the family is allowed the indulgent total of two beers a week in the food budget. By this standard, a family of four would have required an annual (before-tax) income of $9,198 in 1974 to live at an adequate level.[8] Although the government does not explicitly collect and publish data by this standard, it appears that roughly 30 percent of all Americans lived in poor families in 1975 according to this higher definition of absolute poverty.[9]

An Editor's Supplement in this chapter summarizes some recent data both on the characteristics of the poor and on trends in poverty.

A *relative* definition of poverty compares the income of those at the bottom of the income distribution with that of more affluent families. Given total output in society and average standards of living, a society can express some preferences about how equally total income should be distributed among its members. One society might wish for nearly perfect equality of income, while another might ac-

[4] *Ibid.* For the original explanation of the definition, see Mollie Orshansky, "Counting the Poor . . .," Social Security Bulletin, January 1965. As Orshansky admits, the Agriculture Department food plan is itself extremely meager, designed for "temporary or emergency use when funds are low." (Orshansky, *ibid.,* p. 12). Politics may have influenced the formulation of the SSA standard substantially. The Council of Economic Advisers originally proposed that anyone with less than $3,000 be considered poor, estimating in 1963 that 34 million persons were poor. "More refined estimates, if they were to be politically acceptable, had to be consistent with CEA's estimate of the size of the problem." (Martin Rein, "Problems in the Definition and Measurement of Poverty," in Louis Ferman *et al.,* eds., *Poverty in America* (Ann Arbor: University of Michigan Press, 1968), rev. ed., p. 125). The final plan and a multiple of three produced an aggregate estimate of poverty very close to the CEA estimate, so they seemed appropriate.

[5] See the further discussion in the Editor's Supplement on "Trends in Poverty" in this chapter.

[6] See the Editor's Supplement for more detail.

[7] See the selection by Rainwater in this chapter.

[8] See Edna B. Branch, "Urban Family Budgets Updated to Autumn 1974," *Monthly Labor Review,* June 1975.

[9] See the Editor's Supplement on "Counting the Underemployed" in Chapter 2 for the basis of this estimate.

cept the degree of inequality already reflected in the final market distribution of income. The more equal the desired income distribution, the higher will be the income level established as the definition of "relative" poverty. A society in favor of considerable income equality might feel, for instance, that any family earning less than 80 percent of the social median family income should be considered relatively poor and should receive some income transferred from more affluent families. The President's Commission on Income Maintenance Programs has argued that relative definitions of poverty become increasingly important as societies become more affluent:

> As a society's general standard of living rises, increasingly expensive consumption patterns are forced on the poor, not in order to catch up, but in order to remain a part of that society. Moreover, as society's normal standard of living rises the poor will seek to emulate it — since they are part of society — and feel increasingly deprived if they cannot.[10]

The United States has rarely considered relative definitions of poverty, and the government has never adopted an official definition of poverty in relative terms. As the next section will suggest, liberal and conservative perspectives informing public policy on poverty have always emphasized absolute rather than relative definitions. Nonetheless, many academicians have found a definition proposed by Victor Fuchs as a rather sensible minimal relative standard. By this relative definition, any family earning less than one half the national median family income would be considered poor. This does not involve very great equality, for it says that families earning as little as $4,500 a year would be included among the nonpoor if the national median income were $8,000. Throughout the period since World War II, the percentage of Americans who were poor by this definition remained constant at roughly 20 percent.[11] Not surprisingly, there are now more Americans considered poor relative to our aggregate affluence than there are Americans considered poor by an absolute measure of the minimum they need to survive.[12]

A third definition of poverty involves interpretation of social efforts to help the poor. In the United States, historically, society has publicly supported only those families whose household head was *unable* to work. If a family head worked but earned very little money, the American public has traditionally been reluctant to consider his family worthy of support. Public assistance, as we have called it, was always intended as "a 'residual program' to aid those considered unable to enter the labor force." [13] In fact, during the 1960s, only one-third of Americans considered poor by the official definition of absolute poverty actually received any kind of public assistance.[14] Lumping all government transfer programs together, including Social Security, unemployment compensation, and public

[10] President's Commission on Income Maintenance Programs, *Poverty Amid Plenty* (Washington, D.C.: U.S. Government Printing Office, 1969), p. 38.

[11] Fuchs, "Comment on Measuring the Low-Income Population," in Lee Soltow, ed., *Six Papers on the Size Distribution of Wealth and Income* (New York: National Bureau of Economic Research, 1969), pp. 198–202; and President's Commission, *Poverty Amid Plenty,* p. 40.

[12] This, however, has been true only recently, since 1960.

[13] *Poverty Amid Plenty,* p. 46.

[14] See Robert Lampman, "Expanding the American System of Transfers to Do More for the Poor," *Wisconsin Law Review,* 2 (1969), pp. 548–49.

assistance, Christopher Green estimated for the early 1960s that transfers filled less than half the total poverty gap (the difference between final market income and absolute poverty level) for those who were still poor in the final income distribution.[15]

According to this implicit social definition of poverty, therefore, Americans have defined poverty more by capacity to work than by market income. If a household head was able to work, the public has felt that he should accept his market income as his final family income.

The Liberal and Conservative Views

Liberal and conservative perspectives on poverty follow precisely from the theories of the State and the normative predispositions of the two paradigms outlined in Chapter 1.

Both perspectives emphasize absolute definitions of poverty. Since they accept the market system as an essentially just system for the allocation of resources, they tend basically to accept the pattern of income distribution resulting from that system. Writers in both perspectives acknowledge, however, that some people are not able to work and that some others earn too little to maintain their families at a "minimum" standard. Conservatives tend to emphasize absolute definitions of poverty more singularly than liberals; some liberals urge a slight equalization of the market distribution, although they do not advocate modification of the market process by which initial incomes are determined.

Both perspectives therefore tend to urge a system of income redistribution which would establish a basic floor to incomes but would disrupt the market system of income determination as little as possible. Both liberal and conservative economists have objected to traditional public assistance programs in this country because they have not effectively established comprehensive or adequate income floors, and because they have tended to undercut the market system of wage incentives. On the former grounds, public assistance programs have historically included only portions of the poverty population, and have provided basic living allowances far below officially accepted absolute poverty standards.[16] On the latter grounds, economists have argued that public assistance programs traditionally provided a disincentive to work; for each dollar of employment earnings, the programs subtracted a dollar from public assistance allowances, imposing an effective 100 percent tax on work income.[17]

Based on those criticisms, liberals and conservatives have joined in suggesting various forms of a basic redistribution scheme — typically called "negative income taxation." [18] Most proposals have suggested a minimum income allowance and a tax rate on additional earnings of only one third to one half of extra work income.[19] In response to this stream of proposals, the Nixon administra-

---

[15] Christopher Green, *Negative Taxes and the Poverty Problem* (Washington, D.C.: Brookings Institution, 1967), p. 33.

[16] The low standards have been especially prevalent in the South. For criticisms on these grounds, see the selection by the President's Commission on Income Maintenance Programs in this chapter.

[17] See *ibid.*

[18] See Green, *Negative Taxes,* or James Tobin, "Raising the Incomes of the Poor," in Kermit Gordon, ed., *Agenda for the Nation* (Washington, D.C.: Brookings Institution, 1968).

[19] For a summary of proposals, see Theodore Marmor, ed., *Poverty Policy: A Sourcebook of Cash-Transfer Proposals* (Chicago: Aldine, 1971).

tion offered its Family Assistance Plan to Congress for approval in 1970. The plan called for $2,400 cash equivalent to a family of four with no income, and would take away 50 percent of any additional earned income. After complicated political tussles, the plan eventually died.[20]

In the long run these proposals would not basically affect the shape of the distribution of income in the United States, since they would tend simply to establish a floor under final income. Liberals and conservatives have tended not to emphasize the issue of relative poverty because they assume that society is not interested in this issue. If society decided that it wanted to equalize the distribution of income, both perspectives imply, then it would be able to pick whatever final distribution it wanted. As Walter Heller wrote in the excerpt included in Chapter 1, the set of liberal theories of the state "points the way to achieving any combination of Government services, income redistribution, and economic redistribution, and economic stability we set our sights on."

Both analyses assume further that the existence of progressive income tax statutes in the United States provides sufficient documentation of general American preference for government redistribution of income from the more affluent to the poor. Otto Eckstein says simply, "Adam Smith argued that taxes should be *proportional* to income. . . . Today, we have gone one step further. We favor *progressive* taxes." [21] Since society favors progressive taxation in general, the perspectives imply, it would be able to establish a *more* progressive system of taxation and transfer if it wanted. Those who favor such redistribution need simply mobilize a majority of public opinion.

The Radical View

The radical perspective on the problem of poverty differs from the liberal and conservative views in two fundamental respects. First, radicals tend to emphasize relative rather than absolute definitions of poverty. Second, radicals argue that any kind of meaningful redistribution of income cannot be achieved in the context of current capitalist institutions. Both of those premises derive directly from the general radical paradigm discussed in Chapter 1.

Radicals argue, first of all, that man cannot be free until society separates man's activities as producer from his needs as consumer. He must be freed, as Max Weber put it, from the "whip of hunger." Although members of society should have widely varying opportunities to engage in different kinds of productive activities, radicals argue, they should receive fundamentally equal allocations of social resources. Thus the famous Marxist dictum, "From each according to his abilities, to each according to his needs." This set of normative predispositions obviously implies a primary concern with the relative shape of the distribution of income, in present societies, rather than with the definition of absolute levels of poverty.[22] The distribution of income and resources, radicals urge, should approach perfect equality (adjusted for need).

This kind of equality cannot possibly be achieved in capitalist societies based on the private ownership of property, according to the radical analysis, for two reasons.

---

[20] For a brilliant account, see D. P. Moynihan, *The Politics of a Guaranteed Income* (New York: Basic Books, 1973).

[21] Eckstein, *Public Finance* (Englewood Cliffs, N.J.: Prentice-Hall, 1964), p. 56.

[22] See the piece by David M. Gordon in Chapter 1.

First, the market distribution of income tends to become increasingly unequal in a market system based on private ownership of property. As James Meade concludes from his extended analysis of the distributional implications of the market system, in most cases

> Efficiency pricing would require that an ever-increasing proportion of output accrued to property owners and the distributional dilemma would to this extent be intensified. . . . The question which we should ask is: What shall we all do when output per man-hour of work is extremely high but practically the whole of the output goes to a few property owners, while the mass of the workers are relatively . . . worse off than before? [23]

Second, radicals argue that the State cannot and will not achieve a fundamental equalization of income in capitalist societies. This argument derives from the radical theory of the State, and was summarized by Paul Sweezy (see Chapter 1), in his exposition of that view: "Let us summarize the principles underlying the use of the state as an economic instrument within the framework of capitalism. In the first place, the state comes into action in the economic sphere in order to solve problems which are posed by the development of capitalism. In the second place, where the interests of the capitalist class are concerned, there is a strong predisposition to use the state power freely. And, finally, the state may be used to make concessions to the working class provided that the consequences of not doing so are sufficiently dangerous to the stability and functioning of the system as a whole."

Radicals suggest that capitalists would oppose a meaningful redistribution and equalization of income for two reasons. First, it would undermine the wage-incentive system in a society where work is fundamentally alienating. If workers can receive a decent income from the State without working, and if their work in society is unsatisfying, why should they work? As John Gurley has put it, "If people were willing to work for non-material reasons — for the sheer love of it, to serve their country, to serve others, to serve God — material incomes . . . could be distributed equitably in the first place." [24]

This State refusal to upset the only potent work incentives in a capitalist society like the United States surfaced in the debates about the Nixon administration proposal for income maintenance. Congress and the Administration were insisting that those able to work must work before they could receive adequate income from the government. In testimony before the Senate, the Secretary of Labor tried to reassure Congress: "If the person has no skills . . . he or she will have to take an unskilled job. . . . We are not remaking the American labor market in this bill and fully realize that people are going to have to do the work that is available in our economy." [25]

Second, radicals also argue that the State would not and could not meaningfully redistribute income in a capitalist society because the State serves the interests of the capitalist class and because capitalists are interested primarily in

[23] Meade, *Equality, Efficiency and the Ownership of Property* (London: Unwin, 1965), p. 26. See also John Gurley, "Maoist Economic Development," *Review of Radical Political Economics,* Winter 1970.

[24] John G. Gurley, "Federal Tax Policy: A Review Article," *National Tax Journal,* September 1967.

[25] Quoted in *New York Post,* August 5, 1970, p. 18. See also the selection by Piven and Cloward in this chapter.

maintaining or increasing their relative share of income. Radicals point to three kinds of evidence about the government impact on the distribution of income to support their argument that the State protects the capitalists' relative share.

1. Although our society nominally prefers progressive taxation, according to liberal views, radicals argue that the net effect of government taxes in this country is plainly not progressive. At best, the total impact of government taxes is proportional, as official government figures summarized by Gabriel Kolko in this chapter would suggest. At worst, as Gurley argues, a more accurate measurement of the impact of government taxes would demonstrate actually regressive patterns of impact.[26]

2. In view of these figures on the impact of taxes, liberals often argue quite justly that one must look at the distribution of government expenditures among income classes (as well as the distributional burden of taxes) in order totally to assess the impact of the State. These analyses pose extremely intractable statistical problems, however, and one can question the assumptions involved in any set of such estimates. How does one allocate among income classes the $80 billion the government spends on national defense, for instance? Does everyone benefit equally from the expenditure, or do defense firms and their owners benefit most? Some estimates of the distributional impact of government expenditures have been made.[27] One summary of such estimates is presented in Table 5 of the Editor's Supplement on "Recent Evidence of Government Impact" among the readings in this chapter. According to that set of estimates, which the government itself supports, the net government impact in 1965 was progressive up to $4,000, proportional from $4,000 to $15,000, and progressive above $15,000.

3. Finally, and most important, radicals argue that such calculations fundamentally misstate the total impact of the State on the distribution of income. These estimates begin from a common starting point, for they both measure government impact on the final market distribution of income.[28] Neither set of statistical calisthenics asks a more important preliminary question: What impact has the government had on determining which citizens end up in which income classes in that final market distribution of income? Michelson states the point directly: "The process by which people receive money . . . is not independent of ordinary government action."[29] He cites one example of the importance of this impact on the *process* of income generation. The government spends money on schools, spending different amounts on different schools. Those who attend the schools learn different amounts, attain different levels of school depending largely on what they learn and how much it is worth, find jobs substantially on how far they have gone in school, and then earn different amounts of money. Standard estimates of the differential impact of government

[26] Gurley, "Federal Tax Policy."

[27] See principally, W. I. Gillespie, "The Effect of Public Expenditures on the Distribution of Income," in R. A. Musgrave, ed., *Essays in Fiscal Federalism* (Washington, D.C.: Brookings Institution, 1968), pp. 122–68; and Larry Sawers and Howard Wachtel, "The Distributional Impact of Federal Government Expenditures," presented to the 13th annual meetings of the International Association for Research on Income and Wealth, Balatonfüred, Hungary, August 1973.

[28] See the further development of this argument in the selection by David M. Gordon in this chapter.

[29] Stephan Michelson, "The Economics of Real Income Distribution," *Review of Radical Political Economics,* Spring 1970, p. 78.

expenditures on education look only at how much money the government spends on schools attended by the children of families with different incomes. But these estimates have nothing to do with the real effect of the government expenditure, and therefore with the real benefits it provides. Michelson summarizes the implications of estimating the impact of eventual benefits from education, rather than looking solely at the distribution of current government expenditures:

> If low-class children are taught that they will be high school graduates at best, then laborers, the finding that these people tend not to go to college surely cannot be written off as exogenously determined taste. Because the chances of going to college vary by income class, and future income is strongly a function of college graduation (for whites), the high-income students are gaining more from their college-preparatory, elementary, and secondary schooling than are the low-income students from their presumably non-college directed schooling.... The result is a biased benefit in favor of the *higher* income classes within each race, and in favor of whites over nonwhites.
>
> Now when these children from high-income families achieve their increment to lifetime income which ... education has provided, they will be taxed at higher rates than the children of the poor, who now earn less.... All will see this money being spent rather equally by race and income in the ... school system, and many will say ... that government has effectuated a redistribution from [the rich] to the poor. Yet their present before-tax income position is itself a direct result of this equal expenditure, which produced a very unequal benefit in their favor when they were in school, and continues in their children's favor now. Thus the analysis taking pre-tax incomes as given leads to exactly the opposite conclusion from that of a correct analysis. And carrying this analysis over two generations shows, I believe, that this class bias in the benefits to education is large enough to dominate the apparent redistribution to the lower classes of the traditional analysis.[30]

Many readings throughout the rest of this book suggest the extensive and important ways in which government expenditures help reinforce the class biases in private-sector institutions. These effects seem large enough, as Michelson argues, not only to undercut the importance of conventional benefit estimates but also thoroughly to support the radical contention about the role of the State. The implication of that contention for the problem of poverty seems clear: although the government may help establish a floor under incomes to help stabilize the system, it will hardly be very conscientious about trying to equalize the distribution of income. If the distribution of income seems unnecessarily unequal now, it will probably seem just as unequal many years from now.

The Readings

The first group of readings provides Impressions, Definitions, and Magnitudes. In a classic piece of journalism, Jimmy Breslin describes his impressions watching the U.S. landing on the moon in 1969 with a welfare family in Brooklyn; the contrasts between all that wealth marshalled toward the moon and the grim poverty back here on earth provide bitter testimony to our country's priori-

[30] *Ibid.,* pp. 82–83.

ties. In the next selection Lee Rainwater summarizes the results of some careful research on peoples' perceptions of poverty standards, arguing that Americans define poverty in largely relative terms. Two Editor's Supplements follow, one summarizing the characteristics of the poor in the United States, the second summarizing trends in poverty.

A second group of readings focuses on the general problems of poverty in our economy. Alice M. Rivlin presents some of the orthodox economists' view of the relationships between the economy and the income distribution. Howard M. Wachtel summarizes the general radical perspective. Herbert J. Gans emphasizes the many different functions that poverty plays in our economy, underscoring the difficulty that the "economy" would have in getting along without the poor.

A third group of readings analyzes welfare programs in this country. The first, from the late-1960s' report of the President's Commission on Income Maintenance, summarizes the different kinds of public assistance programs and reviews common objections to those programs. In the following selection Michael C. Barth, George J. Carcagno, and John L. Palmer review evidence on the coverage of the transfer system, showing how small a portion of the real poverty population receives adequate public assistance under the present programs. Christopher Green carefully presents the basic features of most common proposals for some kind of more universal income maintenance. In their long selection, finally, Frances Fox Piven and Richard A. Cloward review the central radical argument about the political economic dynamics of the welfare system. Welfare has never been intended as a purely benevolent system under capitalism, they argue, but has always served certain control functions through the economy's own cyclical paths of development.

The final group of selections reviews the relationship between the government and the distribution of income. In the first selection, David M. Gordon summarizes both orthodox and radical views of government policies affecting the distribution of income. Gabriel Kolko summarizes historical evidence suggesting that the government has never tried to equalize the distribution of income, and an Editor's Supplement summarizes more recent data that seem to confirm this impression.

MOONWALK ON SUTTER AVENUE

Jimmy Breslin

Breslin watches the moon landing with a family on welfare in Brownsville, a rapidly decaying slum in New York City. Better than any statistics, the selection illustrates the distribution of income in this country. Though the piece was written in 1969, nothing has changed in Brownsville.

The article is reprinted in its entirety from *New York Magazine.* Breslin formerly wrote a regular column for *The New York Post,* and recently wrote a best-selling novel, *The Gang That Couldn't Shoot Straight.*

It began raining in the early evening of Sunday, July 20, 1969. The kids crowded under the marquee of the Premier, the movie-house on the corner of Sutter Avenue and Hinsdale Street in Brownsville, which is in Brooklyn. The marquee said the movie showing inside was *Las Sicodalics.* The smeared showcase windows had glossy photos of Puerto Rican girls in undergarments. When somebody pushed open one of the Premier's doors, a thick, sour smell came out of a lobby which must have been ornate in the thirties and forties. The smell from the lobby mixed with the smell of the wet garbage in the gutter in front of the Premier. None of the kids standing under the marquee noticed the smell.

Ralph DuBois, who is 15, twirled a long, varnished stick that had rows of finger-width notches carved into it. He stopped twirling it long enough to show you the knobbed head of the stick. He had burned an evil-looking face into the wood.

"That's Africa, like you see," Ralph said.

"Oh."

"It was hard to do," he said. He began twirling the stick. "I made it in school."

"What school are you in?"

"A 'special' school."

"What special school is that?"

"My *personal* 'special' school." They all laughed.

"What are you doing for the summer?" he was asked.

"Work," he said. He held the stick up to your face and spun it with a flourish. "Wanna know where I work at?"

"Where?"

"Nearest crap game."

"Where is the nearest crap game?" he was asked.

"Usually right around the corner. But it rainin' now, so we got to wait for dry sidewalk."

"Isn't the moon landing on television now?" he was asked.

"Guess so," he said.

Gregory Dyer, who is 12 and who was wearing a wine polo shirt and a pink beret, stepped forward. "They got peoples on the moon, I know that," he said.

"They do?"

"Yeah. They all look like me. The peoples on the moon all like me. So you through when you get to the moon. Y'unnerstan? On the moon, you gotta look like me. Black. Black on the moon, black on Mars, black on the stars."

"Why aren't you watching television to see if there are men on the moon?" he was asked.

"I can't, account of my mother, she watchin' Alfred Hitchcock."

When the rain let up a little, I went across the street to Borinquen's grocery store to buy a pen. The cramped area in front of the counter was crowded, so I stepped back and leaned against the meat counter and waited. Only one of the trays in the window of the meat counter had meat on it. The meat was a thin slab which once was red but now had gray in it. The sides were curling up. The tray next to it had green peppers and two cans of Ballantine beer. On the other trays, flies covered the dried meat blood on the wax paper.

Alongside the grocery store was the Cuchifritos, a stand that sold Spanish food. Next to the food stand was an empty corner lot, enclosed with a high chicken-wire fence. The kids had come over from the Premier movie house and were standing at the fence and throwing rocks into the lot. The lot was covered with mounds of garbage. Each time a kid threw a rock into the lot, a rat would come out of the garbage and make his way over to the wall and disappear through an opening into the Cuchifritos stand.

Ralph DuBois poked his carved stick through the wire fence and began rapping it on an empty beer can. A rat came out from under the beer can and in one motion headed toward the wire fence. DuBois was wearing sneakers and the tips of his feet were sticking through the wire fence. "Eeeyahhh!" he shouted. He jumped back from the fence.

The rat changed direction. It moved with this quick, but not fast, scurry to the wall of the Cutchifritos stand. Then it disappeared. All the kids picked up rocks and began throwing them into the lot, and everywhere there were these shapes moving through the garbage to the wall. Twenty to twenty-five rats showed themselves.

"More rats here than in the whole world," DuBois said.

"Big rats, little rats, baby mice," one of the kids said.

"You should see when the Cuchifritos closes and everybody goes home," DuBois said. "The rats run around inside the stand. Then they come out here on the sidewalk. They are all over the corner. You come home late and you come to the corner here and there are hundreds of rats on the sidewalk."

The corner traffic light was red and Spanish music came from two of the three cars waiting for it to change. In the third car, an old red convertible, the voice on the radio was saying, ". . . man's incredible initial conquest of the universe, a 240,000-mile flight through space — and now, the unbelievable, a lunar landing . . ."

Angelo Cora, who is 35, was leaning against the car parked at the curb. He wore a dark blue polo shirt, black pants and sandals. His arms were folded cross his chest. When I introduced myself to him, he unfolded his arms to shake hands. The streetlight caught these little streaks of scar tissue on the inside of his elbows. Needle marks. He saw me looking at them, and he smiled.

"Two months home now," he said.

"Where were you?"

"Hospital for bein' an addict. But no more addict, man. I'm two months home now. I go to the Civic Center Clinic. It's at 44 Willoughby. They help all the addicts there. It's a good thing. This is the first time in my life I ever felt good."

"How long were you on it?"

He smiled again. "Fourteen years."

"How much of a habit?"

"Twenty, twenty-five dollar a day," he said.

"How did you get it?"

"Crack cribs. You know, go into apartments and steal. I got caught a few times. Between prison and hospitals, I was off the streets three years. Now, man, I'm two months home and I really don't need it. But, man, this whole neighborhood. It's addicts."

"Are these kids addicts?" I asked, pointing to the ones by the fence.

He shrugged.

"Any of you kids use narcotics?" I called out.

"Why, you got somethin' for me?" one of them said. They all laughed.

Angelo held out his hands. "You see, you can't say anything to them. Like you couldn't say anything to me, either. I never thought about gettin' caught. I was just contented. You go 'round contented. Everything is beautiful, man. The street here, the rats there, it don't mean nothin'. You get contented. You're out of it. It's very hard to tell somebody he shouldn't try. Because when he does, he likes it so much."

There was another red light and one of the car radios was saying, ". . . at this moment, Neil Armstrong is preparing to be the first man to walk on the moon . . ."

"Hey, didn't they do that yet?" Cora said.

"I guess they didn't," I said.

"We ought to go watch it on television someplace," he said. "It's a terrific thing. We beat the Russians to the moon. It makes me happy, man."

There was a bar on the opposite corner, but there was no television set inside. Cora said he knew a place where we could watch the men walk on the moon. The sister of a girl who had been his wife lived on Sheffield Street and Cora said she would let us come in. We got into a car and began driving there.

At night, the streets of Brownsville are like a well-bombed target. On each block there are half-demolished buildings. Their corroded insides of staircases and broken walls and sagging floors are outlined by the car headlights. Most of the streetlights are broken, and with no light coming from the houses, you drive on some blocks through complete darkness. On many of the streets, the rows of four- and five-story houses have been almost abandoned. Windows and doorways have tin sheets nailed over them. Here and there in a block, a lone light will show. One person, or one family, will be living with the rats in the building. The people in these lone apartments must keep somebody awake all night, because the kids from the neighborhood come into these buildings and set fires in the empty apartments. The firehouse serving the neighborhood, Ladder 103, is so busy that the company rarely comes back to the station after a call. It stays out on the streets, going from fire to fire, sometimes two and three in a single block.

It has been like this for a long time in Brownsville. A year and a half ago, I went to visit the nuns working at the Good Shepherd center on the corner of Hopkinson and Sutter. The stores on the corners were empty and the apartments over the stores were empty and the broken glass from the windows covered the sidewalks. And here, in the rain on this Sunday night, the corners were as they were, except now stripped cars sat there. One of the cars had crashed into the light pole. It sat on rusted haunches on the sidewalk. Several buildings down Hopkinson Avenue, the faint blue light of television showed from an apartment window. When you looked in the window, you could see a woman sitting on a kitchen chair in a bare room and watching the moon coverage on a small television set. There was a noise behind you at the curb. Something had moved in one of the trash cans sitting in the sprawl of spilled garbage.

Here and there in the ruins of Brownsville there are neatly painted wooden signs proclaiming that a housing project will be erected on the spot. Under the proclamation is the name of the politician, and of the various urban experts, in charge of the housing program. These signs have been standing in Brownsville for many, many months. Just as the same signs have been standing for the same months and months on Roosevelt Avenue in Chicago and Twelfth Avenue in Detroit and Joseph Avenue in Rochester. The story of a city in this nation in the 1960s is a sign with a politician's name on it, and only the name on the sign changes.

As we drove, the news announcer on the car radio was talking about the technical skill it took to get the lunar landing ship down onto the surface with its four legs evenly touching.

The place Angelo took us to was a frame house sitting in a lot that was filled with old cars. He went to a door with a torn screen and called in Spanish. A woman opened the door.

"I was asleep," she said. She had a sundress thrown over a nightgown. Her name was Clara Pagan. She was plump and her face looked 40. She is only 26.

A clock in the small, clean kitchen said it was 10:45. In a box-like bedroom off the kitchen two teenage nieces of Clara Pagan sat on a bed and watched a small portable television.

"Columbia, this is Houston . . ."

"They coming out now," one of the girls said.

"They haven't been out yet?" Angelo said. The girls shook their heads. "Wow, we're in time," Angelo said. He clapped his hands and sat on the bed.

Clara Pagan leaned in the doorway and watched.

"You tell your mailman?" Angelo said to her. She shrugged. "You better," he said. "I told you, the new rule says that if the mailman puts the check in your mailbox and somebody steals it, then they won't replace the check anymore."

On the television, there still was the "simulated" tag across the screen. Walter Cronkite talked in fatherly tones to the country, and every few seconds the metallic, mechanical voices of the spacemen — "Houston, this is Eagle . . ." — came through.

"I have to watch for the mailman because this is bad out here," Clara said. "They steal, they do everything. This gang of kids. The Devils. Very bad. Coloreds and Puerto Ricans. They steal and beat up people. You can't go out at night. They stab you. Last night they were running down the street all covered with somebody's blood."

"How much relief do you get?" she was asked.

"I get $115.95 every two weeks," she said. "It's supposed to be more, but now I don't know. They going to cut down."

"They used to give carfare to the people going to clinics," Angelo said. "Now they don't give that anymore. They cut out carfare for people on relief."

"How long have you been on relief?" she was asked.

"For a year. I have two children. The baby is only a year old. I worked all my life, but I cannot go and leave the baby. My husband leave me a year ago. He went home to Puerto Rico. So now I stay home." She made a face. "Relief is no good."

"Why isn't it good?" she was asked.

"They come and look. They always *axt* you about a husband. They come to house one time at 6:30 in the night. I was surprised. She didn't say anything to me. She just walked by me and she look in the draws and the closets. She look all over."

"She look for a man's clothes," Angelo said. "To see if she's living with a man."

"I don't like relief," Clara said.

On the television, the "simulated" line suddenly said "live from the surface of the moon." The picture was upside down. It was fixed. Now you could watch the simple, staggering act of a man coming down a stepladder and onto the surface of the moon.

Clara Pagan kept talking. "I was on relief when I was with my mother," she said. "She had TB. My father died. I was with my brothers and sisters. Relief, it was no good then. No good now."

Images skipped across the screen. The astronauts romped on the moon.

"Smell it?" Clara said.

"Smell what?"

"The dogs. The old lady downstairs keeps dogs in the cellar and she never cleans. The smell makes you sick. The rats and the roaches come."

". . . Eagle, this is Houston. Can we get you two together so we can see the two of you . . ."

"Look at this," Clara Pagan said. "They have them pose for pictures like children in the park."

"Look at it, you can't believe it," Angelo Cora said, holding out his arms. In the bright light of the room, you could see that he has needle scars all up and down the insides of his arms.

Clara Pagan walked over to the stove and lit a cigarette. She came back to the doorway with the cigarette in her mouth and she watched American men walk on the moon.

"Some day I'm going to get off relief," she said.

PERCEPTIONS OF POVERTY AND ECONOMIC INEQUALITY

Lee Rainwater*

The government has defined poverty absolutely and has concluded that poverty has been declining. (See the Editor's Supplement following this selection.) Rainwater summarizes a growing body of evidence suggesting that most people actually view poverty in relative terms. Rainwater concludes from popular perceptions of poverty and inequality that poverty has not declined at all over the last thirty years.

This selection is excerpted from a longer article, published in *Working Papers for a New Society*, entitled "Economic Inequality and the Credit Income Tax." Further evidence about popular perceptions of poverty and inequality is provided in Rainwater's book *What Money Buys*.

Rainwater is professor of sociology at Harvard University and a faculty associate of the Joint Center for Urban Studies at Harvard and M.I.T. He has written several other books about urban problems.

Source: "Perceptions of Poverty and Economic Inequality" by Lee Rainwater excerpted from "Economic Inequality and the Credit Income Tax" published in *Working Papers for a New Society*, I, 1, Spring 1973.

* The research on which this paper is in part based has been supported by a Public Health Service grant, MH-18635, and earlier by MH-15567. In the development of the ideas presented here I have profited greatly from discussions over the years with several of my colleagues,

Reflection on the past decade of the war on poverty produces many paradoxes.[1] The most central is that while "poverty" has been reduced by almost half, we have no sense of a change for the better in the prevalence of the human problems associated with poverty. The proportion of all persons living below the poverty line decreased year by year from 1959 to 1969 from 22.4 to 12.2 percent of all persons.[2] In

particularly Richard P. Coleman, Phillips Cutright, Herbert J. Gans, and Martin Rein.

[1] The lessons of the 1960s war on poverty have been analyzed in Joseph E. Kershaw, *Government Against Poverty* (Washington: The Brookings Institution, 1970); Robert A. Levine, *The Poor Ye Need Not Have With You: Lessons from the War on Poverty* (Cambridge: M.I.T. Press, 1970); Peter Marris and Martin Rein, *Dilemmas of Social Reform* (Chicago: Aldine-Atherton, revised edition in press); Daniel P. Moynihan, *Maximum Feasible Misunderstanding* (New York: The Free Press, 1969); James Sundquist, *On Fighting Poverty* (New York: Basic Books, 1969); and Gilbert Y. Steiner, *The State of Welfare* (Washington: The Brookings Institution, 1971).

[2] U.S. Bureau of the Census, Current Population Reports, Series P-60, No. 81, *Characteristics of the Low Income Population 1970* (Washington: U.S. Government Printing Office, 1971), Table A, p. 2.

the 1971 recession this decline halted and poverty increased slightly. No more elaborate explanation of this decline is necessary than to say that the people at the bottom of the heap got their usual share of the increasing affluence, and this shift in their income moved almost half of them above the poverty line. If economic growth continues at its long-term rate, it is not overly risky to predict the near elimination of poverty by around 1980.

But we know that is ridiculous. Any speaker is likely to meet with audience disbelief if he argues that in 1973 the poverty problem is only half of what it was in 1959. His listeners will be quick to point to the undiminished intensity of a broad range of human and social problems.

If we leave aside the statistical indicators of problems and look instead at the families at the lower end of the socio-economic scale we see that the quality of their lives seems to have changed hardly at all over longer periods of time than a decade. The people who would have been considered poor on an "eyeball to eyeball" basis in 1959 still seem poor today. The people who felt themselves poor and deprived, oppressed and wasted by society in 1959 still seem to feel poor, deprived, oppressed, and wasted today. Indeed a reader who systematically compares community studies carried out in low-income slum or ghetto communities in the 1930s with recent studies is struck by the tremendous similarity across that time span in the style of life and in the kinds of human difficulties and problems that confront people in those communities. No one who was acquainted with the lower-lower class described in 1930s studies by such researchers as Warner, Davis and Gardner, or Whyte would feel at all surprised by the style of life in Boston's white slums of today.[3] And no one acquainted with Negro lower

class life as dealt with by authors such as Cayton and Drake or Allison Davis would find basic change in the style of life of today's ghettos (although he might be surprised by the quality of ideological and political expression).[4] Yet the material base for life has changed dramatically. Today's low-income person has available to him perhaps two-and-a-half times as much in the way of goods and services as was true of his 1930 counterpart. If we look for what has not changed in the economic situation of the poor, we do not have far to go. Although the incomes of people at the bottom (as in the middle and at the top) of the income hierarchy have changed dramatically, the degree of inequality in income distribution has changed only marginally since before World War II.[5] There is some reason to believe that there was a slight shift toward a more equal distribution during the depression and through World War II. Since 1947, however, there seem to have been hardly any changes in the distribution of income. The proportion of the population with incomes less than half the median family income was 18.9 percent in 1947, and it was still 18.9 in 1970. (It had reached a high of 20.9 percent in 1954 and a low of 18.3 percent in 1968.)[6]

---

[3] See for earlier descriptions of lower-class family and community life W. Lloyd Warner, et al., *Yankee City*, one-volume abridged edition (New Haven, Conn.: Yale University Press, 1963); Allison Davis, Burleigh B. Gardner, and Mary R. Gardner, *Deep South* (Chicago: University of Chicago Press, 1941); Allison Davis, "The Motivation of the Underprivileged Worker," in W. F. Whyte (Ed.), *Industry and Society* (New York: McGraw-Hill, 1946); Allison Davis, *Social Class Influences Upon Learning* (Cambridge: Harvard Univ. Press, 1948); William Foote Whyte, *Street Corner Society* (Chicago: University of Chicago Press, 1943). For studies after World War II, see Herbert J. Gans, *The Urban Villagers* (New York: The Free Press, 1962); Gerald E. Suttles, *The Social Order of the Slum* (Chicago: University of Chicago Press, 1968); Lee Rainwater, Richard P. Cole-

man, and Gerald Handel, *Working Class Wife* (Dobbs Ferry, N.Y.: Oceana Publications, 1959); Lee Rainwater, *And The Poor Get Children* (Chicago: Quadrangle Books, 1960).

[4] For studies of lower-class black communities, see Davis, Gardner, and Gardner, op. cit.; Davis, op. cit.; Horace Cayton and Sinclair Drake, *Black Metropolis* (New York: Harper and Row, 1962); John Rohrer and Monro Edmundson, *The Eighth Generation Grows Up* (New York: Harper and Row, 1960); Hylan Lewis, *Blackways of Kent* (Chapel Hill: University of North Carolina, 1955); Kenneth Clark, *Dark Ghetto* (New York: Harper and Row, 1965); Elliot Liebow, *Tally's Corner* (Boston: Little, Brown, 1967); Ulf Hannerz, *Soulside* (New York: Columbia Univ. Press, 1969); Lee Rainwater, *Behind Ghetto Walls* (Chicago: Aldine-Atherton, 1970); and David Shultz, *Coming Up Black* (Englewood Cliffs, N.J.: Prentice-Hall, 1969).

[5] U.S. Bureau of the Census, *Income Distribution in the United States* by Herman P. Miller, 1960 monograph (Washington: U.S. Government Printing Office, 1966), pp. 12–28; and U.S. Bureau of the Census, Current Population Reports, Series P-60, No. 80, *Incomes in 1970 of Families and Persons in the United States* (Washington: U.S. Government Printing Office, 1971), Table 14, p. 28.

[6] Victor R. Fuchs, "Comments on Measuring the Low Income Population," in Lee Soltow (Ed.), *Six Papers on the Size Distribution of Income* (New York: National Bureau of Economic Research, 1969), p. 200; and Current Population Survey, *Incomes in 1970*, op. cit.

The Council of Economic Advisers at the beginning of the War on Poverty defined the poor as "families who do not have the resources to provide minimum satisfaction of their own particular needs." But the Council went on to observe that "by the standards of contemporary American society most of the population of the world is poor, and most Americans were poor a century ago. But for our society today a consensus on an approximate standard can be found." [7] In fact, however, it is not possible to find a consensus based on absolute logic. If we define the poor, as the Council does, as "those who are not now maintaining a decent standard of living — those whose basic needs exceed their means to satisfy them," then we must recognize that what society defines as a "decent" standard of living depends on what most members of the society can afford, and that the cost of meeting "basic needs" depends on how society as a whole defines such needs. The standards involved must therefore be relative rather than absolute. This can be demonstrated by looking at historical changes in both official definitions of minimum budgets and popular definitions of what it takes to get along economically.

Official Definitions

Oscar Ornati has carried out an historical survey of living standards budgets at three levels — "minimum subsistence," "minimum adequacy," and "minimum comfort" for the period 1905–1960.[8] An examination of his findings suggest that the three budgets served as dividing points between three classes of people, all of whom were seen to live below the mean income level for the society. These classes were:

■ A "Charity" Class

These budgets Ornati called "minimum subsistence." Except in the early part of the 1905–1960 period these budgets have been used almost exclusively for charity purposes — to establish "minimum decency" or "minimum for physical efficiency" standards. In the few cases where the budgets have

[7] *Economic Report of the President,* January 1964.

[8] Oscar Ornati, *Poverty Amid Affluence* (New York: The Twentieth Century Fund, 1966). See also the discussion of changing consumption and styles of life from the 19th into the 20th century by Dorothy S. Brady in Davis, Easterlin, Parker, et al., *American Economic Growth: An Economist's History of the United States* (New York: Harper and Row, 1972).

been used for wage determination it has been with a characterization (e.g., "lowest bare existence") which indicates that the budget is not supposed to provide more than what is regarded as the minimum daily resources for staying alive and functioning. Charity has become more public and more bureaucratized; now the principal versions of the minimum subsistence budget are the state AFDC budget standards.

■ A "Poor-But-Honest-Worker" Class

The budgets that Ornati called "minimum adequate" seem to have been established principally to fix a kind of floor for membership in the established working class. These budgets were almost all related to wage determination; when they were used by charitable institutions it was for the purpose of establishing the point at which clients could be expected to begin to pay for social agency services. Characterizations of the budgets suggest that the focus was on a kind of minimum "social" subsistence rather than a presumed minimum physical subsistence — budgets were characterized as representing "a fair living wage," "the working margin," "minimum wholesome living," "minimum but reasonable."

■ The Average-American-Worker Class

These budgets were for purposes of wage determination and comparison. Many of the budgets were prepared for establishing the wages of civil service workers, a further indication of the "averageness" of the class the budget level was to denote. Interestingly enough, however, the budgets tended to be characterized by their developers much more in terms of some presumed necessity than otherwise. Thus many of the budgets are said to represent the consumption necessary for "health and decency" or "minimum health and comfort." Occasionally, however, the budget makers were a little more forthright. Thus the 1923 budget for Eastern Massachusetts Street Railway wage determination characterized the budget only as representing an income that was "proper and suitable." And in 1926 and 1927 when the National Industrial Conference Board established a standard for industrial workers in 12 industrial cities the standard was characterized simply as "a fair American standard." Again as the matter has become bureaucratized (in this case at the U.S. Bureau of Labor Statistics) the point of the budget has become somewhat more obvious. Thus the minimum comfort budget Ornati used for the later years of his survey is the Bureau of Labor Statistics' "interim city worker's family budget" which is characterized as "modest but adequate" by "prevailing standards." The "prevailing standards" introduces much more directly the relative emphasis for this budget.

The higher two of the three budgets were explicitly relative in their logic — the budget makers sought to construct budgets that would enable families to live at a particular consumption level relative to the average for the society as a whole. To a certain extent these budgets were a substitute for accurate family income statistics. In the absence of such statistics the budget makers could make budgets for one level of living ("minimum comfort") near the median for the society, and another level of living ("minimum adequacy") below the median, but not so far below as to represent great deprivation.

The logic of the charity-class budget, however, is somewhat different. The budget makers tended to describe charity-class budgets as "subsistence budgets" with the note that they represented the minimum goods and services for the family simply to continue to exist. Such budgets were often considered as for emergencies rather than for a consistent level of living.

In fact, however, all three budget levels tended to increase in fairly constant ratio as the overall level of affluence of the society increased.

Over the 1905–1960 period all three budgets increased in constant dollar value, with the minimum comfort budget increasing the most (120 percent) and the minimum adequate close behind (111 percent). The minimum subsistence budget did not increase quite so dramatically — only 93 percent — and after 1930, it increased much more slowly than the others, suggesting that the further professionalization of welfare has tended to dampen the growth of charity-class budgets in line with the "absolute" logic of subsistence.

In the period since 1935 there seems to have been a very stable relationship between the minimum subsistence budgets and the average income for families of our people. If one ignores the World War II years, from 1935 to 1963 the minimum charity-class budgets range from 42 percent of average family income on the high side to 34 percent on the low side. There is no discernible linear trend during this period. It is only after 1963, when the new Social Security poverty index was fixed except for price changes, that this relationship to a minimum

subsistence budget begins to change. By 1971, the SSA poverty index amounted to only 29 percent of [average] family disposable income.

Popular Definitions

More important than standard of living budgets made by the experts are the standard of living conceptions held by people themselves. A useful historical series on public conceptions of living standards is provided by a Gallup Public Opinion Poll question which has been asked in exactly the same form since 1946: "What is the smallest amount of money a family of four needs to get along in this community?" Table 1 presents the mean responses of national samples for 21 surveys during the 1946–1969 period, and relates those responses to median family income, per family consumption (per capita income times four) and the average weekly spendable income for workers with three dependents in private non-agricultural industries.[9] It is apparent that there is a constant relationship with family consumption. The relationship to workers' earnings seems also quite stable. There is a slight downward trend in the proportion the "get along" amount represents of median family income — perhaps reflecting the slight increase in the proportion of family income attributable to wives' earnings.

From 1959 to 1970 per family consumption and the Gallup get-along figure both increased by about two-thirds. In contrast, the consumer price index and the low-income "poverty" budget which is tied to it increased by only 27 percent.

The Gallup get-along question produces results which match very closely with the amounts in Ornati's minimum adequacy budgets, a budget represented today by the Bureau of Labor Statistics' "lower standard" budget for an urban family. Over the 1946–1969 period the Gallup get-along amount for the country as a whole averaged 107 percent of the minimum adequacy budget (the range was from a high of 125 percent to a low of 99 percent). "Get-

[9] Data on the get-along questions and several other Gallup and Roper questions discussed here are available in the files of the Roper Public Opinion Research Center. We wish to thank Professor Phillip K. Hastings and his staff for their assistance in detailed tabulation of Gallup questions for surveys from 1937 to 1969. Claude Fischer and Sally Nash carried out further calculations to prepare Gallup and the Boston Social Standards Survey data for this presentation.

TABLE 1. "What Is the Smallest Amount of Money a Family of Four Needs to Get Along in This Community?"

Date of Survey	Current Dollars	Constant Dollars (1969)	% of Median Family Income	% per Family Consumption	% Average Weekly Spendable Earnings †
Jan. 1946	42.80	80.30	—	55	—
Aug./Dec. 1947 *	45.20	74.00	78	53	101
June 1948	51.93	78.80	85	56	107
May 1949	49.73	76.40	83	54	100
Feb. 1950	47.98	73.00	75	50	92
Apr./Dec. 1951 *	55.00	77.20	86	57	101
Oct. 1952	62.00	85.50	83	58	107
Mar. 1953	59.80	82.00	73	54	99
Apr. 1954	63.85	87.90	79	57	105
Nov. 1957	74.77	97.10	78	59	110
May 1958	82.17	103.70	69	54	114
Aug. 1960	81.54	101.10	75	59	112
Jan. 1961	83.23	101.20	76	59	111
Jan. 1962	83.13	100.80	73	57	108
Apr. 1963	83.24	99.40	71	55	106
Nov. 1964	85.35	100.70	68	53	103
Dec. 1967	109.16	119.20	71	57	120
Feb./Oct. 1969 *	119.72	119.72	66	55	107

* Indicates average of two surveys
† In private nonagricultural industries for a worker with three dependents

ting along" seems to mean having a standard of living that puts you just inside the mainstream, a level that places you in the lower part of the working class.

In the Boston Social Standards Survey,[10] carried out in the spring of 1971 by Richard Coleman and me, respondents were asked to specify how much income was necessary for a family to live at various qualitatively defined levels — "poverty," "enough to get along," "comfortable," "prosperous and substantial," and "rich." Subsamples were asked about each of these living levels for families with different numbers of children varying from none through five. The geometric means for each of the combinations of living level and family size are given in Table 2.

Starting with the comfortable level as a midpoint and setting that arbitrarily at 100, a regression analysis of the data in Table 2 suggests that the income

[10] The Boston Social Standards Survey involved a sample of 600 respondents representing the Boston metropolitan area. The survey was carried out by the Survey Research Program of the Joint Center for Urban Studies and we wish to thank the staff for their able response to the challenge of a highly complex questionnaire.

amounts tied to these different levels seem to be in the following ratios:

Living Levels	Ratio to a Comfortable Level
Poor	48%
Get-along	69%
Comfortable	100%
Prosperous-substantial	128%
Rich	209%

Apparently you are poor if you have about half the money necessary to be comfortable. You have enough to get along if you have 70 percent of what is necessary to be comfortable. And you are rich when you have twice as much as is necessary to be comfortable.

These findings are quite interesting in terms of policy. Many federal and state programs vary income limits or benefits in terms of family size. These variations reflect differences in the resources welfare workers believe families of different sizes need to live at a given level. They presumably assume that

TABLE 2. Incomes Appropriate for Living Levels and Family Sizes (Geometric Means)

| Living Levels | Number of Children | | | | | |
	None	1	2	3	4	5
Poverty (highest income to be considered living in poverty)	$ 4,036	$ 4,477	$ 4,508	——*	$ 5,458	$ 5,848
Get-along (lowest income to still have just enough to get along)	5,794	6,683	7,586	$ 8,298	8,356	9,419
Comfortable (lowest income to have a comfortable level of living)	9,141	——*	11,402	10,864	11,912	12,882
Prosperity (lowest income to have a prosperous, substantial level of living)	——*	11,967	14,158	15,560	15,996	15,922
Rich (lowest income to be considered rich)	17,498	21,380	24,717	21,878	26,122	——*

* No questions asked for these combinations of level and family size

the public generally accepts the idea that families need different amounts to have "equal welfare." In fact, however, the public does not seem to think large families need as much extra money as welfare experts think such families need. Table 3 shows the

TABLE 3. Comparison of Incomes Necessary for Equal Welfare of Different Family Sizes with Poverty Line and FAP Family Size Variations in Payment by Family Size

Family Size	Equal Welfare Ratios	Social Security Administration Low Income Threshold Ratios (Non-Farm)	Payment Ratios in FAP
Two	1.00	1.00	1.00
Three	1.13	1.19	1.30
Four	1.23	1.52	1.60
Five	1.32	1.79	1.90
Six	1.39	2.01	2.20
Seven	1.46	2.48	2.50

rate of income increase required to maintain "equal welfare" according to our informants, the Social Security Administration's official poverty index, and the 1969 version of the Family Assistance Plan (EAP). Our informants feel that a family of seven persons requires about 46 percent more income than a family of two persons to be at an equal living level. The SSA poverty index and the earlier versions of the FAP proposal assume that a family of seven needs 148–150 percent more income than a family of two. If our respondents' logic mirrors even roughly the national consensus, government standards considerably overestimate the "poorness" of large families and underestimate the "poorness" of small families.

Detailed analysis of two surveys in 1969 indicates that regional variations are not significant after community size is controlled for, while community size is an important variable in all regions. Until the early 1960s the amount needed to get along in the largest cities was, on the average, about 45 percent higher than the amount needed in farm and rural areas. By the mid and late 1960s that difference seemed to have narrowed somewhat, with about 35 percent more needed in the larger cities than in the country-side.

These results point to the necessity of paying systematic attention to relative incomes if we are to properly understand the meanings of "poverty" and inequality for families and individuals. One way of seeing the implications of this is to project the historic relation of poverty lines and per capita personal income into the future. In 1985, according to Herman Miller's projections, mean family income will be around $18,700 in 1971 dollars, and median family income will be around $17,100.[11] The historical relation of the "poverty" or "minimum subsistence" line to personal income suggests that we will consider $8,300 as the poverty line for a family of four in 1985. Today, two-fifths of all families fall below this line. Those who fall just below it do not call themselves poor. They are still in the mainstream. But by 1985, average living standards will have risen to the point that $8,300 is a bare minimum for participating in American life. Yet if the present distribution persists, as it has since 1945, about 18 percent of all families will have less than $8,300. "Poverty," as popularly understood, will be no less than it is today.

Popular Conceptions of Fair Wages

The foregoing evidence suggests that both official and popular definitions of poverty are relative rather than absolute. The evidence also suggests that there is considerable agreement about how such poverty should be eliminated. For three decades, whenever the American people have been consulted by public opinion polls, they have preferred providing people with jobs to any other strategy for eliminating poverty. Yet the fact is that many jobs do not now provide a family of four with enough to get along at what the public regards as an adequate level.

In order to probe people's feelings about this issue more closely, we asked respondents in the Boston Social Standards Survey two kinds of questions dealing with what they would regard as a fair distribution of wages. One set of questions was concerned with a fair minimum wage or salary for persons who worked full time and the other was concerned with a fair distribution of wages among persons at different occupation and skill levels.

In order to understand what our respondents felt was a fair wage for a full-time worker, no matter how low his skills, we asked respondents what they felt should be "the lowest amount" any man at each of six different ages should learn if he worked full time, no matter what his job was. We also asked what he should receive in retirement. The results for our sample are presented in Table 4. The pattern of responses suggests that there are no significant differences in the minimum annual wages thought appropriate for male workers between 32 and 52. People do think it appropriate that both 22-year-olds and 62-year-olds earn less than other workers, even though they work full time. They think a retired worker should receive about three-fourths as much income as he received in the years just before his retirement, or two-thirds of what he received from 32 to 52.

In general the results for 32, 42, and 52-year-old men are consistent with an underlying logic that the minimum wages should be close to the get-along level for a family with two children. The amounts are almost 50 percent above the amount that our respondents consider poverty for a family with two children. The younger worker is expected to have to get by on lower wages — perhaps on the logic that he is still learning the job, perhaps also on the assumption that he does not yet have enough family responsibilities (at least, if he's "sensible") to need as much in the way of income. His minimum "fair" wage runs a little over 80 percent of that of men in the mature years. According to our respondents' logic, that is not quite enough to support a wife (perhaps they assume that she will work) and certainly not enough to support a family.

[11] Herman P. Miller, *Rich Man, Poor Man* (New York: Thomas Crowell, 1971), pp. 234–246; and Lee Rainwater, "Post 1984 America," *Society*, February 1972.

TABLE 4.   Recommended Minimum Annual Wage

Age of Worker	Mean Fair Minimum	Estimated Median Income for Boston Men Empl. Full-time, All Year	Fair Amount as % of Median for Boston Workers
22 years old	$5,715	$ 7,720	74%
32 years old	6,886	10,038	69
42 years old	7,170	11,284	64
52 years old	6,819	10,924	62
62 years old	6,010	9,978	60
Retired Man	4,667	—	—

Overall, then, one can say that conceptions of minimum wages are about the same as conceptions of an income sufficient for families to get along. For everyone who is willing to give full-time effort, employment is supposed to produce an income that allows one to approximate the mainstream. If this turns out not to be the case, people believe something is wrong — either the individual hasn't tried hard enough or has some fundamental flaw, or the system is not working right — because the system should produce a decent living for the well-motivated person.

In order to get some idea of how men and women thought about the equity of relative shares for different occupational groups, we developed a complex question in which respondents were asked about a hypothetical community with 1,000 workers distributed at several different skill and occupational levels.

50 are top management level
150 are at the middle management and professional level
250 are at an average white collar level
400 are at an average working man level
150 are at a lower skill level

Respondents were then asked to specify appropriate earnings for each group. Table 5 shows that on the average the respondents thought that top management salaries should be almost four times the wages of the lowest skilled group. The least skilled workers are assigned incomes about two-thirds the mean income, the average working man is assigned about 78 percent of the mean, the average white collar worker about 90 percent of the mean. The

average middle management and professional person receives 150 percent of the mean, and the average top management person receives more than 250 percent of the mean. Clearly our respondents are willing to accept a marked dispersion of income.

The income considered fair by our respondents is quite close to the actual average incomes of *full-time year-round* male workers at different occupational levels in the U.S. in 1970. When we compare our sample's proportions with those for *all* employed males, however, we see large differences. This suggests that unemployment is the major factor responsible for differences between what our respondents judge to be fair and actual average compensation in a given category.

In fact, the relevance of these findings to the real world is limited, however. The variance in income due to occupation, or to amount of unemployment, is only a minor part of the pattern of income inequality. Christopher Jencks has calculated that if inequality among occupations were eliminated while the dispersion of incomes within occupations remained the same, income inequality would be reduced by only 20 percent.[12] The dispersion within occupations turns out to be much greater than that between them.

Yet it is clear from our interviews that people think of income inequality and equality in terms of relative earnings by persons with different kinds of jobs. The rationale for income variations within occupations is a much more subtle issue and our respondents tend to avoid it. Given their specifica-

[12] Christopher Jencks, et al., *Inequality* (New York: Basic Books, 1972).

TABLE 5. Popular Estimates of Fair Incomes in a Hypothetical Community

Level of Worker	Estimates for:		
	Mean Income (Geomean)	All U.S. Male Workers (median)	U.S. Full-Time Male Workers (median)
150 Lowest Skill	$ 6,427 (85) *	$ 3,500 (82)	$ 7,000 (82)
400 Average Workingmen	7,482 (100)	6,400 (100)	8,500 (100)
250 Average White Collar	8,831 (118)	7,250 (113)	9,500 (111)
150 Middle Management	14,454 (193)	14,200 (221)	15,000 (176)
50 Top Management	24,717 (330)	24,500 (382)	28,000 (329)

* Figures in parentheses give ratio of amount specified to amount for average workingman level.

tions on minimum incomes however, it is clear that they believe that a just income distribution would sharply truncate the low side of the dispersion of earnings. Note that the best paid fifth of all workers would earn about 140 percent more than the worst paid fifth in our hypothetical community. In the real world, the best paid fifth of full-time year-round workers earns about 700 percent more than the worst paid fifth.

We can summarize the results for this question by saying that respondents do not find gross inequity in the way income is distributed among occupational categories. But they want minimum incomes for workers that range from somewhat under $6,000 for young men just starting out, to over $7,000 for mature workers. This means that they want a minimum wage — at least for adult males — of $3.00 to $3.50 an hour. The present minimum is [$2.25]. Even $3.50 an hour would not suffice in occupations which cannot provide full-time year-round employment.

CHARACTERISTICS OF THE POOR

Editor's Supplement

Many different kinds of people are more likely than others to suffer poverty. Our society makes adequate subsistence an intolerably difficult accomplishment for women, minorities, the elderly, and other victims of discrimination. This Editor's Supplement reviews the data on the composition of the poor population and changes in the characteristics of the poor over the past fifteen years.

Table 1 summarizes some relevant data. The data are based on the official government definition of poverty — the SSA "absolute poverty" standard. While that definition of poverty seems much too low, for reasons which the chapter introduction and the following supplement suggest, these data nonetheless help identify who suffers the most severe poverty most frequently.

Looking at the first half of the table — Columns 1 through 4 — we can draw some specific conclusions about the composition of the poor population in 1973.

First, column 2 makes clear that certain specific groups are most likely to experience poverty: families headed by women, by blacks, living in central cities and on the farm, headed by younger and older people, with large numbers of children, and headed by people who are unemployed or out of the labor force.

Second, columns 1 and 3 help remind us that, although those disadvantaged groups are most likely to suffer poverty, poverty is not confined to those kinds of families alone. Two-thirds of all poor families are headed by whites, for instance, and 42 percent are headed by white men.

Third, a comparison of columns 3 and 4 — a comparison of the composition of the poverty population and the nonpoverty population makes clear that the characteristics of the poor differ in some important respects from the characteristics of the rest of the population. Many more poor families are headed by blacks and headed by females, many more of the poor are concentrated in central cities, and disproportionate numbers of poor families are headed by people not in the labor force.

If we compare the first half of the table with the second half — by comparing columns 1 through 4 with columns 5 through 8 — we can begin to sketch some of the changes in the composition of poor people that have taken place recently.

Between 1958 and 1973, specifically, the following changes in the characteristics of poor people in the United States seem most important.

- While the absolute numbers of poor families declined, the absolute numbers of poor families headed by women actually increased. The percentage of female-headed families who are poor also increased.

TABLE 1.   Selected Characteristics of Families Below the Poverty Level in 1973 and 1959 (Numbers in thousands)

	1973 Percent Distribution				1959 Percent Distribution			
Selected Characteristics	Number Below Poverty Level (1)	Percent Below Poverty Level (2)	Below Poverty Level (3)	Above Poverty Level (4)	Number Below Poverty Level (5)	Percent Below Poverty Level (6)	Below Poverty Level (7)	Above Poverty Level (8)
Sex and Race of Head								
Total	4,828	8.8	100.0	100.0	8,320	18.5	100.0	100.0
Male head	2,635	5.5	54.6	87.6	6,404	15.8	77.0	80.0
Female head	2,193	32.2	45.4	12.4	1,916	42.6	23.0	10.0
White	3,219	6.6	66.6	88.5	6,185	15.2	74.3	90.5
Male head	2,029	4.6	42.0	79.7	4,952	13.3	59.5	83.1
Female head	1,190	24.5	24.6	8.8	1,233	34.8	14.8	7.4
Black[a]	1,527	28.1	31.6	9.9	2,040	52.1	24.5	8.7
Male head	553	15.4	11.4	5.5	1,373	45.8	16.5	6.7
Female head	974	52.7	20.2	3.4	661	72.6	8.0	2.0
Residence								
Total	4,828	8.8	100.0	100.0	8,320	18.5	100.0	100.0
Nonfarm	4,533	8.6	94.4	95.4	6,624	16.1	79.6	94.3
Central City	4,062	29.6	84.1	24.3	3,816	40.8	45.7	20.6
Farm	295	11.6	5.6	4.6	1,696	44.6	20.4	5.7
Age of Head								
Total	4,828	8.8	100.0	100.0	8,320	18.5	100.0	100.0
14 to 24 years	676	15.8	14.0	7.1	622	26.9	7.5	4.6
25 to 54 years	2,731	8.1	56.6	63.8	4,752	16.0	57.1	68.0
55 to 64 years	593	6.9	12.3	16.0	1,086	15.9	13.1	15.6
65 years and over	829	10.5	17.2	14.0	1,860	30.0	22.4	11.8
Size of Family								
Total	4,828	8.8	100.0	100.0	8,320	18.5	100.0	100.0
2 persons	1,697	8.2	35.1	37.1	2,850	19.6	34.2	31.7
3 and 4 persons	1,604	7.5	33.2	41.5	2,420	12.8	29.1	44.9
5 and 6 persons	988	10.5	20.4	16.8	1,793	20.2	21.6	19.3
7 persons or more	539	20.8	11.2	4.1	1,257	45.6	15.1	4.1
Employment Status of Head								
Total	4,828	8.8	100.0	100.0	8,320	18.5	100.0	100.0
Employed	1,983	2.0	41.2	79.2	4,536	12.8	54.5	84.3
Unemployed	263	19.5	5.4	2.2	559	33.1	6.7	3.0
In Armed Forces or not in labor force	2,576	21.6	53.4	18.6	3,225	40.8	38.8	12.7

[a] Data for "Blacks" do not include "other races"; the "white" and "black" figures, therefore, do not total 100 percent of all families.

Source: U.S. Bureau of the Census, *Current Population Reports,* Series P-60, No. 98, January, 1975.

- Although the percentage of black-headed families suffering poverty declined, a growing proportion of poor families are black. One-quarter of poor families were headed by blacks in 1958, for instance, while almost one-third were headed by blacks in 1973. The proportion of poor families headed by black women increased from 8.0 per cent to 20.2 per cent.
- More and more, poor people live in central cities. (You can't keep them down on the farm.) Less than half of poor families lived in central cities in 1958, while five-sixths of poor families lived in central cities in 1973.
- Many fewer older families suffered poverty in 1973 than in 1958, reflecting the substantial increase in Social Security benefits over that period. The percentage of families headed by people sixty-five years and older who suffered poverty dropped from 30 percent in 1958 to only 10.5 percent — or just above the national average — in 1973.
- The problem of poverty became more and more concentrated among families headed by people not in the labor force. However, this conclusion depends heavily on the definition of poverty. If one looks at some of the other definitions of poverty mentioned in the chapter introduction, there is much less evidence that working people are less and less likely to experience "poverty."

TRENDS IN POVERTY

Editor's Supplement

As the chapter introduction suggested, analysts use varying measures and definitions of poverty. Many definitions of poverty are proposed, each intended as a refinement of its predecessor.[1] Within each definition, analysts employ slightly different statistical assumptions or statistical sources to produce real estimates of incidence. For political purposes, writers on poverty typically choose to emphasize those measures that best support their conclusions.

It would take volumes to review all these discussions of poverty trends adequately. This supplement has more limited aspirations: first, to present a bare skeleton of estimates, most of them rather widely accepted, suggesting some of the less disputed measures in trends in poverty; and, second, to offset some conventional conclusions about poverty that seem unjustifiably optimistic. The supplement concentrates on three means of measurement: absolute poverty, relative poverty, and relative wealth.

Trends in Absolute Poverty

As described in the chapter introduction, measures of the incidence of absolute poverty count the number of people whose incomes fall below a strictly defined poverty threshold, a dollar measure of the income necessary for minimum subsistence. For the United States, many analysts have accepted the Social Security Administration's definition of poverty, which had reached $5,008 for a family of four in 1974.[2]

Using that definition of poverty, or a rough counterpart, most analysts tend to argue that the United States experienced an enormous reduction in the incidence of poverty over the past fifty years and especially in the more recent post-World War II era. In the 1969 *Economic Report of the President*, the Council of Economic Advisers concluded, "With the general rise in family incomes in the postwar period,

[1] See the bibliography at the end of this chapter for references.

[2] U.S. Bureau of the Census, *Current Population Reports*, Series P-60, No. 93, July 1975.

the incidence of poverty . . . has declined sharply." [3] Although the decline is indisputable, its extent and significance should be very carefully questioned.

First, the evidence about long-run trends in poverty is difficult to interpret. The Social Security Administration's definition of poverty has been applied only since 1959. For estimates of poverty trends before 1959, analysts have resorted to a wide variety of definitions and statistics. The most important differences in long-term estimates of poverty involve a single issue: Should estimates reflect our current definitions of poverty, themselves a function of currently available, institutionally determined commodity baskets, or should they incorporate historical standards of poverty, which are based on the quantity and kind of goods necessary for subsistence in earlier periods? The difference between the two definitions produces profoundly varying historical estimates of the poverty population. For instance, Oscar Ornati estimated that roughly 39 percent of the population in 1929 lived below a "subsistence" level defined by 1960 standards, while only 26 percent would have been considered poor by 1929 standards. I personally prefer estimates based on historical — rather than current — standards of poverty, principally because the variety, availability, and quality of goods necessary for minimum subsistence change radically over time. As the poverty population becomes more urban, for instance, the poor must pay for much more of their food, rather than growing it. And as society becomes more bureaucratic, telephones increasingly become a necessity for everyone, including the poor, in order to negotiate bureaucratic channels.

Table 1 presents a set of historical estimates of absolute poverty that seem reasonable. [4] They depend on historically determined definitions of poverty, and include two separate definitions of poverty, a "subsistence" definition and an "adequacy" definition. In 1960, the "subsistence" standard for a family of four was $2,660, the "adequacy" standard $4,350. The Social Security Administration's definition for 1960 considered roughly $3,000 as the appropriate poverty standard. The two historical standards therefore

[3] *Economic Report of the President,* January 1969 (Washington, D.C.: U.S. Government Printing Office, 1969), p. 153.

[4] For an intelligent summary of a variety of historical estimates and their problems, see Herman Miller, "Changes in the Number and Composition of the Poor," in Margaret S. Gordon, ed., *Poverty in America* (San Francisco: Chandler, 1965).

TABLE 1. Trends in Absolute Poverty, 1929–1960

Year	Below "Minimum Subsistence" Level		Below "Minimum Adequacy" Level	
	Number of Persons (millions)	Percent of Households	*Number of Persons (millions)*	Percent of Households
1929	31.8	26	52.2	43
1935–36	33.9	27	57.3	46
1941	21.6	17	41.5	32
1944	12.1	10	19.2	15
1947	21.3	15	38.1	27
1950	20.1	14	41.8	28
1951	18.9	12	37.4	25
1952	17.8	12	33.2	22
1953	22.7	14	35.7	23
1954	23.0	14	42.7	27
1955	19.9	12	45.3	28
1956	18.1	11	42.4	26
1957	17.7	10	42.9	25
1958	22.7	13	49.0	28
1959	21.3	12	46.8	27
1960	19.9	11	46.1	26

Note: The marked discontinuity in numbers and percentages between 1941 and 1944 and between 1944 and 1947 is due to the combination of the following factors: the table deals with civilian population only; there was a significant change in income distribution during these years; and there was a large upgrading of budget standards between 1944 and 1947 while between 1941 and 1944 budget standards remained relatively unchanged.

Source: Oscar Ornati, *Poverty Amid Affluence* (New York: The Twentieth Century Fund, 1966), p. 158.

bound the SSA definition. Table 1 suggests four important conclusions about trends in absolute poverty defined by historically determined standards, conclusions about which I find relatively little disagreement in the literature:

1. Between 1929 and the end of World War II, the number of Americans living in absolute poverty declined absolutely, although the singular nature of the Depression and war years makes it difficult to pinpoint exactly when those declines occurred.
2. The percentage of families in poverty declined even more sharply during that period, since the population itself grew.
3. Between 1947 and 1960, the number of poor

Americans remained roughly constant, barely dropping by the "subsistence" measure and increasing by the "adequacy" measure.

4. Since the population grew between 1947 and 1960, this relative constancy in numbers of poor reflected a slight decline in the percentage of Americans who were poor. By the "subsistence" standard, the incidence of poverty decreased from 15 percent to 11 percent; by the "adequacy" standard from 28 percent to 26 percent.[5]

After 1960, many agree on the usefulness of applying the official SSA definition, but many differ substantially in interpreting the results of that application. Table 2 summarizes figures on the number of poor, and the percentage of families in poverty. They suggest a substantial decline in absolute poverty, from 22.4 percent to 11.6 percent of the population between 1959 and 1974. Government officials have cited these figures with pride. "This is the key to what happened in the 1960's" as Daniel P. Moynihan, a chief adviser on urban problems in the early 1970s, put it. "Opportunities opened to those equal to them, for the white poor as well as for the black." [6]

As noted in the Editor's Introduction, the SSA definition of absolute poverty, like any other, embodies many arbitrary assumptions. Criticisms of the level of the SSA definition were mentioned in the introduction — for instance, that the definition understates the poverty threshold. More important for the purposes of this supplement, the use of the same definition to measure trends over the past fifteen

TABLE 2.   Trends in Absolute Poverty, 1959–1968

Year	Number of Poor (in thousands)	Percentage of Population
1959	39,490	22.4
1960	39,851	22.2
1961	39,628	21.9
1962	38,625	21.0
1963	36,436	19.5
1964	36,055	19.0
1965	33,185	17.3
1966 [a]	28,510	14.7
1967	27,769	14.2
1968	25,389	12.8
1969 [b]	24,147	12.1
1970	25,420	12.6
1971	25,559	12.5
1972	24,460	11.3
1973	22,973	11.1
1974	24,260	11.6

[a] After 1966, the data rely on a different procedure for processing income data. The new procedures reduced the estimate of poor people in 1966 by about 6.2 percent. In other words, the 1974 estimate of the poor as a percentage of the population might be about 12.6 percent, rather than 11.6 percent, if based on the earlier methods.

[b] After 1969, the data rely on new procedures for collecting income data. It is not clear what effect these changes have had on the estimates of the poverty population.

Source: U.S. Bureau of the Census, *Current Population Reports,* Series P-60, No. 99, July 1975, pp. 17, 18.

years has also been severely criticized as sketching too rosy a picture of the decline in poverty.

Current criticisms focus on two related issues.

First, the SSA definition continues to rely on a calculation assuming that poor families need money at a constant food-costs-to-total-income ratio of one to three.[7] This ratio was derived from a Department of Agriculture study made in 1955. Various strands of evidence suggest that the costs of non-food expenditures for poor families rose during the late 1950s and 1960s. This ought to have meant that a higher income to food ratio should have been used for later dates. By 1960–61, one study already suggested that the ratio should more properly be ap-

[5] This conclusion in particular differs from those based on the current definitions of poverty, which suggest a much more substantial decline in the incidence of poverty. Backcasting the 1960 standard of $3,000 (in constant dollars), for instance, the Council of Economic Advisers estimated a decline in the percentage of families who were poor from 32 percent in 1947 to 21 percent in 1960. As noted in the text, however, this backward application of current standards of poverty ignores the substantially increased costs (in constant dollars) of maintaining minimum subsistence standards over time as a result of technology and migration; large flows of black migration from the rural South to the urban North came between 1947 and 1960, for instance, substantially increasing the constant dollar costs to those blacks of reaching a given standard of living. For CEA estimates, see *Economic Report of the President,* January 1964, p. 57.

[6] Daniel P. Moynihan, *The Politics of a Guaranteed Income* (New York: Random House, 1973), p. 37.

[7] See especially Michael Harrington, "The Betrayal of the Poor," *Atlantic,* January 1970, pp. 71–72, and Martin Rein, "Problems in the Definition and Measurement of Poverty," in Louis Ferman *et al.,* eds., *Poverty in America,* rev. ed. (Ann Arbor: University of Michigan Press, 1968), pp. 123–25.

proximately one to four.[8] During the 1960s themselves, non-food prices rose more rapidly than food prices did.[9] By the late 1960s, at least, it appears that the costs of the "economy food plan" should have been multiplied by a factor of four, not three, in deriving the SSA poverty threshold.

If this were true, it would suggest that the recent SSA poverty definitions should be adjusted upward to reflect this increase in the non-food costs of subsistence. We can provide a rough measure of the significance of this adjustment for 1973. Using the same cost of food in 1973 prices and a one-to-four food-to-income ratio, we compute a weighted 1973 poverty threshold of $6,020 for a family of four. Applying this definition to the 1973 income distribution, we can estimate that approximately 36.0 million Americans suffered absolute poverty in 1973 — not 24.3 million as Table 2 suggests — or roughly 18 percent of the population.[10] Referring both to Tables 1 and 2, we see that the decline in the numbers of poor Americans has been slight. It was essentially these same calculations that led Michael Harrington, writing in 1970, to conclude: "The fact is that society has taken to celebrating paper triumphs over poverty. . . . By using the erroneous assumptions of the Eisenhower fifties, the government abolished the poverty of 12 million Americans who were still poor." [11]

Second, many would argue that the continuing upward drift in the absolute cost of the "real" social necessities of "minimum subsistence" has left the SSA definition far behind. In the preceding selection, Lee Rainwater traces the levels of these "popular conceptions" of poverty thresholds. If we apply these popular conceptions against the income distribution

by family size, we find, as Rainwater notes, virtual constancy in the numbers of Americans who earn incomes below this level. According to these standards, there has been no real decline in the numbers of Americans who are "absolutely" poor.[12]

Trends in Relative Poverty

Two measures of relative poverty are usually applied. One common measure of relative poverty calculates the percentage of total personal income earned by the poorest fifth among all families. Trends in this measure over time represent relatively unbiased estimates of the effect of changes in the income distribution on those at its bottom end.

With this measure, one finds fairly close agreement about historical trends in relative poverty. First, it appears that relative poverty declined slightly between 1929 and 1947, as Table 3 shows. The share of the poorest 40 percent increased from 12.5 per cent to 16.0 per cent of total income. Between 1935–36 and 1947, the share of the poorest fifth barely increased, from 4.1 percent to 5.0 percent. Since World War II, however, relative poverty remained roughly constant in the United States: the share of the poorest fifth fell from 5.0 percent in 1947 to 4.7 percent in 1961, and then rose back to about 5.4 percent in 1974. Table 3 summarizes the shape of the income distribution and the extent of relative poverty between 1929 and 1974, presenting estimates for the shares of aggregate money income among quintiles of families and among the richest 5 percent of families. Table 3 clearly belies a central illusion about the American income distribution, the illusion that it has become much more equal over time as the country has grown more prosperous. Quite simply, it has not.

A second measure gained currency during the late 1960s. Following the initial proposals of Victor Fuchs, many argued that those families earning less than one-half the national median family income suffered relative poverty.[13] Table 4 presents data on

---

[8] Despite the fact, for instance, that the later study documented a decline in the food/income ratio of 5.6 percent during the 1950s. See Alan Haber, "Poverty Budgets: How Much Is Enough," *Poverty and Human Resources Abstracts,* I, No. 3, 1966, p. 6.

[9] For these figures, see the U.S. Bureau of Labor Statistics, "Consumer Price Index," for any recent year.

[10] This estimate derives from the following sources: for the official poverty thresholds by poverty size, see U.S. Bureau of the Census, *Current Population Reports,* Series P-60, No. 98, January 1975, p. 162; and for the 1973 income distribution by family size and for unrelated individuals, see U.S. Bureau of the Census, *Current Population Reports,* Series P-60, No. 97, January 1975, pp. 56 and 110 respectively.

[11] Harrington, "Betrayal," pp. 71–72.

[12] For greater detail, see Lee Rainwater, *What Money Buys: Inequality and the Social Meanings of Income* (New York: Basic Books, 1974).

[13] For the initial proposal, see Victor Fuchs, "Comment on Measuring the Low-Income Population," in Lee Soltow, ed., *Six Papers on the Size Distribution of Wealth and Income* (New York: National Bureau of Economic Research, 1969), pp. 198–202.

TABLE 3.   Percentage Distribution of Aggregate Money Income Among Families 1929–1968

Year	Lowest Fifth	Second Fifth	Third Fifth	Fourth Fifth	Highest Fifth	Top 5%
1929	——	12.5	——	13.8	19.3	54.4	30.0
1935–36	4.1	9.2	14.1	20.9	51.7	26.5
1947 *	5.0	11.0	16.0	21.8	46.1	21.3
1947 *	5.1	11.8	16.7	23.2	43.3	17.5
1948	5.0	12.1	17.2	23.2	42.5	17.1
1949	4.5	11.9	17.3	23.5	42.8	16.9
1950	4.5	11.9	17.4	23.6	42.7	17.3
1951	4.9	12.5	17.6	23.3	41.8	16.9
1952	4.9	12.2	17.1	23.5	42.2	17.7
1953	4.7	12.4	17.8	24.0	41.0	15.8
1954	4.5	12.0	17.6	24.0	41.9	16.4
1955	4.8	12.2	17.7	23.4	41.8	16.8
1956	4.9	12.4	17.9	23.6	41.1	16.4
1957	5.0	12.6	18.1	23.7	40.5	15.8
1958	5.1	12.4	17.8	23.7	41.0	15.8
1959	4.9	12.3	17.9	23.8	41.1	15.9
1960	4.8	12.2	17.8	24.0	41.3	15.9
1961	4.7	11.9	17.5	23.8	42.2	16.6
1962	5.0	12.1	17.6	24.0	41.3	15.7
1963	5.0	12.1	17.7	24.0	41.2	15.8
1964	5.1	12.0	17.7	24.0	41.2	15.9
1965	5.2	12.2	17.8	23.9	40.9	15.5
1966	5.6	12.4	17.8	23.8	40.5	15.6
1967	5.5	12.4	17.9	23.4	40.4	15.2
1968	5.5	12.4	17.7	23.7	40.5	15.6
1969	5.6	12.4	17.7	23.7	40.6	15.6
1970	5.4	12.2	17.6	23.8	40.9	15.6
1971	5.5	12.0	17.6	23.8	41.1	15.7
1972	5.4	11.9	17.5	23.9	41.4	15.9
1973	5.5	11.9	17.5	24.0	41.1	15.5
1974	5.4	12.0	17.6	24.1	41.0	15.3

* The first estimates for 1947 come from Source (a) below; the second come from (b).

Sources: (a) 1920–1947: U.S. Census Bureau, *Historical Statistics of the United States, Colonial Times to 1957.*

(b) 1947–1973: U.S. Bureau of the Census, *Current Population Reports,* Series P-60, No. 97, January 1975, p. 43.

(c) 1974: U.S. Bureau of the Census, *Current Population Reports,* Series P-60, No. 99, July 1975, p. 8.

trends in relative poverty measured by this definition. As with the previous definition, there is clear evidence that relative poverty has remained roughly constant — decreasing slightly during wartime periods like those during the Korean and Vietnam war years, increasing slightly during periods of recession. The illusions of increasing equality suffer another blow.

Trends in Relative Wealth

The distribution of wealth in the United States has always been much less equal than the distribution of income. Trends in the distribution of wealth are difficult to estimate, since data on its distribution are hard to develop.

One recent study sought to make various esti-

TABLE 4. Percentage of Families Receiving Less Than Half the National Median Income, 1947–1974

Year	Percent of Families
1947	18.9
1948	19.1
1949	20.2
1950	20.0
1951	18.9
1952	18.9
1953	19.8
1954	20.9
1955	20.0
1956	19.6
1957	19.7
1958	19.8
1959	20.0
1960	20.3
1961	20.3
1962	19.8
1963	19.9
1964	19.9
1965	20.0
1966	19.5
1967	19.1
1968	18.6
1969	18.7
1970	19.0
1971	19.5
1972	19.7
1973	19.6
1974	19.4

Source: (a) 1947–1965; Victor Fuchs, "Comment on Measuring the Low-Income Population," in Lee Soltow, ed., *Six Papers on the Distribution of Wealth and Income* (New York: National Bureau of Economic Research, 1969), p. 200.

(b) 1966–1973: U.S. Bureau of the Census, *Current Population Reports,* Series P-60, No. 97, January 1975, pp. 25, 30.

(c) 1974: U.S. Bureau of the Census, *Current Population Reports,* Series P-60, No. 99, July 1975, p. 8.

mates of the distribution of wealth consistent with each other over the years. Table 5 presents these estimates of the share of total American wealth controlled by the wealthiest 0.5 per cent of the population. As the authors of this recent study conclude, "the distribution of wealth (1) became significantly more equal in the 1930's and early 1940's, two periods of massive government intervention in the changed since 1945, and (2) has remained essentially unchanged since 1945." [14]

[14] James D. Smith and Stephen D. Franklin, "The Concentration of Personal Wealth, 1922–1969," *American*

TABLE 5. Share of Personal Sector Wealth Held by Top 0.5 Percent of Adults, 1922–1969

Year	% Held by Top 0.5%
1922	29.8
1929	32.4
1933	25.2
1939	28.0
1945	20.9
1949	19.3
1953	22.7
1956	25.0
1958	21.7
1962	21.6
1965	23.7
1969	19.9

Source: 1922–1956: Robert J. Lampman, *The Share of Top Wealth-Holders in National Wealth* (Princeton: National Bureau of Economic Research, 1962), p. 24.

1958–1969: James D. Smith and Stephen D. Franklin, "The Concentration of Personal Wealth, 1922–1969," *American Economic Review,* May 1974, p. 166. (The Smith and Franklin estimates for these years were constructed in order to remain consistent with the Lampman estimates of the earlier years. The Series for 1958–1969 actually understates the degree of concentration in any given year." (*Ibid.,* p. 163).

These data help support conclusions based on other measures of "poverty" above; measured in wealth terms, there is no evidence of recent movements toward increasing equality. Moreover, the principal authors of this study[15] suggest that the figures presented in Table 5 dramatically understate the actual concentration of wealth in this country in recent years. For 1969, for instance, the authors propose a "best estimate" that the wealthiest 0.5 per cent of the population controlled about 25 percent of the country's wealth — or nearly 15 percent higher than the estimates presented in Table 5. Whatever the actual numbers, the data provide little support for the illusion that "people's capitalism" has been approaching.

Economic Review, May 1974, p. 162; the estimates for the years up to 1956 come from the classic study by Robert J. Lampman, *The Share of Top Wealth-Holders in National Wealth* (Princeton: National Bureau of Economic Research, 1962).

[15] Smith and Franklin, "Concentration."

INCOME DISTRIBUTION – CAN ECONOMISTS HELP?

Alice M. Rivlin

This piece is written for orthodox economists by a liberal economist. Rivlin takes seriously the
problem of explaining the shape of the income distribution and doing something about it — something few
orthodox economists did until the late 1960s. She admits that orthodox economics has trouble explaining
many of the facts associated with the income distribution. And she admits that orthodox economists now find
it difficult to provide politically meaningful economic
advice about redistributive policy. Hesitantly, almost
timidly, she expresses the hope that a growing pragma-
tism among economists "may presage . . . some real
albeit incremental, movement in the direction of a more
equal income distribution."

This selection comes from a longer essay presented
as the Ely Lecture to the American Economics Association in December 1974.

Formerly associated with the Brookings Institution,
Alice Rivlin was appointed in 1975 as director of the
new Congressional Budget Office, supervising economic research designed to provide Congress with its
own budgetary expertise.

Why Things Are as They Are

It seems only reasonable that those concerned with
the size distribution of income should ask economists
why they think the distribution is so unequal.[1] Why
do so many have so little while a few have so much?

Economists have made some valiant efforts to answer this question. Vilfredo Pareto even thought he
had discovered a natural law that accounted for the
shape of income distributions in a wide variety of
places in various time periods. Pareto was concerned
with the distribution of total income, but most of the
other theorists who have tackled the problem have
confined their attention to the distribution of earnings, especially full-time male earnings. Indeed, it is
something of a paradox that what economists think
of as "income distribution theory" relates to the dis-

tribution of earnings of fully employed males, while
what they think of as "income distribution policy"
means almost everything else.

Over the years various theorists have offered explanations of the puzzling fact that the abilities of
individuals, whether physical or intellectual, are distributed normally while the earnings distribution is
more nearly normal in the logs. This observation suggested that some multiplicative factor related ability
and earnings; for example, that several different kinds
of abilities determine earnings and that they are multiplicative in their effects, or that individual earnings, initially proportional to some index of ability,
are subject to a series of random proportional shocks.
These theories were intriguing, but devoid of any
policy significance. Indeed, only within the last fifteen years has economics produced a theory — the
human capital theory — that both offers a credible
explanation of the shape of the earnings distribution
and some potentially testable hypotheses about how
one might intervene to change that distribution.

Human capital theory was appealing to scholars
not only because it offered hope of accounting for
the shape of the earnings distribution, but also because it accounted for part of the unexplained variation in earnings among individuals, regions, and sub-
groups in the population.[2] It even answered some
questions that no one had thought needed asking,
like why people tend to get their education when
they are young.

But an even stronger appeal of the human capital
approach was to people with an interest in policy
and a predisposition to the belief that education was
a good thing and ought to be better funded. (Economists tend to fall in this category, not only because
they have invested so much in their own education,
but because they so frequently earn their living educating the young.)

First, of course, the human capital approach provided a rationale for education spending in a growth-
oriented society. The exact calculations were not im-

Source: American Economic Review, LXV, 2, May 1975.
Reprinted with permission of the author and the American Economic Association.

[1] For a good general review of income distribution
theory, see Martin Bronfenbrenner and Jacob Mincer
(Mar. 1970).

[2] See, for example, Gary S. Becker (both references),
Mincer, and Barry R. Chiswick.

portant — no one cared much whether social rates of return on additional education were 5 percent or 15 percent as long as they seemed to be positive. If one was proeducation, one could imagine all manner of external benefits of education — from reduction of crime to more intelligent behavior in the voting booth — that had not been counted in the rates of return. The point was that education could be thought of as an investment and therefore a worthy use of resources, not a wasteful frivolity that consumers wanted only for their own enjoyment or for impressing their neighbors. This basic idea may have done as much as Sputnik to convince legislators of the 1950s and 1960s that increasing education spending (more than was dictated by population increases alone) was in the public interest.

Second, the human capital approach suggested that subsidies for education and training could be used to alter the income distribution in one of two distinct ways: (1) raising the relative position in the income distribution of people whose parents were near the low end; and (2) narrowing income differentials in the coming generation compared with what they would otherwise have been.

It is important to be clear that these are not the same thing. Improving the relative position of some small fraction of the next generation (i.e., their own children) is what motivates parents who scrimp and save to move into a neighborhood where the schools are better or to take a second job to send the kids to college. Parents are not trying to narrow income differentials among the next generation; on the contrary, they think large differences between the incomes of the well educated and the poorly educated are just fine as long as their own kids make it into one of the top groups. The motivation behind the education and training components of the 1960's war on poverty appears to have been similar to that of parents seeking to improve the chances of their kids. The notion was that additional public resources could be concentrated on a fairly small number of young people (or even adult workers) who would otherwise be likely to have low incomes, and that this additional investment would improve the relative position of the recipients. It might, of course, be more efficient to improve their relative position by giving them money, but the education route had more political sex appeal.

Success in this endeavor requires: (1) that the additional resources devoted to the education of the disadvantaged actually do some good, in the sense that the students or trainees actually increase their skills or acquire valuable credentials, and (2) that there not be so many people with the new skills or credentials that the wages they command fall and the income advantage diminishes.

Alternatively, however, the public policy objective might actually be to narrow disparities in the distribution of income among the next generation. Human capital theory suggests that one way to do this — again not necessarily the most efficient way — is to increase the proportion of people attaining higher levels of education and training. Other things being equal, this would increase the competition for jobs with high education or skill requirements and lower the wages those jobs command. At the same time, wages of jobs requiring less skill and training would tend to rise, and disparities in income among education and skill levels would be reduced.

Such allegations are hard to prove, but I suspect that narrowing disparities in income was *not* among the significant motivations for the major expansion in public subsidies for higher education that occurred in the last fifteen years nor for the education and training programs of the war on poverty. The proponents of these programs were focused on giving all young people including the children of the poor a chance to improve their expected income, *not* on reducing inequality per se. They hoped, in fact, that the income differentials between education groups would remain large rather than erode under the impact of the policies. There would then be no losers, only gainers.

One of the minor economic mysteries of the 1960s was that these hopes were not disappointed. Despite substantial increases in high school graduation rates and in the ratio of college to noncollege workers, income differences did not narrow at all. In 1960, for example, men aged 35–44 with four years of college had 1.91 times the median earnings of those with only eight years of schooling; in 1970 the comparable ratio was 1.92 — another one of those "stuck" statistics.[3]

At the time an explanation seemed in order and several have been offered. First, technology may be changing in such a way that the demand for employees with the skills acquired in education is shifting upward at about the same rate as the supply. Second, labor markets may not actually work in the

[3] See U.S. Bureau of the Census, "Educational Attainment," 1963, and "Educational Attainment," 1973.

neoclassical way that human capital theorists have assumed they do. Alternate theories of labor market functioning abound at the moment and several have been used to explain why income differentials among income groups did not narrow in the 1960s. The most drastic explanation simply rejects the human capital theorists' contention that education enhances productivity, and suggests that the only reason that education is correlated with income is that the combination of ability, motivation, and personal habits that it takes to succeed in education happens to be the same combination that it takes to be a productive worker. If one takes this view, then changes in the supply of people with various amounts of education are simply irrelevant to the distribution of earnings and there is no reason to expect one to predict the other.

An intermediate explanation may be that those aspects of education that count in the labor market are not actually being equalized as much as the data on years of schooling would suggest. There may be a basic number of years of schooling that society expects everyone to have and that counts for nothing in the labor market because all but the subnormal have it. Much of the shift in education in recent years can be construed as a shifting upward of the base level, rather than a change in the proportions of workers having significant amounts of education beyond the base level.

Whatever the merits of these hypotheses, more recent data suggest that the decline in the relative earnings of recent college graduates, expected in the 1960's, is actually occurring in the 1970's and that the delay may have been attributable to the fact that such a large fraction of the college graduates of the 1960s flowed into graduate and professional schools and did not hit the labor market immediately (Richard B. Freeman). It is too soon to tell, but if the drop in relative earnings of highly trained people does continue, it will be somewhat harder to use education as a tool for enhancing social mobility. It will be good news, however, for those who see education as a way of narrowing disparities in income.

Even if one accepts human capital theory and conventional views of labor market operation as, so far, the best explanation of the earnings distribution that we have, one cannot make a strong case for relying on educational investment as a primary tool for changing the income distribution. At best the effects of education are slow in appearing, the proportion of the variance in income explained by education is not large, and firm empirical evidence is weak that increased expenditure for education of particular students actually increases their future income. Alternate views of the labor market and alternate explanations of the correlation between income and education — such as the queuing, screening, and dual labor market models — offer even less support for education as a tool for increasing income equality.[4]

What Can We Do About It?

The pay-dirt question, of course, is what policies might change the distribution of income — presumably in the direction of greater equality, since no one is likely to advocate less equality as an explicit objective. How would such policies work? What would they cost?

There has been a major accumulation of useful knowledge in this area in the last ten or fifteen years and economists have good reason to be proud of their contributions. They have put tremendous effort into the study of redistributional policies and have learned a great deal that ought both to improve politicians' abilities to make informed choices and the workability of any programs that are chosen. It is not economists' fault that the real world is so complicated and that much of what has been achieved is an elaborate documentation of the fact that there are no quick and easy solutions to problems that have been around for a long time.

It can be argued, of course, that it is better not to know so much, because knowledge of the complexity of the problem paralyzes action. But the history of the 1960s teaches the opposite lesson: naive hopes and hastily designed programs can produce a disillusionment with public intervention in general that is itself paralyzing.

So let us suppose that there is a new High Wizard in Washington — you may identify him as a President or a Congress or both — who has a landslide election behind him and an interest in fairness and in improving the lot and the future chances of those below the middle of the economic ladder. The Wizard calls his Trusty Economic Adviser (TA) and says: You and your colleagues have been working on this problem for a long time and I want to know what you have learned. What policy choices do we really have? Trusty Adviser, of course, starts by say-

---

[4] See, for example, Kenneth J. Arrow and Lester C. Thurow and Robert E. B. Lucas.

ing that he needs another ten years to work on the problem and a lot more money for research, but the Wizard won't buy that — he wants to know what is known *now*. OK, says TA, but first, tell me what you want to happen. Three things, replies the Wizard. First, I'd like the very poor to be better off — closer to the average. Second, it doesn't seem fair to me that there should be such concentration of income in the hands of the families at the top. And third, I think there ought to be more chance for people at the bottom to move up or at least to see their children move ahead. It's bad when people get stuck at the same level with no hope of improving their position. You want to do all three? asks TA. I'd at least like to make some progress, says the Wizard, but of course I have some constraints. The people who elected me are not socialists or anything. So just tell me what's possible without making the government very much bigger than it is now. What would be done with taxes and government programs? Let's start with education.

Education may be a good thing to spend more resources on, says the TA, and there certainly won't be much upward mobility unless low-income children have access to education. But I have to warn you that increasing education spending is probably a slow and relatively ineffective way to change the income distribution. You could, of course, try spending substantially larger sums on the education of children from families in the lower part of the distribution. You could reach them earlier through pre-school programs; you could buy them more teachers, better facilities, and special "compensatory" programs in elementary and secondary school. All this would make their lives a bit less grim, and in theory this would improve their performance in school and increase their chances of earning more money later on.

Why do you say "in theory"? interjects the Wizard. Because in practice no one knows how to do this. One thing that makes it difficult is that your national government does not control how local schools spend money, but the main problem is that no one knows what to tell the schools to do. Statistical studies do not prove that higher spending for schools is associated with better performance of children — as long as the children's home background is held constant — and evaluations of special new educational programs have not yet shown convincingly that any of them lead to permanent increases in the school performance of low-income children or

any other children. Of course, a bigger research effort on teaching and learning might lead to a breakthrough that would make education spending more effective. Such a breakthrough might help low-income children more than others — the way control of contagious diseases helped the poor more than the rich — but there is also the risk that it might be of most help to those who need it least.

Are you saying, asks the puzzled Wizard, that spending more per child in elementary and secondary school is a waste of money? Not at all, replies TA. I'm just saying that economists cannot prove that the additional spending will raise children's test scores or incomes. But we can't prove that increments in most public expenditures have measurable effects especially on income. Good education is something most people want for themselves and their children. You politicians have to figure out how much they want it and how to distribute it fairly and I'm afraid you aren't going to get much help from economists.

But, says the persistent Wizard, how about encouraging students from low-income families to stay in school longer, especially making it financially possible for them to go to college? We're on firmer ground here, admits TA. Making the college option available to students from all income levels is bound to increase mobility from one generation to the next. If a lot more students go on to higher levels of education, there may be more competition for high status jobs and the distribution of income may even become more equal. Of course, you may have to deal with some disappointed people. Some of those who thought a college education was going to guarantee them a professional or managerial job and a high income may feel they were misled. Also it is my duty as an economist to point out that the education purveyed by our colleges and universities is expensive and if your objectives are to raise the relative income of the poor or to narrow income differentials (not just to facilitate upward mobility in status or occupation) it might be cheaper to do it by taxing higher income people and supplementing the incomes of those who earn less.

Ah yes, says the Wizard, you economists developed something called a negative income tax to solve this problem. Should I try that?

You certainly ought to consider it, replies TA. A lot of economists got excited about the negative income tax in the early 1960s because it seemed to be such a clean, elegant solution to several problems at once. It would put a floor under everyone's income — indeed, the floor could bear some relation to average income, as you suggested — without destroying incentives to work. Combined with reform of the positive tax system, to raise average effective tax rates on high-income people, it could not only raise the share of those at the bottom of the income distribution, but could also reduce the concentration of income among those at the top. In the last decade we economists have done a lot of hard practical work on this general idea. Besides theoretical and statistical studies of the usual sort, we have designed and analyzed actual experiments and have helped lay out detailed plans for turning the government's welfare system into something resembling a negative income tax or having the tax authorities take on these new responsibilities.

That's nice, says the Wizard, a little impatiently, but what have you learned from all of this that will help me decide what to do? I was coming to that, says TA. First, the experiments proved that a negative income tax was not just a crackpot idea; it was actually possible to administer one. Moreover, male family heads did not quit working just because they were getting the payments, although some of their wives did. We still don't know, of course, how the results of a real long-term national program would differ from those of a short-term local experiment. Second, all the work on legislative proposals revealed that it was very difficult and expensive to use a negative income tax both to supplement the wages of low earners and to support families with no earners at all; that it was hard to start a national program when wage levels and public attitudes in various parts of the country were so different; and that a lot of complex tangles have to be straightened out before a negative income tax can be made to mesh with the positive tax system and other existing government activities.

Are you telling me, asks the Wizard, that economists don't favor a negative income tax anymore? No, no, replies TA patiently, lots of them, including economists of very different political persuasions, still think that a negative income tax, plus reform and simplification of the positive tax system, is the best approach to reducing the concentration of income and improving the position of the poor. It's just that we now realize that a negative income tax is no easy panacea, and we are increasingly skeptical of our ability to explain it to politicians and the public and persuade them it is a good idea. Some of us tried that in a recent presidential campaign and it didn't

work out too well. Hence, many of us are leaning to more eclectic solutions.

Tell me what you mean by that, demands the Wizard. Well, a lot of economists used to be purists about redistributing income in cash so that recipients of the benefits could choose freely how to spend them — presumably buying what they needed most. But some of us have realized that the public may be more willing to pay taxes to ensure that everyone has the basic essentials, such as food, housing, and medical care, than to hand over cash to people whose spending priorities may differ from their own (Thurow and James Tobin). So you may be more successful with your redistribution program if it features health insurance and housing assistance, rather than just a negative income tax. Of course, there are problems with this too. If people are eligible for a lot of different benefits, each of which is related to their income, they may in effect be facing very high marginal tax rates on their income. There is also a problem of deciding what form assistance should take. Most economists believe in markets so they usually favor giving the equivalent of a voucher to the consumer and letting him choose among suppliers; but, of course, suppliers like it better when the subsidy goes directly to them.

Actually, if you are serious about your objectives, you might try all these policies at once: education, negative income tax and positive tax reform, plus greater efforts to ensure everyone such essentials as medical care. Is that a recommendation? asks the Wizard. Oh, I don't make recommendations, replies TA, I just tell you what the choices are.

This facetious-sounding conversation comes close to mirroring, as I perceive it, what the TA's have to tell the Wizards right now. Of course, the contributors of advice include only those who hold some hope for change within the system and do not view all government actions as part of a conspiracy of the few to oppress the many. Moreover, at the moment most of the Wizards are not listening.

Clearly, economists have done a lot to make the policy discussion more informed and constructive than it was ten or even five years ago. We may have contributed to the loss of innocence, but we have also accumulated some practical knowledge that can be used to effect change if a political Wizard with a passion for fairness and a will to change the income distribution asks for advice.

Actually, however, Wizards don't ask — they generally have to be persuaded that a problem exists whose solution would be popular, at least with substantial numbers of the electorate, and, more important, that change is possible. Once that happens they may even pick up a half-formed policy proposal and run with it too hard and too fast. Although some economists may bemoan the lack of influence of our breed, my own view is that in the income distribution area the political world grabbed some economic hypotheses — such as human investment as a cure for low earnings or negative income tax as a solution to income inadequacy — before the economists were quite ready to turn them into proposed laws. The result was disillusionment that turned people away from the objectives, rather than causing them to renew their efforts to find solutions. If the new eclecticism among economists means, among other things, a new willingness to work hard on the details and possible limitations of policy proposals, it may presage an end to the enthusiasm-disillusionment cycle of recent years and some real, albeit incremental, movement in the direction of a more equal income distribution.

REFERENCES

K. J. Arrow, "Higher Education as a Filter," *J. of Pub. Econ.*, 1973, 2.

G. S. Becker, *Human Capital and the Personal Distribution of Income: An Analytical Approach*, Woytinsky Lecture No. 1, Ann Arbor 1967.

———, *Human Capital*, Nat. Bur. of Econ. Res., 4th printing, New York 1972.

M. Bronfenbrenner, *Income Distribution Theory*, 2d printing, Chicago 1970.

B. R. Chiswick, *Income Inequality: Regional Analysis within a Human Capital Framework*, Nat. Bur. of Econ. Res., New York 1974.

J. Mincer, "The Distribution of Labor Incomes: A Survey with Special Reference to the Human Capital Approach," *J. of Econ. Lit.*, Mar. 1970, 8, 1–26.

———, *Schooling, Experience, and Earnings*. Nat. Bur. of Econ. Res., New York 1974.

A. Okun, *Equality and Efficiency: The Big Tradeoff*, Washington, forthcoming 1975, ch. 1.

V. Pareto, *Manual of Political Economy*, Clifton 1971, 7, 11–31.

J. Rawls, *A Theory of Justice*, Cambridge, Mass. 1971.

L. C. Thurow, "Cash Versus In-Kind Transfers," *Amer. Econ. Rev. Proc.*, 1974, 64, 190–96.

——— and R. E. B. Lucas, *The American Distribution of Income: A Structural Problem*, U.S. Congress, Joint Econ. Comm., Mar. 17, 1972, Washington 1972.

J. Tobin, "On Limiting the Domain of Inequality," *J. of Law and Econ.*, Oct. 1970, 13.

U.S. Bureau of the Census, *U.S. Census of the Population, 1950*, Special Reports, Part 2, Ch. D, "Marital Status (1953)," Tables 1 and 2, Washington, 4.

———, *U.S. Census of the Population, 1960*, Subject Reports, "Educational Attainment," Final Report PC(2) 5B 1963, Table 6, Washington.

———, *U.S. Census of the Population, 1970*, Subject Reports, "Educational Attainment," Final Report PC(2) 5B 1973, Table 7, Washington.

LOOKING AT POVERTY FROM A RADICAL PERSPECTIVE

Howard M. Wachtel

This article summarizes many of the main points of the radical perspective on poverty. It emphasizes the difference between descriptions of the symptomatic characteristics of poverty — which leads to "blaming the victim" — and analyses of the underlying structural causes of poverty.

Wachtel teaches economics at American University and has written many articles on poverty, the labor market, and the role of the state.

Poverty is a condition of society, not a consequence of individual characteristics.* If poverty is a condition of society, then we must look to societal institutions to discover the cause of poverty rather than to the particular individual characteristics of the poor. The societal institutions which have been of particular importance for western industrialized countries are the institutions of capitalism — markets in labor and capital, social stratification and class, and the state.

The interaction of these institutions of capitalism manifest themselves in a set of attributes and problems that we normally associate with the condition of poverty in society. These *attributes* of poverty, however, are incorrectly viewed as the causes of poverty. For example, income distribution, the living conditions of the poor, education, health, and the personal characteristics of the poor are merely surface manifestations (the superstructure) of a systemically caused problem. It is important to differentiate between these manifestations of poverty — normally called "the poverty problem" — and their underlying causes. We return to this theme later, but

first let us contrast this formulation with the orthodox view of poverty and its causes.

Since the industrial revolution commenced in Great Britain and spread to other western nations, the poor have been blamed for their own poverty. The causes of poverty have been assigned to the characteristics of the individual rather than to societal institutions. In nineteenth century America this was given a crude formulation within the industrializing ideology of individualism. The New Deal provided a temporary break from this tradition. However, this ideology has reappeared in the more sophisticated mid-twentieth century liberalism in which we now reside. Public policy has mirrored these trends in social ideology, starting with the Elizabethan Poor Laws and their American counterparts down to the Great Society's poor laws.

Social science research has mirrored our social ideology. Virtually all of the last and contemporary social science research has concentrated on the characteristics of individuals who are defined as poor by the federal government. Being poor is associated with a set of individual characteristics: age, sex, race, education, marital status, etc. But these are not *causes* of poverty. There have been dozens of studies of the so-called "causes of poverty"; not surprisingly, these studies merely associate the "cause" of poverty with a particular set of individual characteristics. For example, if you are poor and have low levels of education, it does not *necessarily* follow that low levels of education are a cause of poverty since education itself is endogenous to the system. The causes of inequality in education and their impact on incomes must be analyzed by examining social class, the role of the state, and the way in which educational markets function.[1]

There has been essentially no social science research in the last ten years on the question of pov-

Source: Howard M. Wachtel, "Looking at Poverty from a Radical Perspective," from *The Review of Radical Political Economics*, Vol. 3, No. 3, Summer 1971, pp. 1–8. Copyright © 1971 by Union for Radical Political Economics. Reprinted with permission.

* For their help in preparing this paper, I thank: David Gordon, Richard Edwards, James Weaver, Jim Campen, Stephan Michelson, Frank Ackerman, and Dawn Wachtel. Many of the ideas in this paper have grown out of conversations with Mary Stevenson and Barry Bluestone.

[1] See, for instance, Samuel Bowles, "Wage Labor and the Contradictions of Higher Education," *Review of Radical Political Economics*, Spring 1974.

erty which has gone beyond a mere cataloging of the characteristics of the poor.[2] A proper formulation of the problem would start with poverty as a result of the normal functioning of societal institutions in a capitalist economy. Given the existence of poverty as a result of the functioning of societal institutions, the next question is: who is poor? Is poverty randomly distributed across the population with respect to various individual characteristics or is it nonrandomly distributed? Poverty research has demonstrated that the incidence of poverty is *nonrandomly* distributed in America. Blacks, Mexican-Americans, Indians, women, the old, etc., have a higher probability of becoming poor than do individuals without these characteristics. The so-called studies of the "causes" of poverty have simply estimated the differential importance of the individual characteristics associated with the poor. The research has only demonstrated which groups of people are affected most adversely by capitalist institutions.

The orientation of this poverty research has not been accidental, and it reveals some interesting insights into the sociology of knowledge. Since the industrial revolution, the poor have been blamed for their own condition. They have been charged with causing squalor. Hence, the research of the 1960s has been rendered compatible with the prevailing ideology of capitalist countries with only a few minor modifications of the crude formulations of earlier centuries to make the ideology more palatable to a supposedly more enlightened populace. In this context, the research has performed an important stabilizing and obfuscating function; it has received wide acceptance precisely because it has been conveniently supportive of existing social arrangements and our prevailing social ideology.

Theories of Poverty

Examined from a perspective of radical political economics, poverty is the result of the normal functioning of the principal institutions of capitalism — specifically, labor markets, social class divisions and the state.

An individual's class status — his or her relationship to the means of production — provides the

point of departure for an analysis of income inequalities and low incomes in an absolute sense. If an individual possesses both labor and capital, his chances of being poor or in a low income percentile are substantially less than if only labor is possessed. For individuals earning incomes under $10,000, nearly all income comes from labor. However, for individuals earning between $20,000 and $50,000 (in 1966), only slightly more than half comes from labor; while for individuals with incomes between $50,000 and $100,000 only a third comes from labor. And if you are rich — earning in excess of $100,000 — only 15 percent comes from wage and salary earnings while two-thirds comes from capital returns (the balance is composed of "small business" income).[3]

More important than the magnitude of capital income is its unequal distribution in our economy. Were we to redistribute this income, we could alleviate the purely financial aspects of low incomes. A direct transfer of income that would bring every family up to the Bureau of Labor Statistics' "Moderate but Adequate" living standard in 1966 (roughly $9,100) would have required $119 billion.[4] This comes to about 20 percent of total personal income, slightly *less* than the proportion of personal income derived from ownership of capital.

Consequently, any meaningful discussion of the causes of income inequalities or low incomes must start with a discussion of Marx's class categories. The plain fact is that the probabilities of being both a capitalist and poor are slim compared with the opportunities for poverty if labor forms the principal means of acquiring income. And under capitalism, there is no mechanism for sharing the returns from capital — it all goes to the private owners of capital.

The individual's relationship to the means of production is only the starting point in the analysis. The labor market is the next institution of capitalism which must be analyzed to understand the causes of poverty. Given the fact that workers have no capital income, the chances of becoming poor are increased. However, not all workers are poor in any sense of that ambiguous term. This leads us to our next concept in the analysis — *social stratification*. Social stratification refers to the divisions within a social

---

[2] For some of the more sophisticated attempts, see the work reflected in Lester Thurow, *Poverty and Discrimination* (Washington: Brookings Institution, 1969), Chapter 3.

[3] Frank Ackerman *et al.*, "Income Distribution in the United States," *Review of Radical Political Economics*, Summer 1971.

[4] Donald Light, "Income Distribution: The First Stage in the Consideration of Poverty," *Review of Radical Political Economics*, Summer 1971.

class as distinct from the class itself. In this context, the divisions among workers in the labor market lead to social stratification among the class of workers which has had important implications for the cyclical and secular movements in class consciousness.

The functioning of labor markets, interacting with individual characteristics of workers, determines the wage status of any particular individual in stratified labor markets. The labor market causes poverty in several important ways. Contrary to conventional wisdom, nearly every poor person is or has been connected with the labor market in some way. Poor individuals sift into several categories. First, there are enormous members of *working poor* — individuals who work full-time and full year, yet earn less than even the government's parsimonious poverty income. These people earn their poverty. Of all poor families attached to the labor force in 1968, about one-third (1.4 million) were fully employed workers. Of the more than 11 million families with incomes under $5,000 in 1968, nearly *30 percent* were headed by a full-time wage earner. The incidence of the working poor is greater among black poor families and families with female heads. About *22 percent* of all black poor families were headed by an individual working full-time in 1968. And a *third* of all black families with incomes under $5,000 worked full-time. The Department of Labor reports that 10 million workers in 1968 (nearly 20 percent of the private nonsupervisory employees) were earning less than $1.60 per hour — the wage rate that yields a poverty if fully employed.[5]

A second significant proportion of the poor are attached to the labor force but are not employed full-time. Some of these individuals suffer intermittent periods of employment and unemployment, while others work for substantial periods of time and then suffer severe periods of long-term unemployment.

A third significant portion of the poor are handicapped in the labor market as a result of an occupational disability or poor health. However, these occupational disabilites are themselves related to a person's earlier status in the labor force. There are greater occupational hazards and opportunities for poor health in low wage jobs. Low incomes can contribute significantly to poor health, especially in the American markets for health care where enormous incomes or proper health insurance are an absolutely essential precondition for the receipt of medical care. Disabilities are widespread throughout the economy. In 1966, nearly *one-sixth* of the labor force was disabled for a period longer than *six months*. Only 48 percent of the disabled worked at all in 1966, while 12 percent of the employed disabled workers were employed only part-time. As a consequence of disability, many households with disabled heads are poor — about 50 percent.[6]

Thus we see that nearly all of these poverty phenomena are endogenous to the system — they are a consequence of the functioning of labor markets in the economy. This argument can be extended to birth defects as well. There is a growing body of evidence which suggests that many forms of birth defects are related to the nutrition of the mother which, in turn, is related to family income (itself dependent upon the class status of the family and the labor market status of the family wage earners). Even with the evidence as tentative as it is, we can say that the probability of birth defects is greater in families with low incomes and the resultant poor nutritional opportunities.[7]

Another category of the poor are not presently attached to the labor market — the aged, the prison population, members of the military, the fully handicapped, and those on other forms of public assistance (principally women with dependent children). Though these individuals are not presently attached to the labor force, in many instances their low income is determined by past participation in the labor force.

For example, the ability of aged persons to cope with their nonemployed status depends upon their wealth, private pension income, savings and public pension income (social security). Each of these, in turn, is related to the individual's status in the labor force during his working years. The one partial exception is social security which is typically cited as an income equalizing programs where payments are only partially related to contributions. But even in

---

[5] A few try to alert us to the plight of the working poor. See, for instance, Barry Bluestone, "The Tripartite Economy: Labor Markets and the Working Class," *Poverty and Human Resources,* July–August 1970.

[6] The President's Commission on Income Maintenance Programs, *Background Papers* (Washington: U.S. Government Printing Office, 1970), pp. 139–42.

[7] See Leon Eisenberg, "Racism, The Family and Society: A Crisis in Values," *Mental Hygiene,* October 1968, p. 512; and R. L. Naeye, N. M. Diener, W. S. Dellinger, "Urban Poverty Effects on Prenatal Nutrition," *Science,* November 21, 1969, p. 1026.

this case, the redistributive effects of social security are not as great as they have been advertised, as we shall see later in this paper. This point aside, the payments for social security are so small that retired people, dependent solely in this source of income, end up in the government's poverty statistics.

The important elements of income for retirees are all associated with past labor force status and with the class status of the individual. High paid professional and blue-collar jobs typically provide private pension supplements to social security, while low paid jobs do not. Individuals with income from capital can continue to earn income from capital beyond the years they are attached to the labor force, while wage earners cannot. High income workers and owners of capital have vehicles for ensuring their security in old age, while medium and low wage earners have only social and financial insecurity to contemplate in their old age.

To a somewhat lesser extent other poor nonparticipants in the labor force attain their poverty as a result of their (or their spouse's) past association with the labor force. Even for the handicapped, the prisoner, or the welfare mother, the labor market is not a trivial determinant of their poverty status.

If labor force status provides such an important and inclusive explanation of poverty among individuals, the next question is: what determines an individual's status in the labor force? For simplicity, we will take occupation as an imperfect proxy for labor force status, bearing in mind that there is substantial variation in wage status within occupational categories as well as among occupational categories.

In broad terms, an individual's wage is dependent upon four types of variables:

1. Individual characteristics over which the individual exercises no control — age, race, sex, family class status, and region of socialization.
2. Individual characteristics over which the individual exercises degree of control — education, skill level, health, region of employment, and personal motivation.
3. Characteristics of the industry in which the individual is employed — profit rates, technology, product market concentration, relation of the industry to the government, and unionization.
4. Characteristics of the local labor market —

structure of the labor demand, unemployment rate, and rate of growth.[8]

One observation is immediately apparent: There are very few variables that lie within the individual's control that affect his labor market status. Even the individual characteristics placed in category 2 are not completely within the control of the individual. For example, as Coleman, Bowles and others have shown, education is heavily dependent upon the socioeconomic status of the family, an attribute which lies outside of individual control.[9] Health is partially endogenous to the system as discussed above. Geographic mobility depends upon income and wealth.

This classification scheme is a useful starting point, but a more formal analysis is needed to understand the way in which these several categories of variables interact in the labor market to yield low incomes.

The occupation an individual enters is *associated with* individual characteristics: educational quantity and quality, training, skills, and health. These attributes are normally defined as the *human capital* embodied in an individual. The differences in these variables among individuals, which influence their entry into occupations, are dependent upon race, sex, age and class status of the family. Although human capital is *defined* by the set of characteristics associated with the individual, the *determinants* of the differing levels of human capital among individuals are found in the set of individual characteristics that lie outside of the individual's control.[10]

The story does not end here; the wage is not solely dependent upon the occupation of an individual. The fact that one person is a janitor, another a skilled blue-collar worker, tells us something about the wage that each will receive but not everything.

[8] This classification of variables is used to analyze low-wage employment in Howard Wachtel and Charles Betsey, "Employment at Low Wages," *Review of Economics and Statistics,* February 1972.

[9] See Bowles, *op. cit.,* and James S. Coleman *et al., Equality of Educational Opportunity* (Washington: U.S. Government Printing Office, 1966). [Ed: See also the supplement on "Class, Race, and Education" in Chapter 4.]

[10] This model borrows from the work in progress of Barry Bluestone and Mary Stevenson. [This work was subsequently published with C. Murphy as *Low-Wages and the Working Poor* (Ann Arbor: University of Michigan Press, 1974).]

There is a substantial variation in wage within each of those occupations that is dependent upon the industry and the local labor market in which an individual works. There are a variety of industrial and local labor market characteristics which yield different wages for essentially the same occupation and level of human capital. The wage will be higher for a given occupation in an industry with high profit rates, a strong union, highly productive technologies, a high degree of product market concentration, and a favorable status with the government.[11] A similar type of analysis holds for the impact of local market conditions.

In sum, the individual has very little control over his or her labor force status. If you are black, female, have parents with low socioeceonomic status, and dependent upon labor income, there is a high probability that you will have relatively low levels of human capital which will slot you into low-paying jobs, in low wage industries, in low wage labor markets. With this initial placement, the individual is placed in a high risk category, destined to end up poor sometime during her working and nonworking years. She may earn her poverty by working full-time. Or she may suffer either sporadic or long periods of unemployment. Or she may become disabled, thereby reducing her earning power even further. Or when she retires, social security payments will place her in poverty even if she escaped this fate throughout her working years. With little savings, wealth, or a private pension income, the retiree will be poor.

In contrast with this radical political-economic theory of the cause of poverty, both conservative and liberal political-economic theories look for the cause of poverty in terms of some individual characteristic over which the individual is presumed to exercise control. The conservative theory of poverty relies upon markets in labor and capital to provide sufficient mobility either within a generation or between generations to alleviate poverty. If one does not avail himself of the opportunities for social and economic mobility through the market, the individual is to blame. The poor cause their own poverty and its continuation. The individual is presumed to be master of his own destiny, and individualism will lead any deserving person out of poverty. (Of course, the people who posit these notions are the nonpoor.) For the undeserving poor, only institutionalization of one form or another will do.[12] These people are trapped by their lower class life styles which prevent them from escaping poverty. If the poor would only work, there would be no poverty. The Elizabethan poor laws and their American counterpart considered unemployment a crime for which the penalty was work. Gilbert and Sullivan were appropriate when they said "let the penalty fit the crime."

The liberal (and dominant) theory of poverty grants some recognition to institutions as partial causes of poverty as well as social class as an intergenerational transmitter of poverty. But rather than seeking remedies by altering these social institutions or searching for ways to break class rigidities, liberals concentrate their energies on trying to find ways to use government either to ease the burden or assist the individual in adapting to prevailing institutions. The liberals reject exclusive reliance upon the market to foster social mobility and attempt to use government to equalize opportunities within the market or assist individuals in coping with their poverty status by direct income transfers. Nonetheless, their commitment to "alleviating" poverty without systemic changes is as deep as any conservative's. Manifestations of this orientation abound. The entire social work profession, born out of liberal social reform, exists principally to help people cope with a rotten personal or family situation. Hungry people are given nutritional advice rather than access to food, which would involve structural changes in agricultural markets.

The objective of liberal social policy is equal opportunity — a random distribution of poverty — though we are far from that goal today. The radical challenge goes as follows: If you start from a position of inequality and treat everyone equally, you end up with continued inequality. Thus the need to create equality in fact rather than in opportunities.

Manpower programs, educational assistance, and the like are the principal policy results of the contemporary liberal human capital approach to social mobility. All of these programs are based on an essentially *untested* view of the labor market: namely, that personal characteristics over which the individual has control are the major causes of un-

[11] Barry Bluestone, "The Characteristics of Marginal Industries," in this book.

[12] Edward C. Banfield, *The Unheavenly City* (Boston: Little, Brown, 1968).

equal and low incomes. The programs are quite similar in their ideological premise to virtually all the poor laws of capitalist society, starting with the Elizabethan poor laws. Poverty is associated with the absence of work for which work is the cure. The poor are incapable of managing their own affairs so they must be "social worked" to adapt to the rigor and needs of an industrialized and urbanized society.

This view of poverty is wrong in theory, in fact,

and in social values. The causes of poverty lie outside the individual's control in markets for labor and capital and class backgrounds. Equally important, something happens both to the people seeking to help the poor and to the poor themselves when we take as our starting point the premise that people are poor because of some manipulable attribute associated with the person.

THE FUNCTIONS OF POVERTY

Herbert J. Gans

Many argue that poverty is a blight, a sore, a "dysfunction." In fact, as Gans argues, the persistence of poverty serves many important social functions, helping provide a glue which holds the society together as it is currently structured. Gans enumerates many of those functions here. As Gans would agree, however, this analysis can be misleading unless coupled with a more dialectical perspective. The system can never work as smoothly as this overpowering list of functions seems to suggest, for these "functional people" — these serviceable poor — also struggle against their oppression. While the system has functions, it also has important contradictions.

This piece comes from one part of a chapter in Gans's recent book, *More Equality.* An earlier version of this analysis first appeared in the late 1960s.

Gans teaches sociology at Columbia University and has written numerous books and articles on the problems of poverty in Western countries.

The conventional view of American poverty is so dedicated to identifying the dysfunctions of poverty, for both the poor and the nation, that at first glance it seems inconceivable that poverty could be functional for anyone. Of course, the slumlord and the loan shark are widely known to profit from the existence of poverty, but they are popularly viewed

as evil men and their activities are, at least in part, dysfunctional for the poor. What is less often recognized, at least in the conventional wisdom, is that poverty also makes possible the existence or expansion of "respectable" professions and occupations, for example, penology, criminology, social work, and public health. More recently, the poor have provided jobs for professional and paraprofessional "poverty warriors," as well as for journalists and social scientists, this author included, who have supplied the information demanded since public curiosity about the poor developed in the 1960s.

Clearly, then, poverty and the poor serve a number of functions for affluent groups — households, professions, institutions, corporations, and classes, among others — thus contributing to the persistence of these groups, which in turn encourages the persistence of poverty in dialectical fashion. These functions are not, however, necessarily the causes of poverty, for functions are, by definition, effects and not causes, and my analysis is more concerned with showing how the functions of poverty aid in the persistence of nonpoor groups than with determining the causes of the persistence of poverty. I shall describe fifteen sets of such functions — economic, social, cultural, and political — that seem to me most significant.

First, the existence of poverty makes sure that "dirty" work is done. Every economy has such work:

physically dirty or dangerous, temporary, dead-end and underpaid, undignified and menial jobs. In America, poverty functions to provide a low-wage labor pool that is willing — or rather, unable to be unwilling — to perform dirty work at low cost.[1] Indeed, this function is so important that in some Southern states, welfare payments have been cut off during the summer months when the poor are needed to work in the fields. Furthermore, many economic activities involving dirty work depend heavily on the poor; restaurants, hospitals, parts of the garment industry, and industrial agriculture, among others, could not persist in their present form without their independence on the substandard wages they pay their employees.

Second, the poor subsidize, directly and indirectly, many activities that benefit affluent people and institutions.[2] For one thing, they have long supported both the consumption and the investment activities of the private economy by virtue of the low wages they receive. This was openly advocated at the beginning of the Industrial Revolution, when a French writer quoted by T. H. Marshall pointed out that "to assure and maintain the prosperities of our industries, it is necessary that the workers should never acquire wealth."[3] Examples of this kind of subsidization abound even today; for example, poorly paid domestics subsidize the upper middle and upper classes, making life easier for their employers and freeing affluent women for a variety of professional, cultural, civic, or social activities. Conversely, because the rich do not have to subsidize the poor, they can divert a higher proportion of their income to savings and investment and thus fuel economic growth. This in turn can produce higher incomes for everybody, including the poor, although it does not necessarily improve the position of the poor in the socioeconomic hierarchy, since the benefits of economic growth are also distributed unequally.

At the same time, the poor subsidize the governmental economy, because many of them pay a higher percentage of their income in taxes than the rest of the population. Although about a third to a half of the poor get welfare benefits and other transfer payments exceeding what they pay in taxes, those who do not get them are thus subsidizing the many state and local governmental programs that serve more affluent taxpayers.[4] The poor who do not get welfare payments also subsidize federal governmental activities, at least in the sense that they help to provide the taxes that are not paid by the rich who receive tax preferences, such as the reduced tax rate for capital gains.[5] In addition, the poor support medical innovation as patients in teaching and research hospitals and as guinea pigs in medical experiments, reducing the risk for the more affluent patients who alone can afford these innovations once they are incorporated into medical practice.

Third, poverty creates jobs for a number of occupations and professions that serve the poor, or shield the rest of the population from them. As already noted, penology would be minuscule without the poor, as would the police, since the poor provide the majority of their "clients." Other activities that flourish because of the existence of poverty are the numbers game, the sale of heroin and cheap wines and liquors, Pentecostal ministers, faith healers, prostitutes, pawnshops, and the peacetime army, which recruits its enlisted men mainly from among the poor.

Fourth, the poor buy goods that others do not want and thus prolong their economic usefulness, such as day-old bread, fruit, and vegetables that would otherwise have to be thrown out, secondhand clothes, and deteriorating automobiles and buildings. They also provide incomes for doctors, lawyers, teachers, and others who are too old, poorly trained, or incompetent to attract more affluent clients.

In addition, the poor perform a number of social and cultural functions:

Fifth, the poor can be identified and punished as alleged or real deviants in order to uphold the

---

[1] On the economic functions of the poor and of welfare, see Frances F. Piven and Richard A. Cloward, *Regulating the Poor* (New York: Pantheon Books, 1971).

[2] Of course, the poor do not actually subsidize the affluent to use the money saved in this fashion for other purposes. The concept of subsidy used here thus assumes belief in a "just wage."

[3] T. H. Marshall, "Poverty and Inequality," unpublished paper prepared for a project on stratification and poverty of the American Academy of Arts and Sciences, n.d., p. 7.

[4] Joseph A. Pechman, "The Rich, the Poor, and the Taxes They Pay," *The Public Interest,* no. 17 (Fall 1969), pp. 21–44, especially p. 33.

[5] For an estimate of how these tax preferences affect different income groups, see Joseph A. Pechman, and Benjamin A. Okner, "Individual Tax Erosion by Income Classes," paper prepared for the United States Joint Economic Committee, January 14, 1972.

legitimacy of dominant norms.[6] The defenders of the desirability of hard work, thrift, honesty, and monogamy need people who can be accused of being lazy, spendthrift, dishonest, and promiscuous to justify these norms, and as Erikson and others following Durkheim have pointed out, the norms themselves are best legitimated by discovering violations.[7]

Whether the poor actually violate these norms more than affluent people is still open to question. The working poor work harder and longer than high-status jobholders, and poor housewives must do more housework to keep their slum apartments clean than their middle-class peers in standard housing. The proportion of cheaters among welfare recipients is considerably lower than among income-tax payers.[8] Violent crime is higher among the poor, but the affluent commit a variety of white-collar crimes, and several studies of self-reported delinquency have concluded that middle-class youngsters can be as delinquent as poor ones. However, the poor are more likely to be caught when participating in deviant acts, and once caught, more likely to be punished than middle-class transgressors. Moreover, they lack the political and cultural power to correct the stereotypes that affluent people hold of them and thus continue to be thought of as lazy, spendthrift, and so on, whatever the empirical evidence, by those who need living proof that deviance does not pay.[9] The actually or allegedly deviant poor have traditionally been described as undeserving, and in more recent terminology, as culturally deprived or pathological.

Sixth, another group of poor, described as deserv-

ing because they are disabled or suffering from bad luck, provide the rest of the population with different emotional satisfactions; they evoke compassion, pity, and charity, thus allowing those who help them to feel that they are altruistic, moral, and practicing the Judeo-Christian ethic. The deserving poor also enable others to feel fortunate for being spared the deprivations that come with poverty.[10]

Seventh, as a converse of the fifth function described previously, the poor offer affluent people vicarious participation in the uninhibited sexual, alcoholic, and narcotic behavior in which many poor people are alleged to indulge, and which, being freed from the constraints of affluence and respectability, they are often thought to enjoy more than the middle classes. One of the popular beliefs about welfare recipients is that they are on a continuous sex-filled vacation. Although it may be true that the poor are more given to uninhibited behavior, studies by Lee Rainwater and other observers of the lower class indicate that such behavior is as often motivated by despair as by lack of inhibition, and that it results less in pleasure than in a compulsive escape from grim reality.[11] Whether the poor actually have more sex and enjoy it more than affluent people is irrelevant; as long as the latter believe it to be so, they can share in it vicariously and perhaps enviously when instances are reported in fictional and journalistic or sociological and anthropological formats.

Eighth, poverty helps to guarantee the status of those who are not poor. In a stratified society, where social mobility is an especially important goal and class boundaries are fuzzy, people need quite urgently to know where they stand. As a result, the poor function as a reliable and relatively permanent measuring rod for status comparison, particularly for the working class, which must find and maintain status distinctions between itself and the poor, much as the aristocracy must find ways of distinguishing itself from the *nouveaux riches.*

Ninth, the poor also assist in the upward mobil-

---

[6] David Macarov, *Incentives to Work* (San Francisco: Jossey-Bass, Publishers, 1970), pp. 31–3. See also Lee Rainwater, "Neutralizing the Disinherited," in Vernon Allen, ed., *Psychological Factors in Poverty* (Chicago: Markham Pub. Co., 1970), pp. 9–28.

[7] Kai T: Erikson, "Notes on the Sociology of Deviance," in Howard S. Becker, ed., *The Other Side: Perspectives on Deviance* (New York: Free Press, 1964), pp. 9–22.

[8] Most official investigations of welfare cheating have concluded that less than 5 percent of recipients are on the rolls illegally, while it has been estimated that about a third of the population cheats in filing income tax returns.

[9] Although this chapter deals with the functions of poverty for other groups, poverty has often been described as a motivating or character-building device for the poor themselves, and economic conservatives have argued that by generating the incentive to work, poverty encourages the poor to escape poverty.

[10] A psychiatrist has even proposed the fantastic hypothesis that the rich and the poor are engaged in a sadomasochistic relationship, the latter being supported financially by the former so that they can gratify their sadistic needs. Joseph Chernus, "Cities: A Study in Sadomasochism," *Medical Opinion and Review,* May 1967, pp. 104–9.

[11] Lee Rainwater, *Behind Ghetto Walls* (Chicago: Aldine Publishing Co., 1970).

ity of the nonpoor, for as William J. Goode has pointed out, "the privileged . . . try systematically to prevent the talent of the less privileged from being recognized or developed." [12] By being denied educational opportunities or being stereotyped as stupid or unteachable, the poor thus enable others to obtain the better jobs. Also, an unknown number of people have moved themselves or their children up in the socio-economic hierarchy through the incomes earned from the provision of goods and services to the poor, as by becoming policemen and teachers, owning "Mom and Pop" stores, or working in the various rackets that flourish in the slums.

In fact, members of almost every immigrant group have financed their upward mobility by providing retail goods and services, housing, entertainment, gambling, and narcotics to later arrivals in America (or in the city), most recently to blacks, Mexicans, and Puerto Ricans. Other Americans, of both European and native origin, have financed their entry into the upper middle and upper classes by owning or managing the illegal institutions that serve the poor, as well as the legal but not respectable ones, such as slum housing.

Tenth, just as the poor contribute to the economic viability of a number of businesses and professions (see function 3 above), they also add to the social viability of noneconomic groups. For one thing, they help to keep the aristocracy busy, thereby justifying its continued existence. "Society" uses the poor as clients of settlement houses and charity benefits, so as to practice its public-mindedness and thus demonstrate its superiority over the *nouveaux riches* who devote themselves to conspicuous consumption. The poor play a similar function for philanthropic enterprise at other levels of the socio-economic hierarchy, including the mass of middle-class civic organizations and women's clubs engaged in volunteer work and fund-raising in almost every American community. Doing good among the poor has traditionally helped the church to find a method of expressing religious sentiments in action; in recent years, militant church activity among and for the poor has enabled the church to hold on to its more liberal and radical members who might otherwise have dropped out of organized religion altogether.

Eleventh, the poor perform several cultural func-

tions. They have played an unsung role in the creation of "civilization," having supplied the construction labor for many of the monuments often identified as the noblest expressions and examples of civilization, for example, the Egyptian pyramids, Greek temples, and medieval churches.[13] Moreover, they have helped to create a goodly share of the surplus capital that funds the artists and intellectuals who make culture, and particularly "high" culture, possible in the first place.

Twelfth, the "low" culture created for or by the poor is often adopted by the more affluent. The rich collect artifacts from extinct folk cultures (though not only from poor ones), and almost all Americans listen to the jazz, blues, spirituals, and country music which originated among the Southern poor — as well as rock, which was derived from similar sources. The protest of the poor sometimes becomes literature; in 1970, for example, poetry written by ghetto children became popular in sophisticated literary circles. The poor also serve as culture heroes and literary subjects, particularly of course for the Left, though the hobo, cowboy, hipster, and mythical prostitute with a heart of gold have performed this function for a variety of groups.

Finally, the poor carry out a number of important political functions::

Thirteenth, the poor serve as symbolic constituencies and opponents for several political groups. For example, parts of the revolutionary left could not exist without the poor, particularly now that the working class can no longer be perceived as the vanguard of the revolution. Conversely, political groups of conservative bent use the "welfare chiselers" and others who "live off the taxpayer's hard-earned money" to justify their demands for reductions in welfare payments and tax relief. Moreover, the role of the poor in upholding dominant norms (see function 5 above) also has a significant political function. An economy based on the ideology of laissez-faire requires a deprived population that is supposedly unwilling to work; not only does the alleged moral inferiority of the poor reduce the moral pressure on the present political economy to eliminate poverty, but redistributive alternatives can be made to look quite unattractive if those who will benefit from them most can be described as lazy, spendthrift, dishonest, and

[12] William J. Goode, "The Protection of the Inept," *American Sociological Review,* vol. 32 (February 1967), pp. 5–19, quotation at p. 5.

[13] Although this is not a contemporary function of poverty in America, it should be noted that today these monuments serve to attract and gratify American tourists.

promiscuous. Thus, conservatives and classic liberals would find it difficult to justify some of their political beliefs without the poor — but then, so would modern liberals and socialists who seek to eliminate poverty.

Fourteenth, the poor, being powerless, can be made to absorb the economic and political costs of change and growth in American society. During the nineteenth century, they did the backbreaking work that built the cities; today, they are pushed out of their neighborhoods to make room for "progress." Urban renewal projects to hold middle-class taxpayers and stores in the city and expressways to enable suburbanites to commute downtown have typically been located in poor neighborhoods, since no other group will allow itself to be displaced. For much the same reason, urban universities, hospitals, and civic centers also expand into land occupied by the poor. The major costs of the industrialization of agriculture in America have been borne by the poor, who are pushed off the land without recompense, just as in earlier centuries in Europe they bore the brunt of the transformation of agrarian societies into industrial ones. The poor have also paid a large share of the human cost of the growth of American power overseas, for they have provided many of the foot soldiers for Vietnam and other wars.

Fifteenth, the poor have played an important role in shaping the American political process; because they vote and participate less than other groups, the political system has often been free to ignore them. This has not only made American politics more centrist than would otherwise be the case, but it has also added to the stability of the political process for the rest of the population. If the 12 percent of Americans below the federal poverty line participated fully in the political process, they would almost certainly demand better jobs and higher incomes, which would require some income redistribution and would thus generate further political conflict between the haves and the have-nots. Moreover, when the poor do participate, they often provide the Democrats with a captive constituency, for they can rarely support Republicans, lack parties of their own, and thus have no other place to go politically. This in turn has enabled the Democrats to count on their votes, allowing the party to be more responsive to voters who might otherwise switch to the Republicans.

FEDERAL PUBLIC ASSISTANCE PROGRAMS

The President's Commission on Income Maintenance Programs

This brief survey summarizes most of the kinds of criticisms leveled at the recent system of public assistance in this country. Many agreed on the criticisms, leading to formulation of more general income maintenance proposals.

The commission was appointed by President Johnson, although it issued its report under President Nixon. It was chaired by Ben Heineman. The report was called *Poverty Amid Plenty: The American Paradox.*

The Origins of Existing Programs

The existing system of income maintenance programs originated in the Depression of the 1930's when mil-

Source: The President's Commission on Income Maintenance Programs. Washington, D.C.: U.S. Government, 1969.

lions were unemployed. As it has evolved over 35 years, it has been based on a three-pronged strategy of employment, social insurance, and Public Assistance. In our society the great majority of people obtain their income and social status through employment. The strategy thus assumed that monetary and fiscal policies would guarantee sufficient employment at adequate wages for most people, while education and training programs would assist others in developing their employment potential. If there were enough jobs, adequate education would assure young people a place in the labor force. In addition, a family or individual would need protection against changes in the unemployment rate and against the crippling losses of income when the breadwinner retires, dies, or becomes disabled. Finally, Public Assistance would be necessary as a "residual program" to aid those considered unable to enter the labor force.

This analysis gave birth to the Social Security System, which provided partial income replacement to workers and their families upon retirement or death. More recently it has provided income to disabled workers and health insurance for the aged. State Unemployment Insurance programs were encouraged by Federal legislation to keep those who were briefly unemployed from becoming paupers. The Public Assistance system was constructed as an optional State program, jointly financed by all levels of government, to provide aid for particular categories of the poor: the blind, the aged, the disabled, and dependent children and their guardians. Generally, able-bodied male workers were ineligible for assistance under any of these programs. Training and manpower programs have been developed to increase the earning power of employables — but only recently. Other transfer programs have been created for special groups deemed deserving and in need — such as veterans — and a variety of subsidized goods and services — such as housing, health, and food — have been made available to various income groups.

The strategy behind the income maintenance programs of the 1930's was aimed at the lack or loss of employment rather than directly at the problem of poverty. Today, however, the context of poverty and our view of it are vastly different from that era. We have learned to manage the economy so that catastrophic unemployment no longer is a significant threat. While the economic growth of recent decades has multiplied vastly the output of the economy, we have learned that a very substantial portion of poverty and unemployment is chronic, beyond the control of individuals or the influence of rising aggregate demand. The American economy holds the promise of continued economic growth, a growth in which all Americans *could* share, but in which some may not.

In the mid-1960's an effort was made to mount a war on poverty; the main emphasis was placed on programs to expand opportunities. Social service, training, counseling, and related programs grew rapidly. But on the income maintenance front we attempted to fight the war with old weapons. We sought to improve old programs by raising benefits, easing eligibility requirements, and extending coverage. Now every month on the average, 24 million Americans receive Social Security checks, 10 million are helped by Public Assistance, and 1.1 million

draw Unemployment Insurance benefits. But many of the poor remain untouched by any of these programs.

Critique of Current Programs

We have done much to help the poor in our midst. But we have not reassessed our theories or changed our program structure. We have not developed a National program which (1) provides economic security to all those in need, not just those in certain categories, (2) provides aid in an efficient, dignified, consistent fashion, and (3) preserves the incentives that have provided much of our unique growth as a Nation and as individuals. The present income maintenance system has not succeeded for several reasons.

■ *Program Focus on the Unemployable Poor*

One of the major obstacles in the development of an adequate National income maintenance program has been the reluctance to supplement the incomes of employed and *potentially* employable persons. We have assumed that the labor market would provide such persons with sufficient income. But many persons are at least intermittently unemployed due to both cyclical and structural reasons. In 1968, a good year in terms of employment opportunities, monthly unemployment averaged 2.8 million persons. During the course of the year, a total of 11 million persons experienced some period of unemployment.

The major program dealing with the temporarily unemployed but employable person is Unemployment Insurance. However, in 1968 this insurance did not provide compensation for nearly two-thirds of total unemployment because of gaps in coverage and expiration of benefits. Not only are payments limited to a specified length of time, but Unemployment Insurance benefits levels are low. In most States they are below the poverty level for families with children.

The program of Aid to Families with Dependent Children is aimed primarily at families with absent or incapacitated fathers. An Unemployed Father component of this program (AFDC–UF) can provide benefits to households headed by unemployed able-bodied men, but the eligibility requirements are stringent. Only 25 States have chosen to implement this program since its enactment in 1961, and less than 100,000 families are benefiting from it.

In 1966 there were 2.6 million poor families

headed by nonaged able-bodied men.[1] These men, and their 10 million dependents, were excluded from Federally-assisted Public Assistance, although a few received locally-financed General Assistance. That exclusion may have weeded out a few potential malingerers and saved a few dollars in the short run, but in the long run it has produced harmful social and economic effects.

The structure of existing welfare programs encourages the real or feigned breakup of poor families, since unemployed or poorly paid fathers generally must leave home if their families are to become eligible for AFDC benefits. AFDC benefits vary by family size and provide a predictable if low income, while wages are subject to the vagaries of a labor market characterized by diminishing need for low-skilled workers.

The employment potential of AFDC recipients — and hence the rationale for treating them separately from working men and women — is unclear. The employability of incapacitated AFDC fathers obviously is limited. The education and skill levels of many AFDC mothers severely limit their employment opportunities in the current job market, especially since the demand for low-skilled workers has been declining. Partially because of this, provisions were enacted recently which allow AFDC recipients to work and still retain part of their grants.

While many AFDC recipients could increase their total income from this provision, the employed poor and the employable poor are put at a further disadvantage vis-à-vis welfare recipients. These work incentives make increasingly frequent the inequitable situation in which a poor family headed by an employed worker may have significantly lower income than an AFDC family which the male head has deserted.

Thus, the lack of a program which aids working men and women not only creates economic disincentives and encourages family breakup; it also is socially divisive, because it is possible for the incomes of some aid recipients to exceed the incomes of low earners of the same family size. The understandable resentment that has developed against welfare programs sometimes has been interpreted to mean that all efforts to assist the poor are resented by the nonpoor and especially by the marginally nonpoor — who have somehow "made it on their own." But ma-

levolence need not be the source of this resentment. Clearly, resentment can spring from a sense of unfairness because programs reverse positions and ranks in the income distribution for no justifiable reason.

The potential for reversing positions in the income distribution exists under the welfare system because we have largely clung to the notion that employment and receipt of welfare must be mutually exclusive. This view is untenable in a world where many employable persons have potential earnings below assistance payment standards. In developing programs to eliminate poverty, exclusion of the employable and the working poor from categories aided by the Government would be justifiable only if all who worked achieved adequate incomes. This is not the case.

■ Social Insurance Benefits Depend on Earnings

Social insurance programs protect workers and their families against the loss of earnings from some of the hazards of industrial life. Each social insurance plan is built around one of several carefully specified risks that have been identified as potential interruptions to earnings. Old Age, Survivors, and Disability Insurance, Unemployment Insurance, Workmen's Compensation, and other forms of social insurance generally pay benefits based on earning levels before employment is interrupted.

These programs have departed somewhat from strict insurance principles because they also provide benefits to some persons who have contributed little or nothing, and the ratio of benefits to contributions declines as the size of contributions increases. Despite this they do not provide adequate benefit levels for the very poor. They pay adequate benefits only to those with strong labor force attachments and relatively high earnings records. Because eligibility for social insurance is related to employment, it cannot reach effectively those who are poorest — those who have fleeting or irregular labor force ties. Moreover, low wage earners will receive low social insurance benefits. The poor worker will become a poor beneficiary. And the system's coverage is still denied to the most poorly paid workers and to the poor who are not employed at all.

■ Programs Deal Differently with Categories of the Poor

Federal assistance and social insurance programs are designed to provide aid to selected categories of the poor. Programs are designed to cover only cer-

[1] U.S. Department of Health, Education, and Welfare, Office of the Assistant Secretary (Planning and Evaluation), *Poverty Status Tabulations, 1966.*

tain risks or to benefit only certain groups, such as persons who are old, blind, or disabled, veterans, and farmers.

One consequence of this categorical approach has been the exclusion from Public Assistance of many who are unquestionably in need of help. Part of this exclusion has been by design, as in the case of the employed or employable poor. Other exclusions result because it is impossible to design categories which can cover all cases of need, anticipate the wide variety of human circumstances, and change in response to new manifestations of need. So, we exclude many and arbitrarily include others.

Similarly, it has proven impossible to spell out and devise social insurance programs for all the possible risks to earnings. While old age, death, severe disability, and involuntary unemployment are fairly obvious risks, others — such as partial mental and physical disorders — are not so obvious or so easily covered. It is more difficult to design programs for those who cannot work due to psychological disorders than for those with physical disabilities, although they may be equally unemployable.

■ *Public Assistance Programs Are State and Local Programs*

Public Assistance was designed as a residual program for unemployable persons which would wither away in the face of effective employment and social insurance programs. Instead it has grown increasingly larger. Employment has not guaranteed economic security to workers. Social insurance does not cover all workers, or provide adequate benefits to those with inadequate earnings. Thus, the primary burden of providing basic economic security for many Americans has fallen on Public Assistance programs. These responsibilities go far beyond those originally intended for the programs.

Public Assistance provides Federal matching funds for State Public Assistance programs that operate within loose Federal guidelines. The programs exist at State option, and the decision to implement or ignore each of the various cash assistance and service programs is left to the States. The Federal Government can provide financial encouragement for participation, but it cannot compel States to offer these programs.

This local option arrangement has consistently thwarted efforts at National welfare reform. The Federal administering agencies simply have not been able to develop uniform practices and procedures in the 50 States. New administrative guidelines may be issued at the Federal level with comparatively little information on how they will be interpreted and instituted at lower levels of government. The multiplicity of governments involved has made effective policy coordination nearly impossible. The major power of the Department of Health, Education, and Welfare for affecting State programs is the power to withhold funds. But the burden of such action falls primarily on the poor rather than on the State, so such a step never has been taken. Hence, it is not surprising, given resource limitations at the State level, that several of the more significant welfare reforms in recent years have been the result of court decisions rather than National legislation or Federal administrative action.

Clearly, it is somewhat misleading to talk of Public Assistance as a single set of program components, since there are at least 50 State programs with considerable intra-State variations. This multiplicity of programs has several effects: program benefits are generally low; program coverage is restricted; administration is subject to local discretion; and programs differ markedly from State to State in benefit levels, program coverage, and administrative practices.

There are wide differences both in the treatment of needy individuals who fall into the same categories — because of variations in State benefit levels — and in the treatment of needy persons in different categories. Within the Aid to Families with Dependent Children Program, in January 1969 for example, average grants per recipient ranged from $10 per month in Mississippi to $65 in Massachusetts. For Old Age Assistance the range was from $36 per person monthly in Mississippi to $115 in New Hampshire.

Average grants reflect the variety of factors taken into account by States in determining payment levels and eligibility. Among these factors are amounts of income from other sources and family composition. The data below, however, show maximum payments for cases with no other income under the various programs.

Type of Case	Maximum Monthly Payment	
	High State	*Low State*
AFDC (4 persons)	$55	$332
AFDC (6 persons)	88	423
OAA (1 person)	50	182

These are the amounts that would be paid if the assistance unit had no other income. Six States set maximum AFDC payments for families of four persons at a level almost identical with those for single aged women under OAA. One State actually pays the family less. Differences in benefit levels by State far exceed cost-of-living variations. These programs thus act to accentuate rather than to reduce the sharp differences in living standards across this Nation.

The administration of Public Assistance stands in marked contrast to other public programs such as Social Security and the Federal personal income tax. In both of those, administrators have little discretion in dealing with individuals and follow objective rules and procedures. The determination of eligibility, need, and grant levels in Public Assistance on an individual case-by-case basis gives a great deal of discretion to officials at the lowest level. They have the power to interpret regulations broadly or narrowly, to give or withhold assistance. Moral fitness requirements not characteristic of more impersonally run programs often are imposed, and administration of the program may be harsh and stigmatizing. While such individual discretion is not misused always or perhaps even generally, the *potential* for abuse and the way in which this potential affects Assistance clients compels us to emphasize here the types of problems we have encountered in the system.

Some recipients of Public Assistance have not had sufficient access to information regarding the rules which govern them or the benefits to which they are entitled. In many areas, this information has been systematically kept from them as well as from the general public. Thus more stringent interpretations of regulations may be made in times of budgetary pressure. Various forms of coercion may be used to impose conditions on the recipient of aid. Recipients may be harassed by investigators and their private lives may be exposed to governmental scrutiny seldom found in an open society.

■ *Programs Provide Benefits-in-Kind*

There are also governmental programs which supplement low incomes through direct provision of goods and services or subsidies to consumers. The major in-kind programs provide subsidized housing, health care, and food.

Federal housing programs reach low and middle-income families through a number of means, including public housing, mortgage insurance, rent supplements, and urban renewal. The limited funds allotted to these programs have restricted their scale. There are approximately 700,000 units of Public Housing, for example, while the number of families potentially eligible as tenants exceeds seven million. These housing programs requires a basic financial capability if families are to repay loans — despite very low interest rates — or to pay rent — even subsidized, modest, below-market rents. Hence, many of the poorest families are excluded.

Two major programs assist families and individuals in paying for health care. The Medicare program, enacted in 1965, provides medical care benefits to those over age 65. Part A, under which virtually the entire aged population is enrolled, primarily covers hospitalization. Part B, under which approximately 90 percent of the aged are enrolled, costs enrollees $4 per month for coverage of physicians' fees. Because of deductibles, co-insurance formulas, limitations of benefits, and non-coverage of out-of-hospital drugs, Medicare pays only 40 percent of the health care costs of aged persons.

The Medicaid program assists States in furnishing medical care under State Public Assistance programs. Many of the poor are screened out of the program due to stringent income tests and a variety of State-imposed non-income eligibility requirements. Medicaid covers a minority of low-income persons, and generally does not provide fully for even this group.

Two major programs have been developed to subsidize food for low-income families: the Commodity Distribution program, which provides for direct distribution of certain commodities, and the Food Stamp program, which sells stamps at a discount to low-income families, with which they can purchase food at commercial grocery stores. Both programs give low-income households an opportunity to supplement their diet, but neither program is designed to assure a participating household of an adequate diet. Moreover, non-food needs go unmet. These needs often deter persons from buying stamps since outlays for stamps tie up scarce dollars and may leave families unable to meet other needs, such as rent. Commodity programs have been unpopular with recipients because the range of foodstuffs generally is limited and many of the commodities are not very palatable. Both the Commodity and Food Stamp programs are administered by local welfare departments and are governed by State Public Assistance eligibility requirements which exclude many of the poor. These exclusions, plus the reluctance or inability of many persons to buy the Food Stamps, have limited program beneficiaries to only one-fourth of the poor.

In-kind programs are a response to both the limitations of the market — which cannot always make available an adequate supply of housing and health services at low cost — and the inadequate incomes of the poor. Government efforts thus far have not compensated successfully for either of these factors. Programs have been funded at low levels, and responsibility for their implementation and operation often rests with the States. Hence, not all of the poor have been reached. Many of those who have participated have had their range of choice severely limited by earmarked benefits. In-kind programs aimed to supplement low incomes generally do so less well than direct cash payments. Programs which provide a money income supplement allow for greater consumer choice, and permit greater flexibility of family resources than governmental programs which attempt to set family priorities and allocate family resources. Moreover, we feel that the market system is more efficient at distributing goods and services than direct governmental distribution.

THE COVERAGE OF THE TRANSFER SYSTEM

Michael C. Barth, George J. Carcagno, and John L. Palmer

This short selection provides some useful data on the relationship between poverty and the welfare system. It catalogues the numbers and kinds of poor people who benefit from transfer payments. As the authors themselves conclude, "the data reveal that the coverage and benefit levels of the current transfer system are considerably less than adequate in terms of raising poor families above poverty threshholds.

The selection comes from a book reviewing the transfer system and proposals for reforming it, *Toward an Effective Income Support System: Problems, Prospects, and Choices.*

The authors have been associated with the Institute for Research on Poverty at the University of Wisconsin. Barth and Palmer have also served in the planning office of the Department of Health, Education and Welfare in Washington, while Carcagno has also served as a vice-president of Mathematica, Inc., in Princeton, New Jersey, a consulting firm involved in several of the most important experiments in income maintenance during the early 1970s.

Data collected recently by the University of Michigan Survey Research Center allows us to compare the incidence of poverty among family types and to evaluate the adequacy of the transfer system in alleviating poverty.[1]

Table 1 shows the number and percentage of families[2] whose incomes before transfers were below the poverty standard in 1971. Clearly, families with

Source: "The Coverage of the Transfer System," by Michael C. Barth, George J. Carcagno, and John L. Palmer, from *Toward an Effective Income Support System: Problems, Prospects, and Choices* published by The Institute for Research on Poverty, University of Wisconsin, Madison, 1974.

[1] The Michigan Survey Research Center (SRC) data were used in preference to figures published by the Bureau of the Census because the SRC data include the bonus value of food stamps in the definition of income and because they allow greater flexibility in presenting data for different family types. However, utilization of Census data would show patterns of coverage similar to the results presented here.

[2] The term "families" as used here includes childless couples and unrelated individuals. The reader is warned that this definition consistently understates the relative importance of families with children in that each such "family" in poverty represents an average of nearly three individuals in poverty.

TABLE 1.   Number and Percentage Families with Incomes Below Poverty Level Before Transfers, and Number and Percentage Receiving Transfers, 1971

	Total Families in U.S.	Families with Incomes Below Poverty Standard Before Transfers*	Percentage Families Below Poverty Standard Before Transfers*	Pretransfer Poor Families Receiving Transfers	Percentage Pretransfer Poor Families Receiving Transfers	Percentage Pretransfer Poor Families Transfers Not Receiving
	(thousands)	(thousands)		(thousands)		
All families	72,046	15,059	21	12,095	80	20
Families with aged head	12,974	6,977	54	6,773	97	3
Families with non-aged, disabled head	3,567	2,041	57	1,823	89	11
Families with non-aged, nondisabled head without children	24,129	2,356	10	1,009	43	57
Families with non-aged, nondisabled male head with children	26,671	1,659	6	815	49	51
Families with non-aged, nondisabled female head with children	4,706	2,027	43	1,676	83	17

Notes: Families include childless couples and unrelated individuals. Transfers are benefits from both social insurance and welfare programs, including state General Assistance.

* This contrasts with our more usual measurements of poverty which show the percentage of families whose incomes including transfers are below the poverty standard.

a non-aged, nondisabled male head were the least likely of all to have private incomes below the poverty standard while those with heads who were aged, disabled and/or female were the most likely to be in poverty.[3]

What percentage of these pretransfer poor families receive any transfers at all? The answer to this question is important because the higher the percentage that receive some transfers, the more one would look to increasing benefits of existing programs to increase the adequacy of coverage. On the other hand, the lower the percentage, the more one might look to broadening categorical eligibility criteria so more poor would be included. Table 1 shows the percentage of pretransfer poor families in each category who receive some transfers. As might be

expected, given the categorical nature of our current transfer system, some poor families are much more likely to receive transfer benefits than others. Coverage is best for the poor aged, disabled, and female-headed families with children; only 3 percent, 11 percent, and 17 percent, respectively, received no transfer payments. In contrast, 51 percent of poor male-headed families with children and 57 percent of poor families with a non-aged, nondisabled head without children received no transfer benefits.

Within the category of those receiving some transfers, there is considerable variation in the number of programs from which families are receiving benefits. For example, a recent survey by the General Accounting Office (GAO) of selected low-income areas[4] (which probably have greater program cover-

[3] These calculations are based upon the Social Security Administration's poverty index for 1971. The poverty threshold in 1971 for a four-person urban family was then $4,113.

[4] The General Accounting Office (GAO) survey was conducted at the request of the Subcommittee on Fiscal Policy of the Joint Economic Committee of Congress. Information was gathered from the records of 100 pro-

age than other areas) found between 60 percent and 75 percent of recipient households benefited from more than one program and between 10 percent and 25 percent received benefits from five or more programs.[5]

How adequate are the transfers (both social insurance and welfare benefits) received by these families? While several measures of adequacy might be used, these tables show the percentage of each family type whose total incomes were raised above the poverty threshold through the receipt of transfer benefits. Table 2 shows the extent of poverty alleviation by the social insurance programs (principally Social Security and unemployment compensation). Not surprisingly, these programs were most effective in the case of the aged. Table 3 allows us

to look at the antipoverty effectiveness of welfare benefits (the cash and food stamp programs) as distinguished from the social insurance programs. It shows the percentage of pretransfer poor families raised out of poverty by social insurance and welfare programs combined. The percentage of poverty alleviation for the total population of pretransfer poor is 32 percent for social insurance programs alone, and is increased only to 43 percent with welfare programs included. The receipt of welfare benefits removes from poverty only 16 percent of the families who would have been poor in the absence of the welfare system. Looking at specific family types, adding in the benefits from the welfare system has very little impact on decreasing the percentage of aged and childless families in poverty. It has the greatest impact on female-headed families with children. The transfer system as a whole raise 39 percent of the pretransfer poor female-headed families with children above the poverty standard. It should be emphasized that these data are not intended to be all-inclusive: benefits from other programs, such

---

grams including public assistance, Social Security, veterans benefits, unemployment compensation, and many programs offering aid in the form of food, health care, housing, child care, and other basic services.

[5] See the Joint Economic Committee, *Studies in Public Welfare*, Paper Nos. 1 and 6.

TABLE 2. Extent of Poverty Alleviation by Social Insurance Programs

	Pretransfer Families with Income Below Poverty Standard	Pretransfer Poor Families Made Nonpoor by Social Insurance Benefits	Percentage Pretransfer Poor Families Made Nonpoor by Social Insurance Benefits	Families Remaining Poor After Social Insurance Benefits	Percentage Pretransfer Poor Families Remaining Poor After Social Insurance Benefits
	(thousands)	(thousands)		(thousands)	
All families	15,059	4,770	32	10,290	68
Families with aged head	6,977	3,629	52	3,348	48 *
Families with non-aged, disabled head	2,041	401	20	1,640	80 *
Families with non-aged, nondisabled head without children	2,356	416	18	1,940	82
Families with non-aged, nondisabled male head with children	1,659	107	6	1,552	94
Families with non-aged, nondisabled female head with children	2,027	216	11	1,811	89

Notes: Families include childless couples and unrelated individuals. Transfers are benefits from social insurance and welfare programs.

* Pattern will shift due to SSI program.

TABLE 3. Antipoverty Effectiveness of Welfare Benefits (Cash Programs and Food Stamps) and Social Insurance Programs Combined

	Families with Pretransfer Income Below Poverty Standard	Pretransfer Poor Families Made Nonpoor by Receipt of Transfers	Percentage Pretransfer Poor Families Made Nonpoor by Receipt of Transfers	Families Remaining Poor After Transfers	Percentage Pretransfer Poor Families Remaining Poor After Transfers
	(thousands)	(thousands)		(thousands)	
All families	15,059	6,432	43	8,627	57
Families with aged head	6,977	4,006	57	2,971	43 *
Families with non-aged, disabled head	2,041	745	36	1,296	64 *
Families with non-aged, nondisabled head without children	2,356	536	23	1,820	77
Families with non-aged, nondisabled male head with children	1,659	355	21	1,304	79
Families with non-aged, nondisabled female head with children	2,027	790	39	1,237	61

Notes: Families include childless couples and unrelated individuals. Transfers are benefits from both social insurance and welfare programs.

* Pattern will shift due to SSI program.

as subsidized housing and Medicaid, are not included. Furthermore, the data may not be precisely accurate: Recipients may be underreporting their transfer incomes.

In summary, Table 3 shows that the transfer system does not remove all recipient families from poverty. In fact, while 80 percent of all pretransfer poor families received some transfer benefits, only 43 percent were raised above the poverty standard by these transfers. Fifty-seven percent of pretransfer poor families remain poor either because they did not receive transfers at all or because the level of transfers was not sufficient to raise their income above the poverty standard.

Table 4 gives us the breakdown by family type of those families that remain in poverty even after transfers. The percentage of poverty incidence is

[6] The SSI program was not in existence and the recent Social Security increases were not in effect when the data were collected. Starting in 1974, the percentage of posttransfer poverty will be somewhat lower for the aged, blind, and disabled.

highest for families with aged or disabled heads[6] and female-headed families with children. The distribution of individuals living in poor families differs from that of the families themselves, as family sizes vary by family type. Table 5 shows the average family size and the number of individuals living in poor families. More than one-half of all individuals living in poor families live in families with children in which the family head is neither aged nor disabled; the majority of these families have both parents present.

In sum, the data reveal that the coverage and benefit levels of the current transfer system are considerably less than adequate in terms of raising poor families above poverty thresholds. The social insurance programs, although not targeted for this purpose, have had considerably more impact than the welfare programs in reducing poverty. Furthermore, the coverage of the current transfer system is very uneven; childless couples with a non-aged, nondisabled head and families with children headed by a non-aged, nondisabled male are the least likely to receive benefits.

TABLE 4.   Types of Families Remaining Poor After Transfers

	Total Families in U.S.	Families Remaining Poor After Transfers	Percentage Families Remaining Poor After Transfers
	(thousands)	(thousands)	
All families	72,046	8,627	12
Families with aged head	12,974	2,971	23 *
Families with non-aged, disabled head	3,567	1,296	36 *
Families with non-aged, nondisabled head without children	26,671	1,820	8
Families with non-aged, nondisabled male head with children	4,706	1,304	5
Families with non-aged, nondisabled female head with children	24,129	1,237	26

Notes: Families include childless couples and unrelated individuals. Transfers are benefits received from both social insurance and welfare programs.

* Pattern will shift due to SSI program.

TABLE 5:   Average Family Size and Number of Individuals in Families Remaining Poor After Transfers

	Families Remaining Poor After Transfers	Average Number of Individuals in Family	Individuals Living in Poor Families *
	(thousands)		(thousands)
All families	8,627	2.77	23,900
Families with aged head	2,971	1.72	5,100
Families with non-aged, disabled head	1,296	3.06	4,000
Families with non-aged, nondisabled male head without children	1,820	1.31	2,400
Families with non-aged, nondisabled male head with children	1,304	5.48	7,100
Families with non-aged, nondisabled female head with children	1,237	4.30	5,300

Notes: Families include childless couples and unrelated individuals. Transfers are benefits received from both social insurance and welfare programs.

* Rounded to nearest hundred.

THE COMMON FEATURES OF
TRANSFER-BY-TAXATION PLANS

Christopher Green

This selection includes all of Chapter 5 of Green's book, *Negative Taxes and the Poverty Problem*. The selection outlines the variables from which one chooses in devising a scheme for generalized income maintenance. It clarifies the nature of that choice, illustrating the interrelationships among minimum allowance level, tax rate, and total program cost. Green is now a professor of economics at McGill University in Canada.

The different types of transfer-by-taxation plans which were discussed in the preceding chapter are basically similar. Furthermore, all transfer-by-taxation contains three basic variables: (1) a guaranteed minimum level of income that varies with family size or family composition or both; (2) a tax rate or rates applied against a tax base; and (3) a breakeven level of income where the tax liability equals the allowance guarantee. Any two of these variables determine the outcome of the third.

The Basic Variables

The interrelationships of these three variables of transfer-by-taxation can be clarified by simple illustrations. If a family is guaranteed $3,000 and a tax rate of 50 percent is applied against the family's income (excluding the guaranteed allowance), the breakeven level of income will be $6,000 for the family. That is, at $6,000 the family's income tax liability of $3,000 (.50 times $6,000) equals the guaranteed allowance of $3,000. Suppose it was desirable to make the family's breakeven level of income $3,000 and to guarantee $1,500. The transfer-by-taxation tax rate would be 50 percent — or some combination of rates which averaged 50 percent on $3,000 of family income. Finally, a breakeven level of income of $3,000 and a 25 percent tax rate

would mean an income guarantee of $750 (.25 times $3,000). Only if the guarantee is $750 is the net allowance[1] reduced to zero by a flat 25 percent tax rate when income reaches $3,000.[2]

Once it becomes clear that the essentials of transfer-by-taxation can be reduced to three basic variables, it is easy to understand why there is, in principle, no difference between the Rhys-Williams social dividend plan, the Lampman or Friedman negative rates taxation plans, and the Tobin plan which is a cross between the two types. The only important difference between these plans lies in the magnitude of the guaranteed minimum income or allowance, the level of the tax rate, and the breakeven level of income.

All the social dividend schemes described in Chapter IV [of Green's book] begin with the choice of a guaranteed minimum income (which varies with family size) and the choice of an income tax rate which will finance the plan. These choices determine the magnitude of the third variable, the breakeven level of income. In simple algebraic terms:

$$(1) \qquad Y_g/t_s = R$$

where

Y_g = guaranteed minimum income,
t_s = social dividend tax rate,
R = the breakeven level of income — or the level of income at which the net allowance is reduced to zero.

The righthand side of equation 1 may be thought of as the "outcome" of sociopolitical decisions involving the magnitudes on the lefthand side of the equation. This does not mean that in social dividend taxation the breakeven level of income, R, is not a matter of concern for policy makers. It simply means that social dividend taxation is characterized by an

[1] The net allowance is equal to the guaranteed allowance less the tax on the family's income.
[2] Throughout this discussion, "income" refers to the family's excluding the allowance.

emphasis upon a guaranteed minimum income and a tax schedule which reduces the guarantee to zero at some point. This is true of the Tobin plan which differs from social dividend taxation in its more modest proportions and in its failure to specify how the cost is to be financed. It is also true of tax credit schemes which would convert the personal exemptions under present tax systems into a credit financed by a tax on income.

The emphasis in negative rates taxation is somewhat different. A breakeven level of income is first determined. In the case of Friedman's plan, the breakeven level of income is the value of exemptions and deductions allowed a family; for the plan by Lampman it is the family's poverty line. When the breakeven level of income is combined with a negative tax schedule, a guaranteed minimum income level is determined. The equation for negative rates taxation might be written as:

$$(2) \qquad\qquad Rt_n = Y_g,$$

where

t_n = the negative tax rate (or rates)

and R and Y_g are the same as in equation 1 above.

The negative rates taxation equation might also have been written as:

$$(3) \qquad\qquad Y_g/R = t_n.$$

The emphasis here is upon a breakeven level of income and a guaranteed minimum income. The outcome is the negative tax rate. It is difficult to say whether proponents of a negative rates plan, after having chosen a breakeven level of income, put more emphasis on the negative tax rate or upon the guaranteed minimum income. The answer probably is "both equally."

The tax base, at first glance, would seem to differentiate negative rates taxation from social dividend taxation or the Tobin plan. In negative rates taxation, the tax base is the gap between some "standard" — such as the value of personal exemptions and minimum standard deductions (hereafter EX-MSD) allowed a family or the family's poverty line —and the family's income. In social dividend taxation and in the Tobin plan the tax base is the family's income before allowance. In fact, this difference is superficial. For example, it is easy to show that a negative rates plan which fills X percent of a family's poverty income gap is the same as a plan which guarantees a minimum income equal to X percent of the family's poverty line and taxes the family's income at an X percent rate. This is shown in Table 1. The first plan shows what happens under a typical negative rates taxation plan with a negative tax rate of 40 percent applied against the family's poverty income gap or the family's unused EX-MSD. The second resembles a social dividend plan in that it guarantees a family of four $1,200 (40 percent of $3,000) and taxes the family's income at a 40 per-

---

TABLE 1. Allowance for a Family of Four under Two Transfer-by-Taxation Plans

Type of Plan	Family's Income Before Allowance				
	$ 0	$ 500	$1,000	$2,000	$3,000
Negative Rates Taxation:					
(1) Poverty income gap or unusued EX-MSD *	$3,000	$2,500	$2,000	$1,000	$ 0
(2) Allowance based on 40% of poverty gap or unused EX-MSD	1,200	1,000	800	400	0
Social Dividend:					
(3) Basic allowance guarantee of $1,200 (equal to 40% of poverty line)	1,200	1,200	1,200	1,200	1,200
(4) Tax liability with 40% income tax rate	0	200	400	800	1,200
(5) Net allowance, (3) — (4)	1,200	1,000	800	400	0

* Both the Lampman poverty line and the value of exemptions and minimum standard deductions (EX-MSD) are $3,000 for a family of four.

cent rate. Lines 2 and 5 show that both plans, given the family's income, produce identical results.[3]

The Similarity of Transfer-by-Taxation and Other Minimum Income Plans

It is interesting to consider whether any plan which guarantees a minimum income differs, in principle, from a transfer-by-taxation plan. That is, if a plan completely unrelated to the tax system is devised, will it not in substance be the same as a transfer-by-taxation plan? The answer would seem to be yes. If, as an example, some federal bureau were established with the duty of assuring all families a minimum income, it would necessarily have to implement a plan consisting of a "tax rate" and a breakeven level of income in addition to the guaranteed minimum. This is because the bureau would be forced to decide on a rate at which the guaranteed allowances are reduced as a family's income rises. Once this is determined, the rate (or rates) in conjunction with the guarantee will determine a breakeven level of income. In addition, the bureau would have to secure financing in some form, even though the means of financing might be completely unrelated to the plan itself.

Some writers, as noted in Chapter IV, have proposed raising the income of families with income deficiencies to some predetermined level.[4] This effectively means equating the minimum income guaran-

[3] The similarity between negative rates taxation and social dividend taxation is further illustrated by comparing their allowance formulas. . . .

[4] See Edward E. Schwartz, "A Way to End the Means Test," *Social Work*, Vol. 9 (July 1964), pp. 3–12; Robert Theobald, ed., *Free Men and Free Markets* (New York: C. N. Potter, 1963), Appendix, pp. 192–197.

tee and the breakeven level of income. The outcome is a 100 percent tax rate on the negative taxable income of allowance recipients. Sometimes modifications are made in order to mitigate the potential disincentive to work produced by a 100 percent tax on earned income. One modification takes the form of an allowance premium equal to some percentage of the family's earned income.[5] If a family is guaranteed $3,000 and has earnings of $2,000, it might be allowed $1,000 (which would fill the gap) plus some percentage of its earned income. The difficulty with this modification is that it produces what tax experts call a "notch" problem. That is, it is possible for some families, whose before-allowance income made them worse off than some other families, to have a higher after-allowance income than that of previously better-off families. For example, suppose two four-member families have, respectively, $2,000 and $3,200 of income before an allowance is made.[6] Assume the guaranteed minimum income for a four-person family is $3,000. The $3,200 family does not qualify for any allowance because its before-tax income is above the guarantee. The $2,000 family qualifies for a $1,000 allowance plus a premium of, say, 20 percent of its $2,000 earnings. Its after-tax and after-allowance income is $3,400.

This notch problem can be remedied by extending eligibility for receiving an allowance to families whose before-tax income is above the guaranteed minimum income level. Schwartz, one of the proponents of the fill-the-gap approach, has suggested such a remedy. Under his modified plan, outlined in Table 2, as earned income rises, the allowance

[5] This approach is taken by Theobald, *op. cit.*

[6] It is assumed for simplicity that the income of these families is composed solely of earnings.

TABLE 2.   The Schwartz Plan

Earned Income	Tax on Income (percent)	Allowance	Total Income
$ 0– 999	60	$3,000–2,400	$3,000–3,399
1,000–1,999	70	2,399–1,700	3,399–3,699
2,000–2,999	80	1,699– 900	3,899–3,999
3,000–3,999	90	899– 0	3,699–3,899
4,000–4,499	100	0	4,000–4,499

* Guarantees a minimum income of $3,000 to all families.

Source: Edward Schwartz, "A Way to End the Means Test," *Social Work*, Vol. 9 (July 1964), page 9.

falls until a breakeven point is reached at $4,000. This plan, aside from the progressivity in the tax schedule, is equivalent to a social dividend plan with a $3,000 guarantee and a 75 percent tax rate on income below the breakeven level of income.

In sum, simply filling the gap is equivalent to a negative rates plan with a 100 percent negative tax rate. If the disincentive effect of such a plan is to be avoided without producing a notch problem, the fill-the-gap plan resembles a social dividend plan. The same analysis may be applied to public assis-

tance, social insurance, and family allowance programs designed to guarantee a minimum income.[7] Although this study is confined to transfer-by-taxation plans, such a limitation is not necessary except to the extent that it reduces the number of specific plans to be examined.

[7] A recent guaranteed minimum income proposal appears in U.S. Department of Health, Education, and Welfare, Advisory Council on Public Welfare, *Having the Power, We Have the Duty* (June 1966).

REGULATING THE POOR

Frances Fox Piven and Richard A. Cloward

In this selection, the authors argue that public assistance systems serve the important functions of "regulating the poor" — cooling out their protests when times are turbulent and forcing them back into the labor market when low-wage markets get too tight. The argument supports some of the broader radical assertions about the role of the state in the capitalist system and poses serious questions about the liberal faith that we can blithely establish whatever kinds of reforms we might choose.

The selection is based on their pioneering book by the same title, first published in 1971. It comes from a separate excerpt prepared by the authors which appeared in *Trans-action* magazine.

Frances Fox Piven and Richard Cloward have written widely about issues of welfare and public policy. She teaches political science at Boston University, and he teaches at the Columbia University School of Social Work.

Aid to Families with Dependent Children (AFDC) is our major relief program. It has lately become the source of a major public controversy, owing to a large and precipitous expansion of the rolls. Between

Source: From *Regulating the Poor*, by Frances Fox Piven and Richard A. Cloward. Copyright © 1971 by Frances Fox Piven and Richard A. Cloward. Reprinted by permission of Pantheon Books, a Division of Random House, Inc.

1950 and 1960, only 110,000 families were added to the rolls, yielding a rise of 17 percent. In the 1960s, however, the rolls exploded, rising by more than 225 percent. At the beginning of the decade, 745,000 families were receiving aid; by 1970, some 2,500,000 families were on the rolls. Still, this is not the first, the largest or the longest relief explosion. Since the inauguration of relief in Western Europe three centuries ago, the rolls have risen and fallen in response to economic and political forces. An examination of these forces should help to illuminate the meaning of the current explosion, as well as the meaning of current proposals for reform.

Relief arrangements, we will argue, are ancillary to economic arrangements. Their chief function is to regulate labor, and they do that in two general ways. First, when mass unemployment leads to outbreaks of turmoil, relief programs are ordinarily initiated or expanded to absorb and control enough of the unemployed to restore order; then, as turbulence subsides, the relief system contracts, expelling those who are needed to populate the labor market. Relief also performs a labor-regulating function in this shrunken state, however, Some of the aged, the disabled and others who are of no use as workers are left on the relief rolls, and their treatment is so degrading and punitive as to instill in the laboring masses a fear of the fate that awaits them should they relax into beggary and pauperism. To demean and punish those who do not work is to exalt by contrast even the meanest labor at the meanest wages. These regulative functions of relief are made necessary by several strains toward instability inherent in capitalist economics.

Labor and Market Incentives

All human societies compel most of their members to work, to produce the goods and services that sustain the community. All societies also define the work their members must do and the conditions under which they must do it. Sometimes the authority to compel and define is fixed in tradition, sometimes in the bureaucratic agencies of a central government. Capitalism, however, relies primarily upon the mechanisms of a market — the promise of financial rewards or penalties — to motivate men and women to work and to hold them to their occupational tasks.

But the development of capitalism has been marked by periods of cataclysmic change in the market, the main sources being depression and rapid modernization. Depressions mean that the regulatory structure of the market simply collapses; with no demand for labor, there are no monetary rewards to guide and enforce work. By contrast, during periods of rapid modernization — whether the replacement of handicraft by machines, the relocation of factories in relation to new sources of power or new outlets for distribution, or the demise of family subsistence farming as large-scale commercial agriculture spreads — portions of the laboring population may be rendered obsolete or at least temporarily maladjusted. Market incentives do not collapse; they are simply not sufficient to compel people to abandon one way of working and living in favor of another.

In principle, of course, people dislocated by modernization become part of a labor supply to be drawn upon by a changing and expanding labor market. As history shows, however, people do not adapt so readily to drastically altered methods of work and to the new and alien patterns of social life dictated by that work. They may resist leaving their traditional communities and the only life they know. Bred to labor under the discipline of sun and season, however severe that discipline may be, they may resist the discipline of factory and machine, which, though it may be no more severe, may seem so because it is alien. The process of human adjustment to such economic changes has ordinarily entailed generation of mass unemployment, distress and disorganization.

Now, if human beings were invariably given to enduring these travails with equanimity, there would be no governmental relief systems at all. But often they do not, and for reasons that are not difficult to see. The regulation of civil behavior in all societies is intimately dependent on stable occupational arrangements. So long as people are fixed in their work roles, their activities and outlooks are also fixed; they do what they must and think what they must. Each behavior and attitude is shaped by the reward of a good harvest or the penalty of a bad one, by the factory paycheck or the danger of losing it. But mass unemployment breaks that bond, loosening people from the main institution by which they are regulated and controlled.

Moreover, mass unemployment that persists for any length of time diminishes the capacity of other institutions to bind and constrain people. Occupational behaviors and outlooks underpin a way of life and determine familial, communal and cultural patterns. When large numbers of people are suddenly barred from their traditional occupations, the entire network of social control is weakened. There is no harvest or paycheck to enforce work and the sentiments that uphold work; without work, people cannot conform to familial and communal roles; and if the dislocation is widespread, the legitimacy of the social order itself may come to be questioned. The result is usually civil disorder — crime, mass protects, riots — a disorder that may even threaten to overturn existing social and economic arrangements. It is then that relief programs are initiated or expanded.

Western relief systems originated in the mass disturbances that erupted during the long transition from feudalism to capitalism beginning in the sixteenth century. As a result of the declining death rates in the previous century, the population of Europe grew rapidly; as the population grew, so did transiency and beggary. Moreover, distress resulting from population changes, agricultural and other natural disasters, which had characterized life throughout the Middle Ages, was now exacerbated by the vagaries of an evolving market economy, and outbreaks of turbulence among the poor were frequent. To deal with these threats to civil order, many localities legislated severe penalties against vagrancy. Even before the sixteenth century, the magistrates of Basel had defined twenty-five different categories of beggars, together with appropriate punishments for each. But penalties alone did not always deter beginning, especially when economic distress was severe and the numbers affected were large. Consequently, some localities began to augment punishment with provisions for the relief of the vagrant poor.

Civil Disorder and Relief

A French town that initiated such an arrangement early in the sixteenth century was Lyons, which was troubled both by a rapidly growing population and by the economic instability associated with the transition to capitalism. By 1500 Lyons' population had already begun to increase. During the decades that followed, the town became a prosperous commercial and manufacturing center — the home of the European money market and of expanding new trades in textiles, printing and metalworking. As it thrived it attracted people, not only from the surrounding countryside, but even from Italy, Flanders and Germany. All told, the population of Lyons probably doubled between 1500 and 1540.

All this was very well as long as the newcomers could be absorbed by industry. But not all were, with the result that the town came to be plagued by beggars and vagrants. Moreover, prosperity was not continuous: some trades were seasonal and others were periodically troubled by foreign competition. With each economic downturn, large numbers of unemployed workers took to the streets to plead for charity, cluttering the very doorsteps of the better-off classes. Lyons was most vulnerable during periods of bad harvest, when famine not only drove up the cost of bread for urban artisans and journeymen but brought hordes of peasants into the city, where they sometimes paraded through the streets to exhibit their misfortune. In 1529 food riots erupted, with thousands of Lyonnais looting granaries and the homes of the wealthy; in 1530, artisans and journeymen armed themselves and marched through the streets; in 1531, mobs of starving peasants literally overran the town.

Such charity as had previously been given in Lyons was primarily the responsibility of the church or of those of the more prosperous who sought to purchase their salvation through almsgiving. But this method of caring for the needy obviously stimulated rather than discouraged begging and created a public nuisance to the better-off citizens (one account

of the times describes famished peasants so gorging themselves as to die on the very doorsteps where they were fed). Moreover, to leave charity to church or citizen meant that few got aid, and those not necessarily according to their need. The result was that mass disorders periodically erupted.

The increase in disorder led the rulers of Lyons to conclude that the giving of charity should no longer be governed by private whim. In 1534, churchmen, notables and merchants joined together to establish a centralized administration for disbursing aid. All charitable donations were consolidated under a central body, the "Aumone-Generale," whose responsibility was to "nourish the poor forever." A list of the needy was established by a house-to-house survey, and tickets for bread and money were issued according to fixed standards. Indeed, most of the features of modern welfare — from criteria to discriminate the worthy poor from the unworthy, to strict procedures for surveillance of recipients as well as measures for their rehabilitation — were present in Lyons' new relief administration. By the 1550s, about 10 percent of the town's population was receiving relief.

Within two years of the establishment of relief in Lyons, King Francis I ordered each parish in France to register its poor and to provide for the "impotent" out of a fund of contributions. Elsewhere in Europe, other townships began to devise similar systems to deal with the vagrants and mobs cast up by famine, rapid population growth and the transition from feudalism to capitalism.

England also felt these disturbances, and just as it pioneered in developing an intensively capitalist economy, so it was at the forefront in developing nation-wide, public relief arrangements. During the closing years of the fifteenth century, the emergence of the wool industry in England began to transform agricultural life. As sheep raising became more profitable, much land was converted from tillage to pasturage, and large numbers of peasants were displaced by an emerging entrepreneurial gentry which either bought their land or cheated them out of it. The result was great tumult among the peasantry, as the Webbs were to note:

> When the sense of oppression became overwhelming, the popular feeling manifested itself in widespread organized tumults, disturbance and insurrections, from Wat Tyler's rebellion of 1381, and Jack Cade's march on London of 1460, to the

Pilgrimage of Grace in 1536, and Kett's Norfolk rising of 1549 — all of them successfully put down, but sometimes not without great struggle, by the forces which the government could command.

Early in the sixteenth century, the national government moved to try to forestall such disorders. In 1528 the Privy Council, anticipating a fall in foreign sales as a result of the war in Flanders, tried to induce the cloth manufacturers of Suffolk to retain their employees. In 1534, a law passed under Henry VIII attempted to limit the number of sheep in any one holding in order to inhibit the displacement of farmers and agricultural laborers and thus forestall potential disorders. Beginning in the 1550s the Privy Council attempted to regulate the price of grain in poor harvests. But the entrepreneurs of the new market economy were not so readily curbed, so that during this period another method of dealing with labor disorders was evolved.

Early in the sixteenth century, the national government moved to replace parish arrangements for charity with a nation-wide system of relief. In 1531, an act of Parliament decreed that local officials search out and register those of the destitute deemed to be impotent and give them a document authorizing begging. As for those who sought alms without authorization, the penalty was public whipping till the blood ran.

Thereafter, other arrangements for relief were rapidly instituted. An act passed in 1536, during the reign of Henry VIII, required local parishes to take care of their destitute and to establish a procedure for the collection and administration of donations for that purpose by local officials. (In the same year Henry VIII began to expropriate monasteries, helping to assure secular control of charity.) With these developments, the penalties of beggary were made more severe, including an elaborate schedule of branding, enslavement and execution for repeated offenders. Even so, by 1572 beggary was said to have reached alarming proportions, and in that year local responsibility for relief was more fully spelled out by the famous Elizabethan Poor Laws, which established a local tax, known as the poor rate, as the means for financing the care of paupers and required that justices of the peace serve as the overseers of the poor.

After each period of activity, the parish relief machinery tended to lapse into disuse, until bad harvests or depression in manufacturing led again to widespread unemployment and misery, to new outbreaks of disorder, and then to a resuscitation and expansion of relief arrangements. The most illuminating of these episodes, because it bears so much similarity to the present-day relief explosion in the United States, was the expansion of relief during the massive agricultural dislocations of the late eighteenth century.

Most of the English agricultural population had lost its landholdings long before the eighteenth century. In place of the subsistence farming found elsewhere in Europe, a three-tier system of landowners, tenant farmers and agricultural workers had evolved in England. The vast majority of the people were a landless proletariat, hiring out by the year to tenant farmers. The margin of their subsistence, however, was provided by common and waste lands, on which they gathered kindling, grazed animals and hunted game to supplement their meager wages. Moreover, the use of the commons was part of the English villager's birthright, his sense of place and pride. It was the disruption of these arrangements and the ensuring disorder that led to the new expansion of relief.

By the middle of the eighteenth century, an increasing population, advancing urbanization and the growth of manufacturing had greatly expanded markets for agricultural products, mainly for cereals to feed the urban population and for wool to supply the cloth manufacturers. These new markets, together with the introduction of new agricultural methods (such as cross-harrowing), led to large-scale changes in agriculture. To take advantage of rising prices and new techniques, big landowners moved to expand their holdings still further by buying up small farms and, armed with parliamentary Bills of Enclosure, by usurping the common and waste lands which had enabled many small cottagers to survive. Although this process began much earlier, it accelerated rapidly after 1750; by 1850, well over 6 million acres of common land — or about one-quarter of the total arable acreage — had been consolidated into private holdings and turned primarily to grain production. For great numbers of agricultural workers, enclosure meant no land on which to grow subsistence crops to feed their families, no grazing land to produce wool for home spinning and weaving, no fuel to heat their cottages, and new restrictions against hunting. It meant, in short, the loss of a major source of subsistence for the poor.

New markets also stimulated a more businesslike approach to farming. Landowners demanded the maximum rent from tenant farmers, and tenant farmers in turn began to deal with their laborers in terms of cash calculations. Specifically, this meant a shift from a master-servant relationship to an employer-employee relationship, but on the harshest terms. Where laborers had previously worked by the year and frequently lived with the farmer, they were now hired for only as long as they were needed and were then left to fend for themselves. Pressures toward short-term hiring also resulted from the large-scale cultivation of grain crops for market, which called for a seasonal labor force, as opposed to mixed subsistence farming, which required year-round laborers. The use of cash rather than produce as the medium of payment for work, a rapidly spreading practice, encouraged partly by the long-term inflation of grain prices, added to the laborer's hardships. Finally the rapid increase in rural population at a time when the growth of woolen manufacturing continued to provide an incentive to convert land from tillage to pasturage produced a large labor surplus, leaving agricultural workers with no leverage in bargaining for wages with their tenant-farmer employers. The result was widespread unemployment and terrible hardship.

None of these changes took place without resistance from small farmers and laborers who, while they had known hardship before, were now being forced out of a way of life and even out of their villages. Some rioted when Bills of Enclosure were posted; some petitioned the Parliament for their repeal. And when hardship was made more acute by a succession of poor harvests in the 1790s, there were widespread food riots.

Indeed, throughout the late eighteenth and early nineteenth centuries, the English countryside was periodically beseiged by turbulent masses of the displaced rural poor and the towns were racked by Luddism, radicalism, trade-unionism and Chartism, even while the ruling classes worried about what the French Revolution might augur for England. A solution to disorder was needed, and that solution turned out to be relief. The poor relief system — first created in the sixteenth century to control the earlier disturbance caused by population growth and the commercialization of agriculture — now rapidly became a major institution of English life. Between 1760 and 1784, taxes for relief — the poor rate — rose by 60 percent; they doubled by 1801, and rose by 60 percent more in the next decade. By 1818, the poor rate was over six times as high as it had been in 1760. Hobsbawm estimates that up to the 1850s, upwards of 10 percent of the English population were paupers. The relief system, in short, was expanded in order to absorb and regulate the masses of discontended people uprooted from agriculture but not yet incorporated into industry.

Relief arrangements evolved more slowly in the United States, and the first major relief crisis did not occur until the Great Depression. The inauguration of massive relief-giving was not simply a response to widespread economic distress, for millions had remained unemployed for several years without obtaining aid. What finally led the national government to proffer aid was the great surge of political disorder that followed the economic catastrophe, a disorder which eventually led to the convulsive voting shifts of 1932. After the election, the federal government abandoned its posture of aloofness toward the unemployed. Within a matter of months, billions of dollars were flowing to localities, and the relief rolls skyrocketed. By 1935, upwards of 20 million people were on the dole.

The contemporary relief explosion, which began in the early 1960s, has its roots in agricultural modernization. No one would disagree that the rural economy of America, especially in the South, has undergone a profound transformation in recent decades. In 1945, there was one tractor per farm: in 1964 there were two. Mechanization and other technological developments, in turn, stimulated the enlargement of farm holdings. Between 1959 and 1961, one million farms disappeared; the 3 million remaining farms averaged 377 acres in size — 30 percent larger than the average farm ten years earlier. The chief and most obvious effect of these changes was to lessen the need for agricultural labor. In the years between 1950 and 1965 alone, a Presidential Commission on Rural Poverty was to discover, "New machines and new methods increased farm output in the United States by 45 percent, and reduced farm employment by 45 percent." A mere 4 percent of the American labor force now works the land, signalling an extraordinary displacement of people, with accompanying upheaval and suffering. The best summary measure of this dislocation is probably the volume of migration to the cities; over 20 million people, more than 4 million of them black, left the land after 1940.

Nor were all these poor absorbed into the urban

economic system. Blacks were especially vulnerable to unemployment. At the close of the Korean War, the national nonwhite unemployment rate leaped from 4.5 percent in 1953 to 9.9 percent in 1954. By 1958, it had reached 12.6 percent, and it fluctuated between 10 and 13 percent until the escalation of the war in Vietnam after 1964.

These figures pertain only to people unemployed and looking for work. They do not include the sporadically unemployed or those employed at extremely low wages. Combining such additional measures with the official unemployment measure produces a subemployment index. This index was first used in 1966 — well after the economic downturns that characterized the years between the end of the Korean War and the escalation of the war in Vietnam. Were subemployment data available for the "Eisenhower recession" years, especially in the slum-ghettoes of the larger central cities, they would surely show much higher rates than prevailed in 1966. In any event, the figures for 1966 revealed a nonwhite subemployment rate of 21.6 percent compared with a white rate of 7.6 percent.

However, despite the spread of economic deprivation, whether on the land or in the cities, the relief system did not respond. In the entire decade between 1950 and 1960, the national AFDC caseload rose by only 17 percent. Many of the main urban targets of migration showed equally little change: the rolls in New York City moved up by 16 percent, and in Los Angeles by 14 percent. In the South, the rolls did not rise at all.

But in the 1960s, disorder among the black poor erupted on a wide scale, and the welfare rolls erupted as well. The welfare explosion occurred during several years of the greatest domestic disorder since the 1930s—perhaps the greatest in our history. It was concurrent with the turmoil produced by the civil-rights struggle, with widespread and destructive rioting in the cities, and with the formation of a militant grassroots movement of the poor dedicated to combating welfare restrictions. Not least, the welfare rise was also concurrent with the enactment of a series of ghetto-placating federal programs (such as the antipoverty program) which, among other things, hired thousands of poor people, social workers and lawyers who, it subsequently turned out, greatly stimulated people to apply for relief and helped them obtain it. And the welfare explosion, although an urban phenomenon generally, was greatest in just that handful of large metropolitan counties where the political turmoil of the mid- and late 1960s was the most acute.

The magnitude of the welfare rise is worth noting. The national AFDC caseload rose by more than 225 percent in the 1960s. In New York City, the rise was more than 300 percent; the same was so in Los Angeles. Even in the South, where there had been no rise at all in the 1950s, the rolls rose by more than 60 percent. And most significant of all, the bulk of the increase took place after 1965 — that is, after disorder reached a crescendo. More than 80 percent of the national rise in the 1960s occurred in the last five years of the decade. In other words, the welfare rolls expanded, today as at earlier times, only in response to civil disorder.

While muting the more disruptive outbreaks of civil disorder (such as rioting), the mere giving of relief does nothing to reverse the disintegration of lower-class life produced by economic change, a disintegration which leads to rising disorder and rising relief rolls in the first place. Indeed, greatly liberalized relief-giving can further weaken work and family norms. To restore order in a more fundamental sense the society must create the means to reassert its authority. Because the market is unable to control men's behavior a surrogate system of social control must be evolved, at least for a time. Moreover, if the surrogate system is to be consistent with normally dominant patterns, it must restore people to work roles. Thus even though obsolete or unneeded workers are temporarily given direct relief, they are eventually succored only on condition that they work. As these adjustments are made, the functions of relief arrangements may be said to be shifting from regulating disorder to regulating labor.

Restoring Order by Restoring Work

The arrangements, both historical and contemporary, through which relief recipients have been made to work vary, but broadly speaking, there are two main ways: work is provided under public auspices, whether in the recipient's home, in a labor yard, in a workhouse or on a public works project; or work is provided in the private market, whether by contracting or indenturing the poor to private employers, or through subsidies designed to induce employers to hire paupers. And although a relief system may at any time use both of these methods of enforcing work, one or the other usually becomes predominant, depending on the economic conditions that first gave rise to disorder.

Publicly subsidized work tends to be used during business depressions, when the demand for labor in the private market collapses. Conversely, arrangements to channel paupers into the labor market are more likely to be used when rapid changes in markets or technology render a segment of the labor supply temporarily maladapted. In the first case, the relief system augments a shrunken labor market; in the other, its policies and procedures are shaped to overcome the poor fit between labor demand and supply.

Public work is as old as public relief. The municipal relief systems initiated on the Continent in the first quarter of the sixteenth century often included some form of public works. In England, the same statute of 1572 that established taxation as the method for financing poor relief charged the overseers of the poor with putting vagrants to work. Shortly afterwards, in 1576, local officials were directed to acquire a supply of raw goods — wool, hemp, iron — which was to be delivered to the needy for processing in their homes, their dole to be fixed according to "the desert of the work."

The favored method of enforcing work throughout most of the history of relief was the workhouse. In 1723, an act of Parliament permitted the local parishes to establish workhouses and to refuse aid to those poor who would not enter; within ten years, there were said to be about fifty workhouses in the environs of London alone.

The destitute have also sometimes been paid to work in the general community or in their own homes. This method of enforcing work evolved in England during the bitter depression of 1840–1841. As unemployment mounted, the poor in some of the larger cities protested against having to leave their communities to enter workhouses in order to obtain relief, and in any case, in some places the workhouses were already full. As a result, various public spaces were designated as "labor yards" to which the unemployed could come by the day to pick oakum, cut wood, and break stone, for which they were paid in food and clothing. The method was used periodically throughout the second half of the nineteenth century; at times of severe distress, very large numbers of the able-bodied were supported in this way.

The first massive use of public work under relief auspices in the United States occurred during the 1930s when millions of the unemployed were subsidized through the Works Progress Administration. The initial response of the Roosevelt administration was to appropriate billions for direct relief payments. But no one liked direct relief — not the president who called for it, the Congress that legislated it, the administrators who operated it, the people who received it. Direct relief was viewed as a temporary expedient, a way of maintaining a person's body, but not his dignity; a way of keeping the populace from shattering in despair, discontent and disorder, at least for a while, but not of renewing their pride, of bringing back a way of life. For their way of life had been anchored in the discipline of work, and so that discipline had to be restored. The remedy was to abolish direct relief and put the unemployed to work on subsidized projects. These reforms were soon instituted — and with dramatic results. For a brief time, the federal government became the employer of millions of people (although millions of others remained unemployed).

Quite different methods of enforcing work are used when the demand for labor is steady but maladaptions in the labor supply, caused by changes in methods of production, result in unemployment. In such circumstances, relief agencies ordinarily channel paupers directly into the private market. For example, the rapid expansion of English manufacturing during the late eighteenth and early nineteenth centuries produced a commensurately expanded need for factory operatives. But it was no easy matter to get them. Men who had been agricultural laborers, independent craftsmen or workers in domestic industries (i.e., piecework manufacturing in the home) resisted the new discipline. Between 1778 and 1830, there were repeated revolts by laborers in which local tradesmen and farmers often participated. The revolts failed, of course; the new industry moved forward inexorably, taking the more dependent and tractable under its command, with the aid of the relief system.

The burgeoning English textile industry solved its labor problems during the latter part of the eighteenth century by using parish children, some only four or five years old, as factory operatives. Manufacturers negotiated regular bargains with the parish authorities, ordering lots of fifty or more children from the poorhouses. Parish children were an ideal labor source for new manufacturers. The young paupers could be shipped to remote factories, located to take advantage of the streams from which power could be drawn. (With the shift from water power to steam in the nineteenth century, factories began to locate in towns where they could employ local children; with that change, the system of child labor became a system of "free" child labor.) The children were also preferred for their docility and for their light touch at the looms. Moreover, pauper children could be had for a bit of food and a bed, and they provided a very stable labor supply, for they were held fast at their labors by indentures, usually until they were twenty-one.

Sometimes the relief system subsidizes the employment of paupers — especially when their market value is very low — as when the magistrates of Lyons provided subsidies to manufacturers who employed pauper children. In rural England during the late eighteenth century, as more and more of the population was being displaced by the commercialization of agriculture, this method was used on a very large scale. To be sure, a demand for labor was developing in the new manufacturing establishments that would in time absorb many of the uprooted rural poor. But this did not happen all at once: rural displacement and industrial expansion did not proceed at the same pace or in the same areas, and in any case the drastic shift from rural village to factory system took time. During the long interval before people forced off the land were absorbed into manufacturing, many remained in the countryside as virtual vagrants; others migrated to the towns, where they crowded into hovels and cellars, subject to the vicissitudes of rapidly rising and falling markets, their ranks continually enlarged by new rural refugees.

These conditions were not the result of a collapse in the market. Indeed, grain prices rose during the second half of the eighteenth century, and they rose spectacularly during the Revolutionary and Napoleonic wars. Rather, it was the expanding market for agricultural produce which, by stimulating enclosure and business-minded farming methods, led to unemployment and destitution. Meanwhile, population growth, which meant a surplus of laborers, left the workers little opportunity to resist the destruction of their traditional way of life — except by crime, riots and incendiarism. To cope with these disturbances, relief expanded, but in such a way as to absorb and discipline laborers by supporting the faltering labor market with subsidies.

The subsidy system is widely credited to the sheriff and magistrates of Berkshire, who, in a meeting at Speenhamland in 1795, decided on a scheme by which the Poor Law authorities would supplement the wages of underemployed and underpaid agricultural workers according to a published scale. It was a time when exceptional scarcity of food led to riots all over England, sometimes suppressed only by calling out the troops. With this "double panic of famine and revolution," the subsidy scheme spread, especially in counties where large amounts of acreage had been enclosed.

The local parishes implemented the work subsidy system in different ways. Under the "roundsman" arrangement, the parish overseers sent any man who applied for aid from house to house to get work. If he found work, the employer was obliged to feed him and pay a small sum (6 d) per day, with the parish adding another small sum (4 d). Elsewhere, the parish authorities contracted directly with farmers to have paupers work for a given price, with the parish paying the combined wage and relief subsidy directly to the pauper. In still other places, parish authorities parcelled out the unemployed to farmers, who were obliged to pay a set rate or make up the difference in higher taxes. Everywhere, however, the main principle was the same: an underemployed and turbulent populace was being pacified with public allowances, but these allowances were used to restore order by enforcing work, at very low wage levels. Relief, in short, served as a support for a disturbed labor market and as a discipline for a disturbed rural society. As the historians J. L. Hammond and Barbara Hammond were to say, "The meshes of the Poor Law were spread over the entire labour system."

The English Speenhamland plan, while it enjoys a certain notoriety, is by no means unique. The most recent example of a scheme for subsidizing paupers in private employ is the reorganization of American public welfare proposed in the summer of 1969 by President Richard Nixon; the general parallel with the events surrounding Speenhamland is striking. The United States relief rolls expanded in the 1960s to absorb a laboring population made superfluous by agricultural modernization in the South, a population that became turbulent in the wake of forced migration to the cities. As the relief rolls grew to deal with these disturbances, pressure for "reforms" also mounted. Key features of the reform proposals included a national minimum allowance of $1,600 per year for a family of four, coupled with an elaborate system of penalties and incentives to force families to work. In effect, the proposal was intended to support and strengthen a disturbed low-wage labor market by providing what was called in nineteenth century England a "rate in aid of wages."

Enforcing Low Wage Work During Periods of Stability

Even in the absence of cataclysmic change, market incentives may be insufficient to compel all people at all times to do the particular work required of them. Incentives may be too meager and erratic, or people may not be sufficiently socialized to respond to them properly. To be sure, the productivity of a fully developed capitalist economy would allow for wages and profits sufficient to entice most of the population to work; and in a fully developed capitalist society, most people would also be reared to want what the market holds out to them. They would expect, even sanctify, the rewards of the market place and acquiesce in its vagaries.

But no fully developed capitalist society exists. (Even today in the United States, the most advanced capitalist country, certain regions and population groups — such as southern tenant farmers — remain on the periphery of the wage market and are only partially socialized to the ethos of the market.) Capitalism evolved slowly and spread slowly. During most of this evolution, the market provided meager rewards for most workers, and none at all for some. There are still many for whom this is so. And during most of this evolution, large sectors of the laboring classes were not fully socialized to the market ethos. The relief system, we contend, has made an important contribution toward overcoming these persisting weaknesses in the capacity of the market to direct and control men.

Once an economic convulsion subsides and civil order is restored, relief systems are not ordinarily abandoned. The rolls are reduced, to be sure, but the shell of the system usually remains, ostensibly to provide aid to the aged, the disabled and such other unfortunates who are of no use as workers. However, the manner in which these "impotents" have always been treated, in the United States and elsewhere, suggests a purpose quite different from the remediation of their destitution. These residual persons have ordinarily been degraded for lacking economic value, relegated to the foul quarters of the workhouse, with its strict penal regimen and its starvation diet. Once stability was restored, such institutions were typically proclaimed the sole source of aid, and for a reason bearing directly on enforcing work.

Conditions in the workhouse were intended to ensure that no one with any conceivable alternatives would seek public aid. Nor can there by any doubt of that intent. Consider this statement by the Poor Law Commissioners in 1834, for example:

> In to such a house none will enter voluntarily; work, confinement, and discipline will deter the indolent and vicious: and nothing but extreme necessity will induce any to accept the comfort which must be obtained by the surrender of their free agency, and the sacrifice of their accustomed habits and gratifications. *Thus the parish officer, being furnished an unerring test of the necessity of applicants, is relieved from his painful and difficult responsibility: while all have the gratification of knowing that while the necessitous are abundantly relieved, the funds of charity are not wasted by idleness and fraud.*

The method worked. Periods of relief expansion were generally followed by "reform" campaigns to abolish all "outdoor" aid and restrict relief to those who entered the workhouse — as in England in 1722, 1834 and 1871 and in the United States in the 1880s and 1890s — and these campaigns usually resulted in a sharp reduction in the number of applicants seeking aid.

The harsh treatment of those who had no alternative except to fall back upon the parish and accept "the offer of the House" terrorized the impoverished masses in another way as well. It made pariahs of those who could not support themselves; they served as an object lesson, a means of celebrating the virtues of work by the terrible example of their agony. That, too, was a matter of deliberate intent. The workhouse was designed to spur men to contrive ways of supporting themselves by their own industry, to offer themselves to any employer on any terms, rather than suffer the degraded status of pauper.

All of this was evident in the contraction of relief which occurred in the United States at the close of the Great Depression. As political stability returned, emergency relief and work relief programs were reduced and eventually abolished, with many of those cut off being forced into a labor market still glutted with the unemployed. Meanwhile, the Social Security Act had been passed. Widely hailed as a major reform, this measure created our present-day welfare system, with its categorical provisions for the aged, the blind and families with dependent children (as well as, in 1950, the disabled).

The enactment of this "reform" signalled a turn toward a work-enforcing function of relief arrangements. This became especially evident after World War II during the period of greatly accelerated agricultural modernization. Millions were unemployed in agriculture; millions of others migrated to the cities where unemployment in the late 1950s reached extremely high levels. But few families were given assistance. By 1960, only 745,000 families had been admitted to the AFDC rolls. That was to change in the 1960s, as we have already noted, but only in response to the most unprecedented disorder in our history.

That families without jobs or income failed to secure relief during the late 1940s and the 1950s was in part a consequence of restrictive statutes and policies — the exclusion of able-bodied males and, in many places, of so-called employable mothers, together with residence laws, relative responsibility provisions and the like. But it was also — perhaps mainly — a consequence of the persistence of age-old rituals of degradation. AFDC mothers were forced to answer questions about their sexual behavior ("When did you last menstruate?"), open their closets to inspection ("Whose pants are those?"), and permit their children to be interrogated ("Do any men visit your mother?"). Unannounced raids, usually after midnight and without benefit of warrant, in which a recipient's home is searched for signs of "immoral" activities, have also been part of life on AFDC. In Oakland, California, a public welfare caseworker, Bennie Parish, refused to take part in a raid in January 1962 and was dismissed for insubordination. When he sued for reinstatement, the state argued successfully in the lower courts that people taking public assistance waive certain constitutional rights, among them the right to privacy. (The court's position had at least the weight of long tradition, for the withdrawal of civil rights is an old feature of public relief. In England, for example, relief recipients were denied the franchise until 1918, and as late as 1934 the constitutions of fourteen American states deprived recipients of the right to vote or hold office.)

The main target of these rituals is not the recipient who ordinarily is not of much use as a worker, but the able-bodied poor who remain in the labor market. It is for these people that the spectacle of the degraded pauper is intended. For example, scan-

dals exposing welfare "fraud" have diffuse effects, for they reach a wide public — including the people who might otherwise apply for aid but who are deterred because of the invidious connotations of being on welfare. Such a scandal occurred in the District of Columbia in 1961, with the result that half of all AFDC mothers were declared to be ineligible for relief, most of them for allegedly "consorting with men." In the several years immediately before the attack, about 6,500 District of Columbia families had applied for aid annually; during the attack, the figure dropped to 4,400 and it did not rise for more than five years — long after that particular scandal itself had subsided.

In sum, market values and market incentives are weakest at the bottom of the social order. To buttress weak market controls and ensure the availability of marginal labor, an outcast class — the dependent poor — is created by the relief system. This class, whose members are of no productive use, is not treated with indifference, but with contempt. Its degradation at the hands of relief officials serves to celebrate the virtue of all work and deters actual or potential workers from seeking aid.

The Current Call for Reform

From our perspective, a relief explosion is a reform just because a large number of unemployed or underemployed people obtain aid. But from the perspective of most people, a relief explosion is viewed as a "crisis." The contemporary relief explosion in the United States, following a period of unparalleled turbulence in the cities, has thus resulted in a clamor for reform. Similar episodes in the past suggest that pressure for reform signals a shift in emphasis between the major functions of relief arrangements — a shift from regulating disorder to regulating labor.

Pressure for reform stems in part from the fiscal burden imposed on localities when the relief rolls expand. An obvious remedy is for the federal government to simply assume a greater share of the costs, if not the entire cost (at this writing, Congress appears likely to enact such fiscal reform).

However, the much more fundamental problem with which relief reform seeks to cope is the erosion of the work role and the deterioration of the male-headed family. In principle, these problems could be dealt with by economic policies leading to full employment at decent wages, but there is little political support for that approach. Instead, the historic approach to relief explosions is being invoked, which is to restore work through the relief system. Various proposals have been advanced: some would force recipients to report regularly to employment offices; others would provide a system of wage subsidies conditional on the recipient's taking on a job at any wage (including those below the federal minimum wage); still others would inaugurate a straightforward program of public works projects.

We are opposed to any type of reform intended to promote work through the relief system rather than through the reform of economic policies. When similar relief reforms were introduced in the past, they presaged the eventual expulsion of large numbers of people from the rolls, leaving them to fend for themselves in a labor market where there was too little work and thus subjecting them once again to severe economic exploitation. The reason that this happens is more than a little ironic.

The irony is this: when relief is used to enforce work, it tends to stabilize lower-class occupational, familial and communal life (unlike direct relief, which merely mutes the worst outbreaks of discontent). By doing so, it diminishes the proclivities toward disruptive behavior which give rise to the expansion of relief in the first place. Once order is

restored in this far more profound sense, relief-giving can be virtually abolished as it has been so often in the past. And there is always pressure to abolish large-scale work relief, for it strains against the market ethos and interferes with the untrammeled operation of the market place. The point is not just that when a relief concession is offered up, peace and order reign; it is, rather, that when peace and order reign, the relief concession is withdrawn.

The restoration of work through the relief system, in other words, makes possible the eventual return to the most restrictive phase in the cycle of relief-giving. What begins as a great expansion of direct relief, and then turns into some form of work relief, ends finally with a sharp contraction of the rolls. Advocates of relief reform may argue that their reforms will be long-lasting, that the restrictive phase in the cycle will not be reached, but past experience suggests otherwise.

Therefore, in the absence of economic reforms leading to full employment at decent wages, we take the position that the explosion of the rolls is the true relief reform, that it should be defended, and that it should be expanded. Even now, hundreds of thousands of impoverished families remain who are eligible for assistance but who receive no aid at all.

TAXATION OF THE POOR AND THE DISTRIBUTION OF INCOME

David M. Gordon

This selection summarizes the general radical critique of prevailing notions about the tax system and its justifications. It argues that conventional theories of taxes do not take account of the real roles of the government. Having made that critique, it reviews the more comprehensive radical analysis of the state and its relationship to the distribution of income.

Source: American Economic Review, LXII, 2, May 1972. Reprinted with permission of the author and the American Economic Association.

The author teaches economics at the New School for Social Research in New York City.

That man is poor who consumes all of his earnings. Rich is the man who consumes only a fraction. In Italy, for no clear reason, consumer goods are taxed to the last cent. But the income tax is a real joke.

I have been told that the economics textbooks call this system of taxation "painless." Painless means that the rich manage to have the poor pay the taxes without the poor noticing it.

— *The Schoolboys of Barbiana.*

American economists have been exhibiting a growing concern about taxation of the poor. Their criticisms have most frequently focused on the effective lack of progressivity in our tax-and-transfer systems. Unfortunately, much of this recent discussion has been plagued by a pervasive confusion about normative issues. No matter how sophisticated our empirical measures of the incidence of government taxes, transfers, and expenditures, we must still be able to evaluate the system's performance. How "progressive" is progressive enough? Should tax systems bear a full and final responsibility for effecting distributional objectives? Economists have been finding fewer and fewer answers about which they could even imagine agreement.

This confusion has largely stemmed, I would argue, from the inadequacy and irrelevance of traditional normative theories of tax incidence. I would join Joseph Pechman in his assessment: "The critical need at this stage is to reevaluate the entire theory of incidence. . . ." In this paper, I try to suggest some initial directions for that process of reconsideration. The first section summarizes the most important failures of traditional normative incidence theory. The second section suggests an alternative view of the nature of the state and taxation in a capitalist economy, drawing on a radical political economic perspective.

A Critique of Traditional Incidence Theory

Most recent economic approaches to the normative theory of tax incidence have dropped the "scientific" trappings of earlier discussions. Many economists now suggest that plain and simple normative preferences about the government's aggregate distributive impact constitute the only valid bases for opinions about the differential burdens of taxation. Three critical assumptions provide an underpinning for most expressions of normative preference about tax incidence. While space limitations preclude a full and rigorous critique of each, a prolegomenon to that critique can be sketched in relatively simple terms.

First, following Richard Musgrave's classic formulation of "a multiple theory of the public household," most economists suggest an analytic separation of the *redistributive* functions of the state from its *allocative* and *stabilizing* functions in order to isolate two alternative justifications for progressive taxation. On the one hand, when users' charges seem inappropriate or impractical, expenditures serving allocative and stabilizing functions should be financed through progressive taxes simply because, as Otto Eckstein states with confidence, "we favor progressive taxes . . ." at this point in our history. On the other hand, society may feel that the government should make some adjustments in the market distribution of income through the policies of the Distribution Branch. Economists usually assume, *ceteris paribus,* that the government ought to dampen market inequalities through taxes and transfers. This second source of preference for progressive taxes reflects what Stephan Michelson has called "the theoretical view of the benevolent exogenous redistributive state."

I would argue, instead, that the distributive, allocative, and stabilizing functions of the state are inextricably intertwined. Any analyses which begin with their presumptive separation disregard the realities of politics and economics in this country. One brief example, focusing directly on the poor, helps illustrate the nature of the fundamental interconnections.

Many of the most important functions of the Distribution and Stabilization Branches are obviously interdependent. Public assistance constitutes the principal mode of government transfer to the non-aged poor in the United States, but its distributive functions are probably not what they seem. Frances Fox Piven and Richard A. Cloward have recently presented a strong case to support the general cyclical hypothesis about public assistance that, as they write, "relief arangements are initiated or expanded . . . to mute civil disorder, and [then abolished or contracted] to reinforce work norms." At the same time, the Stabilization Branch has become increasingly important over the years as it has sought, through alternative tools, to cope with and temper some of the same problems of economic instability. The policies of the two branches can therefore be seen as *functional complements,* for they serve some of the same political economic objectives. The government can choose some combination of both kinds of policies to perform the same functions.

The second critical orthodox assumption concerns the determinants of labor incomes. Economists generally assume, no matter how much they may relax classical or neoclassical axioms about market mechanisms, that the variation in individual market earnings roughly corresponds to the variation of individual marginal productivities and that, in the Paretian sense, the market distribution of income from labor reflects a (relatively) efficient equilibrium solution. As a result, they believe that public taxation policies, justified for whatever purposes, should involve, as Musgrave writes, "a minimum interference in the allocation of resources as determined by the pricing system." This perspective places a strong normative emphasis on the preservation of the ordinal ranking of individual labor incomes as one moves from the market to the post-tax-and-transfer distribution.

This second assumption seems essentially archaic. As Lester Thurow has written: "There is practically no direct information on whether or not labor is paid its marginal product. Economists take it as an article of faith. . . ." A contrasting view of income determination and distribution would suggest that the variation of individual market incomes corresponds, at the first approximation, to variations in individual access to market power, status, and hierarchy — that individual "productivities" *and* incomes both flow from the market positions which individuals are able to gain as a result of their nominal, rather than productive, characteristics.

The processes which distribute individuals among those points of access involve private and public political economic power, and I have not yet seen a convincing argument that the ordinal ranking of individual incomes which results from inequalities in such power are either efficient or legitimate. While one cannot yet describe those political economic processes comprehensively, a recognition of their determinant importance seems at least to undermine the validity or relevance of the traditional normative assumption that initial ordinal rankings ought in all circumstances to be preserved.

Third, economists have conventionally ignored the extent to which, as Michelson writes, "the process by which people receive money income . . . is not independent of ordinary government action." As far as I can tell from my knowledge of the literature, this assumption has never been supported by any empirical evidence that the differential distributive impact of government expenditures on initial factor earnings is sufficiently insignificant to warrant its exclusion from the analysis. This unsupported presumption, nonetheless, provides a central justification for a willingness to make summary normative judgments about tax systems solely with respect to the movement from initial market earnings to final income.

This third assumption also seems archaic. In modern industrial societies, the state has sweeping distributive impact on the lives of its citizens. Only a few of those distributive effects result from tax-and-transfer adjustments of the market distribution of income. The government not only pays wages and profits to individual "owners" of labor and capital, but it also confers various rights to engage in economic activities differentially among individuals. Indeed, as Charles Reich argues in his analysis of the "new property," "more and more of our wealth takes the form of rights or status rather than of tangible goods." The government has become a principal source and guarantor of these rights; as Reich writes, "[it] pours forth . . . money, benefits, services, contracts, franchises, and licenses." Nearly all of these munificent activities have distributive biases, and we should no longer pretend that our normative judgments about the government's impact on the distribution of income can be limited to its marginal adjustments of the market distribution. As much or more than any other social institution, the government helps *create* and *maintain* that "market" distribution.

A Radical View of Tax Incidence

Can we replace traditional incidence theory with a more useful view of taxation and the state? In this section, I sketch an alternative view of normative tax incidence criteria which builds from the perspectives of radical political economics. According to that view, any "normative" theory of tax incidence seems meaningless. The irrelevance of such theories can be suggested by analysis at both the "positive" and the "normative" levels.

One sees the superfluity of incidence theory at the positive level by beginning with the general radical theory of the state. In the radical view, the state in capitalist societies serves the critical function of preserving and stabilizing the property relations of the capitalist economy. While not simply a "tool" of the capitalist class, it is dominated by their interests. The state may act to solve economic problems posed by capitalist development, and it may occasionally make concessions to the working classes when its failure to do so might threaten the stability of the system. Within that general functional framework, marginal variations in the evolution of state policies will be affected by changes in relative class power and the changing dialectics of class conflict, on the one hand,

and will be mediated through what radicals call "superstructural" forces — the influence of custom, religion, ideology, and so on — on the other hand.

What do these general hypotheses about government activities imply about the specific structure and incidence of taxes applied in order to finance those activities? Two hypotheses seem most important. First, the range of the tax system's potential distributive impact will be bounded by two different kinds of constraints. On the one hand, capitalists will try to apply their power to guarantee that the net real effects of the tax system do not compromise their primary drive for continuing capital accumulation. Toward this end, capitalists may be content with a tax system which merely protects their relative share, rather than one which actually increases it. On the other hand, capitalists will be influenced as they seek to channel government tax policies by the critical necessity of forestalling worker bitterness and unrest. The "capitalist state" can never appear too unfair to workers or they may revolt. Capitalists will therefore be inclined to accept statutes which share the burden of taxes between owners and workers; they will favor certain kinds of taxes which permit the shifting of the tax to consumers and workers while appearing to tax capital; and they will help legitimize certain standards of vertical and horizontal "equity" which seem to encodify some principles of justice.

A second principal hypothesis about the political economy of taxes seems equally important. Inequalities in income play a critical role in helping stabilize capitalist economies and the power of the capitalist class. In particular, inequalities help induce workers to tolerate alienating work. As a result, capitalists will obviously try to ensure that income inequalities will not be disturbed as it becomes necessary to impose taxation. In more rigorous language, this amounts to the obvious hypothesis that the tax-and-transfer system will not fundamentally alter the ordinal ranking of individual workers in the market distribution of labor income, however differentially it may tax those with different incomes.

Finally, what do these hypotheses imply about the extent and structure of taxes levied on the poor? On the one hand, because the poor may be the most (potentially) disruptive workers in society, many tax-and-transfer policies will seek to forestall potential unrest among the poor. Although the poor may be powerless and too weak to gain tax-and-transfer advantages on their own, they may nonetheless be tempted by various relief policies designed to under-cut their potential anger. Second, it may become increasingly true in a market economy that many unskilled, relatively "unproductive" workers seem superfluous to the owners of production. The imperative of preserving work incentives may become irrelevant with these members of the underclass. As a result, the tax-and-transfer function of muting disorder may begin to dominate the constraint of work incentives; relatively cheap transfer policies, making use of 100 percent work disincentives, may emerge. Because this involves differential tax-and-transfer treatment of these groups, "categorical" programs which define these groups as deserving differential treatment provide a convenient framework for this imperative.

This outline of a radical analysis of the state and taxation, however brief, serves a single central purpose for this discussion: it obviously implies that universal standards for evaluating the incidence of taxation have no relevance for the "positive" analysis of taxes and the poor. A universal social welfare function is tautologically absurd from the radical perspective, since different classes with fundamentally competing interests battle for influence over the state. Members of each of those classes will have, on the average, completely different preferences about taxation. The dynamics of their conflicts will determine which preferences acquire what kinds of influence. The specific (cross-sectional) incidence of a particular tax system will simply emerge as a by-product of that historical conflict. It is not and could not be produced by some single set of exogenous social preferences.

At the normative level, radicals would make a different kind of argument about the irrelevance of normative theories of tax incidence. Most radicals would argue that ethics about the distribution of resources and income are purely "situational," that the ethics of distribution are rooted in a society's particular relations of production and exchange. In capitalist economies, Marx argued, workers lose control of their labor power because they are forced to sell it to obtain the means of survival. If capitalists are able to extract surplus labor from a worker, they have every "right" to that surplus because they have purchased his–her labor power for their own use. In his classic analysis of the inevitable conflict over the length of the working day, Marx argues that each party to the conflict is trying to exercise an equally valid right: "There is here, therefore, an antinomy, right against right, both equally bearing the seal of the law of exchanges." In the conflict, force decides the issue. And thus the "situational" character of radical ethics: as Marx puts it, "Right can never be higher than the economic structure of society and its cultural development thereby determined." Robert C. Tucker summarizes the argument:

> In short, the only applicable norm of what is right and just is the one inherent in the existing economic system. Each mode of production has its own mode of distribution and its own form of [distributional] equity, and it is meaningless to pass judgment on it from some other point of view.

In this sense, it seems pointless to demand a more "equitable" distribution of income than that distribution which emerges from the power relations of capitalist production and the state. To argue that the poor "ought" to be treated more progressively is to bequeath them a set of "rights" from some other economic system. The changing historical dimensions of class conflict may eventually lead to a new set of distributional ethics among the poor (or other strata), and they may begin to demand an entirely different distribution of economic welfare, but we can hardly presume, as economists, to transcend the historical dialectics through which consciousness about normative issues evolves.

TAXATION AND INEQUALITY

Gabriel Kolko

This selection provides some of the historical evidence used by radicals to argue that the government does not seek to redistribute income from the rich to the poor. Kolko sketches the origins of heavily progressive taxation in the New Deal, and shows that the progressivity of the tax system is primarily an illusion. The wealthy are typically able to evade most of the heavy burden of statutory tax rates for upper-income brackets. Kolko's book *Wealth and Power in America,* from which this has been reprinted, was published in 1962. More recent figures supporting Kolko's earlier data are summarized in the Editor's Supplement following this selection.

Kolko, who teaches history at the State University of New York at Buffalo, has written several other books about twentieth-century America.

It is widely believed that, as Ernest van den Haag and Ralph Ross put it, "the effect of progressive income taxes in diminishing the income of the upper brackets is too plain to need rehearsing." [1] But the impact of Federal income taxes on the actual distribution of wealth has been minimal, if not negligible. The desire to avoid the burden of high taxes has given rise to new factors in the distribution of wealth, which have so complicated the picture that a change in form has been mistaken by many for a basic change in content. A careful study of the topic will hardly sustain this illusion.

Contrary to common belief, heavy taxation of upper-income groups did not begin with the advent of the New Deal; it began only with the approach of United States involvement in World War II. Higher income taxation came as a response of the Roosevelt Administration to world events and not as a result of a conscious commitment to a social policy of reducing inequalities in the distribution of wealth.

As a matter of historical record, the New Deal was not seriously interested in taxation as a means

Source: From *Wealth and Power in America: An Analysis of Social Class and Income Distribution* by Gabriel Kolko. © 1962 by Frederick A. Praeger, Inc., New York. Reprinted by permission.

[1] Ralph Ross and Ernest van den Haag, *The Fabric of Society: An Introduction to the Social Sciences* (New York: Harcourt, Brace, 1957), p. 398.

of income equalization — despite its frequent assertions that it was. Roosevelt actively supported the Revenue Act of 1934, but his support for the somewhat stronger 1935 Act was equivocal and was finally obtained only because he feared the growing appeal of Huey Long's "Share-the-Wealth Clubs" and attacks by progressives in Congress. Even so, in a number of important areas, the provisions of the two Acts were hardly designed to redistribute wealth effectively or reduce the capital accumulations of the rich. The estate-tax rates, which the 1932 Act set at 2 percent for each bracket above $70,000, were raised to 3 percent on amounts above $70,000 and up to $4.5 million, after which the rate dropped to 2 percent. The corporate income tax was raised from 12 percent to 15 percent in 1936, to 19 percent in 1939; not until 1942 was it raised to 40 percent.[2]

Before 1941, the New Deal practice on personal-income taxation was, despite its difference in verbiage, essentially a continuation of that of the Hoover Administration. In 1929 and 1940, when the national personal income was almost the same, Federal receipts from personal income taxes were virtually identical—$1,323 billion in 1929 and $1,393 billion in 1940. But in 1941, the Federal personal income tax, increased because of the growing military budget, produced revenue one-half more than in 1940, although personal income increased only 14 percent. In 1944, personal income was twice the 1940 level, but the tax yield was twelve times as great.[3] While much of this increased burden fell on the upper-income groups — enough to stimulate their search for new ways to avoid the highest tax brackets — the major weight fell on income groups that had never before been subjected to the income tax.

Thus, the ironic fact is that the extension of the income tax to middle- and low-income classes was the only original aspect of the New Deal tax policy.

Taxation: Theory and Practice

The feature of the income-tax structure that purportedly has had a major impact is the extremely steep tax rates (up to 91 percent) on the very largest incomes. Actually, the resulting varied and ingenious methods of tax avoidance have substantially lessened the importance of these theoretically high rates.

Since 1951, members of the economic elite have attempted to receive their income in nontaxable forms or to postpone receiving it until retirement, when they will be in lower income brackets. There has been a strong downward shift in income-bracket levels, with an increasing proportion in the $25,000–$100,000 bracket, and in some years there has been an absolute drop in the number of returns reporting more than $100,000. More important, however, has been the trend away from the forms of income subject to high tax rates (salaries, wages, and certain types of property income) and toward tax-free interest, capital gains, and many other forms of income taxed at much lower rates or not at all. The proportionate importance of these forms of income to total income rises sharply in every income category over $10,000 a year.

Under Roosevelt, up to 1941, the actual, as opposed to the theoretical, tax rates on very high incomes were not very different from those under Herbert Hoover. Theoretically, the statutory tax is levied on straight income, none of which is derived from capital gains or other sources taxed at lower rates, from which no deducations are made, and no evasion attempted. In 1932, the highest possible tax rate on incomes of $1 million and up was 54 percent, but only 47 percent was actually collected. In 1938, the maximum theoretical tax rate had increased to 72 percent, but only 44 percent was collected. By 1957, the highest possible tax rate was 91 percent, but only 52 percent was collected.[4] As J. Keith Butters, Harvard economist, has written in his major study of taxation and the rich, *Effects of Taxation — Investment by Individuals* (1953), "By far the most striking and significant feature . . . is the large excess of theoretical over actual tax rates on upper bracket individuals when these rates are computed for income inclusive of all net capital gains"[5]

[2] Roy G. and Gladys C. Blakey, *The Federal Income Tax* (New York: Longmans, Green & Co., 1940), pp. 366–73; and Louis Eisenstein, "The Rise and Decline of the Estate Tax," *Federal Tax Policy for Economic Growth*, p. 830 ff.

[3] Office of Business Economics, *National Income, 1954* (Washington, D.C.: Government Printing Office, 1954), p. 471.

[4] All calculations from data in Bureau of Internal Revenue, *Statistics of Income for 1939, Part I* (Washington, D.C.: G.P.O., 1943), pp. 63 64, and *Statistics of Income — Individual Income Tax Returns for 1957* (Washinton, D.C.: G.P.O., 1959), p. 20.

[5] J. Keith Butters *et al., Effects of Taxation — Investment by Individuals* (Boston: Harvard Business School, 1953), p. 85.

TABLE 1. Percentage of National Personal Income, Before Taxes, Received by Each Income-Tenth *

	Highest Tenth	2nd	3rd	4th	5th	6th	7th	7th	8th	9th	Lowest Tenth
1947	33.5	14.8	11.7	9.9	8.5	7.1	5.8	5.8	4.4	3.1	1.2
1948	30.9	14.7	11.9	10.1	8.8	7.5	6.3	6.3	5.0	3.3	1.4
1949	29.8	15.5	12.5	10.6	9.1	7.7	6.2	6.2	4.7	3.1	0.8
1950	28.7	15.4	12.7	10.8	9.3	7.8	6.3	6.3	4.9	3.2	0.9
1951	30.9	15.0	12.3	10.6	8.9	7.6	6.3	6.3	4.7	2.9	0.8
1952	29.5	15.3	12.4	10.6	9.1	7.7	6.4	6.4	4.9	3.1	1.0
1953	31.4	14.8	11.9	10.3	8.9	7.6	6.2	6.2	4.7	3.0	1.2
1954	29.3	15.3	12.4	10.7	9.1	7.7	6.4	6.4	4.8	3.1	1.2
1955	29.7	15.7	12.7	10.8	9.1	7.7	6.1	6.1	4.5	2.7	1.0
1956	30.6	15.3	12.3	10.5	9.0	7.6	6.1	6.1	4.5	2.8	1.3
1957	29.4	15.5	12.7	10.8	9.2	7.7	6.1	6.1	4.5	2.9	1.3
1958	27.1	16.3	13.2	11.0	9.4	7.8	6.2	6.2	4.6	3.1	1.3
1959	28.9	15.8	12.7	10.7	9.2	7.8	6.3	6.3	4.6	2.9	1.1

* In terms of "spending units."

Source: Previously unpublished data for 1947–58 are reproduced by permission of the Board of Governors of the Federal Reserve System, and data for 1959 by permission of the Survey Research Center.

The income of the richest tenth is reduced less than 10 percent by Federal income taxes. And, of course, the other tenths also show a net reduction in earnings after income taxes. Thus, it should come as no surprise that the distribution of income by tenths after Federal income taxes, shown in Table 2, is practically the same as the distribution before taxes [shown in] Table 1. . . . The slight changes in income-shares effected by the income tax have benefited income-tenths in the upper half almost as frequently as income-tenths in the lower half. These fundamental facts have been ignored by those who interpret the tax system on the basis of their arbitrary preconceptions rather than on the basis of its actual effects.

The Revolution in Taxation

Now we see that progressive taxation of incomes has not been applied to the economic elite sufficiently to change the distribution of income-shares, and that although the economic elite has been subject to heavier Federal income taxation since 1941, the same factor that stimulated a higher tax rate on the rich also produced, for the first time in American history, permanent and significant income taxation of low- and middle-income earners.

In 1939, only 4.0 million families or persons were subject to Federal income taxation; in 1940, 7.5 million; in 1941, 17.6 million; in 1944, 42.4 million;

TABLE 2. Percentage of National Personal Income Received by Each Income-Tenth After Federal Income Taxes

	Highest	2nd	3rd	4th	5th	6th	7th	8th	9th	Lowest
1947	31(−2)*	15	12	10	9	8(+1)	6	5(+1)	3	1
1949	28(−2)	15	13(+1)	11	9	8	7(+1)	5	3	1
1950	27(−2)	15	13	11	10(+1)	8	7(+1)	5	3	1
1951	28(−3)	15	13(+1)	11(+1)	9	8	7(+1)	5	3	1
1952	27(−3)	15	13(+1)	11	10(+1)	8	7(+1)	5	3	1
1953	28(−3)	15	12	11(+1)	9	8	7(+1)	5	4(+1)	1
1954	27(−2)	15	13	11	9	8	7(+1)	5	4(+1)	1
1955	27(−2)	16	13	11	10(+1)	8	6	5(+1)	3	1

* Numbers in parentheses indicate change in percentage points from before-tax income.

Source: Bureau of the Census, *Statistical Abstract of the United States — 1957* (Washington, D.C.: Government Printing Office, 1957), p. 309. These data, collected by the Survey Research Center, include capital gains but exclude income-in-kind.

and in 1957, 46.9 million.[6] Similarly, the share of the national personal income subject to Federal income taxes was 10 percent in 1939, 24 percent in 1941, and 43 percent in 1957.[7] The net effect, since there was a fairly stable distribution of income over that period, was to tax lower- and middle-income classes that had never been taxed before. This was done by reducing the minimum tax exemption and extending the tax scale. In 1957, 66 percent of all reported incomes were taxed at the base rate of 20 percent. For married couples, taxable income began at $3,500 in 1929, $2,500 in 1935 and 1936, $1,500 in 1941, $1,000 in 1944, and $1,200 from 1948 on. Inflation sharply increased this trend by reducing the value of both incomes and exemptions, and its influence continues. The percentage of Federal revenue yielded by personal-income taxes increased from a scant 9 percent in 1916 to 18 percent in 1941, 41 percent in 1946, and 53 percent in 1960. At the same time, the percentage of Federal revenue yielded by corporate-profits taxes grew from 8 percent in 1916 to 26 percent in 1941, and 30 percent in 1946, and fell to 28 percent in 1960.[8]

In this process of incorporating more and more of the American population into the Federal income tax system, a moderate degree of progressive taxation has been maintained. The income tax is practically the only major tax that is not basically regressive. Nevertheless, the income tax paid by the average family in the lowest income-fifth — in 1957, amounting to 3.3 percent of their income — constitutes a greater hardship for those living on an emergency budget than does the tax burden of 13.7 percent paid in the same year by the average family in the richest income-fifth.[9]

The basic tax rate on taxable income (i.e., income after all deductions for dependents, charitable donations, medical expenses, etc.) begins at 20 percent. A major proportion of legitimate expenses is unclaimed annually, and most of this can, we know, be attributed to low- and middle-income families.[10] Fewer than 10 percent of those earning less than $2,000 take credit for deductible expenditures beyond their dependents and the flat 10 percent allowed on the short form.[11] This failure is due in large part to the complexity of filling out a "long form" for deductions. Deductions, it should be pointed out, must be quite high before they will save a family anything. For example, a family that can claim no deductions for interest, state taxes, donations, casualty losses, or the like must have medical expenses amounting to at least 13 percent of its total income before it will save anything.

Joint-filing provisions for husbands and wives, intended to lower their tax burden, were of no benefit in 70 percent of the joint returns filed in 1957, which were from low- and middle-income groups.[12] In the upper-income brackets, however, the joint return can be of enormous benefit. On an income of $35,000, it can realize a peak saving of 40 percent of the tax bill.[13]

The Combined Impact of All Taxes

Most recent commentators who have credited the Federal income tax with redistributing income have ignored the fact that it is only one of a number of taxes — and the only one that is in some measure progressive. Therefore, any discussion of distribution of income after taxes must consider the consequences of all taxes.

[6] Daniel Creamer, *Personal Income During Business Cycles* (Princeton, N.J.: Princeton U. Press, 1956), p. 153; Bureau of Internal Revenue, *Statistics of Income — Individual Returns for 1957*, p. 23.

[7] Joseph A. Pechman, "What Would a Comprehensive Individual Income Tax Yield?" *Tax Revision Compendium*, I. 258.

[8] William Crum *et al.*, *Fiscal Planning for Total War* (New York: National Bureau of Economic Research, 1942), pp. 172, 174; *Economic Report of the President — 1958*, p. 174; Tax Foundation, *Reexamining the Federal Corporation Income Tax* (New York: Tax Foundation, 1958), p. 22; *The Budget of the U.S. Government for the Fiscal Year Ending June 30, 1960* (Washington, D.C.: G.P.O., 1959), p. M-12.

[9] Selma F. Goldsmith, "Income Distribution by Size — 1955–58," *Survey of Current Business*, April 1959, p. 16.

[10] C. Harry Kahn, "Personal Expense Deductions," *37th Annual Report, National Bureau of Economic Research, 1957*, p. 49.

[11] Daniel M. Holland and C. Harry Kahn, "Comparison of Personal Taxable Income," in U.S. Senate, Jt. Committee on the Economic Report, *Federal Tax Policy for Economic Growth and Stability*, 84th Cong., 1st Sess. (Washington, D.C.: G.P.O., 1955), 331 32.

[12] Bureau of Internal Revenue, *Statistics of Income — 1957*, p. 37; Lawrence H. Seltzer, "The Individual Income Tax," *39th Annual Report, National Bureau of Economic Research, 1959*, p. 74.

[13] Holland & Kahn, *op. cit.*, p. 333.

TABLE 3. Percentage of 1958 Total Income Paid in Federal, State, and Local Taxes,* by Income Class

Income Class (in dollars)	Share of Taxes (in percent)		
	Federal	State and Local	Total †
0– 2,000	9.6	11.3	21.0
2,000– 4,000	11.0	9.4	20.4
4,000– 6,000	12.1	8.5	20.6
6,000– 8,000	13.9	7.7	21.6
8,000–10,000	13.4	7.2	20.6
10,000–15,000	15.1	6.5	21.6
15,000–plus	28.6	5.9	34.4
Average	16.1	7.5	23.7

* Social-insurance taxes are not included.
† Because of rounding, items do not always add up to totals.

In general, local and state taxes are regressive. More than half — 59 percent in 1958 — of all state tax revenues come from sales taxes. About one-half of the expenditures of an average spending unit earning a cash income of less than $1,000 a year are subject to general sales or excise taxes, but only one-third of the expenditures of those earning $10,-000-plus are so taxed.[14] In effect, corporations present the public with additional hidden taxes. The corporation income tax is, as the *Wall Street Journal* puts it, "treated by the corporations as merely another cost which they can pass on to their customers."[15] It has been variously estimated that one-third to one-half of this tax is shifted to the consumers. Furthermore, at least two-thirds of American corporations add all payroll-tax costs to their prices.[16]

The Tax Foundation has calculated actual taxes paid as a percentage of income for all income classes in 1958 (see Table 3). Its figures show that state and local taxes are regressive, and that all Federal taxes combined, although tending to be progressive, fall much more substantially on the low-income classes than is generally realized. Included in its calculations are all local, state, and Federal personal-income taxes; inheritance, estate, and gift taxes;

corporate-profit taxes (it assumes that one-half of this is shifted to the public); excise and sales taxes; customs and property taxes. Excluded are the highly regressive social-insurance taxes, which take 7.3 percent of the total income of those earning $2,000 or less but only 1.5 percent in the $15,000-plus class.

These Tax Foundation data indicate that the combined American tax system is scarcely "progressive" and hardly in accord with the image of it nourished by most social scientists and students of contemporary America.[17] If, despite innumerable loopholes, the Federal income tax has introduced a moderately progressive but greatly misunderstood and overemphasized taxation, the Federal excise and customs — and most major local and state — taxes have seriously lessened its impact. The income tax paid by the lower-income classes is, for the most part, money that would otherwise go for essential personal and family needs; in this light, the tax burden is substantially heavier for the lower-income classes than for the higher-income classes.

Welfare and Income Inequality

Theoretically, it would be possible for the revenues from regressive taxation to be directed to welfare expenditures for lower-income groups, and for the inequality of income distribution to be reduced thereby by a significant extent. This has actually been achieved, in the eyes of a number of proponents of the income-redistribution thesis. "Through a combination of patchwork revisions of the system — tax laws, minimum wage laws, subsidies and guarantees and regulations of various sorts, plus labor union pressures and new management attitudes — we had repealed the Iron Law of Wages," wrote Frederick Lewis Allen in *The Big Change.* "We had brought about a virtually automatic redistribution of

[14] Tax Foundation, *Federal Excise Taxes* (New York: Tax Foundation, 1956), p. 47.
[15] *Wall Street Journal,* 5 May 1958, p. 1.
[16] Lewis H. Kimmel, *Taxes and Economic Incentives* (Washington, D.C.: Brookings Institution, 1950), p. 182.

[17] Even this inadequate progression is an improvement over the distribution of the total Federal, state, and local tax burden in 1938–39. In that fiscal year, the total Federal tax burden as a percentage of the income of every income class was about equal in every income class up to $10,000 (roughly equal to $20,000 in 1958), when it began to rise steeply. State and local taxes, as a whole, were mildly regressive. See Temporary National Economic Committee, *Who Pays the Taxes?* (Washington, D.C.: G.P.O., 1940) Monograph #3, p. 6.

income from the well-to-do to the less well-to-do." [18] The plausibility of this thesis has only been strengthened by the attacks of conservatives on the alleged "welfare state" created by the Roosevelt Administration.

However, this viewpoint is not sustained by a careful examination of the motives for the revisions in the tax structure: The reason for high taxation, at least since 1933, has been not to redistribute income but to pay for extraordinary costs — primarily military from 1940 on — in the most expeditious way. We have not taxed the rich to give to the poor; we have taxed both the rich and the poor and, at least since 1940, contributed only a small fraction of the proceeds to the welfare of the poor.

Consider, for example, 1958. In that year, Federal revenue from person-income, estate and gift, corporate-profit, and excise and customs taxes, excluding the self-financing social-insurance program, amounted to $69 billion.[19] The families and unattached individuals in the $0–2,000 class contributed $1.066 billion, those in the $2,000–$4,000 class contributed $4.971 billion. But the Federal government spent only $4.509 billion on what by the most generous definition may be called "welfare." Included were all expenditures for public assistance, public

[18] Frederick Lewis Allen, *The Big Change* (New York: Harper & Brothers, 1952), p. 286.
[19] Tax Foundation, *Allocation of the Tax Burden by Income Class*, pp. 14–15; Bureau of the Census, *Statistical Abstract — 1959*, p. 368.

health, education, and "other welfare," and half of the outlay for farm parity prices and income, and public housing. In 1949, Federal expenditures for welfare were $2.037 billion; in 1954, they were $2.451 billion, and in 1955, $4.062 billion. In each of these years, however, the total Federal tax payments of the spending units earning less than $4,000 were greater than these welfare expenditures. If all Federal welfare expenditures went to the $0–$4,000 class — which was certainly not the case — this class more than paid for them.

In brief, welfare spending has not changed the nature of income inequality, nor raised the standard of living of the lowest-income classes above what it would have reached if they had not been subjected to Federal taxation. It might be claimed that these classes must assume some responsibility for the nation's "larger obligations," but this is not an argument advanced by those who assert that we have redistributed income through taxation and welfare measures. . . .

The complexity of the effect of taxation should not be allowed to obscure the basic trends — the growing tax burden on the low- and middle-income classes, and the huge disparity between theoretical and actual tax rates for the wealthy. The conclusion is inescapable: Taxation has mitigated the fundamentally unequal distribution of income. If anything it has perpetuated inequality by heavily taxing the low- and middle-income groups — those least able to bear its burden.

RECENT EVIDENCE OF GOVERNMENT IMPACT

Editor's Supplement

Since Kolko revised his book in 1962, more recent figures have become available on the net impact of government taxes and expenditures on the American income distribution. Although several changes both in the tax structure and in tax rates were implemented during the 1960s and the level of government expenditures increased enormously during the same period, none of Kolko's conclusions was affected significantly by subsequent developments. The following five tables, all taken from a useful summary article by Joseph Pechman, published in late 1969, summarize the most recent evidence available at the time of writing. Their implications seem clear. At the end of the 1960s, just as at the beginning, available evidence provided no support for the contention that one of government's functions in the United States was to correct the market distribution of income by substantial redistribution from the rich to the poor.

Source for all five tables is Joseph Pechman, "The Rich, the Poor, and the Taxes They Pay," *The Public Interest*, No. 17, Fall 1969, pp. 23, 24, 27, 28, and 33 respectively.

TABLE 1. Before-Tax Income Shares, Census Data (Percent)

Year	Top 5 Percent of Families	Top 20 Percent of Families
1952	18	42
1957	16	40
1962	16	42
1967	15	41

Source: Bureau of the Census. Income includes transfer payments (e.g., social security benefits, unemployment compensation, welfare payments, etc.), but excludes capital gains.

TABLE 2. Before-Tax Income Shares, Tax Data (Percent)

Year	Top 1 Percent of Tax Units	Top 2 Percent of Tax Units	Top 5 Percent of Tax Units	Top 10 Percent of Tax Units	Top 15 Percent of Tax Units
1952	9	12	19	27	33
1963	8	12	19	28	35
1967	9	13	20	29	36

Source: Statistics of Income. Income excludes transfer payments, but includes realized capital gains in full.

TABLE 3. Effective Federal Tax Rates on Total Income (Percent)

Year	Top 1 Percent of Tax Units	Next 1 Percent of Tax Units	Next 3 Percent of Tax Units	Next 5 Percent of Tax Units	Next 5 Percent of Tax Units
1952	33	20	16	14	12
1963	27	20	16	14	13
1967	26	18	15	13	12

Source: Statistics of Income. Total income is the sum of adjusted gross income and excluded capital gains, dividends, and sick pay.

TABLE 4. Shares of Total Disposable (i.e., After-Tax) Income (Percent)

Year	Top 1 Percent of Tax Units	Top 2 Percent of Tax Units	Top 5 Percent of Tax Units	Top 10 Percent of Tax Units	Top 15 Percent of Tax Units
1952	7	10	16	24	30
1963	7	10	17	26	33
1967	7	11	17	26	34

Source: Statistics of Income. Disposable income is total income less federal income tax paid.

TABLE 5.   Taxes and Transfers as Percent of Income, 1965

Income Classes	Federal	State and Local	Total	Transfer Payments	Taxes Less Transfers
Under $2,000	19	25	44	126	−83 *
$ 2,000– 4,000	16	11	27	11	16
4,000– 6,000	17	10	27	5	21
6,000– 8,000	17	9	26	3	23
8,000–10,000	18	9	27	2	25
10,000–15,000	19	9	27	2	25
15,000 and over	32	7	38	1	37
Total	22	9	31	14	24

Header: Taxes spans Federal, State and Local, Total.

* The minus sign indicates that the families and individuals in this class received more from federal, state, and local governments than they, as a group, paid to these governments in taxes.

Source: Economic Report of the President, 1969. Income excludes transfer payments, but includes realized capital gains in full and undistributed corporate profits.

BIBLIOGRAPHY

I. IMPRESSIONS, DEFINITIONS, AND MAGNITUDES

A. Impressions

Richard Conot. *Rivers of Blood, Years of Darkness.* New York: Morrow, 1968.
Robert Coles. *Children of Crisis,* Vol. III. Boston: Houghton Mifflin, 1973.

B. Definitions
1. *Absolute Poverty*

Mollie Orshansky. "Counting the Poor: Another Look at the Poverty Profile," in L. A. Ferman *et al.,* eds., *Poverty in America,* rev. ed. Ann Arbor: University of Michigan Press, 1968. Explains the original SSA definition.
Martin Rein. "Problems in the Definition and Measurement of Poverty," *ibid.* Reviews and criticizes that definition.
Sar A. Levitan and Robert Taggart. "Employment and Earnings Inadequacy: A Measure of Worker Welfare," *Monthly Labor Review,* October 1973. A broader definition.

2. *Relative Poverty*

Victor Fuchs. "Redefining Poverty and Redistributing Income," *The Public Interest,* Summer 1967.
Lee Rainwater. *What Money Buys.* New York: Basic Books, 1974.

C. Magnitudes

U.S. Bureau of the Census. "Characteristics of the Low-Income Population, 1973," *Current Population Reports,* Series P-60, No. 98, January 1975.

Herman Miller. "Changes in the Number and Composition of the Poor," in Margaret S. Gordon, ed., *Poverty in America.* San Francisco: Chandler, 1965. Longer-term historical data.

II. ANALYSES OF POVERTY

A. Orthodox Economic Perspectives

Lester Thurow. *Poverty and Discrimination.* Washington, D.C.: Brookings Institution, 1969.

Bradley Schiller. *Poverty.* New York: Prentice-Hall, 1972.

B. Radical Perspectives

Charles Sackrey. *The Political Economy of Urban Poverty.* New York: Norton, 1973.

Barry Bluestone *et al. Low Wages and the Working Poor.* Ann Arbor: University of Michigan — Wayne State University, 1973.

III. PAST AND FUTURE PROGRAMS

A. Past Programs

1. *Public Assistance*

President's Commission on Income Maintenance Programs. *Poverty Amid Plenty.* Washington, D.C.: U.S. Government, 1969.

2. *Antipoverty Programs*

Sar Levitan. *The Great Society's Poor Law.* Baltimore: Johns Hopkins, 1969.

Daniel P. Moynihan. *Maximum Feasible Misunderstanding.* New York: Basic Books, 1969.

Frances Fox Piven and Richard Cloward. *Regulating the Poor.* New York: Pantheon, 1971.

B. Future Programs

Theodore Marmor, ed. *Poverty Policy: A Sourcebook of Cash-Transfer Proposals.* Chicago: Aldine, 1971.

Christopher Green. *Negative Taxes and the Poverty Problem.* Washington, D.C.: Brookings Institution, 1967.

Michael C. Barth *et al. Toward an Effective Income Support System: Problems, Prospects, and Choices.* Madison, Wis.: Institute for Research on Poverty, 1974.

6

CRIME

EDITOR'S
INTRODUCTION

What is there to say? We've got a living to earn. There wouldn't be any prostitution if there weren't a demand for it.

— New York City prostitute[1]

The poor youth growing up in the slum has little incentive to emulate Abraham Lincoln when he sees the homage which society pays to the corrupt. Such a boy will probably never have the opportunity to embezzle funds from a bank or to promote a multimillion dollar stock fraud scheme. The criminal ways which we encourage him to choose will be those closest at hand — from vandalism to mugging to armed robbery. And, if he is very successful at these, perhaps he can work his way through the rackets to the high level where he, too, can open a Swiss bank account.

— Robert Morgenthau[2]

Most people who live in large cities have experienced those fearful moments. Walking down the street at night. Footsteps behind begin to quicken. The pulse throbs. A furtive glance over the shoulder. Two kids are running. . . .

It is easy to joke about our fears of crime. Although the problem is real, our paranoia sometimes seems excessive. We are beginning to get caught in the tides of our own rhetoric. One side screams for law and order; another side decries the erosion of civil liberties. "A coincidence of events has heightened the traditional tensions between the forces of enforcement and of justice," Fred Graham has written, "and has greatly increased the likelihood of a constitutional crisis somewhere down the line." [3]

The debate about urban crime cannot be ignored. Our views about the sources and solutions of the problem will critically determine our political future. Conservative and liberal views have dominated the debate in the past. A radical perspective on crime and social justice has begun to emerge. In this introduction, I summarize the dimensions of the problem, outline the three views,

[1] Quoted in *The New York Times,* May 29, 1970.
[2] Robert M. Morgenthau, "Equal Justice and the Problem of White Collar Crime," *The Conference Board Record,* August 1969, p. 20.
[3] Fred P. Graham, "Black Crime: The Lawless Image," *Harper's,* September 1970, p. 71.

and provide a brief introduction to the contents and purposes of the reading selections.

Definitions and Magnitudes

The problem of urban crime involves elements of both myth and reality. Factually, a great deal of serious crime occurs in large central cities, much of it committed by young blacks. Subjectively, many Americans have blown the problem out of proportion, tending to view certain kinds of urban crime as the major threat to law and order in this country, although these crimes account for small proportions of death, injury, and property loss.

The reading selections on definitions and magnitudes provide some useful introductory summaries of the problem of urban crime. A few conclusions from those selections should be underscored.

First, crime is everywhere. There are more crimes than we can count. As the President's Commission on Law Enforcement and the Administration of Justice wrote in 1967:

> There are more than 2800 Federal crimes and a much larger number of State and local ones. Some involve serious bodily harm, some stealing, some public morals or public order, some governmental revenues, some the creation of hazardous conditions, some the regulation of the economy. Some are perpetrated ruthlessly and systematically; others are spontaneous derelictions. Gambling and prostitution are willingly undertaken by both buyer and seller; murder and rape are violently imposed upon their victims. Vandalism is predominantly a crime of the young; driving while intoxicated, a crime of the adult.[4]

Second, nearly everyone commits a "crime" sometime, somewhere. Our laws are so pervasive that one must virtually retire to hermitage to avoid committing a crime. According to a national survey conducted in 1965, 91 percent of all adult Americans "admitted that they had committed acts for which they might have received jail or prison sentences."[5] The same study showed that more than two million Americans are in jail or on probation. Criminal behavor seems more clearly like the norm than an aberration.

Third, it appears that we focus our fears and paranoia on only a small set of crimes. These crimes are essentially covered by the FBI Index of Crime. The Index Crimes include willful homicide, forcible rape, aggravated assault, robbery, burglary, larceny (involving more than $50), and motor vehicle theft. As the reading selections show, these crimes account for small proportions of total personal harm and property loss in the United States. According to data compiled in 1967, willful homicide accounts for only one-twelfth the number of deaths attributed to four more frequent causes of "unnatural" death — car accidents, other accidents, suicide, and falls. The economic losses attributable to Index

---

[4] From the selection by the President's Commission on Law Enforcement and the Administration of Justice in this chapter, p. 367.

[5] President's Commission on Law Enforcement and the Administration of Justice, *The Challenge of Crime in a Free Society* (Washington, D.C.: U.S. Government Printing Office, 1967), p. v.

Crimes against property are only one-fifth the losses attributable to embezzlement, fraud, and commercial theft.[6]

Although we fear them for their violence, the Index Crimes are largely motivated by desire for economic gain. As Ramsey Clark has concluded, "their main purpose is to obtain money or property."[7] The risk of fatal injury from Index Crimes against property has been greatly exaggerated. One survey of crimes in the District of Columbia found that less than one-half of 1 per cent of robberies and roughly 1 percent of forcible rapes resulted in homicide.[8] Most Index assaults, indeed, are committed by family members, friends, or persons previously known to their victims — not by strangers creeping out of the darkness.[9] Despite our fears, in short, the FBI Index traces a primarily economic phenomenon, not a violent scourge.

The data suggest that, as our mythology recounts, these Index Crimes are primarily urban problems. In the mid-1960s, crime rates in large cities were twice as high as the national average. (Since then, crime rates in the suburbs have been increasing more rapidly.) Within large cities, Index crimes occur most frequently in ghetto areas.[10]

The data also suggest that another element of the conventional wisdom is partly true. Black youths commit more than their share of property crimes measured by the FBI Index. In 1966, for instance, the arrest rate for blacks was about four times higher than for whites.[11] In the public mind, however, these figures appear to be further exaggerated: public attitudes often appear to presume that *all* the Index Crimes are committed by blacks and that *every* black male is on the verge of committing a crime.

These statistical summaries measure only part of the problem of urban crime. They focus on the "criminal" — a person whose acts are defined by the State as illegal. There is another fundamental dimension to the problem of urban crime: the *government,* whose edicts declare that illegality and whose institutions arrest, prosecute, process, and imprison the "criminal offender."

The government is a "part of the problem" for two reasons. First, the government plays a central role in the selectivity of our attention to crime. The government devotes most of its attention to a few crimes, traces a few crimes statistically, and prosecutes only some "criminal offenders." Many seem to agree that we have a dual system of justice in this country. Public agencies concentrate on crimes committed by the poor, while crimes by the more affluent are left to private auspices. Our prisons function, as Ronald Goldfarb has noted, like a "national poorhouse," swallowing the poor, chewing them up and occasionally spitting them back at the larger society.[12] When the more affluent get in trouble, the state almost always manages, it appears, to "let them off."

Second, the government is "part of the problem" because it appears that the government actually makes the problem of crime worse. Rapid increases in government expenditures have not curbed the rapid rise in crime rates. Many argue

---

[6] See the selection by the President's Commission on Law Enforcement and the Administration of Justice, Table 3 (p. 370).

[7] Ramsey Clark, *Crime in America* (New York: Simon & Schuster, 1970), p. 38.

[8] See the selection by the President's Commission on Law Enforcement and the Administration of Justice in this chapter, p. 368.

[9] *Ibid.,* p. 368.

[10] From the selection by the National Advisory Commission on Civil Disorders, p. 372.

[11] *Ibid.,* p. 374.

[12] See the selection by Goldfarb in this chapter.

that our courts and prisons actually exacerbate the criminality that they are supposed to be controlling. The prisons themselves are veritable "factories of crime." Ramsey Clark has concluded: "Jails and prisons in the United States today are more often than not manufacturers of crime. Of those who come to jail undecided, capable either of criminal conduct or of lives free of crime, most are turned to crime." [13] Roughly half of those released from prison eventually return, and fully 80 percent of serious crime is committed by "repeaters" — by those who have been convicted of crime before.

These conclusions clearly outline the main questions that any analysis of crime must answer: Why is there so much crime? Why has it been increasing? Why does the government focus so selectively on just a few crimes? And why do our billions of dollars fail so miserably to curb the crime problem — apparently contributing, in fact, to its increase?

Liberal and Conservative Views

Conventional public perspectives on crime have often bobbed in murky waters. As Andrew Hacker wrote recently, "writers and politicians no longer speak confidently on the subject." [14] In contrast, some orthodox economists are beginning to write with consummate confidence about crime. Their analyses are beginning to provide a more rigorous support for some conventional views. Given this contrast in conviction, it seems most useful to summarize the conventional public analyses first and then to move on to the recent orthodox economic contributions.

■ Conventional Public Analyses

Conventional liberal and conservative approaches to crime begin from some relatively similar views of society and its governments. They diverge more and more widely as they debate the specifics of crime prevention and control.

To each view, crime against person and property represents an individual aberration from basic social norms. As Chapter 1 noted, both perspectives view the social "order" as ultimately rational. Governmental laws, in their view, harmoniously reflect the interests of all rational people. Those who violate the social order can therefore be regarded as irrational citizens and social misfits. As such, these "criminals" should be punished in some way or another.

Both perspectives also agree that society pays such close attention to "urban crimes" because they are more "violent." Neither perspective would accept the radical contention, outlined in this chapter, that society pays differential attention to some crimes because the government seeks to "control" members of the lower classes, for neither perspective accepts the radical argument that the State favors one class over another.

From those points of agreement, the two perspectives begin to diverge.

The conservative perspective displays an appealing simplicity.[15] Most conservatives believe that criminals should be punished regardless of the social forces that may well have produced their criminality. They represent a threat to

---

[13] Clark, *Crime in America,* p. 212.

[14] Andrew Hacker, "Getting Used to Mugging," *New York Review of Books,* April 19, 1973, p. 9.

[15] For one statement of the perspective, see Edward Banfield, *The Unheavenly City Revisited* (Boston: Little, Brown, 1974), Chapter 8.

the safety and property of those who act with civility and reason. They should be isolated until society can be certain of their good behavior. The more violent the crimes, the more seriously we must regard their consequences and the more stringently we must punish their perpetrators. Because conservatives tend, in general, to regard irrational criminals as "diseased," they do not place much hope in the prospects for their rehabilitation.

These several assumptions inform conservative attitudes about the best solutions to urban crime. Since criminals act irrationally, we can deter and prevent their actions only by communicating through a "language they can understand" — principally by the threat or application of raw force. Toward that end, conservatives typically engage in two kinds of policy calculations.

First, they discuss the potential deterrence of a variety of crime-prevention techniques. If only enough deterrent force could be mustered, they argue, crime could certainly be stopped. Typically, they argue more police and more equipment to prevent crime. In Hacker's words, the police "would be so omnipresent that would-be criminals would forebear from assaulting anyone, in view of the extremely high chances of getting caught."[16] They also tend to urge stringent penalties for convicted criminals; if current sentences do not deter crime, then harsher sentences seem necessary.

Second, conservatives are willing to consider the possibility of preventive detention — locking up those who are "very likely" to commit crimes but have not yet committed them — as a necessary means of protecting the social order from the threat of probable criminality. They marshall their arguments on relatively pragmatic terrain. Edward Banfield has summarized the logic:

> In any event, if abridging the freedom of persons who have not committed crimes is incompatible with the principles of free society, so, also, is the presence in such society of persons who, if their freedom is not abridged, would use it to inflict serious injuries on others. There is, therefore, a painful dilemma. If some people's freedom is not abridged by law-enforcement agencies, that of others will be abridged by law breakers. The question, therefore, is not whether abridging the freedom of those who may commit serious crimes is an evil — it is — but whether it is a lesser or a greater one than the alternative.[17]

Liberals' policy prescriptions build upon somewhat more complicated premises. While they agree with conservatives that the social order is rational and that its violators are irrational, liberals argue that the question cannot be so simply stated. Other factors intervene. First, liberals regard the interactions of individuals with society as extremely complex processes, fraught with imperfections in the allocation and distribution of social rewards. Because of those imperfections and inequalities, some individuals are much more likely than others to be *pushed* toward the irrationality of criminal behavior by factors *beyond their individual control*. Criminality should be regarded as irrational, but we should nonetheless try to avoid *blaming* all criminals for their irrational acts. Second, as Chapter 1 noted, liberals tend to view all people as potentially decent. If criminals are pushed toward criminality by one set of social circumstances, then another set of social circumstances might permit their shedding

---

[16] Hacker, "Getting Used to Mugging," p. 9.
[17] *The Unheavenly City* (Boston: Little, Brown, 1970), p. 184.

their uncharacteristically *un*-decent behavior. It is possible to "rehabilitate" criminals, according to this liberal premise, if only we devote enough energy and resources to the task.

These premises together inform three basic policy orientations among most liberals.

- Because such complex social forces create the soil from which criminality springs, no single set of policy prescriptions can ever deal adequately with all the different kinds of crime we confront. As the President's Commission on Law Enforcement and the Administration of Justice put it in 1967, "No single formula, no single theory, no single generalization can explain the vast range of behavior called crime." [18]
- Because individuals may not actually be "responsible" for their criminal actions, we must be especially careful not to trample the civil liberties of individuals in reckless pursuit of law and order. While conservatives might resolve Banfield's difficult question by judging potential criminality the greater evil, liberals often judge the abridgement of civil liberties as the greater evil.
- Because social factors help cause crime, liberals argue that we cannot ultimately solve the problem of crime until we change these social factors. "We will not have dealt effectively with crime," the President's Commission argued, "until we have alleviated the conditions that stimulate it." [19]

Can we do nothing until the magic moment of those "drastic changes" arrives? Liberals offer some tentative reassurance. They argue that we can marginally improve our prevention of crime if we can at least marginally rationalize our system of enforcement and administration of justice. We need more research, more analysis, more technology, more money, better administration, and more numerous and professional personnel. As in other areas, liberals argue that more money will produce better results. As the President's Commission on Violence concluded in 1970, "We reiterate our previous recommendations that we double our national investment in the criminal justice process." [20]

As in other areas, this liberal faith has been sorely tested in recent years. Government expenditures have increased, but crime rates appear to have increased, too. Rising public fears about street crime have been testing the liberals' balanced prescriptions. If varied, "soft," civil libertarian, rehabilitative policies have failed, are we not forced to move toward the conservatives' emphasis on harsh penalties and preventive detention? "The delicacy of their position has undoubtedly led many liberals to change their tone in recent years," Andrew Hacker concludes. "More and more, liberals are beginning to argue that a conservative's emphasis on law and order is perfectly consistent with their liberalism." [21]

■ Orthodox Economic Analyses

Orthodox economists have devoted substantial attention in recent years to the problems of crime and punishment. They have trumpeted their conclusions

[18] See President's Commission, *The Challenge of Crime in a Free Society*, p. v.
[19] *Ibid.,* p. 15.
[20] National Commission on the Causes of Violence, *To Establish Justice, to Ensure Domestic Tranquility* (New York: Bantam, 1970).
[21] Hacker, "Getting Used to Mugging," p. 9.

with ringing self-confidence. Gary Becker, a pioneer in the orthodox analysis of crime, explains how simply we can understand it all: "... a useful theory of criminal behavior can dispense with special theories of anomie, psychological inadequacies, or inheritance of special traits and simply extend the economists' usual analysis of choice." [22]

The central and most important tenet of the orthodox analysis is that criminal behavior, like any other economic activity, is eminently rational. In this respect, the economists differ fundamentally with conventional liberal and conservative public analyses. Becker summarizes this central contention:

> ... a person commits an offense if the expected utility to him exceeds the utility he could get by using his time and other resources at other activities. Some persons become "criminals," therefore, not because their basic motivation differs from that of other persons, but because their benefits and costs differ.[23]

Individuals are assumed to calculate the returns to, and the risks of, "criminal" activity. These are compared with the returns to and the risks of "legitimate" employment. If people are able to earn more income (at equal risk) or equivalent income (at less risk) through criminal activity, then they will become criminals. As George Stigler concludes: "The details of occupational choice in illegal activity are not different from those encountered in the legitimate occupations." [24]

Given this simple reformulation of criminal behavior, orthodox economists argue that we can construct some "optimal" social policies to combat crime. The analysis has several stages. First, one assumes that there is some social calculus through which the costs and benefits of criminal offenses can be translated into a common sum or deficit for the entire society. (In economics, this is called the "social welfare function.") Second, given this function, society can minimize the "social loss" from criminal offenses by choosing an appropriate level of crime prevention and punishment expenditure. By balancing the costs of crimes actually committted against the costs of preventing them, society can choose (through its government) some combination of punishment levels and social expenditures that will make us happiest: if we moved from that optimal combination, the gains (from further reductions in crime) would be less than the costs (of further taxes to finance additional government activity to produce that reduction in crime).

The major policy emphasis of the orthodox analysis flows clearly from its structure. Since criminals are rational, balancing the costs of conviction against the benefits of successful transgression, there will be less crime if punishments become more severe. They conclude, from a variety of empirical studies, that deterrence works.[25] They conclude, from both logical argument and empirical evidence, that rehabilitation does not work. The implications seem clear. As one leading economist, Gordon Tullock, puts it: "We have an unpleasant method —

[22] Gary Becker, "Crime and Punishment: An Economic Approach," *Journal of Political Economy,* March/April, 1968.

[23] *Ibid.,* p. 176.

[24] George J. Stigler, "The Optimum Enforcement of Laws," *Journal of Political Economy,* May/June 1970, p. 530.

[25] These studies are collected in William Landes, ed., *Essays in the Economics of Crime and Punishment* (New York: National Bureau of Economic Research, 1974).

deterrence — that works, and a pleasant method — rehabilitation — that (at least so far) never has worked. Under the circumstances, we have to opt either for the deterrence method or for a higher crime rate." [26]

With these arguments, the orthodox economists are joining policy hands with the conservatives. The pressures on forgiving liberals mount. "Writing off any human being certainly seems wrong," as Hacker writes of the liberals' dilemma, "but then our New Deal parents never faced Saturday Night Specials." [27]

A Radical Perspective

Like orthodox economists, radicals had neglected the problem of crime until recently. Recent radical analyses clearly outline the radicals' position. Radicals argue that we cannot understand the crime problem without understanding its roots in the structure of American economic and political institutions. They suggest that we cannot realistically expect to "solve" the problem of crime in the United States without first effecting a fundamental redistribution of power in our society.

Several of the reading selections present the radical perspective. Their main arguments can be briefly summarized.

First, radicals argue that our conceptions of crime are not immutable. Our definitions of crime and punishment change from one epoch to another, they suggest, and our current definitions emerged with the rise of capitalism and the "rational" state. Mark Kennedy writes about this period of transition that "in aligning itself with capital and the interests of capital, the State came to guarantee as law both the ethic and the practices which had emerged among merchants prior to the alliance." Apart from older crimes, he concludes, "criminal laws were established primarily for the protection and development of the institutions of capitalism. . . . With power fully behind this [capitalist] class, any act could become criminal simply by fixing a penal sanction to it and processing it through a growing judicial machinery." [28]

Second, radicals argue that people commit crimes in natural response to the competitiveness and insecurity of capitalist societies. Capitalist societies depend on competition and inequality. Individuals must fend for themselves, finding the best available opportunities for themselves and their families. Some of these opportunities may, in fact, violate the law. Three different kinds of crime in the United States illustrate these rational responses: ghetto crime, organized crime, and corporate crime.

Third, radicals argue that many of the important difference among crimes — given this similar response to competition and insecurity — flow from the structure of class institutions in our society and from the class biases of the state. Different individuals, living in different class situations, will find it necessary to commit different kinds of crimes in order to gain the same reward. And the State, ultimately serving and protecting the interests of the dominant class, largely protects ruling-class criminals while it prosecutes lower-class criminals. That differential attention often drives many lower-class criminals into the kind of violence that seems necessary to protect themselves.

[26] Gordon Tullock, "Does Punishment Deter Crime?" *The Public Interest*, Number 36, Summer 1974, p. 110.

[27] Hacker, "Getting Used to Mugging," p. 9.

[28] See the selection by Kennedy in this chapter.

Fourth, radicals argue that this duality in the criminal justice system has itself grown up out of the complicated relationships between the State and different classes in the capitalist system. In any class society, a government arises that mainly protects the interests of a dominant class. In capitalist societies, the State arises primarily to serve the interests of the capitalist class. Its institutions of crime prevention, prosecution, and imprisonment have grown through that history. We cannot take them as given, like orthodox economists, but must clearly analyze their biases and complicated dialectics.

Finally, radicals argue that these patterns cannot be changed without fundamentally transforming our society. Reform is implausible, they conclude, unless we change the basic institutions upon which capitalism in the United States depends. Capitalism depends upon the preservation of competition and inequality, themselves principal causes of crime. Capitalism also depends centrally, in this country at least, on the continuing racism that so clearly feeds the sources and consequences of crime. Moreover, current patterns of crime and punishment clearly serve important functions. Many vested interests benefit from current practices. Even more important, current practices and ideologies help legitimize the economic system by reinforcing common beliefs about "legitimate" and "illegitimate" economic activities. Were we to "solve" the problems of crime and punishment, we would ultimately undermine the stability of the capitalist economic system and the institutions upon which it depends. It is in that ultimate sense of causality, radicals argue, that we must somehow change the entire structure of institutions in this country in order to eliminate the causes of crime.

This summary of the radical perspective helps clarify the similarities and differences between the radical view and more conventional liberal and conservative views. Like orthodox economists, radicals argue that criminal activity represents a "rational" response to conditions in capitalist societies, differing with the liberal and conservative conventional wisdom. At the same time, radicals differ fundamentally with several premises of the orthodox economic analysis. The history of the State makes it clear, radicals contend, that we cannot take some neutral "social welfare function" for granted. State policies, in fact, reflect a complicated history. The history of the State clearly suggests, moreover, that government actions and policies primarily serve the needs and interests of one class over those of others. The idea of society-wide "optimal" policies seems to overlook the class biases of the State. In particular, radicals continue, the orthodox view of State expenditures on crime prevention and punishment seems extremely simplistic. The orthodox perspective suggests that such expenditures are motivated exclusively by their prospective benefits to the rest of society — to the prospective victims of crime. In fact, the radicals argue, State activities are designed as much to serve the more general purposes of social "control" as they are to protect the majority of citizens.

The Readings

The first group of readings provides Impressions, Definitions, and Magnitudes. Claude Brown and Arthur Dunmeyer talk about the kinds of experiences in black ghettos that tend to breed crime. Roger Feldman and Glenn Weisfeld present an interview with a young white who talks in somewhat similar terms, partly suggesting that some of the economic roots of crime cross racial lines. The two following selections provide useful summaries of the kinds of crime prominent in urban areas and the relative importance of that crime. As both selections clearly show, urban crime constitutes only a small part of total crime in the country.

The second group of readings reviews different analytic perspectives. Richard F. Sullivan gives the orthodox economic approach to crime and prevention. David M. Gordon summarizes the general radical perspective on crime. Mark Kennedy focuses on the historical relationship between the rise of capitalism and the origins of crime — a central element in the radical analysis. In the final selection, Ronald Goldfarb focuses on our modern poorhouses, on the jails where, as radicals argue, we dump those in our society for which we have no other use.

A WAY OF LIFE IN THE GHETTO

Claude Brown and Arthur Dunmeyer

In 1966 the "Ribicoff subcommittee" held a long series of hearings on urban problems, inviting both academic experts and many city residents. One of the most dramatic testimonies of the entire hearings involved Claude Brown, author of *Manchild in the Promised Land,* and Arthur Dunmeyer, a friend of Brown's from Harlem. Both of them had grown up poor and black in the center of a ghetto, and both had long records of crime and arrest as teenagers. Better than more detached analysis, their testimony underscored a basic fact of ghetto life — crime often offers more status, income, and dignity to many ghetto residents than "legitimate" employment does. No matter how hard the ghettos are policed, this implies, the links to crime for many in the ghetto cannot really be broken until the nature of "legitimate" employment opportunities radically improves.

SENATOR RIBICOFF: What is the impact on the Negro from the rural South who comes up to the slums of New York? What happens to them physically, emotionally, mentally, morally? What do you find happens when they have to make their change? Your parents came and you were born here, or you were just a child in arms, and now you are older and you observe this. What happens to them then?

MR. BROWN: Once they get there and become disillusioned, they can see the streets aren't paved with gold, and there exist no great economic opportunities for them, they become pressured. Many of the fathers who brought the families can't take the pressure any more, the economic pressure. How can you support a family of five kids on $65 a week? So he just leaves. He just ups one day and leaves, maybe becoming an alcoholic. Maybe he just goes out one night and he is so depressed because he missed a day's pay. During the week — he was sick. He couldn't help it. And he wasn't in the union, and this depression leads to a sort of touchiness, I

Source: Claude Brown and Arthur Dunmeyer, "A Way of Life in the Ghetto," from *The Federal Role in Urban Affairs,* Hearings Before the Subcommittee on Executive Reorganization of the Committee on Government Operations. U.S. Senate, 89th Congress, 2d Session, August 29–30, 1966.

will say—to become more mundane, where in a bar a person can step on his foot and he or the person gets his throat cut.

Somebody is dead. The other is in jail. He is going to the electric chair. It won't happen in New York today since they have abolished capital punishment. But this was one of the reactions.

Many of the physical reactions — they took out their frustrations on their kids — they beat the hell out of them. My father used to beat me nearly to death every day. Still they take it out on their wives. They beat their wives. It is just frustration that they feel. . . .

Or maybe the number runner on the corner digs Mama or something. She has got a couple of kids. He can give her $25 a week. All her husband can make is, say, $60 at most a week, and it isn't enough, and the $25 helps because she wants her kids to have the things that TV says that they should have.

You know, these are many of the reactions. And, then, there is the shooting. The guy comes home. He is trying. He comes home. He hears about his wife and he goes out one day, picks up a gun, he says "Oh, Lord, I have tried so hard. It is just not for me. It is my lot to always be a day late and a dollar short. But, this guy has been making it with my woman and he has got to die. This is an affront to my masculinity."

So he kills him. Then he is in jail. His family is on welfare or he is in the electric chair. These are emotional and physical reactions.

I will turn it over to you, Arthur.

MR. DUNMEYER: I would like to bring this up also. In some cases this is the way you get your drug dealers and prostitutes and your numbers runners. You get people that come here and it is not that they are disillusioned. They see that these things are the only way that they can compete in the society, to get some sort of status. They realize that there aren't any real doors open to them, and so, to commit crime was the only thing to do, they can't go back. There is nothing to go back to. This is understood. This is why they came.

The only thing to do is to get something going to

benefit yourself. It is a way to live, a way to have enough to keep your wife from going to bed with the butcher. It is a way to keep from killing the butcher. You kill him in small ways, by taking him off, by holding him up, by seeing that he don't hang out in the neighborhood after the store is closed. It is cheating. It is stealing. These things are just a way of life that come from this one particular thing.

This Negro comes to the promised land, as he says, and he finds that it isn't a promised land and he finds that there is nowhere else to go. There is nothing else to do. And he has the physical and the mental ability to do this particular thing. So he does it as a way of life.

Society has made this law to protect itself, not to protect this man in any way, just to protect itself so there is a law that he can't do this, and he doesn't recognize this law. Really, he doesn't recognize anything in society, because of this one particular thing. He sees there are no doors really open to him; and until these doors can be open to this man and this woman, there is going to be the same thing over and over again.

It is a matter of getting caught. Not a matter of taking or doing anything. It is a matter of getting caught and this is where it comes from.

MR. BROWN: I would like to add something more to this. In the Harlems throughout the Nation, it is like the crimes which society considers crimes, that the Negro who has migrated to the North has to resort to. My father he started — as it is related in the book — one of my most pronounced recollections is seeing my father cut a man's throat when I was at the age of 5. My father and I never got too close because there never was time. He beat the hell out of me quite often, and that was it. We couldn't talk. He had too many problems, too many frustrations. And there were times when I would be bothering my sisters. I would hit them or something. They'd say, "I'm going to tell Daddy on you and he's going to cut your throat," and I say, "No, he ain't." But I never believed that he wasn't because I had seen him do it.

Anyway, my father started when he came, the only thing he knew was what his father had taught him as a trade, considered illegitimate by Internal Revenue Service, of course, but it was making corn liquor in the bathtub — White Light, King Corn, perhaps you heard of it in those terms. And so he did this and ran his parlor parties and his crap games.

When I was coming up I wanted things, too, as a child, that my parents couldn't give me because my father he wanted to be with his family, he wasn't going to jail and had to give up his way of life, and at this time he was making a little more money. Of course, by the age of 40 or 42 he was making, say, $75 a week, because he had been working on the job for about 15 years at that time and this was a big deal to him. But still, he couldn't afford to give me the things, buy the sport jackets and things that the kids were wearing at the time to go along with the fad of the community. Anyway, I took to selling drugs.

SENATOR RIBICOFF: How old were you when you started selling drugs?

MR. BROWN: I was selling drugs at 13.

SENATOR RIBICOFF: Thirteen?

MR. BROWN: Yes; heroin. Anyway, it is like, in the community, in the Negro ghettos throughout the country, these things that are considered criminal by society, the solid citizen, aren't considered criminal. It is like a war between them and us, the society which oppresses us, and us, the oppressed. When a guy goes to jail, it is OK. You are looked up to, if you are a successful hustler, you have a big Cadillac and you have always got $300 in your pocket, you are taking numbers, you are selling drugs, you are a stickup artist, you are anything, you are a prostitute, anything you may be doing, you are a con man, a hustler. Anybody you heard of, Jim Smith, the mayor, or somebody from Arkansas, this is the way you come up in Harlem. You learn these games at certain ages.

At 13 I learned how to cut drugs, how much quinine to put in cocaine. At the age of 15 I learned how to "Murphy" somebody. The "Murphy" is the flimflam. Anyway, had I been in the South, had I been in a better society, I would have been learning. I would have been in school and learning how to make it legitimately, but I wasn't. I was learning how to make it illegitimately, but these were the best possible ways to make it financially, to establish a decent place for yourself in America's greatest metropolis.

The TV's were saying, yes, get this, you know, have a car. Everybody should have a car. Even color TV, how are you going to get it? You can get it selling drugs. You can get it taking numbers. You know, you can get it playing the Murphy. You can get it if you ran around taking off people, sticking up people, this sort of thing. As long as you were making it, as long as you were a success, that is why in Harlem people respect the guy who is always clean.

You know, he has on a $200 silk suit every day, $55 alligator shoes and this sort of thing. He drives a big Cadillac, and, they know he is winning the war. He is a soldier, he is a real soldier. He is a general in the community. If he gets busted, well, he is just a prisoner of war. That is the way it is looked upon.

MR. DUNMEYER: Or you have a situation where you have got a white fellow from downtown. He is a gangster, and high in society. He can bring the dope in town. He imports it. He brings it uptown. He makes me feel important. I have the money that he has. I can dress the way he dresses. I can drive a car like he drives. I can take care of my family the way

he takes care of his. And he is white. So if it is recognition by the white standards, then, I am getting recognition by the white. And this is very important, you are being looked up to in your community. It is just a way of life. So when you get struck, you take it until you get struck again. That is the way it is.

It is not a matter of a guy saying, "I want to go to jail. I am afraid of jail." Jail is on the street just like it is on the inside. The same as, like when you are in jail, they tell you, "Look, if you do something wrong you are going to be put in the hole." You are still in jail, in the hole or out of the hole. You are in jail in the street or behind bars. It is the same thing. . . .

"I DON'T LIKE NOBODY WITH MONEY ANYWAY"

Roger Feldman and Glenn Weisfeld

Two sociologists conducted a series of interviews with an experienced young white robber. The following excerpts suggest clearly that whites pursue the same ends that blacks do in their lives of crime — mostly they want to make money.

Tom is white. He is virtually illiterate but highly intelligent. He is about twenty-four. For most of his life he has lived independently, "on the street." He learned to fight in reform school. Fighting helped him win the presidency of the Bel Airs, a club in the Logan Square neighborhood of Chicago's Northwest Side. He has been in trouble with the police regularly — for acts of violence and occasional property crimes and because he was a potentially powerful man in the community. He served one year in

Source: From "An Interdisciplinary Study of Crime," by Roger Feldman and Glenn Weisfeld. Reprinted, with permission of the National Council on Crime and Delinquency, from *Crime & Delinquency,* April 1973, pp. 150–62.

jail for involuntary manslaughter and is now on parole. He lives with his wife and daughter and is no longer active as a gang leader.

We first discussed some sociological and psychological explanations of crime. In general Tom discounts the importance of such factors, or else makes comments that can be subjected to more than one interpretation.

He concedes that there may be individuals with a personality structure that predisposes them toward crime. He is familiar with the word *kleptomaniac*; though he thinks that persons to whom this label is applied exist, he has never met any.

TOM: There is people that like to steal — kleptos, you know. You know that, right?
ROGER FELDMAN: Yeah.
TOM: Them people I couldn't talk about. I couldn't tell you about it, because I don't know any kleptos. I know people that steal for a living — steal because they have to steal, because they can't get nothing else better to do. . . .

Is it theft per se which is valued, or is it the ability of the successful thief to acquire material goods — the income-earning factor — which is valued? Tom clearly indicates that the second interpretation is more important.

RF: Do you get a reputation from stealing. . .

Tom: Sure you do.

RF: . . . or do you get it more from fighting?

Tom: Look at Bobby Beagle, he's got a reputation from stealing. But not the kind of reputation. . .

RF: Well, he's kind of notorious, but do people look up to him?

Tom: The kids look up to him. You know, they hear about him. "There goes Beagle."

RF: I remember, Dave pointed him out to me the first time I saw him and that's just what he said. "That's Beagle, he's a good thief."

Tom: He's a good car thief. There's a difference. He steals cars. And all he can get out of it — maybe 45 bucks out of the car, right? He's not a good *thief*. He's a good *car* thief. He's not a good *thief*. In other words, he's not making enough to rate as a professional thief.

RF: What makes a professional thief?

Tom: A professional thief is somebody that brings back two grand. Between six hundred and two and a half a day. John Doe used to bring back three, four, five thousand a day. He got so big, man, they didn't know what to do with him. California was going crazy.

RF: You mean Shakespeare? [Shakespeare is the name of the local police district. The station house is located on California Avenue.]

Tom: No, California. California, the state of California, they were going nuts. Chicago too. They were going crazy. They couldn't catch him. The guy used to take jets back and forth. They couldn't ever catch him. And finally when they did catch him they caught him ten years later. He was burglarizing something like twenty-five years. . . .

Tom: There's different kinds of respect, man. You're talking about reputation and you're talking about respect. A man with a reputation has never got no respect. He's got people afraid of him. So this fear brings respect to him because everybody's too scared to tell him what they really think. Then you've got the man with respect. The man who works every day and brings home a decent living, you know, a decent pay. Who lives good. You know. Not none of this church bullshit. Lives with his family. Now me, I had respect because I'd stick by a lot of people and a lot of people hated me. But a lot of people dug me because I really stuck by them. Not because they were scared of me but because I got my head busted for them a lot of times.

Tom: Now a lot of kids they all got different reasons why they're stealing. Like one might think, I'm stealing to be with some club, you know, and the rest of the club is out stealing cars all night, joyriding. No reason at all, right? You're just getting in the car and running around. You could get forty bucks and buy a car, right, and joyride all you want for free, right? Without going to jail. But they rather go and steal a car, you know, a beat-up old Chevy and drive it and get busted and go to jail. And that's the kind of guy who wants to belong, you know, and the only way he can do it was to go out and steal with them. . . .

Tom talked at length about his dislike for wealthy people. He traced out a coherent theory of exploitation, as well as arguing that wealthy people deserve to get ripped off because they treat the poor with less than decent respect.

RF: When people go out and do crimes in the suburbs, how much do they feel that they're getting back at the people who live out there for doing wrong to them? Sort of like Robin Hood?

Tom: No. It's not none of that Robin Hood bullshit. That's all fairytales. Ain't nobody that steals from the rich and gives to the poor. They steal from the rich and put it in their pockets.

DF: But you talk about Capone [Al Capone] that way.

Tom: Capone *wasn't* a Robin Hood. He was a millionaire. And he made a millionaire out of himself by the poor, by booze. But — when he did make it big he didn't forget the poor. He didn't forget himself being poor. What he did, he opened up soup kitchens. He opened up on Madison Street some hundreds of joints to feed the people that couldn't afford to eat, you know. But he wasn't no Robin Hood. He just fed the people, but he took their money too. He had millions.

GW: What about what Roger said earlier, about whether they think they're getting back at the people in the suburbs, when they rip them off?

Tom: Every kid that lives in this neighborhood hates people that live in the suburbs. Since I remember, there was always like dupers, greasers, gousters. You know what I mean?

GW: What are gousters?

Tom: Gousters is dudes that got something going up here [points to his head]. Greasers are the type of dude with the leather coat and black tight pants and walk around with chains. And dupers are the gym-shoed creeps with bobby sox and white levis, out in the suburbs. I never went for it, myself. *But*, they hate all suburbs, man. You laugh at it. It doesn't matter. They hate anybody that got more than they do.

RF: You could hate them because they're better off or your could hate them because they took it from you.

Tom: No, we hate them because — like me, I'm a roofer, but when I go out there to do one of the roofs, you know, they sit there on the patio or something and drink Pepsi-Cola, Jack, when you're sweating your ass off, man, and they look at you like you're some kind of creep, man, and they stick their nose up in the air. If you ask them a question — one time one girl told me. "Don't talk to me; talk to my husband." I went to talk to him and he just walked away. They're creeps, man. They get a little bit of bread and then they move out to some little-bitty suburb and then they act like they're some kind of president or something. Too good to talk to anybody. And the same deal goes for their kids. When their kids come into Chicago they walk down the street like some kind of sissy and expect you to do something. They just stick it to me. I don't like them.

I don't like nobody with money anyway. Because they don't get money. Most of them own businesses, like Breits — Breits supermarket, Leslies department store, all them, right? The way they got up there, man, they robbed people, right? But they robbed them in a way where they couldn't get arrested for it. Only they're good people. To society they're good people. . . .

MF: Would you rather steal in a rich neighborhood than in a non-rich? You know what I mean?

Tom: Of course. Why would you steal from somebody that ain't got nothing, like you? That would be like me living down Madison Street and Halsted [Skid Row] and robbing the guy's house next door. Trying to steal something what he ain't got, you know. All right, let's say you were going to a beautician shop; would you go to one that doesn't know how to fix your hair? You'd go to the one that does, right? OK, it's the same with them burglaries. You don't want to burglarize someone that ain't got nothing. You want to go out and burglarize someone that got something. What are you doing, just running around for tricks, just burglarizing to find out what was happening? . . .

Tom draws the distinction between "high" and "low" crime. His criteria are mainly in terms of size,

type of crime, and the different people involved. High crimes involve millions of dollars; they are typically white-collar theft or the sale of illegal goods (narcotics, gambling); they are done by politicians, police, the syndicate, and businessmen. Low crimes are small jobs for property articles committed by people for whom society normally reserves the word "criminals." But to Tom there is no *fundamental* difference. Both high and low crimes are done for financial reward.

Tom: You talk about the syndicate. That *is* the syndicate — the mayor. There is too much crime in Chicago. I mean, not penny-ante bullshit that dudes pull on the street. I'm talking about high-class crime, you know. Like that million dollar embezzlement ring in Zenith [Zenith Radio Corporation]. Shit, like millions of dollars just don't get up and disappear without somebody listening to it or somebody hearing about it. You know what I mean? Too many ears closed up, man.

RF: What's the relationship between the two machines, the politics machine and the syndicate machine?

Tom: They're the same machine. There ain't no two machines.

RF: The same people?

Tom: Leo Peppitone, the alderman out at, ah, not the alderman — what do they call that out at the neighborhoods?

DF: Precinct captain?

Tom: Precinct captain. He grew up on Madison Street and his brother used to run with a club called the Packer Gang. A hit man for the syndicate, in the beginning. And he's the precinct captain in the neighborhood over there, you know. And he's nothing but a hood.

MF: You're making the distinction between high crime. What would be the low crime that you talked about? Like, petty crime?

Tom: Petty crime? Why people do petty shit, right? What you want to know, actually, is why, like, I jump up and steal something. Or why would Bobby Beagle steal a car. I don't know, man. There ain't no difference in it actually. The syndicate, all they are is a high-class thief. And guys like me and Beagle and Poker or Tommy or any of us, you know, we steal for a reason. It's the same reason they do: to make money.

DF: Of all the people that you know who were involved in small crime, how many of them at this point have continued on a serious basis — continued in some crime in any way? Do most of them just stop or do they do a little bit or do they go into some other. . .

Tom: Nobody never stops. Everybody in the world has stole. Everybody has. What you're talking about. . .

DF: I haven't [laughter].

Tom: What you're talking about is steadily doing it every day and then *stopping*, right? You don't stop. Now, they might act like they stop. They try to stop, but when they see an opening, they'll steal anyway. Even me. Sure. If I see an opening where I can pick up some bread, I'll take it.

CRIME IN THE UNITED STATES

The President's Commission on Law Enforcement and the Administration of Justice

This brief selection (from what is often referred to as the Crime Commission Report) outlines the magnitude of various kinds of crime in the United States. Pulling together varieties of official statistics on national crime, it makes clear that what we think of as "urban crime" constitutes only a small proportion of total crime. For the nation as a whole, many other causes of death and injury account for much more personal harm than do the FBI Index Crimes against persons, and many other kinds of crime have much larger economic impact than do Index Crimes against property.

The Amount of Crime

There are more than 2,800 Federal crimes and a much larger number of State and local ones. Some involve serious bodily harm, some stealing, some public morals or public order, some governmental revenues, some the creation of hazardous conditions, some the regulation of the economy. Some are perpetrated ruthlessly and systematically; others are spontaneous derelictions. Gambling and prostitution are willingly undertaken by both buyer and seller; murder and rape are violently imposed upon their victims. Vandalism is predominantly a crime of the young; driving while intoxicated, a crime of the adult. Many crime rates vary significantly from place to place.

Source: The President's Commission on Law Enforcement and the Administration of Justice. Washington, D.C.: U.S. Government, 1967.

The crimes that concern Americans the most are those that affect their personal safety — at home, at work, or in the streets. The most frequent and serious of these crimes of violence against the person are willful homicide, forcible rape, aggravated assault, and robbery. National statistics regarding the number of these offenses known to the police either from citizen complaints or through independent police discovery are collected from local police officials by the Federal Bureau of Investigation and published annually as a part of its report, "Crime in the United States, Uniform Crime Reports." The FBI also collects "offenses known" statistics for three property crimes: Burglary, larceny of $50 or over and motor vehicle theft. These seven crimes are grouped together in the UCR to form an Index of serious crimes. Table 1 shows the totals for these offenses for 1965.

■ *The Risk of Harm*

Including robbery, the crimes of violence make up approximately 13 percent of the Index. The Index reports the number of incidents known to the police, not the number of criminals who committed them or the number of injuries they caused.

The risk of sudden attack by a stranger is perhaps best measured by the frequency of robberies since, according to UCR and other studies, about 70 percent of all willful killings, nearly two-thirds of all aggravated assaults and a high percentage of forcible rapes are committed by family members, friends, or other persons previously known to their victims. Rob-

TABLE 1. Estimated Number and Percentage of Index Offenses, 1965

	Number	Percentage
Murder, non-negligent manslaughter	9,850	0.4
Forcible rape	22,467	0.8
Robbery	118,916	4.3
Aggravated assault	206,661	7.4
Burglary	1,173,201	42.2
Larceny, $50 and over	762,352	27.4
Motor vehicle theft	486,568	17.5
Total, crimes against person	357,894	12.9
Total, crimes against property	2,422,121	87.1
Grand Total	2,780,015	100.0

Source: *Uniform Crime Reports*, 1965, p. 51.

[Ed.: In the Commission Report, this table is actually presented as a bar graph. I present it as a table, to save space, and I added the percentages.]

bery usually does not involve this prior victim-offender relationship.

Robbery, for UCR purposes, is the taking of property from a person by use or threat of force with or without a weapon. Nationally, about one-half of all robberies are street robberies, and slightly more than one-half involve weapons. Attempted robberies are an unknown percentage of the robberies reported to the UCR. The likelihood of injury is also unknown, but a survey by the District of Columbia Crime Commission of 297 robberies in Washington showed that some injury was inflicted in 25 percent of them. The likelihood of injury was found higher for "yokings" or "muggings" (unarmed robberies from the rear) than for armed robberies. Injuries occurred in 10 of 91 armed robberies as compared with 30 of 67 yokings.

Aggravated assault is assault with intent to kill or for the purpose of inflicting severe bodily injury, whether or not a dangerous weapon is used. It includes all cases of attempted homicide, but cases in which bodily injury is inflicted in the course of a robbery or a rape are included with those crimes rather than with aggravated assault. There are no national figures showing the percentage of aggravated assaults that involve injury, but a survey of 131 cases by the District of Columbia Crime Com-

mission found injury in 84 percent of the cases; 35 percent of the victims required hospitalization. A 1960 UCR study showed that juvenile gangs committed less than 4 percent of all aggravated assaults.

Forcible rape includes only those rapes or attempted rapes in which force or threat of force is used. About one-third of the UCR total is attempted offense. In the District of Columbia Crime Commission survey of 151 cases, about 25 percent of all rape victims were attacked with dangerous weapons; the survey did not show what percentage received bodily harm in addition to the rape.

About 15 percent of all criminal homicides, both nationally and in the District of Columbia Crime Commission surveys, occurred in the course of committing other offenses. These offenses appear in the homicide total rather than in the total for the other offense. In the District of Columbia Crime Commission surveys, less than one-half of 1 percent of the robberies and about 1 percent of the forcible rapes ended in homicide.

Some personal danger is also involved in the property crimes. Burglary is the unlawful entering of a building to commit a felony or a theft, whether force is used or not. About half of all burglaries involve residences, but the statistics do not distinguish inhabited parts of houses from garages and similar outlying parts. About half of all residential burglaries are committed in daylight and about half at night. A UCR survey indicates that 32 percent of the entries into residences are made through unlocked doors or windows. When an unlawful entry results in a volent confrontation with the occupant, the offense is counted as a robbery rather than a burglary. Of course, even when no confrontation takes place there is often a risk of confrontation. Nationally such confrontations occur in only one-fortieth of all residential burglaries. They account for nearly one-tenth of all robberies.

In summary, these figures suggest that, on the average, the likelihood of a serious personal attack on any American in a given year is about 1 in 550; together with the studies available they also suggest that the risk of serious attack from spouses, family members, friends, or acquaintances is almost twice as great as it is from strangers on the street. Commission and other studies, moreover, indicate that the risks of personal harm are spread very unevenly. The actual risk for slum dwellers is considerably more; for most Americans it is considerably less.

Except in the case of willful homicide, where the

figures describe the extent of injury as well as the number of incidents, there is no national data on the likelihood of injury from attack. More limited studies indicate that while some injury may occur in two-thirds of all attacks, the risk in a given year of injury serious enough to require any degree of hospitalization of any individual is about 1 in 3,000 on the average, and much less for most Americans. These studies also suggest that the injury inflicted by family members or acquaintances is likely to be more severe than that from strangers. As shown by Table 2, the risk of death from willful homicide is about 1 in 20,000.

TABLE 2.   Deaths from Other Than Natural Causes, 1965 (Per 100,000 Inhabitants)

Motor vehicle accidents	25
Other accidents	12
Suicide	12
Falls	10
Willful homicide	5
Drowning	4
Fires	4

Source: National Safety Council, "Accident Facts," 1965; Population Reference Bureau.

Criminal behavior accounts for a high percentage of motor vehicle deaths and injuries. In 1965 there were an estimated 49,000 motor vehicle deaths. Negligent manslaughter, which is largely a motor vehicle offense, accounted for more than 7,000 of these. Studies in several States indicate that an even higher percentage involve criminal behavior. They show that driving while intoxicated is probably involved in more than one-half of all motor vehicle deaths. These same studies show that driving while intoxicated is involved in more than 13 percent of the 1,800,000 nonfatal motor vehicle injuries each year.

For various statistical and other reasons, a number of serious crimes against or involving risk to the person, such as arson, kidnapping, child molestation, and simple assault, are not included in the UCR Index. In a study of 1,300 cases of delinquency in Philadelphia, offenses other than the seven Index crimes constituted 62 percent of all cases in which there was physical injury. Simple assault accounted for the largest percentage of these injuries. But its victims required medical attention in only one-fifth of the cases as opposed to three-fourths of the ag-

gravated assaults, and hospitalization in 7 percent as opposed to 23 percent. Injury was more prevalent in conflicts between persons of the same age than in those in which the victim was older or younger than the attacker.

■ Property Crimes

The three property crimes of burglary, automobile theft, and larceny of $50 and over make up 87 percent of Index crimes. The Index is a reasonably reliable indicator of the total number of property crimes reported to the police, but not a particularly good indicator of the seriousness of monetary loss from all property crimes. Commission studies tend to indicate that such non-Index crimes as fraud and embezzlement are more significant in terms of dollar volume. Fraud can be a particularly pernicious offense. It is not only expensive in total but all too often preys on the weak.

Many larcenies included in the Index total are misdemeanors rather than felonies under the laws of their own States. Auto thefts that involve only unauthorized use also are misdemeanors in many States. Many stolen automobiles are abandoned after a few hours, and more than 85 percent are ultimately recovered, according to UCR studies. Studies in California indicate that about 20 percent of recovered cars are significantly damaged. . . .

Economic Impact of Individual Crimes

The information available about the economic cost of crime is most usefully presented not as an overall figure, but as a series of separate private and public costs. Knowing the economic impact of each separate crime aids in identifying important areas for public concern and guides officials in making judgments about priorities for expenditure. Breakdowns of money now being spent on different parts of the criminal justice system, and within each separate part, may afford insights into past errors. For example, even excluding value judgments about rehabilitative methods, the fact that an adult probationer costs 38 cents a day and an adult offender in prison costs $5.24 a day suggests the need for reexamining current budget allocations in correctional practice.

Table 3 represents six different categories of economic impacts both private and public. Numerous crimes were omitted because of the lack of figures. Estimates of doubtful reliability were used in other cases so that a fuller picture might be presented.

TABLE 3.   Economic Impact of Crimes and Related Expenditures (Estimated in Millions of Dollars)

General Class of Crime	Component	Amount Component	Class Total
1. Crimes Against Person (loss of earnings, etc.)	Homicide	750	
	Assault and Other	65	
			815
2. Crimes Against Property (transfers and losses)	Unreported Commercial Theft	1,400	
	Index Crimes (robbery, burglary, larceny $50+, auto theft)	600	
	Embezzlement	200	
	Fraud	1,350	
	Forgery and Other	82	
	Property Destroyed by Arson and Vandalism	300	
			3,932
3. Other Crimes	Driving Under Influence of Alcohol	1,816	
	Tax Fraud	100	
	Abortion	120	
			2,036
4. Illegal Goods & Services	Narcotics	350	
	Loan-sharking	350	
	Prostitution	225	
	Alcohol	150	
	Gambling	7,000	
			8,075
5. Public Law Enforcement, Criminal Justice	Police	2,792	
	Corrections	1,034	
	Prosecution and Defense	125	
	Courts	261	
			4,212
6. Private Costs Related to Crime	Prevention Services	1,350	
	Prevention Equipment	200	
	Insurance	60	
	Private Counsel, Bail, Witness Expenses	300	
			1,910

Estimates do not include any amounts for pain and suffering. Except for alcohol, which is based on the amount of tax revenue lost, estimates for illegal goods and services are based on the gross amount of income to the seller. (Gambling includes only the percentage retained by organized crime, not the total amount gambled.) The totals should be taken to indicate rough orders of magnitude rather than precise details.

The picture of crime as seen through cost information is considerably different from that shown by statistics portraying the number of offenses known to the police or the number of arrests:

• Organized crime takes about twice as much income from gambling and other illegal goods and services as criminals derive from all other kinds of criminal activity combined.

- Unreported commercial theft losses, including shoplifting and employee theft, are more than double those of all reported private and commercial thefts.
- Of the reported crimes, willful homicide, though comparatively low in volume, yields the most costly estimates among those listed on the UCR crime Index.
- A list of the seven crimes with the greatest economic impact includes only two, willful homicide and larceny of $50 and over (reported and unreported), of the offenses included in the crime Index.
- Only a small proportion of the money expended for criminal justice agencies is allocated to rehabilitative programs for criminals or for research.

Employee theft, embezzlement, and other forms of crime involving business, which appear in relatively small numbers in the police statistics, loom very large in dollar volume. Direct stealing of cash and merchandise, manipulation of accounts and stock records, and other forms of these crimes, along with shoplifting, appear to constitute a tax of one to two percent on the total sales of retail enterprises, and significant amounts in other parts of business and industry. In the grocery trade, for example, the theft estimates for shoplifting and employee theft almost equal the total amount of profit. Yet Commission and other studies indicate that these crimes are largely dealt with by business itself. Merchants report to the police fewer than one-quarter of the known offenses. Estimates for these crimes are particularly incomplete for nonretail industries.

Fraud is another offense whose impact is not well conveyed by police statistics. Just one conspiracy involving the collapse of a fraudulent salad oil empire in 1964 created losses of $125–$175 million. Fraud is especially vicious when it attacks, as it so often does, the poor or those who live on the margin of poverty. Expensive nostrums for incurable diseases, home-improvement frauds, frauds involving the sale or repair of cars, and other criminal schemes create losses which are not only sizeable in gross but are also significant and possibly devastating for individual victims. Although a very frequent offense, fraud is seldom reported to the police. In consumer and business fraud, as in tax evasion, the line between criminal conduct and civil fraud is often unclear. And just as the amount of civil tax evasion is much greater than the amount of criminal tax fraud, the amount of civil fraud probably far exceeds that of criminal fraud.

Cost analysis also places the crimes that appear so frequently in police statistics — robbery, burglary, larceny, and auto theft — in somewhat different perspective. The number of reported offenses for these crimes accounts for less than one-sixth the estimated total dollar loss for all property crimes and would constitute an even lower percentage if there were any accurate way of estimating the very large sums involved in extortion, blackmail, and other property crimes.

This is not to say, however, that the large amounts of police time and effort spent in dealing with these crimes are not important. Robbery and burglary, particularly residential burglary, have importance beyond the number of dollars involved. The effectiveness of the police in securing the return of better than 85 percent of the $500 million worth of cars stolen annually appears to be high, and without the efforts of the police the costs of these crimes would doubtless be higher. As with all categories of crime, the total cost of property crimes cannot be measured because of the large volume of unreported crimes; however, Commission surveys suggest that the crimes that are unreported involve less money per offense than those that are reported.

The economic impact of crimes causing death is surprisingly high. For 1965 there were an estimated 9,850 homicide victims. Of the estimated 49,000 people who lost their lives in highway accidents, more than half were killed in accidents involving either negligent manslaughter or driving under the influence of alcohol. An estimated 290 women died from complications resulting from illegal abortions (nearly one-fourth of all maternal deaths). Measured by the loss of future earnings at the time of death, these losses totaled more than $1½ billion.

The economic impact of other crimes is particularly difficult to assess. Antitrust violations reduce competition and unduly raise prices; building code violations, pure food and drug law violations, and other crimes affecting the consumer have important economic consequences, but they cannot be easily described without further information. Losses due to fear of crime, such as reduced sales in high crime locations, are real but beyond measure.

Economic impact must also be measured in terms of ultimate costs to society. Criminal acts causing property destruction or injury to persons not only result in serious losses to the victims or their families but also the withdrawal of wealth or productive capacity from the economy as a whole. Theft on the other hand does not destroy wealth but merely transfers it involuntarily from the victim, or perhaps his insurance company, to the thief. The bettor purchasing illegal betting services from organized crime may easily absorb the loss of a 10-cent, or even 10-dollar, bet. But from the point of view of society, gambling leaves much less wealth available for legitimate business. Perhaps more important, it is the proceeds of this crime tariff that organized crime collects from those who purchase its illegal wares that form the major source of income that organized crime requires to achieve and exercise economic and political power.

CRIME IN URBAN AREAS

The National Advisory Commission on Civil Disorders

This second set of basic figures on crime provides a more specific picture of crime in urban areas and especially in urban ghettos. It emphasizes that crime rates within cities bear a fairly clear relationship to the poverty of urban neighborhoods, and that the victims of crime in poor neighborhoods are usually the neighborhood residents themselves, not random citizens living in other parts of the city.

Nothing is more fundamental to the quality of life in any area than the sense of personal security of its residents, and nothing affects this more than crime.

In general, crime rates in large cities are much higher than in other areas of our country. Within such cities, crime rates are higher in disadvantaged Negro areas than anywhere else.

The most widely used measure of crime is the number of "index crimes" (homicide, forcible rape, aggravated assault, robbery, burglary, grand larceny, and auto theft) in relation to population. In 1966, 1,754 such crimes were reported to police for every 100,000 Americans. In cities over 250,000, the rate was 3,153, and in cities over one million, it was 3,630 — or more than double the national average. In suburban areas alone, including suburban cities, the rate was only 1,300, or just over one-third the rate in the largest cities.

Source: Report of the National Advisory Commission on Civil Disorders. Washington, D.C.: U.S. Government, 1968.

Within larger cities, personal and property insecurity has consistently been highest in the older neighborhoods encircling the downtown business district. In most cities, crime rates for many decades have been higher in these inner areas than anywhere else, except in downtown areas themselves where they are inflated by the small number of residents.

High crime rates have persisted in these inner areas even though the ethnic character of their residents continually changed. Poor immigrants used these areas as "entry ports," then usually moved on to more desirable neighborhoods as soon as they acquired enough resources. Many "entry port" areas have now become racial ghettos.

The difference between crime rates in these disadvantaged neighborhoods and in other parts of the city is usually startling, as a comparison of crime rates in five police districts in Chicago for 1965 illustrates. Taking one high-income, all-white district at the periphery of the city, two very low-income, virtually all-Negro districts near the city core, both including numerous public housing projects, and two predominantly white districts, one with mainly lower-middle-income families, the other containing a mixture of very high-income and relatively low-income households, the table [on p. 373] shows crime rates against persons and against property in these five districts, plus the number of patrolmen assigned to them per 100,000 residents.

These data suggest the following conclusions:

Incidence of Index Crimes and Patrolmen Assignments per 100,000 Residents in 5 Chicago Police Districts, 1965

Number	High-Income White District	Low-Middle-Income White District	Mixed High and Low-Income White District	Very Low-Income Negro District No. 1	Very Low-Income Negro District No. 2
Index crimes against persons	80	440	338	1,615	2,820
Index crimes against property	1,038	1,750	2,080	2,508	2,630
Patrolmen assigned	93	133	115	243	291

- Variations in the crime rate against persons within the city are extremely large. One very low-income Negro district had 35 times as many serious crimes against persons per 100,000 residents as did the high-income white district.
- Variations in the crime rate against property are much smaller. The highest rate was only 2.5 times larger than the lowest.
- Both income and race appear to affect crime rates: the lower the income in an area, the higher the crime rate there. Yet low-income Negro areas have significantly higher crime rates than low-income white areas. This reflects the high degree of social disorganization in Negro areas described in the previous chapter, as well as the fact that poor Negroes, as a group, have lower incomes than poor whites, as a group.
- The presence of more police patrolmen per 100,000 residents does not necessarily offset high crime in certain parts of the city. Although the Chicago Police Department had assigned over three times as many patrolmen per 100,000 residents to the highest-crime area shown as to the lowest, crime rates in the highest-crime area for offenses against both persons and property combined were 4.9 times as high as in the lowest-crime area.

Because most middle-class Americans live in neighborhoods similar to the more crime-free district described above, they have little comprehension of the sense of insecurity that characterizes the ghetto resident. Moreover, official statistics normally greatly understate actual crime rates because the vast majority of crimes are not reported to the police. For example, a study conducted for the President's Crime Commission in three Washington, D.C., precincts showed that six times as many crimes were actually committed against persons and homes as were reported to the police. Other studies in Boston and Chicago indicated that about three times as many crimes were committed as were reported.

Two facts are crucial to understand the effects of high crime rates in racial ghettos: most of these crimes are committed by a small minority of the residents, and the principal victims are the residents themselves. Throughout the United States, the great majority of crimes committed by Negroes involve other Negroes as victims, just as most crimes committed by whites are against other whites. A special tabulation made by the Chicago Police Department for the President's Crime Commission indicated that over 85 percent of the crimes committed by Negroes between September 1965 and March 1966 involved Negro victims.

As a result, the majority of law-abiding citizens who live in disadvantaged Negro areas face much higher probabilities of being victimized than residents of most higher-income areas, including almost all suburbs. For nonwhites, the probability of suffering from any index crime except larceny is 78 percent higher than for whites. The probability of being raped is 3.7 times higher among nonwhite women and the probability of being robbed is 3.5 times higher for nonwhites in general.

The problems associated with high crime rates generate widespread hostility toward the police in these neighborhoods for reasons described elsewhere in this Report. Thus, crime not only creates an atmosphere of insecurity and fear throughout Negro neighborhoods but also causes continuing attrition of the relationship between Negro residents and police. This bears a direct relationship to civil disorder.

There are reasons to expect the crime situation in these areas to become worse in the future. First, crime rates throughout the United States have been rising rapidly in recent years. The rate of index crimes against persons rose 37 percent from 1960 to 1966, and the rate of index crimes against property rose 50 percent. In the first nine months of 1967, the number of index crimes was up 16 percent over the same period in 1966 whereas the United States population rose about one percent. In cities of 250,000 to one million, index crime rose by over 20 percent, whereas it increased four percent in cities of over one million.[1]

Second, the number of police available to combat crime is rising much more slowly than the amount of crime. In 1966, there were about 20 percent more police employees in the United States than in 1960, and per capita expenditures for police rose from $15.29 in 1960 to $20.99 in 1966, a gain of 37 per-

cent. But over the six-year period, the number of reported index crimes had jumped 62 percent. In spite of significant improvements in police efficiency, it is clear that police will be unable to cope with their expanding workload unless there is a dramatic increase in the resources allocated by society to this task.

Third, in the next decade the number of young Negroes aged 14 to 24 will increase rapidly, particularly in central cities. This group is responsible for a disproportionately high share of crimes in all parts of the nation. In 1966, persons under 25 years of age comprised the following proportions of those arrested for various major crimes: murder — 37 percent; forcible rape — 60 percent; robbery — 71 percent; burglary — 81 percent; larceny — about 75 percent; and auto theft — over 80 percent. For all index crimes together, the arrest rate for Negroes is about four times higher than that for whites. Yet the number of young Negroes aged 14 to 24 in central cities will rise about 63 percent from 1966 to 1975, as compared to only 32 percent for the total Negro population of central cities.[2]

---

[1] The problem of interpreting and evaluating "rising" crime rates is complicated by the changing age distribution of the population, improvements in reporting methods, and the increasing willingness of victims to report crimes. Despite these complications, there is general agreement on the serious increase in the incidence of crime in the United States.

[2] Assuming those cities will experience the same proportion of total United States Negro population growth that they did from 1960 to 1966.

THE ECONOMICS OF CRIME:
INTRODUCTION TO THE ORTHODOX LITERATURE

Richard F. Sullivan

As the chapter introduction notes, orthodox economists have recently developed their analysis of crime. In this short selection, an economist with legal training and experience in the field of criminology digests the orthodox approach for a lay audience — specifically for those working in the criminal justice

Source: Reprinted, with permission of the National Council on Crime and Delinquency, from *Crime & Delinquency,* April 1973, pp. 138–144.

system. Sullivan's summary presents the orthodox conclusions with somewhat more hesitation than the orthodox analysts themselves have done.

This article was prepared as an introductory piece for a special issue of *Crime & Delinquency* on economic approaches to the problem of crime.

Sullivan received a master's degree in economics, taught economics and law, worked in a probation department, and served as an economic consultant to the Solicitor General of Canada.

The recent onrush of academic economists into the field of criminology may be expected to increase our understanding of how criminal laws and sanctions function in our society and to explain the motivations and goals of criminals. In the short run, however, the picture is not quite so promising.

At one extreme, economists are saying that most concepts taught by schools of criminology are irrelevant and that individuals planning careers as probation officers, parole officers, or institutional correctional officers, with the intention of "rehabilitating" criminals, are suffering from delusions. According to economists, the intervention skills that these individuals are learning will largely fail because they are being implemented by the wrong people against the wrong people and for the wrong reasons. In other words, some economists seem to be saying that society would be better off if criminology students packed up their bags, went home, and urged elected representatives to do two things: (1) re-allocate law enforcement expenditures to increase the probability that a criminal will be caught and (2) increase the severity of punishment to make prisons less pleasant places to live in.

Economics for Criminologist

Until very recently, economists generally ignored the field of crime and law enforcement. They now contend, however, that their explanation of criminal behavior is superior to psychological or sociological explanations. The implications of this development for criminologists are profound. For the past generation, economic analyses and predictions on a wide variety of issues have been extremely useful to government policy-makers. Furthermore, of all the social scientists, the economists have been most successful in selling the idea that they are the most scientific: their methods of model-building, their adaptations of mathematical and statistical analyses, and their procedures for hypothesis-testing more closely aproximate those of the physical sciences, and where they do not, economists design analytic and predictive techniques that facilitate our understanding of how society works and of how government policies should be changed to achieve specific goals. As a result, economic researchers have always been able to obtain a very large share of foundation grants and government research money.

Academic economists are beginning to swarm into the field of criminology. . . . Large numbers of economists and nearly all of the larger economic research centers are importuning foundations and governments for research funds to conduct a wide variety of criminological studies. They will probably be successful in obtaining them. This means that in the next few years economic studies dealing with criminology will receive a great deal of attention both because of their volume and their novel approach to the field and because many professional criminologists will feel compelled to refute or elaborate on these explanations.

Although I have had experience in both worlds — as a probation officer and, more recently, as an academic economist — a short time ago I learned just how naïve I had been. In a lecture I stated that "an economist would be well advised to ignore the case of the man who murders his wife in a drunken, jealous rage and should leave sadists and revolutionaries to psychiatrists and political theorists." I had underestimated the skills of my new colleagues. That week's mail brought a manuscript written by an economist of international reputation in which he claimed that he could explain all three cases *and* point out how to control them.[1]

Adam Smith, Jeremy Bentham, Beccaria-Bonesana, Karl Marx, and William Bonger wrote about economics and crime, but their observations have been largely ignored by recent generations of economists. Before 1968, some academic criminologists in North America and England adapted economic techniques to the study of criminology. This was also true of some civil servants working within various branches of the criminal justice system. But the current interest in the economic approach to criminology began in 1968 with the publication of a major article by Gary S. Becker in the *Journal of Political Economy*.[2] Since then, the stage has been set for a vigorous academic dialogue with far-reaching policy implications.

Becker's article is important because it is the first major statement on crime by the current generation of economists. It has not been refuted in print or seriously modified and has provided the model for a

---

[1] This may be an extreme interpretation of the paper by Gordon Tullock, "Two Hypotheses on Crime," presented at the meeting of the Southern Economics Association, Savannah, Ga., November 1971, and his forthcoming "The Economics of Repression" and "The Paradox of Revolution."

[2] Gary S. Becker, "Crime and Punishment: An Economic Approach," *Journal of Political Economy*, March–April 1968, pp. 169–217.

rash of econometric[3] studies and will continue to do so. Consequently, it has been responsible for the shifting of scarce research money from other types of criminological studies to those having to do with the economics of crime. This article may have considerable influence on government policy-makers, although some important criminologists believe it to be, if not outright wrong, terribly oversimplified. Understandably, these criminologists are apprehensive about the potential influence of this particular school of economics. Important modifications are beginning to be formulated. The work done by Carr-Hill, Stern, and their associates in England should prove particularly helpful in this regard.

The Economists' View Simplified

Becker states that "a useful theory of criminal behavior can dispense with special theories of anomie, psychological inadequacies, or inheritance of special traits and simply extend the economists' usual analysis of choice" and that "the general criterion of social loss is shown to incorporate as special cases, valid under special assumptions, the criteria of vengeance, deterrence, compensation, and rehabilitation that historically have figured so prominently in practice and criminological literature." [4]

Becker is saying that for a broad range of criminals everything we have been told — that they are sick, abnormal, deviant, or deprived — is wrong. Criminals are relatively simple, normal people like the rest of us, and any attempt to treat them as abnormal or deviant or to "rehabilitate" them is doomed to fail.

Traditional explanations of criminality have applied the concepts of depravity, insanity, deviance, abnormality, and deprivation. Economists maintain that criminals are rational and normally calculating people maximizing their preferences subject to given constraints. This is a psychological explanation that economists prefer over nearly all other explanations of criminal behavior.

Opportunity Cost

Economists use the term *opportunity cost* to refer to whatever it is that must be sacrificed to acquire something else. The opportunity cost of war is peace; of

[3] A subdiscipline that utilizes mathematical techniques in testing and applying economic theories.

[4] Becker, *supra* note 2, p. 170.

the constraints of marriage, the freedoms of being single; of the earnings in one career, the earnings in another; of choosing legally obtained income, obtaining illegal income. In accordance with this reasoning, a heroin addict is no more abnormal or deviant than a nicotine addict. Through a historical accident, the act of possessing heroin has been declared criminal while the act of possessing the dangerous drug nicotine has not. The nature of the addictions is not so very different, in that, given our present knowledge, the heroin user is no less rational than the nicotine user. The law has simply driven up the price for the heroin addict's article of consumption, and, as a result, has often forced the addict to resort to illegitimate earnings. Change the law and the behavior of many heroin users would become similar to that of many nicotine addicts. They court death in different ways but otherwise lead normal lives — giving lectures, driving trucks, raising children, running governments — obliviously smoking or shooting away.

All of us have insatiable desires that we cannot accommodate because of our limited wealth and incomes. Within these constraints of wealth and income, we try to maximize our satisfaction in keeping with our preferences and tastes. Preferences and tastes differ among individuals, and constraints vary according to levels of wealth and income. We choose occupations that can provide us with the highest income or at least the greatest combination of monetary income and nonmonetary rewards. For some, the occupation itself has satisfaction features. All men are not born equal in regard to genetic endowments or social and economic opportunities. From the outset some individuals have more choices than others.

To avoid complications, I will restrict the discussion to various forms of theft. According to the economic explanation of criminality, the individual calculates (1) all his practical opportunities of earning legitimate income, (2) the amounts of income offered by these opportunities, (3) the amounts of income offered by various illegal methods, (4) the probability of being arrested if he acts illegally, and (5) the probable punishment should he be caught. After making these calculations, he chooses the act or occupation with the highest discounted return. To arrive at a discounted return he must include among his cost calculations the *future costs* of going to prison if he is apprehended. It is in this sense that the criminal is understood to be a normal, rational, calculating individual.

Parents, police, probation and parole officers, and judges are always saying, "If you keep it up, you will end up in jail (or in jail again)." Economists believe that this kind of admonition is irrelevant. The individual knows perfectly well that he will probably end up in jail, but he still reasons that he will be better off than were he to go "straight." He has already calculated the costs and benefits. If he is not caught or sent to jail, so much the better. But even if he pays the cost of a stretch in jail, he is still ahead of the game — according to his own calculations. His calculations are not assumed to be accurate: he may overestimate the income to be received or he may underestimate the costs — just as many graduate students in recent years overestimated the material benefits of graduate study.

The "amateur" criminal who overestimates the pay-off from a certain job or underestimates the probability of being apprehended and thus the cost to himself may be considered "irrational" and short-sighted. Many of the individuals who come through our court systems can be characterized this way. But their miscalculations are no more irrational than those of the consumer who gets too much in debt, the worker who does not save in anticipation of lay-offs, the man who squanders a week's pay on a whim, or the businessman who goes bankrupt. In all of these cases, there has been a miscalculation in the discounting of future costs. The basic economic assumption does not maintain that people do not make mistakes but rather that they do their best given their reading of present and future possibilities and given their resources.

Since criminals calculate costs and benefits the economist concludes that we must increase the cost to them by increasing the probability that they will be caught or by increasing the punishment if they are caught. Most of the evidence so far — if it can be called evidence — seems to indicate that criminals are more responsive to the probability of apprehension than to the extent of the punishment. This is not encouraging since it is highly doubtful that the proportion of solved crimes will dramatically increase given our scarce resources, the state of technology in the field of criminology, and the constraints of the law.

Econometric Studies

Many econometric studies adhere too simplistically to the Becker model. The relations postulated are too simple — they relate the number of petty thefts to the length of prison terms for petty theft, the number of burglaries to the jail sentences for burglary — and rely primarily on global statistics, statistics for an entire state or an entire nation. Some economists, contrary to their training, are ignoring in their studies the long-run social costs of some of these relations.

To estimate the costs of crime and our methods of combating it, we must device a method of relating the present sentences for petty theft to the future incidence of grand larcency, armed robbery, and murder. The economists should include in their studies the sociological variables, such as age, race, education, and social history, used by crimonologists to develop their predictive techniques.

An Economic View of Recidivism

If it is valid, the economic explanation of criminality has profound implications not only for all our correctional institutions but for our entire society and, in particular, for every employer. If a man goes to prison, he goes there after making a rational choice. He has surveyed all his opportunity costs and has chosen this path. In most prisons he serves dead time or, if anything at all, acquires additional criminal skills. And when he is released from prison, he faces rational employers who are understandably reluctant to hire him because of the high recidivism rate among ex-convicts.

The high recidivism rate makes perfect sense to an economist. A man made a rational choice before he went to prison, acquired further criminal skills in prison, and faced rational, hostile employers when he was released. Given these circumstances this man would be irrational if he did *not* return to crime.

Academic criminologists and practitioners have initiated a strong movement for prison reform. The economic view should reinforce drastic reform of prison-education programs, and it should argue for a social insurance system that would guarantee reimbursement for any financial loss incurred by hiring an ex-convict. This would be a minimal guarantee and there could be many variations on such a scheme.

The economist believes that the criminal is a rational human being making rational choices according to his constraints, opportunities, and preferences. To alter his calculations we must change his opportunities, increase his opportunity costs, and teach him to discount the future more realistically. Consequently, any "rehabilitative" program that assumes the criminal is abnormal, deviant, inadequate, irrational, or characterized by anomie is doomed to failure.

The economist takes tastes and preferences for granted and assumes that an individual maximizes satisfaction subject to constraints of wealth given his reading of his opportunities. The non-economist might assert that it is not enough to change an individual's opportunity costs or to teach him to read or discount his future costs more realistically; his "tastes" or "preferences" must be changed by effective programs of "rehabilitation" or "punishment.'

CLASS AND THE ECONOMICS OF CRIME

David M. Gordon

This selection summarizes the basic radical analysis of crime. It argues that capitalism breeds crime and that we would have to transform our underlying institutions before we could make meaningful progress toward eliminating crime.

The selection is excerpted from a longer article with the same title, which originally appeared in 1971.

The author teaches economics at the New School for Social Research in New York City.

This section outlines the structure of a radical analysis of crime in the United States. Many points in the argument will seem quite obvious, simple elaborations of common sense. Other points will bear some important similarities to one or another of the views described in the preceding sections. Taken all together, however, the arguments in the following analysis seem to me to provide a more useful, coherent, and realistic interpretation than the more conventional models. In the analysis, I have tried as simply as possible to apply some general hypotheses of radical economic analysis to a discussion of the specific problem of crime in this country. My intention, quite clearly, is to argue that we cannot realistically expect to "solve" the problem of crime in the United States without first effecting a fundamental redistribution of power in our society.

Source: David M. Gordon, "Class and the Economics of Crime," from *The Review of Radical Political Economics*, Vol. 3, No. 3, Summer 1971, pp. 50–75. Copyright © 1971 by Union for Radical Political Economics. Reprinted with permission.

I have divided the analysis into five separate parts. The first sketches the major hypotheses of the general radical framework through which I have tried to view the problem of crime. The second tries to explain a basic behavioral *similarity* among all the major kinds of crime in the United States. Given that fundamental similarity, the third part seeks to explain the most important dimension of *difference* among various crimes in this country. Given a delineation of the sources of difference among crimes, the fourth part attempts a historical explanation of the origins of those sources of difference — an analysis, as it were, of the underlying causes of some immediate causes of difference. The fifth part argues that we cannot easily reverse history, cannot easily alter the fundamental social structures and trends that have produced the problem of crime today. A final paragraph provides a brief summary of the central hypotheses of the entire argument.

Some General Assumptions

The radical analysis of crime outlined in this section applies several basic radical assumptions or hypotheses.[1] It presumes, first of all, that the basic structure of social and economic institutions in any society fundamentally shapes the behavior of individuals in that society and, therefore, that one cannot in

[1] [Ed.: These assumptions are spelled out in Chapter 1 of this book.]

fact understand the behavior of individuals in a society like the United States without first understanding the structures and biases of the basic "system-defining" institutions in this country. It argues, furthermore, that the "social relations of production" in capitalist societies help define an economic class structure and that one cannot therefore adequately understand the behavior of individuals unless one first examines the structure of institutionally determined opportunities to which members of the respective economic classes are more or less confined. The analysis depends, at another level, on the radical theory of the State, according to which radicals hypothesize that the activities of the State in capitalist societies serve primarily to benefit members of the capitalist class—either directly, by bestowing disproportionate benefits upon them, or indirectly by helping preserve and solidify the structure of class inequalities upon which capitalists so thoroughly depend. The radical analysis expects, finally, that various social problems in capitalist societies, although they may not have been created by capitalists, cannot easily be solved within the context of capitalist institutions because their solution would tend to disrupt the functioning of the capitalist machine. If the disruptive potential of solutions to such problems therefore inclines the State to postpone solution, one can expect to solve those problems only by changing the power relationships in society so that the State is forced to serve other interests than those of the capitalist class.

Each of these general hypotheses underlies all of the more specific hypotheses about crime which follow.

Competitive Capitalism and Rational Crime

Capitalist societies depend, as radicals often argue, on basically competitive forms of social and economic interaction and upon substantial inequalities in the allocation of social resources. Without inequalities, it would be much more difficult to induce workers to work in alienating environments. Without competition and a competitive ideology, workers might not be inclined to struggle to improve their relative income and status in society by working harder. Finally, although rights of property are protected, capitalist societies do not guarantee economic security to most of their individual members. Individuals must fend for themselves, finding the best available opportunities to provide for themselves and

their families. At the same time, history bequeaths a corpus of laws and statutes to any social epoch which may or may not correspond to the social morality of that epoch. Inevitably, at any point in time, many of the "best" opportunities of economic survival open to different citizens will violate some of those historically determined laws. Driven by the fear of economic insecurity and by a competitive desire to gain some of the goods unequally distributed throughout the society, many individuals will eventually become "criminals." As Adam Smith himself admitted, "Where there is no property, . . . civil government is not so necessary." [2]

In that respect, therefore, radicals argue that nearly all crimes in capitalist societies represent perfectly *rational* responses to the structure of institutions upon which capitalist societies are based. Crimes of many different varieties constitute functionally similar responses to the organization of capitalist institutions, for those crimes help provide a means of survival in a society within which survival is never assured. Three different kinds of crime in the United States provide the most important examples of this functionally similar rationality among different kinds of crime: ghetto crime, organized crime, and corporate (or "white-collar") crime.[3]

It seems especially clear, first of all, that ghetto crime is committed by people responding quite reasonably to the structure of economic opportunities available to them. Only rarely, it appears, can ghetto criminals be regarded as raving, irrational, antisocial lunatics.[4] The "legitimate" jobs open to many ghetto

[2] Adam Smith, *The Wealth of Nations* (New York: Modern Library, 1937), p. 670.

[3] This is not meant to imply, obviously, that there would be no crime in a communist society in which perfectly secure equal support was provided for all. It suggests, quite simply, that one would have to analyze crime in such a society with reference to a different set of ideas and a different set of institutions.

[4] Our knowledge of ghetto crime draws primarily from the testimony of several ex-ghetto criminals, as in Claude Brown, *Manchild in the Promised Land* (New York: Macmillan, 1965); Eldridge Cleaver, *Post-Prison Writings and Speeches* (New York: A Ramparts Book by Random House, 1969); George Jackson, *Soledad Brother* (New York: Bantam Books, 1970); and Malcolm X, *Autobiography* (New York: Grove Press, 1964). For more analytic studies, see Clifford Shaw and Henry McKay, *Juvenile Delinquency and Urban Areas* (Chicago: University of Chicago Press, 1969); and Marvin E. Wolfgang and Franco Ferracuti, *The Subculture of Violence* (New York: Barnes and Noble, 1967). For interesting evidence

residents, especially to young black males, typically pay low wages, offer relatively demeaning assignments, and carry the constant risk of layoff. In contrast, many kinds of crime "available" in the ghetto often bring higher monetary return, offer even higher social status, and—at least in some cases like numbers running—sometimes carry relatively low risk of arrest and punishment.[5] Given those alternative opportunities, the choice between "legitimate" and "illegitimate" activities is often quite simple. As Arthur Dunmeyer, a black hustler from Harlem, has put it:

> In some cases this is the way you get your drug dealers and prostitutes and your numbers runners.... They see that these things are the only way that they can compete in the society, to get some sort of status. They realize that there aren't any real doors open to them, and so, to commit crime was the only thing to do, they can't go back.[6]

The fact that these activities are often "illegal" sometimes doesn't really matter; since life out of jail often seems as bad as life inside prison, the deterrent ef-

fect of punishment is negligible. Dunmeyer expresses this point clearly as well:

> It is not a matter of a guy saying, "I want to to go to jail [or] I am afraid of jail." Jail is on the street just like it is on the inside. The same as, like when you are in jail, they tell you, "Look, if you do something wrong you are going to be put in the hole." You are still in jail, in the hole or out of the hole. You are in jail in the street or behind bars. It is the same thing. . . .[7]

In much the same way, organized crime represents a perfectly rational kind of economic activity.[8] Activities like gambling and prostitution are illegal for varieties of historical reasons, but there is a demand for those activities nonetheless. As Donald Cressey writes: "The American confederation of criminals thrives because a large minority of citizens demands the illicit goods and services it has for sale."[9] Ramsey Clark makes the same point, arguing that organized crimes are essentially "consensual crimes . . . , desired by the consuming public."[10] The simple fact that they are both illegal and in great demand provides a simple explanation for the secrecy, relative efficiency, and occasional violence of those who provide them. In nearly every sense the organization of the heroin industry, for example, bears as rational and reasonable a relationship to the nature of the product as the structures of the tobacco and alcoholic beverages industries bear to the nature of their own products.[11]

---

on the different attitudes toward crime of poor and middle-class youth, see Leonard Goodwin, "Work Orientations of the Underemployed Poor," *Journal of Human Resources,* Fall 1969. For a bit of "analytic" evidence on the critical interaction between job prospects and rates of recidivism, see Robert Evans, Jr., "The Labor Market and Parole Success," *Journal of Human Resources,* Spring 1968.

[5] One often finds informal support for such contentions. A Manhattan prostitute once said about her crimes, "What is there to say. We've got a living to earn. There wouldn't be any prostitution if there weren't a demand for it." Quoted in the *New York Times,* May 29, 1970. A black high school graduate discussed the problem at greater length with an interviewer in Herb Goro, *The Block* (New York: Random House, 1970), p. 146: "That's why a lot of brothers are out on the street now, stinging, robbing people, mugging, 'cause when they get a job, man, they be doing their best, and the white man get jealous 'cause he feel this man could do better than he doing. 'I got to get rid of him!' So they fire him, so a man, he lose his pride. . . . They give you something, and then they take it away from you. . . . And people tell you jobs are open for everybody on the street. There's no reason for you to be stealing. That's a lie! If you're a thief, I'd advise you to be a good thief. 'Cause you working, Jim, you ain't going to succeed unless you got some kind of influence."

[6] Claude Brown and Arthur Dunmeyer, "A Way of Life in the Ghetto." [In this chapter.]

[7] *Ibid.,* p. 293. A friend of Claude Brown's made a similar point about the ineffectiveness of the threat of jail. "When I go to jail now, Sonny, I live, man. I'm right at home. . . . When I go back to the joint, anywhere I go, I know some people. If I go to any of the jails in New York, or if I go to a slam in Jersey, even, I still run into a lot of cats I know. It's almost like a family."

[8] For two of the best available analyses of organized crime, see Donald Cressey, *Theft of the Nation: The Structure and Operations of Organized Crime* (New York: Harper & Row, 1969); and Norval Morris and Gordon Hawkins, *The Honest Politician's Guide to Crime Control* (Chicago: University of Chicago Press, 1969).

[9] Cressey, *op. cit.,* p. 294.

[10] Clark, *Crime in America* (New York: Simon & Schuster, 1970), p. 68.

[11] As Cressey (*op. cit.*) points out, for instance, it makes a great deal of sense in the heroin industry for the supplier to seek a monopoly on the source of the heroin but to permit many individual sellers of heroin at its final destination, usually without organization backing, because the risks occur primarily at the consumers' end.

Finally, briefly to amplify the third example, corporate crime also represents a quite rational response to life in capitalist societies. Corporations exist to protect and augment the capital of their owners. If it becomes difficult to perform that function one way, corporate officials will quite inevitably try to do it another. When Westinghouse and General Electric conspired to fix prices, for instance, they were resorting to one of many possible devices for limiting the potential threat of competition to their price structures. Similarly, when Ford and General Motors proliferate new car model after new car model, each differing only slightly from its siblings, they are choosing to protect their price structures by what economists call "product differentiation." In one case, the corporations were using oligopolistic power quite directly; in the other, they rely on the power of advertising to generate demand for the differentiated products. In the context of the perpetual and highly competitive race among corporations for profits and capital accumulation, each response seems quite reasonable. Sutherland made the same points about corporate crime and linked the behavior of corporations to lower-class criminality:

> I have attempted to demonstrate that businessmen violate the law with great frequency. . . . If these conclusions are correct, it is very clear that the criminal behavior of businessmen cannot be explained by poverty, in the usual sense, or by bad housing or lack of recreational facilities or feeblemindedness or emotional instability. Business leaders are capable, emotionally balanced, and in no sense pathological. . . . The assumption that an offender must have some such pathological distortion of the intellect or the emotions seems to me absurd, and if it is absurd regarding the crimes of businessmen, it is equally absurd regarding the crimes of persons in the lower economic class.[12]

Class Institutions and Differences Among Crimes

If most crime in the United States in one way or another reflects the same kind of rational response to the insecurity and inequality of capitalist institutions, what explains the manifold differences among different kinds of crimes? Some crimes are much more violent than others, some are much more heavily prosecuted, and some are much more profitable. Why?

As a first step in explaining differences among crimes, I would apply the general radical perspective in a relatively straightforward manner and argue quite simply that many of the most important differences among different kinds of crime in this country are determined by the *structure of class institutions* in our society and by the *class biases* of the State. That argument has two separate components.

First, I would argue that many of the important differences among crimes in this society derive quite directly from the different socio-economic classes to which individuals belong. Relatively affluent citizens have access to jobs in large corporations, to institutions involved in complicated paper transactions involving lots of money, and to avenues of relatively unobtrusive communication. Members of those classes who decide to break the law have, as Clark puts it, "an easier, less offensive, less visible way of doing wrong."[13] Those raised in poverty, on the other hand, do not have such easy access to money. If they are to obtain it criminally, they must impinge on those who already have it or direct its flow. As Robert Morgenthau, a former federal attorney, has written, those growing up in the ghetto "will probably never have the opportunity to embezzle funds from a bank or to promote a multimillion dollar stock fraud scheme. The criminal ways which we encourage [them] to choose will be those closest at hand — from vandalism to mugging to armed robbery."[14]

Second, I would argue that the biases of our police, courts, and prisons *explain* the relative violence of many crimes — that many of the differences in the degree of violence among different kinds of crime do not cause the selectivity of public concern about those crimes but *are* in fact *caused by* that selectivity. For a variety of historical reasons, as I noted above, we have a dual system of justice in this country; the police, courts, and prisons pay careful attention to only a few crimes. It is only natural, as a result, that those who run the highest risks of arrest and conviction may have to rely on the threat or commission of violence in order to protect them-

---

[12] Edwin H. Sutherland, "The Crime of Corporations," in David M. Gordon, ed., *Problems in Political Economy* (Lexington, Mass.: D. C. Heath, 1971), p. 310.

[13] Clark, *op. cit.*, p. 38.
[14] Robert Morgenthau, "Equal Justice and the Problem of White Collar Crime," *The Conference Board Record*, August 1969, p. 20.

selves. Many kinds of ghetto crimes generate violence, for instance, because the participants are severely prosecuted for their crimes and must try to protect themselves however they can. Other kinds of ghetto crimes, like the numbers racket, are openly tolerated by the police, and those crimes rarely involve violence. It may be true, as Clark argues, that "violent crime springs from a violent environment," [15] but violent environments like the ghetto do not always produce violent crimes. Those crimes to which the police pay attention usually involve violence, while those which the police tend to ignore quite normally do not. In similar ways, organized crime has become violent historically, as Cressey especially argues,[16] principally because its participants are often prosecuted. As long as that remains true, the suppliers of illegal goods require secrecy, organization, and a bit of violence to protect their livelihood. Completely in contrast, corporate crime does not require violence because it is ignored by the police; corporate criminals can safely assume they do not face the threat of jail and do not therefore have to cover their tracks with the threat of harming those who betray them. When Lockheed Aircraft accountants and executives falsified their public reports in order to disguise cost overruns on the C-5A airplane in 1967 and 1968, for instance, they did not have to force Defense Department officials at knife-point to play along with their falsifications. As Robert Sherrill reports in his investigation of the Lockheed affair, the Defense Department officials were entirely willing to cooperate.[17] "This sympathy," he writes, "was reflected in orders from top Air Force officials to withhold information regarding Lockheed's dilemma from all reports that would be widely circulated." If only local police were equally sympathetic to the "dilemmas" of street-corner junkies, the violent patterns of drug-related crimes might be considerably transformed.[18]

In short, it seems important to view some of the most important differences among crimes — differences in their violence, their style, and their impact — as fundamental outgrowths of the class structure of society and the class biases of our major institutions, including the State and its system of enforcement and administration of justice. Given that argument, it places a special burden on attempts to explain the historical sources of the duality of the public system of justice in this country, for that duality, coupled with the class biases of other institutions, plays an important role in determining the patterns of American crime.

The Sources of Duality

One can explain the duality of our public system of justice quite easily, it seems to me, if one is willing to view the State through the radical perspective. The analysis involves answers to two separate questions. First, one must ask why the State ignores certain kinds of crimes, especially white-collar crimes and corporate crimes. Second, given that most crimes among the poor claim the poor as their victims, one must ask why the State bothers to worry so incessantly about those crimes.

The answer to the first question draws directly from the radical theory of the State. According to the radical theory, the government in a capitalist society like the United States exists primarily to preserve the stability of the system which provides, preserves, and protects return to the owners of capital. As long as crimes among the corporate class tend in general to harm members of other classes, like those in the "consuming" class, the State will not spontaneously move to prevent those crimes from taking place. On the other hand, as Paul Sweezy has especially argued,[19] the State may be pressured to prosecute the wealthy if their criminal practices become so egregiously offensive that their victims may move to overthrow the system itself. In those cases, the State may punish individual members of the class in order to protect the interests of the entire class. Latent opposition to the practices of corporations may be forestalled, to pick several examples, by token public efforts to enact and enforce antitrust, truth-in-lending, antipollution, industrial safety, and auto safety legislation. As James Ridgeway has most clearly shown in the case of pollution,[20] however,

[15] Clark, *op. cit.*, p. 39.

[16] Cressey, *op. cit.*

[17] Robert Sherrill, "The Convenience of Being Lockheed," *Scanlan's Monthly*, August 1970, p. 43.

[18] It is possible to argue, as this point suggests, that heroin addicts would not be prone either to violence or to crime if heroin were legal and free. The fact that it is illegal and that the police go after its consumers means that a cycle of crime and violence is established from which it becomes increasingly difficult to escape.

[19] See the article by Sweezy in Chapter 1 of this book.

[20] James Ridgeway, *The Politics of Ecology* (New York: Dutton, 1970).

the gap between the enactment of the statutes and their effective enforcement seems quite cavernous.[21]

The answer to the second question seems slightly more complicated historically. Public responses to crime among the poor have changed periodically throughout American history, varying according to changes in the patterns of the crimes themselves and to changes in public morality. The subtlety of that historical process would be difficult to trace in this kind of discussion. But some patterns do seem clear.

Earlier in American history, as Clark has pointed out,[22] we intended to ignore many crimes among the poor because those crimes rarely impinged upon the lives of the more affluent. Gambling, prostitution, dope, and robbery seemed to flourish in the slums of the early twentieth century, and the police rarely moved to intervene. More recently, however, some of the traditional patterns of crime have changed. Two dimensions of change seem most important. On the one hand, much of the crime has moved out of the slums: "Our concern arose when social dynamics and population movements brought crime and addiction out of the slums and inflicted it on or threatened the powerful and well-to-do." [23] On the other hand, the styles in which ghetto criminals have fulfilled their criminal intent may have grown more hostile since World War II, flowing through what I have elsewhere called the "promised land effect." [24] As Claude Brown points out, second-generation Northern blacks — the slum-born sons and daughters of Southern migrants — have relatively little reason to hope that their lives will improve. Their parents migrated in search of better times, but some of those born in the North probably believe that their avenues for escape from poverty have disappeared.

> The children of these disillusioned colored pioneers inherited the total lot of their parents — the disappointments, the anger. To add to their misery, they had little hope of deliverance. For where does one run to when he's already in the promised land? [25]

Out of frustration, some of the crime among younger ghetto-born blacks may be more vengeful now, more concerned with sticking it to whitey. Coupled with the spread of ghetto crime into other parts of the city, this symbolic expression of vengefulness undoubtedly heightens the fear that many affluent citizens feel about ghetto crime. Given their influence with the government, they quite naturally have moved toward increasing public attention to the prevention and punishment of crimes among the poor.

Once the patterns of public duality have been established, of course, they acquire a momentum and dynamic all their own. To begin with, vested interests develop, deriving their livelihood and status from the system. The prison system, like the defense industry, becomes a power of its own, with access to public bureaucracies, with workers to support, and with power to defend. Eldridge Cleaver has made special note of this feature of our public system:

> The only conclusion one can draw is that the parole system is a procedure devised primarily for the purpose of running people in and out of jail — most of them black — in order to create and maintain a lot of jobs for the white prison system. In California, which I know best — and I'm sure it's the same in other states — there are thousands and thousands of people who draw their living directly or indirectly from the prison system; all the clerks, all the guards, all the bailiffs, all the people who sell goods to the prisons. They regard the inmates as a sort of product from which they all draw their livelihood, and the part of the crop they keep exploiting most are the black inmates.[26]

---

[21] This rests on an assumption, of course, that one learns much more about the priorities of the state by looking at its patterns of enforcement than by noting the nature of its statutes. This seems quite reasonable. The statutory process is often cumbersome, whereas the patterns of enforcement can sometimes be changed quite easily. Furthermore, as many radicals would argue, the State in democratic societies can often support the capitalist class most effectively by selective enforcement of the laws rather than by selective legislation. For varieties of relatively complicated historical reasons, selective enforcement of the law seems to arouse less fear for the erosion of democratic tradition than selective legislation itself. As long as we have statutes which nominally outlaw racial inequality, for instance, inadequate enforcement of those laws seems to cause relatively little furor; before we had such laws in this country, protests against the selective statutes could ultimately be mounted.

[22] Clark, *op. cit.*, pp. 55–56.

[23] *Ibid.*, p. 55.

[24] Gordon [this book], Chapter 2.

[25] Brown, *op. cit.*, p. 8.

[26] Cleaver, *op. cit.*, p. 185.

In much the same way, the police become an interest and a power of their own.[27] They are used and manipulated by the larger society to enforce the law selectivity: "We send police to maintain order, to arrest, to jail — and to ignore vital laws also intended to protect life and to prevent death. . . ." [28] As agents of selective social control, the police also inevitably become the focus of increasing animosity among those they are asked selectively to control. Manipulated by the larger society, hated by those at the bottom, the police tend to develop the mentality of a "garrison." [29] They eventually seek to serve neither the interests of the larger society nor the interests of the law but the interests of the garrison. One reaches the point, finally, where police interests interject an intermediate membrane screening the priorities of the state and society on the one hand and the interests of their victims on the other. "When enforcement of the law conflicts with the ends of the police, the law is not enforced. When it supports the ends of the police, they are fully behind it. When it bears no relation to the ends of the police, they enforce it as a matter of routine." [30]

The Implausibility of Reform

One needs to ask, finally, whether these patterns can be changed and the trends reversed. Can we simultaneously eradicate the causes of crime and reform our dual system of justice? At the heart of that question lies the question posed at the beginning of this essay, for it simultaneously raises the necessity of explaining the failures of our present system to prevent the crime it seeks most systematically to control.

I would argue, quite simply, that reform is implausible unless we change the basic institutions

upon which capitalism in the United States depends. We cannot legitimately expect to eradicate the initial causes of crime for two reasons. First, capitalism depends quite substantially on the preservation of the conditions of competition and inequality. Those conditions, as I argue above, will tend to lead quite inevitably to relatively pervasive criminal behavior; without those conditions, the capitalist system would scarcely work at all. Second, as many have argued, the general presence of racism in this country, though capitalists may not in fact have created it, tends to support and maintain the power of the capitalists as a class by providing cheap labor and dividing the working class. Given the substantial control of capitalists over the policies and priorities of the State, we cannot easily expect to prod the State to eliminate the fundamental causes of racism in this country. In that respect, it seems likely that the particular inequalities facing blacks and their consequent attraction to the opportunities available in crime seem likely to continue.

Given expectations that crime will continue, it seems equally unlikely that we shall be able to reform our systems of prosecution and punishment in order to mitigate their harmful effects on criminals and to equalize their treatment of different kinds of crime. First and superficially, as I noted above, several important and powerful vested interests have acquired a stake in the current system and seem likely to resist efforts to change it. Second and more fundamentally, the cumulative effect of the patterns of crime, violence, prosecution, and punishment in this country plays an important role in helping legitimize and stabilize the capitalist system. Although capitalists as a class may not have created the current patterns of crime and punishment, those patterns currently serve their interests in several different ways. We should expect that the capitalists as a class will hardly be able to push reform of the system. Given their relative reluctance to reform the system, we should expect to be able to push reform only in the event that we can substantially change the structure of power to which the State responds.

The current patterns of crime and punishment support the capitalist in three different ways.

First, the pervasive patterns of selective enforcement seem to reinforce a prevalent ideology in this society that individuals, rather than institutions, are to blame for social problems. Individuals are criminally prosecuted for motor accidents because of negligent or drunken driving, for instance, but auto man-

[27] For some useful references on the police, see Paul Chevigney, *Police Power* (New York: Pantheon, 1969); William Westley, *Violence and Police* (Cambridge, Mass.: M.I.T. Press, 1970); and James Q. Wilson, *Varieties of Police Behavior* (New York: Basic Books, 1969). For a review of that literature, with some very interesting comments about the police, see Murray Kempton, "Cops," *New York Review of Books,* Nov. 5, 1970. For one discussion of the first hints of evidence that there may not, in fact, be any kind of identifiable relationship between the number of police we have and their effectiveness, see Richard Reeves, "Police: Maybe They Should Be Doing Something Different," *New York Times,* Jan. 21, 1971.

[28] Clark, *op. cit.,* p. 137.

[29] Westley, *op. cit.*

[30] *Ibid.*

ufacturers are never criminally prosecuted for the negligent construction of unsafe cars or for their roles in increasing the likelihood of death through air pollution. Individual citizens are often prosecuted and punished for violence and for resisting arrest, equally, but those agents of institutions, like police and prison guards, or institutions themselves, like Dow Chemical, are never prosecuted for inflicting unwarranted violence on others. These patterns of selectivity reinforce our pervasive preconceptions of the invulnerability of institutions, leading us to blame ourselves for social failure; this pattern of individual blame . . . plays an important role in legitimizing the basic institutions of this kind of capitalist society.

Second, and critically important, the patterns of crime and punishment manage "legitimately" to neutralize the potential opposition to the system of many of our most oppressed citizens. In particular, the system serves ultimately to keep thousands of men out of the job market or trapped in the secondary labor market by perpetuating a set of institutions which serves functionally to feed large numbers of blacks (and poor whites) through the cycle of crime, imprisonment, parole, and recidivism. The system has this same ultimate effect in many different ways. It locks up many for life, first of all, guaranteeing that those potentially disaffected souls keep "out of trouble." As for those whom it occasionally releases, it tends to drive them deeper into criminality, intensifying their criminal and violent behavior, filling their heads with paranoia and hatred, keeping them perpetually on the run and unable, ultimately, to organize with others to change the institutions which pursue them. Finally, it blots their records with the stigma of criminality and, by denying them many decent employment opportunities, effectively precludes the reform of even those who vow to escape the system and to go "straight."[31]

The importance of this neutralization should not be underestimated. If all young black men in this country do not eventually become criminals, most of them are conscious of the trap into which they might fall. The late George Jackson wrote from prison: "Blackmen born in the U.S. and fortunate enough to live past the age of eighteen are conditioned to accept the inevitability of prison. For most of us, it simply looms as the next phase in a sequence of humiliations."[32] And once they are trapped, the cycle continues almost regardless of the will of those involved. Prison, parole, and the eventual return to prison become standard points on the itinerary. Cleaver has written:

> I noticed that every time I went back to jail, the same guys who were in Juvenile Hall with me were also there again. They arrived there soon after I got there, or a little bit before I left. They always seemed to make the scene. In the California prison system, they carry you from Juvenile Hall to the old folks' colony, down in San Luis Obispo, and wait for you to die. Then they bury you there. . . . I noticed these waves, these generations . . . graduating classes moving up from Juvenile Hall, all the way up.[33]

And those who succeed finally in understanding the trap and in pulling themselves out of it, like Malcolm X, Claude Brown, Eldridge Cleaver, and George Jackson, seem to succeed precisely because they understood how debilitating the cycle becomes, how totally dehumanizing it will remain. Another black ex-con has perfectly expressed the sudden insight which allowed him to pull out of the trap:

> It didn't take me any time to decide I wasn't going back to commit crimes. Because it's stupid, it's a trap, it only makes it easier for them to neutralize you. It's hard to explain, because you can't say it's a question of right and wrong, but of being free or being trapped.[34]

If the system did not effect this neutralization, if so many of the poor were not trapped in the debilitating system of crime and punishment, they might gather the strength to oppose the system that reinforces their misery. Like many other institutions in this country, the system of crime and punishment serves an important function for the capitalist class by dividing and weakening those who might potentially seek to overthrow the capitalist system. Although the capitalists have not created the system, in

[31] For a devastating story about how the neutralization occurs to even the most innocent of ghetto blacks, see Eliot Asinof, *People vs. Blutcher* (New York: Viking, 1970).

[32] Jackson, *op. cit.*
[33] Cleaver, *op. cit.*, pp. 454–55.
[34] Bell Gale Chevigny, "After the Death of Jail." *Village Voice,* July 10, 1969.

any direct sense, they would doubtlessly hate to have to do without it.[35]

The third and perhaps most important functionally supportive role of the current patterns of crime and punishment is that those patterns allow us to ignore some basic issues about the relationships in our society between institutions and individuals. By treating criminals as animals and misfits, as enemies of the state, we are permitted to continue avoiding some basic questions about the dehumanizing effects of our social institutions. We keep our criminals out of sight, so we are never forced to recognize and deal with the psychic punishment we inflict on them. Like the schools and the welfare system, the legal system turns out, upon close inspection, to be robbing most of its "clients" of the last vestiges of their personal dignity. Each one of those institutions, in its own way, helps us forget about the responsibilities we might alternatively assume for providing the best possible environment within which all of us could grow and develop as individuals. Cleaver sees this "role" of the system quite clearly:

> Those who are now in prison could be put through a process of real rehabilitation before their release. . . . By rehabilitation I mean they would be trained for jobs that would not be an insult to their dignity, that would give them some sense of security, that would allow them to achieve

some brotherly connection with their fellow man. But for this kind of rehabilitation to happen on a large scale would entail the complete reorganization of society, not to mention the prison system. It would call for the teaching of a new set of ethics, based on the principle of cooperation, as opposed to the presently dominating principle of competition. It would require the transformation of the entire moral fabric. . . . [36]

By keeping its victims so thoroughly hidden and rendering them so apparently inhuman, our system of crime and punishment allows us to forget how sweeping a "transformation" of our social ideology we would require in order to begin solving the problem of crime. The more we forget, the more protected the capitalists remain from a thorough reexamination of the ideological basis of the institutions upon which they depend.

It seems useful to summarize briefly the analysis outlined in this section, in order both to emphasize the connections among its arguments and to clarify its differences with other "models" of crime and punishment. Most crimes in this country share a single important similarity — they represent rational responses to the competitiveness and inequality of life in capitalist societies. (In this emphasis on the rationality of crime, the analysis differs with the "conventional public analyses" of crime and resembles the orthodox economic approach.) Many crimes seem very different at the same time, but many of their differences — in character and degree of violence — can usefully be explained by the structure of class institutions in this country and the duality of the public system of the enforcement and administration of justice. (In this central deployment of the radical concepts of class and the class-biased State, the analysis differs fundamentally with both the "public" and the orthodox economic perspectives.) That duality, in turn, can fruitfully be explained by a dynamic view of the class-biased role of public institutions and the vested interests which evolve out of the State's activities. For many reasons, finally, it seems unlikely that we can change the patterns of crime and punishment, for the kinds of changes we would need would appear substantially to threaten the stability of the capitalist system. If we managed somehow to eliminate ghetto crime, for instance, the competitiveness, inequalities, and racism of our insti-

[35] One should not underestimate the importance of this effect for quantitative as well as qualitative reasons. In July 1968, for instance, an estimated 140,000 blacks were serving time in penal institutions at federal, state, and local levels. If the percentage of black males in prison had been as low as the proportions of white men (by age groups), there would have been only 25,000 blacks in jail. If those extra 115,000 black men were not in prison, they would likely be unemployed or intermittently employed. In addition, official labor force figures radically undercount the number of blacks in the census because many black males are simply missed by the census-taker. In July 1968, almost one million black males were "missed" in that way. On the conservative assumption that one-fifth of those "missing males" were in one way or another evading the law, involved in hustling, or otherwise trapped in the legal system, a total of 315,000 black men who might be unemployed were it not for the effects of the law were not counted in "measured" unemployment statistics. Total "measured" black male unemployment in July 1968 was 317,000, so that the total black unemployment problem might be nearly twice as large as we "think" it is were it not for the selective effects of our police, courts, and prisons on black men.

[36] Cleaver, *op. cit.*, pp. 179, 182.

tutions would tend to reproduce it. And if, by chance, the pattern of ghetto crime was not reproduced, the capitalists might simply have to invent some other way of neutralizing the potential opposition of so many black men, against which they might once again be forced to rebel with "criminal acts." It is in that sense of fundamental causality that we must somehow change the entire structure of institutions in this country in order to eliminate the causes of crime.

CRIME AND THE EMERGENCE OF CAPITALISM

Mark C. Kennedy

This selection provides a central element of analytic and historical support for the general argument developed by Gordon in the preceding selection. Kennedy develops the historical view that almost all of our present conception of the relationship between the individual and the state, manifested in the laws and criminal codes, arose with the emergence of capitalism, commercial exchange, and the "rational state." The historical contingency of our present notions of "law" and our present treatment of "criminals" helps suggest the possibility of alternative conceptions of the relationship between people and their governments.

This selection comes from a longer essay by Kennedy, originally published in 1970, called "Beyond Incrimination." Like the rest of the essay, this selection is somewhat difficult to read because it uses formal, abstract terms with which to develop its argument. Because the point of view developed is so important, however, it is well worth the effort that it demands.

Crime is here defined as a violation, by act or omission, of any criminal law. According to that law, it is also a specific conduct leading to a harm and is an act construed as a harm against a State. It follows that deviation from norms which are not criminal laws are not crimes. It also follows that in any society where such laws are absent there is no crime. Crime, then, is unique behavior. To understand this calls for some knowledge of the characteristics of criminal law as unique law.

Punishment is an intended harm imposed by one or more parties upon an individual over whom those who impose that harm have assumed or have been granted jurisdiction as a right — a right contingent upon superior coercive power or upon collectively given power to exempt an offender from any reprisal for his offense. Penal sanction is a special case of punishment, and both are special cases of intended harms generally. They differ from acts of war, for example, only insofar as reciprocal acts of war assume political equality between contenders.

Crime and Criminal Law in Relation to the State

Under criminal law no act is crime until it violates a norm having the following characteristics: uniformity, specificity, politicality, and penal sanction. Procedurally, these characteristics become *criteria* for legal classification of any act as crime versus not-crime. In legal procedure, uniformity is more an assumption than a working criterion, thus we are concerned only with the latter three characteristics. Any law failing to detail the conduct proscribed lacks specificity, and violating it is not a crime. Any law neither created nor recognized by the State as a bona fide part of its legal order and which fails to define the proscribed act as a harm against the State lacks politicality, its violation is not a crime. Any law in which a punishment is not prescribed lacks penal sanction, and its violation is not a crime.[1]

Source: "Beyond Incrimination," from *Catalyst*, No. 5, Summer 1970. Reprinted with permission.

[1] E. H. Sutherland and D. R. Cressey, *Principles of Criminology*, 7th ed. (New York: J. B. Lippincott, 1966), pp. 10–13.

It follows that any society having no laws like this has no crime, and that crime is a unique class among all violations of conduct norms. Since politicality and penal sanction (the decisive characteristics of criminal law) presuppose a State, there can be no crime in any society which has no State.[2] The latter are still abundant in parts of the world yet untouched by Western political and economic institutions.[3]

While Stateless societies have emerged apart from Western influence, they are rare, and societies having what Weber described as "formally rational States" are either Western or have come by such political communities through Western influence. Since the formally rational State is, roughly, a post-fifteenth-century development of Western culture,[4] it follows that crime in its present character did not exist before that period and at the advent of feudal States — apart from Roman law — crime as such did not exist. The same is true of penal sanction. Both are linked to the formal laws of the State and to civil institutions supported by it. Both types of law are managed by the State as a monopoly.

But while both are unique in contrast with those norm violations and punishments common to societies without States, neither seems behaviorally different from the other — in part because both crime and punishment are intended harms, and in part because both emerged historically with and are now founded upon individualism as a common ideology or value system which has as its basic premise the belief that each individual (and not social institutions) is fully responsible for his own conduct and its consequences.[5] While the era of individualism is now at an end in the West, its hold is still very evident in the State, in citizenship, in criminal law and legal procedures,

and in the dominance of penal sanctions over the use of the power to pardon.

Historical Conditions of the Advent of Crime and Penal Sanction

It is an oversimplification to say that these two classes of harms arose together in post-fifteenth-century Europe as a function of the advent of formally national States, but what finally took place, beginning with the thirteenth century, amounts to that. What was fundamental to the birth of crime and penal sanction was fundamental to political, economic, religious, and familistic transformation generally, and essential to the transformations of these institutions was the transformation of the ethic of shared responsibility for individual conduct (the co-operative ethic) to the ethic of individual responsibility.

In part as the legacy of the collapse of feudalism and in part as a consequence of the rise of institutions of capitalism which this collapse afforded, individualism as a generalized social movement emerged from a fact of institutional chaos to a social philosophy and a normative order and transformed, as it grew, the whole of Western society and its culture. Early or late, it came eventually to find social expression in religion as Protestantism; in philosophy as empiricism and idealism; in scholastic inquiry as deductive and inductive methods of natural science; in economy as new institutions of private property, the market, entrepreneurship, rational accounting, and the redivision of labor along new social lines.

It found social expression politically with the birth of formally rational States, citizenship, the theory of social contract, and the rise and diffusion of two interlinked bodies of calculable law (civil and criminal). Just as egoism came to play a major part in psychological inquiry. All the while, kinship was being nucleated and dispossessed, and religion was atomized and made impotent as a social control. On every side, with each new expression of individualism, the society based earlier on the ethic of shared responsibility for individual conduct vanished from the scene. When fealty was for sale, altruism was dead.[6]

The emergence of individualism, in transforming all social institutions, transformed the relation of in-

[2] This point was first made by C. R. Jeffery in his Ph.D. dissertation, "An Institutional Approach to a Theory of Crime," Indiana University, 1954, ch. I.

[3] E. E. Evans-Pritchard and M. Fortes, *African Political Systems* (London: Oxford University Press, 1958). See introduction and last three chapters.

[4] Max Weber, *General Economic History*, trans. by Frank Knight (New York: Collier, 1961), pp. 232–258. "Roughly" is used here because the foundations of Weber's formally rational state appeared incipiently in the twelfth century but did not appear in full until the time Weber specified.

[5] *Ibid.*, p. 232. See references to "citizenship" and to the internalization of the "alien ethic" or commercial principle into each European country — as sharply contrasting with cooperative values — making each individual citizen, apart from his clan, responsible for his own conduct in market behavior.

[6] Marc Bloch, *Feudal Society*, trans. by L. A. Manyon, vol. 1 (Chicago: University of Chicago Press, 1964), pp. 208–210.

dividuals to each other, of each individual to society, and created a new relation between each person and the emergent State. In all these relations, the legal fiction that each citizen is alone responsible for his own conduct and its consequences, good or bad, became reified both at the level of self or personality and at the level of law and judicial practice. Individualism as an attitude of self is basic to guilt, and as a premise of both civil and criminal law it is elemental to the whole legal practice of incrimination. What we witness in the advent of crime and penal sanction is but one facet of the total transformation of institutional life. Remembering this, we now must look at crime and punishment in a more singular and comparative way.

Feudal Institutions in Relation to Harms and Their Disposal

Between the period of the last invasion of Moslems, Hungarians, and Scandinavians, and the middle of the eleventh century, Europe developed what came to be called the institutions of feudalism. This period, in Bloch's astute analysis, was the first feudal age — the second feudal age extending from the middle of that century roughly to the thirteenth.[7] In the present analysis, the first feudal age is important because its normative order and institutional systems were founded on the ethic of shared responsibility for individual conduct. Criminal law and penal sanctions had not emerged, and no territorial power had been able successfully to obtain from local social worlds the power to pardon an offender his harms; citizenship and the formally rational State were absent, and so were the institutions of capitalism. Customary law and the oral tradition prevailed and were imbedded in the religious mentality, the epic, and the folk memory.[8] Kinship and vassalage were knit by companionage — so greatly that fealty was meaningful in a double sense. Vassalage and kinship were unthinkable without friendship or companionage. Public authority had not emerged, and while vassalage meant subjection, subjection was personal and of a quasi-family character. Feudal society differed as much from those based wholly on kinship as it differs from societies dominated by the State.[9]

The second feudal age is important because in it

the ethic of shared responsibility began to give way, and its normative order and institutions began to transform. A vernacular literature emerged and the oral tradition and customary law began to wane. Calculable law began to emerge, along with a host of other changes which account for the rise of citizenship, the formally rational State, and the increasing scope of the institutions of capitalism. Profound changes in economic institutions took place as the ethic of individual responsibility began to find reality in one's relation to himself, to others, and to society and State.

The thesis which will be supported historically and cross-culturally is simply that crime and penal sanction are twin products of the origin and continuity of the State and citizenship, that these institutions, founded on emergent civil and criminal law, emerged as a cluster of new institutions (entrepreneurship, private property, and the market system) all of which were originally the social manifestations of the ethic of individual responsibility for individual behavior. Thus, it follows that in absence of the State, in the absence of its laws, crime and penal sanction do not exist, and in the absence of the institutions of capitalism, the special features cannot exist.

During the first feudal age, the legal system was the rule of custom and oral tradition. It rested on the belief that whatever has been has the right to be.[10] Precedent, not innovation, ruled. It was the normative foundation of feudal society — finding its expression not in hierarchy as we know that word today in the mutually binding obligations of mutually given oaths all the way up the feudal scale. Land, the only real capital, was tied up solidly by customary obligations and could not for that reason become a commodity for sale in any market. Labor had the same provisions. The whole notion of exclusive propriety rights was repugnant to people generally. As Bloch put it:

> For nearly all land and a great many human beings were burdened at this time with a multiplicity of obligations differing in nature, but all apparently of equal importance. None implied that fixed proprietary exclusiveness which belonged to the conception of ownership in Roman law. The tenant who — from father to son, as a rule — ploughs the land and gathers in the crop; his im-

---

[7] *Ibid.*, vol. 1, parts I and II.
[8] *Ibid.*, pp. 72–103.
[9] *Ibid.*, vol. 2, pp. 443–444.

[10] *Ibid.*, vol. 1, pp. 109–116 ff.

mediate lord, to whom he pays dues and who, in certain circumstances, can resume possession of the land; the lord of the lord, and so on right up the feudal scale — how many persons there are who can say, each with (equal) justification . . . "That is my field." [11]

While landed wealth was differentially though mutually shared, its usufruct did not pass from hand to hand in any important way through any market system. Just as private property was absent, so was trade — except in a marginal and irregular way. While buying and selling was not unknown, no one lived by it unless they were the few who were generally scorned as banished persons or pariahs. Even barter was peripheral, for the chief means for the distribution of goods and services — as demanded by customary law — was "aid" or tallage, and the corvee or boon work in return for protection. In such a system wages were meaningless. "The corvee furnished more laborers than hire." [12] Customary law possessed no norms which bore any similarity to civil and criminal laws of post fifteenth-century Europe, and certainly it possessed none having the decisive characteristics of criminal law — politicality and penal sanction. Both State and citizen were absent as continuous elements of society. These presume an ethic not present in the first feudal age — that of individual responsibility for one's conduct.

Just as the ethic of shared responsibility found institutional expression in vassalage, feudal land tenure, and the feudal system for the distribution of goods and services, so was it the basis for kinship solidarity and the restoration of peaceful relations between offenders and the wronged. What linked vassalage to the kinship system was companionage or friendship, but friendship which carried a profounder meaning by far than it carries today. People united by blood were not necessarily friends, but friendship did not exist unless people were united by blood. Moreover, friendship obligations were weakened by the fact of differential status between friends of blood. If anything, this gave them strength. Any harm falling upon one fell upon all. Any avengement suffered by one was suffered by all members of the companionage. [13] *Treue* and fealty have their meaning here.

Even when infrequently a man was brought before a court, the ethic of shared responsibility found

expression in *compurgation* or oath-helping. A collective oath was enough to clear a man accused or to confirm a complaint brought against the accused. If compurgation should result in a draw, the dispute could be settled either by trial by battle or by voluntary compensation. A defeated champion in trial by battle might be either the accused or the plaintiff, but his defeat was also the defeat of the companionage who "stood surety" for him. *Punishment was an act of war and was collective.* Those of a companionage who were not killed in battle were often hanged upon defeat. Guilt was never established until defeat was received as the verdict of God. This did not mean, however, that guilt was not felt or feared. It meant only that the "structure" of guilt was different then than now. Guilt was the fear of bringing shame upon one's kindred, not shame for having killed (for example) a member of another kindred. It had nothing to do with conscience but everything to do with honor. And the dishonor of one was the dishonor of all. [14]

Perhaps nothing better exemplifies the cooperative ethic more than the extrajudicial and quasi-judicial vendetta or *faida*. Kinship vengeance neatly balanced kinship protection of the accused from vengeance. [15] In any feud it was impossible to distinguish acts of punishment from acts of war; it was also impossible to distinguish acts of crime from acts of war. Crime and punishment were never known until after the battle was over, and when over, the guilty had already been punished. Feudal justice did not require the death of the individual who had done the killing. It did not require the death of one or more of his kinsmen who protected him. Guilt was more of a projection than a feeling on the part of the killer, unless the killer had slain one of his own. In that case, punishment was self-imposed if imposed at all.

Feuds might be forestalled or terminated by arbitration and compensation, but in a social climate where "the very corpse cried out for vengeance . . . and hung withering in the house till the day when vengeance was accomplished" arbitration and compensation were ordinarily futile gestures — at least in the early stages of the feud. But a rotten corpse or even one whose bones are white may be ample inducement later on for accepting compensation. As the will for avenging the dead waned, the desire for

---

[11] *Ibid.*, p. 116.
[12] *Ibid.*, p. 67.
[13] *Ibid.*, pp. 123–125.

[14] *Ibid.*, p. 125.
[15] *Ibid.*, p. 126. See Bloch's distinction between active and passive solidarity.

reconciliation with indemnity heightened and the adage "buy off the spear or feel it in your breast" had practical results.[16]

Judicial procedures, Bloch observes, were little more than "regularized vendettas" and were used only when relatives preferred that means to the feud or compensation.[17] The role of public "authority" in all matters of harms and counterharms and their settlements was negligible. No territorial authority could intervene to impose punishment on an individual without becoming, under custom, the object of a collective vendetta. Penal sanction was absent because it assumes something that did not exist — that the individual and not the kindred of the individual is responsible for the conduct of the individual. In the first feudal age, any "law" having politicality and penal sanction would have been scorned as an attempt by outsiders to profane the bonds of kinship and companionage.

But even well into the second feudal age these customs persisted as did the ethic on which they rested. In the thirteenth century, courts still recognized that any act done by one individual involved all his kindred. In Paris, Parlement still recognized the right of a man to take his vengeance on any relative of his assailant. In cases where such a victim took action in court on the grounds that he had not been involved, those grounds would not have been recognized. The assailant would have been freed.[18] The idea that each man is a citizen of the State and is alone responsible for his own conduct and its consequences was not to be found either in court procedure, in the characteristics of custom, or in judicial decision. The State could not lodge and process complaints. That was a prerogative of the relatives alone.[19]

The power to pardon a man for any offense whatever rested not in the State or in any public authority. Forgiveness was fully a matter to be settled or granted or arranged with indemnity between disputant clans. In Flanders as in Normandy, even down to the thirteenth century, a murderer could not receive his pardon either from the King or the judges until he had first been reconciled with the kindred of the slain.[20] It is easy to pass over the significance of the power to pardon, but doing so would be a major error. For whoever has the power to pardon or to forgive also holds the power to mete out penal sanctions or to punish, and prior to the emergence of formally rational States and citizenship the power to forgive without punishment resided among the kindreds — and punishment without forgiveness was an act of war in interclan disputes. It follows that neither crime nor penal sanctions can have any meaning until the power to pardon becomes the clear monopoly of the State — until the ethic of individual responsibility and citizenship become sociocultural facts.

Rusche and Kirchheimer observe that even to the mid-sixteenth-century the power to pardon still reposed with the offended party and not with the State. In cases punishable by law the offender could keep his harm out of court by compensating the offended party. Even a man sentenced to punishment by the State could avoid punishment by compensating the victim.[21] The power to pardon shifts ever so slowly to a territorial power when custom and the cooperative ethic is strong. In this connection, Weber observed that in ancient India and China the "State" was devoted to making verses, literary masterpieces and was without power to punish or to pardon offenders, due to the deeply imbedded customs of strong peasant clans. The same applied in Europe until Roman law broke the power of similar kindreds.[22]

In the second feudal age down to 1250, repopulation and the makings of an economic revolution took shape. Given the persistence of customary law the commercial principle or what Weber called "the alien ethic"[23] grew not internally but externally and toward the East. Cloth centers emerged nearly everywhere — Flanders, Picardy, Bourges, Languedoc, Lombardy — but from the end of the eleventh century, with the creation of artisans and merchants on a vastly larger scale, in urban places, internal trade came into its own. With it came the institutionalization of private property, citizen-entrepreneurship, and the market system. Men of commerce began to compete with each other with the same unabashed ruthlessness as had characterized international trade prior to the internalization of this ethic.[24] Under the market ethos, since society

[16] *Ibid.*, p. 129.
[17] *Ibid.*, p. 128.
[18] *Ibid.*, pp. 128–129.
[19] *Ibid.*
[20] *Ibid.*, p. 129.

[21] Rusche and Kirchheimer, *Punishment*, p. 213.
[22] Weber, *General Economic History*, pp. 250 ff.
[23] *Ibid.*, p. 232.
[24] *Ibid.*

could not share one's risks and costs, it could not share one's opportunities and gains. Each man as an entrepreneur was responsible for himself, his conduct, and its consequences good or bad. This ethic came eventually to expression in civil and criminal law and in the rational State. But in judicial processes, especially in criminal law procedures, this ethic held little significance because States had not yet developed a clear monopoly over the power to pardon, and few of the ruthless practices common to the newly developing world of commerce had come to be proscribed under any legal order. Whether acts of war or of punishment and crime, the only intended harms proscribed were for the most part "blood harms" and had little to do with violations of private property, breaches of market contracts, and entitlement to allodial (private) property.[25]

Which acts of intended violence, in feuds or war or in trials by combat, are crimes and which are punishments? In the absence of any singular, dominant State capable of continually reducing feuds to crime and penal sanction, crime and penal sanction disappear, and where kinship solidarity between kindreds is strong, war disappears. Interclan marriages may have preserved solidarity in the first feudal age. Certainly no State functioned to do this. In the twelfth century, crime was held not to exist during an interregnum — not even when destruction of royal palaces was involved. In any such power vacuum, people, as usual, relied on customary means of terminating disputes. The rationale was stated simply enough: "We served our emperor while he lived; when he died, we no longer had a sovereign." [26]

Collective reprisals against feudal principalities in the second feudal period were commonplace. In 1127, for example, the Duke of Brittany confessed inability to protect his monasteries from assaults by his own vassals. Evidently the expansion of feudalism by subinfeudation reduced certain marriages up and down the feudal scale, and with this, fealty and companionage were reduced to meaninglessness. Incentives for settling feuds by indemnity had thus vanished, and the feud along with other acts of feudal justice ceased to restore solidarity. In the absence of fealty the strength of authority collapsed and no principality could muster sufficient military force, eventually, to fill the void.[27]

Throughout both feudal ages there emerged no clear distinction between a personal leader or champion and the abstract idea of power. Not even kings were able to rise above family sentiments.[28] Against the force of custom and shared responsibility for individual conduct, States of the first feudal age were weak. With the force of custom and shared responsibility, they were strong. As bonds of fealty waned with the expansion of feudal estates — from top to bottom of the feudal scale — the ethic of shared responsibility for conduct collapsed. Feuds, wars, petty violence increased in frequency and savagery. The forms of tradition remained *as forms,* but interpersonal sentiments favoring peace gave them no meaning. What gave them meaning was the temper of violence and irreparably wounded honor. In all this, traditional authority, stripped of fealty and companionage, was powerless. Toward the close of the second feudal age, feudalism of old had collapsed, and feudal authority in the midst of chaos was on the threshold of transformation. Under the ethic of shared responsibility, crime and penal sanction did not exist. Without it, and before the development of citizenship and the formally rational State — toward the end of feudalism — only reprisals and counterreprisals existed. In neither situation was there criminal law or a force strong enough to impose it on each individual as an individual. Individualism without ethic and without institutions to regularize it was born of the collapse of feudal institutions.

Rational Institutions and Their Relation to Crime and Penal Sanction

The institutional chaos of the latter Middle Ages — extending well into the fourteenth century — and the steady decline of the ethic of shared responsibility left feudal authority impoverished and impotent to arrest the increasing savagery of interminable feuds, wars, petty violence and brigandage. The vassalage, tied to landed interests, could no longer rely on fealty and tallage from lesser ranks for their politi-

[25] Bloch, vol. 2, pp. 365 ff.
[26] *Ibid.,* p. 409 ff. Acts like this were regular in this period, because principalities were weak — no longer holding consensus and strong military forces. Under weak principalities "crime" meant only the clash of armies. Upholding custom in feuds led inadvertently (with other causes) to individuation of society through loss of fealty, meaningful epics, and the obsoleteness of the folk memory.

[27] *Ibid.,* Chapter 30, pp. 408–421.
[28] *Ibid.,* p. 10 ff.

cal and economic support. Nor could perpetuity of landed wealth be relied upon from the fourteenth century on. Royal revenues and power were drying up as fealty declined, and of necessity royal authority sought revenues elsewhere, if only to raise armies to put down recalcitrants in the realm.

Not all was chaos. Petty merchants throughout Europe, once objects of scorn, had already begun to develop, with their artisans, the institutions of private property, exchange of titles to property in markets growing steadily in the second feudal age, and a labor force freed from feudal ties. Even by the thirteenth century, these merchants had become dedicated to the business of creating opportunities for continued, renewable gains — calling for stern rejection of sentiment and sympathy for any who might lose heavily in trade relations. It called for monklike pursuit of gain. Initially banished, outside the feudal city, these pariahs grew with every decline of feudal institutions, and with them grew the ethic of individual responsibility. In the midst of feudal anomie, this ethic — expressed institutionally in market contracts — finally supplanted the cooperative ethic. It did so with the eventual alliance between European monarchs and the rising merchant class.

The alliance created the formally rational State and citizenship and had direct bearing upon the advent of crime and penal sanction. Petty merchants throughout Europe gained fantastic wealth and with it power directly in consequence to the wars and feuds of the landed nobility. Such wars, in absence of fealty and tallage, had to be financed from outside the system. War loans, using land as collateral, were made to such nobles by merchants. Lands once held by nobles in perpetuity under laws of primogeniture and entail were regularly mortgaged by both parties in conflict. Every war meant that the land of one of the parties in conflict would fall to the merchant making the loan and not to the winner of the battle. Dobb observed that from the Wars of the Roses onward, the landed wealth of Europe fell in this manner into the hands of merchants like fish into their nets.[29] As most wealth had been landed wealth held out of the market by laws of primogeniture and entail, this transfer of land to the merchant class made land a commodity for buying and selling *as private property* in the interest of profit. Any labor attached

to such land under serfdom was freed from feudal ties to that land, and so were the nobles themselves. Human relations underwent profound transformation.

The plight of monarchs in raising revenues became more acute since revenues had come previously from landed nobles all the way up the feudal scale. Now in the hands of merchants, changing hands with every sale, land came to resemble mobile capital. It became clear that the destiny of monarchs was at once the prosperity of merchants. In this way the State cut its bond with family relations. The kinship aspects of the feudal State vanished. Tied to the interests of an entrepreneurial world, authority and power became abstract. In aligning itself with capital and the interests of capital, the State came to guarantee as law both the ethic and the practices which had merged among merchants prior to the alliance.

The annuity bond arising from personal debts and war loans, the stock certificate, the bill of exchange, the commercial company, the mortgage, trust deeds, and the power of attorney — all were practices of merchants which grew with the collapse of feudal institutions and which became guaranteed in law with the alliance between monarchs and the entrepreneurial class.[30] With this alliance the remnants of shared responsibility for gains and losses were bypassed along with the social control value of customary law, kinship as a restraint upon power, and the sentiments of fealty and companionage. Local feudal worlds such as kindreds and medieval cities lost all autonomy and authority as the nation-state emerged. Everywhere cities in Europe came under the power of competing national States as a condition, Weber observed, of perpetual struggle for power in peace and war:

> This competitive struggle created the largest opportunities for modern capitalism. The separate States had to compete for mobile capital, which dictated to them the conditions under which it would assist them to power. Out of this alliance of the state with capital, dictated by necessity, arose the national citizen class, the bourgeoisie in the modern sense of the word. Hence, it is the closed national State which afforded to capitalism its chance for development — and as long as the national state does not give to a world empire capitalism also will endure.[31]

---

[29] Maurice Dobb, *Studies in the Development of Capitalism,* chap. 5, rev. ed. (New York: International Publishers, 1963), especially pp. 186–198.

[30] Weber, *General Economic History,* pp. 247–253 ff.
[31] *Ibid.,* p. 249.

Just as the national State came to recognize and guarantee, as well as create, civil laws relating to market relations, private property, labor, imports, exports, tariffs, it likewise came to have full power to create and impose criminal laws which related to the same institutions of capitalism. Under the ethic of individual responsibility, any citizen, even one forgiven by his kin or community, could be penally sanctioned as an individual by an abstract State and without much probability of reprisal against the State on the part of those who had forgiven him. With the advent of the formally rational State, punishment was no longer an act of war. And any violation of criminal law — defined by the State — came to be seen as a harm against the State.

With authority behind the institutions of capitalism, and as the commercial principle became intense and diffused through the commercial and industrial revolutions, criminal law proscribed far more behaviors as crimes that had ever existed even in the second feudal age. In addition to the short list of blood harms, fornication, and adultery which had been dealt with on the shared responsibility basis, the State created new crimes and punishments directly as the institutions of capitalism advanced. Moreover, the older blood harms — including the older forms of justice — became criminal in that the State now specifically proscribed them and fixed to them penal sanctions. Thus the State obtained a monopoly over the processing of acts of violence.

Apart from the older harms criminal laws were established primarily for the protection and development of the institutions of capitalism. The reference here is not simply to penal sanctions levied against robbery, theft, burglary, or other violations of private property. It is to penal sanctions which directly controlled the manner in which social structure would develop in cities. It is to penal sanctions which had direct bearing on determining the organization of the division of labor in society and consequently upon the class structure of commercial settlements.

Criminal laws strangled the ability of lower classes (those alienated from landed feudal ties who had migrated to cities as "free labor") to possess tools or capital goods, raw materials, and also, on pain of heavy penal sanction, forbade association with guild masters.[32] In short, upward mobility became a crime unless guild masters themselves chose to elevate the status of an artisan. Thus penal sanctions guaranteed by the State guaranteed a continuous labor force (whether employed or not) and created two classes of citizens — one bound by criminal laws and penal sanctions, and another bound only by nonpunitive civil laws. The situation is hardly different today in this respect.[33] Under the formally rational State, second-class citizens are never in a position to be governed only by civil laws — they are never, therefore, beyond incrimination.

[32] Rusche and Kirchheimer, chap. 2. See reference made to R. H. Tawney and to the latter's support of the above statement where the State is described as a class State whose criminal laws protected only the interests of large capitalistic guild masters and held labor captive.

[33] E. H. Sutherland, *White Collar Crime* (New York: Holt, Rinehart, Winston, 1949).

JAILS

Ronald Goldfarb

Goldfarb reports here on the state of jails in this country. As the radical analysis suggests more abstractly, he finds concretely that "the jail is for the poor, the street is for the rich."

The selection combines several excerpts from a longer book by the same title.

The author, an attorney in Washington, D.C., has written numerous books and articles on the criminal justice system.

Jail: The Nation's Dumping Ground

A jail is not a prison. A prison houses convicted criminals; no untried people go to prisons. A jail is essentially a pretrial detention center used to hold people until they are tried. But to complicate matters, the jail also has come to be used both as a short-term correctional institution for misdemeanants, and a way station for a random mélange of other defendants. Sometimes people are lost and forgotten in the jails for weeks and months after they could have been legally released. Men convicted but awaiting sentence or appeal, defendants on their way across the country to trial or prison, defendants being moved from one institution to another, immigrants awaiting deportation, military arrestees, people held as material witnesses to a forthcoming trial also crowd the jails, adding to the confusion and the bedlam and complicating the mission of these institutions.

The jail population is composed predominantly either of people who are denied bail because of the seriousness of the offenses with which they were charged or who, because they are poor, cannot afford bail and are forced to waste in jail waiting for a distant trial.

One stark fact of life is that generally people of means never see the inside of a jail. Wealthy people can make bail, get medical treatment, make restitution, pay fines, and generally find alternative techniques to resolve their problems. Noah Pope, a per-

ceptive convict, once told me: "The jail is for the poor, the street is for the poor, the street is for the rich." . . .

Proliferation of Jails

Our jails touch the lives of more people in the community than all other correctional institutions. One of the nation's leading correctional experts, Hans Mattick, has said that jails are the most important part of the correction system "in terms of numbers and impact." They hold "the highest percentages of innocent and inoffensive persons." Jails are, as the 1967 President's Crime Commission noted, the beginning of the correctional continuum, the distributor and the key filtering point for the criminal justice system. . . .

The jail houses a disparate collection of social outcasts and underprivileged people in desperate need of unavailable social services. The jail of any American city is in one author's words, "the traditional dumping ground for the untried, the petty offender, the vagrant, the debtor and beggar, the promiscuous, and the mentally ill." It is the "forgotten, residual institution" for "the public nuisance, the sick and the poor, the morally deviant, and the merely troublesome and rejected." [1] Alcoholics filled half of many jails until recently. A 1967 survey of one city jail and three large county workhouses in one state revealed that more than half of the prisoners sentenced to jail for commission of a crime were there for drunkenness. Huge numbers of narcotics addicts are thrown into jails at random. Others are in jail because they cannot pay a fine; men are there on work release; youngsters and first offenders who could be reached and corrected are thrown together with inveterate criminals who ought to be segregated; mentally ill individuals, and social delinquents like alimony dodgers, all compose parts of this often nightmarish mélange. . . .

[1] Edith Flynn, "Jails and Criminal Justice," in *Prisoners in America* (Englewood Cliffs: Prentice-Hall, 1973), p. 2.

There are about 400 prisons in the United States, but a survey conducted in 1967 for the President's Crime Commission estimated that there were about 3,500 jails.[2] There are actually many more since the figure of 3,500 appears to have been derived from the number of counties in the United States; the city jails and workhouses that do not hold prisoners for the counties, are excluded. A recent survey of jails in Illinois found 160 jails in that state (excluding police lockups), of which the Crime Commission survey presumably included only 102 (the number of Illinois counties). If this considerable undercounting of the jails by the Crime Commission was true of other states, one might extrapolate from its figures and arrive at an estimated total of at least 5,250 jails. . . .

The 1967 President's Crime Commission reported more than one million convicted offenders, mostly misdemeanants, served sentences in jails in 1965. The average daily population then serving sentences was 141,303. Although some of these people undoubtedly served more than one jail term in a year and thus were counted more than once, the figure still represents a gross underestimate of the entire jail population, since this survey excluded prisoners serving sentences in facilities where convicted offenders could not serve sentences of at least thirty days. Add to this an unknown annual number of pretrial defendants who comprise more than half of the population of most jails — and persons in jail for violations of motor vehicle laws and other civil offenses, and one could speculate that jails hold from three to four million people annually — perhaps thirty-five times the number handled by all state and federal prisons.

High turnover rates and poor record keeping make accurate data impossible but, according to Professor Mattick, himself a former Cook County Jail official, "the best estimate of the number of jail commitments in the United States each year is at least one and a half million, and may be as many as five and a half million"; the most likely accurate estimate "is probably around 3 million." [3] . . .

Staffing patterns also are revealing. In 1965, more than 19,000 people were employed in the jails surveyed for the Crime Commission, of whom only 500, less than 3 per cent, performed any sort of rehabilitative functions. There was only one social worker for each 850 inmates, one psychologist for each 4,300 and one academic teacher for each 1,300. Some of these professionals worked in jails only part time, and most were concentrated in the large institutions.

The LEAA survey reported that in March 1970, there were 5,676 part-time employees and 28,911 full-time employees in the country's jails. Of the full-timers, more than 30 per cent worked in New York and California; their average earnings were $617 per month. It is not surprising that two thirds of the jails surveyed by LEAA said they had no rehabilitative programs at all. (If institutions receiving no prisoners with sentences greater than thirty days were included, the proportion of jails with no programs doubtless would be considerably higher.)

The LEAA survey reported that 86 per cent of the larger jails (3,319) had no facilities at all for exercise or recreation; nine out of ten had no educational facilities; almost half had no medical facilities; a quarter of them had no visiting facilities; in fact, forty-seven jails in twenty-one states had no toilet facilities.

Philadelphia's superintendent of prisons concedes the problem: "Our problem basically is that we are overwhelmed with detentioners. We are so busy receiving and discharging and sending detentioners to court every day that we have very little time left for our staff to devote to program development." . . .

The Heroin Epidemic and Criminal Risk

Chronic, compulsive self-administration of narcotic drugs today is generally regarded as a disease.[4] Yet most addicts are not under treatment in hospitals, community mental health clinics or physicians' offices. They are on the streets or behind bars. Dr. John Kramer, a psychiatric authority on the treatment of addicts, has observed cynically: "The only treatment modality available everywhere is prison or jail." [5]

[2] President's Commission on Law Enforcement and Administration of Justice, *Task Force Report: Corrections* (Washington, D.C.: U.S. Government Printing Office, 1967), p. 75.

[3] Hans Mattick, "The Contemporary Jails of the United States," in D. Glaser, *Handbook in Criminology* (Chicago: Rand McNally, 1974), p. 47.

[4] See, e.g., Joint Committee of the American Bar Association and the American Medical Association, *Drug Addiction: Crime or Disease* (Bloomington: Indiana Univ. Press, 1961); President's Advisory Commission on Narcotic and Drug Abuse Report (Washington, D.C.: Government Printing Office, 1963).

[5] Statement of Dr. John C. Kramer in "Narcotics Research, Rehabilitation and Treatment," Hearings before

Certain addicts are protected by status from prosecution. "Professional addicts" — physicians and nurses, who favor the synthetic narcotics such as Demerol — are seldom arrested or jailed. Rarely are patients of private physicians who prescribe narcotics for non-medical purposes exposed and punished. "Medical addicts" — who receive authorized maintenance dosages of various opiumlike drugs for pain relief — are beyond the reach of the law. It is the "street addicts," primarily the poor and unprotected, who are convicted as criminals because of their habit or activities related to securing a supply of drugs to satisfy that habit. Hence, punitive treatment of drug users is selective as to race and class and economic circumstances. . . .

Despite the advice of reputable medical authorities, the typical "street" addict is treated not as a sick person but as a criminal.[6] Although the United States Supreme Court ruled in *Robinson* v. *California*[7] that the status of addiction, in itself, cannot be punished as a crime, every other aspect of an addict's life-style — including sale, possession or use of narcotic drugs, and possession of narcotics "paraphernalia" (syringes, glassine envelopes, improvised "cookers," etc.) — is penalized under federal, state and local criminal laws. In a number of jurisdictions, mere association with narcotics addicts has been made punishable.[8] But the middle-class or affluent

users generally escape detection. Police seldom invade their homes and they need not resort to the streets for supply.

Poverty makes criminals of many addicts. The suburban teenagers habit may be financed by his parents directly or indirectly. But the ghetto youth, like the adult, often is unemployed or without resources, and thus moves into an endless round of acquisitive criminality to finance his habit. Heroin, the favored drug of "street addicts," is available only in the illicit market. Data on the cost of street heroin are derived almost exclusively from the reports of addicts themselves; even though the quest for prestige or the desire to obtain preferential medical treatment may lead addicts to overstate the price of their drug use, the average cost of a heroin habit ranges between twenty-five and fifty dollars per day.[9]

Data compiled by economist John Holahan suggest that only a tiny minority of the heroin customers, probably fewer than 5 per cent, support their habits legally.[10] Between 15 and 30 per cent traffic in drugs (taking the profits in cash or in kind), or perform services for dealers or traffickers to finance their personal needs. Thus from 65 to 80 per cent or more must support their habits primarily through other criminal activities. For female addicts, prostitution is a typical choice; many male addicts specialize in burglaries. Minor property crimes which yield hard cash or readily salable merchandise — shoplifting, pickpocketing and other larcenies — also are common among addicts.

Because criminality is a symptom of the disease of addiction, the jails today are housing many of its victims. According to a 1969 study of the District of Columbia Jail, 45 per cent of all its inmates were

the Select Committee on Crime of the House of Representatives, 92d Cong., 1st sess., 665 (1971).

[6] Throughout the following discussion, the term "addict" will be used to describe those inmates who come to local short-term prisons or detention facilities from the subculture of narcotics use. The term necessarily conceals the diversity of this population. Recognizing that some men and women involved in heroin use are either light or erratic consumers, some authorities favor general use of the broader label "addict-user." But the mere "user" is less likely than the compulsive consumer to be jailed, and does not require the same special treatment services. Alternative labels for the jailed heroin user's disease — ranging from the World Health Organization's preferred "drug dependence of the morphine type" to the fashionable euphemism "drug abuse" — are in some respects less serviceable than "addiction." Although the term "addict" does carry pejorative overtones, it is regularly employed by those who deal with narcotics users on a day-to-day basis; its use here should not be taken to imply a lack of compassion for the "addict," or a failure to recognize the complexity of the disease with which he is afflicted.

[7] 370 U.S. 660 (1962).

[8] See Eldridge, *Narcotics and the Law*, pp. 149–93, for state laws forbidding "resort" to places where narcotics are used.

[9] In most cities, narcotics are the only habit-forming illicit drugs so expensive that large numbers of users must commit non-drug crimes. Where heroin use is suppressed, however, secondary crackdowns on once inexpensive drugs substituted by former heroin addicts — such as amphetamines — may produce new drug-related crime by driving up street prices. The tendency of former heroin addicts to substitute non-opiate drugs has been documented; there is no clear indication as to the effect this tendency ultimately may have on the price structure of the illicit market, or on the criminal conduct of its customers.

[10] John F. Holahan, "The Economics of Heroin," *Dealing with Drug Abuse* (Drug Abuse Survey Project, 1972), pp. 255, 289–93, citing Mark Moore, *Policy Concerning Drug Abuse in New York State*, Vol. III: *Economics of Heroin Distribution*, Croton-on-Hudson, N.Y.: (1970), p. 66.

addicted to heroin, probably a significant increase over previous years.[11] About forty "known addicts" — persons already familiar to law enforcement officials as heroin users — were booked into the D.C. Jail in 1958. By 1968, the number of annual "known addict" bookings was over 420, still only an undetermined fraction of the total number of addicts booked. Of this increase of 1,000 per cent in a decade, only a part can be attributed to improvements in police and custodial information gathering.

New York City's commissioner of correction stated in mid-1970 that of a one-day population of 14,324 jailed prisoners, 42 per cent of the men and 70 per cent of the women were "hard-core" narcotics addicts. Addiction rates among sentenced prisoners were roughly the same.[12] In late 1971 the city's Department of Correction estimated that half of its prisoners were addicts. . . .

It is a fact of street life that, at some point in his career, almost every street addict — that is, the urban poor, especially the minority group poor — will be jailed. Of 750 New York City addiction treatment patients ranging from twenty to fifty years of age, each of whom had used heroin for at least four years, 91 per cent had been jailed in the past.[13]

The user-victims of the drug trade are punished, but the commercial wholesalers of the trade, the major dealers and victimizers, remain almost immune from arrest and jailing. Their reliance on subordinates and their private arrangements with corrupt law enforcement personnel often insulate major dealers. They will remain immune until new intensified efforts to reduce the heroin supply through vigorous investigation and prosecution of suppliers and wholesalers, like those of the new federal Drug Enforcement Agency (DEA), produce substantial results. Thus, the jails are used to punish those who are sick and in need of treatment. Those who have nurtured and spread the disease too often go free. . . .

[11] Nicholas J. Kozel, Barry S. Brown and Robert L. DuPont, "A Study of Narcotics Addicted Offenders at the D.C. Jail," *Int'l. J. Addictions* 7 (1972):443. Adams, Meadows, and Reynolds, "Narcotic-involved Inmates in the Department of Corrections" (D.C. Department of Corrections Research Report No. 12, 1969).

[12] "Crime in America — Heroin Importation, Distribution, Packaging and Paraphernalia," Hearings before the Select Committee on Crime of the House of Representatives, 91st. Cong., 2d sess., 215 (1970).

[13] Vincent P. Dole, Marie E. Nyswander, and Alan Warner, "Successful Treatment of 750 Criminal Addicts," *J.A.M.A.* 206 (1968): 2708, 2710.

Alcoholics

Striking ironies in the treatment of alcoholic offenders reflect the class bias characteristic of society's response to drunkenness begun a century and a half ago. Furthermore, enforcement policies also ignore the public safety element of law enforcement. The laws against the genuinely menacing offense of driving under the influence are grossly underenforced as the statutes prohibiting public drunkenness are overenforced. If drinking drivers actually cause 180 million auto accidents annually, or about 500,000 a day (as the National Safety Council has estimated), an annual total approaching only 800,000 DWI arrests appears as nothing more than a modest gesture toward controlling this dangerous behavior.

The DWI arrestee can expect to receive a reasonably fair trial, and ordinarily will not be jailed after a conviction. He generally will have been out on bail awaiting trial. He is likely to receive a revocation of his driver's permit, a suspended sentence, or a fine in an amount which he is able to pay.

A simple drunkenness offender will be held in jail, will be sentenced usually on a guilty plea without a trial and will serve a jail sentence sufficient to disrupt whatever tenuous order exists in his personal life. He usually is committed to jail or fined an amount he cannot pay or both.

The sanctions most commonly applied to the DWI offender have little or no impact on his future misconduct. According to a California survey, as many as 85 per cent of those penalized for driving under the influence by license revocation simply continue to drive.

The aberrant drinking behavior of motorists is a genuine threat to public safety; simple drunkenness usually is not. It is a paradox then that offenders who are more dangerous to society are thus punished less severely and less summarily than those who are generally of no danger at all. . . .

Beverage alcohol is America's drug of choice. How many people use it is impossible to determine. How many misuse it is also difficult to ascertain. In 1962, Mark Keller of the Rutgers Center for Alcohol Studies estimated that 4.5 million Americans could be classified "alcoholics." [14] Don Cahalan, an authority

[14] Keller, "The Definition of Alcoholism and the Estimation of its Prevalence" in D. Pittman and C. Snyder, eds., *Society, Culture and Drinking Patterns* (New York: J. Wiley, 1962), pp. 310, 312. This estimate is based on mortality rates for cirrhosis of the liver and corresponds

on drinking problems, states that 9 per cent of the population (approximately 6,500,000 persons) are seriously afflicted heavy drinkers.[15] A special federal task force recently found that "about 9 million men and women are alcohol abusers and alcoholic individuals."[16] Alcoholism is the third most serious American public health problem (after cancer and heart disease).

Legal and social responses to deviant drinking are heavily biased against certain social classes, yet drinking and alcoholism are classless. "Heavy drinkers" exist in comparable percentages in all economic, educational and professional classes. (In the most comprehensive recent survey of alcohol use in America, only upper-middle-class persons over sixty years of age showed a markedly lower rate of "heavy drinking" than members of other groups.)[17]

Yet, the laws against drunkenness have come to be applied discriminately to lower-status persons, primarily.

The costs generated by problem drinking throughout American society are high, totaling $15 billion by one recent estimate.[18] About $10 billion of this is in lost work time. According to the General Accounting Office, the U. S. Army alone loses the equivalent of $120 million annually through the absenteeism and impaired productivity of alcoholic personnel. $3 billion takes the form of property damage, private medical expenses and other direct losses. According to the National Safety Council, alcoholic-related traffic accidents in themselves generate costs of $1.8 billion annually, along with half of all traffic fatalities. The remaining $2 billion is expended in cash or kind through public service programs for alcoholics and their families. The indirect costs of alcohol abuse —

the personal suffering and social disruption — cannot be assigned a dollar value.

Buried somewhere in the national bill for alcohol abuse is a relatively small but shockingly anomalous item: the costs of enforcing the public drunkenness laws. The most comprehensive study of this expense item was made in Atlanta, Georgia, during 1961. For roughly 50,000 arrests, the cost of apprehending, detaining, trying and jailing drunkenness offenders totaled about $870,000.[19] If Atlanta's examples were typical of the costs of drunkenness law enforcement, the nation's bill for expenses stemming from two million arrests for intoxication and equivalent offenses would be about $35 million. But Atlanta is not typical: a drunk arrest is estimated to take fifteen minutes in Atlanta, but in some cities it may consume up to three hours of police time. Because Atlanta prosecutes so many drunkenness offenders, court processing is cost-efficient. And while the average cost of maintaining a sentenced inmate in Atlanta's jails was estimated in 1961 at $1.69, other jails today report a cost as high as eight or nine dollars. Estimating a conservative four dollars per inmate-day, the direct cost of jailing convicted drunkenness offenders alone may approach $50 million annually in the 1970s. If Atlanta is viewed as a city where drunkenness law enforcement is exceptionally efficient and if a decade of cost inflation is taken into account, the national cost of such enforcement overall appears to be in the hundreds of millions of dollars. This expense is incurred in an ineffective attempt to control the behavior of an unfortunate minority of Americans who make up no more than 10 to 15 per cent of the total population of serious problem drinkers. It is one by-product of a pattern of legal discrimination against lower-class alcohol abusers which is as old as the nation itself. . . .

Impressed, and Unpaid, Labor

All total institutions — particularly penal institutions and most particularly jails — may be said to be run for the convenience and benefit of the staff and administrators, rather than the welfare of the inmates. Where the relationship between the ordinary misdemeanant and his jailer-employer often is one of ex-

---

to a relatively restrictive definition of "alcoholism" which excludes many other drinkers, whose day-to-day functioning is impaired by alcohol use.

[15] D. Cahalan, *The Problem Drinkers.* (New York: Jossey-Bass, 1970). The class of "problem drinkers" — men and women who experience some medical or social difficulty because of alcohol use — may number as many as thirty million.

[16] U.S. Department of Health, Education and Welfare, *First Special Report to the U.S. Congress on Alcohol and Health* (Washington, D.C.: Government Printing Office, 1971), p. viii.

[17] D. Cahalan, J. Cisin, and H. Cressley, *American Drinking Practices* (1969), pp. 26–27.

[18] U.S. Department of Health, Education, and Welfare, *First Special Report to the U.S. Congress on Alcohol and Health,* p. viii.

[19] See President's Commission on Law Enforcement and Administration of Justice, *Task Force Report: Drunkenness* (Washington, D.C.: Government Printing Office, 1967), pp. 98–99.

ploitation, the relationship between the jailed drunk and his taskmaster is perversely symbiotic. The jail administrator who drafts prisoners as servants gets free labor; the drunk finds he is needed temporarily. Despite the verbal abuse he receives from some quarters, the drunk's status in jail is high. A medium- or large-sized jail requires kitchen help, laundry workers, groundkeepers and other staff. The drunk makes a passive non-rebellious worker. And among the inmates with whom a drunk identifies, status in jail society is largely a function of the job assignment.

A job that is useful, that is physically undemanding, that carries responsibility and implies the trust of jail authorities; a job that provides extra or special food, reading matter, additional tobacco rations, more freedom of movement — that job has status in jail. Such jobs are precisely those to which confined drunks are likely to be assigned. I remember being shown around one jail by a proud warden. When we got to an empty immaculate kitchen, he pointed with pride to a shiny, polished chrome stove. "We've got an alky," he told me, "who is in here every month. Whenever he comes, his project is that stove. He loves it and keeps it in that shape for us."

The population of jailed drunks, and particularly its older and more familiar members, provides a valuable labor pool for the management and maintenance of otherwise underfinanced and understaffed institutions. The typical drunk is sentenced with dependable regularity and often for increasingly long terms; he submits readily to authority and responds positively to insignificant rewards; he seldom is troubled by sexual deprivation, since active sexuality has ceased to be a focus of his free existence; and — since he is not a clinical alcoholic but a chronic drunk — he is little troubled by enforced sobriety after the first few days of his sentence. He is a prized asset. The more often he is sentenced, the closer he comes to being the ideal jail laborer; the younger drunkenness offender must work his way up the job-status scale.

The Toronto Alcoholism and Drug Addiction Research Foundation's study of its local jail disclosed a highly elaborate caste system and jail hierarchy based on occupational prestige.[20] Jobs assigned to

drunks ranged from the highly desirable positions of the "Governor's men" (the warden's houseboys), the "tea room gang" (men assigned to serve the guards), and barbers; through positions of intermediate desirability, such as the clothing details and the garden gang; down to the lowly garbage detail. The best jobs, and most of the fringe benefits, went to the most thoroughly confirmed recidivist drunks.

In the Seattle City Jail, drunks compete for especially desirable job assignments:

It was discovered that there were about 60 categories (of "trusties") who work at an enormous number of jobs; they staple targets and mow lawns, mop floors, clean boats, clean toilets, make coffee, usher in the court, care for the sick, make pastries, wait on bulls, carry messages, wash pots, run elevators, cut hair and a variety of other tasks. In this jail, which has a capacity for approximately 500 inmates, nearly 150 trusties are required each day to work. It was estimated by one police official that 80 percent of the inmates at any time are those charged with public drunkenness and that these are the men chosen to become trusties. . . .[21]

Such exploitation of free labor sometimes extends to a form of "recruitment":

Penal officials like police officers don't consider public drunkenness offenders as serious criminals. It is simple enough to observe that many of the men when sober are steady workers . . . Much of the janitorial work in the jails is assigned to them. There are many instances where especially good workers with skills needed by the jail system are picked up by the police specifically to fill the jail's need.[22]

The drunks Spradley interviewed in Seattle told of being shanghaied in this manner in jurisdictions through Washington and California. One man, while working in the kitchen of the Seattle Jail, "overheard the cook ask an officer where a certain man was who had been a good cook. The officer replied that they knew his whereabouts and would pick him up in a few days." [23]

[20] Alcoholism and Drug Addiction Research Foundation of Toronto, "The Chronic Drunkenness Offender: The Jail" (Research Report No. 6, unpublished, n.d.) The findings of this study, conducted during 1960–61, are cited here with the kind permission of the foundation.

[21] James Spradley, *You Owe Yourself a Drunk* (Boston: Little, Brown, 1970), p. 84.
[22] Sidney Cahn, *The Treatment of Alcoholics* (New York: Oxford Univ. Press, 1967), p. 47.
[23] Spradley, *You Owe Yourself a Drunk,* p. 85.

A 1970 survey of California county jails found that the general view that drunks should be removed from the penal system was tempered by administrators' reliance on these dependable — and dependent — prisoners:

Even when faced with the obvious problem of handling and caring for these individuals, a few sheriffs were reluctant to suggest removing all such persons from their jurisdictions. They based their opposition on their present needs for trustees to do custodial, maintenance and kitchen duty. Experienced jail supervisors know that the older alcoholics are docile, amiable and obedient workers when sober, as well as experienced in the ways of an institution. Some of these same supervisors are reluctant to change the system which provides such workers when no alternative sources of labor are available.[24]

The work drunks do in the jail cannot be rationalized as a kind of improvised vocational rehabilitation. Any correspondence between the labor needs of a jail and the demands of the job market is accidental. Like every other facet of the drunk's experience as an inmate, his institutional work prepares him for only one career — chronic recidivism.

[24] California State Board of Corrections, "A Study of California County Jails" (April 1970), pp. 129–30.

BIBLIOGRAPHY

I. IMPRESSIONS, DEFINITIONS, AND MAGNITUDES

A. Impressions

Eliot Asinof. *People v. Blutcher*. New York: Viking, 1970.

B. Definitions and Magnitudes

Marvin Wolfgang. "Urban Crime," in James Q. Wilson, ed., *The Metropolitan Enigma*. Cambridge: Harvard University Press, 1968.
President's Commission on Law Enforcement and the Administration of Justice. *The Challenge of Crime in a Free Society*. Washington, D.C.: U.S. Government, 1967.

II. ANALYTIC PERSPECTIVES

A. Orthodox Economic Perspectives

Gary Becker. "Crime and Punishment: An Economic Approach," *Journal of Political Economy,* April 1968.
William Landes. *Essays in the Economics of Crime and Punishment*. New York: National Bureau of Economic Research, 1974.

B. Liberal and Conservative Approaches

Ramsey Clark. *Crime in America*. New York: Simon & Schuster, 1970. A decent liberal's perspective.
James Q. Wilson. *Thinking about Crime*. New York: Basic Books, 1975. More conservative than Clark, with more emphasis on deterrence.

C. Radical Perspectives

David M. Gordon. "Capitalism, Class, and Crime," *Crime and Delinquency,* June 1973.

Richard Quinney. *Critique of Legal Order. Boston:* Little, Brown, 1974.

III. POLICY PERSPECTIVES

A. The Criminal Justice System

James Q. Wilson. *Varieties of Police Behavior.* New York: Basic Books, 1969.

Jerome Skolnick. *Justice Without Trial.* New York: Wiley, 1966. On the prevalence of pretrial settlement.

Marvin Frankel. *Criminal Sentences: Law Without Order.* New York· Hill and Wang, 1972. A leading judge condemns the sentencing system.

Jessica Mitford. *Kind and Usual Punishment: The Prison Business.* New York: Knopf, 1973.

Calvert R. Dodge, ed. *A Nation Without Prisons.* Lexington, Mass.: D. C. Heath, 1975. Possible alternatives to the current system of criminal justice.

HEALTH

EDITOR'S
INTRODUCTION

...a "health care crisis" ... does not exist.

Insofar as medical science can control illness and death, the United States in the 1970s has a population enjoying the best health and greatest longevity in the nation's history.

— Harry Schwartz[1]

The American health crisis became official in 1969. President Nixon announced it in a special message in July. Liberal academic observers of the health scene ...hastened to verify the existence of the crisis. Now the media is rushing in with details and documentation. ...

[But for] the great majority of Americans, the "health care crisis" is not a TV show or a presidential address; it is an on-going crisis of survival.

— Barbara and John Ehrenreich[2]

By the end of the 1960s, many Americans were experiencing a crisis of health. Some people still treasured their visions of a happy and healthy society, of course, but many were beginning to wonder whether their society was healthy at all. It is probably not coincidental that criticisms reached their peak in 1969 and 1970. If we could drop men on the moon with such astonishing ease, why could we not apply our technological wizardry to heal the sick? The contrasts seemed dazzling. As one Boston doctor put it:

> The teaching hospital has become the nub of the medical universe. On its upper floors we have the very best that American medicine can offer. And down on the street floor — or in the basement — we have that great medical soup kitchen, that cafeteria of clinics, that Siberia of medical care, the old-fashioned outpatient department.[3]

[1] Harry Schwartz, *The Case for American Medicine* (New York: McKay, 1972), pp. 1, 57.
[2] Barbara and John Ehrenreich, *The American Health Empire* (New York: Random House, 1970), p. 3.
[3] Quoted in Selig Greenberg, *The Quality of Mercy: A Report on the Critical Condition of Hospital and Medical Care in America* (New York: Atheneum, 1971), p. 103.

Most critics of the health care system, insulted by the obscenities of disease amidst wealth and waste, framed their attacks in the rhetoric of personal outrage. Senator Edward M. Kennedy typified the health crusaders:

> I am shocked to find that we in America have created a health system that can be so callous to human suffering, so intent on high salaries and profits, and so unconcerned for the need of our people. . . . The health care industry seems by its nature to give most freedom and power to the providers of care — and very little to the people. . . . It is an industry which strongly protects the profits and rights of the provider, but only weakly protects the healing and the rights of the people.[4]

The rhetoric carried over from criticisms to policy prescription. Advocates of different medical care solutions battled each other like convention orators supporting their favorite politicians: their own pet programs offered eternal cure. Their opponents' programs would feed the fat and neglect the needy. Slogans filled the chambers. "Socialized medicine!" "Hospital empires!" "Plutocratic physicians!"

And still, the positions remain essentially the same. When the air clears, advocates cluster in the usual clumps. Conservatives, liberals, and radicals remain true to their perspectives. No matter how we define and measure the crisis in health, we tend to analyze its causes and suggest its solutions through the same lenses that we use with most of our other urban problems.

This chapter outlines the nature of the disagreement. In this introduction, I first describe the problems, then sketch the respective analyses of the different perspectives, and finally introduce the readings.

Definitions and Magnitudes

Health problems are easy to define. An individual is healthy when he is not sick. A society is aggregately healthy when few of its citizens are sick. Typically, a wide variety of indices are deployed to measure the "health" of a society. Infant mortality rates are frequently measured, total mortality rates are often compared, and relative mortality rates within certain segments of the population are also charted. Finally, the prevalence of preventable or curable diseases is also studied.

By almost any general standard, the United States fares poorly in international health comparisons. The U.S. ranks 15th in infant mortality rates, with an infant mortality rate 50 percent higher than Sweden's. During the 1960s, the U.S. slipped from 13th to 22nd place in the rankings of countries for male life expectancy rates.[5] In general, indices of American health are not improving. "After a long period of decline in the mortality rate," as one analyst concludes, "there has been no significant change in the rate since 1950. . . . Overall morbidity rates . . . show little change from year to year." [6]

Worse than this, the United States has developed a dual health system. Some

---

[4] Edward M. Kennedy, *In Critical Condition: The Crisis in America's Health Care* (New York: Simon & Schuster, 1972), pp. 16–17.

[5] See William H. Stewart, "Health Assessment," in B. Jones, ed., *The Health of Americans* (Englewood Cliffs, N.J.: Prentice-Hall, 1970).

[6] *Ibid.*, p. 63.

people have few health problems and have access to decent (if expensive) care. Many poor people, many blacks, many who live in our central cities — millions of Americans — are condemned to poor health and poorer treatment.

• *Blacks* have higher death rates than whites do from several diseases, like pneumonia and tuberculosis. Infant mortality rates for black infants are three times higher than those for white infants. Black maternal mortality rates are four times higher.[7]

• The *poor* also suffer. Between 1963 and 1965, for instance, poor families suffered four times as many chronic disabilities as did families earning over $7,000 a year.[8]

• These two effects combine most dramatically in large *central-city ghettos.* "There is a slum neighborhood in Boston," Selig Greenberg writes, "where infant mortality exceeds the level of the Biblical plague inflicted in ancient Egypt, when every tenth newborn child died."[9] Similar conditions recur in large ghettos around the country. Comparing poverty and nonpoverty areas in Chicago, one study found that the poverty area had 60 percent higher infant mortality, 200 percent higher incidence of premature births, 550 percent more new cases of venereal disease, and so on.[10] Another study found that ghetto blacks in San Francisco had infant mortality rates three times greater than central-city whites.[11]

• Some of these same kinds of differences show up in data on prevention and treatment:

• Data show that ghetto residents visit doctors less frequently for regular checkups than other citizens do, follow less nutritional diets, and often have trouble finding and/or traveling to medical facilities.[12]

• The poor are susceptible to some special illnesses common to their environments. For example, at least 400,000 poor children had lead poisoning in the United States in 1969, most of them in older ghetto communities in the Northeast; they contract the poisoning from eating chipped, lead-base paint in deteriorating housing.[13] Also there were 14,000 cases of rat-bite in the United States in 1965, most of these in ghetto communities where rats feast on garbage and hide in rotten buildings.[14]

• When ghetto residents do become ill, they receive much less adequate medical service. They must wait longer for attention, must often use inferior hospital facilities, and must often solicit service from inexperienced or incompetent medical personnel.[15]

In general, health is a condition that few poor people experience with any

[7] Ruth Covell *et al., The Delivery of Health Services for the Poor* (Washington: Dept. of Health, Education and Welfare, December 1967).

[8] Harold S. Luft, "Poverty and Health: An Empirical Investigation of the Economic Interactions," Ph.D. Dissertation, Harvard University, 1972, p. 48. In his study, poverty was defined to include families earning below $3,000 in 1966.

[9] Greenberg, *The Quality of Mercy,* p. 97.

[10] Mark H. Lepper *et al.,* "Approaches to Meeting Health Needs of Large Poverty Populations," *American Journal of Public Health and the Nation's Health,* July 1967, p. 1154.

[11] *City Health Officers News,* Vol. 8, No. 3, January 1968, p. 3.

[12] See Lawrence Bergner and Alonzo Yerby, "Low Income and Barriers to Use of Health Services," *New England Journal of Medicine,* March 7, 1968, pp. 541–46.

[13] An article in *Look* magazine, October 21, 1969, estimated 400,000.

[14] *Report of the National Advisory Commission on Civil Disorders* (New York: Bantam Books, 1968), p. 273.

[15] See evidence on this in the selection by Lashof in this chapter.

regularity. A relatively recent Blue Cross survey reached some candid conclusions:

> "Living sick" is the prevailing condition of poverty in America today. For two out of every three people in the population, when they are "feeling fine" it means that nothing is the matter with them. But for nearly two out of every three ghetto blacks in the inner city . . . , "feeling fine" means literally "not as sick as usual." [16]

The same survey reported that more than half of black ghetto residents feel that their health has deteriorated, that it was worse than that of their parents or grandparents.

And that, to say the least, adds up to a "health problem."

Conservative and Liberal Views

As much as in any other area, conservatives and liberals tend to suggest different policy orientations toward the solution of some of these health problems. Their analyses begin, as usual, from some of the same analytic foundations. But their policy prescriptions quickly diverge.

Both conservatives and liberals begin from the orthodox economist's emphasis on *choice*. We cannot have perfect health care in this country, they warn us, because health care is expensive, there are scarce resources, and there are other competing demands on those resources. We must carefully weigh the relative improvement in our social welfare from health reforms, they argue, against the opportunity costs of spending that money somewhere else.[17]

Conservatives and liberals also emphasize that health reforms should interfere with the private market mechanism as little as possible. If the government were totally to nationalize health insurance, for instance, they warn that health care provision would be inefficient and wasteful.

But how much should the private market be protected, and how much should the government interfere? Where should the balance be struck? Here conservatives and liberals quickly diverge.

Conservative perspectives on health tend to be dominated by the American Medical Association and its core of private doctors. They have largely benefited from the system in the past, earning high incomes and enjoying professional power. In his selection Robert R. Alford aptly summarizes their perspective.

This perspective builds from several explanations of current health problems. First, health cost inflation has simply involved too much demand for a limited supply of services; we should slowly increase the supply of health care services, they admit, but there is no reason to tamper with the system's underlying structure. Second, the poor do have trouble financing health care, and we should continue to find the right mix of health care subsidies, like Medicare and Medicaid.[18] Third, conservatives argue that many health care inefficiencies have resulted from government intervention, rather than private power; we will

---

[16] Quoted in Greenberg, *The Quality of Mercy,* p. 116.

[17] See the selection by Fuchs in this chapter.

[18] Conservatives have been pushed to this position, in fact, and have largely abandoned their earlier opposition. Why? A cynic would answer that doctors found out how much they could earn under the system of Medicare and Medicaid billing.

all benefit, as economist Charles Baird concludes, "if the resulting impetus for change is channeled into efforts to improve the health market by making it more open and competitive."[19]

Through all these responses, conservatives insist that our past and present system should be preserved precisely because it is premised on free-market principles. As a competitive market system, Marvin Edwards writes, it is "simple, relatively inexpensive, and efficient. And it preserves the freedoms and privacy of both patient and doctor." As Edwards continues:

> Unfortunately, this system of private enterprise medicine is so familiar to most of us that we seldom stop to marvel at its classic simplicitly. Yet, despite its simplicity, it *is* a system — and a system that has worked to provide high quality health care to the American people at a reasonable cost.[20]

Liberals are much more critical of the health care system. They argue that substantial reforms are needed and that those reforms should move in a particular direction.[21]

Liberals do not intend their criticisms to reflect badly upon free enterprise. They merely argue that the health system in the United States does not fit the conventional model of a competitive market system.

First, they argue that health is not a *commodity* like many other goods. Consumers of health care cannot evaluate the product, liberals argue, since they do not have the expertise; suppliers — the doctors and surgeons — control basic decisions about how much of the product should be demanded. Second, liberals argue that it makes little sense to think of the health system as *competitive*. Doctors maintain a monopoly on the provision of service, keeping the supply of doctors very low. Given the organization of health care around fee-for-service, both physicians and hospitals have a strong incentive to oversupply medical care; patients do not pay for the health care they get, but for the services of the professionals. Finally, liberals argue that the system is hardly a *system* at all, but a crazy-quilt patchwork of sensible and senseless practices.

These analyses combine to convince liberals that a major reform of the health care system is necessary. These calls for reform are dominated by the major institutional forces in the nation's largest medical complexes. As Alford notes in his selection, they constitute a group of "bureaucratic reformers."

They call for two kinds of basic reforms. First, they urge the "rationalization" of the health care system. They call for expanded hospital services, more systematic treatment through hospital centers, more advanced technology, more reliance on "professional" services. Second, they urge an expanded system of national health insurance, guaranteeing everyone the same basic rights to health care subsidy, through the consolidation of the private health care insurance system.

All we need to do is spend more money, more systematically — without upsetting the basic private character of the system — and the liberals argue that

[19] Charles Baird, "A Reply," *Journal of Human Resources,* Winter 1971, p. 129.

[20] Marvin Henry Edwards, *Hazardous to Your Health: A New Look at the "Health Care Crisis" in America* (New Rochelle, N.Y.: Arlington House 1972), pp. 107–8. (Emphasis in the original.)

[21] See the book by Kennedy, *In Critical Condition,* for one statement of this liberal view.

most of our health care problems would be solved. As Senator Edward Kennedy has himself written:

> the comprehensive health service organization would offer all essential health services to its enrollees, frequently in the same building or complex. . . . Moreover, by encouraging affiliations between health care institutions, and by requiring coordinated planning of what facilities are built and where, all Americans will benefit from better balanced services.[22]

The Radical View

The radical analysis of health problems suggests that the entire structure of social and economic institutions in this country tends to preclude the adequate provision of health care to many Americans. Increasingly, the provision of health care has been tied to the priorities of profit-making institutions. As this has occurred, the institutions dominating the health care sector have become less and less concerned with the very human needs of patients.[23]

Traditionally, critics of medical care in this country have focused their complaints on the American Medical Association and the orientation of physician payment toward fees for service. But since World War II, and especially in the last decade, the character of the health sector has changed radically. Now, the provision of medical care is growing more and more intertwined with the structure of big business in this country. Large enterprises like Blue Cross/Blue Shield provide health insurance. Large drug companies provide increasing proportions of medical supplies. And huge, frequently profit-making, hospital complexes become more and more tied to the price structures of huge medical suppliers. These developments have several implications.

The post-World War II period of growth has created a new health care system, radicals argue, with four major components, all interacting in a complicated political economic dynamic.

1. At the center are the private hospital "empires."[24] The more these empires grow, the more bureaucratized and impersonal they become. Their priorities become more and more absorbed in profit-making, professional prestige, and internal politics. As systems, these empires are less and less capable of worrying about the health needs of human patients.

2. Closely intertwined are the large corporations of the "medical-industrial complex." Drug companies, hospital supply companies, health technology suppliers — all these corporations have strong interests in promoting the centralization of health care. The more centralized the buyers of their products, the more likely they will be to obtain cost-plus contracts and to avoid competition.

3. The private insurance companies hold the system together. They finance the inflated health care costs generated by the imperial dynamics. They make those who need more care — usually the poor — pay more in order to avoid the higher risks of those more prone to sickness. They structure the entire system of health care finance to satisfy their own drive for profits.

4. And there are the public hospitals and impoverished facilities on which many Americans must rely. These facilities feed into the systemic dynamic.

---

[22] *Ibid.*, p. 248.

[23] The following draws heavily on Barbara and John Ehrenreich, *The American Health Empire.*

[24] For a detailed review of these empires, see *ibid.*

They help provide patients as subjects for medical research. They provide a dumping ground for those whose sicknesses seem to offer no interesting scientific possibilities. They create the illusion of health care so that many may be less likely to revolt over the revolting health care conditions with which they are provided. "The two-class system will continue," Health-PAC concludes, "as long as there are low-income people who cannot pay for their health care or cannot find care in their communities." [25]

This analysis has several important implications for the evaluation of various proposals for health care reform.

First, public subsidy of health care costs for the poor will have increasingly little effect. As monopoly powers gain more and more control over the price mechanisms within the health sector, they will be able to match increases in demand with price increases, preventing an increase in the supply of service. [26]

Second, as private health insurance plans like Blue Cross/Blue Shield consolidate their control of that particular market, it becomes increasingly difficult to advocate universal public insurance plans. And the difference between private and public insurance seems clear. With private, profit-making insurance plans, patients always face the possibility that the companies will raise their prices, refuse to cover certain costs, or refuse to insure certain high-risk categories of patients. Automobile insurance companies have fought frantically against proposals for a "no-fault" car insurance system; private health insurance companies would probably do the same. [27]

Third, as the provision of health care becomes increasingly dominated by large organizations, it becomes less likely that preventive programs sensitively geared to the subtle differences among residential communities can be developed. The problem of lead poisoning among small children in ghettos was ignored for years, for instance, mainly because middle-class doctors and large hospital organizations were not able to imagine that the problem could be serious. Public action against lead poisoning has been taken only after community groups have forced the medical establishment to pay attention.

Finally, and most important, it becomes less likely that the needs of patients will be considered as the health sector becomes more dominated by large corporations. The Ehrenreichs, in their article on the "medical-industrial complex," intend the analogy with the "military-industrial complex" quite directly. In both cases, corporations have been searching for safe, large, stable, effectively guaranteed outlets for their capital. Decisions about research, construction, supply, and allocation within the health sector will increasingly be tied to profitability criteria.

And as the "medical-industrial complex" emerges, it becomes less and less possible over time to effect the kind of radical institutional transformation of the health sector that we seem to require. Formerly, one could somehow have envisioned public pressure pushing the government toward assumption of important planning, administrative, and financial responsibilities in health — not completely socialized medicine perhaps, but an extension of public power comparable to the government's role in England and Scandinavia. Now with the new and apparently permanent involvement of major corporations in health, it is be-

[25] *Health-PAC* Bulletin, No. 51, April 1973, p. 2.

[26] Louise Lander, *National Health Insurance*, A Health-PAC Report (Health-PAC, 7 Murray St., New York, N.Y.).

[27] See the selection by Ehrenreich and Fein in this chapter.

coming increasingly improbable that the United States can redirect its health priorities without at the same time changing the ways in which American industry is organized and the ways in which monopoly capitalism works. To quote the Ehrenreichs, to try fundamentally to change the health care system in this country will be increasingly

> to challenge some of the underlying tenets of the American free enterprise system. If physicians were to become community employees, if the drug companies were to be nationalized, then why not expropriate the oil and coal industries, or the automobile industry? There is an even more direct antipathy to nationalizing the health industry: a host of industries, including the aerospace industry, the electronic industry, the chemical industry, and the insurance industry, all have a direct stake in the profitability of the medical care system.[28]

The Readings

The first group of readings provides Impressions, Definitions, and Magnitudes. Fred J. Cook describes the kind of health care problems plaguing people in central-city ghettos, while a registered nurse describes the kind of health care she got — or rather did not get — in what was supposed to be one of the nation's best hospitals. Joyce C. Lashof presents some basic data on health conditions in central-city ghettos, and Robert Hill reviews the health problems of blacks. Although both selections describe the 1960s, there is no indication that conditions have improved; indeed, with cutbacks during the economic crisis of the mid-1970s, they have probably deteriorated somewhat.

The second group of readings presents different analytic perspectives. The selection by Victor R. Fuchs presents a clear overview of the orthodox economic perspective, summarizing the kinds of choice issues that mainstream economists think are most important in framing our health care problems. The next four selections sketch elements of the radical analysis. "The Structure of American Health Care," by Health-PAC, sketches the structure of the system. Robert R. Alford elaborates some of the main objectives of the dominant interest groups in that system. Barbara and John Ehrenreich present more detail on one of the most important sectors — the "medical-industrial complex." Using that analysis of the system and the role of health insurance companies, finally, John Ehrenreich and Oliver Fein argue that current proposals for "national health insurance" would make little difference — unless they fundamentally attack the structures of private power on which the entire system rests.

A final reading presents a "vision." Joshua Horn describes the simple but fundamentally effective steps that the People's Republic of China was able to implement in attacking some of its basic health problems. The Chinese did not rely on technology or centralized bureaucracies. They relied on people and, according to Horn, got results that were healthy for "children and other living things."

[28] Barbara and John Ehrenreich, *The American Health Empire.*

THE DOOMED OF WATTS

Fred J. Cook

This excerpt from Cook's book, *The Plot Against the Patient,* illustrates the many ways in which residents of poor urban neighborhoods encounter health problems. They suffer not only because they are poor and eat relatively less nutritional food, for instance, but also because the public health facilities provided for their neighborhoods are woefully inadequate.

He was born in Watts in August 1964, the youngest of five children and a welfare case. Dr. Sol White, a county health commissioner and a pediatrician, saw him for the first time four months after birth. Already the boy (let's call him C.J.) was a tiny bundle of suffering. He had bronchitis, eczema, cow's milk allergy, an umbilical hernia and a right anal hernia. The last required immediate surgery.

But C.J. was born in Watts.

Watts is the ghetto of southeast Los Angeles that was literally torn apart in the summer of 1965 in the nation's worst race riot. It is a sprawling warren with the population of a fair-sized city — 344,000 residents, 50 percent of them fifteen years old or younger. Thirty-three percent of the 18–45 year group are unemployed. In the hard-core area of Watts, there is no hospital of any kind. Around the periphery are eight proprietary hospitals, only two of which are accredited. There is no emergency service available to the 344,000 residents of Watts except in unaccredited hospitals or in hospitals miles beyond its borders. There is no place in Watts for a four-month-old boy like C.J. to go for a hernia operation. The only alternative is Los Angeles' huge County General Hospital.

County General is a two-hour ride and six bus changes away from Watts, and it is chronically overwhelmed trying to treat and succor the human flotsam that daily flows through its doors. What hope is there for a four-month-old baby needing a hernia operation? Dr. White sighed and telephoned County General, trying to set up an appointment for C.J.

"I had to make the appointment for the next surgical date," Dr. White explained long afterwards. "If I had sent the mother and child to the hospital right away, they would have had to get there at seven in the morning in order to be seen around 10 A.M. in the regular clinic. Then they would have been referred to the evening clinic, and they wouldn't have been through until four or five in the afternoon — and then they would be put on a waiting list."

The waiting list at County General at times seems infinite. When Dr. White saw C.J. again on December 29, 1964, no appointment had yet been made for surgery — C.J. was still on the waiting list. A few weeks later, in January, 1965, examining C.J. again, Dr. White found that, in addition to all his earlier ailments, he had a scalp infection and had developed a heart murmur. He sent the mother and baby to a pediatric cardiologist 20 miles away.

On January 28, 1966, a full year later, Dr. White saw C.J. again. The boy's heart murmur was still present. He also had tonsilitis, an ear infection and mild but persistent bronchitis. He had had incomplete immunization shots. He still had the hernias; he still had not had the needed operation. County General had been so swamped with cases, it had been working through such a backlog, that C.J.'s case had been postponed and postponed until the mother, Dr. White indicated, had eventually just given up.

Perhaps today, with greatly expanded federal medical programs — not just Medicare but the treatment of youthful indigents like C.J. under the California program that takes advantage of the Title XIX amendment to the Kerr-Mills Act — it might be easier for C.J. to get his much needed operation. He would at least be able to get a specialist who could assure him some continuity of care. But there is still no hospital in Watts. He would still have to go to County General, with its still long waiting list. It was, as one observer described it, "a helluva situation."

This nation has two kinds of medicine. One kind for those with insurance and money; one kind for those with nothing. It is not true that those with nothing get nothing. But they do sometimes get very close to nothing.

This, needless to say, is not the view of the medical establishment. Organized medicine has long trumpeted that Americans get "the best medical care in the world" and that "anyone can get care." Even in the aftermath of the bloody riots in Watts, one heard the same old refrains. One of the most prominent hospital authorities in Southern California acted as if Watts was just a lower class Beverly Hills, without hospitals of its own from choice. Why, he said, residents of the area could go to County General or Harbor General, and then there were those eight proprietaries scattered around the periphery of Watts.

"Every region is well served, if you travel," he said.

Fortunately, the report on the Watts riots prepared by the commission headed by John A. McCone, millionaire businessman and former director of the Central Intelligence Agency, tells a different and more candid story. The McCone commission wrote:

"Statistics indicate that health conditions of the residents of south central Los Angeles are relatively poor, and facilities to provide medical care are insufficient. Infant mortality, for example, is about one and one-half times greater than the city-wide average. Life expectancies are considerably shorter. A far lower percentage of the children are immunized against diphtheria, whooping cough, tetanus, smallpox and poliomyelitis than in the rest of the county.

"As established by the comprehensive reports of consultants to the Commission, the number of doctors in the southeastern part of Los Angeles is grossly inadequate as compared with other parts of the city. It is reported that there are 106 physicians for some 252,000 people, whereas the county ratio is three times higher. The hospitals readily accessible to the citizens in southeastern Los Angeles are also grossly inadequate in quality and in numbers of beds. Of the eight proprietary hospitals, which have a total capacity of 454 beds, only two meet minimum standards of professional quality. The two large public hospitals, County General and Harbor General, are both distant and difficult to reach. The Commission recognizes that the motivation of patients to take advantage of the medical facilities is an important factor in health conditions, but it appears that the facilities in the area are not even sufficient to care for those who now seek medical attention."

Statistics make this general description even more grim. A poverty report prepared by the Institute of Industrial Relations at UCLA for the Los Angeles County Commission on Human Relations found that in 1960, the Watts area contained only 17 percent of the city's population, but in category after category it harbored nearly 50 percent of the city's ills. It had 48.5 percent of amoebic infections, 42 percent of food poisoning, 44.8 percent of whooping cough, 39 percent of epilepsy, 42.8 percent of rheumatic fever, 44.6 percent of dysentery, 46 percent of venereal diseases, 36 percent of meningitis and 65 percent of reported tuberculin reactors. The death rate in Watts was 22.3 percent higher than for the remainder of the city.

It was clear that in health, as in all else, Watts existed in a vacuum of deprivation and suffering. There were only three specialists — two pediatricians and one radiologist — in the entire greater Watts area inhabited by 344,000 persons. And the first of these, Dr. Sol White, had come to the area only in 1959.

With no hospital of its own, Watts had no emergency service worthy of the name. The nearest approved emergency facility was in St. Francis Hospital in Lynwood, miles beyond its borders. The proprietary hospitals scattered around the periphery of Watts maintained walk-in clinics, but had no organized outpatient or emergency service. They had at the most a doctor or a nurse, who might be summoned and who *might* arrive sometime to give a patient in dire need some cursory attention. If the patient had insurance (less than one-fourth of the population of Watts did), he would, of course, be hospitalized if he needed it, and sometimes even if he didn't. But if he lacked resources of any kind, the most normal circumstance in Watts, he would usually be told to travel on to County General.

Three of the unaccredited hospitals in the Watts area had contracts with the city to provide some kind of emergency care, but Dr. White and others who had observed the situation at close hand were contemptuous of the quality of that care.

"If you can breathe and you're conscious, they send you on," Dr. White said in one interview. "Sometimes they don't even take X-rays or sew up an open wound."

The kind of things that happen in proprietary

hospitals, where profit too frequently overrides humanity, is illustrated by some Los Angeles cases. In June, 1964, a four-year-old girl was scalded in the bathtub in her home. The accident happened on a Monday, and the parents did nothing until Thursday when they decided they had better take the child to a hospital. They found one private hospital's doors closed. Two other proprietaries refused aid, the family later said, because it was "too early in the morning." The child was finally taken to County General, where she died.

In another case, a seventy-two-year-old woman suffering from internal hemorrhaging was rushed to a hospital holding a city service contract. The hospital, learning she was on Social Security, which meant that it would receive only the small city contract fee, insisted her family take her on to County General. The family, not familiar with the city streets, got lost on the way, wandered around, finally arrived at County General, fortunately with the woman still alive.

On the other hand, Dr. White cites the case of a family that was well-fortified with hospitalization insurance. The parents took their five children to one of the proprietary hospitals, and they were all promptly slapped into hospital beds and kept there for days on end. What was the strange malady that had felled all five children at the same time? According to Dr. White: ringworm.

Such incidents brought the entire medical profession into disrepute in the disadvantaged and disgruntled world of Watts.

"We are not reaching the people," Dr. White conceded. "There is no image. I'm referred to as the 'eight to four.'" . . .

Built in 1932, County General is poorly planned, by modern standards. Its laboratories and X-ray departments are usually hopelessly inadequate to meet the burdens they must handle. It has a 3,000 bed capacity, and is chronically overcrowded. It is afflicted, like most hospitals in its circumstances, with an acute and growing shortage of nurses and other personnel. In an atmosphere of perpetual crisis, where the medical staff seems about to be buried under an avalanche of patients, County General treats the afflicted, administers to the maimed and saves lives.

The figures dealing with its operations are phenomenal. In mid-1965 County General had 6,351 employees and nearly 3,000 doctors, including volunteers. The attending medical staff, all private private practice specialists, comprised one-fifth of the entire doctor population of Los Angeles, and these doctors donated on an average of two mornings a week without pay to County General patients. In 1964, the hospital cared for 121,071 bed patients, who stayed an average of eight days each. It performed 14,254 surgeries, saw 15,739 babies born. Outpatient visits totaled an incredible 892,800, and the emergency wards handled 205,529 cases — an average of one every three minutes around the clock, seven days a week. It all cost Los Angeles County $38,777,775.

The sheer pressure of numbers puts at times an almost insupportable burden upon the hospital staff. The staff handles 90 percent more patients per employee than the average of the four largest teaching hospitals in the United States, and Local 434 of the Los Angeles County Employees Union (AFL-CIO) has long contended that such figures spell out an understaffing crisis. In 1959, the union created a brief public flurry when it dramatized its case with an illustrative horror anecdote. The incident took place in Olive View Sanitarium, part of County General, when, according to a union spokesman, "a woman nursing attendant overseeing 50 male patients was recently attacked and almost killed in a darkened room."

The outcry engendered by the deed was purely temporary; the headlines died and nothing changed. Alfred Charlton, general manager of Local 434, insisted in early 1966 that the crisis in understaffing was as bad as ever, despite his union's years-long battle. He blamed budget limitations on hospital expenditures and deaf ears. The argument his union most often hears, Charlton said, is shocking from a humane view: it must face the fact, it is told, that its members are serving indigent patients who can't expect to receive top quality care.

There is an urgent need, Charlton insists, to double hospital staffs, a goal that might seem a bit of overblown union press-agentry, except for the acknowledged fact that in County General the staff handles 90 percent more persons per employee than the average in top-graded hospitals that are probably themselves somewhat shorthanded. Under existing circumstances, there is simply no leeway in County General or other county hospitals if someone becomes ill, has an accident or for some other reason misses a day of work. Then one attendant may have to do the work of four instead of two. Charlton says one employee may be left to take care of 52 persons, all of whom need to be tended and turned over every couple of hours. When the crush reaches such proportions, care inevitably is inadequate, and accidents happen.

Charlton cited the case of a 105-pound woman attendant who tried by herself to lift a heavy patient. The patient twisted in her arms, and in struggling to prevent a fall, the attendant strained herself and suffered a heart attack. There was some dispute about whether this was an industrial accident, but the woman attendant was finally awarded $18,000 in compensation and medical care for the rest of her life. Charlton has a thick dossier of similar cases. In 1962, he declared, the insurance premium for county hospital employees cost over $3 million; by 1964, it had doubled. When the Board of Supervisors became alarmed about this staggering cost factor, Charlton suggested that it might be cheaper to hire the number of hospital employees actually needed. "But that fell on deaf ears," he recalled.

DEAR DR. POMRINSE

Nancy Shamban

A registered nurse became ill. She sought treatment at Mt. Sinai Hospital in New York City, described by *New York Magazine* as "one of New York's great teaching hospitals, . . . a primary hospital for its community. . . . Emergency department is highly recommended." Shamban found otherwise. Her report on her experiences helps convey a central message of the radical analysis of health problems. The crisis does not involve just a few isolated pockets in central-city ghettos. It involves the entire system.

The selection, slightly excerpted, first appeared in *Health-PAC Bulletin*, a newsletter about health problems.

Nancy Shamban is a registered nurse in New York and has a master's degree.

Dear Dr. Pomrinse:

From Thursday evening, November 15, 1973, to Monday, November 19, I was an inpatient at Mt. Sinai Hospital. I am writing to you about my stay because of your position and the fact that I am a graduate of the Mt. Sinai Hospital School of Nursing and devoted close to five years of working experience to Mt. Sinai after my graduation in Adult and Child Psychiatry.

Source: From *Health-PAC Bulletin*, No. 60, September–October 1974, pp. 7–10.

On Wednesday, November 14, I went to see my own physician because of a leg infection which had become quite severe. On Wednesday evening I had cold, shaking chills and a temperature of 103.6 degrees. On Thursday afternoon, I phoned my doctor and he urged me to go to the Emergency Room of Mt. Sinai and be admitted. He notified the Emergency Room and the chief medical resident there.

I went into the ER, informed them who I was and that I was to see the chief resident. They stated that they had no knowledge of this matter, became quite belligerent and hostile to me and told me I had to go to the admitting office. I stood there with my friend (also a former staff member) at a loss. After some minutes, a volunteer agreed to call the chief resident. She returned in a few moments to inform me that he had stated that he didn't know anything about it. At that point the doctor walked by, heard the conversation and ignored it. Some minutes later, my friend went to the door of the staff area and asked what was to be done, and at that point the chief resident acknowledged having spoken to my doctor and took me into the treatment area. He informed me that he did not think I should be admitted. He said he could either admit me or we could wait until he spoke with my doctor on the phone to discuss it.

The Agony of Admission

At this point, I should say that I was very ambivalent about admission. I felt physically ill and had a great deal of leg pain, making it almost impossible to walk; however, I was in great financial difficulties and knew a hospitalization would be a great added burden at this point.

Five months ago I completed my graduate degree in Psychological Counseling. While a student I worked part-time in nursing and other capacities to support myself. From last June until about two weeks before hospitalization, I had been unemployed, working only part-time as a nurse-counselor in an abortion facility, and had no health or hospital coverage. I had incurred many debts, including government loans necessary to see me through graduate school. Two-and-a-half weeks before hospitalization, I had begun working as an individual and family therapist at a facility for adolescents. Hospital coverage in this position would not begin until February, 1974, and of course I was concerned as well with whether I would be allowed to keep my position or get sick time benefits since I had just begun working. For these reasons, I told the resident I would wait until he conferred with my doctor. The resident then disappeared for over an hour and I sat and waited. On his return, the resident got in touch with my doctor, who had been trying to return his call for some time.

After consultation, it was decided that I should have an incision and drainage and if most of the difficulty was due to an abscess, I should be sent home; if, however, most of the problem was from the cellulitis in my leg, I should be admitted. The resident took me to a surgical intern. I had blood cultures drawn and an incision and drainage. Up to this point, the only person who had spoken to me as a human being was the surgical intern. It was obvious that the emotional as well as physical trauma I was experiencing was of no consequence to any member of the Emergency Room staff.

The surgical intern felt, after doing the incision and drainage, that I should be admitted. The majority of the inflammation was cellulitis. He looked for and paged the medical resident, who never appeared and could not be found. The intern told me the surgical resident (who had walked into the treatment room for approximately 60 seconds, looked at the incision and drainage and left) had stated that I should not be admitted but would have to return daily to the ER to have my leg taken care of, packing changed, etc. I informed the intern that this was not feasible for two reasons: I refused to be put through such a dehumanizing and degrading experience daily and I live alone on the fifth floor of a walkup apartment, and going up and down those stairs was not possible in my condition. The resident said that was my problem, there was nothing he could do about it if I wanted treatment. The surgical intern suggested that I go home; he could not find the medical resident and saw that I was obviously in pain, feverish and distraught. I accept my mistake in having left at this point.

On returning home, I called my doctor and told him of my experiences. He called the resident, and I was told to return to the emergency room for admission. I refused, feeling physically and emotionally drained and having no desire to see that staff again. I was told to go directly to 4 North. When I arrived there, I was told to go to admissions. This was approximately 10 or 10:30 p.m. I could hardly walk, I had not eaten for some time and I was quite weak and upset. I asked if someone from admissions could come over there and without investigation was told no.

I went to admissions and was informed that unless I was prepared to pay $1,400, I could not be admitted. I explained my financial situation and informed them that I was a graduate of the School of Nursing. After again conferring with my doctor, I returned to the Emergency Room on foot. I was at this point put in a wheelchair, to be brought to 4 North. Up to that point the only thing I had been given was a $10 ER bill. I arrived on 4 North at 1:30 a.m. Friday.

The Inpatient as Outcast

I was given the usual physical and a case history was taken. I also informed the doctors of my history of reactions to medications. I was given no medication, although I had been put on Oxycillin by my doctor. Finally, at 11 a.m., after inquiring of both nursing and medical personnel, I was given my first dose of Oxycillin since arriving.

I had met several of the house staff but had no idea who was in charge of my case and soon found out that there a complete lack of communication between any of the staff. If I asked about the medication or anything else, I was put off or told that "the doctor" would be told. He (whoever he was) never was informed. For the three days I was hospitalized, it was only by hitting the right person by luck that anything was communicated. Even then frequently nothing was done.

By Friday afternoon I had severe, explosive diarrhea and severe nausea. I had not eaten anything for some time and never did eat during the entire hospitalization. I asked to see the doctor about these symptoms, and many hours later kaopectate was ordered. The doctor never acknowledged what I had told him about the nausea and retching except to say that my symptoms weren't dramatic enough for him to do anything about, it was just the infection. I have had this type of reaction with other antibiotics, but he would not believe it was from the medication. When I told him I had eaten nothing (he had not been told by the nursing staff, although they had removed my trays and commented about it during these three days), he laughed and said, "You haven't eaten?" He told me he would give me nothing. His manner was always flippant, arrogant, patronizing and egotistical. This seemed to be the attitude of several of your medical house staff from my observation of their behavior toward myself and my roommates.

I discovered also that the nursing staff, especially on evenings, were totally uninvolved and uncaring of the patients. I received remarks to the effect that I could change my own dressing. Although at home I kept my leg elevated, fixed a cradle to keep the blankets off my bed, fixed a doughnut to keep my heel from being irritated, kept myself on bedrest and made some clear fluids, in the hospital I was for the most part ignored and none of these things were done or even offered. Even my temperature and blood pressure, which were ordered four times a day, frequently were not checked more than twice a day. Twice during my stay, in the evenings, I put on my light to ask for something for nausea. The bell was turned off at the nurses' station, and no one ever acknowledged it. My roommates had to help me back to bed from the bathroom several times.

Friday evening I went to the nurses' station to ask the chief resident what was happening. I stood there, talking to the resident; another resident came by and interrupted our discussion. They then proceeded to go off together. The chief yelled back over his shoulder, "Oh, I'll be back in a while." I was dumbfounded. I was angry and stated that I wasn't finished talking. He was not being called away for

an emergency, he just seemed totally uninvolved in talking to a patient.

Saturday morning, when a few doctors made rounds, I again asked for something for the nausea. They looked at me and said, "Nausea, since when are you nauseated?" They didn't know. I don't know if there was anything written in my chart by either nursing or medicine, whether they hadn't read it or whether they just weren't concerned. They left with, "We'll order something," and that was the last time I heard anything about it.

At this point I should say that I was very emotionally upset about this whole experience. When I was in nursing school we learned that sick people, especially patients in a hospital, are more vulnerable and need help not only physically but also emotionally, socially, religiously and sometimes economically. We were taught to see and respect the whole person. What I was seeing was a lack of concern about any of these areas, including the physical. I know I wasn't the sickest patient at Mt. Sinai, but there is no excuse for the lack of concern and caring on the part of all disciplines of the supposed team.

Saturday afternoon I did by chance meet a very nice resident, whom I begged to help me. Having been a patient at Mt. Sinai himself on previous occasions, he seemed to understand and spent a few moments talking with me and did order something for my symptoms. Finally Saturday evening the antibiotic was discontinued. This was done only because my own doctor had come up to the unit and I informed him of my symptoms. The house staff had told him nothing, despite the fact that he was the attending [physician] on the unit. . . .

Enter the Bill Collector

On Monday I asked to see the social worker. I told her of my financial difficulties, and she told me to go to patients' accounts. I was still not well and still shaky on my feet. I walked to patients' accounts, was kept waiting for some time, was passed from one person to another. I told the man who finally spoke to me about my financial situation and asked about Medicaid. He excused himself, saying he was going for a pad of paper; he returned 20 minutes later to inform me not only that I could not receive Medicaid, but also that he had spoken to my place of employment and stated that I was employed there. (I had not denied that I had started working there two-and-a-half weeks before.) He then informed me in a very nasty tone that I owed Mt. Sinai $200 per month until my bill was paid. I told him this was impossible, asked if the payments could be less per month and again explained my financial difficulties. He refused to compromise in any way and would not let me go until I signed a paper stating that I owe Mt. Sinai $200 per month. . . .

This experience was a nightmare for me; it angers me, it dehumanized me. I know it was worse for me because I am a nurse with medical knowledge of what can be done for patients; because psychology is my field and I'm aware of feelings and attitudes more in myself and others; because I'm a woman who felt surrounded by men who haven't begun to understand people; because I spent three

years being educated at Mt. Sinai, learning and believing everything in the opposite way from the way I was treated; and because I speak up for what I believe in and this, I am sure, was a threat to a lot of the staff.

I am left with three things after my hospitalization. The first is an eight-pound weight loss (which I appreciate), the second is information I am utilizing in writing an article and the third is the sad knowledge that one does not enter a hospital to get better, one enters to not get worse — hopefully!

Yours with concern,

Nancy Shamban, R.N., M.A.

MEDICAL CARE IN THE URBAN CENTER

Joyce C. Lashof

This short piece sketches the dimensions of various sources of health problems in central cities, and particularly the inadequacy of facilities available to the poor for health care. Dr. Lashof is the director of the community medicine section of Presbyterian–St. Luke's Hospital in Chicago.

The private practice of medicine in our inner cities has been declining steadily in recent years. Physicians in increasing numbers have left the inner city for the suburbs, and the community areas served by the urban hospitals have changed. A study of four community areas in Chicago showed a decline of 40 to 60 percent in the number of physicians practicing in these areas in 1966 as compared with 1953. One of these communities of 26,300 persons had only 4 doctors practicing in its area in 1965.[1] The number

of physicians in the Chicago area as a whole has increased at only half the rate that the population has grown.[2] Such a study illustrates the changing pattern of *medical care* in urban areas.

The distribution of physicians is clearly related to the socioeconomic and racial changes in urban centers. The migration into urban areas of both the Appalachian white and southern Negro and the flight of the prior urban white population have led to steady enlargement of poverty areas in the inner city. A large discrepancy in available medical manpower now exists between the poverty and nonpoverty areas, both quantitatively and qualitatively. In Chicago in 1965 there were 1.26 physicians per thousand population in nonpoverty areas of the city but only 0.62 per thousand in poverty areas. The ratio of board-certified specialists per thousand was 0.53 for the nonpoverty areas and only 0.18 for the pov-

Source: Joyce C. Lashof, "Medical Care in the Urban Center," *Annals of Internal Medicine,* 68:2, pp. 242–244.

[1] Rees, P. H.: Numbers and movement of physicians in southeast Chicago 1953–1965. Working Paper no. 1. 13. Chicago Regional Hospital Study, July 1967.

[2] Rees, P. H.: The movement and distribution of physicians. Working Paper no. 1. 12. Chicago Regional Hospital Study, June 1967.

erty areas.[3] Studies carried out by the Hospital Planning Council of Chicago indicate that whereas suburban hospitals draw the majority of their patients from the immediate surrounding community many of the urban hospitals draw from a much larger service area with a minority of patients coming from the area in which the hospital is located.[4] Much of the patient distribution is related to the economic and racial changes that have occurred in the area. The difference in hospitals used by the poverty and nonpoverty groups is striking. Thirty percent of all admissions from the poverty communities in Chicago in 1965 were to Cook County Hospital. Among patients in one community 15 miles distant from the County Hospital 47 percent of hospital admissions occurred at County Hospital. This concentration is in sharp contrast to the diffusion of care provided to residents of the nonpoverty areas among whom no one hospital accounted for over 4 percent of all admissions.[5]

One cannot look at medical practice in the urban setting without also considering the rising cost of medical care. In 1950 medical care expenditures totaled $12.9 billion but rose to $43 billion in 1966, of which $10.9 billion came from public funds.[6] These rising costs have served to widen the gap between the medical care available to the affluent and to the poor. They also have made it increasingly difficult to define medical indigency. At the same time there has been a decay of the tax base in the city, while the demands for health and social services have increased.

The large poverty areas in our inner city have produced health problems that we have not solved. Infant mortality, which has generally been accepted as a sensitive indicator of health conditions, has steadily risen in Chicago from 1958 to 1965. The average yearly infant mortality rate for the years 1958 to 1961 was 22.7 per 1,000 for whites and 37.9

per 1,000 for nonwhites. By 1965 the rate had risen to 28.8 per 1,000 for whites and 48.1 per 1,000 for nonwhites. Comparing morbidity and mortality statistics between the city and the state as a whole, Somers found that Trenton's tuberculosis and venereal disease rates were three to five times as high as those of New Jersey as a whole.[7] In addition, death rates from virtually all major causes — cancer, heart disease, accidents, etc. — in Trenton were higher than state and national rates. Dr. George James has calculated that 15,000 deaths in New York in 1964 could be attributed to poverty.[8]

Efforts to meet the problems posed by these changes have been made over the past two decades. Hospital outpatient departments have expanded, emergency room services have increased, board of health clinics have multiplied, and welfare medical care programs have developed. Unfortunately, these efforts have taken the form of piecemeal, uncoordinated, stopgap measures designed to meet the most obvious needs of the moment. This has resulted in a complex range of facilities and disease-oriented clinics. When we now look at what is available in our cities we find prenatal clinics, well-child clinics, family-planning clinics, tuberculosis clinics, mental health clinics, disease-detection programs, school health programs, and so forth, none of which are quantitatively adequate. In public health nursing alone, in some cities one can find board of health nurses, visiting nurse association nurses, teacher nurses, and tuberculosis control nurses. Funding may also come from different agencies of local, state, and federal government as well as from private voluntary agencies and foundations.

The dual system of medical care is most obvious when one compares the patterns of obtaining medical care followed by the indigent with those of the more affluent sector of our population. The basis of medical practice is a personal physician who takes responsibility for the total care of the patient, including preventive and curative services, coordination of speciality care, and arrangement for hospitalization when indicated. This concept, however, has not been part of our medical care system for the poorer

[3] Preliminary report on patterns of medical and health care in poverty areas of Chicago and proposed health programs for the medically indigent. *Chicago Board of Health Medical Care Report,* 1966, p. 16.

[4] Chicago Hospital Planning Council: Hospital discharge study 1965. IBM print-out sheets.

[5] Preliminary report on patterns of medical and health care in poverty areas of Chicago and proposed health programs for the medically indigent. *Chicago Board of Health Medical Care Report,* 1966, pp. 19–22.

[6] Blue Cross Reports. *Hosp. Cost Trends* 5: May–June, 1967.

[7] Somers, A. R.: An American city and its health problems: a case study in comprehensive health planning. *Med. Care* 5: 129, 1967.

[8] James, G.: Poverty and public health — new outlooks. I. Poverty as an obstacle to health progress in our cities. *Amer. J. Public Health* 55: 1757, 1965.

segment of our society. Approximately 40 percent of people interviewed in four poverty communities of Chicago indicated that they had no family physician.[9] This segment depends on the numerous facilities listed above for their care. No one person takes the responsibility for coordinating care and evaluating total health needs. Thus, a population with the least sophistication is left on its own to determine the appropriate time and place to seek care. The physician seeing those patients usually takes care of acute needs but does little in health counseling or preventive services. If hospitalization is necessary the physician can merely refer a patient to a hospital, but it is not his decision as to whether the patient is admitted. It is estimated that not more than 40 percent of the physicians in Chicago who take care of welfare patients have hospital staff appointments. If the referring physicians feels consultation is necessary or specialized workup is indicated he may give the patient a list of places where this may be obtained. Here, again, it becomes the responsibility of the patient to work his way through the maze and to have himself accepted for treatment. We have encountered families who had been attending five different hospitals and agencies, both public and private, in an effort to have their families' health needs met. Dr. Yerby[10] summarized the health care of the disadvantaged as being "piecemeal, often inadequate, underfinanced, poorly organized and provided without compassion or concern for the dignity of the individual."

Although it is probably true that there has never been enough medical care for any group, medical technology before World War II was such that the difference in care given by the voluntary sector and the public sector was not as great as it is at present. In the last two decades the deficits in the dual system have become obvious in that the voluntary vector has had the resources to exploit the scientific breakthrough while the "charity" system has been overwhelmed.

In an attempt to deal with the financial aspects of the problem, Congress enacted both Titles XVIII and XIX of the Social Security Act in 1965. Indeci-

sion in social policy is clearly reflected by the diametrically opposed approaches of these two laws. Title XVIII is based on the social insurance principle with all persons over 65 years of age eligible on the basis of having in the past paid taxes. Title XIX, on the other hand, provides a mechanism by which the states may provide health services for persons whom they define as unable to meet their medical bills on the basis of a means test. The accomplishments and problems presented by these laws are beyond the scope of this discussion, but clearly the effects of Titles XVIII and XIX are far-reaching, and a decision as to which approach will become dominant is not far off. The implications and the effect on social policy are clearly analyzed by Eveline Burns.[11]

In an effort to deal with the fragmentation of care, to improve accessibility of care, and to experiment with new models for delivery of health services, the Office of Economic Opportunity has nurtured and given financial support to the development of the neighborhood health center. The first such centers were developed by Tufts Medical School in Boston, and the Department of Health and Hospitals in Denver. Centers are now also open in New York (under the auspices of Morissania-Montefiore Hospitals), Chicago (under the auspices of Presbyterian–St. Luke's and Mt. Sinai Hospitals), and in Los Angeles (sponsored by the University of Southern California). An additional 36 centers have been funded in 26 cities. These centers are designed to bring a core of physicians, public health nurses, social workers, and community health aides together with other ancillary services into an organized group to attack the health problems of defined communities. The experiences of these centers should help define the health problems of the urban centers and, hopefully, offer one solution. Other experimental models are badly needed.

At the White House Conference on Health, Marion Folsom stated. "Health is a basic human right. Comprehensive, continuous and personal care should be available to all." [12] To reach this goal in our urban centers is a challenge to the medical profession.

[9] Preliminary report of medical and health care in poverty areas of Chicago and proposed health programs for medically indigent. *Chicago Board of Health Medical Care Report*, 1966, p. 41.

[10] Yerby, A. S.: The disadvantaged and health care. *Amer. J. Public Health* 56: 5, 1966.

[11] Burns, E. M.: Social policy and the health services: the choices ahead. *Amer. J. Public Health* 57: 199, 1967.

[12] Proceedings of the White House Conference on Health, Nov. 3 and 4, 1965, Washington, D.C., p. 7.

HEALTH CONDITIONS OF BLACK AMERICANS

Robert Hill

This brief selection reviews data on the many dimensions of inequality in health conditions and health care confronting black Americans. The survey was published in 1973.

Robert Hill has been research director for the National Urban League.

In his recent budget message cutting back on social spending for the poor, the President said life is getting better for Americans, and that we had turned the corner on the nation's urban problems.

An analysis of the health conditions of black Americans today, from the most recent available census and national health surveys, shows a different picture.

The average *life expectancy* of a black man has declined over the last decade. In 1960 it was 61.1 years. In 1969 it was 60.5 years.

White males born 30 years ago had a greater life expectancy than black males do now: whites' was 63.2 years in 1944.

Mortality Rates

Infant mortality is another indicator of health conditions.

In 1971, black infants were dying at the rate of 30 for every 1,000 born alive. Twenty-three years ago, in 1950, white babies died at a lower rate — 27 out of a thousand — and today their death rate is 17 out of a thousand.

In families with incomes under $5,000, mortality rates for black infants are one-and-a-half times greater than those for white infants.

The gap between black and white *maternal death* rates has increased in the last 30 years. Today, at 63.6 black childbirth and pregnancy-related deaths per 100,000, it is four times greater than the rate for white women. In 1940, mortality rates for black mothers was less than two-and a-half times that of white mothers.

Source: "Health Conditions of Black Americans" by Robert Hill, *Urban League News,* May 1, 1973. Reprinted with permission.

There is also a higher proportion of premature births among blacks. In 1963, 10 percent of black babies were born prematurely compared to 5 percent of white babies. These babies have both higher mortality and morbidity rates.

Infant mortality, premature births, and maternal death rates can be lowered by improved maternity care.

Yet in 1964–65, almost two-thirds of the mothers of black children had no maternity care insurance. 63 percent of white mothers *had* coverage.

From 1968 to 1970, the U.S. Public Health Service conducted a *nutrition* study in ten states, which found malnutrition most frequently among blacks: 38 percent had hemoglobin deficiencies, compared to 18 percent among American Indians who were the next highest group.

Recent studies indicate that there is a consistent correlation between malnutrition and mental retardation.

Leading Death Causes

Nine of the *ten leading causes of death* are common to blacks and whites, but the mortality rate for blacks is higher in six of them.

In 1969, the most recent year for which statistics are available, the ten leading causes of death among blacks were (in order): heart disease (280.1 per 100,000 population), malignant neoplasm (134.9), cerebrovascular diseases (106.1), accidents (70.2), early childhood diseases (43.6), influenza and pneumonia (43.2), homicide (34.1), diabetes (23.6), cirrhosis of the liver (19.0), and arteriosclerosis (9.6).

Blacks die from accidents, cerebrovascular diseases, influenza and pneumonia, early childhood diseases, cirrhosis of the liver and diabetes, at rates substantially higher than whites do — and at all ages.

Homicide, the fifth highest cause of death among black men, is not among the top ten causes of death among whites. Blacks have a death rate of 58.1 per 100,000 population due to homicide. This is ten times the rate for whites.

Health Care

In 1970, almost two-fifths (39.3 percent) of the black population under 65 had no hospital insurance coverage. Low income families earning under $5000 a year were least insured: (62.7 percent) had no coverage.

A national health survey by the U.S. Public Health Service in 1968 showed that blacks see doctors less often, and in hospital clinics and emergency rooms rather than as private patients in their offices.

That year, 21 percent of blacks had not seen a doctor in two years or more, compared to 18 percent for whites.

Seventy-one percent of whites saw doctors in their offices, whereas only 61 percent of blacks did. On the other hand, 23 percent of blacks saw their doctors in hospital clinics or emergency rooms. Only nine percent of whites did.

Forced to go to hospital clinics, unable to afford (and sometimes to find) private doctors nearby,

black people lose more time from work because of poor health than do whites — and to compound their difficulty, are less likely to be reimbursed by their employers for the time lost.

In 1968, blacks working in private industry received only 25 percent reimbursement of pay for the time they lost because of illness or disability. Whites, who averaged better jobs and insurance coverage, fared better: 48 percent of their pay for days lost from work was reimbursed.

As for the amount of time lost getting medical attention, the average American takes about an hour getting to and from his private doctor's office and waiting to see him.

But of those who go to hospital clinics — and most blacks are among them — fully a third have to wait an hour or more to see a doctor, quite apart from the time they spent getting to the clinic. And 10 percent of those who go to hospital clinics have to travel over an hour each way to get there.

WHO SHALL LIVE? HEALTH, ECONOMICS, AND SOCIAL CHOICE

Victor R. Fuchs

Orthodox economists have been turning more and more to problems like health, as the introduction to this chapter notes, applying the basic tools of microeconomics to complicated social questions. The following selection presents a clear statement of the framework within which orthodox analyses of health problems proceed. As with other economic problems, tradeoffs are formulated and choices outlined. Both the possibilities for and limitations to reform of the health system are carefully explored.

This selection comes from a short book by Fuchs with the same title. The discussion reprinted here introduces the book, and then Fuchs proceeds to develop

detailed analyses around several of the main questions identified here.

Fuchs is one of the leading scholars in health economics in the United States. Author of *The Service Economy,* he has written widely on problems of health and other services. He currently holds a joint appointment as professor of economics at Stanford University and of community medicine at the Stanford Medical School.

The Choices We Must Make

An appreciation of the inevitability of choice is necessary before one can begin to make intelligent plans for health-care policy, but more than that is required. Some grasp of the variety of levels and kinds of choices we make is also essential. All of us, as

Source: From pp. 17–29, "The Choices We Must Make," from *Who Shall Live?: Health, Economics, and Social Choice* by Victor R. Fuchs, © 1974 by Basic Books, Inc., Publishers, New York.

individuals, are constantly confronted with choices that affect our health. In addition, some choices must be exercised collectively, through government.

■ Health or Other Goals?

The most basic level of choice is between health and other goals. While social reforms tell us that "health is a right," the realization of that "right" is always less than complete because some of the resources that could be used for health are allocated to other purposes. This is true in all countries regardless of economic system, regardless of the way medical care is organized, and regardless of the level of affluence. It is true in the communist Soviet Union and in welfare-state Sweden, as well as in our own capitalist society. No country is as healthy as it could be; no country does as much for the sick as it is technically capable of doing.

The constraints imposed by resource limitations are manifest not only in the absence of amenities, delays in receipt of care, and minor incoveniences; they also result in loss of life. The grim fact is that no nation is wealthy enough to avoid all avoidable deaths. The truth of this proposition is seen most clearly in the case of accidental deaths. For instance, a few years ago an airplane crashed in West Virginia with great loss of life. Upon investigation it was found that the crash could have been avoided if the airport had been properly equipped with an electronic instrument-landing device. It was further found that the airport was fully aware of this deficiency and that a recommendation for installation of such equipment had been made several months before the crash — and turned down because it was decided that the cost was too high.

Traffic accidents take more than fifty thousand lives each year in the United States, and because so many of the victims are young or middle-aged adults,[1] the attendant economic loss is very high. As a first approximation, the relative economic cost of death can be estimated from the discounted future earnings of the deceased if he had lived. According to such calculations, the death of a man at twenty or thirty is far more costly than death at seventy. Many of these traffic deaths could be prevented, but some of the most effective techniques, such as the elimination of left turns, are extremely expensive to implement. The same is true of deaths from other

causes — many of them are preventable if we want to devote resources to that end. The yield may be small, as in the case of a hyperbaric chamber[2] that costs several million dollars and probably saves a few lives each year, but the possibilities for such costly interventions are growing. Current examples include renal dialysis, organ transplants, and open-heart surgery. Within limits set by genetic factors, climate, and other natural forces, every nation chooses its own death rate by its evaluation of health compared with other goals.

But surely health is more important than anything else! Is it? Those who take this position are fond of contrasting our unmet health needs with the money that is "wasted" on cosmetics, cigarettes, pet foods, and the like. "Surely," it is argued, "we can afford better health if we can afford colored telephones." But putting the question in this form is misleading. For one thing, there are other goals, such as justice, beauty, and knowledge, which also clearly remain unfulfilled because of resource limitations. In theory, our society is committed to providing a speedy and fair trial to all persons accused of crimes. "Justice delayed is justice denied." In practice, we know that our judicial system is rife with delays and with pre-trial settlements that produce convictions of innocent people and let guilty ones escape with minor punishment. We also know that part of the answer to getting a fairer and more effective judicial system is to devote more resources to it.

What about beauty, natural or manmade? How often do we read that a beautiful stand of trees could be saved if a proposed road were rerouted or some other (expensive) change made? How frequently do we learn that a beautiful new building design has been rejected in favor of a conventional one because of the cost factor? Knowledge also suffers. Anyone who has ever had to meet a budget for an educational or research enterprise knows how resource limitations constrain the pursuit of knowledge.

What about more mundane creature comforts? We may give lip service to the idea that health comes first, but a casual inspection of our everyday behavior with respect to diet, drink, and exercise belies this claim. Most of us could be healthier than we are, but at some cost, either psychic or monetary. Not only is there competition for resources as con-

---

[1] The motor accident death rate reaches its peak in the late teens and early twenties.

[2] A specially constructed facility for raising the oxygen content of air in order to treat more effectively certain rare diseases.

ventionally measured (i.e., in terms of money), but we are also constantly confronted with choices involving the allocation of our time, energy, and attention. If we are honest with ourselves there can be little doubt that other goals often take precedence over health. If better health is our goal, we can achieve it, but only at some cost.

Stating the problem in this fashion helps to point up the difference between the economist's and the health professional's view of the "optimum" level of health. For the health professional, the "optimum" level is the highest level technically attainable, regardless of the cost of reaching it. The economist is preoccupied with the *social optimum,* however, which he defines as the point at which the value of an additional increment of health exactly equals the cost of the resources required to obtain that increment. For instance, the first few days of hospital stay after major surgery might be extremely valuable for preventing complications and assisting recovery, but at some point the value of each additional day decreases. As soon as the value of an additional day's stay falls below the cost of that day's care, according to the concept of social optimum, the patient should be discharged, even though a longer stay would be desirable if cost were of no concern. The cost reminds us, however, that those resources could be used to satisfy other goals.

The same method of balancing *marginal benefit* and *marginal cost* [3] is equally applicable in choosing the optimum number of tests and X rays, or in planning the size of a public health program, or in making decisions about auto-safety equipment. Indeed, the concept of margin is one of the most fundamental tools in economics. It applies to the behavior of consumers, investors, business firms, or any other participant in economic life. Most decisions involve choosing between a little more or a little less — in other words, comparing the marginal benefit with the marginal cost. The optimum level is where these are equal and the marginal cost is increasing faster (or decreasing slower) than the marginal benefit.

■ *Medical Care or Other Health Programs?*

But weighing individual and collective preferences for health against each and every other goal is only the first choice. There is also a range of choices

[3] Marginal (or incremental) benefits and costs are those resulting from small changes in inputs.

within the health field itself. Assume that we are prepared to devote x amount of resources to health. How much, then, should go for medical care and how much for other programs affecting health, such as pollution control, fluoridation of water, accident prevention, and the like? There is no simple answer, partly because the question has rarely been explicitly asked. In principle, the solution is to be found by applying the economist's rule of "equality at the margin." This means relating the incremental yield of any particular program to the incremental cost of the program and then allocating resources so that the yield per dollar of additional input is the same in all programs.

Expenditures for any type of health-related activity, be it a hyperbaric chamber for a hospital or a rat-control program in the ghetto, presumably have some favorable consequences for health which can be evaluated. It is not easy to measure these consequences, but we could do a lot better than we are doing and thus contribute to more rational decision making.

Note that decisions about expanding or contracting particular programs should be based on their respective *marginal* benefits, not their *average* benefits. Thus, while a particular health program — say, screening women once a year for cervical cancer — may be particularly productive (that is, yield a high average benefit per dollar of cost), it does not necessarily follow that expanding that program twofold — for example, screening women twice a year — will be twice as productive. Some other program — say, an antismoking advertising campaign — might not show as high an average return as the screening program, yet the marginal return to *additional* expenditures might exceed that obtainable from additional cancer screening. In the following hypothetical numerical example, cancer screening has a higher average benefit than the antismoking campaign at every expenditure level, but the *incremental* yield from additional expenditures at any level above $40,000 is higher for the antismoking program. Thus if both programs were at the $40,000 level, it would be preferable to expand the second one rather than the first.

An objection frequently raised to such an approach is that "we can't put a price on a human life." One answer to this is that we implicitly put a price on lives whenever we (or our representatives) make decisions about the coverage of a health insurance policy, the installation of a traffic light, the extension of a food stamp program, or innumerable other items.

Hypothetical Illustration of Distinction between Average and Marginal Benefit

	Expenditures	Value of Benefits	Average Benefit Per Dollar of Expenditures	Marginal Benefit Per Dollar of Expenditures
Cancer Screening Program	$10,000	$ 50,000	$5.00	
	20,000	80,000	4.00	$3.00
	30,000	100,000	3.33	2.00
	40,000	120,000	3.00	2.00
	50,000	130,000	2.60	1.00
	60,000	135,000	2.25	.50
Antismoking Program	$10,000	$ 30,000	$3.00	
	20,000	50,000	2.50	$2.00
	30,000	70,000	2.33	2.00
	40,000	90,000	2.25	1.50
	50,000	105,000	2.10	1.00
	60,000	115,000	1.92	

A second answer is that it may be possible to choose from among health programs *without* placing a dollar value on human life; it may be sufficient to compare the marginal yield of different programs in terms of lives saved in order to determine the allocation of resources that yields the more significant social benefits.

■ Physicians or Other Medical Care Providers?

But that is not the whole story. Even if we could make intelligent choices between medical care and other health-related programs, we would still be faced with a significant range of decisions concerning the best way to provide medical care — that is, the best way to spend the medical care dollar. One of the most important of these decisions, which will be discussed in Chapter 3 [of Fuchs's book], concerns the respective roles of physicians and such other medical care providers as physician assistants, nurses, clinicians, midwives, and family-health workers. A related set of decisions concerns the optimal mix between human inputs (whether physicians or others) and physical capital inputs, such as hospitals, X-ray equipment, and computers.

In short, if we are concerned with the best way to produce medical care, we must be aware that the solution to the problem requires more than medical expertise. It requires consideration of the relative prices, of various medical care inputs, and of their contribution (again at the margin) to health. The argument that these inputs must be used in some technologically defined proportions is soundly refuted by the evidence from other countries, where many health systems successfully utilize doctors, nurses, hospital facilities, and other health inputs in proportions that differ strikingly from those used in the United States.

■ How Much Equality? and How to Achieve It?

One of the major choices any society must make is how far to go in equalizing the access of individuals to goods and services. Insofar as this is a question of social choice, one cannot look to economics for an answer. What economic analysis can do is provide some insights concerning why the distribution of income at any given time is what it is, what policies would alter it and at what cost, and what are the economic consequences of different distributions.

Assuming that some income equalization is desired, how is this to be accomplished? Shall only certain goods and services (say, medical care) be distributed equally, or should incomes be made more equal, leaving individuals to decide how they wish to adjust their spending to take account of their higher (or lower) income?

For any given amount of redistribution the welfare of all households is presumably greatest if there is a general tax on the income of some households and grants of income to others, rather than a tax on particular forms of spending or a subsidy for particular types of consumption. Common sense tells us that if a household is offered a choice of either a hundred dollars in cash or a hundred dollars' worth of health care, it ought to prefer the cash, because it can use the entire sum to buy more health care or health insurance (if that is what it wants) or, as is usually the case, increase consumption of many other commodities as well. By the same reasoning, if a household is offered a choice between paying an additional hundred dollars in income tax or doing without a hundred dollars' worth of health care, it will opt for the general tax on income, and then cut back spending on the goods and services that are, in its opinion, most dispensable.

Despite the obvious logic of the foregoing, many nonpoor seem more willing to support a reduction in inequality in the consumption of particular commodities (medical care is a conspicuous example) than toward a general redistribution of income. In England, for instance, everyone is eligible to use the National Health Service, and the great majority of the population gets all of its care from this tax-financed source. At the same time, there is considerable inequality in other aspects of British life, including education and income distribution in general.

Support for the notion that medical care ought to be available to all, regardless of ability to pay, is growing in the United States. There is, however, also growing recognition of marked disparities in housing, legal services, and other important goods and services. Whether these disparities should be attacked piecemeal or through a general redistribution of income is one of the most difficult questions facing the body politic. . . .

■ *Today or Tomorrow*

One of the most important choices every individual and every society has to make is between using existing resources to satisfy current desires or applying them to capital-creating activities in anticipation of future needs. Economists call the former *consumption* and the latter *investment*.

This broad concept of investment should not be confused with the narrow use of the term in financial transactions — e.g., the purchase of stock. Broadly speaking, investment takes place when a tree is planted, when a student goes to school, when you brush your teeth, as well as when you build a house, a factory, or a hospital. Any activity that can be expected to confer future benefits is a form of investment. (To be sure, sometimes a single activity — such as education — will have elements of consumption — that is, provide current satisfaction — along with those of investment.)

Such investment can be in both physical or human capital.[4] Thus health is a form of capital: health is wealth. Investment in health takes many forms. Immunization, annual checkups, exercise, and many other activities have current costs but may yield health benefits in the future. Medical education and medical research, both involving expenditures of billions of dollars annually, are prime examples of investment in the health field that results in the diversion of resources (physicians and other personnel) from meeting current needs in order to reap future rewards.

How far should we go in providing for tomorrow at the expense of today? As with all economic decisions, price plays a role here, too. Specifically, in making decisions concerning health investments, we must somehow take into account the fact that people discount the future compared with the present. Using the concept of the special kind of price called *rate of interest* or *rate of return* answers that need.

No investment in health is undertaken unless the investor believes it will yield a satisfactory rate of return. Health professionals frequently despair over the failure of some people to invest in their own health; such behavior, they assert, is irrational. But this need not be the case. If a person discounts the future at a high rate, as evidenced by a willingness to pay 20 or 30 percent annual interest for consumer loans or installment credit, it would not be rational for him to make an investment in health that had an implicit return of only 15 percent.

It is abundantly clear that people differ in their attitudes toward the future; that is, they have different *rates of time discount*.[5] The reasons for these differences are not known. They may be related to perceptions about how certain the future is, and they may depend upon how strongly rooted is one's sense of the past. Young children, for instance, characteristically live primarily in the present; they lack both a historical perspective and a vision of the future. Thus it is often difficult to get children to undertake some unpleasant task or to refrain from some pleasureable activity for the sake of a beneficial conse-

---

[4] The development of the theory of human capital by Gary Becker, Jacob Mincer, T. W. Schultz, and others and its application in fields such as education and health is one of the great advances in economics in the past quarter-century.

[5] *Rate of time discount* is a measure of how willing people are to incur present costs or defer present benefits in order to obtain some benefit in the future.

quence five or ten years away. Some adults, too, set very little store in the future compared with the present; they have a very high rate of time discount.

Most health-related activities — smoking, exercise, diet, periodic checkups and so forth — have consequences which are realized only after long periods of time. One possible reason for the high correlation between an individual's health and the length of his schooling (see Chapter 2 [of Fuchs's book]) is that attending to one's health and attending school are both aspects of investment in human capital. Thus the same person who has accumulated a great deal of human capital in the form of schooling may, for the same reasons, have made (or had made for him) substantial investments in health.

■ *Your Life or Mine?*

Suppose a small private plane crashes in an isolated forest area and no one knows whether the pilot is dead or alive. How much of society's resources will be devoted to searching for him? How much "should" be devoted to the search? If the pilot is a wealthy or prominent man, the search is likely to be longer and more thorough than if he is not. If he is wealthy, his family's command over private resources will make the difference; if he is a prominent government official, it is likely that publicly owned resources will be utilized far more readily than if the pilot were unknown and poor.

We see in this simple example one of the basic dilemmas of modern society. On the one hand, we believe that all people should be treated as equals, especially in matters of life or death. Against this we have what Raymond Aron calls the imperative "to produce as much as possible through mastery of the forces of nature," a venture requiring differentiation, hierarchy, and inevitably unequal treatment. The problem arises in all types of economic systems, and in all systems the response is likely to be similar.

If the family of a wealthy man wants to devote his (or their) wealth to searching for him, thereby increasing his probability of survival, is there any reason why the rest of society should object? (If the family used their command over resources for some frivolous consumption, would anyone else be better off?) Suppose, however, that instead of a plane crash the threat of death came from an ordinarily fatal disease? Would the same answers apply? The capacity of medical science to intervene near the point of death is growing rapidly. Such interventions are often extremely costly and have a low probability of

long-term success — but sometimes they work. Whose life should be saved? The wealthy man's? The senator's? Society cannot escape this problem any more than it can avoid facing the other choices we have discussed.

A related dilemma concerns the allocation of resources, either for research or care, among different diseases and conditions. The potential for social conflict here is high because the relative importance of different diseases is perceived differentially by groups according to their income level, race, age, location, and other characteristics.

A particularly striking example of this problem is sickle-cell anemia, a disease which in the United States affects primarily blacks. Recently there has been a substantial increase in the amount of funds available for research on this as-yet-incurable disease, primarily as a result of the growing political strength of the black community.

Many other diseases have a particularly high incidence among specific groups. Thus cigarette smokers have a much greater stake in research or services for lung cancer than do nonsmokers. And in the case of occupation-related diseases, the interests of workers and employers directly affected are much greater than those of the general public.

Economics cannot provide final answers to these difficult problems of social priorities, but it can help decision makers think more rationally about them. In allocating funds for medical research, for instance, economic reasoning can tell the decision maker what kind of information he ought to have and how to arrange that information so as to find the probable relative value of various courses of action.

Contrary to the opinion of many medical researchers, the criterion of "scientific merit" is not sufficient to form the basis for a rational allocation of medical research funds. Certainly decision makers should consider the relative importance the scientific community attaches to particular problems. But other kinds of information — such as the number of persons affected by a particular disease, the economic cost of the attendant morbidity[6] and mortality, and the cost of delivering preventive or therapeutic services if research is successful — should also be considered. The last item is particularly important when funding applied [research] as opposed to basic research, because the development of a "cure" that is enormously ex-

---

[6] *Morbidity* is the extent of an illness in the population.

pensive to implement probably has a low return and creates many serious social problems as well. For example, if a cure for cancer were discovered tomorrow but cost $150,000 per case to implement, the resulting controversies over the method of financing and the selection of cases to be cured might be so great as to make one view the cure as a mixed blessing.

■ The Jungle or the Zoo?

One of the central choices of our time, in health as in other areas, is finding the proper balance between individual (personal) and collective (social) responsibility. If too much weight is given to the former, we come close to recreating the "jungle" — with all the freedom and all the insecurity that the jungle implies. On the other hand, emphasizing social responsibility can increase security, but it may be the security of the "zoo" — purchased at the expense of freedom. Over the centuries man has wrestled with this choice, and in different times and different places the emphasis has shifted markedly.

Nineteenth-century Western society idealized individual responsibility. This was particularly true in England and the United States, where a system of political economy was developed based on the teachings of Locke, Smith, Mill, and other advocates of personal freedom. As this system was superimposed on a religious foundation which exalted hard work and thrift, the result was an unprecedented acceleration in the rate of growth of material output. Each man's energies were bent to enhancing his own welfare, secure in the knowledge that he and his family would enjoy the fruits of his efforts and in the conviction that he was obeying God's will.

That the system worked imperfectly goes without saying. That the outcome for some individuals was harsh and brutal has been recounted in innumerable novels, plays, histories, and sociological treatises. But when set against man's previous history, the material benefits and the accompanying relaxation of social, religious, and political rigidities were extraordinary.

By the beginning of this century, however, reactions to such uninhibited "progress" had arisen in most Western countries. Since then a variety of laws have been passed seeking to protect individuals from the most severe consequences of unbridled individualism. Laissez-faire is dead, and only a few mourn its passing. In fact, the attitude of many intellectuals and popular writers on political economy seems to have swung to the other extreme. In the 1920s R. H. Tawney, surveying the eighteenth- and nineteenth-century attitudes toward poverty, wrote that "the most curious feature in the whole discussion . . . was the resolute refusal to admit that society had any responsibility for the causes of distress." Some future historian, in reviewing mid-twentieth-century social reform literature, may note an equally curious feature — a "resolute refusal" to admit that individuals have any responsibility for their own distress.

From the idealization of individual responsibility and the neglect of social responsibility we have gone, in some quarters, to the denial of individual responsibility and the idealization of social responsibility. The rejection of any sense of responsibility for one's fellow men is inhuman, but the denial of any individual responsibility is also dehumanizing.

Moreover, with respect to health such a view runs contrary to common sense. As Henry Sigerist, an ardent advocate of socialized medicine and other expressions of social responsibility, has observed: "The state can protect society very effectively against a great many dangers, but the cultivation of health, which requires a definite mode of living, remains, to a large extent, an individual matter." Most of us know this is true from personal experience. As long as we believe that we have some control over our own choices, we will reject theories that assume that "society" is always the villain.

A great deal of what has been written recently about "the right to health" is very misleading. It suggests that society has a supply of "health" stored away which it can give to individuals and that it is only the niggardliness of the Administration or the ineptness of Congress or the selfishness of physicians that prevents this from happening. Such a view ignores the truth of Douglas Colman's observation that "positive health is not something that one human can hand to or require of another. Positive health can be achieved only through intelligent effort on the part of each individual. Absent that effort, health professionals can only insulate the individual from the more catastrophic results of his ignorance, self-indulgence, or lack of motivation." The notion that we can spend our way to better health is a vast oversimplification. At present there is very little that medical care can do for a lung that has been overinflated by smoking, or for a liver that has been scarred by too much alcohol, or for a skull that has been crushed in a motor accident.

The assertion that *medical care* is (or should be) a "right" is more plausible. In a sense medical care is to health what schooling is to wisdom. No society can truthfully promise to make everyone wise, but society can make schooling freely available; it can even make it compulsory. Many countries have taken a similar position with respect to medical care, although the compulsory aspects are sharply limited. Our government could, if it wished to, come close to assuring access to medical care for all persons. But no government now or in the foreseeable future can assure health to every individual.

Because utilization of medical care is voluntary, the mere availability of a service does not guarantee its use. The discovery of polio vaccine was rightly hailed as a significant medical advance, but in recent years there has been a sharp drop in the proportion of children receiving such vaccinations. At present, probably one-third of the children between 1 and 4 years of age are not adequately protected. The problem is particularly acute in poverty areas of major cities, where as many as half the children probably are without full protection against polio. There are undoubtedly many difficulties facing poor families that make it more difficult for them to bring their children to be vaccinated, but the service itself is available in most cities.

Another example of a gap between availability and utilization comes from a study of dental services covered by group health insurance. The study reported that white-collar workers and their families used significantly more preventive services than their blue-collar counterparts even though the insurance policy provided full coverage for all participants. The only dental service used more frequently by blue-collar families was tooth extraction — a procedure which is usually a consequence of failure to use preventive services, such as repair of caries.

If people have a *right* to care, do they also have an *obligation* to use it? This complex question will assume greater significance as the collective provision of care increases. In our zeal to raise health levels, however, we must be wary of impinging on other valuable "rights," including the right to be left alone. Strict control over a man's behavior might well result in increased life expectancy, but a well-run zoo is still a zoo and not a worthy model for mankind.

As we attempt to formulate responsible policy for health and medical care, we should strive for the balance advocated by Rabbi Hillel more than two thousand years ago when he said, "If I am not for myself, who will be for me, but if I am for myself alone, what am I?"

The preceding discussion of the choices that face our society helps to put the major problems of health and medical care in proper perspective. These problems, as perceived by the public, are high cost, poor access, and inadequate health levels. In order to attack them intelligently, we must recognize the scarcity of resources and the need to allocate them as efficiently as possible. We must recognize that we can't have everything. In short, we need to adopt an economic point of view.

The discussion of choices also reveals some of the limits of economics in dealing with the most fundamental questions of health and medical care. These questions are ultimately ones of value: What value do we put on saving a life? on reducing pain? on relieving anxiety? How do these values change when the life at stake is a relative's? a neighbor's? a stranger's?

Nearly all human behavior is guided by values. Given the values, together with information about the relationship between technological means and ends, about inputs and constraints (resources, time, money), economics shows how these values can be maximized. To the extent that individual behavior attempts to maximize values, economic theory also possesses significant power to predict behavior. If and when values change and these changes are not taken into account, however, economics loses a good deal of its predictive power. The most difficult part of the problem is that values may change partly as a result of the economic process itself.

According to one well-known definition, "economics is the science of means, not of ends": it can explain how market prices are determined, but not how basic values are formed; it can tell us the consequences of various alternatives, but it cannot make the choice for us. These limitations will be with us always, for economics can never replace morals or ethics.

THE STRUCTURE OF AMERICAN HEALTH CARE

Health–PAC

This introductory selection provides an overview of the American health care system from the radical perspective. Health-PAC, which stands for Health Policy Advisory Council, is a collective of people working on health care issues in New York City. They publish the *Health-PAC Bulletin* and occasional pamphlets.

The health-care system seems so chaotic, so unplanned, so uncoordinated, that many people call it a nonsystem. To cure the health care crisis, they conclude, we must turn it into a system. Specifically, they argue, some form of national health insurance would provide financially shaky hospitals with a stable income. Doctors should be encouraged to form group practices to increase efficiency — the equivalent of corner grocers banding together to open a supermarket. And hospitals and medical schools should be linked together into regional networks which would be able efficiently and rationally to plan for the medical needs of an entire region. More money, more planning, more coordination — that is the standard prescription for the ailing American health system.

But careful examination of the structure of health care indicates that, in fact, there is a health care system; it is not totally chaotic and unplanned. It seems chaotic only if it is described in terms of private doctors. Years ago, the doctors did dominate and control health care; but now health care is dominated by institutions — hospitals, medical schools, research laboratories, drug companies, health insurance companies, health planning agencies, and many others. Many people don't even have a private doctor any more; the hospital clinic and emergency room have become their doctor. Less than 20 percent of the nation's health expenditures now go for private doctors; most of the rest goes to institutions. And, more than nine out of ten health workers these days

Source: Revised and updated from *Health Care in Crisis,* a Health-PAC publication (1972). Reprinted from *Prognosis Negative: Crisis in the Health Care System,* a Health-PAC anthology, David Kotelchuk, ed. (New York: Vintage, 1976).

are not doctors at all, but workers employed by health care institutions — nurses, dieticians, X-ray technicians, orderlies, laboratory technicians, etc. The health institutions are big and growing rapidly and as they grow they are becoming more and more interconnected to form a system.

There are three major components to the existing American health-care system: medical empires, the financing-planning complex and the health-care profiteers, especially the medical-industrial complex.

Medical Empires

Medical empires are the primary units. They are privately controlled medical complexes, usually but not always organized with a medical school at the hub. From these centers, radiating out like spokes on a wheel, are a network of affiliations to smaller private hospitals, city hospitals, state mental hospitals, neighborhood health centers and subspecialty programs such as alcoholism, rehabilitation or prison health. To each of these affiliated programs, the medical center provides professional personnel in return for healthy rake-offs of the affiliated programs' resources. In fact, the benefits of such arrangements are often so highly weighted in favor of the medical center that *exploitation* is the only fair description of the relationship — thus the term "empires." These networks of medical centers with their far-reaching affiliations resemble a mother country's relationship to its colonies. This resemblance has been exacerbated by the fact that many of the affiliation relationships are with hospitals, neighborhood centers and special programs in poor communities, most often populated by blacks, Puerto Ricans, Chicanos, Asians or Appalachians.

The empires have their own priorities. Some of these are related to expansion and profit-making, others are related to research and teaching, and still others are concerned with control — influencing policy both locally and nationally. How much any of these priorities relate to patient care is the critical question. The answer is complicated and in many instances not yet fully understood. On balance, however, these priorities are the basis for the exploitative relationship between the medical center and its affiliates.

For example, take Einstein College of Medicine (a medical school) and Montefiore Hospital and Medical Center (a close ally). Together they have come to control most of the medical resources in the Bronx, an entire borough of New York City. Through affiliation contracts, Einstein/Montefiore monopolizes care at three out of the four city hospitals in the Bronx, the only state mental hospital in the borough, several neighborhood health centers, prison health services, several private voluntary hospitals and numerous nursing homes. Of the 6,670 beds in general care hospitals in the Bronx, 4,500 are controlled by Einstein/Montefiore; most doctors practicing in the Bronx are affiliated with Einstein/Montefiore.

What has this arrangement meant for patients? Perhaps — and this has not been proven — the technical-scientific management of hospitalized patients has improved. But the price for this questionable improvement — questionable both in terms of money and in terms of distorted priorities — is enormous:

- In sheer dollars, the affiliation of the city hospitals to Einstein/Montefiore has increased the money coming into those hospitals by over $37 million a year.
- In the outpatient departments of the affiliated hospitals, sub-specialty clinics have proliferated — in some cases to more than 100 in number. Patients have found their care fragmented, with no single doctor taking responsibility. On the one hand, the patient has no one to see for a common cold; on the other hand, when he or she has a more complicated illness, it takes a visit to three or four separate clinics before a diagnosis can be made, and even then a different doctor may supervise the patient's treatment each visit.
- In the inpatient services, (i.e., hospitalized patients), all of the hospitals were converted through affiliations into teaching institutions. Patients frequently find themselves subjected to unnecessary and occasionally dangerous procedures. Liver biopsies (removal of tissue from the liver), for example, are performed primarily to teach interns how to do the procedure; Caesarean sections and hysterectomies are performed when their medical necessity is ques-

tionable at best, so that the residents can gain more experience in performing these operations.
- In research, the affiliations have brought more academic interest to the affiliated hospitals, but not necessarily more patient-oriented controls. In one such hospital, patients admitted for a routine tubal ligation (sterilization) were given medication prior to the operation and then had their ovaries biopsied to determine the effect of the medication on the ovaries. The patients were not asked for their informed consent. Moreover, it turned out that no research proposal had been submitted, as required, to the hospital's research committee.

Besides elevating the medical center's priorities without regard for patient's priorities, medical empires tend to institutionalize the unequal relationship between the mother-medical center and the colony-affiliated hospital. This is done in overt ways, with the medical center extracting natural resources from the affiliated hospital. Patients with interesting or rare diseases are taken from the affiliated hospital and brought to the medical center, while patients with mundane medical problems are "dumped" by the medical center onto its affiliates. Likewise, talented medical teachers and researchers located in the affiliated hospitals are asked to spend unpaid teaching time at the medical center. This means that their talents are utilized by the medical center while their salary continues to be paid out of the affiliated hospital's budget. When the affiliated hospital, on the other hand, wants the expertise of a researcher at the medical center, it has to pay handsomely for a lecture or consultation.

In addition to such overt discrimination, there are more subtle ways in which inequalities within a medical empire are institutionalized. Patients being referred from the affiliated hospital to the medical center for some specialized procedure, such as cardiac catheterization or cobalt therapy, may end up on waiting lists for months. The scheduling priorities are explicit: Private patients come first, clinic patients from the medical center come second and the affiliated hospital's patients come third. Another example is the fact that pension programs and other fringe benefits for the professional personnel on the medical center's staff are significantly more generous than those for the affiliated hospital's staff. The list could go on and on.

Some people may minimize the importance of

medical empires. "It hasn't happened here," they will say, "The county medical society is still the strongest force in town." While such an observation may be accurate in many rural and some suburban communities, the nationwide trend is very clear: In Cleveland, Case Western Reserve Medical School controls many of the medical resources. In Baltimore, it's Johns Hopkins Medical School; in Seattle, it's the University of Washington; in North Carolina, it's Duke University and the University of North Carolina. And everywhere the results are the same: The structure of health care is organized around the institutional priorities of the medical center and not the health-care needs of the patient. And that disparity of priorities is most accentuated when the individual is not an affluent private patient at the medical center but a poor or uninsured ward or clinic patient at one of its affiliated institutions.

The Financing-Planning Complex

The second main part of the health care system is the financing-planning complex. The most important part of this complex is the multibillion dollar Blue Cross operation, whose insurance plans cover 80 million people, four of every ten Americans. Through the publicly funded Medicare and Medicaid programs, Blue Cross administers insurance benefits for an additional 32 million people. Altogether, Blue Cross disburses about half of all hospital revenues.

Because it is by far the nation's largest single health insurer, Blue Cross also plays a very important role in setting health policy: Its leaders sit on governmental advisory committees, advise congressional committees, and, together with representatives of the big private hospitals, set up and run area-wide comprehensive health planning agencies.

Blue Cross is closely allied with the big hospitals. It was set up during the Depression by financially starved hospitals to provide them a guaranteed income, and it continues to be dominated by the major hospitals. Nearly half of the members of the boards of directors of local Blue Cross plans (Blue Cross operates in 74 localities) are hospital representatives. Needless to say, hospitals and health consumers often have very different interests. Consumers want high-quality, low-cost, relevant health care; hospitals, on the other hand, are often more interested in institutional expansion and the prestige gained through the acquisition of well-known researchers, fancy medical equipment and new and larger buildings. This is why the hospital-dominated Blue Cross has consistently failed to support consumer concerns such as cost and quality control.

The Health-Care Profiteers

The third part of the health system are the health-care profiteers, especially the medical-industrial complex. An alliance exists between the providers of health care (doctors, hospitals, medical schools and the like) and the companies that make money from people's sickness (drug companies, hospital supply companies, hospital construction companies, commercial insurance companies, and even companies that provide medical services for profit — profit-making proprietary hospitals, chains of nursing homes for old people, laboratories, etc.). Health care is one of the biggest businesses around, and one of the fastest-growing.

The magnitude of the medical-industrial complex is hard to believe. For example, in 1969 drug companies (Abbott, Upjohn, Merck, etc.) had after-tax profits of about $600 million. The drug industry rated first, second, or third in profitability among all U.S. industries during the 1960s, causing *Forbes Magazine*, a financial journal, to call it "one of the biggest crap games in U.S. industry."

Hospital supply companies (Becton-Dickinson, American Hospital Supply, etc.), which sell hospitals and doctors everything from sheets and towels and bedpans to surgical instruments, X-ray machines and heart-lung machines, had after-tax profits of $400 million in 1969. Proprietary (profit-making) hospitals and nursing homes earned nearly $200 million. (There are even nationwide chains of hospitals and nursing homes run by such businesses as Holiday Inns.)

The commercial insurance companies and the construction firms which build hospitals make additional millions, and, of course, the doctors themselves are still the highest paid people around. Even the banks are getting in on the act, with loans to hospitals both for building and for operating expenses. The patient at one of New York's prestigious hospitals, for example, finds that $3 a day of his hospital bill doesn't go for services at all; it goes to the banks for interest payments.

The System in Health

And not only do all of these empires, insurance people, financiers, businessmen and doctors make a lot of money from people's bad health, they do it with to-getherness. Their mutual needs coincide: Prestigious medical empires require the manufacture of expensive equipment and the presence of large construction companies; and, of course, only large institutions can afford the expensive products of the medical equipment and drug manufacturers. And all of these groups require the stable, lenient financing of Blue Cross, Medicare and Medicaid and other medical insurers. Their growing interdependence is evident. Increasingly drug and medical equipment executives, banking and real estate/construction company executives sit on boards of trustees at academic medical centers. Meanwhile, hospital and medical school professionals moonlight as consultants to drug and hospital supply companies and sometimes sit on their boards of trustees.

The best thing about the health business is that the profits are sure (as long as you're not a patient or taxpayer, that is). Blue Cross, Medicare and Medicaid hand the doctors and hospitals a virtual blank check. The hospital, in effect, simply tells Blue Cross how much its expenses are, and Blue Cross pays the bill. In the boom years of the 1960s there was no cost control to speak of. The inflation in health-care costs that resulted has led to some belt-tightening more recently. But the accepted definition of a necessary health-care cost remains very generous.

Some costs of course may be necessary for better patient care. But they also may be "necessary" for the purchase of seldom-used and expensive equipment that is available in another hospital across the street; for plush offices and high salaries for doctors and hospital administrators; for expenses incurred in fighting off attempts by unions to organize hospital workers; or for hiring public relations firms to clean up the hospital's poor image in the community. The health industry and the doctors get rich; the consumer and the taxpayer pay the bill.

Even the so-called nonprofit hospitals get in on the fun. All that "nonprofit" means is that such hospitals do not have to pay out their excess income to stockholders. They also do not have to pay it back to their patients in the form of cheaper rates. Instead, they use it to grow; to buy more fancy (even if unnecessary) equipment, more plush offices, more public relations; to pay staff doctors even higher salaries; to buy up real estate, tear down poor people's housing, and build new pavilions for private patients.

There is, then, a health care *system*. Its components are, in addition to the doctors, the vast network of health care resources that make up the medical empires; the financing and planning complex of agencies dominated by Blue Cross; and the medical-industrial complex. But if American health care is provided by such a big, well-organized, interconnected, business-like system, why is it so poor? The answer is that *health care is not the aim of the health-care system*. The health-care system exists to serve its own ends. The aims of big medical centers are teaching and research. The hospitals and medical schools seek to expand their real estate and financial holdings. And everyone, from hospitals and doctors to drug companies and insurance companies, wants to make profits. Health care for patients is a means to these ends, but is not the sole end in itself. And so the patient sees a system which is expensive, which is fragmented into dozens of specialties, which has no time to treat him in a dignified way, and which doesn't even take care of him very well.

HEALTH CARE INTEREST GROUPS

Robert R. Alford

This selection reviews the political economic interests of the major competing groups in the
health area. People do not approach the problems of
the health system from dispassionate concern, Alford
suggests, but rather on the basis of their material relationship to the system.

This is an excerpt from a longer article that traces
these themes in somewhat more detail.

Alford teaches sociology at the University of California at Santa Cruz and has written widely on health
problems and other social policy issues.

Introduction

Health care in the United States is allegedly in a
state of crisis.* High and rising costs, inadequate
numbers of medical and paramedical personnel, a
higher infant mortality rate in 1969 than thirteen
other countries, a lower life expectancy in 1965 for
males than seventeen other countries, and poor emergency room and ambulatory care are among the diverse facts or allegations which have justified a wide
variety of proposed reforms. And yet the numbers of
health personnel, the proportion of the gross national
product spent on health care, and the sheer quantity

of services rendered have grown considerably faster
than the economy as a whole.[1]

If health care is in "crisis" now, then it was in
crisis ten, twenty, and forty years ago as well. Several qualified observers have commented on the similarity between the 1932 analysis by the Committee
on the Costs of Medical Care[2] and reports issued
thirty-five or more years later. Dr. Sumner N. Rosen,
an economist on the staff of the Institute of Public
Administration in New York City, has said that the
"catalogue of problems drawn up almost forty years
ago strongly resembles the latest list — inadequate
services, insufficient funds, understaffed hospitals.
Virtually nothing has changed."[3] Economist Eli
Ginzberg, summarizing the results of his study of
New York City, concludes that "While changes have
occurred in response to emergencies, opportunities,
and alternatives in the market place, the outstanding
finding is the inertia of the system as a whole."[4]

The overwhelming fact about the various reforms
of the health system that have been implemented or
proposed — more money, more subsidy of insurance,
more manpower, more demonstration projects, more
clinics — is that they are absorbed into a system
which is enormously resistant to change. The reforms which are suggested are sponsored by different
elements in the health system and advantage one or
another element, but they do not seriously damage
any interests. This pluralistic balancing of costs and
benefits successfully shields the funding, powers, and

Source: "Health Care Interest Groups," from an article in
Politics & Society, Winter 1972, by Robert R. Alford.
Reprinted with permission.
* This paper was prepared under a grant to the Center
for Policy Research, New York, from the National Center
for Health Research and Development, National Institute
of Mental Health. I am indebted to the Center for Policy
Research for providing research facilities, and particularly
for making it possible for Ann Wallace to serve as my research associate during 1970–71.

I wish to thank the National Conference of Social
Welfare for permission to use part of an earlier version
which appeared in The Social Welfare Forum (New
York: Columbia University Press, 1971).

Too many friends and colleagues have commented on
the paper by this time to allow their names to be mentioned here, but I hope they will recognize their impact
on the final version and realize that their sometimes
severe criticisms have been appreciated if not always
heeded.

[1] For a collation of a wide variety of health statistics,
see the Committee on Ways and Means, U.S. House of
Representatives, Basic Facts on the Health Industry
(Washington, D.C.: U.S. Government Printing Office,
June 28, 1971).

[2] Medical Care for the American People, the final report of the Committee on the Costs of Medical Care,
adopted October 31, 1932. (Reprinted, 1970, by the U.S.
Department of Health, Education and Welfare.)

[3] Sumner N. Rosen, "Change and Resistance to
Change," Social Policy I (January/February 1971): 4.

[4] Eli Ginzberg et al., Urban Health Services (New
York: Columbia University Press, 1971), p. 224.

resources of the producing institutions from any basic structural change.

This situation might well be described as one of "dynamics without change." This paper argues that both the expansion of the health care industry and the apparent absence of change are due to a struggle between different major interest groups operating within the context of a market society — professional monopolists controlling the major health resources, corporate rationalizers challenging their power, and the community population seeking better health care.

Although the paper generalizes from the scholarly literature as well as from documents and from interviews which took place in New York City, it should be regarded as a set of "outrageous hypotheses," in the spirit of Robert S. Lynd's classic *Knowledge for What?*,[5] rather than as a theory inferred from reliable empirical findings.

Market Versus Bureaucratic Reform

Pressures for change come largely from three types of reformers, of which the first two are most important. The first, whom I shall call the "market reformers," would expand the diversity of facilities available, the number of physicians, the competition between health facilities, and the quantity and quality of private insurance. Their assumptions are that the public sector should underwrite medical bills for the poor and that patients should be free to choose among various health care providers. The community population is regarded as consumers of health care like other commodities and is assumed to be able to evaluate the quality of service received. Market pressures will thus drive out the incompetent, excessively high priced or duplicated service, and the inaccessible physician, clinic, or hospital. The market reformers wish to preserve the control of the individual physician over his practice, over the hospital, and over his fees, and they simply wish to open up the medical schools to meet the demand for doctors, to give patients more choice among doctors, clinics, and hospitals, and to make that choice a real one by providing public subsidies for medical bills.

These assumptions are questioned by the "bureaucratic reformers." They stress the importance of the hospital as the key location and organizer of

health services and wish to put individual doctors under the control of hospital medical boards and administrators. The bureaucratic reformers are principally concerned with coordinating fragmented services, instituting planning, and extending public funding. Their assumption is that the technology of modern health care requires a complex and coordinated division of labor between ambulatory and in-hospital care, primary practitioners and specialists, and personalized care and advanced chemical and electronic treatment. The community population is regarded as an external constituency of the health providers to be organized to represent its interests if necessary to maintain the equilibrium of the system. . . . These two contrasting diagnoses, images of the future, and proposals for reform of health care are not opposing political ideologies which can be accepted or rejected only in terms of one's moral and political values. They are also analyses of the structure of health care resting upon different empirical assumptions about the nature of and power of the medical profession, the nature of medical technology, the role of the hospital, and the role of the patient (or the "community") as passively receiving or actively demanding a greater quality and quantity of health care.

Major Interest Groups

Strategies of reform based on either "bureaucratic" or "market" models are unlikely to work. Each type of reform stresses certain core functions in the health system and regards others as secondary. But both neglect the way in which the groups representing these functions come to develop vital interests which sustain the present system and vitiate attempts at reform.

For the market reformers, supplying trained physicians, innovating through biomedical and technological research, and maintaining competition between diverse health care producers are the main functions to be maintained. They view the hospitals, medical schools, and public health agencies as only the organizational framework which sustains the primary functions of professional health care and biomedical research. However, these types of work become buttressed through institutional mechanisms which guarantee professional control, and come to constitute powerful interest groups which I shall call the "professional monopolists." Because these interest groups are at present the dominant ones, with their powers

[5] Robert S. Lynd, *Knowledge for What?* (Princeton: Princeton University Press, 1939).

and resources safely embedded in law, custom, professional legitimacy, and the practices of many public and private organizations, they do not need to be as visibly active nor as cohesively organized as those groups seeking change.

For the bureaucratic reformers, the hospitals, medical schools, and public health agencies at all governmental levels perform the core functions of organizing, financing, and distributing health care. Hospitals are seen ideally as the center of networks of associated clinics and neighborhood health centers, providing comprehensive care to an entire local population. The bureaucratic reformers view physicians and medical researchers as performing crucial work, but properly as subordinated and differentiated parts of a complex delivery system, coordinated by bureaucrats, notably hospital administrators. However, these large-scale organizations also become powerful interest groups, which I shall call the "corporate rationalizers." These interest groups are at present the major challengers of the power of the professional monopolists, and they constitute the bulk of the membership of the various commissions of investigation and inquiry into the health care "crisis."

A third type of reformer is relatively unimportant in the American context as yet: the "equal-health advocates," who seek free, accessible, high-quality health care which equalizes the treatment available to the well-to-do and to the poor. They stress the importance of community control over the supply and deployment of health facilities, because they base their strategies upon a third set of interest groups: the local population or community affected by the availability and character of health personnel and facilities. The community population is not as powerful or as organized as the other two sets of interest groups, but has equally as great a stake in the outcomes of the operations of health institutions.

Each of these three major interest groups is internally heterogeneous. The professional monopolists include biomedical researchers, physicians in private or group practice, salaried physicians, and other health occupations seeking professional privileges and status, who differ among themselves in their relationships to each other, as well as to hospitals, medical schools, insurance plans, and government agencies, and thus their interests are affected differently by various programs of reform. But they share an interest in maintaining professional autonomy and control over the conditions of their work, and thus will — when that autonomy is challenged — act together in defense of that interest.

The corporate rationalizers include medical school officials, public health officials, insurance companies, and hospital administrators, whose organizational interests often require that they compete with each other for powers and resources. Therefore, they differ in the priority they attach to various reform proposals. But they share an interest in maintaining and extending the control of their organizations over the conditions of work of the professionals (and other employees) whose activities are key to the achievement of organizational goals.

The community population constitutes a set of interest groups which are internally heterogeneous with respect to their health needs, ability to pay, and ability to organize their needs into effective demands, but they share an interest in maximizing the responsiveness of health professionals and organizations to their concerns for accessible, high-quality health care for which they have the ability to pay.

My assumption in making these key distinctions is that the similarities of structural location and interests vis-à-vis each other of each of these interest groups warrant an emphasis on the common interests within each group rather than on their differences. If my concern were to explain the actions of various individuals and groups with respect to a particular piece of legislation or administrative decision, lumping these diverse groups and individuals together into three such internally diverse groups would be entirely too crude. But for explaining the main contours of the present system and its resistance to change, finer distinctions would entail a short-term time perspective. Differences which are extremely important for tactics may be relatively unimportant in the long run.[6]

[6] I assume also that there is a reasonably high correlation between ideologies and personal incentives of doctors, researchers, administrators, and the organizational interests of the medical profession, hospitals, or public health associations. That is, there is a high probability that elites will take a public position consistent with the interests of their organization. Career incentives probably require that collective myths be publicly sustained, even if there is considerable private cynicism or disbelief. More detailed analyses of particular events and conflicts would require taking into account contradictions and discrepancies between ideology, personal incentives, and organizational interests.

A further distinction can also be drawn between the objective interests of an individual or group (the con-

The danger of this mode of analysis, however, is that the internal contradictions within each interest group may be the source of potential strategic alliances which may have great long-term implications. For example, the vision of an ideal health system which erases the distinction between those who pay and those who don't is held up by the bureaucratic reformers as well as by the equal-health advocates. And, in the abstract, both the value of personalized care (defended by one group as viable only through fee-for-service medicine) and the value of coordinated, comprehensive care (defended by another group as possible only through hospital-organized health care) are hard to question.

But whether or not these values of personalized service and comprehensive care are sheer ideological rationalizations by one or another interest group of its power and privileges may be irrelevant if they can be used as a weapon for critical attack upon the inadequacies of health care. The corporate rationalizers properly accuse the professional monopolists of not providing the personalized care which justifies their claim to fee-for-service practice. The professional monopolists properly accuse the corporate rationalizers of not being concerned with personalized care in their drive for efficient, high-technology health care. The contradictions in both cases between rhetoric and performance provide an opportunity to the equal-health advocates to show the deficiencies in analysis and program of the dominant interest groups.

Differences between these interest groups should not be overemphasized, because both the professional monopolists and the corporate rationalizers are operating within the context of a market society. Both have a concern to avoid encroachments upon their respective positions of power and privilege, which depend upon the continuation of market institutions: the ownership and control of individual labor, facilities, and organizations (even "nonprofit" ones) by autonomous groups and individuals, with no meaningful mechanisms of public control. (The instruments of alleged political control available to the community population are discussed later.)

The corporate rationalizers may thus favor certain market reforms, if that will provide them with more doctors for their hospitals, more researchers for their medical schools, and more potential workers for medical corporations, and will subject these workers to market pressures which in turn will make them tractable employees. The professional monopolists may thus favor certain bureaucratic reforms, particularly those aspects of planning and coordination which safeguard their interests, or administrative rules in hospitals which guarantee their continued dominance of medical practice.

Nor should the seeming rationality implied by the term "interest group" be overemphasized, because one basic consequence of the plurality of interest groups is that health institutions in a real sense are out of control of *both* the professionals and the bureaucrats. A hospitalization that could be terminated in one week lasts two, because there is a week's waiting time for a barium enema. Or one-third of a high-cost ward may be occupied because convalescent or chronic care facilities are unavailable. These failures of "coordination" or "planning" are not due to a conspiracy, vested interests (except in a very narrow sense), or failures of information (the horror stories are endless).[7]

---

sequences of certain policies) and its subjective interests (beliefs about those consequences). A group may be affected in important ways by the operations of an institution, but its members may not be conscious of those consequences and thus may not act either to defend themselves or to change the structure which produces the consequences. Or even if conscious of the consequences, the members may be unwilling or unable to act for a variety of reasons. See Isaac D. Balbus, "The Concept of Interest in Pluralist and Marxian Analysis," *Politics and Society* I (February 1971): 151–177, for a recent discussion of this point, and for an earlier but similar statement, Harry Eckstein, *Pressure Group Politics: The Case of the British Medical Association* (Stanford: Stanford University Press, 1960), pp. 9–12.

[7] I am indebted to Dr. Joel Hoffman for some of these points.

THE MEDICAL-INDUSTRIAL COMPLEX

Barbara and John Ehrenreich

This long selection clearly documents the emergence of a new "medical-industrial complex" in this country. The implications of that emergence are clear. If we desire a basic reorganization of our health care system, then we shall have to contend with an increasing domination of that system by large corporations in pursuit of profit.

The selection appeared originally as Chapter 7 of *The American Health System: Power, Profits, and Politics*, a Health-PAC book prepared by Barbara and John Ehrenreich. The Health Policy Advisory Center (Health-PAC) is a collective of radicals in New York City who do research and organizing on health care issues. Barbara and John Ehrenreich are members of the group.

Ever since Florence Nightingale, medical care has had an aura of selflessness and self-imposed poverty. The great modern hospital center, for instance, projects itself as a "non-profit" institution where "the few toil ceaselessly that the many might live." But behind the facade of the helpless sick and dedicated healers lies the 1960s greatest gold rush, a booming "health industry" churning out more than $2.5 billion a year by 1969 in after-tax profits.

In 1969 the nation spent over $62 billion on medical care, up more than 11 percent over [1968] and twice the 1960 level. $6 billion of this flowed into the hands of the drug companies; almost $10 billion went to the companies that sell doctors and hospitals everything from bed linen to electrocardiographs; $35 billion was spent on "proprietary" (profit-making) hospitals and nursing homes. The nation purchased $6 billion worth of commercial health insurance and construction companies built about $2 billion worth of hospitals. Additional billions were raked in by private physicians. The health industry is big business, profitable business, and booming business. Stockbroker Goodbody and Company clued in its customers earlier this year: "Steady growth of the health industry ... is as certain as anything

can be" — as certain as death and taxes, in any event.

The great boom of the 1960s in the health industries is largely the product of government subsidization of the market. For years the government has directly or indirectly fed dollars into the gaping pockets of the dealers in human disease. In addition to direct payments for health care, for educating health manpower, and for hospital construction, it has granted tax deductions to individuals for their medical expenses, making their health dollars cheaper. It has expanded the purchasing power of "non-profit" hospitals by granting them tax exemptions, and, until recently, by not applying minimum wage or labor relations laws to them. It has directly supported basic biological and chemical research to the tune of billions of dollars as well as sponsoring the dramatic advances in electronics. These technologies underlie many of the most profitable sectors of the health industry. And in 1966, the biggest government subsidy of all — Medicare and Medicaid — got going. By 1969 federal, state and local governments directly picked up more than a third of the tab for the nation's health needs, and all signals were go for a steadily increasing government-guaranteed market. One likely mechanism: government subsidized national health insurance, to underwrite the entire medical care market.

Only a small part of the new money being spent on health has gone to improve health care. For instance, community hospitals spent 16 percent more money in 1968 than they did in 1967. But they provided only 3.3 percent more days of inpatient care and 3.7 percent more outpatient visits. (Nobody noticed any 13 percent increase in the quality of care.) A large fraction of the new money for the health care delivery system has, for all social purposes, simply vanished — as inflated costs for drugs, supplies and equipment, and as profits for doctors and hospitals.

In this section we take a look at the money for health which has surged through the delivery system of doctors, hospitals and drug stores to fuel an unprecedented boom in the health "industry" — the private companies which supply, equip, finance, build for and (sometimes) manage the health delivery system. Here, the dollar-for-dollar return as health benefits is, first, shockingly low, and second, perhaps not even that "healthy." From the outset, the aim of the health industry is not to promote the general well-being (in the long run, that would be self-defeating), but to exploit existing profitable markets and create new ones. The emphasis, then, is not on products and services which would improve basic health care for the great mass of consumers, but on what are essentially luxury items: computerized equipment for intensive cardiac care units, hyperbaric chambers, hospitals which specialize in elective surgery for the rich, expensive combination drugs, etc. Under the pressure of the industry's barrage of packaged technology, the health care delivery system is increasingly distorted towards high-cost, low-utilization, inpatient services.

Most of the money which flows through the delivery system to the health industry's drug and hospital supply and equipment companies never returns to the delivery system in any medically useful form, or in any form at all. First, a good 5 to 10 percent is raked off directly as profits, and these by and large vanish into the larger economy, going to stockholders and going to finance the companies' expansions into other enterprises. More and more of the health industry firms are conglomerates, whose holdings in drugs or hospital supplies help finance their acquisitions in cosmetics, catering or pet food.

Profits are only part of the story. There is no way of auditing the health industry companies to determine how much of their "costs" actually represents medically wasted, privately managed, surplus income. Prices are high, the health companies claim, not on account of profits, but because of the enormous cost of research, skilled manpower, meeting exacting standards, etc. But how much of the industry's research goes into a needless and dangerously confusing proliferation of marginally different products — like drugs which differ only in flavor, electronic equipment which differs only in console design, etc.? How much goes to plan the planned obsolescence in expensive hospital hardware? How much of the costs go for the design of appealing packaging? How much for million-dollar advertising and promotion campaigns? Money spent on these causes is not simply wasted. The needless proliferation of dazzlingly advertised and packaged products is a health hazard. It prevents the buyer, whether he is a doctor, a hospital administrator, or a patient, from making informed choices among products and mystifies him to the point where he will accept unquestioningly the industry's definition of what he needs and what he must pay for it.

Drugs

The drug industry likes to think of itself as a sort of public service — dispensing life and comfort and at the same time upholding the American, free-enterprise way. *Forbes* magazine, which likes to think of itself as the "capitalist tool," much more honestly describes the drug industry as "one of the biggest crap games in U.S. industry." Any way you cut it, the drug industry is big and on the way to being bigger:

- $6 billion worth of drugs (prescription and nonprescription) were sold in 1969, $6.5 billion will be sold in 1970, and so on, increasing at about 9 percent a year.
- There are 700 drug firms. Control is concentrated in the top fifteen, who sell more than half of all drugs.
- 200,000 people are employed by drug companies all over the world. 100,000 of these are Americans and 20,000 of them are the "detail men" who push prescription pills to private doctors.
- The American drug industry is worldwide. Foreign sales are growing faster than domestic, as drug companies expand their foreign subsidiaries. The two leading drug imperialists are Pfizer, with 48 percent of its business abroad, and Merck, with 37 percent industry-wide; more than one quarter of sales are abroad.
- The industry spends one and a half billion dollars a year on advertising, twenty-five cents out of every sales dollar and more than three times as much as its spends on its much-heralded research and development effort.

What makes drugs the "biggest crap game," however, is profits. For the last ten years, the drug industry has held either first, second or third place among all U.S. industries in terms of profitability, outdistancing such obvious moneymakers as the cosmetics, aerospace, recreation and entertainment industries.

But the drug industry has seen better days. Earlier leaps in profits grew out of major breakthroughs: antibiotics in the late '40s, tranquilizers in the late '50s and early '60s and birth control pills in the early and mid-'60s. Nothing big has come along since "the pill" and even it is something of a disappointment. Efforts to push the pill beyond the 20 percent of eligible women who now use it have been checked by growing mutters about annoying and often lethal side effects. "We're in a trough right now," says a top Merck man, and some companies are beginning to wonder whether it's worth gambling on another wave of wonder drugs.

According to the industry's own probably inflated estimates, a really new drug takes about 10 years and $7 million worth of research. Hence more and more "new" drugs are not new at all. Over half released in the last 10 years are what are called "me, too" drugs: minor chemical modifications of old drugs, combinations of old drugs, old drugs released in chewable form, time capsule form, half-dose form, in handy dispensers, and so on in endless, meaningless elaboration. Meanwhile some of the old bestsellers are threatened with patent expirations and anti-trust suits. Parke Davis has become too dependent on chloromycetin, and began to slip in profitability when the antibiotic's patent expired a couple of years ago. Similarly, Pfizer has lost an anti-trust suit which will loosen its grip on tetracycline. Overall drug industry profits slipped below 10 percent of sales in 1968 for the first time in years. (That's still way ahead of most industries.)

Then, as if the drug companies didn't have enough problems of their own, the federal government has shown increasing signs of being serious about regulating drug costs and quality. The Kefauver investigations into drug prices and the resulting federal drug law amendments had drug companies, by their own admission, "running scared" in the early sixties. The stiffer scrutiny of new drugs required by the 1962 law caused a sharp drop in the rate at which new products were introduced, and pushed many companies to expand abroad, in countries where drug-testing laws are more permissive.

But the most potentially far-reaching affront to the drug companies' independence was Medicare. Drug companies knew from the start that a healthy chunk of Medicare funds would find its way to their pockets. What they feared was that there might be some strings attached. The Pharmaceutical Manufacturers Association, in their right-wing public relations throwaway "Medicine at Work," editorialized in early 1965:

> What is the logic in socializing medical care (via Medicare) when health insurance programs can function so effectively and are expanding every day, in fact already covering most of our citizens? . . . If private initiative disappears there may never be enough time to repair the damage that will ensue . . . .

But a few months later the Pharmaceutical Manufacturers Association, at their national convention, spent a whole day in seminars on Medicare. When they emerged, *The New York Times* reported with cautious optmism that "some companies have accepted the fact that Medicare is here and with it has come a new opportunity for the industry."

Even though they reluctantly accepted Medicare (and of course Medicare money for their pills), the drug companies saw the handwriting on the wall. Like the AMA, the drug industry knows that government subsidy can lead to government scrutiny. Drug costs are a big bill to swallow, and have already become the subject of repeated Congressional inquiry. If the government role in financing medical care expands beyond Medicare and the ruins of Medicaid, the government might begin to insist on generic drugs (as opposed to much more expensive but chemically identical brand-name drug) price-setting, or other forms of profit-regulation.

When the neighborhood pusher feels the heat coming on him he begins to turn to new, but related, rackets. So with the drug companies, menaced by real or imagined regulation, the answer has been to diversify into anything which their technology and marketing skills prepare them for. As if by free association, drug companies have been turning to cosmetics, chemicals, hospital supplies and electronic equipment for hospitals. American Cyanamid which owns Lederle Labs now owns Breck (shampoo). Pfizer has bought Coty, Barbasol, Pacquin and Desitin (baby powders and oils). Richardson-Merrill acquired Clearasil; Smith, Kline and French has Sea and Ski; Syntex, Upjohn and Merck are all reaching into chemicals. Upjohn, Searles and Smith, Kline and French are all into medical electronics, with Searle, for instance, betting on Medidata, which makes computers for futuristic mechanized mass screening devices. Parke Davis, Abbott and Cutter Labs are getting into the booming hospital supplies industry.

All this diversification by the once-staid drug manufacturers does not represent a flight from drugs. Prescription drugs remain the most profitable line of the diversified companies, and the drug habit, once established, is hard to break. In fact, the most interesting trend in the drug industry is not diversification of the old guard, but the influx of new industries, all potential drug addicts. Chemical companies are leading the way. Dow Chemicals, of Saran Wrap and napalm fame, began buying up small drug companies in 1960, and is now a major contender in the measles vaccine market. Other chemical newcomers are 3M (formerly Minnesota Mining and Manufacturing, the conglomerate which makes, among other things, Scotch Tape), Rohm and Haas, Union Carbide, Malinckrodt and DuPont. Cosmetic and soap companies, such as Bristol Meyers, Colgate Palmolive, and Helene Curtis are not far behind in the rush for the drug markets. Revlon now owns U.S. Vitamin and Pharmaceuticals; Cheeseborough, Pond has acquired Pertussin. One other industry which is being invaded by the drug firms has begun a counteroffensive, the medical supplies industry. Baxter, Becton-Dickinson and Johnson and Johnson have all bought into the drug industry.

You don't have to be a member of the chemical/drug/cosmetics axis to get in on the drug action. For instance, American Home Products, Inc., maker of Boyardee foods, Gulden's mustard and Gay-pet products for animals also serves up nonprescription drugs such as Preparation H, Quiet World (a tranquilizer) and Sudden Action (breath freshener), and has become a big shot in the ethical drug world, owning Wyeth Labs as well as several smaller drug companies. Then there's Squibb-Beechnut which makes gum, babyfoods, candy, coffee, pastry, airlines' meals and operates drive-ins and snack bars, in addition to prescription drugs. Anybody who makes anything which can be swallowed, inhaled, absorbed or applied would like to make drugs . . . and vice versa.

Hospital Supplies and Equipment

The story of the growth of the hospital supplies industry is the story of the explosive growth of the hospital as the central institution in the delivery of health care in America. In 1950 the nation spent $3.8 billion on hospital care. By 1965, the figure had risen to $13.8 billion, and in 1969, three years after Medicare and Medicaid, hospital expenditures were running at a $20 billion a year clip. About $7.5 billion of this went for goods and services. Much of it's mundane — food, bed linen, and dust mops, but billions went for more specifically medical equipment, from scalpels, syringes and catheters to X-ray equipment, electronic blood cell counters, and artificial kidneys. In addition to the hospital market, physicians, dentists, nursing homes, and medical research labs spend huge sums, measured in the billions of dollars, on similar supplies.

The risks in the hospital supply industry appear to be as low as the profits are high. Medicaid may have its ups and downs, but Medicare, at least, is here to stay. And only a gambler with a compulsion for losing would bet against the likelihood of continued growth in hospital expenditures and increased subsidy of the market by the government. The hospital supply companies have gotten the message. "The start of IPCO's new financial year on July 1, 1966," said the annual report of one of the major distributors and manufacturers of hospital goods, "also marked the beginning of the Federal Medicare program and supplementary state health programs [Medicaid]. The enormous increase in demand for institutional care . . . will, we believe, create a growing demand for the type of products IPCO distributes and manufactures." Like the man said, in the last dozen years IPCO's earnings have increased at a compound annual rate of 22 percent. In the same vein, an executive of the paper manufacturer of Kimberly-Clark, which has applied its technology to disposable bed linen and uniforms for hospitals, said, "The type of care usually provided under Medicare is the type that creates new opportunities for disposables." In 1951, $14 million worth of disposable products (including needles, syringes, and such standbys as paper plates) were sold. By 1965, the last pre-Medicare year, the market hit $100 million, and 1970 sales are expected to reach $300 million.

The stock market has been hot on the track. The month Medicare went into operation, stockbrokers Burnham and Co. prepared an analysis of the industry for their customers. One year later, the Value Line Investment Survey spoke of one hospital supply company as "operating in a sector of the economy that is virtually recession-proof." (The company, American Hospital Supply, has seen its earnings grow at 16 percent per year for the last decade. In the first half of 1969, earnings were up 19 percent over the corresponding period of 1968.) And despite the Medicaid flip-flops United Business Service listed eight hospital supply companies on its fall 1969 list of 200 top-growth stocks.

The traditional hospital supply companies — C. R. Bard, Becton-Dickinson, Baxter Labs, Sherwood Medical, Johnson and Johnson, IPCO, and American Hospital Supply — have been the big winners in the Medicare sweepstakes, with earnings up 15 percent to 25 percent a year over the last few years. But the soaring profits and wide-open market are attracting new contenders, as well. Through acquisitions of existing hospital supply companies or through applying the technology of other markets to medical supplies, many of the big guns of American industry are out for a piece of the pie. 3M Company is getting in through its mastery of cellophane — it makes peel-open packages of sterile surgical supplies as well as surgical tapes and drapes and masks. Soapmaker Procter and Gamble goes for germicidal soaps and cleansers, rubbermaker B. F. Goodrich for anti-bacterial mattresses, and chemical company W. R. Grace for carbon dioxide absorbants for anesthesiology. Other big non-medical companies buying in are, for instance, American Cyanamid and the Brunswick Corporation (a conglomerate). Companies with past experience in medical technology are especially active, with such big drug companies as Smith, Kline and French, Searle, Parke Davis, Abbott, and Warner Lambert going into everything from blood bank equipment to cardiac pacemakers.

Supplies aren't the only thing booming in the hospital products industry. Medical electronics is moving out of the realm of science fiction and into the *Wall Street Journal*. A convergence of several factors has created a market currently running at about $350 milion a year and expected to reach $1–$1.5 billion a year by the mid-1970's. For one thing, hospitals are buried under an increasing patient load. The volume of every service, from laundry to lab tests, from medical record-keeping to financial record-keeping, from diagnosis to intra-hospital communications, is growing at a staggering rate. At the same time, the cost of the labor to perform these functions is rising sharply, under the impact of the hospital workers' unionization movement, newly applicable minimum wage legislation, and an acute shortage of skilled medical manpower. The need of hospitals for cost-cutting technology has created a good sales pitch for the industry.

At the same time, years of government expenditures on defense and on medical research are flowering into a wealth of new technology to apply to hos-

pitals. The new technology is expensive — out of reach of the solo practitioner — but the large hospital has both the volume to effectively use it and the financial resources to afford it. And the costs can be passed along to the government in the form of Medicare and Medicaid depreciation allowances. "Medicare is the computer manufacturer's friend," exults one trade journal.

Finally, some sectors of the electronics industry, at least, are under pressure to find new markets. The aerospace industry, for one, is in a trough, with NASA expenditures on the decline since 1965, Vietnam production past its 1968 peak, and a lag in new orders from the commercial airlines. Health — another government subsidized market — looks like a good pasture to head for.

One big chunk of the hospital electronic market is in computers. There are three types: general computers for business use (billing, accounting, payrolls, etc.); small machines built into other apparatuses (such as patient monitors); and computers for medical information and practice (diagnosis, medical record-keeping, and "total hospital information systems"). This last type of computer has not grown as rapidly as expected, due in part to the inherent irrationality of many hospital operations. (Installation of a major computer must be preceded by a thorough systems analysis of the hospital and rationalization of its procedures — often by experts supplied by the computer company.)

Most of the major computer companies are out for a share in the hospital market. They are joined by such outsiders as United Aircraft, Lockheed, Motorola, Xerox, and American Optical. Industry spokesmen estimate that upwards of a billion dollars' worth of computers will have been installed in hospitals by 1975.

The general medical electronics industry is growing even more rapidly. Practically everybody who knows an oscilloscope from a stethoscope is out for this one — Litton Industries, GE, International Rectifier, TRW, RCA, Varian and Siemens, among the big ones. Perhaps the most intriguing product is produced by Fairchild Space and Defense Systems Division of Fairchild Camera and Instrument. It's a "foreign body locator" patterned after mine detectors, for locating pieces of shrapnel bullets, or the safety pin baby has swallowed. As with the parent electronics industry, a plethora of smaller companies like those lining Route 128 around Boston are appearing on the fringes. Hospital journals feature ads for such companies as Astro Associates, Spacelabs, Inc., Laser Systems and Electronics, Inc., and Medidata Services, Inc.

Like drugs in an earlier era, medical electronics has the potential to revolutionize medical practice. At one level, new vistas in diagnosis and treatment are opened up by the electron microscope, fiber optics, high energy radiation sources, computer analysis of electrocardiograms, and the like. At a second level, the potentials of computer diagnosis may lead to new roles for the doctor and other health workers. Finally, the need for systems analysis to accompany the fully effective use of computers may have fallout in the form of partial rationalizations of hospital operations. There is no guarantee, of course, that any of these changes will work to the favor of the patient. Like the drug companies' "me too" drugs, innovations may rebound mainly to the favor of the manufacturers.

Health Insurance

The growth of private health insurance is superficially one of the great success stories of American business. In 1940 only 12 million Americans had the most common form of medical insurance, coverage for hospital expenses. By 1967, no less than 175 million, or 83 percent of the civilian population, were covered by private hospital insurance. 100 million of these were covered by commercial, profit-making insurance companies, the rest by Blue Cross, Blue Shield, and independent plans. Many of these subscribers were insured for other kinds of medical expenses than hospitalization, as well. The private companies collected premiums totaling $5.86 billion and paid out $4.84 billion in benefits, administrative and selling expenses comprising much of the remainder.

Demand for health services has risen sharply since the forties, just as the cost of those services skyrocketed beyond the reach of the average consumer. Some sort of insurance against the financial catastrophe of getting sick has become a necessity. Meanwhile, the courts were recognizing fringe benefits as a legitimate area for collective bargaining, and mass purchasers of health insurance in the form of union and employer health and welfare plans emerged. For these reasons, the health insurance industry grew explosively in the late 1940s and early 1950s. By now more than a thousand companies, mainly life insurance companies, write health insurance. But the business is still dominated by a few giants: eight companies do almost two thirds of the business.

The companies get a huge gross income from their health insurance business, but the profit picture is a bit muddy. Insurance companies earn money in two ways: directly, from premiums paid by consumers, and indirectly, from the investment of premiums in corporate and government securities. On a direct sales of health insurance to individuals, the companies generally make an underwriting profit. But on group policies (e.g., policies covering all the employees of a certain firm), the industry claims to lose money overall — about a quarter of a billion dollars in 1967. And the investment income which the companies attribute to their health insurance business is, according to their claim, barely adequate to cover the underwriting loss.

Don't believe that the industry is writing health insurance for charity, though. Industry-wide, the companies take an apparent underwriting loss, but most of the bigger companies report substantial profits. The losses probably reflect the trouble smaller companies have had in predicting expenses in the face of escalating medical prices. Industry giants, such as Equitable, Prudential, Metropolitan, have all showed net underwriting gains over the last five years. And the two big companies that did not, Aetna and Connecticut General, had one bad year that outweighed substantial gains in the other years.

The real profits in health insurance may be very different. Insurance companies are good jugglers. Almost all companies link sales of health insurance to sales of life insurance, sometimes refusing to sell the one without the other. Thus the problems of allocating profits and costs between individual life, group life, individual health, group health and various other kinds of policies are enough to turn even an honest accountant's hair grey.

Finally, the insurance companies see health insurance, in the words of one insurance executive, as "not so much a separate product but rather another of the client's needs." In many cases, health insurance is thrown in at a low price as a sweetener or "loss leader" for a highly profitable package including life insurance, disability, and even casualty insurance. The industry trade journals are full of such success stories as "Health Insurance — the Door Opener," and "Company Growth through Health Insurance."

For all these reasons, it is hard to say anything quantitative about the profits in the business. But health insurance is clearly an important component of the overall business of the life insurance companies. Health premiums alone account for 15–45 percent of the total gross income (including investments and all sorts of premiums) of the major companies. The entire life insurance industry had an after-tax income in 1967 of $9.1 billion, and had assets of $180 billion. The availability of such huge funds for investment makes control of the top companies a major source of corporate wealth and power. The health insurance business thus represents a significant piece of a very large pie indeed.

Despite its great size, the health insurance industry is about as functional as a dinosaur. Most Americans do have some kind of basic hospitalization insurance, but relatively few are covered for other medical expenses (40 percent for home or office physician visits, 9 percent for nursing home care, 2 percent for dental expenses). Moreover, the insurance companies, along with their non-profit buddy, Blue Cross, are caught in a cost squeeze: as prices for medical services rise, either the cost of insurance must go up or the expenses covered must be limited. Since commercial insurance companies set their premiums according to the medical experience of the individual group they are insuring, it is the elderly and other relatively high-risk groups who are squeezed out first.

The first consequence of the failures of commercial insurance came in 1965 when the companies were forced to relinquish older customers to Medicare. The companies' screams in response to Medicare had something of a theatrical quality. After all, the companies were ridding themselves of their least profitable customers. In fact, the year following Medicare saw a drop in company premiums but a much larger drop in benefit payments to consumers. But, as one company official said, "Most of us feel the loss of the over-65 market is not the important thing, but rather what Medicare will do to the business in 10 or 15 years." They feared that "Medicare has brought the country a giant step closer to socialized medicine" which could "all but eliminate the need for health insurance as it is sold today." According to *The New York Times*, the companies, "generally inspired more by the wish to discourage government expansion of Medicare than by the desire for the business that would be generated," cooperated with the government in setting up the program. About fifteen companies now serve as intermediaries in the administration of the program.

By 1968 it was again becoming evident that the health insurance companies were not able to provide adequate protection for many Americans. Under the influence of problems affecting other aspects of the insurance industry and under pressure from consumer groups, the companies' attitudes toward the government were shifting. Some industry figures openly hoped that the government would serve as guarantor of the companies' market rather than as a competitor. One plan for national health insurance, for instance, would have used government funds to subsidize the purchase of private health insurance by employers and employees. According to the president of Aetna: "A program of universal health insurance offers one way to spread the cost of medical care [between employer, employee and government]. It could be structured to retain the advantages of competition and the profit incentive. . . . I have full confidence in our ability to work successfully in partnership with government."

Nursing Homes and Hospitals

The age-old way of profiting from illness is by selling health services themselves. Doctors have always done it; so have what are called "proprietary" (profit-making) hospitals and nursing homes. During all the fuss about glamorous health hardware and electronics industries, old-fashioned health service profiteering hasn't been going out of style. If anything, nursing homes and hospital chains have become, at least to the adventurous investor, the hottest things going in the entire health industry, if not the entire stock market. Brokers and investment advisors liken the current boom in nursing homes and hospital chains to the boom in bowling alleys a few years ago or to that in computer software and fried chicken drive-ins today. In 1969 the nursing home industry, almost all of which is proprietary, grossed $2.8 billion, up 21 percent over 1968 and up 529 percent from 1960. Proprietary hospitals trailed with $720 million in total "sales."

Only four years ago, the nursing home and hospital business was still a cottage industry. A family added a wing to their home and called it a nursing home. A doctor or group of doctors bought and ran their own hospital for their own patients. Four years ago, only five nursing homes and one hospital company were "publicly owned," i.e., sold stock on the open market. Now there are 50 publicly owned nursing home companies and six hospital companies. For both hospital and nursing home chains profits are running at about 5 percent of "sales," after taxes.

What put the profit into the traditionally "charitable" nursing home and hospital business? Medicare, more than anything else, is underwriting the boom. The expansion of Blue Cross and commercial insurance coverage has helped, of course, to create hosts of paying customers for the health service business. Clever management is another factor. Nursing home and hospital companies are able to cut costs through economies of scale, such as bulk purchasing for an entire chain of facilities, centralized administration, etc. But the voluntary (private, nonprofit) health sector also did much to set the stage for the entrance of the energetic profit-makers. Local voluntary hospital establishments, working with Blue Cross and the regional health planning agency, have done much to keep down the number of hospital and nursing home beds — creating a shortage which the profit-makers are eagerly filling.

Nursing homes are the ideal way to cash in on Medicare and Medicaid. Every oldster is at least partially covered and every oldster is a potential customer. Some of the largest publicly owned nursing home companies are: Extendicare, Four Seasons Nursing Centers of America, Medicenters of America (a franchise system owned by Holiday Inns), and American Automated Vending Corp. All are expanding: for instance, Four Seasons projects 100 additional homes per year. Some buy existing homes; others build their own. Some operate their own homes; others are selling franchises.

If hotels are profitable, nursing homes ought to be profitable. But hospitals would seem to be another matter. Costs are wild; manpower is scarce and frequently irascible; funds are unreliable. To make a profit out of hospitals, you would have to forget all the old voluntary-sector inhibitions about hospitals as "a sacred trust" and a public service. This is exactly what the new hospital companies are doing: They select well-to-do neighborhoods and turn away any nonpaying patients who might find their way in. They avoid outpatient and emergency services insofar as possible. They encourage short-term patients in order to gain a high turnover rate (the first few days in the hospital pay the most). They avoid expensive and difficult technology, by concentrating on simple illnesses and elective surgery, and by contracting out for services such as pathology and radiology.

Wherever they spring up, profit-making hospitals offer stiff competition for the local voluntaries. First they sell stock to local doctors, guaranteeing themselves a large medical staff and plenty of private patients. And of course the doctor/stockholders have a special interest in keeping the hospital running efficiently and profitably. Once in operation, the profit-maker skims off the cream of the local patient crop from nearby voluntaries — the not-too-sick, able-to-pay patients. Having cut costs in all the ways listed above, the profit-maker is then able to lure nurses away from local voluntaries by offering higher salaries.

What's most insulting is for a profit-maker to parasitize off a local voluntary — setting up shop near a voluntary which can handle patient-rejects and unprofitable services like obstetrics and outpatient care. This happened recently in Fort Myers, Florida, where the Hospital Corporation of America (HCA) decided to locate a new 150-bed profit-maker near the already-underutilized voluntary Lee Memorial Hospital. When Lee Memorial protested against being left with the dregs of the patient supply, HCA president responded, "As proprietary hospitals we pay taxes. These taxes help support the tax-supported hospitals [voluntaries] which are in business to care for the nonpaying patient and were established for that purpose." Lee Memorial never intended to be that charitable, and is ganging up with the local power structure to drive out Nashville-based HCA. A recent *Fort Myers News Press* editorial was entitled, "No Fast-Buck Hospital Needed Here."

If the hospital boom continues, it is likely to run into more and more organized opposition from voluntaries. Much of the opposition will be, on the surface at least, on moral grounds, although it is not clear why profits made by hospitals are any less "moral" than profits made by drug and hospital supply companies. The voluntary hospital leaders in many localities may be especially resentful because the men who head up hospital companies are not, by and large, the kind of men who would ever be chosen as trustees and directors of voluntaries. American Medicorp, which does business primarily in the South and Midwest, was founded by a couple of young Jewish lawyers from the North. The chairman and founder of HCA is an ex-retail druggist who made his first fortune in the Kentucky Fried Chicken chain of drive-ins. To fight the profit-making intruders, voluntaries may have to swallow their traditional antipathy to government "interference," and lobby for tougher laws regulating licensing and operation of hospitals.

In case government regulation is in the cards, many profit-making hospital companies are already one step ahead of the game — busily diversifying into hospital-related businesses. Beverly Enterprises, which owns 18 hospitals and nursing homes, is forming Career Development Corp., to train health personnel at a profit. Metrocare Enterprises, owner of nine acute-care hospitals, has purchased a construction firm and plans to build complete medical centers. Other companies are developing firms to provide ancillary services to hospitals. For instance, American Medical Enterprises, Inc. owns Cario-Pulmonary Services of America, Inc. (inhalation therapy); American Medicorp, Inc. has purchased Metropolitan Diagnostic Labs, Inc.

Coming from the other direction, a number of outside companies are diversifying into the profitable nursing home and hospital field. American Hospital Supply Corp. owns American Health Facilities, Inc., which constructs and furnishes nursing homes. Computer Research, Inc., runs Mental Retardation Centers, Inc.; and Cenco Instruments, Inc. has joined a nursing home consortium in Milwaukee.

The health industry has come a long way from the days of the one-horse patent medicine peddler with his line of liver pills and elixirs. Replacing him are the mammoth internationalist drug companies, whose corporate medicine chests are increasingly likely to include hospital supplies, computers and cosmetics along with a growing profusion of pills. Health insurance, which can trace its origins to pre-trade union workers' welfare funds, is now a key element of the nation's vast insurance industry. The hospital supply industry has outgrown its Band-Aid days and is branching into catheters, computers and artificial organs. Proprietaries, which used to be the dark horse of the delivery system, are forging multi-state chains and moving into more and more investors' portfolios. Two other components of the modern health industry bear watching: the hospital construction industry and the health policy consulting business. The "health consultant" of fifty years ago was likely to be the neighborhood barber; today such consultants include defense-oriented think tanks like Rand, the Institute for Defense Analysis and Research Analysis Corporation.

The health industry has changed rapidly in the last five or ten years, that is, in the short period that the federal government has begun to play an important role in regulating and subsidizing health services and products. Changes in the future may be just as rapid and unpredictable, but two trends seem to be almost built-in: First, the health industry will move increasingly into the mainstream of American industry. Corporate giants like Dow, DuPont, TRW, Lockheed are busily staking out their claims on the profit-rich health turf. Drug companies, once the heavy-weights of the health business, will be challenged by these newcomers. Second, the health industry will be pulling itself together into a more and more integrated monolith. The drug, hospital supply and hospital equipment industries have already begun to blur into a single "health products" industry. Profit-making hospital chains are creating vertical chains including construction and supplies and equipment. Insurance companies, so far aloof from the promiscuous merging in health products, may be about to take the plunge into hospital operation, following the lead of nonprofit innovators like Kaiser and HIP.

These developments in the health industry may have more impact on health services delivery than anything that happens in the next decade of medical research. What is emerging is an increasingly unified, significant sector of the U.S. economy with a major direct stake in the organization and finances of health services. In the past, drug companies dominated the health industry and they picked up their policy line from between the drug ads in the AMA publications: up with solo, fee-for-service practice, down with government intervention of any sort. There's more to the health industry today than drugs, and many of the booming newcomers have market perspectives which reach far beyond the traditional, doctor-centered delivery system. And diversification into Medicare-subsidized, hospital-oriented products has seriously compromised the purity of the policy line of the drug companies.

It was Medicare that transformed the old bogey-man of government "interference" into a Santa Claus for the health industry. The drug industry and even the commercial insurance industry have found that they can live more than comfortably with Medicare and Medicaid. And of course it was Medicare that sent the hospital supply, equipment and proprietary chain industries spiraling giddily into a boom. Within a few years the health industry may begin to outweigh organized consumer groups as the most powerful force lobbying for increased government subsidy for health services. The industry's interest, however, will be in subsidy with a minimum of regulation, as outlined, for instance, in some of the current proposals for a national health insurance. With national health insurance, the health industry could settle down to the kind of guaranteed security which the defense and aerospace industries enjoyed during the heyday of cold war spending.

When it comes to the health services delivery system, the health industry is again likely to line up with the medical "liberals" as opposed to the AMA-rear-guard. Although only the proprietaries (hospitals and nursing homes) actually deliver services themselves, all segments of the health industry have an interest in increasing the productivity and efficiency of the delivery system. Insurance companies, which foot part of the bill, want to see health services become cheaper, or at least to see people utilize more of the cheaper services (e.g., clinic visits, as opposed to hospital stays). Drug and supply and equipment dealers have an interest in increasing the total volume of health services delivered, since, for almost every provider/consumer encounter, a prescription is written, equipment is used, or a disposable is disposed of. This interest is not compatible with a fixation on solo physician practice — the least productive means for delivering health services. In fact, as far as the industry is concerned, there is no reason why the dispenser of drugs or the user of supplies and equipment should be a physician at all. The health industry may eventually join the ultra-liberal faction of the medical world in advocating group practice and extensive use of paraprofessionals (if not machines) in direct patient contacts.

The hospital equipment industry has an even more immediate interest in the development of more centralized, institutionalized health services delivery systems. The market for heavy hardware such as computers, patient-monitoring devices, multi-phasic screening equipment, etc., is necessarily health facilities which serve a large number of patients — rather than private offices. Furthermore, in order to absorb such equipment, health facilities must be moderately rational in their internal operations. (There's no point in getting a computer unless some of the hospital's operations are at least rational enough to program into it.) Looking beyond the individual facility, computer and electronics companies even have an interest in rationality at the regional level, i.e., in the development of multi-facility, regionally integrated health systems. The multi-hospital medical empire is the ideal market for computers to book admissions, for super-specialty hardware, and

for TV systems to link outposts with centralized technical staff.

The danger in increasingly centralized, institutionalized health delivery networks is, of course, that they will eventually get wise to the health products industry. Bulk buyers of pills, supplies and equipment could begin to exert significant leverage over prices and quality even before government regulation becomes a serious threat. However, if government subsidy of the health services delivery system is generous enough, hospitals will probably go on as they are now — hardly bothering to ask the price of pills and supplies. So long as the government is standing by to pick up the tab, the health industry's interest is in a delivery system which is boundlessly productive and mindlessly extravagant: organ transplants should be prescribed as frequently as tranquilizers are today; normal people should periodically have their blood cleaned out with an artificial kidney machine; "search and destroy" operations should become part of normal diagnostic work-ups; and so on.

To say that the health industry has an interest in a certain kind of delivery system is one thing; whether it can do anything about it is another question. So far the answer is yes — the health industry is developing increasingly effective ways of influencing public and private policy in health services delivery. At the most obvious level, the very existence of equipment which can be used only in hospitals, of insurance which can be used only in hospitals, of insurance which can be used only for hospital care, etc., gives hospitals an edge over non-institutional delivery modes. At the level of government policy, the health industry can always join oil as an industry-wide lobby, testify in Congressional hearings, etc. Already, health industry people are beginning to show up regularly on important governmental panels and commissions. For instance, the McNerney Task-force on Medicaid and National Health insurance includes the Director of Prudential Life Insurance Company. New York's 1966 Piel Commission, which was the launching pad for New York City's new Health and Hospitals Corporation (a public authority set up to run the municipal hospitals) included the chairman of the board of the Systems Development Corporation, a leading consulting firm in health.

There are more direct and intimate ways in which the health industry influences and interacts with the delivery system. Trustees and upper-level staff of medical schools and hospitals are always welcome on the boards and top staffs of health industry firms. Many hospital and medical school professionals moonlight as consultants to the health industry, thus acting as human bonds between the two worlds. Consulting in the other direction, industry to nonprofit delivery institutions, is more important in terms of volume and potential policy impact. For instance, Technomics Corporation, a consulting firm with links to the defense hardware industry, did much of the staff work for the Piel Commission. [Ed.: The Piel Commission recommended the formation of a nonprofit public corporation to assume administrative responsibility for New York City's public hospitals. The plan was implemented in 1970.] Another consultant, MacKinsey Corp., is under contract to get the New York City Hospital Corporation off the ground. Interestingly enough, such consultants' recommendations invariably feature heavy use of computers and other expensive hardware.... And as hospitals install more and more sophisticated "sys-tems," executives with backgrounds in health industry firms are increasingly moving into jobs in hospital administration.

No one seems to be too alarmed about the growing rapport between the health industry and the health services delivery system. Far from it, it's become fashionable to look to the profit-motivated health industrial forces to lead the way out of the health services crisis. According to this view, what's been wrong with health services all along is that they've been isolated from the business world, cut off from "hard-headed management thinking," and of course, without the profit motive, "unstimulated to really produce." But there is no reason yet to trust that the "rationalizations" that the health industry brings to health services will look like rationalizations to the consumer. Judging from America's experience with the drug industry — the consumer can expect no mercy from the new Medical-Industrial Complex.

NATIONAL HEALTH INSURANCE: THE GREAT LEAP SIDEWAYS

John Ehrenreich and Oliver Fein

Many now expect some kind of national health insurance program soon in the United States. Will it solve our health problems? In this selection Ehrenreich and Fein forcefully argue, within the radical perspective, that national health insurance will make relatively little difference — an important step in some respects, but with marginal impact on many of our most basic health problems.

Both have worked with Health-PAC in New York. Ehrenreich now teaches at the State University of New York at Old Westbury. Fein, a medical doctor, works both at Health-PAC and in medicine.

Source: "National Health Insurance: The Great Leap Sideways," by John Ehrenreich and Oliver Fein, from *Social Policy* (January/February 1971), Vol. 1, No. 5, pp. 5–9. Published by Social Policy Corporation, New York, N.Y. 10010. Copyright 1971 by Social Policy Corporation.

It is evident that the inadequate delivery of health care — to the poor, in particular — is one of the most pressing of America's domestic crises. There are, in fact, two health crises: one shortchanging consumers, the other crippling suppliers.

The present system fails to deliver adequate medical services to its users at any price. Both middle-class and lower-class clients have begun to raise many of the same questions, prompted by soaring costs, long waits in overcrowded waiting rooms, and a growing awareness that despite the wonders of heart transplants, it is increasingly difficult to find a doctor to treat ordinary ills. Poor people — Black and Puerto Rican community groups, in particular — go so far as to demand control over health institutions they hold directly responsible for what they perceive as services wholly unaccountable and irresponsive to the pressing health needs of the community. Medical care, they say, is fragmented and isolated from the social, economic, and environmental causes of pathology; the services are little more than a supply store for "teaching material" and subjects for medical experiments.

Those who provide and pay for health care face a different crisis, namely, the breakdown of the old systems of financing. The hospitals are near collapse as costs skyrocket and financing fails to keep pace. This threatens not only the institutions themselves but also the multibillion-dollar drug and hospital supply companies that depend on the hospitals as a retail outlet for their products. At the same time that the hospitals weep over "inadequate" funds, the providers of funds groan under the weight of the hospitals. Blue Cross is forced to raise its rates and face its enraged subscribers. The trade unions find themselves having to allocate an ever-increasing portion of wage hikes to medical care merely to maintain their present level of health benefits. Employee health plans cut an ever-bigger bite out of corporate profits. Even the government feels the pinch as Medicare and Medicaid costs knock the budget for a loop.

Since the providers respond only to that part of the overall problem they themselves directly experience, they tend generally to ignore the consumers' experience of crisis. The various plans for health insurance proposed by such groups and figures as the AMA, the late Walter Reuther, the AFL-CIO, Nelson Rockefeller, Blue Cross President Walter McNerney, the American Hospital Association, and Senators Javits and Kennedy are all equally careless of the prospective patients, who become simply "programs" to put the financing of medical care on a sounder basis. The debated issues — coverage, benefits, sources of financing, administrative mechanisms, etc. — all attempt to answer just one question: how to finance existing services.

What is most significant about the current wave of national health insurance proposals is the strength of the army forming to force them through. Proposals for national health insurance are not at all new to the nation's health history. In 1914, the American Association for Labor Legislation submitted a model plan to state legislatures across the country; not a single state acted. In 1935, national health insurance was successfully kept out of the Social Security Act, largely by AMA pressure. Another plan, the Wagner-Murray-Dingle Bill, proposed in 1943 without Ad-

ministration support, never made it out of Congressional committee. Again, in 1948, the bill was pushed, this time with backing from President Truman; but it died in committee. It was only in 1965 that a nationwide health insurance scheme (Medicare), limited in coverage to the elderly, was adopted. Now labor, management, the hospitals, Blue Cross, the companies that manufacture and sell hospital supplies, and local and state governments all see one or another brand of national health insurance as a solution to their own special health-care crises.

Why National Health Insurance?

Labor wants national health insurance to eliminate the hassle at the bargaining table over health fringe benefits. In 1965, in the steel industry, 19 cents an hour, or 4 percent of the average steelworker's total wages and benefits, went for health and life insurance. Today, because medical prices have risen two to three times as fast as prices in general, as much as 8 to 10 percent of any new wage and benefits package must go to health and life insurance, just to maintain existing benefits. At a time when the real disposable income of American workers has stopped growing for the first time in 35 years (due largely to inflation and increased taxes because of the Vietnam war), labor is desperate to find ways to augment workers' wages. Relegating health insurance to the government would leave more dollars and cents for wage increases.

Management also wants national health insurance, because health insurance premiums have become a significant and rapidly rising component of overall labor costs. Although management is not unified on the issue, those that count in big business and industry are certainly for it.

Of the medical-industrial complex, the hospital supply and equipment companies, the medical electronics and computer companies, and at least those drug companies that are diversified and produce hospital supplies would all benefit from national health insurance. Their experience with Medicare and Medicaid has been profitable. As *Value Line Investment Survey* points out, because of programs like Medicare the hospital supply industry is "operating in a sector of the economy that is virtually recession-proof." The annual report of one major hospital supply company announces: "The enormous increase in demand for institutional care (caused by Medicare) will, we believe, create a growing demand for the type of products IPCO distributes and manufactures." National health insurance, like Medicare before it, would provide the dollars to guarantee the demand.

For the voluntary (private, nonprofit) hospitals, almost any program of national health insurance would be better than the present Medicaid program. Eligibility has become so restricted under Medicaid that many patients are no longer covered. That leaves the hospitals stuck with the bills of patients who are too well off for Medicaid but too poor to pay. A national health insurance program would allow the possibility of universal coverage without eligibility restrictions. Equally important, national health insurance would stabilize hospital income by guaranteeing a certain level of reimbursement. The government would be reluctant to cut a program that affected a large cross section of Americans. Of course, the voluntary hospitals would prefer a plan that merely subsidized their operations, with minimal interference from government. But almost any form of national insurance would be better than none.

Blue Cross/Blue Shield, the fiscal intermediary of the voluntary hospitals, wants a particular brand of national health insurance: one that would expand Blue Cross hegemony over the health insurance market. Although Blue Cross enrollment has burgeoned in recent decades, its percentage of the health insurance market has been declining. In 1945, Blue Cross claimed 61 percent of the hospital insurance market, compared with the commercial insurance companies' 33 percent. Today, those figures are reversed for the population under age 65, Blue Cross garnering only 34 percent of the hospital insurance market, compared with the commercial carriers' 60 percent. However, Medicare and Medicaid gave Blue Cross a big boost, since virtually every state turned over administration of its program to Blue Cross. It is just such a relationship with national health insurance that Blue Cross would like to foster. With Walter McNerney, president of the Blue Cross Association of America, serving as chairman of the President's task force to investigate national health insurance, there is little doubt that Blue Cross's interests will be represented.

Parenthetically, it should be noted that even the commercial insurance companies are not totally opposed to national health insurance. The president of Aetna has said: "A program of universal health insurance . . . could be structured to retain the advantages of competition and the profit incentive. . . . I have full confidence in our ability to work successfully in partnership with government."

Finally, local and state governments see rising costs for their health programs (state and city hospitals, Medicaid, etc.) as an unlimited drain on already scarce funds. Any program that shifts part of the burden from their backs is welcome. As a result, even the most ardent states' righters voted enthusiastically to support New York Governor Nelson Rockefeller's national health insurance proposals at the 1969 National Governors Conference.

To reiterate: this newly forming coalition of labor, management, parts of the medical-industrial complex, the voluntary hospitals, Blue Cross, and local governments that supports national health insurance actually takes little account of the health needs of the public. However, such an unprecedented coalition foreshadows both the inevitability of national health insurance and the form it may take.

Three Plans

Three major plans have been proposed for "universal" or "national" health insurance, and many others appear to be on the drawing boards. Each plan is best designated by the name of the individual or group that originated it: the AMA plan, the Rockefeller plan, and the Reuther plan.

The AMA plan is not really a program of national health insurance at all. Rather, it is a national system of incentives to encourage people to purchase private (commercial or Blue Cross) health insurance *voluntarily*. The incentive would be in the form of income tax credit. The AMA public relations men call it "medicredit." A person who purchased health insurance would have the right to deduct a certain fraction of the insurance premiums from his federal taxes, the percentage depending on the total tax due. The 30 percent of the population with the lowest tax liability would receive vouchers entitling them to purchase health insurance at government expense. People slightly better off might be able to count 70 percent of the dollars they paid for health insurance as if they were dollars paid in taxes. The more affluent would get credit for a smaller percentage of their premiums; and those with a very high income, and hence a very high tax liability, would get no tax credit at all. In effect, the government would be paying for a variable fraction of the health insurance people chose to buy — directly for the very poor and indirectly, by foregoing part of its tax revenues, for others.

The AMA plan would interfere least with the way medicine is now practiced. There would be no cost controls and no new administrative apparatus (both patients and providers would continue to deal directly with insurance companies). Commercial insurance companies are expected to favor the AMA plan, which would subsidize their customers but entail little risk of regulation for them.

The Rockefeller plan revolves around mandatory purchase of private health insurance (Blue Cross, Health Insurance Plan, or commercial). It differs from the AMA plan primarily in that it is compulsory and is thus "universal health insurance." Insurance premiums for working people would be paid by employer and employee contributions. Premiums for the unemployed and the poor would be paid by the government out of general tax revenues. Medicare would continue as it is. As with the AMA plan, there would be need for little in the way of a new administrative apparatus, since patients and providers would deal directly with private insurance companies. With Blue Cross and commercial insurance companies running the show, cost controls would probably be minimal.

The American Hospital Association, representing 7,000 voluntary hospitals and nursing homes, had not yet released its plan at the time of writing. It is almost certain to favor a Rockefeller-type plan. Ray Brown, past president of the AHA, has said, "We've got to find the additional support for our hospital system, and, I think, our whole medical care system, in the private sector. The one way to do this is to . . . set a national standard for minimum benefits for health coverage, then mandate . . . that every employer have this minimum coverage for everyone . . . he employs."

It is expected that the McNerney task force, representing Blue Cross, will also support a Rockefeller-type plan, just as the National Governors Conference of 1969 has already come out in favor of the Rockefeller plan.

The Reuther plan for national (rather than "universal") health insurance would be "an integral part of the national social insurance system." It would be compulsory health insurance for everyone, with the government acting as the insurer. The program would supplant most of the coverage now offered by private companies (Blue Cross and the commercial firms). The Reuther plan would be paid for by employer, employee, and government contributions: tentatively, two-thirds of the cost would come from employer-employee contributions, and one-third would come from general tax revenues. Medicaid would be eliminated, and Medicare would be integrated into the national plan. The Reuther plan, unlike the AMA and Rockefeller plans, would require a new administrative apparatus, resembling that for Medicare. Whether the government would administer the entire program itself or would turn over much of this role to private companies, such as Blue Cross (as it does with Medicare), remains to be decided.

The Reuther plan envisions comprehensive benefits, although these might be introduced in stages. Contrary to the other plans, the Reuther plan acknowledges the need for reorganization of the health-delivery system, but advances no concrete proposals beyond the vague idea of "incentives" to encourage group practice, regional planning, cost controls, etc. The proposal that $1 billion be creamed off the top of the first year's collections and allocated to solving delivery-system problems appears no more than an afterthought. And many of the forms of reorganization of the delivery system envisioned (e.g., hospital-based group practices) seem to be motivated more by their cost-saving potential than by their implications for patient care.

Regardless of these shortcomings, the Reuther plan has been dubbed the most progressive of the three and thus has attracted the support of such health liberals as Michael DeBakey, heart specialist and originator of the Regional Medical Programs; Mary Lasker, the philanthropist who guided the development of the National Institutes of Health; and Whitney Young, director of the Urban League. The AFL-CIO has not yet announced its plan, but it is expected to be similar, in most respects, to the Reuther plan.

Still other proposals are being developed. Senator Jacob Javits (R-N.Y.) is reported working with former HEW Secretary Wilbur Cohen (architect of the Medicare Program) on a proposal that will resemble Medicare. At this time it is uncertain how the Javits plan will differ from the Reuther plan. Recently, Senator Edward Kennedy (D-Mass.) sketched broad outlines for a national health insurance program that would be introduced in stages, similar to the Reuther plan, but based primarily on general tax revenues.

The More We Change . . .

Liberal critics have seen major shortcomings in all the plans advanced to date.

All the plans would reinforce the fee-for-service system. So long as doctors can choose to be reimbursed on a fee-for-service basis within a national health insurance system, this fragmented, inefficient, and costly form of delivering care will be preserved; and the political strength of this *status-quo*-oriented sector will be reinforced.

All the plans would leave the system dependent on private health insurance companies. Even the Reuther plan, in which the government is the insurance "company," would probably use Blue Cross to administer the plan.

The presently proposed national health insurance plans offer no workable and equitable mechanism for controlling costs, and would merely fuel the inflationary fire now consuming the health-care system.

Most of the proposals, including the labor-backed plans, are based on regressive methods of taxation. Flat-rate, employee-employer, payroll taxes take a bigger proportional bite out of the wages of low-paid workers than of higher-paid ones.

None of the plans makes any provision for significant consumer-community participation in program planning or budgeting.

But even these criticisms, as many medical students and younger professionals (active in organizations such as the Medical Committee for Human Rights and the Student Health Organization) have argued, beg the question. No national health *insurance* system, they point out, is going to solve the basic problems of the American health-care system. National health insurance might well be a useful reform for many Americans, helping some people pay for medical services they would otherwise not get, and shoring up some hospitals, in low-income areas, whose total collapse would be an immediate tragedy for the people of the community. But it would make no inroad on the root problems, and might even have regressive effects.

The problem is that national health insurance would be a mechanism for funneling money out of the pockets of workers and taxpayers into the hands of the people who now run (and misrun) the health-service delivery system — the doctors, the hospital administrators, and the medical-industrial complex that fattens off people's illness. It would thus strengthen those forces that insist that all health care must cen-

ter on the doctor and the hospital, rather than those that want to totally reorganize the delivery of health care.

At the same time, national health insurance would throw a cloud over what was really happening. To liberals, for whom national health insurance has long been a goal, it might appear that the problems of the medical system were being solved. Middle-class doubts about the organization of care might quiet down temporarily if part of the bill were paid by someone else. An aura of goodwill and liberalism would surround President Nixon. The accelerating movement for more fundamental reorganization of the medical-care system for the great majority of poor and middle-class people would be defused, at least for a while.

The hopes of some insurance-plan advocates that the medical-care system could be reorganized through incentives linked to the insurance scheme's repayment system would almost certainly be dashed. For example, one plan has proposed giving hospitals incentives to operate efficiently. This might save money; but at best it would have no effect on the patterns of care in the institutions, on the relations of the institution to the community on the quality of care, etc. In fact, unless very stringent community controls were introduced, the likely result would be that the hospital would cut down on service in order to save money and pick up its incentive reward. For another thing, economic incentives can conquer only economic obstacles to change. They have no power over the other pillars of the two-class medical system. For example, economic incentives might encourage a hospital to be more economical, but they would be unlikely to persuade a hospital to accept community control, or to convince $50,000-a-year doctors to put care of the indigent ahead of prestigious research. Finally, incentives are slow. We can't wait 20 or 30 years just to get doctors into group practices.

Furthermore, national health insurance, as we have seen in the past few years with respect to Medicaid and Medicare, might well feed galloping medical inflation. The mechanisms are clear: the medical establishment, which commands the use of the funds, employs them for its own priorities — prestigious and expensive and "interesting" medical technology, and high salaries for doctors and administrators. As a result, Medicare and Medicaid costs soared, while patient care improved only slightly, if at all. We still have no workable cost-control law, land we continue to confront hospital administrators whose impulse seems to be to cut costs at the expense of patients and hospital workers. It is entirely conceivable that by 1975, under a national health insurance scheme, the nation will be spending $90 billion a year instead of the present $60 billion for health services, and $200 a day for a hospital bed, without realizing any significant improvement in the quality of care for the average citizen.

The problem with national health insurance is, in a very real sense, that it would be, literally, national health insurance — that is, the application of *public* funds to defray the costs of *private* services. No matter how liberal such an insurance mechanism might be, and no matter how hard the public insurers tried to persuade the controllers of the private delivery system to change that system, no attempt would be made to take control away from them. This eliminates the key issues from discussion about the health system right from the start.

The only way to effect fundamental change in the health system so that it will provide adequate, dignified care for all is to take power over health care away from the people who now control it. National health insurance would *not* be a move in the direction of a national health *system;* it would be more of a shuffle sideways.

AWAY WITH ALL PESTS

Joshua Horn

This selection provides a vision of a different relationship between health care and the larger society. When the People's Republic of China was established in 1949, the Chinese suffered many of the health problems common to underdeveloped countries. They mobilized themselves, in both common and ingenious ways, to attack those problems. Horn tells here the story of some of their successes. In the United States, the wealthiest country in the world, epidemics of venereal disease persist. In China, one of the poorest when it began its revolution thirty years ago, venereal disease has been conquered. Socialism makes a difference.

The selection comes from Horn's classic book by the same title. He spent many years as a doctor in China, one of the few Westerners not only privileged to remain there after the revolution but also to continue working with the Chinese in a fully productive capacity.

The History of Venereal Disease in China

Until 1504, venereal disease was unknown in China, and this was not because it had not yet been cor-

Source: From *Away with All Pests* by Joshua Horn. Copyright © 1971, Monthly Review Press. Reprinted with permission of Monthly Review Press.

rectly diagnosed, for at that time Chinese Traditional Medicine was already well advanced and hundreds of diseases had been accurately described in manuscripts which are still extant.

In that year, the old colonialists introduced syphilis into Canton and it soon spread widely throughout the whole land.

Syphilis is a "social disease" — that is, a disease whose incidence and spread (and, as we shall see, its decline and eradication) are dependent on social and political factors. What were the political and social factors responsible for the hold it gained in China?

Firstly, imperialism and colonialism, the forcible occupation of her territory by invading countries, the subjugation of her people and the wrecking of her economy. In 1877, more than three hundred years after the introduction of syphilis into Canton, the British Admiral in Shanghai, concerned about the mounting incidence of venereal disease among the sailors under his command, summoned his Surgeon-Commander and between them they devised a scheme to protect them. They instituted a totally illegal system of compulsory medical examination of prostitutes with a fee for examination and a money fine for non-compliance. In the first year the revenue from fines and fees totalled 2,590 taels of silver. But the syphilis rate was unchanged.

Secondly, war, inseparable from imperialism and from the fragmentation of Chinese society consequent upon it.

Invading armies, and indigenous armies in the service of exploiters and oppressors, habitually loot, ravage and rape. They become infected with syphilis and they spread syphilis. The Kuomintang armies had a syphilis rate of about twenty percent.[1] The incidence of syphilis in Chinese villages was directly proportional to the size and the duration of stay of invading US, Japanese and Kuomintang armies.

Thirdly, poverty, a result of feudal and capitalist exploitation and of the economic backwardness and insecurity they caused.

The editorial of the National Medical Journal of China for September 1920, entitled "Vice, Famine and Poverty," reads as follows:

"... The year 1920, will, we fear, be marked by much suffering, especially in the North where the long drought killed most of the crops and thus brought 20 *million* people to the verge of starvation. The present famine will swell the ranks of slave girls and prostitutes." [2]

Fourthly, drug addiction. Until the British East India Company sent the first big shipment of Indian-grown opium into China in 1781, the drug was almost unknown in China. For many years before then, British merchants had bought Chinese tea, silk, cotton-textiles, porcelain and manufactured goods of a quality and variety unknown elsewhere, but in return, China imported very little. Replying to a proposal for wider trade, the Emperor Chien Lung wrote to King George III of England: "We possess all things. I set no value on things strange or ingenious and have no use for your country's manufactures." So the British merchants had to pay for China's exports in the silver which they had obtained by selling slaves in silver-rich Mexico and Peru. To halt this drain on their silver, the British East India Company extended the cultivation of the opium poppy in Northern and Central India and boosted sales to China. By 1820, profits from the sale of opium accounted for twenty per cent of the revenue of the British government of India. China's annual imports of opium rose from 2,000 chests (140–160 pounds in each) in 1800 to 40,000 chests in 1838, and silver flowed out of China at such a rate that, between 1832 and 1835, twenty million ounces left the country.

In self-preservation, the Chinese rulers had to act. On 3 June, 1839, Lin Tse-hsu, the special commissioner for Canton, forced the British and American opium merchants to hand over 20,000 chests of opium which he publicly burned. The result was the First Opium War ending in the humiliating Treaty of Nanking (1842) which ceded Hong Kong, opened the door wide to imperialist penetration and guaranteed a huge and exceedingly profitable market for the sale of narcotics.

"Legal" importation of opium into China continued until 1917 and after that "illegal" importation continued until Liberation in only slightly reduced amounts and at a very much higher rate of profit.

Dr. L. T. Wu, engaged in Narcotic Control in 1920, complained: "What can Chinese government regulations do when advanced countries like Britain and the USA produce and export unlimited quantities of morphine and heroin without any question or supervision of their destination and when there are post-offices throughout China over which the Chinese Government has no control? ..." [3]

Drugs and prostitution are co-partners in depravity. Most brothels were also opium dens and the girls, who had been sold into prostitution at an early age and who were not free to leave, also became addicts and lost their will to resist.

Fifthly, an attitude to women characteristic of class society which sees women as inferior to men, as their chattels and playthings. In feudal society with its polygamy, concubinage, child-marriage and a complete absence of legal and property rights for women, there was no attempt to disguise the inequality between the sexes. In Western capitalist society, where the legal trappings of equality exist to a greater or lesser degree, the inferior status of women still persists in a concealed form, and organs for moulding public opinion, from glossy magazines to television, inculcate an obsessive preoccupation with sex and present a picture of woman as little more than the sum total of her vital statistics.

---

[1] Lai, D. G., et al. "Incidence of syphilis among Chinese Soldiers in Swatow," *Chinese Med. Journal*, 42, 557, 1928.

[2] *Nat. Med. Journ. of China*, Sept. 1920. Vol. VI, No. 3.

[3] *Nat. Med. Journ. of China*, No. 6, 1920, p. 66.

World-Wide Trends in Venereal Disease

We have seen that the spread of venereal disease in China was closely connected with policies pursued by "advanced" imperialist countries.

What was happening within these countries themselves? In 1905, Paul Ehrlich, after 606 experiments, discovered the world's first chemotherapeutic drug, Salvarsan, which he named 606. It was thought that one dose would cure syphilis and it was hailed as a beneficent contribution to civilization. Some, however, were less enthusiastic. If venereal disease can be so easily cured, they argued, then this drug will become a license for lechery; veneral disease will disappear but fornication will flourish. They need not have worried. Venereal disease did not disappear. Neither did it after Penicillin, a much more potent drug, was discovered. It takes more than drugs to eliminate syphilis just like, as the Vietnamese are showing, it takes more than weapons to win a war.

Since 1957, syphilis has continually increased in the USA where there are at least 1.2 million *untreated* cases.[4]

According to minimal official estimates, the venereal disease rate among the invading US forces in Vietnam in 1966 was ten per cent[5] although other estimates put the figure as high as forty per cent. The incidence is still increasing, for in the first six months of 1967, 46,561 *new* cases of venereal disease were reported among US troops in Vietnam as compared with 27,701 cases for the same period the previous year.[6] Venereal disease ranks highest of six major diseases among US troops in Vietnam.

There has been a huge increase in veneral disease in Australia in the past six years.

A Christchurch specialist, Dr. W. M. Platts, states that "last year sixty per cent of New Zealand girls attending VD clinics were under the age of twenty — a proportion approached only by Sweden.... In 1955 the disease seemed to be under medical control ... but since then the incidence of gonorrhoea has passed the peak reached in the 1930s. It had risen not only in New Zealand but in most parts of the world."

VD in Britain, especially among teenagers, has been rising alarmingly and is now the second largest group of notifiable diseases after measles. The incidence of gonorrhoea doubled in a decade and that of infectious syphilis trebled in the six years up to 1965. Venereologist Dr. Catterall of the Middlesex Hospital, London, describes the world-wide epidemic of venereal disease as "one of the major health problems of the second half of the twentieth century."

In 1963, Ambrose King and Claude Nichol, president and vice-president respectively of the International Union against VD, stated:[7] "Shortly after the Second World War there were high hopes that the venereal diseases were nearing extinction, and it has been a surprise to many that in a settled and prosperous society at peace and with potent therapeutic agents to hand, these diseases should be causing anxiety. In recent years there has been an increase in the incidence of syphilis and gonorrhoea in many countries.... At any rate, it seems that the problem of the venereal diseases is with us for the foreseeable future."

The Incidence of VD in pre-Liberation China

Since the Kuomintang health authorities left behind no reliable official statistics, estimates of its pre-Liberation incidence must be based either on figures published at the time by individual research workers or on conditions which were found to exist soon after Liberation.

In most National Minority areas[8] the incidence of syphilis was more than ten per cent. There were many reasons for this very high incidence including poverty, ignorance, superstition and oppression by their own feudal rulers, by Han landlords and merchants and by marauding war-lords. Many of these National Minority societies were very primitive and, in some, slavery was only abolished after Liberation. Feudal lords and religious leaders (the latter nominally celibate) took what women they wished and spread venereal disease far and wide. There were no

---

[4] Clark, E. G. "Untreated Syphilis and Natural Course." *Proceedings 12th International Congress of Dermatology*, 2, 855. Washington.

[5] *US News and World Report*, May 1966.

[6] *US News and World Report*, 16 October 1967, p. 37.

[7] King, A., and Nichols, C. *Venereal Diseases*, ed. I, pp. 7–9, Cassel, London, 1964.

[8] These are regions of the People's Republic of China where the majority of the inhabitants are of non-Han nationality. They have their own language, dress, religion and customs. Although they number no more than 6% of the Chinese people, the territories in which they have regional autonomy cover some 60% of the area of the Chinese People's Republic and 14.6% of deputies to the National People's Congress are members of National Minorities.

medical services to speak of and what there were, were beyond the reach of ordinary persons.

The offspring of the feudal or religious aristocracy were habitually put out to be wet-nursed by slave or serf women and, if the babies had congenital syphilis, they infected their wet-nurses.

In cities and urban areas, the incidence was five per cent and in the countryside it averaged between one and three per cent. However, in those rural areas ravaged by the Kuomintang armies, it was much higher.

When one recalls that China has a population of seven hundred million, the magnitude of the problem becomes clearer. There were some tens of millions of syphilitics scattered throughout the country, most of them suffering from latent syphilis but many still potentially infectious.

The Present Venereal Situation in China

The present position can be stated in one short sentence.

ACTIVE VENEREAL DISEASE HAS BEEN COMPLETELY ERADICATED FROM MOST AREAS AND COMPLETELY CONTROLLED THROUGHOUT CHINA.

This is a sweeping statement but I am convinced that it is true. I now give some fragments of the vast mass of facts on which it is based.

In Peking it is impossible to find active syphilitic lesions to demonstrate to medical students. A generation of doctors is growing up in China with no direct experience of syphilis but this is of little consequence for the disease will never return.

At a conference held in the Research Institute of Dermatology and Venereal Disease of the Chinese Academy of Medical Sciences in January 1956,[9] specialists from eight major cities reported that a total of only twenty-eight cases of infectious syphilis had been discovered in their areas in the four years 1952–55. An investigation of infectious syphilis in seven major cities between 1960 and 1964 showed that by the end of this period, the early syphilis rate was less than twenty cases per hundred million of population per year; that is, it had very nearly reached the point of extinction.

In the National Minority areas, especially in those where the syphilis rate had been highest, a striking

9 Dr. Ma Hai-teh, *China's Medicine*, No. 1, Oct. 1966.

fall occurred in the ten years between 1951 and 1960. In the Wulatechien Banner of Inner Mongolia, where the syphilis rate had been nearly fifty per cent in 1952, not a single case of infectious syphilis was found among 3,158 persons examined at random in 1962. In the Jerimu Banner of the Djarod League, which had shown a sero-positivity rate of thirty-five per cent in 1952, ninety-seven per cent of the whole population was tested for syphilis and not a single new, infectious or congenital case was found.

Before Liberation, one of the harmful effects of the widespread syphilis in Minority areas was a progressive depopulation resulting from lowered fertility, a high miscarriage rate and the large number of babies born dead.

For example, the Ikechao League in Inner Mongolia, which had a population of 400,000 in the seventeenth century, was reduced to 80,000 persons by the time of Liberation. The Hulunbu League, which numbered 10,386 in 1933, had fallen to 7,670 in 1950 and an investigation of 2,334 nomadic families revealed that fifty-eight per cent were childless.

Following the anti-syphilis campaign this depopulation trend was reversed. In the Djarod Banner the population increased from 2,548 to 3,343 in ten years. In the same period, 390 herdsmen's families in Hulunbu League, Wusumu, registered increases of from 14.1 per cent to 21.6 per cent.

My friend Dr. Ma Tai-teh, who has actively participated in the anti-syphilis campaign since its inception and to whom I am indebted for much of the material in this chapter, tells me of a Mongolian woman suffering from syphilis who had been married for five years but had not given birth to a live child. She was given a course of treatment in 1952 and the following year she demanded more injections because after the first course she had given birth to a fine baby boy and she wanted another. Tests showed that she had been cured and she was not seen again until the ten-year follow-up when she appeared with eight children, having left one at home. This time she stated flatly that whatever the doctors said, she would have no more injections. She now had a big enough family and was satisfied!

In the rural areas, intensive search shows that the disease has been virtually eliminated. In Hsingku and Ningtu counties in Kiangsi province, a follow-up study five years after the anti-syphilis campaign revealed no new cases or recurrences. In 1960, a complete dermatological examination of the entire population in Chaoan county (population 746,495)

Kwangtung province, and Haian county (population 225,305) Kiangsu province, revealed only one case of secondary recurrent syphilis, and a re-survey of fifty per cent of the population of these two counties in 1964 showed not a single infectious case.

How the Victory Was Won

Since, as has been shown, the spread and persistence of syphilis in any country is due to social and political factors, it can only be eliminated by tackling these factors. That is to say, only an all-round political, as opposed to a purely technical, medical or legislative aproach, can ever solve the problem.

The conquest of syphilis in China within a few years of the conquest of power by the Chinese working class is an outstanding example of the decisive role of politics in tackling major health problems.

There were two essential preconditions for the elimination of syphilis from China. The first was the establishment of the socialist system which ended exploitation and made the oppressed masses the masters of their fate. The second was the equipping of all those involved in the campaign, whether lay or medical, with a determination to serve the people and help socialist construction, with the method of thinking of Mao Tse-tung, so that they would be able to surmount all difficulties confronting them.

The following measures were carried out on the basis of these two prerequisites:

The Elimination of Prostitution

Within a few weeks of Liberation, most of the brothels were closed down by the direct action of the masses. The vast majority of the people recognized that prostitution was harmful and that it constituted crude exploitation of the prostitutes who, for the most part, had been driven into prostitution by poverty or by brute force. Brothel keepers who were scoundrels, drug-peddlers or gangsters were dealt with directly by the angry masses or handed over to the Public Security forces. The few remaining brothels were closed down by Government order in 1951 when prostitution was made illegal.

The prostitutes were treated as victims of an evil social system. First it was necessary to cure the venereal diseases which affected more than ninety per cent of them and then to embark on their social rehabilitation. Those who had been prostitutes for only

a short time were encouraged to go home and were found jobs. It was patiently explained to their families that no shame was attached to having been a victim of the old society and that now everyone who did an honest job was worthy of respect. Those who were deep rooted in prostitution were asked to enter Rehabilitation Centres where they studied the policy of the Government towards them, the nature of the new order, the reasons why they had become prostitutes and the new prospects which were opening up for them providing they themselves were willing to make a contribution. The flood-gates of the past were opened at "Speak Bitterness" meetings which revealed the reasons for their former oppression and degradation. At the same time they were taught a trade and spent part of the day in productive work for which they were paid at the same rate as other workers. They were free to leave whenever they wished and were encouraged to organize their own committees for study, work and recreation. Those who were illiterate learned to read and write. Those who could sing, dance, act or write plays gave performances in their own centres and in others in different parts of the country. Visits from family members were encouraged. When their rehabilitation was complete, they were either found jobs in the city or returned to their native villages where their economic security was guaranteed. One of them, Lu Shen Li, ex-prostitute from Kiangsu province, wrote a most moving letter in which she said, "People in different societies have different fates. The old society made people into devils; the new society makes devils into people."

Now the Rehabilitation Centres have all closed down for there is no further need for them. Some have been converted into factories and among their veteran workers are ex-prostitutes, most of whom have married and some have joined the Communist Party.

The Transformation of the Position of Women

The closure of brothels and legislation outlawing prostitution cannot, of course, be equated with the elimination of prostitution or with the complete emancipation of women. The only fundamental way to do this is first to change the structure of society and then change the thinking of those who comprise it. The first found expression in the Common Programme of the Chinese People's Political Consultative Conference of 1949 and the Marriage Law of

1950 which freed women from feudal bondage and gave them equal rights with men.

Changing the moral values and deep-rooted customs of millions of people takes a very long time and necessitates unremitting effort. Great progress has been made since Liberation and Chinese women are now approaching genuine equality with men. They occupy important posts in every sphere of governmental, political, productive and cultural work, and sex relations based on inequality are disappearing. Although it would be an exaggeration to say that they have already achieved 100 per cent emancipation, it can be confidently stated that history has never before witnessed such a transformation in the status of women as has happened in China since 1949.

The Elimination of Poverty

Although China is still a poor country, it is possible to talk of the elimination of poverty because poverty is relative and only has meaning in relation to the productive level and social system of a given country at a given time. Certainly a situation such as that quoted above, in which twenty million people were described as being on the verge of starvation and in which an influx of girl slaves and prostitutes into the cities was regarded as inevitable, cannot recur. No one in China is allowed to fall below a subsistence level, to starve, to become homeless or to be without adequate clothing. No one is forced to beg or steal in order to stay alive. No one is burdened down by debt. Millions of new jobs have been created and a widespread system of social security is being built up. A clause in the Constitution reads: "Working people in the People's Republic of China have the right to material assistance in old age and in case of illness or disability."

The economic roots of prostitution and crime have been cut for ever.

Mass Campaigns Against Syphilis

The First National Health Conference in August 1950 adopted four guiding principles:

- Health work should primarily serve the masses of the labouring people.
- Chief emphasis should be placed on the prevention of disease.
- Close unity should be fostered between traditional and modern doctors.
- Health work should, whenever appropriate, be conducted by mass campaigns with the active participation of medical workers.

In the same year the Ministry of Health organized teams to investigate the venereal disease situation throughout the country and to work out plans for prevention and treatment. The following year an assault on venereal diseases in the National Minority regions was started.

In 1954, the Central Research Institute of Dermatology and Venereology was established to coordinate the field work and initiate appropriate research and training programmes.

In 1958, the Research Institute organized pilot projects in eight different provinces and when some initial successes had been scored, the Ministry of Health called a nation-wide conference to study the experience gained in Ningtu county, Kiangsi. Characteristically, the conference was held in the little township where the work had actually been done and where participants could see it with their own eyes, discuss it with the local people and gain first-hand experience of its successes and problems.

Mobilizing an Army of Fighters Against Syphilis

To find and treat millions of cases of syphilis and change the attitude of tens of millions of ordinary folk towards venereal disease, the existing corps of medical personnel was totally inadequate. A new approach was needed involving the mobilizing and training of thousands of paramedical workers and immediately a number of highly controversial questions arose. What sort of people should be trained? What minimal educational standards should they possess? How, where and in what should they be trained? Were qualified doctors from the old society able to train others or did they themselves need to learn more before they could teach?

In the course of prolonged and at times heated discussions it gradually became clear that to meet the challenge of eliminating venereal disease from the world's most populous country, the basic necessity was for medical workers to acquire a new philosophy, and a new style of work based on the thinking of Mao Tse-tung.

At the same time, they needed to become familiar with the signs and symptoms of venereal disease, with the technique of blood testing and with methods of treatment.

This combination of political and professional qualifications is in China called becoming "Red and Expert."

Once agreement had been reached on these basic principles, it was easy to find the answers to the controversial questions concerning methods of training and recruitment.

As the work progressed, and particularly as the formerly backward Minority regions caught up with the rest of China, the training and composition of medical teams underwent a change. For example, in 1952 when the first medical team went to Inner Mongolia, all its sixty members came from Peking, for there were not yet any Mongolian doctors. They lived and worked in yurts, a sort of felt-covered wigwam. In 1962, for the much bigger task of re-surveying the entire population, all but six of the team were Mongolians and they had access to first-class laboratory facilities in the newly built medical school in Paotow. In 1962, there were 177,418 primary and secondary school students and 2,517 college students in Mongolia whereas, at the time of Liberation, ninety per cent of Mongolians had been illiterate.

The teachers had, for the most part, been trained in the old society as private practitioners and so they, together with the trainees, studied politics and especially the "Three Old Articles," [10] learned to mix with ordinary people and tried to get rid of their old feelings of conceit and superiority for, as Chairman Mao put it, "To be a teacher of the people, one must first be a pupil of the people."

Gradually, on the basis of a common political outlook, unity was established between teachers and pupils, between traditional and modern doctors, between the masses and the whole body of medical and paramedical workers, and this unity was further strengthened during the course of actual work.

New Methods of Case Finding

To find the millions of cases of latent syphilis scattered throughout the country was an immense undertaking which could not be tackled along orthodox lines.

Opinions were divided as to how it could be done. Those with conservative, stereotyped thinking urged greater working efficiency, more personnel, better and speedier methods of blood testing and more expenditure. Theirs was a purely technical approach. Those who could think in a bold, revolutionary way urged a political approach, with reliance on the initiative of the masses as the key to success. The political approach won out, although not without a struggle. . . .

In a county in Hopei province, after prolonged discussions between political and medical workers, a form was drawn up asking ten questions, an affirmative answer to any one of which would suggest the possibility of syphilis. These ten questions contained "clues" such as a history of a skin rash, falling hair, genital sore or exposure to the risk of infection. To draw up the questionnaire was one thing; to persuade tens of thousands of people to fill it in, honestly and conscientiously, was quite another thing. To do this intensive propaganda and education was carried out by anti-syphilis fighters who were able to make close contact with the people, give them the concept that they should liberate themselves, and enlist them as allies in the struggle. Propaganda posters were put up in the village streets, one-act plays performed in the market place, talks given over the village radio system and meetings, big and small, held night after night at which the purpose of the questionnaire was explained and the co-operation of the peasants gradually won. The opening talk would be brief and to-the-point and would go something like this: "Comrades, syphilis is a disease that was bequeathed to us by the rotten society we have thrown out. It's no fault of yours if you have syphilis and no shame should be attached to it. It's only shameful if you cling to your syphilis when you can easily get rid of it. We've got rid of the landlords and the blood-sucking government that looked after *their* interests and now we have a government that looks after *ours*. We have a Party that speaks for us and shows us how to go forward. Now it calls on us to get rid of syphilis and we should seize the opportunity. This form asks ten questions and you should answer them honestly. We will be glad to help any of you who can't read or write. If you don't remember the answers to some of the questions, ask your friends and relatives. In fact, there's nothing wrong with friends and relatives jogging your memories

[10] "In Memory of Norman Bethune." Mao Tse-tung, *Selected Works,* Vol. II, p. 337; "Serve the People." Mao Tse-tung, *Selected Works,* Vol. III, p. 227; "The Foolish Old Man Who Removed Mountains." Mao Tse-tung, *Selected Works,* Vol. III, p. 321.

even when they're not asked. This is *our* country now and we shoul⸱ all be concerned about the well-being of everyone else.

"Comrades, we're going forward to Communism and we can't take this rotten disease with us."

At first in some places the response was slow; few villagers filled in the questionnaire and some of those who did so, concealed one or other of the "clues." More propaganda was done and more meetings were called at which the main speakers were those who had already been diagnosed as having syphilis and had been cured by a few injections. They told of the mental struggles they had gone through before admitting to the clues, and of their feelings after they had been cured. They recalled the brutality and indifference of the old days and contrasted it with the present.

The trickle of diagnosed cases increased until it became a torrent. News of the questionnaire, spread by political workers, attracted peasants from far and wide who came to the treatment centres eager to be diagnosed and treated.

All those having clues were given a blood test and it was found that one in twenty of them actually had syphilis. This reduced the problem of case finding to manageable proportions, but the sceptics were not convinced. They said this method was too crude, that it was not scientific, that politics couldn't diagnose syphilis, that it wasn't known how many cases had been missed. Accordingly, the Research Institute decided to test the method, improved in the light of experience, in Ningtu county, Kiangsi province, where the VD rate was known to be high.

The People's Communes assembled three thousand volunteers, some of whom, after suitable study, were given the political task of mobilizing the people to regard the fight against syphilis as their own fight. The remainder were given a seven-day course on the principles of diagnosis and treatment, at the end of which they examined some 3,000 people under the scrutiny of experts, who checked on their results, questioned them, and watched them perform blood tests. Eighty per cent of the trainees passed this stringent practical and theoretical examination and thereby qualified to work independently. One old professor, who had been particularly sceptical, examined a trainee for twenty minutes without getting a wrong answer to his probing questions. He then graciously expressed his complete approval in the classical Chinese phrase, "I bow to the ground with all the five points of my body."

The campaign went on for two months, covering not only syphilis, but also such diseases as ringworm of the scalp, leprosy and malaria. Forty-nine thousand cases were examined and treated.

Then the results were checked. Some 30,000 people who had been "processed" by the trainees on the basis of the questionnaire were given a full clinical and serological examination by qualified doctors. It was found that 90.2 per cent of all sufferers from venereal disease had been discovered.

The value of the mass line method had been conclusively proved and the baffling problem of finding one case in a hundred or one case in a thousand among 500 million peasants had been solved.

In the National Minority areas, this method was not suitable and total population surveys were carried out.

In the cities, several case-finding methods were used including examination of selected age groups, of service trade groups, of army entrants, of those about to marry, of pregnant women and of residents in particular lanes and localities. In some cities, the whole population was covered; in others, only those sections who were particularly at risk. In Shanghai, where the VD rate at the time of Liberation was as high as five per cent, the whole population was tested and to do this some 3,600 technicians were trained to perform the rapid fresh blood side test for syphilis, which gives an answer of ninety-two percent accuracy within twenty minutes and which requires only two drops of blood from a prick in the ear.

Active Treatment

Once the sufferers from syphilis had been discovered, treatment was a relatively simple matter although this, too, aroused some controversy around the question as to whether or not trainees with little knowledge and experience should be allowed to give treatment. Some elderly doctors with a strong "closed-shop" mentality, argued that it would be unethical and unwise to allow such people to carry out treatment. But the Ningtu experience refuted their arguments and, moreover, it was obvious that for many years to come there would not be enough fully qualified doctors to carry the work load.

Penicillin was proved to be superior to all other forms of treatment and Chinese antibiotic factories were by now producing enough to supply all domestic needs, leaving a surplus for sending to impoverished newly-emerging nations.

Criteria of Cure

The new approach to syphilis demanded a concept of cure which extended beyond the individual to include the whole community. The criteria for community cure were strict. They included the finding and treatment of all existing cases, a total absence of new cases appearing in the community, disappearance of congenital syphilis in new-born babies, and normal pregnancies and pregnancy outcomes in previously treated mothers. When these criteria had been fulfilled and maintained for five years, the community was considered to be cured. This has already been achieved in most areas and soon, with continued follow-up measures to detect the rare case of recurrent or congenital syphilis, it will undoubtedly be reached throughout the country.

That is how China, once the so-called "sick man of Asia," became the first country in the world to conquer syphilis.

BIBLIOGRAPHY

I. IMPRESSIONS, DEFINITIONS, AND MAGNITUDES

A. Impressions

Selig Greenberg. *The Quality of Mercy: A Report on the Critical Condition of Hospital and Medical Care in America.* New York: Atheneum, 1971.

B. Definitions and Magnitudes

William H. Stewart. "Health Assessment," in B. Jones, ed., *The Health of Americans.* New York: Prentice-Hall, 1970.

John Kosa and Leon S. Robertson. "The Social Aspects of Health and Illness," in J. Kosa et al., eds., *Poverty and Health: A Sociological Analysis.* Cambridge: Harvard University Press, 1969.

U.S. Congress. *Basic Facts on the Health Industry.* 92nd Congress, 1971.

II. ANALYTIC PERSPECTIVES

A. Orthodox Economics

Victor Fuchs. *Who Shall Live?* New York: Basic Books, 1975.

Herbert Klarman. *The Economics of Health.* New York: Columbia University Press, 1965.

B. Radical Political Economics

Sander Kelman. "Toward the Political Economy of Medical Care." *INQUIRY,* September 1971.

Barbara and John Ehrenreich. *The American Health Empire: Power, Profits and Politics.* New York: Random House, 1970.

III. POLICY PERSPECTIVES

A. Health and the Poor

Ruth Covell. *Delivery of Health Services for the Poor.* U.S. Department of Health, Education, and Welfare, 1967.

Harold Luft. "Poverty and Health: An Empirical Investigation," *Journal of Human Resources,* Fall 1975.

B. The Policy Perspectives

Robert R. Alford. *Health and the Politics of Power.* Chicago: Aldine, 1975.

David Kotelchuk, ed. *Prognosis Negative: Crisis in the Health-Care System.* A Health-PAC anthology. New York: Vintage Paperback, 1976.

C. The Debate over National Health Insurance

Louise Lander. *National Health Insurance: A Health-PAC Report,* Health-PAC, 1975; available from Health-PAC, 7 Murray St., New York, N.Y.

Medicare and Medicaid: Problems, Issues and Alternatives, Report of the Staff to the Committee on Finance, U.S. Senate, 1970.

HOUSING

The shortage of housing is so real ... that families may actually begin a squatters' movement in order to find a place to live. It has not come to living in autos yet, but it could happen here.

— Cleveland public housing official

People are looking all over for good homes and we have thousands of these empty ones around.

— Detroit buildings official [1]

In early 1970, a *New York Times* reporter was describing an area near the center of Washington, D.C.:

> On a winter afternoon, the area seems to be a ghost town occupied by children at play. This scene of premature decay and abandonment provides visual evidence of a trend that is evident in large cities across the country.
> While the nation is undergoing the most critical housing shortage since World War II, structurally sound dwellings in the inner cities are being abandoned in increasing numbers to vandalism and demolition.[2]

The juxtaposition of the housing shortage and abandoned buildings reflects the paradoxical allocation of resources in the housing sector. Fancy homes are being built in the suburbs, but the central cities are decaying. Rows of houses stand vacant while thousands of families search for decent housing.

The causes of this imbalance are complex, but the problem reflects a simple phenomenon. The private sector is not building housing in central cities. In particular, it is neither building nor renovating any low-cost housing. Apparently, corporate investment is ignoring the low-cost housing market because it cannot profit from low-cost units. Experience with government efforts to construct housing for the poor has also been disappointing.[3] The volume of public housing construction falls consistently below projected Congressional goals. Why?

[1] Quoted in *The New York Times,* June 4, 1970, and February 9, 1970, respectively.
[2] *The New York Times,* February 9, 1970.
[3] See the selections by Sawers and Wachtel and by Friedman in this chapter.

This chapter directly explores that question. The introduction has four sections: a discussion of problem definitions and magnitudes; a summary of liberal and conservative views; an outline of the radical approach to the problem; and an introduction to the readings.

The Dimensions of the Problem

The urban housing crisis has two principal physical or structural dimensions. First, many Americans live in housing of miserable quality, defined by absolute standards. Second, many Americans suffer relatively desperate housing problems, as a result principally of their race.[4]

On the first level, we conventionally use three measures of the absolute quality of housing:

1. Housing is considered substandard if its basic structure is physically dilapidated or if it lacks basic plumbing facilities.[5] By government standards, roughly 4.7 million American housing units were substandard in 1970.[6]

2. Many consider housing to be overcrowded if it provides less than one room per person for its occupants. By this hardly luxurious criterion, a family of three requires at least a living room, a kitchen and one bedroom to satisfy its space demands. Roughly 5.2 million families lived in overcrowded housing in 1970.[7]

3. Families are expected to pay no more than 25 percent of their total income for housing. If the cost of their housing exceeds that percentage of family income, it is considered too expensive. At least 11 million households paid more than 25 percent of their income for housing in 1970; we do not know how many of them lived either in substandard or overcrowded units.[8]

Summing up the three definitions of absolute housing quality, we can estimate that a minimum of 11 million households — or one-sixth of all households in the country — could not find adequate housing in 1970 by one or more of these criteria.[9] And of these poorly housed families, at least half lived in metropolitan areas, primarily in central cities.[10]

At the second level, some Americans suffer relatively severe housing problems. Blacks in central cities face these "relative" problems most frequently.

---

[4] For summary definitions, see President's Committee on Urban Housing, *A Decent Home* (Washington, D.C.: U.S. Government Printing Office, 1968.)

[5] See U.S. Bureau of the Census, *Measuring the Quality of Housing . . .*, Working Paper No. 25 (Washington, D.C.: U.S. Government Printing Office, 1967).

[6] U.S. Bureau of the Census, *General Housing Characteristics — U.S. Summary* (Washington, D.C.: U.S. Government Printing Office, 1971).

[7] *Ibid.*

[8] *Ibid.*

[9] This minimum presumes that all those paying more than 25 percent are exactly the same families who live in substandard and/or overcrowded units. This presumption is obviously absurd, but it does provide a minimum estimate.

[10] The estimates for metropolitan areas are based on data in *A Decent Home*. In all, to replace currently inadequate housing and to meet all new housing needs (for new household units and other demands) by 1980, we would have to build 26 million units, or 2.6 million a year. At its highest, private construction of housing reached 1.6 million units a year during the 1960s. See Anthony Downs, "Moving Toward Realist Housing Goals," in Kermit Gordon, ed., *Agenda for the Nation* (Washington, D.C.: Brookings Institution, 1968), and *A Decent Home*.

As a result of racial discrimination in the housing market, blacks suffer two kinds of relative housing problems:

For the same quality of housing, blacks pay more on the average than do whites. In an analysis of the St. Louis housing market, for instance, two economists concluded that blacks must pay roughly 5 to 10 percent more than whites do for the same quality of housing.[11]

For the same price, blacks invariably get housing of lower quality than do whites. In 1960, for instance, 57.1 percent of black central-city residents paying between $50 and $79 per month for one- or two-room apartments were living in substandard units. Only 24.6 percent of whites in the same city/rent/room class were living in substandard units.[12]

Finally, the urban housing crisis has a single but critical nonphysical dimension. Increasingly in many urban areas, the character of housing and neighborhoods is becoming hopelessly standardized. Housing tends more and more to appear in environments that serve the simple physical need for shelter but that ignore other important human needs — the need for variety; the need for pleasant surroundings; the need for various, unexpected, and intimate human contact.[13] In the suburbs, tract homes proliferate, spreading conformity, homogeneity, and compartmentalized living. In the central cities, high-rise luxury apartments and huge prisonlike public housing abound, replacing older, more varied environments. For many Americans, the physical quality of housing has improved but the strength of community has been fractured.[14]

The Liberal and Conservative Views

Among most liberal and conservative analysts of the urban housing market, one finds a surprising degree of consensus about the range of causes of current housing problems. Experts tend to agree less about the relative importance of these forces. Four principal perspectives dominate explanations of housing problems; most disagreements about policy and the wisdom of current programs evolve from the implications of these four perspectives.

1. Most basically, nearly everyone agrees that current levels of housing construction costs make it impossible for builders to profit from the construction of housing cheap enough for poor families without some kinds of government subsidies. Several important factors seem to explain the level of these costs and their recent rapid rate of increase.[15]

[11] John Kain and John Quigley, *Housing Markets and Racial Discrimination* (New York: National Bureau of Economic Research, 1975).

[12] Chester Rapkin, "Price Discrimination Against Negroes in the Rental Housing Market," in John Kain, ed., *Race and Poverty* (Englewood Cliffs, N.J.: Prentice-Hall, 1969), p. 119.

[13] Far varied statements of this basic criticism, see Jane Jacobs, *The Life and Death of Great American Cities* (New York: New American Library, 1961), and Richard Sennett, *The Uses of Disorder* (New York: Knopf, 1970).

[14] Herbert Gans has traced the process, first describing the destruction of a rich, varied urban community in Boston, *The Urban Villagers* (New York: The Free Press, 1962), and then very sympathetically describing a rather more standardized suburban working-class community, *The Levittowners* (New York: Pantheon, 1967).

[15] For a good discussion of the building industry, see National Commission on Urban Problems, *Building the American City* (Washington, D.C.: U.S. Government Printing Office, 1968).

• The power of the building trades unions has both limited the supply of labor and has pushed up the level of wages in the construction industry.

• The building industry has always been one of the least concentrated industries in the economy. This low level of concentration has had two important effects. First, firms are apparently so small that they cannot realize economies of scale in construction. Second, they cannot afford the development of radically new cost-saving technologies.

• Because housing construction is so capital-intensive, its costs vary directly with the cost of capital (and therefore with the rate of interest) in the economy. Over the period of economic crisis in the late 1960s and mid-1970s, rates of interest have been kept at extremely high levels to try to reduce the rate of inflation.

2. Analysts of housing focus on the operation of what they call the "filtering" or "turnover" process.[16] Typically, in this view, low-cost housing becomes available indirectly through the housing market as a result of new high-cost construction and the impact of that new construction. Older stock is said to "trickle down" through the income scale, "turning over" rapidly enough to satisfy lower-income families before it deteriorates.[17] This perspective provides an essential link in the formulation of many housing policy recommendations. If costs prohibit the private construction of new low-cost housing, then one way the private sector can increase the supply of housing for the poor comes through its construction of new high-cost units and the operation of the filtering process. As one economist put it recently:

> The turnover process does make sound housing available to income groups which cannot afford new construction. It is this process that is largely responsible for the fact that, in 1960, a majority of families at the lowest income levels were living in standard housing.[18]

3. Many view the operations of the housing market from the perspective of "location theory" and its implications for changes in residential location.[19] According to this set of theories, the location of industry in metropolitan areas determines the location of residential housing. With everything else equal,

[16] For the best discussion of this process, see William Grigsby, *Housing Markets and Public Policy* (Philadelphia: University of Pennsylvania Press, 1963).

[17] Essentially, the filtering process works in the following way: new construction of high-cost housing increases the supply and thereby lowers the relative price of high-cost housing; many relatively higher-income families move out of their older housing into the new stock. This in turn decreases the demand for their older housing segment of the market (with supply constant), lowering the relative prices of that sector. With lower relative prices, this stock is now within the reach of families with slightly lower income. These families move out of their relatively lower-quality houses, thereby lowering demand and consequently relative prices for their old houses. This in turn opens those houses to the pocketbooks of still lower-income families. And so on down to the lowest-quality houses and the poorest families.

[18] Irving H. Welfeld, "Toward a New Federal Housing Policy," *The Public Interest,* No. 19, Spring 1970, p. 34.

[19] For a good discussion of these forces, see John Meyer, John Kain, and Martin Wohl, *The Urban Transportation Problem* (Cambridge: Harvard University Press, 1965), Chapters 2–3, pp. 9–55; and Richard Muth, *Cities and Housing* (Chicago: University of Chicago Press, 1969).

workers will try to live as close to their jobs as they can in order to minimize transportation costs. Since the turn of the century — and especially since World War II — industry has been moving out of the central cities into the suburbs.[20] As jobs have decentralized, demand for land in the central cities has declined and demand for suburban locations has increased. In the face of sharply reduced demand, relatively older central city housing stock has deteriorated rapidly. And large business interests in the central cities, trying to protect the value of their land holdings, encourage the demolition of old decaying residential housing, hoping for and investing in new luxury units or new office space.[21]

As a result of this process, those who live predominantly in the central city, and especially those blacks who are trapped there because of housing market discrimination, must contend with dilapidated housing. Their incomes — and therefore their effective demand for housing — cannot sustain the prices necessary to spur renovation of the stock.

4. Finally, everyone admits that pure racial discrimination exists in the housing market, that its effects are widespread, and that it explains many of the housing problems of blacks in the cities. Few can agree, however, on a satisfactory explanation of housing segregation. One writer who has studied the problem extensively concludes: "Until we know how and why segregation exists on its current scale and what its social impacts are, we can accomplish little in healing the breach between the two societies."[22] In any case, segregation continues. Since World War II, it has been increasing in many Northern cities. If we cannot adequately explain its mechanisms, we must nevertheless try to deal with its consequences.

By any possible standard, the federal government has totally failed to solve our urban housing problems. In 1949 Congress declared the urgent goal "of a decent home and a suitable living environment for every American family." As the figures on housing problems cited above should testify, it has not come close to its objective. Arguments about the failures of past policy and the priorities for future policy usually center around four related questions:[23]

1. Should we rely on the filtering process indirectly to provide low-cost housing while we concentrate on increasing the rate of new construction of high-cost units? Or should we also increase the rate of direct construction of low-cost units?

2. If we build low-cost units directly, should the government build the units or should the private sector be provided with subsidies to build them?

3. In the case of either answer to either question, what emphasis should be placed on new construction, and what emphasis should we put on renovation of the older housing stock, in our efforts either to speed the turnover process or directly to increase the supply of low-cost housing?

4. Finally, should we accept the facts of housing market segregation, building low-cost housing primarily in central-city ghettos, or should we try to

[20] See Kain, "The Distribution and Movement of Jobs and Industry," in James Q. Wilson, ed., *Metropolitan Enigma,* (Cambridge: Harvard University Press, 1968).

[21] For a historical view of the way this process evolves, see Edgar Hoover and Raymond Vernon, *Anatomy of a Metropolis* (Garden City, N.Y.: Doubleday Anchor, 1961).

[22] Anthony Pascal, "The Analysis of Residential Segregation," in J. P. Crecine, ed., *Financing the Metropolis* (New York: Sage Publications, 1970).

[23] See Arthur Solomon, *Housing the Urban Poor* (Cambridge: MIT Press, 1974).

break the cycle of increasing segregation by building low-cost housing in the suburbs?

Answers (or combinations of answers) to these questions vary widely. Many assert that we should pursue a more diversified set of strategies, opening a wider set of alternative housing choices. At the same time, certain elements of priority appear in the liberal and conservative literature on housing policy, and it seems important to highlight those areas.

In answer to the first question, many agree that it would be most efficient to rely principally on the turnover process. This argument contends that costs of new construction render direct provision of low-cost units inefficient, that the turnover process does reach the poorest families, and that those who still must pay more than 25 percent of their incomes can receive general income maintenance or specific rent supplements.[24]

In answer to the second question, nearly everyone argues that we should rely on the private sector because recent history has proved that the public sector cannot build low-cost housing efficiently. This set of historical contentions includes the following components: First, that the failure of public housing programs to produce a sufficiently high volume of construction can be attributed to the inefficiency of government bureaucracy and the difficulty of public construction in effecting technological innovation;[25] second, that the public urban renewal program, through which the government has provided some subsidies to private industry for reconstruction of central cities, has failed to increase the stock of low-cost housing because the government subsidies were not substantial enough to build housing cheap enough for the poor;[26] and third, that only the private sector — and especially large corporations — have the capacity to apply management expertise, technological wizardry, and appropriate economies of scale to the reduction of housing costs.[27]

In answer to the third question, many argue that both new construction and renovation are needed. But since so many new units are necessary to solve our housing problems, renovation is regarded as too slow a process, affecting too few units, to warrant high priority.

Finally, in answer to the fourth question, most agree that it would be ideal if we could build low-cost housing in the suburbs because blacks could then choose to live closer to suburban employment sites. Disagreements about the importance of effecting suburban construction evolve from differing views of its political feasibility and of the positive value of preserving the integrity and political power of black communities in central-city ghettos.[28]

[24] For one position close to this view, see Welfeld in this chapter.

[25] See the references in the selection by Lawrence Friedman in this chapter.

[26] For the strongest statement of the case against urban renewal, see Martin Anderson, *The Federal Bulldozer* (Cambridge: MIT Press, 1964), and for arguments about the program, see James Q. Wilson, ed., *Urban Renewal: The Record and the Controversy* (Cambridge: MIT Press, 1966).

[27] In *A Decent Home,* this argument is made extensively.

[28] In one strong statement on the problem, Kain and Persky have argued that all the inefficiencies engendered throughout the metropolitan market by the continued presence of the ghetto require that we try to dissolve it even if the costs are high. "Alternatives to the Gilded Ghetto," *The Public Interest,* No. 14, Winter 1969. In another apposite view, Piven and Cloward argue that the objective of integrating housing in the suburbs has so aroused

The Radical View

The radical analysis of urban housing problems consists of two fairly simple arguments. Radicals contend first of all that trends in the structure of American social and economic institutions are making it increasingly unlikely that absolute and relative physical housing problems can be solved within the context of those institutions. They also argue that the structure of those institutions makes it unlikely that housing in this country will provide *both* adequate physical shelter *and* an enriching community environment for everyone. I have summarized the two arguments in order.

Radicals agree with many of the liberal and conservative analyses of absolute housing problems. They argue especially that the structure of the housing industry and the necessary rates of profit in that industry make it virtually impossible for industry directly to construct low-cost housing. Further, radicals suggest that several trends in this country have reinforced that impossibility. First, the intensified quest by all large corporations for stability and security of investment opportunities has made low-cost housing construction increasingly unattractive compared to other kinds of investments.[29] Low-income populations move constantly, and low-income areas change their characters rapidly. Since large-scale housing investments must be amortized over long periods of time in order to return a stable and competitive rate of profit, the viability of investment in low-income housing may be threatened by sudden movements of low-income populations or sudden shifts in the demand for low-income housing. Second, the long-run shifts in the political-economic structure of metropolitan areas have also undercut possibilities for new low-income housing.[30] On the one hand, with substantial metropolitan decentralization (from central cities to suburbs), many relatively affluent citizens have been able to incorporate their own homogeneous, protected suburban enclaves, escaping from the jurisdiction of central-city governments. It is often in the interests of these affluent communities to establish protective zoning ordinances, in order to keep out low-income families with heavy requirements for public services. As the metropolitan areas have become increasingly balkanized, those urban governments with the greatest wealth have screened out low-income units, while those governments with the greatest concentrations of low-income families have lost the tax base on which they could afford public construction of low-income housing. And central-city financial interests have found it increasingly important to preserve the value of their central-city land holdings (in the face of suburbanization and declining demand for central-city space) by tearing down low-income housing and replacing it with high-rise luxury apartments (in order to attract wealthy families back to central-city areas). All these developments seem to lessen the possibili-

---

opposition to public housing that it has vitiated the program; at least by building in the ghetto, they argue, we can get some housing built. "Desegregated Housing: Who Pays for the Reformers' Ideal?" in Kain, ed., *Race and Poverty.*

[29] For statements of the intensity of this quest, see Paul Baran and Paul Sweezy, *Monopoly Capital* (New York: Monthly Review Press, 1966), or J. K. Galbraith, *The New Industrial State* (Boston: Houghton Mifflin, 1967).

[30] For this argument, see Larry Sawers, "Urban Form and the Mode of Production," *Review of Radical Political Economics,* Spring 1975; and David M. Gordon, "Capitalism and the Roots of Urban Crisis," in R. Alcaly and D. Mermelstein, eds., *The Fiscal Crisis of American Cities* (New York: Random House, 1977).

ties that private or public construction of low-income housing will increase in the normal course of events.

Liberals and conservatives tend to reply to those arguments by citing the importance of the "turnover" process. They insist that none of these trends precludes the provision of decent housing to the poor as an indirect result of new housing construction for higher-income families. Radicals reply with two arguments. First, most evidence seems to suggest that the black poor do not benefit very much from the "turnover" process, that the persistence of segregated housing markets prevents the normal filtering of higher-quality housing in the white market into the lower-income black market. In the most recent study of the filtering process, Lansing, Clifton, and Morgan provide especially strong evidence of this market separation.[31] Since the black poor constitute an increasing percentage of those living in substandard housing in cities, one has less and less faith that the turnover process can solve the absolute (or relative) housing problems of the urban poor. Second, as public pressure increases in the United States against overt and explicit racial discrimination, the functional economic importance of housing segregation increases. For instance, the schools play an important economic role in channeling blacks into lower-class jobs and in preparing blacks for lower-class status. In the South, the school system could perform this function through the preservation of legally segregated schools. As a result of the civil rights movement, legal segregation in education is no longer possible. But Northern schools perform the same functions as long as housing segregation solidifies the *de facto* segregation of schools. And as the importance of racism persists, the importance of *de facto* housing segregation as the least explicit form of discrimination increases simultaneously. One can expect fewer and fewer private and public efforts to desegregate the housing market over time.[32]

All these points suggest that radically increased efforts by the government to provide better housing for the poor constitute the only avenue toward solution of absolute and relative housing problems. But the radical theory of the State, summarized in Chapter 1, implies that the government will not directly aid the poor (unless such assistance becomes necessary to help stabilize the system). Liberals and conservatives tend to reply that the government has already provided substantial housing assistance to the poor, and that the radical argument must therefore be considered absurd. Look at all the government housing programs, they say — at urban renewal, public housing, public subsidies, public subsidies of low-income housing, and so on.[33]

In fact, radicals reply, government housing programs have never been used to help the poor.[34] One should look at program effects, radicals argue, not program intentions, in order most accurately to judge the possibilities for effective public action. In the case of housing, the evidence on the effects of housing programs seems clear. Contrary to liberal and conservative claims, the two

[31] See their book, *New Homes and Poor People* (Michigan: Survey Research Center, 1970).

[32] See the chapters on education, employment, and race in this book for some other comments on the importance of racism.

[33] See the selection "Federal Housing Programs," by the President's Committee on Urban Housing, among the readings in this chapter.

[34] See Sawers and Wachtel in this chapter.

principal government housing programs in the last twenty years — public housing and urban renewal — have failed to improve housing for the poor not because they were run by entangled, inefficient, cumbersome bureaucratic organizations. They failed because dominant institutions never intended that those programs should provide housing for the poor. The urban renewal program has been dedicated to the preservation of central-city land values; it has sought to accomplish this by ripping down slum housing and constructing new luxury and middle-income housing.[35] In many cities, critics have given urban renewal a more accurate name: the "Negro removal" program.

Equally, the public housing program was never intended to provide housing for the poor.[36] It was initiated during the Depression to provide low-cost housing for the temporarily indigent middle class, and to provide a countercyclical category of direct federal expenditure. Since World War II, the white middle and working classes have been able to find their own housing, and the Cold War has established the defense budget as the principal fiscal tool for stabilization. Congress has never appropriated enough money to make public housing work, local public housing authorities have not even spent what little money the federal government has authorized, and those to whom our institutions have given control over public housing have no intention of redirecting the program in order dramatically to improve its contribution to the low-income housing stock in urban areas. Hartman and Carr conclude from their survey of local public housing authorities:

> Our survey has shown that the men and women who make basic public housing policy at the local level are in no sense representative of the client group the programs are intended to serve. A substantial proportion of the commissioners do not favor adding to the stock of publicly subsidized housing, nor use of newer forms of public housing, nor many of the "liberalization" trends, including increased tenant participation. . . . [The authority] inserts, at a critical level of internal decision-making, an intervening layer of part-time, lay commissioners who act as a brake on the program by failing to keep abreast of new trends and techniques and by representing a microcosm of middle-class, white views about the poor, their housing, and the responsibilities of government.[37]

Those authorities reflect the real balance of institutional power in this country and, despite the profusion of good intentions at the federal level, will continue to block public construction of low-income housing until the balance of power shifts.

Suppose, despite all these barriers, that the government was suddenly forced, *mirabile dictu,* radically to increase its efforts to provide low-cost housing. Even if that happened, which radicals strenuously doubt, it seems nearly certain that the housing product would be imprisoning and oppressive, that physically adequate structures would barely compensate for the inhumanity of the design, environment, and community surrounding those structures. This seems certain

---

[35] For basic statistical evidence, see Anderson, *The Federal Bulldozer.* For the debate about urban renewal, see Wilson, ed., *Urban Renewal.*

[36] See the selection by Friedman among the readings in this chapter.

[37] Chester Hartman and Gregg Carr, "Housing Authorities Reconsidered," *Journal of the American Institute of Planners,* January 1969, pp. 18–19.

if the housing were constructed either directly by the government or indirectly by private industry with the help of government subsidy.

Government housing would continue to consist of tall, standardized, prison-like structures completely isolated from other communities and other facilities. This has been true in the past, and seems likely to be true in the future. With the balkanization of suburban governments and corporate attempts to revive central cities, pressures have consolidated against the government to keep the poor out of sight because they depress property values. Furthermore, because of the depletion of the treasures of most large central cities, governments would have to build the most inexpensive housing possible in order both to have money and to minimize the land subtracted from the private property tax base.[38]

Privately constructed low-cost housing, if it materialized on a large scale, seems even more likely to ignore community needs for housing conducive to, rather than oppressive of, human development. In order to attract private industry into the low-cost housing field, it seems apparent that we shall have to provide large financial incentives for research and development in housing construction technology; the current state of construction technology simply does not permit profitable construction of low-cost housing even with substantial government subsidy. Given the power of large corporations, their apparent interest in attracting government subsidy for research and development, and the current state of public and government opinion about the housing market, it seems certain that the R&D subsidies would go to very large corporations. And it seems probable that large corporations will be interested in low-cost housing development only if they can be guaranteed extremely stable, extremely large investment possibilities. To protect their investments, they will probably insist on subsidy arrangements with the government similar to those the government has provided defense firms — cost-plus or cost over-run contracts through which the firm cannot possibly suffer a loss. Finally, large corporations will undoubtedly seek to "delocalize" the housing market, developing standardized, nationally marketable housing designs to permit mass production and prefabrication. All of these probabilities suggest that privately constructed low-cost housing would be provided by an emergent "housing-industrial complex" — a concentration of housing construction in the hands of a few large corporations, subsidized by the government, building on extremely large scales and providing housing designed according to abstract, cost-saving, "delocalized" criteria. The consequent housing would bear almost no relationship to the communities for which it was built, and communities would be able to play little or no role in its planning, design, and construction. Housing policies would be determined by corporate profitability criteria and by corporate requirements for guaranteed investment outlets, not, as one might vainly hope, by publicly determined standards of quality, accessibility, beauty, suitability, or community.

What is the alternative? There are no alternatives, the radical argument suggests, in the context of current social and economic institutions. In another context, it should be simple enough to involve people in the planning and design of housing suited for individual communities — to build housing affording variety, community, interaction, and a certain intimacy. It should also be simple enough to provide housing for all, regardless of ability to pay, according to

---

[38] For one depressing account of these kinds of housing projects, see Lee Rainwater, *Behind Ghetto Walls: Black Family Life in a Federal Slum* (Chicago: Aldine, 1970).

need. If society didn't spend so much money on war, space, obsolescent cars, useless luxury goods, and pure waste, there could be plenty for decent, human, relevant housing supportive of community development.

The Readings

The first four readings provide some Impressions, Definitions, and Magnitudes. The short selection from Joseph P. Lyford's book, *The Airtight Cage,* illustrates the failure both of landlords and of the public bureaucracies to respond to human needs for decent housing. The selection from the Report of the National Advisory Commission on Civil Disorders sketches the dimensions of housing problems in central cities. The first selection from the report of the President's Committee on Urban Housing provides some estimates of total American housing needs. And the second selection from the same report describes the plethora of federal housing programs, candidly admitting that they do not suffice to provide housing for the truly poor.

The second group of readings provides analytic perspective on these housing problems. Irving H. Welfeld represents the liberal-conservative perspective, arguing that housing policies should combine incentives to private industry to construct high-cost housing — to speed up the "trickle down" process — with housing allowances to the poor. In the next five selections, elements of the radical analysis are represented. Michael E. Stone reviews the central importance of mortgage bankers to the housing market — and through them, of the profit motive. Larry Sawers and Howard M. Wachtel summarize the evidence that federal housing programs have not benefited the poor. Lawrence M. Friedman echoes that general conclusion in his more detailed review of the history of the public housing program. Chester Hartman and Dennis Keating also reflect that general perspective in their debunking of the liberal-conservative panacea — housing allowances. In the last selection, Matthew Edel adds a dimension to the analysis that is missing entirely in the liberal and conservative views — the class conflict involved in fights over "turf."

THE AIRTIGHT CAGE

Joseph P. Lyford

This brief story describes the dedicated but ultimately futile efforts of one New York City tenant to obtain adequate housing for his family. It illustrates the striking indifference of both landlords and government bureaucracies. José Rodriguez had to battle both and, despite his tenacity, he lost.

The episode comes from Lyford's book about an urban renewal area on the Upper West Side in Manhattan, *The Airtight Cage.* Lyford lived in the area while he was writing the book. He has been a staff member of the Center for the Study of Democratic Institutions.

José Rodriguez . . . is one of those uninfluential citizens whose fate helps illustrate the nature of man's relationship to his government in the twentieth century. The Rodriguez family's personal education about the democratic system began in earnest when José, his wife Christine, and their two young children moved into a rooming house in the West Nineties and acquired a notoriously callous landlord. The Rodriguezes liked their new location because it was just across the street from a new elementary school, and only a couple of blocks from a junior high school. Local authorities also had reason to be pleased with the advent of the Rodriguezes. Although both parents were employed, they took an interest in local affairs. On several occasions Rodriguez helped out with special events at public schools and hospitals, and both children quickly made an excellent impression on their teachers.

Rodriguez's income and that of his wife, who worked in a laundry, enabled them to pay on time each month their $110 rent for the new place, which consisted of two and a half rooms on the basement floor. It became apparent soon after they moved in that they were not getting anywhere near their money's worth. The apartment, no better and no worse than hundreds of decomposed compounds which flourished under the city's so-called rent control program, was badly in need of painting and

Source: From pp. 308–312 of *The Airtight Cage* by Joseph P. Lyford. Copyright © 1966 by Joseph P. Lyford. By permission of Harper & Row, Publishers, Inc.

plastering. Holes in the floor were covered by carpet or cardboard, and a large opening under the kitchen sink produced frequent visits from rats in the basement. Rodriguez also found that the toilet bowl was coming loose and water ran over the bathroom floor. The apartment was also overrun with cockroaches. Rodriguez asked for exterminator service, to which he was entitled. The landlord refused it. Nor did the landlord pay for a stove and kitchen sink which Rodriguez had bought for the kitchen, although the original equipment had been so decayed as to be unusable.

When Rodriguez found that he could not get his landlord to clean the filthy hallways or get rid of the vermin, he phoned the Department of Health until a department official told him curtly to buy himself a can of insecticide and stop bothering the department. Next he complained to the office of Area Services North, a local agency of the Housing and Redevelopment Board, which was charged with seeing that private landlords in the urban renewal area maintained their buildings properly and kept them free of code violations. Rodriguez's experience with Area Services North was typical; nothing happened.

So he wrote to Chairman Mollen [of the New York City Housing and Redevelopment Board] himself. When the chairman also refused to do anything about the complaint, Rodriguez decided to write to the then candidate for the U.S. Senate, Robert Kennedy. The letter described the family's living conditions and declared that city agencies entrusted with the enforcement of health and building codes had failed to cooperate with the tenants.

"How much can a human being take?" Rodriguez concluded. "Please, Mr. Kennedy, help us."

A week or so later, he received an answer.

"I was shocked to hear of your plight," wrote Kennedy, "and I am certainly going to do everything I can to help you and your fellow tenants." What Kennedy meant by "help" was that he had referred Rodriguez's letter to Chairman Mollen, "who has assured me that he will have your situation thoroughly investigated."

Five weeks later, Rodriguez received a letter from Mollen describing the results of the "thorough investigation" the chairman had promised Mr. Kennedy.

"A check, both at our office and with the Department of Buildings, revealed that certain violations existed on said premises." Mollen also wrote that the attorney for the landlord had stated that several violations had been removed and that other violations existed because of Rodriguez's continued refusal to allow repairmen to enter his apartment.

Chairman Mollen then proceeded to give the back of his hand to the family Rodriguez. "In your complaint to Senator-elect Kennedy you stated that various city agencies involved in code enforcement had neglected to cooperate with the tenants. I am certain that if you cooperate the city will do all it can to see that conditions are improved."

At no time during Mollen's "investigation" did any representative of the Housing and Redevelopment Board or of any code-enforcement agency take the trouble to talk to Rodriguez or to look at his apartment to see if, in fact, any violations had been removed. Nor was Rodriguez ever given an opportunity to respond to the charges — which were untrue — that he had refused entry to any workman hired by the landlord. By his own admission Chairman Mollen's sole source of information was the landlord's attorney. Apparently no city official had the time to make an on-the-spot investigation. However, shortly before he wrote to Rodriguez, Chairman Mollen attended a tree-planting ceremony a few blocks from the apartment, at which occasion his photograph was taken for the Spanish newspaper *El Diario*.

Such rebuffs as Mollen's letter dealt the Rodriguez family a double blow. Not only did it mean they could expect little help from the authorities, but it also was the signal to the landlord that he could harass them with impunity. This landlord was not accustomed to having his tenants complain, and he decided to get rid of the troublemakers as quickly as possible. Until their arrival he had operated the building and another even more decrepit one on the same street in defiance of all manner of fire, occupancy, building, and health regulations without any protest from his tenants. Most of them were Puerto Ricans, desperate for a place to live, who were jammed into these buildings in violation of occupancy regulations; any complaints about their treatment would have meant their immediate eviction. A measure of the landlord's control over the tenants

was the fact that he even distributed their mail. There were no regulation mailboxes in the Rodriguezes' house: the postman dropped the mail into the slot of a padlocked box to which the landlord had the only key. Rodriguez protested to the U.S. Post Office, but the postal authorities did nothing about it.

For nearly a year the landlord carried out a campaign of harassment to drive the Rodriguez family out of the house. He served several eviction notices, and on more than six different occasions he appeared at the door of their apartment with summonses charging Rodriguez with assault, theft, disorderly behavior, nonpayment of rent, or threats of violence. On most of these occasions, he was accompanied by a policeman who had been told by the landlord that Rodriguez was dangerous. To answer each summons or notice of eviction, Rodriguez had to take the better part of a day to find a lawyer, prepare a defense, call witnesses, and travel downtown to criminal court or the agency where a hearing was to be held. The summonses forced him to absent himself from his union hiring hall, thereby losing a chance at any employment opportunity which might turn up that day.

The truth of the landlord's charges can be judged by the fact that in some cases he did not even appear to press his complaint, and in all cases the charges against Rodriguez were dismissed. But, although he lost each time, the landlord succeeded in irritating and worrying the family, keeping it in a constant state of insecurity, using up Rodriguez's time, causing him expense, and interfering with his employment.

In the opinion of this observer, Rodriguez won his rounds in court in spite of the judicial procedure because he could speak English (although with a heavy accent), because he kept his temper both in and out of court, in spite of considerable provocation in both places, and because he kept a complete file of documents bearing on his case. Finally, he had some friends who were occasionally able to get him a lawyer without charge. Had he lacked any of these assets, it is difficult to say whether he would be a free man today. The proceedings in court had very little resemblance to the administration of justice as it is discussed in bar association meetings. Rodriguez was merely one of a long line of people — largely Negroes and Puerto Ricans — who were handled on an assembly-line basis by an overworked, harried judge who sometimes did not appear to understand the charges. There would be a "Now what's this all about?"; then, after a few moments of confused argument, the magistrate would berate both plaintiff and defendant, tell them to stop picking on each other, and threaten them both with jail if they ever appeared before him again. Or he might just postpone things by granting the landlord an adjournment, thereby prolonging Rodriguez's discomfort a little longer.

On one occasion when Rodriguez took the offensive and filed charges against the landlord for failing to render services and correct violations, the head of a city agency appeared as a witness for the landlord himself, appealing to the judge to postpone a decision on the case until her agency had had time to make an inspection of the Rodriguez apartment — a plea which came months after Rodriguez had vainly appealed to her agency and to her boss, Chairman Mollen, for just such an inspection. When the inspection was finally held, the two inspectors became angry at Rodriguez for having invited one of his friends to be present as a witness, and Rodriguez was never allowed to see the report of the inspection.

The conclusion to the harassment of Rodriguez could have been predicted. For one thing, Rodriguez began to run out of lawyers. Friendly attorneys were willing to help on a one-shot basis, but when the next summons was served they were always too busy. Rodriguez appealed to local civil rights groups, to Puerto Rican organizations, to the FDR-Woodrow Wilson Democratic Club, and got promises of help, but the help never materialized.

One night Rodriguez was arrested and arraigned in the 24th Precinct police station, charged by the landlord with assault. This case was also thrown out of court, but it was Rodriguez's last victory. During a summer rainstorm a few weeks later, a marshal knocked at the Rodriguez door with a court order evicting the family for nonpayment of rent. The order had been signed without Rodriguez's ever having had a hearing on the charges, which were false. So the Rodriguez family and all its belongings were moved out onto the sidewalk, and all a handful of friendly neighbors could do was to cover the furniture with plastic to keep it dry. Then the Rodriguezes were transported to a fifth-floor walkup apartment in a frightful city-owned building a block or so away.

HOUSING PROBLEMS IN CENTRAL CITIES

The National Advisory Commission on Civil Disorders

The following excerpt provides an interesting series of figures on the range and intensity of housing problems in central cities, especially in black ghettos. The figures support the conclusion that, for many in the central cities, "the goal of a decent home and suitable environment is as far distant as ever." The selection (from what is often referred to as the Riot Commission Report) was published in 1968. In central cities, at least, conditions have not improved much since then.

Source: Report of the National Advisory Commission on Civil Disorders. Washington, D.C.: U.S. Government, 1968.

The passage of the National Housing Act in 1934 signalled a new federal commitment to provide housing for the nation's citizens. Fifteen years later Congress made the commitment explicit in the Housing Act of 1949, establishing as a national goal the realization of "a decent home and suitable environment for every American family."

Today, after more than three decades of fragmented and grossly under-funded federal housing programs, decent housing remains a chronic problem for the disadvantaged urban household. Fifty-six percent of the country's nonwhite families live in central cities today, and of these, nearly two-thirds live in neighborhoods marked by substandard [1] housing and general urban blight. For these citizens, condemned by segregation and poverty to live in the decaying slums of our central cities, the goal of a decent home and suitable environment is as far distant as ever.

During the decade of the 1950s, when vast numbers of Negroes were migrating to the cities, only 4 million of the 16.8 million new housing units constructed throughout the nation were built in the central cities. These additions were counterbalanced by the loss of 1.5 million central-city units through demolition and other means. The result was that the number of nonwhites living in substandard housing increased from 1.4 to 1.8 million, even though the number of substandard units declined.

Statistics available for the period since 1960 indicate that the trend is continuing. There has been virtually no decline in the number of occupied dilapidated units in metropolitan areas, and surveys in New York City and Watts actually show an increase in the number of such units. These statistics have led the Department of Housing and Urban Development to conclude that while the trend in the country as a whole is toward less substandard housing, "There are individual neighborhoods and areas within many cities where the housing situation continues to deteriorate." [2]

Inadequate housing is not limited to Negroes. Even in the central cities the problem affects two and a half times as many white as nonwhite households. Nationally, over 4 million of the nearly 6 million occupied substandard units in 1966 were occupied by whites.

It is also true that Negro housing in large cities is significantly better than that in most rural areas — especially in the South. Good quality housing has become available to Negro city dwellers at an increasing rate since the mid-1950s when the postwar housing shortage ended in most metropolitan areas.

Nevertheless, in the Negro ghetto, grossly inadequate housing continues to be a critical problem.

[1] The Department of Housing and Urban Development classifies substandard housing as that housing reported by the United States Census Bureau as (1) sound but lacking full plumbing, (2) deteriorating and lacking full plumbing, or (3) dilapidated.

[2] Hearings before the Subcommittee on Executive Reorganizations of the Committee on Government Operations, United States Senate, 89th Congress, 2nd session, August 16, 1966, p. 148.

Substandard, Old, and Overcrowded Structures

Nationwide, 25 percent of all nonwhites living in central cities occupied substandard units in 1960 compared to 8 percent of all whites. Preliminary Census Bureau data indicate that by 1966, the figures had dropped to 16 and 5 percent respectively. However, if "deteriorating" units and units with serious housing code violations are added, the percentage of nonwhites living in inadequate housing in 1966 becomes much greater.

In 14 of the largest U.S. cities, the proportions of all nonwhite housing units classified as deteriorating, dilapidated, or lacking full plumbing in 1960 (the latest date for which figures are available), were as follows:

Nonwhite Housing in 14 Cities

City	Percentage of Nonwhite Occupied Housing Units Classified Deteriorating or Dilapidated, 1960	Percentage of Nonwhite Occupied Housing Units Classified Deteriorating, Dilapidated, or Sound but Without Full Plumbing, 1960
New York	33.8	42.4
Chicago	32.1	42.8
Los Angeles	14.7	18.1
Philadelphia	28.6	32.0
Detroit	27.9	30.1
Baltimore	30.5	31.7
Houston	30.1	36.7
Cleveland	29.9	33.9
Washington, D.C.	15.2	20.8
St. Louis	40.3	51.6
San Francisco	21.3	34.0
Dallas	41.3	45.9
New Orleans	44.3	56.9
Pittsburgh	49.1	58.9

Source: U.S. Department of Commerce, Bureau of the Census.

Conditions were far worse than these citywide averages in many specific disadvantaged neighborhoods. For example, a study of housing in Newark, New Jersey, before the 1967 disorders, showed the following situation in certain predominantly Negro neighborhoods as of 1960:

Percentage of Housing Units Dilapidated or Deteriorated in Selected Areas of Newark, 1960

Area Number	Population	Percentage Nonwhite	Percentage of All Housing Units Dilapidated or Deteriorating
1	25,300	75.5	91.0
2	48,200	64.5	63.8
3A	48,300	74.8	43.1

Source: George Sternlieb, *The Tenement Landlord* (New Brunswick, N.J.: Rutgers, 1966), pp. 238–241.

These three areas contained 30 percent of the total population of Newark in 1960, and 62 percent of its nonwhite population.

The Commission carried out special analyses of 1960 housing conditions in three cities, concentrating on all Census Tracts with 1960 median incomes of under $3,000 for both families and individuals. It also analyzed housing conditions in Watts. The results showed that the vast majority of people living in the poorest areas of these cities were Negroes, and that a high proportion lived in inadequate housing:

higher percentages of nonwhites than whites occupied units built prior to 1939.

Percentage of White and Nonwhite Occupied Housing Units Built Prior to 1939 in Selected Metropolitan Areas

Metropolitan Area	White Occupied Units	Nonwhite Occupied Units
Cleveland	33.2	90.6
Dallas	31.9	52.7
Detroit	46.2	86.1
Kansas City	54.4	89.9
Los Angeles — Long Beach	36.6	62.4
New Orleans	52.9	62.2
Philadelphia	62.0	90.8
Saint Louis	57.9	84.7
San Francisco — Oakland	51.3	67.6
Washington, D.C.	31.9	64.9

Source: U.S. Department of Commerce, Bureau of the Census.

Finally, Negro housing units are far more likely to be overcrowded than those occupied by whites. In U.S. metropolitan areas in 1960, 25 percent of all nonwhite units were overcrowded by the standard measure (that is, they contained 1.01 or more persons per room). Only 8 percent of all white-occupied units were in this category. Moreover, 11 percent of all nonwhite-occupied units were seriously overcrowded (1.51 or more persons per room), compared

Analyses of Housing Conditions, 1960

Item	Detroit	Washington, D.C.	Memphis	Watts Area of Los Angeles
Total population of study area	162,375	97,084	150,827	49,074
Percentage of study area nonwhite	67.5%	74.5%	74.0%	87.3%
Percentage of housing units in study area:				
Substandard by HUD definition	32.7%	23.9%	35.0%	10.5%
Dilapidated, deteriorating or sound but lacking full plumbing	53.1%	37.3%	46.5%	29.1%

Source: U.S. Department of Commerce, Bureau of the Census.

Negroes, on the average, also occupy much older housing than whites. In each of ten metropolitan areas analyzed by the Commission, substantially

with 2 percent for white-occupied units. The figures were as follows in the ten metropolitan areas analyzed by the Commission.

Percentage of White and Nonwhite Occupied Units with 1.01 or More Persons Per Room in Selected Metropolitan Areas

Metropolitan Area	White Occupied Units	Nonwhite Occupied Units
Cleveland	6.9	10.3
Dallas	9.3	28.8
Detroit	8.6	17.5
Kansas City	8.7	18.0
Los Angeles — Long Beach	8.0	17.4
New Orleans	12.0	36.1
Philadelphia	4.9	16.3
Saint Louis	11.8	28.0
San Francisco — Oakland	6.0	19.7
Washington, D.C.	6.2	22.6

Source: U.S. Department of Commerce, Bureau of the Census.

Higher Rents for Poorer Housing

Negroes in large cities are often forced to pay the same rents as whites and receive less for their money, or pay higher rents for the same accommodations.

The first type of discriminatory effect — paying the same amount but receiving less — is illustrated by data from the 1960 Census for Chicago and Detroit.

In certain Chicago census tracts, both whites and nonwhites paid median rents of $88, and the proportions paying various specific rents below that median were almost identical. But the units rented by nonwhites were typically:

- Smaller (the median number of rooms was 3.35 for nonwhites versus 3.95 for whites).
- In worse condition (30.7 percent of all nonwhite units were deteriorated or dilapidated units versus 11.6 percent for whites).
- Occupied by more people (the median household size was 3.53 for nonwhites versus 2.88 for whites).
- More likely to be overcrowded (27.4 percent of nonwhite units had 1.01 or more persons per room versus 7.9 percent for whites).

In Detroit, whites paid a median rental of $77 as compared to $76 among nonwhites. Yet 27.0 percent

of nonwhite units were deteriorating or dilapidated, as compared to only 10.3 percent of all white units.

The second type of discriminatory effect — paying more for similar housing — is illustrated by data from a study of housing conditions in disadvantaged neighborhoods in Newark, New Jersey. In four areas of that city (including the three areas cited previously), nonwhites with housing essentially similar to that of whites paid rents that were from 8.1 percent to 16.8 percent higher. Though the typically larger size of nonwhite households, with consequent harder wear and tear, may partially justify the difference in rental, the study found that nonwhites were paying a definite "color tax" of apparently well over 10 percent on housing. This condition prevails in most racial ghettos.

The combination of high rents and low incomes forces many Negroes to pay an excessively high proportion of their income for housing. This is shown dramatically by the following chart, showing the percentage of renter households paying over 35 percent of their incomes for rent in ten metropolitan areas:

Percentages of White and Nonwhite Occupied Units with Households Paying 35 Percent or More of Their Income for Rent in Selected Metropolitan Areas

Metropolitan Area	White Occupied Units	Nonwhite Occupied Units
Cleveland	8.6	33.8
Dallas	19.2	33.8
Detroit	21.2	40.5
Kansas City	20.2	40.0
Los Angeles — Long Beach	23.4	28.4
New Orleans	16.6	30.5
Philadelphia	19.3	32.1
Saint Louis	18.5	36.7
San Francisco — Oakland	21.2	25.1
Washington, D.C.	18.5	28.3

Source: U.S. Department of Commerce, Bureau of the Census.

The high proportion of income that must go for rent leaves less money in such households for other expenses. Undoubtedly, this hardship is a major reason many Negro households regard housing as one of their worst problems.

AMERICAN HOUSING NEEDS

The President's Committee on Urban Housing

This set of analyses and tables provides some further evidence on the magnitude of housing problems in the United States. Based on work done for the special committee on urban housing, the selection includes some of the most recent available estimates of housing needs. Given our avowed goal of providing a decent home for everyone, the selection outlines the enormity of fulfilling that objective.

The selection comes from the report of the President's Committee on Urban Housing, *A Decent Home,* published in 1968.

- How many American families are too poor to afford the market rate price for adequate housing? Are their numbers increasing or declining?
- How many existing homes are unfit for occupancy by the Nation's standard of living?
- How many homes must be built to meet the growing needs of the total population?

When this Committee received its charge from the President in June, 1967, reliable statistics for answering such questions were so difficult to obtain that TEMPO, General Electric's Center for Advanced Studies, was commissioned to make an in-depth computerized study of current and future U.S. housing construction and subsidy requirements. In addition the Committee reviewed an independent study by Robert Gladstone and Associates prepared for a Committee member. . . .

26 Million New or Rehabilitated Housing Units

TEMPO began by analyzing National population trends reflected in the 1950 and 1960 U.S. Censuses and then projected to 1978 the Nation's urban and rural population growth, new household formation, and racial characteristics. The basic trends can be seen in Table 1. With these projections determined, TEMPO next analyzed the fate of today's 66 million

Source: The President's Committee on Urban Housing, "American Housing Needs," from *A Decent Home.* Washington, D.C.: U.S. Government, 1968.

housing units over the next decade: how many will be lost by demolition, destruction and merger? How many will deteriorate? How many must be demolished or rehabilitated if all substandard housing is to be eliminated by 1978?

By coupling the population trends (Table 1) with the projected fate of existing housing, TEMPO produced estimates of total gross construction needs, both to accommodate the growing population and for replacement or rehabilitation of all substandard units.

TEMPO's findings on construction needs can be found in Table 2.

TEMPO found our Nation must build and rehabilitate 26 million houses and apartments in the next decade to provide for all the new households forming, to allow enough vacancies for our increasingly mobile population, to replace houses destroyed or demolished, and to eliminate all substandard housing. Gladstone, using a different approach emphasizing market analysis, estimates 10-year construction needs at a comparable level. [Table 3 presents a detailed breakdown of projected substandard units.]

The total figure of 26 million presents two major challenges to the Nation:

- Greatly expanded production for families who can afford adequate housing without government assistance.
- Measures to relieve the severe shortage of adequate housing for the poor.

The latter, a more immediate social problem and the primary subject of the Committee's work, is set in the context of the former. The housing market and the housing industry are all of a piece with each of the several parts affecting the others. Finding and producing housing for the urban poor is made more difficult if more resources must also be devoted to provide added housing for the total population. If the housing needs of middle-income citizens are not met, then it will be impossible to meet the housing needs of the great mass of the poor.

To meet this projected total need for the coming decade there must be a vast increase of the Nation's

TABLE 1. Population and Household Characteristics of the United States and Percentages of Selected Population Classes — 1950, 1960, 1966, 1968, 1978

	1950	1960	1966	1968	1978
Population (millions):					
Total	151.3	178.5	194.1	201.8	235.2
White	135.1	158.1	170.8	177.3	204.3
Nonwhite	16.2	20.4	23.3	24.5	30.9
Central City:					
White	45.5	47.5	46.6	46.1	44.9
Nonwhite	6.3	10.3	12.8	13.5	18.8
Households (millions):					
Total	42.9	53.0	58.9	60.9	74.3
White	39.0	47.9	53.0	54.8	66.3
Nonwhite	3.9	5.1	5.9	6.1	8.0
Percentages of U.S. population:					
Inside SMSA: *					
White [1]	59	62	64	64	65
Nonwhite [2]	56	64	68	70	77
Central City:					
White [1]	34	30	27	26	22
Nonwhite [2]	43	51	55	55	61
Nonwhite as percent of total Central City	12	18	22	23	30

* Standard Metropolitan Statistical Area.
[1] Relative to the total United States white population.
[2] Relative to the total United States nonwhite population.

TABLE 2. U.S. Housing Construction Needs — 1968 to 1978 (Millions of Units)

Construction of new standard units:	
Units for new households	13.4
Replacement of net removals of standard units	3.0
Allowance for vacancies	1.6
Subtotal	18.0
Replacement or rehabilitation of substandard units:	
Units becoming substandard during 1968–78	2.0
Replacement of net removals	2.0
Other substandard units in the inventory in 1966	4.7
Subtotal	8.7
Total Construction Needs	26.7

Source: GE TEMPO, *United States Housing Needs: 1968–1978.*

TABLE 3. Occupied Substandard Housing Units — 1950 to 1978 (Thousands of Units)

Category	1950	1960	1966 [1]	1978 [1]
Total units	15,256	9,007	6,727	4,300
By location:				
Inside SMSA	5,426	2,761	2,088	2,150
Outside SMSA	9,830	6,246	4,639	2,150
SMSA	35	31	30	50
Percent inside				
By condition:				
DILAP [2]	3,708	3,083	2,663	1,900
NDIP [3]	11,548	5,924	4,064	2,400

[1] TEMPO projections.
[2] DILAP means "dilapidated with adequate plumbing."
[3] NDIP means "not dilapidated with inadequate plumbing."

Source: GE TEMPO, *United States Housing Needs: 1968–1978.*

housing production. The average of 2.6 million new and rehabilitated units required for each of the 10 years, in order to meet this objective, compares with the current annual rate of 1.5 million new housing units per year. Recently the Nation has produced only about 50,000 subsidized units a year — in 10 years at that rate, only half a million. Production of both subsidized and unsubsidized housing must clearly be expanded to rid the cities of substandard housing by 1978.

Six to Eight Million Units for the Poor

Over the next 10 years, assuming that current economic trends and National policies continue without marked change, the number of American households unable to afford decent housing will remain almost constant. . . . TEMPO, besides calculating the housing construction levels required to eliminate substandard housing in the next decade, also carried out the complementary task of projecting the number of families who are, and will be, unable to afford adequate housing without government assistance. Its estimates on these "noneffective demand households" are shown in Table 4.

▪ *When Does a Family Need a Subsidy?*

To speak of millions of families who "cannot afford decent housing" implies a standard of what is reasonable or fair for a family to pay for shelter.

TEMPO found that (1) the average relation of housing expenditures to income for the U.S. total population is about 15 percent but (2) that white families earning between $4,000 to $5,000 a year spend an average of 20 percent of their income for housing. It employed this 20 percent figure to reach its estimate and projection of families unable to afford standard housing without some form of subsidy. Gladstone, on the other hand, applied the Federal rent supplement program's criterion, under which a family must allocate 25 percent of their gross monthly income for shelter costs. In many European countries, the percentage of income paid by families in subsidized housing is considerably smaller than either figure. . . .

▪ *A Look at These Nearly Eight Million Needy Families*

One may divide the families requiring housing subsidies into two broad income groups:

TABLE 4.   United States Noneffective Demand Households (in Millions)

	White households			Nonwhite households			
Year	Inside SMSA	Outside SMSA	Total	Inside SMSA	Outside SMSA	Total	Total households
1960	3.6	2.5	6.1	1.0	1.2	2.2	8.3
1968	3.4	2.2	5.6	1.0	1.2	2.2	7.8
1978	3.4	1.9	5.3	1.1	1.1	2.2	7.5

Source: GE TEMPO, *United States Housing Needs: 1968–1978.*

The number of house-poor families will decline only slightly in the coming decade, if help is not forthcoming. One family in eight is now house-poor, and only slow improvement is in sight. Massive government assistance is essential not only to enable these families to afford adequate quarters, but also to make the production target of 26 million units feasible as an economic matter. We estimate that six to eight million families must be receiving housing assistance by 1978, if all Americans are to be living in decent housing by that time.

- Those below the Federal government's poverty line (called "low income" for purposes of Federal housing programs), and
- Those above the poverty line but who would still have to pay more than 20 to 25 percent of their income for decent housing in the absence of a subsidy (called "moderate income" for purposes of Federal housing programs).

Economic characteristics.   Among low- and moderate-income families requiring a subsidy, the great-

TABLE 5.   Income Distribution of Households Inside All SMSAs, 1960 and 1978

Annual income ($1,000)	1960 Households in —		1978 Households in —	
	Thousands	Percent	Thousands	Percent
Less than 2.0	5,014	14.7	5,246	10.5
2.0 to 2.9	2,541	7.5	2,960	5.9
3.0 to 3.9	2,932	8.6	2,824	5.6
4.0 to 4.9	3,482	10.2	3,072	6.1
5.0 to 5.9	4,015	11.8	3,285	6.6
6.0 to 6.9	3,557	10.5	3,640	7.1
7.0 to 9.9	6,930	20.4	8,685	17.3
10.0 or more	5,538	16.3	20,434	40.7
Total	34,009	100.0	50,145	100.0

Source: Derived from GE TEMPO, *United States Housing Needs: 1968–1978.*

est need, perhaps not surprisingly, is that of the poorest of the poor. What is surprising is that their needs have not received priority.

Table 5 presents TEMPO's projection of the income distribution of households in metropolitan areas in 1978. The table suggests that while the percentage of urban families earning less than $4,000 a year will decline from 31 percent in 1960 to 22 percent in 1978, their absolute numbers will *increase* slightly. Even in 1978, almost half of the urban families with incomes under $4,000 will be earning less than $2,000.

TABLE 6.   Distribution of Noneffective Demand Households by White and Nonwhite Head, Inside All SMSAs — 1960, 1968, 1978

Year	White head		Nonwhite head	
	Thousands	Percent [1]	Thousands	Percent [2]
1960	3,612	11.8	1,017	29.2
1968	3,374	9.6	989	23.4
1978	3,380	7.7	1,132	18.3

[1] Relative to all white families in SMSAs.
[2] Relative to all nonwhite families in SMSAs.

Source: GE TEMPO, *United States Housing Needs: 1968–1978.*

Racial characteristics. About 70 percent of the six to eight million families unable to afford housing will be white, and about 30 percent will be non-white. The nationwide proportionate need among nonwhites will be almost three times more acute than among the white majority. In 1978, one in every four nonwhite families will need housing assistance, compared to only one in every 12 white families. Also in 1978, as Table 6 shows, 18 percent of all *urban* nonwhite families will require some form of housing subsidy, compared to only about 8 percent of all urban white families. [Table 7 presents more detailed figures.]

The nonwhite family must pay an economic penalty because of racial discrimination. "Nonwhites," TEMPO concluded after amassing data on National housing cost patterns, "must earn approximately one-third more annual income than whites, irrespective of household size, to assure [themselves of] standard housing." . . .

Geographic characteristics. The six to eight million families in need of housing assistance live in rural America as well as in what the President called "the corroded core of the American city."

TABLE 7.   Percentage of White and Nonwhite Households in Specific Income Groups Occupying Substandard Housing, Inside and Outside SMSAs — 1960

Annual income: [1] Household characteristics (dollars in thousands)	Inside SMSAs		Outside SMSAs	
	White (per-cent)	Non-white (per-cent)	White (per-cent)	Non-white (per-cent)
Under 2.0	21	45	45	87
2.0 to 2.9	15	35	33	77
3.0 to 3.9	12	28	25	65
4.0 to 4.9	9	21	18	56
5.0 to 5.9	6	16	13	49
6.0 to 6.9	4	14	10	43
7.0 to 9.9	2	9	7	36
Over 10.0	1	7	4	31
All incomes	7	28	23	77

[1] Income is for the calendar year 1959, and is limited to that received by the primary family or primary individual.

Source: GE TEMPO, *United States Housing Needs: 1968–1978.*

According to TEMPO, only about 56 percent of today's house-poor families live in metropolitan areas with populations of 50,000 or more (Standard Metropolitan Statistical Areas). TEMPO's projections indicate that subsidy requirement in these areas will increase to 60 percent of total requirements by 1978, however, because the numbers of needy urban dwellers will remain relatively constant while the numbers of their rural counterparts will decline.... About one-eighth of the house-poor families in 1978 will be nonwhite households living in the central cities.

This report emphasizes urban housing needs. It is not our intention, however, to minimize or ignore the sizable housing problems of rural America for both needs are tightly related. A recurring factor in the life of urban slums has been a steady trek of rural poor — black and white — from the countryside to the nation's big industrial cities.

The elderly. One of the largest and neediest groups among the poor are the elderly — couples, widowers, bachelors, widows — living on social security, meager savings, a pension, or welfare. TEMPO projects that nearly half of the 3.4 million white urban households needing housing assistance in 1978 will be headed by a person aged 65 or older. These older Americans make up a much larger part of the American poor than is the impression sometimes given by the current literature on poverty. In 1960, 77 percent of all persons over 65 who lived alone had incomes of less than $2,000 — making them one of the largest of all the subgroups of the poor.

FEDERAL HOUSING PROGRAMS

The President's Committee on Urban Housing

These excerpts outline the features of major federal housing programs designed to provide housing for the poor. The selection makes clear that policy is tending more and more toward subsidy to private industry for low-cost housing construction and that even the most recent subsidy programs do not provide sufficient subsidy to induce housing for the truly poor.

Like the preceding selection, this comes from *A Decent Home.* This selection has been heavily excerpted; many small administrative and operational details about each program have been delated.

There are a great many Federal housing programs. Most are administered by HUD, but the Veterans Administration, the Farmers Home Administration, and the Department of Defense all have significant housing programs of their own. Many of the HUD

Source: The President's Committee on Urban Housing, "Federal Housing Programs," from *A Decent Home.* Washington, D.C.: U.S. Government, 1968.

programs, like the traditional mortgage insurance programs of FHA, do not involve the subsidization of housing costs. The major HUD housing subsidy programs are outlined below....

Public Housing

Although the layman may refer to all Government-assisted housing as "public housing," the term is used by housing professionals only to denote the specific program begun in 1937. The Public Housing program, as it has traditionally operated, places responsibility for development, ownership, and management of subsidized rental projects in the hands of independent local government agencies called housing authorities. A local housing authority cannot receive Federal assistance without the approval of both its local government and the Housing Assistance Administration, a subdivision of the Department of Housing and Urban Development. Some state laws go further and require local government approval of specific sites. Some jurisdictions, like the entire states of California and Texas, require that the Federal contract to support Public Housing projects be approved by local voters in referenda. Although practically all large cities have established housing authorities, many small jurisdictions, particularly suburban ones, do not participate in the program. For example, in 1967 less than half of the localities with populations between 25,000 and 50,000 had housing authorities. . . .

Rents in Public Housing are lowered through a number of subsidies, both Federal and local. The cost of project development is financed with long-term tax-exempt local bonds. This tax exemption lowers direct debt retirement costs. The Federal Government makes annual contributions to the local housing authority which cover all costs of retiring the bonds. The Federal Government is also authorized to pay a local authority an additional $120 per year for the benefit of each family which is elderly, displaced, extremely poor, or contains four or more children. Lastly, public housing projects do not pay normal local real estate taxes but instead pay lower amounts in-lieu-of-taxes.

Because of these substantial subsidies, admission to public housing projects is restricted to families whose incomes are below limits established by the local housing authority under statutory Federal guidelines. At the end of 1964 the median income limit for admission for a family of two adults and two children, in localities within urbanized areas, was $4,000. The highest limit ($5,760) was in New York City. The median income of all families admitted to Public Housing in recent years has been roughly $2,500. The median rent for all public housing units is approximately $45. Roughly one-half of all public housing units are occupied by Negro tenants and one-third by elderly persons. Given the inadequate coverage and size of welfare payments, there are still millions of families who are too poor to live in public housing projects. Even those who live there may have to commit a disproportionate share of their incomes to pay the low rents. . . .

In 1967, the Public Housing program included some 650,000 units which housed almost 2.4 million persons. This figure dwarfs production totals under the other programs described below, principally because Public Housing was the only housing subsidy program in the United States until the last decade. Table 1 presents production figures for all Public

TABLE 1. Low-Rent Public Housing Units Completed, Acquired, or Leased for Calendar Years 1939–67

Year	Units	Year	Units
1939	4,960	1954	44,293
1940	34,308	1955	20,899
1941	61,065	1956	11,993
1942	36,172	1957	10,513
1943	24,296	1958	15,472
1944	3,269	1959	21,939
1945	2,080	1960	16,401
1946	1,925	1961	20,965
1947	466	1962	28,682
1948	1,348	1963	27,327
1949	547	1964	24,488
1950	1,255	1965	30,769
1951	10,246	1966	31,483
1952	58,258	1967	38,756
1953	58,214		

Source: Housing Assistance Administration.

Housing programs between 1939 and 1967. Production has been rather erratic, at least until recent years; the highest production peaks were reached in 1941 and 1952–53.

202 and 221(d)(3) Below Market Interest Rates Programs

These two low-interest loan programs, although differing in details, use the same subsidy technique and are best analyzed together. The 202 program begun in 1959 is administered by the Housing Assistance Administration which is also responsible for Public Housing. The subsidy used is a direct loan from HUD to sponsoring nonprofit corporations, originally at an interest rate based on the outstanding Federal debt and since 1965 at a flat 3 percent interest rate. Profit-motivated sponsors are not permitted to own these projects; only elderly or handicapped persons may live in 202 projects. Current income limits for tenant eligibility are the lesser of: (1) $4,500 per year for single persons, and $5,400 per year for two person families; or (2) 80 percent of the appropriate 221(d)(3) BMIR limits. Under this program, HUD also provides the interim financing needed for construction, again at a 3 percent rate of interest. The permanent loans may have a term of up to 50 years and can cover up to 100 percent of the costs of a project. Projects built under 202 are *not* restricted to jurisdictions which have HUD-approved Workable Programs.

TABLE 2.   Average or Minimum Required Rentals on Newly Constructed One- and Two-Bedroom Apartments Under Different Federal Housing Programs and the Required Family Income Implied at Specified Rent-Income Ratios *

| | | | Required income at rent-income ratios of 20 or 25 percent for families occupying — | | | |
| | Required annual (monthly) rentals on units with — | | One bedroom | | Two bedrooms | |
Program	One bedroom	Two bedrooms	20 percent	25 percent	20 percent	25 percent
207 average (no subsidy)	$2,270 ($189)	$2,719 ($227)	$11,350	$9,080	$13,595	$10,876
Public Housing average	905 (75)	1,161 (97)	4,525	3,620	5,805	4,644
Rent Supplement minimum	472 (39)	540 (45)	2,360	1,888	2,700	2,160
236 minimum	1,472 (123)	1,763 (147)	7,360	5,888	8,815	7,052
221(d)(3) BMIR average	1,664 (139)	1,993 (166)	8,320	6,656	9,965	7,972

* The calculations apply to Detroit in 1967 and cities with similar cost levels. Within the group of cities with more than 2 million inhabitants, Detroit had the lowest dwelling construction cost limits for Public Housing in 1966. They were at the same level as those in Dallas (population 1.1 million in 1960). Development cost limits in all other cases except the Rent Supplement program (RS) were assumed to be equal to those specified for 221(d)(3) BMIR. These were $14,150 for one-bedroom and $16,950 for a two-bedroom dwelling unit. No rent supplement projects have been completed in Detroit by 1967.

Source: Von Furstenberg and Moskof: *Federally Assisted Rental Housing Programs: Which Income Groups Have They Served or Whom Can They Be Expected to Serve?*

The 221(d)(3) Below Market Interest Rate program (221(d)(3)BMIR), a considerably broader program than 202 in terms of eligible sponsors and eligible tenants, was begun in 1961. FNMA is now authorized to purchase 221(d)(3) mortgages bearing interest rates of 3 percent. . . .

Table 2 presents projections of the rent levels achievable in Detroit with the 221(d)(3) BMIR, Public Housing and Rent Supplement programs and compares them with those achievable in nonsubsidized housing represented by the Section 207 program. It also indicates the incomes needed to support the required rents for 20 and 25 percent rent-income ratios. While this table is based only on Detroit cost data and contains some assumptions which may not be generally applicable, it does serve to illustrate that housing cannot be generally built for rents which low-income groups can be expected to pay without subsidies at least as great as those provided by the Rent Supplement program.

As of June 1967, 62,000 units of 221(d)(3) BMIR housing had been completed or were under construction. Roughly one-half of these units had been built by profit-motivated developers and about one-half by non-profit and cooperative sponsors. . . .

Rent Supplement

The Rent Supplement program was offered by the Administration in 1965 as a substitute for 221(d)(3) BMIR. Under the rent supplement technique, the tenant family pays 25 percent of its income toward rent, while the Federal Government pays directly to the landlord the difference between economic rent levels and the tenant's contribution. This approach has the advantages of keying the amount of subsidy to the tenant's need and of spreading the cost to the Federal Government over a long period. In its deliberations on the Housing Act of 1965, Congress did not accept the Administration's recommendation that the Rent Supplement program be aimed at moderate-income families as well as low-income families. Instead, it adopted the Rent Supplement program only after restricting eligibility for supplements to families whose incomes on admission are below the eligibility limits for Public Housing in the same locality. In addition, Congress continued the 221(d)(3) program instead of substituting the Rent Supplement program for it as the Administration had recommended.

In essence, the Rent Supplement program attempts to shift the responsibility for building and operating low-rent housing projects from the local housing authorities (relied on in the Public Housing program) to private groups, both profit-motivated and nonprofit. After receiving approval of a proposed project from FHA (which administers the program), the private housing owner finances his project with a private mortgage at the market interest rate. On completion of construction, the housing owner rents units in the project to any family he chooses. However, not all tenants in a project are eligible for supplements. To be eligible, a family must have a low income (one below limits established by the Secretary of HUD which themselves must be below the limit for admission to Public Housing in that area), have few assets, and be a member of one of the following deserving groups: elderly, handicapped, displaced by Government action or natural disaster, or now living in substandard housing. As mentioned, these eligible tenants pay 25 percent of their income toward rents and the Federal Government pays any remainder directly to the landlord. Tenants who are not eligible for supplements pay the entire rent themselves. As a tenant's income rises, his supplement is reduced. For this reason, a family whose income rises substantially after admission to a Rent Supplement project is not required to leave it.

Congress passed the Rent Supplement program by the smallest of margins in 1965 and has since limited its implementation in a number of ways. The program has received few appropriations; in fact it has barely survived attacks during the appropriations stage. To mollify Congressional pressures HUD has been forced to impose regulations on the program which have made it increasingly unworkable. One regulation requires that in no instance may a tenant receive a supplement which exceeds 70 percent of the fair market rental of the unit. Other regulations which have proved to be very damaging to the program establish specific dollar limits on construction costs and on maximum fair market rental. These low maximums inhibit production and force those who do build to produce rather austere projects. Still other regulations flatly prohibit even some of the limited amenities allowed in 221(d)(3) BHIR projects....

The basic rent supplement approach, emphasizing flexible subsidies as well as private ownership, private financing, and private management, has many advantages. As Table 2 illustrates, this pro-

gram can reach rather low income levels. If Congressional limits were removed, this program could serve the full range of families in need and could be used effectively by private business.

Section 236 Rental Housing Program

The new 236 program, part of the Housing Act of 1968, is designed to replace eventually both the 202 and 221(d)(3) programs. Like the Rent Supplement program, it relies on private developers — both nonprofit and profit-oriented — or rental or cooperative housing. The subsidy technique is similar to that used in the Rent Supplement program: tenants pay 25 percent of their income toward rent, and the Federal Government pays a supplement which makes up the difference between a tenant's payment and market rents. There is, however, a crucial difference. The maximum Federal payment on a unit lowers the rent to the level which would be achieved had the project been financed with a 1 percent mortgage. Thus, the primary difference between 236 and the Rent Supplement program is that the subsidy under 236 is not as deep.

The maximum Federal subsidy to a tenant per month will be about $50 to $60. This is not enough to reach the poorest families. To be eligible, a family's income (less $300 per child) must not exceed 135 percent of the limits for admission to Public Housing projects. Thus, 236 will serve primarily families whose incomes range between $4,000 and $6,500 per year. Table 2 indicates that in high cost area, such as Detroit, tenant incomes must be higher unless families chose to allocate more than 25 percent of gross income to housing. To alleviate this problem partially, 20 percent of the units of a 236 project can be occupied by tenants receiving Rent Supplement payments and who thus might have lower incomes....

Homeownership Program — Section 235

The Homeownership program contained in the Housing Act of 1968 is a major landmark in the history of Federal housing legislation. Prior to its enactment, all major housing subsidy programs were limited to rental units, with cooperative housing units permitted in a few instances.

Assistance under the new Homeownership program generally will be restricted to new or substantially rehabilitated units. Private homebuilders will plan the housing and have it approved by FHA for inclusion in the program prior to the beginning of construction. When built, the houses will be sold to eligible buyers who will finance their purchases with FHA-insured market rate mortgages from private lenders. The subsidy technique used is similar to that in the Section 236 rental program. The Federal Government contracts to pay part of the homebuyer's mortgage payments. The maximum Government subsidy reduces the homebuyer's payment to that which he would owe if his purchase had been financed with a mortgage bearing an interest rate of 1 percent. Translated into dollars, the maximum subsidy will be about $40 to $70 a month, depending on the value of the house and the market interest rate. The actual amount of the subsidy may be somewhat less, depending on the income of the family buying the house. All families must devote at least 20 percent of their income to paying off the mortgage. (This figure of 20 percent is lower than the 25 percent used under the rental programs because the homebuyer must bear all utility charges, maintenance, and repair expenses himself.) As family income rises, the Federal payments due to the lender consequently will be gradually reduced and eventually eliminated.

Because the maximum Federal subsidy is limited, the program will not be of much help to families with very low incomes. However, it will provide assistance to those in the broad range of incomes between $3,000 and $7,000 a year. . . .

This brief description of the major Federal housing programs reveals that a striking acceleration in the innovation of new programs has occurred in the last decade and particularly in the last five years. Even the conventional Public Housing program, the only Federal housing subsidy program in existence between 1937 and 1959, has been rejuvenated with recent innovations. The basic trends in policy developments are:

- Increased reliance on private development, private financing, private ownership, and private management of subsidized housing;
- Greater subsidization of homeownership (and membership in cooperatives or condominiums) and less exclusive emphasis on rental buildings;
- Less reliance on low interest loans and greater reliance on periodic Federal subsidies;
- Less emphasis on particularized programs . . . in favor of broadly applicable programs; and
- More emphasis on subsidy programs for families somewhat above the very lowest income levels.

AMERICA'S HOUSING PROBLEMS

Irving H. Welfeld

Reflecting the liberal and conservative perspectives, Welfeld argues in this selection that housing problems can be solved through a judicious combination of programs to encourage private production of housing and a federal program of financial assistance to the poor. The selection comes from a longer book by the same title. In the book, Welfeld spells out specific proposals that would meet the criteria he outlines here.

The author has served as a policy analyst in the U.S. Department of Housing and Urban Development.

The basic goal of national housing policy was set forth in the Housing Act of 1949.

Source: Reprinted with permission from Irving H. Welfeld, *America's Housing Problem: An Approach to Its Solution* (Washington, D.C.: The American Enterprise Institute for Public Policy Research, 1973).

The Congress hereby declares that the general welfare and the security of the Nation and the health and living standards of its people require

. . . the realization as soon as feasible of the goal of a decent home and a suitable environment for every American family. . . .[1]

To accomplish this goal, two things must be done. First there must be enough housing units so that decent housing exists for every family. If there are not enough units, it will be necessary to produce more. Second, every household must be able to afford decent housing. If this is not the case, it will be necessary to provide financial assistance to some households.[2]

Unfortunately, the distinction between housing production and financial assistance has been blurred in the framing of American housing subsidy programs. The basic programs have attempted to solve the "housing problem" by constructing dwelling units for those who cannot afford them. On the production side, the current approach has led to programs that are inefficient, that lack general applicability and market discipline, and that maximize federal involvement, inequity to nonrecipients, and opportunities for fraud. On the assistance side, the current approach has led to programs that serve little more than 10 percent of the households in need of assistance.

A new approach is needed — an approach that recognizes the distinction between housing production and financial assistance.

Why Produce Housing?

Even if one accepts the goal of a "decent" home for every American, the necessity for a program of housing production is questionable on two grounds. First, it may be asked — and this is a question of fact — is there a housing shortage? Second, it may be asked — and this is a question of policy — even if there is a housing shortage, would a financial assistance program adequately stimulate increased production without unacceptable side effects?

■ *The Question of Fact*

Using as its standard of adequacy the existence of a full complement of plumbing facilities (hot and cold indoor piped water, plus an indoor flush toilet and bathtub or shower for the exclusive use of the unit's occupants), the 1970 Census counted 4,668,303 inadequate, year-round housing units (6.9 percent of the existing stock).[3] Of these, 1,699,682 units were in urban areas and 2,985,539 were in rural areas. Inadequate housing in urban areas represented 3.4 percent of total urban housing units, and inadequate housing in rural areas constituted 16.9 percent of total rural housing units.[4]

In addition to the inadequate units, a sizable number of adequate units were overcrowded.[5] Defining overcrowding as more than 1.5 persons per room, 1,028,291 units were overcrowded.[6] Defining overcrowding as more than 1.0 persons per room, 4,464,376 units were overcrowded. Depending on the definition of overcrowding, the sum of inadequate (those lacking complete facilities) and overcrowded adequate units was either 9.1 or 5.7 million units in 1969.

This does not imply that the goal of adequate housing cannnot be accomplished by private enterprise without a federal presence. Since the passage of the Housing Act of 1949, housing production has far outpaced new household formation. Over the twenty-year period from 1950 through 1970, approximately 1.5 new housing units were constructed for each new household formed despite the even more rapid growth in households than in population. (The median size of households declined from 3.1 to 2.7 persons during this period.) Inadequate housing

---

[1] Housing Act of 1949, Section 2, 42 U.S.C. Section 1441 (1964).

[2] As used in this monograph, an assistance strategy denotes one intended to enable poor households to pay for decent housing. It does not denote the manner in which a subsidy is delivered. For example, the current rent supplement program assists poor families even though the subsidy payment is made to the landlord.

[3] U.S. Bureau of the Census, *General Housing Characteristics — United States Summary* (Washington: U.S. Government Printing Office, 1971), Table 1.

[4] *Ibid.,* Table 2. The statistics include vacant as well as occupied units. The vacancy rate was 10.1 percent (1,778,848 units) in rural areas and 4.9 percent (2,427,971 units) in urban areas. *Ibid.,* Table 10. Approximately 97 percent of the urban vacant units and 88 of the rural vacant units were adequate. U.S. Bureau of the Census, *Current Housing Reports — Housing Vacancies* (Washington: U.S. Government Printing Office, August 1972), Table 7 (data for vacant units inside and outside of S.M.S.A.'s). There are, therefore 1,626,843 occupied inadequate urban units (3.4 percent) and 2,77,2077 occupied inadequate rural units (17.4 percent).

[5] *Ibid.,* Table 4.

[6] *Ibid.*

(units lacking a full complement of plumbing facilities) dropped from 37 percent of the housing stock in 1950 to 17 percent in 1960 to 7 percent in 1970. The incidence of overcrowding (more than one person per room) dropped from 16 percent in 1950 to 12 percent in 1960 to 8 percent in 1970.[7]

This, indeed, occurred during a period when the net effect of government action on the housing stock was negative — that is, government programs destroyed more units than they built.[8] The main causes of the housing improvement were (1) the productivity of private enterprise in building and rehabilitating and (2) the federal bulldozer, insofar as it demolished (through the urban renewal, public housing and highway programs) more substandard than standard units.

Only within the last five years has federally subsidized construction been significant. Housing produced under federal programs totaled 163,360 units in 1968, increased to 430,990 units in 1970, 433,480 in 1971 and an estimated 452,300 in 1972.[9] This level of federal activity need not be an enduring feature of the housing scene since the basic problem is not the private sector's inability to produce an adequate supply of decent housing. The problem is not on the supply side but on the demand side.

■ A Question of Policy

Even with the present shortage of decent units, the need for a direct federal presence in production is not self-evident. Why not attempt to kill two birds with one stone? If housing allowances were given to poor families, would not these families be able to pay for standard units? In response to the increase in demand, would not suppliers produce more units?

There are at least five possible scenarios for an assistance program which (1) increases the number of poor households covered and (2) provides payments at a level sufficient to permit the poor to bid

for higher quality housing but is not so generous as to enable them to afford new housing.

1. The poor outbid lower middle-income households for standard units. The latter move into the units vacated by the poor.
2. The poor do not outbid lower middle-income households for standard units and remain residents of their original units.
3. Either (1) or (2) is the case and landlords raise prices on the units originally occupied by the poor.
4. Either (1) or (2) is the case and landlords raise prices on the units originally occupied by the poor but also improve their quality.
5. The poor pay more and obtain the standard apartments of lower middle-income households. The latter in turn pay more[10] and obtain better housing. This ripple effect ends when builders add to the housing supply inasmuch as the price of the new units is competitive with the rent of older units.

The scenarios are simplified. It is likely that the actual result of the assistance program defined above might be some combination of the third, fourth and fifth scenarios. However, it is clear that the possibility that some nonpoor households end up in poorer housing or suffer higher housing costs reduces the attractiveness of a housing policy that relies exclusively on assistance.

Why Give Financial Assistance?

A government housing production strategy would move in the opposite direction from a strategy of financial assistance. With an increase in the supply of housing, the ripple effect (more commonly referred to as the filtering or turnover process) would tend to lower housing costs to lower income households in relative if not absolute terms. If this in fact were the result of a production program, would a program of financial assistance be necessary? As production was increased to a level where the housing gap is closed, would not the housing problem of the poor be solved?

---

[7] *Message from the President of the United States, Fourth Annual Housing Report on National Housing Goals* (Washington: U.S. Government Printing Office, 1972), pp. 21–23; hereinafter cited as *Fourth Annual Report.*

[8] National Commission on Urban Problems, *Building the American City: Report to the Congress and the President of the United States* (Washington: U.S. Government Printing Office, 1968), pp. 80–82; hereinafter cited as *Douglas Commission Report.*

[9] *Fourth Annual Report,* p. 46.

[10] Homeowners, who constitute roughly two-thirds of the occupants of housing, would not be burdened by rising rents.

Based on the evidence of the recent past, the answer to the last question is no. Increases in the number of units and decreases in population during the past twenty years have substantially improved the housing situation of the poor in central cities. In this regard middle class blight is often the same phenomenon as an increase in housing opportunities for lower class families. Nevertheless, despite the improvement in the supply situation for the poor, the price of standard, uncrowded, unsubsidized housing to a poor family is high relative to its income, leaving little for other necessities.

In 1970, the median rent/income ratio in the United States, for renter households with incomes of less than $5,000, was 35 percent.[11] This compares with a median rent/income ratio of 18.9 percent for households with incomes between $5,000 and $9,999, of 13.9 percent for households with incomes between $10,000 and $14,999, and 10.7 percent for households with incomes of $15,000 or more.[12] . . .

Of course, not all poor families pay such a high relative price for their housing. But when they do not, the housing stock and the neighborhood suffer. Elderly homeowners who scrimp by saving on maintenance are milking their property in the same way as the proverbial slum landlord (who often turns out to be an elderly widow) and have the same effect on the housing stock. The poor families who default on their FHA-insured mortgages are behaving in the same manner as the managers of public housing units who find themselves unable even to cover their operating costs. In this way much of the production effort to increase the supply of housing is undercut.

As a result of increases in supply, standard housing "filters down." But, if poor households cannot (or will not) pay the amounts necessary to cover the basic expenses of ownership and operation, housing will "filter out" through disinvestment and abandon-ment. This is illustrated not only by the abandonment of private housing in the central cities, but also by the massive disinvestment through deferred maintenance by local housing authorities (LHAs). Thus, without a program of financial assistance, the gains brought about by increased production are offset by a lack of effective demand.

■ The Political Answer

If assistance is necessary, the obvious economic question is why should it be given in the form of housing dollars rather than cash? Would not the taxpayer and the family be far better off with unrestricted direct cash payments? Would not a single cash payment be a more efficient way of dispensing welfare than a series of separate programs? Would not the poor family have greater freedom and dignity if it were allowed to decide how to spend the money?

The obvious practical answer is that the unrestricted cash payment is not popular with voters. After a four-year effort, the family assistance plan, which embodies a $2,400 minimum for a family of four, went down to defeat under a hail of criticism from left and right. The $2,400 minimum was both too low (for people unable to work) and too high (for people unwilling to work). Depending on one's political perspective, the family assistance plan represented a giant leap forward, or a long step backward, from the present "unworkable and undesirable" welfare system.[13] In either case, it was politically unfeasible.

There are political advantages to restricting the cash transfer to specified essentials. As James Tobin has written, "The social conscience is more offended by severe inequality in nutrition, and basic shelter . . . than by inequality in automobiles, books, clothes, furniture. . . ."[14] Even from a purely economic point of view, restricted transfers may have advantages when viewed within a broadened analytical framework. As Roger Scott has written in a recent article:

> I have taught my students that such taxes and subsidies were "economically inefficient." Now,

[11] Rent to income ratios for low-income households overstate the burden of rent since many low-income households have temporarily dropped into that category from higher income categories to which they will return, particularly in a period of cyclical downturn such as 1970. See George J. Stigler, *The Theory of Price* (New York: The Macmillan Company, 1966), pp. 35–38; Milton Friedman, *A Theory of the Consumption Function* (New York: National Bureau of Economic Research, 1957).

[12] U.S. Bureau of the Census, *Population & Housing Characteristics for the United States, by State 1970* (Washington: U.S. Government Printing Office, 1972), Table H-2.

[13] See, for example, statements of Senator Long and Senator Ribicoff during Senate debate on the "Social Security Amendments of 1972," *Congressional Record*, vol. 118, pp. S 16238–16248.

[14] James Tobin, "On Limiting the Domain of Inequality," *Journal of Law and Economics*, vol. 13 (October 1970), p. 263.

suddenly, I fear I may have been mistaken. For the world of interdependence forces me to recognize that the framework for analysis of economic inefficiency that I once used ignored an important systematic interdependence of utilities.

If a starving moron freely spends his money on balloons instead of food, who am I to say he is irrational in his behavior? I am forced to presume that his happiness is best served by his "revealed preference." But if I am to be asked to help pay for his care, then should my preferences have no weight in deciding what he will consume? [15]

Policy Criteria

A decision regarding a basic structure for the subsidy system is only the first step. With the basic structure set, it is still necessary to determine the specific programs. We must look at the criteria for judging the efficaciousness and efficiency of housing programs and see how fully the existing programs satisfy these criteria.

■ Housing Production

A well-designed production program must, in the author's view, satisfy tests on performance, efficiency, general applicability, effective incentives, reduction of federal presence, consumer choice, minimized opportunity for fraud, and minimum inequity.

Performance. The program should be capable of enticing builders and landlords to construct and upgrade more units than would have been built or rehabilitated in its absence. It should not result simply in substituting the production of subsidized units for units which would have been built with no subsidy.

Efficiency. The program should result in the production of housing services at a low cost to the taxpayer.

General Applicability. The program should be operable in all areas of the country and should take into account regional differences in incomes and housing costs.

Effective Incentives. The program should not enable a profit to be reaped if housing is built where no need exists or is below par in terms of location, structural quality or price. The subsidy should not bail out a poor builder or manager.

Reduction of Federal Presence. The program

[15] Roger Scott, "Avarice, Altruism and Second Party Preferences," *The Quarterly Journal of Economics,* vol. 86 (February 1972), p. 17.

should require no more than a minimu[m] mental regulation and supervision. This closely related to the effective incentive cr[iteria;] the extent incentives are effective, the direc[t govern-]ment role can be reduced. Much of the pap[er work,] processing, and regulation in federal housin[g pro-]grams results from the absence of effective incen[tives.] When it turned out in the late 1940s that develo[pers] could obtain large profits by building rental proje[cts] which had to be repossessed by the FHA because [of] the lack of tenants, the ensuing scandal brought ad[-]ministrative requirements that are now criticized as bureaucracy and red tape. The paper work and supervision often amount to an administrative patchwork on a surface undermined by structural defects.

Consumer Choice. The program should offer a choice in price, building type, unit size and location.

Minimized Opportunity for Fraud. The program should not provide a few developers and builders with the equivalent of a grant of hunting privileges in a game preserve. When a subsidy allocation becomes a bounty rather than a license, it also becomes an invitation to corrupt the gamekeeper.

Minimized Inequity. There are three aspects to this problem. The program should minimize unfairness between the beneficiary and his economic peers, between the beneficiary and those above him on the economic totem pole, and between the beneficiary and those below him in economic level.

Although traces of unfairness will always be present in any nonuniversal subsidy, there are, nevertheless, ways to minimize its extent and intensity. If the opportunity to benefit is available to all and the selection process is fair, the pain may be no worse than the pain of "losing" a lottery that an economic equal has "won." If the subsidy enables the recipient to obtain better housing but at a greater effort (a higher rent/income ratio) than a household with higher income, the higher income household may overlook the recipient's good luck. If the subsidy assists the higher income household to acquire new housing, any sting of unfairness to those lower on the totem pole can be salved if there is also a benefit to them in the form of increased housing opportunities — that is, if they can move into the house from which the higher income family moved.

■ Financial Assistance

With differences where appropriate, the criteria for a well-designed assistance program are like those listed above:

[Torn corner with partial text:]

...m should enable every
...e of decent housing.
...ld produce this re-
...xpayer with mini-
...sing to others.

...he program should be
...e country and should take
...differences in incomes and

...*entives.* The program should re-
...lord who meets the housing demands
...of the poor. The program should not en-
...consumer to pay such a high percentage of
...income that he has little left for necessities nor
...trap a poor family (by requiring only a nominal
investment) into purchasing a home it is unable to
maintain.

Minimized Federal Presence. The program should
require no more than a minimum of federal regulation and supervision.

Consumer Choice. The program should offer a
choice in price, building type, unit size, and location.

Minimized Opportunity for Fraud. The program
should put the barrier of self-interest in the path of
those who would be tempted to fraud.

Minimized Inequity. The benefits of the program should be available to all poor households. The
program should not enable a lower income household to obtain a more expensive unit than a higher
income household unless the lower income household
tries harder (has a higher rent/income ratio). . . .

[Welfeld next argues that existing programs do
not meet these standards and that new programs are
necessary.]

Alternative Production Programs

The objective of the three programs proposed [in
Welfeld's book] is to produce more housing as long
as the need for additional units exists. Their justification is the need for additional dwellings up to the
point where a decent unit exists for every family.
They are intended to eliminate the shortage of decent housing by enabling private builders to build
for markets that would not exist without the programs. Unlike present programs they are not subsidies to bridge the gap between what the builder
must receive to produce new dwellings and what the
poor can afford to pay.

The main feature of the three programs is their
use of the subsidy as a lever to widen the market.

In two of them, maximum leverage is obtained by
harnessing the subsidy to the income cycle of young,
mobile households. The programs retain the basic
checks and balances of the marketplace. By dissolv-
ing the distinction between subsidized and nonsubsidized developments, they minimize the need for
federal regulation and supervision. The government
becomes the beneficiary of the market relationship
between consumer and producer.

Since the proposed programs are national in character, they are neutral with respect to issues of community development. No attempt is made to engage
in social restructuring by altering the locational decisions of target households. These are decisions better made at the state and local level. The proposed
subsidies are designed so that they can be supplemented by state and local subsidies that have explicit community development objectives.

New programs in the sales, rental, and elderly
fields are set forth below. Each approach will be described and evaluated in terms of the production
policy criteria. . . .

Alternative Assistance Programs

The objective of the assistance program proposed [in
Welfeld's book] is to enable every household to pay
for decent housing. Its justification is the assumption
that the community has an obligation for the general
welfare of all its citizens. The program differs from
existing housing assistance in that it has no production component. It is intended to provide poor households with the means to pay for decent existing units,
not to directly produce new units. Indeed, it is assumed that the source of units for the program would
be the existing stock of 60 million standard units,
and that substandard housing would be destroyed or
upgraded as the occupants moved out. The production programs suggested in Chapter 3 [of Welfeld's
book] can be expected to increase the stock of housing directly whereas the assistance program discussed
here would work to that end indirectly.

The primary target of the program is the "poor."
The "poor" could be defined as either those households with incomes below the Social Security Administration's poverty thresholds or those with incomes below 50 percent of the median income level
in the local housing market area. Either definition
would be workable for a housing assistance program.
Use of the SSA's poverty threshold might be prefer-

able, because the proliferation of eligibility requirements is one factor that complicates the development of a coherent national strategy against poverty.

The proposed assistance program is meant to encompass all eligible households, not just the small percentage now benefited by existing federal housing programs. Coverage could be extended to this full constituency in stages to enable the phasing out of existing programs and to soften the initial impact on the federal budget.

The program would provide poor households with the widest possible choice of housing. Subsidies are designed to reward the family that chooses to upgrade its housing substantially. However, if a family wishes to limit its expenditure for housing and, as a result, chooses substandard quarters, its decision would be accepted. The government would have fulfilled its obligation by providing the family with the means to pay for decent housing. For the government to go further and force families into rigid expenditure patterns would be a cure more unpleasant than the illness.

Willingness to grant the poor a choice in housing (and not to require that assisted households live in standard units) is entirely consistent with a local government policy of eliminating substandard units through code enforcement and other means. Indeed, a housing assistance program that provided poor households (many of which are currently living in substandard units) with the means to pay for upgraded units meeting code requirements would remove one of the main stumbling blocks to local upgrading efforts. Although the program is not focused on housing conservation, the availability of housing dollars for the poor would almost certainly result in improving the nation's housing stock by increasing the demand for well-maintained, older properties even in low-income areas. . . .

Vicious Cycles or Virtuous Circles?

An attempt to reach the national housing goal by reliance solely on production stimulus through consumer demand or solely on the assistance approach is, as a practical matter, impossible. The thirty-five year history of housing subsidy programs shows that by attempting too much, too little is produced. Existing production programs, by striving to produce large numbers of new housing units for the poor, have managed to antagonize a substantial segment of the population. To redress their grievances, those antagonized worked changes that crippled the programs' capacity to produce many units or to help many of the poor. In each case, the expectations of the poor are disappointed and new legislation is demanded, which starts the vicious cycle in motion again.

The approach suggested in this paper relies on both housing production and housing assistance programs, but it separates subsidies to bring about new production and subsidies to households unable to pay for decent housing. By separating these strategies, political interests could be brought into close harmony and a more efficient system could be created. The result might even be called a virtuous circle. Housing production programs that made the cost of new housing attractive to middle-income families would have obvious appeal in a predominantly middle-income society. The large volume of new production could also provide substantial benefits to lower-income families by allowing good used housing to flow down to them through the filtering process. This in turn would make housing assistance to the poor more attractive politically and more feasible economically — thereby, one may hope, achieving the goal of a decent home for all American families.

MORTGAGE BANKERS AND THE POLITICS OF HOUSING

Michael E. Stone

Stone argues in this selection that many of our housing problems can be traced to the central role of banking institutions. America's housing market depends centrally on, and is therefore dominated by, mortgage lenders. Their priorities frame the growth and development of the housing industry. If certain kinds of housing are not suitable for private mortgage finance, they are unlikely to develop. Until the capitalist basis of those mortgage finance institutions is transformed, Stone concludes, many of our housing problems are likely to persist.

Stone teaches at the University of Massachusetts in Boston and has worked with many different tenant groups.

The United States is in the midst of a severe housing crisis. There are not enough dwelling units in decent condition, at appropriate locations, with required amenities and secure tenure and at bearable prices. While the present situation is particularly severe and great public concern is being voiced about it, this country has had a persistent housing problem which it has never shown itself capable of solving. Even at the times when the absolute number of housing units has been nearly sufficient, families have still had to pay an enormous percentage of their incomes for housing and millions still have had to live in squalid miserable conditions. The housing problem is not new; it has just persisted and worsened. Indeed it is unlikely that much progress will be made toward its solution unless widespread political and economic changes take place in America.

The crucial decisions in the housing sector — as in most major areas of this society — are not made primarily on the basis of human needs. Instead, the important decisions revolve around the flow of investment capital into housing, and these decisions of course are made on the basis of opportunities for profit. Due to the intrinsic nature of housing and to

Source: "The Politics of Housing: Mortgage Bankers," by Michael E. Stone. Published by permission of Transaction, Inc., from *Society*, Volume 9, no. 9. Copyright © 1972, by Transaction, Inc.

the structure of ownership in this country, housing investment is primarily by means of mortgage borrowing. Mortgage-lending institutions are the dominant force in the housing sector and contribute directly to the existence and maintenance of the housing problem.

The Housing Market

Housing possesses certain characteristics which, taken together, make it quite distinctive as an economic good. These characteristics make housing particularly vulnerable to the profit-making structure of capitalism and therefore make housing a particularly good example of the injustices and inefficiencies of the present economic order.

One of the most distinguishing qualities of housing is its durability. If reasonably well built and maintained, housing can last for generations. As a result, the stock of housing turns over and is replaced only very slowly. In any given year newly constructed housing is only about 2 to 3 percent of the total supply. In 1968, for example, there were about 66 million dwelling units in the United States and a total of about 1.5 million housing starts — 2.3 percent of the housing stock was therefore new. Last year [in 1972] housing starts reached the highest rate this country has ever seen — nearly 2.1 million units. Since there were a total of about 69 million units at the beginning of the year, new housing was 3 percent of the total stock. Even if the stated national goal of an average of 2.6 million housing starts for the ten-year period 1968–1978 were met (it was met last year, if mobile homes are included), each year new housing would still be less than 4 percent of the total.

In addition, housing is an extremely bulky commodity — a characteristic with two important aspects. First, the total construction time for new housing tends to be at least a year. Second, housing is tied to land and possesses locational advantages or disadvantages. Together, the durability and bulkiness of housing make its supply extraordinarily stable and unresponsive to changes in demand. They also make it extremely hard for equivalent or comparable replacement housing to enter the market.

The relative fixity of housing supply would probably not be terribly significant were it not for certain important features of the demand for housing. First, the need for housing is constantly expanding. The number of households is continually growing, while at the same time housing is being lost through age, neglect, disasters and clearance for highways and urban renewal. Growing competition for the existing housing drives up its price, but, in the short run at least, there is no compensating increase in supply. The market mechanism is thus rather ineffective in adjusting housing supply to housing demand.

In addition, housing is a necessity in this society. As demand increases and prices rise as a result, consumers generally have no choice but to pay. Because of climatic and social conditions in this country, people cannot choose to do without housing and live on the streets or in the woods. Because of legal constraints they cannot successfully opt out of the housing market by squatting in vacant buildings or erecting their own structures on vacant land.

The increasing and unavoidable need for a bulky commodity of relatively fixed supply inevitably drives housing expenses up as high as consumers can possibly bear, that is, to a very high proportion of every family's income. Housing is by far the largest single consumption expenditure in this country. For the population as a whole, on average 15 percent of family income goes for housing. For most poor families, housing expenditures exceed 25 percent of their already meager incomes. Over 80 percent of the residents of metropolitan areas with annual incomes of below $2,000 spend more than 35 percent of their incomes for rent. About two-thirds of households with incomes between $2,000 and $3,000 and nearly one-half of households between $3,000 and $4,000 must spend over 25 percent. At the same time, these poor families are relegated by the market to the worst housing because of their inability to compete for more costly better housing. For no other item, except perhaps medical care, are the injustices of the market economy so great and the burdens so heavy.

Given the market-determined system of monthly housing expenses, who benefits from these housing payments? Many studies reveal that typically, for both renters and for so-called homeowners, about one-quarter of monthly occupancy expenses goes for property taxes and one-quarter for utilities, maintenance, repairs, and overhead. The other half represents profits for the investors in the property — the owner of record and the mortgage lender or lenders.

At present nearly every purchase of residential real estate is financed in part by mortgage loans. Because of the long economic life of most housing and as a result of state support for mortgage lenders, the loans usually amount to about 70 to 90 percent of the purchase price and are for terms of 25 to 40 years. This means that during the first few years of ownership nearly all the investment profits go directly to the mortgage lender in the form of interest payments. Indeed, over the entire period of the loan, total payments for interest are generally much greater than the loan principal itself. For example, on a 30-year 7-percent loan, the borrower will pay in interest 1.4 times the amount of the loan.

Mortgage lenders are clearly major beneficiaries of the scarcity and resulting high prices of housing. The political significance of these benefits becomes clearer when the scope of the housing sector and the nature of mortgage lenders is considered. Dwellings and the land they occupy comprise almost one-third of the wealth of this country, and despite the slow turnover of stock, new housing represents over one-quarter of the nation's annual capital investment. Home mortgages outstanding at the end of 1970 were worth nearly $340 billion, about the same as total publicly held government debt and almost one-and-a-half times the value of all outstanding long-term bonds of nonfinancial corporations. In a typical year over four million new mortgages are written, with a net increase of mortgage debt of over $25 billion.

The collective power of mortgage-lending institutions is obviously enormous. What makes this power even more formidable is its distribution. Rather than being dispersed among a diverse and heterogeneous group of relatively small investors, it is concentrated in five major types of savings institutions. Three of these are "depository institutions" — savings and loan associations, mutual savings banks, commercial banks — and together they hold about 70 percent of outstanding mortgage debt. The two others are "contract savings institutions" — life insurance companies and retirement funds.

Each type of lending institution has an enormous scope and power. In addition, the different types have much in common and wield their power very much in concert. What is especially noteworthy about all of them is that their enormous power comes from control of wealth which they do not even own. They collect and direct the savings of tens of millions of people. Thus, the power over this wealth and much of the profits that flow from it accrue to those who do not even own it. This is a remarkable feature of modern capitalism in general as well as of the housing sector, and it has come about only relatively recently and with the active support of the federal government.

Changes in Housing Supply

Although mortgage lenders are the principal beneficiaries of the large expenditures which people must make for housing services, it might be argued that these burdensome expenditures are simply the result of excessive demand relative to supply and not the result of any action by mortgage lenders. If the supply of housing were to increase significantly, consumers would have more choices available and sellers of housing would have to compete for buyers by lowering their rents and sale prices. In fact, there are definite reasons why a housing shortage persists, and mortgage lenders play a crucial role in maintaining this shortage.

Although the supply of housing is relatively fixed, the supply does gradually change as builders and developers pursue profit opportunities created by increasing demand. What determines whether new housing gets built, however, is the cost of producing new housing relative to the price of existing housing. Thus, even though a shortage of housing drives up the price of existing housing and apparently creates a market for new housing, not much new housing will get built if production costs also rapidly increase and sharply reduce developer's potential profits. This is in fact what has been happening.

As rents rise in response to scarcity, housing investment becomes attractive to would-be landlords who hope to profit from high rents and would-be homeowners who want to escape from paying rent. As the demand for residential real estate increases, sales prices rise and the size of and demand for mortgage loans increase. Although mortgage interest rates are largely determined by the overall supply of and demand for credit in the economy, increased demand specifically for mortgage money does tend to push up interest rates. Higher interest rates and larger loans combine to produce higher monthly mortgage

payments. These higher payments will partially offset the financial attraction of buying property and thereby reduce demand somewhat. This in turn has a depressing effect on the price of houses. Mortgage lending thus prevents scarcity-induced rent increases from being fully translated into increases in sale prices for existing housing. Mortgage lending therefore inhibits the impact of increased demand on new construction.

The Cost of New Housing

In producing new housing, a developer's costs, both for single-family and multifamily housing, are roughly distributed as follows:

Site		20%
Land acquisition	10%	
Grading, sewers, etc.	10%	
Building		55%
Labor	20%	
Materials	35%	
Developer's Overhead and Profit		15%
Construction Financing		10%

It is commonly believed that labor is the main factor causing increased housing-production costs. The cost increases are allegedly attributed to the archaic closed-shop practices of the unions, low productivity and high wage settlements. This is in fact a union-busting tactic designed to divide the working class and divert attention from the major sources of cost increases — profiteering by land speculators and bankers.

Hourly wages of workers in the building trades have risen extremely rapidly when compared with other industries. What is never added though is that the average construction worker has a job only two-thirds of the year, and for the past few years there has been little enough construction work of any sort. Indeed, ever since World War II the annual average unemployment rate in the construction industry has been about twice as high as in all nonagricultural industries; since the mid-1950s it has been even more than twice as high. The apparently high wage settlements have in fact not kept annual incomes of construction workers up with workers in manufacturing.

In addition, careful studies have revealed that from 1947 to 1965 real output per man-hour in the construction industry actually increased at an average annual rate of 3.4% — quite comparable with manufacturing. According to the President's Committee on Urban Housing, labor today represents only about 20 percent of the cost of new housing, and between 1950 and 1966 the labor share of housing costs actually decreased. This relative decrease can be attributed to "rising labor productivity, transfer of many activities formerly performed on building sites back into factories, and extremely rapid increases in land prices." The assertion that labor has been the prime source of construction-cost increases is clearly a myth.

The most rapidly rising components of housing costs in recent years have actually been land costs, financing charges and closing costs. During the last few decades land has been the fastest rising major element in the cost of new housing. On average, each parcel of urban land in the U.S. more than doubled in value between 1950 and 1965. This increase refers to raw land alone and does not reflect additional increases in the cost of land development and site preparation. In the same period, for single-family FHA homes, site value (including land development) went on average from 12 to 20 percent of total house value.

As land prices rise, there is a multiplier effect on total construction costs. Developers generally tend to put more expensive or larger houses on higher-priced land. In addition, increases in land prices are generally related to increases in housing demand and housing prices. As the value of housing goes up, the value of both occupied and potentially occupied land also goes up. To the extent that land speculation is financed by mortgage borrowing, lenders contribute to and profit from increased land values.

The incredible inflation in urban land values can also be traced in a very direct way to the changes in mortgage-lending practices caused by federal intervention in the housing sector. By inducing the creation of long-term low-down-payment mortgage loans which resulted in the post-war boom in single-family home construction, state intervention encouraged land speculation, created the present scarcity and high price of land in metropolitan areas and yielded immense profits to speculators and lenders.

The other area of major cost increase is associated with profits made by the financial institutions that invest in housing production. Since housing developers rarely supply much of the capital themselves, they must go through an elaborate process to obtain the funds to build. A study by the National

Association of Home Builders of housing-cost increases from 1960 to 1964 directed sharp attention to construction financing in attributing "the greatest percentage cost increases to the factors of financing (higher interest rates and larger discounts on interim loans) and closing costs (title search, recording fees, escrow fees, title insurance, and the like)."

The market for construction financing tends automatically to limit the rate of construction of new housing. As developers compete for construction money, interest rates and/or discount points rise. Depending upon the general scarcity of money and upon the total time of construction, financing charges can add 5 to 12 percent to the cost of new housing. In addition, interim lenders, which are usually commercial banks, often will not make a construction loan unless a developer already has a commitment from another lender for a long-term mortgage loan following construction. In view of the vested interest of lenders in limiting the rate of construction so as to protect the values of their investments in existing housing, this commitment process can have a great deal of leverage over new construction.

Finally, closing costs may add another 10 percent to the price of housing. These costs, which largely represent fees received by banks and lawyers for excessive and often unnecessary paperwork, of course add to the price of existing housing as well as new housing. However, the effect of these costs is to increase the price of housing to potential buyers without passing on any of the increase to potential sellers. The net result is thus to stifle housing-market activity and thereby reduce incentives to developers for new construction.

Both in the operations of the housing market generally and in the production of new housing, financial institutions are seen to play a decisive role.

The controlling influence of mortgage-lending institutions on housing has not always existed. In fact, it really began at the start of this century and has grown mainly during the past 40 years, primarily as a result of federal intervention. In this process, an incredible thicket of agencies, structures, programs, devices and regulations has been created, designed to make housing investment profitable and secure especially for the mortgage lender.

The importance of mortgage financing for residential real estate developed from the quest for new profit opportunities by banks. According to Charles Abrams, "With the dawn of the twentieth century, funds of financial institutions swelled. New outlets for their investment had to be found. Undermortgaged real estate provided one source, new building another." Buyers still had to put up a sizable share of the purchase price and faced the traditional risks of business ventures, while mortgage terms were only three to five years, much less than the economic life of the mortgaged buildings.

The growing importance of mortgage credit for housing was at the time exerted most strongly through the supply side. By the 1920s suppliers of mortgage credit, mostly banking institutions, had already become the locus of power in housing production. As Abrams has said, "Concentration of lending power in institutions having a common interest and a common idiom gave them the power to stimulate or depress building activity. Since building activity vitally influences recovery and depression, the decisions of these institutions to lend or not to lend react upon the national welfare." Inevitably then, when the depression of the 1930s occurred, lending institutions were in the key position for action in the housing sector.

The Trigger for State Intervention

The initial shock of the Depression struck the housing sector, and especially the system of mortgage finance, with particular severity. The collapse was essentially a simple cycle that fed on itself. When the depression struck, homeowners lost their sources of income and landlords could not command high rents. Property owners therefore could not keep up their mortgage payments without drawing on their savings. But when they went to the banks to withdraw their savings the banks did not have the cash. Their assets were frozen in outstanding mortgage loans.

Unable to make their mortgage payments, owners had their properties foreclosed by the banks, and the banks were then left with houses that they could not sell. In addition, in those cases where banks did have some funds available to satisfy depositors, the withdrawal of these funds eliminated the possibility of new mortgage loans and thereby brought the housing market to a virtual standstill. The need for retooling and for state assistance was therefore obvious and compelling.

In the housing sector the restructuring took place primarily through the creation of permanent supports for the institutions supplying mortgage credit, with no benefits for the masses of people. Apart from

a few minor alterations and several additions, the basic form of these supports has remained as originally conceived.

Federal attention toward the housing sector in the 1930s resulted in three main types of structures to aid mortgage lenders. First was the creation of a central banking system for home-loan banks, comparable to the Federal Reserve System for commercial banks, along with governmental insurance of deposits for all types of banks. This system was designed to create a national mortgage market by centralizing, stabilizing and insuring mortgage-banking operations. Its purpose was to make mortgage banking more efficient, predictable and profitable and at the same time to free mortgage lenders from liability to their depositors, the very people whose money they profit from.

Passed in 1932, the Federal Home Loan Bank Act was the first major federal support for the housing sector. The Act created the Federal Home Loan Bank Board which oversees a system of 12 regional Home Loan Banks and also directs the Federal Savings and Loan Insurance Corporation. Membership in the system is open to all state and federally chartered financial institutions other than commercial banks that engage in long-term financing. Savings and loan associations have made up the great majority of membership in the system. The various regional banks act as reserve banks for their members, accepting deposits from them and making loans to them as they pursue profitable investments. Thus the system puts the credit of the federal government behind the member banks, enabling them to borrow cheaply to maintain their profit position.

In addition, the Federal Savings and Loan Insurance Corporation was intended to attract funds into member banks by promising savers that they could get their money back, virtually on demand, regardless of how poorly the bank has operated, As a result, the member banks have been able to obtain greatly increased funds for investment while at the same time reducing their obligation to the suppliers of these funds.

Since 1945 the total capital in savings and loan associations has increased over twentyfold to almost $150 billion in 1970. This fantastic growth has provided needed funds for housing, but has done so at great cost in the form of lenders' profits. And it has done so at virtually no risk to the lending institutions because of the second main feature of federal assistance — mortgage insurance.

Mortgage Insurance

The Federal Housing Administration (FHA) was established by the National Housing Act of 1934. It is in the business of insuring mortgage lenders against the risk of financial loss occurring from default on approved mortgage loans. The costs of running the business and the funds for paying off claims do not come from taxes nor from the lenders who receive the insurance. They come from the borrower, who is insured against nothing. Once again, the federal government created a device to stimulate the housing sector by reducing risk and guaranteeing profits.

The FHA mortgage-insurance system and Veterans Administration (VA) mortgage-guarantee system which was added in 1944 were together an ingenious device for greatly increasing the power and profits of mortgage lenders. Essentially the scheme was one of promoting a boom in housing sales and increasing the role of approved mortgage lenders in each housing transaction. To promote purchases the system reduced the down payment to 10 percent or less and greatly extended the loan term to at least 25 years. This in and of itself would have vastly increased the relative importance of lenders but lenders would not liberalize their loan terms in this way unless their risk could be reduced as well.

Risk reduction was provided by the insurance or guarantee of the mortgage by a federal agency, and so the system was built around this feature. Its results are well known: the vast postwar suburban boom, creating the illusion of homeownership for millions of people, while the actual owners are the mortgage lenders. The putative homeowner pays rent to the bank and also pays an insurance premium to the government. Then if he cannot make his mortgage payments, the government insurance repays the outstanding part of the loan to the mortgage holder and the government is left owning the property.

The FHA scheme has been very successful in enlarging and consolidating the power of institutional mortgage lenders. By standardizing the mortgage instrument and requiring mortgages to meet certain standards for approval, the system facilitated participation by large-scale institutions and discouraged or prevented individual lenders from participation.

It was originally expected, or at least declared, that the ceiling on interest rates for insured loans would tend to keep down interest rates on conventional loans. In fact, conventional rates have driven up to insured rates, attesting to the power of mortgage lenders and their quest for profits. Part of the power over interest rates is revealed in real adjustments up and down of the maximum interest rates FHA will permit on insured loans. A more subtle and profitable adjustment is effected, though, by the lenders themselves — through the institution of "points," a system of hidden surcharges on VA and FHA-backed mortgages which effectively circumvents the interest ceiling.

The FHA housing-subsidy programs have been built around the established formula and represent no real departure from the basic mortgage-insurance system. In these programs FHA not only provides the mortgage insurance, but also pays part of the interest on the mortgage loan. The loan is made by an approved mortgagee at the market rate, and so the lender's profits are as high as ever. Although the home buyer or tenant pays less, the lender receives his usual share. The programs thus use tax dollars to subsidize the profits of mortgage lenders, an approach quite consistent with the basic FHA philosophy.

Secondary Mortgage Markets

One problem with mortgage lending in general and especially with the long-term lending induced by FHA and VA policies is that the investment is not very liquid. If new investment opportunities come along, it is normally not very easy for a mortgage lender to convert his holdings into cash for the new investment. He certainly cannot call in the unpaid balance from the borrower since it was the borrower's own illiquid position that caused him to borrow in the first place. To overcome this difficulty of mortgage lending and to provide a means for lenders to pursue profitable opportunities as they appear, the state provided its third major structural addition in the housing sector — the national secondary mortgage market.

Prior to the 1930s there did exist some secondary markets for mortgages in which lenders would sell off their holdings to other investors. However, due to the great variation in mortgage characteristics and the great potential risk faced by such secondary investors, this market never became very large. One of the principal results of federal mortgage insurance was to provide the needed uniformity and security to make mortgages potentially more liquid.

The standardization and insurance of mortgages did not, however, result in the creation (by private capital) of national mortgage associations to act as secondary trading posts for insured mortgages. Mortgage lenders wanted to be able to sell their holdings as desired, but they did not want to be bothered with having to peddle their mortgages themselves. They wanted a ready buyer always there to serve them.

In response to this desire by the powers of the mortgage business, in 1938 Congress created the Federal National Mortgage Association (FNMA), provided it with an initial capitalization of $10 million and ordered it to buy insured mortgages. In purchasing mortgages from approved lending institutions FNMA permitted the original lenders to continue to service the loans and to receive a fee of 0.25 percent to 1 percent for doing so. In addition, FNMA was authorized to raise additional capital for its operations by issuing notes backed by the federal government.

FNMA thus made the housing sector more profitable in several ways. First, it gave mortgage lenders the liquidity they desired and still enabled them to make some profits on their mortgages even after the mortgages had been sold off. Second, by creating a large-scale, national pool of insured mortgages, FNMA was able to offer shares in this pool on a short-term basis in the securities markets, thereby making housing finance profitable for another whole group of investors.

Although initially the mortgage lenders had wanted the federal government to underwrite the costs and risks of establishing FNMA, by 1954 it had become so successful that there was great pressure for it to become privately owned and operated. The FNMA Charter Act of 1954 began the transfer process by authorizing the sale of stock to finance the secondary-market operations of FNMA. The Housing Act of 1968 completed the process and now FNMA is virtually private.

This sequence of events is one of the clearest examples of the intermeshing of the state and private business under modern capitalism. A national facility, greatly needed and desired by private business to reduce its risks and assure it of ready markets for its products, is first created and nurtured at public expense. Once it becomes established and begins to repay its costs, the facility is turned over to private interests so that its success can produce profits for them.

In the process of reorganizing FNMA in 1968, the secondary-market operations of FNMA were separated from more risky functions of special assistance, management and liquidation of holdings, which were left with a new government-underwritten corporation known as the Government National Mortgage Association. Thus the pattern of activity continues.

Finally, until 1970 FNMA was limited to purchasing government-insured mortgages. For a number of years after World War II a majority of new residential mortgages were either FHA or VA loans. In recent years the proportion has decreased to under one-fifth, mainly because the interest-rate ceiling on these loans remained somewhat below the market rate for long-term uninsured mortgage loans. This led to pressure for a secondary market for conventional mortgages. The Emergency Home Finance Act of 1970 provided for not one but two secondary-market structures for conventional mortgages: first, FNMA was authorized to purchase conventional mortgages; and second, the new Federal Home Loan Mortgage Corporation, set up under the Home Loan Bank Board, can purchase both conventional and insured mortgages from any federally insured banking institution.

Public Housing: The Exception?

The one apparent departure from the pattern of federal involvement in housing is the public-housing program. On closer examination, however, it turns out not to be so great a departure. Enacted in 1937 primarily as a job-creation program, public housing was initially opposed by mortgage lenders because it is not financed by conventional mortgage loans. Nor, however, is it financed directly by public funds. Rather, local housing authorities raise funds by selling tax-exempt federally secured bonds to private investors. In fact, the vast majority of such bonds are held by commercial banks. The federal government then makes annual payments for interest and bond retirement. In financing terms the scheme is thus not so different from the FHA subsidy.

Public housing simply provides an additional way for private investors, most particularly commercial banks, to make profits in housing with the state assuming the risk. Additionally, in market terms public housing has offered very little competition to private housing, amounting to only about 1 percent of all housing in the country and serving families too poor to compete in the private market. Finally, recent additions to the public-housing program (Turn-key I and Leased Housing) have channelled funds to private developers and landlords and thereby indirectly to mortgage lenders.

It should be emphasized that within the housing sector the crucial area of housing finance has very much participated in the transformation to a modern capitalist economy. The construction industry, which has only just begun the process of restructuring, is an important aspect of the housing sector but not the most important. Housing finance, in the shape of mortgage lending institutions, remains the dominant factor in and will undoubtedly continue to be the central and focal point of power in American housing. This will be so and millions of American families will continue to live in substandard homes and neighborhoods and continue to pay exorbitant sums for housing until and unless there are radical changes in the American political economy.

WHO BENEFITS FROM FEDERAL HOUSING POLICIES?

Larry Sawers and Howard M. Wachtel

The authors review the distributional impact of the major government housing programs. Virtually without exception, they conclude, government housing programs benefit those whose housing problems are least severe. This evidence casts doubt, they argue, on the idea that our housing policies are actually designed to help the poor.

Both authors teach economics at American University in Washington, D.C. Each has written numerous articles on various urban and social problems.

A wide variety of federal programs influence the housing market. By examining what the federal government does — not what it says — one can isolate three major themes: 1) virtually every federal program which affects housing benefits mortgage lenders, the construction industry, and land speculators; 2) the most important federal housing programs encourage home ownership, especially for those with above average income; and 3) a small amount of federal housing subsidies have gone for brief periods to groups in the population which were temporarily insurrectionary (i.e., urban low-income populations in the late 1960s). This paper will survey the major federal housing programs — mortgage market reorganization, tax subsidy of housing, public housing, urban renewal, and rental and mortgage assistance for the poor — in an attempt to elucidate their distributed impact.

Source: This selection first appeared as one section of "Activities of the Government and the Distribution of Income in the United States," a paper presented to the General Conference of the International Association for Research in Income and Wealth, September 1973. Professor Sawers has reorganized the original text and incorporated some additional material in preparing the paper for this volume.

Mortgage Credit

Beginning in the 1930s, the federal government created a number of credit institutions which have profoundly altered the mortgage market. By insuring lenders against default and assisting the secondary mortgage market, they have increased the profitability of mortgage lending. Several credit institutions have been created to insulate the housing mortgage market from other credit markets, thus protecting the housing industry from the tight money policies followed by the Federal Reserve Board. The long-term, low down-payment mortgage created by federal credit institutions has brought about an enormous increase in effective demand for housing, thus benefiting the above-average income household which could afford to buy its own home as well as benefiting lenders, developers, and builders.

The Federal Housing Administration (FHA), created in the midst of the Great Depression, has been perhaps the single most important housing program of the federal government. Housing construction had ground to a virtual standstill when in 1935 FHA first began insuring mortgages. (Housing starts had fallen 90 percent from 1929 to 1934). The contemporary practice was for mortgage lenders to require high down-payments (35 percent or more), short repayment periods (seven to ten years), and payments to include only interest with the principal due at the loan's expiration. The FHA began insuring mortgage lenders against default on mortgages with 10 percent down-payments and twenty-five year repayment periods with the principal amortized over the life of the loan. By the 1960s, some mortgages could be insured with only 1 percent down and thirty years to repay. At one stroke, the federal government created a *national* mortgage market instead of a local one and enormously increased the willingness of investors to enter the home mortgage market by removing virtually all risk involved. Since 1965 only about 15 percent of all mortgages have been insured by FHA, but federal mortgage guarantees have revolutionized the mortgage market. Furthermore, FHA provides high-ratio, short-term construction mortgages to developers and builders on FHA-approved single and multiple family dwellings. This permits profitable housing construction with little or no initial investment on the part of the developers and builders. In 1944 the Veterans Housing Administration was created to insure mortgages for veterans.

In 1938 the Federal National Mortgage Association (FNMA or Fannie Mae) was set up to expand substantially the secondary mortgage market (the repurchase of existing mortgages). FNMA increased the liquidity of lenders by allowing them to sell off mortgages and encouraged new money to enter the mortgage market by offering its shares on the short-term securities market. Here again, the effect was to make the mortgage market a national instead of local one, and thereby greatly increase the flow of funds into the housing industry. FNMA was so profitable that in 1968 it was turned over to private investors while the Government National Mortgage Association was created to take over FNMA's unprofitable activities.

The federal government has also created another set of credit institutions aimed at insulating the mortgage market from other credit markets. Savings and Loan Associations and Mutual Savings Banks are permitted to pay higher interest rates on passbook savings than commercial banks; in turn they have invested most of their depositors' money in housing mortgages. These banks are regulated by the Federal Home Loan Bank Board and depositors are insured by the Federal Savings and Loan Insurance Corporation.

These federal credit institutions have enormously increased the flow of money into the mortgage industry, thereby boosting the profits of mortgage lenders. Developers, builders, and those families affluent enough to buy their own homes have also benefited from these programs. These programs have not been primarily a cash subsidy (except for the insurance premium on mortgages for veterans), but together their benefits have most likely exceeded those of any other federal housing program.

Tax Subsidies of Housing

The largest cash subsidy of housing goes to landlords and the more affluent households which own their own homes. Landlords are subsidized via the federal income tax structure because they are allowed to deduct from their income a fictitious expense called accelerated depreciation. (See Stern, Chapter 9.) Instead of depreciating their buildings for the same amount each year, landlords are able to depreciate more in earlier years and less in later years through several formulas allowed by the Internal Revenue Service. The total depreciation cannot exceed the value of the asset, but by selling off the asset after a few years and purchasing another (which in turn is depreciated at an artificially high rate) the landlord can avoid a significant amount of taxes. Even if the asset is not sold, accelerated depreciation amounts to an interest-free loan from the U.S. Treasury. If the investor maintains a steady rate of investment, the "loan" need never be repaid. In fact, even straight-line depreciation generally exceeds the true rate of depreciation of rental housing. Housing, if well built and properly maintained, will last indefinitely; if so, the only depreciation is from obsolescence.

A second major way in which the federal tax system subsidizes housing is through various deductions allowed homeowners. Homeowners are allowed to deduct interest on mortgages and property taxes which constitute the majority of housing costs for homeowners. In addition, the imputed rental income of the house and most capital gains are untaxed. These subsidies amount to about ten billion dollars per year. (Stern, p. 357.) Since poor and low-income persons normally cannot afford to purchase a house, these tax deductions go largely to families with above-average income. Furthermore, the same deduction is worth more to those with higher tax rates; higher-income persons tend to fall in higher tax brackets and thus benefit disproportionately. The homeowners' preferences are worth on the average only 66 cents per year to the lowest income group but over $6,000 to the higher income group. (Stern, p. 359.) These provisions benefit the "average" taxpayer by offsetting about 15 percent of his/her annual housing costs and about one-third of the much higher housing costs for those at the $50,000 income level. (Douglas Commission, p. 400.)

Public Housing

The first federal sponsorship of public housing came during the depression of the 1930s. By 1937 the public housing program had achieved its present form. Local government housing authorities were authorized to pay private contractors to build public housing financed by the sale of tax-exempt bonds. The federal government services the debt and gives the local housing authority money to subsidize rents for the elderly, the very indigent, and those with large families. The program originally had several groups of beneficiaries. The construction industry benefited directly. Credit markets were bolstered because of the increased borrowing. The first tenants were from the temporarily indigent middle class. During World War II, public housing was seen as part of the mobilization effort, and was used to build housing, much of it temporary in nature, for workers in war materiel factories. The program was very nearly ended by Congress in 1949. The Korean War gave the program new life by exacerbating housing shortages; public housing construction reached a peak in 1951 that it would not match again until the late 1960s. The Eisenhower Administration was decidedly hostile to public housing, but its construction increased gradually in the late 1950s and early 1960s. It was not until the urban racial insurrections

of the mid-1960s forced the government to act that public housing again found favor in Washington as a part of the "war on poverty." Construction of public housing increased. In 1969, the federal government raised its operating subsidies so that no tenant paid more than 25 percent of his or her income in rent. When Nixon was re-elected to the presidency, his administration ended all funding of new public housing construction projects and cut back on the liberalized subsidies that had been instituted only four years earlier.

In the last two decades, public housing has been the largest single federal subsidy of housing directed primarily at the poor. Two and one-half million people live in federally subsidized public housing, and over three-quarters of the households living in public housing have incomes of less than $4,000 per year. (Aaron, pp. 108, 115.) A 1966 study showed that housing tenants received a subsidy of over one-half a billion dollars as measured by the difference between rents charged public housing tenants and equivalent private housing. (Aaron, p. 123.) Benefits have risen substantially since 1966 as the number of units of public housing has increased, but are meager when compared with the tax subsidies of housing received by the well-to-do.

Public housing is a grudging gift to the poor for another reason. Housing projects "almost inevitably consist of tall, standardized, prison-like structures completely isolated from other communities and other facilities." (Gordon, p. 362.) Operating subsidies are so stingy and construction so shoddy that public housing projects are instant slums. In seeming contradiction, "most projects have extremely low vacancy rates and long waiting lists for admission." (Aaron, p. 108.) Public housing, despite its many drawbacks, meets a crying need of the poor for better and more housing.

Public housing is commonly seen as a major attempt to relieve the housing problems of the poor — a perception which stands in sharp contrast to the facts. Instead, we see that:

> Congress has never appropriated enough money to make public housing work. Local public housing authorities have not even spent what little money the federal government has authorized, and those to whom our institutions have given control over public housing have no intention of redirecting the program in order to improve dramatically its contribution to the low-income housing stock in urban areas." (Gordon, p. 361.)

Urban Renewal

Urban renewal is normally thought of as a program which is essentially housing-oriented, and additionally, a program designed to increase the supply of housing for low-income households. In actual fact, neither of these popular conceptions is true.

Urban renewal, begun in 1949, is a program which buys up urban land, clears the property, builds needed infrastructure, and then sells the land to private developers. The subsidy goes to the developers, the new users of the land and their creditors. The subsidy comes from several sources. First, plans for urban renewal are normally announced considerably ahead of time, often years, before the acquisition of the land takes place. As soon as an area is designated for renewal, property owners understandably reduce their maintenance and repair outlays and the neighborhood begins to deteriorate physically. As residents move out, it becomes increasingly difficult to find new tenants. Rising vacancy rates lead to vandalism and accelerated deterioration. Businesses begin to close their doors. In short, the community that has existed in the urban renewal area disintegrates and property values fall. When the urban renewal authority takes possession of property, it pays the current market value, not the value of the property at the time that the area was designated for urban renewal. Property owners often bear a considerable loss which becomes in effect a subsidy to the new users of the land.

A second source of subsidy arises from the fact that the property owners are forced to sell their land whether or not they wish to. For the first time in the history of this country, the government's right of eminent domain has been used to acquire land from one set of private owners in order to give the land to another set of private citizens. Property owners are remunerated at the "fair market value," as determined ultimately by the courts, but it is clear that many property owners would not choose to sell if they had the choice. Another way of saying the same thing is that the price they would voluntarily accept for their property is higher than the amount they are forced to accept, and this difference therefore is a subsidy to the new users of the land.

A third source of subsidy arises from the fact that businesses are reimbursed for only the physical assets which it loses. A small shop may have spent a generation building a clientele within a community and its "goodwill" is by far its most important asset. If it

leases a store front and holds its inventory on credit, the shop may have only a few hundred dollars in tangible assets. Yet it would be obviously impossible to start up a new business elsewhere with only that much cash. Thus the shop-keeper is wiped out. One study has shown that over three-fifths of the 750 small businesses displaced by one urban renewal project never reopened. (Cited in Ives, p. 75.) The size of the subsidy to the new owners is the difference between what the shop-keepers would voluntarily accept as payment to move and the far smaller sum which they actually do receive.

The fourth source of subsidy is the actual "write-down" which is the difference between the urban renewal authority's outlay for acquisition, clearance, and site improvement of the land and the smaller sum which the private developers pay. The federal government pays two-thirds to three-quarters of the write-down, depending on the size of the sponsoring jurisdiction. By 1967, the federal government had spent over $6 billion on the program. But most of the subsidy of the new property owners was paid by the former property owners; not the government.

The new uses of urban renewal land are typically commercial facilities, upper-middle income or upper-income housing, and the cultural facilities which service these income groups. Some low and moderate income housing has been built, but this has not been the thrust of the program. (See Edel, Kessler and Hartman.)

Urban renewal, in fact, has reduced the supply of low-cost housing and thereby driven up rents in the remaining units. Renewal did not even remove the worst dwelling units from the housing stock! From the early fifties, urban renewal concentrated on the "gray" areas rather than on the slums *per se*. (Douglas Commission, p. 156.) By displacing blacks, urban renewal also exacerbated racial divisions within the working class, thereby strengthening the power of employers.

By the late 1960s, in response to popular uprisings by the urban poor, minor reforms in the administration of the urban renewal program — such as increased community input — were instituted. The thrust of the program, however, remained the same. Categorical grants for urban renewal were ended in 1973 and are being replaced by revenue sharing for community development. LeGates and Morgan argue that this will: 1) increase the flow of federal funds to small towns and suburbs at the expense of large, deteriorated central cities; 2) reduce overall spending for community development as revenue sharing funds are used to lower local taxes; 3) work to reduce progressive elements of urban renewal administration such as community participation and relocation benefits; and 4) lead to a rise in the non-residential use of urban renewal land. Thus the meager benefits that the urban poor received from urban renewal in the 1950s and 1960s will be further reduced.

The major beneficiaries of urban renewal have been developers, builders, and lenders as well as the new users of renewed land who have only rarely been the poor. The latter have received very few benefits from urban renewal and have born a major share of its costs.

Other Housing Subsidies of the Poor

In the last fifteen years the federal government has sponsored a number of programs other than public housing which have subsidized housing for the poor. It was not until 1968, however, that these subsidies achieved substantial levels. By 1972 the housing assistance programs set up under the Housing Act of 1968 subsidized the poor by about $450 million, (Aaron, p. 579) or by about half the government's outlays on public housing. The 1968 legislation was an attempt to bail out bankers and builders hard hit by the credit squeeze and consequent recession in the housing industry. In addition, these subsidies can be seen as an attempt to buy off the dissent of angry blacks who were burning the nation's cities in the mid-sixties.

Low-income groups probably did not receive the major share of the subsidy from these programs. In purchasing a house under the Section 235 program, the family paid a fixed amount no matter how much the house cost and the federal government paid the rest. This allowed real estate speculators to buy up nearly worthless property and sell it to unsophisticated purchasers — often with hardsell tactics — at exorbitant mark-ups. The new owners often did not have the resources to pay the enormous repair and maintenance expenditures on a dwelling that was unfit for habitation. The new owners defaulted, giving themselves a bad credit rating. FHA picked up the tab.

A recent government study on abuses of the program concluded that "speculator profits of 60–70 percent on houses held for less than 8 weeks are not uncommon." (Committee on Government Operations, p. 4.) In 1972 HUD was expected to own

240,000 largely worthless, repossessed dwellings and stood to lose $2.4 billion. (Downie, p. 50.) Thus the subsidy of real estate speculators through FHA insurance exceeded the subsidy to homeowners. There is clear evidence that FHA collaborated with the mortgage industry in this raid on the Treasury. (Committee on Government Operations, pp. 4–6.)

The Section 236 program provides below-market interest rate loans on multifamily housing, and has been subject to many of the same difficulties. The program was quite profitable to developers and financiers, largely because of the special depreciation provisions which offered high-income investors lucrative shelters from the federal income tax. (Solomon, p. 90.) The precursor to Section 236 was ended, according to one authority on federal housing subsidies, because of its limited appeal to profit-oriented investors. Developers were limited to 6 percent return on equity and the rental subsidy law was successfully revised to allow greater profits. (Aaron, p. 132.)

In 1972 upon his re-election, Nixon ended all federal housing subsidies to the poor except in cases where construction of a project had already begun. In the years that followed, lawsuits by members of Congress and others have forced Nixon and Ford to spend some of the money which they had impounded. What will happen to these programs is thus in doubt, but it seems unlikely that even the meager funding levels of the early 1970s will be attained in the future.

Conclusion

Political economists argue that the government is largely the instrument of the wealthy, the owners of income-generating property. If this is the case, then governmental activity would either benefit directly the owners of large amounts of wealth or would benefit them indirectly by favoring the stability of the social and economic system from which they receive a disproportionate share of the benefits. Federal housing programs fit easily into either or both of these categories.

As we have seen, every federal housing program benefits directly the wealthy in important ways. The reorganization of mortgage markets has been an enormous boon to builders, developers, and of course mortgage bankers. The income tax laws produce a significant tax subsidy to owners of property. Public housing, urban renewal, and the Housing Act of

1968 have bestowed huge benefits on the real estate industry and those that finance it.

Federal housing programs have fostered social and political stability — thereby benefiting the wealthy who receive the lion's share of society's spoils — through either encouraging home ownership among middle-income groups or "buying off" the dissent of lower income groups. The reorganization of mortgage markets and various federal income tax provisions encourage households to purchase a home. The Douglas Commission (p. 401) has made explicit the benefits to the "community" from widespread homeownership:

> Home ownership encourages social stability and financial responsibility. It gives the homeowner a financial stake in society with a built-in inflation hedge . . . It helps eliminate the "alienated tenant" psychology.

The net effect of these government programs to encourage homeownership has been to raise the proportion of owner-occupied units from 44 percent of all units in 1940 to 63 percent in 1970. In those three decades, the number of rental units increased only 20 percent while the number of owner-occupied units nearly tripled.

A second way in which some federal housing programs have fostered social stability is by quelling the dissent of disadvantaged, militant groups. During the latter half of the 1960s, the federal government pursued a number of programs aimed at either repressing dissent through various legal and illegal means or buying off the dissent through anti-discrimination laws, manpower programs, expansion of welfare rolls, housing subsidies, and the like. The housing subsidies of the poor were either public housing (which was originally designed for the temporarily indigent middle class), or rental subsidies and mortgage assistance, most of which were funded under 1968 legislation. In the 1950s, the only one of these programs then in force was public housing and it received very little funding. During the sixties, as the civil rights movement gained strength and insurrection swirled through the nation's cities, funding of federal housing programs for the poor steadily expanded, reaching their peak in the early 1970s. But the civil rights movement and the urban racial riots were largely over by 1968 and there was no longer any need for these subsidies. When Nixon was assured (or so he thought) of a second four years in office, he dis-

banded the entire federal "war on poverty" and the housing subsidies of the poor that were an important part of it. There remain important disagreements among the powerful about whether the "carrot" is still needed to entice dissidents back into the great American consensus, and the Nixon-Ford administration has been forced into spending some of the money that the Congress appropriated for housing subsidies of the poor.

Two remaining points should be made. First, all government-assisted housing programs employ private sources of funding and private profit-oriented construction companies. The federal government has virtually refused to involve itself in any part of the housing industry where there is a potential for private profit. Federal housing programs thus cannot be viewed as attempting to socialize or nationalize the housing industry, but rather as collaborating with private industry in order to increase its profitability. Second, there is no federal housing program which severs the worker's link to the labor market. As with all public assistance to the poor — from food stamps to unemployment compensation —the worker must supply some cash of his or her own before receiving a government subsidy. (The only exception is Aid to Families with Dependent Children, but even here there are periodic attempts to force welfare mothers to work for extremely low wages.) The public housing tenant must pay some rent; the beneficiaries of the Housing Act of 1968 must pay some of their rent or mortgage payments. Thus these programs can be easily seen as subsidies of the *employers* of low-wage workers rather than the workers themselves (Engels). These companies are able to pay less than starvation wages because the government picks up part of the tab. Thus even those programs which appear to be directed solely at the poor, on closer examination can be seen to yield substantial benefits to capitalists, some of whom have no direct connection with the housing industry.

REFERENCES

Henry J. Aaron, *Shelter and Subsidies*, (Washington: The Brookings Institution, 1972).

The Douglas Commission (The National Commission on Urban Problems), *Building the American City*, U.S. Congress, House, 91st Cong., 1st Ses., (House Document No. 91–34), (Washington: Government Printing Office, 1968).

Leonard Downie, Jr., *Mortgage on America: The Real Costs of Real Estate Speculation*, (New York: Praeger, 1974).

Matthew Edel, "Urban Renewal and Land Use Conflicts," *Review of Radical Political Economics*, 3, 3, (Summer, 1971), p. 76–89.

Frederick Engels, *The Housing Question.*

David M. Gordon, (ed.), *Problems in Political Economy: An Urban Perspective*, (Lexington, Mass.: D. C. Heath and Co., 1971).

Ralph Ives, Gary W. Lloyd, and Larry Sawers, "Mass Transit and the Power Elite," *Review of Radical Political Economics*, IV, 2, (Summer, 1972), pp. 68–77.

Robert P. Kessler and Chester W. Hartman, "The Illusion and the Reality of Urban Renewal: A Case Study of San Francisco's Yerba Buena Center," *Land Economics*, 1973, p. 440–53.

Richard T. LeGates and Mary C. Morgan, "The Perils of Revenue Sharing for Community Development," *American Institute of Planners Journal*, July 1973, p. 254–64.

Arthur P. Solomon, *Housing the Urban Poor*, Cambridge, Mass.: MIT Press, 1974).

Philip M. Stern, *The Rape of the Taxpayer*, (New York: Vintage, 1974).

Michael Stone, "Federal Housing Policy: A Political-Economic Analysis," in Jon Pynoos, *et al.*, *Housing Urban America*, (Chicago: Aldine, 1973), p. 423–32.

U.S. Congress, House Committee on Government Operations, "Defaults on FHA-Insured Home Mortgages — Detroit, Michigan," 92nd Congress, 2nd Session, (Washington: GPO, 1972).

U.S. League of Savings Associations, *Savings and Loan Fact Book: 1974*, (Chicago: 1974).

PUBLIC HOUSING AND THE POOR

Lawrence M. Friedman

The following discussion provides a critically important historical perspective on the federal public housing program. The program has been generally abandoned and has failed to provide very much housing for the poor, as Friedman notes, because it was never intended to serve the housing needs of the poor. Given this history, it seems much more difficult to argue that public housing has failed to meet an objective that it never intended to achieve.

The selection represents the first portion of a longer article, "Public Housing and the Poor: An Overview." Friedman is a professor of law at the University of Wisconsin Law School.

Public housing became a reality in the United States only in the days of the New Deal.* There were some

Source: Lawrence M. Friedman, "Public Housing and the Poor: An Overview," *California Law Review*, 54, 642–649 (1966). Copyright © 1966, California Law Review, Inc. Reprinted by permission.
* Some of the material on which this paper is based was gathered in the course of interviews. Some individu-

gingerly steps toward public housing during the First World War, and a few more in the states in the Twenties, but a serious, living program had to wait for the days of the great depression.[1] The major piece of federal legislation on housing was the Wagner-Steagall Act of 1937 [2] which, despite a gloss of amendments, remains on the statute books today, hardly altered in its basic design. On September 1,

als who were interviewed would prefer not to be quoted directly. Some of the information supplied must be treated as confidential. Consequently, supporting authorities for some statements have been omitted.

[1] On the forerunners of the Wagner-Steagall Act, see Fisher, *Twenty Years of Public Housing* (1959); a good short account is Riesenfeld & Eastlund, "Public Aid to Housing and Land Redevelopment," 34 *Minn. L. Rev.* 610 (1950). On the Wagner-Steagall Act itself, see see McDonnell, *The Wagner Housing Act: A Case Study of the Legislative Process* (1957).

[2] 50 Stat. 888 (1937), as amended, 42 U.S.C. §§ 1401–30 (1964), as amended, 42 U.S.C. §§ 1402–21b (Supp. I, 1965).

1937, President Roosevelt signed the bill [3] which was to begin a "new era in the economic and social life of America." [4] Hopes ran high in the early years of the program. The wall of resistance to federally supported housing had been breached. A "real start" would be made "at last" toward "wiping out . . . city slums." [5] The states passed enabling legislation, local housing authorities were formed, and the flow of cash into public housing began in earnest. "In city after city," wrote Nathan Straus in 1939, "the sound of the wrecker's hammer is heard, sites are being cleared, the excavators are at work, and the superstructures are going up . . . . [By] next summer . . . five thousand families will be moving from the slums into new and decent homes." [6] In the years since then, public housing has become a familiar aspect of the urban landscape. By the end of 1965 every state had some public housing units in planning or operation,[7] and more than 2,100,000 people lived in low-rent public housing.[8] In New York City more than half a million people lived in public housing units built with the aid of federal, state, or city money.[9] The overwhelming majority of these units were products of the federal program. New York City had more public housing than any other city; but every major city and a host of minor ones ran more or less substantial programs of their own.[10] As of October 1964, 26,175 people lived in public housing in Detroit, Michigan; Duluth, Minnesota, at the end of 1964, operated three hundred units divided into three separate projects.[11] Whatever else these figures signified, they meant that vast tracts of slum wasteland had been cleared and that millions of people over the last thirty years had been rehoused in units which met at least minimum sanitary and spatial standards.

But to judge by some newspaper and magazine accounts — and even by the words of housing experts — the public housing program had betrayed its fond expectations. In 1937 Catherine Bauer, a highly respected expert on housing, praised the Wagner-Steagall Act as "progressive legislation" — a hopeful first step toward the goal of good housing for all.[12] Twenty years later, in 1957, Miss Bauer returned to the subject in an article in *Architectural Forum*. The title was significant: "The Dreary Deadlock of Public Housing." [13] She found little to praise in the program as it had evolved. Rather, she saw rigidity and paternalism in management, crudity and segregation in project design, and a deplorable fragmentation of over-all housing policy. In the following issue of the magazine, eleven housing experts commented on her article and made suggestions for change.[14] Not one of the eleven disagreed with her general thesis: that the public housing movement was stagnant; that politically the program was at a standstill; that existing projects were badly conceived and perhaps did more harm than good; and that the whole program needed radical reformation. This was the twentieth anniversary of the Wagner-Steagall Act.

It was a bad time for the image of public housing. Harrison Salisbury, Russian correspondent for *The New York Times*, came home to write his reactions to the domestic scene. What he saw in New York's housing projects profoundly shocked him — for example, the "stench of stale urine that pervades the elevators" in Fort Greene Houses, Brooklyn.[15] He had other things to report about the "new ghettos," as he called them. They were "human cesspools worse than those of yesterday." [16] Fort Greene and

---

[3] *N.Y. Times,* Sept. 3, 1937, p. 1, col. 3.

[4] Letter from Franklin D. Roosevelt to Nathan Straus, Administrator of the United States Housing Authority, March 17, 1938, quoted in Straus & Wegg, *Housing Comes of Age* 189 (1938).

[5] *N.Y. Times,* Sept. 3, 1937, p. 16, col. 3.

[6] Straus, "Housing — A National Achievement," *Atlantic Monthly,* Feb. 1939, pp. 204, 210.

[7] As of the end of 1963, Utah, Wyoming, and Iowa had no units of public Housing. *Housing and Home Finance Agency, Annual Report* 306 n.1 (1963). Iowa since has passed enabling legislation. *Iowa Code Ann.* § 403A (Supp. 1964). At the end of 1964, every state had one or more local public housing authorities, except Oklahoma and this state had two projects federally owned and operated. *Housing and Home Finance Agency, Annual Report* 235, 239, Tables IV-1, IV-3 (1964).

[8] *Id.* at 235.

[9] New York City Housing Authority, Project Statistics 26, Dec. 31, 1964.

[10] Every city of more than one million population ran a public housing authority aided housing program, and 89% (42 out of 47) of the cities of more than a quarter million and less than a million. Sixty-three percent of the cities with more than fifty thousand and less than two hundred fifty thousand had programs. *Housing and Home Finance Agency, Annual Report* 240 (1964).

[11] Information supplied by the respective housing authorities.

[12] "Now, at Last: Housing," *The New Republic,* Sept. 8, 1937, pp. 119, 121.

[13] Bauer, "The Dreary Deadlock of Public Housing," *Architectural Forum,* May 1957, p. 140.

[14] "The Dreary Deadlock of Public Housing — How to Break It," *Architectural Forum,* June 1957, p. 139.

[15] Salisbury, *The Shook-Up Generation* 74 (1958).

[16] *Id.* at 75.

similar projects were "monsters, devouring their residents, polluting the areas about them, spewing out a social excrescence which infects the whole of our society." [17] The slums themselves had rarely felt such a tongue-lashing.

Salisbury's conclusions were published in book form and widely read. They were by no means the last such attack on public housing. Readers of the *Chicago Daily News*, in April 1965, were invited to share a sense of wrath and dismay toward public housing. A sensational series of articles excoriated the Robert R. Taylor homes, Chicago's "$70 Million Ghetto." Taylor was the "world's biggest and most jam-packed housing development," an "all-Negro city within a city," a "civic monument to misery, bungling and a hellish way of life," a "'death trap,' a concentration camp." Its tenants — who sometimes called their home "the Congo Hilton" — lived in misery, "grappling with violence and vandalism, fear and suspicion, teen-age terror and adult chaos, rage, resentment, official regimenting." [18] In the same year, a tenant of the Syracuse Housing Authority described her home as "nothing but a prison camp." In Syracuse, under the impetus of the war against poverty, the Negro poor organized to do battle with those they identified as their oppressors. Prominent among these oppressors were officials of the local housing authority. To judge by the outcry, public housing in Syracuse was also worse than the slums. [19]

Public housing does not totally lack defenders, but they have spoken softly of late. It is hard to think of any prominent housing figure outside of government who defends the program as it is. Politically, the program has little appeal. Appropriations for additional units have been grudgingly voted in Congress; time and time again requests have been scaled down. What is perhaps more significant, authorizations have often gone begging because local government agencies have not been interested in applying for federal grants — authorized units have "washed away." [20] This is perhaps the darkest symptom of all: A program must be genuinely unpopular if free federal money is spurned. The unpopularity of public housing need not be left to oblique inference. In scores of cities and small towns, public housing has been put to the test by the voters. Where it is legally possible, opponents have demanded referenda on the question. In a distressing number of cases, bond issues to finance the program have failed or public housing has been voted out of town. [21]

Where does the trouble lie? Is it in the conception, the shape of the public housing program? Is it in its mode of administration? Perhaps the problems lie in both. The indictment is clear: Public housing, ostensibly designed to clear the slums and to alleviate the sufferings of the poor, has failed to do either. We turn now to the facts.

Conception and Design

The public housing law is one of a vaguely defined group of statutes called "social" or "welfare" legislation.

It would be a mistake to suppose (if anyone did) that the Wagner-Steagall Act [22] arose solely out of a gradual persuasion of decent-minded people that the slums were odious, crowded, and evil, and that the federal government had a duty to relieve the sufferings of the poor. The social and economic conditions in the slums provided the opportunity, the background, and much of the emotive power of the law. Yet reformers had long dreamed in vain of public housing. And the slums were surely no worse than they had been in the nineteenth century, though possibly they were larger.

In 1937 the country was suffering from a deep and dangerous depression. Fully one-quarter of the work force was unemployed during the worst days of the depression. In the spring of 1933, thirteen to fifteen million were unemployed. [23] Millions of families were barely making a living. The number of "poor people" in the country had been vastly increased; indeed, many of the "poor people" were formerly members of the middle class, who had enjoyed prosperity in the twenties. They retained their middle-class culture and their outlook, their articu-

[17] *Id.* at 77.

[18] *Chicago Daily News*, April 10, 1965, p. 1, col. 1.

[19] The tenant quotes are from *The Tenants Report, Public Housing: Syracuse Style, This Is the Way It Is*, 1965. Materials on the Syracuse movement were supplied to me by Professor Warren C. Haggstrom of Syracuse University.

[20] Seligman, "The Enduring Slums," in *The Exploding Metropolis* 92, 105 (1958).

[21] *E.g.*, in elections in April and June 1961, Rapid City, South Dakota, and Marin County, California, turned down low-rent proposals. 18 *J. of Housing* 289 (1961).

[22] 50 Stat. 888 (1937), as amended, 42 U.S.C. §§ 1401–30 (1964), as amended, 42 U.S.C. §§ 1402–21b (Supp. I, 1965).

[23] Brown, *Public Relief* 1929–1939, at 65 (1940).

lateness, their habit of expressing their desires at the polls. There were, therefore, millions of candidates for public housing who did not belong (as later was true) to the class of the "problem poor"; rather they were members of what we might call the submerged middle class. The attractiveness of public housing was enormously enhanced because the potential clientele was itself enormous, composed of millions of relatively articulate citizens, angry and dispirited at their unjust descent into poverty. Public housing was not supported by the dregs of society; a discontented army of men and women of high demands and high expectations stood ready to insist on decent housing from government or at least stood ready to approve and defend it. The political climate was receptive to federal planning and federal housing — not so much as a matter of radical ideology, but out of a demand for positive programs to eliminate the "undeserved" privations of the unaccustomed poor.

Moreover, business was stagnant in the thirties. Programs of social welfare and relief were tested by their ability to create new jobs and prime the business pump as much as by their inherent welfare virtues. Public works programs were exceedingly popular for this reason.[24] A vast federal program of house building naturally received the enthusiastic support of manufacturers of building supplies and workers in the building trades. The normal opposition to "socialized" housing made its appearance in debate,[25] but it was weak and somewhat muted. Nonetheless, business support for the act was conditioned upon the act being so structured as to avoid any actual government competition with business. Homes would be built only for those who could not possibly afford to buy them on their own. A clear wall must separate the public and private sector. This too was only partly ideological. Government, it was felt, should not cut into the markets of private industry; it must stimulate fresh demand and make fresh jobs — otherwise the effect of the program on the economy would be wasted.

During the depression, the volume of private housing construction was very low. In 1925, 900,000 housing units were constructed; in 1934, only 60,-000.[26] Yet in one sense no housing shortage developed. During much of the depression, plenty of apartments stood vacant.[27] People who were poor doubled up with relatives, lived in "Hoovervilles" and shanties, returned to rural areas, and in general failed to consume the housing supply. Rents were extremely low. The high vacancy rate posed a potential danger for the program. If public construction increased the housing supply during a period in which many dwellings stood vacant, rents would decrease still more and vacancies would increase. In a decade willing to kill baby pigs and impose acreage controls on farmers, one could hardly expect to see government flooding the housing market with new units. And in fact, the Wagner-Steagall Act was careful to avoid the problem of oversupply. No units were to be built without destroying "dwellings . . . substantially equal in number to the number of newly constructed dwellings provided by the project."[28] This provision — the so-called "equivalent elimination" provision[29] — killed two birds with one stone. It neutralized potential opposition from landlords and the housing industry by removing the danger of oversupply; at the same time, by making slum clearance a part of the law, it appealed to those whose desire for public housing stemmed from their loathing of the slums and slum conditions. The Wagner-Steagall Act was thus shaped by the force of concrete social conditions; what emerged was a program geared to the needs of the submerged middle class, tied to slum clearance, and purged of any element of possible competition with business.[30]

Constitutional difficulties played a part in determining one of the most notable features of the program — its decentralization. From 1933 on, the Public Works Administration had run its own public housing program.[31] In 1935 a federal district court

[24] Mitchell, *Depression Decade* 314–38 (1947).

[25] *E.g.*, 81 *Cong. Rec.* 8079 (1937) (remarks of Senator Walsh).

[26] Brookings Institution, *The Recovery Problem in the United States* 183–84 (1936).

[27] *Id.* at 184–85.

[28] 50 Stat. 891 (1937), as amended, 42 U.S.C. § 1410(a) (1964), as amended, 42 U.S.C. § 1410(a) (Supp. I, 1965).

[29] Robinson & Altman, "Equivalent Elimination Agreements in Public Housing Projects," 22 *B.U.L. Rev.* 375, 376 (1942).

[30] The 1949 act, to make the point crystal clear, provided that no annual contribution contract be entered into unless the local agency demonstrates "that a gap of at least 20 per centum . . . has been left between the upper rental limits for admission to the proposed low-rent housing and the lowest rents at which private enterprise unaided by public subsidy is providing . . . decent . . . housing." 63 Stat. 422 (1949), as amended, 42 U.S.C. § 1415 (7)(b)(ii) (1964).

[31] Fisher, *Twenty Years of Public Housing* 82–89 (1959).

case held that the federal government had no power under the constitution to clear land and build public housing. It was not proper, said the court, for the federal government "to construct buildings in a state for the purpose of selling or leasing them to private citizens for occupancy as homes." [32] The federal government never appealed this decision. In 1935 the government's prospect of sympathetic treatment by the United States Supreme Court seemed bleak; attempting to overturn the adverse housing decision might risk the whole program of public works. On the other hand, no important legal barriers stood in the way of a decentralized program. Washington could supply money and a certain amount of benign control; title to property and the motive force in condemnation could remain vested in local public agencies. A key New York state decision strengthened this view, distinguishing the federal cases as inapplicable to state power.[33] Moreover, decentralization was politically attractive to those who dreaded further expansion of the "federal octopus."

Financial considerations had an important impact on the design of the housing law. If the federal government had made outright grants to local authorities to build houses, immense amounts of money would have been immediately required. Under the act, however, local authorities were invited to borrow money through bond issues; with the proceeds, they were to acquire sites, clear them, and put up houses. The federal government would enter into "contracts" with local housing authorities, under which the federal government would agree to make annual contributions for a long period of time. The federal government would pay (in essence) enough money for the interest on the bonds and the amortization of the principal. Operating expenses for the housing projects would come out of current rents. In this way, federal contributions would be kept relatively small; housing could be built on the installment plan, and paid for over a period of fifty or sixty years.[34]

Note, too, that the tenants were only partially subsidized. They were not given "free" housing. Each tenant had to pay his rent. Project rents had to be sufficient to pay operating costs — maintenance, administration, and payments in lieu of taxes to local government for fire and police protection and other municipal services.[35] Though the federal act was discreetly silent on the subject, the rent requirement meant that the unemployed and the paupers were not welcome in public housing. They could not pay the rent, any more than in private housing. There are "some people," said Senator Wagner, "who we cannot possibly reach; I mean those who have no means to pay the rent.... [O]bviously this bill cannot provide housing for those who cannot pay the rent minus the subsidy allowed." [36] The projects were for poor but honest workers — the members of the submerged middle class, biding their time until the day when they regained their rightful income level. The tenants were not to receive any "charity." The difference between a dole and a subsidy is psychologically powerful, whether or not the distinction is good economics. The working class residents of public housing were not to receive a gift from the government, but their rightful due as citizens. Public housing, arguably, was no more "charitable" than the free land of the Homestead Act of 1862 — an earlier form of middle-class subsidy. Decent, sanitary apartments were a stepping-stone to a free simple cottage — the American dream. Perhaps a radical fringe of housing reformers looked on public housing as something more fundamentally "public"; but the core of support lay in an old and conservative tradition.

If this general analysis is correct, what would happen to public housing if a rising standard of living released the submerged middle class from dependence on government shelter? Public housing would be inherited by the permanent poor. The empty rooms would pass to those who had at first been disdained — the unemployed, "problem" families, those from broken homes. The program could adapt only with difficulty to its new conditions, because it had been originally designed for a different clientele. To suit the programs to the needs of the new tenant would require fresh legislation; and yet change would be difficult to enact and to implement precisely be-

[32] United States v. Certain Lands, 9 F. Supp. 137, 141 (W.D. Ky.), *aff'd*, 78 F.2d 684 (6th Cir.), *dismissed*, 294 U.S. 735 (1935), 297 U.S. 726 (1936). See also United States v. Certain Lands, 12 F. Supp. 345 (E.D. Mich. 1935).

[33] New York Housing Authority v. Muller, 270 N.Y. 333, 1 N.E.2d 152 (1936).

[34] 50 Stat. 892 (1937), as amended, 42 U.S.C. §§ 1410(b), (c) (1964), as amended, 42 U.S.C. § 1410(c) (Supp. I, 1965).

[35] The so-called "in-lieu" payments. See 63 Stat. 428 (1949), as amended, 42 U.S.C. § 1410(h) (1964), as amended, 42 U.S.C. § 1410(h) (Supp. I, 1965).

[36] 81 *Cong. Rec.* 8099 (Aug. 1937).

cause the new clientele would be so poor, so power-less, so inarticulate. The political attractiveness of public housing would diminish. Maladaptations to reality in the program would disenchant housing re-formers; they would declare the program a failure and abandon it to search out fresh cures for bad housing and slums.

All this is precisely what has happened. . . .

THE HOUSING ALLOWANCE DELUSION

Chester Hartman and Dennis Keating

Liberals and conservatives have focused increasingly on housing allowances as a potential policy to solve urban housing problems. In this article, Hartman and Keating relate those proposals to an analysis of housing problems from a radical perspective. They conclude that housing allowances, by themselves, offer little promise of substantial solution of housing problems.

As urban planner and lawyer respectively, Hartman and Keating have been working on the National Housing and Economic Development Law Project at the University of California at Berkeley.

The newest panacea for solving the nation's enduring slum problem is a national program of housing allowances. The theory is: since the nonpoor are able to get decent housing without the need for government bureaucracy or subsidy,[1] the government should give the poor direct cash grants to spend on housing so that, as housing consumers, they will no longer be poor; it is expected that the slum problem will then dissolve.

Proponents of this approach assume that the housing allowance will have the following advantages for the recipient of housing subsidies and for the housing stock itself.

1. It will expand consumer choice with respect to housing type, location, and landlord. The recipient of a housing allowance would be free to seek out housing anyplace in the housing market. In contrast, existing production-oriented subsidies (those which serve to create subsidized housing units) limit the recipient to residency in particular units — primarily public housing and FHA projects.
2. By providing the landlords with sufficient revenue for repairs, it will encourage them to maintain their buildings and remove housing code violations. The undermaintenance and abandonment of buildings in many large cities are, according to recent views, attributable to the inability of low-income occupants to afford the rents required to pay the ongoing costs of owning and maintaining a building.
3. Administrative simplicity is touted as well. By giving subsidies directly to the poor and allowing them to seek out their own housing, there is no need for large and expensive bureaucratic intermediaries like local public housing authorities. Moreover, the direct grant approach permits benefits to be given to persons who do not live in jurisdictions served by local housing

Source: "The Housing Allowance Delusion," by Chester Hartman and Dennis Keating, from Social Policy (January/February 1974) Vol. 4, No. 4, pp. 31–37. Published by Social Policy Corporation, New York, N.Y. 10010. Copyright 1974 by Social Policy Corporation.
[1] The nonpoor do in effect get subsidized through the income tax system which permits those who own their own homes to exempt from taxes all they spend on mortgage interest and property taxes. In 1971 the benefits received from these "tax breaks" totaled $3.1 billion for families earning over 15,000 per year, and only $244 million for families in the $3–7,000 bracket. However, in the peculiar American folk logic, such tax features are not considered subsidies. Only that which we give to the poor is so labeled. Housing Affairs Letter (Washington, D.C.), July 28, 1972; Henry J. Aaron, Shelter and Subsidies (Washington, D.C.: The Brookings Institution, 1972), p. 223.

authorities — which amounts to half of the nation's total population.

4. Apart from these assumed advantages to housing consumers and the housing supply, it is also generally put forth that a housing allowance program will be less expensive than current approaches.

The administration's January 1973 moratorium on federal housing and community development aid set the stage for introduction of a whole new approach to federal housing subsidies to replace the complex pastiche of programs built up over the past four decades. The Nixon administration is known to want a simple substitute for the current array of aids. An elaborate series of housing allowance pilot projects directed by HUD, the Urban Institute, and several of the country's leading urban research groups, is currently under way in a dozen cities, involving 15–20,000 families. These experiments will test the effect of allowances on housing supply and demand and alternative forms of administrative arrangements. Some $150 million will be expended during these pilot projects which are scheduled to last from two to five years.[2]

On September 19, 1973, President Nixon, jumping the gun on these experiments, submitted to Congress a series of housing policy proposals; chief among them was a program of housing allowances for low-income households, starting with the elderly. In submitting this program, the President stated the following objective:

> . . . to make decent housing available for *all* low-income families without the housing "project" stigma, the loss of freedom of choice and the inordinately high costs of current programs by . . . identifying direct cash assistance as the most promising approach to help such families. . . .[3]

The federal government has been in the low-income housing business since the mid-1930s, and over that time has spent or committed, according to administration calculations, almost $90 billion. In the

[2] See Robert Beckham, "The Experimental Housing Allowance Program: An Old Idea Will Get a New Kind of Test in 1973," *Journal of Housing*, January 1973, pp. 12–17.

[3] Office of the White House Press Secretary, "Housing Policy Recommendations Fact Sheet," and text of President's message to Congress, September 19, 1973.

past four years alone the government has subsidized almost 1.6 million new housing units and over 400,-000 existing and rehabilitated housing units. These units alone could eventually cost the taxpayer $50 billion.

In his housing statement President Nixon asks: "But what have we been getting for all this money?" Indeed, what *have* we been getting? What *are* we getting? And what *will* we be getting if the housing allowance program is adopted?

What Have We Been Getting?

It may be useful to look first at what has been done in the past, for in the world of housing subsidies there is little new under the sun. One program not usually regarded as a housing program but which is remarkably similar to housing allowances is public welfare. Under the welfare program families receive a lump sum with a specified portion of that amount earmarked for housing.

Some 14 million persons in the United States receive welfare payments. Not very much exists in the way of systematic data on the housing conditions of welfare recipients, but what there is indicates that such families are among the worst housed in the whole society. The Department of Health, Education and Welfare found that at least one-half of all welfare recipients live in substandard housing.[4]

Why the welfare program is such a failure in the housing area is crystal clear: not enough money is given to recipients to enable them to get decent housing; there is widespread discrimination against welfare families on the part of landlords; and welfare officials have no mechanism for insuring that recipients secure decent housing. Those few states with laws permitting a welfare agency or recipient to withhold rent if the recipient's housing is substandard have found such controls totally ineffective in view of the following realities of the housing market: the high cost of decent housing; the overall shortage of standard, inexpensive housing; and the ability of landlords to pick and choose among applicants so as to secure the most "desirable" tenants.

A second public program that resembles housing allowances is leased public housing. Under the public housing program, local housing authorities have

[4] HEW, *The Role of Public Welfare in Housing* (Washington, D.C., 1969).

since 1965 been able to use the federal subsidies they administer to lease units from private owners and sublease them to eligible low-income families. This is in contrast to the traditional approach of construction, ownership, and operation of specialized developments (projects) for low-income households. In effect, this amounts to a housing allowance of the type proposed, the only major difference being that instead of the individual household seeking out the apartment on its own, receiving the subsidy, and making all arrangements directly with the private landlord, the local housing authority acts as intermediary.

The evaluations of the leased housing program paint a disturbing picture of how low-income tenants fare in the private market. A 1972 audit report by the Department of Housing and Urban Development found widespread evidence that much of leased public housing was substandard. The HUD report also found that local housing authorities either were not making the required prelease inspections or, in cases where the owner was required to make repairs, they were not actually carried out. In addition to poor housing conditions, the HUD report found that local housing authorities were paying private landlords rents in excess of prevailing market levels.[5]

The presence of a public agency as intermediary should, if anything, produce results more beneficial to the low-income tenant than the proposed housing allowance system, which would leave the poor and powerless tenant to bargain directly with the landlord. Based on the serious shortcomings of the leased housing program, it seems inevitable that the low-income tenant armed with only his housing allowance will have little protection against landlords who charge excessive rents, fail to make repairs, or otherwise exert the power inherent in a seller's market.

Finally, the failure of the home ownership program for lower-income families made available under Section 235 of the 1968 Housing Act provides ample evidence of how the private housing sector behaves toward subsidized consumers. Under these programs of interest-rate subsidies, moderate-income families have been able to purchase new, existing, or rehabilitated homes. A raft of exposés by the House Banking and Currency Committee, the General Accounting

Office, and the Civil Rights Commission[6] have uncovered shocking scandals in these programs in city after city, which led HUD to take the unprecedented step of suspending Section 235 for a time. House prices were sharply inflated, with realtors purchasing older, dilapidated homes at panic-sale prices in areas undergoing racial transition, then reselling them immediately at huge profits. Any interim repairs were at best cosmetic in nature. Government supervision of the program proved totally incompetent. According to the congressional report, "FHA has allowed real estate speculation of the worst type to go on in the 235 program and has virtually turned its back to these practices" and is "insuring existing homes that are of such poor quality that there is little or no possibility that they can survive the life of the mortgage." Many of the existing houses "have no resale value, and even minimal repairs will place such a burden on the homeowner's income that the congressional purpose of affording decent, safe, and sanitary housing for low- and moderate-income individuals not only has been thwarted but amounts to sheer fraud."

HUD has had to repossess nearly a quarter of a million of these homes and has now become the nation's biggest slumlord. Although these interest-subsidy programs were for homeowners rather than renters — the group to be served by the housing allowance program — this experience shows clearly the behavior of the real estate industry's fast-buck artists in the so-called free market and the inability of moderate-income (let alone low-income) consumers to exert an effective countervailing force.

These three programs — public welfare, leased public housing, and the interest-subsidy home ownership program — provide a clear demonstration of some of the limitations of the housing allowance approach. Proponents of housing allowances have been

---

[5] HUD, Office of Audit, "HUD Monitoring of Local Authority Management of Section 23, Leased Housing Program," Region I, July 20, 1972.

[6] Reports on the Section 235 home ownership program are: U.S. Congress, House, Committee on Banking and Currency, *Investigation and Hearings of Abuses in Federal Low- and Moderate-Income Housing Programs: Staff Report and Recommendations*, 91st Cong., 2d sess., December 1970; Committee on Government Operations, *Defaults on FHA-Insured Home Mortgages — Detroit, Michigan*, 92d Cong., 2d sess., June 20, 1972, H. Rept. 92–1152; and U.S. Commission on Civil Rights, *Home Ownership for Lower Income Families: A Report on the Racial and Ethnic Impact of the Section 235 Program* (Washington, D.C.: U.S. Government Printing Office, June 1971).

unable to state convincingly why and how their pet idea would not meet the same fate.

What Are We Getting and What Will We Get with a Housing Allowance Program?

Because of the failures of our past programs, we should look closely at the housing market as it exists today before embarking on a new program. The shortcomings of the past programs inhere in the nature of the housing market itself. The failure of the so-called private market to meet the nation's housing needs is amply demonstrated by the fact that, by contemporary housing, environmental, and ability-to-pay standards, we have not moved very far from President Roosevelt's 1937 lament that one-third of the nation is ill-housed. And the reason for this does not lie solely in the fact that many persons don't have enough income to rent or buy decent housing for themselves. While the maldistribution of income is a principal (and probably the central) cause of slum housing, a host of other realities about the housing market temper this simple cause-and-effect relationship and alert us to what can be expected if all that is done is to put additional housing consumption income into the private market in the form of housing allowances.

Five major defects in the housing market, apart from inadequate incomes, stand out as serious barriers to attaining decent living conditions for all Americans. These are: inadequate total number of housing units at prices or rents the poor can afford and located where they want to live; the substandard conditions prevalent in the low-income housing sector, urban and rural; widespread discrimination against many classes of housing consumers; rising and uncontrolled rents; and the pattern of legal relationships between landlords and tenants.

■ *Not Enough Existing Housing*

In most areas of the United States, there is a severe shortage of decent housing in the low- and moderate-rent categories. Urban renewal, highways, and other public programs which annually demolish (and do not replace) tens of thousands of units, as well as demolitions by private owners seeking more profitable uses for their property, add constantly to this shortage. The housing allowance program, confined to use for existing units, will do nothing to add to the total supply of housing and can therefore be

effective only in those few areas where there is an abnormally high vacancy rate for low- and moderate-income housing. Allowances may induce some owners to upgrade their units — that is, transfer them from the substandard category to the standard category — but wherever possible, landlords will attempt to capture the additional consumer income made available by allowances without doing renovation or by making minimal and nondurable repairs. Any housing allowance program must therefore be joined to a large-scale program to increase the total housing supply available to low- and moderate-income families.

■ *Prevailing Slum Conditions*

The past several decades have seen a marked decline in housing conditions in a great many inner-city and rural areas. Landlords in these areas for the most part simply have not kept up their properties, nor have they had to. The short supply of available housing has created a seller's market for landlords, and local housing code officials have been unable to enforce minimum housing standards. Landlords who desire to maintain decent conditions were often deterred by deterioration in the surrounding neighborhood — created through a combination of neglect by fellow landlords and the city's failure to provide proper levels of municipal services — and by "redlining" practices of banks and insurance companies, which effectively cut whole areas off from badly needed renovation capital. The cumulative result of these years of neglect will not be obliterated simply by giving current housing consumers more rent money to spend.

Housing allowances are to be available only for rental of units that meet minimum housing code standards. But it is hard to see how this can be enforced, given prevailing housing conditions in the areas where low-income consumers will be forced to seek out housing. Code enforcement agencies are inadequately staffed, generally work with a poor set of laws and uncooperative courts, and are understandably reluctant to enforce the code when the result may be the eviction of tenants and abandonment or demotion of needed housing. If pushed, landlords may respond by making minimal cosmetic repairs, but it is unlikely that they can be forced to maintain decent conditions for long. Tenants will not report substandard conditions if by doing so they run the risk of being evicted or having their allowance revoked. Few cities have mounted serious programs of housing code enforcement, and landlords generally have been able to evade code requirements. The situation will be little different with the introduction of housing allowances.

An instructive example of how landlords will respond to the added rent revenue made available through housing allowances is provided by New York City's recent experience under its MBR (maximum base rent) program. Based on Rand Institute studies of New York's housing market which showed that the costs of maintaining housing were exceeding rent revenues permitted under the city's rent-control statutes, the city administration introduced a new concept of treating rental housing as a public utility, with rates (rents) to be set by determining the actual costs of maintaining a rental unit and permitting landlords an 8.5 percent return on their investment. The amount needed to provide this revenue is the "fair rent" for an apartment and the maximum that may be charged. Landlords are permitted to increase existing rents 7.5 percent annually until the MBR is reached. There is no government subsidy involved and tenants must bear the full brunt of these rent increases. The theory was that landlords previously were unable to afford to keep their properties up to code standards, but that with increased rents they could and would maintain their buildings properly. Although they had no choice in the matter, tenants would at least receive better housing for their increased rents.

In order to qualify for the MBR increases, the landlord had to certify by June 30, 1971, that he had corrected all of the "rent-impairing" violations on record and 80 percent of other housing code violations outstanding as of January 1, 1971. By October 1971, the landlord had to certify that he was maintaining all "essential services" for the building. However, since there was no mechanism for preinspection of the more than one million rent-controlled units in New York City eligible for MBR increases, the city relied on the honesty of landlords (and tenant protests of housing code violations or inadequate services) to insure that MBR increases would indeed provide improved housing. An analysis of the impact of MBR by the New York State Study Commission for New York City revealed the following:

... HDA [The New York City Housing and Development Administration] inspected buildings with violations on the books [as of January 1,

1971]; of the 36,000 certifications which landlords reported as free of violations, 17,000 were found upon inspection to be false.. . .

If HDA inspections of violations showed that almost *half* of the certifications were *false*, it could well be imagined what an inquiry into "essential services" might produce.

Given the final form of the MBR program and its subsequent administration, it is obvious that it has become primarily a mechanism for increasing rents paid.[7]

The New York City experience gives no support to the hypothesis put forth by housing allowance advocates that landlords will correct violations upon receiving increased rent revenues.

■ *Housing Discrimination*

In the housing market to a degree that exists nowhere else in our society, some kinds of money talk louder than others. The extent of discrimination against nonwhite consumers throughout the entire housing network — landlords, real estate and rental agents, those selling their homes, bankers, insurance companies — is too widely documented and recognized to need elaboration. But housing discrimination is exercised for many reasons other than race. Amount and source of income (particularly receipt of public welfare), number of children, number of parents, age, and life-style are grounds for systematic discrimination on the part of landlords and others who control the allocation of housing. Merely having the ability to pay the rent or sale price by no means guarantees that the housing consumer will get what he wants to buy. Federal, state, and local fair housing laws, landmark court decisions, and various "affirmative action" programs haven't made a serious dent in the problem.

The implications of this discriminatory market for the housing allowance program are clear, based on what we know of prevalent patterns of discrimination against racial minorities and welfare recipients. Landlords will covertly charge a premium to housing allowance recipients for the privilege of being accepted as tenants. Realtors and agents will steer minority families to older, racially changing neigh-

[7] New York State Study Commission, *The Management of the Maximum Base Rent (MBR) Program by the Housing and Development Administration of New York City, from June 1970 to October 1972* (1972), pp. 37, 70, 81. (Emphasis in original.)

borhoods which offer the possibility of profitable blockbusting. Despite increased rent rolls, landlords will refuse to invest in major repairs because the influx of poor and minority tenants make it a "bad neighborhood" in which to invest. Lenders will continue to red-line these neighborhoods when considering repair loans and refinancing. The housing allowance program, with its emphasis on the so-called free market and minimal intervention, is not likely to use the power of government effectively to limit or end housing discrimination.

▪ Spiraling Rents

The widespread shortage of low- and moderate-income housing has led to unprecedented rent rises over the past few years. In the current market, with landlords for the most part free to charge what the traffic will bear, the poor, near poor, and even the middle-class are being badly squeezed. Pressures to stop the rent spiral have led to the institution of rent controls of one form or another in a growing number of cities. Even the Nixon administration was reluctantly forced to institute temporary rent limitations during its Phase 2 price stabilization program.

The design of the housing allowance experiments does not call for any form of rent control. But it is beyond question that the introduction of housing allowances will lead to further rent increases. With a tight housing supply and rampant discrimination in the rental of available units, the response of landlords will be to inflate rents as much as possible. Former FHA Commissioner Philip N. Brownstein acknowledged this critical limitation in December 1972, in testimony before the Joint Economic Committee.

I would question the advisability of housing allowances in areas where the existing housing stock cannot adequately meet current demands of low- and moderate-income consumers. To provide housing subsidies in such communities would simply increase inflationary pressures on prices and rents of existing units. . . . It is indeed defeating to provide housing allowances so landlords can charge higher rental for the same units.

Inflation of this sort not only transfers part or all of the housing allowance benefits from the recipient to the landlord's pocket, but it also may harm other low- and moderate-income families who do not receive such subsidies by leading to price rises in the rental market as a whole.

Reliance on voluntary cooperation of the real estate industry in exercising restraint on their profit-taking instincts bears too much of a resemblance to fox-and-chicken-coop analogies. The strong support for housing allowances from the powerful National Association of Real Estate Boards is based precisely on the presumed absence of controls and the government's willingness to allow the private market to function "normally."

In short, without some form of rent controls, housing allowances will benefit landlords far more than low-income families. Yet the basis of support for a housing allowance program and the nature of administration thinking and economic philosophy rule out any such measures.

▪ Landlord-Tenant Laws

It is inconceivable that low-income tenants armed only with housing allowances can succeed in the housing market, given the current state of landlord-tenant legal relationships throughout most of the country. In most parts of the United States tenants are legally vulnerable to the caprice of their landlords regarding the condition of the housing they lease and the terms and rules of tenancy. In the absence of a written lease (and most low-income tenants have no such protection), a landlord may raise the rent without limitation and on short notice. Landlords may evict a tenant without a lease for no stated reason with only thirty days notice. The tenant is not permitted to raise as a defense against eviction the dilapidated condition of the premises. In such a legal context, the notion of a "sovereign consumer" and a true bargaining relationship between landlord and low-income tenant is laughable.

Only a very few states have developed a set of laws which attempt to change the one-sided legal relationships in the housing field. Among these recent reforms are:

- Protection against retaliatory eviction of tenants who report housing code violations to government authorities or who engage in tenant organizing activities.
- An implied warranty of habitability, incorporated into every lease (oral as well as written), which can be raised by the tenant as a valid defense to eviction for nonpayment of rent.
- Court appointment of receivers to collect rents and effect repair and rehabilitation of sub-

standard units where the landlord has refused or is unable to make the required repairs.

- Creation of special housing courts to deal with landlord-tenant disputes.
- Regulation of tenant security deposits.
- Creation of mandatory landlord security deposits.
- "Repair and deduct" statutes, a self-help remedy enabling tenants (after reasonable notice) to arrange on their own for repair of vital facilities and pass the cost of repair on to the landlord by way of deduction from the next rent payment.

But the fear of eviction is a psychological factor which outweighs a lot of paper and legal protection. Many low-income tenants have little knowledge of the legal remedies available to them and would be reluctant to use them if they did. This is compounded by their lack of access to lawyers. And in the vast majority of states, landlord-tenant law still reflects feudal concepts. The low-income family *cum* housing allowance will be as much at the mercy of these legal realities as are other low- and moderate-income tenants in the current housing market.

An irony of the move away from public housing and toward housing allowances is that in the past few years, tenants in public housing (and to a lesser extent in FHA rental housing) have won some major advances through litigation and political pressure. Three million poor families in public housing are now protected by a lease and grievance procedure that stipulates: no arbitrary fines; no arbitrary evictions; hearing rights; right to rent abatement if substandard conditions exist; limits on rent increases and limits on the landlord's rights of entry. These advances, however, are cut short with the advent of the housing allowance program.

Without dramatic changes in the housing market itself — changes which even the most optimistic observers of the U.S. housing scene would not predict — the government cannot hope to insure that recipients of housing allowances will live in decent housing if it is not willing to attach some kind of legal protections to that allowance. One device that would go a long way toward such assurances is a federal model lease that would embody the bulk of landlord-tenant reforms which now exist in the more progressive states and would be a prerequisite to receipt by a landlord of federal housing allowance funds. A federal model lease of this type would have to provide for a warranty of habitability, protection against retaliatory eviction, and protection for tenant organizing activities. However, it is clear that the federal government is not about to attach any such requirements to its housing allowance program; devotion to states' rights principles in this area and to the general interests of the property-owning class preclude such a step.

In sum, the housing allowance approach is only part of a solution to the nation's slum problem. Its useful elements are the notion of free choice and its potential universal applicability to all households in need of assistance. But in the current housing market, freedom of choice can be enhanced only by more intervention, not through illusory free choice in an illusory free market. And commitment to providing all Americans with a decent place to live will cost a great deal more than we have been paying in the past — more than $25 billion annually, according to cogent estimates made recently by the Rural Housing Alliance.[8] This money is needed in large part to increase the supply of low- and moderate-income housing in order to expand real choice, reduce inflationary rent pressure and discrimination by landlords, and create true market pressures on owners to renovate and maintain their buildings. For all its defects, the public housing program was the one program that directly added to the supply of low-income housing — one million units since its inception in 1937 — and was a program that provided subsidies "deep" enough to reach truly poor people. In fact, it was the various amendments to the public housing laws of 1969, 1970, and 1971, increasing subsidies to cover the gap between the real operating costs of public housing and what poor people can afford, which have led to the conclusion that the program is "too costly." Public housing subsidies represent the true costs of providing poor people with a decent place to live, and the introduction of housing allowances as an alternative to expensive public housing is in large part an attempt at buying our way out of the housing problem cheaply.

As presently conceived, housing allowances are bound to fail those who need help in getting a decent place to live, just as they are bound to bring windfall profits to those who control the housing

8 Clay Cochran and George Rucker, "Every American Family: Housing Need and Nonresponse," in Donald J. Reeb and James T. Kirk, eds., *Housing the Poor* (New York: Praeger, 1973).

market. Further, the housing allowance approach does not touch the larger issue of eradicating slum neighborhoods and environments and improving community facilities and municipal services. Until we are willing to deal with the question of how and by whom housing resources — in particular, land and mortgage money — are controlled; until we face the conflict between the profit instincts of those who control the housing market and the human right to live decently; until we are willing to pay the necessary costs to make up for the decades of neglect of our existing housing stock and our failure to build a sufficient number unit for low- and moderate-income households, we will not even come close to meeting the national housing goal (first promulgated by Congress in 1949 and reiterated in 1968) of "a decent home and a suitable living environment for every American family."

URBAN RENEWAL AND LAND USE CONFLICTS

Matthew Edel

Conventional analysts have usually treated urban renewal and other government housing programs as politically neutral solutions to "technical" economic problems. In this selection, Edel argues that urban land use involves fundamental political class interests. Many recent examples of land-use conflicts help demonstrate, in Edel's view, that "neutral turf" does not exist in our cities.

Edel teaches economics and urban studies at Queens College in the City University of New York. He has written widely on urban problems and coedited *Urban Economics: Text and Readings.*

I

Opposition to urban renewal and to land acquisition by universities has been the basis of many political actions by students and community groups in the past decade. Defense of neighborhood "turf" has been a potent organizing issue in a number of cases. This article discusses the economic context of recent conflicts over urban land in the United States. The aim is both to criticize existing theories of urban land use and renewal, which ignore the role of conflict among economic classes, and to provide a framework for discussing the political potential of organization around land-defense issues.

Economic critiques of urban renewal have used two lines of argument. In most cases, the replacement of old neighborhoods by new buildings for business, institutional or higher-value residential use is accepted as a proper function of government, but the failure of the authorities to provide new low-income housing or adequate monetary compensation for those evicted is condemned.[1] Conservatives like Martin Anderson have attacked government land-taking as an interference with the market for the benefit of special interests, implying that blocking urban renewal would strengthen capitalism.[2] Neither critique, however, places urban renewal within a

Source: Matthew Edel, "Urban Renewal and Land Use Conflicts," from *The Review of Radical Political Economics,* Vol. 3, No. 3, Summer 1971, pp. 76–89. Copyright © 1971 by Union for Radical Political Economics. Reprinted with permission. An expanded version appears in Matthew Edel and Jerome Rothenberg, *Readings in Urban Economics* (New York: Macmillan, 1972).

[1] Jewel Bellush and Murray Hausknecht, eds., *Urban Renewal: People, Politics and Planning* (Garden City: Anchor Books, 1967) contains a good selection. See also Jerome Rothenberg, *Economic Evaluation of Urban Renewal* (Washington: Brookings Institution, 1967).

[2] Martin Anderson, *The Federal Bulldozer* (Cambridge: M.I.T. Press, 1964).

overall description of land use changes in a metropolitan area or within a description of interest between classes.

II

One description of the metropolitan economy which considers both land uses and the existence of an "elite," if not of explicit classes, is that of Raymond Vernon, former director of the New York Metropolitan Region Study.[3] Vernon assumed away conflict among the classes described, and failed to predict the conflicts that occurred in the nineteen-sixties. But a critique of his analysis is a useful point of departure for an understanding of what did happen.

Professor Vernon's argument was that urban expansion on the basis of a private market left most Americans satisfied that their housing conditions were improving. He saw metropolitan expansion through construction of high cost homes in new subdivisions as enabling lower-income groups to move into better dwellings left behind by those moving to the suburbs. Because of this filtering process, Vernon contended that many supposed urban problems were actually myths. "The clear majority of Americans who in urban areas look on their lifetime experience as one of progress and improvement, not as one of retrogression . . . they see their lot as being better than that of their parents and confidently expect their children to do better still." Therefore, he did not expect that the mass of the population could be aroused to crisis policies for the city. Indeed, he predicted in 1961 that even problems of taxation could not bring the middle class "shouting into the streets," not that, given filtering and some consequent decrease in slum population density, serious trouble was likely in the ghetto. "The trend," he wrote, "is not clearly retrogressive. Once more there is no clear evidence of the taut stretching of a rubber band close to its breaking point."

That these predictions failed is no news. But why were they wrong? A standard description of an urban housing market holds that low income forces workers to live near the centers of cities if they are to have money left over for expenditures other than housing and transport. By living crowded into neighborhoods which are near the center of the job market, and where buildings are old, they can save on commuting and rent. On the other hand, according to this description, the middle class and the rich prefer to acquire more space and newer housing as their incomes rise. They move toward the edge of the city. Land there is inexpensive enough for low-density living and building anew does not require clearing old structures. As incomes rise, more people move to the suburbs, and the housing they leave behind "filters down" to people of lower incomes.[4]

Vernon accepted this model, and saw the process as continuing indefinitely. As long as vacant land remained around the cities.

> Once more, the rich will be pushed outward. . . . Once more, the middle-income group will move on, placidly pulling their job market with them. Once more, the poor will spread out, in the expanded leavings of their financial betters.

According to Vernon, the overwhelming majority of Americans would be satisfied with the process. The only ones dissatisfied were the monied and the intellectual elites. These groups had interests in the central city. Their jobs and cultural institutions were there. Banks, company head offices, newspapers, universities, museums, concert halls and other facilities represented heavy investments in or near downtown areas. Nor could they be decentralized. Their scale required that they serve the entire metropolitan area, and the need for face-to-face contacts in their operations prevented them from moving to separated parts of the city. As the city grew, these elites had to absorb greater and greater commuting costs, in money and time, to satisfy their need for space (and indeed for security which the central city also came to lack). They would complain of an urban crisis, Vernon predicted, but their cries would fall on deaf ears. Since nobody else shared their complaint, they would adjust. That those few burdens created by urban spread fell on the rich was if anything equitable. They could bear it best.

As historical description, this vision of harmony left out some embarrassing detail. Expansion of the

---

[3] Unless otherwise stated, references to Vernon refer to a series of lectures given in 1961, published as Raymond Vernon, *The Myth and Reality of Our Urban Problems* (Cambridge: Harvard University Press, 1964).

[4] William Alonso, *Location and Land Use* (Cambridge: Harvard University Press, 1964); Lowdon Wingo, Jr., *Transportation and Urban Land* (Washington: Resources for the Future, 1961); Chester Rapkin, Louis Winnick and David M. Blank, *Housing Market Analyssi* (Washington: U.S. Government Printing Office, 1953).

suburban fringe often involved special favors to speculators who benefited from assignment of transit franchises or inside knowledge of highway routes. Often families buying land at high prices were later subjected to high costs when subdividers ceased supporting transit routes once the land was sold, or when taxes to support the entire metropolitan area were levied on middle and low income areas, but not on suburbs. Zoning of neighborhoods to exclude low-income residents had long involved what Vernon admitted was "warfare, not planning." Amendments of proposed federal housing legislation in the 1930s and 1940s diverted federal support from construction of public housing for low-income families to subsidy for higher income land users, ensuring that filtering of old neighborhoods would remain the only source of middle and low income dwellings.[5] Yet as a gross description of the way the housing market worked, at least in peacetime prosperity (1900s, 1920s, 1950s), Vernon's description was not completely wrong. Filtering was providing homes to many families, home-ownership was increasing, and many home-owners did appear content in their castles, despite the jokes about houses looking alike, and the complaints about commuting that Vernon dismissed as the grumbling of the elite.

Vernon's prognosis ignored several economic and political factors. He underestimated the extent to which new migration from the South would increase pressure on housing in the ghetto. He also failed to predict the extent to which businesses, universities and other institutions would seek to expand within the central city. Business, in the nineteen fifties, was being dispersed toward the suburbs, seeking vacant land and following population, and Vernon expected this trend to continue.[6] However, some businesses, particularly requiring face-to-face contact between their officers and those of other firms, could not leave central business districts. Universities and some other institutions were too rooted in central districts to move easily, and because of their nonprofit status could not be driven out by increased taxes. As the financial and nonprofit sectors of the economy expanded, these firms and institutions sought more space. Thus, big business and elite institutions, as

well as low-income black neighborhoods, came to demand more inner city land than had been expected.

More fundamentally, Vernon neglected the fact that if the rich and powerful find a situation not to their liking they are likely to do more than just complain. They have money and access to credit, with which they may try to buy their way out of the situation. If that fails, they may try to use non-market institutions, especially the government. In recent years, rising incomes, the pressure of increasing urban populations on commuting, and the formation of record numbers of new families have led the group Vernon called the "elite" to action more concrete than the deploring of exurbanite living prevalent in the fifties. They have led to attempts to reconvert downtown areas to luxury residences. Increased commuting effort, and the attractions of downtown businesses, universities and other urban institutions make the well-to-do ready to give up some space in return for proximity to work and cultural institutions. This is true at least for families without young children. Rehabilitated town houses, large apartments, and luxury high-rise condominiums, rather than slums, became the highest value use for downtown tracts of land, if these families bid on them.

III

The reconversion of central city land to elite institutional, business or residential uses cannot, however, proceed through ordinary market operations. In the first place, the land is already in what are perceived as slums. A potential resident, although he has the wherewithal to bid away a single building, or lot from its previous users. will probably not do so if it would make him the only member of his ethnic or economic group to enter a neighborhood. The one exception to this is the entry of some single individuals or childless couples — generally students, architects, and other "bohemians" — into run-down neighborhoods with structurally sound buildings.[7] These individuals repair their own housing, getting some satisfaction from the work itself as well as from the moderate costs. If enough such residents enter a neighborhood, it may eventually "tip" back to upper income use, as families can enter without feeling they are moving into a slum. Few people have the

[5] Elliott Sclar and the author are presently investigating the extent to which these phenomena have increased wealth disparities in Boston.

[6] Raymond Vernon, *Metropolis 1985* (Cambridge: Harvard University Press, 1960).

[7] Examples of such renovation include the South End in Boston, and Brooklyn Heights in New York.

spirit to take part in this entering wedge, so spontaneous reconversion has been limited to a few localities. The only possibility for widespread upgrading is, as Vernon stated,

> that of recapturing and redeveloping urban neighborhoods in vast parcels — by the square mile rather than by the acre. Once a piece of real estate has been acquired which is so large as to insulate it utterly from the moldering neighborhood around it — once it is sufficiently large to be equipped with its own parks, schools, libraries, stores and social structure — then the possibility of reusing the land for middle-income living increases considerably.

Such large residential districts, or large institutional clusters or business districts, may not be developed unless large parcels of land are put together. Here, a second problem arises. Most urban land is held in very small parcels. If it is known that a developer is planning a large project, each of the many small landowners will hold back his parcels of land, hoping to be the last to sell, and to capture a larger share of the increase in value. The Douglas Commission report gave several examples of this:

> George Washington University acquired an entire block, with the exception of a one-half interest in a single house. The owner refused to sell, and it took the university nearly 15 years to acquire the site and complete the development. In Denver, assembly was attempted for a bank expansion and an apartment complex. Assembly at the beginning was "deceptively smooth." Most owners were glad to cooperate and wanted only fair prices. But problems arose as the assembler approached his goal. In one block, the owner of a single key lot had tentatively agreed to a price which was, in fact, more than he expected to receive. Then a real estate man, seeing the significance of the property to the whole assembly program, advised the landowner of his leverage, and the assembler ended up paying $50,000 more than the landowner originally thought satisfactory.[8]

The need to assemble large parcels, and the difficulty in doing so through the market may take

[8] National Commission on Urban Problems, *Building the American City* (Washington: Government Printing Office, 1969).

reconquering downtown expensive for the elite. Projects may even be vulnerable to outright refusal to sell by some residents who do not wish to leave, even if offered a high price. Private land assembly has sometimes been possible, to be sure. One way this has been accomplished is through purchases through a variety of "fronts," so that property owners do not guess the identity or intentions of the actual purchaser. But at best, this method is risky. The difficulty of private large scale assembly was enough to convince Vernon that the elites would be unable to do more than stay in their suburbs, and grumble about an urban crisis.

However, the elite has one more weapon, that Vernon overlooked. They may use the government. Under the urban renewal laws of the United States, a local government, with federal support can declare a section of a city a redevelopment area, and take by eminent domain that land which is not voluntarily sold. Generally, the land, once assembled and cleared, is sold to private developers at a subsidized price. The 1965 housing act, and previous urban renewal laws, require local agencies to "make every reasonable effort" to buy property through negotiation. But much of the land ends up taken through eminent domain. According to the Douglas Commission Report, in Washington, one quarter of the parcels acquired for urban renewal were taken through condemnation proceedings due to price disagreements.

Urban renewal is thus a new way of taking land from old users, and selling it in large quantities to new ones, at a much lower price than would otherwise prevail. When it is used to take land which has been used for low-income housing, for use in luxury dwellings or by businesses and institutions, its effect is to lower the cost of evicting the poor. When those removed are low-income homeowners or small businesses, the use of eminent domain proceedings to transfer wealth from the old owners to those more wealthy than they are is obvious. When the people evicted are tenants, which is a more usual case, the effect is similar, although less obvious. Reducing the supply of old, centrally located housing means that more families are competing for each apartment. Rents rise, and all families whose jobs and income levels require them to seek cheap downtown housing are left worse off. Criticism of urban renewal has often been limited to its failure to find vacant apartments for the specific families evicted. But even if the relocation agencies do function for these individuals, the net effect on low income families is adverse.

The conversion of land to new uses through urban renewal, or through private assembly through fronts where it is possible, is thus a form of conflict between two classes. One group must make a deliberate decision to take the land from another, and to use either deceit or authority to carry out its project. The group taking the land will benefit, and the group losing land will be left worse off. The desire of some upper-income groups and elite institutions to take land has been growing in recent years for the reasons apparent in examining Vernon's argument. How the battle has gone so far, and what its importance may be in the future, may now be examined.

IV

Two examples, both of which actually date from before Vernon's predictions, give an idea of the kind of conflict which takes place, and the role of governments and such elite institutions as select citizens-committees and university administrations in this process. In one case the land was taken for high income housing; in the other, for use by a university.

The Gratiot neighborhood of Detroit "129 acres of the city's worst slum," with nearly 2,000 black families as residents, was razed after World War II over the objection of white neighborhoods which feared the influx of relocated families.[9] The original intention was to rehouse many of the families in public housing within the project area. Most demolished dwellings had been one or two family houses. Good-quality but higher-density housing would avoid massive dispersal, and clear some of the tract for new uses, and improve housing standards for the poor. The evicted residents were told, "Many hundreds of new dwellings will be built. Some of it will be rental housing and some will be available for purchase. Many of you will undoubtedly move back into the area when redevelopment is completed, as either renters or owners of a dwelling." The St. James Baptist Church, which had a black congregation, was left standing in the expectation that its parishioners would return.

Once clearance was begun, however, other groups

[9] The following account is based on Robert J. Mowitz and Deil S. Wright, *Profile of a Metropolis* (Detroit: Wayne State University, 1962).

began to take an interest in the land. The director of the Detroit Housing Commission stated that along with rehousing the previous residents, he would consider "the desire of many middle-income groups to live close to the downtown area. These people should be provided for, and, in doing so, we minimize the danger of establishing economic ghettos through our redevelopment program." The original plan for mixed land uses could have acomplished this, but for marketing problems. A survey of possible demand, made in 1955 by the Real Estate Research Corporation, confirmed in this particular case what our general model has predicted. There was a market for downtown housing among well-paid business-district employees, but there was not as much demand for housing in mixed projects.

> The analysts distributed 6,061 forms to employees in the central business district, 5 percent of those employed in the area. The key question stated that investors were considering a fine, modern development on the Gratiot site, and respondents were asked if they would be interested in living in such a development, with rents ranging from $85 a month for an efficiency apartment to $145 for a three-bedroom unit. Twenty-three percent answered in the affirmative. The next question asked whether occupancy by both colored and white tenants would make the development less attractive, more attractive or have no effect. Among those who said they were interested in the area, 1,244 were whites and 125 were Negroes. Seventy-six percent of the white respondents said that the mixed occupancy would make the project less attractive to them, and so did two percent of the Negroes. (p. 63)

Detroit thus faced an either-or choice of land use: low-income housing for blacks, or high-income housing, with the original residents permanently displaced. The conflict could not be resolved through new public housing elsewhere, because no white neighborhood would accept it. Low-cost housing on the site would also have required public construction; private developers judged it could not be profitable. The city, however, lost interest in public housing, in part because the federal government made funds for this hard to obtain, in part out of concern for its tax base. Arguments against building segregated housing could also be made by opponents of public projects. In addition, proponents of middle or high income construction organized directly. A Citizens Redevelopment Committee was appointed by the mayor, including representatives of a major department store, banks, building firms and other businesses, and the president of the United Auto Workers. They recommended private development of a high-rent development, which allowed for some less costly housing at the edges of the project, but not for absorption of many of the former residents.

Once its report was made, the Citizens Committee actually took over the project. It was reorganized into a nonprofit Redevelopment Corporation, which received contributions from the big three automobile companies, several other manufacturing and utility corporations, the Hudson Department Store, the National Bank of Detroit, and the United Auto Workers. This corporation in collaboration with a private company purchased and developed the land. The project as finally completed included high-income apartments and single-family houses. The plans for public housing in part of the area were abandoned completely: the committee did not want one boundary of the site to consist of a large black neighborhood. In the first building opened, monthly rents ranged from $85–$120 for efficiency apartments to $190–$210 for two-bedroom units. Four percent of the tenants were black. The St. James Baptist Church sold its land to the developers and moved.

A second case illustrates the role of universities in the conflict over land. Redevelopment struggles have centered around universities for several reasons. Their location in older cities is often in areas which have become slums after the university was built. They have an incentive to seek the conversion of surrounding land back to more congenial uses. Secondly, universities have been expanding in recent years, both to increase their enrollment, and to take on new research functions. Their expansion also leads to new private demand for residences and commercial properties near them. Finally, universities have good connections; their alumni often hold positions in government or financial institutions which can influence land use. Their faculties have legal, planning and bargaining skills. When universities wish to recapture territory, they can sometimes wield considerable power for this purpose.

For example, when the University of Chicago wished to acquire land, its lawyers interested the state legislature in the passage of a bill to charter local redevelopment corporations, with the power of eminent domain over neighborhoods in which owners of 60 percent of the property agreed to renewal.

This removed the problem of parcel assembly, when the university wished to replace a 14½ acre tract of slums with apartments for students. The local corporation was formed over a somewhat larger neighborhood, in which owners of 61 percent of the land agreed to the project. This 61 percent figure included holdings by the university itself. The racial composition of the blocks razed, 79.9 percent black, as opposed to 54.3 percent in the corporation area and 36.7 percent in the entire Hyde Park-Kenwood area adjacent to the university, became a central grounds for dispute.

A study of this renewal project, by two University of Chicago sociologists,[10] also shows uses of power by Julian Levi, the administrator of the South East Chicago Commission which the university had established.

> The Commission hired two full-time private policemen to investigate a lake-front hotel that had become known in the community as the locale of various criminal activities, and the information was then given by Julian Levi to the insurance company that insured the hotel. . . . Foreclosure forced out the operators of the hotel, and, understandably, the new managers took pains to remove the criminal elements. . . . .

> When a real estate speculator purchased a six-family apartment house and promptly moved in nine Negro families, the local block group of the Hyde Park-Kenwood Community Conference spotted the move and reported it. . . .

> Julian Levi visited the speculator, threatened him with legal action for violating the housing code, and confronted him with evidence of overcrowding; at the same time a generous offer to buy was made by the University real estate office. The speculator sold the apartment dwelling to the University on the next day, and one day later the nine Negro families were moved out by the University's real estate managers. Had this purchase and eviction not been possible, legal action through municipal channels would at best have achieved the levying of fines against the speculators. . . . Levi was able to obtain tighter controls on the issuance of building permits, which include conversion construction. In this effort, Levi effectively brought to bear his own legal skills and executive abilities. Identical efforts had been made with less success by the Hyde Park Planning

[10] Peter N. Rossi and Robert A. Dentler, *The Politics of Urban Renewal* (Glencoe: The Free Press, 1959).

Association earlier, and by the volunteer legal panel of the Community Conference. (pp. 81–83)

University land clearance methods have recently been attacked by students who first learn of such activities, and who charge that plots are afoot to drive out low-income neighbors. Since, in urban renewal, uses of secrecy or authority are often present, revelations are often easy to make. The student pamphlets usually underline the propositions that redevelopment requires explicit (public or private) planning, and that it involves the transfer of land from use by one group to use by another, so that a conflict is in fact involved.

The Chicago authors, Rossi and Dentler, present an interpretation which de-emphasizes conflict. They see the controversies surrounding renewal on the area near the university as failures in a public relations process, a failure to achieve consensus. They do recognize that *"Any plan that would attempt to remove slums, modernize community facilities, revamp the grid street pattern, and reduce total available housing would inevitably clash with individual interests. Any plan would also alter the population composition."* (p. 56) The emphasis is on the italicized first sentences: the interests harmed are seen as individual, not groups at the losing end of an inter-group conflict. The impression given is that by better communication, appropriate compensation could have been agreed to and consensus established. But the second sentence at least admits possibilities of conflict.

V

Variations of this scenario have been enacted in many cities.[11] Perhaps the most famous is New Haven, where the mayor organized urban renewal through the use of a Citizen's Action Committee, which he called:

> ... the biggest set of muscles in New Haven. ... They're muscular because they control the wealth, they're muscular because they control the indus-

tries, represent the banks. ... They're muscular because they're articulate, because of their financial powers, and because of the accumulation of wealth and prestige which they have built up over the years.[12]

In New Haven, which has received more urban renewal funding per-capita than any other city, more than three times as many housing units have been torn down than there have been public housing units erected in the urban renewal program. The urban renewal program is considered a great achievement by the local establishment, including Yale University. But it is referred to as "Negro Removal" by those on the receiving end.

The general effect of urban renewal has been similar in most cities. Statistics prepared by the Douglas Commission show that in 74 cities, between 1949 and 1967, 320,392 housing units were demolished by urban renewal programs, but only 230,795 units were built under public programs. The ratio is not as great as in New Haven, but the total reduction in the number of housing units is substantial. The difference, 89,597 units, is an underestimate of the reduction in low-rent downtown housing availability, however, because some public housing is in middle income price ranges, or is far enough from job-market centers for commuting to be costly. To be sure, the amount of land thus reconquered for elite uses has thus far been relatively small. In 1961, Vernon could say the amount of reclamation, viewed from the air, was so small as to be insignificant. Between 1949 and 1961, nonetheless, 127,136 families had been removed from their dwellings by urban renewal. Thereafter the pace accelerated. In the next three years, 58,045 more families were evicted. In Boston, more than 10 percent of the city's area is now officially in urban development programs.

Recently, however, communities have begun to defend their turf. Because urban renewal requires the use of the state, attempts by the elite to take land by this means can be spotted and fought more readily than can control through indirect market mechanisms. One of the first instances of resistance came when the University of Chicago attempted to expand to the south. The Woodlawn neighborhood, which had the organizational assistance of Saul D. Alinsky and which had also seen the experience of

---

[11] In many cases with the additional factor that city planners, attempting in their own view to serve the good of all, presented plans which redesigned the city from a perspective close to that of the elite. A good general critique of city planning is contained in the forthcoming book by Robert Goodman, *After the Planners: Politics, Architecture and Liberation.*

[12] Cited in Robert Dahl, *Who Governs?* (New Haven: Yale University Press, 1961).

the redevelopment of Hyde Park-Kenwood on the other side of the campus, was able to limit expansion, and secure renovation of some low-income homes, in their existing sites, as a price for permitting the taking of a few blocks. In 1960, the university had announced plans for a major project in Woodlawn, and told local small businessmen they could "either accept the plan and help or sit back and watch it go through." They, however, joined with the tenants Alinsky had organized. In spite of university claims that "there is nobody to speak for the community," a community does exist in Woodlawn. The Woodlawn Organization mustered enough strength to convince Mayor Daley it was expedient to make the university bargain with the community organization.[13]

Turf power organization has been able to stall off urban renewal in a number of other cases since then. Sometimes the resistance is spontaneous; at other times community organizers, including those from SDS in its early days, helped catalyze it. Of course, political conflict is more often than not weighted toward the side of those well-to-do groups and elite institutions, which seek to recapture central city land from residence by the poor. They have more experience with politics, more ties to or control of key institutions. For example, these groups are not likely to face denials of mortgage credit or insurance by financial institutions. Successful defense of a neighborhood against urban renewal may also be subverted by property tax increases which drive residential costs up in inner-city neighborhoods.

In San Francisco, the Mission Coalition, a community organization, has won control over urban renewal in part of the city. But the rest of the downtown area is being rebuilt, and connected to the suburbs by the BART rapid transit system.

To pay off BART and urban renewal . . . corporate leadership will continue to rely on the same tax base that it has bled for all urban functions — taxation on property. The value of properties adjacent to BART in the center of the Mission and adjacent to other newly developed areas will increase because there will be an increased commercial demand for the property. The assessor, as a "neutral bureaucrat, simply reflects the invisible hand of the profit-oriented market. The higher taxes will . . . force up rents on the already deteri-

orated low income housing. The market will continue to do its thing, inexorably: commercial developers will buy out the already squeezed-out owners and build new houses. . . . The process may not be so neat or quick as a bulldozer disposing of the neighborhood in one fell swoop. The result will be the same.[14]

Land value increases will not work this way in all cities. If a ghetto is big enough, and viewed as dangerous enough, business (as well as upper-income housing) will fail to bid on land, unless massive clearance takes place. But at best, defending downtown neighborhoods is obviously difficult. Furthermore, because of the defensive nature of community demands for stopping demolition, the potential of these battles in the development of a radical movement is sometimes doubted. That the War on Poverty has sometimes supported organizers or advocacy planners who have worked against urban renewal has fed this suspicion, and it is clear enough that Saul Alinsky views the defense of neighborhoods as a means toward eventual consensus between them and the elite, rather than a means toward revolution. Yet the success of turf power demands may be important from a radical perspective.

Most suggested strategies for social revolution in America, whether they envision change as nonviolent or as involving armed conflict, point to the need for unity between black communities and low-income or working-class whites, in order to form a winning coalition. Turf power organization appears at first glance to be irrelevant to the need for such a coalition. In the United States, because urban neighborhoods are segregated, community organizations which are formed to resist urban renewal are normally made up of members of only one ethnic group. In at least one case, Back of the Yards, in Chicago, a community organization formed by Alinsky helped to prevent blacks from entering an all-white neighborhood. Yet the importance of defense against urban renewal is apparent if one asks what will happen when urban renewal proceeds unopposed.

When neighborhoods are cleared for urban renewal, their residents must seek housing in other high-density, low-income neighborhoods. Often this involves the entry of displaced blacks into previously white neighborhoods. At other times, it still results in

---

[13] Charles E. Silberman, *Crisis in Black and White* (New York: Random House, 1964), pp. 335–345.

[14] Danny Beagle, Al Haber and David Wellnan, "Turf Power and the Tax Man," *Leviathan* I:2 (April, 1969), p. 32.